LAND USE PLANNING AND DEVELOPMENT REGULATION LAW

Third Edition

By

Julian Conrad Juergensmeyer

Professor and Ben F. Johnson Jr. Chair in Law
Georgia State University College of Law
Adjunct Professor in City and Regional Planning
Georgia Institute of Technology

Thomas E. Roberts

Professor of Law Emeritus
Wake Forest University

HORNBOOK SERIES®

A Thomson Reuters business

Mat #41378465

© West, a Thomson business, 1998, 2003, 2007
© 2013 Thomson Reuters

      610 Opperman Drive
      St. Paul, MN 55123
      1-800-313-9378

Printed in the United States of America

ISBN: 978–0–314–28647–5

To the late Donald G. Hagman, whose enormous contributions to land use law have guided our work.

J.C.J. and T.E.R.

To Ewa, Conrad, Erik, Krissy, Josh, Jonah, Jeremiah, Julia, and Jesse

J.C.J.

To Mary Ellen, Scott, Beth, and Mark

T.E.R.

Preface

This hornbook, with the same title, is an abridgment of Land Use Planning and Development Regulation Law, Practitioner Series Third Edition (2012) and is intended to be more manageable for student use. Numerous footnotes and some text have been omitted; therefore, readers doing land use law research should consult the Practitioner Series Third Edition.

This hornbook owes its origins to Hagman, Urban Planning and Land Development Control Law originally published in 1971. Its author, Professor Donald Hagman, was an important figure in the land use planning and control field during the 1960s and 1970s as the field moved into its modern era. After Don's tragic and untimely death in 1982, Professor Juergensmeyer began the preparation of a second edition, which was published in 1986. Those interested in Professor Hagman's many accomplishments may wish to read the dedications to him at 29 UCLA Law Review 772 (1982).

JCJ & TER

Summary of Contents

Table of Contents

LAND USE PLANNING AND DEVELOPMENT REGULATION LAW

Third Edition

Chapter 1

AN INTRODUCTION TO LAND USE PLANNING AND CONTROL LAW*

Analysis

§ 1:1   The Development of Land Use Planning and Control Law

Land use planning and control law is a relatively new area of the law in our legal system even though governmental and private regulation of the use of land can be found in virtually all legal systems and societies since the beginning of history. Certainly, land use laws, court decisions, and private agreements can be found at the very beginning of our common law system. The tenure and estates concepts which formed the basis of property law at the birth of our legal system in Norman England in 1066 were means of land use regulation as well as the conceptual foundations of property ownership. Even in the colonial period of the United States and the early years of nationhood, governments and individuals used the legal system to substantially regulate the use of land.[1]

Nonetheless, land use planning and control law as a separate and distinct area of law did not begin to emerge until the early zoning ordinances and judicial decisions concerning them in the 1920s. Even then, little evidence supported the recognition of land use control as a legal specialty or distinct area from a conceptual and subject matter viewpoint. Planners and municipal law specialists began to think of "zoning" as a "special" area in the 1930s, 40s, and 50s, but few treatises, hornbooks, casebooks, manuals or law school courses were devoted to the subject before the 1960s.

In the final quarter of the twentieth century the growth in importance and scope of land use regulatory law was astounding and that growth is continuing to accelerate in the early years of the 21st century. Today, few, if any law schools are without at least one course devoted to the topic, the land use "Bar" numbers in the thousands

---

* For more detailed discussion and more extensive citations of authority of the issues covered in this chapter, see Juergensmeyer and Roberts, Land Use Planning and Development Regulation Law, Practitioner Treatise Series (3rd ed. 2012).

[1] Hart, Land Use Law in the Early Republic and the Original Meaning of the Takings Clause, 94 Northwestern Univ. L. Rev. 1099 (2000).

even in individual states, and the number of judicial decisions on point seems to increase exponentially. The interest of the American public in land use regulation has expanded at least as rapidly. Today it is unusual to find a political campaign in which land use regulation and its cohort, environmental protection, are not crucial issues. City Councils' handling of such issues as the entry of big box retailers, sign controls, and housing matters frequently receive front page newspaper coverage and evening TV news attention.

§ 1:2   Scope of This Book

It is inevitable that there be uncertainty and disagreement over the scope of the subject matter of a new and rapidly changing and developing area of the law. Land use control law has matured enough for there to be general agreement that the core of this subject is planning and regulation of land use by governmental entities through the police power. Thus, zoning and subdivision control should make everyone's list of land use control law subtopics. No one, it seems, would confine land use control law to zoning and subdivision control. The uncertainty centers around how many related areas should be included.

The predecessor to this book, as explained in the preface, was Urban Planning and Land Development Control Law by Donald Hagman, a giant in the field. That book, published originally in 1971, reflected Professor Hagman's interest in urban law developments.[2] While urban problems are as serious now as when Professor Hagman wrote, significant changes have occurred to cause us to de-emphasize urban development in this book. One factor is the withdrawal of the federal government from significant participation in urban development, which began in the early 1970s and accelerated rapidly in the 1980s. A second factor is the growing realization of the environmental and social ills caused by sprawl development into the countryside. This book, in contrast to its predecessor, focuses predominantly on these issues.

The scope of this work is best analyzed on a chapter by chapter and topic by topic basis.

• *Planning Law* [Chapter 2]

Planning and land use control law have always been recognized as closely interrelated. Unfortunately, that recognition until recently was more theoretical than actual and plans had few legal consequences. The recent advent of statutes requiring state, regional and local planning and the formulation of the consistency requirement, have created planning law as distinguished from planning theory. Since one of the principal tenets of planning law is that planning should precede any and all land use regulations this chapter is strategically located as the first substantive chapter. Planning principles are discussed in subsequent chapters in relation to particular land use control devices.

• *Zoning* [Chapters 3, 4, and 5]

---

[2] A second edition of Professor Hagman's book was prepared and published after his death: Hagman & Juergensmeyer, Urban Planning and Land Development Control Law (2d ed. 1986).

The traditional "core" of land use control law is included within these chapters. They are critical to understanding the process by which land use development decisions are made.

• *Exclusionary Zoning* [Chapter 6]

One of the negative consequences of local governmental control of land use is that the power can be used to exclude persons and types of land uses that are perceived as threats to the homogeneity of the community. Exclusion may be based on any number of factors such as wealth, race, religion, political unpopularity, or stereotypes. Beyond the harm suffered by the excluded individual, there are widespread regional implications to parochial actions by local governments.

• *Subdivision Control* [Chapter 7]

Subdivision control law is almost as old as zoning law in this country and is a well recognized part of the land use control law "core." The planned unit development concept which is closely tied conceptually and procedurally to subdivision regulation has become an important subtopic of subdivision control.

• *Building and Development Codes* [Chapter 8]

Building codes are even older than zoning and subdivision control laws. Housing codes are more recent but both are closely related to zoning. Their land use regulation consequences have traditionally been indirect. This promises to change because of their potential for being direct land use control devices through building specifications that make some uses impossible on certain types of tracts—for example coastal areas, flood plains, and environmentally sensitive and unstable land. The increased popularity of "green" building standards such as the LEED Green Building Rating System have made them a focal point for efforts designed to promote sustainability and environmental responsibility. Also, the issuance of building permits has increasingly become the regulatory stage at which many growth management techniques such as impact fees are imposed for developer funding of infrastructure.

• *Growth Management* [Chapter 9]

The present direction of land use planning and control law is its reformulation to fit and serve growth management and smart growth objectives. Although all land use planning concepts can be used as growth management tools, this chapter is designed to assimilate planning law, zoning law, subdivision control law, infrastructure finance, and, in fact, all aspects of land use planning and control law and focus it on growth management. The "smart growth" movement and "new urbanism" are new labels and new directions for growth management from both a planning and regulatory perspective. Their legal implications are considered.

• *Constitutional Limitations* [Chapter 10]

The greatly increased frequency and severity of land use restrictions in recent years has made judicial determinations of the limits of governmental power more important. For many years litigation over land use control regulations was confined almost exclusively to the state courts. Beginning in the 1970s, the interest of the Supreme Court and other federal courts in land use control law—an interest which was dormant for decades—awakened and remains active.

The limitation imposed on government by the Fifth Amendment's takings clause is a dominant issue in American land use law. There is a sharp debate over the Court's interpretation of the Fifth Amendment and the meaning of property in our legal system and our society. Beyond the takings issue, there are frequent issues of arbitrary and discriminatory government action in regulating land use, some of which affect speech, religion, and privacy rights.

• *Protection and Preservation of the Natural and Built Environment: Environmental Protection, Aesthetic Regulation, Historic Preservation, Farmland Preservation* [Chapters 11, 12 & 13]

Perhaps the fastest growing area of land use control law is that relevant to, and at times overlapping with that of, protection of the natural and built environments. Environmental law is even newer than land use law and in its early days it ran parallel to rather than intertwining with land use planning and control. Today, environmental protection and land use regulation overlap to such a great degree on many points that it is impossible to entirely separate the two. Chapter 11 covers the integration of environmental and land use control law in the regulation of ecologically sensitive lands. Chapter 12 focuses on the "built environment" through consideration of aesthetic regulation and historic preservation. Chapter 13 treats farmland and open space preservation problems and the land use planning and control techniques for their accomplishment. The newly important issues raised by urban agriculture are also considered.

• *Nuisance Law* [Chapter 14]

Nuisance law was the earliest form of land use control, one affected by the courts, rather than the legislature. Though reliance on it diminished significantly through the twentieth century, it remains an important cog in the land use regulation machine. It is of particular relevance to the definition of property rights in the constitutional sense. There is no property right to conduct a nuisance and to the extent that land use directs itself to nuisance activities, no constitutional problem is present. Determining when that point is reached is, however, a point of difficulty.

• *Private Land Use Control* [Chapter 15]

Private individuals have for centuries regulated the use of land even absent governmental activities or interest. Privately created land use restrictions continue to function as significant and often effective means of controlling the use of land. Public land use regulation has in many regards made private methods more rather than less important and the ever frequent use of traditionally private devices (restrictive covenants for example) have revitalized the importance of "private" land use control techniques.

• *Power of Eminent Domain* [Chapter 16]

The power of eminent domain can be conceived of as the ultimate land use control power possessed by governmental entities since as long as the entity is willing to pay compensation, the government has the power to take title to the land for a wide variety of public uses and purposes.

§ 1:3   Issues for the 21st Century

The chapters that follow focus on hundreds of issues. Some are old and have been discussed and disputed since the beginnings of land use control law. Others are quite recent in origin. Most, if not all, are interrelated so that it is difficult if not impossible to solve one without raising another. In this subsection, we set out our questions and concerns about what we see as leading issues to aid readers' reflection on what land use planning and control law will be like in the 21st century. The list that follows is not designed to be clever, exhaustive, or innovative. It is simply designed to establish greater rapport between the authors and readers so that the latter can read the balance of the book with some insight into what the authors "worried" about when the chapters which follow were written.[3]

• *What Will Become of Traditional Euclidean Zoning?*

Traditional zoning was indicted many years ago by John Reps in a seminal analysis.[4] Others have called for the abolition or minimalization of zoning.[5] The anti-mixed use bias of zoning has been labeled a major cause of sprawl by "smart growth" advocates. Certainly Euclidean zoning in its cumulative, static and negative sense should not and probably will not survive this century. Even a more enlightened noncumulative and mixed use oriented zoning system is of questionable value. But, what will replace it? Will local governments—especially those with severe budget and staff limitations—be able to effectively, efficiently and equitably administer point systems, development order systems and performance standards?

• *Will Mediation of Land Use Disputes Increase and Will It Alter the Practice of Land Use Law?*

The resolution of land use disputes is increasingly occurring through mediation rather than litigation as a choice of the parties and because many courts encourage or even require mediation.[6] Will this affect the way land use law is practiced? Will less frequent judicial resolution of land use disputes adversely affect the development of precedent in an area of the law so dependant upon judicial law-making?[7]

---

[3] For another list, see Netter, Land–Use Law: Issues for the Eighties (1981).

[4] Reps, Pomeroy, Memorial Lecture: Requiem for Zoning Paper presented at the 1964 ASPO National Planning Conference. Planning 1964. American Society of Planning Officials.

[5] Krasnowiecki, Abolish Zoning, 31 Syracuse L. Rev. 719 (1980). See also Ziegler, The Twilight of Single—Family Zoning, 3 UCLA J. Envtl. L. & Policy 161 (1983); Nelson, Privatizing the Neighborhood: A Proposal to Replace Zoning with Private Collective Property Rights to Existing Neighborhoods, 7 Geo. Mason L. Rev. 827 (1999); Hall, Divide and Sprawl, Decline and Fall: A Comparative Critique of Euclidean Zoning, 68 U. Pitt. L. Rev. 915 (2007).

[6] Florida has a statute designed to encourage alternate dispute resolution of land use disputes. The Florida Land Use and Dispute Resolution Act. Fla. Stat. Ann. § 70.51.

[7] The Lincoln Institute of Land Policy has been a leader in sponsoring publications and conferences concerning mediating land use disputes. Three of its leading publications are Lawrence Susskind, Ole Amundsen and Masahiro Matsuura, Using Assisted Negotiation to Settle Land Use Disputes: A Guidebook for Public Officials (1999), Lawrence Susskind, Mieke van der Wansem, and Armand Ciccarelli, Mediating Land Use Disputes: Pros and Cons (2000), and Patrick Field, Kate Harvey, and Matt Strassberg, Integrating Land Use Decision Making: A Study of Vermont (2010). Information on the subject is available on the Institute's website: http://www.lincolninst.edu.

• *Will Impact Analysis Become the Universal Antidote to Land Use Complaints and Will Land Use Regulatory Fees Based on That Analysis Rescue Local Governments From Their Infrastructure Funding Crisis?*

Fred Bosselman raised the question in the mid 1980s.[8] Since then, conditioning development approval on impact analysis and the payment of impact, linkage and mitigation fees or participation in mitigation and transferable development rights programs have become common place. In an era in which tax revenues are less and less adequate to permit governments to pay for capital improvement needs, the revenue potential of land use regulation looms as a major fiscal resource for local governments and thereby a new function to be served by land use regulations.

• *Will the Coordination of Planning and Land Use Regulation and the Requirement That Land Use Regulations Be Consistent With Comprehensive Plans Become the Norm in All Jurisdictions?*

Nothing would seem more basic and essential than that land use regulations should be consistent with and implement comprehensive plans. Yet, only a few states have this requirement. Why is it taking so long to be accepted? Can there be any validity to land use regulations not based upon comprehensive planning? Surely not.

• *Will the Quiet Revolution Continue?*

In 1972, Fred Bosselman and David Callies wrote of the revesting of land use control power in state government.[9] Will the trend continue or will there be a revitalization of local government home rule power? Will regional planning authorities replace both state and local governments as the key players in land use planning and regulation? In fact, are county and municipal governments anachronistic in large urban areas because they are unable to operate on a jurisdictional scale adequate to control sprawl and related problems?[10]

• *Will Judicial and Legislative Takings Limitations Seriously Restrict the Future Exercise of the Land Use Control Power?*

The Supreme Court's land use decisions in the 1980s and 1990s appeared to tighten the reins on government regulation of land use by an expansion of the regulatory takings doctrine. While an expansion did occur, it has been less dramatic than initially thought and in the early years of the 21st century the Court has stepped back. Will the Court revert to its expansionist tendency, and if so, how stringently will it limit government? What will be the long range effect of private property protection measures enacted by various state legislatures, Oregon [Measure 37] and Arizona [Measure 207]

---

[8] Bosselman, Linkage, Mitigation and Transfer: Will Impact Analysis Become the Universal Antidote to Land Use Complaints? (1985).

[9] F. Bosselman and D. Callies, The Quiet Revolution in Land Use Control (1972).

[10] See Arthur C. Nelson & Robert E. Lang, Megapolitan America: A New Vision for Understanding America's Metropolitan Geography (2011); Ziegler, The Case for Megapolitan Growth Management in the 21st Century: Regional Urban Planning and Sustainable Development in the United States, 41 Urb. Law. 147 (2009); see also Griffith, Smart Governance for Smart Growth: The Need for Regional Governments, 17 Ga. St. L. Rev. 1019 (2001).

in particular,[11] that are designed to award compensation to land owners economically affected by land use regulations? Will they effectively destroy the growth management programs of those states and the programs of any other states which adopt them? Without detracting from the importance of constitutional guarantees of due process and of compensation for property that is regulated or taken for a public use, if governments are not allowed to effectively plan and regulate the use of land and resources in the long run society will suffer. In our view, the limitation of rights to use real property should not be equated with essential freedoms such as speech, press, and religion.[12] Many occupy both sides of the divide between those who lean toward government and those who lean toward property rights. Will one view prevail? Can a balance or accommodation be reached?

- *Will Federal Control of Land Use Continue to Increase?*

In a wide array of areas, such as fair housing for the handicapped, telecommunications, clean water, and endangered species, Congress has stepped into areas traditionally the province of local government.

- *Will Environmental Regulation and Land Use Regulation Merge or Continue to Overlap and Conflict?*

In spite of considerable overlap in goals, principles and approaches, the land use and environmental regulatory systems often work at cross purposes to the great detriment of landowners and society. What should happen is that one permit-performance (or impact analysis) system should develop for the unified implementation of both systems.

- *Environmental Justice: What is it? Is There a Solution?*

Many have charged that locally unwanted land uses, such as landfills, are sited predominantly in minority and low-income communities. Numerous studies in recent years have attempted to determine whether the charge is true and, if so, what causes such disproportionate siting, and how more equitable sharing of the harms from such uses could be achieved.

- *Will "Smart Growth" Redirect Land Use Planning and Land Use Control Law?*

The smart growth movement and the new urbanism concepts upon which it is based have rapidly moved to the forefront of land use planning and land use control law.[13] What at first seemed only a new "buzz word" is thought by many to be a new direction and a new approach to nearly every aspect of the way planners and planning

---

[11] See Kusy and Stephenson, Regulatory Takings Initiatives: The Stories Behind the November 2006 Election, 59 Plan. & Env. L. 3 (Jan. 2007); G. Homsy, Sons of Measure 37: Lessons from Oregon's Property Rights Law, Planning 14 (June 2006).

[12] Contrast the position taken in Krotoszynski, Fundamental Property Rights, 85 Geo. L.J. 555 (1997).

[13] See the "monumental" (over 1400 pages!) work prepared by the American Planning Association, Growing Smart Legislative Guidebook: Model Statutes for Planning and the Management of Change, (2002 Edition) which has 2 volumes of accompanying work papers and its own user manual: Jerry Weitz, Growing Smart User Manual (APA 2002). See also Salkin, Sustainability and Land Use Planning: Greening State and Local Land Use Plans and Regulations to Address Climate Change Challenges and Preserve Resources for Future Generations, 34 Wm. & Mary Envtl. L. & Pol'y Rev. 121 (2009).

lawyers approach the issues of land use regulation, sprawl, and growth management. Is it a substantive or only cosmetic change?

• *Is There a Solution to Sprawl?*

America has become a nation of urban sprawl. Megacities sprawl into each other creating urban areas that cover hundreds of miles. Smart growth promises approaches to development that can at least lessen future sprawl but can anything or anybody cure the urban blight already created?[14]

• *Will Sustainable Development Become Integrated Into the Substance of Environmental and Land Use Law Thereby Emphasizing a "Land Ethic" Basis for Land Use and Environmental Law? Could Such a Development Counter the Private Property Rights Protection Movement?*

The importance placed on the concept and goal of global sustainable development by the United Nations publication *Our Common Future* [15] catapulted that concept into the forefront of the international political, social, economic and environmental agenda. Although the concept is no stranger to American land use and environmental law, the ramifications for domestic law are only beginning to be considered in the United States. The statutory and jurisprudential changes needed in our land use and environmental regulatory goals to implement the concept could be one of the headline stories for many years to come.

A small indication of a judicial awakening in this regard can be glimpsed in Minnesota where three judicial decisions consider that the Minnesota Legislature through its environmental legislation has given the "land ethic" of conservationist Aldo Leopold the "force of law."[16]

That "Land Ethic" adopted by the Minnesota courts merits quoting as a reference point for land use and environmental regulation in the 21st century:

All ethics so far evolved rest upon a single premise: that the individual is a member of a community of interdependent parts. His instincts prompt him to compete for his place in the community, but his ethics prompt him also to co-operate (perhaps in order that there be a place to compete for).

The land ethic simply enlarges the boundaries of the community to include soils, waters, plants, and animals, or collectively: the land. In short, a land ethic changes the role of Homo sapiens from conqueror of the land community to plain member and a citizen of it. It implies respect for his fellow members, and also respect for the community as such.[17]

---

[14] See Symposium on Urban Sprawl, 17 Ga. St. L. Rev. 4 (2001).

[15] The World Commission on Environment and Development, Our Common Future (1987).

[16] *Freeborn County by Tuveson v. Bryson*, 309 Minn. 178, 243 N.W.2d 316, 322 (1976); *Application of Christenson*, 417 N.W.2d 607, 18 Envtl. L. Rep. 20947 (Minn. 1987); *McLeod County Bd. of Com'rs as Drainage Authority for McLeod County Ditch No. 8 v. State, Dept. of Natural Resources*, 549 N.W.2d 630 (Minn. Ct. App. 1996).

[17] Aldo Leopold, A Sand County Almanac 203 (1949).

§ 1:4   Characteristics of Land Use Planning and Control Law

Several characteristics of land use planning and control law can be noted which assist in understanding the field.

• There are a relatively small number of cases, which are frequently discussed and cited in the literature and in judicial opinions. The lexicon of the land use lawyer must include, and the lawyer must be familiar with, the Supreme Court cases of *Pennsylvania Coal*,[18] *Euclid*,[19] *Nectow*,[20] *Penn Central*,[21] *Lucas*,[22] *Nollan*,[23] *First English*,[24] *Tahoe-Sierra*[25] and *Lingle*,[26] as well as the state courts cases of *Mt. Laurel*,[27] *Ramapo*,[28] and *Fasano*.[29]

• There are a handful of leading and influential states. Traditionally land use planning and control law has been almost exclusively state as opposed to federal law. New York and New Jersey were in the forefront of land use planning for many years and remain so but many newer issues and approaches come from sunbelt and coastal states where development pressures generate controversies which in turn generate cases and statutes. Within the sunbelt/coastal category, there are leaders. Note how many recent citations throughout the book are to material from California, Florida, and Oregon.

• The inter-disciplinary nature of land use law is increasingly important. Hardly any major land use regulation program or litigation is handled exclusively these days by lawyers or planners. Usually both are integrally involved as well as engineers and economists. The multi-disciplinary nature of the work is beginning to influence the content and subject matter of land use literature and consequently its study and practice.

---

[18] *Pennsylvania Coal Co. v. Mahon,* 260 U.S. 393, 43 S. Ct. 158, 67 L. Ed. 322, 28 A.L.R. 1321 (1922).

[19] *Village of Euclid, Ohio v. Ambler Realty Co.,* 272 U.S. 365, 47 S. Ct. 114, 71 L. Ed. 303, 4 Ohio L. Abs. 816, 54 A.L.R. 1016 (1926).

[20] *Nectow v. City of Cambridge,* 277 U.S. 183, 48 S. Ct. 447, 72 L. Ed. 842 (1928).

[21] *Penn Cent. Transp. Co. v. City of New York,* 438 U.S. 104, 98 S. Ct. 2646, 57 L. Ed. 2d 631, 11 Env't. Rep. Cas. (BNA) 1801, 8 Envtl. L. Rep. 20528 (1978).

[22] *Lucas v. South Carolina Coastal Council,* 505 U.S. 1003, 112 S. Ct. 2886, 120 L. Ed. 2d 798, 34 Env't. Rep. Cas. (BNA) 1897, 22 Envtl. L. Rep. 21104 (1992).

[23] *Nollan v. California Coastal Com'n,* 483 U.S. 825, 107 S. Ct. 3141, 97 L. Ed. 2d 677, 26 Env't. Rep. Cas. (BNA) 1073, 17 Envtl. L. Rep. 20918 (1987).

[24] *First English Evangelical Lutheran Church of Glendale v. Los Angeles County, Cal.,* 482 U.S. 304, 107 S. Ct. 2378, 96 L. Ed. 2d 250, 26 Env't. Rep. Cas. (BNA) 1001, 17 Envtl. L. Rep. 20787 (1987).

[25] *Tahoe-Sierra Preservation Council, Inc. v. Tahoe Regional Planning Agency,* 535 U.S. 302, 122 S. Ct. 1465, 152 L. Ed. 2d 517, 54 Env't. Rep. Cas. (BNA) 1129, 32 Envtl. L. Rep. 20627, 10 A.L.R. Fed. 2d 681 (2002).

[26] *Lingle v. Chevron U.S.A. Inc.,* 544 U.S. 528, 125 S. Ct. 2074, 161 L. Ed. 2d 876, 35 Envtl. L. Rep. 20106 (2005).

[27] *Southern Burlington County N.A.A.C.P. v. Mount Laurel Tp.,* 67 N.J. 151, 336 A.2d 713 (1975).

[28] *Golden v. Planning Bd. of Town of Ramapo,* 30 N.Y.2d 359, 334 N.Y.S.2d 138, 285 N.E.2d 291, 2 Envtl. L. Rep. 20296, 63 A.L.R.3d 1157 (1972).

[29] *Fasano v. Board of County Com'rs of Washington County,* 264 Or. 574, 507 P.2d 23 (1973) (disapproved of by, Neuberger v. City of Portland, 288 Or. 585, 607 P.2d 722 (1980)) and (rejected by, Quinn v. Town of Dodgeville, 120 Wis. 2d 304, 354 N.W.2d 747 (Ct. App. 1984)) and (rejected by, Hampton v. Richland County, 292 S.C. 500, 357 S.E.2d 463 (Ct. App. 1987)).

• A standard list of issues is omnipresent in many land use controversies. It is hard to imagine a major land use case that does not raise several, if not most, of the following issues:

1.   Does the action or proposed action of the governmental entity in question constitute an exercise of the police power?

2.   Has the police power been exercised reasonably?

3.   Has the governmental entity—if it is other than the State—been delegated the power to do what it has done or proposes to do?

4.   Has there been an unlawful delegation of legislative authority by the governmental entity?

5.   Has there been a denial of equal protection?

6.   Have notice and hearing requirements been respected?

7.   Is the action of the governmental unit legislative or quasi judicial? Will the fairly debatable standard or some stricter standard of review be applied to it?

8.   Has there been a taking?

§ 1:5   Research Sources

While we hope that this book will serve as a beginning step for research in land use law issues, in depth studies will require one to look at additional material. Fortunately, an array of sources is available.

A.   *Westlaw*

An appendix to this book contains a guide on the research of land use law through Westlaw. This data base includes not only all state and federal cases and statutes, but also includes numerous recent law review articles, specialty journals, and daily newspapers that cover land use developments.

B.   *One Volume Treatises*

There are several other one volume reference books available. Those with a primary focus on land use law include: Daniel R. Mandelker, Land Use Law (5th ed. Michie Co. 2003) and Peter W. Salsich, Land Use Regulation: Planning, Zoning, Subdivision Regulation, and Environmental Control (2d ed. 2004).

In the related area of environmental law, the leading book is by Professor William H. Rodgers, Jr. Environmental Law (updated 2011). Professor Linda A. Malone also has an excellent book, Environmental Regulation of Land Use (2d ed. 2000, annual updates).

C. Multi-Volume Treatises

Several extensive multi-volume works are available. They are all updated regularly.

Edward H. Ziegler, Jr., Rathkopf's the Law of Zoning and Planning (4th ed. updated 2007, annual updates) (5 volumes); Patricia Salkin, American Law of Zoning (5th ed.2006, annual updates) (4 volumes);

Patrick J. Rohan and Eric Damian Kelly, Zoning and Land Use Controls (1977) (9 volumes);

Norman Williams, Jr. and John M. Taylor, American Planning Law: Land Use and the Police Power (2003, annual updates) (6 volumes); and

James A. Kushner, Subdivision Law and Growth Management (2009, annual updates) (2 volumes).

In the area of eminent domain the standard reference work is Julius Sackman and Patrick J. Rohan, Nichols' The Law of Eminent Domain (3d ed. 1976) (14 volumes).

D. Law Reviews

Law school law reviews regularly carry land use articles. The breadth of coverage has significantly increased in recent years. Articles are available through Westlaw dating back to the mid 1980s with more complete coverage starting in the early 1990s. Among the law reviews carrying numerous land use articles are:

The Urban Lawyer, published four times a year by the Section of State and Local Government Law of the American Bar Association through the University of Missouri—Kansas City School of Law;

The *Journal of Land Use and Environment Law* published twice a year by Florida State University College of Law; and

The *Washington University Journal of Urban & Contemporary Law* published semi-annually by the Washington University School of Law.

E. Newsletters

The American Planning Association publishes a monthly journal, *Planning and Environmental Law,* which contains a short lead article on a topic of current interest as well as briefs of recent cases and statutes.

A monthly newsletter, *Zoning and Planning Law Report,* is published by Thomson West. Like the APA digest noted above, it contains a short lead article on a topic of current interest as well as briefs of recent developments.

A bi-weekly newsletter, *Land Use Law Report,* is published by Business Publishers, Inc. The report contains case briefs as well as news of legislative developments around the country.

F. On-Line: Internet Sources

Web sites, too numerous to list and ever growing, contain valuable information on land use topics. A few of interest include:

The Section of State and Local Government Law of the American Bar Association has a web site, http://www.abanet.org/statelocal/home.html, with articles on land use. It also hosts an e-mail discussion group used by students, practitioners and academics.

The American Planning Association also has planning and land use information. It can be accessed at http://www.planning.org/. Of particular current interest to land use lawyers and planners is the APA's Growing Smart Legislative Guidebook: Model Statutes for Planning and the Management of Change, 2002 Edition which can be downloaded from the website.

The Lincoln Institute of Land Policy, a nonprofit institute that studies land policy, including land economics and land taxation, has a website at http://www.lincolninst. edu.

The codes of hundreds of municipalities around the country are available through the site State and Local Government on the Net, http://www.statelocalgov.net/. The federal government maintains links to state and local law: http://www.usa.gov/ Agencies/Local.shtml.

Cyburbia (formerly called PAIRC-The Planning and Architecture Internet Resource Center) contains a comprehensive directory of internet resources relevant to planning, architecture, built environment, http://www.cyburbia.org/.

The United States Department of Housing and Urban Development's (HUD) site has information on a broad spectrum of real estate and housing issues, http://www.hud. gov/.

Chapter 2

COMPREHENSIVE PLANS AND THE PLANNING PROCESS*

Analysis

I.   PLANNERS AND PLANNING

---

* For more detailed discussion and more extensive citations of authority of the issues covered in this chapter, see Juergensmeyer and Roberts, Land Use Planning and Development Regulation Law, Practitioner Treatise Series (3rd ed. 2012).

I. PLANNERS AND PLANNING

§ 2:1   The Practice of Planning

There is no universally accepted definition of planning, nor is there a definition of "planner" which would be endorsed by all those who now practice urban planning. Currently, only two states, New Jersey[1] and Michigan,[2] as well as the Commonwealth of Puerto Rico,[3] have legislation concerned with defining or licensing the urban planner as a professional. Nevertheless, those involved with urban planning would generally agree that the planner who deals with land use regulation has several principal characteristics.[4]

First, the planner has technical training at the undergraduate or graduate school level, often in one of the many university urban planning programs, or possibly in another discipline such as engineering, architecture or landscape architecture.

Second, the planner is future-oriented. The urban planner believes that by analyzing existing conditions, forecasting future trends, and establishing normative goals and policies, an optimum path for the development or redevelopment of a geographic area may be formulated. This process usually results in a "plan." In addition, many urban planners perform independent projections, statistical analyses, studies of housing needs and conditions in blighted or underdeveloped areas, and draft municipal ordinances for zoning, aesthetic regulation, and environmental protection. These studies are often done in conjunction with the process of preparing a plan.

Third, the planner acts as a catalyst in the political process by which plans and land use regulations are developed, adopted, and implemented by a local government such as a county or city. This catalytic role arises from the planner's function as an analyst of conditions and trends in development or decline, and as a proponent of alternative means to guide the development, or redevelopment, of urban and rural areas. As the proponent of new regulations and of the plan, the planner exerts an influence through the legislative and administrative processes by which local governments plan for, and regulate, development.

Planners are most often employees of governmental agencies. According to a 2012 APA/AICP Survey:

> The typical (median) planner is 44 years old and has been in the planning field for 14 years. Almost all (95%) planners indicated at least one area of specialization, the most common being community development and redevelopment (51%), and land-use or code enforcement (45%). Other common areas of specialization include transportation planning (30%), environmental and natural resources planning (26%), economic planning and development (25%), urban design (22%), and sustainability (20%). 71% of planners work in public agencies and 22% in private con-

---

[1] N.J. Stat. Ann. 45:14A-1 et seq.

[2] Mich. Comp. Laws Ann. §§ 339. 2301 et seq.

[3] P.R. Laws Ann. tit. 20, § 3501(e).

[4] For information on the profession and practice of planning, see generally The Practice of Local Government Planning (So and Getzels eds.1998); Hall, Urban and Regional Planning (4th ed. 2002); Cullingham, Planning in the USA: Policies, Issues, and Processes (2003); Levy, Contemporary Urban Planning (7th ed. 2005); Institutions and Planning (Ninaj Verma, ed.) (2007).

sulting firms. 62% of planners report their principal place of employment is located in a city, another 21% indicated a suburb, 12% a small town, and 4% a rural area.[5]

The planning profession has been seeking recognition as a profession for several decades. Engineers, architects, and landscape architects are often found in planning positions, but many colleges and universities now offer bachelor, masters, and doctoral degrees in urban planning. Curricula in these academic programs range from a technical, design-oriented approach, termed "physical planning" by planning theorists, to a more policy-oriented approach at the opposite extreme. Considerable intermixing of the two disciplines in planning occurs in practice.

In an effort to foster professionalism, the American Institute of Certified Planners (the professional component of the American Planning Association)[6] administers an examination and certification program for urban planners. Passing the application and examination criteria entitles the planner to present himself as a "certified planner." Increasingly, government agencies seeking to fill positions request applicants with such certification. However, it has not yet become a thoroughly-established prerequisite for the practice of urban planning in either government or the private sector.

Thus, the planner may be educated in a field other than planning, and if so, is likely to be a licensed engineer, architect, or landscape architect. In truth, these professionals have not recently invaded the field of urban planning. Rather, the modern science of urban planning grew out of the efforts of individuals in these fields to design cities to accommodate the rapid growth that has consistently characterized the history of the United States. A debate continues to take place among these professions regarding their respective entitlements, and qualifications, to practice planning. Thus, when a state undertakes to regulate or register planners, litigation may ensue regarding the rights of other professionals to qualify as planners.[7]

A coming of age sign for the planning profession is the attention given by the United States Supreme Court in recent years. The attention, however, has not been benign. On several occasions, the Court has voiced concern over what it perceives as abusive treatment of property owners by planners acting for local government.[8] Exemplifying this is the rhetorical question posed by Justice Brennan in his *San Diego Gas & Electric Co. v. City of San Diego* dissent, that "[a]fter all if a policeman must know the Constitution, then why not a planner?"[9]

---

[5] http://www.planning.org/salary/summary.htm.

[6] See http://www.planning.org/aicp/.

[7] See, e.g., *New Jersey Chapter, Am. Institute of Planners v. New Jersey State Bd. of Professional Planners,* 48 N.J. 581, 227 A.2d 313 (1967) (state statute licensing planners did not violate equal protection clause by exempting, from examination requirements, any licensed engineer, land surveyor or registered architect of New Jersey).

[8] See *Lucas v. South Carolina Coastal Council,* 505 U.S. 1003, 112 S. Ct. 2886, 120 L. Ed. 2d 798 (1992) (beach set back law suspected as pressing "private property into some form of public service under the guise of mitigating serious public harm"). See also *Nollan v. California Coastal Com'n,* 483 U.S. 825, 107 S. Ct. 3141, 97 L. Ed. 2d 677 (1987) (beach easement program labeled "extortion"), discussed infra §§ 10:5 to 10:6.

[9] *San Diego Gas & Elec. Co. v. City of San Diego,* 450 U.S. 621, 661, 101 S. Ct. 1287, 1309, 67 L. Ed. 2d 551 (1981). The point of the comment was that a monetary remedy was necessary to compel planners, as government officials, to abide by the Constitution. The Court subsequently decided that compensation was the mandatory remedy for a Fifth Amendment taking. See *First English Evangelical Lutheran Church of Glendale v. Los Angeles County, Cal.,* 482 U.S. 304, 107 S. Ct. 2378, 96 L. Ed. 2d 250 (1987).

The consequence of this concern is that the Supreme Court and lower courts review the administration of land use regulatory programs with heightened scrutiny. This increases the likelihood that courts will find that municipalities have violated constitutional rights. When municipalities violate constitutional rights, planners, along with other government officials, may be held personally liable for money damages under federal law.[10]

The Court is not uniformly hostile to land use regulation; nor is it always skeptical of planners' motives. The Court has given wide latitude to government to enact laws protecting the environment, open space, and historic preservation. Indeed, in *Dolan v. City of Tigard,* the Court acknowledged that "[c]ities have long engaged in the commendable task of land use planning, made necessary by increasing urbanization . . . . "[11] More recently, the Court took a strong pro-planning stance in regard to the use of moratoria in *Tahoe-Sierra Preservation Council, Inc. v. Tahoe Regional Planning Agency.*[12] Still, the overall thrust of the Supreme Court's cases since 1987 is that the actions of government, and its planners, are less likely to be given the benefit of the doubt, particularly in cases challenging the means chosen to achieve admittedly legitimate public ends. More than in the past, courts today require planners to support the reasonableness of regulations affecting private property.

II. ANTECEDENTS OF LOCAL GOVERNMENT PLANNING

§ 2:2   The Colonial Planning Era[13]

Town planning in the United States, from early colonial days, resembled the modern science of subdivision design. At this stage in the early development of the American city, the planning of frontier settlements was dominated principally by civil engineers and land surveyors. The seminal town plan during the colonial era was the plan for the new City of Philadelphia, commissioned by William Penn and drawn up in 1681.[14] A site between two rivers was selected, and a gridiron system of streets was devised. Open spaces in the central area of the city were set aside, and uniform building spacings and setbacks were prescribed. Penn's engineer, Thomas Holme, prepared this plan, which became the model for most early city plans prepared for other colonial-era towns and cities. The Philadelphia Plan thus left its gridiron-street imprint on many cities planned later.

Such early town plans were invariably drawn by surveyors and engineers, and so the man-made aspects of cities took the rectilinear forms preferred by those professions. A notable departure from this approach was the first plan for Washington, D.C., commissioned in 1791 by the new federal government, and prepared by engineer Pierre L'Enfant that year. This plan superimposed an impressive diagonal-street and radial-thoroughfare system upon a traditional gridiron street system, thus incorporating elements of French civil design. Today, L'Enfant's plan can still be seen in the broad, sweeping vistas that characterize the nation's capital.

---

[10] See discussion infra § 10:9 and §§ 10:23 to 10:26.

[11] *Dolan v. City of Tigard,* 512 U.S. 374, 396, 114 S. Ct. 2309, 2322, 129 L. Ed. 2d 304 (1994).

[12] Tahoe-Sierra Preservation Council, Inc. v. Tahoe Regional Planning Agency, 535 U.S. 302, 122 S. Ct. 1465, 152 L. Ed. 2d 517 (2002).

[13] For discussions of land use regulation during the colonial period, see Hart, Land Use Law in the Early Republic and the Original Meaning of the Takings Clause, 94 Nw. U. L. Rev. 1099 (2000).

[14] W. Goodman & E. Freund, Principles and Practice of Urban Planning 9–10 (1968).

The Philadelphia and Washington plans are only two well-known examples of early town planning. Many other plans were prepared, some taking a different, smaller-scale approach.[15] Most of these city plans were no more than early forms of land subdivision control, since they were usually maps showing street right-of-way lines, parcel boundaries, open spaces and water bodies. The towns themselves were often no larger than modern tract subdivisions, but they accommodated that era's primitive technology and simple, agrarian economy.

After the American Revolution, power became more centralized in state governments, with a corresponding loss of autonomy by cities. With the adoption of state constitutions, cities henceforth derived powers of self-government usually by an act of the state legislature delegating that power. Thus, without a delegation of specific powers to control land uses, municipalities, mere creatures of the state, could not exert broad, effective control over the use, and intensity of use, of private property. During this time, the reach of municipalities in regulating the use of land was largely confined to prevention of nuisances.[16] Land speculation became a new industry, and the practice of maximization of economic returns upon land investments made it difficult to implement the open space and civic design elements of city plans such as those for Philadelphia and the District of Columbia.

§ 2:3   The Sanitary Reform Movement

Along with the advent of widespread land speculation came the era of city-building. Factories were built in existing towns, attracting workers from abroad and from agrarian areas. Slowly, American cities became aware that urbanization might be a contributing factor to disease and poor sanitation. Because their growth had been unplanned (and perhaps unanticipated), no American cities had ever comprehensively addressed the problems of drainage and disposal of wastes. The typical American city, by the 1840's, was characterized by filth, stench and stagnant water in the streets, backyard privies, dampness, and the absence of sunlight in residential space. As a result, deadly diseases such as yellow fever, cholera, typhoid, typhus, scarlet fever and diphtheria were commonplace.[17] Backyards, gullies, and even public streets became repositories of all kinds of waste matter, and drainage ditches became choked with debris, including fecal matter and animal carcasses.

There was a remedy to this serious danger to the public health. English sanitary reformer Edwin Chadwick, commencing in 1842, began to champion the construction of "water-carriage sewerage systems." By use of an egg-shaped pipe, flushed with water, Chadwick learned, sewage and even the carcasses of animals could be carried away from homes and cities, and channeled into water bodies in which, presumably, they would disappear. The system required the construction of public potable water supply systems, and sewer lines to carry away wastes. Chadwick's ideas took root in the United States, during a brief period before the Civil War now referred to as the era of the Sanitary Reform Movement.

---

[15] W. Goodman & E. Freund, Principles and Practice of Urban Planning at 10–14.

[16] See infra §§ 14:1 et seq., for discussion of land use regulation through nuisance law.

[17] J. A. Peterson, The Impact of Sanitary Reform upon American Urban Planning, 1840–1890, in Introduction to Planning History in the United States 13–17 (D. Krueckeberg ed. 1983).

New York City opened its first public water piping system in 1842, recognizing early on the need to provide an adequate water supply system. Boston opened its first system in 1848. The delivery of water obviously led to the need to pipe it away again, laden with wastes. By 1865, New York City had constructed about 125 miles of sewerage pipelines; Boston completed about 100 miles of sewers by 1873.[18] These early systems were mostly unplanned, and constructed in response to pressures from landowners and political interest groups. Thus, a sort of incrementalist, project-by-project approach typified these early efforts at sanitation reforms.

Installation of sanitary sewers grew more widespread after the Civil War, and by 1875 sanitary engineering was firmly established as a profession in the United States. During this time period, there was also a virtual renaissance in the development of the design professions: in 1866, the American Institute of Architects was formed and in 1871 the engineering professions were first organized.[19] However, none of these professions engaged in comprehensive planning for the future, in the modern sense. The first major, comprehensive American effort to plan for future public health was spurred by the spread of a massive yellow-fever epidemic in the lower Mississippi River Valley in 1878. The epidemic killed over 5,000 people in Memphis, Tennessee, then a city of only 45,000.

In 1879, in response to the plague, Congress created a National Board of Health to advise state governments and to regulate quarantines. By 1880, the Board, at the request of Tennessee authorities, completed an exhaustive, unprecedented study of physical and structural conditions in the City of Memphis, a study that filled 96 volumes and made over 12,000 recommendations for improvements of a remedial nature on property in Memphis—principally nuisance abatements.

The recommendations also included major proposals for a new sanitary public water supply, a sewerage system, destruction of substandard buildings, enactment of a sanitary code for the entire city requiring elevation of buildings whose floors were less than two feet above the ground, repaving of many streets, ventilation of all city houses, and the appointment of a city sanitation officer to oversee all future sanitary work.

This scheme is regarded by modern observers as the first major example of the modern "comprehensive" approach to urban problems, although limited to the goals of prevention of disease and sanitation problems caused by unregulated growth of an urban area. The Memphis scheme did not address many concerns now regarded as properly within the purview of urban planning, such as planning vehicular circulation, districting of incompatible land uses, and recreation space planning. But it was a sign of things to come.

A prophetic expression of the broad approach the planner of urban areas must take was expressed during this era by at least one writer. Horace Bushnell, in his essay "City Plans," observed in 1864 that:

> Considering the immense importance of a right location, and a right planning for cities, no step should ever be taken by the parties concerned, without employing

---

[18] J. A. Peterson, The Impact of Sanitary Reform upon American Urban Planning, 1840–1890, in Introduction to Planning History in the United States at 19.

[19] D. Krueckeberg, The Culture of Planning, Introduction to Planning History in the United States 13–17 (D. Krueckeberg ed. 1983).

some person who is qualified by a special culture, to assist and direct. Our engineers are trained by a very different kind of service, and are partly disqualified for this by the habit of a study more strictly linear . . . . The qualifications of surveyors are commonly more meagre still . . . . We have cities for the new age that has come, adapted to its better conditions of use and ornament. So great an advantage ought not to be thrown away. We want, therefore, a city planning profession. . . .[20]

§ 2:4   The City Beautiful Movement

The consciousness of a new age, with new opportunities for civic improvement, was not limited to those who advocated sanitary reforms. With the increasing congestion of urbanizing areas came a growing awareness that aesthetics also plays a role in the evolution of urban form and function.

American cities grew rapidly during the 19th century. In 1840, the census showed only twelve American cities with populations of over 25,000 and of these only three had populations of over 100,000. But as industry grew, so grew American cities. By 1880, 77 cities had populations of over 25,000 and twenty cities had more than 100,000 residents. This rapid centralization of population in cities, where job opportunities were, led to an increased awareness of the need for civic beauty and amenities in America's unplanned urban areas.

The proponents of civic beauty would hardly have claimed the title, but their agitations for greater attention to aesthetics in city planning later became known as the City Beautiful Movement, the precursor to modern urban planning. The movement was really a groundswell, grass-roots concern with the physical appearance of towns and cities. Because they were largely the product of unrestrained private enterprise, towns across the United States were, before the advent of the 20th century, largely unattractive, muddy, cluttered clusters of buildings. Individual residences sported trash-strewn alleys and yards, and there was little monumental civic architecture. But if sanitary reform could be planned, many believed, so could aesthetics.

The origin of the City Beautiful Movement is commonly traced to the Chicago World's Fair of 1893, a massive celebration of technology, art and architecture in which Americans were first introduced *en masse* to classical design via the Columbian Exposition. The exposition was an array of neo-classical structures and sculpture forming part of the Chicago World's Fair. But the World's Fair exposition was only a symbol of a growing consciousness of the importance of the physical appearance of towns.

In villages and towns across the country, "village improvement associations," usually ad-hoc committees of townspeople, were being created during the 1890s. The village improvement associations championed street lighting, paving of dirt streets and sidewalks, the cleaning up of private yards and alleys, planting of public and private gardens, and setting aside of public, urban parks. By 1901, over 1,000 such improvement associations had sprung up across the United States, advocating both urban aesthetics and sanitation.[21]

---

[20] H. Bushnell, Work and Play 196 (1864).

[21] Introduction to Planning History in the United States 46–49 (D. Krueckeberg ed. 1983).

The City Beautiful Movement, like the Sanitary Reform Movement, was oriented to physical improvements to rectify a perceived evil: the lack of order and cleanliness in American towns. Well-kept streets, beautiful parks, attractive private residences, fresh air and sanitary improvements became its hallmarks. Many of the village associations were persuaded to join the National League of Improvement Associations, which crusaded for these causes. Renamed the American League for Civic Improvement in 1901, the national association created advisory panels of experts in municipal art, sanitation, recreation and related concerns. To a great extent the City Beautiful Movement reflected the ideals of the Progressive Era of reform in which it flourished. But it also planted the seeds for a more comprehensive view of the science of planning urban spaces.

City Beautiful proponents caused a great deal of municipal expenditure for civic architecture and municipal improvements. But the proponents of beautification did not necessarily espouse comprehensive regulation of land uses and development. In fact, there was a fear of governmental regulation, rooted in a fundamental aversion to the limitation of private enterprise by local government. As one early commentator observed:

> In America it is the fear of restricting or injuring free and open competition that has made it so difficult for cities to exercise proper and efficient control over their development. The tendency therefore has been to promote those forms of civic improvement which can be carried out without interfering with vested interests. . . .[22]

§ 2:5   The Advent of Planning Commissions

Proponents of the City Beautiful advocated the creation of citizens' advisory planning commissions, which were the precursors to modern local government planning commissions. The early advisory planning commissions were composed, usually, of locally-prominent merchants and professionals who had an interest in civic beautification, the construction of parks, and the financing of municipal outdoor art. Frequently, these early planning commissions engaged prominent architects and landscape architects to prepare advisory "plans" for civic improvement. These early plans by consultants were non-legal documents, principally maps and lists of suggestions for civic improvements. Several of the early advisory plans, however, attempted to achieve a comprehensiveness of scope that was similar to the modern local government comprehensive plan.[23]

The citizens' advisory planning commissions, in some instances, achieved the status of organs of municipal government. Hartford, Connecticut in 1907 created the first city planning commission. Milwaukee, Wisconsin initiated its city planning commission in 1908. In 1909, Chicago, Illinois appointed a 328-member city planning commission. These commissions, without powers conferred by statute or ordinance, could only recommend the plans they produced as guidelines for decision making by the local municipal legislative body.

---

[22] J. Nolen, New Ideals in the Planning of Cities, Towns and Villages 133–34 (1919).

[23] J. Nolen, New Ideals in the Planning of Cities, Towns and Villages 133–34 (1919).

In 1909, Chicago became the first city in the United States to voluntarily adopt, only as a non-legal, advisory document, a "comprehensive plan" for its future development. The plan was prepared by famed architect Daniel H. Burnham, who had been director of works for the Columbian Exposition at the 1893 Chicago World's Fair. Backed by wealthy commercial interests in Chicago, and with a budget of $85,000, Burnham prepared a long-range plan for the Chicago region more comprehensive in scope than any plan previously prepared for an American city.

The Chicago plan addressed transportation and recommended a system of regional highways extending far outside the city. It made suggestions for improvement of traffic circulation within the city limits, including the development of new collector streets and consolidation of regional railroad terminals. It recommended new city shipping docks, new parks and beaches on Lake Michigan, and construction of a new city civic center. While the plan was to remain principally advisory in nature, it was nonetheless adopted as the official General Plan of Chicago, by the city's advisory planning commission, in 1911. Ultimately, implementation of its recommendations depended upon the degree of political influence over city government exercised by the businessmen who were members of the Chicago Planning Commission.

§ 2:6   Early Conceptions of the City Plan

In 1909, the First National Conference on City Planning and the Problems of Congestion was convened in Washington, D.C., and attended by many of the design professionals who were working, at that time, as consultants to advisory planning commissions across the United States. At this conference, Frederick Law Olmsted, a prominent landscape architect and planning consultant, described the city plan as a compendium of all regulations on building, physical development, "districting" of land, health ordinances, and "police rules" for the use and development of land. Olmsted drew many of his ideas on plans from earlier experiments in town planning in Germany and Switzerland.[24]

In 1911, Olmsted, again addressing the National Conference on City Planning, said the plan was a forecast of the best path for development to take, which should be followed by the local legislative body in making land use and development-related decisions:

> We must cultivate in our minds and in the minds of the people the conception of the city plan as a device or piece of . . . machinery for preparing, and keeping constantly up to date, a unified forecast and definition of all the important changes, additions, and extensions of the physical equipment and arrangement of the city which a sound judgment holds likely to become desirable and practicable in the course of time, so as to avoid as far as possible both ignorantly wasteful action and . . . inaction in the control of the city's physical growth. It is a means by which those who become at any time responsible for decisions affecting the city's plan may be prevented from acting in ignorance of what their predecessors and their colleagues in other departments of city life have believed to be the reasonable contingencies.[25]

---

[24] M. Scott, American City Planning Since 1890, at 97 (1969).

[25] Proceedings of the Third National Conference on City Planning, Philadelphia, Pennsylvania, 1911, as reprinted in W. Goodman & E. Freund, Principles and Practice of Urban Planning 352 (1968).

Olmsted's conception of the city plan was prophetic of today's plans, in focusing on the role of the plan as a rational, policy document by which development-related decisions by successive, elected city officials should be guided. Later, Alfred Bettman, a land use attorney from Cincinnati, reinforced the concept of the city plan as a master development guide for the city or town. Addressing the National Conference on City Planning in 1928, Bettman said:

> A city plan is a master design for the physical development of the territory of the city. It constitutes a plan of the division of land between public and private uses, specifying the general location and extent of new public improvements, grounds and structures . . . and, in the case of private developments, the general distribution [of land areas] amongst various classes of uses, such as residential, business and industrial uses.[26]

III. RELATIONSHIP OF PLANNING AND ZONING

§ 2:7   The Promulgation of Zoning Ordinances

The comprehensive plan's emphasis on setting the distribution of classes of land uses caused some confusion by many local governments over the difference between comprehensive *plans* and comprehensive *zoning ordinances*. Unlike the plans adopted during this era, which were advisory documents of a policy nature, zoning ordinances were local ordinances establishing land-use districts for residential, commercial, industrial and agricultural activities, and usually prescribing standards within each district for building height and bulk, setbacks from lot lines, and density or intensity of the use of individual lots within each district. When faced with the choice of either preparing a comprehensive plan, followed by adoption of a zoning ordinance to implement the policies in the plan, or just preparing and adopting a "comprehensive zoning ordinance," most local governments opted for the latter alternative.

The first modern, comprehensive zoning ordinance was enacted by New York City in 1916. The ordinance classified land uses and created zones for these uses, depicted on zoning maps. The purposes of zoning were to segregate residential uses from more intensive uses of land, such as industrial, and thereby to provide safer, quieter areas for family life. By 1921, zoning had become fashionable: its advocates had persuaded almost half of the state legislatures to adopt zoning enabling acts, conferring upon municipalities the power to adopt and enforce zoning ordinances.

The popularity of zoning was given a boost by the preparation of a model zoning enabling act by the United States Department of Commerce. The Act, published in 1924, was entitled the Standard State Zoning Enabling Act.[27] It provided a ready-made model for legislatures to follow in delegating police power to municipalities to prepare, adopt, and administer zoning codes. The act authorized the appointment of zoning commissions by local governments, which would set district boundaries and regulations, hold a public hearing on the proposed zoning ordinance, and submit it to the city

---

[26] Planning Problems of Town, City and Region: Papers and Discussions of the Twentieth National Conference on City Planning, reprinted in W. Goodman & E. Freund, Principles and Practice of Urban Planning at 352–53.

[27] Issued in draft form in 1922 and first published in mimeographed form in 1923, the Act was revised and printed for the first time in 1924, and reprinted in 1926. By the time the final version was released in 1926, 43 states had enacted it.

council for final hearings and enactment into law. Without such an enabling act, a municipal zoning ordinance was in danger of being invalidated as *ultra vires* if challenged in court.

By 1926, 564 cities and towns had adopted zoning ordinances, and several state courts had upheld zoning as a valid exercise of police powers delegated by states to their municipalities. In that year, the United States Supreme Court upheld the use of the police power to zone. In *Village of Euclid v. Ambler Realty Co.,*[28] the Court heard a challenge by an Ohio landowner of a "comprehensive zoning plan" adopted by the city council of Euclid, Ohio. The ordinance established districts for land use, and district regulations for building heights and minimum lot sizes. The ordinance, the Supreme Court held, did not violate due process, and bore a rational relationship to valid governmental interests in preventing congestion and in segregating incompatible land uses.

But the attractiveness of zoning to the general public was due principally to the fact that a new zoning ordinance tended to validate existing land use patterns by including them on the zoning map, and also provided the opportunity to over-zone for profitable industrial and business uses. The comprehensive zoning ordinance of the City of New York, the first such ordinance in the nation, set aside enough land in business and industrial zones to accommodate an eventual city population of some 340 million persons.[29] Hence, zoning appeared to be a welcome device for facilitating land speculation and validating the existing pattern of land uses.

§ 2:8   Zoning Displaces Planning

While "comprehensive zoning" proliferated, planning remained principally the province of advisory planning commissions. Few cities had created full-time planning staffs. By 1929, only 46 cities had an annual city planning budget of more than $5,000.[30] Most city plans were prepared by consultants, and typically addressed a half-dozen principal elements of city design:

1. A land use plan or zoning plan.

2. A plan for streets.

3. A plan for public transit.

4. An element addressing rail and water transportation.

5. A plan addressing parks and public recreation.

6. An element addressing civic art or civic appearance.[31]

---

[28] *Village of Euclid, Ohio v. Ambler Realty Co.,* 272 U.S. 365, 47 S. Ct. 114, 71 L. Ed. 303 (1926). *Euclid* is discussed in depth in Ch.3 and § 10.12 infra.

[29] R. Walker, The Planning Function in Urban Government 11 (1941).

[30] Principles and Practice of Urban Planning 23 (W. Goodman & E. Freund, eds. 1968).

[31] M. Scott, American City Planning Since 1890, at 228 (1969). Compare the list of required elements for local government comprehensive plans in Florida's Local Government Comprehensive Planning and Land Development Regulation Act: capital improvements; intergovernmental coordination; future land use plans; traffic circulation; general sanitary sewer, solid waste, potable water, and natural ground water aquifer re-

These plans exerted an influence upon the drafters of the first model act for planning, the Standard City Planning Enabling Act of 1928. The earlier Standard State Zoning Enabling Act had made little mention of planning. However, the Standard City Planning Enabling Act, also prepared by the U.S. Department of Commerce, addressed only city planning. The Act enabled local governments to prepare plans for five principal urban concerns (streets, public grounds, public buildings, utilities, and zoning) via a municipally-appointed planning commission:

§ 6. General Powers and Duties—It shall be the function and duty of the commission to make and adopt a master plan for the physical development of the municipality . . . [showing] the commission's recommendations for the development of said territory, including, among other things, the general location, character, and extent of streets, viaducts, subways, bridges, waterways, water fronts, boulevards, parkways, playgrounds, squares, parks, aviation fields, and other public ways . . . [and] the removal, relocation, widening, narrowing, vacating, abandonment, change of use or extension of any of the foregoing . . . as well as a zoning plan for the control of the height, area, bulk, location and use of buildings and premises. . . . The commission may from time to time amend, extend, or add to the plan.

§ 7. Purposes in View—In the preparation of such plan the commission shall make careful and comprehensive surveys and studies of present conditions and future growth of the municipality . . . . The plan shall be made with the general purpose of guiding and accomplishing a coordinated, adjusted, and harmonious development of the municipality . . . as well as efficiency and economy in the process of development. . . .

Thus, the Standard City Planning Enabling Act envisioned a more comprehensive approach to regulating land uses and providing municipal services for future growth than zoning could attempt. Zones for land uses were to be only one concern in preparation of the plan, and efficient provision of utilities, transportation and other public services figured as prominently as land use districting.

The Act, however, contributed to the confusion over the differences between city plans and zoning ordinances, by stating that the plan should include a zoning element. As a result of this confusion and because of the growing interest in zoning, many communities prepared and adopted zoning ordinances without ever making the general, comprehensive plan upon which zoning was supposed to be based. This practice tended to divert attention from the future-oriented, general policies of city planning in favor of squabbles over the details which dominated individual zoning decisions and controversies.[32]

In addition, under the Act planning was not mandatory, but optional. While the Act implied that zoning was distinct from planning, it did not expressly state that zoning should be enacted in accordance with an existing comprehensive plan document. The Standard State Zoning Enabling Act did expressly state that zoning should be en-

---

charge; conservation; recreation and open space, housing; and coastal management (if coastal). Fla. Stat. Ann. § 163.3177.

[32] Principles and Practice of Urban Planning (W. Goodman & E. Freund, eds. 1968) at 353.

acted "in accordance with a comprehensive plan,"[33] but in view of the fact that planning was optional under the Standard City Planning Enabling Act, most courts addressing this question have held that the plan with which zoning must be in accord could be found in the entirety of the zoning ordinance. A separate plan was generally not required.[34] However, a growing number of states are requiring their municipalities to prepare comprehensive plans with specific "elements" therein, and in a growing minority of these jurisdictions zoning ordinances and other land use regulations are required to be "in accordance with," or consistent with, policies and provisions of the comprehensive plan.[35]

The federal government has also supplied strong incentives to municipalities to prepare comprehensive plans. Under the Housing Act of 1949,[36] municipalities applying for federal financial assistance in slum clearance were required to prepare a comprehensive plan before funds would be provided. Later, Congress provided federal funds to municipalities to finance preparation of such plans, under the Housing Act of 1954.[37] As a result of both federal and state initiatives, many local governments across the nation now maintain planning departments and routinely prepare and revise comprehensive plans.

IV. THE PROCESS OF PLANNING COMPREHENSIVELY

§ 2:9   The Function of the Plan

Traditionally, land use regulations such as zoning and subdivision ordinances adopted by local governments were written and promulgated without reference to any prior comprehensive plan. However, in a growing number of states, the adoption of such regulatory ordinances in the absence of a general comprehensive plan may cast doubts upon the validity of the ordinances. The comprehensive plan, once viewed as primarily an advisory document to the local legislative body, is in many states becoming a legal, binding document as well as a prescription for future development patterns.

The plan serves as an overall set of goals, objectives, and policies to guide the local legislative body in its decision making in regard to the physical development of the community.[38] When particular regulatory decisions are made by the county commission or the city council, the comprehensive plan's policies, goals, and objectives may be invoked as the "rational basis" upon which local government exercises of the police power to zone must be based. Planners have encouraged the use of the comprehensive plan as a rational basis for land-use decisions, and, in an effort to promote planning as a new

---

[33] A Standard State Zoning Enabling Act, § 3 (1926): *"Purposes in view.* Such regulations shall be made in accordance with a comprehensive plan . . . . "

[34] A minority of states requires that plans be enacted and that zoning be in accordance with comprehensive plans. For a detailed discussion of this trend, see § 2:13 infra.).

[35] See § 2:14 infra; DeGrove, Planning Policy and Politics: Smart Growth and the States (2005). See also *Trail v. Terrapin Run, LLC,* 403 Md. 523, 943 A.2d 1192 (2008).

[36] 42 U.S.C.A. §§ 1441 et seq.

[37] 42 U.S.C.A. §§ 1450 to 1469(c).

[38] See, generally, Principles and Practice of Urban Planning 349 (W. Goodman & E. Freund, eds. 1968).

profession, have developed a theory of urban planning as a rational process of choice between different policy alternatives.[39]

§ 2:10   The Rational Planning Process

An overall definition of "comprehensive plan" has become necessary. The comprehensive plan is generally defined as an official public document preferably (but often not) adopted as law by the local government as a policy guide to decisions about the physical development of the community. Usually it sets forth, in a general way, using text and maps, how the leaders of local government want the community to develop in the future. The length of the future time period to be addressed by a comprehensive plan varies widely from locale to locale, and is often set by state legislation enabling or requiring local governments to plan.

The growing importance of the comprehensive plan in local land-use decisions prompted urban planning practitioners and theorists to develop a theory of planning as a "rational process." The rational, comprehensive planning process has four principal characteristics. First, it is *future-oriented,* establishing goals and objectives for future land use and development, which will be attained incrementally over time through regulations, individual decisions about zoning and rezoning, development approval or disapproval, and municipal expenditures for capital improvements such as road construction and the installation of municipal utilities.

Second, planning is *continuous,* in that the plan is intended not as a blueprint for future development which must be as carefully executed as the architect's design for a building or the engineer's plan for a sewer line, but rather as a set of policies which must be periodically reevaluated and amended to adjust to changing conditions. A plan that is written purely as a static blueprint for future development will rapidly become obsolete when circumstances change.

Third, the plan must be based upon a *determination of present and projected conditions* within the area covered by the plan. This requirement ensures that the plan is not simply a list of hoped-for civic improvements, as were many of the plans prepared during the era of the City Beautiful Movement. Substantial efforts have been made by public planning staffs, university planning departments, and planning consulting firms, to develop useful techniques for gathering data, analyzing existing conditions, and projecting future trends and conditions within the geographic area covered by a comprehensive plan. This body of methods, procedure and models is generally termed *planning methodology.*

Fourth, planning is *fair.* Traditional regulations used to control development patterns often give rise to practices that many would view as arbitrary, uncertain, and exclusionary.[40] Comprehensive planning on the state, regional, and local levels, however, advocates a "framework of collective, community-wide decision-making" so that

---

[39] For additional information on planning theory see generally Burchell and Sternlieb, Planning Theory in the 1980s (1978). For comprehensive planning, see generally, Branch, Comprehensive City Planning, Introduction & Explanation (1985); Kaiser, Godschalk, and Chapin, Urban Land Use Planning (4th ed. 1996); Nelson, Estimating Land Use and Facility Needs and Impacts (1998); Arthur C. Nelson & Robert E. Lang. The New Politics of Planning: How States and Local Governments are Coming to Common Ground on Reshaping America's Built Environment (2009); Arthur C. Nelson & Robert E. Lang, Megapolitan America: A New Vision for Understanding America's Metropolitan Geography (2011).

[40] For a discussion of exclusionary practices, see infra §§ 6:1 et seq.

landowners are treated fairly, exclusionary practices and tactics are resolved, and a greater amount of certainty is attached to the regulation of the use of land.[41]

Fifth, planning is *comprehensive*. In the past, architects, and engineers who became involved in solving urban problems, such as those attacked in the Sanitary Reform Movement, tended to identify one problem perceived to be solvable by one solution. Having targeted that problem, these early planners preferred to develop and advocate one solution, usually expressed as a static blueprint which, if fully implemented, would solve that problem. This problem-solution approach was the product of the project orientation that was typical of traditional civil engineering and architecture.

Planning theorists over the past several decades have observed that this approach has led to a phenomenon termed "disjointed incrementalism," in which successive governmental problems such as drainage, traffic circulation, or sewage treatment might be incrementally "solved" without reference to related concerns of local governments. For example, sewer systems in the era of the Sanitary Reform Movement were usually designed without reference to any overall plan for the optimum future locations, and densities, of different land uses to be served by them. Highways were often laid out without reference to any long-range plans for the types of land uses they were to serve in the future.

The recognition, starting after World War II, that the entire range of municipal land use, transportation, and growth problems were all interrelated, led to advocacy of comprehensive plans as a means of identifying the key problems in land use regulation, and recommending alternative solutions to these problems which were the product of a rational planning process. The courts have recognized this role of planning, in defining planning as concerned with:

> the physical development of the community and its environs in relation to its social and economic well-being for the fulfillment of the rightful common destiny, according to a "master plan" based on "careful and comprehensive surveys and studies of present conditions and the prospects of future growth of the municipality," and embodying scientific teachings and creative experience.[42]

The rational planning process essentially subsumes four discrete steps: *data gathering and analysis, setting of policies, plan implementation,* and *plan re-evaluation.* Rather than resulting in a final plan effective for all time, the process is instead reiterative over a period of years: re-evaluation of the plan starts the process over again, resulting in a new set of policies to be implemented, and the success of the new plan is again evaluated at a future date. Thus the rational planning process is both reiterative and continuous.

During the first step of the process, the planner preparing the comprehensive plan performs research and analysis of a wide range of present and projected physical, economic, and sociological conditions of the municipality, aided by a wide variety of planning methodologies. Statistical surveying, population forecasting, mapping of existing conditions in land use, transportation, and environmentally-sensitive areas, mathe-

---

[41] See American Planning Association Policy Guide on Smart Growth Planning Structure, Process, and Regulation, No. 7 (APA, 2002), available at http://www.planning.org/policy/guides/smartgrowth.htm.

[42] *Angermeier v. Borough of Sea Girt,* 27 N.J. 298, 142 A.2d 624, 629 (1958).

matical modeling of economic trends, analysis of traffic flows on major highways, and techniques borrowed from other professions such as economics, geography, and engineering are some of the methods employed by planners in data gathering and analysis.

The data-gathering and analysis phase of the process usually results in the identification of present and potential future concerns in land use, transportation, environment, utilities, housing, and other areas to be addressed in the plan. Thus, following the first stage of the process, the planner may identify and prioritize a range of municipal problems and opportunities which should be addressed in the policy-formation stage of the planning process.

Analysis of the data then leads naturally to the second phase, setting of policies for the plan. In this phase, the planner ceases being a data gatherer, and assumes a policy formation role. Working closely with the planning commission and sometimes the local legislative body, the planner examines and proposes alternative means of solving or averting the problems identified in the first phase of the process. Through communication with the local legislative body and the planning commission (if one exists), the planner develops a set of policies, goals, and objectives which constitute the principal, future-oriented sections of the comprehensive plan. Thus, for example, the policies may include a provision that sewage-treatment services must be expanded to accommodate new development; that the legislative body should initiate a program to stimulate new economic development in the declining downtown; and that steps should be taken to prevent further flood-prone development in low-lying areas adjoining rivers and streams.

As a supplement to these general policies, or goals, of planning, the planner may suggest means of achieving these goals. In setting the goals and recommending alternative objectives, the planner may refer to standards and principles widely-accepted in the planning profession: that excessive use of septic tanks rather than public sewers tends to pollute groundwater; that decay of the central business district leads to devaluation of the tax base; that development in flood-prone areas is detrimental to public safety by exposing buildings and their occupants to flood hazards.

The mere statement of policies and objectives will not, in itself, ensure that action is taken. Thus, the third stage of the planning process, implementation of the plan, becomes the most important stage. Implementation involves three discrete steps: developing public support for the plan by means of various forms of citizen participation and a series of public hearings and media coverage; securing adoption of the plan, either as an advisory document (as in many states) or as a legally-binding ordinance (as in a growing number of states); and action by the legislative body to implement the policies and objectives. Not only is this one of the most important stages of the planning process, but it is also one of the most difficult goals for the planner to achieve. Planners often face harsh opposition to proposed changes in development patterns. As a result it is helpful for the planner to clearly lay out the causal nexus between the implementation of the plan and positive outcomes for the community in order to gain popular support.

Upon adoption of the plan, the adopting agency espouses the policies and objectives of the plan as guidelines for daily decision-making. Thus, to return to our three examples of policies, the local legislative body will undertake revisions of the municipal zoning map to bring it into accordance with the land-use recommendations of the plan.

Similarly, the governing body may prepare plans for expansion of sewers and construction of new roads to serve new development. The legislative body may appoint a downtown revitalization authority to oversee efforts to attract new businesses back into the central business district. The governing body may authorize the city attorney to draft a new flood-plain protection ordinance prohibiting careless construction of new buildings in low-lying areas adjoining streams and rivers.[43]

V. THE LEGAL STATUS OF THE COMPREHENSIVE PLAN

§ 2:11   Plans as Optional Policy Documents

The majority of the states whose legislation enables the preparation of comprehensive plans do not *require* local governments to prepare plans, and comprehensive plans in these states are principally land use policy documents without the force of law.[44] The justification frequently given for the lack of legal status is that urban planning has not yet proven itself capable of solving urban problems, and there is no consensus among the states over what elements of urban development plans should always address. Furthermore, some commentators believe that the comprehensive plan serves an important "visionary function," unlike the regulatory function of ordinances and statutes, and that to require the plan to be a painstakingly-drafted, regulatory document would prevent plans from being suggestive and boldly-innovative.[45]

The fact that plans are usually neither mandated by state laws nor given the force of law is traceable to the standard planning and zoning legislation promulgated by the United States Department of Commerce in the 1920s. The Standard State Zoning Enabling Act required that zoning regulations and zoning decisions be made "in accordance with the comprehensive plan," but failed to address the obvious question of what a comprehensive plan was. Later, the Standard City Planning Enabling Act of 1928, while boldly setting forth suggested "elements" of comprehensive plans, and the manner in which a city might prepare and adopt them, failed to strictly define the legal relationship between plans and zoning ordinances. In addition, plans were optional under the Standard City Planning Enabling Act.[46]

Many states adopted these acts verbatim or only in slightly-altered form. The task of defining the relationship between local zoning statutes and local comprehensive plans (if one existed at all) naturally fell to the courts. In the majority of states, since a separate plan was not required, courts considering challenges to zoning ordinances as

---

[43] This synopsis of the process represents a synthesis of current theories on the planning process. For a more detailed discussion, see F. Chapin & E. Kaiser, Urban Land Use Planning 68–104 (3d ed. 1979).

[44] A slightly different approach to classifying states according to the status of comprehensive plans—or lack thereof—is found in the periodic review of comprehensive planning cases compiled by Edward J. Sullivan and published by the *Urban Lawyer:* 'These cases fall into three major categories. The first category, the 'unitary view,' reflects what still may be the majority rule, i.e., that there is no requirement for a plan that is separate from the zoning regulations and that any existing plan has no legal effect. The second category gives the plan some significance as a factor, but not the exclusive or even the most significant one, in evaluating land use regulations and actions. The weight to be given to the plan varies from state to state and from case to case. Finally, the third category comprises those cases in which the plan is described as a quasi-constitutional document that governs the regulatory ordinances and actions of the local government implementing the plan..'' Sullivan, Recent Developments in Comprehensive Planning Law, 38 Urb. Law. 685, 686–87 (2006). See also Sullivan, Recent Developments in Comprehensive Planning Law, 43 Urb. Law. 823 (2011).

[45] See DiMento, The Consistency Doctrine: Continuing Controversy, F. Strom, ed., 1982 Zoning and Planning Law Handbook 77.

[46] See § 2:8 supra.

not "in accordance with a comprehensive plan" looked to the overall land-use policies of the zoning ordinance, if an optional comprehensive plan did not exist.

The classic case taking this position is *Kozesnik v. Montgomery Township.*[47] The case arose before New Jersey enacted legislation requiring municipalities to prepare plans.[48] The existing zoning enabling legislation required zoning decisions to be "in accordance" with a plan, but the defendant township in the case had not prepared any plan. The state supreme court noted that New Jersey's zoning enabling legislation (like that of most states) predated the adoption of its planning enabling legislation. Inferring from this that the legislature could not have possibly required zoning to be in accordance with non-existent "plans," the court concluded that the plan with which zoning had to accord could "readily be revealed in . . . the zoning ordinance . . . and no more is required by the statute."[49] Thus, although it appears to be a somewhat circular reasoning process, the court was willing to measure individual zoning decisions—even those that altered the community's zoning maps—for their "accordance" with the master zoning code for the municipality, which included the maps. This amounted to no more than a process of "discovering" a comprehensive plan and policies for land use within the dictates of a zoning code.

This process, which has been followed by the majority of states,[50] does not always result in a validation of rezoning decisions when challenged. Indeed, it may be no more than a reflection of the general requirement, under substantive due process, that exercises of municipal police powers be reasonable. However, the majority position appears to be largely the result of the historical accident of zoning becoming a widespread practice before the advent of comprehensive planning. The result of this doctrine, however, has been to perpetuate the "optional" nature of comprehensive plans in most states, because zoning codes so often became the "comprehensive plan" against which individual rezoning decisions had to be measured for conformity.

In a variation on this position, the New York Superior Court in *Udell v. Haas* required that "accordance" between rezoning and the overall zoning plan be "rational" as well. Reviewing a challenge to a zoning decision regarding an individual lot of land, the court observed that:

> the comprehensive plan is the essence of zoning. Without it, there can be no rational allocation of land use. It is the insurance that the public welfare is being served and that zoning does not become nothing more than just a Gallup poll.[51]

§ 2:12   Incentive Based Comprehensive Planning

A recent development in some states which do not mandate comprehensive plans is to nonetheless strongly encourage their adoption by offering incentives to those local

---

[47] *Kozesnik v. Montgomery Tp.,* 24 N.J. 154, 131 A.2d 1 (1957).

[48] N.J. Stat. Ann. 40:55D-62 partially overruled *Kozesnik,* requiring elements of a formal plan and consistency unless set aside by a majority vote of the full membership of the governing body.

[49] 24 N.J. at 166, 131 A.2d at 7. See also *Iowa Coal Min. Co., Inc. v. Monroe County,* 494 N.W.2d 664, 669 (Iowa 1993) (plan need not be reduced to writing and can be found in ordinance itself).

[50] See 3 R. Anderson, American Law of Zoning § 21.01 et seq. (1977); but see *Forestview Homeowners Ass'n, Inc. v. Cook County,* 18 Ill. App. 3d 230, 309 N.E.2d 763 (1st Dist. 1974) (holding that the presumption of validity usually accorded zoning is shifted or weakened in the absence of a comprehensive plan).

[51] 21 N.Y.2d 463, 469, 288 N.Y.S.2d 888, 893, 235 N.E.2d 897, 900 (1968). See also *Palatine Nat. Bank v. Village of Barrington,* 177 Ill. App. 3d 839, 127 Ill. Dec. 126, 532 N.E.2d 955 (2d Dist. 1988).

governments that do adopt them. The State of Georgia, for example, has employed a framework of planning that provides for certain incentives and disincentives designed to encourage the planning process.[52] Utilizing the funding incentives directed at them, nearly all of Georgia's counties have "voluntarily" adopted comprehensive plans.[53] Illinois, in 2002, adopted the Local Planning Technical Assistance Act to encourage its local governments through funding and other incentives " to engage in planning, regulatory, and development approaches that promote and encourage comprehensive planning."[54]

§ 2:13   Plans as Mandatory Policy Documents

The traditional position, that individual zoning decisions could be compared to the general zoning code to determine whether they are "in accordance with a comprehensive plan," had a circularity of reasoning which did not make sense to planning advocates. Many urged reform of the planning enabling statutes so as to clarify the role and status of the comprehensive, or master, plan. Thus, Harvard Law School Professor Charles Haar wrote in 1955:

> While the statutory references [to planning by municipalities] are cast in large and hopeful terms, they assign no clear legal position to the plan. The legal impact of planning is significant only as it imports governmental control of physical development . . .   [and] no consistent pattern of interpretation of the effect of the plan on the real world has yet emerged in the legislation or judicial opinions . . . . The requirement in the Zoning Enabling Act that the zoning ordinance shall be made "in accordance with a comprehensive plan" has apparently carried the courts no further than requiring that the ordinance be reasonable and impartial so as to satisfy the *constitutional* conditions for the exercise of a state's police power . . . . Some acts do not even require the adoption of the master plan in order to exercise subdivision controls.[55]

Clearly, Haar said, the plan ought to have some legal significance, and it ought to be a separate document from zoning ordinances. The states that have adopted this approach, by requiring a separate comprehensive plan, have escaped from the confusion, caused by the standard planning and zoning acts, over the role of the comprehensive plan.[56] In these jurisdictions, a zoning challenge does not draw the court into a process of "discovering" a comprehensive plan inside a general zoning ordinance. As a result, in these states the comprehensive plan is the "constitution" for the jurisdiction's land use regulations. The legal concept for implementing this recently accepted status for comprehensive plans in the "consistency" requirement.[57]

---

[52] See Ga. Code Ann. § 50-8-2(a)(18).

[53] One of the incentives is the power to adopt certain impact fees. The Georgia system is described more fully infra § 9:11D.

[54] 20 Ill. Comp. Stat. Ann. 662/1.

[55] Haar, The Master Plan: An Impermanent Constitution, 20 Law & Contemp. Probs. 353, 366 (1955) (emphasis in original).

[56] Those states, by statute or by court decision, include California, Delaware, Florida, Kentucky, Maine, Nebraska, Nevada, New Jersey, Oregon, South Dakota, and Vermont. See Sullivan and Pelham, Comprehensive Planning and Growth Management, 28 Urb. Law. 819 (1996).

[57] See, generally, Sullivan, Recent Developments in Comprehensive Planning Law, 43 Urb. Law. 823 (2011).

§ 2:14   The Consistency Requirement

A.   *The Meaning of Consistency*

In a broad sense, consistency refers to the relationship between planning and land use regulations. The concept can be traced back to the Standard State Zoning Enabling Act's (SZEA) requirement that zoning be "in accordance with a comprehensive plan."[58] Controversy regarding the term's precise meaning has existed for many years.[59] Much of this confusion stems from a difference in terminology used in the SZEA, referring to a comprehensive plan, and in the Standard City Planning Enabling Act (SPEA),[60] calling for a "master plan."[61] The SPEA provided for establishment of a local planning commission whose duty was to produce a master plan, to be used as a guide for orderly future development. The master plan was meant to serve as a substantive document, stating the goals of a locality to direct subsequent implementing legislation.[62] Because the SPEA's master plan was not considered binding, and because it has not traditionally been equated with the SZEA's comprehensive plan, implementation of the consistency mandate has been slow and controversial.

An unfortunate effect of this confusion has been a judicial tendency to interpret the "in accordance with" directive as meaning nothing more than that land use regulation ordinances be comprehensive or uniform in scope and coverage. Thus many courts have looked to the zoning ordinance itself to fulfill the requirement and have regarded as sufficient elements of internal consistency and rationality within the ordinance. This is a fairly common judicial response to the consistency requirement in those jurisdictions which do not statutorily mandate consistency.[63]

The scope of the consistency doctrine today is wide, and a number of different forms of the requirement have evolved. As noted above, consistency refers to the relationship between a comprehensive plan and its implementing measures. Not only does this mean that the plan and regulations promulgated under it must be consistent, it also means, in a growing number of jurisdictions, that any development orders and permits issued must be consistent with the local plan.[64] From a practical standpoint, the plan—implementation form is probably the most important type of consistency. It is from this relation that the bulk of inconsistency challenges are mounted.[65]

---

[58] U.S. Dep't of Commerce, A Standard State Zoning Enabling Act § 3 (1926). See also supra § 2:11.

[59] See, generally, Haar, In Accordance with a Comprehensive Plan, 68 Har. L. Rev. 1154, 1158 (1955).

[60] U.S. Dep't of Commerce, Standard City Planning Enabling Act (1928).

[61] An explanatory note to the SZEA indicated the comprehensive plan's purpose: "This will prevent haphazard or piecemeal zoning. No zoning should be done without such a comprehensive study." U.S. Dep't of Commerce, Standard City Planning Enabling Act (1928) § 3.

[62] See J. DiMento, The Consistency Doctrine and the Limits of Planning, 9 n. 1 (1980). (Portions of this work are reproduced herein with the author's permission.).

[63] See, generally, J. DiMento, J. DiMento, The Consistency Doctrine and the Limits of Planning, 9 n. 1 (1980).

[64] See e.g. Cal. Gov't Code § 65567 mandating that development requiring a building permit, subdivision approval, or open space zoning be consistent with the local open space plan. Curtin & Talbert, Curtin's California Land Use and Planning Law 18 (26th ed. 2006). See, generally, the Florida Environmental Land and Water Management Act of 1972, Fla. Stat. Ann. ch. 380, in particular, § 380.04(1) (defining development) and § 380.06 (mandating local and regional review of developments of regional impact and requiring that such projects be consistent with state and local comprehensive plans before development approval).

[65] See, generally, J. DiMento, J. DiMento, The Consistency Doctrine and the Limits of Planning, 9 n. 1 (1980).

Jurisdictions that statutorily mandate planning frequently also require that the individual elements of the plan be consistent with one another. As one commentator has noted:

> [i]nternal consistency refers to compatibility within the general plan—that is, dimensions of planning are to be addressed with cognizance of other dimensions. Where several separate plan elements are mandated, for example, integration of elements is required.[66]

Thus, internal consistency requires coordination between the various elements of a plan so that they can operate in an effective and comprehensive manner.

Still another form of consistency, appearing with greater frequency, is the type mandated between local, regional, state, and even federal[67] comprehensive plans. A number of state planning acts now require this form of consistency.[68] This has caused a certain amount of controversy as some regard it as an affront on local land use autonomy.[69] Although the purpose of this form of consistency is to assure that individual local and regional plans operate in a rational and coordinated manner, the effect has been to place even greater control over local land use policy in the hands of state government.[70]

The consistency doctrine did not exist at common law and is purely a creature of statute and case law.[71] Attempts to define the concept precisely have proven largely unsuccessful. As Professor DiMento notes:

> [e]ven in those states where legislation has been passed to effect consistency, there is no generally accepted understanding of the term in affected local governments. This is certainly a common state of affairs in statutory interpretation; however, differences in terminology need to be addressed if other issues surrounding the legal effect of the comprehensive plan are to be resolved.

In California, for example, several attempts have been made to clarify the cryptic language in the consistency statutes. The major consistency mandate notes:

> A zoning ordinance shall be consistent with a city or county general plan only if:
>
> (i) The city or county has officially adopted such a plan, and

---

[66] Roddewig, Recent Developments in Land Use, Planning and Zoning, 21 Urb. Law. 769 (1989).

[67] See e.g., The National Coastal Zone Management Act of 1972, 16 U.S.C.A. § 1456(c)(1), requiring that federal activity affecting coastal zones be consistent with state management programs. Section 1456(d) makes the act cut in both directions by requiring state and local coastal activities to be consistent with the federal plan as a prerequisite to receiving federal assistance.

[68] See e.g. Cal. Gov't Code § 65030.1 (stating that local growth decisions should proceed within the framework of officially adopted state-wide goals and policies); Or. Rev. Stat. § 197.251 (creating an acknowledgement process wherein local plans are tested by a state agency for compliance with statewide planning goals); Fla. Stats. Ann. ch. 186 (the state and regional planning act, mandating state and regional plans with which local plans must be consistent).

[69] See, e.g., F. Bosselman & D. Callies, The Quiet Revolution in Land Use Controls (1971).

[70] F. Bosselman & D. Callies, The Quiet Revolution in Land Use Controls (1971); Attkisson, Note: Putting a Stop to Sprawl: State Intervention as a Tool for Growth Management, 62 Vand. L. Rev. 979 (2009).

[71] See e.g., *Fasano v. Board of County Com'rs of Washington County,* 264 Or. 574, 507 P.2d 23 (1973) (disapproved of by, Neuberger v. City of Portland, 288 Or. 585, 607 P.2d 722 (1980)).

(ii) The various land uses authorized by the ordinance are compatible with the objectives, policies, general land uses and programs specified in such a plan.[72]

This definition is neither very helpful nor clear, as zoning deals with more than just uses.[73] If consistency is limited to uses—as the definition suggests—then an ordinance permitting greater density than the plan might not be within the scope of the requirement, and as such might not be regarded as inconsistent with the plan.[74]

The difficulty in defining consistency has undoubtedly been influenced by the use of similar terms; the "in accordance with" requirement of the SZEA, for example. Other synonymous terms include "substantially consistent with," "in conformity with," "in furtherance of," "closely attuned to," and "in basic harmony with" a comprehensive plan. None of these, however, has provided much in the way of progress toward an understanding of the term's meaning.

Another uncertain aspect of the doctrine concerns the phasing of consistency. Some jurisdictions might be willing to allow as consistent a less intensive use than the one contemplated by the plan on the theory that this type of development will lead toward achievement of the planned goal; for example, single family homes in an area with a plan designation approximating multifamily residential would be considered consistent. This holding zone approach reflects the planner's awareness of timing constraints, and recognizes the validity of interim development measures not inconsistent with the plan's long-term objectives.[75] Other jurisdictions might reject this as inconsistent, favoring instead a more literal one-to-one relationship between planning and zoning. A number of different approaches to the phasing problem have been suggested: i) requiring revision of the zoning ordinance to occur when the plan is adopted, ii) resolving the question through litigation on a case-by-case basis, iii) allowing a reasonable transition period, and iv) applying the comprehensive plan in a prospective manner only.[76]

Almost every zoning challenge contains an allegation that the contested action is inconsistent with some aspect of the comprehensive plan. Until recently, however, such challenges were seldom based solely on the grounds of inconsistency. In 1973, the Oregon Supreme Court in *Fasano v. Board of County Commissioners*[77] held that the state's planning act required that zoning ordinances and decisions be consistent with the adopted comprehensive plan. The court invalidated a rezoning which was determined to be inconsistent with the comprehensive plan. *Fasano* is seen by many as one of the

---

[72] Cal. Gov't Code § 65860(a). See J. DiMento, supra note 5, at 18.

[73] See Hagman & DiMento, The Consistency Requirement in California, 30:6 Land Use L. & Zoning Dig. 5, 6 (1978); Curtin & Talbert, Curtin's California Land Use and Planning Law Ch. 2 (26th ed. 2006); Ziegler, Rathkopf's The Law of Zoning and Planning § 14:8 (4th ed.).

[74] But see *Twain Harte Homeowners Assn. v. County of Tuolumne,* 138 Cal. App. 3d 664, 188 Cal. Rptr. 233, 254 (5th Dist. 1982), where the state planning act was held to require that population density be expressed numerically, and not merely in terms of uses (e.g., dwelling units per acre).

[75] See J. DiMento, The Consistency Doctrine and the Limits of Planning (1980), at 22.

[76] See J. DiMento, The Consistency Doctrine and the Limits of Planning, 9 n. 1 (1980), at 22.

[77] *Fasano v. Board of County Com'rs of Washington County,* 264 Or. 574, 507 P.2d 23 (1973) (disapproved of by, Neuberger v. City of Portland, 288 Or. 585, 607 P.2d 722 (1980)) and (rejected by, Quinn v. Town of Dodgeville, 120 Wis. 2d 304, 354 N.W.2d 747 (Ct. App. 1984)) and (rejected by, Hampton v. Richland County, 292 S.C. 500, 357 S.E.2d 463 (Ct. App. 1987)).

earliest and strongest judicial endorsements of both consistency and comprehensive planning.[78]

Finally, an additional insight into the meaning of consistency can be gained by a consideration of some of the arguments for and against the doctrine. Proponents of consistency argue that the effectiveness of planning as a rational mechanism for allocating public resources will be weakened considerably by failure to mandate consistency. They additionally argue that planners can identify community objectives through a variety of means and present alternatives for rational and informed decisionmaking.[79] It has further been suggested that consistency helps prevent the taking challenge by putting landowners on notice well in advance as to what types of uses can be made of their property.[80] Thus proponents contend that only if consistency—the "missing link" between planning and zoning—is mandated can rational planning find any hope of successful implementation.

On the other hand, opponents of consistency argue forcefully that the doctrine creates more problems than it solves.[81] An interesting counter to one of the proponent's views is the argument that not only does mandatory consistency not prevent the taking challenge, it actually moves forward the point in time at which the taking occurs. Opponents suggest that if consistency really means that the plan controls, then planning is in reality regulatory, and such regulation results in "planning blight," potentially giving rise to claims of inverse condemnation.[82] They also contend that consistency does not prevent the spot zoning problem, but instead causes "spot planning."[83] Thus, rather than isolating planning from outside forces, consistency in reality subjects planning to the pressures of political and economic influence.[84]

The consistency debate continues today. Although only a relatively small number of states currently have legally enforceable consistency requirements,[85] it is significant that several of these—California, Florida and Oregon—are regarded as innovators in land use and environmental law. Uncertainty about its true meaning will undoubtedly continue to plague the concept, but a growing number of statutory and judicial interpretations should help make a practical understanding of the concept possible.

---

[78] The case is perhaps better known for the surprising approach it took in regard to judicial review of local land use decisions. See infra § 5:9.

[79] See, generally, Long, Making Urban Policy Useful and Corrigible, 10 Urb. Aff. Q. 379 (1975). See also J. DiMento, The Consistency Doctrine and the Limits of Planning (1980), at 45.

[80] See Housing for All Under Law: New Directions in Housing, Land Use and Planning Law, Report of the A.B.A. Advisory Comm'n on Housing and Urban Growth, 379 (Fishman ed. 1978).

[81] See, generally, Tarlock, Consistency with Adopted Land Use Plans as a Standard of Judicial Review: The Case Against, 9 Urb. L. Ann. 69 (1975).

[82] See, generally, DiMento, "But It's Only Planning": Planning and the Taking Issue in Land Development and Environmental Control Law, 1984 Zoning and Planning Law Handbook, ch. 5 (Clark Boardman 1984).

[83] Spot planning occurs when instead of adhering to the existing plan designation, a locality allows both a comprehensive plan amendment and a zoning change to occur simultaneously without valid justification. Another definition was recently suggested in an article on Florida's new growth management legislation; spot planning, the practice of post-hoc consistency by amending plans or planning maps to coincide with or follow individual rezoning approvals. Davidson, Florida Restructures State and Local Growth Management Laws, 9:5 APA Planning & Law Div. Newsletter 7, 10 (Sept. 1985).

[84] See, generally, J. DiMento, The Consistency Doctrine and the Limits of Planning (1980), ch. 3.

[85] See e.g., Cal. Gov't Code § 65860; D.C. Code § 5–414 (1981); Fla. Stat. Ann. § 163.3194; Ky. Rev. Stat. Ann. § 100.213; Neb. Rev. Stat. § 23–114.03; N.J. Stat. Ann. 40:55D-62; Or. Rev. Stat. § 197.010(1); Wash. Rev. Code Ann. § 36.70A.040.

B. Judicial Enforcement of the Consistency Requirement

As a practical matter, the meaning of consistency is in large part determined by what action courts will take for failure to meet the mandate. Remedies available include a reprimand,[86] injunctive relief, development moratoria,[87] and invalidation of the zoning ordinances.[88] It is clear that the impact of consistency will be greatly blunted unless an effective set of judicially enforceable remedies exists.[89] Thus the statutory remedies available for failure to meet the mandate will play an important role in defining consistency in a given jurisdiction.

Thus far, the most dramatic instance of judicial "enforcement" of the consistency requirement occurred in Florida as a result of the construction of a residential development which was found to be inconsistent with Martin County's comprehensive plan.[90] Neighboring property owners challenged the county board's approval of an apartment development and sought injunctive relief and removal (i.e. destruction) of the newly constructed apartment complex. Although the developer prevailed in the circuit court, the District Court of Appeal ordered a trial de novo to determine the consistency issue.[91] The Circuit Court on trial de novo issued an injunction against further development and ordered demolition of the apartments even though the loss to the developer would be approximately $3,300,000, and the loss in market value to the adjoining property owner (plaintiff) was only $26,000. On re-appeal the District Court found the development inconsistent with the comprehensive plan and held that the lower court's order to destroy the apartments was an appropriate remedy.[92] The apartments were, in fact, demolished pursuant to the court order in September of 2002.[93]

C. Consistency and the Standard of Judicial Review

Courts in states with mandatory local comprehensive planning and legally enforceable consistency requirements have begun to reexamine the traditional rules and procedures by which land use decisions are reached and judicially reviewed. Traditionally, courts have viewed zoning decisions as legislative decisions, subject to deferential review under the fairly debatable rule.[94] However, there is growing judicial recognition that local government decision-makers are not always equivalent to state and national legislatures, particularly where local governments are statutorily required to apply the standards and policies of the local plan in reaching land use decisions.[95] Challenges to the consistency of those decisions with the comprehensive plan have prompted some

---

[86] See J. DiMento, The Consistency Doctrine and the Limits of Planning (1980), at 24.

[87] *Allen v. Flathead County,* 184 Mont. 58, 601 P.2d 399 (1979).

[88] *Manley v. City of Maysville,* 528 S.W.2d 726 (Ky. 1975).

[89] See J. DiMento, The Consistency Doctrine and the Limits of Planning (1980), at 23.

[90] *Pinecrest Lakes, Inc. v. Shidel,* 795 So. 2d 191 (Fla. 4th DCA 2001).

[91] 700 So. 2d 163 (Fla. 1997).

[92] The language of Judge Farmer indicates the strong role assigned by the court to the consistency requirement: "The statute says that an affected or aggrieved party may bring an action to enjoin an inconsistent development allowed by the County under its Comprehensive Plan. The statutory rule is that if you build it, and in court it later turns out as inconsistent, it will have to come down." 795 So. 2d 191 (2001).

[93] For an analysis of the importance of the case to implementation of the consistency requirement in Florida, see Grosso, The Pinecrest Lakes Case: the Demolition Heard "Round the State" http://www. nsulaw.nova.edu/faculty/documents/Pinecrest%20Analysis.pdf. See also, Land Planning: Demolition of Buildings Permitted, 31-MAR Real Est.L.Rep 2 (2002).

[94] See infra § 5:9.

[95] See *Fasano v. Board of County Com'rs of Washington County,* 264 Or. 574, 580 (1973); § 5:9 infra.

courts to characterize certain local land use decisions as quasi-judicial, subject to greater judicial scrutiny than legislative decisions.

In *Board of County Commissioners of Brevard County v. Snyder,*[96] the Florida Supreme Court held that while comprehensive rezonings affecting a large portion of the public are legislative in nature, rezoning actions which entail application of general rules or policies to specific individuals, interests, or activities are quasi-judicial, and subject to strict scrutiny review. *Snyder* involved a landowner's request to rezone a one-half acre parcel in an area designated for residential use under the county's comprehensive plan. The parcel was zoned for single-family residences and the requested zoning classification would allow fifteen units per acre. While either classification was considered potentially consistent with the residential use designation under the comprehensive plan, the county denied the rezoning.

The court held that a landowner seeking to rezone property has the burden of proving the proposal is consistent with the comprehensive plan. Upon demonstrating such consistency, however, the landowner is not presumptively entitled to such use. Instead, the burden thereupon shifts to the local government to demonstrate that maintaining the existing zoning classification accomplishes a legitimate public purpose.[97]

In 1997, Florida courts shed further light on the distinction between planning and zoning explaining the scope of judicial review with respect to amendments of local comprehensive plans. In *Martin County v. Yusem,*[98] the Florida Supreme Court held that amendments to a comprehensive land use plan are legislative decisions subject to the fairly debatable standard of review. The court further held that the fairly debatable standard applied even when such plan amendments are being sought as part of a rezoning application in respect to only one piece of property. The court found that amendments to a comprehensive land use plan, like the adoption of the plan itself, result in formulation of policy, rather than application of policy, and, since amendments to comprehensive plans are legislative actions, the "fairly debatable" standard of review applies in these cases.

As future opinions illuminate the extent of quasi-judicial land use decision making, the courts seem likely to confront and clarify the procedural responsibilities of local governments in reaching such decisions. At present, these procedural requirements are not well-developed in state law.

§ 2:15   Smart Growth and New Urbanism

The role of comprehensive plans—and indeed of planners themselves—has intensified in the first years of the twenty-first century as a result of the "smart growth" and "new urbanism" movements.[99] Without comprehensive and legally enforceable plans

---

[96] Board of County Com'rs of Brevard County v. Snyder, 627 So. 2d 469 (Fla. 1993).

[97] Although the local government is not required to make findings of fact in denying the application for rezoning, upon review the circuit court must be shown that there was competent substantial evidence presented to the local government to support its ruling. *Board of County Com'rs of Brevard County,* 627 So. 2d at 476.

[98] *Martin County v. Yusem,* 690 So. 2d 1288 (Fla. 1997).

[99] Both movements are discussed in detail infra § 9:1. See, generally, New Urbanism: Comprehensive Report and Best Practices Guide (2001); Codifying New Urbanism (APA Planning Advisory Service, Report No.526, 2004).

conceived and implemented by and through planning techniques and principles, neither movement could exist. In fact,

> *Smart growth means using comprehensive planning* to guide, design, develop, revitalize and build communities for all that have a unique sense of community and place, preserve and enhance valuable natural and cultural resources, equitably distribute the costs and benefits of development, expand the range of transportation, employment and housing choices in a fiscally responsive manner, value long range, regional considerations of sustainability over short term incremental geographically isolated actions; and promotes public health and healthy communities.[100]

New urbanism is equally dependent on comprehensive plans and planning principles to achieve urban reconfiguration.[101]

A related recent development in regard to comprehensive plans and the planning process is the increasing importance of *regional comprehensive plans*.[102]

---

[100] American Planning Association Policy Guide on Smart Growth (adopted April 4, 2002 by Chapter Delegate Assembly and ratified April 15, 2002) [emphasis supplied]; Andres Duany et al., The Smart Growth Manual (2010).

[101] See Charter of the New Urbanism (Michael Leccese and Kathleen McCormick, ed. 2000).

[102] See infra § 9:5, Growth Management Through Regional Planning and Regulation. See also Arthur C. Nelson & Robert E. Lang, Megapolitan America: A New Vision for Understanding America's Metropolitan Geography (2011).

Chapter 3

LAND USE CONTROLS: HISTORY, SOURCES OF POWER, AND PURPOSES

Analysis

I.   INTRODUCTION

I. INTRODUCTION*

§ 3:1   Introductory Note

Public and private land use controls have a long history in Anglo/American law, dating back to at least Elizabethan times. Modern public controls, our emphasis in this book, date back to the early 20th century. While zoning, the division of land into areas according to use, building height and bulk, remains the core tool of land use control, its inability to deal with the explosion of land use development which began in the last quarter of the 20th century and gradual recognition of the environmental effects of intense development led to the adoption of new controls and significant changes in zoning itself. Though this chapter focuses primarily on zoning, other land use controls are covered in other chapters, such as the planning process, building codes, subdivision control law, and growth management systems. These are often so intertwined with zoning that drawing a clear division between them is difficult. Thus, much of what is said here relates not solely to zoning but to the land use control power in general.

Alternatives to zoning have been suggested over the years. The Model Land Development Code integrates zoning and subdivision controls and provides state oversight of local control of developments of regional impact. Drawbacks from the parochial effects of localism have prompted greater use of state and regional controls. Finally, and more fundamentally, use of the regulatory power to limit land use has been challenged. Some critics would simply, or essentially, omit government from the field, while others would zone using the power of eminent domain in combination with the police power.

II. THE HISTORY OF LAND USE CONTROLS

§ 3:2   Pre-20th Century

Land use regulations date back to colonial America, and earlier.[1] In the earliest days, colonists treated land as a community resource to be used in the public interest. For example, a 1632 Cambridge, Massachusetts ordinance provided that no buildings could be built in outlying areas until vacant spaces within the town were developed. Roofs had to be covered with slate or board rather than thatch. Heights of all buildings

---

* For more detailed discussion and more extensive citations of authority of the issues covered in this chapter, see Juergensmeyer and Roberts, Land Use Planning and Development Regulation Law, Practitioner Treatise Series (3rd ed. 2012).

[1] *Tahoe-Sierra Preservation Council, Inc. v. Tahoe Regional Planning Agency,* 535 U.S. 302, 122 S. Ct. 1465, 1494, 152 L. Ed. 2d 517 (2002) (Rehnquist, C.J., dissenting).

had to be the same. Lots were forfeited if not built on in six months. Finally, buildings could only be erected with the consent of the mayor.[2]

The Cambridge ordinance is typical of laws found throughout colonial America. Many restricted the location of dwellings, imposed affirmative obligations of use, compelled the fencing of agricultural land, required owners of wetlands to share the cost of drainage projects, and allowed the public to hunt on private land.[3] Over the following centuries, land use ordinances were enacted to deal with specific problems. For example, they excluded certain kinds of buildings and uses from particular areas of the city, such as wooden buildings, horse stables, and cemeteries, and imposed bulk requirements providing for setbacks and yards, and set height limits.

§ 3:3   Comprehensive Zoning

Zoning became prevalent in the 20th century. New York City enacted the first comprehensive zoning ordinance in 1916. It was comprehensive in the sense that it classified uses and created zones for all uses, which zones were then mapped, and it included height and bulk controls. Four years after enactment, the ordinance was upheld in *Lincoln Trust Co. v. Williams Building Corporation.*[4]

Zoning proved enormously popular and spread rapidly. By the time the Supreme Court upheld its constitutionality in 1926 in *Village of Euclid v. Ambler Realty Co.,*[5] some 564 cities and towns had enacted zoning.[6] After the *Euclid* decision, so-called Euclidean or use zoning swept the country. The zoning was Euclidean in two senses—the kind of zoning adopted was similar to that used in the Village of Euclid—and the landscape was divided into a geometric pattern of use districts.

While the Euclidean origins of most present-day zoning ordinances can be recognized, there have been many changes. Most notably, they allow for a flexibility in the development approval process not present in early ordinances. Basic use zoning and the flexibility devices used today are discussed in Chapter 4.

§ 3:4   Early Constitutional History of Zoning

A.   Pre-Comprehensive Zoning Cases

The Supreme Court decided a number of land use cases on its way to sustaining comprehensive zoning. From 1885 to 1922, the Court upheld a San Francisco ordinance restricting the hours of operation of laundries in certain locations,[7] but invalidated another ordinance prohibiting laundries in wooden buildings unless permission was obtained from the Board of Supervisors, where it was applied exclusively against Chinese.[8] The Court upheld an ordinance designating certain areas of a city for prostitu-

---

[2] The ordinance is reprinted in Gallagher, Report of Committee on Zoning and Planning, 18 NIMLO Mun. L. Rev. 373 (1955).

[3] Hart, Colonial Land Use Law and Its Significance for Modern Takings Doctrine, 109 Harv. L. Rev. 1252 (1996).

[4] Lincoln Trust Co. v. Williams Bldg. Corporation, 229 N.Y 313, 128 N.E. 209 (1920).

[5] *Village of Euclid, Ohio v. Ambler Realty Co.,* 272 U.S. 365, 47 S. Ct. 114, 71 L. Ed. 303 (1926).

[6] See supra § 2:7.

[7] *Barbier v. Connolly,* 113 U.S. 27, 5 S. Ct. 357, 28 L. Ed. 923 (1884); *Soon Hing v. Crowley,* 113 U.S. 703, 5 S. Ct. 730, 28 L. Ed. 1145 (1885).

[8] *Yick Wo v. Hopkins,* 118 U.S. 356, 6 S. Ct. 1064, 30 L. Ed. 220 (1886).

tion,[9] a Massachusetts statute setting height limitations in Boston,[10] and an ordinance precluding further burials in existing cemeteries.[11] The Court also invalidated an ordinance allowing neighbors to establish setback lines,[12] upheld an ordinance excluding stables from a commercial district,[13] upheld a Los Angeles regulation that precluded the operation of an existing brickyard within an area zoned to exclude them,[14] upheld an ordinance prohibiting signs in residential neighborhoods unless neighbors consented,[15] held invalid race-based zoning,[16] upheld an ordinance that precluded the storage of oil and gasoline within 300 feet of a dwelling house,[17] and invalidated a state statute that banned underground coal mining where it would cause subsidence of homes.[18]

In sum, during this turn of the century era, the Court found that the police power was "one of the most essential powers of government-one that is the least limitable. * * * * There must be progress, [said the Court,] and if in its march private interests are in the way, they must yield to the good of the community."[19] Regulations, however, did have a constitutional limit, and if they went "too far," they would be recognized as takings.[20]

B. *Constitutional Parameters of Comprehensive Zoning:* **Euclid** *and* **Nectow**

While the string of late nineteenth and early 20th century cases noted above demonstrated the Court's view that the police power could be used to impose significant limitations on land use, there was still some doubt as to the validity of a comprehensive land use control system. In the early 1920s, several state courts addressed the issue, and, though most had upheld comprehensive zoning, some found it invalid, generally on the basis that it interfered with the free market.[21]

In 1926 the Court handed down the seminal land use decision of *Village of Euclid v. Ambler Realty Co.,*[22] where against a facial attack it upheld the general validity of an ordinance that set use, height, and bulk restrictions for an entire town. Key to the case was the use of a deferential standard of judicial review of municipal zoning. Urbanization, said the Court, had brought a set of problems that justified governmental intervention to protect the public. While there could be differences of opinion on the separation of residential, commercial, and industrial use in specific situations, as a general proposition the separation of uses made sense. Furthermore, said the Court, if all that

---

[9] *L'Hote v. City of New Orleans,* 177 U.S. 587, 20 S. Ct. 788, 44 L. Ed. 899 (1900).

[10] *Welch v. Swasey,* 214 U.S. 91, 29 S. Ct. 567, 53 L. Ed. 923 (1909).

[11] Laurel Hill Cemetery v. City and County of San Francisco, 216 U.S. 358, 30 S. Ct. 301, 54 L. Ed. 515 (1910).

[12] *Eubank v. City of Richmond,* 226 U.S. 137, 33 S. Ct. 76, 57 L. Ed. 156 (1912).

[13] *Reinman v. City of Little Rock,* 237 U.S. 171, 35 S. Ct. 511, 59 L. Ed. 900 (1915).

[14] *Hadacheck v. Sebastian,* 239 U.S. 394, 36 S. Ct. 143, 60 L. Ed. 348 (1915).

[15] *Thomas Cusack Co. v. City of Chicago,* 242 U.S. 526, 37 S. Ct. 190, 61 L. Ed. 472 (1917).

[16] *Buchanan v. Warley,* 245 U.S. 60, 38 S. Ct. 16, 62 L. Ed. 149 (1917).

[17] Pierce Oil Corp. v. City of Hope, 248 U.S. 498, 39 S. Ct. 172, 63 L. Ed. 381 (1919).

[18] *Pennsylvania Coal Co. v. Mahon,* 260 U.S. 393, 43 S. Ct. 158, 67 L. Ed. 322 (1922).

[19] *Hadacheck v. Sebastian,* 239 U.S. 394, 36 S. Ct. 143, 60 L. Ed. 348 (1915).

[20] *Pennsylvania Coal Co. v. Mahon,* 260 U.S. 393, 415, 43 S. Ct. 158, 160, 67 L. Ed. 322 (1922). See infra §§ 10:1 et seq. for discussion of constitutional issues.

[21] *Village of Euclid, Ohio v. Ambler Realty Co.,* 272 U.S. 365, 390, 47 S. Ct. 114, 119, 71 L. Ed. 303, (1926), discussing state court cases.

[22] *Village of Euclid, Ohio v. Ambler Realty Co.,* 272 U.S. 365, 47 S. Ct. 114, 71 L. Ed. 303 (1926).

could be said of a law was that it was "fairly debatable, the legislative judgment must be allowed to control."[23]

The Court tempered the reach of *Euclid* two years later in *Nectow v. City of Cambridge,*[24] when it held a zoning ordinance invalid as applied to a particular parcel because it found that the public good was not promoted by the zoning classification. In the end, though, it was the deferential review of *Euclid* rather than the closer scrutiny of *Nectow* that created the climate that allowed comprehensive zoning to flourish.[25]

C. The Current Generation of Cases

After setting constitutional guidelines for zoning in the 1920s, for almost fifty years the Court did not address zoning issues. Since the early 1970s, however, the Court has acted on a wide array of land use and zoning controls under the First Amendment's speech clause, the Fifth Amendment's takings clause, the 14th Amendment's due process and equal protection clauses, and the commerce clause. These developments are covered in detail in Chapter 10.

III. SOURCES OF POWER

§ 3:5   In General

Public land use controls, including zoning, subdivision regulation, building codes and growth controls, are exercises of the police power. Though broad, this power to enact laws to promote the health, safety, morals, and general welfare is limited by the federal and state constitutions. State legislatures can delegate their power to regulate land use and by and large have done so. In the early years, almost complete power was delegated to local governments, but over the past few decades, a number of state legislatures have limited local rule and instituted statewide controls.

Among local governments, the delegated police power is distributed to municipal corporations—cities, villages and towns—and to counties. These terms generally are used inter-changeably in this book to refer to any political subdivisions that have land use control power. Limited purpose governments, such as utility districts and school districts, are seldom given the power to zone or otherwise regulate land use.

Though the source of power to control land use in most states is by way of a zoning enabling act, the power may come from other sources. In a number of states, the state constitution provides for home rule to distribute state power to local governments. Home rule power is also sometimes granted by legislation. Land use control power can also be implied from a law generally authorizing the exercise of the police power by local government. Rarely, land use control power may also be based on a doctrine of inherent powers, meaning that the mere creation of a political subdivision confers power to do the kinds of things local governments need to do, such as zone.

Generally, the power to zone is delegated to the legislative bodies of local governments. When the source is the enabling act, the power is sometimes divided among legislative and administrative bodies, such as planning commissions and boards of ad-

---

[23] 272 US. at 388, 47 S. Ct. at 118.

[24] *Nectow v. City of Cambridge,* 277 U.S. 183, 48 S. Ct. 447, 72 L. Ed. 842 (1928).

[25] See discussion infra § 10:12.

justment.[26] In many states, the people retain the power of initiative and referendum and may use them to control land use.

Finally, many states have enabling acts establishing or authorizing land use control systems for special situations, such as airport zoning, flood plain zoning, historic districting, landmark preservation, or watershed management. The following sections cover these matters in more detail.

§ 3:6   Standard Zoning Enabling Act

The popularity of Euclidean zoning was aided significantly by the fact that there was a good model: the Standard State Zoning Enabling Act (SZEA). Released in 1924, the SZEA resulted from the work of an Advisory Committee appointed by Herbert Hoover, then Secretary of Commerce.[27] Few model or uniform laws have enjoyed such widespread adoption or influence. All 50 states eventually adopted enabling acts substantially patterned on the Standard Act. Many regard the Act as outdated and some commentators suggest radical reform, but the basic provisions still apply in many states.

The first three sections of the SZEA state the purposes of zoning and define its scope.[28]

Section 1.   Grant of Power.—For the purpose of promoting health, safety, morals, or the general welfare of the community, the legislative body of cities and incorporated villages is hereby empowered to regulate and restrict the height, number of stories, and size of buildings and other structures, the percentage of lot that may be occupied, the size of yards, courts, and other open spaces, the density of population, and the location and use of buildings, structures, and land for trade, industry, residence, or other purposes.

Sec. 2.   Districts.—For any or all of said purposes the local legislative body may divide the municipality into districts of such number, shape, and area as may be deemed best suited to carry out the purposes of this act; and within such districts it may regulate and restrict the erection, construction, reconstruction, alteration, repair, or use of buildings, structures, or land. All such regulations shall be uniform for each class or kind of buildings throughout each district, but the regulations in one district may differ from those in other districts.

Sec. 3.   Purposes in View.—Such regulations shall be made in accordance with a comprehensive plan and designed to lessen congestion in the streets; to secure safety from fire, panic, and other dangers; to promote health and the general welfare; to provide adequate light and air; to prevent the overcrowding of land; to avoid undue concentration of population; to facilitate the adequate provision of transportation, water, sewerage, schools, parks, and other public requirements. Such regulations shall be made with reasonable consideration among other things, to the character of the district and its peculiar suitability for particular uses, and

---

[26] Boards of Adjustment are frequently called Boards of Appeal.

[27] See Edward M. Bassett, Zoning: The Laws, Administration, and Court Decisions During the First Twenty Years 28–29 (1940).

[28] Dep't of Commerce (1926). The Act, with official commentary, is reprinted in full in 8 Zoning and Land Use Controls § 53.01[1] (P. Rohan and E. Kelly eds. 1997).

with a view to conserving the value of buildings and encouraging the most appropriate use of land throughout such municipality.

Subsequent sections provide a procedure for adopting zoning and making amendments, including provision for protest by neighbors. The Act calls for the establishment of a zoning or planning commission, which makes recommendations on zoning. The Act also permits the establishment of a Board of Adjustment to hear appeals from enforcement of the ordinance, to hear and decide special exceptions (i.e., special permits) and to grant variances. Finally, the Act contains provisions for enforcement of the regulations.

The American Planning Association, which began a "Growing Smart" Project in 1994 to update the standard planning and zoning enabling acts of the 1920s,[29] has a created the Growing Smart Legislative Guidebook with various model statutes.[30] The Association has published drafts of model smart growth codes covering such topics as mixed-use, town centers, affordable housing density bonuses, a unified development permit review process, transferable development rights, cluster development, and pedestrian overlay districts.[31] Despite the SZEA's shortcomings, many states still use it, although they have enacted piecemeal modifications over the years.

In addition to ultra vires challenges to zoning enactments that fall outside the scope of the enabling act,[32] zoning can also be held invalid if the procedures established by the enabling act are not followed.

§ 3:7   Inherent and Implied Powers

Local governments, as creatures of the state, lack inherent powers, and judicial construction of local powers granted by state legislatures generally has been tight.[33] With this history of limited construction of municipal powers, it is not surprising that the power to zone is usually not implied from typical legislation conferring general police power on a municipality.[34]

Dillon's Rule, which limited municipal powers, prevailed in state courts throughout the country from the mid-nineteenth to mid-20th century and is still used in a few states today.[35] The rule provides that "a municipal corporation possesses and can exercise the following powers and no others: first, those granted in express words; second, those necessarily or fairly implied in or incident to the powers expressly granted; third, those essential to the accomplishment of the declared objects and purposes of the corporation, not simply convenient, but indispensable."[36] While the "fairly implied" lan-

---

[29] The Department of Commerce published the Standard City Planning Enabling Act in 1928.

[30] The Guidebook provides commentary with legislative alternatives and suggestions for implementation. See http://www.planning.org/growingsmart/.

[31] See http://www.planning.org/research/smartgrowth/.

[32] See infra § 3:13.

[33] See, generally, Sands, Libonati, and Martinez, Local Government Law § 4:01; Briffault, Our Localism: Part I-The Structure of Local Government Law, 90 Colum. L. Rev. 1 (1990).

[34] *M.S.W., Inc. v. Board of Zoning Appeals of Marion County,* 29 Kan. App. 2d 139, 24 P.3d 175 (2001) (municipality has no inherent power to enact zoning laws).

[35] Schefer v. City Council of City of Falls Church, 279 Va. 588, 691 S.E.2d 778, 780–81 (2010); Arnwine v. Union County Bd. of Educ, 120 S.W.3d 804, 807 (Tenn. 2003).

[36]John F. Dillon, Commentaries on the Law of Municipal Corporations, § 237 (5th ed. 1911), as quoted in *Homebuilders Ass'n of Charlotte, Inc. v. City of Charlotte,* 336 N.C. 37, 442 S.E.2d 45 (1994).

guage would have lent itself to reading grants broadly, the courts treated Dillon's Rule to dictate narrow construction.

This narrow view of local authority has been relaxed by court giving a broad reading of state enabling acts,[37] and by the establishment of home rule authority.[38] Enabling acts themselves frequently authorize liberal interpretation. One statute provides, for example, that:

> It is the policy of the General Assembly that the cities of this State should have adequate authority to execute the powers, duties, privileges, and immunities conferred upon them by law. To this end, the provisions of this Chapter and of city charters shall be broadly construed and grants of power shall be construed to include any additional and supplementary powers that are reasonably necessary or expedient to carry them into execution and effect * * *.[39]

Though Dillon's Rule has been formally rejected in most states,[40] it still lurks behind the scenes to strike on occasion. Applying the above statute, which expressly authorizes broad construction, the North Carolina supreme court invalidated a city's stormwater utility ordinance, finding that the city exceeded the grant of authority.[41]

§ 3:8   Charter

A charter is the basic document of a local government, akin to a constitution. The state legislature can confer power on a city in a charter, including zoning power.[42] Sometimes home rule powers [43] can be obtained only by adopting a charter, that is, the zoning enabling act governs unless there is a charter.

§ 3:9   Home Rule

While local governments lack inherent powers, in many states a degree of independence exists by virtue of home rule powers conferred by state constitution or state statute.[44] The courts of the various states are not in agreement as to whether home rule power authorized by state constitution or legislation is a source of zoning power.[45] In California and Ohio,[46] for example, power to make and enforce local regulations is

---

[37] *Almquist v. Town of Marshan,* 308 Minn. 52, 245 N.W.2d 819 (1976).

[38] *Home Builders Ass'n of Lincoln v. City of Lincoln,* 271 Neb. 353, 711 N.W.2d 871 (2006) (Dillon's rule does not apply to a city operating under home rule charter.); *South Carolina State Ports Authority v. Jasper County,* 368 S.C. 388, 629 S.E.2d 624 (2006). See also § 3:9.

[39] N.C. Gen. Stat. § 160A-4.

[40] Briffault, Our Localism: Part I-The Structure of Local Government Law, 90 Colum. L. Rev. 1, 8 (1990).

[41] *State v. Jones,* 350 N.C. 822, 539 S.E.2d 639 (1999).

[42] Society Created to Reduce Urban Blight (SCRUB) v. Zoning Bd. of Adjustment of City of Philadelphia, 729 A.2d 117 (Pa. Commw. Ct. 1999).

[43] See infra § 3:9.

[44] *Condominium Ass'n of Commonwealth Plaza v. City of Chicago,* 399 Ill. App. 3d 32, 338 Ill. Dec. 390, 924 N.E.2d 596 (2010).

[45] Baker and Rodriguez, Constitutional Home Rule and Judicial Scrutiny, 86 Denv. U. L. Rev. 1337 (2009).

[46] Brougher v. Board of Public Works of City and County of San Francisco, 205 Cal. 426, 271 P. 487 (1928).

interpreted as authorizing zoning, whereas in New York, the constitutional power of municipalities to enact local laws does not authorize zoning.[47]

Even where zoning power is authorized by home rule, it only applies to local matters not in conflict with state law.[48] Conflict with zoning enabling legislation is possible, particularly on procedural issues. Due to a great state interest in procedural uniformity, the latter typically controls. A state requirement that cities adopt plans has been held to be of such statewide concern that home rule cities must comply.[49] Local zoning measures often implicate substantial state interests. Thus, the Colorado Supreme Court rejected, as a home rule measure, an affordable housing mitigation ordinance that addressed a matter of mixed local and statewide concern.[50]

§ 3:10 Initiative and Referendum

In a few states, the people can enact legislation through use of the initiative, and in many states, can revoke legislative acts by referendum.

The initiative and referendum are discussed in detail in Chapter 5.

§ 3:11 Special Enabling Acts

Authority for some kinds of zoning may be provided by a separate enabling act. Airport zoning and flood plain zoning, both of which were stimulated by federal legislation, are two examples. Enabling acts have also been amended, or special acts passed, to permit the creation of districts to preserve historic and architecturally significant areas.[51]

Peculiar aspects of airport operations have led to the passage in many states of specific airport zoning enabling legislation.[52] Airport zoning has also been encouraged by the federal government, which has helped fund airport construction provided that uses adjacent to the airport are so regulated as to preclude interference with airport operation.

A state's participation in the National Flood Insurance Program requires that certain regulatory measures be adopted to exclude or limit building on flood plains.[53] While some local governments implement these requirements through general zoning enabling legislation, a number of states have specific flood plain legislation.[54]

---

[47] See *DJL Restaurant Corp. v. City of New York*, 96 N.Y.2d 91, 725 N.Y.S.2d 622, 749 N.E.2d 186 (2001).

[48] Rispo Realty & Development Co. v. City of Parma, 55 Ohio St. 3d 101, 564 N.E.2d 425 (1990).

[49] *City of Los Angeles v. State of California*, 138 Cal. App. 3d 526, 187 Cal. Rptr. 893 (1982). But see *Moore v. City of Boulder*, 29 Colo. App. 248, 484 P.2d 134 (App. 1971) (low cost housing a matter of purely local concern).

[50] Town of Telluride v. Lot Thirty-Four Venture, L.L.C., 3 P.3d 30 (Colo. 2000).

[51] See, e.g., Mass. Gen. Laws Ann. ch. 40C, § 2; Mo. Ann. Stat. § 89.040.

[52] See e.g., Cal. Gov't Code §§ 50485 to 50485.14. See also infra § 4:29 for discussion on zoning for airports.

[53] 42 U.S.C.A. §§ 4001 et seq. See infra § 11:16.

[54] See, e.g., Ala. Code §§ 11–19–1, et. seq.

§ 3:12　Geographical Reach

A.　*Extraterritorial Zoning*

The Standard Zoning Enabling Act did not provide for extraterritorial zoning. The act also only empowered municipalities to zone. Counties were excluded, and without county power to zone, the fringes of city areas could be developed without zoning control. The power to zone eventually was extended to counties in most states, but extraterritorial concerns persisted.

Some states grant the power to zone extraterritorially.[55] Such power is frequently conferred only on larger cities and is limited in terms of miles from the city.[56] It may be permitted only where the county does not zone or where the county approves. In metropolitan areas, overlapping extraterritorial jurisdiction is usually solved by limiting power to points equidistant between the municipalities exercising the power. Regionalization of zoning in metropolitan areas remains a major problem, and the prospective loss of zoning power is one of the major reasons why municipalities in metropolitan areas resist metropolitan government. The extraterritorial impact of a local exclusionary ordinance is discussed in Chapter 6.

B.　*Annexation and Prezoning*

If extraterritorial zoning power is lacking, problems can arise upon annexation. Previous zoning regulations usually terminate upon annexation, leaving the land unzoned.[57] While the area can now be zoned, uses inconsistent with the plan for the area may become vested in the time that it takes to implement new zoning.

The Standard Zoning Enabling Act created no mechanism for zoning territory in advance of annexation, and states have handled the problem in a variety of ways. In California, cities are permitted to prezone territory to be annexed so that the zoning ordinance takes effect immediately upon annexation.[58] A zoning ordinance also may be part of the annexation ordinance.[59] Interim zoning also has been used. In other states, statutes provide that upon annexation the area, if already zoned, will retain that classification for a period of time.[60] Ordinances sometimes provide that upon annexation the territory is automatically zoned to the most restrictive zone available under the zoning ordinance, pending reclassification.

IV. PURPOSES

§ 3:13　In General

The purposes for which zoning may be enacted are as broad as the source of power from the state allows. Whether by enabling act or home rule, the power may extend to the full limits of the police power of the state, or it may be more limited.

---

[55] Wis. Stat. § 62.23(7a). See *Village of DeForest v. County of Dane,* 211 Wis. 2d 804, 565 N.W.2d 296 (Ct. App. 1997).

[56] See, e.g., Ark. Code Ann. § 14–56–413.

[57] Ben Lomond, Inc. v. City of Idaho Falls, 92 Idaho 595, 448 P.2d 209 (1968).

[58] Cal. Gov't Code § 65859.

[59] *Beshore v. Town of Bel Air,* 237 Md. 398, 206 A.2d 678 (1965).

[60] Ohio Rev. Code §§ 303.18, 519. 08.

Section 1 of the Standard Act broadly grants the power to zone to municipalities "for the purpose of promoting health, safety, morals, or the general welfare of the community." Section 3, set out above,[61] then lists various "purposes in view." Official commentary to the act observes that Section 1 "defined and limited the powers" conferred, while Section 3 "contain[ed] a direction from the [legislature] as to the purposes * * * [and] constitut[ed] the 'atmosphere' under which zoning [was] to be done."[62] The New York Court of Appeals has read Section 1 as merely providing the "constitutional predicate" for zoning, and not as conferring the full police power of the state. To be valid, a zoning ordinance must be authorized, expressly or implicitly, by Section 3.[63]

Zoning may be invalid because it is beyond the power conferred by the enabling act.[64] The general language of the SZEA has led some courts to judge ultra vires challenges by reference to a reasonableness test that is the same as that used to determine whether an act is beyond the police power. This finds support not only in the fact that Section 1 of the SZEA provides a grant of power in language that equals the full reach of the police power, but in the long list of "purposes in view" of Section 3. Additional leeway exists since most courts will imply powers that are fairly related, or incident, to powers expressly granted.[65]

Courts have upheld numerous ordinances that lack precise grounding in the "purposes in view" list. In *Golden v. Planning Board of Town of Ramapo,*[8] the court found that an ordinance that limited growth based on the availability of public services and infrastructure for an 18 year period was within the Standard Act's language that permits zoning "to avoid undue concentration of population [and] to facilitate the adequate provision of transportation, water, sewerage, schools, [and] parks, * * *."[66] Single-use zoning covering an entire municipality has been upheld even though a narrow reading of the enabling act arguably requires multiple districts.[67] Conditional zoning has also been upheld despite the lack of express language authorizing such a technique.[68]

Where a zoning ordinance is unrelated to the achievement of land use objectives, it will be invalidated. For example, a moratorium imposed on cellular telephone antennas enacted for the health of a village's residents was found to be outside the enabling act where there was not a scintilla of evidence to support the claim of a health hazard.[69] Revocation of a permit to operate a nursing home to "quell community opposition"[70] or to prevent riots[71] also has been held outside the enabling act.

---

[61] See supra § 3:6.

[62] SZEA, § 3, n. 21.

[63] *Golden v. Planning Bd. of Town of Ramapo,* 30 N.Y.2d 359, 334 N.Y.S.2d 138, 285 N.E.2d 291 (1972).

[64] An ordinance may be sustained under another source of power. See, e.g., *T.J.R. Holding Co., Inc. v. Alachua County,* 617 So. 2d 798 (Fla. 1st DCA 1993).

[65] *Giger v. City of Omaha,* 232 Neb. 676, 442 N.W.2d 182, 193 (1989).

[8] *Golden v. Planning Bd. of Town of Ramapo,* 30 N.Y.2d 359, 334 N.Y.S.2d 138, 285 N.E.2d 291 (1972).

[66] SZEA § 3.

[67] *Valley View Village v. Proffett,* 221 F.2d 412, 416 (6th Cir. 1955). See discussion infra § 6:9 for contrary authority.

[68] *Giger v. City of Omaha,* 232 Neb. 676, 442 N.W.2d 182 (1989).

[69] Cellular Telephone Co. v. Village of Tarrytown, 209 A.D.2d 57, 624 N.Y.S.2d 170 (1995).

[70] *Belle Harbor Realty Corp. v. Kerr,* 35 N.Y.2d 507, 364 N.Y.S.2d 160, 323 N.E.2d 697 (1974).

[71] *DeSena v. Guide,* 24 A.D.2d 165, 265 N.Y.S.2d 239 (1965).

Regardless of the breadth of the delegated power, zoning for a particular purpose may be invalid because the exercise of power constitutes an act that is beyond the scope of the police power. For example, if zoning is exercised to lower the market value of property so that a governmental body can acquire it more cheaply by eminent domain, exercise of the power for that purpose would be unconstitutional.[72]

In the sections that follow, some of the purposes of zoning are considered in further detail. A particular zoning action often effectuates several purposes and the purposes often overlap.

§ 3:14   Preservation of Property Values

The preservation of property values is often cited as an important, if not primary, purpose of zoning. While preservation is not an explicitly stated purpose, the Standard Zoning Enabling Act does speak of "conserving values." While none would likely quarrel with the preservation of value as a legitimate factor in zoning, it cannot stand alone. Value is a consequence of action or inaction, and it is the action or inaction that matters. Nonetheless, some courts say that is an independent interest. In a leading case in the area of aesthetic controls, the Wisconsin Supreme Court stated that "[a]nything that tends to destroy property values of the inhabitants of the village necessarily adversely affects the prosperity, and therefore the general welfare, of the entire village,"[73] is within the reach of the zoning power. The court's statement goes too far, and fails to recognize that one must ask what it is that affects value, and whether the regulation of that activity or occurrence is valid. That which causes the value to go down might be a commercial use in a residential neighborhood or the building of an architecturally unusual structure. It also might be the fact that a controversial radio talk show host wants to move into the neighborhood or that a nonmainstream religious group wishes to establish a place of worship in a neighborhood where other religious uses are located. The former, but not the latter two, could be restricted.[74]

Courts ought not allow a goal to preserve property values to obscure an unarticulated illegitimate motive. The Michigan Supreme Court recognized this when it held that the "conservation of property values is not by itself made a proper sole objective for the exercise of police power under the statute."[75] The court proceeded to invalidate an ordinance specifying a minimum house size enacted solely to preserve the value of existing homes.

The mere fact that zoning depresses values of particular buildings or parcels does not render it invalid.[76] Similarly, the zoning of a parcel can be valid though the value of neighboring property is adversely affected by the zoning.[77] In any event, to the extent zoning is effective, the sum total of real property values in a city should be increased by orderly rather than haphazard development.

The "maintenance of property values" purpose is sometimes used to support zoning that preserves the property tax base and to justify controls designed to preserve or

---

[72] See, e.g., *Robyns v. City of Dearborn,* 341 Mich. 495, 67 N.W.2d 718 (1954).

[73] State ex rel. Saveland Park Holding Corp. v. Wieland, 269 Wis. 262, 69 N.W.2d 217, 224 (1955).

[74] See infra §§ 10:12, 10:14, and 10:18.

[75] *Elizabeth Lake Estates v. Waterford Tp.,* 317 Mich. 359, 26 N.W.2d 788, 792 (1947).

[76] Parking Ass'n of Georgia, Inc. v. City of Atlanta, Ga., 264 Ga. 764, 450 S.E.2d 200 (1994).

[77] *Fritts v. City of Ashland,* 348 S.W.2d 712 (Ky. 1961).

promote aesthetics, or historic or natural areas. These matters are discussed separately.[78]

§ 3:15   Preservation of Character and Aesthetics

The Standard Act indicates that the zoning should take into consideration the character of the district. "Character" is a vague and loaded term. It may refer to the physical appearance of an area to justify architectural or other aesthetic controls.[79] It also may be "code" language to reflect "snob zoning," to exclude housing for persons of low and moderate income. The validity of such exclusionary ordinances is explored in Chapter 6.

Some ordinances indicate that zoning is to stabilize neighborhoods. Though the phrase is not in the Standard Act, perhaps the "character" language implies that zoning should not upset the status quo. Neighbors unhappy with a proposed zoning change often argue that they have a right to have the zoning affecting them remain unchanged. They do not. While zoning should provide some stability, it is not a guarantee against change.[80]

The vagueness of the "character of a district" is apparent in zoning ordinances deemed to promote aesthetics, typically the regulation of signs and the imposition of architectural controls.[81]

§ 3:16   Traffic Safety

The Standard Act provides that regulations should be made to lessen congestion in the streets and to facilitate adequate provision of transportation.[82] The location and dimension of streets are typically not controlled by zoning. However, there are several aspects of zoning related to traffic. This purpose is used to argue against nonresidential development in residential areas because of the danger to children in street crossing. The purpose is also effectuated by front yard and setback requirements, so that vision will not be impaired at street corners. Density controls, such as minimum lot sizes, can be used to lessen the amount of traffic generating activity.[83]

Off-street parking requirements are also justified to promote public safety and to maintain the traffic capacity of streets.[84] While generally held valid,[85] off-street parking requirements have been opposed because they add expense to construction and limit use of a lot for its primary purpose.[86] Subject to constitutional limitations,[87] municipalities may require the dedication of land for streets as a condition for the granting of

---

[78] See infra §§ 12:1 et seq.

[79] See infra §§ 12:1 et seq.

[80] *Lamb v. City of Monroe,* 358 Mich. 136, 99 N.W.2d 566 (1959).

[81] §§ 12:1 et seq. covers aesthetic and sign regulation in detail.

[82] Jarvis Acres, Inc. v. Zoning Commission of Town of East Hartford, 163 Conn. 41, 301 A.2d 244 (1972).

[83] Flora Realty & Inv. Co. v. City of Ladue, 362 Mo. 1025, 246 S.W.2d 771 (1952).

[84] *Grace Baptist Church v. City of Oxford,* 81 N.C. App. 678, 345 S.E.2d 242 (1986).

[85] *Stroud v. City of Aspen,* 188 Colo. 1, 532 P.2d 720 (1975).

[86] See Zoning: Residential Off-Street Parking Requirements, 71 A.L.R.4th 529.

[87] See infra § 9:8.

development permission. Such dedications relate to the purpose of lessening congestion in the streets caused by the development.

Traffic relates to zoning in at least two other ways. First, a substantial increase in traffic along a street may be a change of condition making a rezoning of a residential area proper. Second, parking is a use of land which, when not on public streets or areas, is a use of land subject to zoning regulation.

§ 3:17 Public Health

Over the years shifts occur in the conceptualization of the purposes sought to be accomplished by land use regulation. For example, "public health" has always been in the litany of police power purposes but for decades the implementation of regulations designed to protect public health were largely confined to measures such as limitation of uses in wooden building in order to reduce fire hazards or to regulate street design and location in order to encourage traffic safety. Today, thanks to the smart growth and new urbanism movements, public health is being interpreted to justify regulations designed to accomplish such goals as reduction of obesity and other sedentary life style grounded diseases by requiring—or at least encouraging—bike paths, neighborhood playgrounds, and mixed use friendly urban design to discourage automobile usage and encourage walking. This recent development is discussed in greater detail in Chapter 9.

§ 3:18 Regulation of Competition

The regulation of competition is often said to be an improper purpose of zoning,[88] but care must be taken not to overstate the matter. In one case, when a city amended its zoning ordinance to allow new types of dry cleaners using particular solvents, it delayed the effective date of the ordinance to give existing businesses a chance to adjust to the new competition. Deeming the purpose improper, the court invalidated the portion of the ordinance that delayed the effective date of the new zoning.[89] Reasoning that zoning should not be used to create a monopoly, some courts also have held zoning invalid if it does not provide space for the establishment of future competitive businesses.[90] On the other hand, the mere act of districting has some effect on competition,[91] and the fact that the control of competition was a factor in the zoning of an area will not necessarily be fatal. An ordinance excluding small retailers from operating in a planned commercial zone in which large operations in the same retail business were allowed was held legitimate since its purpose was to preserve economic viability of the downtown business district, rather than to serve any impermissible private anticompetitive purpose.[92] We discuss potential federal antitrust liability in Chapter 10.

The big box phenomenon has led to the adoption of various anti-big box measures such as architectural controls, size limitations,[93] minimum wage and benefits' laws,[94]

---

[88] See, e.g., *Coleman v. Southwood Realty Co.,* 271 So. 2d 742 (Miss. 1973).

[89] *Wyatt v. City of Pensacola,* 196 So. 2d 777 (Fla. 1st DCA 1967).

[90] *In re White,* 195 Cal. 516, 234 P. 396 (1925).

[91] *City of Columbia v. Omni Outdoor Advertising, Inc.,* 499 U.S. 365, 111 S. Ct. 1344, 113 L. Ed. 2d 382 (1991).

[92] *Hernandez v. City of Hanford,* 41 Cal. 4th 279, 59 Cal. Rptr. 3d 442, 159 P.3d 33 (2007).

[93] See infra § 4:13D, discussing big box retailers in the context of building size.

and exclusions. Unsurprisingly, adversely affected big box stores object to and often challenge such regulations. In *Wal-Mart Stores, Inc. v. City of Turlock*,[95] the anti-competitive effect of an ordinance banning discount superstores did not lead to its invalidation. The court found it was rationally related to the public welfare inasmuch as it was designed to protect against urban and suburban decay, increased traffic, and reduced air quality.[96]

If the exclusionary effect of an ordinance is incidental to an otherwise legitimate zoning purpose, it will be held valid.[97] The desire to achieve stability and balance in the provision of services is a legitimate goal, even though competition is suppressed.[98] Furthermore, a zoning ordinance enacted pursuant to a comprehensive plan is more likely to survive attack.[99]

The improper regulation of competition argument is often used to attack spacing requirements between such uses as gasoline stations and bars.[100] Similarly, spacing requirements may be upheld for gasoline stations on the grounds of an undesirable increase of traffic or fire hazards, or even on the ground that there are already a sufficient number of stations in the area to serve the public need.[101]

§ 3:19 Fiscal Zoning to Increase Tax Base

Fiscal zoning to increase the tax base, provide for employment, or otherwise plan the local economy has met with mixed reaction in the courts. In some states the enabling act provides that protecting or enhancing the tax base is a purpose of zoning.[102] In those states with the SZEA, which has no express provision regarding tax considerations, the purpose might be inferred from the "conserving values" clause.[103] A non-fiscal purpose also may be found to support zoning that is alleged to be fiscally motivated.[104]

A number of courts have recognized the desire to stimulate the local economy as a valid purpose of zoning. In one case, a court upheld a rezoning based on the county's findings that the result would lead to the employment of eighty-seven people from the community and would produce tax revenues constituting 25% of the city's budget.[105]

For many courts, the goal of increasing the tax base and providing employment opportunities is not fatal, but it cannot stand alone. There must be other legitimate

---

[94] George Lefcoe, The Regulation of Superstores: The Legality of Zoning Ordinances Emerging from the Skirmishes Between Wal-Mart and the United Food and Commercial Workers Union, 58 Ark. L. Rev. 833 (2006).

[95] *Wal-Mart Stores, Inc. v. City of Turlock*, 138 Cal. App. 4th 273, 41 Cal. Rptr. 3d 420 (2006).

[96] See also *In re Wal-Mart Stores, Inc.*, 167 Vt. 75, 702 A.2d 397 (1997); Hernandez v. City of Hanford, 2007 WL 1629830 (Cal. 2007).

[97] See *In re Wal-Mart Stores, Inc.*, 167 Vt. 75, 702 A.2d 397 (1997).

[98] *In re Wal-Mart Stores, Inc.*, 167 Vt. 75. The vast majority of states hold that one whose goal is to prevent competition with an existing business lacks standing to challenge a zoning action. *Earth Movers of Fairbanks, Inc. v. Fairbanks North Star Borough*, 865 P.2d 741, 744 (Alaska 1993) (collecting cases).

[99] *Ensign Bickford Realty Corp. v. City Council*, 68 Cal. App. 3d 467, 137 Cal. Rptr. 304 (1977).

[100] *Mazo v. City of Detroit*, 9 Mich. App. 354, 156 N.W.2d 155 (1968).

[101] *Van Sicklen v. Browne*, 15 Cal. App. 3d 122, 92 Cal. Rptr. 786 (1971).

[102] Utah Code Ann. § 10-9a-102.

[103] See supra § 3:14.

[104] *Putney v. Abington Tp.*, 176 Pa. Super. 463, 108 A.2d 134 (1954).

[105] See *Watson v. Town Council of Town of Bernalillo*, 111 N.M. 374, 805 P.2d 641 (Ct. App. 1991).

reasons.[106] Some courts, however, roundly condemn fiscal zoning, declaring it to be "totally violative of all the basic principles of zoning."[107]

Fiscal considerations often explain the use of exclusionary zoning devices, such as minimum lot sizes. The validity of such measures is discussed in Chapter 6.

§ 3:20 Promotion of Morals

It is unusual for zoning ordinances to rely expressly on morals as a purpose, and the degree to which such a purpose is permissible is uncertain. Section 1 of the Standard Act provides that local government has the power to promote morals through zoning, but Section 3 does not list morals as an express purpose. Some early cases that authorized the banning of billboards did so on the barely credible rationale that immoral activities could be conducted behind them.[108] This presumably was a makeweight argument for courts that accepted, but were unwilling to acknowledge, the fact that aesthetics was the real purpose. This was necessary since aesthetics was once deemed an improper, or inadequate, purpose for which to exercise the police power.[109]

Some zoning ordinances provide that liquor stores and bars must be a certain distance from schools and churches. In one case, a town actually created an overlay "inebriate" district.[110] Other ordinances regulate the location of sexually oriented businesses. These are arguably based, at least in part, on a morals purpose, as well as directed at the secondary effects of such uses. Municipalities that regulate adult uses on "morals" grounds run some risk of running into First Amendment violations if the measure suppresses protected speech.[111]

§ 3:21 Managing Growth

The Standard Act makes no reference to timing and sequencing controls used today to manage growth. Enabling act problems can be encountered with respect to both short and long-term timing controls.

A. Short-Term Controls: Interim Zoning[112]

When an area is not zoned or is zoned but under comprehensive study for rezoning, a significant time delay may occur from the beginning of the planning process to the ultimate adoption of the zoning ordinance.[113] Meanwhile, developers can emasculate the proposed controls by developing in a manner inconsistent with the proposed ordinance. In order to prevent such development, legislative bodies use temporary or interim zoning to freeze or stringently limit land use. The need for speedy enactment of the interim control means that standard procedural safeguards of notice, hearing, referral to planning commissions and the like are usually not possible.

---

[106] *Griswold v. City of Homer,* 925 P.2d 1015, 1023 (Alaska 1996).

[107] Concerned Citizens for McHenry, Inc. v. City of McHenry, 76 Ill. App. 3d 798, 395 N.E.2d 944, 950 (1979).

[108] St. Louis Gunning Advertisement Co. v. City of St. Louis, 235 Mo. 99, 137 S.W. 929 (1911).

[109] See infra §§ 12:1 et seq.

[110] Jachimek v. Superior Court In and For County of Maricopa, 169 Ariz. 317, 819 P.2d 487 (1991).

[111] See discussion infra § 10:18B.

[112] See related discussion infra §§ 5.28 and 9.5.

[113] See Tahoe-Sierra Preservation Council, Inc. v. Tahoe Regional Planning Agency, 535 U.S. 302, 122 S. Ct. 1465, 152 L. Ed. 2d 517 (2002).

The SZEA did not provide for temporary or interim zoning. In earlier years, some courts invalidated interim zoning for lack of express authority.[114] Other courts, recognizing that proper zoning cannot be done quickly, found implied authority for interim ordinances and upheld it where the time delay was reasonable.[115] Several states now authorize interim zoning by special legislation.[116] The acts generally limit the period of time during which the interim ordinances are effective.

B.   Long-Term Growth Management

As is true with the short-term problem of stopping development pending completion of a planning process, municipalities face long-term growth concerns. During the 1960s and 1970s, the objectives of land use control expanded to include consideration of a community's appearance, open space preservation and phased growth. At this time, zoning came under attack as being inflexible, as discouraging innovation, and inadequately dealing with environmental and housing affordability issues. New mechanisms were introduced to implement long-term growth management plans. For instance, in the leading case of *Golden v. Planning Board of Town of Ramapo,*[117] the New York Court of Appeals found that the state's enabling act, patterned after the SZEA, authorized controls on the timing and sequencing of development. A number of states specifically authorize growth management, which is covered in detail in Chapter 9.

§ 3:22   Zoning to Lower Condemnation Costs

Where zoning limits the use of land to fewer uses than those for which the market creates a demand, the value of the land is reduced. The effect of zoning on land is taken into account in determining just compensation in eminent domain proceedings.[118] If government yields to the temptation to use zoning to depress values to lower future condemnation costs, the zoning will be held invalid.[119] Since courts do not generally inquire into motives, the circumstances surrounding the zoning must be considered before concluding that the purpose of zoning was to lower values rather than some legitimate purpose. An improper purpose may be evidenced when land that is rezoned is coextensive with land to be condemned, as distinguished from zoning that affects a large number of landowners or is part of a comprehensive rezoning.[120]

Zoning and condemnation proceedings that are substantially concurrent may reveal an improper purpose. When a court suspects that zoning is being used to depress values, it may hold the zoning invalid on other grounds without giving the real basis for its decision. For example, if an "island" is rezoned for agricultural uses in an area the government intends to acquire as an airport, the court may hold it invalid spot zoning.

---

[114] *Alexander v. City of Minneapolis,* 267 Minn. 155, 125 N.W.2d 583 (1963); *State ex rel. Kramer v. Schwartz,* 336 Mo. 932, 82 S.W.2d 63 (1935).

[115] Miller v. Board of Public Works of City of Los Angeles, 195 Cal. 477, 234 P. 381 (1925).

[116] See, e.g., Colo. Rev. Stat. § 30–28–121; Utah Code Ann. § 10-9a-504.

[117] *Golden v. Planning Bd. of Town of Ramapo,* 30 N.Y.2d 359, 334 N.Y.S.2d 138, 285 N.E.2d 291 (1972).

[118] See infra § 16:12.

[119] *U.S. v. 480.00 Acres of Land,* 557 F.3d 1297 (11th Cir. 2009).

[120] *Kissinger v. City of Los Angeles,* 161 Cal. App. 2d 454, 327 P.2d 10 (1958).

Official maps, which restrict the right to build in the pathway of planned streets, parks and other public sites, and setback provisions [121] imposed so that streets can be widened without the necessity of paying for buildings, are examples of other regulations that may limit costs of acquisition in some circumstances. [122]

V. ALTERNATIVES

§ 3:23   Alternatives to Euclidean Zoning and the Standard Act

The Standard Zoning Enabling Act (SZEA) remains the basic enabling act in many states, but it, and its planning counterpart, the Standard Planning Enabling Act, are criticized as outdated. Many shortcomings in zoning enabling laws have been cured or improved upon by piecemeal changes to the SZEA. [123] There have been efforts at more revolutionary change, some more successful than others. As noted earlier, some call for deregulation, preferring to allow land use to be determined by market forces, limited only by the common law of nuisance. [124] Other alternatives are explored in the following sections.

The American Planning Association began a "Growing Smart" Project in 1994 to update the standard planning and zoning enabling acts. This led to the creation of the Growing Smart Legislative Guidebook with various model statutes. [125] The Association has published drafts of model smart growth codes covering such topics as mixed-use development, town centers, affordable housing with density bonuses, a unified development permit review process, transferable development rights, cluster development, and pedestrian overlay districts. [126]

§ 3:24   The Model Land Development Code

A major effort to modernize the land development process at one fell swoop began in 1963 when the Ford Foundation financed an American Law Institute effort to develop a model code for land development. Completed in 1976, [127] the Model Land Development Code (MLDC) deals with the physical development of land, so as to maximize social and economic objectives. [128] The MLDC is based on the same assumptions underlying the Standard State Zoning Enabling Act, (SZEA) and its companion, the Standard City Planning Enabling Act (SPEA), which provides powers for planning, control of subdivisions, official maps and regional planning. These assumptions are, first, that government should control privately initiated development rather than be the primary development agency itself as it is in some countries, and, second, that local government should exercise most of the control.

Nevertheless, the MLDC offers significant changes to the land development process. The drafters thought that changes were needed since land use was being regulat-

---

[121] See infra § 4:13.

[122] Regarding official maps, see infra § 7:9.

[123] See, e.g., Liebmann, The Modernization of Zoning: Enabling Act Revision as a Means to Reform, 23 Urb. Law. 1 (1991).

[124] See supra § 3:1. See also Krasnowiecki, Abolish Zoning, 31 Syracuse L. Rev. 719 (1980).

[125] The Guidebook provides commentary with legislative alternatives and suggestions for implementation. See http://www.planning.org/growingsmart/.

[126] http://www.planning.org/research/smartgrowth/.

[127] American Law Institute, A Model Land Development Code (1976).

[128] Model Land Development Code, Art. 3, Commentary at 111–112.

ed by standard acts, "product[s] of the twenties, that notwithstanding a mass of encrustations failed to provide the necessary guidance"[129] to the legislators, administrators, planners, developers, judges, and lawyers involved in the process. Ad hoc rulings left parties unable to predict what would be allowed. The standard acts also were based on outdated views of lot by lot development that impeded growth. The drafters intended to deal with these weaknesses and to reverse parochial decisionmaking that disregarded regional concerns.

The MLDC integrates zoning and subdivision regulations under the concept of a development ordinance and streamlines the process of obtaining development permission. The most important definition in the MLDC is that of "development," which essentially is any material change in the appearance of a parcel of land or in its shape.[130]

Land development, not planning, is the focus of the act. The position of the drafters was that comprehensive planning was desirable, but was beyond the scope of the MLDC.[131] While the Code does not mandate planning, it encourages it by providing local governments with additional powers if a plan is adopted. Regulation of the state and regional effects of local development practices is a major component of the MLDC. In the more than twenty years that have passed since promulgation of the MLDC, there has been little in the way of direct adoption. Its greatest effect has been its approach to regional controls. Early on, Florida adopted Section 7 of the Model Code that deals with control over developments of regional impact and protection for areas of critical state concern.[132] A few other states have enacted provisions dealing with specific areas that use the MLDC approach.[133] The MLDC has also been influential as persuasive authority in several leading cases supporting growth management[134] and condemning exclusionary zoning.[135]

§ 3:25 Wipeout Mitigation and Windfall Recapture

Police power controls impose losses and create gains that generally go unrecognized. In recent years there has been a spate of legislative proposals around the country to compensate landowners who suffer economic loss from land use controls.[136] While only a few have been enacted, the concern with the losses sustained persists and deters the adoption of new controls needed to protect the public welfare. A notable omission from these proposals, and usually absent from the debate, is the question of recapturing for the public the gains conferred on landowners by virtue of public improvements and government regulation. Recently, however, commentators have raised for consideration the equity of windfall recapture, often citing to the nineteenth century writings

---

[129] Model Land Development Code, Foreword at x.

[130] Model Land Development Code, § 1–202.

[131] Model Land Development Code, Art. 3, Commentary at 114.

[132] See Pelham, Regulating Developments of Regional Impact: Florida and the Model Land Development Code, 29 U. Fla. L. Rev. 789 (1977).

[133] See the Cape Cod Commission Act, 1989 Mass. Acts 716, noted in Epstein, Where Yards Are Wide: Have Land Use Planning and Law Gone Astray?, 21 Wm. & Mary Envtl. L. & Pol'y Rev. 345, 379, n. 107 (1997).

[134] *Golden v. Planning Bd. of Town of Ramapo,* 30 N.Y.2d 359, 334 N.Y.S.2d 138, 146, 285 N.E.2d 291, 297 n.6 (1972).

[135] *Southern Burlington County N.A.A.C.P. v. Mount Laurel Tp.,* 67 N.J. 151, 210, 336 A.2d 713, 743 n.132 (1975); *Associated Home Builders etc., Inc. v. City of Livermore,* 18 Cal. 3d 582, 135 Cal. Rptr. 41, 65, 557 P.2d 473, 497 (1976).

[136] See discussion of takings legislation infra § 10:11.

of Henry George, particularly his classic work Progress and Poverty, and to the late 20th century work of Donald Hagman.[137]

Donald Hagman, coauthor of the precursor to this book,[138] was an ardent student and advocate of addressing the fairness of land use controls by systems of wipeout mitigation and windfall recapture. Hagman and Dean Misczynski published through the Planners Press of the American Planning Association a major collection of essays in 1978 entitled Windfalls for Wipeouts: Land Value Capture and Compensation that serves as a major resource in the area.

§ 3:26 Wipeouts Defined and Illustrated

See Donald Hagman and Dean Misczynski, Windfalls for Wipeouts: Land Value Capture and Compensation (Planners Press 1978). See last paragraph of §3.25.

§ 3:27 Windfalls Defined and Illustrated

See Donald Hagman and Dean Misczynski, Windfalls for Wipeouts: Land Value Capture and Compensation (Planners Press 1978). See last paragraph of §3.25.

§ 3:28 Implementing Land Value Capture and Compensation Programs

See Donald Hagman and Dean Misczynski, Windfalls for Wipeouts: Land Value Capture and Compensation (Planners Press 1978). See last paragraph of §3.25.

§ 3:29 Zoning by Special Assessment Financed Eminent Domain (ZSAFED)

One windfalls and wipeouts technique goes by the name of zoning by special assessment financed eminent domain (ZSAFED). It was used in the early years of the 20th century when there were doubts about validity of zoning under the police power.[139] Under this system, when the right to develop was restricted causing an economic loss, compensation was paid. Money to pay those restricted came from assessments that were levied on land benefited by the restrictions. The practice was never widespread, and not surprisingly, when the Supreme Court held zoning via the police power valid under the constitution, its use faded quickly. There are vestiges of the practice. Some parts of Minneapolis and St. Paul, and of Kansas City, Missouri are still zoned by eminent domain.[140]

---

[137] Williams, Recovering the Full Complexity of Our Traditions: New Developments in Property Theory, 46 J. Legal Educ. 596, 606 (1996); Byrne, Ten Arguments for the Abolition of the Regulatory Takings Doctrine, 22 Ecology L.Q. 89, 126–127, n. 240 (1995).

[138] Donald G. Hagman and Julian Conrad Juergensmeyer, Urban Planning and Land Development Law (2d ed. 1986).

[139] Anderson, Zoning in Minnesota; Eminent Domain vs. Police Power, 16 Nat'l Mun. Rev. 624 (1927). See, generally, Validity and construction of "zoning with compensation" regulation, 41 A.L.R.3d 636.

[140] Minn. Stat. Ann. §§ 462.12 to 462.17. *City of Kansas City v. Kindle,* 446 S.W.2d 807, 41 A.L.R.3d 620 (Mo. 1969) (upholding such zoning).

Chapter 4

ZONING BASICS*

Analysis

I. INTRODUCTION

---

* For more detailed discussion and more extensive citations of authority of the issues covered in this chapter, see Juergensmeyer and Roberts, Land Use Planning and Development Regulation Law, Practitioner Treatise Series (3rd ed. 2012).

I.   INTRODUCTION

§ 4:1   Types of Zones: In General

The core principle of use zoning or Euclidean zoning, as it is often called, is "everything in its place." The name stems from the case in which the Court upheld the constitutionality of zoning, *Village of Euclid v. Ambler Realty Co.*[1] As James Metzenbaum, the attorney for the village, argued to the Court, "zoning is nothing more than good housekeeping."[2] Paraphrasing what the Supreme Court said in Euclid, "the pig belongs in the barnyard, not the parlor." Zoning, like nuisance law, prohibits an otherwise legitimate use from locating in the wrong place.

New York City's 1916 ordinance is usually credited as the first comprehensive zoning ordinance, but it was the 1922 Standard State Zoning Enabling Act that became the standard nationwide by the mid-1920s.[3] Indeed, the act still is used in a number of states albeit significantly augmented by other legislation.[4] While enabling acts and codes have had to respond to new development pressures in ways not envisioned in the 1920s, the kinds of regulations authorized by the Act still constitute the basic approach to controlling land use.

The Standard Act empowers a legislative body to:

---

[1] *Village of Euclid, Ohio v. Ambler Realty Co.*, 272 U.S. 365, 47 S. Ct. 114, 71 L. Ed. 303 (1926).

[2] James Metzenbaum, 1 Law of Zoning 56–60 (1955).

[3] Anderson's American Law of Zoning § 2.21 (4th ed. 2006, Kenneth H. Young ed.).

[4] See §§ 3:1 et seq.

regulate and restrict the height, number of stories, and size of buildings and other structures, the percentage of a lot that may be occupied, the size of yards, courts, and other open spaces, the density of population, and the location and use of buildings, structures and land for trade, industry, residence, or other purposes.[5]

To do so:

[T]he local legislative body may divide the municipality into districts of such number, shape and area as may be * * * best * * * and within such districts it may regulate and restrict the erection, construction, alteration, repair, or use of buildings, structures, or land.[6]

The authority provided is the basis for four kinds of controls: use, height, bulk and density. Use zones for "trade, industry, residence or other purposes" are designated and defined by the ordinance, which then incorporates a precise map showing the areas. Typically, there are several kinds of residential zones, e.g., single-family, two-family, and various multi-family classifications such as garden apartments and high-rise apartments, several kinds of office and commercial zones, and a few industrial categories. Normally, there are also specialized use zones for institutional uses, historic areas, airports, and the like. While early ordinances had few zones (New York City's 1916 ordinance had three; Euclid, Ohio's 1922 ordinance had six), it is common today to find 30 or more zones.

An ordinance may establish a variety of height limitations for structures in the various use zones. Height regulations may be stated in terms of maximum permitted heights or number of stories or both. In some instances separate height zones may be adopted. Where this is done, the height zones generally have the same boundaries as the use zones.

While height regulations control building size by vertical measurement, bulk controls primarily deal with horizontal measurements such as minimum lot size, percentage of a lot that may be occupied, and yard requirements. Ordinances generally tie bulk controls to use zones, so that the zone boundaries for all three are the same.

Use, height, and bulk provisions can control population densities. Most zoning ordinances also control density by limiting areas to use by a specific number of families or living units per acre or per lot.[7] Building or housing codes may also regulate density by establishing the number of persons who can occupy the habitable floor area based on its square footage.

Recent years have seen a move away from the focus on how land is used to how it looks, i.e., that form is more important than use. Form based zoning is discussed infra, Ch. 8.2 B, under "Smart Growth and New Urbanism Codes."

---

[5] Standard State Zoning Enabling Act (SZEA) U.S. Dept. Commerce (1926).

[6] Id, at § 2.

[7] *Conlin v. Scio Tp.,* 262 Mich. App. 379, 686 N.W.2d 16 (2004) (density restrictions upheld).

II. USE ZONES

§ 4:2   Use Zoning

A. *In General*

Operating from the "everything in its place" principle, zoning is the comprehensive division of a city into different use zones. Use zoning is also known as Euclidean zoning, taking the name from the leading case of *Village of Euclid v. Ambler Realty Co.,*[8] which upheld its validity. While use zoning has its detractors [9] and is typically supplemented by other techniques, it remains the primary tool that local governments use to regulate land use.

In the typical zoning ordinance each zone has three varieties of uses: permitted, accessory and conditional. Ordinances may also specifically prohibit some uses.

B. *Permitted Uses*

There may be many permitted uses in a zone, any one of which may be engaged in as a matter of right within the zone. For example, the Office and Institution I District of the City of Raleigh, North Carolina lists 34 uses, beginning with accountant and ending with veterinary hospital.[10] The Buffer/Commercial District of that city allows forty-two uses, ranging from antique shops and banks to toy stores and variety stores. There are five other commercial zones in the ordinance. Many city ordinances have lists that are longer. The theory behind these groupings is that the uses are compatible and share reciprocal benefits or at least do not cast major external costs on other uses permitted in the zone.

Since it would take an imaginative drafter a long time to list every conceivable compatible use, in many ordinances the permitted use list will close with language such as "and any other similar uses." Even if the phrase is not in the ordinance, the building inspector or other administrator or administrative body may be given authority expressly or by practice to permit similar uses. Whether a particular use is similar to a use listed in the ordinance is frequently litigated.[11] Favoring free land use, courts generally construe similar use questions in favor of the least restrictive use.[12] One troubling tendency of courts when determining whether a use is permitted is to look to decisions defining the term in a non-zoning context. For example, a court permitted an ice-making plant to remain in a business district from which manufacturing was prohibited by finding the plant was not a manufacturing use. To reach this conclusion the court referred to opinions from other states involving tax issues, which had nothing to do with proper zoning considerations.[13]

---

[8] *Village of Euclid, Ohio v. Ambler Realty Co.,* 272 U.S. 365, 47 S. Ct. 114, 71 L. Ed. 303 (1926).

[9] See Ohm, Reforming Land Planning Legislation at the Dawn of the 21st Century: The Emerging Influence of Smart Growth and Livable Communities, 32 Urb. Law. 181 (2000); Haar, The Twilight of Land-Use Controls: A Paradigm Shift?, 30 U. Rich. L. Rev. 1011 (1996); Krasnowiecki, Abolish Zoning, 31 Syracuse L. Rev. 719 (1980). See also supra § 3.1.

[10] Raleigh City Code § 10–2033 (as amended 1980).

[11] See, e.g., *Appeal of Chatelain,* 164 Vt. 597, 664 A.2d 269 (1995) (an emergency medical facility held not to be "meeting hall" permitted in residential zone because it was not like other uses such as museums, art galleries, and libraries in terms of impact on neighbors.

[12] Gangemi v. Zoning Bd. of Appeals of Town of Fairfield, 255 Conn. 143, 763 A.2d 1011 (2001).

[13] *Atkinson v. City of Pierre,* 2005 SD 114, 706 N.W.2d 791 (S.D. 2005).

An ordinance may specifically prohibit a use to avoid the finding that it is similar to permitted uses. For example, if not specifically prohibited, a mobile home might be found to be a single-family dwelling allowable in a residential zone.[14] Occasionally, the lists of permitted and prohibited uses in the various zones are such that a particular use is not permitted anywhere in the city. Total exclusion of a use, however, may not be valid.[15]

C. *Regulating Use, Not Ownership*

Zoning regulates how property is used and who uses it, not who owns it or how title is held.[16] Thus, ordinances terminating nonconforming use status when the owner transfers title to the land are invalid.[17] Some courts have also rejected municipal efforts to preserve rental housing by adopting ordinances that preclude conversion of apartments to condominiums.[18]

Distinguishing between owners and non-owners has also been held invalid.[19] Thus, a New Jersey court found that a municipality could not prohibit an owner from renting residential housing. The town's goal of changing its character and demographics was not a permissible zoning measure.

The bar, however, is not absolute. The city of Provo, Utah relaxed its code to allow homes in single-family zones (where occupiers were required to be related) to rent accessory apartments to no more than four persons, related or unrelated, in order to accommodate the need for university student housing. Investors then began acquiring homes in the area, renting the principal dwelling to persons qualifying as a family and renting the accessory apartment to unrelated persons. Concluding that neighborhood stability was deteriorating, the city amended its code to require owner-occupancy of the primary unit if there was an accessory apartment. The state supreme court upheld the owner-occupancy requirement, finding it a reasonable method of accommodating the need for student housing while maintaining the residential character of the neighborhood.[20] Other courts have upheld zoning ordinances that ban short term rentals in resort towns designed to preserve the residential character of areas for permanent residents.[21]

While zoning ordinances cannot normally be based on the ownership interest in the land, they are often based on who uses the land.[22] Thus, an ordinance that zones

---

[14] See *Puls v. Meyer,* 195 Wis. 2d 680, 538 N.W.2d 860 (Ct. App. 1995) (mobile homes expressly excluded). As to the validity of excluding mobile homes, see infra § 6:5.

[15] *South Whitford Associates, Inc. v. Zoning Hearing Bd. of West Whiteland Tp.,* 157 Pa. Commw. 387, 630 A.2d 903 (1993). See infra § 6:9 as to the validity of total exclusion of particular uses.

[16] FGL & L Property Corp. v. City of Rye, 66 N.Y.2d 111, 495 N.Y.S.2d 321, 485 N.E.2d 986 (1985).

[17] *Town of Seabrook v. Tra-Sea Corp.,* 119 N.H. 937, 410 A.2d 240 (1979).

[18] *Appeal of Lowe,* 164 Vt. 167, 666 A.2d 1178 (1995).

[19] *City of Wilmington v. Hill,* 189 N.C. App. 173, 657 S.E.2d 670 (2008); *Coalition Advocating Legal Housing Options v. City of Santa Monica,* 88 Cal. App. 4th 451, 105 Cal. Rptr. 2d 802 (2001).

[20] *Anderson v. Provo City Corp.,* 2005 UT 5, 108 P.3d 701 (Utah 2005).

[21] *Ewing v. City of Carmel-By-The-Sea,* 234 Cal. App. 3d 1579, 286 Cal. Rptr. 382 (1991).

[22] *Dvorak v. City of Bloomington,* 796 N.E.2d 236 (Ind. 2003).

land for single-family use and defines family as persons who are related regulates who can use the land.[23]

§ 4:3 Cumulative and Exclusive Use Zoning

A. *Higher and Lower Use Zones*

Euclidean or use zoning creates a hierarchy of uses with the detached, single-family residence at the top level. From the highest zone, the ordinance moves down the ladder, cumulatively adding zones of lower uses. The single-family zone is the highest zone in the sense that it is the most restricted area, the one needing and deemed deserving of protection from other uses. After single-family use, a Euclidean code permits other uses, beginning with higher density residential uses, continuing on to commercial uses, and ending with heavy industrial uses at the bottom.

The phrase "highest zone" is not the equivalent of the common appraisal phrase, "the highest and best use of land," where it means the use that will confer the highest market value on the land. It refers instead to society's value of the use from a broad perspective. Land zoned for single-family use generally will have a lower value than if zoned for more intensive uses. An argument that property should be rezoned from residential to commercial because commercial use is the highest and best use of land may be considered as a factor in the rezoning request, but it is by no means determinative, and usually is not persuasive. Planning and zoning focus on the appropriate use of the land for the community and are concerned with many factors beyond maximizing the market value for each parcel.

Confusion may result from the customary practice of referring to a rezoning from commercial to residential as a "downzoning." This language does reflect the market in that the property usually will drop in value when its use becomes more restricted. In contrast, an "upzoning" refers to the value increase when the intensity of allowable uses increases. This custom is inconsistent with the hierarchical value scheme noted above that treats residential use as the highest use.[24]

B. *Intensive and Unintensive Use Zones*

An "intensive use zone" is one that permits heavy industry, or a large variety of activities or uses, high and large buildings, great densities, and requires little open space. The least intensive use zones are large lot, single-family zones and agricultural zones.

C. *Exclusive and Cumulative Use Zones*

From zoning's inception the single-family zone has been essentially an exclusive zone. Uses permitted in other zones are not permitted in the single-family zone. Protecting homes, particularly single-family homes, from nonresidential intrusions is paramount. Indeed, for many, it is the *raison d'etre* of zoning.

---

[23] See infra § 4:5. Such provisions may run afoul of state constitutional privacy rights. *Coalition Advocating Legal Housing Options v. City of Santa Monica,* 105 Cal. Rptr. 2d 802 (2001).

[24] In a very few instances, courts call a rezoning from commercial to residential an upzoning, see *Munnelly v. Town of East Hampton,* 173 A.D.2d 472, 570 N.Y.S.2d 93 (2d Dep't 1991), but the almost universal practice labels such a rezoning as a downzoning.

Under Euclidean zoning, all other zones are cumulative, that is, they permit all uses permitted in any higher, less intensive use zone and exclude uses permitted in lower, more intensive use zones.[25] For example, the light commercial zone will permit those uses permitted in single-family and multi-family zones and exclude those uses permitted in heavy commercial, light industrial and heavy industrial zones.

The anomaly of cumulative zoning is that it allows the people in the parlor to join the pigs in the barnyard. Since cumulative zoning does not preclude residences in commercial and industrial areas, it does not protect people from their own foibles. Perhaps the difference is explainable by reference to legal concerns prevalent when zoning originated. Zoning proponents, who feared courts would be inclined to declare zoning invalid on due process grounds, recognized that judges would more likely sustain such restrictions where strong and universally held values such as the sanctity of the home were involved. For all other uses, cumulative zoning represented less restraint on property, and thus was less offensive. Early zoning commissioners might also have assumed that since the land in intensive use zones would have high value, residential uses could not compete. Further, to the extent that zoning was, as often alleged, motivated by snobbery, a scheme that kept commerce and industry from upper and middle class residential enclaves, while allowing the poor and minorities to keep company with industrial and other intensive uses was consistent with the allegation. The practice has spawned an environmental justice movement with the goal of correcting or preventing such inequities.[26]

By allowing uses with significantly different characteristics in the same zone, cumulative zoning causes several problems. Sensitive land uses permitted in intensive use districts may be harmed by locating there. In turn, the harmed sensitive use may claim the intensive use is a common law nuisance.[27] While often not persuasive,[28] the possibility of this occurring may deter the establishment of more intensive uses in the very zone where the community wants them. Consequently, the trend is against cumulative zoning and in favor of creating exclusive zones for uses beyond single-family residential.

§ 4:4   Accessory Uses and Home Occupations

A   Historical Basis and Modern Status

Ordinances generally allow accessory activities that are necessary or convenient to principal, permitted uses. Edward Bassett noted that "from time immemorial,"[29] people had used parts of their homes for office and other non-residential purposes, and that from their inception, zoning codes acknowledged this tradition. Considerations of personal liberty also require concessions about what one can do at home.[30] Disagreement, nonetheless, remains as to what non-residential activities can be pursued in the home

---

[25] For a description of such a scheme, see Cunningham v. Board of Aldermen of City of Overland, 691 S.W.2d 464, 468 (Mo. App. 1985).

[26] See infra § 6:9 regarding environmental justice concerns.

[27] See infra §§ 14:1 et seq.

[28] Bove v. Donner-Hanna Coke Corp., 236 A.D. 37, 258 N.Y.S. 229 (1932).

[29] Edward Bassett, Zoning 100 (2d ed. 1940). Bassett has been described as the "father of zoning." Seymour Toll, Zoned American 143 (1969).

[30] See Roberts, The Regulation of Home Occupations Under Zoning Ordinances: Some Constitutional Considerations, 56 Temp. L.Q. 49 (1983).

without unduly harming neighbors. Such disputes may increase as the revolution in telecommunications makes it easier for people to work at home, leading to greater use of the home for nontraditional purposes. Communities must be concerned both with under-regulation, failing to adequately protect neighbors, and over-regulation, excessively restricting personal freedom.[31]

There are accessory uses in all use zones. The predominant accessory use is the home occupation. Ordinances vary in what qualifies as a home occupation, but they often allow such customary uses as sewing and clothing alterations, childcare, teaching of music, and part-time offices for doctors, lawyers, real estate agents, and hairstylists. Though a code normally lists allowable accessory uses, where it fails to enumerate them, courts have implied such rights.[32] Most disputes deal with activities in residential areas: home occupations, recreational uses (e.g., tennis courts, swimming pools),[33] and accessory residential use (e.g., relatives, boarders, servant quarters).[34] Expansions of non-residential use in residential zones by religious organizations and educational institutions are also common.[35]

B. Incidental and Customary Use

An accessory use must be subordinate or incidental to the principal use. A part-time business use allowed as accessory to residential use must be incidental to the principal home use. If the business use predominates, it is disqualified. The incidental requirement may be controlled by limitations or prohibitions on outside employees, limits on the percentage of floor space the activity can occupy, and prohibitions on the sale of products.[36]

In addition to being incidental to the principal use, accessory uses typically must be "customary" or "customarily incidental." It is an unfortunate requirement. Applying it is difficult since a strict definition precludes new uses from ever gaining legal status. For example, placing a large satellite dish in the sideyard would never qualify as customary.[37] An adult cabaret might not be deemed customarily incidental to a restaurant and bar. While those decisions may well elate some, they may also unfairly and unnecessarily prohibit activities in which people expect to be able to engage. Maintaining a stable for horses was customary at one time, and it is not clear when that status was lost, if ever. Applied with a view to the past, the requirement may confer nonconforming use status on uses that were once, but are no longer, customary. By and large, the courts have not taken that approach. One judicial method of liberalizing the customary

---

[31] See Stelle Garnett, On Castles and Commerce: Zoning Law and the Home-business Dilemma, 42 Wm. & Mary L. Rev. 1191 (2001).

[32] Graff v. Zoning Bd. of Appeals of Town of Killingworth, 277 Conn. 645, 894 A.2d 285 (2006).

[33] See Thomas v. Zoning Bd. of Adjustment of City of University Park, 241 S.W.2d 955 (Tex. Civ. App. 1951).

[34] See, e.g., *Acorn Montessori School v. Bethlehem Tp. Planning Bd.*, 380 N.J. Super. 216, 881 A.2d 784 (Law Div. 2005).

[35] See, e.g., National Cathedral Neighborhood Ass'n v. District of Columbia Bd. of Zoning Adjustment, 753 A.2d 984 (D.C. 2000).

[36] See, e.g., *Town of Sullivans Island v. Byrum,* 306 S.C. 539, 413 S.E.2d 325 (Ct. App. 1992).

[37] Local regulation of satellite dishes is partially preempted by FCC regulation. See *Hunter v. City of Whittier,* 209 Cal. App. 3d 588, 257 Cal. Rptr. 559 (1989).

requirement is to focus on a broad geographical area that reaches beyond the city to determine the customary nature of a use.[38]

At best, the customary requirement is a rough measure of compatibility: neighbors haven't complained often about the activity so it must be okay. With that lukewarm endorsement, the better course is to eliminate the customary requirement. There are better ways to measure compatibility, such as performance standards and specific limitations on outside employees, sales of goods, and limitations on hours to receive clients.

Not only is the customary requirement problematical to apply, it does not rationally advance a legitimate interest. The goal is to allow greater personal freedom of use while avoiding an adverse impact on neighbors. New uses, however, might be inoffensive and customary ones may have become offensive over time with changing tastes.

The customary requirement also unfairly discriminates against some. In one case, a court denied a barber a right to have a part time shop in his home because it found that cutting hair in the home was not customary. Sewing and cooking would be fine, said the court, but not barbering.[39] In reaching that conclusion, the court failed to take note of the inequality of the result. Although the use was incidental, posing no harm to the neighbors, the court denied the barber the ability to work at home while anyone else in the neighborhood could operate a sewing or cooking business.

C. *Accessory Residential Use*

Accessory living units are a source of affordable housing.[40] These units, often labeled accessory apartments,[41] are created by the subdivision of existing single-family homes. They may also be separate structures. While generally controlled by local ordinance, some state legislatures have preempted local control. California, for example, by statute requires that municipalities allow second units on existing single-family lots in order to help meet the need for new housing.[42] Where no provision is made to permit accessory housing, illegal conversions of single-family dwellings are common in areas where affordable housing is scarce.[43]

A common method to limit the use of accessory housing is to limit occupancy to persons who are related to the owners of the principal unit by blood, marriage, or adoption. Such restrictions, though, may run afoul of constitutional privacy rights under some state constitutions.[44]

Non-residential users may also provide accessory housing. In a recent case, for example, the Ohio supreme court held that a religious organization was permitted to es-

---

[38] See, e.g., Atlantic Refining & Marketing Co. v. Whitpain Tp. Zoning Hearing Bd., 656 A.2d 598 (Pa. Commw. Ct. 1995).

[39] *Gold v. Zoning Board of Adjustment,* 393 Pa. 401, 403, 143 A.2d 59, 60 (1958).

[40] See Weinstein, The Challenge of Providing Adequate Housing for the Elderly . . . Along with Everyone Else, 11 J.L. & Health 133, 140 (1996–97).

[41] Also known as "granny flats" and "mother-in-law units."

[42] Cal. Govt. Code § 65852.2.

[43] *Sherman v. Frazier,* 84 A.D.2d 401, 446 N.Y.S.2d 372 (1982). But see *Anderson v. Provo City Corp.,* 2005 UT 5, 108 P.3d 701 (Utah 2005), discussed supra § 4:2(C).

[44] Coalition Advocating Legal Housing Options v. City of Santa Monica, 88 Cal. App. 4th 451, 105 Cal. Rptr. 2d 802 (2001).

tablish transitional apartments for homeless women and their children in a former convent even though the convent was in a residential zone.[45]

D. *Professional Offices*

A troubling limitation in many home occupation ordinances is the allowance only for offices of "professionals." A lack of standards or the use of improper ones leads to unjustifiable discrimination. One court held that a music teacher was a professional,[46] while another court denied a management consultant that status.[47] Ordinances often expressly recognize doctors, lawyers, and clergy as "professionals." Others who want to claim status as professionals, such as real estate or insurance agents, musicians, or artists often must attempt to prove that they have specialized training, follow a code of ethics, and render a public service. These factors, derived from dictionaries defining "professional," are irrelevant to proper zoning considerations. The customer's car driven to the house of the part-time management consultant is no noisier than the car driven to the lawyer's house. Municipalities should eliminate the elitist and unnecessary requirement that the home occupation be that of a professional.

§ 4:5   Single-Family Use

A. *The Single-Family Exclusive Zone*

Preservation of the home in suburbia protected by zoning from multi-family, commercial and industrial uses, has been, and remains in many communities, the goal of zoning. As the California Supreme Court said, in upholding the exclusion of multifamily buildings from a single-family zone:

> we do not wish to unduly emphasize the single-family residence as a means of perpetuating the home life of a people, [but] a single family home [is] more desirable for the promotion and perpetuation of family life than an apartment, hotel, or flat. * * * The establishment of such districts is for the general welfare because it tends to promote and perpetuate the American home. * * * The character and quality of manhood and womanhood are in a large measure the result of the home environment.[48]

Veneration of the single-family home continues, but it has many critics who point to its tendency to increase housing costs, to consume more land and destroy more of the natural environment than necessary, to unnecessarily mandate conformity in lifestyles, and to exclude persons on socioeconomic, and sometimes racial, grounds.[49] We explore these criticisms below.[50]

---

[45] *Henley v. Youngstown Bd. of Zoning Appeals,* 90 Ohio St. 3d 142, 2000-Ohio-493, 735 N.E.2d 433 (2000).

[46] *People ex rel. Fullam v. Kelly,* 255 N.Y. 396, 175 N.E. 108 (1931).

[47] Simon v. Board of Appeals on Zoning of City of New Rochelle, 208 A.D.2d 931, 618 N.Y.S.2d 729 (1994).

[48] *Miller v. Board of Public Works of City of Los Angeles,* 195 Cal. 477, 492–93, 234 P. 381, 386–87, 38 A.L.R. 1479 (1925).

[49] See, e.g., Ziegler, The Twilight of Single-Family Zoning, 3 UCLA J. Envtl. L. & Pol'y 161 (1983); Richard F. Babcock, The Egregious Invalidity of the Exclusive Single-Family Zone, Land Use Law & Zoning Digest 4 (July 1983).

[50] Some residential exclusionary zoning practices are invalid. See infra §§ 6:1 et seq.

B. Who Constitutes a Family?

Who can legally live in a single-family zone turns on the ordinance's definition of "family." Ordinances usually define single-family use to require that persons live together as a "single housekeeping unit," or they specify that persons be related by blood, marriage, or adoption. If there is no statutory requirement that the persons be related, the test is a functional one. Some cases are easy. In one case, a court found that a married couple, their two biological children, and their foster children did not violate the family definition of a zoning ordinance because they were found to "bear the generic character of a family."[51]

Cases involving groups of unrelated persons, such as college students, are more difficult. Under an ordinance that allowed families of "one or more persons * * * who are living together as a stable and permanent living unit," 10 unrelated college students were deemed a family upon proof that they ate together, shared household chores, paid expenses from a common fund, and intended to live together for three years.[52] In contrast, another court found seven unrelated college students who shared a house for convenience and economics did not meet the statutory requirement of a relationship of a "permanent and distinct character with a demonstrable and recognizable bond characteristic of a cohesive unit."[53] Groups of unrelated adults, other than students, who live together for economic reasons or convenience, may also be challenged.[54]

The exclusion of non-traditional groups increases when municipalities define "family" to require that persons be related by blood, marriage, or adoption. In *Village of Belle Terre v. Boraas*,[55] the Supreme Court held that a municipal zoning ordinance limiting the occupancy of one-family dwellings to related persons or to groups of not more than two unrelated persons passed constitutional muster. Finding that the group of six unrelated college students presented no issue involving a fundamental right, such as association, privacy, or travel, the Court applied a relaxed standard of review, and upheld the restriction since it was conceivable that the village adopted it to secure the quality of the environment of single-family areas.

While the *Belle Terre* ordinance allowed two unrelated persons to constitute a family, there is little reason to believe an ordinance without that provision would be found unconstitutional.[56] At least one court has found that the state interest in marriage and in preservation of the biological or legal family justifies excluding unmarried couples.[57]

Critical to the validity of ordinances that ban the unrelated from living together is the determination as to whether such laws affect a fundamental right. With some success, complainants have pressed state courts to reject the reasoning of *Belle Terre*, which found no fundamental rights affected, and to interpret state constitutional pro-

---

[51] *City of White Plains v. Ferraioli*, 34 N.Y.2d 300, 357 N.Y.S.2d 449, 313 N.E.2d 756 (1974).

[52] *Borough of Glassboro v. Vallorosi*, 117 N.J. 421, 568 A.2d 888 (1990).

[53] *Stegeman v. City of Ann Arbor*, 213 Mich. App. 487, 540 N.W.2d 724 (1995).

[54] *City of Santa Barbara v. Adamson*, 27 Cal. 3d 123, 164 Cal. Rptr. 539, 610 P.2d 436, 12 A.L.R.4th 219 (1980) (12 unrelated adults in 24 room, 10 bedroom, six bathroom house protected by state right of privacy).

[55] *Village of Belle Terre v. Boraas*, 416 U.S. 1, 94 S. Ct. 1536, 39 L. Ed. 2d 797 (1974).

[56] *Hollenbaugh v. Carnegie Free Library*, 439 U.S. 1052, 99 S. Ct. 734, 58 L. Ed. 2d 713 (1978).

[57] *City of Ladue v. Horn*, 720 S.W.2d 745 (Mo. Ct. App. E.D. 1986). For a more in depth discussion of the constitutional issues, see infra §§ 10:12 and 10:14.

visions to offer more protection to alternate living arrangements. State courts are divided on the question. Several have recognized a right of unrelated persons to live together as protected under their state constitutions, and have invalidated zoning ordinances restricting the size of unrelated families.[58] More courts, however, have refused the request and, instead, followed the *Belle Terre* rationale.[59]

An ordinance that targets related persons is unlikely to survive judicial scrutiny. In *Moore v. City of East Cleveland*,[60] the Court struck down a housing code restriction that limited occupants of residences to individuals with specified degrees of consanguinity. The ordinance had the effect, in the case before the Court, of making it a crime for a grandmother to have two of her grandsons live with her since the boys had different parents. In a 5–4 decision, a plurality of justices found the definition of relatedness flawed on substantive due process grounds as an invasion of the sanctity of the family.

§ 4:6   Group Homes as Single-Family Use

Attempts to provide more normal living environments for persons in need of supervised care by placing them in group homes frequently lead to struggles with neighbors and local zoning authorities. Often, group homes for the elderly, troubled teenagers, HIV infected persons, rehabilitation centers for persons recovering from drug abuse, and halfway homes for prisoners run afoul of "single-family" definitions found in zoning codes.[61] However, recent judicial and legislative intervention limits the ability of local government to exclude such homes. The federal Fair Housing Act provides a powerful tool for those who qualify as disabled under the Act.[62]

Many single-family neighborhoods have refused to extend the welcome mat to group homes, and contentious zoning struggles often ensue when a group home seeks to "invade" a neighborhood. In some cases, the government has prosecuted neighborprotesters, or threatened them with prosecution, on the basis that the neighbors are violating the federal Fair Housing Act's proscription against intimidating or interfering with the right of the disabled to be free from discriminatory treatment in their pursuit of housing. Unsurprisingly, these prosecutions have raised First Amendment concerns.[63]

The argument in favor of allowing the disabled to live in group homes in single-family areas is that society, whether government by zoning or private parties by covenant, ought not deny such persons the opportunity to enjoy at least a semblance of a way of life that is often characterized as "the American dream." The arguments against group homes vary. While the mere fact that the individuals in a home will be unrelated seems a petty objection, others are not necessarily so. These include the number of residents, the frequency of resident turn-over, whether the residents are likely to engage in antisocial behavior, and the traffic and activity that will be generated by outside supervisors or health providers. The issue is whether or when these concerns justify relegating those who would live in the group homes to live elsewhere in town or in crowded

---

[58] See *McMinn v. Town of Oyster Bay,* 66 N.Y.2d 544, 498 N.Y.S.2d 128, 488 N.E.2d 1240 (1985).

[59] *Dvorak v. City of Bloomington,* 796 N.E.2d 236 (Ind. 2003).

[60] *Moore v. City of East Cleveland, Ohio,* 431 U.S. 494, 97 S. Ct. 1932, 52 L. Ed. 2d 531 (1977).

[61] Albert v. Zoning Hearing Bd. of North Abington Tp., 578 Pa. 439, 854 A.2d 401 (2004).

[62] See infra §§ 4:7 and 6:8.

[63] *White v. Lee,* 227 F.3d 1214 (9th Cir. 2000). See also discussion and cases infra § 5:2.

institutions or on the streets. Undoubtedly, in some instances, reasons advanced by neighbors are pre-textual, masking unexpressed prejudices based on irrational stereotyping.

Many states divest local authorities from using the zoning power to differentiate between residential use and certain types of group homes.[64] North Carolina, for example, provides that "family care homes," defined as adult care for not more than six disabled persons, are residential uses for local zoning purposes. Under the statute cities cannot require that such homes obtain special permits, but they can prohibit new homes from locating within a one-half mile radius of an existing home.[65] Even where such a statute is lacking, group homes operated by a governmental entity or licensed by the state may be immune from local zoning.

Differential zoning treatment of some group homes may be subject to exacting rational basis scrutiny. In *City of Cleburne v. Cleburne Living Center*[66], the Supreme Court held that a special permit requirement imposed on homes for the mentally retarded, but not imposed on similar semi-institutional uses, such as fraternity houses and nursing homes, violated the equal protection clause. The *Cleburne* Court refused to classify the mentally retarded as a "quasi-suspect class," which would have triggered intermediate scrutiny. Nonetheless, the Court invalidated the ordinance purportedly using the rational basis test.[67] The type of review used, however, was not the historically highly deferential conceivable basis standard, but one that required some degree of proof by the city that its treatment was justified. Numerous parties have unsuccessfully sought *Cleburne-like* review, and, for group homes, courts have reached different results using the *Cleburne* test.

The holding of *Village of Belle Terre v. Boraas,*[68] permitting the exclusion of unrelated persons, survives the *Cleburne* decision. Nothing in *Cleburne* suggests that the equal protection clause prohibits municipalities from defining "family" to include related persons only. However, some state court holdings offset the limited federal constitutional protection.[69] In defining "family," these courts apply a higher level of scrutiny than did the Court in *Belle Terre*. In one case, a lower New York court invalidated on state due process grounds an ordinance that excluded a group home for up to 10 adolescents because a rotating professional staff, rather than house parents, supervised the residents.[70] The court said that whether such a home was the functional equivalent of a biological family was irrelevant, since no limit on the unrelated could stand if there was no corresponding limit on related persons.[71]

The need for group homes for disabled persons to seek constitutional protection from stringent zoning by trying to use or expand *Cleburne* receded in importance with

---

[64] See Kanter, A Home of One's Own: The Fair Housing Amendments Act of 1988 and Housing Discrimination Against People with Mental Disabilities, 43 Am. U. L. Rev. 925, 975 (1994).

[65] N.C. Gen. Stat. § 168–22. See discussion infra § 6:8 regarding the validity of numerical limits and of such dispersal requirements under the Fair Housing Act.

[66] *City of Cleburne, Tex. v. Cleburne Living Center,* 473 U.S. 432, 105 S. Ct. 3249, 87 L. Ed. 2d 313 (1985).

[67] See infra § 10:14 regarding equal protection.

[68] Discussed supra § 4:5.

[69] See supra § 4:5.

[70] *Children's Village v. Holbrook,* 171 A.D.2d 298, 576 N.Y.S.2d 405 (1991).

[71] Id.

the protection afforded the disabled under the federal Fair Housing Amendments Act of 1988.[72]

§ 4:7 Federal Disabilities Laws and Use Zoning

A *Fair Housing Amendments Act*

Federal law limits the exercise of the zoning power with respect to persons with disabilities. The primary restraint is the Fair Housing Amendments Act of 1988 (FHAA).[73] In that act, Congress extended the protection of the 1968 Fair Housing Act to the handicapped or disabled[74] and significantly altered the legal environment for group homes. The Fair Housing Act, discussed in detail in Chapter 6,[75] has become the major vehicle used by group homes to challenge zoning ordinances that affect persons the act defines as disabled.

B. *Americans with Disabilities Act*

The Americans with Disabilities Act (ADA)[76] also limits zoning. The ADA provides that no person with a qualifying disability shall, "by reason of such disability, * * * be denied the benefits of the services, programs, or activities of a public entity, or be subjected to discrimination by such entity."[77] A public entity must make reasonable modifications in policies when necessary to avoid discrimination on the basis of disability, unless the entity can demonstrate that to do so would fundamentally alter the nature of the activity. A protected person under the ADA is "an individual with a disability who, with or without reasonable modifications * * *, meets the essential eligibility requirements for the receipt of services or the participation in programs or activities provided by a public entity." Thus, entities subject to the act may not discriminate and must make reasonable accommodations that are necessary to provide the protected person with an equal opportunity to receive the services provided by such entities. While ADA claimants will often also be able to state Fair Housing Act claims, the availability of the ADA is vital in non-housing cases.

The first federal circuit court case applying the ADA to zoning was *Innovative Health Systems v. City of White Plains.*[78] The Second Circuit held that the second and disjunctive phrase of the prohibitory section of the ADA plainly prohibits discrimination by a public entity, making it unimportant whether zoning is a program, activity or service. Examining the city's conduct in the permitting process, the court found it likely that the plaintiff could show that the city had discriminated based on the disabilities of the plaintiffs patients and, thus, would prevail on the merits. Applicability of the ADA, of course, does not guarantee success to the claimant. Only reasonable accommodations are required. A "but for" causation standard is used to show the requested accommodation is necessary, meaning that without the accommodation, the plaintiff will

---

[72] 42 U.S.C.A. §§ 3610 et seq., discussed infra §§ 4:7 and 6:8.

[73] 42 U.S.C.A. §§ 3610 et seq.

[74] The Act uses the term "handicapped," but the regulations use the term "disabled," reflecting currently accepted terminology to avoid stereotypes and patronizing attitudes that accompany the word "handicapped." 28 C.F.R., § 36.104, Pt. 36, App. B.

[75] See infra § 6:8.

[76] 42 U.S.C.A. §§ 12101 et seq.

[77] 42 U.S.C.A. § 12132.

[78] Innovative Health Systems, Inc. v. City of White Plains, 117 F.3d 37 (2d Cir. 1997).

be denied an equal opportunity to obtain the housing of her choice.[79] For example, in a case following its decision in *Innovative Health Systems,* the Second Circuit held that a city need not permit construction of an assisted living facility on land zoned for commercial use where the evidence showed that a special use permit would not be granted to any residence of similar size whether intended for persons without disabilities or not.[80]

Section 504 of the Rehabilitation Act of 1973[81] may also be used to challenge zoning actions that deny permits to the disabled. The Rehabilitation Act, in language similar to the ADA, prohibits the denial of benefits or discrimination against the disabled. It differs in one significant respect from the ADA in that it applies only to "any program or activity receiving Federal financial assistance."[82] While all cities likely receive some federal funds, to prevail the plaintiff must show a nexus between the federal funds and the allegedly discriminatory program or activity.[83] Remedies under these two federal acts are provided by reference to other acts. The ADA incorporates the remedies of the Rehabilitation Act.[84] That act, in turn, incorporates the remedies of the Civil Rights of 1964.

§ 4:8   Agricultural Uses

Early zoning was urban oriented. Only cities and incorporated villages received the power to zone by the Standard Zoning Enabling Act and the use zones contemplated by the act were for "trade, industry, residence, or other purposes."[85] The country still had much open space, and prime agricultural land was not regarded as a limited resource. Urban sprawl had not yet struck, and automobile and transit facilities were not so extensive as to allow the "leapfrogging" of urban development far out into the countryside. Agricultural use was not an issue of concern. In small towns, and in some areas of larger cities, the poor and those of moderate means often kept a garden and perhaps a few chickens. These modest agricultural uses were permissible since they were not considered industrial or commercial uses.

Over the years, this picture has changed in almost every respect. Farmland preservation is a major national concern,[86] and agricultural zoning is common.[87] Agricultural zoning is usually unintensive use zoning, though it will normally permit industrialized agriculture, such as intensive stock feeding, canneries and other uses associated with an agricultural economy. Typically, agricultural zoning is also nonexclusive, allowing single-family homes on large lots. But, it will prohibit, or allow only as special uses,[88] conventional subdivisions and other urban uses that encroach upon the

---

[79] Wisconsin Community Services, Inc. v. City of Milwaukee, 465 F.3d 737, 749, 918 (7th Cir. 2006). See also Smith & Lee Associates, Inc. v. City of Taylor, Mich., 102 F.3d 781, 795 (6th Cir. 1996) and Lapid-Laurel, L.L.C. v. Zoning Bd. of Adjustment of Tp. of Scotch Plains, 284 F.3d 442, 460 (3d Cir. 2002).

[80] Forest City Daly Housing, Inc. v. Town of North Hempstead, 175 F.3d 144 (2d Cir. 1999).

[81] 29 U.S.C.A. § 794.

[82] 29 U.S.C.A. § 794(a).

[83] *U.S. v. City of Charlotte, N.C.,* 904 F. Supp. 482, 486 (W.D. N.C. 1995).

[84] 42 U.S.C.A. § 12117. Discovery House, Inc. v. Consolidated City of Indianapolis, 319 F.3d 277 (7th Cir. 2003).

[85] Standard State Zoning Enabling Act § 1 (1926).

[86] §§ 13:1 et seq. infra covers the topic in detail.

[87] See infra §§ 13:1 et seq. for discussion of farmland preservation and agricultural zoning.

[88] See, e.g., *Henley v. Zoning Hearing Bd. of West Fallowfield Tp.,* 155 Pa. Commw. 306, 625 A.2d 132 (1993).

preservation of the prime agricultural resource.[89] An agricultural zone may work as a holding zone[90] to contain urban areas and force denser development to infill developed areas rather than allowing sprawl and destruction of agricultural areas.[91] Some communities make agricultural zones exclusive, prohibiting even low-density residential use.

The courts have upheld both exclusive and nonexclusive agricultural zoning, finding the preservation of farmland to be a legitimate exercise of the police power.[92] As-applied taking problems will arise if the permitted agricultural use is not economically viable, but typically zoning does not have that effect and survives a takings challenge.[93]

The growth in agricultural zoning has been accompanied by a trend to ban certain agricultural uses from residential zones. Most residential zones ban commercial farming operations and the keeping of farm animals such as chickens, cows, goats and horses, and such ordinances generally pass constitutional muster.[94] It is not always clear what "farm animal" includes. Pet Vietnamese pot-bellied pigs have been found not to be farm animals, allowing their owners to keep them in residential areas.[95] A horse, however, was found not to be a "household pet."[96] All zones, including residential zones, typically permit the growing of crops.[97]

§ 4:9   Industrial and Commercial Uses

Variations in industrial and commercial zones are considerable. The present complexity of zoning codes is exemplified by the numerous commercial districts found in many cities. Where an early zoning ordinance would have one general business district and one industrial district, today's ordinances often have separate districts for neighborhood retail businesses, office and institutional uses, and shopping centers. Industry is often divided into light and heavy use zones.

In contrast to the early years of zoning, many industrial and commercial zones today are non-cumulative. Industrial zones commonly exclude residential uses for, just as industry can be a nuisance in residential zones, prime industrial land may be lost by the intrusion of residential uses. Furthermore, allowing homes in industrial zones may subject industry to nuisance actions.[98]

---

[89] Lewis County v. Western Washington Growth Management Hearings Bd., 157 Wash. 2d 488, 139 P.3d 1096 (2006).

[90] See infra § 4:20.

[91] See infra §§ 9:1 et seq. on Growth Management and Planning.

[92] See infra § 13:8.

[93] See, e.g., *Gardner v. New Jersey Pinelands Com'n,* 125 N.J. 193, 593 A.2d 251 (1991); *Nelson v. Benton County,* 115 Or. App. 453, 839 P.2d 233 (1992). See also Cordes, Takings, Fairness, and Farmland Preservation, 60 Ohio St. L.J. 1033 (1999).

[94] *Greater Chicago Combine and Center, Inc. v. City of Chicago,* 431 F.3d 1065 (7th Cir. 2005) (ban on keeping pigeons in residential areas constitutional).

[95] *City of Peoria v. Ohl,* 262 Ill. App. 3d 522, 201 Ill. Dec. 597, 636 N.E.2d 1029 (1994).

[96] Kaeser v. Zoning Bd. of Appeals of Town of Stratford, 218 Conn. 438, 589 A.2d 1229 (1991).

[97] Farming is not always allowed outside agricultural zones. See *Borough of Kinnelon v. South Gate Associates,* 172 N.J. Super. 216, 411 A.2d 724 (App. Div. 1980).

[98] See infra §§ 14:1 et seq.

While cumulative zoning represented the early practice, the Standard Zoning Enabling Act did not require it, and exclusive industrial or commercial zoning does not conflict with a typical enabling act.[99] Litigation challenging exclusive districts has been based on arguments that it is beyond the police power to protect lower uses from higher uses and that exclusive industrial zoning is unreasonable as applied to particular property. The former ground has failed as courts have upheld commercial and industrial districts that exclude residential uses.[100] The courts reason that just as residential areas exclude industrial uses to promote the public welfare, people can be protected from themselves by precluding them from moving into industrial areas. Furthermore, courts may uphold exclusive industrial zoning to promote and protect industrial uses.[101] In states allowing fiscally-motivated zoning,[102] exclusive industrial zoning may also be justified as a measure to attract uses that will increase the tax base.[103]

Exclusive industrial or commercial zoning may be invalid as applied. Communities are frequently "overzoned" for commercial and industrial uses, that is, there is no demand for the quantity of land so zoned. Where the zoning is cumulative, it usually does not unreasonably burden the property owner, whose land can be devoted to some use for which there is a market. But when exclusive industrial zoning is used and there is no demand for using the property in that manner, it is in effect zoned for nonuse, which is unreasonable and does not serve the public health, safety and welfare.[104]

In addition, or as an alternative, to use zoning, performance standards may regulate industrial uses. A performance zoning ordinance provides standards to measure the external effects produced by industrial activities. Specific standards may be established for smoke, noise, dust, toxic emissions, glare, vibration, radioactivity, electrical disturbance, heat, and odors.[105] If the standards are met, the manufacturing use is permitted within the zone.[106]

§ 4:10 Enterprise Zones and Tax Incentives

Certain "zones," such as enterprise zones, are not zones at all in the Euclidean sense that refers to areas of land use classifications. Still, enterprise zones, as redevelopment tools, may override other planning concerns and may result in the intensification of land use.

Enterprise zones, which three-fourths of the states authorize,[107] are economically deteriorating areas into which government incentives attract commercial activity.[108] Though they have most often been directed toward urban renewal, enterprise zones

---

[99] *Kozesnik v. Montgomery Tp.,* 24 N.J. 154, 131 A.2d 1, 9 (1957).

[100] See *Grubel v. MacLaughlin,* 286 F. Supp. 24, 27 (D.V.I. 1968).

[101] People ex rel. Skokie Town House Builders, Inc. v. Village of Morton Grove, 16 Ill. 2d 183, 157 N.E.2d 33 (1959).

[102] See supra § 3:20.

[103] Power, The Unwisdom of Allowing City Growth to Work Out Its Own Destiny, 47 Md. L. Rev. 626, 671 (1988).

[104] *Corthouts v. Town of Newington,* 140 Conn. 284, 99 A.2d 112 (1953).

[105] See, e.g., DeCoals, Inc. v. Board of Zoning Appeals of City of Westover, 168 W. Va. 339, 284 S.E.2d 856 (1981).

[106] See infra § 4:19 for a discussion of performance zoning.

[107] See Williams, The Enterprise Zone Concept at the Federal Level: Are Proposed Tax Incentives the Needed Ingredient?, 9 Va. Tax Rev. 711, 721–22 (1990).

[108] See, generally, Boeck, Enterprise Zone Debate, 16 Urb. Law. 71, 73–77 (1984).

increasingly target rural areas as well. Generally, the enterprise zones contain reductions of tax rates or fees, attempts to increase the level and efficiency of local services, provisions to streamline government regulation, and incentives to obtain commitments from the private sector to provide jobs and job training for low income residents. Income tax incentives for businesses may be split between employers and employees. Virginia's plan, for example, provides for tax incentives to encourage business participation in designated areas, and allows some regulatory flexibility at the local level by use of special zoning districts, ordinance exemption and permit process reform.[109]

Tax incentives may violate the dormant commerce clause if they discriminate against interstate economic activity. In *Cuno v. DaimlerChrysler,*[110] the Sixth Circuit found Ohio's franchise tax credit unconstitutional. The defect in the statute, said the court, was that it rewarded businesses already subject to the tax that expanded locally rather than out-of-state. A company that chose to expand out-of-state paid a higher franchise tax than one that chose to expand in-state. While the United States Supreme Court vacated the decision, finding the taxpayers who challenged the act lacked standing, the circuit court's opinion raises concern for incentive programs across the country.[111]

While some 500 enterprise zones exist in cities around the country via state legislation,[112] there is federal involvement as well. Federal enterprise zone legislation was debated fairly continuously beginning in the early 1980s. Congress finally acted in 1993. Using the label "empowerment zones," Congress created nine zones: five in large urban centers, one in a medium size city, and three in rural areas.[113] Tax incentives amounting to $2.5 billion were provided as wage credits that entitled an employer to take credits equal to 20% of the first $15,000 of each employee's wages with a maximum of $3,000. The legislation also provided $720 million for social service grants for child care, education, and job training. Finally, the zones were granted the power to use tax-exempt bonds to finance businesses. In addition to the empowerment zones, 95 "enterprise communities" (65 urban, 30 rural) received the tax-exempt bond powers of the empowerment zones and $280 million for social service grants.[114] Another program, the New Market Tax Credits, was enacted as part of the Community Renewal Tax Relief Act of 2000.[115] It is designed to encourage capital investment in low-income communities by providing tax incentives to investors who make qualified equity investments in qualified entities.

Some question whether enterprise and empowerment zones really attract business and revitalize an area. Assessments of the federal programs are mixed and inconclu-

---

[109] Va. Code Ann. §§ 59.1–270 to 59.1–284 (expired 2005).

[110] *Cuno v. DaimlerChrysler, Inc.,* 386 F.3d 738 (6th Cir. 2004), judgment vacated in part, 547 U.S. 332, 126 S. Ct. 1854, 164 L. Ed. 2d 589 (2006), vacated *DaimlerChrysler Corp. v. Cuno,* 547 U.S. 332, 126 S. Ct. 1854, 164 L. Ed. 2d 589 (2006) (taxpayers lacked standing).

[111] See Iyer, Recent Development, Cuno v. DaimlerChrysler, Inc.: Dormant Commerce Clause Limits State Location Tax Incentives, 40 Harv. C.R.-C.L. L. Rev. 523, 537 (2005).

[112] See Williams, The Enterprise Zone Concept at the Federal Level: Are Proposed Tax Incentives the Needed Ingredient?, 9 Va. Tax Rev. 711, 721–22 (1990).

[113] 26 U.S.C.A. § 1391. See Hyman, Empowerment Zones, Enterprise Communities, Black Business, and Unemployment, 53 Wash. U. J. Urb. & Contemp. L. 143 (1998).

[114] For data on the program, see "Empowerment Zones" Showing Progress, Wash. Post, March 8, 1997, 1997 WL 9338470.

[115] Pub. L. No. 106–554, § 314(f), 114 Stat. 2763A-643 (2000).

sive.[116] The British experience suggests that tax breaks and regulatory simplification alone are insufficient.[117] Yet, there is some evidence of success.[118]

Though not denominated a "zone," a related redevelopment tool is tax increment financing.[119] Authorized by enabling legislation in 38 states,[120] tax increment financing uses the increase in value that results from redevelopment, which the public financed in whole or in part. The *ad valorem* taxes levied on a redevelopment area are divided into two parts. That levied on the base value (assessed value at the time a project begins) is allocated to cities, counties, schools and other taxing districts, as usual. The tax levied on the increment (excess of assessed value over base value) goes to the redevelopment authority where the money may be used to finance the public costs of the redevelopment or to repay bonds previously issued to raise revenue for the redevelopment.

§ 4:11 Buffer Zones

Land on the periphery of a zone may suffer adverse effects from neighboring uses in a more intensive zone. Euclidean zoning attempts to reduce these effects by transition or buffer zoning, which puts the next lower, more intensive zone as the adjacent zone. Thus, a single-family zone is in theory next to a two-family zone, which is next to a four-family zone and so on. Buffering is not always possible to that degree, but it is common for a multi-family zone to be placed between a single-family zone and an industrial zone to shield the single-family zone from industrial uses.[121] The result is anomalous in the sense that it places more people closer to the presumed harmful industrial use, but it is consistent with the zoning hierarchy that places single-family use at the top of the pyramid.

Buffer zones are valid so long as the property in the zone can be devoted to a profitable use.[122] If the buffer zone classification renders the land useless, the zoning may be found invalid or found to be a taking.[123]

Buffering is also achieved by height and bulk controls. For example, where commercial areas abut single-family residential areas, the commercial uses may be limited in height and greater than ordinary setbacks may be required.[124]

Buffer conditions are frequently imposed as part of the grant of development permission with rezonings, variances, or special permits. Typically, these conditions take

---

[116] See Forbes, Using Economic Development Programs as Tools for Urban Revitalization: A Comparison of Empowerment Zones and New Markets Tax Credits, 2006 U. Ill. L. Rev. 177 (2006).

[117] Callies and Tamashiro, Enterprise Zones: The Redevelopment Sweepstakes Begins, 15 Urb. Law. 231 (1983).

[118] Wolf, An "Essay in Re-Plan": American Enterprise Zones in Practice, 21 Urb. Law. 29 (1989); Rubin and Trawinski, New Jersey's Urban Enterprise Zones: A Program That Works, 23 Urb. Law. 461 (1991).

[119] See Tomme, Note: Tax Increment Financing: Public Use or Private Abuse?, 90 Minn. Rev. 213 (2005).

[120] See Winter, Tax Increment Financing: A Potential Redevelopment Financing Mechanism for New York Municipalities, 18 Fordham Urb. L.J. 655, 656 (1991).

[121] See *Village of Arlington Heights v. Metropolitan Housing Development Corp.*, 429 U.S. 252, 97 S. Ct. 555, 50 L. Ed. 2d 450 (1977), where the policy of the village was to only allow multifamily use where it served this buffering purpose.

[122] *Evanston Best & Co. v. Goodman*, 369 Ill. 207, 16 N.E.2d 131 (1938).

[123] *Janesick v. City of Detroit*, 337 Mich. 549, 60 N.W.2d 452 (1953) (found unreasonable).

[124] *Big Creek Lumber Co. v. County of San Mateo*, 31 Cal. App. 4th 418, 37 Cal. Rptr. 2d 159 (1995).

the form of fencing, landscaping or open space requirements to protect neighbors from the external effects of noise and view of the new, more intensive development.[125]

III. HEIGHT, BULK, AND SETBACK CONTROLS

§ 4:12 Height Controls

Height regulations state maximum heights either in terms of feet or number of stories or both. The Supreme Court accepted their general validity long ago in *Welch v. Swasey*.[126] Today, when litigation arises, courts question their validity as applied. Height regulations effectuate purposes of the Standard Act, namely "to secure safety from fire," "to provide adequate light and air" and "to prevent the overcrowding of land."[127] They may also promote aesthetics.[128] Denver, for example, has a height limitation in certain zones to preserve the view of the mountains from several city parks.[129]

Minimum height requirements are less common. Historically they have fared less well than maximum height limits. When courts first confronted minimum height requirements, they invalidated them. For example, where an ordinance required all facades of buildings to be at least 15 feet in height in a commercial area, the court held the regulation had no relation to the public health, safety and welfare.[130] These cases invalidating minimum height requirements, however, were decided in an era when courts refused to recognize aesthetics as a legitimate zoning aim. Today, the reverse is true,[131] and aesthetics may justify minimum height requirements.[132]

Problems with height controls may develop as applied to particular building features. Some ordinances anticipate this, by excepting roof top protrusions, such as elevator towers and heating and air-conditioning units and vents. Where height is measured by stories, the ordinance must be checked to determine whether a basement counts as a story, and "story" must be defined.[133] Cases construing ordinance provisions as to the level from which heights are measured are common.[134] Where practical difficulties or undue hardship will result from strict application of an ordinance, a variance may be sought. Height variances, as a type of area variance,[135] are usually less consequential than use variances and thus easier to obtain.[136]

---

[125] *Quirk v. Town of New Boston*, 140 N.H. 124, 663 A.2d 1328 (1995) (upholding 200 foot buffer).

[126] *Welch v. Swasey*, 214 U.S. 91, 29 S. Ct. 567, 53 L. Ed. 923 (1909).

[127] See, e.g., *Quality by Father & Son, Ltd. v. Bruscella*, 174 Misc. 2d 664, 666 N.Y.S.2d 380 (1997).

[128] See infra § 4:14 (floor area ratios); supra § 3:11 and infra § 4:26 (airport/flight plane zoning); § 4:12 (height restrictions).

[129] *Landmark Land Co., Inc. v. City and County of Denver*, 728 P.2d 1281 (Colo. 1986).

[130] *City of North Miami v. Newsome*, 203 So. 2d 634 (Fla. 3d DCA 1967).

[131] See infra §§ 12:1 et seq.

[132] See, e.g., *City of Green Ridge v. Kreisel*, 25 S.W.3d 559 (Mo. Ct. App. 2000).

Fiscal considerations may also be involved. See, e.g., *Allright Auto Parks, Inc. v. Zoning Bd. of Adjustment of City of Philadelphia*, 107 Pa. Commw. 448, 529 A.2d 546 (1987).

[133] *Hiner v. Hoffman*, 90 Haw. 188, 977 P.2d 878 (1999).

[134] *Katcher v. Home Sav. and Loan Ass'n*, 245 Cal. App. 2d 425, 53 Cal. Rptr. 923 (1966).

[135] See infra § 5:15.

[136] *Wilcox v. Zoning Bd. of Appeals of City of Yonkers*, 17 N.Y.2d 249, 270 N.Y.S.2d 569, 217 N.E.2d 633 (1966).

§ 4:13   Bulk and Setback Controls

Bulk regulations provide a zoning envelope for buildings by horizontal measurement. They include such regulations as minimum lot size, minimum frontage of lots, the area of a lot that may be covered, setbacks, and floor-area ratios (FARs).

A.   *Minimum Lots and Frontages*

Minimum lot size and lot frontage requirements control densities and preserve view and open space. They are sometimes regulated by the subdivision ordinance instead of, or in addition to, the regulations in a zoning ordinance.[137] Reasonable frontage requirements are valid[138] as are minimum lot size requirements.[139] Since both increase housing costs by raising the price of lots, they may be challenged as exclusionary zoning.[140] Details of application may also pose problems. Where the lot frontage is not straight, for example on a cul-de-sac, the proper construction of ordinances requiring minimum footage sometimes leads to litigation.[141] Rarely, a property owner may seek to meet a frontage requirement where the particular lot has a non-continuous frontage. While the common understanding is that "frontage" means a single, continuing property line on a public way, there is little authority on the point.[142] Questions may also arise as to what constitutes a lot.[143]

B.   *Setback and Lot Coverage*

The Standard Zoning Enabling Act provides that a community may regulate the percentage of a lot that may be occupied and the size of yards. A typical ordinance, for example, may provide that in a multi-family zone, not more than 60% of the lot shall be covered by buildings. Most ordinances go beyond regulating the percentage of the lot that is covered, and mandate building location by requiring minimum front, side and rear yards in residential districts. A 40,000 square foot minimum lot size in a residential zone may be accompanied by the requirement that any building on the lot be at least 40 feet from the front street, 30 feet from the rear line, and 10 feet from the side property lines.[144]

Setback and lot coverage requirements provide space, light and air, and safety from fire. Setbacks have several other purposes. They are used to reserve future street sites.[145] Flood plain zoning is a kind of setback provision,[146] as are provisions for set-

---

[137] See infra §§ 7:1 et seq.

[138] Procter v. City of Raleigh Board of Adjustment, 140 N.C. App. 784, 538 S.E.2d 621 (2000).

[139] Minimum lot sizes of 5,000 square feet, 26,000 square feet, 40,000 square feet, as well as two, three and five acres are common and have been upheld often. See cases cited infra § 6:2.

[140] See infra § 6:2.

[141] See Annot., Validity and construction of zoning regulations prescribing a minimum width or frontage for residence lots, 96 A.L.R.2d 1367.

[142] See *Valcourt v. Zoning Bd. of Appeals of Swansea,* 48 Mass. App. Ct. 124, 718 N.E.2d 389 (1999).

[143] *North Shore Realty Trust v. Com.,* 434 Mass. 109, 747 N.E.2d 107 (2001).

[144] § 10–2062, Zoning Code of Raleigh, N.C.

[145] See infra § 7:11.

[146] See infra § 11:16.

back of outdoor advertising signs and beachfront construction. In addition, setbacks may be used to keep buildings from active earthquake fault lines.[147]

In *Gorieb v. Fox*,[148] the United States Supreme Court upheld the general validity of setbacks to further the general goals of open space, light and air, and safety from fire.[149] Still, setbacks may be invalid as applied, and if the property owner is left with no room to build, a Fifth Amendment taking may be found.[150] In *Lucas v. South Carolina Coastal Council*,[151] the Supreme Court examined a statute that prohibited building on a beachfront lot in front of a setback line established in part to prevent erosion. The Court held that where the effect of compliance with the setback prevented the property owner from engaging in any economically viable use of the lot, a taking had occurred. The state was required to pay compensation unless it could prove that state nuisance or property law justified the requirement. These conventional requirements reflect traditional housing patterns prevalent in zoning's early days. In many areas today there remains a deeply embedded preference for single-family detached homes surrounded by front, side, and back yards. Many have criticized excessive reliance on the single-family detached house for several reasons. It increases housing costs, consumes substantial open space, and limits personal choice.[152] Some have even questioned the legitimacy of mandating conformity to the single-family detached house style.[153] To avoid these kinds of problems and to offer options to developers, most ordinances provide for planned unit developments, cluster zoning, and neotraditional development.[154]

C. *Setback Lines for Street Widening Purposes*

Setback lines may facilitate the subsequent widening of streets, since the land can be acquired for less expense when buildings have not been erected on the site.[155] The validity of such a setback is suspect since the lowering of condemnation costs is not a proper purpose of zoning.[156] However, the courts are often not precise over the distinction between setbacks for street widening and setbacks for front yards, and the generally accepted validity of the latter has led to approval of the former under the police power, particularly if the setbacks are part of the zoning ordinance or a comprehensive plan.[157]

---

[147] See *Better Alternatives for Neighborhoods v. Heyman*, 212 Cal. App. 3d 663, 260 Cal. Rptr. 758, 54 Ed. Law Rep. 1273 (1989).

[148] *Gorieb v. Fox*, 274 U.S. 603, 47 S. Ct. 675, 71 L. Ed. 1228 (1927).

[149] In an earlier case the Court invalidated an ordinance that allowed neighbors to establish the setback. *Eubank v. City of Richmond*, 226 U.S. 137, 33 S. Ct. 76, 57 L. Ed. 156 (1912).

[150] *Giambrone v. Aurora*, 85 Ohio App. 3d 758, 621 N.E.2d 475 (1993).

[151] *Lucas v. South Carolina Coastal Council*, 505 U.S. 1003, 112 S. Ct. 2886, 120 L. Ed. 2d 798 (1992), discussed infra § 10:6.

[152] Ziegler, Jr., The Twilight of Single-Family Zoning, 3 U.C.L.A. J. Envtl. L. & Pol'y 161 (1983).

[153] Richard F. Babcock, The Egregious Invalidity of the Exclusive Single-Family Zone, Land Use Law & Zoning Digest 4 (July 1983).

[154] See infra §§ 7:15 to 7:19.

[155] A setback line used to reserve future street sites is similar to an official map provision, a distinction being that official maps reserve new street sites as well as sites for widening existing streets. See infra § 7:11.

[156] See supra § 3:22, regarding zoning to lower condemnation costs.

[157] *Palm Beach County v. Wright*, 641 So. 2d 50, 53 (Fla. 1994).

D. *Building Size*

In addition to limits imposed by controlling the percentage of a lot that may be occupied,[158] zoning authorities may set minimum and maximum size for buildings, both residential and nonresidential. Size requirements for houses are generally based on aesthetic and community character concerns. Considerations of affordable housing may lead to minimum or maximum house size regulations, with the former excluding it and the latter promoting it. For non-residential development, limits on the size of big box stores are increasingly common for a variety of reasons.

The Standard State Zoning Enabling Act expressly authorizes government to regulate the "height, number of stories, and size of buildings [and] the percentage of lot that may be occupied. . . . "[159] Yet, regulations must further the purposes of the act, which, while broad and general,[160] are not unlimited. Courts suspecting illegitimate motives will not always defer to assertions of valid purposes. This is especially true of minimum house size ordinances, which have not fared well in the courts. Arguments by cities that bans on small houses prevent overcrowding and preserve community character have been seen as makeweight reasons designed to obscure the intent to exclude persons of lower income. We discuss this technique and judicial reactions to it in Chapter Six dealing with exclusionary zoning.[161]

Maximum house size regulations are fairly new and are a response to the building of so-called monster homes. Estimates of the average house size in the United States in 1970 range from 1,300 to 1,500 square feet. Estimates of average size in 2000 ranged from 2,100 to 2,260 square feet.[162] At the high-end of the scale are monster homes, also known as McMansions or starter castles, which are generally considered those from 5,000 square feet and up.[163] They can soar to the truly super-sized. In one case, a proposed 29-bedroom, 40-bathroom, 55,000 square foot home with a 75 car garage and a 10,000 square foot playhouse on a 63-acre tract led to the adoption of an ordinance limiting houses to 20,000 square feet. The ordinance came too late to prevent this proposal as the court found the owner had a vested right to complete his "house."[164] Putting aside the vested rights problem in that case, limits on size have been upheld by the courts.

The trend of building larger homes has reversed itself. By 2015, the average new house is predicted to be 2,152 square feet.[165] In addition to harsh economic realities, many people want smaller homes. Lifestyles have changed. Studies show that younger homebuyers want to live in pedestrian friendly urban settings.

---

[158] See supra § 4:13B.

[159] SZEA, § 1, set out supra § 3:6.

[160] See SZEA, § 3, set out supra § 3:6.

[161] See infra § 6:3.

[162] Ironically, average household size decreased from 3.14 in 1970 to 2.62 in 1998. U.S. Dept. of Commerce, http://www.bts.gov/publications/the_changing_face_of_transportation/html/table_05_02.html.

[163] See, generally, Garvin and LeRoy, Design Guidelines: The Law of Aesthetic Controls, 55 Land Use Law & Zoning Dig. 3 (Apr. 2003).

[164] *Association of Friends of Sagaponack v. Zoning Bd. of Appeals of the Town of Southampton,* 287 A.D.2d 620, 731 N.Y.S.2d 851 (2001).

[165] NAHB Study: New Homes in 2015 Will Be Smaller, Greener and More Casual, March 7, 2011. http://www.nahb.org/news_details.aspx?newsID=12244&fromGSA=1.

Caps are set on houses by local governments who believe that such hefty houses have an adverse impact on the supply of affordable housing and are out of place with the character of the community. In *Rumson Estates, Inc. v. Mayor & Council of the Borough of Fair Haven*,[166] the New Jersey supreme court upheld a zoning ordinance that limited house size to 2,200 square feet. The borough defended its cap as a measure to ensure "proportionality of new construction to other homes in the zone and providing affordable housing." The court found that the goal of assuring "a desirable visual environment, [by preventing] 'homes built to a scale completely out of keeping with the homes in the surrounding area'" was valid under state enabling legislation similar to the Standard Act.

In *Board of County Commissioners of Teton County v. Crow*,[167] an 8,000 square feet cap on housing size foiled a homeowner in his attempt to expand his existing home to 11,000 square feet The county's goal in limiting house size was twofold: to preserve its small-town, rural, and western character and to promote social and economic diversity through housing affordability. The former, said the court, "lay at the very heart of zoning and planning legislation," and the latter was a justifiable effort to carry out the delegated power to promote the general welfare.

Like houses, big box retailers have grown ever larger over the past 15 to 20 years. One study groups these stores as "discount department stores," such as K-Mart, Target and Wal-Mart, ranging from 80,000 to 130,000 square feet, "category killers," such as Home Depot and Lowe's, ranging from 20,000 to 120,000 square feet, and "warehouse clubs," such as Costco and Sam's, ranging from 100,000 to 170,000 square feet. "Power centers," groupings of several big boxes, top the list at 250,000 square feet.[168]

As with residences, the express enabling authority to regulate height, number of stories and size of buildings and other structures, along with the presumption of validity accorded ordinances, make a challenger's job to show an ordinance is ultra vires or arbitrary a difficult one.[169] Courts have upheld caps of 20,000, 25,000 and 52,000 square feet.[170] Limitations on size range from fairly stringent limits such as 4,000 square feet in some San Francisco zones, to 80,000 square feet in New Mexico, and on to efforts to keep out only the truly immense stores of over 100,000 and 150,000 square feet.[171]

The purposes generally offered by towns include promotion of orderly development of shopping areas, the relationship of buildings and open spaces, pedestrian circulation, traffic control, and, in general, preservation of community character and aesthetics.[172]

---

[166] *Rumson Estates, Inc. v. Mayor & Council of Borough of Fair Haven,* 177 N.J. 338, 828 A.2d 317 (2003).

[167] Board of County Com'rs of Teton County v. Crow, 2003 WY 40, 65 P.3d 720 (Wyo. 2003).

[168] Managing Maryland's Growth: "Big Box" Retail Development, Md. Dept. of Planning (2001), www.mdp.state.md.us/mgs/bigbox/bigbox_v3.pdf.

[169] *C&K Real Estate, LLC v. Guilford Planning and Zoning Com'n,* 2003 WL 21384646 (Conn. Super. Ct. 2003) (25,000 square feet maximum upheld).

[170] *C&K Real Estate, LLC, 2003 WL 21384646; Samben Realty Co., Inc. v. Watertown Planning & Zoning Com'n,* 1999 WL 494106 (Conn. Super. Ct. 1999) (upholding maximum gross floor area of 10,000 square feet).

[171] See Merriam, Breaking Big Boxes: Learning from the Horse Whisperers, 6 Vt. J. Envtl. L. 7 (2004–2005).

[172] See *Savings Bank of Rockville v. Town of Tolland,* 18 Conn. L. Rptr. 275, 1996 WL 686902 (Conn. Super. Ct. 1996).

In addition, economic protection of local business[173] and local employees, particularly union workers in grocery stores,[174] may drive adoption of a cap. Controls other than those on size may include architectural requirements to make the stores less boring and out and out exclusion of big boxes.[175]

§ 4:14   Floor-Area Ratio (FAR)

FAR, meaning floor-area ratio, is a device that combines height and bulk provisions and provides an inducement to a developer to leave more open space by allowing a higher building. Generally, it is defined as the sum of the area of all the floors of the building compared to the area of the site. Under FAR, an ordinance designates a floor-area ratio for a particular zone. If the ratio is 1:1, a one story building can cover the entire buildable area of the lot, a two-story building can cover half the buildable area, a four-story building can cover one-fourth of the buildable area and so on. In commercial office areas in large cities the ratio may be 10:1, which allows a twenty-story building on half the buildable area of the lot. Some cities induce developers to leave more open space by offering increases in FAR in return for on-site public facilities, such as plazas.[176]

FAR may be used with maximum height limits and other bulk controls, so that in a 10:1 area, it may not be possible to build a 200-story building on 1/20th of the buildable area of a lot or to eliminate yards entirely and build a 10-story building up to all lot lines. Nevertheless, FAR does give the builder some flexibility.

FAR has been assumed to be valid, but, as with other bulk controls, problems develop with specific applications. Taking the general definition from above (the sum of the area of all the floors of the building compared to the area of the site), questions may arise as to whether the basement is included as building floor, and whether the area of the site means to total area or the buildable area. Where state law defined FAR as "the sum of the area of all floors of buildings or structures compared to the total area of the site," a municipality's attempt to exclude environmentally sensitive areas from calculations, thus reducing allowable development, was held ultra vires.[177] The statute, the court said, required use of the "total area." In another case, a court rejected a city's attempt to include the open space beneath a second story in calculating FAR.[178] In contrast, a developer was unable to convince a court that the appropriate measure against which to calculate its building allowance included its fee interest in an abutting street.[179]

---

[173] See *Wal-Mart Stores, Inc. v. City of Turlock,* 138 Cal. App. 4th 273, 41 Cal. Rptr. 3d 420 (5th Dist. 2006).

[174] Lefcoe, The Regulation of Superstores: The Legality of Zoning Ordinances Emerging from the Skirmishes Between Wal-Mart and the United Food and Commercial Workers Union, 58 Ark. L. Rev. 833 (2006).

[175] See Dwight H. Merriam and Robert I. McMurry, Regulating McMansions, Starter Palaces and Homes on Steroids, SK002 ALI-ABA 1081 (2004). See § 6:9 on exclusion of non-residential uses.

[176] See infra § 4:18 on bonus and incentive zoning.

[177] *Crow-New Jersey 32 Ltd. Partnership v. Township of Clinton,* 718 F. Supp. 378 (D.N.J. 1989) (disapproved of by, Rumson Estates, Inc. v. Mayor & Council of Borough of Fair Haven, 177 N.J. 338, 828 A.2d 317 (2003)).

[178] *Baker v. Town of Islip Zoning Bd. of Appeals,* 20 A.D.3d 522, 799 N.Y.S.2d 541 (2005).

[179] *Mall, Inc. v. City of Seattle,* 108 Wash. 2d 369, 739 P.2d 668 (1987).

IV. ZONING WITH FLEXIBILITY

§ 4:15   The Need for Flexibility

Euclidean or use zoning[180] proved too rigid to meet changing community needs and development pressures.[181] Difficulties arose in determining the compatibility of different uses. Increased numbers of use districts with fewer permitted uses of right in each district, along with underzoning, limited developers' options.[182] This led to many rezoning requests, but change, at least in theory, was difficult.[183] Government approval involved an all or nothing decision to grant or deny development permission. A grant of permission left neighbors of the newly authorized use unprotected and allowed environmentally sensitive lands to be destroyed since the authorities lacked the capacity to impose site-specific controls. On the other hand, denial of permission left the land possibly underused, and the landowner unnecessarily restricted.

Over the years governments developed a variety of techniques to inject flexibility into the process to remedy these deficiencies.[184] These include the use of floating zones, conditional zoning, increased reliance on the special permit process,[185] site review controls, performance zoning, planned unit developments,[186] interim zoning, and overlay zoning.

§ 4:16   Floating Zones

A floating zone is an unmapped district with detailed and conditional use requirements. Metaphorically, the zone "floats" over the city until affixed to a particular parcel.[187] Floating zones generally involve predictable uses that have significant community impacts such as shopping centers and planned unit developments, or uses that the city wishes to encourage such as industrial parks, affordable housing, and housing for the elderly.

Use of the floating zone involves a two-step process. The city first creates a zone with listed characteristics, for example, a planned unit development with minimums set for acreage, open space, and a mix of uses. This ordinance provides that land meeting these characteristics may be so zoned by a second ordinance when a property owner applies for it, if the action will otherwise promote the public interest. Upon receipt of an application meeting the criteria of the initial ordinance, the zone floats down to the surface by enactment of the second ordinance. Once affixed, it is similar to any other zone, except that the invitation remains open to apply it wherever an applicant meets the conditions.

---

[180] Use zoning is described supra §§ 4:1 to 4:9. See discussion in *Campion v. Board of Aldermen of City of New Haven,* 278 Conn. 500, 899 A.2d 542 (2006).

[181] Another major deficiency was the lack of mandatory planning under the Standard Zoning Enabling Act, which meant that many codes were not based on a thoughtful assessment of the community's future needs. See supra §§ 2:1 et seq.

[182] Lane Kendig, Performance Zoning 9 (Planners Press 1980).

[183] See infra §§ 5:1 et seq. for methods of change.

[184] Porter, Phillips & Lassar, Flexible Zoning: How It Works (1988).

[185] See infra § 5:24.

[186] Discussed infra §§ 7:15 to 7:19.

[187] *Campion v. Board of Aldermen of City of New Haven,* 278 Conn. 500, 899 A.2d 542 (2006).

Rodgers v. Village of Tarrytown[188] upheld the floating zone technique. In that case, an ordinance provided that parcels of 10 acres or more could be rezoned to a BB district permitting multiple family dwellings if certain standards were met. The ordinance required a 10-acre minimum and imposed height, setback, and open space requirements. The BB zone floated since no parcel on the zoning map was so designated. At the request of a landowner, a tract zoned residential A was rezoned BB. When a neighbor challenged the rezoning, the court upheld it, noting that the village had acted to fill a need for multi-family housing to keep young families in the area. Thus, rather than being for the primary benefit of the owner, the zoning promoted the general welfare. The court also held that the ordinance set sufficient standards for the zone, and exemplified a considered, comprehensive scheme.

The floating zone's invitation to landowners to seek rezonings was the primary objection of *Eves v. Zoning Board of Adjustment of Lower Gwynedd Township*,[189] the leading case invalidating floating zones. *Eves* involved a floating limited industrial zone applied to a 103-acre tract in a residential neighborhood. The court held the scheme invalid because, in the court's view, there was no plan. It viewed the failure of the legislative body to map land for industrial use in the first instance as an abdication of the power to zone. Development itself, as solicited by individuals, would become the plan. The court thought the process carried evils akin to spot zoning, and was particularly concerned with neighboring property owners who had no way of foreseeing changes resulting from floating zones. Perhaps the fact that the rezoned tract was to be used as a sewage treatment plant and that there were 300 neighbors who had objected accentuated the court's concern.

The objections of the *Eves* court have not troubled other courts, who recognize that the marketplace subjects zoning authorities to constant pressure to change. Even without floating zones, landowners and developers are usually the ones who initiate rezoning requests to intensify land use and neighboring property owners have no better chance of foreseeing that these types of changes may occur. Consequently, courts generally approve the idea of floating zones.[190]

The second or mapping step of the floating zone process, like any rezoning, can present problems. A floating zone may be held invalid as spot zoning.[191] There also may be contract-like features of the floating zone that make it invalid as contract zoning.[192] Or, if the ordinance lacks sufficient criteria to guide decisionmaking, it may be held unconstitutional as an invalid delegation of legislative authority.[193]

A floating zone also may be held invalid because it does not "accord with a comprehensive plan."[194] Floating zones may not be in accord where courts construe the comprehensive plan exclusively to mean the zoning plan as evidenced by the zoning

---

[188] *Rodgers v. Village of Tarrytown,* 302 N.Y. 115, 96 N.E.2d 731 (1951).

[189] *Eves v. Zoning Bd. of Adjustment of Lower Gwynedd Tp.,* 401 Pa. 211, 164 A.2d 7 (1960).

[190] *Treme v. St. Louis County,* 609 S.W.2d 706 (Mo. Ct. App.1980).

[191] See infra § 5:10. See also Kristine Cordier Karnezis, Annot., Zoning: regulations creating and placing "floating zones," 80 A.L.R.3d 95.

[192] See infra § 5:11.

[193] See infra § 5:4. See also *Friends of Great Southern, Inc. v. City of Hollywood ex rel. City Com'n,* 964 So. 2d 827 (Fla. 4th DCA 2007) and *City of Miami v. Save Brickell Ave., Inc.,* 426 So. 2d 1100 (Fla. 3d DCA 1983).

[194] See *Eves v. Zoning Bd. of Adjustment of Lower Gwynedd Tp.,* 401 Pa. 211, 164 A.2d 7 (1960).

map. In this instance, a floating zone appears as an "island," as spot zoning does. However, where zoning need accord only in the sense that it is not arbitrary, or may accord to a master plan (and the master plan has embodied floating zones),[195] floating zones should be held valid.[196] Rather than showing a lack of planning, the mere creation of the floating zone is some evidence that the legislative body has thought the matter through. Furthermore, the fact that legislators take the first step in a neutral setting, without a specific rezoning request, eliminates the fear that private interests are driving the decision to invite applications for the particular use in question.

Use of a floating zone process may lead to greater judicial deference than is the case with the similar technique of the special use permit. The latter, an administrative process, is subject to close judicial review, while the former, a legislative act, traditionally enjoys a presumption of validity and more deferential review.[197] Also, a jurisdiction that requires proof of mistake or change in circumstances to uphold a standard rezoning may not apply that stringent rule to a floating zone.[198]

§ 4:17   Conditional Zoning

Conditional zoning provides flexibility to the basic use zoning system. While conditional zoning takes a variety of forms and lacks a precise definition, its use stems from the need for site-specific control of rezoned land.[199]

A.   *Inadequacy of General Rezoning Process*

Zoning classifications typically contain many uses permitted of right.[200] A general rezoning of land allows all listed uses without regard to site-specific concerns that might suggest that some of those uses would be harmful to neighboring uses within the same zone or in adjacent zones. This is often the case as the theoretical compatibility of the uses may not accord with political reality and the needs of the specific area in question. Aware of this, zoning authorities have an unending interest in knowing a developer's specific plans. But, general rezonings leave the authorities with no commitment that the developer will use the land as indicated during the rezoning process.

A general rezoning request is an all or nothing proposition. When a city grants a general rezoning without limiting conditions, all permitted uses in the zoning classification are available. Assume that a developer says that it wishes to build a flower shop on a parcel and seeks rezoning to a commercial zone that allows numerous uses including flower shops, antique shops, banks, toy stores, and gas stations. The legislative body of the city finds the idea of a flower shop unobjectionable and rezones the property to the general commercial use category. The property owner then builds a gas station. The neighbors have a fit, but the property is zoned for such use, and the gas station stays. Theoretically, a city should not rezone the parcel unless it is willing to permit any of the uses that are listed in the commercial zone. But, without the authority

---

[195] See supra §§ 2:1 et seq. for discussion of relation of zoning to planning.

[196] See *Floyd v. County Council of Prince George's County,* 55 Md. App. 246, 461 A.2d 76 (1983).

[197] *Homart Development Co. v. Planning and Zoning Com'n of Town of Watertown,* 26 Conn. App. 212, 600 A.2d 13, 15 (1991).

[198] *Rockville Crushed Stone, Inc. v. Montgomery County,* 78 Md. App. 176, 552 A.2d 960, 962 (1989).

[199] See *Chrismon v. Guilford County,* 322 N.C. 611, 370 S.E.2d 579, 584 (1988).

[200] See supra § 4:2.

to impose conditions, a city must rezone for any listed commercial purpose or not rezone.

B. *Conditional Zoning as a Solution*

Conditional zoning is tailor-made zoning, designed to provide an escape from the dilemma of open-ended general rezonings. With conditional zoning, the property is rezoned to the more intensive zone, but a condition in the rezoning ordinance [201] or in a separate contract[202] limits the kinds of uses permitted. Using the example from above, if the legislative body is willing to permit any commercial uses at the site except gas stations, the land might be rezoned for commercial uses subject to the condition that the otherwise permitted gas station use is prohibited. If the city wishes to allow flower shops only, then the condition can preclude all other normally permitted uses. A condition requiring the planting and maintenance of a landscaped buffer may also be added. With this method, the legislative body can create an almost unlimited number of different kinds of zones.

Substantial, and some would say excessive, flexibility is obtained by combining the features of conditional zoning and floating zones. Floating above the general, and mapped, use districts, are special use districts created to parallel the general use districts. A property owner seeking a change in classification can apply for either general or special use rezoning. A general use rezoning allows all permitted uses of right, while a special use rezoning limits use to a specified, detailed project. For example, if R-2 zoning contains four permitted uses (say single-family, two-family, garden apartments, and institutional uses), an R-2-S special use, or floating zone, option exists so that a developer intending to build garden apartments can have its property specifically zoned for such use or can seek a general rezoning.

In applying for general R-2 zoning the property owner may be precluded from making known its intended use, which is irrelevant since the rezoning will allow any of the four permitted uses, and the legislative body is obligated to find that any of the four uses are appropriate at the site. In contrast, for an R-2-S rezoning for garden apartments, the developer must submit to specific site plan review of its project by the legislative body. Protective conditions will also be imposed on the special use district to conform to site problems detected during the review process.[203] The fact that the city knows and can closely control the use to take place in the special use district make a developer's chances of success much greater than with general rezonings.

Conditional zoning presents difficulties in some jurisdictions. The enabling act may not authorize it. It may be proscribed under the rubric of contract or spot zoning since it may appear to a court that private deal making, rather than the public interest, motivated the action. It also may violate the uniformity clause of the Standard Act. We explore these issues in detail elsewhere in this treatise.[204]

---

[201] *Goffinet v. Christian County,* 65 Ill. 2d 40, 2 Ill. Dec. 275, 357 N.E.2d 442 (1976).

[202] *Sylvania Elec. Products, Inc. v. City of Newton,* 344 Mass. 428, 183 N.E.2d 118 (1962).

[203] See *Chrismon v. Guilford County,* 322 N.C. 611, 370 S.E.2d 579 (1988), describing such a system authorized by special enabling legislation.

[204] See infra § 5:11 discussing contract zoning and § 5:13 discussing uniformity.

C. Automatic Zoning Conditions

Rezonings sometimes occur automatically. Like common law shifting and spring-ing executory interests, property may be downzoned or upzoned upon the happening of a future event. Reversionary zoning is sometimes used where a community wishes to assure itself that a developer engages only in the use granted by a rezoning. To do so, it may provide that if no one develops the property for a specific use within a set time or if the newly allowed use ceases, the property's zoning classification will revert to its prior classification.

Reverter provisions pose problems. Since the property's classification moves auto-matically from one zoning classification to another, no notice is given and no hearing may be held. Some courts find this a violation of both due process and the enabling act requirement that a zoning enactment occur upon notice and public hearing.[205] Other courts uphold reversionary conditions by implying an obligation on the zoning authori-ties to provide notice and a hearing.[206] Still, even if the authorities follow procedural safeguards, a substantive objection exists since the process assumes the prior classifi-cation, to which the land reverts, is still valid. With the passage of time and changing circumstances, however, that may not be the case. The reclassification should focus on current, not past, needs.

Another automatic zoning process may be used to meet different community con-cerns. An ordinance might provide that the happening of certain events will reclassify the property for a different use. For example, the ordinance might provide that proper-ty zoned agricultural will be zoned residential upon the opening of a major street. This "potential classification zone" has the advantage of giving property owners and others some indication of the plans of the city. As with reverter provisions, substantive and procedural defects may exist with this technique. The new street may have opened, triggering the rezoning, but other intervening developments may have occurred that suggest uses other than residential would be preferable. There also may be no provi-sion for notice and hearing.

§ 4:18   Incentive Zoning

Incentive zoning obtains public benefits or amenities from private developers.[207] A city may offer a developer an incentive, such as a density bonus, in return for the de-veloper agreeing to provide a desired amenity. Typical amenities include public plazas, off-street parking, access sites to rapid transit, day care centers, and theaters.[208] New York City, for example, has granted incentives to development along the Fifth Avenue shopping area to provide hotel and residential uses above the street level commercial use. Washington, D.C. granted a planned unit development on Dupont Circle an in-crease in height and density to provide a two-level pedestrian arcade and mini park.

Incentive zoning is similar in some respects to conditional zoning, discussed in the previous section. As part of the development permission process, a condition is at-tached that grants added development rights and requires construction of, or payment

---

[205] *Spiker v. City of Lakewood,* 198 Colo. 528, 603 P.2d 130 (1979).

[206] *Perry v. Planning Commission of Hawaii County,* 62 Haw. 666, 619 P.2d 95 (1980).

[207] See, generally, Terry Lassar, Carrots and Sticks: New Downtown Zoning (1989).

[208] See e.g., Va. Code Ann. § 15.2–2201 (allows incentive zoning in the form of density bonuses for a de-veloper providing desired "features or amenities" to the locality).

for, some public facility. However, they have dissimilar goals and effects. Conditional zoning generally arises from the desire to accommodate development while protecting neighbors from a presumably more intensive use or to impose exactions or fees to cover infrastructure needed to handle the new development. With incentive zoning, the acquisition of the amenity is the driving force, and while the neighbors might benefit from the amenity provided, it is acquired for the public at large. In fact, the neighbors may suffer more from the increased density allowed by the bonus than they do from the amenity.

One may attack the validity of incentive zoning on several fronts.[209] If authority from the state is not express,[210] a court may not imply the right to use it. The deal-making nature of incentive zoning may make it suspect as a species of spot or contract zoning.[211] Constitutional objections under the due process and taking clauses must be considered as well. If the incentive program is a voluntary option, a developer can hardly object to the consequences of its own choice. Even if participation in the program is mandatory, government typically designs the size of the bonus to more than offset the cost of the amenity, leaving the developer better off economically with the incentive than without it.[212] This likely solves some of the potential constitutional infirmities. This assumes, however, that the incentives are truly bonuses. If, in fact, the incentive zoning program is preceded by a downzoning of property, which is done to make the "incentive" attractive, the provision is an improper use of the police power.

An incentive program also may be vulnerable to the charge that it does not legitimately advance a public purpose. From one perspective incentive zoning is "zoning for sale,"[213] as the city trades its zoning restrictions for the amenity. If the city allows the developer to build a larger building and the costs of the amenity are not too high, the developer wins. The city wins as well, since it acquires a public amenity. Yet, if there is no such thing as a free lunch, someone must be paying a cost. The public suffers harm from the greater building density, which exceeds the base zoning, and the city must still defend the base zoning as appropriate because it is the base zoning that creates the bonus that brings the developer to the bargaining table. The neighbors in the community surrounding the bigger building pay the highest cost. For them, the congestion from the more intensive use may outweigh any benefit they receive from the amenity, but the city is entitled to decide that the gain of the amenity for the public at large more than offsets the loss to the neighbors from congestion. If a legal challenge brought on due process or equal protection grounds by either a developer or a neighbor is tested by a deferential standard of judicial review, it would likely fail.[214]

Higher scrutiny may come by way of a nexus challenge under the takings clause if a mandatory condition results in a physical exaction of the developer's property. Thus, a new shopping center will generate more traffic, and that may well justify requiring the developer to use part of its land for new traffic lanes. No bonus or incentive is likely

---

[209] See Alan C. Weinstein, Incentive Zoning, 2 Zoning and Land Use Controls, § 8.04.

[210] See N.Y. Village Law § 7–703 authorizing incentive zoning.

[211] See *Municipal Art Soc. of New York v. City of New York,* 137 Misc. 2d 832, 522 N.Y.S.2d 800 (1987). See also §§ 5:10 to 5:11.

[212] See *Montgomery County v. Woodward & Lothrop, Inc.,* 280 Md. 686, 376 A.2d 483 (1977).

[213] See, e.g., Kayden, Zoning for Dollars: New Rules for an Old Game?, 39 Wash.U. J. Urb. & Contemp. L. 3 (1991).

[214] See *Asian Americans for Equality v. Koch,* 72 N.Y.2d 121, 531 N.Y.S.2d 782, 527 N.E.2d 265 (1988). See, generally, infra §§ 10:12 and 10:14.

necessary. But, if the shopping center developer is told to build a performing arts center, the link or nexus to the shopping center disappears or is certainly harder to see than a requirement to build traffic lanes. Thus, the requirement to build the arts center may constitute a taking. We explore these constitutional arguments elsewhere.[215]

§ 4:19   Performance Zoning

An alternative to use zoning is performance or impact zoning.[216] Avoiding the rigidity of use classifications, performance zoning concerns itself with the spillover effects of land use activities. Performance zoning establishes criteria to measure such effects, and if the criteria are met, the activity is allowed.

The most prevalent use of performance zoning involves industrial activities. First used in the 1950s, it is widespread today. Instead of, or in addition to, specifically listed uses, the industrial performance zoning ordinance provides standards to measure the external effects produced by industrial activities. It may establish specific standards for smoke, noise, dust, toxic emissions, glare, vibration, radioactivity, electrical disturbance, heat, and odors.[217] If the manufacturing operation meets the standards, it is permitted within the zone.

Performance standards are used increasingly in dealing with nonindustrial activities. Performance zoning even achieved the status of being "one of the trendiest topics"[218] of land use in the 1990s. Such natural resource features as floodplains, woodlands, steep slopes, and groundwater can be protected by performance standards. An ordinance might protect steep slopes by limiting the percentage of slopes of certain grades from being developed or stripped of vegetation. Topographical features may limit the density of development. These include such features as depth to bedrock and the seasonal high water table, factors that concern the possibility of sewage effluent polluting groundwater. Set percentages of vegetation and trees that must remain on site are another example.[219] Noise controls also can be applied to any use.

Performance zoning has met with judicial approval so long as the standards are reasonably set.[220] While the enforcement of such standards may produce development lots of varying size, courts have held them not to violate the uniformity requirement because they treat similar property similarly. As with any ordinance, overbreadth and vagueness may be concerns. For example, a noise standard of "plainly audible" was held invalid on these grounds.[221]

Whether performance standards do their job well is another matter. One commentator actually uses the scarcity of legal challenges as proof of their ineffectiveness.[222]

---

[215] See § 9:8 regarding exactions and impact fees, and § 10:5 regarding the nexus test.

[216] See, generally, Duersken, Modern Industrial Performance Standards: Key Implementation and Legal Issues, 18 Zoning and P. L. Rep. 33 (May 1995).

[217] See, e.g., *DeCoals, Inc. v. Board of Zoning Appeals of City of Westover,* 168 W. Va. 339, 284 S.E.2d 856 (1981).

[218] See Duersken, Modern Industrial Performance Standards: Key Implementation and Legal Issues, 18 Zoning and P. L. Rep. 33 (May 1995).

[219] *Chrin Bros., Inc. v. Williams Tp. Zoning Hearing Bd.,* 815 A.2d 1179 (Pa. Commw. Ct. 2003).

[220] *Jones v. Zoning Hearing Bd. of Town of McCandless,* 134 Pa. Commw. 435, 578 A.2d 1369 (1990).

[221] *Easy Way of Lee County, Inc. v. Lee County,* 674 So. 2d 863 (Fla. 2d DCA 1996).

[222] See Jaffe, Redesigning Industrial Performance Standards, 47 Land Use Law & Zoning Dig. 3 (Nov.1995).

Regardless of whether that is a justifiable conclusion, problems do exist. The systems are not as devoid of discretionary decisionmaking as theory envisions. Drafting workable standards can be difficult, and some standards are highly subjective, creating concerns of arbitrary application. Performance zoning also requires more administrative time than does use zoning.

Still, performance zoning is viable, possibly as an alternative or particularly as a supplement to use zoning. Studies show that communities that employ performance standards, usually in industrial design, and environmental matters, have reached some level of satisfaction with them.[223] Pre-stated performance criteria produce better design and site control in a less confrontational manner than traditional use zoning. If federal and state governments eliminate or decrease environmental controls, one local option to deal with the resultant void will be to increase environmental performance standards.

Form based zoning is another tool that supplants, or predominates over, use zoning.[224]

§ 4:20   Interim Zones and Moratoria

Interim zoning or moratoria are used to freeze or limit development while new comprehensive plans, zoning ordinances, or growth management programs can be adopted and implemented.[225] Interim zoning may also freeze development pending the solution of problems of overburdened public services, such as schools, water, and sewer or be used to prevent a proliferation of particular uses that a city finds itself unprotected against, such as adult entertainment uses,[226] fast food restaurants,[227] or cellular towers.[228]

Interim zoning is vital in preserving the integrity of the planning and zoning processes. Without a moratorium on development, building activity may occur that will defeat the plan's purposes before it is enacted. The publicity that will necessarily be a part of the planning process may in fact trigger a race by developers to build or at least achieve a vested right to build before new controls, which they fear may be more intrusive than current ones, are adopted.[229] Interim zoning is controversial since, to be effective, it must be enacted without the usual notice and hearing that accompany the adoption of land use controls. Still, authority to enact interim controls is often ex-

---

[223] Porter, Phillips & Lassar, Flexible Zoning: How It Works 82 (1988).

[224] See infra § 8:2 B.

[225] Interim zoning is also discussed infra § 5:28 regarding vested rights, § 9:6 regarding growth management and at § 10:8B regarding constitutionality.

[226] See, e.g., *City of Renton v. Playtime Theatres, Inc.,* 475 U.S. 41, 106 S. Ct. 925, 89 L. Ed. 2d 29 (1986).

[227] See, e.g., *Schafer v. City of New Orleans,* 743 F.2d 1086 (5th Cir. 1984).

[228] Lopata, Monumental Changes: Stalling Tactics and Moratoria on Cellular Tower Siting, 77 Wash. U. L.Q. 193 (1999).

[229] See § 5:28 regarding vested rights.

press.[230] Where not so provided, courts are divided over whether there is an implied power.[231]

In spite of much recent litigation, the best summary of the requirements for a valid moratorium can be found in the 1976 decision of the Supreme Court of Minnesota in *Almquist v. Town of Marshan.*[232] That court opined that a moratorium on building permits is valid if:

(1) It is adopted by the local government in good faith;[233]

(2) It is not discriminatory;[234]

(3) It is of limited duration;

(4) It is for the purpose of the development of a comprehensive zoning plan; and

(5) The local government acts promptly to adopt such a plan.

Where interim zoning is not authorized, there are alternative, albeit less effective, techniques cities may use. One technique is to enact a quick downzoning while another is to administratively deny a permit request.

Upon learning of a proposed unwanted development, or fearing such development may be in the offing, a municipality may hastily pass what purports to be a permanent zoning classification, downzoning property to prohibit the use. Such action, not supported by a planning process, is ill-advised. Such an ordinance also may be invalid in a jurisdiction with a meaningful consistency requirement.[235]

Administrative denial, an informal way to freeze land use, is another technique. Here, the zoning or building inspector withholds action on a permit request where the city expects the proposed development to be inconsistent with upcoming changes in the law. If the permit is delayed long enough to permit passage of the new ordinance, the inspector can deny the permit based on the new law. Courts differ over the validity of this technique. Some courts uphold the denial where convinced that the city acted to further the general welfare and did not arbitrarily single out the permit applicant.[236] In other states, courts will only uphold the denial if the newly enacted ordinance was pending at the time of the denial.[237] In some jurisdictions, the technique will not work.

---

[230] See, e.g., Cal. Gov't Code § 65858; Colo. Rev. Stat. § 30–28–121; Utah Code Ann. § 10-9a-504 (authorizing six month ordinance without public hearing).

[231] Implying such power, see *CEEED v. California Coastal Zone Conservation Com.,* 43 Cal. App. 3d 306, 118 Cal. Rptr. 315 (1974) (Coastal Conversation Act);. Refusing to imply power, see *City of Sanibel v. Buntrock,* 409 So. 2d 1073 (Fla. 2d DCA 1981).

[232] *Almquist v. Town of Marshan,* 308 Minn. 52, 245 N.W.2d 819 (1976).

[233] See *Lake Illyria Corp. v. Town of Gardiner,* 43 A.D.2d 386, 352 N.Y.S.2d 54 (1974).

[234] See *Stubblefield Construction Co. v. City of San Bernardino,* 32 Cal. App. 4th 687, 38 Cal. Rptr. 2d 413 (1995).

[235] See supra § 2:13. Also, such a hasty downzoning may raise a claim of spot zoning. See infra § 5:10.

[236] *Spector v. Building Inspector of Milton,* 250 Mass. 63, 145 N.E. 265 (1924).

[237] *Action Outdoor Advertising JV, LLC v. City of Destin, FL,* 2005 WL 2338804 (N.D. Fla. 2005); *Ben Lomond, Inc. v. City of Idaho Falls,* 92 Idaho 595, 448 P.2d 209 (1968). The pending ordinance rule is discussed infra § 5:28F.

There may, for example, be a vested right to develop pursuant to the law in effect at the time of the permit application despite a subsequent change in the law.[238]

Property owners may suffer economic loss from an interim control which stringently limits or freezes use. If, after the adoption of the new ordinance, the property owner may proceed with development as before the freeze, the fact that the control was temporary mitigates the harm. If, however, the new ordinance prohibits the owner's intended use, the loss will be greater. If the loss is severe, a property owner may raise a regulatory takings claim. Constitutionally, a property owner is guaranteed a reasonable use over a reasonable period of time. The mere loss of the present right to use land is not a taking.[239] The longer the duration of the control, the more likely it is to be found a taking.[240]

§ 4:21 Overlay Zoning

An overlay zone places property simultaneously in two zones. Most often this occurs where the use of the property affects two distinct municipal concerns, such as compatibility of use with surrounding lands and the preservation of sensitive lands or protection from problem uses. An overlay zone often implements historic preservation, for example, since historically significant areas near urban centers frequently encompass contiguous commercial and residential areas.[241] In this fashion, the commercial and residential classifications are continued while the overlay imposes historic controls on the portion of the properties within those two zones that comprise the historic area. Another use of overlay zones is to protect environmentally sensitive land. Thus, land zoned for single-family homes may be undevelopable because of an overlay zone showing the land to be on a steep hillside. Other examples include land beneath the flight paths, which may be placed in an airport overlay, and floodplain zoning.

The "overlay" term is sometimes used in a sense reverse from above where cities lift or reduce restrictions from a certain part of a zoned area. This may be done in order to encourage reuse of declining urban areas or to allow greater freedom of use to generate diversity.

Overlay zones may run afoul of the uniformity clause of the Standard State Zoning Enabling Act.[242] The City of Phoenix created an "inebriate district" as an overlay in a large commercially zoned area. In this bizarrely, but perhaps aptly, named zone, establishments selling alcohol, pawn shops, blood banks, second hand stores, and missions were required to get special permits. Those same uses in the commercial zone, but outside the overlay, were permitted of right. A property owner, whom the city denied a permit to operate a pawn shop in the inebriate zone, challenged the law on uniformity grounds. In *Jachimek v. Superior Court in and for County of Maricopa,*[243] the court agreed with the property owner, holding that the city could not create an overlay in

---

[238] See infra § 5:28 for a discussion of vested rights.

[239] *Tahoe-Sierra Preservation Council, Inc. v. Tahoe Regional Planning Agency,* 535 U.S. 302, 122 S. Ct. 1465, 152 L. Ed. 2d 517 (2002.

[240] The takings issue is discussed in full, infra §§ 10:4 to 10:10. See § 10:8B with particular reference to moratoria as takings.

[241] *A-S-P Associates v. City of Raleigh,* 298 N.C. 207, 258 S.E.2d 444 (1979).

[242] See infra § 5:13 for discussion of uniformity.

[243] *Jachimek v. Superior Court In and For County of Maricopa,* 169 Ariz. 317, 819 P.2d 487 (1991).

which use permits were required for certain uses that were not required for the same uses in the same underlying zone elsewhere within the city.[244]

Not all courts agree with the literal view of *Jachimek. In AS-P Associates v. City of Raleigh,*[245] the court found an historic overlay that subjected commercial property to restrictions not suffered by other commercially zoned land did not violate the uniformity clause. Giving the enabling act a more relaxed reading than the court in *Jachimek,* the *A-S-P* court acknowledged that the regulations of a particular use district must be uniform, but found that rule not to prohibit overlay districts despite the fact that they imposed additional regulations on some property. After all, said the court, the overlay did "not destroy the uniformity of the regulations applicable to the underlying use-district."[246] Whether one views an overlay as violating the uniformity clause, it does create a new use district subjecting the land to dual controls. If doubt exists over whether overlays are authorized, a city can achieve the same effect by creating a new zone that contains the controls of the prior underlying zone and the newly desired controls that would otherwise be imposed by overlay.

V. GOVERNMENTAL AND COMMUNITY USES

§ 4:22   Favored Status

Among the vast number of potential land uses, some are thought to generate special benefits to the public, which may result in their being regulated differently than similar private uses. They include government uses and such community facilities as schools, public utilities, airports, religious uses, and medical facilities. These uses, while perhaps as objectionable to their immediate neighbors as other kinds of uses, are often treated more leniently.

The special treatment afforded to, or sought by, these uses results in a substantial amount of litigation. Government owned or operated uses often claim immunity from the zoning of lower or coequal levels of government. If the government use is immune, uses that are similar to the governmental use, but not allowed by local law, may then object on uniformity or equal protection grounds to the dissimilar treatment. Regulatory schemes of states and the federal government may authorize or license private uses that conflict with local zoning. Where that occurs, the private licensee will attempt to establish that state law has preempted the local zoning.

Zoning codes may permit public uses in a zone, but ban otherwise identical private uses. They may allow nonprofit private uses that are similar to the permitted public use, but disallow for-profit uses. These distinctions are often unrelated to the land use effects of the various owned and organized uses, but many courts allow them nonetheless.

---

[244] Accord, *Boerschinger v. Elkay Enterprises, Inc.,* 32 Wis. 2d 168, 145 N.W.2d 108 (1966).

[245] *A-S-P Associates v. City of Raleigh,* 298 N.C. 207, 258 S.E.2d 444 (1979).

[246] 298 N.C. at 230, 258 S.E.2d at 458.

§ 4:23 Immunity for Governmental Uses

A. *General Considerations*

The superior sovereign, by virtue of that status, is immune from control by subordinate units of government. The supremacy clause of the constitution prevents the application of state or local zoning laws to the federal government. Likewise, local zoning does not bind a state. Courts presume that when the state delegates police power functions to local governments, it does not intend to waive the immunity it has as a sovereign. Thus, the delegated power cannot be used against the state.[247]

Immunity is essential for numerous government functions that are unwanted in many locales such as waste disposal, correctional facilities, and homeless shelters. While operating a governmental use in noncompliance with local zoning may result in harm to the residents of the city or at least to the immediate neighbors, the carrying out of an essential state function benefits the public at large. If local controls were permitted to exclude these uses, they might have nowhere to go.

Whether immunity attaches depends on the purpose of the land use, not the ownership.[248]

Privatization of government functions ought not cause a loss of zoning immunity. In *City of Louisville v. Gailor,*[249] the county contracted with a private corporation to house some of its inmates. The company's chosen site was within the city. While the city's board of adjustment granted a conditional use permit, the trial court overturned it on appeal. The high court, however, held that the privately operated jail enjoyed the same immunity as a county run jail. The key to zoning and to immunity is use, not ownership, said the court. Use for a prison, even where delegated to private parties, is still governmental.[250]

B. *Federal*

The supremacy clause of the constitution prevents the application of state or local zoning laws to federally operated land uses.[251] Federal regulatory schemes also may preempt local law.[252] The federal government, of course, can consent to be governed by local law. Where it recognizes the desirability of some local control, it generally does so by directing federal agencies to consult with local authorities. The agency, though, retains final decisionmaking power. Federal urban land use policy, for example, requires that agencies cooperate with local authorities by directing that actions taken "shall be consistent with zoning and land use practices and with the planning and development objectives of local governments and planning agencies."[253]

---

[247] See, e.g., *Aviation Services v. Board of Adjustment of Hanover Tp.,* 20 N.J. 275, 119 A.2d 761 (1956).

[248] *Crown Communication New York, Inc. v. Department of Transp. of State,* 4 N.Y.3d 159, 791 N.Y.S.2d 494, 824 N.E.2d 934 (2005) (immunity of state-owned telecommunications towers from zoning extends to private telecommunications providers).

[249] *City of Louisville Bd. of Zoning Adjustment v. Gailor,* 920 S.W.2d 887 (Ky. Ct. App. 1996).

[250] *Crown Communication New York, Inc. v. Department of Transp. of State of New York,* 309 A.D.2d 863, 765 N.Y.S.2d 898 (2003).

[251] *U.S. v. Gardner,* 107 F.3d 1314 (9th Cir. 1997).

[252] See, e.g., *Blockbuster Videos, Inc. v. City of Tempe,* 141 F.3d 1295 (9th Cir. 1998).

[253] 40 U.S.C.A. § 901.

With respect to the federal government it does not matter whether the government owns the property in fee or is the lessee of property. In neither case is its use governed by local regulation. Private lessees of federally owned property may also be exempt if they are carrying out a government function.

C. State and Local Government

A state's immunity extends not only to departments and agencies of the state,[254] but includes local governments when exercising state functions and private licensees operating pursuant to comprehensive state regulatory programs.[255] Immunity problems also arise between governmental subunits of the state, such as cities, counties, and school districts, where one unit attempts to use land under the zoning control of another unit. Statutes may expressly confirm immunity for a specific use or expressly subject the activity to local control, but legislatures usually fail to deal expressly with immunity, leaving resolution of the issue to the courts. The Standard State Zoning Enabling Act, for example, is silent with respect to regulation of government uses.

The courts have employed several tests to decide whether immunity attaches. The early tests used include the superior sovereign test, the eminent domain test, and the governmental-proprietary test. All have their shortcomings, and are frequently, and derogatorily, referred to as mechanical. The superior sovereign and eminent domain tests embody "might makes right" philosophies and, while having the advantage of simplicity, they ignore the fact that the power or status that confers immunity is unrelated to the purposes of the delegated zoning power.

The governmental-proprietary distinction, likely the most popular early test, is frequently unhelpful because it varies depending on the context in which courts apply it. A governmental activity for purposes of determining municipal tort liability may not be a governmental activity for purposes of determining immunity from zoning regulations, yet courts are not always careful to avoid mixing precedent. Moreover, no unanimity exists as to what is a governmental function even in the zoning context.

A growing number of courts, dissatisfied with early cases that they regarded as too permissive in exempting state activities from local zoning,[256] have instituted a balance of interests test.[257] The balance of interests test places a heavier burden on government to justify its claimed immunity than is the case under the mechanical tests. Even where a use is found immune, the right may not be absolute, as some courts review the use to see that it is operated reasonably.[258] This gives the recipient community some protection that it might not otherwise enjoy. Even the application of a mechanical superior sovereign test may not result in absolute immunity, as the court may subject the state to local laws aimed at public safety.[259]

---

[254] *Town of Bloomfield v. New Jersey Highway Authority,* 18 N.J. 237, 113 A.2d 658 (1955).

[255] See infra § 4:24.

[256] *Witzel v. Village of Brainard,* 208 Neb. 231, 302 N.W.2d 723, 726 (1981) (Hippe, J. dissenting).

[257] See *Native Village of Eklutna v. Alaska R.R. Corp.,* 87 P.3d 41 (Alaska 2004) (listing 14 states as adherents).

[258] *Blackstone Park Imp. Ass'n v. State Bd. of Standards and Appeals,* 448 A.2d 1233, 1239 (R.I. 1982).

[259] *City of Hattiesburg v. Region XII Com'n on Mental Health & Retardation,* 654 So. 2d 516 (Miss. 1995).

As with the mechanical approaches, dissatisfaction exists with the balancing approach.[260] Some courts find that it confers too much land use policymaking authority on the courts and lacks predictability.[261]

Likely the better approach is to do what several courts do and simply refrain from confusing the issue with any of the above tests by simply acknowledging that the question is one of legislative intent, calling for the court to use its standard rules of statutory interpretation.[262] Some apply the intent test with a bias in favor of local control and demand a clear expression of intent to find a use immune.[263]

D. Local Government's Self-Exemption

Local governments often exempt their own uses from the operation of their zoning laws. Even where a municipality does not expressly exempt municipal uses, many courts find the municipality is not bound to follow its own ordinances.[264] Some, however, presume that if the code is silent, the city must follow its own ordinances.[265] Courts have upheld these exemptions, reasoning that if it is a governmental use, it necessarily promotes the public interest.[266] However, if they follow the governmental/proprietary distinction, the latter activities would not be exempt.[267]

§ 4:24 Preemption of Local Law

Local law may also be preempted by state law for various types of activities, such as airports, alcohol sales, nuclear facilities, cemeteries, group homes, hospitals, and waste disposal facilities. While preemption for the licensee is similar to a finding of immunity for a state agency or other governmental body,[268] prevailing on the theory is often more difficult. A governmental use may be immune simply by virtue of the superior sovereign status of the state or by the user's possession of the power of eminent domain. The relative infrequency of preemption leaves many land uses subject to multiple permitting processes. Our federal system, and preference for a local role in land use decisions, may justify this, but a cost results. Multiple permitting increases the possibility of a total denial of the requested use. The mere requirement of seeking multiple permits subjects the applicant to the prospect of conflicting conditions. If the conditions imposed by the subordinate government conflict with the higher level or if the former denies a use that the latter allows at a specific location, the subordinate's decision is preempted. But, even if there is no denial and they impose no additional conditions, the process of multi-permitting adds to the cost and the time for development approval.

---

[260] See Reynolds, The Judicial Role in Intergovernmental Land Use Disputes: The Case Against Balancing, 71 Minn. L. Rev. 611 (1987).

[261] *Macon Ass'n for Retarded Citizens v. Macon-Bibb County Planning and Zoning Com'n,* 252 Ga. 484, 314 S.E.2d 218 (1984).

[262] *Byrne v. State,* 463 Mich. 652, 624 N.W.2d 906 (2001).

[263] *Macon Ass'n for Retarded Citizens v. Macon-Bibb County Planning and Zoning Com'n,* 252 Ga. 484, 314 S.E.2d 218 (1984).

[264] *Glascock v. Baltimore County, Md.,* 321 Md. 118, 581 A.2d 822 (1990).

[265] *Clark v. Town of Estes Park,* 686 P.2d 777 (Colo. 1984).

[266] *Sinn v. Board of Selectmen of Acton,* 357 Mass. 606, 259 N.E.2d 557, 559 (1970).

[267] *Hunke v. Foote,* 84 Idaho 391, 373 P.2d 322 (1962) (electrical substation found proprietary).

[268] See supra § 4:23.

§ 4:25   Public Utilities

A.   *General Rules*

Public utilities are often exempt from local zoning control. If governmentally owned, they may be immune from local zoning as are other governmental uses.[269] If privately owned, the state law that grants the utility its franchise and regulates its operations may preempt local law. States usually deem exemption from local law necessary to assure that the utility can meet its service obligations, which may be regional, state, or national in character. While local authorities and neighbors may not want an electric substation or oil pipeline in a residential area, the desire for efficient provision of service may compel insulating the utility from local law. Courts are often bothered by the scenarios they foresee if local law were to apply. As the Florida Supreme Court said in a case involving a local government's attempt to require an electric utility to underground its lines: "If 100 such municipalities each had the right to impose its own requirements with respect to installation of transmission facilities, a hodgepodge of methods of construction could result and costs and resulting capital requirements could mushroom."[270]

State law typically vests authority over public utilities in a state commission and precludes local regulation. Immunity may be automatic or the state commission may be empowered to grant exemptions. In Ohio, for example, the zoning enabling act does "not confer any power on any board of county commissioners or board of zoning appeals in respect to the location, * * * use, or enlargement of any buildings or structures of any public utility."[271] Massachusetts law authorizes a public utility to seek an exemption from local zoning.[272] A state commission may also be authorized to review and reverse local zoning decisions.[273]

Even exempt utilities may not be able to act with impunity toward local interests. Where a utility must petition the state utility commission for an exemption, the local community has input to assert its interest. This does not guarantee that the local government will have its way, and in considering a request the state commission must weigh all aspects of the public interest and not merely the local interest,[274] but at least the local government has an opportunity to be heard. State commissions may also attach conditions to utility land uses and activities to protect the local interest.[275]

In some jurisdictions certain utilities are expressly subject to zoning law.[276] Where local authority exists, they frequently permit utilities only in commercial and industrial areas. Where authorities allow utilities in residential zones, they handle them as special uses. The special permit technique is useful because it allows a unique use to be conditioned for minimal disruption to the neighborhood.

---

[269] See, e.g., *Forsyth County v. Georgia Transmission Corp.*, 280 Ga. 664, 632 S.E.2d 101 (2006). See also supra § 4:23.

[270] *Florida Power Corp. v. Seminole County*, 579 So. 2d 105, 107 (Fla. 1991).

[271] Ohio Rev. Code Ann. § 303.211.

[272] Mass. Gen. Laws ch. 40A, § 3.

[273] *Newport Elec. Corp. v. Town of Portsmouth*, 650 A.2d 489 (R.I. 1994).

[274] Planning Bd. of Braintree v. Department of Public Utilities, 420 Mass. 22, 27, 647 N.E.2d 1186, 1190 (1995).

[275] *Appeal of Milford Water Works*, 126 N.H. 127, 489 A.2d 627 (1985).

[276] Ind. Code § 8–1–2–89 (b); Or. Rev. Stat. § 221.420.

Where state law is ambiguous or silent, courts must determine whether state law impliedly preempts local law. While generalizations may be imprudent for an issue that turns on non-uniform state regulatory regimes, the cases seem to weigh in favor of implied preemption in the public utility area.[277] This tendency is in contrast to the reluctance to find preemption of local law in many other areas that the state regulates.[278] A concern that the parochial views of multiple localities would destroy effective and low-cost utility service presumably explains this tendency.[279]

B. *What Constitutes a Public Utility*

What constitutes a public utility for the purposes of preemption depends first on the state statutory definition, which may be general or precise, and may itself contain express exemptions. To the extent that a court must construe legislative intent, the fundamental question is whether the efficient and continuous supply of the public service requires that the utility not be subject to multiple levels of government control.[280] Where this test is met, courts have shown a willingness to confer immunity on entities that do not precisely fit specific statutory language. Thus, while state law may regulate and exempt "public service corporations," courts are likely to include private corporations that otherwise meet the concept of a public utility.[281] By the same rationale, a public entity that is not, in form, a corporation, such as a municipal electric department, transit authority or water commission, may be treated as a "public service corporation" for the purposes of a preemption determination.[282] Many disputed classifications involve radio and other communication facilities, and the case results vary.[283]

Even if an entity is not a public utility under state utility law, it may meet the definition of a public utility for state zoning law purposes and be entitled to preferential treatment.[284]

C. *Cellular Towers and Other Telecommunications Facilities*

Our insatiable demand for cellular telephones and other advanced communication devices has fueled the need to build more, and taller, towers. The towers are unpopular with those who have to look at them or live near them. While some have health concerns,[285] the dominant objection is that the towers are aesthetically offensive, which may result in a lowering of property values.

The federal Telecommunications Act of 1996 partially preempts zoning of cellular towers by providing that local zoning may not unreasonably discriminate among pro-

---

[277] See, e.g., *Howard County v. Potomac Elec. Power Co.,* 319 Md. 511, 573 A.2d 821 (1990).

[278] See discussion supra §§ 4:23 to 4:24.

[279] See *Florida Power Corp. v. Seminole County,* 579 So. 2d 105 (Fla. 1991).

[280] For varying formulations of this test, see *Cellular Telephone Co. v. Rosenberg,* 82 N.Y.2d 364, 604 N.Y.S.2d 895, 898, 624 N.E.2d 990, 993 (1993).

[281] *Save the Bay, Inc. v. Department of Public Utilities,* 366 Mass. 667, 680, 322 N.E.2d 742 (1975).

[282] *Planning Bd. of Braintree v. Department of Public Utilities,* 420 Mass. 22, 27, 647 N.E.2d 1186, 1189 (1995).

[283] *Campanelli v. AT&T Wireless Serv., Inc.,* 85 Ohio St. 3d 103, 706 N.E.2d 1267 (1999).

[284] The fact that an entity is not a public utility for state utility law purposes also does not preclude it from meeting the local zoning definition of that use. Finding cellular use to be a public utility, see *Bellsouth Carolinas PCS, L.P. v. Henderson County Zoning Bd. of Adjustment,* 174 N.C. App. 574, 621 S.E.2d 270 (2005).

[285] See *Hawk v. Zoning Hearing Bd. of Butler Tp.,* 152 Pa. Commw. 48, 618 A.2d 1087, 1090 (1992).

viders of functionally equivalent services and that zoning cannot have the effect of totally prohibiting such services.[286] The Act precludes consideration of the environmental effects of radio frequency emissions if the facility complies with federal regulations concerning such emissions. The Act has significant procedural provisions as well: (1) it requires that permit requests be acted on in a reasonable time, (2) it provides for expedited judicial review of adverse rulings by state or local government bodies, and (3) it requires that permit denials be in writing, supported by a written record of substantial evidence. While some have suggested that the Act may violate the Tenth Amendment,[287] courts have thus far rejected the argument.[288]

In the first decade since its passage, the Act has generated a great deal of case law over the question of unreasonable discrimination among functionally equivalent services, and, in particular, total exclusion.[289] The not-in-my-backyard syndrome is evident in municipal reactions to tower siting requests and, likely for that reason, courts have gradually increased their scrutiny of local decisions.[290] Although, in the only case to reach the Supreme Court, the remedies for providers suffering violations of the Act were limited. In *Rancho Palos Verdes v. Abrams,*[291] the Court held that § 1983 is not available as a remedy in an action brought under the Act.

Decisions on total denial range from the pro-local government approach of the Fourth Circuit, which holds that only a blanket ban on all wireless facilities constitutes a prohibition of service[292] to the more nuanced and less predictable approaches of the First and Third Circuits, which hold that individual denials of service may effectively constitute a total denial. The Third Circuit asks whether the proposed facility would fill a significant existing gap in service generally, not just for the provider seeking the facility, and whether the proposal is the least intrusive on local interests.[293] The First Circuit expressly rejects what it calls the "any service equals no effective prohibition."[294] Thus, the act is violated if the applicant is prevented from filling a significant gap in its own service network.[295] The Federal Communications Commission has issued a ruling rejecting the Third Circuit approach.[296]

---

[286] 47 U.S.C.A. § 332(c)(7)(B)(i)(I) and (II).

[287] *Petersburg Cellular Partnership v. Board of Sup'rs of Nottoway County,* 205 F.3d 688 (4th Cir. 2000) (Niemeyer, J., concurring).

[288] *Southwestern Bell Wireless Inc. v. Johnson County Bd. of County Com'rs,* 199 F.3d 1185 (10th Cir. 1999).

[289] See Foster and Carrel, Tell Me What You Really Think: Judicial Review of Land Use Decisions on Cellular Telecommunications Facilities Under the Telecommunications Act of 1996, 37 Urb. Law. 551 (2005).

[290] Id. See also Steven J. Eagle, Wireless Telecommunications, Infrastructure Security, and the NIMBY Problem, 54 Cath.U.L.Rev. 445 (2005) (arguing in favor of congressional amendment to more clearly limit local control).

[291] *City of Rancho Palos Verdes, Cal. v. Abrams,* 544 U.S. 113, 125 S. Ct. 1453, 161 L. Ed. 2d 316 (2005).

[292] *USCOC of Virginia RSA #3 v. Montgomery County Bd. of Sup'rs,* 343 F.3d 262 (4th Cir. 2003).

[293] *Nextel West Corp. v. Unity Township,* 282 F.3d 257 (3d Cir. 2002).

[294] *Second Generation Properties, L.P. v. Town of Pelham,* 313 F.3d 620 (1st Cir. 2002).

[295] *MetroPCS, Inc. v. City and County of San Francisco,* 400 F.3d 715, 731 (9th Cir. 2005) (extensive discussion of various views; ultimately adopting the First Circuit view).

[296] *In the Matter of Petition for Declaratory Ruling to Clarify Provisions of Section 332(C)(7)(B) to Ensure Timely Siting Review and to Preempt Under Section 253 State and Local Ordinances That Classify All Wireless Siting Proposals as Requiring a Variance,* 24 F.C.C.R. 13994, 14017, 2009 WL 3868811 (F.C.C. 2009), petition for review denied, 668 F.3d 229 (5th Cir. 2012), discussed in *Sprint Spectrum L.P. v. Zoning Bd. of Adjustment of Borough of Paramus, N.J.,* 51 Communications Reg. (P & F) 1267, 2010 WL 4868218 (D.N.J. 2010).

In addition to federal limits, the power of local authorities to regulate these uses turns on whether the service provider is exempt under state law as a public utility. The towers may be treated as "inherently beneficial" public utilities since mobile telephone service enhances personal and commercial communications and is valuable for emergency services.[297]

Even if not public utilities under state utility law, cellular towers may be treated as public utilities for state and local zoning law purposes and be entitled to the preferential treatment they afford to such uses. The New York Court of Appeals, for example, has found the towers to be "inherently beneficial" uses subject to a relaxed variance test.[298] While several courts also have found cellular towers to qualify as public utilities under local law,[299] cellular phone businesses lack essential features of traditional public utilities. For example, a court found a cellular tower did not qualify as a use permitted by special exception under a provision that permitted "public utility buildings and structures (including storage yards)" since the communications provider did not show that it would serve all members of the public, and was not required to file tariffs or discontinue service only with the approval of a regulatory agency.[300]

D. Underground Utility Lines

Another issue of controversy is whether local government can require utilities to underground their services. Aesthetics generally is the reason undergrounding is desired, though issues of safety may also be alleged. An undergrounding requirement is likely within the police power,[301] but courts differ over the preemption issue.[53] Cost is the problem from the utilities' perspective. In a Missouri case, the court noted that while the cost of 1.8 miles of overhead lines was roughly $300,000, it soared to $2,000,000 if the lines were put underground.[302] Lacking local control, the state utility commission may be able to require undergrounding.[303]

§ 4:26 Public-Private and Profit-Nonprofit Distinctions

Privately owned facilities and those operated for gain are often denied use rights granted to publicly owned facilities and to nonprofit facilities. To the extent that these distinctions are based on the form of ownership of an operation, they are at odds with

---

[297] See *Pennsylvania Cellular Telephone Corp. v. Zoning Hearing Bd. Buck Tp.*, 127 F. Supp. 2d 635 (M.D. Pa. 2001) (wireless telecommunication not a public utility within meaning of special use ordinance).

[298] *Cellular Telephone Co. v. Rosenberg*, 82 N.Y.2d 364, 604 N.Y.S.2d 895, 624 N.E.2d 990 (1993). But see *Smart SMR of New York, Inc. v. Borough of Fair Lawn Bd. of Adjustment*, 152 N.J. 309, 704 A.2d 1271 (1998).

[299] See supra § 4:25B.

[300] *Pennsylvania Cellular Telephone Corp. v. Zoning Hearing Bd. Buck Tp.*, 127 F. Supp. 2d 635 (M.D. Pa. 2001).

[301] *U.S. West Communications, Inc. v. City of Longmont*, 948 P.2d 509 (Colo. 1997).

[53] Invalidating application of local law: *Florida Power Corp. v. Seminole County*, 579 So. 2d 105 (Fla. 1991); *Union Elec. Co. v. City of Crestwood*, 499 S.W.2d 480 (Mo. 1973).

Allowing application of local law, see, *Arizona Public Service Co. v. Town of Paradise Valley*, 125 Ariz. 447, 610 P.2d 449 (1980); *Benzinger v. Union Light, Heat & Power Co.*, 293 Ky. 747, 170 S.W.2d 38 (1943).

[302] *Union Elec. Co. v. City of Crestwood*, 499 S.W.2d 480 (Mo. 1973). In a more recent case a utility estimated that undergrounding, if required by all jurisdictions through which the line passed, would cost $2.5 billion. *Florida Power Corp. v. Seminole County*, 579 So. 2d 105, 106 (Fla. 1991).

[303] *Sleepy Hollow Lake, Inc. v. Public Service Commission*, 43 A.D.2d 439, 352 N.Y.S.2d 274 (1974).

the general rule of zoning that ownership is not a legitimate basis for use zoning.[304] To the extent they are based on the organization's purpose and its use of revenue, they are on shaky grounds of enabling act legitimacy. To the extent they are based on the effects of the use of land, they are legitimate.

A. Public v. Private Uses

Many courts tolerate the public-private distinction without seriously examining the justification.[305] Government may achieve the discriminatory treatment by expressly either allowing its own public use and banning like private uses, or banning all uses and then exempting itself from its own ordinance.[306]

The distinction between public and private use has arisen frequently in the context of schools, where it has most often been found wanting.[307] In one case, the court noted that the city offered no reason for prohibiting private schools when it allowed public ones, probably "for the very good reason that none exist [ed]."[308] One case upholding the exclusion of private schools from zones that permitted public schools did so on the ground that private schools do not serve all comers from the community.[309]

If the reason supporting the classification is that the public facility is for the benefit of the public at large, the validity may turn on whether the private use is open to the public.[310] Where a city allowed public museums, a court struck down an ordinance banning private museums, noting the private museum, like the public one, would be open to serve the public.[311]

Favoring public use over private use, though it lacks a land use justification, may be justified for other reasons. If high density housing is viewed as imposing negative externalities, a city might choose to limit the amount of such housing by permitting only public housing.[312] The same can be said for schools, and most other uses. From a federal equal protection standpoint, a classification based on factors unrelated to the legislative purpose is likely constitutional. In review of mere socioeconomic regulation, not involving a fundamental right or suspect class, the Supreme Court applies a highly deferential, rational basis rule of review that virtually assures the law will be upheld.[313] Limiting negative externalities by excluding private uses does not affect a suspect class or a fundamental right.[314]

---

[304] See supra § 4:2 regarding ownership, and § 4:23, regarding government immunity, particularly § 4:23D on local government self-exemption.

[305] *Cameron v. Zoning Agent of Bellingham*, 357 Mass. 757, 260 N.E.2d 143 (1970).

[306] *Jefferson Nat. Bank of Miami Beach v. City of Miami Beach*, 267 So. 2d 100 (Fla. 3d DCA 1972), as interpreted in *City of Kissimmee v. Ellis*, 431 So. 2d 283 (Fla. 5th DCA 1983).

[307] *Catholic Bishop of Chicago v. Kingery*, 371 Ill. 257, 20 N.E.2d 583 (1939). See also discussion of schools infra § 4:27.

[308] *City of Miami Beach v. State ex rel. Lear*, 128 Fla. 750, 175 So. 537, 539 (1937).

[309] *State ex rel. Wisconsin Lutheran High School Conference v. Sinar*, 267 Wis. 91, 65 N.W.2d 43 (1954). The distinction of *Sinar* was labeled "doubtful" by a later Wisconsin court. *State ex rel. Warren v. Renter*, 44 Wis. 2d 201, 221, 170 N.W.2d 790, 799 (1969).

[310] *Golf, Inc. v. District of Columbia*, 67 F.2d 575 (App. D.C. 1933).

[311] *City of Kissimmee v. Ellis*, 431 So. 2d 283 (Fla. 5th DCA 1983).

[312] *Cameron v. Zoning Agent of Bellingham*, 357 Mass. 757, 260 N.E.2d 143 (1970).

[313] See discussion infra § 10:14.

[314] The more sympathetic treatment given to tax supported uses may be perceived like grandfathering nonconforming uses because of their built-up reliance interests, which the Court has upheld. *City of New*

Some courts, employing greater scrutiny than is necessary as a matter of federal constitutional law, have invalidated unequal treatment of private land uses. [315]

B. Profit v. Nonprofit Uses

A distinction similar to the public-private one is the permission given to uses that are nonprofit. As with the private versus public distinction, the profit versus nonprofit distinction is not an invidious one, and will be upheld where a court applies a deferential rule of review.[316] In *Town of Huntington v. Park Shore Country Day Camp of Dix Hills, Inc.,*[317] the New York Court of Appeals upheld the exclusion of a for-profit tennis club in a district that allowed nonprofit clubs. The court thought it "a point too obvious to belabor that the separation of business from nonbusiness uses"[318] was appropriate. The court's point is problematical, however, since the distinction was not between business and non-business, but between profit and nonprofit.

Applying a deferential test, the New York court suggested that for-profit uses might be more harmful to an area than nonprofit uses. The former, said the court, were interested in making money and would likely expand, bringing more noise and traffic.[319] The for-profit operation was also more likely to become an eyesore in tough times, pumping good money after bad. In contrast, a nonprofit club, the court thought, was more likely to consider the long term benefits to the community than the for-profit group, and the nonprofit would probably have stronger ties to the neighborhood.

Zoning authorities and courts would do well to reexamine the reason for the nonprofit distinction, and to explore what it means to be nonprofit. If it is state corporation law or federal tax law that defines nonprofit status, they should study the relevancy of those statutory regimes to land use considerations. For example, if state corporation law creates a special nonprofit category to establish a different rule of liability or a different process of dissolution, the fact that the reasons supporting these differences have nothing to do with land use should lead a court to ignore them.

§ 4:27   Schools

A. Schools as Neighbors

Schools, as neighbors, have positive and negative features. Schools, particularly if they serve local residents, provide a sense of community. This is less true today than once was the case, as most schools no longer serve their immediate neighborhood but draw students from the wider community. On the downside, the noise and traffic attendant to school use make residential locations that are adjacent to or very close by the school less attractive. Historically, municipalities and courts have often ignored the negatives or presumed that the positives outweigh them. Furthermore, the educational atmosphere of schools, particularly elementary schools, is generally considered to bene-

---

Orleans v. Dukes, 427 U.S. 297, 96 S. Ct. 2513, 49 L. Ed. 2d 511 (1976). See discussion infra § 4:31 regarding nonconforming uses.

[315] *Mahony v. Township of Hampton,* 539 Pa. 193, 651 A.2d 525 (1994).

[316] See *Lykins v. Hohnbaum,* 2002 WL 32783973 (D. Or. 2002).

[317] *Town of Huntington v. Park Shore Country Day Camp of Dix Hills, Inc.,* 47 N.Y.2d 61, 416 N.Y.S.2d 774, 390 N.E.2d 282 (1979).

[318] Id.

[319] Conditions on size of use, though, could be imposed to limit growth.

fit from a residential location. Consequently, schools have been granted favored status in zoning.

Nonexistent or lax regulation has allowed virtually unchecked expansion of schools. Universities and colleges, in particular, have taken advantage of this unregulated environment. This expansion, along with increases in the size of schools, their tendency to serve students from outside the neighborhood, and increased use of cars and buses have led to a reexamination of the notion that schools are inherently benign land uses.[320]

Several school zoning issues arise. First, is whether government can exclude schools from certain zones and, if not, the degree to which it can regulate them. A second question is whether government can separately classify private schools and treat them differently than public schools. Finally, is the question of what is a "school" for the purposes of a zoning code.

Total exclusion of schools from certain zones is highly suspect. While one might well imagine the exclusion of educational uses from a heavy industrial zone, an ordinance that limited schools to intensive use zones almost certainly will fail. The New York Court of Appeals invalidated a municipality's effort to absolutely bar educational uses from a historic district.[321] Reasoning that a "decision to restrict a proposed educational use can only be made after the intended use is evaluated against other legitimate interests, with primary consideration given to the over-all impact on the public welfare,"[322] the court held that government is obligated to provide applicants, at a minimum, with an opportunity to be heard. Typically, this occurs by way of a special use permit process.[323]

Subjecting schools to a special permit process, though it may be closely scrutinized, is valid. One of the more protective courts, the New York Court of Appeals, limits zoning authorities from assessing the need for a school to locate at a given site or to expand. However, "once those institutions have identified their own needs and presented those interests in a special permit application, zoning officials have the flexibility to consider other means of accommodating those needs if the negative impacts of the proposed use outweigh its beneficial effects."[324]

B. *Public Schools*

Most ordinances permit public schools to locate as a matter of right in even the most restrictive residential districts. Usually, this occurs because of the philosophy noted above that schools need, and have a positive affect on, residential areas. However, local zoning authorities likely have no choice since public schools, as with other gov-

---

[320] See the sentiments expressed in *Cornell University v. Bagnardi,* 68 N.Y.2d 583, 510 N.Y.S.2d 861, 865, 503 N.E.2d 509, 513 (1986).

[321] *Trustees of Union College in Town of Schenectady v. Members of Schenectady City Council,* 91 N.Y.2d 161, 667 N.Y.S.2d 978, 690 N.E.2d 862 (1997). Indeed, total exclusion from commercial districts as well has been invalidated. See *Albany Preparatory Charter School v. City of Albany,* 31 A.D.3d 870, 818 N.Y.S.2d 651 (2006).

[322] Id., 690 N.E.2d at 865, 667 N.Y.S.2d at 981.

[323] See, e.g., *Council Rock School Dist. v. Wrightstown Tp. Zoning Hearing Bd.,* 709 A.2d 453 (Pa. Commw. Ct. 1998).

[324] *Pine Knolls Alliance Church v. Zoning Bd. of Appeals of Town of Moreau,* 5 N.Y.3d 407, 804 N.Y.S.2d 708, 838 N.E.2d 624 (2005).

ernmental uses,[325] are normally immune from zoning. Immunity may be based on the state constitution or statutory powers granted to schools.[326]

C. *Private Schools: Secular and Religious*

Where a zoning code permits public schools but excludes private schools, a question of the legitimacy of the unequal treatment arises. The courts differ over the question, but most require that private schools be permitted if public schools are.[327] This makes sense from a land use perspective as the impact on the community will not differ based on the ownership of the school. The noise and traffic from private students are not greater than from public students.

Differences between private and public schools exist. Whether they justify harsher zoning treatment of private schools is another matter. The leading case upholding the exclusion of private schools from zones where public schools were permitted did so on the ground that private schools do not serve all comers from the community. Most courts have held that the First Amendment does not insulate religious schools from zoning controls,[328] but in a few older cases courts held to the contrary.[329] Courts that otherwise might invalidate or closely scrutinize the regulation of religious uses are less likely to favor religious schools since they are more intensive land uses than most religious uses.[330] Distinguishing between religious use and religious educational use, though, is fraught with difficulty.[331]

D. *Qualifying as a School*

Zoning codes may define schools as buildings used for educational or instructional purposes or by reference to whether state or local school officials certify the use as meeting state educational requirements. Where not defined, or where the ordinance is general and must be construed, the courts have little difficulty recognizing certain uses as schools. A school for Jewish children was easily found the equal of other public and private schools that were permitted.[332] In another case, an ordinance that permitted all schools in an apartment district except nursery schools was held invalid. The court found that a nursery school was so similar to other schools that the exclusion was unreasonable.[333] Accessory uses are also typically allowed.[334]

---

[325] See supra § 4:23.

[326] *Town of Atherton v. Superior Court In and For San Mateo County,* 159 Cal. App. 2d 417, 324 P.2d 328 (1958).

[327] *Catholic Bishop of Chicago v. Kingery,* 371 Ill. 257, 20 N.E.2d 583 (1939). For a collection of such cases, see *Creative Country Day School of Sandy Spring, Inc. v. Montgomery County Bd. of Appeals,* 242 Md. 552, 567, 219 A.2d 789, 796 (1966).

[328] *Abram v. City of Fayetteville,* 281 Ark. 63, 661 S.W.2d 371 (1983).

[329] *Jewish Reconstructionist Synagogue of North Shore, Inc. v. Incorporated Village of Roslyn Harbor,* 38 N.Y.2d 283, 379 N.Y.S.2d 747, 342 N.E.2d 534 (1975). See infra § 10:19 for discussion of First Amendment protection of religious uses.

[330] *Abram v. City of Fayetteville,* 281 Ark. 63, 661 S.W.2d 371 (1983).

[331] See discussion of religious uses infra § 4:28.

[332] *Brandeis School v. Village of Lawrence,* 18 Misc. 2d 550, 184 N.Y.S.2d 687 (Sup. 1959).

[333] *City of Chicago v. Sachs,* 1 Ill. 2d 342, 115 N.E.2d 762 (1953).

[334] See, e.g., *Acorn Montessori School v. Bethlehem Tp. Planning Bd.,* 380 N.J. Super. 216, 881 A.2d 784 (Law Div. 2005).

While some private schools are very much like typical public or religious schools, some operations may be called schools by their proprietors only to obtain favorable zoning treatment.[335] The cases range widely.[336] It is not likely that a court would find a ceramics factory and store to have the favorable status of a school merely because the owner conducted classes in ceramics there.[337] A school "for the study of the Holocaust" in a single-family home was found not to be a school under the zoning code because it lacked certification from the state board of regents.[338] Courts denied school status to a "horse riding school,"[339] and a halfway house for recovering alcoholics.[340] However, a court allowed a private dance school in a residential zone under an ordinance that permitted educational or cultural facilities.[341]

§ 4:28 Religious Uses

The use of property for religious purposes[342] traditionally has been considered beneficial to a community. Religious buildings may provide a community focal point, giving a neighborhood a sense of identity. In older urban areas, religious institutions may also provide a base for community rebuilding efforts.[343] Still, religious institutions are not desirable neighbors in all respects. Like schools,[344] they generate noise and traffic and, thus, may depreciate property values in neighboring areas. Their ability to serve as a community resource is also diminished if their membership is not drawn from the neighborhood. The growth in recent years of the "mega-church," occupying more land, bringing more people from outside the community, and engaging in increasingly diverse activities under a religious rubric has led to frequent zoning disputes. While neighbors often have legitimate complaints about large institutional use, in some instances the protests appear levied against non-mainstream religious groups who are feared, disliked, or distrusted because they are different.[345]

Religious use zoning is more suspect than school zoning due to religious freedom guarantees in the federal and state constitutions. The First Amendment and its state counterparts prevent zoning laws from unduly interfering with the free exercise of religion. The adoption of so-called "religious freedom restoration acts" at both the federal and state levels is due, in large measure, to the perception that zoning unduly limits religious freedoms, and that courts have been overly deferential to local government.[346]

---

[335] Qualifying as an accessory use to a school is another avenue to gain permission. Jay M. Zitter, Annotation, What constitutes accessory or incidental use of religious or educational property within zoning ordinance, 11 A.L.R.4th 1084.

[336] Annot., What constitutes "school," "educational use," or the like within zoning ordinance, 64 A.L.R.3d 1087.

[337] *City of Chicopee v. Jakubowski,* 348 Mass. 230, 202 N.E.2d 913 (1964).

[338] *Boldman v. Taney County Com'n,* 179 S.W.3d 427 (Mo. Ct. App. 2005).

[339] *Incorporated Village of Asharoken v. Pitassy,* 119 A.D.2d 404, 507 N.Y.S.2d 164 (1986).

[340] *Couriers v. Zoning Hearing Bd. of Chippewa Tp.,* 88 Pa. Commw. 625, 491 A.2d 304 (1985).

[341] *Sarti v. City of Lake Oswego,* 106 Or. App. 594, 809 P.2d 701 (1991).

[342] Many zoning codes and cases refer to "church" use reflecting the country's dominant Christian tradition. Despite such usage, the First Amendment requires that the term be understood to include all religious institutional names and uses of any faith, such as temples, synagogues, mosques, fellowship halls, churches, or other such names or uses.

[343] *Great Lakes Soc. v. Georgetown Charter Tp.,* 281 Mich. App. 396, 761 N.W.2d 371 (2008).

[344] See supra § 4:27.

[345] See Pearlman, Zoning and the Location of Religious Establishments, 31 Cath. Law. 314 (1988); Rice, Re-evaluating the Balance Between Zoning Regulations and Religious and Educational Uses, 8 Pace L. Rev 1 (1988).

[346] The federal religious land use act is discussed infra 10:19B along with constitutional considerations.

In many cases discussed below that favor religious uses, courts refrain from express determinations that the First Amendment has been violated, but they often admit that their decisions are influenced by the importance of religious freedom in this country.[347]

Three basic approaches are used in zoning religious uses: (1) allow them in any district as a matter of right, (2) allow them in any residential district only if they obtain a special permit, or (3) exclude them from some residential zones. The first approach dominated early zoning ordinances, but the second is the technique employed most often. The third is the least practiced, and is invalid in many states. A fourth possibility is total exclusion from the community. This is likely a rare occurrence and, if attempted, almost certainly invalid under state and federal law.[348] Where litigated, that has been the result.[349]

Allowing religious uses in all districts, particularly all residential districts, as a matter of right, is premised on the notion that religious use is inherently beneficial. Several cases reflect this belief and, where true, an attempt to exclude religious uses from residential areas will be held invalid.[350] Typically in these cases, most of which are dated, the courts invalidate the zoning on due process grounds finding that the police power does not extend to the banning of such highly regarded uses. The growth in size and divergence in use of religious institutions has caused courts to reexamine whether this routine deference is justified,[351] and one should be wary of relying heavily on older authority that grants or intimates absolute protection. Whether the surge of interest in the tension between land use controls and religious uses exemplified by the religious freedom restoration acts will lead to a reestablishment of religious uses as uses that are close to immune from regulation remains to be seen.[352]

By far the most common regulatory approach is to permit religious uses in some or all residential districts by special permit. Courts have upheld this technique as against charges that the mere requirement to apply for a permit is an undue burden on religion.[353] Some municipalities, however, do exempt religious uses from the special permit process that they apply to similar uses, and such exemptions have survived establishment clause challenges.[354]

§ 4:29 Airports

Airports, particularly large ones, have a dramatic and widespread impact on a community. With the continuous increase in air travel communities can expect new airports and expansions of existing airports. Airports produce an enormous amount of noise, adversely affecting nearby residential uses, and are a safety concern to all. While these issues of land use, noise, and safety are typically ones handled by local government, airports, as vital links in national and international trade and travel, are also

---

[347] See infra 10:19.

[348] Regarding federal law, see infra 10:19.

[349] *North Shore Unitarian Soc. v. Village of Plandome,* 200 Misc. 524, 109 N.Y.S.2d 803 (1951). See infra, 10:19B.

[350] *Ellsworth v. Gercke,* 62 Ariz. 198, 156 P.2d 242 (1945).

[351] *Congregation Kol Ami v. Abington Township,* 309 F.3d 120, 144 (3d Cir. 2002).

[352] See infra 10:19B.

[353] *Pine Knolls Alliance Church v. Zoning Bd. of Appeals of Town of Moreau,* 5 N.Y.3d 407, 804 N.Y.S.2d 708, 838 N.E.2d 624 (2005).

[354] See infra 10:19D.

regulated by the federal government. This overlapping regulation at times leads to conflict. Takings issues also arise with airport use by the invasion of private airspace and the loss of value of property subject to the noise.[355]

The leading preemption case is *City of Burbank v. Lockheed Air Terminal, Inc.,*[356] in which the Supreme Court held a municipal ordinance that imposed a curfew on flights between 11 p.m. until 7 a.m. was preempted by federal regulations. The Court implied preemption since it found that federal control of flights would be jeopardized by local regulation. *Burbank's* preemption of local law applies only to controls relating to the noise from aircraft operations.

§ 4:30   Hospitals and Medical Facilities

Like other uses described in this chapter, many hospitals and other medical facilities are either publicly owned or are owned by nonprofit groups, and provide necessary social services. Provision of health care comes through a variety of uses, from large medical complexes to group homes for persons in need of supervised care. The zoning treatment of these uses varies.

Particularly in earlier days, hospitals dealing with tuberculosis, mental disorders, and the disabled mothers were frequently separately classified by ordinance, and excluded or confined to less restricted zones. As with other land uses like cemeteries and funeral parlors,[357] though to a lesser degree, hospitals and various treatment centers may encounter resistance as reminders of death, disease and other social ills.

VI. NONCONFORMING USES

§ 4:31   In General

Nearly all zoning ordinances provide that a use that would be unlawful if established after the passage of an ordinance may continue if it lawfully preexists the adoption of the ordinance. "Nonconforming use" is a generic term covering all these uses, but separating nonconforming situations into four types is useful: (1) nonconforming buildings, (2) conforming uses of nonconforming buildings, (3) nonconforming uses of conforming buildings, and (4) nonconforming uses of land. For example, a building built at the front lot line is a nonconforming building after passage of an ordinance establishing a front yard setback requirement. An office building is a nonconforming building in a multi-family zone although it has been abandoned for office use and is occupied by several families. If a single-family house is used for manufacturing furniture in a single-family zone, the building conforms though the use does not. Land used for a pig farm, with the land containing no structures rising to the dignity of buildings, would be nonconforming use of land. Certain consequences concerning the expansion and termination of nonconformities may depend on these classifications.

The distinction between a non-conforming building and a non-conforming lot is not always clear and to some the attempt to distinguish between the two can lead to illogical results. In one case owners of a single-family residence on an undersized, non-

---

[355] See, generally, Zambrano, Comment: Balancing the Rights of Landowners with the Needs of Airports: the Continuing Battle Over Noise, 66 J. Air L. & Com., 445–497 (2000).

[356] *City of Burbank v. Lockheed Air Terminal Inc.,* 411 U.S. 624, 93 S. Ct. 1854, 36 L. Ed. 2d 547 (1973).

[357] See infra § 6:9.

conforming lot sought to reconstruct their house, doubling its footprint. The zoning inspector denied a permit based on the ordinance, which provided "where alteration, reconstruction, extension or structural change to a single family or two family residential structure does not increase the non-conforming nature, neither public hearing nor Special Permit from the Board of Appeals is required . . . . "[358] The inspector concluded the proposal increased the house's non-conforming nature, requiring a special permit, which was then denied by the board. The owners argued that there was no increase in the non-conforming nature of the structure but only the presence of a conforming structure on a nonconforming lot.

The high court affirmed the board's denial of the permit and concurring justices argued that "where an undersized lot exists, the proposed reconstruction may be allowed without special permit only if the proposed new residence does not intensify existing nonconformities." They found that the expansion would reduce the open space previously existing on the lot and increase the density of the residential neighborhood. "Creating a distinction in treatment between a nonconforming structure and a nonconforming lot is one that analytically and practically should not be made. The two concepts are intertwined and separating them would permit a landowner to circumvent valid and useful minimum lot area requirements."

Protection of existing uses was important goal from zoning's onset. First, zoning was considered a prospective control, whose primary purpose was to control land as it developed and to maintain that control rather than to change existing development. Second, while the purist Euclidean zoner aimed to divide the landscape into districts having a place for everything and everything in its place, convincing pragmatists that a few nonconforming uses were totally contrary to the public health, safety and welfare was hard. After all, even the purists contemplated cumulative rather than exclusive zones.[359] Thus, while a mom and pop grocery store is a nonconforming use in a single-family zone, the necessity for its termination is not compelling. Third, while proponents could convince the body politic of the wisdom of zoning applied prospectively, the political forces against adoption of zoning would have been much stronger if zoning had been applied to require existing uses to comply with new laws. Fourth, the validity of zoning as a police power measure was in doubt in zoning's early years and the risk of unconstitutionality would have been greater if preexisting uses had been terminated.[360] It, thus, became customary to exempt existing uses to avoid the question.[361]

While the Standard State Zoning Enabling Act makes no provision for the treatment of existing uses, some enabling acts require that nonconforming uses be allowed to continue.[362] Even where not mandated by state law, zoning ordinances almost universally permit nonconforming uses to continue. Where not so allowed, some courts

---

[358] Bransford v. Zoning Bd. of Appeals of Edgartown, 832 N.E.2d 639, 641 (2005).

[359] See supra § 4:3.

[360] Earlier cases upholding retroactive applications of zoning-like regulations which terminated preexisting uses dealt with land uses that had nuisance or near-nuisance features. See, e.g., *Hadacheck v. Sebastian,* 239 U.S. 394, 36 S. Ct. 143, 60 L. Ed. 348 (1915).

[361] *Hansen Brothers Enterprises, Inc. v. Board of Supervisors,* 12 Cal. 4th 533, 48 Cal. Rptr. 2d 778, 789, 907 P.2d 1324, 1335 (1996).

[362] See N.H. Stat. Ann. § 674:19.

have held retroactive application invalid as having no substantial relation to the public health, safety and welfare,[363] or as not authorized by enabling acts.[364]

§ 4:32   Lawful Existence

In order for nonconforming uses to continue, they must be lawfully established at the time the ordinance making them nonconforming takes effect. The stakes are high, and litigation on the matter is frequent. If the use is not "in existence" at the critical time, expenses incurred in construction will be lost and more expense will be encountered in removing illegal structures that were built. Benefit may also flow from securing legal nonconforming use status due to the monopoly position that it might confer. For example, to be the only flower shop permitted near a cemetery because of nonconforming status is an enviable position for the flower shop owner.

The law of vested rights, discussed elsewhere,[365] controls the establishment of lawful existence that protects a use from zoning changes. Difficulties are often encountered when a race ensues between a developer attempting to establish a use and a municipality in the process of enacting a new zoning ordinance that might declare the developer's use illegal. Under the law of vested rights, the one to cross the finish line first does not necessarily prevail. Generally, to acquire immunity from a newly enacted law, a developer must engage in substantial expenditures in good faith reliance on a validly issued building permit. The municipality must also act in good faith, and unreasonable delay in issuing a permit may preclude it from applying a newly enacted law.[366]

§ 4:33   Restrictions on Nonconforming Uses

While lawful nonconforming uses are allowed to continue, they are at most tolerated. Unless precluded by state law, municipalities typically place numerous limitations on nonconforming uses designed to achieve conformance as soon as practicable and reasonable.[367] These include limitations on changes in use,[368] on repairs and alterations,[369] on rebuilding in the event of destruction,[370] and on resuming use after a period of abandonment.[371] Most courts construe rights conferred on nonconforming uses narrowly to promote the goal of early elimination.[372]

§ 4:34   Change in Use

Generally, protected status is lost upon change in use.[373] The rule, however, is hardly absolute. Ordinances may permit some change, reflecting a tension between effectuating the goal of eliminating nonconforming uses at the earliest opportunity and

---

[363] *Jones v. City of Los Angeles,* 211 Cal. 304, 295 P. 14 (1930).

[364] *Bane v. Pontiac Tp., Oakland County,* 343 Mich. 481, 72 N.W.2d 134 (1955).

[365] See infra § 5:27.

[366] See infra § 5:28.

[367] *Kaloo v. Zoning Bd. of Appeals for City of Chicago,* 274 Ill. App. 3d 927, 211 Ill. Dec. 31, 654 N.E.2d 493 (1995).

[368] See § 4:34.

[369] See infra § 4:35.

[370] See infra § 4:38.

[371] See infra § 4:38.

[372] See *Rotter v. Coconino County,* 169 Ariz. 269, 818 P.2d 704 (1991).

[373] *Altpa, Inc. v. North Huntingdon Tp. Zoning Hearing Bd.,* 67 Pa. Commw. 60, 445 A.2d 1358 (1982).

allowing the owner of the nonconforming use some degree of flexibility. Furthermore, a mere change in ownership does not end the nonconforming use.[374]

A. More Intensive Use

In the absence of an ordinance permitting it, a nonconforming use cannot be expanded. Some ordinances flatly provide that no nonconforming use "shall be enlarged or intensified."[375] Others may be less sweeping in their interdiction. For example, an increase in the volume of activity was allowed under an ordinance that provided that "nonconforming uses shall not be enlarged, increased or extended to occupy a greater area of land * * *."[376] Some ordinances allow "limited expansion."[377]

B. Similar or Less Intensive Use

Some ordinances and courts allow a change of use to one of less intensity.[378] On first impression permitting changes that move a use in the direction of conformity seems sensible. However, if there is a desire to change, it may be that economics has dictated that the present use should not be continued, making it likely that without permission to change it would be abandoned, resulting in full conformity.[379] Furthermore, if the city permits a new use that is only in the direction of conformity, the new nonconforming use is likely to prevail for a longer time.

C. Natural Growth: Right of Expansion

A few courts allow what they call "normal" expansion.[380] As one court put it, "[a]n ordinance which would allow the housing of a baby elephant cannot evict the animal when it has grown up, since it is generally known that a baby elephant eventually becomes a big elephant."[381]

In most states where normal expansion is allowed, courts allow a mere increase in the volume of business by natural growth but prohibit changes amounting to a new or different use.[382] In Pennsylvania, the courts go one step further and hold that there is a constitutional right to natural expansion. The right is grounded in the court's view that under the state's substantive due process guarantee it would be "inequitable to prevent [an owner] from expanding the property as the dictates of business or modernization require."[383]

---

[374] *Triangle Fraternity v. City of Norman, ex rel. Norman Bd. of Adjustment,* 63 P.3d 1 (Okla. 2002).

[375] See county ordinance cited in *Hansen Brothers Enterprises, Inc. v. Board of Supervisors,* 12 Cal. 4th 533, 48 Cal. Rptr. 2d 778, 803, 907 P.2d 1324, 1349 (1996). But see *Land v. Village of Wesley Chapel,* 206 N.C. App. 123, 697 S.E.2d 458, 466 (2010).

[376] *Town of Gardiner v. Blue Sky Entertainment Corp.,* 213 A.D.2d 790, 623 N.Y.S.2d 29 (1995).

[377] See *Rotter v. Coconino County,* 169 Ariz. 269, 818 P.2d 704 (1991).

[378] *Malakoff v. Zoning Bd. of Adjustment of City of Pittsburgh,* 78 Pa. Commw. 178, 467 A.2d 97 (1983).

[379] See infra § 4:38.

[380] *Conway Lake Resorts, Inc. v. Quisisana Resort,* 899 A.2d 815 (Me. 2006).

[381] *Appeal of Associated Contractors, Inc.,* 391 Pa. 347, 138 A.2d 99, 102 (1958).

[382] *Conway Lake Resorts, Inc. v. Quisisana Resort,* 2006 ME 77, 899 A.2d 815 (Me. 2006).

[383] *Silver v. Zoning Bd. of Adjustment,* 435 Pa. 99, 255 A.2d 506 (1969).

A right of natural expansion is contrary to the prevailing weight of authority that calls for strict limits on changes.[384]

D. *Natural Resources Diminishing Assets Doctrine*

The rule prohibiting expansion of a nonconforming use poses particular problems with respect to natural resource extraction where the nature of the use necessarily involves expansion. In quarrying, for example, the operator must either widen or deepen the pit to continue operations.

Many courts apply a diminishing assets doctrine that permits a nonconforming extractive process to expand its mining operation beyond the area mined at the time the activity became a nonconforming use.[385] In effect, they define the nonconforming use to include "all that land which contains the particular asset and which constitutes an integral part of the operation, notwithstanding the fact that a particular portion may not yet be under actual excavation."[386]

There are limitations. Generally, a miner must show by objective evidence that it intended to mine the contemplated area at the time the zoning changed. Thus, a New York court held that a nonconforming gravel operation could expand to cover its entire parcel where it was established that the operator had removed gravel from various portions of the entire parcel, had built service roads throughout the parcel, and had built a processing plant in the center of the property.[387]

§ 4:35   Repairs and Alterations

Most ordinances allow repairs to a nonconforming use.[388] If not, courts will typically permit repairs. Such permission makes sense, because there is a general policy, particularly as represented by housing codes, to have buildings in good repair. Generally, the repairs allowed are modest. Ordinances sometimes permit repairs as measured by a percentage of the appraised or assessed value of the building to provide a standard that will permit repairs but eliminate substantial alterations. Assessed values, however, frequently have little relation to market values and values may change over time, both of which can make application of the standard difficult or unfair.

Alterations and structural repairs are usually prohibited on the theory that they will prolong the life of the nonconforming use.[389] Deciding what is a permitted repair and a prohibited alteration is sometimes difficult, but, beyond the specifics of the applicable ordinance, the goal of early elimination determines the issue.[390] Replacing old billboards with new ones, for example, has been disallowed in several cases.[391] Though the new signs might improve the appearance of the nonconforming property, such changes, if allowed, could indefinitely continue a nonconforming use. Meanwhile, of

---

[384] See *Rotter v. Coconino County,* 169 Ariz. 269, 818 P.2d 704 (1991).

[385] *City of University Place v. McGuire,* 144 Wash. 2d 640, 30 P.3d 453 (2001).

[386] *Du Page County v. Elmhurst-Chicago Stone Co.,* 18 Ill. 2d 479, 165 N.E.2d 310, 313 (1960).

[387] *Syracuse Aggregate Corp. v. Weise,* 51 N.Y.2d 278, 434 N.Y.S.2d 150, 414 N.E.2d 651 (1980).

[388] Annot., Zoning: right to repair or reconstruct building operating as nonconforming use, after damage or destruction by fire or other casualty, 57 A.L.R.3d 419.

[389] *Marris v. City of Cedarburg,* 176 Wis. 2d 14, 498 N.W.2d 842 (1993).

[390] See, e.g., *Mossman v. City of Columbus,* 234 Neb. 78, 449 N.W.2d 214 (1989).

[391] *Gannett Outdoor Co. of Arizona v. City of Mesa,* 159 Ariz. 459, 768 P.2d 191 (Ct. App. Div. 1 1989).

course, the general community, and particularly the immediate neighborhood, has to suffer from older signs or structures that are deteriorating.

Ordinances may allow alterations that are "necessary to assure the safety of the structure"[392] or otherwise required by law. In one case, for example, a court held that a nonconforming nursing home operated in a frame building could be replaced with a new fireproof structure if it did not increase the scale of the nursing home operations.[393] The new structure was necessary for the home to continue to be licensed.

§ 4:36   Conversion to Administrative Permission [Section Appears Only in Juergensmeyer and Roberts, Land Use Planning and Development Regulation Law (3rd ed.2012)]

§ 4:37   Termination of Nonconforming Uses: In General

A nonconforming use is not entitled to continue in perpetuity. Fire, flood, or other cause beyond the owner's control may destroy it and permission for restoration may not be given. The owner's abandonment may terminate the nonconforming use. The municipality may terminate it through amortization, or a court may find that the nonconformity constitutes a nuisance. We discuss these matters in the following sections of this chapter.

§ 4:38   Destruction and Abandonment

As a general proposition, a destroyed or abandoned nonconforming use cannot be rebuilt.[394] While fairness supports protecting investments in existing uses from newly enacted zoning laws, once the nonconforming use is gone, whether by destruction or abandonment, the investment is lost. At that point, the owner of the land may have to stand on equal footing with the neighbors and comply with current zoning.[395] Some legislatures[396] and courts[397] require non-use and intent.[398]

A.   Destruction

If destruction is involuntary and partial, ordinances often allow rebuilding.[399] Most, however, prohibit rebuilding where destruction, voluntary or involuntary, is substantial.[400] They usually measure substantiality by the percentage of value destroyed.[401] For example, in *Moffatt v. Forrest City,*[402] an ordinance provided that one

---

[392] See ordinance interpreted in *Christy v. Harleston,* 266 S.C. 439, 223 S.E.2d 861 (1976).

[393]*"Application of O'Neal,* 243 N.C. 714, 92 S.E.2d 189 (1956).

[394] *Red Garter, Inc. v. Cleveland Bd. of Zoning Appeals,* 100 Ohio App. 3d 177, 652 N.E.2d 260 (1995).

[395] See *Pelham Esplanade, Inc. v. Board of Trustees of Village of Pelham Manor,* 77 N.Y.2d 66, 563 N.Y.S.2d 759, 761, 565 N.E.2d 508, 510 (1990).

[396] Conn. Gen. Stat. Ann. § 8–2.

[397] *S & S Auto Sales, Inc. v. Zoning Bd. of Adjustment for Borough of Stratford,* 373 N.J. Super. 603, 862 A.2d 1204 (App. Div. 2004).

[398] See also infra § 4:38B.

[399] *Manhattan Sepulveda, Ltd. v. City of Manhattan Beach,* 22 Cal. App. 4th 865, 27 Cal. Rptr. 2d 565 (2d Dist. 1994).

[400] *City of Las Cruces v. Neff,* 65 N.M. 414, 338 P.2d 731 (1959).

[401] See *Manhattan Sepulveda, Ltd. v. City of Manhattan Beach,* 22 Cal. App. 4th 865, 27 Cal. Rptr. 2d 565 (1994).

[402] *Moffatt v. Forrest City,* 234 Ark. 12, 350 S.W.2d 327 (1961).

could not rebuild a building if it were destroyed by more than 60% of its value. The residential part of a building located in a residential zone was totally destroyed although the third of the building used as a meat market was not. The court held the building was more than 60% destroyed, so that it could no longer be used for a meat market.

B. Abandonment, Discontinuance and Merger

If the owner abandons the use, lawful nonconforming status is lost.[403] Most courts require proof of an overt act and an intention permanently to abandon.

Requiring proof of intent has been criticized. Not only is it difficult for a court to deal with subjective intentions, but also "because it encourages property owners who have actually abandoned their nonconforming use to commit perjury."[404] Furthermore, the burden of proving intent is on the municipality, and it is a difficult one to carry.[405] The job is made easier in some states which presume intent to abandon upon expiration of a specified time period.[406]

A compulsory and temporary cessation does not constitute abandonment if the stoppage is not due to acts within the owner's control. For example, in *City of Fontana v. Atkinson,*[407] the county health department ordered the owner of a nonconforming dairy to rebuild corral fences. When they tore down the fences temporarily to permit rebuilding, the city claimed that removal of the fences constituted abandonment. The court found no abandonment. Similarly, abandonment may not be found if the use stops due to wartime restrictions, economic depression, and the like-providing the property is devoted to its nonconforming use as soon as reasonably possible.[408] If the owner's misconduct is the cause of a restraining order requiring that the use cease for a period of time, nonconforming status may be lost.[409]

Some ordinances provide that if a nonconforming use ceases or is discontinued for a stated period of time, the use may not resume. Periods of six months and one year are common and have been found reasonable.[410] These discontinuance or cessation ordinances may be distinguished from abandonment ordinances. Under the former, proof of intent may not be required. While most courts have treated the word "discontinue" as the equivalent of "abandon," and transported an intent element into discontinuance ordinances,[411] several courts reject this view, relying either on the plain language of the ordinance or the goal of early elimination of nonconforming uses.[412] In some cases, the dispensation of the intent element is broader and applies to "abandonment" language as well.[413]

---

[403] See *County of Du Page v. K-Five Const. Corp.,* 267 Ill. App. 3d 266, 204 Ill. Dec. 702, 642 N.E.2d 164 (1994).

[404] *City of Glendale v. Aldabbagh,* 189 Ariz. 140, 142–43, 939 P.2d 418, 420–21 (1997).

[405] *Van Sant v. City of Everett,* 69 Wash. App. 641, 849 P.2d 1276 (1993).

[406] *Williams v. Salem Tp.,* 92 Pa. Commw. 634, 500 A.2d 933 (1985).

[407] *City of Fontana v. Atkinson,* 212 Cal. App. 2d 499, 28 Cal. Rptr. 25 (1963).

[408] *Southern Equipment Co., Inc. v. Winstead,* 80 N.C. App. 526, 342 S.E.2d 524 (1986).

[409] *City of Glendale v. Aldabbagh,* 189 Ariz. 140, 939 P.2d 418 (1997).

[410] *City of New Orleans v. Hamilton,* 602 So. 2d 112 (La. Ct. App. 1992).

[411] *Boles v. City of Chattanooga,* 892 S.W.2d 416 (Tenn. Ct. App. 1994) (collecting cases on both sides of the issue).

[412] *City of Glendale v. Aldabbagh,* 189 Ariz. 140, 939 P.2d 418 (1997).

[413] *Villari v. Zoning Bd. of Ad. of Deptford,* 277 N.J. Super. 130, 649 A.2d 98 (App. Div. 1994).

Ordinances may also require that non-conforming lots be held under separate ownership from adjacent lots. If a conforming and non-conforming merge into single ownership, non-conforming status may be lost.[414]

§ 4:39 Amortization

Amortization provisions require the termination of a nonconforming use after the passage of a period of time from when the use becomes nonconforming or from the time of passage of the amortization ordinance.[415] Amortization is an attractive tool for local government since it is proactive.[416] The city need not wait an indefinite time for a nonconforming use to be abandoned or destroyed.

The length of the amortization period varies depending on the significance of the investment and the harmful nature of the use. Nonconforming uses of land, like junkyards, are typically given relatively short periods, since there is little or no investment in buildings to recoup. Except for uses that consume the land such as mines and quarries,[417] nonconforming uses of land theoretically can move elsewhere. The loss (or possibly gain) may be small or large. Relatively short periods of amortization also may be appropriate for nonconforming uses of conforming buildings particularly where they can be converted to conforming uses without substantial cost.

The periods are typically longest for nonconforming buildings, particularly those that feasibly can serve but one purpose, such as an oil refinery. The period of amortization may also depend on the type of construction, so that the period would be longer for brick or concrete high-rise buildings and less for temporary, low-rise, inexpensively constructed warehouses. Periods range from 30 days for portable flashing signs,[418] 90 days for adult entertainment businesses,[419] three years for junkyards,[420] five years for billboards,[421] and 20 to 40 years for nonconforming buildings.[422]

While amortization was upheld as early as 1929,[423] it did not enjoy substantial use until the 1960s. Over the years it has also produced substantial litigation. Almost all courts have upheld amortization in principle and have examined the reasonableness of specific applications on a case by case basis.[424]

The validity of amortization, its accounting-sounding lineage aside, does not depend on a precise mathematical analysis.[425] Courts may question particular techniques. In one case, the court invalidated an amortization schedule that set varying

---

[414] *John B. DiSanto and Sons, Inc. v. City of Portland,* 2004 ME 60, 848 A.2d 618 (Me. 2004).

[415] See, generally, Collins, Methods of Determining Amortization Periods for Non-conforming Uses, 3 Wash. U. J.L. & Pol'y 215 (2000).

[416] Michaels, Amortization and the Constitutional Methodology for Terminating Nonconforming Uses, 41 Urb. Law. 807, 807–29 (2009).

[417] See supra § 4:34 and infra § 6:9.

[418] *Art Neon Co. v. City and County of Denver,* 488 F.2d 118 (10th Cir. 1973).

[419] *Northend Cinema, Inc. v. City of Seattle,* 90 Wash. 2d 709, 585 P.2d 1153 (1978) (provision upheld).

[420] *State v. Joyner,* 286 N.C. 366, 211 S.E.2d 320 (1975).

[421] *Art Neon Co. v. City and County of Denver,* 488 F.2d 118 (10th Cir. 1973).

[422] See *City of Los Angeles v. Gage,* 127 Cal. App. 2d 442, 274 P.2d 34 (1954).

[423] *State ex rel. Dema Realty Co. v. Jacoby,* 168 La. 752, 123 So. 314 (1929).

[424] *Trip Associates, Inc. v. Mayor and City Council of Baltimore,* 392 Md. 563, 898 A.2d 449 (2006).

[425] See Collins, Methods of Determining Amortization Periods for Non-conforming Uses, 3 Wash. U. J.L. & Pol'y 215 (2000).

periods from two to five years on signs based on replacement value.[426] The court found sign replacement value irrelevant to the question of the overall loss to the owner's business.

Another question explored in assessing reasonableness is the justification for eliminating the use. Some nonconforming uses for which short amortization periods are upheld have nuisance-like qualities, such as junkyards and signs. A billboard that is a traffic hazard can be immediately removed, but signs targeted due to their unattractive qualities provide a less compelling reason for immediate termination.[427]

Signs are popular targets of amortization. This is presumably because many cities have intensified their sign regulations in recent years, rendering many signs nonconforming.[428] While traffic hazards and portable signs can be terminated with short or no amortization period, billboards are given a longer time. Most billboards are successfully amortized in three to seven year periods. A few courts hold amortization schemes invalid on their face.[429]

§ 4:40   Immediate Termination of Nuisance

When a use is a nuisance, courts can order immediate termination, despite the loss of value sustained. Since there is no property right to maintain a nuisance, there can be no Fifth Amendment taking.[430] Courts have also upheld ordinances that provide for immediate termination of uses with nuisance-like qualities without judicial determinations that the uses are common law nuisances.[431]

In several cases the Supreme Court sustained ordinances that immediately terminated obnoxious uses. In *Reinman v. Little Rock*[432] it upheld a regulation that prohibited stables as applied to a preexisting stable in a business area. In *Hadacheck v. Sebastian*,[433] an ordinance prohibited brickyards in an area designated for residential use, and, though the property was reduced in value from $800,000 to $60,000, the Court held it valid as applied to an existing brickyard. "A vested interest," said the Court, "cannot be asserted against [the police power] because of conditions once obtaining."[434] In *Goldblatt v. Town of Hempstead*,[435] a restriction on the operation of a quarry rendered its continued operation all but impossible. The Court upheld the regulation, pointing out that where health and safety are involved, a large loss is justified.

In contemporary takings jurisprudence, the fact that none of these cases involved a total economic loss of use is significant since the Court has held that a presumptive

---

[426] *Art Neon Co. v. City and County of Denver,* 488 F.2d 118 (10th Cir. 1973).

[427] *Modjeska Sign Studios, Inc. v. Berle,* 43 N.Y.2d 468, 402 N.Y.S.2d 359, 366, 373 N.E.2d 255, 261 (1977).

[428] See discussion of signs infra § 10:16 and § 12:2.

[429] *PA Northwestern Distributors, Inc. v. Zoning Hearing Bd. of Tp. of Moon,* 526 Pa. 186, 584 A.2d 1372 (1991).

[430] *Lucas v. South Carolina Coastal Council,* 505 U.S. 1003, 112 S. Ct. 2886, 120 L. Ed. 2d 798 (1992). See infra § 10:6.

[431] See, e.g., *People v. Miller,* 304 N.Y. 105, 106 N.E.2d 34 (1952) (ordinance precluding keeping of pigeons in residential area valid as applied to preexisting uses).

[432] *Reinman v. City of Little Rock,* 237 U.S. 171, 35 S. Ct. 511, 59 L. Ed. 900 (1915).

[433] *Hadacheck v. Sebastian,* 239 U.S. 394, 36 S. Ct. 143, 60 L. Ed. 348 (1915).

[434] *Hadacheck, 239 U.S. at 409, 36 S. Ct. at 145.*

[435] *Goldblatt v. Town of Hempstead, N. Y.,* 369 U.S. 590, 82 S. Ct. 987, 8 L. Ed. 2d 130 (1962).

taking only occurs where a police power control deprives a landowner of all economically viable use.[436] In such a case, the state can only avoid paying compensation under the takings clause if it can show that the ordinance's prohibition duplicates the result it could obtain in the state courts under the common law of nuisance or other property law principles.[437] Where the economic loss is not total, the *Penn Central* test will apply.[438]

---

[436] *Lucas v. South Carolina Coastal Council,* 505 U.S. 1003, 1026 n.13, 112 S. Ct. 2886, 120 L. Ed. 2d 798 (1992).

[437] *Lucas, 505 U.S. 1003.* See also infra § 10:6.

[438] See infra § 10:6B.

Chapter 5

ZONING PROCESS: OBTAINING OR RESISTING DEVELOPMENT PERMISSION*

I. INTRODUCTION

---

* For more detailed discussion and more extensive citations of authority of the issues covered in this chapter, see Juergensmeyer and Roberts, Land Use Planning and Development Regulation Law, Practitioner Treatise Series (3rd ed. 2012).

I.   INTRODUCTION

§ 5:1   Zoning "Forms of Action"

After a zoning ordinance implements a comprehensive plan, the process of zoning is normally directed toward the acquisition of development permission for specific tracts. In his seminal work, The Zoning Game,[1] Richard Babcock observed that the name of the zoning game is change. The "players" in the game include the property owner/developer, the local government, and the neighbors. Occasionally others may be involved, such as environmental organizations, historic preservation societies, builders' associations, and other governmental units with overlapping authority.

The local government often sets the stage by initially underzoning its territory, placing much of the undeveloped land in highly restrictive zones. This means the developer must initiate matters by requesting a change. The neighbors typically play a reactive role, usually resisting the change sought by the developer. They may also be proactive. Vigilant current residents, who anticipate the possibility of development contrary to their interests, may employ a preemptive strike to have the zoning changed to preclude intensive uses. The government approaches the game with several concerns. It must judge a proposal's consistency with the community's comprehensive plan and determine whether the development will impose costs on the community that exac-

---

[1] Richard F. Babcock, The Zoning Game (1966).

tions or impact fees might mitigate. In some instances, the government may also act as a de facto mediator between neighbors and the developer.

An owner or developer who wishes to use property in a manner that would be improper as presently zoned may have various ways to secure permission. Options include seeking a legislative change through a textual or zoning map amendment, proceeding administratively to seek a variance or special permit, seeking a judicial declaration that the land is improperly or unconstitutionally zoned, or attempting to qualify the property as a nonconforming use. More than one approach may be appropriate and each is peculiar in its requirements and procedure. To highlight the point, Professor Donald Hagman aptly described the options, by analogy to our common law heritage, as the "zoning forms of action."[2]

The primary choice among the forms of action is between legislative, administrative, and judicial relief. Generally, the latter is available, if at all, only after pursuing one or both of the others. As with common law forms of action, choice of form dictates the allegations to be made, decision makers involved, subject matter jurisdiction, evidence to be presented, standing requirements of the parties, kinds of relief allowed and availability of an appeal. Res judicata-like effects may differ, as will opportunities to merge or split "causes of action" or "plead in the alternative." The advocates who customarily appear (for example, lawyers or lay persons) may differ. Depending on the needs of the property owner, one zoning form of action may be preferable to another when alternatives are available. This chapter considers these forms of action, except the nonconforming use, which is separately considered.[3]

§ 5:2   Coping With the Cost of Land Use Disputes

Whatever the form of action pursued, the costs of the zoning game may be high. Most obvious are the costs to the moving party, typically the developer, who will have acquisition costs for land, financing costs, and planning, architectural and legal fees. Most of these will increase if the permitting process is a prolonged one. There are also financial costs to the neighbors and to the government in responding to the developer's request. The adversarial nature of the process also takes an emotional toll on all concerned. If the game has a loser, as most games do, the loser will not be happy. Subsequent relations between the players may well be strained.

Two opposing tools exist to lessen these costs. First, a developer may bring a so-called SLAPP suit (strategic lawsuit against public participation) against neighbors. Second, the parties may employ mediation.

A.   *Lawsuits to Deter or Retaliate Against Public Participation*

Developers may attempt to recover losses inflicted on them by neighbors' opposition to development.[4] Usually, the effort takes the form of a tort action for defamation or wrongful interference with business relations, and seeks damages suffered as a consequence of the neighbors' obstreperousness. Questioning the authenticity of the devel-

---

[2] Donald G. Hagman and Julian Conrad Juergensmeyer, Urban Planning and Land Development Control Law 163 (2d ed. 1986).

[3] See supra §§ 4:31 to 4:40.

[4] See Tate, California's Anti-Slapp Legislation: A Summary of, and Commentary on, Its Operation and Scope, 33 Loy. L.A. L. Rev. 801 (2000).

opers' motives, commentators often denominate such suits "strategic lawsuits against public participation," or SLAPPs. The mere threat of such an action may deter citizen opposition, and, if filed, the suit may quickly deplete citizen resources and thus remove them as obstacles. A SLAPP suit may also be used after the fact to retaliate against those who obstructed the project. Neighbors who are sued may then "SLAPP-back," by bringing abuse of process suits.[5]

SLAPP suits implicate the First Amendment's right to petition the government for grievances. The Supreme Court has interpreted the First Amendment as giving citizens immunity from liability for damages caused by them while exercising their right to petition. There is, however, no absolute right to defame another or bring unfounded litigation. In the antitrust field, for example, the Supreme Court provides immunity from damages to those urging government to take anticompetitive action under the *Noerr-Pennington* doctrine.[6] A "sham exception" to such immunity provides that liability can attach to petitioning activity that merely hides a direct attempt to interfere with a competitor.[7] While one may sue in tort against the speech or writings of another, the defendant may interpose the First Amendment and thereby elevate the burden on the plaintiff. *New York Times v. Sullivan,*[8] for example, requires that in libel actions brought by public officials, a plaintiff must prove that the defendant published a defamatory statement with actual malice.

Similar rules govern SLAPP suits in the land use context. While the label given these suits, "lawsuits against public participation," assumes the conclusion that they are motivated to silence or punish the opposition, whether that is in fact the case can only be resolved by litigation. The neighbors usually raise the issue as a First Amendment defense. *Protect Our Mountain Environment, Inc. v. District Court*[9] exemplifies the problem and the process. There, a developer obtained a rezoning of a 500-acre tract for a planned unit development. Several neighbors, organizing themselves as *Protect Our Mountain Environment, Inc. (POME),* sued, challenging the rezoning on a number of grounds including illegal spot zoning and inconsistency with the county plan. While the spot zoning challenge was pending, the developer sued POME and its attorney contending they had abused the legal process by challenging the rezoning. When POME and its attorney sought dismissal on First Amendment grounds, the trial court, without a hearing and based solely on the pleadings, denied the motion, finding POME's motion a sham, not entitled to First Amendment protection. The Colorado Supreme Court reversed the denial of the motion to dismiss, finding that the neighbors' First Amendment rights to petition the government entitled them to greater protection than that afforded by the trial court. The court held that when a defendant raising the First Amendment defense files a motion to dismiss, the plaintiff is then required to prove that the defendant's actions fall outside the scope of protection afforded by the First Amendment.[10] Not all anti-developer statements are protected. They must be "aimed at procuring favorable governmental action."[11] Thus, statements made to potential home

---

[5] See *Morse Bros., Inc. v. Webster,* 2001 ME 70, 772 A.2d 842 (Me. 2001).

[6] *Eastern R. R. Presidents Conference v. Noerr Motor Freight, Inc.,* 365 U.S. 127, 144, 81 S. Ct. 523, 533, 5 L. Ed. 2d 464 (1961).

[7] *Manistee Town Center v. City of Glendale,* 227 F.3d 1090 (9th Cir. 2000).

[8] *New York Times Co. v. Sullivan,* 376 U.S. 254, 84 S. Ct. 710, 11 L. Ed. 2d 686 (1964).

[9] *Protect Our Mountain Environment, Inc. v. District Court In and For Jefferson County,* 677 P.2d 1361 (Colo. 1984).

[10] Protect Our Mountain Environment, Inc., 677 P.2d 1369.

[11] *Penllyn Greene Associates, L.P. v. Clouser,* 890 A.2d 424, 432 (Pa. Commw. Ct. 2005).

buyers and real estate agents that a site was contaminated by Agent Orange were not protected communications since they were not made for the purpose of influencing government action.

Several states have anti-SLAPP statutes protecting the right of citizens to petition the government without fear of retribution.[12] Generally, the statutes take the form of the procedure authorized in the Colorado *POME* case and put the burden on the plaintiff to show the neighbors' action in resisting the development was in bad faith.[13]

Department of Housing and Urban Development investigations of discrimination under the Federal Fair Housing Act raise SLAPP-like concerns. Increased applications to put group homes in residential areas, largely sparked by the 1988 amendment to the Fair Housing Act to include protection for the disabled,[14] resulted in increased efforts by neighbors to block the homes by petitioning the government to deny the necessary permits. This neighborhood opposition may be chilled or thwarted by HUD threatening fines and undertaking investigations pursuant to the Fair Housing Act that makes it unlawful to intimidate person in exercise of housing rights.[15]

Ironically, or perhaps fittingly, Berkeley, California, which gave birth to the free speech movement in the 1960s, is the home of one of the most controversial investigations by HUD. When a proposal was made to convert a motel to a home for recovering substance abusers, the neighbors took action. They wrote letters to the local government officials and spoke at public meetings. While the neighbors contended that the home as planned lacked adequate staff for proper operation, the proponents accused them of opposing the home because it was to be occupied by disabled persons. HUD investigated. It demanded the neighborhood group's membership list, correspondence, meeting minutes and tapes of meetings. It threatened the neighbors with fines of $50,000. After a seven-month investigation, HUD concluded the neighbors had not violated the act.

The neighbors sued HUD and won. In *White v. Lee*,[16] the court found that HUD violated the neighbors' First Amendment right to petition the government. Section 3617 of the Fair Housing Act,[17] which makes it illegal to interfere with another's housing rights protected by the FHA, can be constitutionally applied only to actions such as fire bombings, exclusionary zoning, or insurance redlining, or to advocacy that is directed to inciting or producing violent acts and which is likely to do so.[18] HUD's investigation of the neighbors' advocacy in this case lacked justification, said the court.

B. *Mediation*

Mediation may avoid or defray the high costs of playing the zoning game.[19] The developer and neighbors may use mediation guided by a city employee or, more often

---

[12] See, e.g., Cal. Civ. Proc. Code § 425.16; Del. Code Ann. tit. 10, §§ 8136 to 8138.

[13] *Gilman v. MacDonald,* 74 Wash. App. 733, 875 P.2d 697 (1994).

[14] See supra § 4:7 and infra § 6:8.

[15] 42 U.S.C.A. § 3617.

[16] *White v. Lee,* 227 F.3d 1214 (9th Cir.2000).

[17] 42 U.S.C.A. § 3617.

[18] 227 F.3d at 1230.

[19] See Davidson, Land Use Mediation: Another Smart Growth Alternative, 33 Urb. Law. 705 (2001) (noting increase in use of mediation in land use matters).

and preferably, by a trained and neutral third party. Neighbors and other governmental entities may also be parties. If the parties agree on a development plan to settle their differences, it must be presented to the legislative or administrative authority for action. Though not binding, a pact between these generally warring factions carries considerable influence with the decisionmakers.

Mediation is useful where zoning authorities have discretion in dealing with land development requests. With the flexible zoning employed today in special use permitting, conditional zoning, and planned unit developments, that discretion often exists. If, however, an all or nothing decision faces the government and there is no room for the parties to suggest a compromise, mediation will not work. If, for example, state law requires that a use variance be based on a finding that the present zoning of the land will not yield a reasonable return and, if the board cannot make that finding, no amount of negotiation will matter.

Several states expressly provide for mediation in land use disputes. California provides that the court may invite the parties to a land use dispute to consider mediation.[20] New Jersey requires mediation to resolve exclusionary zoning disputes.[21] North Dakota requires it between jurisdictions in annexation matters.[22] In the absence of statutory authorization, developers and neighbors are nonetheless free to mediate a dispute. Without state enabling legislation, mediation of a dispute by a local government could prompt contract zoning concerns.[23]

A settlement reached through either a formal statutory mediation or one conducted privately will not bind the government.[24] If planning or other government officials are involved, state open meetings laws might apply. The California act provides, for example, that its open meetings law and normal hearing procedures do not apply if the mediation involves less than a quorum of the legislative body or a state body.

Under Florida's Land Use and Environmental Dispute Resolution Act[25] a property owner who believes a development order with respect to land use to be unfair or unreasonable can compel the governmental entity issuing the order to mediate the dispute before a special master.[26] If the parties do not agree, the special master must determine whether the governmental action is unfair or unreasonable, and may recommend alternative solutions to the government.

Arbitration, which differs from mediation in that it results in a binding decision, may also be used in land use matters. In contrast to mediation, where the parties may be inclined to settle, arbitration is used between parties who cannot negotiate a settlement. Traditionally, its use by government has involved areas where the government role is akin to a private party, such as labor disputes, construction contracts, and eminent domain valuation. Its use in zoning, which implicates the government's police

---

[20] Cal. Gov't Code §§ 66030 to 66034. See also Me. Rev. Stat. Ann. tit. 5, § 3341.

[21] N.J. Admin. Code tit. 5, §§ 5:97 to 10.5.

[22] *City of Horace v. City of Fargo ex rel. City Com'n,* 2005 ND 61, 694 N.W.2d 1 (2005).

[23] See Tomain, Land Use Mediation for Planners, 7 Mediation Q. 163, 166 (1989.

[24] The California act provides that the mediation process authorized does not preclude the parties from entering mediation outside the act. Cal. Gov't Code § 66031(d).

[25] Fla. Stat. Ann. § 70.51.

[26] See Powell, Rhodes, and Stengle, A Measured Step to Protect Private Property Rights, 23 Fla. St. U. L. Rev. 255, 296 (1995).

power, is less common.[27] Several states, though, expressly authorize arbitration in disputes over the siting of hazardous waste facilities.[28]

II. LEGISLATIVE AND ADMINISTRATIVE POWERS

§ 5:3   Legislative and Administrative Actions

A.   *Delegation to Administrative Body*

State legislatures empower the local legislative body to zone, and expressly or implicitly, the power to amend. Under the Standard State Zoning Enabling Act, municipalities are not forced to zone, but if they do, the Act requires appointment of a zoning commission to make recommendations.[29] The commission can be a planning commission or the legislative body itself. A planning commission's role is limited to making recommendations.[30]

The Standard State Zoning Enabling Act allows the legislative body to delegate power to an administrative body by establishing a board of adjustment. Section 7 of the Act provides that the board of adjustment:

[m]ay, in appropriate cases and subject to appropriate conditions and safeguards, make special exceptions to the terms of the ordinance in harmony with its general purpose and intent and in accordance with general or specific rules therein contained.

It further provides that the board of adjustment shall have the following powers:

1.   To hear and decide appeals where it is alleged there is error in any order, requirement, decision, or determination made by an administrative official in the enforcement of this act or of any ordinance adopted pursuant thereto.

2.   To hear and decide special exceptions to the terms of the ordinance upon which such board is required to pass under such ordinance.

3.   To authorize upon appeal in specific cases such variance from the terms of the ordinance as will not be contrary to the public interest, where, owing to special conditions, a literal enforcement of the provisions of the ordinance will result in unnecessary hardship, and so that the spirit of the ordinance shall be observed and substantial justice done.

Most states have similar provisions in their state enabling acts, though the board may carry a different name, such as a board of appeals.

There is considerable confusion regarding the terminology used in Section 7 to describe the relief that the board of adjustment may grant. A board may grant three kinds of relief: it may reverse or modify the decision of an administrative officer under subsection 1; it may grant what the Standard Act describes as a "special exception" under subsection 2, which practitioners more commonly know as a conditional or spe-

---

[27] Fla. Stat. Ann. § 51A.04[1].

[28] R.I. Gen. Laws § 23–19.7–10; Wis. Stat. Ann. § 144.445.

[29] U.S. Dep't of Commerce (rev.ed. 1926).

[30] In a few state, zoning commissions are granted the power to zone. See, e.g., Conn. Gen. Stat. § 8.2.

cial use permit; and it may grant a variance under subsection 3. Unfortunately, the lay public, and some lawyers and courts, use the term "special exception" to refer to all three forms of relief. This confusion stems from the wording of the Standard Act.

The first sentence of Section 7 apparently uses the term special exception in a generic sense to describe all the forms of relief that the board may grant, while subsection 2 uses the term to describe a specific form of relief.[31] The special exception provided for in subsection 2 permits certain uses in a zone if the applicant meets the terms of the ordinance. If so, the board will issue what it might term a special permit, special use permit, conditional use permit or a special exception, all of which are synonymous.[32] Generally, we use the term special permit in this chapter.

Subsection 3 authorizes the issuance of variances. A variance is permitted only by sufferance, that is, the board grants one when because of "special conditions," the property owner suffers "unnecessary hardship."[33]

The variance and the special permit provisions have generated a vast body of law, probably for four major reasons: first, the grant or denial of permission can frequently have substantial economic consequences and is a matter worth fighting over; second, thousands of administrative bodies make decisions; third, these bodies are frequently composed of persons with greater political, economic and practical sense than technical expertise, who frequently overstep the bounds of their quasi-judicial functions; and, fourth, recognizing the inadequacies of the boards, courts are not as willing to defer to boards' judgments as they are to more expert administrative bodies, and this lack of deference invites a judicial rehash of the issues involved.

A board's exercise of these powers leads to problems over the propriety of the delegation of the power by the legislative body.[34] There are two major questions that arise with respect to delegation. One is whether the administrative body or officer acted within the scope provided by the enabling act or the ordinance. A second question is whether the enabling act or the local legislative body provided sufficient standards to guide the discretion of administrative bodies or officials. A municipal governing body may violate its zoning enabling act by delegating excessive authority to its lay bodies,[35] or by imposing no standards to guide lay decisionmaking.[36] The validity of a delegation of power may depend upon the body to which it transfers that power.[37] While courts vary with respect to these matters, in many states they do not tolerate the very vague standards tolerated in federal administrative law. This may be a reflection of the reality or perception that these local bodies often have little expertise and, unless controlled judicially, are peculiarly apt to make decisions that are arbitrary, based on improper bias, dictated by conflicts of interest, or made because of bribery or other corrupt mo-

---

[31] The term "exception" may also be used to describe one aspect of the authority of an administrative officer which may be reviewed by the board under subsection 1.

[32] See infra § 5:24.

[33] See infra § 5:14.

[34] Some codes empower zoning administrators to decide simpler cases within the jurisdiction of a board of zoning appeals, thus raising questions as to the propriety of delegation of power to them. A city may also employ hearing examiners to receive evidence and make recommendations. See 4 K. Young, Anderson's American Law of Zoning § 30.02 (4th ed. 1996); Note: Administrative Discretion in Zoning, 82 Harv. L. Rev. 668 (1969).

[35] *Lutz v. City of Longview*, 83 Wash. 2d 566, 520 P.2d 1374 (1974).

[36] *People v. Perez*, 214 Cal. App. 2d Supp. 881, 29 Cal. Rptr. 781 (App. Dep't Super. Ct. 1963).

[37] *Appeal of Moreland*, 1972 OK 87, 497 P.2d 1287 (Okla. 1972).

tives.[38] Most of the work of the board of adjustment deals with special permits and variances, discussed in greater detail below.[39]

B.   *Characterization of Actions*

The characterization of zoning actions as legislative, quasi-legislative, quasi-judicial, or administrative has significant consequences in several contexts. First, the initiative and referendum are only available for legislative actions.[40] Second, issues of absolute and qualified immunity turn on these characterizations.[41] Third, the scope of judicial review and the demands of due process differ depending on the kind of action taken. Fourth, the process by which the action is taken may differ. Since the legislative body is capable of acting in various capacities, it is often unclear in which capacity a challenged action was made. Characterization is also imprecise, which is unsurprising where courts find it necessary to use the term "quasi" in the first place.

Moving beyond its traditional and expected role of creating policy for the jurisdiction by the adoption of ordinance, the legislative body may also act in a quasi-judicial capacity. The action may be expressly authorized by an ordinance with the legislative body retaining the powers that might otherwise be delegated to a board of adjustment.[42] Some courts accept at face value the proposition that actions by the legislative body are legislative and, consequently, entitled to a presumption of validity. Other courts, looking at substance over form, treat some actions that are nominally legislative as quasi-judicial in character. In such cases, the action is viewed as quasi-judicial and not entitled to the same presumption of validity that attaches to true legislation.[43]

Actions by nominally administrative bodies may be administrative or quasi-judicial, with the former referring to ministerial actions of a zoning administrator, and the latter referring to adjudicatory findings by a board of adjustment.[44] Administrative or quasi-judicial acts are usually entitled to a presumption of validity, but it is a weaker presumption than that accorded legislation.[45]

Some courts use the term "quasi-legislative." In the zoning context, "quasi-legislative" most often refers to actions by non-elected planning commissions and, on occasion, to boards of adjustment. If the court decides the decision involved a weighing of interests and the adoption of a general policy, the action by the nominally administrative body will be labeled quasi-legislative and conferred with the presumption of validity. If found to be adjudicatory, the action will be labeled quasi-judicial and the court will scrutinize the decision. In *Marine Forests Soc. v. California Coastal Commission,*[46] the court observed that the Commission acts in administrative capacity when carrying out legislative policies, in a quasi-legislative capacity when it engages in rulemaking and a quasi-judicial function when it passes upon applications for devel-

---

[38] For a court expressing some of these suspicions, see *Topanga Assn. for a Scenic Community v. County of Los Angeles,* 11 Cal. 3d 506, 113 Cal. Rptr. 836, 522 P.2d 12 (1974).

[39] See infra §§ 5:14 and 5:24.

[40] This is true under state law, not under the federal constitution. See supra § 5:5.

[41] See discussion of immunity from civil rights act liability, infra § 10:26.

[42] See infra § 5:25.

[43] See infra § 5:9.

[44] See *County of Lancaster, S.C. v. Mecklenburg County, N.C.,* 334 N.C. 496, 434 S.E.2d 604 (1993).

[45] See infra § 5:37.

[46] 36 Cal. 4th 1, 30 Cal. Rptr. 3d 30, 113 P.3d 1062 (2005).

opment permits. Yet caution is in order as courts are known to have used "legislative" and "quasi-legislative" in the same case, indeed the same paragraph, to mean the same thing, or to use the term without explanation.

§ 5:4   Delegation to Property Owners

Property owners near a proposed development often carry significant political clout in whether a board grants a development request. Protestors packing the meeting hall may sway legislators who not only are concerned with the effect their action will have on a neighborhood but also the effect it will have on their reelection.[47] Recognizing the reality of this political power, it may seem prudent simply to delegate the legal power to decide to the property owners in the vicinity.

Though not a profile in courage, the impulse to delegate decisionmaking power to the neighbors is understandable. It allows those most directly affected to decide the matter. This may be appropriate if the spillover effects of the use are limited to the neighbors who have the delegated power. However, the benefits of granting or denying the proposed use may spread beyond the confines of the neighborhood. Since the legislators have stepped out of the picture to avoid making what might be an unpopular decision, no one may be guarding the public interest. A delegation to neighbors also has the potential of subjecting proponents of change to their neighbors' arbitrary whims, and raises due process concerns.[48]

Several United States Supreme Court cases deal with neighborhood consent ordinances. In a 1912 decision, *Eubank v. Richmond,*[49] the Court reviewed an ordinance that required the municipality to establish a setback line if two-thirds of the property owners abutting a street requested it. A property owner of a lot who wished to build a house 11 feet from the street was prevented from doing so when his neighbors, by petition, established the setback at 14 feet. The Court held the delegation to violate the due process clause since it contained no standards, allowing the neighbors to act capriciously in their own interests. Three years later, in *Thomas Cusack Co. v. Chicago,*[50] the Court reviewed an ordinance that prohibited signs on public streets where more than half of the buildings were used for residential purposes unless the applicant obtained the consent of a majority of the owners of property on the street. The Court upheld this ordinance. It reasoned that since the ordinance prohibited signs, the owner wishing to put up a sign only stood to gain by being able to seek consent. *Eubank* was distinguished because the restriction was imposed by the property owners. In *Cusack,* in contrast, they waived an existing restriction.

Finally, in *State of Washington ex rel. Seattle Title Trust Co. v. Roberge,*[51] the ordinance provided that a home for the elderly poor could be built in an area only if neighbors consented. Despite the similarity between the ordinances in *Cusack* and *Roberge,* the *Roberge* Court considered the signs in *Cusack* and the home for the elderly

---

[47] The filing of a protest petition by neighbors also imposes a super-majority voting requirement on the decisionmakers. See infra § 5:7.

[48] A delegation to a private party is permissible only if there are adequate safeguards to protect against arbitrary decisionmaking. *Moore v. City of Kirkland,* 2006 WL 1993443 (W.D. Wash. 2006).

[49] *Eubank v. City of Richmond,* 226 U.S. 137, 33 S. Ct. 76, 57 L. Ed. 156 (1912).

[50] *Thomas Cusack Co. v. City of Chicago,* 242 U.S. 526, 37 S. Ct. 190, 61 L. Ed. 472 (1917).

[51] *State of Washington ex rel. Seattle Title Trust Co. v. Roberge,* 278 U.S. 116, 49 S. Ct. 50, 73 L. Ed. 210 (1928).

of *Roberge* to be distinguishable. Signs were viewed as nuisances, justifying greater control by property owners. Homes for the elderly, in contrast, had not been determined to be inimical to other uses, and the Court thus invalidated the delegation.

Many courts take these three cases to establish the rule that granting neighbors the power to impose a control violates due process, but granting them the power to waive an existing limitation does not. The cases have, however, "posed a long-standing puzzle to legal theorists,"[52] and many are critical of the rule derived from them. Some courts also find it troubling. As the Supreme Court of Illinois said, the distinction "between 'creating' and 'waiving' a restriction" is too subtle and in any event, each "leave[s] the ultimate determination of * * * the public welfare in the discretion of individuals rather than the city."[53] In one case a court invalidated a so-called consent provision pursuant to which a city ban on horse drawn carriage stands within 100 feet from any restaurant could be waived by the restaurant owner. It was impermissible, said the court, to allow the restaurant owner to determine when public health required enforcement of the ban.[54] Despite the critics, the test enjoys some support in the case law, and under it, improper delegation is limited to instances where the neighbors can impose the regulation. Where the ordinance prohibits uses unless the applicant obtains consent, the ordinance is more likely valid.

An alternative approach is found in *Hornstein v. Barry,*[55] where a divided District of Columbia Court of Appeals upheld an ordinance that prohibited conversion of rental units to condominiums without the consent of a majority of the renters. The majority viewed the matter as controlled by *Cusack,* the billboard case, to which it gave a broad reading. The court found that *Cusack* was not limited to delegations involving nuisances but applied to any instance where the legislative body specifically found that the use was contrary to the public interest.[56] Then, beginning with the assumption that the city could have banned conversions completely, the court held that the provision allowing conversions to proceed only if consented to by the tenants could only benefit the owners of apartments. The court acknowledged that the tenants might act arbitrarily and in their own self-interest in voting, but that did not matter. In fact, the court assumed that the city passed the ordinance with the idea that the owner would buy out the tenants at attractive prices. This, of course, meant that conversions would occur, defeating the purpose of the law, which was to prevent the loss of rental housing. The court, though, regarded the wisdom of the scheme to be a legislative question, and thought the owner had no basis to complain about the choice confronting him.

The *Hornstein* dissent viewed *Roberge* as controlling, reading that case as allowing delegation to a few only where the use was a nuisance. *Roberge,* the court noted, came after *Cusack,* and had distinguished *Cusack* solely with the explanation that it involved a nuisance.[57] Where that is the case, there is no property right. For the dissent, the key concern of *Roberge* and *Eubank,* the cases where the Court invalidated delega-

---

[52] Michelman, Political Markets and Community Self-Determination: Competing Judicial Models of Local Government Legitimacy, 53 Ind. L.J. 145, 164 (1977–78).

[53] *Drovers Trust & Sav. Bank v. City of Chicago,* 18 Ill. 2d 476, 478–79, 165 N.E.2d 314, 315 (1960).

[54] *American Chariot v. City of Memphis,* 164 S.W.3d 600 (Tenn. Ct. App. 2004).

[55] *Hornstein v. Barry,* 560 A.2d 530 (D.C. 1989) (en banc 5 to 4 decision).

[56] Hornstein, 560 A.2d at 536.

[57] Hornstein, 560 A.2d at 540. See also *Minton v. City of Fort Worth Planning Com'n,* 786 S.W.2d 563 (Tex. App. 1990) (ordinance that prevented replatting without neighbors' consent invalid).

tions, was that the neighbors controlled the use and could do so arbitrarily. Consequently, the conversion consent requirement should have been set aside.

The approaches of the *Hornstein* majority and dissent are preferable to the deceptively simplistic imposition/waiver analysis. Having the constitutionality of neighborhood consent ordinances turn on a subtle variation in wording between consent and waiver is unfortunate. In both instances, a few property owners decide how their neighbor's land will be used. The *Hornstein* arguments focus on two more fundamental propositions. One view is that courts should defer to legislative decisions, and if the city could ban the proposed use outright, no due process injury occurs if neighbors have the power to waive. The other is that judicial intervention is appropriate where the delegation allows arbitrary action, unless the sought-after use is a nuisance.

§ 5:5 Initiative and Referendum

In some states, the electorate can use initiative and referendum powers to carry out or veto zoning changes.[58] The predominant use of what has become known as ballot box zoning[59] is to prevent growth that the legislative body would otherwise allow. In the typical initiative scenario, a developer announces its intent to develop land presently zoned for an intensive use. Local citizens, realizing their vulnerability to this unwanted development, place an initiative on the ballot to downzone the land before the developer acquires a vested right.[60] Sometimes those who wish to prevent growth act first, passing by initiative a no, or slow, growth ordinance in advance of any specific development project announcement. The referendum, in contrast, is reactive. Citizens who disagree with an approved upzoning must petition to place the issue on the ballot, hoping to rescind the rezoning at the polls. Usually, the referendum process is permissive, but some communities hold a mandatory referendum on all rezonings. Careful drafting of an initiative or referendum is critical. The language must not confuse or mislead voters. Many states also require that a ballot measure deal with a single subject.

The use of these powers is controversial, and their validity differs around the country based on state constitutional and statutory provisions. While some applaud ballot box zoning as the essence of direct democracy, others worry that its use may serve to mask illegitimate exclusionary zoning, may render planning efforts superfluous, and may undermine the due process rights of property owners who are subjected to the cy of the voters.[61]

A majority of states disallow zoning by initiative,[62] but a fairly even split exists with respect to overturning legislative zoning acts by referendum.[63] Most of those disal-

---

[58] An initiative is the enactment of legislation by direct vote while a referendum is the rejection or ratification of legislation that has already been enacted.

[59] Callies, Neuffer, and Caliboso, Ballot Box Zoning in Hawaii: Initiative, Referendum and the Law, 39 J. Urb. Contemp. L. 53 (1991).

[60] See discussion regarding vested rights infra §§ 5:27 to 5:29.

[61] Selmi, Reconsidering the Use of Direct Democracy in Making Land Use Decisions, 19 UCLA J. Envtl. L. & Pol'y 293 (2001–2002).

[62] See, e.g., zoning by initiative disallowed in *Transamerica Title Ins. Co. Trust Nos. 8295, 8297, 8298, 8299, 8300 and 8301 v. City of Tucson,* 157 Ariz. 346, 757 P.2d 1055 (1988) and zoning by initiative allowed in *Swetzof v. Philemonoff,* 203 P.3d 471 (Alaska 2009). For complete listing, see §5.5 of the Practitioner's edition of this treatise.

lowing voter action find the absence of notice and hearing required by zoning enabling legislation to be fatal.[64] Some courts that allow such action reason that the affected landowner obtains the equivalent of a public hearing through the debate that ensues with the campaign.[65] It is, however, doubtful that there is anything resembling a campaign for the typical initiative or referendum of a specific parcel.[66] If the zoning problem does not involve a community wide issue, it is likely that there will be little debate and that the only ones who will vote will be those living near the parcel in issue.

The concern over notice and hearing explains why courts treat initiatives less favorably than referenda. Arizona, for example, prohibits zoning by initiative because of the absence of notice and a hearing,[67] but allows zoning by referendum on the theory that the zoning process that precedes the referendum provides notice and a hearing.[68] If a state constitutional provision reserves the initiative and the referendum to the people, it will trump a statutory mandate regarding notice and hearing.[69]

Opponents question whether zoning by the electorate must or can comply with statutes that call for zoning to be in accord with a comprehensive plan.[70] The South Carolina supreme court, for example, found the "obvious incompatibility between the initiative and referendum process and the comprehensive [zoning and planning] provisions indicates the Legislature did not intend to allow voters to enact more complex zoning measures by initiative and referendum."[71] The New Jersey high court thought the use of the initiative and referendum would lead to a piecemeal, noncomprehensive approach to land use control.[72] Besides the question of whether voters possess sufficient expertise to apply planning principles and to consider the ramifications of their decisions, the planning process may also require certain functions that voters cannot perform. In *Snohomish County v. Anderson,*[73] for example, a state statute directed "the legislative authority" to hold meetings and create procedures for implementing a growth management program. The court, noting that these responsibilities could not be performed by a yes or no vote on a ballot, held that the term "legislative authority" did not include the electorate.[74]

The effect that electoral zoning has on the planning process is not necessarily negative. If the legislative body itself does not live up to the charge that it zone in accord with a comprehensive plan,[75] it may make little difference if the voters also fail in that respect. The voters in fact may be free from the influence of special interest groups,

---

[63] Zoning by referendum disallowed as to legislative acts, see, e.g., *Sparta Tp. v. Spillane,* 125 N.J. Super. 519, 312 A.2d 154 (App. Div. 1973).

[64] See, e.g., *Transamerica Title Ins. Co. Trust v. City of Tucson,* 157 Ariz. 346, 757 P.2d 1055 (1988).

[65] See, e.g., *Margolis v. District Court, In and For Arapahoe County,* 638 P.2d 297 (Colo. 1981); but see *City of Winter Springs v. Florida Land Co.,* 413 So. 2d 84 (Fla. 5th DCA 1982), decision approved, 427 So. 2d 170 (Fla. 1983).

[66] Callies et al., supra note 59 at n. 35.

[67] *Transamerica Title Ins. Co. Trust v. City of Tucson,* 157 Ariz. 346, 757 P.2d 1055 (1988).

[68] *Queen Creek Land & Cattle Corp. v. Yavapai County Bd. of Sup'rs,* 108 Ariz. 449, 501 P.2d 391 (1972).

[69] *Garvin v. Ninth Judicial Dist. Court ex rel. County of Douglas,* 118 Nev. 749, 59 P.3d 1180 (2002).

[70] *Sustainable Growth Initiative Committee v. Jumpers, LLC,* 122 Nev. 53, 128 P.3d 452 (2006).

[71] *I'On, L.L.C. v. Town of Mt. Pleasant,* 338 S.C. 406, 526 S.E.2d 716, 721 (2000).

[72] *Sparta Tp. v. Spillane,* 125 N.J. Super. 519, 312 A.2d 154 (App. Div. 1973).

[73] *Snohomish County v. Anderson,* 123 Wash. 2d 151, 868 P.2d 116 (1994).

[74] Snohomish County, 123 Wash. 2d 151, 868 P.2d at 118.

[75] See supra § 2:11 regarding jurisdictions where the plan is advisory only.

known sometimes to wield significant behind-the-scenes power in city hall. The planning process also can be judicially protected by requiring that the results of a voter enacted or rescinded ordinance meet state planning law.[76] The efficacy of judicial protection of the planning process is undermined, though, if the courts apply a deferential level of review. If they use higher scrutiny, a greater likelihood exists that the voters will be unable to upset the planning process.[77]

A few property owners near the land rezoned or proposed for rezoning might determine the result of an initiative or referendum that does not generate community-wide interest. If they will be the only ones directly affected, they may be the only ones who vote. This makes the action appear like a delegation to neighbors that courts sometimes condemn as a violation of due process.[78]

The Supreme Court dealt with the issue in *City of Eastlake v. Forest City Enterprises,*[79] where the city charter required that any land use change be approved by 55% of the voters in a specially held referendum. A developer sought to put a high rise housing project in an area zoned for light industrial use. The city council approved the rezoning, but a supermajority of voters did not agree. The developer challenged the referendum requirement, basing its claim on those cases holding that standardless delegations of legislative power to property owners violated due process.[80] The Court held that since the Ohio constitution expressly reserved the referendum to the people, it was a reservation of power by the people, not a delegation of power to them. This rendered inapposite the line of cases relied on by the developer.

The *Eastlake* majority enthusiastically endorsed the referendum as an important means of direct political participation giving "'citizens a voice on questions of public policy.'"[81] It is precisely this point that leads to questions as to whether the procedure should be available for parcel-specific rezonings or other acts that do not raise broad questions of community policy. Justice Powell, in his *Eastlake* dissent, noted that the rezoning involved a small parcel and suggested that "[t]he 'spot' referendum technique appears to open disquieting opportunities * * * to bypass normal protective procedures for resolving issues affecting individual rights."[82] Believing that the owner subjected to the referendum has no realistic opportunity to be heard by the electorate, Justice Powell found the process fundamentally unfair.

The Supreme Court continues to refuse to recognize a federal constitutional distinction between administrative and legislative matters on referenda. In *City of Cuyahoga Falls v. Buckeye Community Hope Foundation,*[83] the voters petitioned to place site plan approval for a low income housing complex on the ballot. Leading up to the election, some residents publicly voiced concerns over the fact that minorities would live in the housing, and, at the polls, the voters overturned the site plan. The Supreme

---

[76] *Merritt v. City of Pleasanton,* 89 Cal. App. 4th 1032, 107 Cal. Rptr. 2d 675, 678 (2001).

[77] See infra § 5:9 and § 5:37, discussing level of review.

[78] See supra § 5:4.

[79] *City of Eastlake v. Forest City Enterprises, Inc.,* 426 U.S. 668, 96 S. Ct. 2358, 49 L. Ed. 2d 132 (1976).

[80] See cases discussed supra § 5:4.

[81] *City of Eastlake v. Forest City Enterprises, Inc.,* 426 U.S. 668, 96 S. Ct. 2358, 49 L. Ed. 2d 132 (1976), quoting *James v. Valtierra,* 402 U.S. 137, 141, 91 S. Ct. 1331, 1333, 28 L. Ed. 2d 678 (1971).

[82] City of Eastlake, 426 U.S. at 680, 96 S. Ct. at 2365.

[83] *City of Cuyahoga Falls, Ohio v. Buckeye Community Hope Foundation,* 538 U.S. 188, 123 S. Ct. 1389, 155 L. Ed. 2d 349 (2003). For *Buckeye's* rejection of an equal protection claim, see infra § 10:14.

Court unanimously upheld the referendum process, reaffirming the *Eastlake* opinion that referenda on administrative land use decisions do not violate due process.

While the federal constitution places no restriction on the submission of administrative land use decisions to the electorate, states prohibit it.[84] Determining whether an action is legislative for submission to the voters has been troublesome since the differences between these actions are blurred.[85] The easier questions involve actions by boards of adjustment and planning commissions, which all agree are administrative or quasi-judicial. As such, variances, subdivision map approvals, and conditional use permits issued by such boards are not subject to direct voter action.[86] A number of states treat site-specific actions by nominally legislative bodies as quasi-judicial and not subject to voter approval. Thus, a city council's approval of site plan for a low-income apartment complex was held to be administrative action not constitutionally subject to referendum.[87]

The major problem is classifying actions by elected local legislative bodies. Local legislatures engage in a variety of acts, some of which are non-legislative, so that close review of an action is necessary to see whether the legislative label is justified.[88] With respect to rezonings, courts have differed. Some accept the nominal legislative label and others treat them as quasi-judicial.[89] In California, which generally treats rezonings as legislative, the court held a rezoning that was a revision of a zoning boundary pursuant to a previously adopted procedure was administrative action,[90] and in Colorado, a court found a conditional use permit issued by city council was legislative.[91]

The unavailability of the initiative and referendum to review or impose administrative or adjudicatory action may be based on state constitutional or statutory provisions that expressly limit the voter's role to legislation and by implication exclude administrative or adjudicatory action. Some courts cite efficiency concerns, fearing that delay and possible revocation by referendum would adversely affect the successful administration of municipal business. The reasoning of these courts suggests that a state might confer administrative or adjudicatory powers on voters, but if that occurs, a due process issue may arise. While notice and hearing to each affected person need not accompany the adoption of a policy applicable to a broad class of persons, those rights do attach when government applies the policy to an individual or a small number of persons. Generally, courts label the former actions adopting policy as legislative, while they label the latter ones applying policy as adjudicatory or quasi-judicial. When ballot box zoning takes action that falls in the latter categories, it will fail if the process does

---

[84] See, e.g., *Margolis v. District Court, In and For Arapahoe County,* 638 P.2d 297, 303 (Colo. 1981); *State ex rel. Marsalek v. S. Euclid City Council,* 111 Ohio St. 3d 163, 855 N.E.2d 811 (2006).

[85] The term administrative may be used interchangeably with the terms quasi-judicial or adjudicatory. See Rose, Planning and Dealing: Piecemeal Land Controls as a Problem of Local Legitimacy, 71 Cal. L. Rev. 837, 866 (1983). See infra § 5:37 for discussion of the characterization issue in the context of judicial review.

[86] *Arnel Development Co. v. City of Costa Mesa,* 28 Cal. 3d 511, 169 Cal. Rptr. 904, 620 P.2d 565 (1980).

[87] *Buckeye Community Hope Found, v. Cuyahoga Falls,* 82 Ohio St. 3d 539, 697 N.E.2d 181 (1998).

[88] See *State ex rel. Zonders v. Delaware Cty. Bd. of Elections,* 69 Ohio St. 3d 5, 630 N.E.2d 313 (1994).

[89] Id.

[90] *Southwest Diversified, Inc. v. City of Brisbane,* 229 Cal. App. 3d 1548, 280 Cal. Rptr. 869 (1st Dist. 1991), reh'g denied and opinion modified, (June 10, 1991) (despite an apparently categorical rule of the state supreme court treating rezonings as legislative).

[91] *Citizens for Quality Growth Petitioners' Committee v. City of Steamboat Springs,* 807 P.2d 1197 (Colo. App. 1990).

not provide adequate notice and hearing. State courts have differed over whether zoning by initiative and referendum meet that test.[92]

The initiative and referendum pose questions of process, not substance. As the Supreme Court said in both *Eastlake* and *Buckeye,* voters cannot, by use of the initiative or referendum power, obtain results otherwise unobtainable by the legislative body.[93] Voters cannot, for example, deny a person the equal protection of the laws or the substantive due process right to be free from arbitrary state action. Thus, the Court in *Hunter v. Erickson* invalidated a racially discriminatory referendum process on equal protection grounds.[94] Still, it is hard to obtain the proof demanded in equal protection cases,[95] and the test for substantive due process is so lax [96] that it is difficult to prevail on either theory. So, the process used may subvert substantive protection.

III. REZONINGS

§ 5:6 Amendments Generally

As Richard Babcock famously pointed out, the name of the zoning game is change,[97] and the major change is the amendment. The Standard State Zoning Enabling Act provides that "regulations, restrictions, and boundaries may from time to time be amended, supplemented, changed, modified, or repealed."[98] The legislative body, a governmental official, or a property owner can initiate amendments. In some states the electorate can also amend through the initiative process.[99] Amendments may be procedural or substantive. Substantive amendments include map amendments that change the zone that applies to a parcel of land and text amendments that change the uses permitted within a zone.

While most amendments are site-specific map amendments, text amendments are also made, typically redefining allowable uses as changing conditions suggest are needed. At times, the text amendment may be a better avenue to pursue for one seeking to develop land. Suppose a property owner wishes to open a group home on land zoned for single-family use, but the city only permits group homes in the office zone. The property owner generally will apply for an upzoning to office uses. If the legislative body grants the request, the property owner might ultimately be foiled since the rezoning might constitute invalid spot zoning.[100] An alternate avenue for the property owner is to seek a text amendment to change the permitted uses within the single-family zone. The text amendment is more appropriate in this situation since the real question

---

[92] See discussion, supra this section.

[93] See *City of Cuyahoga Falls, Ohio v. Buckeye Community Hope Foundation,* 538 U.S. 188, 123 S. Ct. 1389, 155 L. Ed. 2d 349 (2003).

[94] *Hunter v. Erickson,* 393 U.S. 385, 89 S. Ct. 557, 21 L. Ed. 2d 616 (1969), but see limitations in *James v. Valtierra,* 402 U.S. 137, 91 S. Ct. 1331, 28 L. Ed. 2d 678 (1971).

[95] See discussion infra § 10:14.

[96] See infra § 10:12.

[97] Richard Babcock, The Zoning Game: Municipal Practices and Policies (1966).

[98] U.S. Dept. of Commerce § 5 (1926).

[99] See supra § 5:5.

[100] See infra § 5:10.

is whether group homes belong in single-family zones rather than, or in addition to, office zones.[101]

The notice, if any, provided to citizens will differ according to the type of amendment sought and on whom it affects. If the amendment relates to specific land and the owner is not the one requesting the rezoning, the owner is generally entitled to personal notice by statute. Most state statutes or city ordinances also require that nearby property owners be notified of proposed changes by mail.[102] Failure to abide by individual notice requirements to neighbors will likely invalidate any approval,[103] and may violate the neighbors' due process rights.[104] If no statute requires notice, due process requires notice and an opportunity to be heard if the action is regarded as adjudicatory.[9] Newspaper publication may meet the demands of due process as to persons who are unknown, but not as to persons whose identity and address are known or discoverable by reasonable efforts.[105] Posting signs on the property that is the subject of the proposal may also be required. In contrast to a map amendment, when a text amendment is to be made, there are no individuals to be given personal notice since it is legislative in nature.[106] Generally, the only notice given will be newspaper publication as required by the enabling act.[107]

§ 5:7   Neighbor Protests: Extraordinary Majority Requirements

In many states, neighbors of a proposed rezoning possess a powerful defense: the protest petition. The Standard Zoning Enabling Act provides that if a certain percentage of property owners in or near the area of a proposed change file a protest, the change can be made only by vote of three-fourths of all the members of the legislative body.[108] Arizona law, for example, provides that a protest petition by 20% of the property owners within 150 feet of the property for which rezoning is sought triggers a supermajority requirement.[109]

The difficulty that a proponent will often encounter in obtaining a supermajority makes the protest petition a significant weapon in the neighbors' arsenal. A drawback is that the filing time for the petition may be short and may have elapsed by the time the neighbors are organized.

---

[101] But see *Albuquerque Commons Partnership v. City Council of City of Albuquerque,* 144 N.M. 99, 114, 184 P.3d 411, 426 (2008) (there is no "bright-line rule that distinguishes between text amendments and map amendments such that the former can never constitute a rezoning would be a classic elevation of form over substance").

[102] Not all require notice, but it may be provided as a courtesy. *Wells v. Village of Libertyville,* 153 Ill. App. 3d 361, 106 Ill. Dec. 193, 505 N.E.2d 740 (1987).

[103] See, e.g., Glen Paul Court Neighborhood Ass'n v. Paster, 437 N.W.2d 52 (Minn. 1989).

[104] See *DuLaney v. Oklahoma State Dept. of Health,* 1993 OK 113, 868 P.2d 676 (Okla. 1993).

[9] *Passalino v. City of Zion,* 237 Ill. 2d 118, 340 Ill. Dec. 567, 928 N.E.2d 814 (2010). See also discussion infra § 5:9.

[105] *Passalino v. City of Zion,* 237 Ill. 2d 118, 340 Ill. Dec. 567, 928 N.E.2d 814 (2010).

[106] *Tillery v. Meadows Const. Co.,* 284 Ark. 241, 681 S.W.2d 330 (1984). See discussion infra §§ 5:9 and 5:37.

[107] Standard State Zoning Enabling Act § 4.

[108] U.S. Dep't of Commerce (rev.ed. 1926). The protest petition is applicable only to amendments, not original zoning enactments.

[109] Ariz. Rev. Stat. § 9-462(G).

Though litigation may ensue over the proper construction and interpretation of specific statutory provisions,[110] courts generally hold the process valid.[111] Direct delegations of the zoning power to property owners, which courts frequently invalidate,[112] must be distinguished. For example, an ordinance providing that a protest petition completely bars a proposed rezoning is an invalid delegation of legislative authority.[113] Courts have held protest provisions constitutional when challenged as unlawful delegations of legislative power since elected officials have the final word on whether to change the zoning.[114]

Those seeking rezonings may avoid the super-majority vote by omitting an area from the rezoning request to create a buffer.[115]

§ 5:8 Grounds for Rezoning

As with the original zoning ordinance, the legislative body must make amendments in "accordance with a comprehensive plan."[116] Under certain circumstances, rezoning should be relatively easy to obtain. If the comprehensive plan for an area designates a use that differs from the existing zoning and if the decision makers find that the future contemplated by the plan has arrived, they should rezone the property. If the area is in an interim zone, the fact that a property owner has a definite use in mind might stimulate permanent zoning by the city, though perhaps not the kind the property owner wishes. If there is a considerable amount of vacant property in the area, and property adjacent to the property to be rezoned is zoned for the use desired, changing the boundaries of the adjacent zone to incorporate the owner's property should be relatively easy. Finally, if an area has developed by way of nonconforming uses, special uses and variances, a rezoning that would make the uses permitted uses is appropriate.

If none of the above circumstances suggesting the propriety of an amendment exist, the property owner may also argue that conditions have changed since the last zoning and that rezoning would be in the public interest. An argument that rezoning should occur because it will increase the value of the parcel may be considered but it will rarely be persuasive. If that is the only argument and the existing restriction is not unreasonably burdensome, the legislative body should not change the zoning. It should make a change only if it benefits the public health, safety or general welfare.

Many changes of circumstances logically support an argument for a change in zoning. For example, a major highway built through an area zoned for agricultural purposes may justify rezoning to permit more intensive uses. Also, as population increases, some property should be rezoned to permit more intensive uses, but such changes should be based on some rational policy or plan.

---

[110] See *City of Springfield v. Goff,* 918 S.W.2d 786 (Mo. 1996).

[111] *Klein v. City of Shawnee,* 1998 WL 231074 (D. Kan. 1998).

[112] See supra § 5:4.

[113] *Cary v. City of Rapid City,* 1997 SD 18, 559 N.W.2d 891 (S.D. 1997). See supra § 5:4.

[114] *Bredberg v. City of Wheaton,* 24 Ill. 2d 612, 620, 182 N.E.2d 742, 746 (1962).

[115] See *Eadie v. Town Bd. of Town of North Greenbush,* 7 N.Y.3d 306, 821 N.Y.S.2d 142, 854 N.E.2d 464 (2006) (seeing "nothing wrong" with creating a buffer zone to avoid protest petition).

[116] See Standard Zoning Enabling Act, § 3.

Zoning concepts or community needs may change, justifying rezoning even where there has been no physical change in an area. Though the city may have regarded strip commercial zoning as desirable at one time, rezoning areas for shopping centers may better serve the public interest in part because it will help avoid problems associated with on-street parking. Zoning for mixed commercial and residential use may be authorized to relieve transportation burdens associated with long commuter trips. Or, a community originally zoned exclusively for single-family homes may decide, or may be convinced by a developer, that the housing needs of those desirous of living in the town require areas zoned for multi-family use. If these changes are in the public interest, courts will uphold the rezoning over claims of neighbors that they have a right to perpetuation of existing zoning.[117]

Rezoning may also be proper when the existing zoning unreasonably burdens the property and is not necessary to safeguard the public interest. The court in *Oka v. Cole*[118] upheld a rezoning of property from single-family to multi-family residential when the property was in an area where land costs rendered single-family use economically unattractive and the change did not affect the public interest.

In sum, a rezoning, as an exercise of the police power, must be rational. If treated as a legislative act, it will be presumed valid and deferentially reviewed. If treated as quasi-judicial, higher scrutiny will apply.[119]

Rezoning is more difficult to justify in a few states that require a showing of a change of physical circumstances or a mistake in the original zoning.[120] A significant consequence of using this "change or mistake" rule is that when neighbors challenge a rezoning, the normal presumption of validity does not apply and the burden of proof shifts to the one proposing the zoning change, similar to what occurs when a court treats a rezoning as quasi-judicial.[121]

§ 5:9   Rezoning: Legislative or Quasi-Judicial Action?

Most states treat, or purport to treat, all zoning changes, whether general or site-specific, as legislative acts and accord them a presumption of validity.[122] Though neighbors can bring a variety of challenges against a site-specific rezoning, such as claims that it is spot zoning, or contract zoning, or not in accord with a comprehensive plan, a court will often allow a rezoning to stand unless the challengers can show that the decision was arbitrary and capricious. As the Supreme Court has held, "if the validity of the legislative classification for zoning purposes be fairly debatable, the legislative judgment must be allowed to control."[123] The burden is on the one seeking to overturn the legislative body's action, and the test is difficult to meet.

---

[117] *Maryland Reclamation Associates, Inc. v. Harford County,* 414 Md. 1, 994 A.2d 842 (2010).

[118] *Oka v. Cole,* 145 So. 2d 233 (Fla. 1962).

[119] See infra § 5:9.

[120] *Mayor and Council of Rockville v. Rylyns Enterprises, Inc.,* 372 Md. 514, 814 A.2d 469 (2002). See also *Harvey v. Town of Marion,* 756 So. 2d 835 (Miss. Ct. App. 2000), listing states pro and con the change/mistake rule and noting that classification is uncertain since courts articulate their test in various ways.

[121] See infra § 5:9.

[122] *Petersen v. Riverton City,* 2010 UT 58, 243 P.3d 1261 (Utah 2010).

[123] *Village of Euclid, Ohio v. Ambler Realty Co.,* 272 U.S. 365, 388, 47 S. Ct. 114, 71 L. Ed. 303 (1926).

Over the years, dissatisfaction with the virtually unrestrained power conferred on local governments by this rule of deference has led some courts to review zoning decisions more closely, particularly those involving relatively small parcels.[124] Courts use several routes to do so. A few apply the "change or mistake" rule, which eliminates the deference and reverses the burden of proof.[125] Other courts, in some states by statutory mandate, demand much more proof than historically has been called for in meeting the requirement that zoning be in accord with a comprehensive plan. In some states the presumption of validity has an evanescent quality and vanishes without comment when the courts are suspicious of wrongdoing.[126] The underlying assumption of these efforts, though not always articulated, is that site-specific rezonings are not entitled to deference because they are adjudicatory in nature, applying, not creating, policy.

A number of courts expressly reject the conventional wisdom that all rezonings are legislative. They look behind the "amendment" label, and if the action under review was in fact quasi-judicial in nature, it is not entitled to the full presumption of validity accorded legislative acts.[127] *Fasano v. Board of County Commissioners*[128] is the landmark case. Some seven years after creating a floating zone[129] for mobile home parks to meet local needs for diverse types of housing, the county commissioners rezoned a 32-acre tract from single-family use to mobile home use pursuant to the floating zone. As traditional law would have it, when the neighbors challenged the rezoning, the county and the developer asserted the presumption of validity and argued that the challengers had to prove that the rezoning was arbitrary. The court, however, turned the tables on the defendants, requiring them to prove that the rezoning was proper.[130] The rezoning, said the court, reflected the application, not the creation, of policy and therefore was not entitled to the full presumption of validity reserved for legislative policymaking. The court's main concern was that deferential review inadequately protected the neighbors' interests. Loss of the presumption would make change more difficult, but that was justified due to "the almost irresistible pressures that can be asserted by economic interests on local government."[131]

Similar concerns of fairness arise for the developer or property owner who seeks, but is denied, a rezoning. In *Board of County Commissioners v. Snyder,*[132] the county denied property owners a rezoning of a one-half acre parcel from single-family use to a classification permitting 15 units per acre. The commissioners gave no reason when voting against the request. When challenged, the county argued that the deferential "fairly debatable" standard insulated its decision from close review. The Florida supreme court disagreed, and found the denial of the rezoning to be quasi-judicial and

---

[124] See Mandleker and Tarlock, Shifting the Presumption of Constitutionality in Land—Use Law, 24 Urb. Law. 1 (1992).

[125] Albuquerque Commons Partnership v. City Council of City of Albuquerque, 144 N.M. 99, 184 P.3d 411 (2008). See also supra § 5:8.

[126] See Michael B. Brough, Flexibility Without Arbitrariness in the Zoning System: Observations on North Carolina Special Exception and Zoning Amendment Cases, 53 N.C.L. Rev. 925, 945 (1975).

[127] See discussion supra § 5:4.

[128] *Fasano v. Board of County Com'rs of Washington County,* 264 Or. 574, 507 P.2d 23 (1973).

[129] See supra § 4:16.

[130] In *Neuberger v. City of Portland,* 288 Or. 155, 603 P.2d 771 (1979), the Oregon supreme court revised *Fasano,* abandoning the requirement that a challenger show that other properties were not as suitable as his own for the proposed development. Consistency with the comprehensive plan is still required. Neuberger, 288 Or. at 170, 603 P.2d at 779.

[131] Fasano, 264 Or. at 588, 507 P.2d at 30.

[132] *Board of County Com'rs of Brevard County v. Snyder,* 627 So. 2d 469 (Fla. 1993).

subject to strict scrutiny. Thus, the court required the county to prove that its refusal to rezone was not arbitrary.

The *Fasano* doctrine is based on the perceived inapplicability of the separation of powers doctrine to site-specific rezoning requests. Federalist Paper No. 10 is its philosophical basis. There, James Madison expressed misgivings about the legislative process being captured by factions who act unfairly and without regard to others.[133] For Madison, this potential abuse would be countered by the large and varied constituency of the national government which would provoke coalitions and alliances, and limit small factions from exercising dominant roles. Respect for this process calls for judicial restraint.

Local legislation is different. While federal and state legislatures have large constituencies, local governments often do not. Capture by factions, as Madison feared, are more likely to occur, making the need for judicial restraint improper. Some commentators go so far as to argue that no acts of local governments should be treated as legislative.[134] *Fasano,* in a more limited vein, takes the position that courts should not presume nominally legislative site-specific rezonings valid.

Under the *Fasano* doctrine the character of the action governs the type of review. A zoning ordinance that lays down a general policy reflects widespread community interest or impact. It is legislative in character, and judicial deference is appropriate. In contrast, a rezoning that carries out or deviates from a previously adopted policy is quasi-judicial. Often, a determination of the use of a specific and relatively small parcel will affect only the parcel owner and the immediate neighbors. When that is the case, limited community interest will mean little or no public debate. This limited interest, in turn, elevates concern over whether the rights of the individuals affected are adequately safeguarded, and deference is inappropriate. The facts in *Fasano* exemplify the rule. The county passed the floating mobile home zone to help fill a county wide housing need, and its passage afforded an opportunity for the public and their elected representatives to debate the wisdom of encouraging such housing. While that first step was legislative, the subsequent site-specific rezoning was an application of the policy. Close judicial scrutiny was needed to assure that the rezoning was a proper application of the policy.

In contrast, in *KOB-TV, L.L.C. v. City of Albuquerque,*[135] the city adopted a zoning ordinance limiting helicopter operations to one zone. A television station had, prior to the enactment of the restrictive zoning, applied to build a helipad in another zone where such operations were then permitted. The station had not achieved vested rights status and thus was subject to the new ordinance. In its lawsuit to overturn the ordinance, the station argued that the ordinance was quasi-judicial in nature. The court, however, found the act to be legislative. Though the ordinance had limited effect, applying to the only two landowners within the affected zones which had helipads, the ordinance applied to all properties within the affected zones. Thus, it reflected general policy, leading to more deferential review.

---

[133] The Federalist No.10, at 77 (James Madison) (Clinton Rossiter ed. 1961). For a thorough discussion, see Rose, Planning and Dealing: Piecemeal Land Controls as a Problem of Local Legitimacy, 71 Cal. L. Rev. 837, 853–857 (1983).

[134] Id. Rose, at 856, n.70.

[135] *KOB-TV, L.L.C. v. City of Albuquerque,* 137 N.M. 388 111 P.3d 708 (Ct. App. 2005).

Treating rezonings or denials of rezoning requests as quasi-judicial has significant procedural implications beyond shifting the burden of proof and subjecting the action to greater scrutiny. While procedural due process rights do not attach to legislative action,[136] when government adjudicates, due process does apply.[137] The requirements of due process vary [138] and their application to quasi-judicial rezonings is not well developed.[139] The Florida court in *Snyder* left the procedures to be followed vague. It did not require findings, but only said there must be substantial evidence to support the ruling.[140] The *Fasano* court said there was a right to be heard and to present evidence, the right to an impartial board (one that has no ex parte communications with the parties), and the right to a record with findings of fact. It may be unrealistic to expect the impartiality of a court in this context. As one court has said, the "concept of impartiality is, by necessity and by function, more relaxed and informal."[141] It proceeded to hold that public statements of decisionmakers opposing an application prior to a hearing did not violate due process. Washington requires not only fairness but also the appearance of fairness.[142]

The *Fasano* doctrine has met with mixed reaction around the country. The American Law Institute's Model Land Development Code adopted it,[143] and numerous states have followed Oregon's lead.[144] Some courts, however, have specifically rejected *Fasano*,[145] because the process of classifying acts as legislative or quasi-judicial is too difficult and would consume too much of the court's time.[146]

§ 5:10   Spot Zoning

Spot zoning is likely the most frequent charge levied against rezonings. To the popular mind, spot zoning means permission to use an "island" of land for a more intensive use than permitted on adjacent properties. In the legal context this definition needs qualification. First, for most courts the term spot zoning is neutral with respect to validity or invalidity and simply describes a certain set of facts. In such jurisdictions, a zone may look like a spot on the zoning map, but it may not be an illegal spot zone. On occasion, however, the spot zoning term is used in a disapproving sense to state a legal conclusion that an act of rezoning is invalid. Second, while spot zoning challenges

---

[136] *Bi-Metallic Inv. Co. v. State Bd. of Equalization,* 239 U.S. 441, 36 S. Ct. 141, 60 L. Ed. 372 (1915).

[137] *Albuquerque Commons Partnership v. City Council of City of Albuquerque,* 144 N.M. 99, 184 P.3d 411 (2008).

[138] See infra § 10:13.

[139] Application to traditional administrative bodies like the board of adjustment is more settled, see, e.g., *State ex rel. Battershell v. City of Albuquerque,* 108 N.M. 658, 777 P.2d 386 (Ct. App. 1989), but problems still arise. See discussion infra at § 5:37.

[140] 627 So. 2d at 474. See Pelham, Quasi-Judicial Rezonings: A Commentary on the Snyder Decision and the Consistency Requirement, 9 J. Land Use & Envtl. L. 16 (1994).

[141] *Hilltop Basic Resources, Inc. v. County of Boone,* 180 S.W.3d 464, 468 (Ky. 2005).

[142] *Chrobuck v. Snohomish County,* 78 Wash. 2d 858, 480 P.2d 489 (1971).

[143] A.L.I. Model Land Development Code, § 2–312(2) and notes (1975).

[144] See, e.g., *Margolis v. District Court, In and For Arapahoe County,* 638 P.2d 297 (Colo. 1981) (applying *Fasano* only to rezonings but treating rezonings as legislative for purposes of referenda). For complete listing see §5.10 Practitioner's Edition of this work: Juergensmeyer and Roberts, Land Use Planning and Development Regulation Law (3rd ed.2012).

[145] See, e.g., *Cabana v. Kenai Peninsula Borough,* 21 P.3d 833 (Alaska 2001). For complete listing see §5.10 Practitioner's Edition of this work: Juergensmeyer and Roberts, Land Use Planning and Development Regulation Law (3rd ed.2012).

[146] See *Arnel Development Co. v. City of Costa Mesa,* 28 Cal. 3d 511, 169 Cal. Rptr. 904, 620 P.2d 565 (1980).

usually involve an island of more intensive use than surrounding property, some involve instances when the city zones the island parcel for less intensive use than its neighbors. Courts sometimes call this reverse spot zoning. Finally, spot zoning usually refers to a legislative act, such as a rezoning, or to a situation in which the original ordinance creates the island. Courts have not normally applied the term to development permission that comes about by administrative actions like a variance or special permit.

Courts often test accusations of illegal spot zoning with reference to the command of the Standard Zoning Enabling Act that zoning be "in accord with a comprehensive plan."[147] A rezoning that looks like a spot on the zoning map raises a "red flag"[148] of suspicion that the rezoning may have been done to serve private, not public, interests. If the rezoning is shown to be in accord with the plan, that concern is dispelled. Jurisdictions differ over the meaning of the comprehensive plan requirement, and they variously interpret it in spot zoning cases as well. Some courts read the plan requirement as referring simply to the zoning map. If the map reveals some plan for the area, and if the challenged zoning creates a different zone without any apparent variation in the parcel that justifies the difference, the court may find it invalid.[149] For some courts, zoning in accord with a comprehensive plan may mean only that zoning should be rational.[150] Thus, a court may look beyond a document denominated as a comprehensive plan to find evidence to justify the spot zone.[151]

In many cases, courts ask generally whether the rezoning promotes the public interest.[152] They also frequently invoke the "fairly debatable" test as the standard of review.[153] The use of this constitutional standard is not surprising since the constitutional basis for scrutinizing spot zoning appears to be the equal protection and due process clause guarantees against unreasonably discriminatory or arbitrary action.[154] Yet, review is not likely to be deferential in a jurisdiction that imposes a stringent planning consistency requirement,[155] or treats the action as quasi-judicial.[156]

Courts use several factors to determine the reasonableness of a zoning change. These include the uses of surrounding and nearby property, whether conditions in the area have changed, the present use of the property, and the property's suitability for other uses.[157] The overriding question is whether the action bears a substantial relationship to the general welfare of the community. If the different treatment can be justified, a court will not hold that it was improper spot zoning. For example, where a property owner obtained a rezoning from single-family to multi-family to build condo-

---

[147] U.S. Dept. of Commerce § 3 (1926).

[148] Reynolds, Jr., "Spot Zoning"-A Spot That Could Be Removed from the Law, 48 Wash. U. J. Urb. & Contemp. L. 117, 120 (1995).

[149] See *Pumo v. Borough of Norristown,* 404 Pa. 475, 172 A.2d 828 (1961).

[150] *Kozesnik v. Montgomery Tp.,* 24 N.J. 154, 131 A.2d 1 (1957).

[151] *Watson v. Town Council of Town of Bernalillo,* 111 N.M. 374, 805 P.2d 641 (Ct. App. 1991).

[152] *Thomas v. Board of Sup'rs of Panola County,* 45 So. 3d 1173 (Miss. 2010).

[153] *Riverview Farm Associates Virginia General Partnership v. Board of Sup'rs of Charles City County,* 259 Va. 419, 528 S.E.2d 99 (2000).

[154] See infra §§ 10:12 to 10:14.

[155] In such states, a rezoning is tested for its fidelity to a statutorily mandated plan that must precede the zoning ordinance. If the change is consistent with the plan, the rezoning will be valid. See supra § 2:11.

[156] See supra § 5:9.

[157] *Little v. Winborn,* 518 N.W.2d 384 (Iowa 1994).

miniums on land that contained a vacant and deteriorated building, the court stressed that the proposed use was not significantly different from other nearby uses and found that the entire neighborhood would benefit from the change.[158] In another case, the evidence showed that by rezoning a residentially zoned area containing gravel to permit quarrying, the municipality would receive more taxes and would put the land to its most appropriate use. The court found these factors to overcome a charge of illegal spot zoning.[159]

Courts often define spot zoning as involving a small parcel, presumably because a large area will simply look less like a spot on the map. Still, while size is a factor in spot zoning cases,[160] one ought not emphasize the element too heavily. Size is relative, and for it to be meaningful in a given case, a court must compare the size of the area rezoned with the size of the larger surrounding area with which it differs. In one case, a court found that 635 acres carved out of 7,680 acres and zoned for heavy industry was improper spot zoning.[21] In another case 40 acres was large enough not to be stricken.[161] Spot zoning also may be invalid when the authorities have rezoned more than one lot.[162] The number of landowners who will benefit from the change may also be considered.[163]

Spot zoning cases are not easily reconciled.[164] The courts of some states are more tolerant of it than those in other states, and even within a state, consistency is sometimes difficult to find. It is also at times difficult to identify a court's rationale for holding spot zoning valid or invalid

§ 5:11 Contract and Conditional Zoning

Zoning authorities often impose conditions on development permission to mitigate harm to neighbors of the development or to protect the public generally. No problem of authority exists when this occurs administratively in the special permit or variance process.[165] Particular conditions may be unreasonable, but the Standard Zoning Enabling Act expressly confers the authority to condition use in this administrative process. However, when the imposition of conditions occurs in the rezoning process, a nominally legislative act, the authority for, and propriety of, the action are often questioned.

Courts that treat rezonings as legislative and confer upon them a presumption of validity may be inclined to do the same with conditional rezonings. However, the site-specific, quasi-judicial nature of contract and conditional zoning decisions suggests that deferential judicial review may not be warranted.

---

[158] *Boland v. City of Great Falls,* 275 Mont. 128, 910 P.2d 890, 73 A.L.R. 5th 777 (1996).

[159] See *Kozesnik v. Montgomery Tp.,* 24 N.J. 154, 131 A.2d 1 (1957) (rezoning held invalid, but for certain technical reasons).

[160] *Plains Grains Ltd. Partnership v. Board of County Com'rs of Cascade County,* 357 Mont. 61, 238 P.3d 332 (2010); *Cannon v. Murphy,* 196 A.D.2d 498, 600 N.Y.S.2d 965 (1993).

[21] *Chrobuck v. Snohomish County,* 78 Wash. 2d 858, 480 P.2d 489 (1971).

[161] *Zopfi v. City of Wilmington,* 273 N.C. 430, 160 S.E.2d 325 (1968).

[162] *Sullivan v. Town of Acton,* 38 Mass. App. Ct. 113, 645 N.E.2d 700 (1995).

[163] *Plains Grains Ltd. Partnership v. Board of County Com'rs of Cascade County,* 357 Mont. 61, 238 P.3d 332 (2010).

[164] See *Watson v. Town Council of Town of Bernalillo,* 111 N.M. 374, 376, 805 P.2d 641, 643 (Ct. App. 1991), discussing ad hoc nature of spot zoning jurisprudence.

[165] See infra §§ 5:22 and 5:26.

A. *Tests of Validity*

Neighbors often levy the accusation of contract zoning against a conditional rezoning because it may have involved, or appeared to have involved, a bargaining process.[166] Settlement agreements that involve promises respecting land use permission also are subject to challenge as illegal contract zoning.[167] The term "contract zoning" is usually pejorative, suggesting that municipalities are not to make deals when making law. Some state courts condemn the practice unless expressly authorized by statute.[168] In many states, however, a rezoning subject to conditions is more favorably received since it provides flexibility to deal with unanticipated problems.[169] As with spot zoning, the basis on which validity hinges lies in whether the court is satisfied that the rezoning serves the public interest. Labels that courts use vary, but often courts call rezonings they find invalid "contract zoning," and call rezonings with conditions, which they find legitimate "conditional zoning."[170]

When courts first confronted conditional rezonings, they balked. The idea that a legislative action would be tailored specifically to a site was contrary to the notion of early Euclidean general use districts where every parcel was subject to the same restrictions. The Standard Act authorized conditions for special permit and variance techniques, but those were limited, administrative solutions for limited problems. Rezonings, however, were legislative and courts thought that the many differences that would result if conditions were attached on an ad hoc, lot by lot, basis would destroy the system.[171] Rezonings were exercises of the regulatory power of government, and contracts, or specific understandings, with individual landowners were thought foreign to that process. Like illegal spot zoning,[172] courts viewed contract zoning as promoting private interests and not in accord with the comprehensive plan. Alternatively, some courts held the uniformity requirement of the Standard Act violated where a condition resulted in different rules for different tracts within the same zone.[173]

Over time courts warmed to the idea of conditional zoning, finding that it made sense. A requirement that all land in a zone be treated exactly the same unduly constrained municipal efforts to accommodate conflicts among neighboring land uses. A city that was unable to deal with unique aspects of certain tracts by imposing conditions on use faced the dilemma of having to pick a winner and loser. The city could grant the rezoning and allow unlimited use, thus inflicting harm on the neighbors, or, it could deny the request, precluding a more intensive use to the detriment of the owner, but benefiting the neighbors. The solution to the dilemma was to upzone with conditions protective of the neighbors. If the city could impose conditions, both parties would

---

[166] See Wegner, Moving Toward the Bargaining Table: Contract Zoning, Development Agreements and the Theoretical Foundations of Government Land Use Deals, 65 N.C. L. Rev. 956 (1987).

[167] *Trancas Property Owners Assn. v. City of Malibu,* 138 Cal. App. 4th 172, 41 Cal. Rptr. 3d 200 (2006).

[168] In Pennsylvania and Maryland, it must be expressly authorized by statute. *Carlino v. Whitpain Investors,* 499 Pa. 498, 453 A.2d 1385 (1982). In several states, specific statutory constraints govern conditional zoning. See Iowa Code Ann. § 358A.7; Minn. Stat. Ann. § 462.358, Subd. 2a.

[169] See discussion supra § 4:15, regarding flexibility in zoning.

[170] But see *Mayor and Council of Rockville v. Rylyns Enterprises, Inc.,* 372 Md. 514, 814 A.2d 469 (2002).

[171] *Mayor and Council of Rockville v. Rylyns Enterprises, Inc.,* 372 Md. 514, 814 A.2d 469, 486 (2002).

[172] See supra § 5:10.

[173] *Board of County Com'rs of Washington County v. H. Manny Holtz, Inc.,* 65 Md. App. 574, 583, 501 A.2d 489, 493 (1985).

gain some and lose some, in a sense, enabling the city to mediate the dispute. Nothing improper was being sold or given away, and as one early favorable decision said,

> Since the Town Board could have, presumably, zoned this * * * corner for business without any restrictions, we fail to see how reasonable conditions invalidate the legislation. * * * All legislation 'by contract' is invalid in the sense that a Legislature cannot bargain away or sell its powers. But we deal here with actualities, not phrases.[174]

As with variances[175] and special permits,[176] "reasonable conditions" are allowed. There must be a connection between the activity being permitted and the condition being imposed.[177] Conditions attached in the public approval process do not need to be recorded in the land registry system to be effective against subsequent purchasers, as long as the conditions are available in the public records.[178]

A few courts differentiate the good from the bad by using a bilateral/unilateral contract distinction. Under this test, valid conditional zoning involves "merely a unilateral promise from the landowner to the local zoning authority as to the landowner's intended use of the land in question, while illegal contract zoning entails a bilateral contract in which the landowner and the zoning authority make reciprocal promises."[179] The test is of dubious value. Often, trying to reconstruct events to see whether there was "merely a unilateral promise from the landowner" will be difficult.[180] More importantly, the test does not answer the central question of whether the action was in the public interest since even a unilateral promise might be improperly induced. Nonetheless, it remains a verbal formula that some courts follow, or at least to which they pay lip service.

Today most courts use a public interest test, similar to that employed in spot zoning cases, to ask whether they should uphold the conditional zoning. Whether by way of the bilateral/unilateral distinction or a test focused on the public interest being served, many courts have upheld zoning with conditions.[181]

The increased comfort level of legislatures and courts with the idea that bargaining of a sort is not necessarily an evil is reflected in the growing number of states that allow municipalities to enter into development agreements.[182] These agreements involve express undertakings of cities to freeze zoning and of developers to provide public services. While development agreements occur in a regulatory setting, accompanied by public hearings, they also embody contractual overtones, and reveal that the law has

---

[174] *Church v. Town of Islip,* 8 N.Y.2d 254, 203 N.Y.S.2d 866, 168 N.E.2d 680 (1960).

[175] § 5:22.

[176] § 5:26.

[177] See *Sprint Spectrum L.P. v. Borough of Ringwood Zoning Bd. of Adjustment,* 386 N.J. Super. 62, 898 A.2d 1054 (Law Div. 2005).

[178] *Story Bed & Breakfast, LLP v. Brown County Area Plan Com'n,* 819 N.E.2d 55 (Ind. 2004).

[179] *Chrismon v. Guilford County,* 322 N.C. 611, 636, 370 S.E.2d 579, 594 (1988).

[180] Even contract law questions the usefulness of the differentiation. The distinction was not used in the Second Restatement because of doubts as to its utility. See Restatement Second, Contracts § 1.

[181] *Haas v. City of Mobile,* 289 Ala. 16, 265 So. 2d 564 (1972). For complete listing, see §5.9A Practitioner's Edition of this work: Juergensmeyer and Roberts, Land Use Planning and Development Regulation Law (3rd ed.2012).

[182] See infra § 5:31.

traveled far from the early objections to contract zoning as bargaining away the police power.

B. Some Examples

A classic use of conditional zoning occurred in *Church v. Town of Islip.*[183] The owner of a corner lot sought a rezoning from residential to business use. The town granted the rezoning on the condition that the owner execute and record a covenant promising that her building would not occupy more than 25% of the lot, and that she would build a fence six feet high near the border with neighboring residential land, and plant shrubs along the fence, allowing them to grow to six feet in height. The neighbors complained that the zoning was invalid contract zoning, but as the court pointed out, the conditions of which they complained were for their benefit. The real question was whether the upzoning to business use was justified. Noting the lot fronted on one side on a busy thoroughfare and that, due to growth, business zoning was inevitable, the court found the rezoning with the condition was in the public interest.

Similarly, in *Chrismon v. Guilford County,*[184] a rezoning of agriculturally zoned land to an industrial zone limited use of the property to the sale of chemicals used in agricultural operations. The county imposed the condition to avoid the harsh impact of blanket approval for industrial use, which would have allowed several more undesirable uses. When upzoning property, conditional zoning makes sense, said the court, to avoid an "unacceptably drastic change" for the neighbors.

Bilateral contracts, where the municipality promises to rezone land in return for a landowner's promise unrelated to the parcel being rezoned, do take place. In *Dacy v. Village of Ruidoso,*[185] for example, a village needed some land for a highway but lacked the funds to condemn it. A landowner wanted a rezoning. They arranged a swap. The landowner deeded the desired land to the village and the village deeded a tract that it owned to the landowner. As part of the deal, the village promised that it would rezone the land it deeded to allow multi-family use. The court held the contract to rezone illegal.[186]

Situations that involve oral assurances or stipulations made in the rezoning process are subject to contract zoning analysis. In *Carlino v. Whitpain Investors,*[187] the neighbors objected to an upzoning of land to multi-family use across the street from their home. At the hearing, it was "stipulated" that there would be a 300' buffer and no access to the apartments from the street that divided the properties. Later when the developer was building the apartments, the city insisted that it build an access road to the street. The neighbors sought to enjoin the breach of the stipulation. The court, however, held that the rezoning was not subject to the condition. "[(Contractually conditioned rezoning,"[188] said the court, had no place in the exercise of the police power.

---

[183] *Church v. Town of Islip,* 8 N.Y.2d 254, 203 NY.S.2d 866, 168 N.E.2d 680 (1960).

[184] *Chrismon v. Guilford County,* 322 N.C. 611, 370 S.E.2d 579 (1988).

[185] *Dacy v. Village of Ruidoso,* 114 N.M. 699, 845 P.2d 793 (1992).

[186] Practices that seek to extract concessions that only marginally relate to the proposed development may be improper uses of the regulatory power. In contrast, exactions and impact fees related to the development can be obtained in most jurisdictions without running afoul of the contract zoning prohibition. See infra § 9:8 for discussion of impact fees and exactions.

[187] *Carlino v. Whitpain Investors,* 499 Pa. 498, 453 A.2d 1385 (1982).

[188] Carlino, 499 Pa. at 504, n.2, 453 A.2d at 1388.

Not all courts are as troubled by zoning based on developer assurances and bilateral agreements. In *Durand v. IDC Bellingham, LLC*,[189] a city let it be known that it needed eight million dollars to build a new high school. A developer then offered the city that amount of money if the city would rezone its land to permit it to build a power plant. The land was rezoned and the money was delivered to the city. While one need not be a cynic to think that the eight million had something to do with the city's favorable rezoning vote, the court held there was nothing amiss.[190] On the face of it, the money was a voluntary contribution. The town did not bind itself to rezone the property. The rezoning was a legislative act to which substantial deference was due and the court refused to question the motives of the city in approving the new zoning.

Many courts are less deferential than the Massachusetts court in *Durand* and more like the Pennsylvania court in *Carlino*. Nonetheless, while the procedure employed in *Carlino* is not a recommended one, it is an overreaction to condemn all conditional zoning based on such cases. An oral representation by a developer that is not memorialized in writing as part of a rezoning may be ill-conceived and, in such event, the condition ought to be unenforceable. Where, however, there is evidence that the city thought through the condition and where it is expressed in writing so that there is no uncertainty, its enforcement may well serve the public interest.

To the extent that oral assurances, whether designed to do so or not, quell neighborhood opposition, the council or board hearing the matter should be careful to guard against the neighbors being misled into assuming the assurance is binding.

C. Conditions Imposed by Private Covenant

Where a city imposes conditions by way of a side agreement that takes the form of a covenant, problems of uncertainty arise. In one case the landowner recorded a restrictive covenant limiting the uses of rezoned land contemporaneously with the rezoning. Years later, after the property had changed hands, a building inspector, unaware of the covenant, issued a permit allowing the new owner to proceed with a use permitted by the relevant business classification.[191] Someone, who recalled that the city had obtained a covenant, brought it to the inspector's attention, and the inspector revoked the permit. The court invalidated the rezoning in part because of the fact that an examination of the records in the zoning inspector's office did not reveal the zoning restrictions applicable to the tract. This uncertainty properly troubled the court.

Some courts have upheld agreements that take the form of private covenants between a city and landowner,[192] or between neighbors and landowner.[193] Still, unless compelled to resort to such a technique by state law, a city should avoid the practice. While the agreements, if recorded, do provide constructive notice to the public, the land records are not where one expects to find zoning laws. Conditions should be set out in the rezoning amendment. Not only is the chance for confusion or surprise diminished, but the open acknowledgment of conditions eliminates the suspicion that there is something to hide that is aroused by undisclosed, or difficult to find, contracts.

---

[189] *Durand v. IDC Bellingham, LLC*, 440 Mass. 45, 793 N.E.2d 359 (2003).

[190] See Wilson, Contract Zoning and Development Exactions: *IDC Bellingham* and Its Implications, Boston Bar Journal, 48-JUN B. B.J. 10 (May/June 2004).

[191] *Cederberg v. City of Rockford*, 8 Ill. App. 3d 984, 291 N.E.2d 249 (1972).

[192] *Sylvania Elec. Products, Inc. v. City of Newton*, 344 Mass. 428, 183 N.E.2d 118 (1962).

[193] *State ex rel. Zupancic v. Schimenz*, 46 Wis. 2d 22, 174 N.W.2d 533 (1970).

"Community benefits agreements" (CBAs) involve direct negotiations between the developer and representatives of affected neighborhoods, as well as environmental or preservation groups. To mollify potential adversaries and buy support, the developer may scale down a project or offer benefits to the community. Though such agreements are not new, they have reappeared in recent years as more far-reaching than their predecessors. They enable the community to extract benefits that would be illegal if required by local government as a condition for approval. Yet the self-appointed people claiming to represent the community may secure benefits that serve a narrow interest. CBAs may adversely affect the public planning process as city planning officials might not be involved in, or even be aware of, the negotiations.[194]

D. Remedies

When an improper rezoning with conditions is found, the remedy may be either to declare the rezoning void, or to allow the rezoning to stand and refuse to enforce the covenant. If a court finds that a rezoning would not have occurred but for the improper introduction of the contract or condition, it holds the rezoning void.[195] In some cases, however, courts have allowed rezonings to stand, apparently on the theory that the rezonings would, or should, have occurred without the condition.[196]

Courts may follow common law contract principles. Thus, if a contract is found illegal, neither party can enforce it. For example, a county entered into a development agreement promising to amend its comprehensive plan to permit rezoning and to "support and expeditiously process" the developer's rezoning application in exchange for the developer's promise to transfer 50 acres to the county for use as a park. When the county changed its mind and refused to perform, the developer sued for damages. The developer lost, as the court found the agreement illegal contract zoning.[197]

Thus, neither damages nor injunctive relief will generally be available, though restitution may be.[198] On the other hand, if an agreement is found not to constitute an illegal bargaining away of the police power, a court may allow the private party damages for a city's breach of contract.[199]

§ 5:12   Piecemeal or Partial Zoning

"Piecemeal zoning" is an imprecise term used by courts in various ways. Most often "piecemeal" refers to the omission of areas from the coverage of a zoning ordinance. It also may refer to a zoning ordinance that regulates fewer than all the usual elements of height, area, and use, or fewer than all uses. Finally, courts may describe small parcel rezonings as piecemeal zoning.[200]

---

[194] See Frank, Yes in My Backyard: Developers, Government and Communities Working Together Through Development Agreements and Community Benefit Agreements, 42 Ind. L. Rev. 227 (2009).

[195] *Cederberg v. City of Rockford,* 8 Ill. App. 3d 984, 291 N.E.2d 249 (1972).

[196] *Sprint Spectrum L.P. v. Borough of Ringwood Zoning Bd. of Adjustment,* 386 N.J. Super. 62, 898 A.2d 1054 (Law Div. 2005).

[197] *Morgran Co., Inc. v. Orange County,* 818 So. 2d 640 (Fla. 5th DCA 2002).

[198] *Dacy v. Village of Ruidoso,* 114 N.M. 699, 845 P.2d 793 (1992).

[199] See, e.g., *Stephens v. City of Vista,* 994 F.2d 650 (9th Cir. 1993), as amended on denial of reh'g, (Aug. 4, 1993) (contract damages allowed to developer for city's breach of settlement agreement).

[200] *Mayor and Council of Rockville v. Rylyns Enterprises, Inc.,* 372 Md. 514, 814 A.2d 469 (2002).

The term appears in the commentary to the Standard State Zoning Enabling Act, which explains that the act's mandate that zoning be in accord with a comprehensive plan "will prevent haphazard or piecemeal zoning * * * and that [n]o zoning should be done without such a comprehensive study."[201] Partial zoning is a term that might be used in place of piecemeal zoning, particularly when referring to geographical reach.

The piecemeal zoning term was first applied to the question of whether the enabling act required municipalities to zone their entire territory when initially embarking on zoning. In his early zoning treatise, Edward M. Bassett points to numerous turn of the century cases invalidating block ordinances, and cautions drafters to zone all the land within their boundaries to avoid this potential pitfall.[202] Bassett, however, did not think it necessarily irrational to omit unpopulated areas from the reach of an ordinance. In fact, Bassett, a principal drafter of the nation's first comprehensive zoning ordinance in New York City, notes that while the city put all of its land in height and area zones, it omitted large portions from the use classifications.

Courts generally do not require that zoning ordinances be all-inclusive in geographical reach,[203] but ordinances that zone a very small portion of the town's area may fail on the ground that they do not carry out a comprehensive plan. Thus, one court held that zoning less than one-tenth of the town invalid where there was no showing that the ordinance was adopted pursuant to a comprehensive plan.[204] Where a court purports to require that an ordinance apply to the whole town, the rule will not apply to subsequent amendments. In *Darlington v. Board of Councilmen*,[205] the court held that an ordinance that merely zoned a newly annexed area was valid where the city had in place a comprehensive zoning ordinance.[206]

A few courts use the term piecemeal zoning essentially as a synonym to spot zoning. Like spot zoning,[207] the key to invalidating a rezoning due to its piecemeal nature is its failure to conform to a comprehensive plan. Thus, an upzoning of a six-acre tract from single-family use to multi-family use, which did not meet the court's test of changed conditions and which would have adversely affected neighboring land, was found to be piecemeal and spot zoning.[208] In contrast, a height limit that applied in all historic districts in the town and not simply to complainant's property was comprehensive in nature and thus escaped the more rigorous review applied to piecemeal zonings.[209] In Louisiana, the courts have said that piecemeal or spot zoning is suspect and is subjected to higher scrutiny, but the burden of proof does not change.[210] In reviewing an upzoning of a 432—acre tract from residential to heavy industry to allow a chemical manufacturing plant, a Louisiana court found it was not invalid piecemeal zoning since

---

[201]Comment to § 3 Standard State Zoning Enabling Act See supra § 3:20 and infra § 9:5.

An ordinance that regulates fewer than the three usual elements, i.e., height, area, and use, might also be piecemeal.

[202] Edward M. Bassett, Zoning 90, n.l (1940).

[203]*Montgomery County v. Woodward & Lothrop, Inc.*, 280 Md. 686, 376 A.2d 483 (1977).

[204]*Connell v. Town of Granby,* 12 A.D.2d 177, 209 N.Y.S.2d 379 (1961).

[205]*Darlington v. Board of Councilmen of City of Frankfort*, 282 Ky. 778, 140 S.W.2d 392 (1940).

[206] *Hawkins v. Louisville and Jefferson County Planning and Zoning Com'n*, 266 S.W.2d 314 (Ky. 1954).

[207] See supra § 5:10.

[208] *City of Texarkana v. Howard,* 633 S.W.2d 596, 597 (Tex. App. 1982).

[209] *Mandel v. City of Santa Fe,* 119 N.M. 685, 894 P.2d 1041 (Ct. App. 1995).

[210] *Palermo Land Co., Inc. v. Planning Com'n of Calcasieu Parish*, 561 So. 2d 482 (La. 1990).

it extended an adjacent industrial zone and thus was in the public interest.[211] In New Mexico, the courts have said that piecemeal zoning changes, meaning small parcel rezonings, are only valid if supported by a showing of change conditions or mistake.[212]

§ 5:13 Uniformity and Classification

The Standard State Zoning Enabling Act provides that "regulations shall be uniform for each class or kind of buildings throughout each district, but the regulations in one district may differ from those in other districts."[213] The requirement is essentially a statutory equal protection command that like uses be treated the same. For many courts, more lenient or harsher treatment of one parcel of land will not violate the uniformity clause if there is a reasonable basis for the distinction.

Singling out one or a few parcels for a use allowed or disallowed to others will violate the uniformity clause. For example, an ad hoc grant of an exception to conduct a commercial use in an agricultural zone was held to violate the uniformity clause.[214] In another case, an ordinance that required a buffer strip for a single lot within a district was found in violation of the uniformity requirement.[215] Yet, differential treatment that stems from a uniform requirement is permissible. For example, where a town used a mathematical formula to determine minimum lot sizes and maximum lot coverage based upon the steepness of slopes did not violate the uniformity requirement even though it created varying results based upon each parcel's physical conditions or characteristics.[216]

Many arguments urging violations of the uniformity clause have dealt with conditional rezonings, and the results are mixed.[217] The lack of uniformity typically relates to uses allowed, with fewer or more uses granted the rezoned parcel. Physical limitations, such as buffering, may also be the basis of complaint. Some courts hold that conditions that do not affect the use of land do not violate the uniformity clause.[218] A California court, taking this view, held that a reversionary clause placed in a rezoning did not violate the uniformity rule since it did not affect use.[219]

Overlay zones also may run afoul of the uniformity clause. In *Jachimek v. Superior Court,*[220] the Arizona Supreme Court held that a city could not create an overlay

---

[211]*Save Our Neighborhoods v. St. John the Baptist Parish*, 592 So. 2d 908 (La. Ct. App. 1991).

[212] *Miller v. City of Albuquerque*, 89 N.M. 503, 554 P.2d 665 (1976).

[213] U.S. Dep't of Commerce, § 2 (1926).

[214] *Neighbors in Support of Appropriate Land Use v. County of Tuolumne*, 157 Cal. App. 4th 997, 1001, 68 Cal. Rptr. 3d 882, 884 (2007).

[215] *Veseskis v. Bristol Zoning Commission*, 168 Conn. 358, 362 A.2d 538 (1975).

[216] *Rumson Estates, Inc. v. Mayor & Council of Borough of Fair Haven*, 177 N.J. 338, 828 A.2d 317 (2003).

[217] Uniformity argument rejected: *Giger v. City of Omaha*, 232 Neb. 676, 442 N.W.2d 182 (1989).

Uniformity clause violated: *Boerschinger v. Elkay Enterprises, Inc.*, 32 Wis. 2d 168, 145 N.W.2d 108 (1966).

[218] See *Board of County Com'rs of Washington County v. H. Manny Holtz, Inc.*, 65 Md. App. 574, 586, 501 A.2d 489, 495 (1985).

[219] *Scrutton v. Sacramento County*, 275 Cal. App. 2d 412, 79 Cal. Rptr. 872 (1969).

[220] *Jachimek v. Superior Court*, 169 Ariz. 317, 819 P.2d 487 (1991). But see *A-S-P Associates v. City of Raleigh*, 298 N.C. 207, 258 S.E.2d 444 (1979), where the court found an historic overlay that subjected commercial property to restrictions not suffered by other commercially zoned land did not violate the uniformity clause.

zone in which it required permits for certain uses in one part of the city but did not require permits for the same uses in the same underlying zone elsewhere within the city.

With flexible zoning techniques such as conditional zoning, cluster zoning, and planned unit developments, uniformity concerns are present because these processes all anticipate some site-specific review and likely involve some negotiation. The results are likely to be non-uniform, and some applicants may get better deals than others.[221] This may be due to differences in the land or due to the skill or influence of the developer doing the negotiating. Some courts note that all who seek rezonings have an equal opportunity to seek out conditions and suggest that this equality of opportunity is all that is needed to satisfy the uniformity requirement.[222]

The major determinants in whether non-uniform zoning will stand are the degree of a court's discomfort with the possibility that differential treatment is unjustified and the willingness of a court to set aside the traditional rule of deferential review. Most courts say that challenges based on lack of uniformity will fail if they deem the difference in treatment justified. Where the burden of proof is placed may spell the difference in outcome. In *Giger v. City of Omaha*,[223] the city rezoned property and entered into a development agreement by which it gave concessions and obtained exactions from a developer that were unique to this development. The neighbor challenging the ordinance failed to cite any evidence that the conditions were unreasonable, and thus lost his bid. In contrast, in *Boerschinger v. Elkay Enterprises, Inc.*,[224] the city zoned one parcel within its industrial district to allow rendering plants. While the court acknowledged that it would allow distinctions within a district, it found no such explanation in the record for according the one parcel greater use rights than the others. This lack of evidence led the court to overturn the rezoning.

Where differential treatment is deemed necessary, a uniformity objection might be avoided by use of special permits and variances.[225] If a city lists a use as a special use, it may impose conditions on the use under the express language of the standard act.[226] Variances may also be accompanied by conditions.[227]

Classification of uses, inevitable in Euclidean zoning, presents problems similar to the uniformity cases.[228] A city may allow restaurants, for example, but prohibit fast food restaurants. A court is likely to uphold such differential treatment if it applies a deferential rule of review.[229] If the difference allows the exclusion or harsher treatment of a religious school [230] or a group home for a protected class,[231] a higher level of judicial scrutiny may apply.

---

[221] *Campion v. Board of Aldermen of City of New Haven*, 278 Conn. 500, 899 A.2d 542 (2006).

[222] *Chrinko v. South Brunswick Tp. Planning Bd.*, 77 N.J. Super. 594, 187 A.2d 221 (Law Div. 1963).

[223] *Giger v. City of Omaha*, 232 Neb. 676, 686, 442 N.W.2d 182, 194 (1989).

[224] *Boerschinger v. Elkay Enterprises, Inc.*, 32 Wis. 2d 168, 145 N.W.2d 108 (1966).

[225] *Board of County Com'rs of Washington County v. H. Manny Holtz, Inc.*, 65 Md. App. 574, 501 A.2d 489, 493 (1985).

[226] *Bell v. City Council of City of Charlottesville*, 224 Va. 490, 297 S.E.2d 810 (1982). See supra § 5:26 regarding special uses.

[227] See supra § 5:22.

[228] Classification issues are discussed supra §§ 4:2 to 4:11.

[229] See *Ben Lomond, Inc. v. City of Idaho Falls*, 92 Idaho 595, 448 P.2d 209 (1968).

[230] See supra § 4:28.

Cases finding classifications valid or invalid are difficult to reconcile. For example, in *Kozesnik v. Township of Montgomery*,[232] a special permit for a quarry was issued on the condition that it not operate within 400 feet of any existing dwelling. The court held the classification invalid since surrounding undeveloped property also should have had the protection of the condition. In *Pierro v. Baxendale*,[233] the same court upheld an ordinance permitting boarding houses but excluding hotels and motels on the ground that the latter appealed to transients as distinguished from the boarding houses. The court in *Kelly v. Mahoney* [234] upheld an ordinance permitting turkey ranches only if the rancher employed dust control methods but permitted chicken ranches without such control. The court did not offer a justification for the classification.

IV. VARIANCES

§ 5:14   Variances: In General

A variance is an administrative authorization to use property in a manner other-wise not allowed by the zoning ordinance. This authorization alleviates the inevitable hardship situations that arise when zoning boundaries drawn across a community do not fit well due to distinctive features of a parcel or area. Under the Standard Act, the power to issue a variance lies with the Board of Adjustment, which the act authorizes to grant:

> such variance from the terms of the ordinance as will not be contrary to the public interest, where, owing to special conditions, a literal enforcement of the provisions of the ordinance will result in unnecessary hardship, and so that the spirit of the ordinance shall be observed and substantial justice done.[235]

While many states follow the Standard Act's language, some add the phrase "practical difficulties" as a standard to accompany "unnecessary hardship."[236] Other states have more detailed standards.[237] In some states, municipalities may impose stricter stand-ards.[238]

Of the various zoning "forms of action"[239] available to obtain development permis-sion, a choice may exist to seek a variance or other relief, such as a rezoning. A vari-ance may be faster and cheaper than a rezoning, and it may require less paperwork and fewer hearings before fewer bodies.[240] A variance, however, is more likely to be

---

[231] See supra § 4:7 and infra § 6:8.

[232] *Kozesnik v. Montgomery Tp.*, 24 N.J. 154, 131 A.2d 1 (1957).

[233] *Pierro v. Baxendale*, 20 N.J. 17, 118 A.2d 401 (1955).

[234] *Kelly v. Mahoney*, 185 Cal. App. 2d 799, 8 Cal. Rptr. 521 (1960).

[235] Standard Zoning Enabling Act § 7. See Owens, The Zoning Variance: Reappraisal and Recommen-dations for Reform of a Much-Maligned Tool, 29 Colum. J. Envtl. L. 279 (2004), for a review of the basics of variance law and recommendations for improvement.

[236] See, e.g., N.C. Gen. Stat. § 153A–345.

[237] See, e.g., Ind. Code Ann. §§ 36–7–4–918.4 and 36–7–4–918.5.

[238] *City of Dallas v. Vanesko*, 189 S.W.3d 769, 772 (Tex. 2006).

[239] See infra § 5:1.

[240] See *Enterprise Citizens Action Committee v. Clark County Bd. of Com'rs*, 112 Nev. 649, 918 P.2d 305, 312 n.7 (1996).

overturned on appeal than is a rezoning,[241] and courts may frown on efforts to obtain a variance if the facts clearly do not support the request.[242]

Stringent rules limit grants of variances.[243] Courts frequently assert that variances are to be granted "sparingly," and they commonly describe the variance as a "safety valve," so that zoning, which would otherwise be unconstitutional as applied, can be made constitutional.[244] Some courts, however, take a slightly more relaxed view.[12]

Despite the judicial admonition for sparing use of variances, conventional wisdom, backed by numerous studies,[245] has it that in practice applicants too easily obtain variances from boards that are untrained and insufficiently independent.[246] Most grants are not challenged but commentators suspect that if challenged, many variances granted would be found invalid. Increased flexibility by way of special permits, floating zones, and conditional zoning lessen the need for variances, particularly use variances. The variance process itself has improved. Many statutes and ordinances today are more specific than early laws regarding findings that need be made, and board members, at least in some states, receive training and have professional planning staffs to assist them so that better decisionmaking should occur. Unfortunately, this expected improvement has not yet come to pass, at least in areas where studies have been conducted.[247]

Suspicions about abuses of the variance power lead some courts to review the granting of variances closely, and grants of variances are subjected to closer scrutiny than denials.[248] Some courts require that the board make findings supporting its decisions.[249] The findings enable the court to determine for itself whether the board obtained the required evidence. The potential for intrusive judicial review calls for a balanced approach. Some courts hesitate to overturn variances too freely for fear of becoming super zoning boards themselves and out of a desire to defer to local community boards. Yet, in some cases, the applicant puts forth little evidence and the board makes

---

[241] The standard of review of administrative actions is traditionally less deferential than with legislative actions. See *Kaufman v. Zoning Com'n of City of Danbury*, 232 Conn. 122, 653 A.2d 798 (1995). See discussion infra § 5:37.

[242] *Enterprise Citizens Action Committee v. Clark County Bd. of Com'rs*, 112 Nev. 649, 918 P.2d 305, 312 (1996).

[243] *Lussier v. Zoning Bd. of Appeals of Peabody*, 447 Mass. 531, 854 N.E.2d 1236 (2006).

[244] See *Bacon v. Town of Enfield*, 150 N.H. 468, 840 A.2d 788 (2004).

[12] *Simplex Technologies, Inc. v. Town of Newington*, 145 N.H. 727, 766 A.2d 713 (2001). See discussion infra § 5:19.

[245] Anderson, Brees and Reninger, A Study of American Zoning Board Composition and Public Attitudes Toward Zoning Issues, 40 Urb. Law. 689 (2008).

[246] Some states authorize the use of trained hearing examiners to assure better decisions. Idaho Code § 67–6520(1).

[247] Owens, The Zoning Variance: Reappraisal and Recommendations for Reform of a Much-Maligned Tool, 29 Colum. J. Envtl. L. 279, 317 (2004).

[248] *Meszaros v. Planning Bd. of City of South Amboy*, 371 N.J. Super. 134, 852 A.2d 236 (App. Div. 2004).

[249] See, e.g., *Topanga Assn. for a Scenic Community v. County of Los Angeles*, 11 Cal. 3d 506, 113 Cal. Rptr. 836, 522 P.2d 12 (1974).

little effort to comply with its obligations. In such cases, judicial reversal is necessary to preserve the integrity of the system.[250]

§ 5:15 Standards: Area or Dimensional Variances v. Use Variances

Under the Standard Zoning Enabling Act, the power to issue a variance lies with the Board of Adjustment, which the act authorizes to grant:

> such variance from the terms of the ordinance as will not be contrary to the public interest, where, owing to special conditions, a literal enforcement of the provisions of the ordinance will result in unnecessary hardship, and so that the spirit of the ordinance shall be observed and substantial justice done.[251]

While many states have adopted the Standard Act's language, some add the phrase "practical difficulties" as a standard to accompany "unnecessary hardship."[252] Other states have more detailed standards.[253] In some states, municipalities may impose stricter standards.[254]

Variances are generally of two kinds: area or dimensional variances,[255] which involve modifications for height and building size or placement, and use variances, which allow a use inconsistent with uses permitted of right. The Standard Act, quoted above, does not create these categories, but courts have done so. While the distinction between these types of variances is commonly recognized, the statutes and judicial decisions in most states apply the same standard to both.[256] However, in a significant number of states, area variances are subject to a less onerous standard than use variances.[257] Where different standards apply, the authority to do so usually stems from statutes which add the phrase "practical difficulties" to the Standard Act's "unnecessary hardship" language.[258] The disjunctive phrasing of "practical difficulties *or* unnecessary hardship," is read to dictate different standards based on the relief sought.[259] Under such a view, a lesser showing of "practical difficulties" suffices for an area variance and is justified on the assumption that it involves a relatively minor deviation.[260] Where such a distinction is drawn, a use variance requires a more stringent showing of "unnecessary hardship."

Some statutes provide greater detail than "practical difficulties" and "unnecessary hardship" in distinguishing use and dimensional variances. Rhode Island's statute, for example, provides that the board satisfy itself that "in granting a use variance the subject land or structure cannot yield any beneficial use if it is required to conform to the

---

[250] See, e.g., *Enterprise Citizens Action Committee v. Clark County Bd. of Com'rs*, 112 Nev. 649, 918 P.2d 305, 312 (1996).

[251] Standard Zoning Enabling Act § 7. See Iowa Code Ann. § 414.12 (2008).

[252] See, e.g., N.C. Gen. Stat. § 153A-345.

[253] See, e.g., Ind. Code Ann. §§ 36–7–4–918.4 and 36–7–4–918.5.

[254] See Ind. Code Ann. § 36-7-4-918.5(a)(3).

[255] Sometimes referred to as bulk, structural, yard, nonuse, or site variances.

[256] See 2 Am. Law. Zoning § 13:8 (Patricia Salkin ed. 5th ed.) listing 18 states.

[257] See, e.g., *Ferraro v. Board of Zoning Adjustment of City of Birmingham*, 970 So. 2d 299 (Ala. Civ. App. 2007). For complete listing, see §5.15 Practitioner's Edition of this work: Juergensmeyer and Roberts, Land Use Planning and Development Regulation Law (3rd ed.2012).

[258] See, e.g., N.C.Gen.Stat. § 153A-345 ("practical difficulties or unnecessary hardship").

[259] *McLean v. Soley*, 270 Md. 208, 310 A.2d 783 (1973).

[260] See the leading case of *Village of Bronxville v. Francis*, 1 A.D.2d 236, 150 N.Y.S.2d 906 (1956).

provisions of the zoning ordinance, * * * and (2) in granting a dimensional variance, that the hardship suffered by the owner of the subject property if the dimensional variance is not granted amounts to more than a mere inconvenience."[261] Where statutes lack the "practical difficulties" language or other language differentiating types of variances, some courts nonetheless construe the "unnecessary hardship" differently for use and area variances.[262] Others apply the same standard to all variances.[263]

States that treat area variances subject to a more relaxed standard do so with good reason: they otherwise may be impossible to *legally* obtain. Differentiation between area and use variances generally accords with the purposes of the variance. The strict standard for obtaining a use variance protects the zoning scheme while allowing an exemption to avoid confiscatory application of the law to an individual. The more relaxed standard for an area variance provides flexibility to alleviate somewhat modest difficulties caused by the law in narrow circumstances.[264] The individual acquires the ability to make reasonable use of his land while the neighbors and the comprehensive plan are protected by limiting a variance to the minimum relief necessary.

The Wisconsin Supreme Court has recognized the merits of a lesser standard for area variances. In 1998, the state supreme court reversed its long standing rule applying a lesser standard to area variances and applied the strict unnecessary hardship rule to all variances.[265] It soon regretted its change, noting in 2001 that area variances had become "almost impossible to obtain."[266] In 2004, the court reversed itself holding that "[w]hen considering an area variance, the question of whether unnecessary hardship . . . exists is best explained as '[w]hether compliance with the strict letter of the restrictions governing area, setbacks, frontage, height, bulk or density would unreasonably prevent the owner from using the property for a permitted purpose or would render conformity with such restrictions unnecessarily burdensome.'"[267]

The distinction makes sense in most cases, but it is hardly universally true that an area variance is minor and a use variance major. A height variance of 10 feet to allow for a taller building might be minor, but a height variance of 200 feet might not. A use variance allowing a factory in a residential zone might have a major impact, but a use variance allowing a part-time home occupation might not.[268]

It is not always easy to decide whether a variance is one of use or area. One can view a density variance, for example, as either. In an area zoned for single-family use on one acre lots, a variance to allow two homes was a use variance in one case (two-

---

[261] R.I. Gen. Laws § 45-24-41(d). See also N.Y. Town Law § 267-b.

[262] *Boccia v. City of Portsmouth,* 151 N.H. 85, 855 A.2d 516 (2004).

[263] See, e.g., *In re Mutschler, Canning and Wilkins,* 180 Vt. 501, 904 A.2d 1067 (2006) (applying Vt. Stat. Ann. tit. 24, § 4468).

[264] *State ex rel. Ziervogel v. Washington County Bd. of Adjustment,* 269 Wis. 2d 549, 676 N.W.2d 401 (2004).

[265] *State v. Kenosha County Bd. of Adjustment,* 218 Wis. 2d 396, 577 N.W.2d 813 (1998) (abrogated by, State ex rel. Ziervogel v. Washington County Bd. of Adjustment, 269 Wis. 2d 549, 676 N.W.2d 401 (2004) and abrogated by, State v. Waushara County Bd. of Adjustment, 271 Wis. 2d 547, 679 N.W.2d 514 (2004).

[266] *State v. Outagamie County Bd. of Adjustment,* 244 Wis. 2d 613, 621, 628 N.W.2d 376, 377 (2001). See also *Krummenacher v. City of Minnetonka,* 783 N.W.2d 721, 732 (Minn. 2010) (bemoaning that restrictive language of statute prohibits flexibility for handling area variances).

[267] *State ex rel. Ziervogel v. Washington County Bd. of Adjustment,* 269 Wis. 2d 549, 676 N.W.2d 401 (2004).

[268] *Board of Adjustment of City of San Antonio v. Levinson,* 244 S.W.2d 281 (Tex. Civ. App. 1951).

family use in single-family zone) and an area variance in another (modification of lot size). Since the effect on the neighbors is the same, the label ought not control, and some courts have criticized the rule.[269] In *Harrington v. Town of Warner,*[270] the court held that a request to expand the number of sites in a manufactured housing park was for a use variance. The ordinance set the maximum number of sites in a park at 25 for any parcel of land 10 acres in size or larger. Since the limit applied regardless of the number of acres, it was a regulation on intensity of use. The court upheld the grant of the variance.

Use variances pose particular problems. Some statutes and ordinances simply do not allow them.[271] In other states, courts refuse to permit use variances on the theory that they constitute rezonings, and rezonings are a legislative function.[272] The authority of a board of adjustment to issue a use variance turns on whether the court finds that the legislature intended to confer such power and whether such a grant of power is an unconstitutional delegation of legislative authority. Some courts find the discretion granted to the board of adjustment adequately controlled to justify the issuance of a use variance.[273] Even where allowed in theory, use variances are likely to be overturned where the change allowed is significant. This may be true for particularly large parcels [274] or where the use allowed by the variance is not otherwise allowed anywhere in town.[275] In such instances, a legislative rezoning is the proper route.

§ 5:16   Unnecessary Hardship

The standards that one must meet before the board issues a variance vary among the enabling acts, though most formulations are similar to provisions in the Standard Act. Where there is no statute or ordinance providing more detailed standards, the courts generally have required a four-part showing: (1) that the land in question cannot yield a reasonable return as currently zoned, (2) that the plight of the landowner is due to unique or unusual circumstances and not conditions generally prevailing through the neighborhood, (3) that the variance requested will not alter the essential character of the neighborhood, and (4) that the variance not issue if it would be contrary to the public interest.[276]

Conspicuously absent from the above criteria is the Standard Act's provision that authorizes a variance where the zoning "will result in unnecessary hardship." There is confusion over whether "unnecessary hardship" is a separate standard or whether it is an overall standard established when the applicant meets the above criteria. Courts are not always clear, but support exists for both views. Some courts use the unnecessary hardship language to describe the overall showing of the elements that the appli-

---

[269] See *Bienz v. City of Dayton,* 29 Or. App. 761, 566 P.2d 904, 919 (1977).

[270] *Harrington v. Town of Warner,* 152 N.H. 74, 872 A.2d 990 (2005).

[271] See Ark. Code Ann. § 14–17–209; Cal.Govt.Code § 65906.

[272] *Cook v. Howard,* 134 Ga. App. 721, 215 S.E.2d 690 (1975).

[273] Compare *Livingston v. Peterson,* 59 N.D. 104, 228 N.W. 816 (1930), with *Matthew v. Smith,* 707 S.W.2d 411 (Mo. 1986).

[274] See *Appeal of Catholic Cemeteries Ass'n of the Diocese of Pittsburgh,* 379 Pa. 516, 109 A.2d 537 (1954).

[275] See *Bradley v. Zoning Bd. of Appeals of Town of Westport,* 165 Conn. 389, 334 A.2d 914 (1973).

[276] The first three components are usually attributed to *Otto v. Steinhilber,* 282 N.Y. 71, 24 N.E.2d 851 (1939). The public interest standard is not a separate test in *Otto,* but is subsumed by the other tests. The public interest component is a separate requirement in some jurisdictions. See *Arndorfer v. Sauk County Bd. of Adjustment,* 162 Wis. 2d 246, 469 N.W.2d 831 (1991).

cant must make.[277] For other courts, it specifically embodies the first element noted above, requiring a showing that the applicant can make no reasonable return from the property as zoned,[278] a requirement discussed in more detail below.[279]

As with any delegation of legislative authority, standards must be sufficiently clear to guide the administrative decisionmaking and prevent the exercise of uncontrolled discretion. Courts have found the "unnecessary hardship" standard to meet this test.[280]

§ 5:17   Consideration of Personal v. Land-Based Factors

Administrative bodies sometimes personalize a variance by allowing their decisions to turn on the needs or actions of the owners rather than the nature of the property. Two related situations arise: the personal hardship and the self-created hardship.

A.   *Personal Hardship*

Personal hardships may present sympathetic appeal, but, absent disability considerations discussed below, they are inappropriate factors in variance proceedings, and where boards grant variances on such grounds, courts uniformly overturn them. Boards grant such variances due to either a lack of understanding of the law or in open disregard of it. Courts overturn these variances because variances must relate to the land, not the person. Examples include the parents who wanted a variance from setbacks to build a deck in their backyard for their child to play,[281] the owner who sought a variance to enclose a porch for an asthmatic child,[282] and one who had an overcrowded garage and needed more room to store his antique cars.[283]

B.   *Disabled Persons Exception*

The federal Fair Housing Act and the Americans with Disabilities Act prohibit public agencies, including cities exercising land use control power, from discriminating against the disabled.[284] These laws include a requirement that cities make reasonable accommodations for the benefit of the disabled. In some cases, this will require that a personal variance be granted.[285]

Mastandrea v. North[286] is illustrative. The Mastandreas put in a brick-in-cement pathway to allow their daughter, who suffered from muscular dystrophy, to enjoy the views of the Chesapeake Bay from her motorized wheelchair. The pathway was placed within the 100 foot buffer of the Chesapeake Bay Critical Area, contrary to state and

---

[277] *Mastandrea v. North,* 361 Md. 107, 760 A.2d 677, 692 (2000); *Otto v. Steinhilber,* 282 N.Y. 71, 75, 24 N.E.2d 851, 852 (1939).

[278] *Maturo v. City of Coral Gables,* 619 So. 2d 455, 456 (Fla. 3d DCA 1993).

[279] See infra § 5:19.

[280] See *Southern Pac. Co. v. City of Los Angeles,* 242 Cal. App. 2d 38, 51 Cal. Rptr. 197 (1966).

[281] *Larsen v. Zoning Bd. of Adjustment of City of Pittsburgh,* 543 Pa. 415, 424, 672 A.2d 286, 290 (1996).

[282] *Appeal of Kline,* 395 Pa. 122, 148 A.2d 915 (1959).

[283] *Allison v. Zoning Bd. of Adjustment of Philadelphia,* 97 Pa. Commw. 51, 508 A.2d 639 (1986).

[284] The ADA protects persons with "disabilities. The FHA protects those with "handicaps." Both acts cover zoning. For the purposes of discussion here, the term "disabilities" is used to cover both. See general discussion of these acts, infra § 6:8 and § 4:7, respectively.

[285] *Tsombanidis v. West Haven Fire Dept.,* 352 F.3d 565 (2d Cir. 2003).

[286] *Mastandrea v. North,* 361 Md. 107, 760 A.2d 677 (2000).

local law. Upon being discovered by the authorities, the Mastandreas sought a setback variance, which the board granted. The state appealed, and the property owners defended on the basis that the ADA compelled the county to issue the variance. While the case was on appeal, the county enacted an ordinance that for all relevant purposes mimicked the ADA. The court found the variance was a reasonable accommodation under the new county ordinance to reduce the otherwise discriminatory effect of the buffer requirement and to allow the daughter reasonable use and enjoyment of the property. While the court did not reach the ADA, the case indicates the kind of variances that the act might call for.

An accommodation is reasonable unless it requires a fundamental alteration in the nature of the program or imposes undue costs. In *Howard v. City of Beavercreek,*[287] a board denied a variance from a front yard setback for a man who wanted to erect a six foot fence on one side of his lot. The applicant, who suffered from post traumatic stress disorder, claimed his neighbors were spying on him. Upon denial of the variance, he brought suit claiming the denial was in violation of the FHA. The court denied the claim. While the city's aesthetic objections and concerns over property values were not legitimate justifications for refusing to accommodate the landowner the city's safety objections were. Furthermore, the court held that the landowner was not denied an opportunity to live in a single-family neighborhood. He continued to live in his house and only said that he might be forced to move.

In cases where the variance would have been denied but for the disability, the variance should terminate when the disability ceases or the disabled person ceases to live on the property. While a variance normally runs with the land because it relates to the land, a variance here is personal and ought not run. In the *Mastandrea* case that would mean the pathway would need to be removed and the land restored to its original state. The cost of removal and restoration would presumably be born by the current owner. One who buys from the Mastandreas then should take such cost into account in determining the purchase price she is willing to pay. A justification for allowing the variance to continue might exist where the cost to reverse the variance would exceed the benefits.

To be sure, the granting of variances under these laws undermines the purity of the zoning plan, but the cost is modest since only reasonable accommodations are required. In contrast, the benefit of allowing the disabled to enjoy a more normal life is great. Nonetheless, one can expect that neighbors will object and litigation will follow.

C. *Self-Created Hardships and Purchase with Knowledge*

Self-created hardships occur in two distinct situations. First, there is the owner who builds in violation of the zoning law, is discovered and cited, and then seeks a variance claiming a hardship based on the investment that will be lost if he must remove the illegal structure. The other involves the person who purchases land with knowledge about how the land is zoned, and then seeks a variance based on a hardship in having to comply with the zoning. The two situations should be treated separately.

---

[287] *Howard v. City of Beavercreek,* 276 F.3d 802 (6th Cir. 2002).

One who builds in violation of the zoning law is not entitled to a variance.[288] To grant a variance in such a situation would reward wrongdoing and encourage others to violate the law. Thus, the owner who built a carport violating setbacks could not obtain a variance to keep the carport after being cited for violating the law;[289] neither could the person who converted a house in a two-family zone to eight rental units.[290] Generally, it does not matter whether the owner had actual knowledge of the law before acting, since constructive notice exists. Even if an owner makes a good faith mistake in reliance on erroneous representations of city officials, a variance is improper.[291] In such a case, a court might estop the city from enforcing its law.[292] Some support exists for a variance of a minimal nature where good faith is shown.[293] In a jurisdiction applying a lesser, practical difficulties standard for area variances, the courts may not treat the self-created aspect of the hardship as an automatic bar,[294] but this concession invites lawless behavior, and no difference exists in this respect between an area and a use variance.

When one purchases property and then applies for a variance on the grounds of unnecessary hardship, a difference of opinion exists as to whether the variance should be denied on the ground of self-induced hardship. Most courts consider the transfer of title irrelevant.[295] If the land suffers the requisite hardship, in that the owner can make no reasonable return from its use as zoned, then the board ought to grant a variance. If not, the land becomes permanently zoned in a useless state.

The reasons used to deny a variance to one who violates the law and then seeks relief are not applicable to one who purchases with knowledge. In the former, the owner creates the hardship; in the latter, the zoning, not the person, creates the hardship.[296] The integrity of the law demands that the one who builds in violation of the law not be able to take advantage of his actions, and it is in accord with zoning principles to grant relief to one who acquires land where unique circumstances have already zoned the land into a state of uselessness.

Some courts hold or suggest that a purchaser knew or should have known of the zoning of the property when she purchased does not suffer an unnecessary hardship.[297] These courts are also troubled by the fact that one who buys with knowledge of zoning and then obtains a variance reaps a windfall from the increase in value that results from the granting of the variance.[298] However, since ownership is normally irrelevant to zoning, the transfer of title ought not affect the issue. As to the windfall, the purchaser takes the risk that a board will agree that the situation for a variance exists.

---

[288] *City of Dallas v. Vanesko,* 189 S.W.3d 769 (Tex. 2006).

[289] *Pierce v. Parish of Jefferson,* 668 So. 2d 1153 (La. App. 1996).

[290] *Mills v. City of Manchester,* 109 N.H. 293, 249 A.2d 679 (1969). See also *Rivera v. City of Phoenix,* 186 Ariz. 600, 925 P.2d 741 (Ct. App. 1996).

[291] *City of Dallas v. Vanesko,* 189 S.W.3d 769 (Tex. 2006).

[292] See infra § 5:29.

[293] *Pyzdrowski v. Board of Adjustment of City of Pittsburgh,* 437 Pa. 481, 263 A.2d 426 (1970).

[294] See, e.g., *De Sena v. Board of Zoning Appeals of Inc. Village of Hempstead,* 45 N.Y.2d 105, 408 N.Y.S.2d 14, 379 N.E.2d 1144 (1978).

[295] See, e.g., *Lamb v. Zoning Bd. of Appeals of Taunton,* 76 Mass. App. Ct. 513, 923 N.E.2d 1078 (2010).

[296] *Murphy v. Kraemer,* 16 Misc. 2d 374, 375, 182 N.Y.S.2d 205, 206 (1958).

[297] *Harrington v. Town of Warner,* 152 N.H. 74, 872 A.2d 990 (2005).

[298] *Sofo v. Egan,* 57 A.D.2d 841, 394 N.Y.S.2d 43 (1977).

How that risk is allocated between the seller [299] and the purchaser will vary. Even if one perceives the result as a windfall, it is not an unjustifiable one vis-a-vis the public, since the situation assumes that land deserves the variance.

A related question is presented when one acquires land with knowledge of an existing restriction and then seeks to recover just compensation on the basis that the zoning restriction effects a taking under the Fifth Amendment. The Supreme Court has held that the right to sue survives the transfer if the restriction deprives the landowner of all economically viable use.[300]

§ 5:18 Effect on Public

A showing that the public interest will not be harmed if the variance is granted is required. This requirement simply restates the general rule that all aspects of zoning must be in the public interest. Many courts do not list "the public interest" as a separate requirement, but the consideration of it enters into the formula by examining the effect of the proposed variance on the surrounding area. If the requested variance will alter the essential character of the neighborhood issuance will not serve the public interest even if the owner suffers from a hardship. Where courts specifically examine the public interest, the burden to show that the variance will not harm the public is on the one seeking it.[301]

An argument that the proposed use would be advantageous to the public, such as the convenience of a shopping center to an area or to meet a need for affordable housing, is not only unnecessary but is usually improper. A board of adjustment lacks the power to decide what the public needs. If the city needs more shopping areas or affordable housing, the legislative body should rezone the land or create a new special use category.[302] The board should not decide the issue by way of variance.[303]

Exceptions exist. New Jersey's statute allows for use variances for "special reasons."[304] This so-called "d variance" does not require a showing of hardship, but requires a showing that the proposed use will be beneficial to the public.[305] In New York, the courts have crafted a lesser test for public utilities requiring a showing of a public need for service, and not economic hardship to land.[306]

§ 5:19 No Reasonable Return

A widely followed rule is that before the board can issue a variance on the ground of unnecessary hardship, the applicant must show that the land as zoned cannot yield

---

[299] Who it is assumed would, or might, have received a variance had she sought it.

[300] *Palazzolo v. Rhode Island,* 533 U.S. 606, 121 S. Ct. 2448, 150 L. Ed. 2d 592 (2001). See discussion infra § 10:7.

[301] *State v. Winnebago County,* 196 Wis. 2d 836, 847, 540 N.W.2d 6, 10 (Ct. App. 1995).

[302] See infra § 5:24.

[303] *Topanga Assn. for a Scenic Community v. County of Los Angeles,* 11 Cal. 3d 506, 113 Cal. Rptr. 836, 522 P.2d 12 (1974).

[304] N.J. Stat. Ann. 40:55D-70d.

[305] See N.J. Stat. Ann. 40:55D-70(d)(1).

[306] *Cellular Telephone Co. v. Rosenberg,* 82 N.Y.2d 364, 604 N.Y.S.2d 895, 624 N.E.2d 990 (1993).

Other courts also refer on occasion to the public benefit to be obtained from a proposed use. See, e.g., *Williams v. District of Columbia Bd. of Zoning Adjustment,* 535 A.2d 910 (D.C. 1988).

a reasonable return.[307] Where not expressly a part of a statute or ordinance,[308] courts have implied the requirement. The leading case of *Otto v. Steinhilber*[309] is widely regarded as formulating the rule, and many courts across the country have followed it. The requirement limits use of the variance power, and accords with the view that the power should be used sparingly.[310]

In applying the reasonable use rule, the question is not whether an owner will have property that is more valuable if the variance is granted,[311] but whether the land can earn a reasonable return as zoned. As courts have starkly put it, the question is whether the land has been "zoned into inutility"[312] or whether it would be an "economic disaster"[313] if used as currently zoned. As such, the test is essentially the Fifth Amendment takings test.[314] Only if the effect of the zoning is so oppressive that it leaves the owner with no economically viable use is a variance to be granted. It thus becomes a rule of expediency. Granting the variance is more efficient for the city than waiting to be sued for compensation and running the risk of a large damage award.

Courts require proof of economic loss, not conclusory allegations.[315] It is necessary to show, in what some courts call "dollars and cents proof,"[316] that compliance with the existing ordinance would not be economically feasible. Dollars and cents proof requires evidence of the amount paid for the property, the present value, and costs for maintenance, taxes, and liens. Proof of an inability to sell is probative.[317] If the situation is sufficiently stark, a court may infer that the owner can make no reasonable return.[318] A physical impossibility of use need not be shown. If commercial uses surround a residentially zoned tract, a person can probably live there, but if no market exists for the land for residential use, the owner has likely met the test to obtain a variance.[319]

Not all courts agree that the barrier should be so high. Moved by its view that an owner ought to be free to use his or her land, subject only to reasonable police power controls, the New Hampshire supreme court relaxed its definition of unnecessary hardship and reasonable return.[320] The court softened its rule to allow a finding of unnecessary hardship with proof that a restriction interferes with an owner's reasonable use of her land considering the unique setting of the property.[321] Under this approach, legal variances should be much more common.

A plausible argument exists against applying the reasonable use requirement to variances. If an applicant for a variance can show that granting the variance would not

---

[307] See *Baker v. Connell*, 488 A.2d 1303 (Del. 1985).

[308] Pa. Stat. Ann. tit 53, § 10910.2.

[309] *Otto v. Steinhilber*, 282 NY. 71, 24 N.E.2d 851 (1939).

[310] See supra § 5:14.

[311] *McGee v. Board of Appeal of Boston*, 62 Mass. App. Ct. 930, 819 N.E.2d 975 (2004).

[312] *Davis Enterprises v. Karpf*, 105 N.J. 476, 481, 523 A.2d 137, 139 (1987).

[313] *Appeal of Girsh*, 437 Pa. 237, 241, 263 A.2d 395, 397 n.3 (1970).

[314] See infra §§ 10:2 to 10:6.

[315] *Matthew v. Smith*, 707 S.W.2d 411 (Mo. 1986).

[316] Matthew, 707 S.W.2d at 416–17.

[317] *Zoning Bd. of Adj. of Hanover Tp. v. Koehler*, 2 Pa. Commw. 260, 278 A.2d 375 (1971).

[318] *Valley View Civic Ass'n v. Zoning Bd. of Adj.*, 501 Pa. 550, 462 A.2d 637 (1983).

[319] See *Valley View*, Valley View Civic Ass'n, 501 Pa. at 560, 462 A.2d at 642.

[320] *Simplex Technologies, Inc. v. Town of Newington*, 145 N.H. 727, 766 A.2d 713 (2001).

[321] Simplex Technologies, Inc., 766 A.2d at 717.

adversely affect the public or the neighbors and that the property is unique, perhaps a variance should issue. After all, if no one could be hurt, the present zoning, and therefore the hardship, is unnecessary. Furthermore, the origins of the rule are shaky. The *Otto v. Steinhilber* court, which created the requirement, did so based on meager authority,[322] and offered no reason for the imposition of this strenuous requirement. The *Otto* court's requirement apparently stemmed from its "safety valve" theory,[323] which equated the denial of a variance with the equivalent of a Fifth Amendment taking.

Strict application of the reasonable use rule makes *legal*[324] variances almost unattainable, but in many states the rule's reach is limited because it is applied only to use variances. In those states, the practical difficulties standard used for area variances does not require a showing of a deprivation of all reasonable use.[325]

§ 5:20   Unique or Unusual Characteristics of Property

Characteristics that are unique or unusual to the property must cause the hardship from which the owner seeks a variance.[326] The premise is that a variance is proper only when the property is different from surrounding property. While courts do not require that the owner suffer uniquely in the strict sense of the word, the hardship ought to be unusual. If the problem suffered is widespread, a legislative rezoning is the appropriate vehicle for change.

If the land is physically unique, the classic circumstances for a variance exist. Where setback lines on the sides of a triangular lot limited the useable space of a lot to 10 square feet, a variance from the setback requirements was proper.[327] Where a deep ravine crossed a lot, it was similarly considered unusual enough to justify a variance.[328] If the physical characteristics are not limited to the parcel for which the variance is sought, then relief is improper. *Topanga Association for a Scenic Community v. County of Los Angeles*[329] is illustrative. The administrative body granted a variance to allow a mobile home park on 28 acres that was zoned light agricultural and large lot single family residential. The California supreme court reversed. While the terrain was rugged and contained three stream beds, the developers had not shown that the property was unlike neighboring parcels.

Property in transitional or deteriorating areas may meet the uniqueness requirement. Many such cases involve lots that are either next to more intensive zones or surrounded by more intensive uses. Unique circumstances are more likely to be found in the latter than the former situation. The mere fact that residentially zoned property is next to property zoned for business purposes does not justify a variance.[330] This result is necessary to preserve Euclidean zoning, for if districting is to be used, lines must be drawn somewhere. On the other hand, if a lot is zoned residential, and all, or many, of

---

[322] The *Otto* court cited Edward M. Bassett, Zoning 168–69 (1940), for the proposition.

[323] 282 N.Y. at 75, 24 N.E.2d at 852.

[324] See discussion regarding lax granting of variances, supra § 5:14.

[325] See infra § 5:23.

[326] *Garrison v. Town of Henniker,* 154 N.H. 26, 907 A.2d 948 (2006).

[327] *Hoshour v. Contra Costa County,* 203 Cal. App. 2d 602, 21 Cal. Rptr. 714 (1962).

[328] *Ferry v. Kownacki,* 396 Pa. 283, 152 A.2d 456 (1959).

[329] *Topanga Assn. for a Scenic Community v. County of Los Angeles,* 11 Cal. 3d 506, 113 Cal. Rptr. 836, 522 P.2d 12 (1974).

[330] *Taylor v. District of Columbia Bd. of Zoning Adjustment,* 308 A.2d 230 (D.C. 1973).

the surrounding uses are commercial, the lot may meet the test of uniqueness.[331] The question usually turns on how widespread the problem is.

The absence of unique or unusual circumstances may not necessarily be fatal. If the property owner establishes that she can earn no reasonable return from the land as zoned, a court may uphold a variance simply out of recognition that, without the variance, a taking may occur. However, where a problem is widespread, then the piecemeal granting of variances to those who step forward will leave the overall zoning problem unfixed. Evidence that other properties share a problem indicates that an amendment covering them all may be the proper solution.

§ 5:21   Effect on Neighborhood

A typical ordinance provides that a board should not grant a variance if it would "alter the essential character of the neighborhood."[332] Even if the ordinance does not so provide, most courts require such proof. The requirement is presumably tied to the Standard Act's command that "the spirit of the ordinance be observed and substantial justice done."[333] A board should not permit a commercial use in a residential zone that is actually committed to residential uses for the change would alter the character of the neighborhood.[334] If, however, a residential zone contains commercial uses, whether they exist as nonconforming uses or were previously granted variances or special use permits, a variance for commercial use will not alter the character of the area.[335] The "no alteration of the character" test may not met if the variance would generate a significant increase in traffic [336] or would otherwise result in a measurable depreciation of property values.[337]

Since local governments employ the variance to relieve hardship, any relief granted by a variance should be the minimum necessary to achieve that purpose. The variance should not confer benefits not enjoyed by neighboring property. For example, an undersized lot zoned for large lot single-family use is not entitled to a variance for multi-family use but only to a variance for single-family use, that being the zoning in the area.[338] A minimum variance rule is often a part of the state statute [339] or ordinance; if not, a court may imply it.[340]

Though the number of protestors and the intensity of the objections should not dictate the result, as a matter of practical administration, boards seldom issue variances when neighbors appear and vigorously oppose the request.[341] The absence of ob-

---

[331] *Valley View Civic Ass'n v. Zoning Bd. of Adjustment,* 501 Pa. 550, 462 A.2d 637 (1983).

[332] *Anon v. City of Coral Gables,* 336 So. 2d 420 (Fla. 3d DCA 1976).

[333] Standard Zoning Enabling Act § 7. See *Consolidated Management, Inc. v. City of Cleveland,* 6 Ohio St. 3d 238, 452 N.E.2d 1287 (1983).

[334] *Wilson v. Borough of Mountainside,* 42 N.J. 426, 201 A.2d 540 (1964).

[335] *Guadagnolo v. Town of Mamaroneck Bd. of Appeals,* 52 A.D.2d 902, 383 N.Y.S.2d 377 (1976).

[336] *Corbett v. Zoning Bd. of Appeals of City of Rochester,* 283 A.D. 282, 128 N.Y.S.2d 12 (1954).

[337] *Greenwich Gas Co. v. Tuthill,* 113 Conn. 684, 155 A. 850 (1931).

[338] *Hamer v. Town of Ross,* 59 Cal. 2d 776, 31 Cal. Rptr. 335, 382 P.2d 375 (1963).

[339] See, e.g., Fla. Stat. Ann. § 163.225(3)(a)(5).

[340] *Duncan v. Village of Middlefield,* 23 Ohio St. 3d 83, 491 N.E.2d 692, 696 (1986).

[341] See *Luger v. City of Burnsville,* 295 N.W.2d 609 (Minn. 1980).

jections from neighbors may also be evidence that there will be no adverse effect on surrounding areas.[342]

§ 5:22 Conditions

Under the express terms of the Standard Act a board can grant a variance with conditions to prevent or mitigate adverse effects on the public or the neighborhood.[343] Even where the statute and ordinance do not confer such authority, a court may imply the power to condition variances.[344]

Conditions must relate to the property.[345] The conditions that boards normally impose, as with conditional rezonings and special permits, are designed to reduce the adverse impact of the variance and protect neighbors. These may include landscape buffers or screening,[346] height or lighting limits,[347] or off-street parking.[348] A variance issued on the condition that a restaurant in a residential zone be closed during certain evening hours has been held valid.[349] A condition also may require use of the variance in a timely manner.[350] A variance also may be limited to a term of years, and then be subject to review.[351] On the other hand, a condition relating to a lot different from the one for which the variance was granted has been held void.[352] A condition that prohibits rental of the property has been held violative of public policy in unreasonably restraining alienability.[353]

A limitation on the number of employees might be valid if related to land use problems such as traffic and parking,[354] but to condition a laundromat by requiring the constant presence of an attendant has been held invalid on the ground that such a regulation is not a zoning matter.[355] The power cannot be used to exact land for public use if no nexus exists between the burden the community must bear from the use allowed by the variance and the land exacted.[356]

---

[342] See *U-Haul Co. of New Hampshire & Vermont, Inc. v. City of Concord*, 122 N.H. 910, 451 A.2d 1315 (1982).

[343] A board "may * * * subject to appropriate conditions and safeguards, make special exceptions to the terms of the ordinance in harmony with its general purpose and intent * * *." Standard Act § 7. The term special exception in this portion of the Standard Act is a generic term that includes a variance.

[344] *Town of Warren v. Frost,* 111 R.I. 217, 301 A.2d 572 (1973).

[345] *Gay v. Zoning Bd. of Appeals of Town of Westport*, 59 Conn. App. 380, 757 A.2d 61 (2000).

[346] *Everson on Behalf of Everson Elec. Co. v. Zoning Bd. of Adjustment of City of Allentown*, 395 Pa. 168, 149 A.2d 63 (1959).

[347] *Miller Pump Service, Inc. v. Worcester Tp. Zoning Hearing Bd.*, 59 Pa. Commw. 21, 428 A.2d 779 (1981).

[348] *Woodbury v. Zoning Bd. of Review of City of Warwick*, 78 R.I. 319, 82 A.2d 164 (1951).

[349] *Montgomery County v. Mossburg,* 228 Md. 555, 180 A.2d 851 (1962).

[350] *Ambrosio v. Zoning Bd. of Appeals of Town of Huntington*, 196 Misc. 1005, 96 N.Y.S.2d 380 (1949).

[351] *Guenther v. Zoning Bd. of Review of City of Warwick*, 85 R.I. 37, 125 A.2d 214 (1956).

[352] *Gay v. Zoning Bd. of Appeals of Town of Westport*, 59 Conn. App. 380, 757 A.2d 61 (2000).

[353] *Gangemi v. Zoning Bd. of Appeals of Town of Fairfield*, 255 Conn. 143, 763 A.2d 1011 (2001).

[354] *National Black Child Development Institute, Inc. v. District of Columbia Bd. of Zoning Adjustment*, 483 A.2d 687, 690 (D.C. 1984).

[355] *De Ville Homes, Inc. v. Michaelis*, 201 N.Y.S.2d 129 (1960).

[356] *Gordon v. Zoning Bd. of Appeals of Town of Clarkstown*, 126 Misc. 2d 75, 481 N.Y.S.2d 275 (1984). See the discussion of the constitutional nexus requirement infra § 10:5.

Issuing a variance on the condition that the property remain under the applicant's ownership is improper. Variances run with the land and conditions attached to variances run as well.[357]

Where a court holds a condition invalid, it must decide whether to revoke the variance or allow it to stand unconditioned. If the court deems the variance irrevocably tainted by the condition in that the board would not have issued it without the illegal condition, it will order revocation.[358] If, however, the board should have issued the variance without the condition, it should remain in force. Such may be the case where a variance is limited to the owner who obtained it,[359] or where the condition violates public policy.[360]

§ 5:23   Practical Difficulties

Many enabling acts and ordinances provide for the issuance of a variance if practical difficulties exist as well as where there is an unnecessary hardship. The phrase is important because, as discussed above,[361] it sometimes leads to the creation of a separate, less stringent test for area variances. For many courts the "practical difficulties" and "unnecessary hardship" terms are interchangeable, and those courts use but one test.[362] Where the statute uses the conjunctive "and," some courts require the applicant to satisfy both requirements. Where the disjunctive "or" is used, separate tests are more likely to be applied.[363]

The elements of a separate "practical difficulties" test are not well defined. As noted, the test is to be less rigorous than for the unnecessary hardship standard. Courts usually toss several factors together in a balancing test between the property owner and the community. They include whether, or to what degree, the owner can pursue the permitted use without a variance, what the financial hardship is, the degree of variation sought, the harm to the neighbors, whether alternatives exist, whether the hardship is self-imposed, and whether the interests of justice will be served by granting the variance.[364] New York has a statutory test for area variances that closely approximates these factors and authorizes a balancing test.[365] The statute, however, does not use the "practical difficulties" language, and the state high court has held that an applicant no longer needs to show practical difficulties as a separate element for an area variance.[366]

Some financial hardship must exist, though how much is not clear. Courts take the position that the mere showing that land could be used more profitably does not suffice.[367] Tests of "significant economic injury"[368] and whether the zoning would "un-

---

[357] *National Black Child Development Institute, Inc. v. District of Columbia Bd. of Zoning Adjustment,* 483 A.2d 687, 690 (D.C. 1984).

[358] *Bora v. Zoning Bd. of Appeals of Town of Norwalk,* 161 Conn. 297, 288 A.2d 89 (1972).

[359] *St. Onge v. Donovan,* 71 N.Y.2d 507, 527 N.Y.S.2d 721, 522 N.E.2d 1019 (1988).

[360] *Gangemi v. Zoning Bd. of Appeals of Town of Fairfield,* 255 Conn. 143, 763 A.2d 1011 (2001).

[361] See supra § 5:15.

[362] *In re Mutschler, Canning and Wilkins,* 180 Vt. 501, 904 A.2d 1067 (2006).

[363] See supra § 5:15.

[364] See, e.g., *Duncan v. Village of Middlefield,* 23 Ohio St. 3d 83, 491 N.E.2d 692 (1986).

[365] N.Y. Town Law § 267-b.

[366] *Sasso v. Osgood,* 86 N.Y.2d 374, 633 N.Y.S.2d 259, 657 N.E.2d 254 (1995).

[367] *Metropolitan Bd. of Zoning Appeals of Marion County v. McDonald's Corp.,* 481 N.E.2d 141 (Ind. Ct. App. 1985).

reasonably prevent the owner from using the property for a permitted purpose or would render conformity with such restrictions unnecessarily burdensome" have been used. Significantly, however, these courts do not apply the onerous requirement of showing economic inutility applied to use variances under the unnecessary hardship test.

V. SPECIAL PERMITS

§ 5:24   Special Permits

A.   *In General*

The special permit process is designed to deal with uses that by their nature are difficult to fit within any use zone where they can operate by right. These uses may be especially sensitive and need special protection or they may pose unusual harm to neighboring land. An administrative process deals with these uses on a case by case basis to take these concerns into account. The term "special" relates to the type of use rather than the uniqueness of the property as with a variance.[369] A more descriptive term might be "unusual uses," a term some courts use.[370] For example, an airport has such unusual characteristics that most ordinances do not list it as permitted by right in any zone but allow it only under particular circumstances. Other uses customarily subject to special permits include religious uses,[371] recreational facilities,[372] schools,[373] hospitals, drug treatment centers, child care facilities, gas stations, landfills, gun clubs, junkyards,[374] and dog kennels.

The law and of special permits developed under Section 7 of the Standard State Zoning Enabling Act, which provides that the Board of Adjustment shall have the power to "hear and decide special exceptions to the terms of the ordinance upon which such board is required to pass under such ordinance." Many states still use this grant of power, and others have similar processes. Under the Standard Act, before the board can exercise the power, the legislative body must list the uses to be treated as special. The board may issue a permit for only those uses listed and only if the conditions set forth in the ordinance are met.[375] The label applied to this permit varies. While some ordinances still employ the standard act's "special exception" language, today most label it a "special use permit," a "conditional use permit," or simply a "special permit," the term we employ here to encompass them all. As a general rule, these terms are used interchangeably in the case law, but the specific ordinance at issue should be checked since some may use the terms in other ways.[376]

Special permit requirements may be found invalid if they operate in a discriminatory or oppressive manner. While the equal protection guarantee applies to all persons,

---

[368] *Doyle v. Amster*, 79 N.Y.2d 592, 584 N.Y.S.2d 417, 594 N.E.2d 911 (1992).

[369] *Mayflower Property, Inc. v. City of Fort Lauderdale*, 137 So. 2d 849 (Fla. 2d DCA 1962).

[370] *Metropolitan Dade County v. Fuller*, 515 So. 2d 1312 (Fla. 3d DCA 1987).

[371] See supra § 4:28.

[372] *Bat-A-Ball, Inc. v. City of Chicago*, 184 Ill. App. 3d 776, 132 Ill. Dec. 881, 540 N.E.2d 803 (1989).

[373] *Appeal of O'Hara*, 389 Pa. 35, 131 A.2d 587 (1957). Cf. *L'Hote v. City of New Orleans*, 177 U.S. 587, 20 S. Ct. 788, 44 L. Ed. 899 (1900).

[374] *Thomas v. Board of Sup'rs of Panola County*, 45 So. 3d 1173 (Miss. 2010).

[375] *Piscioneri v. Zoning Hearing Bd. of Borough of Munhall*, 523 Pa. 597, 568 A.2d 610 (1990).

[376] *In re Thompson*, 896 A.2d 659 (Pa. Commw. Ct. 2006).

greater judicial scrutiny is invoked to protect some more than others. Where fundamental or important rights or suspect or quasi-suspect classes are involved, courts may review special permit requirements closely.[377] In *Cleburne v. Cleburne Living Center, Inc.,*[378] the Supreme Court faced an ordinance that subjected group homes for the mentally-retarded to a special permit process, but allowed such uses as fraternities, multi-family use, hospitals, sanitariums, and nursing homes to operate by right. Finding no rational basis to treat group homes more harshly than these similar, permitted uses, the Court invalidated the ordinance on equal protection grounds.[379] Courts may also invalidate special permit requirements as applied to persons protected by the Fair Housing Act.[380]

B. *Distinguishing Features*

Like a variance, a special permit normally involves an administrative process.[381] The two are fundamentally different, however. A variance is permission to engage in an otherwise prohibited act because of hardship.[382] In contrast, a special permit allows a use specifically authorized by the legislative body. A showing that pre-stated standards are met is required for a special permit, but a hardship showing is not necessary.[383]

The special permit also differs from a rezoning. A rezoning is a legislative change in use classification. Issuance of a special permit does not change the underlying zone. It is an administrative act taken with respect to a particular use. For example, a special permit may allow a supermarket of a certain size with required parking and screening in a high density residential zone, but the land retains its residential zoning classification. However, with a general rezoning of the property from residential to commercial with the listing of supermarkets as permitted by right, the new zoning would permit a supermarket by right and would also permit use of the property for any other listed commercial use. The greater the effect that a development will have on a community the more likely the community will handle it by way of amendment, rather than the special permit process.[384]

The legislative-administrative difference becomes clouded where the legislative body retains the power to issue special permits. Floating zones, which are legislative acts, closely resemble special permits.[385] In both instances, certain uses deemed important or proper for the community are allowable but, due to some unusual aspect or need, those interested in pursuing them are subjected to an ad hoc approval process. The greater or more widespread the anticipated impact on the community, the more likely it is that a floating zone will be used.

---

[377] See discussion §§ 10:12 and 10:14 to 10:15.

[378] *City of Cleburne v. Cleburne Living Center,* 473 U.S. 432, 105 S. Ct. 3249, 87 L. Ed. 2d 313 (1985).

[379] See infra § 10:14.

[380] See supra § 4:7 and infra § 6:8.

[381] The power to issue the permit may be retained by the legislative body. See § 5:3.

[382] See supra § 5:14.

[383] *President and Directors of Georgetown College v. District of Columbia Bd. of Zoning Adjustment,* 837 A.2d 58, 183 Ed. Law Rep. 887 (D.C. 2003).

[384] See *Neighborhood Bd. No. 24 v. State Land Use Commission,* 64 Haw. 265, 639 P.2d 1097 (1982).

[385] See supra § 4:16.

C. Growth in Use

From the inception of zoning, the use of the special permit has grown. Its increased and widespread use is part of the transition from rigidity to flexibility,[386] or, as critics fearing too much discretion might say, the evolution of zoning to nonzoning. When an ordinance provides for numerous special permits, cities make decisions on an ad hoc discretionary basis, and districting becomes less evident and less important. This practice resembles the British approach to land use, which historically has not been a districting system. Instead, in a system somewhat like our special permit process, the British have not allowed development generally of right, and property owners must obtain specific permission to use land for most purposes.[387]

A court may invalidate an ordinance that handles all or most uses by special permit. In *Rockhill v. Township of Chesterfield*,[388] the authorities zoned the entire township for agricultural and residential uses, and no other use was possible without issuance of a special permit. The court found the ordinance beyond the scope of the enabling statute since the zoning was neither uniform nor comprehensive. It placed too many uses subject to "local discretion without regard to districts, ruled by vague and elusive criteria, [and was] . . . the antithesis of zoning."[389] The *Rockhill* court's objection is overstated. If the standards are adequate and written into the ordinance, there is no reason to require control of land use by districting rather than a case by case regulatory scheme.

§ 5:25 Standards

The most frequent objection to the issuance of special permits is that the local legislative body failed to provide adequate standards for guiding administrative discretion, violating state law or due process.

Typically, an ordinance listing potential special uses requires that the board find that the applicant meets specific predetermined conditions. For example, an ordinance may permit airports only if a tract of 200 acres is available, the flight path is not over any areas zoned for multi-family use, there are no schools under the flight path, and there is an industrial buffer zone around the airport. The ordinance may also contain more general standards requiring the board to find that the use will not materially endanger the public health and safety, that it will not substantially impair the value of adjoining property, and that the use will be in harmony with the surrounding area. It is with these generalized standards that problems of vagueness or improper delegation may occur.[390]

Standards "may not be so general or tautological as to allow unchecked discretion"[391] by the administrative body. In *Kosalka v. Town of Georgetown*,[392] the Maine

---

[386] See *Town of Rhine v. Bizzell,* 311 Wis. 2d 1, 751 N.W.2d 780 (2008).

[387] See Callies and Grant, Paying for Growth and Planning Gain: An Anglo-American Comparison of Development Conditions, Impact Fees, and Development Agreements, 23 Urb. Law. 221, 226 (1991).

[388] 23 N.J. 117, 128 A.2d 473 (1957). See also *Town of Rhine v. Bizzell,* 311 Wis. 2d 1, 751 N.W.2d 780 (2008).

[389] Id. at 127, 128 A.2d at 479.

[390] See also discussion of delegation problem with respect to variances, supra § 5:16.

[391] *Tandem Holding Corp. v. Board of Zoning Appeals of Town of Hempstead,* 43 N.Y.2d 801, 802, 402 N.Y.S.2d 388, 389, 373 N.E.2d 282, 284 (1977).

[392] *Kosalka v. Town of Georgetown,* 2000 ME 106, 752 A.2d 183 (Me. 2000).

supreme court found that requiring the board to determine that a proposed development will "conserve natural beauty" was an unconstitutional delegation of legislative authority. As the court observed:

> all development, to some extent, destroys or impairs "natural beauty." If the provision means that all natural beauty must be conserved, then all development must be banned. Because the provision cannot reasonably be interpreted to ban all development, the question becomes: How much destruction is okay? . . . Neither developers nor the [board] are given any guidance. Instead, developers are left guessing at how much conservation is necessary, and the [board] is free to grant or deny permits as it sees fit.[393]

Agreement is lacking on how specific the standards must be so as not to allow unchecked discretion. If an ordinance simply provides that the board of adjustment shall find that the granting of the special permit "will not adversely affect the public interest," a court may invalidate the grant as an unlawful delegation of legislative power to an administrative body.[394] Under such a standard, a court may see the legislative body as abdicating to an administrative body the ultimate question of public interest that the legislature is to decide for itself. In contrast, an ordinance that requires the board to find that the use "will not adversely affect the value of adjacent property" is more likely to be upheld.[395] The specific focus on value of the adjacent area is narrower and less subjective than a broad charge to "determine the public interest."

Many courts tolerate fairly vague standards.[396] To do otherwise might demand the impossible. The mere fact that the legislative body does not employ precise standards does not necessarily mean that it is simply avoiding the hard thinking necessary to establish standards which anticipate many situations. Predicting all types of problems that may arise is difficult, if not impossible. Furthermore, detailed standards may unduly reduce discretion and curb flexibility. While some flexibility is a good thing, there are limits. To the extent discretion is uncontrolled, the potential for arbitrariness increases, and due process concerns arise.[397]

In some jurisdictions, the legislative body may issue special permits.[398] Legislative bodies often establish a dual system where they retain authority to issue special permits for uses that will have a large impact on the city, and delegate to the administrative board those special uses with lesser impact.[399] While "the clear weight of authority in the United States holds that a legislative body acts administratively when it rules on applications for special use permits,"[400] the question of the appropriate standard of judicial review is complicated in some states where courts may review acts by legislative bodies with greater deference than they would accord acts by administrative bod-

---

[393] Id. at 187.

[394] See, e.g., *Jackson v. Guilford County Bd. of Adjustment,* 275 N.C. 155, 166 S.E.2d 78 (1969).

[395] See *Gorham v. Town of Cape Elizabeth,* 625 A.2d 898 (Me. 1993).

[396] See *Rolling Pines Ltd. Partnership v. City of Little Rock,* 73 Ark. App. 97, 40 S.W.3d 828 (2001).

[397] For some courts, there is no property right if there is discretion. See infra § 10:12.

[398] See infra § 5:24.

[399] See, e.g., City of Pittsburgh Code § 993.01, described in *Klein v. Council of City of Pittsburgh,* 164 Pa. Commw. 521, 539, 643 A.2d 1107, 1116 (1994).

[400] *Oak Grove Jubilee Center, Inc. v. City of Genoa,* 347 Ill. App. 3d 973, 979, 283 Ill. Dec. 610, 808 N.E.2d 576, 583 (2004).

ies.[401] Thus, guidelines in an ordinance that provided for issuance of special permits by the legislative body as long as the use met "minimum requirements adopted to promote the health, safety, morals, comfort, prosperity and general welfare of the town * * * " were held sufficient to overcome a vagueness challenge.[402] The rationale for more deferential review is that since the legislative body may amend the ordinance if it likes, it makes no sense to require it to adhere to the standards. However, this rationale fails to see beneath the surface.

The practice of legislative bodies deciding whether to grant special permits troubles some.[403] As Justice Klingbiel of the Illinois Supreme Court argued "it is not part of the legislative function to grant permits * * * or decide particular cases. Such activities are * * * judicial in character [and] to place them in the hands of legislative bodies * * * is to open the door completely to arbitrary government."[404] In accord with this conviction, the majority of courts treat special permit decisions as administrative for the purposes of the standard of review regardless of the body that hears the matter.[405]

In determining whether to issue a special permit, an administrative board is not to substitute its judgment for the legislative judgment and is not to impose unlisted criteria.[406] The legislative body's listing of a use in a special permit category creates a "presumption of compatibility"[407] that the general welfare is served by the allowance of such a use.[408] While the burden of proof is on the permit applicant,[409] it is, as one court has said, a "limited evidentiary burden" to show that the proposed use meets the prescribed standards. Notably, the applicant does not have the burden of showing that the use accords with the general welfare. If the legislative body determines that a particular use is a permissible special use, the board cannot use the inherent attributes of the use to deny a permit.

§ 5:26 Conditions

As with variances, boards can condition special permits. The ordinance may list specific conditions, but it may expressly confer the authority to impose additional conditions under more general language. Alternatively, a court may imply the authority from the nature of the special permit.[410] The Standard Zoning Enabling Act provides for "appropriate conditions and safeguards."[411]

In *Montgomery County v. Mossburg*,[412] the ordinance allowed special permits if the use was compatible with the general development plan for the neighborhood, would not adversely affect the health and safety of residents in the area and would not be detri-

---

[401] See *Board of Sup'rs of Rockingham County v. Stickley*, 263 Va. 1, 556 S.E.2d 748 (2002).

[402] *Town of Richmond v. Murdock*, 70 Wis. 2d 642, 235 N.W.2d 497 (1975).

[403] See also discussion supra § 5:9 regarding the treatment of site-specific rezonings as quasi-judicial.

[404] *Ward v. Village of Skokie*, 26 Ill. 2d 415, 186 N.E.2d 529, 533 (1962) (concurring opinion).

[405] See *Oak Grove Jubilee Center, Inc. v. City of Genoa*, 347 Ill. App. 3d 973, 283 Ill. Dec. 610, 808 N.E.2d 576, 583 (2004) and cases there cited.

[406] See *West Texas Water Refiners, Inc. v. S & B Beverage Co., Inc.*, 915 S.W.2d 623 (Tex. App. 1996).

[407] *Montgomery County v. Butler*, 417 Md. 271, 9 A.3d 824 (2010).

[408] *In re Brickstone Realty Corp.*, 789 A.2d 333 (Pa. Commw. Ct. 2001).

[409] *Thomas v. Board of Sup'rs of Panola County*, 45 So. 3d 1173 (Miss. 2010).

[410] *Pearson v. Shoemaker*, 25 Misc. 2d 591, 202 N.Y.S.2d 779 (1960).

[411] Section 7, Standard State Zoning Enabling Act (1926).

[412] *Montgomery County v. Mossburg*, 228 Md. 555, 180 A.2d 851 (1962).

mental to development of adjacent properties or the general neighborhood. The court held such language sufficient to justify a condition imposing early closing hours on a special permit to expand a nonconforming restaurant. In *Whittaker & Gooding Co. v. Scio Township*,[413] the court upheld a five-year time limit on the operation of gravel removal operation on the grounds that the community had a right to limit the activity to a definite period. Other common conditions include off-street parking, minimum acreage, access, and landscaping.

Conditions must be reasonable. For example, it has been held improper for a zoning board to require a university to monitor off-campus enforcement of various sanitation and housing regulations, to require creation of a process to hear neighbors' complaints about students, and to require the university to report violations of its code of conduct to students' parents or guardians.[414]

Conditions likewise must relate to the use allowed by the permit.[415] Thus, a condition requiring the recipient of a special permit to dedicate land for a public road and pay to build the road was held invalid where the special permittee's use of the land would not generate the traffic problem addressed by the condition.[416] If courts see issuance of a permit as a privilege rather than a right, they allow greater discretion. As a result, even if the validity of conditions is doubtful, the courts may estop an owner who accepts the special permit with conditions from a later attack on the conditions.[417] As is true with variances, conditions normally ought not be based on the person seeking the permit, but the federal Fair Housing Act and the Americans With Disabilities Act in some instances may require accommodations that would be impermissible under state law.[418]

An ordinance may require a board to impose conditions. For example, in *Chambers v. Zoning Board of Adjustment*,[419] the property owner applied for a permit to construct a housing project. The ordinance authorized a permit if on-site garage or other satisfactory automobile storage space was provided. The board waived the condition on the ground that street parking was adequate, but the court held the waiver improper since the ordinance gave the board no discretion to waive the condition.

VI. VESTED RIGHTS AND DEVELOPMENT AGREEMENTS

§ 5:27 The Vesting Issue

When the legislative body changes the law, a key question is whether the change applies to development proposals in the permit processing mill. When challenges arise about what development rights exist vis-a-vis a new ordinance, the traditional rule is that a court applies the law that exists at the time of its decision.[420] This, of course, will

---

[413] *Whittaker & Gooding Co. v. Scio Tp.,* 122 Mich. App. 538, 332 N.W.2d 527 (1983).

[414] *President and Directors of Georgetown College v. District of Columbia Bd. of Zoning Adjustment*, 837 A.2d 58 (D.C. 2003).

[415] See *Steuben County v. National Serv-All, Inc.,* 556 N.E.2d 1354 (Ind. Ct. App. 1990).

[416] *Cupp v. Board of Supr's of Fairfax County*, 227 Va. 580, 318 S.E.2d 407 (1984)

[417] *Exxon Co., U.S.A. v. State Highway Admin., Maryland Dept. of Transp.*, 354 Md. 530, 731 A.2d 948 (1999).

[418] See supra § 5:17.

[419] *Chambers v. Zoning Bd. of Adjustment of Winston-Salem*, 250 N.C. 194, 108 S.E.2d 211 (1959).

[420] *People ex rel. Eitel v. Lindheimer*, 371 Ill. 367, 21 N.E.2d 318 (1939).

be the new law, which the municipality will have enacted by the time the challenge reaches the court. Knowing this, developers, fearing that potentially more restrictive laws may be enacted, may seek to hurry the permit process and, once a permit is obtained, build quickly before the law is changed. If successful, the doctrine of nonconforming uses will protect them.[421]

This scenario sets off a "race of diligence"[422] between the municipality seeking to change the law and the developer seeking to build.

Notwithstanding the traditional rule, courts may refuse application of a new law based on considerations of fairness or equity. Thus, even short of establishing a nonconforming use by completing a project, at some point it will be too late for the government to change the rules of the game with respect to it. Determining the point in time when a project is far enough along to acquire immunity from changing laws is the subject of the law of vested rights and estoppel.[423]

The common law vested rights rule developed from, or is explainable by reference to, the due process clause of the Fourteenth Amendment.[424] Government cannot divest property rights arbitrarily, and at some point in the development process a developer's right to proceed achieves constitutional protection. While due process is the foundation of vested rights law, the discussion here deals with state statutory and common law that provides equal or greater protection. The main focus of vested rights is on the actions of the developer.[425] Under the majority rule, to acquire a vested right, and therefore immunity from a newly enacted law, a developer must (1) engage in substantial expenditures (2) in good faith reliance (3) on a validly issued building permit.[426]

The doctrine of estoppel, drawn from equity, focuses on instances when, due to the nature of the government conduct, applying a newly enacted law to a developer would be inequitable. A common statement of the rule is that courts will estop government from applying a new law when a developer (1) makes a substantial change of position or engages in substantial expenditures (2) in good faith reliance (3) upon some act or omission of the government (4) so that applying a new law would be highly inequitable.[427]

While the lineage and focus of vested rights and estoppel doctrines differ, a comparison of the elements listed above shows them to be quite similar. The labels are, in fact, often used interchangeably [428] so that efforts to keep the doctrines separate may be futile. It is also typically unnecessary to distinguish between them since fairness is the premise of both and since the results of applying the two tests are most always the same. In some instances, estoppel may provide relief that vested rights would not since

---

[421] Zoning changes do not apply to uses lawfully in existence at the time a change becomes effective. See supra § 4:31.

[422] *Downham v. City Council of Alexandria*, 58 F.2d 784, 788 (E.D. Va. 1932).

[423] See, generally, Hanes, On Vested Rights to Land Use and Development, 46 Wash. & Lee L. Rev. 373 (1989).

[424] *Town of Paradise Valley v. Gulf Leisure Corp.*, 27 Ariz. App. 600, 557 P.2d 532 (1976).

[425] To the extent that the issue is treated as one of due process, the strength of the public interest must be considered. See infra § 10:12.

[426] *Avco Community Developers, Inc. v. South Coast Regional Com.*, 17 Cal. 3d 785, 132 Cal. Rptr. 386, 553 P.2d 546 (1976).

[427] *The Florida Companies v. Orange County, Fla.*, 411 So. 2d 1008, 1010 (Fla. 5th DCA 1982).

[428] See, e.g., *Kauai County v. Pacific Standard Life Ins. Co.*, 65 Haw. 318, 653 P.2d 766 (1982).

estoppel does not necessarily require a permit.[429] In the material that follows, we treat cases involving reliance on permits under the vested rights label (though courts in some of the cases use estoppel terminology along with or instead of vested rights). In a separate section entitled estoppel we cover cases that turn on conduct not based on a permit.[430]

§ 5:28   Vesting Under Building Permits

In most states, a building permit standing alone does not vest a right to continue if the law changes. Under the majority rule to acquire a vested right a developer must (1) show substantial expenditures, obligations, or harm (2) incurred in good faith reliance (3) on a validly issued building permit.[431] If the authorities have issued a permit, they may revoke it if the zoning classification changes before the developer incurs substantial expenditures under the permit.

A. *Substantial Reliance*

Under the majority common law rule, landowners must show substantial reliance on a validly issued permit.[432] In considering expenses or other harm sustained by the landowner, courts generally do not consider the purchase price of the land since its use to vest rights would allow the developer to freeze zoning.[433] While some courts require that actual construction commence,[434] many courts consider other reliance as well, such as contract obligations.[435] The harm that would follow if compliance with the new law is required must be a "serious loss, rendering the improvements essentially valueless."[436]

In *Vulcan Materials Co. v. Greenville County Board of Zoning Appeals,*[437] a mineral lessee expended nearly two million dollars to find granite, arranged for the removal of 15 acres of overburden to expose the granite for extraction, and was awaiting a mine operating permit from state when, at the urging of the neighbors, the county downzoned the land. The lessee was held to have a moved beyond mere contemplated use and preparation so as to acquire a vested right.

Courts measure substantial reliance in various ways. Many courts hold that a landowner must have invested a certain amount of money in the project. To avoid difficulty in setting an arbitrary amount, some courts adopt a ratio approach, and require that expenditures already made be substantial compared with the total project cost. In *Clackamas County v. Holmes,*[438] however, the court stated that though a developer

---

[429] *Sahl v. Town of York,* 2000 ME 180, 760 A.2d 266 (Me. 2000).

[430] Infra § 5:29.

[431] See *Avco Community Developers, Inc. v. South Coast Regional Com.,* 17 Cal. 3d 785, 132 Cal. Rptr. 386, 553 P.2d 546 (1976).

[432] But see *Crown Media, LLC v. Gwinnett County,* 380 F.3d 1317 (11th Cir. 2004).

[433] See *Gallup Westside Development, LLC v. City of Gallup,* 135 N.M. 30, 84 P.3d 78 (Ct. App. 2003); *North Georgia Mountain Crisis Network, Inc. v. City of Blue Ridge,* 248 Ga. App. 450, 546 S.E.2d 850 (2001).

[434] *Town of Sykesville v. West Shore Communications, Inc.,* 110 Md. App. 300, 677 A.2d 102 (1996).

[435] *Hussey v. Town of Barrington,* 135 N.H. 227, 604 A.2d 82 (1992); *Town of Hillsborough v. Smith,* 276 N.C. 48, 170 S.E.2d 904 (1969).

[436] *Town of Orangetown v. Magee,* 88 N.Y.2d 41, 643 N.Y.S.2d 21, 25, 665 N.E.2d 1061 (1996).

[437] *Vulcan Materials Co. v. Greenville County Bd. of Zoning Appeals,* 342 S.C. 480, 536 S.E.2d 892 (Ct. App. 2000).

[438] *Clackamas County v. Holmes,* 265 Or. 193, 508 P.2d 190 (1973).

must have incurred substantial costs toward completion of the job, vesting of rights should not be based solely on the ratio of expenditures to total project cost. The defendants had taken actions to ready the property for chicken farming, but the county rezoned the property to residential use before they could secure a building permit. The court found that the type of preparations made by a property owner should be considered. It concluded that a right to proceed had vested since the defendants had acted in good faith and since the expenses incurred were substantial and directly related to its intended uses.

B. *Good Faith*

Developers must make expenditures in good faith. Engaging in expenditures or incurring obligations when aware of the fact that an ordinance that would prohibit the use is pending and that adoption is imminent is in bad faith.[439] While acts made in "unseemly haste" just before the effective date of an ordinance have been found in bad faith,[440] mere knowledge that the municipality might make a change has been held insufficient.[441] If it is shown that the developer misled the government or acted in reliance on a permit known to be invalid, no rights will vest.[442]

If the city or the neighbors take an appeal alleging invalidity of the permit or the underlying law on which it is based, expenses incurred during appeal will not be in good faith.[443] Waiting for the appeal time to run its course may place a serious strain on the economic viability of a project, but a developer who proceeds during appeal does so at risk, as courts can, and do, order buildings razed.[444] Since the time to appeal may not start running until the aggrieved party receives notice, the developer may be left in limbo. Extremely short limitations periods substantially aid the developer.[445] One court suggests that neighbors protesting a permit who plan to appeal take steps to assure notice such as filing of lis pendens, quick service of process, and injunctive relief.[446] The stalled developer might attempt to protect itself by seeking to have the neighbors post a bond.

A similar problem may arise if voters seek a referendum to amend the law on which a permit is based before the developer incurs substantial expenses. In *County of Kauai v. Pacific Standard Life Insurance Co.,*[447] the Hawaii supreme court said that a referendum process initiated after final discretionary action by the government would not alter a vested right, but that permits issued after the referendum process is started are not safe to rely on. When voters get into the act, the referendum vote becomes the final discretionary act. This is apparently true even if the election is a year or two

---

[439] *Town of Hillsborough v. Smith,* 276 N.C. 48, 170 S.E.2d 904 (1969).

[440] *Billings v. California Coastal Com.,* 103 Cal. App. 3d 729, 163 Cal. Rptr. 288 (1980).

[441] *Application of Campsites Unlimited, Inc.,* 287 N.C. 493, 215 S.E.2d 73 (1975).

[442] See *City of Coral Gables v. Puiggros,* 376 So. 2d 281 (Fla. 3d DCA 1979). See also discussion of illegal permits infra § 5:28.

[443] *Powell v. Calvert County,* 368 Md. 400, 795 A.2d 96 (2002).

[444] *Pinecrest Lakes, Inc. v. Shidel,* 795 So. 2d 191 (Fla. 4th DCA 2001).

[445] See discussion infra § 5:36.

[446] *Petty v. Barrentine,* 594 S.W.2d 903, 905 (Ky. Ct. App. 1980).

[447] *Kauai County v. Pacific Standard Life Ins. Co.,* 65 Haw. 318, 653 P.2d 766 (1982).

away. Concerns over long-term delay and the court's use of the final discretionary action rule,[448] have prompted criticism of the Hawaii decision.[449]

C. Permit Requirement

Avco Community Developers, Inc. v. South Coast Regional Commission,[450] illustrates the permit requirement. Developer Avco owned some 8,000 acres upon which it planned to construct a planned community. Developing in phases, Avco obtained permits from the county to subdivide and grade 74 acres. As Avco was in the process of installing storm drains, streets, and other utilities, and had spent or incurred liabilities of $2.7 million, the state's coastal act became effective, requiring that it obtain a permit from the coastal commission. Seeking to avoid this new regulatory hoop, Avco claimed a vested right to proceed. The court held against the developer since it had not obtained a final building permit from the county by the date the new permit requirement became effective.

The permit requirement should not turn on labels, and a "building permit or its functional equivalent" should suffice.[451] Whether that flexibility exists is not clear. The *Avco* court rejected the charge that it was being obdurate in denying a vested right because no building permit had issued. The conceded that there might be instances when something less than a final building permit would vest rights.

Some courts relax the demand for a final building permit by vesting rights upon the happening of the final discretionary act.[452] In several cases the issuance of a special permit has been found to vest rights although the city had not yet issued a building permit.[453] Approval of a site plan, seen by some as having "virtually replaced the building permit as the most vital document in the development process,"[454] also has been found sufficient.

D. Right to Obtain Permit Based on Existing Zoning

There is no right to a development permit based on the zoning that existed when the developer acquired the land in the majority of states.[455] If a developer purchases land to build an industrial plant and the city rezones the land for residential use on the day following purchase, the developer has no right to a permit to build an industrial plant. The property may be worth much less than the purchase price if the buyer paid a price based on the assumption that it could develop according to existing zoning. Thus, acquisition costs and pre-application spending must take into account the risk that development permission might not be obtained due to a future downzoning.

---

[448] See discussion of final discretionary action rule infra § 5:28.

[449] See Callies, Nukolii and Vested Rights, 36 Land Use L. & Zoning Dig. 14 (1983).

[450] *Avco Community Developers, Inc. v. South Coast Regional Com.*, 17 Cal. 3d 785, 132 Cal. Rptr. 386, 553 P.2d 546 (1976).

[451] *Hermosa Beach Stop Oil Coalition v. City of Hermosa Beach,* 86 Cal. App. 4th 534, 103 Cal. Rptr. 2d 447 (2d Dist. 2001).

[452] *Wal-Mart Stores, Inc. v. County of Clark*, 125 F. Supp. 2d 420 (D. Nev. 1999).

[453] *Town of Stephens City v. Russell,* 241 Va. 160, 399 S.E.2d 814 (1991).

[454] *Board of Sup'rs of Fairfax County v. Medical Structures, Inc.*, 213 Va. 355, 192 S.E.2d 799, 801 (1972).

[455] See, e.g., *Avco Community Developers, Inc. v. South Coast Regional Com.*, 17 Cal. 3d 785, 132 Cal. Rptr. 386, 553 P.2d 546 (1976).

In a significant and growing number of jurisdictions rights vest under the law in existence at the time of permit application.[456] In these states, which find the uncertainty of the majority rule detrimental to the public interest and the individual property owner, a showing of expenditures in reliance on a permit is not required.[457] Some states employ a date certain approach.[458] Others, such as Utah, have a qualified approach. In the leading case *Western Land Equities, Inc. v. City of Logan,* the Utah supreme court held that an applicant for a building permit is vested as of that date "unless there are pending changes in zoning ordinances which would prohibit the use applied for,[459] or unless the municipality or county could show a compelling, countervailing reason for exercising its police power retroactively to the date of application."[460] The application must be complete. In one case, a builder emailed the zoning office of its intent to excavate a drainage ditch and harvest trees on its property. When the city had the owner enjoined based on the fact that no permit had been properly applied for, the owner argued that the date of the injunction constituted the date of vesting. The court flatly rejected this noting that in the "absence a proper application, it would be difficult to state with certainty what rights, exactly, had vested as to a particular party, or when."[461]

E. Municipal Good Faith

Municipalities, like developers, must act in good faith. Courts that otherwise follow the majority late-vesting rule make an exception if a municipality changes its law primarily to thwart a particular development without clear justification.[462] Most instances of governmental bad faith are encountered where authorities drag their feet and mislead or otherwise hinder an applicant in the permitting process. If a permit is willfully withheld by deceptive conduct, a new intervening law will not apply,[463] and an action for damages may lie.[464] Courts do not, however, universally treat action taken in response to a particular development proposal as bad faith. If a court finds that protection of the general welfare motivated a new law, the court will apply the law even where permit issuance triggered its passage.[465]

F. Pending Ordinance Doctrine

Under the pending ordinance doctrine if a change in the law is pending at the time of application, no rights may vest.[466] This is clearly true in a majority rule state since time of application is not a vesting event. Nevertheless, even in jurisdictions inclined to vest rights earlier, a number uphold denial of a permit based on a later-adopted ordinance that was pending at the time the developer filed the application.[467] If the gov-

---

[456] See discussion infra § 5:30.

[457] See *Zaremba Dev. Co. v. Fairview Park,* 84 Ohio App. 3d 174, 616 N.E.2d 569 (1992).

[458] See, e.g., Tex. Loc. Gov't Code Ann. § 245.002(a)(2)(a-l).

[459] See infra § 5:29 for discussion of pending ordinance rule.

[460] 617 P.2d 388, 396 (Utah 1980).

[461] *In re Keystone Development Corp.,* 186 Vt. 523, 973 A.2d 1179, 1180 (2009).

[462] See, e.g., *Smith v. Winhall Planning Commission,* 140 Vt. 178, 436 A.2d 760 (1981).

[463] *Figgie Intern., Inc. v. Town of Huntington,* 203 A.D.2d 416, 610 N.Y.S.2d 563 (1994).

[464] *Mission Springs, Inc. v. City of Spokane,* 134 Wash. 2d 947, 954 P.2d 250 (1998). See discussion infra § 5:28.

[465] *Manalapan Realty, L.P. v. Township Committee of Tp. of Manalapan,* 140 N.J. 366, 658 A.2d 1230 (1995).

[466] *In re John A. Russell Corp.,* 176 Vt. 520, 838 A.2d 906 (2003).

[467] See *Sherman v. Reavis,* 273 S.C. 542, 257 S.E.2d 735 (1979).

ernment has announced its intent to consider a change, courts following the pending ordinance rule recognize that no sound justification exists to confer benefits on a property owner who has not yet incurred obligations based on existing law, particularly where the government set in motion changes in the law before the developer's appearance on the scene. Coupled with the power to divest rights due to serious public health or safety concerns, the pending ordinance rule is a compromise between fairness to developers and the need to protect the public interest.[468]

G. Moratoria to Protect Planning Process

To prevent a race between a developer, trying to secure a permit and quickly begin building, and a city, trying to hastily enact a new code, the proper course for government is to pass an interim ordinance freezing development before the race begins.[469] Protection of the planning process requires this for without it developers could defeat the plan before it begins by inconsistent vested uses. A moratorium allows the city to avoid hastily enacting an ordinance without adequate consideration.

The Supreme Court has upheld the facial validity of moratoria that deny all use or value of land against takings challenges.[470] Moratoria that are unreasonable, however, may be found to be as applied takings. In some jurisdictions, authority to impose a freeze or moratorium on development may be questionable.[471] Even if unable formally to impose a freeze, administrative action by a municipality to delay approval, while new studies are completed and the new law enacted, is likely to prevent vesting in most states if the action is not deceptive.

H. Illegally Issued Permit

As a general proposition, no rights vest pursuant to an illegally or erroneously issued permit.[472] As one court has observed, "[the] legislative prerogative would be undermined if a government agent could—through mistake, neglect, or an intentional act—effectively repeal a law by ignoring, misrepresenting, or misinterpreting a duly enacted statute or regulation."[473] An applicant for a permit cannot blindly rely on the statements or actions of government officials that purport to authorize a use. Everyone is presumed to know the extent of power of local officials,[474] and courts impose an obligation on an applicant to exercise reasonable diligence to find out whether an authorized action is legal.[475]

Parkview Associates v. City of New York [476] is a dramatic illustration of the rule. There, a city official issued a permit allowing a 31-story building based on an incorrect reading of the zoning map, and the building was constructed. The proper height con-

---

[468] See Steinwascher, Statutory Development Rights: Why Implementing Vested Rights Through Statute Serves the Interests of the Developer and Government Alike, 32 Cardozo L. Rev. 265 (2010).

[469] See *Williams v. Griffin,* 91 Nev. 743, 542 P.2d 732 (1975).

[470] *Tahoe-Sierra Preservation Council, Inc. v. Tahoe Regional Planning Agency,* 535 U.S. 302, 122 S. Ct. 1465, 152 L. Ed. 2d 517 (2002).

[471] See discussion infra § 9:5.

[472] *Thomas v. Town of Hooksett,* 153 N.H. 717, 903 A.2d 963 (2006).

[473] *City of White Settlement v. Super Wash, Inc.,* 198 S.W.3d 770 (Tex. 2006).

[474] *Miller v. Board of Adjustment of Town of Dewey Beach,* 521 A.2d 642 (Del. Super. Ct. 1986).

[475] See *Lehman v. City of Louisville,* 967 F.2d 1474 (10th Cir.1992).

[476] *Parkview Associates v. City of New York,* 71 N.Y.2d 274, 525 N.Y.S.2d 176, 519 N.E.2d 1372 (1988).

trol, however, limited the building to 19 stories. Noting that only very rare cases justify estoppel against a city, the court held that an applicant cannot assume the city officials know or are properly following the law. If "reasonable diligence by a good-faith inquirer would have disclosed the facts and the bureaucratic error,"[477] no defense exists.[478] The court sustained a demolition order and the builder removed the top 12 stories.

However, the rule is not ironclad. Some courts use a doctrine of "honest error" to preclude permit revocation in situations involving a good faith mistake by an official, made within the apparent scope of authority.[479]

While courts are reluctant to let the public interest suffer, as it presumably will if actions conceded to be illegal are allowed to persist, the strength of the public interest may matter. For example, a court is not likely to prevent a city from enforcing a flood plain ordinance where concerns with public safety are at issue, but enforcement of an aesthetics-based ordinance is not as compelling.[480] Further, though exceptional circumstances must exist, there are numerous cases where rights in illegal permits have been found to have vested or municipalities have been estopped.[481] We deal with estoppel and illegal permits in more detail below.[482]

I. *Municipal Liability for Wrongfully Issued Permits*

While a property owner may fail to establish a vested right in an improperly issued permit, all is not necessarily lost for a property owner may have a damage action in tort for the loss sustained because of the wrongfully issued permit.[483] Municipalities are generally immune for liability in tort for governmental or discretionary actions,[484] but exceptions exist. In *L.A. Ray Realty v. Town of Cumberland,*[485] for example, the court held that the town's adoption and enforcement of an illegal ordinance constituted intentional interference with a developer's contractual relations. The town lost its governmental immunity because the court found that its actions were egregious. However, since the actions were nonetheless governmental in nature, liability was capped at $100,000 under the state Tort Liability Act. Government may also be liable for mere negligence where its actions are ministerial.[486]

Washington provides a statutory damage remedy where an "action is unlawful or in excess of lawful authority only if the final decision of the agency was made with knowledge of its unlawfulness or that it was in excess of lawful authority, or it should reasonably have been known to have been unlawful or in excess of lawful authority."[487]

---

[477] Id. at 176.

[478] *Turco v. Town of Barnstead,* 136 N.H. 256, 615 A.2d 1237 (1992).

[479] *City of Berea v. Wren,* 818 S.W.2d 274 (Ky. Ct. App. 1991).

[480] See *Hansel v. City of Keene,* 138 N.H. 99, 634 A.2d 1351, 1354 (1993).

[481] Cases dealing with illegal permits often speak of estoppel, as opposed to vested rights, as the basis for examining whether to allow revocation. The result, regardless of label, is the same.

[482] See cases discussing estoppel infra § 5:29.

[483] A wrongful refusal to process grading permit may also lead to liability under § 1983. See *Mission Springs, Inc. v. City of Spokane,* 134 Wash. 2d 947, 954 P.2d 250 (1998).

[484] See, e.g., *Gleason v. Nuco, Inc.,* 774 So. 2d 1240 (La. Ct. App. 2000).

[485] *L.A. Ray Realty v. Town Council of Town of Cumberland,* 698 A.2d 202 (R.I. 1997).

[486] *Snyder v. City of Minneapolis,* 441 N.W.2d 781 (Minn. 1989).

[487] Wash. Rev. Code Ann. § 64.40.020. See *Isla Verde Intern. Holdings, Ltd. v. City of Camas,* 147 Wash. App. 454, 196 P.3d 719 (2008).

The so-called public duty doctrine is used in a number of states to immunize government from liability. Under this rule a municipality and its agents are viewed as acting for the benefit of the general public and not for a specific individual when exercising its statutory police powers. Since no duty is owed to the individual, there can be no tort liability for negligence.[488] Thus, a county was not liable for negligence where a developer bought and sold lots in reliance on the planning board's approval of its development plan only to be denied septic tank permits by the health department on ground that their lots were unsuitable for purposes of obtaining such permits.[489]

J.   *Zoning Change Invalid*

An alternative argument in dealing with a vested rights issue is to focus on the validity of the later-enacted downzoning. A court may preserve the rights of the permittee by holding the rezoning invalid.[490]

§ 5:29   Estoppel

Courts generally say that estoppel requires that a landowner or developer (1) make a substantial change of position or engage in substantial expenditures (2) in good faith reliance (3) upon some act or omission of the government (4) so that applying a new law would be highly inequitable.[491] When the public health, safety and welfare are at stake, successfully asserting such a claim is difficult. Courts are reluctant to leave the public unprotected due to an error by a governmental body or official.[492] Consequently, courts usually apply the elements of estoppel from a government-protective perspective.

As noted above,[493] some confusion exists as to whether estoppel differs from vested rights, and if so how. In several cases discussed in the prior section on vested rights, the courts referred to estoppel as the, or a, basis for decision. Most of those cases, however, involved complaints of reliance on valid permits. The cases discussed in this section deal with instances where an illegally issued permit followed by government acquiescence may lead to estoppel and where government conduct other than a valid permit was the focus of concern.

The length of time that the city permits a landowner to engage in action pursuant to an illegally issued permit and the clarity of the illegality may make a difference in whether the developer may proceed.

Where the development is clearly illegal, the courts are not inclined to favor the violator. For example, in *City of Raleigh v. Fisher*,[494] the city had allowed the defendant to conduct a bakery business in a house in a residential zone for several years. The building inspector had issued several permits for additions and improvements with knowledge that the use violated the zoning ordinance. The city had also collected a

---

[488] See, generally, Speir, Comment: The Public Duty Doctrine and Municipal Liability for Negligent Administration of Zoning Codes, 20 Seattle U. L. Rev. 803 (1997).

[489] *Derwort v. Polk County,* 129 N.C. App. 789, 501 S.E.2d 379 (1998).

[490] *Gruber v. Mayor and Tp. Committee of Raritan Tp.,* 39 N.J. 1, 186 A.2d 489 (1962).

[491] *The Florida Companies v. Orange County, Fla.,* 411 So. 2d 1008, 1010 (Fla. 5th DCA 1982).

[492] *Healey v. Town of New Durham Zoning Bd. of Adjustment,* 140 N.H. 232, 665 A.2d 360, 367 (1995).

[493] See supra § 5:27.

[494] *City of Raleigh v. Fisher,* 232 N.C. 629, 61 S.E.2d 897 (1950).

privilege license tax for eight years. When the city decided to enforce its ordinance, the court upheld the city. If the result were otherwise, an employee of the city could deliberately misconstrue the law, frustrating public policy.

If the "illegality" of the permit was ambiguous when granted and the applicant proceeded in good faith, some courts have refused to allow a city to revoke the permit. In Crow v. Board of Adjustment of Iowa City,[495] for example, after receiving a supporting opinion from the city attorney, the building inspector issued a permit to a property owner to build a veterinary hospital in a district that permitted hospitals. The property owner purchased a lot, demolished a house on it, began excavating, purchased materials and entered into contracts. Objecting citizens appealed the issuance of the permit to the board of adjustment, which ruled that hospitals did not include veterinary hospitals. The court held that the ordinance was ambiguous and that in such a case the issuance of the permit conferred a vested right where the permittee had materially changed his position.

Governmental tolerance of an illegal use over a long term forms the basis for many estoppel cases. A long time lapse alone, however, even when coupled with governmental notice of the illegal activity, normally will not give rise to estoppel. To win, a property owner must show some municipal action, typically the erroneous issuance of a permit. Where property was used for business purposes in a residential zone for 20 years, no estoppel arose because, while the city knew of the violation, no "active acquiescence" by the municipality existed.[496] However, where 44 years passed without enforcement and where the city had erroneously issued a building permit 27 years earlier, the city was estopped.[497] Even two years of inaction, coupled with express permission, was sufficient for estoppel in one case.[498] Generally, the statute of limitations is not available as a defense since the illegal use is a "continuing crime."[499]

In a rare case, no permit at all need be issued. In *Town of Largo v. Imperial Homes Corp.,*[500] the developer bought two parcels of property relying on assurances that the town would zone to allow construction of multi-family dwellings. Of two tracts purchased on such assurances, one tract was zoned for multifamily use, and the other left unzoned, permitting any use. Municipal review of the developer's master plan evoked no objections, and a planner hired by the town to study its ordinance for comprehensive amendment recommended high-density zoning for the developer's land. The town tentatively approved this proposed zoning, but because of resident objections, it ultimately zoned the parcels for the most restrictive single family use. When challenged, the town argued that the developer had not obtained a building permit thus no rights had vested. The court said a permit was not needed to estop the town, and held that the builders had a right to rely on actions of the governing body taken over a four-year period.

---

[495] *Crow v. Board of Adjustment of Iowa City*, 227 Iowa 324, 288 N.W. 145 (1939).

[496] *Appeal of Crawford,* 110 Pa. Commw. 51, 531 A.2d 865 (1987).

[497] *Knake v. Zoning Hearing Bd. of the Borough of Dormont,* 74 Pa. Commw. 265, 459 A.2d 1331 (1983).

[498] *Caporali v. Ward,* 89 Pa. Commw. 621, 493 A.2d 791 (1985).

[499] See, e.g., *People v. Fletcher Gravel Co., Inc.,* 82 Misc. 2d 22, 368 N.Y.S.2d 392 (1975).

[500] *Town of Largo v. Imperial Homes Corp.*, 309 So. 2d 571 (Fla. 2d DCA 1975).

Avco Community Developers, Inc. v. South Coast Regional Commission,[501] discussed above regarding a permit issue,[502] also involved a separate estoppel issue. The developer had agreed to sell some land to the county at below market price in return for county approval of the project. Noting that the state had approved the agreement, the developer argued that the court should estop the state from enforcing the new law. The court held that the agreement as construed by the developer was unenforceable as "a contracting away of the police power." It would not estop the government from enforcing the new act based on an agreement that was contrary to public policy.

§ 5:30   Statutory Solutions to Uncertainty

The case-by-case, equitable determinations of vested rights and estoppel are difficult to reconcile and result in great uncertainty, particularly for the development community. Large-scale development that takes a long time to get underway and complete has not fared well under the common law vesting rule. Unfortunately, municipal planning is often inadequate or out of date, and the ill-advised nature of the present controls only comes to the attention of governmental decision makers when someone applies for developmental permission. The late-vesting common law rule affords government a chance to correct its mistakes by changing the rules and then denying development permission.

Some see the common law rule as anti-development and have called for change. Professor Hagman, in proposing legislation on the subject, complained that the rule is "excessively protective of the right of government to change its mind," that this "luxury of irresponsibility" chilled desirable development, and that the government ought to "learn to play fair."[503] As noted,[504] some courts have changed the common law rule to be more developer protective. Legislatures also increasingly have stepped into the fray to pass statutes that enhance developer rights.

The scope of protective statutes varies. Under a Pennsylvania statute, "no subsequent change or amendment in the zoning, subdivision, or other governing ordinance" can be applied to adversely affect the right of one with an approved plan for five years.[505] In one case when a municipality increased water and sewer connection fees, a developer sought exemption based on the statute. The court agreed, finding the utility charges were "other governing ordinances" that the city could not apply against the developers.[506] Yet, under the same statute, approval of an industrial park developer's subdivision plan did not vest any right to public sewer service.[507] Under Washington's law, a transportation impact fee was found not to be a "land use control ordinance" within the meaning of the vesting statute.[508]

---

[501] *Avco Community Developers, Inc. v. South Coast Regional Com.*, 17 Cal. 3d 785, 132 Cal. Rptr. 386, 553 P.2d 546 (1976).

[502] See supra § 5:28.

[503] Hagman, The Vesting Issue: Rights of Fetal Development vis-a-vis Abortions of Public Whimsey, 7 Envtl. L. 519, 539 (1977).

[504] See supra § 5:27.

[505] Pa. Stat. Ann. tit. 53, § 10508(4)(ii).

[506] *Board of Com'rs of South Whitehall Tp. v. Toll Bros., Inc.*, 147 Pa. Commw. 298, 607 A.2d 824 (1992).

[507] *Pequea Tp. v. Herr,* 716 A.2d 678 (Pa. Commw. Ct. 1998).

[508] *New Castle Investments v. City of LaCenter*, 98 Wash. App. 224, 989 P.2d 569 (1999).

Massachusetts law provides that if a developer submits a subdivision plan to a planning board for approval, and gives written notice of the submission to the town clerk before the effective date of a new ordinance, the law in effect at the time the plan was submitted governs the plan. If the board approves the plan, the same law will apply for eight years from the date of approval.[509]

Massachusetts also provides that the holder of a building permit may complete construction if the permit was granted before notice of a hearing on a subsequent zoning change was made, construction commenced within six months of issuance of the permit, and construction proceeded in good faith, continuously to completion.[510] Under the statute, the permit issued must be valid. If found invalid on appeal, the permit is void ab initio and a new zoning law applies.[511]

If a vested right statute confers immunity on one with "a building permit," a court may need to determine what "permits" qualify. A permit denominated a "zoning permit" properly issued allowing a quarry operation in a residential zone was held not to be a "building permit" in one case.[512] The statute in that case defined a building permit as one that contained a finding of compliance with the state building code, which the quarry permit lacked. Thus, the statute did not protect the holder of the quarry permit from the effect of an amendment to the code banning quarry use enacted after the permit was issued.

Generally, statutory vested rights laws do not abrogate the common law rule, which remains an alternative argument for one who does not gain protection from the statute. In the above case, for example, the court said that the quarry permit holder was entitled to try to establish a common law right by showing good faith substantial reliance on the permit.

The immunity that exists may be limited to new laws directed specifically at the development in question. Under the Colorado statute, a vested right remains subject to new laws "which are general in nature and are applicable to all property."[513] Under North Carolina's statute, an approved plan is not immune from new "overlay zoning which imposes additional requirements but does affect the allowable type or intensity of use."[514]

§ 5:31   Development Agreements

One solution to the vagaries of vested rights is the use of development agreements, which fix the rights of developers and municipalities as of a certain date and limit the power of government to apply new ordinances to approved projects.[515] Development agreements not only bring greater certainty for the developer, who obtains a promise

---

[509] Mass.Gen.Laws Ann. c. 40A, § 6. *Massachusetts Broken Stone Co. v. Town of Weston,* 430 Mass. 637, 723 N.E.2d 7 (2000).

[510] Mass. Gen. Laws Ann. ch. 40A, § 6.

[511] *Smith v. Building Com'r of Brookline,* 367 Mass. 765, 328 N.E.2d 866, 870 (1975).

[512] *Simpson v. City of Charlotte,* 115 N.C. App. 51, 443 S.E.2d 772, 775 (1994).

[513] Colo. Rev. Stat. Ann. § 24–68–105(2).

[514] N.C. Gen. Stat. § 160A–385.1(e)(2).

[515] See generally, Callies and Tappendorf, Unconstitutional Land Development Conditions and the Development Agreement Solution: Bargaining for Public Facilities after Nollan and Dolan, 51 Case W. Res. L. Rev. 663 (2001).

by the municipality to freeze the regulations on the site for a period of time, but they also may enhance the ability of municipalities to impose exactions and conditions. A number of several states have passed statutes specifically enabling development agreements.[516] At least one court has implied the authority.[517]

The California act provides that government may enter into an agreement with a property owner that deals with permitted uses, density or intensity of use, height and size of buildings, and the reservation or dedication of land for public purposes.[518] The agreement may specify a duration of apparently any length, but it is subject to annual review to determine developer compliance. The law that exists at the time of the execution of the agreement applies to the project during the agreement's duration. The government cannot apply newly enacted laws to the project that are inconsistent with the agreement. The rights under the agreement may also be assignable.

The idea of a "development agreement ordinance" is oxymoronic under the view of early decisions that condemned contract zoning. Yet, times have changed, and, as with the trend to accept conditional zoning, legislatures and courts increasingly accept development agreements as legitimate planning tools. The development agreement idea, however, is not entirely new. In some jurisdictions, annexation agreements have been used to achieve planning objectives. The development agreement also finds support in the vested rights statutes that confer immunity from zoning changes for a fixed period. While those statutes may not refer to an "agreement" being made, the legislatures that passed them likely understood that a city would engage in some form of bargaining or negotiation before it approved a plan that it knew would freeze development rights on the parcel.

The development agreement is not a contract in the common law sense, or at least, not simply a contract. California's statute declares a development agreement to be a legislative act, while Hawaii's declares it an administrative act.[519] If legislative, the land is in effect rezoned to permit a specific use pursuant to the terms of the agreement/ordinance. If administrative, the action is similar to the issuance of a special permit. Questions of validity may hinge on whether the focus is on the agreement's contractual or regulatory aspects.

Even if statutorily authorized, a development agreement can be seen as an illegal "bargaining away of the police power" violative of the reserved powers doctrine or, as a species of spot zoning not in the public interest and violative of due process. A governmental promise not to change the zoning of a tract, perhaps in an agreement in which the developer promises to dedicate land, may trouble some courts. Such a practice, however, is not revolutionary, and differs from conditional zoning only in degree and in terminology. The idea of a freeze may be justified by the need to meet due process rights of property owners as identified in some of the vested rights and estoppel cases. The question of whether the public interest, on balance, is served can be tested in the courts where resolution should follow the principles used in cases dealing with contract

---

[516] See, e.g., Ariz. Rev. Stat. Ann. § 9–500.05. For a complete listing, see §5.31 in the Practitioner's Edition of this work: Juergensmeyer and Roberts, Land Use Planning and Development Regulation Law (3rd ed.2012).

[517] *Giger v. City of Omaha,* 232 Neb. 676, 442 N.W.2d 182 (1989).

[518] Cal. Gov't Code § 65865.2.

[519] Cal. Gov't Code § 65867.5 and Haw. Rev. Stat. §§ 46–121 to 46–132.

and conditional zoning.[520] In California, the birthplace of the development agreement, a court has rejected the argument that a freeze on zoning pursuant to a development agreement is an unconstitutional surrender of the police power.[521]

The validity of a freeze may depend on the agreement's duration. Somewhat surprisingly, the California and Hawaii statutes set no time limit. In contrast, the Florida act sets 10 years as the maximum length.[522] If the agreement has no cutoff date, it is likely to cause problems when the parties attempt to enforce it decades after they executed it.

To overcome the argument that it has made an improper bargain, a legislative body may aid its case by identifying broad public benefits beyond the more obvious benefits to developers. The preamble of the California act, for example, notes the need for certainty to avoid the waste of resources, the discouragement of investment, and the increase in the cost of housing that occurs when local government halts development in mid-course. Florida law emphasizes as well the need to assure the provision of adequate public facilities.

A question may arise as to whether government termination, on grounds other than developer noncompliance, constitutes a taking under the Fifth Amendment requiring payment of compensation, or, in contract terms, whether it is a breach justifying an award of damages. If the reason for termination involves public health or safety, there is likely no breach since most statutes authorize termination or modification for such reasons of health or safety.[523] If no reservation of power is incorporated into the contract by the statute and if not otherwise express in the contract, a court might imply such a power to protect vital public interests without requiring the payment of compensation or damages. If, however, the agreement is terminated on grounds that would not meet the statutory grounds of health and safety, a regulatory taking might be found. The developer could point to specific expectations based on the contract, an important factor in takings cases.[524] Whether the loss sustained would be great enough would be fact-specific, requiring an examination of whether a reasonable use remained.

Another constitutional problem may arise with conditions or exactions that are a part of the agreement. If the agreement contains a provision that a developer will agree to deed land to the government or pay impact fees to support infrastructure needs, it is not clear whether the constitutional nexus test applies.[525] If the agreement is viewed purely as a police power measure, the test should apply, but it should not apply if the contractual aspects control. If the nexus test does not apply, and the government can bargain well, the government may obtain exactions it could not constitutionally impose by regulation. In enforcing settlement agreements, there is support for using contract theory.[526] In *Leroy Land Development v. Tahoe Regional Planning Agen-*

---

[520] See *Giger v. City of Omaha,* 232 Neb. 676, 442 N.W.2d 182 (1989).

[521] *Santa Margarita Area Residents Together v. San Luis Obispo County*, 100 Cal. Rptr. 2d 740 (Cal. App. 2000).

[522] Fla. Stat. Ann. § 163.3229.

[523] Cal. Gov't Code § 65865.3(b) (health or safety).

[524] See infra § 10:7.

[525] See infra § 10:5.

[526] See Callies and Tappendorf, supra note 515, at text accompanying n.131, for the view that the nexus test does not apply.

cy,[527] for example, the court held that the nexus test did not apply to a negotiated settlement agreement.[528]

VII. JUDICIAL REVIEW

§ 5:32 Introduction[529]

Provisions for judicial review of land use controls vary from state to state depending not only on the type of action being challenged but also on general state statutes relating to judicial review, specific zoning enabling act requirements, administrative review acts, and local ordinance provisions. A key determinant in the nature of judicial review is whether the challenged action is legislative or quasi-judicial.

The Standard State Zoning Enabling Act has no provision for review of legislative decisions, but some states do.[530] In the absence of special statutory provisions, parties usually obtain review of such decisions through a *de novo* action for injunctive relief or a declaratory judgment.

Many states authorize an appeal from the quasi-judicial decisions of local zoning boards or planning commissions under the same procedures available for appeals from state administrative agencies. If courts treat nominally legislative, site specific rezonings as quasi-judicial decisions, similar appeals may be available. Zoning and planning boards may or may not be included within the state administrative acts' provisions for judicial review of administrative decisions.

After an appropriate action is filed, the litigants face numerous issues. These include questions of standing and ripeness as well as defenses such as statutes of limitations. The standard of review and the type of relief available must also be addressed.

§ 5:33 Types of Actions

A. *Certiorari*

In most states, review of an administrative body's decision is by writ of certiorari. Developed at early common law, certiorari is an extraordinary writ issued by an appellate court directing a lower court to deliver the record in the case for review. Since the writ is designed to review decisions of lower judicial bodies, it is appropriately applied to boards of adjustment.

When the legislative body decides a matter ordinarily entrusted to a zoning board, it is exercising an adjudicatory function rather than a legislative function, so a writ of certiorari to it is appropriate. Some states provide for this by statute. For example, in North Carolina if a local city council issues special permits, the statute provides for review by writ of certiorari.[531] Others do so by judicial decision.[532] The writ of certiorari

---

[527] *Leroy Land Development v. Tahoe Regional Planning Agency,* 939 F.2d 696 (9th Cir. 1991).

[528] See also *Stephens v. City of Vista,* 994 F.2d 650 (9th Cir. 1993).

[529] Sections 5:32 to 5:36 and 5:38 to 5:40 are edited, modified and updated versions of Chapter 23 of Donald G. Hagman and Julian Conrad Juergensmeyer, Urban Planning and Land Development Control Law (2d ed. 1986). Chapter 23 was written by Fred Bosselman and Clif Weaver and we thank them for their permission to use these sections, as modified, here. Any errors occurring in the modification and editing process are ours.

[530] See, e.g., N.C. Gen. Stat. § 160A-364.1.

[531] N.C. Gen. Stat. §§ 160A-381(c) and 160A-388(e2).

is not generally available to review actions of legislative bodies where they are acting in a legislative capacity.[533] Review of such decisions is usually by injunction or declaratory judgment.[534] Certiorari is not the proper form of action to challenge the validity or constitutionality of an ordinance.[535]

In most states review is based on the record in accord with the common law, but some states by statute allow the court to hear new evidence and a few permit a trial de novo.[536] Under the common law the writ is discretionary, but it is by right under most statutes. The time to file a petition for certiorari is generally very short, often only from 10 to 30 days.[537] Most often, certiorari review is limited to reviewing whether the board acted within its jurisdiction, committed no errors of law, did not act in an arbitrary manner, and based its decision on substantial evidence of record.[538] Remand is generally the proper remedy allowing local zoning officials the opportunity to correct their error.[539]

B. Appeal

The term appeal is often used to describe any route to judicial review of a local board's decision. More narrowly, the term is applied to a provision for court review created by statute. Statutes differ from state to state, but usually, as with writs of certiorari, the term applies to judicial review of acts of administrative bodies when exercising quasi-judicial functions,[540] and review is on the record.[541] Caution, however, is in order since treatment of, and differences between, certiorari and appeal are highly state-specific. Thus, in some states appeal is de novo, where review is broader than under certiorari. In Pennsylvania, for example, "the purpose of an appeal *de novo* is to give a litigant a new trial without reference to the record established in the minor court, whereas *certiorari* connotes a review of the record established in the minor court with an eye to cure defects in procedure and legal error."[542]

C. Mandamus

A writ of mandamus is usually available to review administrative decisions that are ministerial, not discretionary.[543] A writ of mandamus requires that, (1) the petitioner has a clear legal right to the relief sought, (2) the respondent has a ministerial duty to perform the requested act without discretion, and (3) the petitioner has no ade-

---

[532] *Higby v. Board of County Com'rs of El Paso County,* 689 P.2d 635 (Colo. App. 1984).

[533] *Geisler v. City Council of City of Cedar Falls,* 769 N.W.2d 162 (Iowa 2009).

[534] *Fallin v. Knox County Bd. of Com'rs,* 656 S.W.2d 338 (Tenn. 1983).

[535] *Miami-Dade County v. Omnipoint Holdings, Inc.,* 863 So. 2d 195, 199 (Fla. 2003).

[536] See e.g., *Tennessee Waste Movers, Inc. v. Loudon County,* 160 S.W.3d 517, 521 (Tenn. 2005).

[537] *Battaglia Fruit Co. v. City of Maitland,* 530 So. 2d 940, 942 (Fla. 5th DCA 1988); *Schultz v. Gately,* 28 Mass. L. Rptr. 93, 2011 WL 768688 (Mass. Super. Ct. 2011) (60 days).

[538] *Merrill v. Town of Durham,* 2007 ME 50, 918 A.2d 1203, 1204 (Me. 2007).

[539] *State ex rel. Moore & Associates, Inc. v. West,* 246 S.W.3d 569, 574 (Tenn. Ct. App. 2005).

[540] *V. S. H. Realty, Inc. v. City of Rochester,* 118 N.H. 778, 394 A.2d 317 (1978).

[541] *DeSomma v. Town of Casco,* 2000 ME 113, 755 A.2d 485 (Me. 2000).

[542] *Gladstone Partners, LP v. Overland Enterprise, Inc.,* 950 A.2d 1011, 1014–15 (2008).

[543] *Mendota Golf, LLP v. City of Mendota Heights,* 708 N.W.2d 162 (Minn. 2006).

quate remedy at law.[544] Parties frequently employ the writ to seek an order directing the issuance of a building permit or restoration of a revoked permit.[545]

Parties frequently employ the writ to seek an order directing the issuance of a building permit, which the city denied them on the assumption their request was not authorized. Mandamus may also be used to order restoration of a revoked permit. If the government abuses its discretion, the writ is also sometimes available. Usually, such matters as issuance of a variance or special permit are discretionary, so the writ may not be an appropriate mechanism for judicial review.[546] However, if the ordinance clearly spells out the standards for a special permit and the applicant definitely meets the standards, a writ of mandamus may be proper.[547]

Mandamus is usually not available with respect to legislative action or inaction. However, when statutorily provided, a party may bring mandamus to require the local legislative body to hold hearings and issue a decision for curative amendments.[548]

D. *Injunction*

The injunction action is also a means of obtaining judicial review of an ordinance, typically in an action for a declaratory judgment. If a person is violating an ordinance or threatening to violate the ordinance, an injunction may be an appropriate mechanism for review.[549] The injunction may also be used where enforcement of the ordinance will result in irreparable damage, such as the threat of being jailed or fined. The injunction can also be used to challenge the constitutionality of the ordinance as applied, or to challenge a development order as being inconsistent with the land use plan.[550] Where there is an adequate remedy at law by a certiorari petition to review an administrative decision, an injunction is not proper.[551]

Injunctions have been used to prevent a city from interfering with a nonconforming use,[552] to test the validity of conditions attached to a permit,[553] and to test a zoning officer's construction of the ordinance.[554] While the injunction might be used to enjoin enforcement, it is usually not available to require or prevent the adoption of an ordinance.[555]

---

[544] *Muschiano v. Travers,* 973 A.2d 515 (R.I. 2009).

[545] *Pigs R Us, LLC v. Compton Tp.,* 770 N.W.2d 212 (Minn. Ct. App. 2009).

[546] *State ex rel. Parks v. Council of City of Omaha,* 277 Neb. 919, 766 N.W.2d 134 (2009).

[547] *Smith v. City of Mobile,* 374 So. 2d 305 (Ala. 1979).

[548] *Board of Sup'rs of East Norriton Tp. v. Gill Quarries, Inc.,* 53 Pa. Commw. 194, 417 A.2d 277 (1980).

[549] *Ramaker v. Cities Service Oil Co.,* 27 Wis. 2d 143, 133 N.W.2d 789 (1965).

[550] *Baker v. Metropolitan Dade County,* 774 So. 2d 14 (Fla. 3d DCA 2000).

[551] *McDonald v. City of Brentwood,* 66 S.W.3d 46, 50 (Mo. Ct. App. 2001).

[552] *London v. City of Detroit,* 354 Mich. 571, 93 N.W.2d 262 (1958).

[553] *Naper Aero Club v. DuPage County,* 30 Ill. 2d 447, 197 N.E.2d 1 (1964).

[554] *Carp v. Board of County Com'rs of Sedgwick County,* 190 Kan. 177, 373 P.2d 153 (1962).

[555] *State ex rel. Michigan City Plan Commission v. Laporte Superior Court No. 1,* 260 Ind. 587, 297 N.E.2d 814 (1973).

E. *Declaratory Judgment*

In many states, a declaratory judgment is the typical method of seeking judicial review of land use controls.[556] There must be an actual controversy—advisory opinions are not rendered in declaratory judgment actions. In most states, a landowner who has been denied a permit or who has been threatened by enforcement of a zoning ordinance is involved in a controversy and can bring a declaratory judgment action. The constitutionality of the ordinance, either on its face,[557] or as applied, is a proper matter for a declaratory judgment action.[558] An action for declaratory judgment is frequently combined with an action for an injunction. If an act is found invalid, its enforcement will be enjoined.[559]

F. *Choices of Remedy*

Mandamus, injunction and declaratory judgment actions may be barred if an alternative remedy is available, such as appeal or certiorari. For example, a Texas statute precludes attacks on most zoning board decisions except by certiorari.[560] Similarly, a California statute requires that no plain, speedy, and adequate remedy exist in the ordinary course before a writ of mandamus can issue.[561]

The general rule is that an injunction will not lie unless there is no adequate remedy at law.[562] An injunction may be available to test the constitutionality of an ordinance even though certiorari would also be a possible route.[563] The fact that the ordinance may be enforced by a criminal proceeding does not bar an injunction action, since the injunction affects property rights that the criminal remedy does not affect.[564] Similar problems of availability of an alternative remedy may apply with respect to declaratory judgment actions. Statutes that expressly authorize a municipality to seek an injunction have been interpreted as dispensing with the requirement of showing no adequate remedy at law.[565]

§ 5:34 Standing

A. *In General*

To bring an action, one must have standing, and the rules of standing may differ among the different kinds of action for review. The standing rules discussed here for state courts are distinct from Article III standing for federal courts, and they are notably less complex.

---

[556] Since an appeal or certiorari is often available for review of administrative decisions, a declaratory judgment might not be available to review administrative decisions. *Triangle Ranch, Inc. v. Union Oil Co. of California,* 135 Cal. App. 2d 428, 287 P.2d 537 (1955).

[557] *Morgenstern v. Town of Rye,* 147 N.H. 558, 794 A.2d 782 (2002).

[558] *Fulton Cama, Inc. v. Trustees of Village of Farmingdale,* 72 A.D.2d 813, 421 N.Y.S.2d 907 (1979).

[559] *Schwartz v. City of Flint,* 426 Mich. 295, 395 N.W.2d 678 (1986).

[560] *City of San Angelo v. Boehme Bakery,* 144 Tex. 281, 190 S.W.2d 67 (1945).

[561] West's Cal.Code of Civil Procedure § 1086.

[562] *Guido v. Town of Ulster Town Bd.,* 74 A.D.3d 1536, 902 N.Y.S.2d 710, 714 (2010).

[563] *Telegraph-Lone Pine Venture Co. v. Bloomfield Tp.,* 85 Mich. App. 560, 272 N.W.2d 136 (1978).

[564] State ex rel. Jacobson v. City of New Orleans, 166 So. 2d 520 (La. Ct. App. 1964).

[565] *Board of County Commissioners of Teton County* 131 P.3d 988, 994 (Wyo. 2006); *Conservation Com'n of Town of Fairfield v. Red 11, LLC,* 119 Conn. App. 377, 987 A.2d 398, 405 (2010).

As for decisions of the zoning board, the Standard Act provides that "[a]ny person * * * aggrieved by any decision of the board of adjustment or any taxpayer" may petition the court.[566] Courts in states that have dropped the phrase "or any taxpayer," may more narrowly construe standing for taxpayers. The Standard Act also gives "proper local authorities of the municipality" standing to "institute any appropriate action or proceedings,"[567] though the conferral of such standing by the statute does not mean that others could not bring an action.[568]

The courts have evolved essentially consistent rules on the standing issue for several different classes of litigants: those with an interest in the property that is the subject of the dispute, neighbors, taxpayers, competitors, citizens' associations, local governments, and extraterritorial litigants. A citizen with no particular interest likely does not have standing.[569]

B. Property Interest

The Standard Act requires that persons be aggrieved.[570] The owner of the property that is the subject of the dispute is an aggrieved person and owners include co-owners, option holders,[571] contract vendees,[572] and contract vendors.[573] Subsequent purchasers also have standing.[574] Mortgagees and long term lessees [575] also are ordinarily aggrieved, though it may be necessary for these plaintiffs to assert they are agents for the owner, that the owner has joined in the action, or that they have suffered special damages different from the main owner. Contract vendees have been found to have standing,[576] but a conditional vendee may not be able to bring a mandamus action because he may not be able to assert a clear and present right to force the concerned official to act as the vendee would have it.[577] In an action for injunctive relief, it is likely that most of the above described persons could meet the test of establishing special damages peculiar to them.

C. Neighbors

Where persons have interests in property that adjoins property which is the subject of a zoning decision, they are likely to be specially interested in and affected by the zoning decision and hence will have standing.[578] Generally, for non-abutting neighbors, the chances that a court will grant standing diminish in proportion to the distance of the property from the parcel directly affected. Persons likely to be granted standing include those in the same subdivision as the parcel whose use is in issue, or within the

---

[566] Standard State Zoning Enabling Act § 7.

[567] Standard State Zoning Enabling Act § 8.

[568] *Blankenship v. Michalski,* 155 Cal. App. 2d 672, 318 P.2d 727 (1957).

[569] *Bremner v. City & County of Honolulu,* 96 Haw. 134, 28 P.3d 350 (Ct. App. 2001).

[570] Standard State Zoning Enabling Act § 7.

[571] *Krmpotich v. City of Duluth,* 474 N.W.2d 392 (Minn. Ct. App. 1991).

[572] *Reinking v. Metropolitan Bd. of Zoning Appeals,* 671 N.E.2d 137 (Ind. App. 1996).

[573] *Appeal of R. & A. Miller, Inc.,* 18 Pa. Commw. 360, 336 A.2d 433 (1975) (contract vendor).

[574] *Santos v. Zoning Bd. of Appeals of Town of Stratford,* 100 Conn. App. 644, 918 A.2d 303 (2007).

[575] *Coastal Outdoor Advertising Group, LLC v. Township of Union, N.J.,* 676 F. Supp. 2d 337, 347 (D.N.J. 2009), aff'd, 402 Fed. Appx. 690 (3d Cir. 2010).

[576] *Sea Island Scenic Parkway Coalition v. Beaufort County Bd. of Adjustments and Appeals,* 316 S.C. 231, 449 S.E.2d 254 (Ct. App. 1994).

[577] *Metroweb Corp. v. Lake County,* 130 Ill. App. 3d 934 474 N.E.2d 900 (1985).

[578] *McGee v. Board of Appeal of Boston,* 62 Mass. App. Ct. 930, 819 N.E.2d 975 (2004).

distance specified in some ordinances for invoking an extraordinary majority vote of the board or legislative body, or persons to whom notice must be given under an ordinance, or persons owning parcels that must be shown on the site plan ac-companying a petition for a zoning change or administrative permission. However, the nature of the proposed use matters more than the distance measurement. While neighbors living 150 feet from a proposed addition to a house lacked standing,[579] those living 1200 feet to a half mile from proposed CAFO (hog farm) were granted standing.[580]

D.   Taxpayers

Generally, mere status as a taxpayer or resident of the jurisdiction is insufficient to confer standing.[581] The Standard Zoning Enabling Act provides that "[a]ny person * * * aggrieved by any decision of the board of adjustment or any taxpayer" may petition the court.[582] Some courts find this provision confers automatic standing on taxpayers,[583] while others do not.[584] Sometimes a statute provides for taxpayer action only if a certain number join in the petition or after the taxpayers have first requested municipal officials to take action.[585] The Pennsylvania Home Rule Act expressly excludes taxpayers.[586]

E.   Competitors

Generally, a competitor, as competitor, does not have standing, though the matter may be confused with the merits of the case, since zoning to regulate competition is generally considered invalid.[587] While the competition may damage the competitor, it is not the kind of damage entitling one to enjoin the activity.[588] The mere fact that a challenger is a competitor ought not be fatal to establishing standing if the challenger qualifies in another category, such as a neighbor. If this is the case, careful drafting the petition to qualify may avoid the problem by removing any taint.

F.   Citizen Associations

Associations have standing on the theory that if its members own property or reside in the area, the association, acting as their agent, is a proper party to sue.[589] In some states, such as Oregon, statewide citizens' organizations are frequent plaintiffs in land use litigation.

Some courts interpret associational standing narrowly,[590] requiring that all members of the association have standing in their own right.[591] Where courts deny standing

---

[579] *Bagnall v. Town of Beverly Shores*, 726 N.E.2d 782 (Ind. 2000).

[580] *Sexton v. Jackson County Bd. of Zoning Appeals*, 884 N.E.2d 889 (Ind. Ct. App. 2008).

[581] *Templeton v. Town of Boone*, 701 S.E.2d 709, 719 (N.C. App. 2010).

[582] Standard State Zoning Enabling Act § 7.

[583] *Jolly, Inc. v. Zoning Bd. of Appeals of City of Bridgeport*, 237 Conn. 184, 676 A.2d 831 (1996).

[584] *Committee for Responsible Development on 25th Street v. Mayor and City Council of Baltimore*, 137 Md. App. 60, 767 A.2d 906 (2001).

[585] N.Y. Town Law § 268.

[586] *Spahn v. Zoning Bd. of Adjustment*, 602 Pa. 83, 977 A.2d 1132 (2009).

[587] See supra § 3:17.

[588] *Ratner v. City of Richmond*, 136 Ind. App. 578, 201 N.E.2d 49 (1964).

[589] *Society Created To Reduce Urban Blight (SCRUB) v. Zoning Bd. of Adjustment of City and County of Philadelphia*, 682 A.2d 1 (Pa. Commw. Ct. 1996).

[590] See *Smithfield Voters for Responsible Development, Inc. v. LaGreca*, 755 A.2d 126 (R.I. 2000).

on the ground that an association is not a property owner and therefore is not an aggrieved person,[592] suing in the name of an association member who is also a property owner who falls within the class of aggrieved persons will avoid the problem.

G. *Local Government Units*

The local government may be aggrieved entitling it to appeal a decision from its own board of adjustment. The same is true of officers of the local government charged with supervision of the ordinance who believe the government has made an error.[593] A body that exercises only a quasi-judicial function ought not have authority to appeal a judicial reversal of its own decision to a higher court because of the general rule that subordinate courts have no standing to appeal a reversal of their own decisions.[594] However, the Maryland high court said that a body that exercises some quasi-judicial functions has standing if it would be adversely affected in carrying out other responsibilities by a judicial ruling on one of its own rulings. In that case, a planning commission was held to have standing to appeal a lower court ruling on the commission's own ruling in a subdivision matter.[595]

The Standard Act allows proper local authorities to institute any appropriate proceedings or actions, and an injunction has often been used for such purposes.[596] In some states a local government may institute an appeal from a final decision of its own zoning board.[597]

H. *Extraterritorial Litigants*

Earlier cases denied standing to extraterritorial litigants. A New York court held that the Town of Huntington was not an aggrieved party that had standing to challenge the issuance of a special permit by the Town of Oyster Bay to build a shopping center on the border of Huntington.[598] This narrow view of standing is understandable given the strong localized origins of zoning but it fails to recognize the irrelevance of imaginary borders to the harm to property owners.[599] Courts also usually denied individual property owners in other municipalities standing.[600]

A federal case, however, *Township of River Vale v. Orangetown,*[601] recognized extraterritorial rights, allowing River Vale to intervene to show that a decision of Orangetown would reduce property tax revenues and increase municipal expenditures.

---

[591] *Northeast Concerned Citizens, Inc. v. City of Hickory*, 143 N.C. App. 272, 545 S.E.2d 768 (2001).

[592] *Stocksdale v. Barnard,* 239 Md. 541, 212 A.2d 282 (1965).

[593] *Township of North Brunswick v. Zoning Bd. of Adjustment of Tp. of North Brunswick*, 378 N.J. Super. 485, 876 A.2d 320 (App. Div. 2005).

[594] *Smith v. Winhall Planning Commission,* 140 Vt. 178, 180, 436 A.2d 760, 760–61 (1981).

[595] *Calvert County Planning Com'n v. Howlin Realty Management, Inc.*, 364 Md. 301, 772 A.2d 1209 (2001).

[596] Standard State Zoning Enabling Act § 8.

[597] *Kline v. Board of Tp. Trustees of Chester Tp.*, 13 Ohio St. 2d 5, 233 N.E.2d 515 (1968).

[598] *Town of Huntington v. Town Bd. of Town of Oyster Bay*, 57 Misc. 2d 821, 293 N.Y.S.2d 558 (1968).

[599] See *Village of Mount Prospect v. Cook County,* 113 Ill. App. 2d 336, 252 N.E.2d 106 (1969).

[600] *Wood v. Freeman,* 43 Misc. 2d 616, 251 N.Y.S.2d 996 (1964) (no); *Miller v. Upper Allen Tp. Zoning Hearing Bd.*, 112 Pa. Commw. 274, 535 A.2d 1195 (1987) (yes).

[601] *River Vale Tp. v. Town of Orangetown*, 403 F.2d 684 (2d Cir. 1968).

In another case a court granted standing to a property owner of an adjacent tract across a town boundary to challenge a rezoning.[602]

The trend is to allow a challenge to zoning decisions both by neighboring governments [603] and by property owners in neighboring jurisdictions.[604] New York neighbors, who lived 100 feet from land approved for a subdivision by Connecticut board, were granted standing to challenge the decision.[605] This trend is consistent with the growing recognition of the regional impact of individual zoning decisions.

Standing in exclusionary zoning cases presents special considerations.[606] Several states grant nonresidents standing to maintain general exclusionary zoning challenges.[607] Unlike federal law, they need not show site-specific injury. In nonresidential exclusionary zoning, excluded groups may also have standing. In *Halfway House, Inc. v. City of Portland*,[608] for example, the court held that an operator of houses for prerelease prisoners and parolees had standing based on economic injury to challenge an ordinance that totally excluded such facilities from the municipality.[609]

§ 5:35   Ripeness

Courts will not entertain a dispute until it is ripe. Generally for a case to be ripe, a plaintiff must obtain a final decision as to how her land may be used and must exhaust administrative remedies.[610] The ripeness requirement is compelled by the justiciability doctrine that courts in our system of jurisprudence are to hear cases where there is an actual controversy which can be resolved by judicial decree. The facts of a case must be sufficiently defined to assure that the challenger is not presenting a hypothetical or speculative matter to the courts.[611] Ripeness is a matter of subject matter jurisdiction.[612] Just as Article III of the federal constitution limits the federal judicial power to actual cases and controversies, most states, by constitution or judicial opinion, similarly limit the judicial power.

§ 5:36   Defenses

A. *Finality and Exhaustion of Remedies*

A defense often raised by government is that the plaintiff had not obtained a final decision as to what she may do with her land and that she has not exhausted administrative remedies.[613] In other words, the contention is that the claim is not ripe. These

---

[602] *Braghirol v. Town Bd. of Town of Chester,* 70 Misc. 2d 812, 334 N.Y.S.2d 944 (1972).

[603] *Northern Trust Bank/Lake Forest, N.A. v. County of Lake,* 311 Ill. App. 3d 332 723 N.E.2d 1269 (2000).

[604] *Scott v. City of Indian Wells,* 6 Cal. 3d 541, 99 Cal. Rptr. 745, 492 P.2d 1137 (1972).

[605] *Abel v. Planning and Zoning Com'n of Town of New Canaan,* 297 Conn. 414, 998 A.2d 1149 (2010).

[606] See infra § 6:10.

[607] See, e.g., *Southern Burlington County N.A.A.C.P. v. Mount Laurel Tp.,* 67 N.J. 151, 336 A.2d 713 (1975)).

[608] *Halfway House, Inc. v. City of Portland,* 670 A.2d 1377 (Me. 1996).

[609] See also *Bossier City Medical Suite, Inc. v. City of Bossier City,* 483 F. Supp. 633 (W.D. La. 1980).

[610] *Molo Oil Co. v. The City Of Dubuque,* 692 N.W.2d 686, 693 (Iowa 2005).

[611] *B & B Enterprises of Wilson County v. City of Lebanon,* 318 S.W.3d 839, 848 (Tenn. 2010).

[612] *Iowa Coal Min. Co., Inc. v. Monroe County,* 555 N.W.2d 418, 431 (Iowa 1996).

[613] *Molo Oil Co. v. The City Of Dubuque,* 692 N.W.2d 686, 693 (Iowa 2005).

requirements generally apply with respect to mandamus, injunction and declaratory judgment actions.[614]

Government must be given an opportunity to consider and reach a final decision with respect to a proposed development. Anticipation of a denial will not suffice.[615] If an officer or board requests additional information or suggests that it might approve the application with some modifications, there has been no final decision. In its regulatory takings cases, the Supreme Court has held that a property owner must submit at least one meaningful application for development.[616] Some states by statute have made the presentation of specific development plans a prerequisite to judicial review.[617] Federal ripeness rules are considered elsewhere.[618]

The doctrine of exhaustion of remedies is concerned with whether parties have pursued *administrative* remedies. For example, under the Standard State Zoning Enabling Act and statutes in most states, appeals alleging an error in any order by an administrative official go to the board of adjustment.[619] If so provided, the appeal must be pursued. If a further appeal may be taken to the local legislative body, which then sits as a superior administrative body, that too must be followed. In addition, if, as is most often the case, a variance procedure is available, one must be requested. While the exhaustion demanded relates to *administrative* remedies, where a court sees the need for the government to have one real opportunity to rule on a development proposal, exhaustion may include seeking a rezoning.[620]

While finality and exhaustion often overlap in that an administrative appeal may result in a final decision, they are different concepts. As the Supreme Court has said:

> While the policies underlying the two concepts often overlap, the finality requirement is concerned with whether the initial decisionmaker has arrived at a definitive position on the issue that inflicts an actual, concrete injury; the exhaustion requirement generally refers to administrative and judicial procedures by which an injured party may seek review of an adverse decision and obtain a remedy if the decision is found to be unlawful or otherwise inappropriate.[621]

A facial attack on the validity of an ordinance is ripe upon the ordinance's adoption since it is the enactment that causes the injury. An example is a challenge to a billboard amortization ordinance where the billboard companies suffer an immediate harm upon passage of the ordinance.[622] The billboards are permitted to stand for a period of time, but their fate is known at the outset. Likewise, a challenger of an ordi-

---

[614] *Sprenger v. Public Service Com'n of Maryland*, 400 Md. 1, 926 A.2d 238, 252 (2007).

[615] *Town of Riverhead v. Central Pine Barrens Joint Planning and, Policy Com'n*, 71 A.D.3d 679, 896 N.Y.S.2d 382 (2010).

[616] *MacDonald, Sommer & Frates v. Yolo County*, 477 U.S. 340, 352, 106 S. Ct. 2561, 91 L. Ed. 2d 285 (1986).

[617] *Appeal of Miller*, 87 Pa. Commw. 254, 487 A.2d 448 (1985).

[618] See infra § 10:10.

[619] Standard State Zoning Enabling Act § 7 U.S. Dept. Commerce (1926).

[620] *Hendee v. Putnam Tp.*, 486 Mich. 556, 786 N.W.2d 521 (2010).

[621] *Williamson County Regional Planning Com'n v. Hamilton Bank of Johnson City*, 473 U.S. 172, 105 S. Ct. 3108, 87 L. Ed. 2d 126 (1985).

[622] See *Capital Outdoor Advertising, Inc. v. City of Raleigh*, 337 N.C. 150, 446 S.E.2d 289 (1994).

nance need not exhaust administrative remedies where the administrative board lacks the power to rule on validity.[623]

There are exceptions. Courts may not require exhaustion where only an issue of law is presented [624] or where one brings mandamus to compel the performance of purely ministerial duties.[625] A statute may permit an action without exhaustion of remedies under certain specified circumstances. If a zoning body fails to follow the spirit of a previous court decision, and zones again in a way that denies the property owner the previous relief, a court is not likely to require the property owner to begin again and exhaust administrative remedies.[626] Administrative remedies are not considered adequate in such a case.

If the plaintiff challenges the jurisdiction of the local agency, exhausting remedies may not be necessary.[627] Where exhaustion would be futile, a party need not attempt it, but no consensus exists in defining futility.[628]

States also require opponents of a development permit to exhaust remedies. If an appeal is available, they must file an appeal before seeking judicial review.[629] Courts differ as to whether parties affected by a government-initiated rezoning of property must seek a variance before bringing judicial proceedings.[630]

When the local government brings a civil proceeding to enforce its ordinance, it need not have exhausted all administrative remedies before commencement of the action.[631] Courts differ on whether the defendant in an enforcement action may raise defenses without having exhausted administrative remedies appropriate to those defenses. Thus, one court held that the right to claim a nonconforming use was lost because the defendant failed to register such use pursuant to the local ordinance.[632] The defendant may, however, assert the invalidity of the ordinance being enforced without exhausting administrative remedies.[633]

B.   Limitations Periods

Statutes of limitations applicable to actions involving land use issues are often much shorter than those one is accustomed to seeing in other areas. The Standard State Zoning Enabling Act, a version of which is used still by many states, requires that a challenge to a decision of the board of adjustment be filed within 30 days.[634] In

---

[623] *City of Amarillo v. Stapf,* 129 Tex. 81, 101 S.W.2d 229 (Comm'n App. 1937).

[624] *Bourgeois v. Town of Bedford,* 120 N.H. 145, 412 A.2d 1021 (1980).

[625] *Dato v. Village of Vernon Hills,* 91 Ill. App. 2d 111, 233 N.E.2d 48 (1968) (conditions).

[626] *Hillsborough County v. Twin Lakes Mobile Home Village, Inc.,* 166 So. 2d 191 (Fla. 2d DCA 1964).

[627] *Social Spirits, Inc. v. Town of Colonie,* 74 A.D.2d 933, 426 N.Y.S.2d 148 (1980).

[628] Compare *Call v. Feher,* 93 Cal. App. 3d 434, 155 Cal. Rptr. 387 (1979) (issuance of adverse agency staff opinion does not make appeal to agency futile) with *Orion Corp. v. State,* 103 Wash. 2d 441, 693 P.2d 1369 (1985) (where grant of relief would be inconsistent with purpose of statute it need not be sought).

[629] *Williams v. City of Kirkwood,* 537 S.W.2d 571 (Mo. App. 1976).

[630] Compare *O'Rourke v. City of Tulsa,* 1969 OK 112, 457 P.2d 782 (Okla. 1969) with *Florentine v. Town of Darien,* 142 Conn. 415, 115 A.2d 328 (1955).

[631] *Bradley v. South Londonderry Tp.,* 64 Pa. Commw. 395, 440 A.2d 665 (1982).

[632] *City of Scranton v. Baiderman,* 74 Pa. Commw. 367, 460 A.2d 1199 (1983).

[633] *Johnson's Island, Inc. v. Board of Tp. Trustees of Danbury Tp.,* 69 Ohio St. 2d 241, 431 N.E.2d 672 (1982).

[634] SZEA § 7. See also N.C. Gen. Stat. § 160A-388(e2).

some states the period may be as short as 10 days,[635] and many fall in the range of two to three months.[636] In some states, one statute applies to both administrative and legislative action. In others, there are separate statutes.

Short statutes of limitations are deemed necessary, particularly for multi-stage development projects, since the process required to obtain approval is often long and expensive. Once a permit is issued, the economic viability of the project often requires that construction commence as soon as possible. Yet, it is unsafe to proceed until the limitations period has expired.[637]

The statute of limitations to challenge zoning ordinances often accrues upon adoption and with administrative acts upon the board's final decision. Since the time period is often very short, it may be that the time will pass before an interested person learns of an action, leaving the possibility that an invalid law will continue in force. In one case, the state policy stressing need for finality led a court to apply a two-month statute of limitations to bar a challenge to a zoning ordinance as ultra vires.[638] But, another court held that "[w]here a local land use agency acts without jurisdiction in approving or denying a site plan, special permit, or other land use application, a challenge to such an administrative action, as ultra vires, is not subject to the 30-day limitations period."[639] While it is in the very nature of a statute of limitations to cut off an untimely claim, we are accustomed to think of private claims where evidence may grow stale with the passage of time. However, where the time bar occurs with zoning actions there is a possible injury to the public that cannot be judicially challenged.

There is nothing necessarily unconstitutional about a time bar for claims against public laws or acts. The Supreme Court has held that challenges of violations of constitutional rights may be time-barred except where to do so is inconsistent with federal policy.[640] A claim alleging a procedural defect affecting notice or due process rights in the enactment of an ordinance may be brought notwithstanding 30-day statutory time limit for challenging the ordinance.[641]

Some courts use a discovery rule to determine the accrual date, which generally extends the time to sue. For example, in *Fox v. Park City,*[642] the court refused to apply the statute limitations to bar a suit in a situation where the time period expired prior to the time interested persons knew or should have known of their rights. Many cases applying a discovery rule involve instances where actions were taken which violated local procedural rules. All too often, local ordinances fail to establish adequate notice requirements or set clear time periods.[643]

---

[635] Utah Code Ann. § 10-9a-704.

[636] N.C. Gen. Stat. § 1–54.1 (two months); Cal. Gov't Code § 65009(c)(1)(B) (90 days).

[637] See *State ex rel. Brookside Poultry Farms, Inc. v. Jefferson County Bd. of Adjustment*, 131 Wis. 2d 101, 388 N.W.2d 593 (1986).

[638] *Schwarz Properties, LLC v. Town of Franklinville*, 204 N.C. App. 344, 693 S.E.2d 271 (2010).

[639] *420 Tenants Corp. v. EBM Long Beach, LLC*, 41 A.D.3d 641, 838 N.Y.S.2d 649, 650 (2007).

[640] *Board of Regents of University of State of N. Y. v. Tomanio*, 446 U.S. 478, 100 S. Ct. 1790, 64 L. Ed. 2d 440 (1980).

[641] *Glen-Gery Corp. v. Zoning Hearing Bd. of Dover Tp.*, 589 Pa. 135, 907 A.2d 1033 (2006).

[642] *Fox v. Park City,* 2008 UT 85, 200 P.3d 182 (Utah 2008).

[643] *Grotto v. Little Friends, Inc.,* 104 Ill. App. 3d 105, 59 Ill. Dec. 848, 432 N.E.2d 634 (1982).

Many land use challenges are brought pursuant to the federal civil rights statute, Section 1983,[644] where the statute of limitations issue is a mixed matter of state and federal law. Since Congress did not create a statute of limitations for § 1983 actions, the Supreme Court filled the gap, finding that such actions are best characterized as torts and holding that the statute of limitations most appropriate for § 1983 actions is the state limitation period for personal injury actions.[645] State personal injury statutes of limitations vary, but periods from one to four years are common. While state law also applies to issues of tolling and extension, accrual of the cause of action is a matter of federal law. The courts hold that the time begins to run on a § 1983 claim when the plaintiff knew or should have known of the injury.[646] This may give injured persons substantially more time to sue to protect constructional rights than they have to challenge actions on state law grounds.

The time to file a facial challenge to an ordinance runs from its adoption and the time to file an as applied action runs from date of decision denying a permit application is denied or an enforcement action is begun.[647] Some courts have held that if a plaintiff timely files an applied challenge, she may raise a facial claim as well.[648] Furthermore, with First Amendment claims, courts often use the continuing injury doctrine in rejecting a statute that provides a time limitation running from adoption.[649] A strong argument has been made that "the facial/as-applied distinction ... characterizes the nature of the arguments on the merits, and bears no relation to the jurisdictional questions of when a plaintiff has been injured by the challenged law or when her lawsuit is timely filed."[650]

Cases challenging the validity of an ordinance should be distinguished from regulatory takings claims. In a regulatory takings claim, unlike an attack on a law's validity, the property owner concedes the validity of the law, but contends the law's impact is so severe that the Fifth Amendment requires that compensation be paid.[651] A regulatory takings claim accrues on the date of an ordinance's enactment if the ordinance itself severely diminishes the value of property.[652] In an as applied regulatory takings claim the statute of limitations will run from the time the government makes a final decision on the land's use.[653]

C. *Laches*

Courts apply the equitable defense of laches, often characterized as a species of estoppel, in situations to which no statute of limitations is applicable. If a party has delayed prosecuting a claim while the other party has proceeded in good faith to construct a building or continue an existing business, laches may bar judicial review. Laches is most frequently employed as a defense by the developer against a suit by

---

[644] 42 U.S.C.A. § 1983.

[645] *Wilson v. Garcia, All* U.S. 261, 105 S. Ct. 1938, 85 L. Ed. 2d 254 (1985).

[646] *Behavioral Institute of Indiana, LLC v. Hobart City of Common Council*, 406 F.3d 926 (7th Cir. 2005).

[647] *County of Sonoma v. Superior Court,* 190 Cal. App. 4th 1312, 118 Cal. Rptr. 3d 915, 918 (2010).

[648] *Gillmor v. Summit County,* 2010 UT 69, 246 P.3d 102, 111 (Utah 2010).

[649] *Santa Fe Springs Realty Corp. v. City of Westminster*, 906 F. Supp. 1341, 136–465 (CD. Cal. 1995).

[650] Sandefur, The Timing of Facial Challenges, 43 Akron L. Rev. 51, 77 (2010).

[651] *Travis v. County of Santa Cruz,* 33 Cal. 4th 757, 16 Cal. Rptr. 3d 404, 94 P.3d 538, 543–44 (2004).

[652] *Colony Cove Properties, LLC v. City of Carson*, 640 F.3d 948 (9th Cir. 2011).

[653] *Kottschade v. City of Rochester,* 760 N.W.2d 342 (Minn. Ct. App. 2009).

neighbors who unduly delayed bringing a challenge to the permit by which the developer obtained the right to build. In such cases the question of when the neighbors obtained legally effective notice is frequently at issue.

In exceptional circumstances laches may bar a local government from enforcement of a zoning ordinance because of a long history of failure to enforce the ordinance. Similarly, laches may bar a developer from claiming the validity of a permit when he took no action in reliance on it for a substantial time.

D.   Indispensable Parties

The failure to join an indispensable party can be a valid defense. This situation sometimes arises when a complex regulatory structure confuses plaintiffs who then choose the wrong agency as the defendant. Local governments most commonly employ this defense when neighbors seeking to invalidate a rezoning or variance sue them. In some states, the property owner who obtained the rezoning or variance must be joined as a defendant in such an action and the failure to do so gives the local government a valid defense.

E.   Estoppel and Waiver

Situations in which courts estop local government from changing a zoning ordinance because of a property owner's reliance on an existing permit are discussed elsewhere. In addition, an estoppel may arise if an agent of the local government acting within the scope of her powers induced an action later found in violation of the ordinance.

Generally, basic concepts of waiver apply to zoning contests. A party who agrees to conditions in order to receive development permission and takes advantage of the permit granted cannot then dispute the validity of the conditions. Some states have exceptions. For example, while California courts follow this basic rule, the legislature has modified it by providing for a residential developer to file a protest petition under limited circumstances. In Connecticut, one who accepts the benefits of a grant of development permission pursuant to an ordinance may, nonetheless, challenge the facial validity of the ordinance in an independent proceeding.

§ 5:37   Standard of Review

Courts have struggled to develop standards of review for land use decisions that balance the need to protect property owners from abuses of power with the desire not unduly to interfere with the legislative process.[654] Courts in zoning's early years often tipped the scales in favor of the latter concern to avoid entangling themselves in the affairs of zoning. In many states that has changed. As courts have grown jaded due to the practice of zoning authorities to both over and under-regulate, they have increased the intensity of their review. This is justified by a growing unease with the appropriateness of treating the actions of zoning authorities as the equivalent of Acts of Congress and acts of state legislatures, and deferring to them under separation of powers doctrine.

---

[654] See, generally, Mandelker and Tarlock, Shifting the Presumption of Constitutionality in Land—Use Law, 24 Urb. Law.1 (1992).

A. Legislative Acts

Traditionally, courts accord legislative actions of local authorities a strong presumption of validity. Using the fairly debatable standard of review enunciated in *Village of Euclid v. Ambler Realty Co.,*[655] the burden placed on the challenger is onerous. Often denominated the rational basis test by the federal courts in its more deferential application, a better name is the conceivable basis test. While the standards in state courts are enunciated in similar language, application varies from state to state. In some states significant deference is given. As the Michigan supreme court has said only if the law "constitutes 'an arbitrary fiat, a whimsical *ipse dixit,* and ... there is no room for a legitimate difference of opinion concerning its [un]reasonableness'"[656] will the law be overturned.

In recent decades, numerous state courts have expressed dissatisfaction with granting deference to local legislation. The most glaring difference is seen with respect to quasi-judicial site-specific rezonings adopted by local legislatures. When nominal legislative acts are so treated, they are disqualified from the deferential review to which true legislation is entitled.[657] Despite enactment by local legislative body, such rezonings in these states are subjected to greater scrutiny.[658]

The presumption of validity typically accorded legislation is reversed and higher scrutiny is used where actions taken affect fundamental rights or suspect classes. This occurs frequently in challenges to exclusionary zoning practices,[659] where special standards for review may be used. A classic example is the complex system for review of exclusionary zoning in New Jersey.[660] Also, in Pennsylvania, a local government that seeks to exclude completely any particular type of land use bears the burden of showing that the prohibition promotes public health, safety, morals or general welfare.[661] Similarly, in some Fifth Amendment takings litigation and First Amendment speech and religion cases, deferential review may not be used.[662]

B. Administrative Acts

In many states, courts review acts by administrative bodies with deference, and many begin review with a presumption of validity, albeit a weaker presumption than with legislation. The justification for deferring to administrative zoning board decisions lies in the judgment that the board members are experts in whom courts ought to place some trust or that they have a familiarity with local conditions that the courts lack. The expertise argument loses some force where, as often happens, there are no specific qualifications for membership on a board. Ruling on relatively vague standards like "unnecessary hardship," the common variance standard, also does not require expertise. Familiarity with local conditions also cuts both ways, as some courts worry that

---

[655] *Village of Euclid, Ohio v. Ambler Realty Co.,* 272 U.S. 365, 47 S. Ct. 114, 71 L. Ed. 303 (1926).

[656] *Kyser v. Township,* 486 Mich. 514, 521–22, 786 N.W.2d 543, 548 (2010).

[657] See *Fasano v. Board of County Com'rs of Washington County,* 264 Or. 574, 507 P.2d 23 (1973) discussed supra § 5:9.

[658] *Board of County Com'rs of Brevard County v. Snyder,* 627 So. 2d 469 (Fla. 1993).

[659] See infra §§ 6:1 et seq.

[660] See *Hills Development Co. v. Bernards Tp. in Somerset County,* 103 N.J. 1, 510 A.2d 621, 644 (1986).

[661] *McKee v. Montgomery Tp.,* 26 Pa. Commw. 487, 364 A.2d 775 (1976).

[662] See infra §§ 10:6 and 10:15 to 10:18.

the familiarity breeds influence peddling and results in lack of objectivity.[663] As the California supreme court has said, zoning boards often employ procedures that are "casual," necessitating meaningful review.[664] As some evidence of this lack of trust, several states provide for de novo review of local zoning board decisions.[665] The Maine courts grant deference to state administrative agencies because they have professional and technical expertise, but they review actions by "local volunteer boards" de novo.[666]

There is potential confusion between the presumption accorded, and deference given, legislative acts and the presumption accorded, and deference given, administrative acts. There are important differences.[667] Judges, after reciting the presumption of validity mantra, and saying, in language that resembles the fairly debatable standard for legislation, that they will not overturn an administrative ruling unless it is arbitrary or capricious, may engage in a review that is less deferential than that accorded legislation.[668] The review may be significantly less deferential. The North Carolina supreme court, for example, has "a very long tradition ... of significant judicial review of [quasi-judicial zoning actions]."[669]

Generally by statute, substantial evidence must support an administrative action.[670] The burden may remain on the challenger, but in many states, the board must make findings so that the court can assure itself that the board has acted properly.[671] In contrast, evidence need not accompany legislative action to sustain its legitimacy [672] and courts following the deferential rule will look for any conceivable reason to uphold a legislative act.

Where the administrative body is engaged in adjudicating rights of individuals, as is usually the case with zoning boards, procedural due process protections apply.[673] While the demands of due process vary, this generally means that those affected have a right to be heard and present evidence, a right to cross examination, and a right to a record with findings of fact.[674] Still, courts are fond of noting that "'procedural informality is the hallmark of administrative hearings.'"[675] Thus, it has been held not violative of due process to take evidence from a witness who is not under oath.[676] But, a court held due process violated when, at a second hearing on a permit application, a board received testimony adverse to the property owner after advising the owner's attorney that he need not attend the hearing since no additional evidence would be

---

[663] See supra § 5:14.

[664] *Topanga Assn. for a Scenic Community v. County of Los Angeles,* 11 Cal. 3d 506, 518, 113 Cal. Rptr. 836, 522 P.2d 12 (1974).

[665] *Roberts v. Southwestern Bell Mobile Systems, Inc.,* 429 Mass. 478, 709 N.E.2d 798, 804 n.15 (1999).

[666] *Isis Development, LLC v. Town of Wells,* 2003 ME 149, 836 A.2d 1285, 1287 (Me. 2003).

[667] *Ralph L. Wadsworth Construction, Inc. v. West Jordan City,* 999 P.2d 1240 (Utah Ct. App. 2000).

[668] *Sunderland Family Treatment Services v. City of Pasco,* 127 Wash. 2d 782, 903 P.2d 986 (1995).

[669] *Coastal Ready-Mix Concrete Co., Inc. v. Board of Com'rs of Town of Nags Head,* 299 N.C. 620, 265 S.E.2d 379, 382 (1980).

[670] See, e.g., Wash. Rev. Code Ann. § 7.16.120(4) to (5) and *Sunderland Family Treatment Services v. City of Pasco,* 127 Wash. 2d 782, 903 P.2d 986 (1995).

[671] *County Council of Prince George's County v. Brandywine Enterprises, Inc.,* 350 Md. 339, 711 A.2d 1346 (1998).

[672] *Jennings v. Dade County,* 589 So. 2d 1337, 1343 n.3 (Fla. 3d DCA 1991).

[673] *Jackson v. Spalding County,* 265 Ga. 792, 462 S.E.2d 361 (1995). See also infra § 10:13.

[674] *Coral Reef Nurseries, Inc. v. Babcock Co.,* 410 So. 2d 648, 652–53 (Fla. 3d DCA 1982).

[675] See *Mohilef v. Janovici,* 51 Cal. App. 4th 267, 58 Cal. Rptr. 2d 721, 734 (1996).

[676] Id.

heard.[677] If action is legislative, rather than adjudicative, procedural due process rights do not apply.[678]

The deal making nature of local zoning, whether labeled legislative or administrative, coupled with enhanced concern of bias and conflict of interest that exists by virtue of the fact that it is a localized process, suggests a need for meaningful judicial oversight.[679]

§ 5:38   Nature of Relief to Be Granted

A.   *Legislative Challenges*

When a legislative decision is found invalid, a court will ordinarily enjoin the operation of the legislation but will not tell the legislative body what new or alternative law it needs to pass deeming such action an "unwarranted intrusion into the legislative function."[680] The risk of this approach is that it allows the local government to avoid any meaningful effect of the court's decision by enacting a new law that continues to frustrate the landowner's desires in a slightly different fashion. Damages may be available, particularly under the federal civil rights statutes.[681]

From the developer's standpoint, the preferred remedy is an order directing the local government to allow the developer's proposed use, and this is available at times. For example, Pennsylvania and New Jersey by statute have made this remedy available in exclusionary zoning cases.[682] The Illinois courts reach the same result without specific statutory authority.[683] These are, however, the exceptions.

A judicial order rezoning property to a specific classification generally is improper if the city has legislative discretion to consider factors not in the record or pursue other avenues.[684] But, in some cases the courts have simply left the parcel unzoned,[685] or reinstated the plaintiff's original zoning.[686]

Courts may deal with the problem of abuse on remand in several ways. Other than the draconian and intrusive act of ordering a rezoning, a court may use its contempt powers to oversee the local government's response. The Georgia supreme court prefers finding a city in civil, or in severe cases of abuse criminal, contempt as a "'safer alternative' to 'the radical action of declaring property free from zoning restrictions,'" which unfairly punishes adjoining landowners.[687]

---

[677] *Sclavenitis v. City of Cherry Hills Village Bd. of Adjustment and Appeals*, 751 P.2d 661 (Colo. App. 1988).

[678] *Bi-Metallic Inv. Co. v. State Bd. of Equalization*, 239 U.S. 441, 36 S. Ct. 141, 60 L. Ed. 372 (1915). See supra § 5:9.

[679] See Mark W. Cordes, Policing Bias and Conflicts of Interest in Zoning Decisionmaking, 65 N.D.L.Rev. 161 (1989).

[680] *Speedway Grading Corp. v. Barrow County Bd. of Com'rs*, 258 Ga. 693, 373 S.E.2d 205, 208 (1988).

[681] 42 U.S.C.A. § 1983. See infra § 5:39.

[682] 53 Penn.Stat. § 11006-A(1).

[683] *Norwood Builders v. City of Des Plaines*, 128 Ill. App. 3d 908, 84 Ill. Dec. 105, 471 N.E.2d 634 (1984).

[684] *Goss v. City of Little Rock, Ark.*, 151 F.3d 861, 864 (8th Cir. 1998).

[685] *Board of Sup'rs of James City County v. Rowe*, 216 Va. 128, 216 S.E.2d 199 (1975).

[686] *H. Development Corp. v. City of Yonkers*, 64 A.D.2d 690, 407 N.Y.S.2d 573 (1978).

[687] *Alexander v. DeKalb County*, 264 Ga. 362, 444 S.E.2d 743 (1994).

A court may give the local government a specific time to develop new zoning for the property.[688] In some states a court may retain jurisdiction to review and approve an amended ordinance.[689] In Virginia courts require the local government to allow the plaintiff's proposed use but permit it to impose reasonable conditions.[690] Whatever relief is made available the court should not permanently enjoin the local government from changing its zoning because conditions may change in the future.[691]

B. Administrative Challenges

When a court reviews an administrative proceeding, such as the decision of a zoning board granting or denying a variance, principles of state administrative law usually govern the nature of the relief. If the court does not affirm the decision below, it will typically remand the case to the administrative board,[692] although in so doing it will sometimes establish principles of law that give the board little choice in deciding the case,[693] or it may direct the board to do or refrain from doing what the law requires.[694] On other occasions the court will find that the record at the initial hearing was inadequate to decide the matter and will remand to the board for new hearings to develop an appropriate record.[695] Generally, courts lack the authority to grant permits or variances.[696]

If the court concludes that no possible set of facts would support the board's decision, it may reverse the board without remanding for a new hearing.[697] Such a disposition would be appropriate, for example, if the court found that the board lacked jurisdiction to issue the decision. Most land use decisions are fact-sensitive, however, and the most common disposition is a remand to the board so that both sides may further develop the facts in a manner consistent with the court's statement of the law.

C. Consent Decrees

When parties settle a land use case, they often embody the settlement in a consent agreement approved by the court. Careful drafting of such decrees is essential.[698] A decision of the California Supreme Court interpreted a consent decree awarding the developer a vested right to proceed with the development of all its property substantially in accordance with an attached master plan. The court held that this decree did not prevent the local government from subjecting the developer to a subsequently enacted growth control ordinance severely limiting the number of building permits to be issued each year.[699] In another such case, the Georgia Supreme Court found that a consent decree between a kennel operator and the local government did not prevent more ex-

---

[688] *City of Atlanta v. McLennan,* 237 Ga. 25, 226 S.E.2d 732 (1976).

[689] See *Sultanik v. Board of Sup'rs of Worcester Tp.,* 88 Pa. Commw. 214, 488 A.2d 1197 (1985).

[690] *City of Richmond v. Randall,* 215 Va. 506, 211 S.E.2d 56 (1975).

[691] *May Dept. Stores Co. v. County of St. Louis,* 607 S.W.2d 857 (Mo. Ct. App. 1980).

[692] *Duggan v. Cook County,* 60 Ill. 2d 107, 324 N.E.2d 406 (1975).

[693] *Framingham Clinic, Inc. v. Zoning Bd. of Appeals of Framingham,* 415 N.E.2d 840 (Mass. 1981).

[694] *Loring v. Planning and Zoning Com'n of Town of North Haven,* 950 A.2d 494, 510 (Conn. 2008).

[695] *McCarron v. Zoning Hearing Bd. of Borough of Lansdale,* 37 Pa. Commw. 309, 389 A.2d 1227 (1978).

[696] *Belvoir Farms Homeowners Ass'n, Inc. v. North,* 355 Md. 259, 734 A.2d 227 (1999).

[697] *Speedway Bd. of Zoning Appeals v. Popcheff,* 179 Ind. App. 399, 385 N.E.2d 1179 (1979).

[698] See Callies, The Use of Consent Decrees in Settling Land Use and Environmental Disputes, 21 Stetson L. Rev. 871 (1992).

[699] *Pardee Construction Co. v. City of Camarillo,* 37 Cal. 3d 465, 208 Cal. Rptr. 228, 690 P.2d 701 (1984).

tensive relief against the kennel operator in a separate suit brought by a homeowners' association.[700]

D. Monetary Liability

Money damages may be available to a property owner or developer on a number of grounds. The Fifth Amendment takings clause requires that just compensation be provided when property is taken, and in some instances excessive regulations can be deemed to be takings.[701] Monetary liability for other constitutional and federal statutory rights is also available under Section 1983, the federal civil rights law.[702]

State tort law may also be the basis for suit for actions deemed ministerial or for governmental actions that are egregious in nature.[703]

§ 5:39   Relief Under Federal Law

Many land use regulations pose issues arising under various clauses of the federal constitution. Increasingly, parties also allege that land use controls conflict with federal statutes, such as the Fair Housing Act.[704]

A detailed analysis of the rules of federal jurisdiction and procedure is beyond the scope of this book. The tactical advantages of the federal versus the state courts to plaintiffs or defendants will vary from district to district. In any claim, however, consideration should be given to the question of whether to bring the case in federal court or state court.

A. Standing

The federal courts have their own complex rules of standing that have frequently tripped up unwary plaintiffs. Attempts to use the federal courts to challenge exclusionary zoning have often been defeated by the absence of a plaintiff who can demonstrate injury within the meaning of the federal requirements.[705]

On the other hand, the federal courts have been very receptive to First Amendment claims,[706] frequently using an "overbreadth" analysis that allows the plaintiff to challenge vague and overly broad regulations without showing that the particular defect will harm the plaintiff.[707]

B. Removal

If the plaintiff brings a land use case in the state courts, but raises federal constitutional or statutory claims in the complaint, the defendant is entitled to remove the

---

[700] *Life for God's Stray Animals, Inc. v. New North Rockdale County Homeowners Ass'n*, 253 Ga. 551, 322 S.E.2d 239 (1984).

[701] See infra §§ 10:2 to 10:11.

[702] See infra § 10:23. See also discussion of the federal fair housing action supra § 4:7 and infra § 6:8.

[703] See discussion supra § 5:28 regarding liability for wrongfully issued permits.

[704] See discussion supra § 4:7 and infra § 6:8.

[705] *Warth v. Seldin*, 422 U.S. 490, 95 S. Ct. 2197, 45 L. Ed. 2d 343 (1975). See discussion infra § 10:14. Standing in state courts is discussed supra § 5:34.

[706] See, e.g., *Schad v. Borough of Mount Ephraim*, 452 U.S. 61, 101 S. Ct. 2176, 68 L. Ed. 2d 671 (1981).

[707] *National Ass'n for Advancement of Colored People v. Alabama ex rel. Flowers*, 377 U.S. 288, 84 S. Ct. 1302, 12 L. Ed. 2d 325 (1964).

case to the federal courts even though there is no diversity of citizenship between the parties.[708] The federal court may not remand the case to the state court if the defendant has completed the steps necessary for a valid removal.[709]

Local government may take advantage of removal. Whenever a plaintiff files a case in the state court raising a federal constitutional or statutory issue, a comparison of the records of the local state and federal courts in regard to that particular constitutional issue will aid the tactical decision to remain in state court or remove the case to federal court. The propriety of removal by local government of takings claims has been questioned since, under Supreme Court rulings, federal courts lack jurisdiction over takings claim not first heard in state courts.[710]

C. Civil Rights Statutes

The federal civil rights statute, Section 1983, forms the basis for many land use cases. We discuss it in detail elsewhere in the book.[711] State courts have concurrent jurisdiction over § 1983 claims and many states have civil rights laws similar to § 1983 that may provide similar relief.[712] Moreover, some state courts may be more willing to award substantial damages in land use cases than most federal courts.[713]

D. Bankruptcy

Land use disputes occasionally arise in bankruptcy proceedings. The developer who seeks the protection of the federal bankruptcy court obtains a powerful ally. The court's power to absolve the developer of his debts includes debts owed by the developer to a local government. Creative bankruptcy lawyers have occasionally characterized a developer's obligation to comply with land use controls as a "debt." Usually, such an obligation would be a debt only if reduced to a money judgment in favor of the local government.[714] A bankruptcy court lacks authority to waive lawful police power regulations.

E. Eleventh Amendment

The Eleventh Amendment limits the jurisdiction of the federal courts involving suits against a state. Plaintiffs may commence such suits in the federal courts only if the state has expressly waived sovereign immunity,[715] or if Congress, acting pursuant to its powers under § 5 of the Fourteenth Amendment, so provides. Beginning in 1996,[716] the Supreme Court has handed down a series of cases that greatly increases the Eleventh Amendment immunity of states. In 2001, the Court held that state em-

---

[708] 28 U.S.C.A. § 1441(b).

[709] *Thermtron Products, Inc. v. Hermansdorfer,* 423 U.S. 336, 96 S. Ct. 584, 46 L. Ed. 2d 542 (1976) (abrogated by, Quackenbush v. Allstate Ins. Co., 517 U.S. 706, 116 S. Ct. 1712, 135 L. Ed. 2d 1 (1996).

[710] See infra § 10:10.

[711] See infra §§ 10:23 to 10:29.

[712] *Bell v. Mazza,* 394 Mass. 176, 474 N.E.2d 1111 (1985).

[713] *Dickerson v. Young,* 332 N.W.2d 93 (Iowa 1983).

[714] *Ohio v. Kovacs,* 469 U.S. 274, 105 S. Ct. 705, 83 L. Ed. 2d 649 (1985).

[715] *Pennhurst State School & Hosp. v. Halderman,* 465 U.S. 89, 104 S. Ct. 900, 79 L. Ed. 2d 67 (1984).

[716] *Seminole Tribe of Florida v. Florida,* 517 U.S. 44, 116 S. Ct. 1114, 134 L. Ed. 2d 252 (1996).

ployees cannot sue their employers for money damages under the Americans with Disabilities Act.[717]

Under most circumstances, local governments are not entitled to claim the benefit of the Eleventh Amendment because the Court does not treat them as agents of the state for that purpose. However, under those land use control programs having a significant element of state supervision, the local government might be able to claim that it was acting as an agent of the state for Eleventh Amendment purposes.[718] Since, however, such instances will be rare, local governments will often be the only governmental entity to sue.

F. Preemption by Federal Law

If a federal regulatory system preempts local regulation, the federal courts may grant injunctive relief against inconsistent local regulations. Preemption may be express or implied from statutory language, from the pervasiveness of the federal regulatory system, or from conflict between federal law and local regulation.[719] In *California Coastal Commission v. Granite Rock Co.,*[720] the Court found that the California Coastal Act was not preempted by federal law because it found no intent by Congress to preempt state or local control. The Court was aided in this finding by noting that the state law at issue was an environmental one, as opposed to land-use statute. While there is an unclear distinction between an "environmental" and a "land use" law, the suggestion that state and local use laws will be more likely to be found preempted in the former instance, creates, some suggest, "a substantial opportunity to state and local governments [to] recharacterize their regulatory processes to shade them toward environmental regulation."[721]

§ 5:40   Enforcement

A. Historical Inadequacies

Despite the theoretical breadth of the powers of enforcement, the enforcement programs of many local governments have historically been so lax that the chance that inspectors will discover many violations is remote.

B. Public Enforcement Actions

Zoning is typically enforced by civil action, but many zoning ordinances provide for criminal penalties.[722] As in other criminal cases, proof must be beyond a reasonable doubt,[723] and the burden is on the state. In several states and ordinances, the provi-

---

[717] *Bd. of Trustees of University of Alabama v. Garrett,* 531 U.S. 356, 121 S. Ct. 955, 148 L. Ed. 2d 866 (2001).

[718] See *Lake Country Estates, Inc. v. Tahoe Regional Planning Agency,* 440 U.S. 391, 99 S. Ct. 1171, 59 L. Ed. 2d 401 (1979).

[719] *Capital Cities Cable, Inc. v. Crisp,* 467 U.S. 691, 104 S. Ct. 2694, 81 L. Ed. 2d 580 (1984). Preemption of local law by federal and state law is discussed in more detail, supra § 4:24.

[720] *California Coastal Com'n v. Granite Rock Co.,* 480 U.S. 572, 107 S. Ct. 1419, 94 L. Ed. 2d 577 (1987).

[721] Kuhse, The Federal Consistency Requirements of the Coastal Zone Management Act of 1972: It's Time to Repeal This Fundamentally Flawed Legislation, 6 Ocean & Coastal L.J. 77 (2001).

[722] See Durham, N.C. City Code § 20.3.3.

[723] *State v. McNulty,* 111 Ohio App. 3d 828, 677 N.E.2d 405 (1996).

sions are in the nature of a civil action to recover a penalty.[724] Thus, where imprisonment is not an option, the rules of criminal proceedings may not apply.[725]

While the Standard Act does not specifically authorize the use of injunctions, the language is broad and general enough to allow them and injunctions are widely used to enforce zoning ordinances.[726] Some statutes specifically authorize injunctive relief.[727] Rather than a criminal sanction, it is the remedy violators would expect to be applied. Typically, the injunction is used to order compliance with the ordinance.[728] A major advantage of the injunction over a criminal proceeding is that the public can take an appeal with respect to the former. That likely will not be possible with respect to criminal proceedings. The violation of a zoning ordinance may well be found to be a public nuisance, or may, by ordinance or statute be a nuisance per se.

C. *Private Enforcement Actions*

Most zoning violations come to the attention of public officials because of complaints of private parties. In a sense then, the private party is the initiator of machinery to enforce the ordinance. The private party may also be the relator in a mandamus proceeding, forcing the public official to take action. Finally, a private person may be able to enforce the ordinance directly.

If a clear violation of the zoning ordinance occurs and the officer empowered to enforce the ordinance has no discretion in the matter, a private party can seek to compel enforcement through mandamus. As with other types of proceedings, there are problems of standing. While the petitioner of a writ must be beneficially interested,[729] enforcement is a matter of public interest that might entitle any citizen to bring the writ.[730] If there is some question as to whether there is a violation, mandamus may not lie. For example, where a city attorney concluded the ordinance had not been violated, the court held a private party unable to compel the attorney to institute a lawsuit.[731] Sometimes mandamus will not lie because the private party can sue directly to seek enforcement.[732] Since legislative bodies usually perform discretionary rather than administrative acts, mandamus does not typically lie against a legislative body.

Perhaps most typically, a private person seeks to enforce a zoning ordinance by bringing an injunction action. The major problem is that of standing. Some ordinances specially provide for standing, allowing a private action where special damages are shown.[733] Special damage could be shown most easily by a neighbor, but, in some instances, a showing can be made without being a neighbor. For example, residents at the beginning of a long road might object to the development of a large quarry at the end of the road that would generate heavy traffic. Taxpayers can bring injunction ac-

---

[724] *City of Palos Heights v. Pakel,* 121 Ill. App. 2d 63, 258 N.E.2d 121 (1970).

[725] *Town of McCandless v. Bellisario,* 551 Pa. 83, 709 A.2d 379 (1998).

[726] *Little Joseph Realty, Inc. v. Town of Babylon,* 41 N.Y.2d 738, 744, 395 N.Y.S.2d 428, 363 N.E.2d 1163 (1977).

[727] Minn. Stat. Ann. § 462.362; Wis. Stat. Ann. § 59.69(11).

[728] See, e.g., *Adams v. Cowart,* 224 Ga. 210, 160 S.E.2d 805 (1968).

[729] See Cal. Civ. Proc. Code § 1086.

[730] *Blankenship v. Michalski,* 155 Cal. App. 2d 672, 318 P.2d 727 (1957).

[731] Id., 155 Cal. App. 2d 672.

[732] *Pansa v. Sitrin,* 27 A.D.2d 636, 275 N.Y.S.2d 689 (1966).

[733] District of Columbia, Zoning Regulations § (105.2).

tions in some states. Notice to city officials demanding they take action and their refusal to do so may be a prerequisite to the taxpayer suit.

A private individual can bring an action on a nuisance theory alleging violation of an ordinance. While an ordinance or statute may only expressly provide for public enforcement, a private party may still be able to bring suit to abate a public nuisance upon a showing of special damages.[734]

A person specially injured can generally bring an action without a prior request to authorities to enforce the ordinance and without seeking a writ of mandate to compel them to do so.[735] If there is a statutory remedy providing private party a judicial route to seek enforcement of the ordinance, or some administrative route, they should pursue that route generally. Frequently, however, a statutory route is not available. In private enforcement actions, there has usually been no administrative or legislative decision that can be made the basis for appeal, and the statutory provisions often are based on such a decision. Mandamus may not be a proper remedy where the plaintiff can proceed directly against a violator of an ordinance.[736]

---

[734] *Towne v. Harr,* 185 Mich. App. 230, 460 N.W.2d 596 (1990).

[735] *Fitzgerald v. Merard Holding Co.,* 106 Conn. 475, 138 A. 483 (1927).

[736] *Pansa v. Sitrin,* 27 A.D.2d 636, 275 N.Y.S.2d 689 (1966).

Chapter 6

EXCLUSIONARY AND INCLUSIONARY ZONING*

Analysis

Sec.

---

§ 6:1   Introduction: The Evils of Exclusionary Zoning

The benign view of zoning is that it is a system with everything in its place and a place for everything. Indeed, early proponents analogized zoning to good housekeeping: keep the piano in the parlor, not the bedroom and the stove in the kitchen, not the pantry.[1] The dark side, however, was recognized by the first federal judge to address zoning's constitutionality, when he concluded that through zoning communities could classify "the population and segregate them according to their income and station in life."[2] As he predicted, zoning has played a significant role in establishing housing patterns that exclude, among others, persons of low and moderate income, racial minorities, and the disabled.

A zoning ordinance may also exclude undesirable nonresidential uses as well, such as mining or adult entertainment, or exclude general categories, such as all industrial uses. The total or near-total exclusion of such uses by very small or rural communities generally is not contested. However, when larger cities and towns in the path of development engage in exclusionary practices, a real impact is felt on the excluded, who then may question whether this is a proper use of the zoning power.

---

* For more detailed discussion and more extensive citations of authority of the issues covered in this chapter, see Juergensmeyer and Roberts, Land Use Planning and Development Regulation Law, Practitioner Treatise Series (3rd ed. 2012).

[1] See James Metzenbaum, 1 The Law of Zoning 9 (2d ed.1955).

[2] *Ambler Realty Co. v. Village of Euclid, Ohio,* 297 F. 307 (N.D. Ohio 1924), rev, 272 U.S. 365, 47 S. Ct. 114, 71 L. Ed. 303 (1926).

Varying, and likely mixed, motives lie behind exclusionary zoning. Some are fiscal in nature as governments want to encourage development of land uses that will produce high tax revenue and to discourage or prevent land uses that will cost government more than the tax revenue they produce. Business and industry typically are positive tax ratables, while high density, lower cost housing is negative. Education is the key cost component a community faces with housing: generally, the more bedrooms, the more school age children. Thus, lower cost single-family homes with four bedrooms are a poor tax deal. High rise luxury apartments with few bedrooms are a good tax deal.

Non-fiscal motivations also exist. High cost zoning requirements may be designed to achieve aesthetic benefits and preserve open space. They may also be used to "preserve property values" and protect the "character" of the community. Often, these are loaded terms that mask class and race discrimination. It is particularly troubling that state enabling acts and local government processes have been and are being used to further racial discrimination. We should expect more from government.

The practice of exclusionary zoning, or snob zoning as it is sometimes called when the exclusion has a socio-economic effect, is enabled by a parochial view of the police power that local governments exercise. Suburban communities look out for themselves. They do not concern themselves with the effects their actions have on other towns nearby. While the Supreme Court in *Village of Euclid v. Ambler Realty Co.*[3] approved the use of zoning to effect economic segregation in housing, it also warned that there were limits to the parochial use of the power. There might be, said the Court, instances "where the general public interest would so far outweigh the interest of the municipality that the municipality would not be allowed to stand in the way."[4]

As the popularity of zoning grew, local governments and courts ignored the regional welfare implications raised by the *Euclid* Court. Courts, in fact, turned regional welfare on its head by allowing suburban areas to justify exclusion based on the availability of land elsewhere in the region to serve the excluded use.[5] The *Euclid* Court's concern about the negative effect on regional welfare, is, as Professor Briffault has observed, paradoxical for if the proper focus of planning is regional, then local government ought not have the power to zone in the first instance.[6] In the ensuing half-century after the 1926 *Euclid* decision, the practice of exclusionary zoning flourished, and the Supreme Court did not restrain it. Indeed, in 1977, well after the practice was deeply entrenched, the Court gave its blessing to parochial zoning practices in *Village of Arlington Heights v. Metropolitan Housing Development Corp.*[7] In so far as the states are concerned, however, times are changing. As the Colorado supreme court has recognized "the growth of one community is tied to the growth of the next, thereby buttressing the need for a regional or even statewide approach."[8]

While nonresidential uses may be wrongly excluded, the exclusion of high density, lower cost housing is far and away the major problem with exclusionary zoning. The

---

[3] *Village of Euclid, Ohio v. Ambler Realty Co.,* 272 U.S. 365, 47 S. Ct. 114, 71 L. Ed. 303 (1926).

[4] Id., 272 U.S. at 390, 47 S. Ct. at 119.

[5] *Duffcon Concrete Products v. Borough of Cresskill,* 1 N.J. 509, 64 A.2d 347 (1949), discussed infra § 6:9.

[6] Briffault, Our Localism: Part II-Localism and Legal Theory, 90 Colum. L. Rev. 346, 369 (1990).

[7] *Village of Arlington Heights v. Metropolitan Housing Development Corp.,* 429 U.S. 252, 97 S. Ct. 555, 50 L. Ed. 2d 450 (1977), discussed infra § 10:14.

[8] *Town of Telluride v. Lot Thirty-Four Venture, L.L.C.* 3 P.3d 30, 39 (Colo. 2000).

increase in the cost of housing that results from the use of exclusionary controls is well documented.[9] The problem, though, goes beyond high cost housing in the suburbs. Exclusionary zoning promotes sprawl and raises the cost of providing municipal services.[10] Furthermore, those left behind find themselves alone in the urban core. Their tax base is diminished by the exodus of middle and upper income persons who have abandoned the city to these sprawl developments on the outskirts. Many businesses move out as well, and inner-city residents who wish to work at the fleeing businesses, are left with long, difficult and expensive commutes to work.

Communities use various methods to exclude low and moderate cost housing. They include regulations mandating a mini-mum lot size and minimum house size, large lot-frontage requirements, and limitations or bans on multi-family housing and manufactured housing. Zoning and subdivision controls are the standard tools used, but building codes requiring the use of expensive materials may also be employed. The gravity of these problems continues to produce proposals for change.[11] The increasing severity of housing shortages due in part to exclusionary zoning has led to the use in some states of the reverse technique of inclusionary zoning.

§ 6:2   Minimum Lot Size

The requirement of large minimum lot sizes is a popular device used by suburban communities. Minimum lot sizes of 5,000 square feet, 20,000 square feet,[12] 40,000 square feet, two, and five acres are common and have been upheld of ten. Courts sustaining these minimums generally do so on the ground that they carry out the standard zoning or subdivision enabling acts' goals of avoiding congestion in the streets, securing safety from fire, preventing overcrowding, and obtaining adequate light and air.

Health and safety justifications are generally makeweights. Communities enact minimum lot controls to preserve the character and tax base of a community. After all, it is called snob zoning for a reason. Still, in the absence of some form of heightened scrutiny, courts sustain minimum lot size requirements. That is certainly the case under federal constitutional law, where, so long as the complaints involve only wealth discrimination and an assertion of a right to adequate housing, courts apply a highly deferential standard of review.[13]

The courts of several states have come to recognize that the principle of "the larger the lot the better" does not promote the public interest. For example, the Massachusetts court invalidated a 100,000 square foot minimum lot size, noting that as lot size requirements increase, "the law of diminishing returns will set in at some point."[14] In suburban, non-agricultural areas, other courts have invalidated minimum lot sizes of one-half acre,[15] two acres,[16] and 2½ acres.[17]

---

[9] See Not in My Back Yard: Removing Barriers to Affordable Housing (Report of Advisory Commission on Regulatory Barriers to Affordable Housing 1991).

[10] See infra §§ 9:1 et seq. on growth management.

[11] See Frug, The Geography of Community, 48 Stan. L. Rev. 1047 (1996); Briffault, The Local Government Boundary Problem in Metropolitan Areas, 48 Stan. L. Rev. 1115 (1996).

[12] *Zanghi v. Board of Appeals of Bedford,* 61 Mass. App. Ct. 82, 807 N.E.2d 221 (2004).

[13] *Ybarra v. Town of Los Altos Hills*, 503 F.2d 250 (9th Cir. 1974).

[14] *Aronson v. Town of Sharon,* 346 Mass. 598, 604, 195 N.E.2d 341, 345 (1964).

[15] *Christine Bldg. Co. v. City of Troy,* 367 Mich. 508, 116 N.W.2d 816 (1962).

In a significant opinion striking down a four-acre minimum lot size, *National Land & Investment Co. v. Kohn,*[18] the Pennsylvania Supreme Court persuasively articulated the case against large lot zoning. Applying a form of heightened scrutiny, the court found the town's justifications wanting. Health factors, said the town, would require on-site sewage disposal. That concern, said the court, was to be dealt with by the town's sanitary board. The roads were alleged to be inadequate, but the evidence showed they would not reach their capacity for another seven years. The town wanted to preserve a greenbelt. Cluster zoning might do the job, said the court, but an area dotted with houses every four acres would not be a true greenbelt. The town's interest in preserving its semi-rural character was viewed as a matter of private, not public, interest. Large landowners, desirous of keeping out higher density housing, the court said, can enter into private controls to achieve their goals.

The town wanted to keep out "those pressing for admittance" and the question was whether the town could "stand in the way of the natural forces which send our growing population into hitherto undeveloped areas in search of a comfortable place to live."[19] The court concluded that its effort to do so did not promote the public interest and invalidated the ordinance on substantive due process grounds. While the ordinance implicated the third party rights of those living in cities, it violated the due process right of the landowner-developer to be free from arbitrary controls.

Large minimum lot sizes are most likely valid in bona fide rural areas where they operate as a technique of agricultural preservation.[20] In that context, courts have upheld minimum lot sizes of 80,[21] and 160[22] acres. So used, they have characterized them as "reverse exclusionary zoning," indicative of efforts by rural communities to prevent developers who cater to middle and upper income buyers from engaging in leapfrog development.

§ 6:3   Minimum Floor Space

Exclusionary zoning is also achieved through minimum floor space requirements. *Lionshead Lake, Inc. v. Township of Wayne*[23] is the most famous, or perhaps infamous, case sustaining the validity of minimum floor space requirements. Wayne Township, New Jersey, required a minimum of 768 square feet for single story houses, 1,000 square feet for two story houses with an attached garage, and 1,200 square feet for two story houses without an attached garage. A builder of houses containing 484 square feet challenged the ordinance. The court noted that small houses might create health problems, but more broadly found that ordinance preserved property values by precluding the construction of what it called "shanties" that could adversely affect the aesthetics and character of the community.

As with minimum lot size, minimum house size ordinances are generally based on makeweight arguments of health and aesthetics. Wayne Township, for example, sought

---

[16] *Board of County Sup'rs of Fairfax County v. Carper,* 200 Va. 653, 107 S.E.2d 390 (1959).

[17] *Du Page County v. Halkier,* 1 Ill. 2d 491, 115 N.E.2d 635 (1953).

[18] *National Land & Inv. Co. v. Kohn,* 419 Pa. 504, 215 A.2d 597 (1965).

[19] 419 Pa. at 532, 215 A.2d at 612.

[20] See infra § 13:10.

[21] *Ada County v. Henry,* 105 Idaho 263, 668 P.2d 994 (1983).

[22] *Wilson v. McHenry County,* 92 Ill. App. 3d 997, 48 Ill. Dec. 395, 416 N.E.2d 426 (1981).

[23] *Lionshead Lake, Inc. v. Wayne Tp.,* 10 N.J. 165, 89 A.2d 693 (1952).

to justify its ordinance in part based on a study showing that minimum house sizes were related to health. Overcrowding is a legitimate health concern, but an ordinance that places no limit on the number of occupants per square feet is a crude method to prevent it. Furthermore, a sliding scale, like Wayne Township's, based on the number of stories and the existence of an attached garage, makes a health argument nonsensical.

An aesthetics goal is closer to the mark, but still unconvincing. A large house is not necessarily pleasing to view, nor is a small one necessarily offensive. The relationship of house size to lot size is a legitimate aesthetic concern, but ordinances such as Wayne Township's do not control that. Size, however, does influence who will buy the house as the larger the house size required, the more affluent the buyers.

The New Jersey Supreme Court implicitly overruled *Lionshead Lake* in *Home Builders League of South Jersey v. Township of Berlin*.[24] *Berlin* held that an ordinance prescribing minimum floor areas for residences was invalid because it appeared to be directed toward economic segregation, rather than the public health or safety or the preservation of the character of neighborhoods.[25]

§ 6:4   Multi-Family Housing

Multi-family housing occupies a special niche in zoning history. In one of the most callous comments in zoning case law, the Supreme Court declared that apartments in districts of "private houses" were "mere parasites."[26] Perhaps the parasite reference was directed solely toward the monolithic, block tenements common in the early years of the twentieth century, but the implication that the occupants of those parasitical buildings were undesirable was inescapable. In fact, the federal district court judge in *Euclid* had held the ordinance unconstitutional in part because he found it classified "the population and segregate[d] them according to their income or situation in life."[27]

Apartment zones historically have served as buffer zones to protect the residents of the single-family home from the noise and traffic of commercial and industrial areas. This practice, of course, means that more people live close to intensive land use activities to protect the few. And, it means that the more numerous children in the apartments serve as buffers for the safety of the fewer children living in single-family homes. If further evidence of the class motive behind the different types of residential districts is needed, consider that the state not only permits people to live in multi-family housing, but the state builds much of it. At the same time, the state holds the power to exclude apartment dwellers from areas occupied by single-family houses on the theory that such exclusion promotes the public, health, safety and welfare. The matter needs reexamination.[28]

Multi-family, high density housing is not simply set apart from single-family detached homes, but is often provided limited land in many cities. It may also be exclud-

---

[24] *Home Builders League of South Jersey, Inc. v. Berlin Tp.*, 81 N.J. 127, 405 A.2d 381 (1979).

[25] See also *Builders Service Corp., Inc. v. Planning & Zoning Com'n of Town of East Hampton*, 208 Conn. 267, 545 A.2d 530 (1988).

[26] *Village of Euclid, Ohio v. Ambler Realty Co.*, 272 U.S. 365, 394, 47 S. Ct. 114, 120, 71 L. Ed. 303 (1926). For an almost equally unflattering view, see *Lewis v. Gollner*, 129 N.Y. 227, 29 N.E. 81 (1891).

[27] 297 Fed. 307, 316 (N.D.Ohio 1924).

[28] See, e.g., Ziegler, Jr., The Twilight of Single-Family Zoning, 3 UCLA J. Envtl. L. & Policy 161 (1983).

ed totally. The degree to which such exclusion is permitted generally tracks the permissibility of large lot zoning and minimum house size ordinances. In Appeal of Girsh,[29] a developer of luxury high rise apartments challenged an ordinance that totally excluded apartments. The Supreme Court of Pennsylvania invalidated the ordinance, and rejected as irrelevant the argument that apartments would burden the town financially. The jobs, said the court, had moved to the suburbs and the people were entitled to move there as well. Small communities that demonstrate credible and legitimate reasons can probably ban multi-family use.[30] The moderate or lower income multi-family housing developer faces an uphill struggle. In the rezoning game, a developer hopes to acquire property zoned for some unintensive use and obtain its upzoning to high density residential use. Once developed, the property generates an income stream that returns a profit on the developer's original investment. If the developer had developed land initially zoned for high density residential use, its profit might be nil or even negative because land so zoned is usually expensive. Therefore, the only profit comes from the public action of rezoning. This rezoning technique is one of the few ways moderate and lower income housing can be built, yet it typically will not work as envisioned since legislative bodies that routinely rezone for others, infrequently rezone for developers of lower income housing. When the legislative body does rezone, the voters often show their displeasure by petitioning for a referendum and then disapproving the rezoning.

§ 6:5   Manufactured Housing

Manufactured housing, which represents an increasing percentage of the country's housing stock, plays an important role in state and municipal planning efforts to ease the affordable housing crisis. Off-site built houses are not inexpensive, but, at a cost that is on the average one-half that of site-built houses, they are clearly more affordable. Also, they do not require government subsidies.

Despite the benefits of manufactured housing, negative attitudes, like those exhibited toward multi-family housing, have resulted in the placement of legal obstacles to limit the use of manufactured housing or mobile homes. While apartments were seen as parasites in single-family neighborhoods, mobile homes were viewed as "slums on wheels" occupied by "[t]railer folk [who] for the most part are nomads at heart."[31]

Communities may ban manufactured housing entirely, or find other ways to keep mobile homes out, such as allowing them for only temporary use, or subjecting them to building codes designed for houses built on-site, which they cannot meet.[32] Another stratagem is to allow mobile homes only in mobile home parks, and then fail to zone any land for such parks. Where not totally excluded, mobile homes may be subjected to onerous special permit processes or confined to such unattractive land that a de facto ban results.

---

[29] 437 Pa. 237, 263 A.2d 395 (1970).

[30] See *Country walk Condominiums, Inc. v. City of Orchard Lake Village,* 221 Mich. App. 19, 561 N.W.2d 405 (1997) (traffic safety).

[31] *Streyle v. Board of Property Assessment, Appeals and Review, Allegheny County,* 173 Pa. Super. 324, 98 A.2d 410 (1953).

[32] Federal law now preempts state or local laws regarding safety standards for manufactured housing. 42 U.S.C.A. §§ 5401 et seq.

The traditional bases of exclusion, that mobile homes and trailer camps are unattractive, unsafe, detrimental to property values and likely to retard city growth along desired lines, are less compelling today than may have once been the case. The perception that the occupants of manufactured housing are transients and undesirable neighbors may persist in some areas, but the reality is otherwise. The industry has changed dramatically. The image of short tubular trailers being towed around the country by people who could find no housing in the immediate post-World War II era is passé.

Mobile homes are no longer mobile. Once in place, only one in 100 is ever moved.[33] They are also safer and more attractive. In 1975, Congress passed the National Manufactured Housing Construction and Safety Standards Act to reduce the personal and property damage suffered due to poorly constructed homes and to improve their quality.[34] As a consequence, safety has greatly increased. The exterior design of manufactured homes is more like conventional houses in appearance. Municipal concerns that children from the mobile homes will overrun them, resulting in burdensome education costs, are imaginary. Most buyers of manufactured homes today have no children living with them.

Following the improvements in safety and appearance of manufactured housing, state laws have changed over the past 20 years. Some 20 states have legislation that deprives local government of the freewheeling ability of the past to discriminate against manufactured housing. These statutes vary in approach. Vermont sweepingly prohibits any zoning regulation that excludes manufactured homes, "except upon the same terms and conditions as conventional housing is excluded."[35] Under a statute in Maine, municipalities must allow the placement of manufactured homes on individual lots in all areas where other single-family homes are allowed and permit new mobile parks to develop and to expand in their current or new environmentally suitable, locations.[36] Others allow specific, but limited, differential treatment of manufactured housing.[37]

In some states, legislation simply prohibits total exclusion.[38] Under such statutes, an acceptable and common method of zoning is to limit manufactured homes to parks that are away from residential areas for site-built homes. However, municipal compliance with these statutes does not immunize the ordinance from review on constitutional grounds. New Hampshire's statute, for example, prohibits total exclusion but gives significant discretion to municipalities as to where manufactured housing can be located.

Courts in some states have held that cities cannot sequester manufactured housing in parks. A leading case is *Robinson Township v. Knoll*,[39] where the court held that a zoning ordinance that limited mobile homes to mobile home parks was an invalid exercise of the police power. Rejecting as outdated the view that mobile homes were nec-

---

[33] *Yee v. City of Escondido, Cal.,* 503 U.S. 519, 523, 112 S. Ct. 1522, 1526, 118 L. Ed. 2d 153 (1992).

[34] 42 U.S.C.A. §§ 5401 et seq.

[35] Vt. Stat. Ann. tit. 24, § 4406(4)(A). See *Appeal of Lunde,* 166 Vt. 167, 688 A.2d 1312 (1997).

[36] 30-A M.R.S.A. § 4358(2). See *Bangs v. Town of Wells,* 2000 ME 186, 760 A.2d 632 (Me. 2000).

[37] Fla. Stat. Ann. § 320.8285(5) (only roofing and siding materials).

[38] See, e.g., N.H. Rev. Stat. Ann. § 674.32; N.C. Gen. Stat. § 160A-383.1.

[39] *Robinson Tp. v. Knoll,* 410 Mich. 293, 302 N.W.2d 146 (1981).

essarily unsafe and unattractive, the court said that off-site built housing could not be subjected to a per se exclusion from other residential areas. Safety and appearance controls, however, were allowable to assure the compatibility of any manufactured home with the site-built homes in the area.

A number of courts, unconvinced that manufactured housing has changed from its darker "trailer" days or preferring to defer to the judgment of the legislative body, uphold limitations on the placement of manufactured homes. Aesthetic justifications are common.[40] Even in jurisdictions where the courts tend to be deferential in this context, some distinctions are beyond the pale. Thus, a court invalidated an ordinance, which prohibited manufactured housing in rural districts while at the same time allowing such uses as commercial stables and kennels, agriculture, and livestock production.[41]

In jurisdictions that allow such exclusionary practices, municipalities interested in excluding off-site built homes from areas of site-built single-family homes still must take care to exclude them specifically. If not specifically prohibited, a mobile home might be found a "single-family dwelling" allowable in a residential zone.[42] That, after all, is a normal reading of the term, and courts often construe zoning ordinances to allow the broadest use of land.

Federal law also limits exclusionary practices. The National Manufactured Housing Construction and Safety Standards Act expressly prohibits states from enacting safety standards that differ from federal ones.[43] Zoning ordinances that determine the permissibility of siting by reference to state or local building or safety codes that differ from the federal standards are preempted.[44] Under this provision, a local law that required manufactured homes to have a roof snow load of 40 pounds per square foot was preempted by the federal standard of 20 pounds per square foot.[45] The act, however, does not preempt ordinances that exclude manufactured housing on the basis that they may diminish property values.[46] Thus an aesthetic-based requirement that housing have a defined roof pitch has been upheld.[47] Courts have also held that a special charge for utility hookups of residential dwellings not meeting local energy efficiency standards was not preempted by federal law since the charge was not a construction standard, but a method to recover additional costs of servicing inefficient dwellings.[48]

Congress recently amended the 1974 Act's preemption clause in the Manufactured Housing Improvement Act of 2000, part of Title VI of the American Homeownership and Economic Opportunity Act. The new preemption clause provides that "[f]ederal preemption * * * shall be broadly and liberally construed to ensure that disparate State or local requirements or standards do not affect the uniformity and comprehensiveness

---

[40] See *Mississippi Manufactured Housing Ass'n v. Board of Sup'rs of Tate County*, 878 So. 2d 180 (Miss. Ct. App. 2004).

[41] *Petition of Carpenter v. City of Petal*, 699 So. 2d 928 (Miss. 1997).

[42] *Ciavarella v. Zoning Bd. of Adjustment of Hazle Tp.*, 86 Pa. Commw. 193, 484 A.2d 420 (1984).

[43] 42 U.S.CA. § 5403(d).

[44] *Scurlock v. City of Lynn Haven, Fla.*, 858 F.2d 1521 (11th Cir. 1988); *Colorado Manufactured Housing Ass'n v. Board of County Com'rs of County of Pueblo, Colo.*, 946 F. Supp. 1539 (D. Colo. 1996).

[45] *Michigan Manufactured Housing Ass'n v. Robinson Tp.*, 73 F. Supp. 2d 823 (W.D. Mich. 1999).

[46] *Texas Manufactured Housing Ass'n, Inc. v. City of Nederland*, 101 F.3d 1095 (5th Cir. 1996).

[47] *Georgia Manufactured Housing Ass'n, Inc. v. Spalding County*, 148 F.3d 1304 (11th Cir. 1998).

[48] *Washington Manufactured Housing Ass'n v. Public Utility Dist. No. 3 of Mason County*, 124 Wash. 2d 381, 878 P.2d 1213 (1994).

of the [federal] standards."[49] Whether this will alter the outcome of disputes remains to be seen.

A significant problem for those who own mobile homes is having to move when a park closes, and closings are on the rise. Parks, once relegated to fringe areas of town, may now be in the path of development. The consequent high land value induces the park owner to sell, leaving the homeowner the choice of moving the "mobile" home or abandoning it. Since relocation costs are high, and have risen dramatically in recent years, the choice may be illusory. In response, some municipalities require the park owner and park purchaser to assist the evicted homeowners by paying a portion of their relocation costs.

Park owners challenged a relocation assistance ordinance of Bloomington, Minnesota, claiming it was a taking. In *Arcadia Development Corp. v. City of Bloomington,*[50] the court rejected the claims. The crux of the takings claim was that the park owners were being forced to solve housing problems that were not of their making. The court disagreed, finding that park owners had reaped a benefit of charging rents for homes based in part on the immobility of the mobile homes.[51] The Washington Supreme Court reached the opposite result under a different rubric. It held the state's relocation act not to effect a taking, but found it did violate substantive due process because it unfairly singled out park owners to bear a social problem not of their making and was unduly oppressive.[52] The Washington court also found that a law giving tenants the right of first refusal was an unconstitutional private taking under the state constitution.[53]

§ 6:6   Fair Share Requirements

Lack of state or regional oversight has allowed local governments to practice their exclusionary ways. The traditional supposition that zoning is a local matter conflicts with the fact that in metropolitan areas local governments are not "islands unto themselves" but are part of a larger socioeconomic region. The consequences of parochial behavior are great, particularly in terms of the housing market. In recognition of this, in 1975, the state supreme courts of New Jersey, Pennsylvania, and New York imposed regional responsibilities on local governments to open their land for the provision of affordable housing.

The landmark case of *Southern Burlington County NAACP v. Township of Mt. Laurel*[54] was the first to require that a municipality's land use regulations provide a realistic opportunity for low and moderate income housing. In the early 1970s, Mt. Laurel Township, which lies seven miles from Camden and 10 miles from Philadelphia, presented the classic picture of a community practicing exclusionary zoning. The township was zoned for low density single-family housing (70%), industrial use (29%) and commercial use (1%). Sixty-five percent of the land was vacant. No land was zoned to permit multi-family housing or mobile homes.

---

[49] 42 U.S.C.A. § 5403(d).

[50] *Arcadia Development Corp. v. City of Bloomington,* 552 N.W.2d 281 (Minn. Ct. App. 1996).

[51] 552 N.W.2d at 286. The court also rejected due process and equal protection claims.

[52] *Guimont v. Clarke,* 121 Wash. 2d 586, 854 P.2d 1 (1993).

[53] *Manufactured Housing Communities of Washington v. State,* 142 Wash. 2d 347, 13 P.3d 183 (2000).

[54] *Southern Burlington County N.A.A.C.P. v. Mount Laurel Tp.,* 67 N.J. 151, 336 A.2d 713 (1975).

Mt. Laurel's zoning scheme was challenged as an illegitimate exercise of the police power. The New Jersey Supreme Court agreed and invalidated the ordinance, finding it to be violative of the due process and equal protection guarantees of the state constitution. Local zoning, the court said, cannot foreclose the opportunity for low and moderate income families to obtain housing, and regulations must affirmatively provide a realistic opportunity for such housing, at least to the extent of the municipality's fair share of the region's needs.

In the same year of the *Mt. Laurel* decision, the high courts of Pennsylvania and New York adopted similar positions. In *Willistown Township v. Chesterdale Farms, Inc.,*[55] the Pennsylvania court held that communities in the path of population growth are obligated to zone land where housing can be built that is affordable to all who wish to live there. In *Berenson v. Town of New Castle,*[56] the New York court held that zoning must provide a balanced and cohesive community, which includes provision of land for middle and lower income persons. The burden to prove an ordinance has an illegal exclusionary effect is onerous. In one case, where it was overcome, a court found a town's rezoning of land from multi-family to single family was exclusionary since it left the town with no land zoned for multi-family use. The court held that the town failed to consider the local and regional need for affordable housing, shifting the burden to the town to justify its action. The town could not carry its burden as it offered only several make-weight arguments similar to those offered by the town in the *National Land* case.[57]

Implementation of these judicially mandated fair share requirements has been inconsistent. The Pennsylvania and New York courts have not followed an activist approach to insure compliance.[58] Only the New Jersey court has done so. When the *Mt. Laurel* case returned to the New Jersey high court eight years after the court's fair share mandate,[59] the court found the township's ordinance remained "blatantly exclusionary," that there was "widespread noncompliance with the constitutional mandate," and it decided "to put some steel into" the original doctrine.[60] In *Mt. Laurel II,* the court enumerated criteria by which communities might determine their fair share. All areas of the state designated as growth areas by the State Development Land Guide were subjected to the *Mt. Laurel* obligation. This replaced the vague label of "developing municipalities." Besides the removal of restrictive barriers, inclusionary devices such as density bonuses and mandatory set asides were to be used. Mobile homes could not be prohibited. Builders' remedies were to be used to reward a successful challenger and provide specific relief that would lead to actual housing being built. All fair share litigation was to be assigned to a specific corps of three judges, and there were special procedures for review of residential exclusionary zoning cases. Once the obligation was met, other zoning measures to maintain high cost areas or to protect environmentally sensitive lands would be permitted.

---

[55] *Willistown Tp. v. Chesterdale Farms, Inc.,* 462 Pa. 445, 341 A.2d 466 (1975).

[56] *Berenson v. Town of New Castle,* 38 N.Y.2d 102, 378 N.Y.S.2d 672, 341 N.E.2d 236 (1975).

[57] Discussed supra, § 6:2.

[58] See *Heritage Bldg. Group, Inc. v. Plumstead Tp. Bd. of Sup'rs,* 833 A.2d 1205 (Pa. Commw. Ct. 2003); *Asian Americans for Equality v. Koch,* 128 A.D.2d 99, 514 N.Y.S.2d 939 (1987).

[59] 92 N.J. 158, 456 A.2d 390 (1983) *(Mt. Laurel II).*

[60] *S. Burlington County N.A.A.C.P. v. Mount Laurel Twp.,* 92 N.J. 158, 456 A.2d 390 (1983).

Mt. Laurel II provoked angry reaction in New Jersey because, in contrast to the toothless *Mt. Laurel I* opinion, it worked. Some praised it. Professor Haar, for example, lauds what he calls the "audacious activism" of the New Jersey court.[61] It also prompted the state legislature to act. In 1985, the state passed its Fair Housing Act, which established the Council on Affordable Housing (COAH) to oversee implementation of the *Mt. Laurel* obligation.[62] The supposed advantage of the act is that it establishes an administrative mechanism that can more efficiently mediate disputes than can the courts through protracted and costly litigation. COAH has the power to define housing regions and establish criteria by which fair share allotments are determined. Municipalities may apply to COAH for approval of their housing plans. While use of COAH is not mandatory, municipalities are encouraged to participate because a certification of approval by COAH creates a presumption of validity in favor the local zoning scheme should it be challenged in court.

COAH's effectiveness, as well as its existence, is in doubt. The agency has "never found political legitimacy."[63] In 2010, a court invalidated a proposed regulation (perhaps adopted due to political pressure by its opponents) that would allow a municipality to meet its fair share obligation by only providing additional affordable housing if job or residential growth actually occurred in the municipality.[64] COAH remains the target of some bent on eliminating it.

Legislative fair share mandates and enforcement mechanisms are used in other states as well. The first state to address the problem was Massachusetts, which in 1969 created a state agency with power to override local zoning decisions.[65] The act, commonly known as the anti-snob zoning act, provides developers of low and moderate cost housing with a special permitting process before local zoning boards. If a permit is denied, a direct appeal to the state Housing Appeals Committee lies.

Several states require that municipalities address housing needs in their comprehensive planning legislation. In California, local governments must prepare a general plan that includes a housing element that provides for the government's share of regional housing needs.[66] The legislation imposes specific limitations on the power of localities to disapprove affordable housing projects.[67] Florida also requires that local governments adopt a housing element as part of their comprehensive plan.[68] Connecticut [69] and Rhode Island [70] have started programs that share and mix the attributes of the Massachusetts and California approaches.

---

[61] Charles M. Haar, Suburbs Under Siege: Race, Space, and Audacious Judges (1996).

[62] N.J.Stat.Ann. §§ 52:27D-301 to 52:27D-329. The court upheld the act in *Hills Development Co. v. Bernards Tp. in Somerset County,* 103 N.J. 1, 510 A.2d 621 (1986).

[63] Mallach, The *Mount Laurel* Doctrine and the Uncertainties of Social Policy in a Time of Retrenchment, 63 Rutgers L. Rev. 849 (2011).

[64] *In re Adoption of N.J.A.C. 5:96 and 5:97,* 416 N.J. Super. 462, 6 A.3d 445 (App. Div. 2010), cert. granted, 205 N.J. 317, 15 A.3d 325 (2011).

[65] Mass. Gen. Laws Ann. ch. 40B, §§ 20 to 23.

[66] Cal. Gov't Code § 65584(a). See also Ariz. Rev. Stat. Ann. § 9-461.05(D); Or. Rev. Stat. § 197.307.

[67] Cal. Gov't Code § 65589.5.

[68] Fla. Stat. Ann. § 163.3177 and § 163.3184.

[69] See Conn. Gen. Stat § 8-30g.

[70] R.I. Gen. Laws §§ 45 to 53.

Local governments tend to resist fair share mandates. There is widespread non-compliance reported in California, for example, despite the fact that the courts have the power to suspend a city's land use powers if noncompliance is shown.[71] The lack of compliance is attributed to the high cost of bringing suit and the lack of organized representation of the people in the need of housing.

A fair share requirement translates into negative and affirmative duties. In the negative sense, a community must not overuse the common zoning techniques of large minimum lot and house size that increase housing costs. These standards must be relaxed for parts of town by rezoning land to permit high density housing. The removal of prohibitions on mobile homes may be necessary. These are essentially passive in that government is not to impede construction of low and moderate cost housing. Active steps may also be necessary. This may include the adoption of a streamlined permitting process for such housing, and the use of inclusionary zoning through mandatory set-asides or density bonuses. Another technique is the imposition of a maximum floor area to "ensure that appropriately sized residences are built on the lots * * * so as to allow for reasonably priced homes."[72]

§ 6:7   Inclusionary Zoning: Set Asides and Housing Trust Funds

Inclusionary housing programs are designed to achieve the actual construction of affordable housing. Often these programs address the needs of workers who cannot afford adequate housing in reasonable proximity to the high cost communities where they are employed. "Workforce housing," as it has come to be called, may be used to fulfill a fair share requirement imposed on local government by the state legislature or judiciary or they may be enacted voluntarily. A carrot or stick approach may be used. A density bonus may be given to a developer who promises to commit part of a development to low or moderate cost housing. Or, the permitting authority may require that an approved development set aside part of the development for low and moderate cost housing or pay a "linkage fee" for government construction of such housing.[73]

A.   *Inclusionary Set-Asides*

As a condition of development permission, a developer may be required to set aside a percentage of units for sale to persons of moderate income. Set-asides, which have ranged from 5% to 35%, most often fall in the 10 to 20% range. The units may be required to be on-site integrated units, or may be permitted off-site. An on-site requirement works as follows. Assuming a 20% set-aside and a 100 unit development, the developer must set aside 20 units. The 20 inclusionary units must be sold below market price, say 60%. Since the inclusionary units are dispersed among the non-inclusionary units, they must be of comparable quality. Sales are limited to persons meeting maximum income guidelines, often set at earning no more than 80% of the area's median income. Since a buyer is paying a below market price of $60,000, covenants in the deeds must impose resale controls to assure continued use by persons

---

[71] Cal. Gov't Code § 65755, discussed in Field, Why Our Fair Share Housing Laws Fail, 34 Santa Clara L. Rev. 35, 49 (1993).

[72] *Rumson Estates, Inc. v. Mayor & Council Of The Borough Of Fair Haven,* 350 N.J. Super. 324, 795 A.2d 290 (App. Div. 2002), judgment aff'd, 177 N.J. 338, 828 A.2d 317 (2003).

[73] See Nelson, Bowles, Juergensmeyer and Nicholas, A Guide to Impact Fees and Housing Affordability (2008).

meeting the income guidelines.[74] An off-site or segregated set-aside allows the developer to build the 20 inclusionary units apart from the other units.

A density bonus may be used to induce a developer to set aside some affordable housing, or it may be used in combination with a mandatory set-aside to mitigate any economic loss the developer might incur. In the 100-unit project with a 20% set-aside, a 20% density bonus would allow a total of 120 units, with 24 of them inclusionary units.

Inclusionary set-asides are most heavily used in New Jersey and California. A recent survey found 121 inclusionary ordinances in California.[75] Their use is spreading across the country.[76] Montgomery County, Maryland has used inclusionary zoning since 1973. A 12.5% set aside is imposed and a 20% density bonus given. The modest use nationwide is likely attributable to the political disinclination to employ what those in power and their constituents may regard as "Robin Hood" schemes.

Authority to enact an inclusionary zoning ordinance may be questioned. The Standard Zoning Enabling Act contains little language to support the implication of such power other than the general recitation of promotion of the general welfare. The authority to enact inclusionary programs is likely to be more easily implied in a "fair share" jurisdiction where local governments are under an obligation to broaden housing opportunities.

In *Board of Supervisors of Fairfax County v. DeGroff Enterprises, Inc.,*[77] the Virginia Supreme Court held that the state's enabling act only permitted zoning directed toward the physical characteristics of land. Just as the court had invalidated large lot zoning that excluded persons for socioeconomic reasons, it was invalid to include persons for such reasons. The court in *Southern Burlington County NAACP v. Township of Mt. Laurel*[78] found the *DeGroff* physical limitation view of zoning unpersuasive. Physical zoning limitations have socioeconomic effects, said the court, and it would be incongruous to suggest that inclusionary zoning was invalid when the need to use such a device had arisen by the employment of exclusionary techniques.

Developers may claim that inclusionary zoning is an uncompensated taking under the Fifth Amendment. While having to meet a set-aside obligation may diminish the profitability of a development, the economic impact will not be so severe as to amount to a taking in most cases. The more difficult question is whether, despite the amount of the loss, the shortage of affordable housing is a burden that is justifiably put on owners of undeveloped land and developers. This raises the nexus issue dealt with by the Supreme Court in the context of land exactions in *Nollan v. California Coastal Commission.*[79] The question to be answered is whether the development upon which the set-aside or fee is imposed generates a need for low and moderate cost housing or other-

---

[74] See *Alto Eldorado Partnership v. County of Santa Fe,* 634 F.3d 1170, 1172–73 (10th Cir. 2011) for a description of a 30% set-aside process.

[75] Talbert, Costa and Krumbein, Recent Developments in Inclusionary Zoning, 38 Urb. Law. 701, 703 (2006).

[76] In addition to California and New Jersey, they are used in Colorado, Florida, Maryland, Massachusetts, New Mexico, South Carolina, Texas, and Virginia. Talbert, Costa and Krumbein, Recent Developments in Inclusionary Zoning, 38 Urb. Law. 701, 703 (2006).

[77] *Bd. of Sup'rs of Fairfax County v. DeGroff Enterprises, Inc.,* 214 Va. 235, 198 S.E.2d 600 (1973).

[78] *Southern Burlington County N.A.A.C.P. v. Mount Laurel Tp.,* 92 N.J. 158, 456 A.2d 390 (1983).

[79] *Nollan v. California Coastal Com'n,* 483 U.S. 825, 107 S. Ct. 3141, 97 L. Ed. 2d 677 (1987).

wise aggravates the affordable housing problem the community faces to a substantial degree.[80]

As applied to residential developers, the nexus is easily met if on-site integrated inclusionary units are required to meet a goal of promoting socioeconomic integration. In such a case, the community has determined that non-integrated housing projects are harmful to the public welfare. Any project that does not contain a socioeconomic mix would exacerbate existing segregation.

The case is less clear for set-aside ordinances that do not require a socioeconomic mix of inclusionary and non-inclusionary units but have the sole aim of providing needed housing. There is disagreement whether that need is created by high cost residential development.[81] Resolution of a takings challenge will probably turn on the scrutiny the court applies in examining the nexus between the developers' activity and the need for affordable housing. The California courts apply a deferential test to fees or set-asides that are generally applicable, but suggest that higher scrutiny may be imposed on ad hoc requirements.[82] The issue of appropriate scrutiny required by federal law remains unanswered by the Supreme Court and lower courts differ.[83]

The easiest nexus showing arises with nonresidential development. Commercial development creates a wide spectrum of housing needs beyond that of highly paid executives. Since nonresidential developers are not in the business of building houses, a fee rather than a set aside is used. In *Commercial Builders of Northern California v. City of Sacramento,*[84] the court found no taking under a program that levied a fee against nonresidential development to be paid into a housing trust fund for the construction of low and moderate cost housing. The city produced "a careful study [that] revealed the amount of low-income housing that would likely become necessary as a direct result of the influx of new workers [from] the nonresidential development."[85] There is also a good chance that a fee, as opposed to a physical exaction of housing units, will not be subjected to a Fifth Amendment takings analysis, but will be tested under substantive due process or equal protection guarantees.[86]

Inclusionary zoning should not have difficulty meeting federal substantive due process or equal protection challenges, since low level scrutiny will normally be used.[87] The goals of increasing the supply of affordable housing and promoting socioeconomic integration are legitimate.[88] Charging those who contribute to the problem is likely a rational means to carry out those goals. Particular ordinances, of course, may be excessive and thus invalid under a substantive due process challenge. In one case, for example, a 50% mandatory set-aside on mobile home parks was invalidated on due process

---

[80] See discussion of the "substantially advances" test infra § 10:5.

[81] *Holmdel Builders Ass'n v. Township of Holmdel,* 121 N.J. 550, 583 A.2d 277 (1990).

[82] See *San Remo Hotel L.P. v. City And County of San Francisco,* 27 Cal. 4th 643, 117 Cal. Rptr. 2d 269, 41 P.3d 87 (2002).

[83] See infra §§ 9:8 and 10:5.

[84] *Commercial Builders of Northern California v. City of Sacramento,* 941 F.2d 872 (9th Cir. 1991).

[85] 941 F.2d at 873.

[86] See infra §§ 10.4 and 10.6.

[87] *Kamaole Pointe Development LP v. County of Maui,* 573 F. Supp. 2d 1354 (D. Haw. 2008); *Mead v. City of Cotati,* 2008 WL 4963048 (N.D. Cal. 2008). See also discussion infra §§ 10:12 and 10:14.

[88] See, e.g., *California Housing Finance Agency v. Elliott,* 17 Cal. 3d 575, 131 Cal. Rptr. 361, 551 P.2d 1193 (1976).

and equal protection grounds because the renters of the non-inclusionary units would have faced significant rent increases.[89]

B. Housing Trust Fund Fees

A fee may be charged instead of a set-aside. Usually called a linkage fee, the money is earmarked for housing trust funds used to construct low cost housing. The fee is particularly appropriate when applied to developers of nonresidential property. When existing affordable housing units are converted to another use, fees may also be charged to mitigate for the loss.

When linkage fees are used, specific enabling legislation may also be needed.[90] Courts may also regard fees as revenue, rather than regulatory, measures. If so, they must meet state law regarding the levying of taxes, and most will fail that test.[91] As noted above, the easiest case in favor of constitutionality can be made for the charging of fees to nonresidential development.

Relocation or conversion fees may be charged where existing affordable housing is eliminated. Several takings claims have been pursued by landowners who have paid these fees. The courts differ over whether the takings clause applies to fees, the degree of scrutiny to apply to such fees and to the propriety of charging them. Numerous states fund their housing trust funds in whole or in part by dedicating to the fund the revenue gained from real estate transfer taxes or recording fees.

In *San Remo Hotel L.P. v. City and County of San Francisco,*[92] owners of a residential hotel that provided housing to long term, low income renters sought permission to convert their existing use to rent to tourists for short term stays. The city required those demolishing or converting such housing to either build affordable replacement units or pay a fee into the city's housing trust fund. After paying the fee, the owners brought a takings challenge seeking a refund. The state supreme court found no taking. First, the court found that a fee requirement was not subject to the higher scrutiny applied by the United States Supreme Court to exactions of land. Then, applying a deferential standard of review, the court found the housing fee bore the necessary reasonable relationship to the loss of housing.[93]

The New York Court of Appeals, in contrast, found a physical and regulatory taking in *Seawall Associates v. City of New York.*[94] There, a city ordinance prohibited the conversion or demolition of single-room occupancy housing and required the rehabilitation and rental of such units. Employing heightened scrutiny, the court found the ordinance constituted a facial taking. Aiding the homeless was a legitimate state interest, but the court reasoned that the ordinance did not substantially advance that goal since the housing units were not earmarked for the homeless. Perhaps recognizing that earmarking the funds would cure that deficiency, the court added that homelessness was

---

[89] *Van Dalen v. Washington Tp.,* 205 N.J. Super. 308, 500 A.2d 776 (Law Div. 1984).

[90] See Merrill and Lincoln, Linkage Fees and Fair Share Regulations: Law and Method, 25 Urb. Law. 223 (1993). See infra § 9:8.

[91] See Wash. Rev. Code Ann. § 82.02.200.

[92] *San Remo Hotel L.P. v. City and County of San Francisco,* 27 Cal. 4th 643, 117 Cal. Rptr. 2d 269, 41 P.3d 87 (2002).

[93] 117 Cal. Rptr. 2d at 292–293.

[94] *Seawall Associates v. City of New York,* 74 N.Y.2d 92, 544 N.Y.S.2d 542, 542 N.E.2d 1059 (1989).

a complex problem and that there was a tenuous connection between the means and the ends making it unfair to single out the property owners to bear the burden of solving the problem.

§ 6:8 The Fair Housing Act

Under the Federal Fair Housing Act it is unlawful to make housing unavailable "because of race, color, religion, sex, familial status, * * * national origin [or disability]."[95] The act applies to discrimination by private [96] and public parties, and over the years it has been increasingly used to challenge exclusionary zoning practices. The bulk of the FHA zoning cases involve racial and disability discrimination. In addition, a few FHA zoning cases have dealt with discrimination on the basis of religion, sex and familial status.[97]

The FHA has had a dramatic effect on local regulation of land use, giving courts the power to override many traditional zoning laws. One study found that those challenging local law under the FHA have won 90% of the cases.[98]

A. Racial Discrimination

It is widely held that a violation of the FHA can be based on a showing of discriminatory intent or discriminatory effect.[99] Recognition of a discriminatory effects test under the FHA is particularly vital in race discrimination cases since the alternative of relying on the equal protection clause is typically not practical.[100] This is due to the Supreme Court's holding that a violation of the equal protection clause based on racial discrimination requires proof of intent, a showing that is difficult to make.[101] Under the FHA, discrimination on the basis of class does not equal discrimination on the basis of race.[102] Even if intent is shown, the government can escape liability if it can show that it would have made the same decision without using race as a factor.[103]

While plaintiffs have shown discriminatory intent in some FHA racial zoning cases,[104] the bulk of the cases rely on an effects or disparate impact test. While a narrow reading of the "because of language in the FHA could be interpreted to require a showing of motivation, most courts have held that proof of discriminatory effect establishes a prima facie violation of the act. The reasoning of the courts is that since most acts of racial discrimination today are not overt, a requirement that a person prove intent would frequently be insurmountable and would eviscerate the congressional goal to promote fair housing. Though the Supreme Court has not clearly endorsed an effects

---

[95] 42 U.S.CA. § 3604. When passed in 1968 the act covered race, color, religion, and national origin. Sex was added in 1974; familial status and disability protection were added in 1988.

[96] See discussion infra § 15:11 regarding private discrimination.

[97] See infra § 6:8.

[98] Salsich, Jr., Federal Influence on Local Land Use Regulations: the Fair Housing Act Amendments, 9 J. Aff. Housing & Community Dev. L. 228, 232 (2000), citing a study by the Judge David L. Bazelon Center for Mental Health Law in Washington, D.C.

[99] See *Macone v. Town of Wakefield,* 277 F.3d 1 (1st Cir.2002).

[100] See infra §10.14E.

[101] *Village of Arlington Heights v. Metropolitan Housing Development Corp.,* 429 U.S. 252, 97 S. Ct. 555, 50 L. Ed. 2d 450 (1977).

[102] *Hallmark Developers, Inc. v. Fulton County, Ga.,* 466 F.3d 1276 (11th Cir. 2006).

[103] See discussion infra § 10:14.

[104] See, e.g., *Dews v. Town of Sunnyvale, Tex.,* 109 F. Supp. 2d 526 (N.D. Tex. 2000).

test under the FHA, it has held that similar language in Title VII employment discrimination legislation does not require proof of intent, and lower courts have followed that lead in interpreting the FHA.[105]

Huntington Branch NAACP v. Town of Huntington[106] illustrates the operation of the disparate impact test. There, the plaintiff challenged a town's refusal to rezone a 14.4 acre parcel from single-family to multi-family to permit construction of a subsidized housing project that would be largely minority in occupancy. Using a disparate impact test, the court found the refusal violated the FHA. The town's population was 95% white and 3.35% black. Seventy percent of the black population lived in two neighborhoods. The town had a shortage of affordable housing, and while 7% of its overall population needed subsidized housing, 24% of its black population needed such housing. There was, however, little land zoned for multi-family housing and the little that was available was in the predominantly minority urban renewal area.

The Second Circuit found the town's rejection of the request imposed disproportionate harm on blacks as a group and had a segregative impact on the community as whole. The town was unable to rebut the prima facie case. To do so, the court said the town must present legitimate, bona fide justifications for its action, and show that less discriminatory alternatives were not available. Seven reasons were offered justifying the refusal to rezone; all were found wanting. Two justifications, that the rezoning was inconsistent with the town's zoning ordinance and contrary to the town's housing plan, both of which relegated the type of housing sought to the urban renewal area, begged the question. Three justifications could be resolved by design modifications. They included parking problems, inadequate recreation areas, and undersized units. Traffic was asserted to be a problem but there was no proof. Finally, health concerns were raised based on the proximity to a railway substation and sewage capacity. There was, however, no proof that the substation posed a health threat, and the sewage problem was not advanced until trial. The court ordered the land rezoned.

B. *Discrimination Against the Disabled*

Congress added protection for the disabled in the Fair Housing Amendments Act of 1988.[107] In contrast to the other classes of persons protected by the FHA, the provisions covering the disability protection are fairly extensive. Discrimination against the disabled is expressly defined to include a refusal to make reasonable accommodations in rules necessary to afford disabled persons an equal opportunity to use a dwelling.[108] The act defines a disability broadly to include "a physical or mental impairment which substantially limits one or more of such person's major life activities."[109] This includes, for example, the mentally ill, recovering addicts, and persons with AIDS. The act does

---

[105] See *Griggs v. Duke Power Co.*, 401 U.S. 424, 91 S. Ct. 849, 28 L. Ed. 2d 158 (1971).

[106] *Huntington Branch, N.A.A.C.P. v. Town of Huntington,* 844 F.2d 926 (2d Cir. 1988), judgment aff'd in part, 488 U.S. 15, 109 S. Ct. 276, 102 L. Ed. 2d 180 (1988) (per curiam).

[107] The acronym FHAA is sometimes used to refer to disability cases. We use FHA to refer to any claim under the original act or any of its amendments.

[108] 42 U.S.C.A. § 3604(f)(3)(B). Defining "dwelling," see *Lakeside Resort Enterprises, LP v. Board of Sup'rs of Palmyra Tp.,* 455 F.3d 154 (3d Cir. 2006) (residents' average stays of 15 days was sufficient to constitute a dwelling).

[109] 42 U.S.C.A. § 3602(h)(1). The statute confers protection on the "handicapped." In line with other similar acts, such as the Americans with Disabilities Act and Rehabilitation Act, the government uses the term "disabled" to avoid stereotypes and patronizing attitudes that accompany the word "handicapped." C.F.R. § 36.104, Pt. 36, App. B. See supra § 4:7.

not protect anyone who is a direct threat to the health or safety of others. A significant amount of litigation involving both private and public defendants has ensued interpreting these provisions.

Most zoning cases involve group homes of unrelated disabled persons seeking to locate in single-family areas. Typically, these homes are for the mentally retarded or for recovering addicts and alcoholics. Not all group homes for persons in need of supervision qualify as disabled under the act. It has been held, for example, that abused, abandoned, or neglected children do not suffer an impairment that substantially limits major life activities.[110]

Group homes often run afoul of zoning codes that limit use by a "family" defined as any number of related persons or unrelated persons up to a certain number.[111] The successful exclusion of group homes by way of such a definition depends on the FHA's exemption for "any reasonable * * * restrictions regarding the maximum number of occupants permitted to occupy a dwelling."[112]

In *City of Edmonds v. Oxford House, Inc.,*[113] the Supreme Court narrowly construed this exemption. The City of Edmonds' zoning ordinance defined a family as any number of persons related by blood, marriage, or adoption, but it allowed only a maximum of five unrelated persons to qualify as a family. Without seeking a variance from this provision, Oxford House opened a home for 12 persons recovering from alcohol and drug abuse in an area zoned for single-family use. The city charged Oxford House with violating its ordinance, and Oxford House claimed the city's ordinance, as applied to it, violated the Fair Housing Act. The city then sought refuge in the statutory exemption that permits occupancy restrictions.

The Court held that the limitation of five unrelated persons was not an occupancy limit within the meaning of the act. Distinguishing between land use restrictions, designed to foster a family environment, and maximum occupancy restrictions, designed to protect health and safety, the Court held that only the latter come with the FHA's exemption. Since the code provision limiting occupancy to five unrelated persons also allowed an unlimited number of related persons to live together, the Court concluded that its goal was preservation of family character, not health and safety. The dissent thought the plain language of the statute, exempting "any" restriction, precluded the Court from only exempting absolute occupancy restrictions.

Though *Edmonds* is important in that it deprived cities of a significant exemption from the disability coverage of the FHA insofar as single-family zoning is concerned, the case did not decide whether a facially neutral code provision that precludes group homes of unrelated disabled persons from living in single-family areas is unlawful or whether allowance of such homes in other zones is a reasonable accommodation under the FHA.[114]

---

[110] See, e.g., *Cohen v. Township of Cheltenham, Pennsylvania,* 174 F. Supp. 2d 307 (E.D. Pa. 2001).

[111] See supra § 4:5.

[112] 42 U.S.C.A. § 3607(b)(1).

[113] *City of Edmonds v. Oxford House, Inc.,* 514 U.S. 725, 115 S. Ct. 1776, 131 L. Ed. 2d 801 (1995).

[114] 514 U.S. at 737, 115 S. Ct. at 1783.

Compliance with the obligation to reasonably accommodate a person generates the most litigation. Most courts require the plaintiff prove the reasonableness of a proposed accommodation.[115] To prevail, a plaintiff must show the requested accommodation is necessary to afford an equal opportunity to use and enjoy housing.[116] It is not sufficient to show the law inconveniences the disabled person.[117] A "but for" causation standard is used, meaning that without the accommodation, the plaintiff will be denied an equal opportunity to obtain the housing of her choice. A reasonable accommodation may require preferential treatment of the disabled.[118] If a requested accommodation fundamentally alters the nature of the program or imposes undue financial or administrative burdens on the city, it is unreasonable.[119]

In examining the merits of a government justification for refusing to accommodate a request, courts disagree on the standard of review. In Oxford House-C v. City of St. Louis,[120] the single-family classification generally allowed up to three unrelated persons, but raised the limit to eight for group homes for the disabled. This was still too limiting for the plaintiff who claimed that the eight person limit would destroy the financial viability of the home. Using the deferential rational basis test borrowed from equal protection jurisprudence, the court concluded the limit of eight was justified by the city's interest in maintaining the quiet of a residential area.[121]

Other courts have found it inappropriate to transport equal protection analysis into an FHA case. In *Bangerter v. Orem City Corporation,*[122] the court noted that while rational basis review is the standard applied with respect to the mentally retarded under equal protection, the fact that the disabled are an expressly protected class under the statute requires placing a heavier burden on government.

Many ordinances subject group homes to a special use permit process. If the process only burdens the disabled it violates the FHA, and likely the equal protection clause as well.[123] Even facially neutral conditions may be deemed unjustified, such as a requirement that a group reapply for a permit every year or a 24-hour supervision requirement.[124]

It has been suggested that a special permitting process that is facially neutral and applies to similar uses may be invalid on the basis that the permitting process itself is stigmatizing.[125] The Seventh Circuit, however, found that towns have a legitimate interest in conducting nondiscriminatory, public hearings.[126] At a minimum, protected

---

[115] *Groner v. Golden Gate Gardens Apartments,* 250 F.3d 1039 (6th Cir. 2001).

[116] *Community Services, Inc. v. Wind Gap Mun. Authority,* 421 F.3d 170 (3d Cir. 2005).

[117] *Wisconsin Community Services, Inc. v. City of Milwaukee,* 465 F.3d 737, 749 (7th Cir. 2006).

[118] See *U.S. Airways, Inc. v. Barnett,* 535 U.S. 391, 122 S. Ct. 1516, 152 L. Ed. 2d 589 (2002). See also discussion supra § 5:17 regarding variances.

[119] *Huberty v. Washington County Housing & Redevelopment Authority,* 374 F. Supp. 2d 768 (D. Minn. 2005).

[120] *Oxford House-C v. City of St. Louis,* 77 F.3d 249 (8th Cir. 1996).

[121] 77 F.3d at 252 (1974), discussed infra § 10:14.

[122] *Bangerter v. Orem City Corp.,* 46 F.3d 1491 (10th Cir. 1995).

[123] See *City of Cleburne, Tex. v. Cleburne Living Center,* 473 U.S. 432, 105 S. Ct. 3249, 87 L. Ed. 2d 313 (1985) discussed supra § 4:6, and infra § 10:14.

[124] *Turning Point, Inc. v. City of Caldwell,* 74 F.3d 941 (9th Cir. 1996).

[125] *Stewart B. McKinney Foundation, Inc. v. Town Plan and Zoning Com'n of Town of Fairfield,* 790 F. Supp. 1197, 1219–20 (D. Conn. 1992).

[126] *U.S. v. Village of Palatine,* 37 F.3d 1230 (7th Cir. 1994).

persons must use available special permit procedures in order to make a reasonable accommodation request. Offsetting the downside of having to endure the public hostility that often erupts at these hearing is the fact that the hearing may provide evidence of discriminatory intent.

Some ordinances require spacing between group homes to promote the deinstitutionalization process and prevent the reisolation of the disabled in new group home ghettoes. For that reason, the Eighth Circuit found that a state mandated dispersal requirement of one quarter mile between group homes did not violate the FHA.[127] In contrast, the Sixth and Seventh Circuits found such a statute violated the FHA.[128] The latter court read an intervening Supreme Court decision in the employment context to reject the idea that the benign desire to help the disabled was not intentional discrimination. The court further found that the state did not carry its burden of proving the necessity of dispersal.

The "fear" that the FHA will spell the end of the single-family zone that lies at the heart of Euclidean zoning has not come to pass. The Court labeled such a fear "exaggerated" in *Edmonds*.[129] While local governments clearly must treat disabled applicants with care, the FHA was not designed, says Judge Posner, as an "engine for the destruction of zoning."[130] Certainly, the Act's reasonable accommodation requirement has a significant impact on the handling of requests for variances.[131] Beyond local governmental restrictions, economics also play a part. It is likely that higher density areas of low and moderate income housing will accept the great majority of group homes. High land values in the more exclusive single-family areas will make them economically unfeasible as sites for such homes even if federal law allows them to locate there.

C. *Familial Status*

The Fair Housing Act prohibits discrimination on the basis of "familial status," which "means one or more individuals (who have not attained the age of 18 years) being domiciled with—(1) a parent or another person having legal custody of such individual or individuals; or (2) the designee of such parent or other person having such custody, with the written permission of such parent or other person."[132] Most cases under this provision have involved the private sphere arising in the landlord tenant context, but a few cases have involved zoning activities.

The definition of "familial status" is intentionally limited. It does not include, as a number of state laws do, discrimination on the basis of marital status. The provision was adopted to stem the tide of discrimination against families with children, but the Act exempts bona fide housing for seniors. Legislative history indicates that Congress was concerned primarily with the plight of single families, not with the plight of families who desired to live communally.

---

[127] *Familystyle of St. Paul, Inc. v. City of St. Paul, Minn.*, 923 F.2d 91 (8th Cir. 1991).

[128] *Oconomowoc Residential Programs v. City of Milwaukee*, 300 F.3d 775 (7th Cir. 2002).

[129] *City of Edmonds v. Oxford House, Inc.*, 514 U.S. 725, 737, 115 S. Ct. 1776, 1783, 131 L. Ed. 2d 801 (1995).

[130] *Hemisphere Bldg. Co., Inc. v. Village of Richton Park*, 171 F.3d 437, 440 (7th Cir. 1999).

[131] See supra §§ 5:14 to 5:23.

[132] 42 U.S.CA. § 3602(k).

Group homes, which may not qualify for protection under the disability provision discussed above, have, by and large, been unsuccessful in claiming to be families. In *Key Youth Services, Inc. v. City of Olathe*,[133] the Tenth Circuit found that a group home for troubled youths did not qualify for protection under the familial status provision. Key Youth Services sought a special permit to open a group home where 10 minors would live, supervised around the clock by a rotating staff. The court found that the staff members were not "domiciled" with the youths as required by the act. The staff members clearly had "homes" elsewhere, and one cannot have two domiciles at the same time. In *Doe v. City of Butler*,[134] the Third Circuit confronted, but did not decide, whether a temporary shelter for battered women and their children were covered by the act. The town in that case had a zoning regulation which limited transitional dwellings to a total of six persons, disqualifying the shelter. While the court remanded the case for the lower court to consider the family status provision, a dissenting judge argued that remand was unnecessary since the provision protected a family, not "'communities' of families."[135]

The FHA exempts "any reasonable local, State, or Federal restrictions regarding the maximum number of occupants permitted to occupy a dwelling."[136] While such restrictions clearly limit where large families can live, attacks on such limitations have failed. In *Fair Housing Advocates Association, Inc. v. City of Richmond Heights*,[137] housing rights advocates challenged the housing codes of three cities, which they claimed established unduly restrictive occupancy standards that discriminated against families with children. One of the codes required a minimum of 200 square feet of habitable space for the first occupant and 150 square feet for each additional occupant.[138] While the court refused to accord the ordinances a presumption of validity and placed the burden on the cities to prove they fell within the exemption, the cities satisfied the court that the limitations were designed to, and had the effect of, promoting health and safety by preventing overcrowding.[139] The Supreme Court in *City of Edmonds v. Oxford House, Inc.*,[140] had provided a good basis for this decision by quoting a congressman from the legislative history as saying the exemption "makes it plain that, pursuant to local prescriptions on maximum occupancy, landlords legitimately may refuse to stuff large families into small quarters."[141]

§ 6:9   Exclusion of Non-Residential Uses: LULUs

A.   *In General*

While almost every use of land is a legitimate use somewhere, many cities entirely exclude or severely limit particular kinds of uses. Bans may be broad, covering all industrial and most commercial uses, or they may be specific, targeting uses known popularly as LULUs (locally unwanted land uses). They include such uses as hazardous waste dumps, sewage treatment facilities, big box retailers, landfills, hog farms, min-

---

[133] *Keys Youth Services, Inc. v. City of Olathe*, 248 F.3d 1267 (10th Cir. 2001).

[134] *Doe v. City of Butler, Pa.*, 892 F.2d 315 (3d Cir. 1989).

[135] Doe, 892 F.2d at 327.

[136] 42 U.S.C.A. § 3607(b)(1).

[137] *Fair Housing Advocates Ass'n, Inc. v. City of Richmond Heights, Ohio*, 209 F.3d 626 (6th Cir. 2000).

[138] The other codes were similar. Fair Housing Advocates Ass'n, Inc., 209 F.3d at 629–630.

[139] Fair Housing Advocates Ass'n, Inc., 209 F.3d at 636.

[140] *City of Edmonds v. Oxford House, Inc.*, 514 U.S. 725, 115 S. Ct. 1776, 131 L. Ed. 2d 801 (1995).

[141] City of Edmonds, 514 U.S. at 725, 115 S. Ct. at 1776, n. 9.

ing operations, junkyards, billboards, cemeteries, funeral parlors, correctional facilities, and adult entertainment. Where fundamental rights are adversely affected by exclusion, there is no presumption of validity, and a higher degree of judicial scrutiny is used. In contrast, in most states the exclusion of nonresidential uses is presumed valid [142] and not subject to fair share requirements that apply to housing.[143]

In an early, leading case, *Duffcon Concrete Products v. Borough of Cresskill*,[144] the New Jersey Supreme Court upheld the total exclusion of heavy industrial uses. The court found that it was not arbitrary for a small town to exclude such uses to preserve its residential character where industrially zoned land was available in the region. Many other courts have followed suit, allowing the exclusion of a variety of uses, many more innocuous than the LULUs listed above.[145]

Single-use zoning, allowing only residential uses, has been held reasonable for the "bedroom community" that lies on the fringe of a larger, metropolitan area where needed services are readily available nearby.[146] While some courts have narrowly interpreted the standard enabling act's directive that "the local legislative body may divide the municipality into districts"[147] as precluding a single zone, that language is generally seen as permissive.

The regional view cuts two ways. Under *Duffcon*,[148] the municipality was allowed to avoid providing for heavy industry because land was available elsewhere in the region for that purpose. However, if all towns in a region, acting in their parochial self-interest entirely exclude a use, the general welfare may be harmed. Thus, in some instances, a municipality may have to accommodate a use to benefit the larger geographical region. Nonetheless, the obligation to take into account the regional welfare that is applied to limit the exclusion of residential uses may not apply to nonresidential uses.

Courts may find a total exclusion of a nonresidential use arbitrary under particular circumstances. A total prohibition of outdoor theaters within a town village was found unreasonable where more than 57% of the land in the town was vacant, there was ample land for residential and industrial development, and the land surrounding the tract on which the challenger wished to build a theater was either unimproved or devoted to heavy industrial uses.[149] A de facto total ban on fast food restaurants, engineered by creating a zone for such restaurants but not zoning any land for them, was also invalidated.[150] The court found traffic considerations might justify denial of such zoning for the challenger's site, but nothing explained the total exclusion.

The numerous ill effects alleged to accompany the entry of big box retailers leads some cities to exclude them. These effects include causing urban decay as small retail-

---

[142] *Marshfield Family Skateland, Inc. v. Town of Marshfield*, 389 Mass. 436, 450 N.E.2d 605 (1983).

[143] *Gernatt Asphalt Products, Inc. v. Town of Sardinia*, 87 N.Y.2d 668, 642 N.Y.S.2d 164, 664 N.E.2d 1226 (1996).

[144] *Duffcon Concrete Products v. Borough of Cresskill*, 1 N.J. 509, 64 A.2d 347 (1949).

[145] See, e.g., *Marshfield Family Skateland, Inc. v. Town of Marshfield*, 389 Mass. 436, 450 N.E.2d 605 (1983) (video arcade).

[146] See *Valley View Village v. Proffett*, 221 F.2d 412 (6th Cir. 1955).

[147] Standard Zoning Enabling Act, § 2.

[148] See supra note 144.

[149] *People ex rel. Trust Co. of Chicago v. Village of Skokie*, 408 Ill. 397, 97 N.E.2d 310 (1951).

[150] *Wenco Management Co. v. Town of Carrboro*, 53 N.C. App. 480, 281 S.E.2d 74 (1981).

ers shut down and increased traffic and reduced air quality. While the big box retailers deny these effects, courts, applying a rational basis standard of review, have upheld the ordinances against due process[151] and equal protection claims.[152]

Big box exclusion ordinances may be vulnerable to claims that they are intended to regulate economic competition. If so, they may be invalid under state zoning law and potentially violative of the dormant commerce clause.[153] An adverse effect on competition is, of course, an inevitable consequence of much zoning districting and, where local economic considerations are but one of several factors behind a regulation, it is usually upheld under state law.[154] For a constitutional claim, if the ordinance simply favors small retailers over large retailers, it may be a form of economic protectionism, but it will not violate the commerce clause if in-state and out-of-state large retailers are equally affected.[155]

B. Exclusion Infringing Fundamental Rights

Excluding certain uses, even for small communities, is less justifiable if the exclusion infringes on a suspect class or a fundamental or important right. This may include signs,[156] religious practices, abortion clinics,[157] adult entertainment,[158] and other uses that implicate First Amendment speech or religion rights or Fourteenth Amendment substantive due process rights.[159] In such cases, the burden is likely to be put on the municipality to justify the restriction. These issues are discussed elsewhere.[160]

C. State Preemption of Local Exclusion

Governmentally owned, operated, or licensed facilities may be immune from local zoning under the doctrine of preemption. Such activities as municipal landfills, correctional facilities, and group homes often fall into this category.[161] These issues are discussed elsewhere.[162]

D. Environmental Justice

In recent years, attention has focused on whether LULUs, primarily hazardous waste facilities and landfills, are disproportionately sited in minority or low-income neighborhoods.[163] An environmental justice movement has sought to prove the charge

---

[151] *Wal-Mart Stores, Inc. v. City of Turlock*, 138 Cal. App. 4th 273, 41 Cal. Rptr. 3d 420 (2006).

[152] *Wal-Mart Stores, Inc. v. City of Turlock*, 483 F. Supp. 2d 987 (E.D. Cal. 2006).

[153] See *Island Silver & Spice, Inc. v. Islamorada*, 542 F.3d 844 (11th Cir. 2008).

[154] *Hernandez v. City of Hanford*, 41 Cal. 4th 279, 59 Cal. Rptr. 3d 442, 159 P.3d 33 (2007).

[155] *Great Atlantic & Pacific Tea Co., Inc. v. Town of East Hampton*, 997 F. Supp. 340, 351 (E.D. N.Y. 1998).

[156] See infra §§ 10:16 and 12:3.

[157] See discussion infra § 10:15.

[158] See infra § 10:17.

[159] See discussion infra § 10:12. Exclusion based on race or disability and, in some states, high density residential exclusion may also trigger strict review. See discussion supra § 6:6.

[160] See infra §§ 10:1 et seq.

[161] Preemption in the context of governmental uses is discussed supra § 4:24.

[162] See infra §§ 10:1 et seq.

[163] See Collin, Review of the Legal Literature on Environmental Racism, Environmental Equity, and Environmental Justice, 9 J. Envtl. L. & Litig. 121 (1994).

and to rectify the siting process to equitably distribute LULUs among the broader population.[164]

Studies produce conflicting conclusions as to whether minority and low-income neighborhoods are disproportionately burdened by LULUs, and, if so, whether it is the siting process that causes this result.[165] Market forces, also play a role. Professor Vicki Been, who has extensively studied the issue,[166] observes that market forces, rather than the siting process, may more often be responsible for lowering land values near LULUs. Thus, it may be that some LULUs have been sited in or near affluent white communities, and, those then living there, in possession of the financial wherewithal to do so, move away, leaving low-cost housing behind for racial minorities and the poor. Furthermore, she notes that if the siting process is to blame in whole or in part, and the "solution" is development of an equitable siting process, market forces may destroy its effectiveness if affluent whites vacate an area that is chosen as a new LULU site.

Legal remedies for siting facilities in minority or low-income communities have been difficult to come by. At first blush, equal protection seems an obvious choice. But discriminatory intent must be shown, and that is difficult to do.[167]

Efforts to use various federal civil rights statutes have not fared well. Title VI of the Civil Rights Act of 1964 prohibits racial discrimination in programs that receive federal assistance.[168] While intent must be shown under the statute, regulations implementing the act use an effects test, and numerous cases sought to proceed on that ground. The Supreme Court, however, has held that there is no private right of action to enforce disparate impact regulations under Title VI.[169] Also, it is unlikely that a disparate impact claim to enforce EPA's Title VI regulations may be brought under § 1983.[170] It has been suggested that the Fair Housing Act, Title VIII, may be used, though linking the siting of a LULU to the provision of services in connection housing is problematical.

Various legislative proposals have been made to require the collection of data on LULU locations, to assure public participation in the siting process, to give "preference" in siting to those areas that at present have no LULUs, and to remove sites from minority communities. An Executive Order issued by President Clinton requires federal agencies to identify and address disproportionately high adverse health effects of LULUs in minority and low-income communities.[171]

To the extent that racial discrimination in the sale and rental of housing or in lending practices makes it difficult for minorities to move out of LULU-affected neighborhoods, strengthening fair housing act enforcement will help. The negative effect of

---

[164] See, generally, Lazarus, Environmental Racism: That's What It Is, 2000 U. Ill. L. Rev. 255 (2000).

[165] See Kevin, "Environmental Racism" and Locally Undesirable Land Uses: A Critique of Environmental Justice Theories and Remedies, 8 Vill. Envtl. L.J. 121 (1997).

[166] Been and Gupta, Coming to the Nuisance or Going to the Barrios?, A Longitudinal Analysis of Environmental Justice Claims, 24 Ecology L.Q. 1 (1997).

[167] Cole, Environmental Justice Litigation: Another Stone in David's Sling, 21 Fordham Urb. L.J. 523, 539–41 (1994).

[168] 42 U.S.C.A. § 2000d.

[169] *Alexander v. Sandoval*, 532 U.S. 275, 121 S. Ct. 1511, 149 L. Ed. 2d 517 (2001).

[170] *South Camden Citizens in Action v. New Jersey Department of Environmental Protection*, 274 F.3d 771 (3d Cir. 2001).

[171] Exec. Order No. 12,898, 59 Fed. Reg. 7,629 (1994).

LULUs, wherever located, also may be mitigated by strengthening environmental laws that regulate them and by enforcing those laws that exist. Finally, to the extent that government decisionmaking is at fault in excessively burdening a small portion of the population with the adverse effects of LULUs, measures to assure equitable distribution of LULUs can be developed. In the end, though, the unyielding effects of market forces likely will still leave the poor worse off than the rich.

There is a downside to using eminent domain to condemn property of the poor. Since the power of eminent domain includes a broad array of government actions to promote public purposes, poor communities where land values may be low are often targeted. According to Justice Thomas, the high degree of deference given to exercises of eminent domain "encourages 'those citizens with disproportionate influence and power in the political process, including large corporations and development firms' to victimize the weak."[172]

E. *Natural Resource Extraction*

Natural resource extraction poses a distinct regulatory problem since it not only uses land, but consumes it, and if the consumption is to occur, it must occur where the resource is located.[173] The land has special value for resource extraction, and zoning which precludes the use destroys that value. Moreover, those deposits close to urbanized areas are likely to be most valuable since transportation costs will be lower.

The use of lands for oil and gas production, mining, quarrying, topsoil removal and sand and gravel operations is as difficult to reconcile with other uses of lands as any. Exploitation of natural resources produces odors, dust, use of heavy equipment, large amounts of truck traffic, noise-and, in the case of oil and gas production-danger of fire and explosion. Moreover, few uses are as unaesthetic as natural resource extraction sites. Therefore, there are a number of grounds on which such activities can be precluded or regulated under the police power. For example, ordinances often only allow resource extraction in agricultural and heavy industrial zones and such uses are frequently handled on a special permit basis even in such zones.

Earlier cases tended to favor extractive industry and used various reasons to allow the extraction. Courts have held prohibitory ordinances invalid where extraction was permitted in more densely populated areas,[174] where the surrounding area was occupied by other intensive uses,[175] where the area involved was not densely populated [176] and where denial of rights to drill to one would confer a monopoly on others.[177] Prohibitory ordinances have also been held invalid where, for example, a quarry preexisted neighboring development,[178] where the value of the property is substantially reduced [179] or on the ground that the operation was temporary and that neighbors could be

---

[172] See Justice Thomas' dissent in *Kelo v. City of New London, Conn.*, 545 U.S. 469, 125 S. Ct. 2655, 2686–87, 162 L. Ed. 2d 439 (2005). *Kelo* is discussed infra § 16:4.

[173] See Kramer, Local Land Use Regulation of Extractive Industries: Evolving Judicial and Regulatory Approaches, 14 UCLA J. Envtl. L. & Policy 41 (1996) for a detailed examination of the topic.

[174] *Pacific Palisades Ass'n v. City of Huntington Beach*, 196 Cal. 211, 237 P. 538 (1925).

[175] *City of North Muskegon v. Miller,* 249 Mich. 52, 227 N.W. 743 (1929).

[176] *Clouser v. City of Norman*, 1964 OK 109, 393 P.2d 827 (Okla. 1964).

[177] *Braly v. Board of Fire Com'rs of City of Los Angeles*, 157 Cal. App. 2d 608, 321 P.2d 504 (1958).

[178] *Herman v. Village of Hillside*, 15 Ill. 2d 396, 155 N.E.2d 47 (1958).

[179] *East Fairfield Coal Co. v. Booth,* 166 Ohio St. 379, 143 N.E.2d 309 (1957).

temporarily inconvenienced in order to permit exploitation of the mineral value of the land.[180] Zoning of a site having natural resources for quarry operations is also not as likely to be held invalid as spot zoning.[181]

More recent cases have concluded that there is no special right to zoning that permits extraction, and the total exclusion of mining has been upheld as a valid exercise of the police power.[182] As stated by the California Supreme Court in *Consolidated Rock Products Co. v. City of Los Angeles:*

> Too many cases have been decided upholding the constitutionality of comprehensive zoning ordinances prohibiting the removal of natural products from lands in certain zones for us now to accept at full value the suggestion that there is such an inherent difference in natural products of the property that in a case where reasonable minds may differ as to the necessity of such prohibition the same power to prohibit the extraction of natural products does not inhere in the legislative body as it has to prohibit uses of other sorts.[183]

It is true that resources must be extracted where they are located, if extracted anywhere, but place has value in other situations too. For example, it is because a downtown area zoned for commercial high rises is there rather than elsewhere, that it has high value. Zoning the site for single-family residential use may take as much value as prohibiting the drilling of oil from the site. A good corner for a filling station may result in unique values that are as substantially impaired by residential zoning as they would be if an ordinance prohibited the removal of sand and gravel which happened to be the makeup of the soil on the corner.

While many ordinances banning mining exempt existing uses under the doctrine of nonconforming uses,[184] the nuisance-like aspects of such operations may justify immediate termination of existing uses. In *Hadacheck v. Sebastian,*[185] the Court upheld an ordinance requiring the immediate termination of an operating brickyard. The brickyard pre-existed other development in the area and the economic effect of the closure was to reduce the value of the land from $800,000 to $60,000. Still, the Court upheld the state court's finding that the negative effects of the brickyard on expanding residential uses in the area justified its termination.

A takings challenge of an act prohibiting mining of a natural resource turns on whether the effect of the act as applied to the land deprives it of all economically viable use, and if so, whether the mining operation can nonetheless be banned as a nuisance.[186] In many instances the initial showing cannot be made since there will be some economic value left for purposes other than mining. If the economic loss is partial, the strength of the public interest must be balanced against the loss sustained.

---

[180] *Village of Terrace Park v. Errett,* 12 F.2d 240 (C.C.A. 6th Cir. 1926).

[181] *Kozesnik v. Montgomery Tp.,* 24 N.J. 154, 131 A.2d 1 (1957).

[182] *Gernatt Asphalt Products, Inc. v. Town of Sardinia,* 87 N.Y.2d 668, 642 N.Y.S.2d 164, 664 N.E.2d 1226 (1996).

[183] 57 Cal. 2d 515, 529, 20 Cal. Rptr. 638, 648, 370 P.2d 342, 351 (1962).

[184] See supra § 4:34.

[185] *Hadacheck v. Sebastian,* 239 U.S. 394, 36 S. Ct. 143, 60 L. Ed. 348 (1915).

[186] See *Keystone Bituminous Coal Ass'n v. DeBenedictis,* 480 U.S. 470, 107 S. Ct. 1232, 94 L. Ed. 2d 472 (1987) (prohibition of coal mining that causes surface subsidence not a taking). See, generally, infra §§ 10:6 and 10:8.

F.   The Death Industry: Cemeteries and Funeral Parlors

Cemeteries may be permitted in residential, commercial or agricultural districts. As reminders of death, however, they may not always be welcome by neighbors. The drop in property values due to the psychological depression of adjacent or nearby residential users may be recognized as a basis to limit cemetery location or operation. Were it not for this reminder of death, the open space and park-like aspect of cemeteries would make them desirable neighbors.

Historically, local governments have been free to limit cemetery location as they would any commercial use. In an early case, the Supreme Court upheld an ordinance that totally precluded burials in a city.[187] Cemeteries are often regulated by the state,[188] and this may lead to the preemption of local law.[189] Though cemetery lands are subdivided and sold, they are not usually subject to ordinary subdivision ordinances.[190]

The regulation of cemeteries operated by religious organizations may pose special considerations. In *McGann v. Incorporated Village of Old Westbury*,[191] a village denied a Catholic Bishop's request for a special permit to establish a cemetery on a 97-acre tract. The court found that a Roman Catholic cemetery was a place of worship it its own right, and that in New York, unlike most states,[192] religious uses of land are deemed presumptively beneficial. The court ordered the village to issue the permit.[193] Other courts hold that there is "nothing inherently" religious about cemeteries or graves.[194]

It is doubtful that the First Amendment would demand the result achieved in *McGann* under state law. In a recent Sixth Circuit case, an association that operated several Roman Catholic cemeteries in the Detroit area, sought a rezoning of an 88-acre for a new cemetery.[195] The city denied the rezoning for reasons relating to traffic impact, loss of tax base, and insufficient buffering. The plaintiff claimed the refusal to rezone violated its First Amendment free exercise rights. The Sixth Circuit rejected the claim. While the court seemed to agree with the city that the cemetery use was not an exercise of religion, the court found that, nonetheless, the zoning law was a neutral law of general applicability and, thus, not subject to strict scrutiny. The city's reasons for denying the rezoning sufficed under the rational basis test. While the Sixth Circuit's ruling is in accord with First Amendment case law, a party in the plaintiff's position might fare better under the Religious Land Use and Institutionalized Persons Act of 2000.[196]

Like most land uses, devoting land to cemetery use is not necessarily a permanent decision. As development pressures grow, so too will the pressure to move non-

---

[187] *Laurel Hill Cemetery v. City and County of San Francisco*, 216 U.S. 358, 30 S. Ct. 301, 54 L. Ed. 515 (1910).

[188] See, e.g., West's Ann. Cal. Bus. & Prof. Code §§ 9600 to 9770.

[189] See discussion of preemption supra § 4:24.

[190] Sometimes special state statutes apply to cemetery subdivisions. See, e.g., Mo. Ann. Stat. § 214.040.

[191] *McGann v. Incorporated Village of Old Westbury*, 186 Misc. 2d 661, 719 N.Y.S.2d 803 (2000).

[192] See also discussion supra § 4:28.

[193] *McGann*, 719 N.Y.S.2d at 807.

[194] *St. John's United Church of Christ v. City of Chicago*, 502 F.3d 616, 632 (7th Cir. 2007).

[195] *Mount Elliott Cemetery Ass'n v. City of Troy*, 171 F.3d 398 (6th Cir. 1999).

[196] See discussion infra § 10:19.

productive uses, such as cemeteries. Those located in areas where property values have risen may be targets for reuse. Highway or other public improvements may also compel their removal. State statutes may regulate the process.[197] There may be religious objections from family members to the disturbance of grave sites, but these have not fared well.[198]

Like cemeteries, funeral homes are often not welcome in residential neighborhoods, and the body of nuisance and zoning law on funeral homes is substantial. A crematory may be construed to be permitted as a "funeral home"[199] or as an accessory use.[200] Some courts conclude that funeral parlors are nuisances per se or can be nuisances in residential areas,[201] so it is not surprising that funeral parlors are not often a permitted use in residential areas. Some ordinances may attempt to exclude them in commercial zones.[202] Despite the fact that they may be nicely landscaped, funeral parlors do generate traffic and may generate feelings of disquietude leading to depression of neighborhood property values. As a result, they are often handled on a special permit basis. Under such handling, the movement of bodies and traffic can appropriately be controlled through the use of screening and off-street parking.

§ 6:10   Standing to Challenge Exclusionary Zoning

Various persons seek standing to challenge the exclusionary effects of a town's zoning ordinance on general or site-specific bases.[203] These include property owners subject to the restriction, residents of the town who have limited housing choices due to the restriction, and nonresidents who cannot acquire property in the town due to the ordinance. These nonresidents may be individuals seeking housing, or developers interested in acquiring property for housing or other uses. Standing rules differ between federal and state courts.

Standing in federal court to attack exclusionary land use ordinances on equal protection grounds is limited.[204] In *Warth v. Seldin*[205] four categories of plaintiffs challenged the Penfield, New York ordinance as exclusionary. The groups included nonresidents unable to find housing in the town; taxpayers in nearby Rochester bearing a disproportionate share of low income costs; Penfield residents denied benefits of living in an integrated community; and associations representing contractors unable to construct low-income housing in Penfield. The Court denied standing to all of them because none could show how they were personally injured by the ordinances. The Court held that two showings must be made. First, there must be but-for causation, that is there must be "specific, concrete facts" proving harm to plaintiffs. Second, the plaintiffs must show a possibility of redress to them by the Court's intervention. With respect to the nonresidents who could find no affordable housing in the area, the Court noted that

---

[197] See *Atilano v. Board of Com'rs of Columbia County*, 273 Ga. 408, 541 S.E.2d 385 (2001).

[198] See *Lyng v. Northwest Indian Cemetery Protective Ass'n*, 485 U.S. 439, 108 S. Ct. 1319, 99 L. Ed. 2d 534 (1988).

[199] *Rabenold v. Zoning Hearing Bd. of Borough of Palmerton*, 777 A.2d 1257 (Pa. Commw. Ct. 2001).

[200] *Ferry v. City of Bellingham*, 41 Wash. App. 839, 844, 706 P.2d 1103 (1985).

[201] See infra §§ 14:1 et seq.

[202] *Sweet v. Campbell*, 282 N.Y. 146, 25 N.E.2d 963 (1940).

[203] General issues of standing in zoning cases are discussed supra § 5:34.

[204] Standing rules under the Fair Housing Act or under the Americans with Disabilities Act may differ. See *Oak Ridge Care Center, Inc. v. Racine County, Wis.*, 896 F. Supp. 867 (E.D. Wis. 1995).

[205] *Warth v. Seldin*, 422 U.S. 490, 95 S. Ct. 2197, 45 L. Ed. 2d 343 (1975).

there was inadequate proof that elimination of exclusionary zoning practices would lead to the construction of affordable housing.

Standing was found in *Arlington Heights v. Metropolitan Housing Development Corp.*[206] where construction of housing on a specific site was in issue. A developer of federally subsidized housing was granted standing on the basis of its preliminary expenditures on the project and its interest in providing low cost housing in areas where it was scarce. Additionally, a black employee of a nearby plant alleged that he was unable to find affordable housing near his place of work. Because his claim was based on a particular project, he proved an injury in fact. In most exclusionary zoning cases, there will be no specific project, and under the rule of *Warth,* standing in federal courts will be lacking.

Several state courts, which are not restricted by Article III as are the federal courts, have rejected *Warth* and developed more liberal standing rules. In New Jersey nonresidents are granted standing to maintain general exclusionary zoning challenges.[207] They need not show site-specific injury. Similar rules are followed in California [208] and New York.[209]

From the opposite perspective, where state legislation encourages affordable housing, neighbors challenging permits for affordable housing projects may face more stringent standing requirements. For example, a neighbor could not rely on the meaning of "person aggrieved" used in cases construing local zoning disputes to establish standing under a state statute. Thus, for a permit issued under a state law designed to overcome local opposition to affordable housing, an allegation of "diminution in value" did not confer standing. The plaintiff had to show that she suffered an injury that the affordable housing law protected.[210]

Those who own property wishing to develop it for low or moderate cost housing have standing to sue on the basis of injury to their property rights.[211] An association may have standing to bring suit on behalf of its members if it meets three conditions: its members would otherwise have standing to sue in their own right, the interests it seeks are germane to the organization's purpose, and neither the claim asserted nor the relief requested requires the participation of individual members in the lawsuit.[212] Under such circumstances a manufactured housing association was permitted to challenge an ordinance that excluded mobile homes from certain zones.[213]

---

[206] 429 U.S. 252, 97 S. Ct. 555, 50 L. Ed. 2d 450 (1977).

[207] *Southern Burlington County N.A.A.C.P. v. Mount Laurel Tp.*, 67 N.J. 151, 336 A.2d 713 (1975).

[208] *Stocks v. City of Irvine,* 114 Cal. App. 3d 520, 170 Cal. Rptr. 724 (1981).

[209] *Suffolk Housing Services v. Town of Brookhaven,* 91 Misc. 2d 80, 397 N.Y.S.2d 302 (1977).

[210] *Standerwick v. Zoning Bd. of Appeals of Andover,* 447 Mass. 20, 849 N.E.2d 197 (2006).

[211] *Cannon v. Coweta County,* 260 Ga. 56, 389 S.E.2d 329 (1990).

[212] *Mississippi Manufactured Housing Ass'n v. Bd. of Aldermen of City of Canton,* 870 So. 2d 1189, 1192 (Miss. 2004).

[213] Id., where court discusses various federal and state tests of associational standing.

Chapter 7

SUBDIVISION AND PLANNED UNIT DEVELOPMENT CONTROL LAW*

Analysis

I.   INTRODUCTION

---

* For more detailed discussion and more extensive citations of authority of the issues covered in this chapter, see Juergensmeyer and Roberts, Land Use Planning and Development Regulation Law, Practitioner Treatise Series (3rd ed. 2012).

I. INTRODUCTION

§ 7:1   Subdivision Control Law: In General

Subdivision regulation parallels zoning from an historic development perspective, and with zoning, constitutes the traditional foundation of American land use planning and control law. Unlike zoning, subdivision regulation has historically focused almost exclusively on residential development and has been applied only to the development of raw land. In recent years, however, subdivision control law in some states has become newly revitalized and its role greatly enhanced. Traditional subdivision regulation approaches and principles are rapidly being replaced by "development codes" which combine zoning, construction and design codes, and planned unit developments and subdivision regulations.[1] Today, in some jurisdictions "[i]t is principally through the process of subdivision approval that communities take a serious look at the problems of growth, the environmental impact of growth, and the availability of adequate facilities and services to accommodate growth" and subdivision regulation has become "the central technique for controlling the extent and rate of urban growth."[2] In other jurisdictions, especially states like Florida that have sophisticated state oriented or mandated growth management programs and procedures for approval of developments of regional impact, subdivision regulation has become less important and plat approval is more of a ministerial act than an implementation of policy.[3]

Subdivision regulation generally refers to controls implemented during the land subdividing stage of the development process and includes such measures as platting procedures and controls, design regulation, improvement requirements, dedication requirements, in-lieu fees, performance bonds and the like. Official mapping is another kind of land use control which implements planning by giving precise locations of future streets, parks and sites for other public facilities within a local jurisdiction. Planned unit developments are residential developments that include multifamily and single-family housing and that may also include commercial development.[4]

In developing an understanding of the land development regulatory techniques discussed in this chapter, it is important to keep their primary residential focus in perspective. While primarily directed toward residential development, they are often cross-matched with complimentary techniques and integrated into the overall land development control law system. For example, although subdivision regulations are generally independent of zoning regulations, planned unit developments, which often include commercial uses, are often found within zoning regulations. It is also important to note the new role that they often play as the focal point for implementing various growth management techniques such as the establishment of urban growth bounda-

---

[1] See Robert H. Freilich and S. Mark White, 21st Century Land Development Code (American Planning Association 2008).

[2] Kushner, Subdivision Law & Growth Management § 1:1 (2d ed.). For a discussion of the extension of subdivision regulations to nonresidential subdivisions, see Kushner, Subdivision Law & Growth Management § 5:5 (2d ed.).

[3] See § 9:13 infra.

[4] In a previous edition we included analysis and discussion of state and federal subdivided land sales regulations and statutes—especially the Interstate Land Sales Full Disclosure Act, 15 U. S. C.A. §§ 1701 et seq. The incidental nature of their role in land use regulation led to their omission from this edition. Recent discussion of the Act in the development context can be found in Proceeding ALI-ABA CLE, Resort Real Estate and Clubs (Aug.17–18, 2006); Proceedings, ALI-ABA CLE, Drafting Documents for Condominiums and New Urbanism Developments: Practices and Principles (March 2–4, 2006).

ries. The increasing popularity of conservation subdivisions introduces many smart growth and new urbanism concepts into the area as well.[5]

II. SUBDIVISION REGULATIONS

§ 7:2   Introduction and History

Subdivision regulation is a land use control based on the police power. As with zoning, a local government may need specific state statutory or constitutional authorization to enact subdivision regulations based on whether the jurisdiction follows a home rule power or Dillon's rule view of local government authority.[6] Unlike zoning, which controls the use of land and remains important before, during and after development, subdivision regulation generally refers to controls implemented during the development process. Once land is subdivided, subdivision regulations have little or no application until redevelopment, at which time re-subdivision may or may not be necessary. Although the subdivision of land occurs early in the development process, its impact on the community is lasting because "[t]he pattern of a subdivision becomes the pattern of a community, which in turn may influence the character of an entire city."[7]

Modern subdivision regulations include such measures as platting procedures and controls; design regulations including such items as layout of streets, street width, street grading and surfacing, drainage, sidewalks, sewers, water mains, lot size and screen plantings; improvement, reservation and dedication requirements; in-lieu fees; performance bonds and the like.

Prior to the 1920s the primary purpose of subdivision regulations was to provide a more efficient method for selling and conveying subdivided land. Early subdivision statutes, or "Maps and Plats Acts" as they were usually called, required that maps or "plats" of the subdivision be recorded in the local land records office. The plat was required to show roads, parks, lots and blocks and the surveyed dimensions of these features.[8] Once recorded, land within the subdivision could be conveyed by reference to the lot number and subdivision name and the page and volume numbers of the plat record books in which the plat in question was recorded. This avoided the expense and possible confusion inherent in using a metes and bounds or government survey description of each individual lot every time it was conveyed.[9] Even though subdivision regulation has moved into another dimension today, most states still have platting statutes which are now often separate from the statutes authorizing subdivision control.[10]

---

[5] See § 7:9, infra.

[6] See *Lemm, Development Corp. v. Town of Bartlett,* 133 N.H. 618, 580 A.2d 1082 (1990); *New Jersey Shore Builders Ass'n v. Township of Marlboro,* 248 N.J. Super. 508, 591 A.2d 950 (App. Div. 1991). For a discussion of the need for zoning power authorization, see supra §§ 3:7 and 3:9.

[7] R. Freilich and M. Schultz, Model Subdivision Regulations Planning and Law 1 (American Planning Association 1995) (This classic work has been "replaced" by a new development code which will add zoning, sustainability, new urbanism and smart growth to subdivision controls. See Robert H. Freilich and S. Mark White, 21st Century Land Development Code (American Planning Association 2008).

[8] See, e.g., Law of Mar. 31, 1885, S.B. 125 (1885) Colo. Laws; Colo. Rev. Stat. § 6603–21 (1908).

[9] It also made deeds a lot shorter!

[10] For references to and capsule analyses of the subdivision and platting statutes of each of the 50 states see E. Yokley, The Law of Subdivisions, Ch. 14 (2d ed. 1981); Kushner, Subdivision Law & Growth Management § Chs. 5 and 7 (2d ed.).

The second period of subdivision regulation evolved from a recognition that subdivision regulations could be expanded to accomplish the substantive objective of controlling urban development.[11] As a result of land speculation in the 1920's, millions of vacant platted lots of such unusable sizes as 20 by 80 feet existed. Lots in these subdivisions were often undeveloped and had different owners. The diverse ownership and partial development prevented effective re-platting though many of the lots were tax delinquent and hence in public ownership. New suburban development "jumped" these unusable, close-in subdivisions and left "slums" of vacant lands. Some of these "slums" could be removed only by condemnation and urban renewal.[12] Some of this platted land was also improved with streets and utilities. Through the 1920's, local governments often provided these improvements from public funds or by special assessments. During the 1930's many of these special assessment bonds were in default.

In response to the problems created by land speculation and premature development, the Department of Commerce published the Standard City Planning Enabling Act in 1928 which contained provisions on subdivision control.[13] This Act [14] shifted the emphasis of subdivision regulations from a device for selling and conveying land to one of providing a means to implement community comprehensive planning. In addition to recognizing the need for a method to transfer lots by reference to a plat, the act also emphasized the need for a method to require internal improvements within the subdivision. The model statute included provisions concerning the "arrangement of streets in relation to other existing or planned streets and to the master plan, for adequate and convenient open spaces of traffic, utilities, access of fire fighting apparatus, recreation, light and air, and for avoidance of congestion of population, including minimum width and area of lots."[15] Following the adoption of state enabling acts patterned after the model statutes, state courts upheld local government use of subdivision regulations as a land use control device to shape the growth of the entire community.[16]

The third period of subdivision regulation began in the late 40s when the pent up demand for housing generated the postwar building boom that became known as "urban sprawl."[17] This period was marked by an increasing awareness of the demands that rapidly expanding suburban areas placed on local government facilities and services. Concern was focused on the needs of the new subdivision residents for parks, recreation facilities and adequate roads. Many local governments experienced great economic pressure to provide these facilities and services to the new development. At

---

[11] For a thorough discussion of the four historical periods of subdivision regulation see R. Freilich and M. Schultz, Model Subdivision Regulations Planning and Law 1–8 (1995).

[12] See, e.g., *People ex rel. Gutknecht v. City of Chicago,* 414 Ill. 600, 111 N.E.2d 626 (1953) (state urban renewal legislation could be used to condemn and reassemble vacant "slum" lands).

[13] Standard City Planning Enabling Act, U.S. Dep't of Commerce (1928) (hereinafter referred to as "SPEA"). Title II of SPEA, Subdivision Control, is reprinted in the American Law Institute, a Model Land Development Code, Tentative Draft No. 1, 224, 244–253 (1968).

[14] In addition to the SPEA, many states base modern subdivision enabling legislation on two other model acts: the Municipal Planning Enabling Act and the Municipal Subdivision Regulation Act. The latter two acts are reprinted in E. Bassett, F. Williams, A. Bettman and R. Whitten, Model Laws for Planning Cities, Counties and States (1935).

[15] SPEA § 14 (1928).

[16] See, e.g., *Mansfield & Swett v. Town of West Orange,* 120 N.J.L. 145, 198 A. 225 (N.J. Sup. Ct. 1938).

[17] For a major governmental report focusing on the need to control urban sprawl as the number one priority in land-use planning see National Commission on Urban Problems (Douglas Commission), Alternatives to Urban Sprawl, Research Report No. 15 (1968). See § 9:18 infra for a discussion of the legal aspects of urban sprawl.

the same time local officials remembered the financial difficulties that were created in the 30's by excessive reliance on special assessments to fund various subdivision improvements.[18] Subdivision regulations were amended to include provisions which required developers to dedicate park and school sites [19] and on-site roads,[20] to widen off-site streets,[21] and to contribute funds where the need for such facilities was in areas outside the subdivision but within the general vicinity.[22] In response to the demand for control of urban sprawl, subdivision regulations have been modified to incorporate new techniques which go far beyond the needs of residents within the subdivision. Subdivision regulations are more frequently being used to delay or deny development where it can be shown that the subdivision will cause serious off-site drainage problems and flooding, reduce environmental quality, or contribute to existing problems of inadequate local government facilities.[23]

The fourth and most recent period of subdivision regulation emphasizes the relationship of the individual subdivision to its external community environment through the local government comprehensive planning process. Current emphasis is being placed on the rate of subdivision development activity. This current period in the history of subdivision regulation is marked by attempts to integrate subdivision regulations into comprehensive growth management and planning programs [24] with the objective of phasing in new development in coordination with the orderly provision of adequate public facilities,[25] the establishment of urban service areas, sprawl containment, and other smart growth programs such as unified development ordinances [26] and green space preservation through conservation subdivisions.[27]

---

[18] In the 1930s, many local governments faced bankruptcy when the economy collapsed and revenues which secured special assessment bonds disappeared. Most local governments assumed that increased property taxes resulting from new development would generate sufficient revenue for maintaining public facilities. The collapse of the development market in the late 1920's demonstrated the uncertainty of the assumption.

[19] See, e.g., *Rosen v. Village of Downers Grove,* 19 Ill. 2d 448, 167 N.E.2d 230 (1960) (dedication of public school site).

[20] See, e.g., *Brous v. Smith,* 304 N.Y. 164, 106 N.E.2d 503 (1952) (dedication of roads internal to subdivision).

[21] See, e.g., *Ayres v. City Council of City of Los Angeles,* 34 Cal. 2d 31, 207 P.2d 1, 11 A.L.R.2d 503 (1949) (dedication of perimeter streets bordering subdivision).

[22] See, e.g., *Jenad, Inc. v. Village of Scarsdale,* 18 N.Y.2d 78, 271 N.Y.S.2d 955, 218 N.E.2d 673 (1966) (in lieu fee for recreational purposes upheld); *Associated Home Builders etc., Inc. v. City of Walnut Creek,* 4 Cal. 3d 633, 94 Cal. Rptr. 630, 484 P.2d 606 (1971) (in lieu fee for recreation and open space upheld).

[23] See, e.g., *Eschete v. City of New Orleans,* 258 La. 133, 245 So. 2d 383 (1971) (drainage); *Pearson Kent Corp. v. Bear,* 28 N.Y.2d 396, 322 N.Y.S.2d 235, 271 N.E.2d 218 (1971) (inadequate off-site roads); *Salamar Builders Corp. v. Tuttle,* 29 N.Y.2d 221, 325 N.Y.S.2d 933, 275 N.E.2d 585, 3 Env't. Rep. Cas. (BNA) 1267 (1971) (environmental protection of off-site water resources).

[24] See infra §§ 9:1 et seq.

[25] See, e.g., *Golden v. Planning Bd. of Town of Ramapo,* 30 N.Y.2d 359, 334 N.Y.S.2d 138, 285 N.E.2d 291, 2 Envtl. L. Rep. 20296, 63 A.L.R.3d 1157 (1972) (constitutionality of subdivision development timing ordinance upheld); see Freilich, Golden v. Town of Ramapo, Establishing a New Dimension in American Planning Law, 4 Urb. Law. ix (Summer 1972); cf. Bosselman, Can the Town of Ramapo Pass a Law to Bind the Rights of the Whole World?, 1 Fla. St. U. L. Rev. 234 (1973).

[26] Barry Hogue, Unified Development Ordinances: A Coordinated Approach to Development Regulations, Zoning News (December 2002).

[27] See § 7:9, infra.

§ 7:3   Relation to Planning

As with zoning, subdivision regulation is a land use control that implements comprehensive planning.[28] The relationship between planning and subdivision control, however, has historically been viewed as closer than in zoning.[29] This close relationship between subdivision regulation and planning stems at least in part from the combination of those two concepts in the Standard City Planning Enabling Act, and the total omission of subdivision regulation and one terse reference to a "comprehensive plan" in the Standard Zoning Enabling Act.[30] More specifically, in the zoning process the legislative body and the Zoning Board of Adjustment (or Board of Zoning Appeals) often have major roles to play while the planning commission acts only in an advisory capacity. In the subdivision control process, the planning commission is usually given a major role in the formulation and implementation of subdivision regulations. The planning commission is also usually given a major role in the drafting and implementation of comprehensive plans.

Furthermore, although in those states which have not yet embraced comprehensive planning and the consistency requirement for all land use regulations, there is no legally required relationship between either zoning or subdivision controls and comprehensive plans,[31] the statutes of some of these states require a comprehensive plan or at least a plan having a major street element before local governments can regulate subdivisions.[32] In other states an official map is required as a prerequisite to subdivision regulation. In some jurisdictions the statutes specifically require that the subdivision review process include findings as to the compatibility of the subdivision plat with the plan or map.[33] In imposing these planning requirements, the statutes generally follow the guidance of one or more of the model or standard acts. At least one court has held that a planning board could rely on a comprehensive plan to disapprove a subdivision plat even though the master plan had not been formally adopted.[34]

While necessary conformity between planning and subdivision control has traditionally been greater than the conformity between planning and zoning, the matter is relative. Much subdivision regulation still takes place without reference to a comprehensive plan.[35] In many jurisdictions, the plan is only a general guide, it is often not legislatively adopted, and property owners may not be afforded a hearing on the plan. In such circumstances subdivision denial based on non-compliance with the plan may

---

[28] See § 2:7 supra; Cunningham, Land-Use Control—The State and Local Programs, 50 Iowa L. Rev. 367, 435 (1965) ("Ideally, both zoning and subdivision controls are tools for effectuating comprehensive land-use plans.").

[29] Cunningham, Land-Use Control—The State and Local Programs, 50 Iowa L. Rev. at 417 (1965).

[30] See supra § 2:8.

[31] R. Freilich and M. Schultz, Model Subdivision Regulations Planning and Law at 2 (1995).

("Just as the zoning requirement contained in the Standard Zoning Enabling Act . . . that zoning 'be in accordance with a comprehensive plan' has never been interpreted to require that a master plan precede adoption of a zoning ordinance . . . a master plan generally has been held not to be required in order to adopt valid subdivision regulations . . . .").

[32] See, e.g., Colo. Rev. Stat. § 31–23–213; Utah Code Ann. § 10–9–302 (1953).

[33] See, e.g., 65 Ill. Comp. Stat. 5/11–12–8 ("the municipality shall determine whether a proposed plat of subdivision or re-subdivision complies with the official map").

[34] *Neiderhofer v. Gustafson*, 45 A.D.2d 812, 357 N.Y.S.2d 196 (3d Dep't 1974); cf. *Lordship Park Ass'n v. Board of Zoning Appeals of Town of Stratford*, 137 Conn. 84, 75 A.2d 379 (1950).

[35] See Nelson, The Master Plan and Subdivision Control, 16 Me. L. Rev. 107 (1964).

be beyond the authority of the plat reviewing agency.[36] The trend for the future is that established by those states which require zoning and subdivision regulation to be consistent with a comprehensive plan.[37] Furthermore, as has been indicated above,[38] the subdivision approval process is increasingly becoming the focal point for the implementation of growth management techniques.[39] Since consistency of all land use actions with comprehensive plans is such a basic growth management principle, it would seem that consistency of subdivision regulations with comprehensive plans will be increasingly required.[40]

The eventual combination of subdivision regulations, zoning, sustainability requirements, new urbanism principles, and smart growth regulations into "development codes" can only serve to strengthen the role of comprehensive plans and consistency requirements designed to give them legal effect.[41]

§ 7:4   Relation to Zoning

It is usually necessary for a developer to comply with both zoning and subdivision regulations.[42] Although the two types of controls are intended to complement each other within the development process, they are often administered by different agencies. They are also often subject to separate enabling statutes each with its own particular requirements. As a consequence, subdivision regulations and zoning are often administered so as to appear to be working at cross-purposes. Some jurisdictions have integrated the two types of controls into a local development code which provides a consolidated procedure for considering both the zoning change and the subdivision proposal.

While the authority to approve subdivisions and the power to zone are usually authorized by separate statutes,[43] some subdivision control legislation requires that a plat conform to zoning regulations.[44] Courts have also held that local government authority to require conformance may be inferred from the general purposes to be served by subdivision control regulation.[45] Where the enabling legislation is silent on the relationship between the two types of controls, the local regulations often require that plats comply with local zoning.

Courts have also held that subdivision proposals may be rejected where they do not conform to zoning regulations.[46] Some courts have held that subdivision review

---

[36] *Lordship Park Ass'n v. Board of Zoning Appeals of Town of Stratford,* 137 Conn. 84, 75 A.2d 379 (1950). But see *Krieger v. Planning Commission of Howard County,* 224 Md. 320, 167 A.2d 885 (1961).

[37] See, e.g., Cal. Gov't Code § 66474(a); Fla. Stat. Ann. § 163.3202; Ill.—S.H.A. Ch. 24, ¶ 11–12–8; *Board of County Com'rs of Cecil County v. Gaster,* 285 Md. 233, 401 A.2d 666 (1979).

[38] See § 7:1.

[39] Kushner, Subdivision Law & Growth Management § 1:1 (2d ed.).

[40] In Florida for example, subdivision approval is required to be consistent with the local government comprehensive plan. See Fla. Stat. Ann. §§ 163.3194 and 163.3164(8).

[41] Robert H. Freilich and S. Mark White, 21st Century Land Development Code (American Planning Association (2008).

[42] *Oakland Court v. York Tp.,* 128 Mich. App. 199, 339 N.W.2d 873 (1983).

[43] For a discussion of zoning enabling acts see supra §§ 3:1 et seq.

[44] See, e.g., N.J. Stat. Ann. 40:55D-38.

[45] See, e.g., *Benny v. City of Alameda,* 105 Cal. App. 3d 1006, 164 Cal. Rptr. 776 (1st Dist. 1980) (disapproved of by, The Pines v. City of Santa Monica, 29 Cal. 3d 656, 175 Cal. Rptr. 336, 630 P.2d 521 (1981)).

[46] See, e.g., *People ex rel. American Nat. Bank & Trust Co. of Chicago v. City of Park Ridge,* 25 Ill. App. 2d 424, 166 N.E.2d 635 (1st Dist. 1960); *Durland v. Maresco,* 53 A.D.2d 643, 384 N.Y.S.2d 503 (2d Dep't

may not be used so as to amend zoning because the exercise of such a power would effectively amount to a usurpation of the authority of the local zoning board.[47] Where the subdivision control ordinance imposes additional requirements, however, courts have held that mere compliance with the zoning ordinance is not sufficient.[48]

Generally, subdivision approval alone will not confer a vested right on the developer to proceed in the face of a change in the law subsequent to the approval. If there has been a good faith reliance on the approval leading to substantial expenditures, a vested right may be acquired.[49] Similarly, where the owner of unsold lots requests a variance, an old subdivision can be forced to comply with new subdivision regulations.[50] On the other hand, vested rights in nonconforming lots are sometimes recognized, particularly where houses have been built on some lots or sewers and water lines installed.[51] Some statutes and ordinances provide that once a subdivision is approved, the municipality is precluded from exercising its powers inconsistent with the approval for a period of time.[52] These statutes have been interpreted, however, to apply to changes in local but not state land use regulations.[53]

§ 7:5   Definition of Subdivision

The Standard City Planning Enabling Act did not define the term "subdivision." As a result, the definition of subdivision in statutes and ordinances varies and is unclear in many states. Most broadly it is the division of one parcel of land into more than one parcel.[54] Many state statutes, however, define the term as a division of land into a minimum number of parcels.[55] Where a definition is omitted from the statute, courts have generally construed the statute to authorize each local government to define the term.[56] Local ordinances, however, may not generally expand the statutory definition.[57]

1976). *Krawski v. Planning and Zoning Com'n of Town of South Windsor,* 21 Conn. App. 667, 575 A.2d 1036 (1990).

[47] See, e.g., *Shapiro v. Town of Oyster Bay,* 27 Misc. 2d 844, 211 N.Y.S.2d 414 (Sup 1961); *Goodman v. Board of Com'rs of South Whitehall Tp.,* 49 Pa. Commw. 35, 411 A.2d 838 (1980).

[48] See e.g., *Shoptaugh v. Board of County Com'rs of El Paso County,* 37 Colo. App. 39, 543 P.2d 524 (App. 1975); *Popular Refreshments, Inc. v. Fuller's Milk Bar & Recreation Center, Inc.,* 85 N.J. Super. 528, 205 A.2d 445 (App. Div. 1964).

[49] See discussion supra § 5:28 and Ziegler, Rathkopf's The Law of Zoning and Planning § 70:24 (4th ed.).

[50] See, e.g., *Blevens v. City of Manchester,* 103 N.H. 284, 170 A.2d 121 (1961).

[51] *Gruber v. Mayor and Tp. Committee of Raritan Tp.,* 39 N.J. 1, 186 A.2d 489 (1962); *Wood v. North Salt Lake,* 15 Utah 2d 245, 390 P.2d 858 (1964); *Western Land Equities, Inc. v. City of Logan,* 617 P.2d 388 (Utah 1980); *Smith v. Winhall Planning Commission,* 140 Vt. 178, 436 A.2d 760 (1981).

[52] See, e.g., Pa. Stat. Ann. tit. 53, § 10508(4) (five years); N.J. Stat. Ann. 40.55D-49 (three years).

[53] *Island Properties, Inc. v. Martha's Vineyard Commission,* 372 Mass. 216, 361 N.E.2d 385, 7 Envtl. L. Rep. 20342 (1977); *Ocean Acres, Inc. v. State, Dept. of Environmental Protection,* 168 N.J. Super. 597, 403 A.2d 967 (App. Div. 1979).

[54] See, e.g., Mass. Gen. Laws ch. 41, § 81L (two or more). For a state-by-state breakdown of the definitions on this point, see Kushner, Subdivision Law & Growth Management § 5:9 (2d ed.).

[55] See, e.g., Conn. Gen. Stat. Ann. § 8–18 (three or more); Wash. Rev. Code Ann. § 58.17.020 (five or more). For a state-by-state breakdown of the definitions on this point, see Kushner, Subdivision Law & Growth Management § 5:8 (2d ed.).

[56] See, e.g., *Delaware Midland Corp. v. Incorporated Village of Westhampton Beach,* 79 Misc. 2d 438, 359 N.Y.S.2d 944, 946 (Sup 1974), judgment aff'd, 48 A.D.2d 681, 369 N.Y.S.2d 378 (2d Dep't 1975), order aff'd, 39 N.Y.2d 1029, 387 N.Y.S.2d 248, 355 N.E.2d 302 (1976).

[57] See, e.g., *Peninsula Corp. v. Planning and Zoning Commission of Town of New Fairfield,* 151 Conn. 450, 199 A.2d 1 (1964); *Dearborn v. Town of Milford,* 120 N.H. 82, 411 A.2d 1132 (1980); *Martorano v. Board of Com'rs of Cheltenham Tp.,* 51 Pa. Commw. 202, 414 A.2d 411 (1980).

In general, the term subdivision is defined so as to require that the division be for the purpose of sale, lease or building development.[58] Division for other purposes may not constitute a subdivision.[59] States are split on whether condominium development and/or the conversion of apartments to condominiums are subject to subdivision regulations.[60] In some statutes the number of divisions may be given a time horizon, so that property is not considered subdivided if no more than three lots are created within any five year period. Some statutes also expressly exempt subdivisions which do not involve creation of new streets[61] or the extension of existing streets,[62] which divide land among family members,[63] or which are the result of partition actions or testamentary divisions of real property.[64]

In many states there are loopholes, and subdividers engage in elaborate schemes to divide in a way which is not a "subdivision."[65] They thereby avoid the required approval and thus may avoid the imposition of subdivision exactions.[66] Avoidance is more common where there are no statutes or ordinances that are designed to cover less significant subdivisions. For example, in *Pratt v. Adams*[67] the court voided a scheme where one parcel was conveyed to several persons in joint tenancy and the persons then "suffered" the creation of 12 parcels through a partition action, the referee setting up an elaborate scheme for roads, easements, buildings restrictions, etc. as part of the partition order.

§ 7:6   The Subdivision Approval Process

The imposition of subdivision improvement requirements occurs during the subdivision approval process. Although many variations exist in the subdivision approval process from state to state, generalizations about the process can be made. The essential requirement of subdivision control is that a subdivider cannot convey subdivided lands without a recorded subdivision plat.[68] The subdivider is prohibited from recording the plat until the approval of the local subdivision approval agency has been ob-

---

[58] See, e.g., Pa. Stat. Ann. tit. 53, § 10107.

[59] See, e.g., Pa. Stat. Ann. tit 53, § 10107 (subdivision for agricultural purposes exempted); N.J. Stat. Ann. 40:55D-7 (land divided into five acres or more for agricultural use is not a subdivision); Conn. Gen. Stat. Ann. § 8–18 (subdivision for municipal, conservation or agricultural purposes exempted).

[60] See, e.g., *Gerber v. Town of Clarkstown,* 78 Misc. 2d 221, 356 N.Y.S.2d 926 (Sup 1974); but see N.H. Rev. Stat. Ann. § 672:14 (condominium development included); Colo. Rev. Stat. § 12–61–401. For a state-by-state discussion of recent decisions on point, see Kushner, Subdivision Law & Growth Management § 5:11 (2d ed.).

[61] See, e.g., *Stoker v. Town of Irvington,* 71 N.J. Super. 370, 177 A.2d 61 (Law Div. 1961); *Donovan v. City of New Brunswick,* 50 N.J. Super. 102, 141 A.2d 134 (Law Div. 1958); *Urban v. Planning Bd. of Borough of Manasquan, Monmouth County, N.J.,* 124 N.J. 651, 592 A.2d 240 (1991).

[62] See, e.g., *Dube v. Senter,* 107 N.H. 191, 219 A.2d 456 (1966).

[63] See, e.g., *Kiska v. Skrensky,* 145 Conn. 28, 138 A.2d 523 (1958).

[64] See, e.g., N.J. Stat. Ann. 40:55D-7; *Metzdorf v. Borough of Rumson,* 67 N.J. Super. 121, 170 A.2d 249 (App. Div. 1961).

[65] See *Gerard v. San Juan County,* 43 Wash. App. 54, 715 P.2d 149 (Div. 1 1986) (sequence of conveyances used to get short plat exemptions to create 18 parcel subdivision struck down).

[66] See infra § 7:8.

[67] *Pratt v. Adams,* 229 Cal. App. 2d 602, 40 Cal. Rptr. 505 (1st Dist. 1964).

[68] One court has held, however, that such a mandatory recordation requirement results in an unconstitutional restraint on alienation. *Kass v. Lewin,* 104 So. 2d 572 (Fla. 1958). Although the case has never been specifically overruled, it has been distinguished and possibly superseded by Florida's growth management regulations. Compare J. Juergensmeyer, Florida Land Use Law § 13.11 (2d ed. 1999) and Rhodes, Haigler and Brown, Land Use Controls, 31 U. Miami L. Rev. 1083, 1115–1118 (1977).

tained.[69] The local subdivision approval agency will have varying requirements that must be met ranging from requiring certain exactions such as new streets and sewer lines[70] to even requiring the developer to assure that an adequate supply of water will be available for the new subdivision.[71]

While most state enabling acts provide for a two-step approval process,[72] some local governments include an additional preliminary step referred to as a pre-application conference. At the conference the local agency or its staff will familiarize the applicant with the subdivision regulations and answer general questions. At the same time the applicant will provide the agency with the basic idea of the proposal.

The submission of a "preliminary plat" follows and constitutes the first formal step in the subdivision approval process. The regulations usually require that the applicant submit a detailed drawing of the proposed subdivision. Included on the drawing are the necessary improvements and indications of which improvements will be dedicated to public use. The local agency may then approve, disapprove, or conditionally approve the preliminary plat, usually after a properly noticed hearing. Reasons for disapproval are usually required to be made in writing and the final decision is subject to judicial review.[73] The decision of the agency ordinarily will be given judicial deference although some courts view the determination of whether or not the proposed subdivision meets the requirements of the ordinance to be a "ministerial" act.[74] Also, the decision may be reversed if an agency member is disqualified for conflict of interest.[75]

In some states, the right to subdivide may vest following approval of the preliminary plat.[76] Preliminary plat approval usually authorizes the subdivider to begin construction of the improvements provided a surety bond for their completion is posted.[77]

After preliminary plat approval, the subdivider usually has a specified time period, which varies from state to state, within which to submit a final plat for approval.[78] Before the final plat is approved the subdivider must demonstrate substantial conformance to the preliminary plat and any conditions that the local agency has imposed. Some statutes require approval of the final plat if all requirements imposed on approval of the preliminary plat are satisfied.[79] Courts often construe such provisions so as to make approval of the final plat a ministerial as opposed to a discretionary act.[80] Once

---

[69] See 4 R. Anderson, Anderson's American Law of Zoning § 25.05 (4th ed. 1995) (supplemented 1997).

[70] See infra § 7:8.

[71] 5 Waters and Water Rights § 62.03(c) (Robert E. Beck ed., 1991 ed.) (supplemented 2001). See Cal. Gov't Code § 66473.7 and discussion thereof at D. Curtin and C. Talbert, California Land Use and Planning Law 107 (26th ed. 2006).

[72] Kushner, Subdivision Law & Growth Management Ch. 7 (2d ed.).

[73] See, e.g., Wash. Rev. Code Ann. § 58.17.180.

[74] See *Youngblood v. Board of Supervisors*, 22 Cal. 3d 644, 150 Cal. Rptr. 242, 586 P.2d 556 (1978) (ministerial duty in regard to final map approval but quasi-judicial act when tentative map approved.

[75] Kushner, Subdivision Law & Growth Management § 8:2 (2d ed.).

[76] See, e.g., *Western Land Equities, Inc. v. City of Logan*, 617 P.2d 388 (Utah 1980); Kushner, Subdivision Law & Growth Management § 10:6 (2d ed.). See also supra § 5:27 in this treatise.

[77] See SPEA, § 14.

[78] See, e.g., Nev. Rev. Stat. 278.360(1) (two years but permitting a one year extension).

[79] See, e.g., Cal. Gov't Code § 66458; Pa. Stat. Ann. tit. 53, § 10508(4). Also see, *Golden State Homebuilding Associates v. City of Modesto*, 26 Cal. App. 4th 601, 31 Cal. Rptr. 2d 572 (5th Dist. 1994).

[80] See, e.g., *Youngblood v. Board of Supervisors*, 22 Cal. 3d 644, 150 Cal. Rptr. 242, 586 P.2d 556 (1978); *Hakim v. Board of Com'rs of O'Hara Tp.*, 27 Pa. Commw. 405, 366 A.2d 1306 (1976).

the final plat is approved, the subdivider may record the plat and legally convey lots within the subdivision.

Many states set time limits within which the local agency must act on either preliminary or final plats.[81] If the agency takes no action within this period, the plat is deemed approved.[82] Approval of the preliminary or final plat, however, does not constitute acceptance by the local government of the dedicated improvements. Such acceptance, and the responsibility for maintaining the improvements, occurs when the local government makes a formal decision to accept.

The subdivision control process may also include devices designed to achieve sufficient flexibility for the modification of subdivision control requirements.[83] Enabling statutes often authorize administrative relief in the form of variances where a strict application of the regulations would cause unusual and unnecessary hardship on the subdivider.[84] However, unlike zoning variances which are usually granted by the board of adjustment upon appeal from the decision of an administrative official, variance relief from subdivision regulations is usually granted by the same agency which originally reviewed the subdivision proposal. Absent a provision authorizing the zoning board of adjustment to grant variances from subdivision regulations, such board has been held without power to do so.[85] When a local agency has authority to vary the strict application of a subdivision ordinance, courts have held it can only do so by making findings of fact supported by evidence.[86]

§ 7:7   Enforcement Methods, Sanctions, and Required Improvement Guarantees

The effectiveness of subdivision regulations, like all land use control devices, depends upon the presence of fair and efficient enforcement methods, sanctions and required improvement guarantees.[87] One of the model enabling statutes provides:

> Whoever . . . sells . . . any land by reference to or exhibition of or by other use of a plat of a subdivision, before such plat has been approved . . . and recorded . . . shall . . . pay a penalty of $100 for each lot . . . . The municipal corporation may enjoin such transfer . . . or may recover the said penalty.[88]

---

[81] See, e.g., 65 Ill. Comp. Stat. 5/11–12–8; N.J. Stat. Ann. 40:55D-1 et seq.

[82] N.J. Stat. Ann. 40:55D-1 et seq. Pursuant to California's Permit Streamlining Act, Cal. Gov't Code § 65943(a) the application is deemed complete if the City fails to act within the statutory time period. D. Curtin and C. Talbert, California Land Use and Planning Law 91 (26th ed. 2006). It has been suggested, however, that it is doubtful that a court will permit a subdivision project to proceed if it will seriously jeopardize public health and safety.

[83] See, e.g., *Canter v. Planning Bd. of Westborough,* 7 Mass. App. Ct. 805, 390 N.E.2d 1128 (1979); *Blevens v. City of Manchester,* 103 N.H. 284, 170 A.2d 121, 124 (1961).

[84] See, e.g., N.J. Stat. Ann. 40:55D-51(a).

[85] See *Noonan v. Zoning Bd. of Review of Town of Barrington,* 90 R.I. 466, 159 A.2d 606 (1960).

[86] See, e.g., *Smith v. Township Committee of Morris Tp.,* 101 N.J. Super. 271, 244 A.2d 145 (App. Div. 1968).

[87] For a detailed discussion of enforcement methods and improvement guarantees see Kushner, Subdivision Law & Growth Management § 9 (2d ed.).

[88] Dep't of Commerce, Standard City Planning Enabling Act § 16 (1928).

In addition to the sanction of civil fine and injunction,[89] statutes in various states provide other sanctions. Sometimes the sale of a lot in an unapproved subdivision is made a criminal act resulting in the imposition of a fine or imprisonment.[90] A local government or purchaser may set aside the conveyance[91] or in some jurisdictions the purchase is allowed to sue the subdivider for damages.[92] Generally, the option of using a metes and bounds provision is not available if the land involved is covered by the subdivision statute because the statute makes a circumventing conveyance by such a description illegal. As a result, if land is sold that is within the definition of a required subdivision, the statute has been violated.[93] The statute may also preclude the issuance of building permits in lands that should be but have not been submitted for subdivision approval.[94] This sanction is the most controversial because it places the penalty not upon the subdivider but upon the buyer of a lot in an unapproved subdivision. Some courts have refused to uphold this type of sanction.[95]

In addition to enforcement methods and sanctions, local governments also utilize performance bonds which protect both the governmental entity and the public against uncompleted improvements required by subdivision regulations. This is appropriate because although subdivision regulations are utilized to implement local planning and as a means of placing the burden of public improvements on the subdivider, local governments are also interested in the livability of the subdivision for prospective buyers who have often been left remediless. For example, in *Hocking v. Title Ins. & Trust Co.,*[96] the buyer sought damages from a title insurance company insuring her lot on the ground that the lot had no access because streets required by ordinance were not built and this constituted a defect in title. Under the ordinance, the city was to have obtained a bond from the subdivider to insure the improvement of streets, but failed to do so. Despite its neglect the city would not issue a building permit. The court concluded that the problem was not one of title. A properly required performance bond, however, would have provided funds to build the street.

The performance bond mechanism also allows the subdivider to obtain building permits and begin the construction and sale of lots so as to develop an income stream that enables him to pay for improvements.[97] Once the reviewing local government has approved the plat, however, such performance bonding requirements may not be imposed.[98] Alternatively, if the final plat is not approved by the local government, a subdivider who has posted a performance bond or deposited money to insure the comple-

---

[89] See *Lake County v. Truett,* 758 S.W.2d 529 (Tenn. Ct. App. 1988) (Developer prohibited by injunction from other sales); *Johnson v. Hinds County,* 524 So. 2d 947 (Miss. 1988) (injunction against developer of illegal subdivision); *Grand County v. Rogers,* 2002 UT 25, 44 P.3d 734 (Utah 2002) (county recorder's acceptance not bar to county obtaining injunction).

[90] See, e.g., Alaska Stat. § 34.55.028 (a) (one to five years if willful, up to six months if unwillful); Wyo. Stat. Ann. § 15–1–511 (1977). See also *NFC Partners v. Stanchfield Cattle Co.,* 274 Mont. 46, 905 P.2d 1106 (1995) (fine and three months in jail for each lot).

[91] See, e.g., Cal. Gov't Code § 66499.32; Wis. Stat. Ann. 236.31(3).

[92] See Kushner, Subdivision Law & Growth Management § 9:10 (2d ed.).

[93] See supra § 7:5.

[94] See, e.g., Wash. Rev. Code Ann. § 58.17.210.

[95] See, e.g., *Keizer v. Adams,* 2 Cal. 3d 976, 88 Cal. Rptr. 183, 471 P.2d 983 (1970); *State ex rel. Craven v. City of Tacoma,* 63 Wash. 2d 23, 385 P.2d 372 (1963).

[96] *Hocking v. Title Ins. & Trust Co.,* 37 Cal. 2d 644, 234 P.2d 625, 40 A.L.R.2d 1238 (1951).

[97] *City of Merced v. American Motorists Ins. Co.,* 126 Cal. App. 4th 1316, 24 Cal. Rptr. 3d 788 (5th Dist. 2005) (discussing public's damage under performance bond).

[98] See, e.g., *McKenzie v. Arthur T. McIntosh & Co.,* 50 Ill. App. 2d 370, 200 N.E.2d 138 (2d Dist. 1964).

tion of plat improvements, may recover the bond or deposit.[99] Since performance bonds generally name the local government as obligee, only the local government may initiate an action to enforce the bond.[100] Neither purchasers of land in the subdivision who are seeking to have the improvements installed nor contractors seeking monies due for construction work rendered in the proposed subdivision may bring such enforcement actions.[101]

§ 7:8   Antiquated Subdivisions

Standards imposed on developers through subdivision regulations have changed dramatically since the early subdivision regulation ordinances enacted in the mid 1900s. Due to the pattern of land booms and land busts common in many parts of the country—especially the Sunbelt—hundreds of thousands of lots were platted but never built on. When market forces now make these "pre-platted lands" desirable for development, difficult issues come to the forefront in regard to whether or not—and if so, how—current subdivision development standards and requirements can be imposed on the land owners.[102]

Subdivisions which were platted before current subdivision requirements went into effect are often referred to as "antiquated" subdivisions, "paper" subdivisions, or "premature" subdivisions. They may contain lots which are too small to meet current setback or minimum lot size requirements, lack adequate road and utility easement dedications, lack water, sewer and other utility access, and may be located on environmentally fragile or dangerous flood plain areas that would not now be eligible for platting. If developer funding of infrastructure is now imposed by the jurisdiction as a prerequisite for plat approval, antiquated subdivisions may escape infrastructure construction and funding requirements that will be imposed on neighboring unplatted land. The amount or type of development they allow may run counter to the land uses permitted for the land in question by current comprehensive plans and thereby pose a consistency dilemma if the development as platted is permitted.[103] Whatever the planning, safety, or infrastructure problems antiquated subdivisions present, "resolution of this problem requires some degree of retroactive application of police power controls"[104] and thereby raises vested rights, takings, and due process issues.

The decision by the Supreme Court of California in *Gardner v. County of Sonoma,*[105] illustrates the strong public policy basis for judicial decisions that, one way or another, allow local governments to impose current requirements on the owners of an-

---

[99] See, e.g., *Cammarano v. Borough of Allendale,* 65 N.J. Super. 240, 167 A.2d 431 (Ch. Div. 1961).

[100] See, e.g., *Town of Stoneham v. Savelo,* 341 Mass. 456, 170 N.E.2d 417 (1960); *Pacific County v. Sherwood Pac., Inc.,* 17 Wash. App. 790, 567 P.2d 642 (Div. 2 1977).

[101] See, e.g., *Gordon v. Robinson Homes, Inc.,* 342 Mass. 529, 174 N.E.2d 381 (1961) (purchasers); *City of University City ex rel. and to Use of Mackey v. Frank Miceli & Sons Realty & Bldg. Co.,* 347 S.W.2d 131 (Mo. 1961) (adjoining property owners); *Weber v. Pacific Indem. Co.,* 204 Cal. App. 2d 334, 22 Cal. Rptr. 366 (1st Dist. 1962) (unpaid contractor).

[102] Rural Development Considerations for Growth Management, 43 Nat. Resources J. 781 (2003); Johnson, The Effect of Historic Parcels on Agriculture—Harvesting Houses, 12 San Joaquin Agric. L. Rev. 49 (2002).

[103] For a discussion of compelling plan compliance in the subdivision context, see Kushner, Subdivision Law & Growth Management § 9:13 (2d ed.). See D. Salvesen, The Ungrateful Dead (Antiquated Subdivisions) 62:5 Planning 8 (May 1996).

[104] D. Callies, R. Freilich and T. Roberts, Cases and Materials on Land Use 198 (4th ed. 2004).

[105] *Gardner v. County of Sonoma,* 29 Cal. 4th 990, 129 Cal. Rptr. 2d 869, 62 P.3d 103 (2003).

tiquated subdivisions. In Gardner, the court held that an 1865 "map" which was adopted as the county's official map did not create legally cognizable parcels. The court explained the policies behind its decision as follows:

> [I]f we were to adopt plaintiff's position and hold that local agencies must issue a certificate of compliance for any parcel depicted on an accurate, antiquated subdivision map, we would, in effect, be permitting the sale, lease, and financing of parcels: (1) without regard to regulations that would otherwise require consistency with applicable general and specific plans and require consideration of potential environmental and public health consequences: (2) without consideration of dedications and impact mitigation fees that would otherwise be authorized . . .; and (3) without affording notice and an opportunity to be heard to interested persons and landowners likely to suffer a substantial or significant deprivation of their property rights.[106]

Various approaches to eliminating antiquated subdivisions can be found. Most involve some form of vacation and annulment of existing plats—a procedure often authorized by the jurisdiction's Maps and Plats or Subdivision Act.[107] Frequently local governments are prevented from vacating plats unless petitioned by landowners to do so.[108] The resulting lack of flexibility in dealing with the preplatted lands problem has led to innovative approaches frequently labeled "land readjustment" or "land assembly" programs. These programs involve the assembly, usually through lot pooling, and resubdivision of lots in premature or antiquated subdivisions to bring them into conformance with modern subdivision regulations. Lot "pooling" is the "collection" of lots which is usually necessary for a jurisdiction to undertake a readjustment program.[109]

§ 7:9   Conservation Subdivisions

Conservation subdivisions, or cluster subdivisions as they are frequently called, are residential or mixed-use developments in which a significant portion of the tract being subdivided is designated as undivided and permanently preserved open space.[110] The lots to be built on are clustered on the remainder of the tract. They are inspired by cluster communities [111] and golf course developments but they are innovative in that the protected open space areas may be forests, meadows, wetlands, aquifer recharge areas, gardens, or even working farms. They thus differ dramatically from the conventional, sometimes called "cookie cutter," approach to subdivision where the entire tract is divided in to buildable lots usually of uniform size with any open space being provided by setback lines within the privately owned lots or home owner association owned active recreational areas. Conservation subdivisions are of relatively recent origin and

---

[106] Id at 1005. For an in depth discussion of the decision and its context and importance in California subdivision regulation law, see D. Curtin and C. Talbert, California Land Use and Planning Law 136–139 (26th ed. 2006).

[107] See Fla. Stat. Ann. § 177.101; Or. Rev. Stat. § 92.225(2). In most states there are statutory limitations designed to protect land owners who have already built on their lots.

[108] See *Harbor View No. 7, Inc. v. Willson,* 120 So. 2d 453 (Fla. 2d DCA 1960).

[109] F. Schnidman, Resolving Platted Lands Problem: The Florida Experience, 1 Land Assembly & Dev. 27 (1987).

[110] Griffith, Green Infrastructure: The Imperative of Open Space Preservation, 42/43 Urb. Law. 259 (2010–11.

[111] See §§ 7:17 and 13:10 infra.

in their current format are attributable to planning implementation of smart growth and new urbanism principles.[112]

The advocates of conservation subdivisions see them as not only friendly to the environment—through protection of open space, environmentally sensitive land, and preservation of historic structures or agricultural operations—but as meaningful growth management and planning tools to promote such principles of new urbanism as provision of on—site passive and active recreation so as to promote health through discouraging obesity and sedimentary life styles.[113] Furthermore, conservation subdivisions are said to be developer friendly ways of achieving planning goals since they lessen infrastructure costs for developers by encouraging clustering of development that reduces infrastructure costs to both developers and the community. They often allow developers to charge more because of the increased amenities they contain and at the same time reduce the need for public funding of green space.[114]

A local government's land use regulatory program often needs revision or amendment to facilitate development of conservation subdivisions. The starting point in mandatory planning or consistency jurisdictions is to provide for their use in the local government's comprehensive plan. A second step is to ensure that local zoning regulations permit mixed uses (if that is to be the policy) and provide for smaller lots and relaxed setback requirements. A third step is the enactment of a conservation subdivision provision in the subdivision regulations or an independent conservation subdivision ordinance so that the major policies and issues can be implemented upon platting or replatting. At a minimum, such an ordinance should cover a statement of purposes, minimum open space requirements, an explanation/definition of acceptable open space, permitted and prohibited activities on the open space, and detailed provisions in regard to the ownership and management of the open space.[115]

The ultimate success of a conservation subdivision is closely tied to how the ownership and management issue is handled in the ordinance. Usually this is accomplished by a dedication of land to a third party who agrees to maintain but not develop the parcel, or by the imposition of a conservation easement [116] on the land before development occurs. If the former approach is followed the best grantee is usually the subdivision's homeowners association. If a conservation easement is imposed, the homeowners association and or local government should have enforcement powers.[117]

Judicial attention to the legal issues raised by conservation subdivisions is sparse due no doubt to the recent origin of the concept. The Pennsylvania Supreme Court re-

---

[112] See Arendt, Conservation Design for Subdivisions: A Practical Guide To Creating Open Space Networks (1996.

[113] "The format offers a means for local planning officials to accommodate residential growth while preserving natural areas, rural features, and wildlife habitat that is typically altered as sprawl spreads outwards from urban centers. These preserved areas become part of the residential community, accessible via trails and pathways." Austin, Resident Perspectives of the Open Space Conservation Subdivision in Hamburg Township, Michigan, 69 Landscape & Urb. Plan. 245 (2004.

[114] H. Frumkin, L. Frank & R. Jackson, Urban Sprawl and Public Health (2004)4

[115] An excellent conservation subdivision model ordinance can be found at S. Wenger & L. Fowler, Conservation Subdivision Ordinances, Atlanta Regional Commission Community Choices Toolkit: Conservation Subdivisions, Appendix B (2002).

[116] Conservation easements are discussed at §§ 13:12, 15:8 and 15:12 infra.

[117] See Conservation Subdivision Model Ordinance 1.4F, note 6 supra. A state statute may cover these matters.

jected takings and exclusionary zoning claims raised as objections to conservation subdivision restrictions designed to protect prime agricultural and environmentally sensitive lands.[118] The Supreme Court of New Hampshire[119] affirmed a lower court decision allowing a local planning board to revoke its conditional approval of an amendment to a cluster subdivision plan which would have violated that state's "cluster" subdivision statute which provides that open space and development restrictions part of a cluster development create a conservation restriction which runs with the land.[120] Lower courts in other jurisdictions have also reacted positively to the purposes to be served by conservation subdivisions.[121]

§ 7:10   Exactions on Subdivision Approval

As a result of the rapid suburbanization of the United States, there has been a growing acceptance of land use regulations to both accommodate suburban growth and maintain the quality of governmental services. The influx of new residents into suburban areas has forced local governments to provide new streets, water and sewer lines, recreational and educational facilities, police and fire buildings and open space. The increased demand for these local government services in turn raises the difficult question of how a community should finance such services and programs without overburdening either the already strained property tax base or existing local residents who have already contributed to the financing of existing improvements.

Many local governments have chosen to cope with growth-induced financial difficulties by employing a variety of means, including subdivision exactions, to shift the cost of providing capital improvements to the new residents who create the need for them. A subdivision exaction has been defined as "one form of subdivision control, which requires that developers provide certain public improvements at their own expense."[122] No aspect of subdivision control law has interested the casebook authors and the law review article writers more than the question of what kinds of conditions, required dedications, payment of fees and improvements can be imposed for subdivision approval.[123] This emphasis reflects the fact that most subdivision litigation these days concerns exactions. Since subdivision exactions are part of the larger issue of developer funding of infrastructure which is one of the key tenets of growth management law, a brief review of the origins of developer funding requirements as part of the subdivision process and their current legal status will be made at this point but the reader is referred to Chapter 9, for a broader and more in depth analysis.[124]

---

[118] *In re Petition of Dolington Land Group,* 576 Pa. 519, 839 A.2d 1021 (2003).

[119] *Simpson Development Corp. v. City of Lebanon,* 153 N.H. 506, 899 A.2d 988 (2006).

[120] N.H. RSA 674:21-a.

[121]   See *Hay v. New Milford Zoning,* 2006 WL 240518 (Conn. Super. Ct. 2006) (rezoning to conservation subdivision upheld over neighboring landowner objections); *Anderson v. Lenz,* 27 A.D.3d 942, 811 N.Y.S.2d 210 (3d Dep't 2006) (change of land designation to conservation subdivision designation upheld over objection that change decreased provision of affordable housing); *Tevis v. Planning and Zoning Com'n of Town of Wilton,* 1991 WL 32127 (Conn. Super. Ct. 1991). See Ortiz, Biodiversity, The City, and Sprawl, 82 B.U.L. Rev. 145, 183 (2002).

[122] Pavelko, Subdivision Exactions: A Review of Judicial Standards, Wash.U. J. Urb. & Contemp. L. 269, 270 (1983).

[123] A list of recent articles which includes discussions of both exactions and impact fees may be found at § 9.9 Growth Management Techniques: Developer Funding of Infrastructure, infra.

[124] See infra § 9:9 specifically.

Required dedications as a prerequisite for subdivision plat approval were the first land use regulations developed to shift the capital expense burden from local governments to the developer and new residents. Dedication involves a conveyance of an interest in land to the government for a public purpose.[125] Dedications required under subdivision regulations should be distinguished from common law dedications. Common law dedication involves an offer to dedicate and a corresponding acceptance by a local government. Under common law dedication a developer is estopped from later questioning the acceptance. In subdivision regulation dedications, however, questions of legislative authority and constitutionality arise.[126]

Early subdivision enabling statutes authorized local governments to adopt subdivision regulations that required developers to provide and dedicate improvements such as streets.[127] These early statutes were designed to eliminate the confusion of disconnected street systems resulting from earlier voluntary dedications and to avoid future public debt like that incurred as a result of subdivisions made defunct by the real estate crash of the 1920s.[128] Courts often upheld these early mandatory dedications on the "privilege" theory, i.e. that the owner of a subdivision voluntarily dedicates sufficient land for streets in return for the advantage and privilege of having his plat recorded.[129]

During the post-World War II land development boom, many local governments began experiencing severe political and economic pressure from the need to provide facilities and services to new development. Increasingly, subdivision regulations were amended to impose new requirements that developers dedicate park and school sites, widen off-site streets, or contribute funds for a wide variety of purposes.[130] During this period the "in lieu" fee developed as a refinement of required dedications.[131] For example, to require each subdivision to dedicate land to educational purposes would not solve the problem of providing school facilities for developing suburban areas because the sites would often be inadequate in size and imperfectly located.[132] The in-lieu fee solves this problem by substituting a money payment for dedication when the local government determines the latter is not feasible.

---

[125] P. Rohan, Zoning and Land Use Controls § 45.04[2] (1982). The dedicated interest may be an easement or a fee entitlement. See Generally Am. Jur. 2d, Dedications § 23.

[126] See Pavelko, Subdivision Exactions: A Review of Judicial Standards, Wash.U. J. Urb. & Contemp. L. 269, 270 (1983).

4 R. Anderson, American Law of Zoning § 23.26 (4th ed. 1995) (supp.1997); See, generally, Kushner, Subdivision Law & Growth Management § 6:20 (2d ed.).

[127] See R. Freilich and M. Schultz, Model Subdivision Regulations Planning and Law, p. 1 (American Planning Association) (1995).

[128] See Note, Money Payment Requirements as Conditions to the Approval of Subdivision Maps: Analysis and Prognosis, supra note 2, at 296; see generally supra § 7:2.

[129] *Ridgefield Land Co. v. City of Detroit,* 241 Mich. 468, 217 N.W. 58 (1928). See also *Brous v. Smith,* 304 N.Y. 164, 106 N.E.2d 503 (1952); *Ayres v. City Council of City of Los Angeles,* 34 Cal. 2d 31, 207 P.2d 1, 11 A.L.R.2d 503 (1949); *Garvin v. Baker,* 59 So. 2d 360 (Fla. 1952); Pavelko, Subdivision Exactions: A Review of Judicial Standards, Wash.U. J. Urb. & Contemp. L. 269, 283 (1983).

[130] See, Kushner, Subdivision Law & Growth Management § 6:20 (2d ed.).

[131] Juergensmeyer and Blake, Impact Fees: An Answer to Local Governments' Capital Funding Dilemma, 9 Fla. St. U. L. Rev. 415, 418 (1981); Arthur C. Nelson, James C. Nicholas and Julian C. Juergensmeyer, Impact Fees: Principles and Practice of Proportionate-Share Development Fees, Ch. 3 (2009).

[132] 4 R. Anderson, American Law of Zoning § 19.42(4th ed. 1995) (supp.1997).

Also during the 1950's, the "privilege" theory of granting governmental benefits and permits came under intense criticism.[133] In response to this criticism the Supreme Court began to enlarge the concept of "property" to include the reasonable expectation of government grants, permits and benefits.[134] Therefore, at the very time that local governments were expanding their use of exactions the privilege theory rationale for mandatory dedication appeared destined for obsolescence as the subdivision of property began to seem more like a right than a privilege.[135]

As a result of increased demands by local governments for more contributions, and increased reluctance to characterize governmental permits as privileges, courts began to draw back from the approval previously given to privilege theory based principles of mandatory dedication. Based on this retrenchment, some commentators suggested that exactions should be permissible only for facilities that are of exclusive benefit to the new subdivision, such as internal subdivision streets, sewers and neighborhood parks.[136] They concluded that facilities whose benefit extends beyond a subdivision, such as arterial roads and regional parks, were not appropriate subjects for exactions even if the facilities were of substantial benefit to the residents of the subdivision as well.

Two early landmark decisions regarding subdivision exactions placed an almost insurmountable burden on local governments seeking money payments for extradevelopment capital spending from developers whose activities necessitated such expenditures. In *Pioneer Trust & Savings Bank v. Village of Mount Prospect,*[137] a developer challenged the validity of an ordinance requiring subdividers to dedicate one acre per 60 residential lots for schools, parks, and other public purposes. In determining whether required dedications or money payments for recreational or educational purposes represented a valid exercise of the police power, the Illinois Supreme Court propounded the "specifically and uniquely attributable" test. The court focused on the origin of the need for the new facilities and held that unless the village could prove that the demand for additional facilities was "specifically and uniquely attributable" to the particular subdivision, such requirements were an unreasonable regulation not authorized by the police power. Thus, where schools had become overcrowded because of the "total development of the community" the subdivider could not be compelled to help fund new facilities.[138]

A related and equally restrictive test was delineated by the New York court in *Gulest Associates, Inc. v. Town of Newburgh.*[139] In that case developers attacked an or-

[133] See Reich, The New Property, 73 Yale L.J. 733 (1964).

[134] See, e.g., *Speiser v. Randall,* 357 U.S. 513, 78 S. Ct. 1332, 2 L. Ed. 2d 1460 (1958); *Flemming v. Nestor,* 363 U.S. 603, 80 S. Ct. 1367, 4 L. Ed. 2d 1435 (1960); *Sherbert v. Verner,* 374 U.S. 398, 83 S. Ct. 1790, 10 L. Ed. 2d 965 (1963); *Goldberg v. Kelly,* 397 U.S. 254, 90 S. Ct. 1011, 25 L. Ed. 2d 287 (1970); *Bell v. Burson,* 402 U.S. 535, 91 S. Ct. 1586, 29 L. Ed. 2d 90 (1971.

[135] See Bosselman and Stroud, Pariah to Paragon: Developer Exactions in Florida 1975–85, 14 Stetson L. Rev. 527, 529 (1985).

[136] See Reps & Smith, Control of Urban Land Subdivision, 14 Syracuse L. Rev. 405 (1963).

[137] *Pioneer Trust and Sav. Bank v. Village of Mount Prospect,* 22 Ill. 2d 375, 176 N.E.2d 799 (1961).

[138] Ironically, a recent Illinois decision interprets the *Pioneer Trust* standard to be consistent with the proportionate share impact fee concept which developed on the basis of the dual rational nexus cases designed to provide an alternative to the *Pioneer Trust* test. *Northern Illinois Home Builders Ass'n, Inc. v. County of Du Page,* 165 Ill. 2d 25, 208 Ill. Dec. 328, 649 N.E.2d 384 (1995).

[139] *Gulest Associates, Inc. v. Town of Newburgh,* 25 Misc. 2d 1004, 209 N.Y.S.2d 729 (Sup 1960), order aff'd, 15 A.D.2d 815, 225 N.Y.S.2d 538 (2d Dep't 1962) and (disapproved of by, Jenad, Inc. v. Village of Scars-

dinance which charged in lieu fees for recreational purposes. The amounts collected were to be used by the town for "neighborhood park, playground or recreation purposes including the acquisition of property."[140] The court held that the fee was an unreasonable regulation tantamount to an unconstitutional taking because the funds collected were not used solely for the benefit of the residents of the particular subdivision charged, but rather could be used in any section of town for any recreational purposes. In essence, the *Gulest* "direct benefit" test required that funds collected from required payments for capital expenditures be specifically tied to a benefit directly conferred on the homeowners in the subdivision which was charged. If recreational fees were used to purchase a park outside the subdivision, the direct benefit test was not met and the ordinance was invalid.

Perhaps the reason behind these initial restrictive approaches was an underlying judicial suspicion that payment requirements for extradevelopment capital expenditures were in reality a tax. Unlike zoning, payment requirements did not fit neatly into traditional conceptions of police power regulations. By applying the restrictive *Pioneer Trust* and *Gulest* tests, courts imposed the substantial requirements of a special assessment on such payment requirements. This was consistent with perceiving them as a tax. Unfortunately, it effectively precluded their use for most extradevelopment capital funding purposes. Despite this early trend, the *Pioneer Trust* and *Gulest* tests became difficult to reconcile with the planning and funding problems imposed on local governments by the constant acceleration of suburban growth. This restrictiveness also became difficult to rationalize with the judicial view of zoning ordinances as presumptively valid. In contrast to the exclusive benefit theory, in 1964, cost-accounting was advocated as a method for evaluating cost-shifting devices in an article published in the Yale Law Journal by Ira Michael Heyman and Thomas K. Gilhool. This article proposed a new way of evaluating the validity of subdivision exactions. "Given a proper cost-accounting approach," said the authors, "it is possible to determine the costs generated by new residents and thus to avoid charging the newcomers more than a proportionate share." The fact that the general public would also benefit from the exaction is immaterial "so long as there is a rational nexus between the exaction and the costs generated by the creation of the subdivision."[141]

The great appeal of this theory lay in its common sense approach. The transaction between developer and municipality was to be evaluated from an accounting standpoint in the same manner as any other business transaction. If it appeared that the costs were fairly apportioned between the affected parties the transaction should survive judicial scrutiny. Such a theory liberated the developers from the fiction that they were obtaining some sort of privilege, but it also provided local government with a flexible theory that could justify demands for payment of money as easily as for dedication of land. Because the theory was not tied to the financing of any particular type of government facility or service, it could be broadly applied across the whole range of government provision of infrastructure.

---

dale, 18 N.Y.2d 78, 271 N.Y.S.2d 955, 218 N.E.2d 673 (1966)). The *Gulest* decision was overruled in *Jenad, Inc. v. Village of Scarsdale,* 18 N.Y.2d 78, 271 N.Y.S.2d 955, 957, 218 N.E.2d 673 (1966).

[140] 209 N.Y.S.2d at 732.

[141] Heyman & Gilhool, The Constitutionality of Imposing Increases Community Costs on New Subdivision Residents Through Subdivision Exactions, 73 Yale L.J. 1119, 1137 (1964).

The turning point in judicial acceptance of exactions came in a 1965 decision by the Wisconsin Supreme Court in *Jordan v. Village of Menomonee Falls*,[32] which is widely recognized as having established the dual rational nexus test. In response to a developer's attack upon an ordinance requiring developers to pay in lieu fees for educational and recreational purposes as both unauthorized by statute and as an unconstitutional taking without just compensation, the court first concluded that the fee payments were statutorily authorized and then focused first on the *Pioneer Trust* "specifically and uniquely attributable" test.

The Wisconsin Supreme Court expressed concern that it was virtually impossible for a local government to prove that money payment or land dedication requirements were assessed to meet a need *solely* generated by a particular subdivision. Suggesting a substitute test, the court held that money payment and dedication requirements for educational and recreational purposes were a valid exercise of the police power if there was a "reasonable connection" between the need for additional facilities and the growth generated by the subdivision. This first "rational nexus" was sufficiently established if the local government could demonstrate that a series of subdivisions had generated the need to provide educational and recreational facilities for the benefit of this stream of new residents. In the absence of contrary evidence, such proof showed that the need for the facilities was sufficiently attributable to the activity of the particular developer to permit the collection of fees for financing required improvements.[142]

The *Jordan* court also rejected the *Gulest* direct benefit requirement, declining to treat the fees as a special assessment. Therefore, it imposed no requirement that the ordinance restrict the funds to the purchase of school and park facilities that would directly benefit the assessed subdivision. Instead, the court concluded that the relationship between the expenditure of funds and the benefits accruing to the subdivision providing the funds was a fact issue pertinent to the reasonableness of the payment requirement under the police power. The *Jordan* court did not expressly define the "reasonableness" required in the expenditure of extradevelopment capital funds; however, a second "rational nexus" was impliedly required between the expenditure of the funds and benefits accruing to the subdivision. The court concluded that this second "rational nexus" was met where the fees were to be used exclusively for site acquisition and the amount spent by the local government in constructing additional school facilities was greater than the amounts collected from the developments creating the need for additional facilities.

This second "rational nexus" requirement inferred from *Jordan,* therefore, is met if a local government can demonstrate that its actual or projected extradevelopment capital expenditures earmarked for the substantial benefit of a series of developments are greater than the capital payments required of those developments. Such proof establishes a sufficient benefit to a particular subdivision in the stream of residential growth such that the extradevelopment payment requirements may be deemed to be reasonable under the police power.

While the dual rational nexus test quickly became the standard view of most state courts, the United States Supreme Court and other federal courts have used somewhat different language when considering the federal constitutional standards which must

---

[142] Heyman & Gilhool, The Constitutionality of Imposing Increases Community Costs on New Subdivision Residents Through Subdivision Exactions, 73 Yale L.J. 1119, 1137 (1964).

be met by exaction programs. In *Nollan v. California Coastal Commission,*[143] the Court spoke of "essential nexus" when striking down a required dedication requirement. In *Dolan v. City of Tigard,*[144] the Court stressed a need for required dedications to meet a "rough proportionality" test. Whether or not "essential nexus" and "rough proportionality" raise or lower the requirements contained in the "dual rational nexus" test and whether they apply to impact fees or only required dedications of land is controversial and has received much commentary.[145] We discuss these issues and the relevant cases in detail in §§ 9:9 and 10:5[146] and §§ 10:1 et seq.[147]

In recent years the exactions field has expanded beyond the subdivision regulation context. Especially in those jurisdictions with comprehensive plan requirements, growth management programs, and smart growth regulations, the number and scope of developer funding of infrastructure requirements have not only increased dramatically but are more focused on later stages of development regulation than platting. The distinction between site or project related infrastructure and non-site or system related infrastructure has become more important and widely recognized.[148]

The definition of "system" and "project" improvements found in the Georgia Statutes gives insight into the distinction and its significance:

(14) "Project improvements" means site improvements and facilities that are planned and designed to provide service for a particular development project and that are necessary for the use and convenience of the occupants or users of the project and are not system improvements. The character of the improvement shall control a determination of whether an improvement is a project improvement or system improvement and the physical location of the improvement on site or off site shall not be considered determinative of whether an improvement is a project improvement or a system improvement. If an improvement or facility provides or will provide more than incidental service or facilities capacity to persons other than users or occupants of a particular project, the improvement or facility is a system improvement and shall not be considered a project improvement. No improvement or facility included in a plan for public facilities approved by the governing body of the municipality or county shall be considered a project improvement.

---

[143] *Nollan v. California Coastal Com'n,* 483 U.S. 825, 107 S. Ct. 3141, 97 L. Ed. 2d 677, 26 Env't. Rep. Cas. (BNA) 1073, 17 Envtl. L. Rep. 20918 (1987).

[144] *Dolan v. City of Tigard,* 512 U.S. 374, 114 S. Ct. 2309, 2317–20, 129 L. Ed. 2d 304, 38 Env't. Rep. Cas. (BNA) 1769, 24 Envtl. L. Rep. 21083 (1994).

[145] See T. Roberts, ed., Taking Sides on Takings Issues, Ch. 13, D. Curtin, & C. Talbert, Applying Nollan/Dolan to Impact Fees: A Case for the *Ehrlich* Approach; Ch. 14, F. Bosselman, *Dolan* Works; Ch. 15, J. Juergensmeyer & J. Nicholas, Impact Fees Should Not Be Subjected to Takings Analysis (2002).

[146] See infra § 9:8.

[147] See infra § 10:5.

[148] The terms "on-site" and "offsite" infrastructure were once in vogue but are inaccurate since "on site," i.e. site-related infrastructure can actually be located "off-site" and vice versa. "Extradevelopment" and "internal" improvements were also once popular ways of referring to the dichotomy but suffer from the same geographical flaw as on-site and off-site.

(19) "System improvements" means capital improvements that are public facilities and are designed to provide service to the community at large, in contrast to "project improvements".[149]

In an ever increasing number of jurisdictions, subdivision exactions are confined to project related infrastructure improvements and impact and mitigation fees, proffers, concurrency requirements, or "negotiated" development infrastructure conditions are used to obtain developer funding of system improvements. One result of this change in many jurisdictions is that judicial and legislative attention to "exactions" are more and more focused on impact assessment based fees and mitigation programs rather than traditional subdivision dedication requirement or fees in lieu thereof.[150]

III. MAPPING FOR FUTURE STREETS AND OTHER PUBLIC IMPROVEMENTS

§ 7:11   In General[151]

Official mapping provisions are another kind of land use control that implements planning. An official map gives precise locations of future streets within and sometimes without a municipality and sometimes also includes sites for parks and other public improvements.[152] The basis for the regulation is that there is hardly any determinant of future land development as important as the location of future streets. If buildings are placed that interfere with the logical extension of streets, the public authorities are put in the unenviable position of placing major streets around scattered existing development or acquiring improvements at great cost.

The Standard City Planning Enabling Act[153] provided that a plat of an area could be adopted showing streets for future acquisition. Adoption of the plat was a reservation of the indicated streets but was neither the opening of a street nor the taking of land. The Standard Act provision was not widely adopted. The means were too expensive since compensation was paid for the reservation for whatever period of time land was reserved. When the street itself was opened, the Act provided that additional compensation would be paid except for buildings erected in contravention of the easement.

In addition to adoption of a major street plat, streets could also be approved under the Standard Act if shown on the master plan, if on an approved subdivision plat, or if specially approved. Unless approved in one of these ways, Section 18 of the Act provided the municipality could not accept, lay out, open, improve, grade, pave, curb or light any street, or lay or authorize water mains or sewers. In addition, buildings could not

---

[149] Ga. Code Ann. § 36–71–2.

[150] See §§ 9:8 and 10:5 infra.

[151] For a comprehensive discussion of official maps, see Salkin, American Law of Zoning §§ 30:1 et seq. (5th ed.).

[152] Professor Beuscher gave a classic explanation: "In essence the official map is a simple device. It is one way, but not the only way, to fix building lines. The official map may plat future as well as existing streets. Where future streets are mapped, subdividers must conform to the mapped street lay-out, unless they can prevail upon the proper officials to amend the map. Public sewer and water will be installed only in the bed of the mapped streets. Even more important, a landowner who builds in the bed of the mapped street may be refused compensation for his building when the street is ultimately opened and the mapped land taken." Kucirek and Beuscher, Wisconsin's Official Map Law, 1957 Wis. L. Rev. 176, 177 (1957).

[153] U.S. Dep't of Commerce, § 21 (1928).

be erected nor building permits issued unless the street giving access to the building had been approved in one of the four ways.

The competitor to the street plat of the Standard Act became known as the official map because the device was so denominated in Section 4 of the Municipal Planning Enabling Act suggested by Bassett and Williams.[154] The Bassett and Williams Act relied on the police power and formed the basis for legislation in many states. Local governments under the Act could adopt an official map showing existing and future streets and parks. No permit for building in the mapped areas could be issued, unless the land affected would not yield a fair return, in which case a permit in the nature of a variance [155] could be issued to relieve the hardship[156] up to the point of permitting a fair return. Provisions were included similar to those in the Standard Act for preventing utilities in streets and for prohibiting the issuance of building permits where access streets to proposed buildings were not shown on the official map. A requirement that access streets be approved and improved as a condition for issuance of a building permit is valid.[157] The theory is that building permits can be conditioned on reasonable requirements for streets meeting minimum planning and construction standards.

The Municipal Mapped Streets Act also served as another model.[158] Amendments to the model act's official map were automatic when streets were shown on an approved subdivision plat. Buildings could be authorized by variance for two reasons: lack of reasonable return or where the interest of the owner in the use of his property outweighed that of the municipality in preserving the integrity of the official map. As with the other models, utilities could not be placed except on approved streets and building permits could not be issued for proposed buildings which did not have access to approved streets. As with the Municipal Planning Enabling Act, the Municipal Mapped Streets Act contemplated that compensation would be paid only if land was actually taken for a street; no compensation was paid upon adoption of the map or for buildings taken that were not permitted by variance. As a practical matter, compensation is seldom paid, particularly for minor streets, since they are usually obtained by dedication required as a condition for subdivision approval.[159]

A few states have statutes which, rather than authorize variances, seek to keep the restriction within the scope of the police power by limiting the period of time that it can apply. For example, under the statute applied in *Miller v. Beaver Falls,*[160] parks could be designated on a map and once designated no compensation would be paid for buildings if the site was acquired. However, the reservation was void if the site was not acquired by the local government within three years. The court held this provision invalid as beyond the scope of the police power and constituting a taking for which compensation should be paid. The court distinguished between street reservations and

---

[154] Reprinted in E. Bassett, F. Williams, A. Bettman & R. Whitten, Model Laws for Planning Cities, Counties, and States 40 (1935).

[155] See supra § 5:14.

[156] See supra § 5:16.

[157] *Brous v. Smith,* 304 N.Y. 164, 106 N.E.2d 503 (1952).

[158] Reprinted in E. Bassett, F. Williams, A. Bettman & R. Whitten, Model Laws for Planning Cities, Counties, and States 89 (1935).

[159] See supra § 7:10.

[160] *Miller v. City of Beaver Falls,* 368 Pa. 189, 82 A.2d 34 (1951).

park reservations, admitting that the reservation would be valid as to streets because they are narrow, well-defined and absolutely necessary.[161]

Statutes often make official map provisions available to state highway departments. Some states also have special statutes authorizing highway reservations.[162]

§ 7:12   Relation to Master Plan and Planning

As with zoning, official maps or something like them preceded master planning, as a historical matter. In some colonial towns there was one proprietor who owned the land and the town was laid out by map showing dedicated public places. The law of dedication then applied.[163] Where many owners were involved, as in the case of L'Enfant's plan for Washington, D.C., commissioners were given authority to plat the town, owners conveyed property in trust, and a plan was adopted with dedicated areas shown. Regulations similar to modern-day official maps protected future streets in New York City as early as 1806.

Modern official map acts sometimes require some master planning as a prerequisite to official mapping. Acts based on the Standard Act and the Municipal Mapped Streets Act require at least a major street plan, though statutes strictly based on the Bassett and Williams model would not require any kind of plan as a prerequisite.[164] The difference between the major street plan and the official map is that the former only gives general locations, whereas the latter specifies locations and widths to survey accuracy and has the legal effects noted in the previous section.

The overall objective of official maps is the legitimate state interest in promoting health, safety, and welfare of the community. Official maps promote orderly community growth and development so as to prevent construction of buildings and infrastructure that bear no relation to future streets. The result is better community planning that falls within the scope of the government's interest in promoting general health, safety, and welfare and is therefore a valid basis for exercise of the police power. Tying them to and making them complementary of comprehensive plans is an important element in judicial recognition of their constitutional validity as land use regulations pursuant to the police power.[165]

§ 7:13   Relation to Zoning

An official map, like zoning, restricts improvements. Unlike zoning it does not restrict uses requiring no improvements. Since official maps can be used to designate future street widths as well as new streets, the official map device bears some resemblance to front yard requirements in zoning.[166] A front yard requirement under zoning is theoretically used to secure air and light, improve appearance, prevent overcrowd-

---

[161] "For further discussion of what constitutes a reasonable time period see § 7:15 infra.

[162] See Fla. Stat. Ann. § 337.243. See also Brown, Reservation of Highway and Street Rights-of-Way by Official Maps, 66 W. Va. L. Rev. 73 (1964); Mandelker, Planning the Freeway: Interim Controls in Highway Programs, 1964 Duke L.J. 439 (1964).

[163] See supra § 7:10.

[164] See supra § 7:11 for descriptions of these model and standard acts.

[165] See § 7:15 infra for a discussion of the key role integration of comprehensive planning and official maps played in the Supreme Court of Florida's finding of constitutionality in *Palm Beach County v. Wright*, 641 So. 2d 50 (Fla. 1994).

[166] See § 7:11.

ing, mitigate problems of traffic safety on intersections and the like. Practically, the front yard requirement can be used as an official map for the purpose of reducing costs of acquisition when streets are widened. Improvements are in fact kept from the front yard. The official map is also related to zoning in that front yards are often measured from the edge of the officially mapped street rather than the actual street.

Setback provisions,[167] which may be part of the zoning, or subdivision ordinance, or a separate ordinance, are also used to keep improvements from beds of existing but to-be-widened streets.[168]

Setback and front yard requirements under private restrictions have some of the effects of official maps, even if not motivated by a desire to ease the financial burden of acquiring street sites.

§ 7:14   Relation to Subdivision Control

Streets are typically shown on subdivision plats and are often approved in conjunction with the subdivision plat approval. As with official maps, subdivision controls provide that unless a street is approved in some way, streets cannot be opened or improved or utilities placed. Likewise, as with official maps, buildings cannot be built in the streets shown on the subdivision plat and building permits cannot be issued.

Subdivisions and official maps are related in another way under statutes following the Bassett and Williams model.[169] It provides the planning commission with authority to approve subdivision plats showing new streets, highways, or freeways, or the widening thereof only after adoption of the official map. Under other statutes, a subdivision can be rejected if it does not comply with an official map.[170] If no official map has been adopted, a major or master street plan[171] does not have that effect, and the subdivision cannot be rejected, although streets are placed differently than on the master plan.[172]

§ 7:15   Constitutionality

Most of the cases on official maps discussed by the treatise writers and included in the casebooks deal with constitutional problems. This recognizes that property owners whose land is affected by mapped reservations often complain that the prohibition against development constitutes a taking. Landowners also argue that the use of official mapping statutes constitutes an improper attempt to depress the value of mapped land until the power of eminent domain can be exercised.

Actually, official map type provisions were more constitutionally secure at an earlier period than in the nearer past. In the very early days, landowners were so delighted to have roads on their property that land could be had by the public for the asking and compensation was seldom heard of. In that tradition, *In re Furman St.*[173] held that

---

[167] See supra § 4:13 supra.

[168] See, generally, R. Black, Building Lines and Reservations for Future Streets (1935), which is a classic study.

[169] See supra § 7:11.

[170] See *Nigro v. Planning Bd. of Borough of Saddle River,* 122 N.J. 270, 584 A.2d 1350 (1991).

[171] See supra § 7:12.

[172] *Lordship Park Ass'n v. Board of Zoning Appeals of Town of Stratford,* 137 Conn. 84, 75 A.2d 379 (1950). But see *Krieger v. Planning Commission of Howard County,* 224 Md. 320, 167 A.2d 885 (1961).

[173] *In re Furman St.,* 17 Wend. 649, 1836 WL 2754 (N.Y. Sup 1836).

the owner of a building subsequently erected in the bed of an officially mapped street in 1819 was not entitled to any compensation for the building when the street was actually opened, even though the statute did not address the question of compensation for buildings built in mapped streets. The court stated that the mapping and orderly development of the area had in effect already compensated property owners in the area due to increased values.

Forster v. Scott,[174] however, led to some doubts about the constitutionality of the official map statute. In that case an entire lot was covered by a street reservation and there was no provision for variance. It was not surprising that the court held the provision invalid, as it would today if a land use restriction makes an entire separately owned parcel virtually unusable.[175] However, the case led many to assume that official mapping was constitutionally risky without payment of compensation.[176]

In *Gorieb v. Fox,*[177] the U.S. Supreme Court upheld the fixing of a setback line along streets. Therefore it was not a major step in *Headley v. Rochester*[178] for the New York court to approve an official map provision which reserved 25 feet from a large lot for a widened street. The court technically reached this result because the landowner did not apply for the variance to relieve hardship authorized by the statute, but the case is read more broadly than that because courts often do not apply an exhaustion of remedies doctrine when a constitutional issue is raised.[179] Similarly, in *State ex rel. Miller v. Manders,*[180] even though a substantial portion of a lot was reserved for a street, and the owner was denied a building permit, the court refused to hold the statute unconstitutional where no variance was first sought.[181]

While compensation is clearly due where a municipality permanently acquires a street, park or other public site, the official map statutes state they intend no taking, and a temporary reservation does not appear to be an undue burden under the police power. Support for the constitutionality of official map statutes and reservations as interim development restrictions can be found in the interim zoning cases.[182] However, courts have held official mapping statutes unconstitutional where the statute authorizes a reservation for a specific number of years.[183] Where the official map statutes operate more like zoning, imposing a restriction against improvements for an indefinite rather than a fixed time, with variances to relieve hardship, the courts are more dis-

---

[174] *Forster v. Scott,* 136 N.Y. 577, 32 N.E. 976 (1893).

[175] But see *Consolidated Rock Products Co. v. City of Los Angeles,* 57 Cal. 2d 515, 20 Cal. Rptr. 638, 370 P.2d 342 (1962).

[176] See infra §§ 10:1 et seq. on constitutional issues.

[177] *Gorieb v. Fox,* 274 U.S. 603, 47 S. Ct. 675, 71 L. Ed. 1228, 53 A.L.R. 1210 (1927).

[178] *Headley v. City of Rochester,* 272 N.Y. 197, 5 N.E.2d 198 (1936).

[179] Compare *Jensen v. City of New York,* 42 N.Y.2d 1079, 399 N.Y.S.2d 645, 369 N.E.2d 1179 (1977) (not required to seek permit) with *59 Front St. Realty Corp. v. Klaess,* 6 Misc. 2d 774, 160 N.Y.S.2d 265 (Sup. 1957) (variance required).

[180] *State ex rel. Miller v. Manders,* 2 Wis. 2d 365, 86 N.W.2d 469 (1957).

[181] See, generally, Waite, The Official Map and the Constitution in Maine, 15 Me. L. Rev. 3 (1963).

[182] See supra § 3:20.

[183] *Miller v. City of Beaver Falls,* 368 Pa. 189, 82 A.2d 34 (1951) (3 year reservation for parks); *Urbanizadora Versalles, Inc. v. Rivera Rios,* 701 F.2d 993 (1st Cir.1983) (14 year reservation for highway); *Lomarch Corp. v. Mayor and Common Council of City of Englewood,* 51 N.J. 108, 237 A.2d 881, 36 A.L.R.3d 745 (1968) (one year reservation for parks); *Joint Ventures, Inc. v. Department of Transp.,* 519 So. 2d 1069 (Fla. 1st DCA 1988), opinion quashed, 563 So. 2d 622 (Fla. 1990) (five years for roads).

posed to approve.[184] The latter kind of statute may actually be a greater burden on the property than the fixed period reservations—the time period may be longer, the landowner has to prove hardship and even if proved he is not entitled to do what he wants, he can only do what must be allowed to reduce the hardship.

Recent litigation and legislative changes in Florida highlight the current issues in regard to the constitutionality of statutory provisions authorizing official maps. The controversy began with *Joint Ventures, Inc. v. Department of Transportation.*[185] The Florida Department of Transportation (DOT) recorded a "map of reservation" pursuant to the relevant Florida statutory provision which precluded the issuance of development permits or construction of improvements for a five year period which could be extended for another five years.[186] A landowner filed suit claiming that the effect of the statutory provision for maps of reservation was to take property without compensation. Although the lower courts dismissed the suit they certified the issue to the Supreme Court of Florida which held in a 4 to 3 decision that the statutory provision was facially unconstitutional because it illegally froze property sales in an attempt to depress property values in anticipation of the exercise of eminent domain and that the map therefore effected a "taking."

Four years later the Supreme Court of Florida decided another mapping case and this time found the use of the map to be a valid exercise of the police power. In *Palm Beach County v. Wright,*[187] the question certified to the court was:

> Is a county thoroughfare map designating corridors for future roadways, and which forbids land use activity that would impede future construction of a roadway, adopted incident to a comprehensive county land use plan enacted under the local government comprehensive planning development regulation act, facially unconstitutional under *Joint Ventures . . .*?

The Supreme Court of Florida answered in the negative and stressed that the map in *Wright* was designed to implement the Palm Beach County comprehensive Plan. The court explained that its decision in *Joint Ventures* was based on the unconstitutionality of the "map of reservation" statute, which violated due process and not because it was a taking per se. The court further reasoned that the fact that the thoroughfare map is not recorded and can be amended twice a year meant that it limited development only to the extent necessary to ensure compatibility with the land use plan. The key distinction to the court was that the purpose of Palm Beach County's map was to serve as a valuable long range planning tool while the statutory map reservation used by the Florida DOT in *Joint Ventures* was designed to freeze and depress property values.

Before *Wright* was decided, the Florida Legislature responded to *Joint Ventures* in 1990 by enacting a provision on "Roadway Corridor Official Maps," which it amended

---

[184] *Palm Beach County v. Wright,* 612 So. 2d 709 (Fla. 4th DCA 1993), decision quashed, 641 So. 2d 50 (Fla. 1994) (Thoroughfare map authorized by comprehensive plan held constitutional.).

[185] *Joint Ventures, Inc. v. Department of Transp.,* 519 So. 2d 1069 (Fla. 1st DCA 1988), opinion quashed, 563 So. 2d 622 (Fla. 1990).

[186] Fla. Stat. Ann. § 337.241(1).

[187] *Palm Beach County v. Wright,* 641 So. 2d 50 (Fla. 1994). See R. Freilich and D. Bushek, Integrating Land-Use and Transportation: The Case of Palm Beach County v. Wright 18 #2 ABA State and Local Law News 1 (Winter 1995).

in 1995.[188] Under this new provision if a local government designates a "transportation corridor" in its comprehensive plan then before it can grant any zoning change or building permit for land located within the map corridor it must give DOT notice after which DOT must inform the land owner whether it intends to acquire the land in question.

The Florida experience suggests that mapping which is part of comprehensive plan implementation will be looked on favorably by the courts as a legitimate exercise of the police power but that state transportation mapping is suspect if there is no purchase plan to implement it.[189]

§ 7:16 Effect of Official Map on Marketability of Title

Generally, a zoning ordinance is not an encumbrance on title that makes property unmarketable, except where property is improved with an illegal nonconforming building. Perhaps because the official map usually designates roads and in some respects is like an easement for roads, the general rule is different in the case of official maps. A widening line has been construed to be an encumbrance as has a future mapped street over part or all of the property (despite the likely unconstitutionality of the official map provision if enforced in the latter case). The official map is an encumbrance as to buildings illegally built in the mapped area.[190] Even where a building preexisted the mapping of the street, the mapping provision was found to be an encumbrance.[191] The difference in the cases may be that the official map provisions appear to be more like easements to the court or that buyers generally would not be on guard for such provisions, as they would or should be in the case of zoning.

IV. PLANNED UNIT DEVELOPMENTS

§ 7:17 Definition and History

The planned unit development (PUD) is a recent and innovative approach to land use development. Its parentage is a union of cluster zoning and subdivision platting.[192] The definition of a PUD which is most frequently encountered is:

> 'Planned unit development' means an area of land, controlled by a landowner, to be developed as a single entity for a number of dwelling units, and commercial and industrial uses, if any, the plan for which does not correspond in lot size, bulk, or type of dwelling or commercial or industrial use, density, lot coverage and required open space to the regulations established in any one or more districts cre-

---

[188] Fla. Stat. Ann. § 337.243. In 1992, the Florida Legislature repealed the map reservation provision disapproved of in *Joint Ventures,* Laws of 1992, Ch. 92–152 § 108.

[189] See Andrews, Official Maps and the Regulatory Takings Problem: A Legislative Solution, 2011 BYU L. Rev. 2251 (2011).

[190] *Bibber v. Weber,* 199 Misc. 906, 102 N.Y.S.2d 945 (Sup 1951), order aff'd, 278 A.D. 973, 105 N.Y.S.2d 758 (2d Dep't 1951). But see *Lansburgh v. Market St. Ry. Co.,* 98 Cal. App. 2d 426, 220 P.2d 423, 21 A.L.R.2d 785 (1st Dist. 1950) distinguishing New York cases.

[191] See, generally, Kucirek and Beuscher, Wisconsin's Official Map Law, 1957 Wis. L. Rev. 176, 201–211 (1957).

[192] The recent popularity of conservation or cluster subdivisions discussed in § 7:9 supra has further mixed the two concepts.

ated, from time to time, under the provisions of a municipal zoning ordinance enacted pursuant to the conventional zoning enabling act of the state.[193]

A PUD which contains only residential uses may be called a planned unit residential development (PURD) and a purely commercial uses planned unit development may be called a planned unit commercial development (PUCD). We use the acronym PUD here to refer to residential, commercial, industrial, and mixed use developments which are developed pursuant to planned unit development concepts. A PUD is primarily an alternative to traditional zoning since it provides a mixing of uses. The location and identification of the permitted uses are provided on the PUD map or plat, which closely resembles a subdivision plat. Development approval is generally granted for the PUD at one time rather than on a lot by lot basis and in that way closely tracks the subdivision approval process.

The planned unit development concept is sometimes traced to a provision contained in Section 12 of Bassett's Model Planning Enabling Act of 1925.[194] Under that section:

the legislative body [could] authorize the planning board to make * * * changes upon approving subdivision plats, when the owner [submitted] a plan designating the lots on which apartment houses and local shops are to be built and indicating the maximum density of population and the minimum yard requirements per lot. Section 12 also limited the average population density and the total land area covered by buildings in the entire subdivision to that permitted in the original zoning district * * *. Upon the approval of the planning board following a public hearing with proper notice, the changes were to become part of the municipality's zoning regulations.[195]

Although available since the 1920's, planned unit development provisions were not widely utilized until the 1960's. The newfound popularity of planned unit developments coincides with large scale development in the post second world war era. By the early sixties the incompatibility of traditional zoning and larger residential developments was recognized, and the push for the adoption of planned unit development ordinances began.[196] Today, large mixed use developments are the rule rather than the exception, and planned unit development (PUD) regulations represent one attempt to avoid the problems of large scale development under conventional zoning notions.

Conventional subdivision regulations often place significant restrictions on a developer's ability to design an attractive and desirable community. For example, typical subdivision regulations might require the developer to construct roads in a certain de-

---

[193] U.S. Advisory Commission on Intergovernmental Relations, ACIR State Legislative Program, 1970 Cumulative Supp. 31–36–00 at 5 (1969).

[194] Bassett, Laws of Planning Unbuilt Areas, in Neighborhood and Community Planning, Regional Survey Vol. VII, 272–73 (1929). Model legislation for PUDs was proposed in 1965. Babcock, Krasnowiecki and McBride, The Model State Statute, 114 U. Pa. L. Rev. 140 (1965). See D. Mandelker, Land Use Law § 9.29 (3rd ed. 1993).

[195] Krasnowiecki, Planned Unit Development: A Challenge to Established Theory and Practice of Land Use Control, 114 U. Pa. L. Rev. 47, 48 (1965).

[196] See, e.g., Goldston and Scheuer, Zoning of Planned Residential Developments, 73 Harv. L. Rev. 241 (1959); Symposium: Planned Unit Development, 114 U. Pa. L. Rev. 1, 1–170 (1965); R. Burchell, Planned Unit Developments (1972); White & Jourdan, Neotraditional Development: A Legal Analysis, Land Use & Zoning Dig. 3 (Aug. 1997).

sign or pattern.[197] When these types of subdivision regulations are coupled with conventional Euclidean zoning,[198] which eliminates commercial uses and mandates lot size, building height, and house placement, the result may be a "cookie cutter" subdivision where the residents have no choice but to drive several miles to purchase a gallon of milk.[199]

To avoid these unwanted developments, local governments may choose to implement planned unit development regulations, which allow the developer to create a community with a desirable combination of both residential and commercial uses,[200] while still requiring the development to pay for its added burdens on the existing community through exactions.[201] Additionally, the local government can use planned unit development approval to insure that the new development is consistent with the government's growth management plan and in order to achieve smart growth.[202]

Planned unit developments are basically designed to permit the development of entire neighborhoods, or in some cases even towns, based on an approved plan. The completed development usually includes a variety of residential types, common open space for recreation, parks, and in some cases, commercial or even industrial areas. Since the entire project is preplanned the completed development can be based upon a logical and coherent mixture of uses.

The PUD principle is that a land area under unified control can be designed and developed in a single operation, usually by a series of prescheduled phases, and according to an officially approved "plan." The plan does not necessarily have to correspond to the property and use regulations of the zoning district in which the development is located.[203] As can be seen from the definition, the planned unit development concept abandons the lot by lot approach to development, and is primarily an alternative to zoning.

The Supreme Court of Oregon in *Frankland v. City of Lake Oswego,*[204] listed to following objectives of planned unit developments:

(1) to achieve flexibility;

(2) to provide a more desirable living environment than would be possible through the strict application of zoning ordinance requirements;

(3) to encourage developers to use a more creative approach in their development of land;

(4) to encourage a more efficient and more desirable use of open land; and

---

[197] Nolon, Local Land Use Controls That Achieve Smart Growth, 31 Envtl. L. Rep. 11025 (2001).

[198] See supra § 4:2.

[199] Nolon, Local Land Use Controls That Achieve Smart Growth, 31 Envtl. L. Rep. 11025 (2001).

[200] See infra § 7:19.

[201] See supra § 7:10.

[202] Mandelker, Managing Space to Manage Growth, 23 Wm. & Mary Envtl. L. & Pol'y Rev. 801 (1999).

[203] See *Alta Vita Condominium Ass'n v. Zoning Hearing Bd. of Tp. of Hempfield,* 736 A.2d 724 (Pa. Commw. Ct. 1999) (holding under Pa. Stat. Ann. tit. 53, § 10711 once a PUD is adopted the districts zoning and subdivision regulations no longer apply).

[204] *Frankland v. City of Lake Oswego,* 267 Or. 452, 517 P.2d 1042 (1973).

(5) to encourage variety in the physical development pattern of the city.[205]

Cluster development and planned unit development are sometimes viewed as the same thing. It is more accurate to define cluster development as a device for grouping dwellings to increase dwelling densities on some portions of the development area in order to have other portions free of buildings.[206] Many planned unit developments use cluster development as a technique but the planned unit development concept typically encompasses more.[207] However, as pointed out at the beginning of this section, the increasing popularity of conservation subdivisions, often called cluster subdivisions, and new urbanism inspired planned cluster developments has blurred the lines between the two approaches and the two concepts increasingly overlap. This trend will no doubt be accelerated by the increasing use of unified developments codes which combine zoning, subdivision, clustering, planned unit development, and smart growth regulation into a single code.[208]

§ 7:18   Relationship to Zoning

Under typical zoning, where there may be no close relation to a plan,[209] the landscape is divided "into districts . . . [and] [a]ll . . . regulations shall be uniform . . . throughout each district. . . . "[210] In planned unit developments, the area is not districted. A commercial use may be next to a residential use and different types of residential uses may be mixed with no intention of placing them in districts. Special conditions and controls may apply without uniformity to some commercial uses and not to others, so as to better integrate the commercial and residential development. Spot zoning[211] (in a descriptive sense of a small parcel of property controlled differently than adjacent parcels) is or may be the rule in a PUD, rather than something to be avoided.

The PUD technique may not be compatible with a typical zoning enabling act, thus leading to difficulties in the implementation of a planned unit development.[212] There may be no territorial districts and uniformity of use within a district under PUDs.[213] Zoning without districting and without uniformity within districts may be held invalid as it was in *Rockhill v. Chesterfield Township*.[214] The whole town was in effect, a single district in which residential and agricultural uses were permitted, but all other uses were permitted only by special permit under a standard of benefit to the general development of the township.[215] Similarly, floating zones have been held inva-

---

[205] Frankland, 517 P.2d at 1047.

[206] *Chrinko v. South Brunswick Tp. Planning Bd.*, 77 N.J. Super. 594, 187 A.2d 221 (Law Div. 1963), is a leading case explaining and upholding cluster zoning.

[207] See, generally, Dyckman, Book Review, 12 UCLA L. Rev. 991 (1965); Urban Land Institute, New Approaches to Residential Land Development, Tech.Bull. No. 40 chs. 1–2 (1961).

[208] See Robert H. Freilich and S. Mark White, 21st Century Land Development Code (American Planning Association 2008); Duany and Talen, Making the Good Easy: The Smart Code Alternative, 29 Fordham Urb. L.J 1445 (2002).

[209] The plan to which zoning is to accord is usually read to mean the scheme of zoning itself. See supra §§ 2:1 et seq.

[210] U.S. Dept. of Commerce, A Standard State Zoning Enabling Act § 2 (1926). See supra § 4:1.

[211] See supra § 5:10.

[212] See Krasnowiecki, Planned Unit Development: A Challenge to Established Theory and Practice of Land Use Control, 114 U. Pa. L. Rev. 47 (1965).

[213] See, generally, Turner and Morgan, Planned Development Zoning: A Texas Perspective, Ch. 5, Inst. Planning, Zoning and Eminent Domain (1992).

[214] *Rockhill v. Chesterfield Tp., Burlington County*, 23 N.J. 117, 128 A.2d 473 (1957).

[215] See, generally, supra §§ 5:24 to 5:26.

lid because they are not pre-applied to a particular area so as to show on a zoning map.[216] A PUD may not involve a precise zoning map. A PUD is often treated as a floating zone under local ordinances.[217] When conditions have been imposed on zoning, giving rise to so-called contract zoning, the courts have sometimes held the zoning invalid. In a PUD, conditions are imposed that may vary from parcel to parcel, and contract zoning issues may also arise.[218]

Therefore, to avoid adverse judicial decisions, to avoid the impairing effects of non-unitary development controls, and to devise schemes permitting more flexibility, PUD developers have sought routes around conventional zoning. In some cases the special use permit is used under the legal fiction that a PUD could be viewed as a single development having such special characteristics as to be appropriate for special permit treatment. The special permit [219] is a device which allows a special use to be established subject to conditions. But more than a few courts did not see anything special about large-scale development.[220] Variances[221] have sometimes also been misused to permit planned unit developments.[222] Other PUD developers have sought to accomplish PUDs under subdivision enabling acts.[223] Those Acts generally had the advantage of providing more administrative than legislative control and of allowing the use of conditions. But stretching the subdivision enabling acts to cover PUDs was fraught with danger when millions of dollars were to be invested in a PUD. Therefore, pressures began to develop for special enabling legislation for PUDs.[224]

The zoning-like provisions for the PUD are described in the model acts. For example, one of the model PUD enabling acts provides:

(a) Permitted Uses. An ordinance adopted pursuant to this Act shall set forth the uses permitted . . . .

(b) . . . (1) An ordinance adopted pursuant to this Act shall establish standards governing the density, or intensity of land use . . . .

(2) Said standards shall take into account that the density, or intensity of land use, otherwise allowable on the site under the provisions of a zoning ordinance previously enacted pursuant to [the general zoning enabling act] may not be appropriate for a Planned Unit . . . Development . . . .[225]

---

[216] *Eves v. Zoning Bd. of Adjustment of Lower Gwynedd Tp.,* 401 Pa. 211, 164 A.2d 7 (1960). *City of Waukesha v. Town Bd. of Town of Waukesha,* 198 Wis. 2d 592, 543 N.W.2d 515 (Ct. App. 1995). See, generally, supra § 4:16.

[217] A "sinking zone" may also be used. See Craig, Planned Unit Development as Seen from City Hall, 114 U. Pa. L. Rev. 127, 130 (1965); see also Selmi, The Contract Transformation in Land Use Regulation, 63 Stan. L. Rev. 591 (2011); supra § 4:16.

[218] See supra §§ 4:17 and 5:11.

[219] See supra §§ 5:24 to 5:26.

[220] See supra *Rockhill v. Chesterfield Township,* note 6.

[221] See supra §§ 5:14 to 5:23.

[222] See Goldston and Scheuer, Zoning of Planned Residential Developments, 73 Harv. L. Rev. 241, 250 (1959).

[223] See supra § 7:2.

[224] See supra § 7:17.

[225] Babcock, Krasnowiecki, McBride, The Model State Statute, 114 U. Pa. L. Rev. 140, 144–145 (1965).

As the commentary on the Act indicates, intensity of land use includes such density concepts as number of dwelling units per acre or minimum square footage of lot area per dwelling unit. But the Act uses intensity of land use more broadly to include a balancing of bulk, height, open space and dwelling units to reach a permitted concentration.

The Act also provides for other zoning-like controls:

(f) . . . An ordinance adopted pursuant to this Act shall set forth the standards and criteria by which the design, bulk and location of buildings shall be evaluated . . . .[226]

The intensity of use is often carried out by a scheme entitled land-use intensity (LUI). Even if the local ordinance does not expressly provide for LUI, a developer may want to conform to LUI in order to qualify the development for FHA insured loans.

The FHA has devised standards for PUDs and it determines the appropriate LUI and assigns a number. The LUI number is based on a planning analysis and a real estate judgment regarding the proposed site, its community, and the market. For example, if the FHA should determine that the area measured in square feet can be developed at an LUI of a designated number, the developer can easily determine from charts available from FHA the proper or required:

(1) Total floor area of all buildings (floor area ratio);[227]

(2) Total open space (open space ratio);

(3) Open space not used for cars (livability space);

(4) Open space planned for active and passive recreation (recreation space);

(5) Total parking spaces for the number of planned dwelling units, some of which may be on the streets (total car ratio); and

(6) Total offstreet parking spaces (occupant car ratio).[228]

§ 7:19   Legal Status of PUDs

PUD ordinances have been upheld even where not specially authorized by enabling legislation. The first clear-cut and still leading case upholding PUDs is *Cheney v. Village 2 at New Hope, Inc.*[229] An ordinance had created a PUD district and another ordinance[230] rezoned an area PUD that had previously been zoned single family. The PUD zone permitted a wide variety of residential uses as well as professional, public,

---

[226] Babcock, Krasnowiecki, McBride, The Model State Statute, 114 U. Pa. L. Rev. 140, 152 (1965).

[227] See supra § 4:14.

[228] Further descriptions of the FHA-LUI are in Henke, Planned Unit Development and Land Use Intensity, 114 U. Pa. L. Rev. 15 (1965); Bair, How to Regulate Planned Unit Developments for Housing—Summary of a Regulatory Approach, 17 Zoning Digest 185 (1985).

[229] *Cheney v. Village 2 at New Hope, Inc.,* 429 Pa. 626, 241 A.2d 81 (1968). See, *Frankland v. City of Lake Oswego,* 267 Or. 452, 517 P.2d 1042 (1973); Zuker & Wolffe, Supreme Court Legalizes PUD: New Hope from New Hope, 2 Land Use Controls No. 2, at 32 (1968). But see *Lutz v. City of Longview,* 83 Wash. 2d 566, 520 P.2d 1374 (1974).

[230] See supra § 4:16 on floating zones.

recreational and commercial uses. The ordinance provided that the buildable land could be developed up to 80% residential and 20% commercial. A minimum of 20% of the land had to be devoted to open space. The residential density could not exceed 10 units per acre, no building could exceed 12 units and no residence could include more than two bedrooms. There were no traditional setback and side-yard requirements, though a distance of 24 feet was required between buildings. The court rejected arguments that the PUD did not accord with a previously adopted comprehensive plan by indicating that a plan can be changed by adoption of the PUD ordinance if done deliberately and thoughtfully.[231] The court also rejected the allegations that the PUD ordinances constituted spot zoning and that there was an improper delegation of legislative authority because the planning commission had to decide exactly where, within a particular PUD district, specific types of buildings should be placed.[232]

The court reviewed in detail whether the planning commission, the legislative body or the board of adjustment could most appropriately handle the details of the development and concluded that the planning commission was appropriate. The legislative body would otherwise involve itself in too much detail. The board of adjustment functions were to hear appeals, to grant variances and to issue special permits. The court did not believe that any of those powers were as appropriate to implementation of PUD details as were the powers conferred on a planning commission. The court regarded final PUD detailed review as not materially different from subdivision approval, a traditional planning commission function.[233]

Cheney might not have been decided favorably to PUDs,[234] since the Pennsylvania court hardly had the reputation of approving novel approaches to land use controls. However, the *Cheney* decision might not be followed in all states. For example, the California court which would have been expected to uphold PUDs,[235] departed from its earlier tradition of authorizing virtually standardless delegation of authority to administrative agencies, and in *Millbrae Association for Residential Survival v. Millbrae* [236] established some important limitations on PUDs.

In California, as in many states, a rezoning can be accomplished only by the local legislature after notice and hearing. In order to comply with that requirement, the City of Millbrae enacted an ordinance which provided a two-step approval of PUDs. In the first step, property was rezoned as a planned development by the legislature after notice and hearing. However, this rezoning was only in the nature of a generalized plan for development. The rezoning provided for only the general size, location and use of proposed buildings and structures, the location and dimensions of streets, parking areas, open areas and other public and private facilities and uses. After the rezoning, the two-step ordinance required the developer to submit a precise plan, which was in the

---

[231] See supra § 5:8.

[232] See supra § 5:10.

[233] Something much like a PUD was approved in *Bigenho v. Montgomery County Council,* 248 Md. 386, 237 A.2d 53 (1968), though the legislative body rezoned particular parts of a large tract, some for local community use, some for commercial office uses, some for industrial uses and some for multiple family uses.

[234] Among other cases, *Eves v. Zoning Bd. of Adjustment of Lower Gwynedd Tp.,* 401 Pa. 211, 164 A.2d 7 (1960) was precedent for holding the PUD invalid. See 2 Zoning Digest 178 (1968).

[235] The California courts generally are more disposed to approve whatever a municipality does including approval of novel land use controls, than the courts of any other state. See e.g., supra §§ 4:16 to 4:19.

[236] *Millbrae Ass'n for Residential Survival v. City of Millbrae,* 262 Cal. App. 2d 222, 69 Cal. Rptr. 251 (1st Dist. 1968). Compare *Peachtree Development Co. v. Paul,* 67 Ohio St. 2d 345, 21 Ohio Op. 3d 217, 423 N.E.2d 1087 (1981); *Mullin v. Planning Bd. of Brewster,* 17 Mass. App. Ct. 139, 456 N.E.2d 780 (1983).

nature of the detailed development plan. The precise plan could be approved by the planning commission alone. But in the precise plan, which was approved by the planning commission without legislative actions, the developer departed from the approved generalized plan and added seven additional apartments to the high-rise buildings, reduced the size of a golf course, increased the number of parking spaces and relocated two high-rise buildings. The plaintiffs alleged that such changes constituted a rezoning which had to be accomplished legislatively. The developer argued that the changes were details that could be authorized by an administrative body as in the case of special permits or variances. The court held:

> while the change in the number of apartments in each of the high-rise buildings would properly be the subject of the precise plan under the ordinance so long as it did not increase the "general size" of the buildings as delineated in the general plan, the other changes amount to a substantial alteration of the general plan since they materially and fundamentally change the location of two of the high-rise buildings and the size of the parking areas and the open areas.[237]

In short, the court upheld the PUD technique in general, but did not permit substantial changes in the planned development plan without legislative action. The California court was thus unwilling to allow delegation to the planning commission to the extent permitted by the Pennsylvania court. The case is notice to developers that some courts will superintend what is "substantial" and not uphold whatever changes the planning commission approves. Since to be safe the developer must go to the legislative body for any "substantial" change between the generalized and the detailed plan (and presumably for any changes of the generalized plan by amendments to the detailed plan), considerable flexibility is lost.

As previously indicated,[238] when courts proved indisposed to allow PUD development under typical zoning enabling legislation, PUD developers began to look for other alternatives. A few states had adopted Bassett's model provisions[239] which appeared to authorize PUDs under subdivision-like authority. But in *Hiscox v. Levine*[240] the court held approval of a development by a planning commission under authority of a statute based on the Bassett model to be invalid. The developer had submitted a plan for a 100-acre subdivision which involved cluster zoning.[241] It showed one house to the half acre rather than one to the acre as called for by the zoning. However, the balance of the 100 acres was dedicated for a park. The court held that the action of the administrative board in allowing lot size reductions for such a large tract was an encroachment on legislative authority. In reviewing the history and language of the Bassett Act, Krasnowiecki concludes that the Hiscox case was improperly decided.[242]

Krasnowiecki also points to language in the subdivision sections of the Standard City Planning Enabling Act which would appear to enable planning commissions to

---

[237] 262 Cal.App.2d at 245, 69 Cal. Rptr. at 267.

[238] Supra § 7:18.

[239] See supra § 7:17.

[240] *Hiscox v. Levine,* 31 Misc. 2d 151, 216 N.Y.S.2d 801 (Sup 1961).

[241] Hiscox, 31 Misc. 2d 151.

[242] Krasnowiecki, Planned Unit Development: A Challenge to Established Theory and Practice of Land Use Control, 114 U. Pa. L. Rev. 47, 80–83 (1965).

approve PUDs in the several states that adopted the provisions. The Act provides that the planning board:

> shall have the power to agree with the applicant upon use, height, area or bulk requirements or restrictions governing buildings and premises within the subdivision, provided such requirements or restrictions do not authorize the violation of the then effective zoning ordinance of the municipality.[243]

The Act also provided:

> regulations may provide for the proper arrangement of streets . . ., for adequate and convenient open spaces for traffic, utilities, access of fire-fighting apparatus, recreation, light and air, and for the avoidance of congestion of population, including minimum width and areas of lots.[244]

The trial court in *Mann v. Fort Thomas*[245] upheld the constitutionality of a PUD ordinance based on the above sections of the Standard Act and sustained a planning commission's denial of an application for a PUD.[246]

Whether PUDs can be authorized under conventional subdivision enabling acts or not, special enabling legislation for PUDs clarifies the matter, and the suggested model acts contain subdivision-like provisions. For example, the model act suggested by the ACIR defines the plan to include "a plat of subdivision . . . private streets, ways and parking facilities, common open space and public facilities . . . ,"[247] all of which matters are part of typical subdivision controls. In other sections the Act calls for the development of standards on "the amount, location and proposed use of common open space,"[248] provisions for municipal acceptance of "the dedication of land or any interest therein for public use and maintenance"[249] and that:

> the authority granted to a municipality to establish standards for the location, width, course and surfacing of public streets and highways, alleys, ways for public service facilities, curbs, gutters, sidewalks, street lights, parks, playgrounds, school grounds, storm water drainage, water supply and distribution, sanitary sewers and sewage collection and treatment, shall be vested in [the body designated to administer the ordinance enacted to implement the Act].[250]

§ 7:20   Scope of Judicial Review

As discussed in the previous section, there is considerable judicial controversy over the choice of local government agency to approve PUDs and the application of general

---

[243] Standard Act § 15. Violation of the zoning ordinance could be avoided through use of a sinking zone. See Craig, Planned Unit Development as Seen from City Hall, 114 U. Pa. L. Rev. 127, 130 (1965).

[244] Standard Act § 14. See § 4:8 on lot size as a zoning or as a subdivision matter.

[245] *Mann v. City of Fort Thomas,* 437 S.W.2d 209 (Ky. 1969).

[246] On appeal, the court did not reach the merits of the issue due to the developer's lack of standing.

[247] U.S. Advisory Commission on Intergovernmental Relations, An Act Authorizing Municipalities to Provide for Planned Unit Development, § 3(4) in 1970 Cumulative ACIR State Legislative Program 31–36–00 at 5 (1969). See Sternlieb, Burchell, Hughes and Listokin, Planned Unit Development Legislation: A Summary of Necessary Considerations, 7 Urb. L. Ann. 71 (1974).

[248] ACIR State Legislative Program § 4(b)(1) at 6.

[249] ACIR State Legislative Program § 34(c)(1) at 7.

[250] ACIR State Legislative Program § 4(e) at 8.

zoning and subdivision regulations to the approval process. The issue has been complicated in several recent decisions by the addition of the legislative versus quasi-judicial dichotomy which has become key to the judicial standards for review in rezoning[251] as influenced by the Fasano[252] and Snyder[253] cases. The reason that this issue is considered by courts when reviewing PUD approval is often attributable to the belief that such approval requires or is considered to be a rezoning. Several recent cases illustrate these issues and their resolution.[254]

In *Evans v. Teton County,*[255] a neighbor challenged approval of a planned unit development and subdivision on the basis of nonconformity with the local plan. The Supreme Court of Idaho discussed the relationship as follows:

> A comprehensive plan is not a legally controlling zoning law, it serves as a guide to local government agencies charged with making zoning decisions . . . . The "in accordance with" language of [the zoning enabling legislation] does not require zoning decisions to strictly conform to the land use designations of the comprehensive plan . . . . However, a board of county commissioners cannot ignore their comprehensive plan when adopting or amending zoning ordinances . . . . Whether approval of a zone change is "in accordance with" the comprehensive plan is a question of fact, which can only be overturned when the factual findings supporting the zone change are clearly erroneous.[256]

The court conducted its review on the basis of a strong presumption of validity and proceeded on the basis that it must affirm the Board of Commissioners unless it violated constitutional or statutory standards, exceeded its statutory authority, followed unlawful procedures, was not supported by substantial evidence, or was arbitrary and capricious. In other words the courts used the fairly debatable standard accorded to legislative decisions. The Supreme Court of Minnesota, in *Dead Lake Association v. Otter Tail County,*[257] reached a similar conclusion in a controversy based on the Lake Association's appeal by writ of certiorari of the grant of a conditional use permit for a PUD. The court held that the attack was on a legislative decision and therefore not reviewable by writ of certiorari.

The standard of review and presumption of validity—or lack thereof—which are determined by the classification of PUD actions as legislative or quasi judicial can easily determine the outcome of the litigation. A recent decision by the Supreme Court of

---

[251] See supra § 5:9.

[252] *Fasano v. Board of County Com'rs of Washington County,* 264 Or. 574, 507 P.2d 23 (1973) (disapproved of by, Neuberger v. City of Portland, 288 Or. 585, 607 P.2d 722 (1980)) and (rejected by, Quinn v. Town of Dodgeville, 120 Wis. 2d 304, 354 N.W.2d 747 (Ct. App. 1984)) and (rejected by, Hampton v. Richland County, 292 S.C. 500, 357 S.E.2d 463 (Ct. App. 1987)).

[253] *Board of County Com'rs of Brevard County v. Snyder,* 627 So. 2d 469 (Fla. 1993).

[254] See D. Mandelker, The Legal Underpinnings for PUDS, PADS, and Other Entitlements for Master Planned Communities, SM004 ALI-ABA 985 (Aug. 2006) (Surveys PUD cases on legislative v. judicial, scope of review, etc.).

[255] See D. Mandelker, The Legal Underpinnings for PUDS, PADS, and Other Entitlements for Master Planned Communities, SM004 ALI-ABA 985 (Aug. 2006) (Surveys PUD cases on legislative v. judicial, scope of review, etc.).

[256] Evans, 73 P.3d at 89. See Sullivan, Recent Developments in Land Use, Planning & Zoning Law: Comprehensive Planning, 36 Urb. Law. 541 (2004).

[257] *Dead Lake Ass'n, Inc. v. Otter Tail County,* 695 N.W.2d 129 (Minn. 2005). See also *BECA of Alexandria, L.L.P. v. County of Douglas ex rel. Bd. of Com'rs,* 607 N.W.2d 459 (Minn. Ct. App. 2000).

Ohio, *Marsalek v. Council of the City of South Euclid,*[258] emphasizes another reason that the classification of a PUD approval as legislative or quasi judicial is important. If the local government's approval of the PUD is considered legislative then in some jurisdictions it may be subjected to initiative or referendum. Not so if it is labeled quasi judicial.[259] In Marsalek, the plaintiff sought a writ of mandamus to submit a resolution which approved a conditional use permit authorizing a residential PUD to referendum. The writ was denied based on the court's conclusion that the Council's adoption of the PUD permit "constituted an administrative act, which is not subject to referendum."[260]

§ 7:21   Planned Unit Development Approval Process

Planned unit development ordinances generally provide a comprehensive review procedure that requires the developer to submit detailed information on the project, including a concept or master plan; and also allow the municipality to condition approval on changes made in the project. Because of the flexibility of the procedure and the opportunity for negotiation between local government and prospective developers, PUD ordinances have been criticized for institutionalizing the bargaining process of land development.[261] However, the flexibility of planned unit development ordinances does allow local government to have input in the development process. Furthermore, by structuring a PUD ordinance to encourage beneficial uses a municipality can develop the future to fit its image.

Most planned unit development ordinances provide for a detailed review procedure. Planned unit development ordinances generally provide for a two-step process in the approval or disapproval of a large scale development.[262] The first step is the establishment of an overlay district or master plan.[263] Planned development districts must be developed in accordance with the officially approved plan.[264]

The application process generally begins with conferences between the developer and the local government planning department and other agencies involved in the approval process. The general purpose of the preapplication conferences is for the developer and the local government officials to assess the relationship of the proposed pro-

---

[258] *State ex rel. Marsalek v. S. Euclid City Council,* 111 Ohio St. 3d 163, 2006-Ohio-4973, 855 N.E.2d 811 (2006).

[259] "Is approval of a PUD a decision to establish a new land use policy (legislative) or a decision to implement a previously-established policy (administrative)? If it is legislative, the referendum is available. When the approval of a PUD is characterized as a rezoning, or when the approval decision is delegated to the legislative body, most courts characterize the approval decision as legislative even though specific criteria control the approval of a PUD." D. Mandelker, The Legal Underpinnings for PUDS, PADS, and Other Entitlements for Master Planned Communities, SM004 ALI-ABA 985 (Aug. 2006).

[260] Marsalek v. S. Euclid City Council, 111 Ohio St. 3d 163, 2006-Ohio-4973, 855 N.E.2d 811 (2006). Contrast *Blakeman v. Planning and Zoning Com'n of City of Shelton,* 82 Conn. App. 632, 846 A.2d 950 (2004) (planning commission PUD decision legislative); *State ex rel. Helujon, Ltd. v. Jefferson County,* 964 S.W.2d 531 (Mo. Ct. App. E.D. 1998) (PUD approval legislative).

[261] Williams and Taylor, American Land Planning Law § 48.02 (2003 Rev. Ed.).

[262] "Under some planned unit development ordinances, the preliminary plan is presented to the legislative body for formal approval and then becomes the precise plan for the development. In the review of minor subdivisions, the process may bypass this step including only sketch plan and final approval" Kushner, Subdivision Law & Growth Management § 7:10 (2d ed.).

[263] See Baers, Zoning Code Revisions to Permit Mixed Use Development, 7 Zoning & Plan. L. Rep. 81, 85 (1984).

[264] A concept plan is a professionally prepared overall concept of the project. See Aloi, Implementation of a Planned Unit Development, 2 Real Est. L.J. 523, 525 (1974).

ject to the existing community. If all goes well, the petitioners for the PUD zoning submit their application along with any required materials.

The developer will then conduct prehearing conferences with the local planning and zoning commission to iron out problem areas and negotiate acceptable compromises. The planning and zoning commission generally can make written proposals for changes in either the petition or the concept plan. After appropriate public notice is given, a public hearing is held before the planning and zoning commission. The planning and zoning commission then makes its official findings and recommends either approval, conditional approval or disapproval.[265] In most jurisdictions, especially those which have not adopted the *Fasano* rule in regard to rezonings,[266] the decision of the legislative body to approve or deny the proposed PUD will most likely be viewed as a legislative act that courts will review with great deference.[267] Therefore, courts usually will uphold the decision,[268] provided that all required criteria set forth in the PUD ordinance are considered.[269] However, courts will reverse the decision if it is made contrary to the underlying zoning regulations,[270] or based on factors not contained in the PUD regulations.[271]

The final step in the initial application process is approval by the local government legislative body. Upon receiving the planning and zoning commission's recommendation, the legislative body holds a public hearing on the application, and may either grant the proposed rezoning to PUD; deny it; or grant the rezoning with conditions or modifications. If the legislative body approves the proposed application for rezoning, the concept plan of development is adopted as an amendment to the zoning code.

After a concept plan has been approved it establishes a master plan of usages. Any area development within the planned community district is a planned unit development. The second step of the large scale development is approval of the individual planned unit developments. Planned unit developments can be rezoned by resolution, after the master development plan has been adopted, since they are now in accordance with the amended zoning code.

The planned unit development procedure offers a number of benefits. First, the local government's polestar in evaluating a project is whether it is in accordance with the planning and development objectives of the jurisdiction. Second, by providing a detailed application procedure and requiring a concept plan, the local government is in a

---

[265] By keeping the planning board in an advisory capacity and deferring the decision to the city council a local government may avoid a delegation of authority challenge. See Aloi, Implementation of a Planned Unit Development, 2 Real Est. L.J. 523, 532 (1974).

[266] See §§ 2:13, 5:9, and 7:20 supra.

[267] See *State ex rel. Helujon, Ltd. v. Jefferson County,* 964 S.W.2d 531, 536 (Mo. Ct. App. E.D. 1998) (holding "approval of PUD classifications" is a legislative act); *City of Tuscaloosa v. Bryan,* 505 So. 2d 330 (Ala. 1987); *Peachtree Development Co. v. Paul,* 67 Ohio St. 2d 345, 21 Ohio Op. 3d 217, 423 N.E.2d 1087 (1981); but see *McCallen v. City of Memphis,* 786 S.W.2d 633 (Tenn. 1990). For standard of review see supra §§ 5:37 and 7:20.

[268] *Sheridan Planning Ass'n v. Board of Sheridan County Com'rs,* 924 P.2d 988 (Wyo. 1996); *Croteau v. Planning Bd. of Hopkinton,* 40 Mass. App. Ct. 922, 663 N.E.2d 583 (1996); *Ford Leasing Development Co. v. Board of County Com'rs of Jefferson County,* 186 Colo. 418, 528 P.2d 237 (1974).

[269] *Cathedral Park Condominium Committee v. District of Columbia Zoning Com'n,* 743 A.2d 1231 (D.C. 2000).

[270] *Citizens for Mount Vernon v. City of Mount Vernon,* 133 Wash. 2d 861, 947 P.2d 1208 (1997).

[271] *RK Development Corp. v. City of Norwalk,* 156 Conn. 369, 242 A.2d 781 (1968); *BECA of Alexandria, L.L.P. v. County of Douglas ex rel. Bd. of Com'rs,* 607 N.W.2d 459 (Minn. Ct. App. 2000).

better position to evaluate the project. Third, the multi-step process affords many opportunities for input from the local government's various planning, zoning and architectural commissions, thus allowing the municipality to structure future developments to conform with its growth plans.

Planned unit development regulations contain substantive standards to ensure that a project will be developed in accordance with the long range development plans. These standards can solve a number of problems. For instance, what assurance does a local government have that the developer will complete the project as it is proposed in the plan? Fortunately, most PUD regulations contemplate that most projects will be staged developments. Most PUD ordinances provide safeguards to guarantee the different stages of the project will be completed. First, since the local government's legislative body still must approve individual PUDs by resolution, it retains some leverage over the developer. Second, most regulations establish timing controls as to when certain facilities must be built, thereby insuring the entire community will be completed. For example, a regulation may require a park to be built before high density, high profit housing can be developed. Finally, the local government may require an annual report from the developer appraising the project's progress.[272]

Many PUD regulations have substantive provisions which can encourage creative and beneficial developments. Generally, the entire project cannot exceed a certain density level. However, individual planned unit developments may have much higher densities. Also, restrictions may allow the developer to transfer excess PUD densities from one parcel to another as long as the density for the whole project remains the same.

Most PUD ordinances require a computed amount of common open space. Since open space reduces the total lot count, it is seldom utilized under traditional zoning regulations. Ordinances may provide the PUD developer with a number of ways to satisfy the open space computation. For example, the computation may prefer areas left in or restored to their natural habitat rather than areas such as golf courses. Accordingly, the percentage of space which would count as open space would be greater for natural habitat than that for golf courses. This type of incentive zoning allows a city to encourage beneficial uses in the ordinance and preserve those areas for the future.

§ 7:22   Private Restrictions

PUDs typically utilize commonly owned facilities and space to a much greater extent than the conventional development. As a result, complicated restrictions and covenants are necessary. The restrictions and covenants are primarily private matters, though the public has an interest in their enforcement.[273] Caution must be taken to ensure that any covenants and restrictions created as conditions for PUD approval are legally binding on future owners. A rather typical scenario, in this regard, was litigated in *Story Bed & Breakfast v. Brown County Area Plan Commission*.[274] The subsequent purchaser of a PUD sought to escape enforcement of covenants imposed as a condition

---

[272] In *Frankland v. City of Lake Oswego*, 267 Or. 452, 517 P.2d 1042 (1973), the Supreme Court of Oregon stressed that although a key aspect of PUDs is flexibility of design and use, "these objectives can be secured only if the planning authority retains its control by, at a minimum, overseeing and approving general development plans of a developer" and that discretion is properly in the hands of the planning authority and not the developer. Frankland, 517 P.2d at 1047.

[273] See §§ 15:10 to 15:15 infra.

[274] *Story Bed & Breakfast, LLP v. Brown County Area Plan Com'n*, 819 N.E.2d 55 (Ind. 2004).

of PUD approval but never recorded. The Supreme Court of Indiana, after a very positive discussion of the role and importance of the PUD concept, held that it was not necessary to decide whether or not a bona fide purchaser would be subject to the restrictions because the plaintiff had constructive notice of the restrictions because it had actual notice of the PUD designation.

The model acts for PUDs [275] also have provisions to protect the public interest in private restrictions. One model act[276] provides that the common open space need not be dedicated to the public but that the local government is authorized to require establishment of an organization to own and maintain the common open space. If the open space is not properly maintained, the Act authorizes the local government to maintain the space and to assess the lot owners.[277]

The elaborate negative and affirmative restrictions, covenants, conditions and easements are typically so extensive that an association or a corporation must be established as the organization to administer the provisions. The powers of the organization may include many of the functions typically performed by the government, so that the organizations created, typically a homes association, have been called private government.[278]

Suggested Legal Documents for Planned—Unit Development[279] a HUD publication, contains recommended forms for a declaration of covenants, conditions and restrictions and articles of incorporation and by-laws for a homeowners' association. The declaration provides that the easements, restrictions, covenants, and conditions run with the land described in the declaration and bind and benefit the owner of each parcel of property. The declaration deals with annexation of additional properties; confers membership in the association to the owner of property subject to assessment by the association; provides for voting rights in the association with suggestions for division of power between the developer and the lot owners; states the rights of the association and the lot owners to use property; provides for maintenance assessments; states the rules applying to party walls (which may be present because of cluster zoning and condominium development); establishes standards; provides that the association will maintain and repair the privately owned buildings and trees, shrubs, grass and the like; states the use restrictions; provides easements and contains general provisions dealing with enforcement, severability and amendment.

As with conventional subdivisions, the complicated covenants and restrictions in PUDs are the source of litigation. For example, in *Mountain Springs Association of New Jersey Inc. v. Wilson* [280] the covenants provided that land could be sold only with consent of the association or to a member of the association. The defendant's grantor sold without complying with the consent provision. The defendant grantee was willing to join the association but was not willing to pay dues for water and garbage collection. The association sued to compel the defendant to pay full dues or to reconvey the land.

---

[275] See § 7:17 supra.

[276] See Babcock, Krasnowiecki and McBride, The Model State Statute, 114 U. Pa. L. Rev. 140, 146–150 (1965).

[277] See infra § 15:13.

[278] See infra § 15:1 on private control and management.

[279] U.S. Dep't of Housing and Urban Development, Federal Housing Administration and Veterans Administration, FHA Form 1400, VA 26–8200 (1973).

[280] *Mountain Springs Ass'n of N. J., Inc. v. Wilson*, 81 N.J. Super. 564, 196 A.2d 270 (Ch. Div. 1963).

The court held the covenant was unenforceable as restricting free alienation and conferring unconscionable power to the association over prospective purchasers.

The lengthy articles of incorporation and by-laws that are contained in the suggested form establish the institution for accomplishing the matters controlled by the declaration and provide for directors, officers, committees, finances and the like.

The amount of powers and responsibility given to the "private government," of course, varies from new town to new town and from PUD to PUD. For example, the association may not have the responsibility to maintain and repair individually owned properties. That may be the responsibility of the individual owner. Moreover, public government may exercise some of the functions, such as architectural control under a zoning or PUD ordinance. Special districts or special assessment districts may be used as an alternative to provision of water and sewage services by the association.[281]

---

[281] For an example of a special district created to maintain open space see Cal. Gov't Code §§ 50575 to 50628. See also Volpert, Creation and Maintenance of Open Spaces in Subdivisions: Another Approach, 12 UCLA L. Rev. 830 (1965).

Chapter 8

BUILDING AND DEVELOPMENT CODES*

Analysis

§ 8:1   In General

Building and housing codes have existed for centuries but most of the evolution of the codes has occurred in recent years.[1] Their modern history in the U.S. began with the adoption of the Tenement House Act for the City of New York in 1901.[2] Traditionally they were not treated as land use control devices because land use controls are focused on land, and the relationship between buildings and land.[3] Building and housing codes, on the other hand, deal with matters of construction and maintenance. Currently, however, the building permit and certificate of occupancy stages of development have become the focal points for many growth management and infrastructure funding regulations thereby bringing at least that aspect of building codes into the mainstream of land use regulation.[4] Furthermore, the increasing popularity and importance of "green" codes and "smart" codes make building and development codes a major focal point for encouraging or requiring new development to be sensitive and responsive to the principles of new urbanism and smart growth.[5]

---

* For more detailed discussion and more extensive citations of authority of the issues covered in this chapter, see Juergensmeyer and Roberts, Land Use Planning and Development Regulation Law, Practitioner Treatise Series (3rd ed. 2012).

[1] Kelly, Fair Housing, Good Housing or Expensive Housing: Are Building Codes Part of the Problem or Part of the Solution?, 29 J. Marshall L. Rev. 349, 350 (1996).

[2] The Act was held constitutional in *Tenement House Department of City of New York v. Moeschen,* 179 N.Y. 325, 72 N.E. 231 (1904), aff'd without opinion, 203 U.S. 583, 27 S. Ct. 781, 51 L. Ed. 328 (1906). See Gilbert, Tenements and Takings: Tenement House Department of New York v. Moeschen as a Counterpoint to Lochner v. New York, 18 Fordham Urb. L.J. 437 (1991).

[3] See infra § 8:3. See, generally, Proceedings of the 1969 Conference on Code Enforcement, Bureau of Government Research, Rutgers University; Bosselman, The Legal Framework of Building and Housing Ordinances, (pts. 1 & 2) II, The Mun. Att'y 39, 67 (1970).

[4] See § 8:7 infra.

[5] See Duany and Talen, Making the Good Easy: The Smart Code Alternative, 29 Fordham Urb. L.J. 1445 (2002); Emerson, Making Main Street Legal Again: The Smart Code Solution to Sprawl, 71 Mo. L. Rev. 637 (2006); Wolf, A Yellow Light For "Green Zoning": Some Words of Caution About Incorporating Green

The basic goal of building and housing codes is to ensure that buildings are safe, sanitary, and increasingly, convenient and efficient.[6] Building codes are primarily derived from structural safety standards and are generally enforced against new construction. Attention to existing properties is usually given only to those which have been severely damaged or have such serious deficiencies as to render them dangerous. Most codes also require existing structures that are being remodeled to include certain improvements.[7] Housing Codes were originally authorized by environmental health laws, and deal primarily with conditions which must be maintained in existing residential buildings to protect the public health, safety and welfare and the well-being of their occupants.[8] Post-construction maintenance of commercial and state-owned buildings is governed by several supplemental codes such as electrical codes, fire codes, mechanical codes, plumbing codes and others.[9]

Building code standards are classified as belonging to one of two types: (1) specification or (2) performance. Most codes rely heavily on standards of the specification or prescriptive type. That is, the code will require the use of a specific type or grade of material to achieve the desired result. Architects are generally opposed to this sort of code, because they believe it stifles innovation and can be counterproductive in some situations.[10] These codes are usually compiled from specifications developed by various building industry trade associations. Performance standards, on the other hand, permit the use of any material that is able to meet a performance standard. Development of performance standards was required as part of the Energy Conservation Standards for New Building Act of 1976.[11] Though performance standards are favored by architects, they are sometimes impractical to use, expensive to administer and tend to centralize the related administrative functions.[12]

Building codes frequently have land use control consequences even though that is not their primary purpose.[13] The relation of buildings to one another is an important aspect of urban land use control and many key tenets of urban design regulation such

---

Building Standards into Local Land Use Law, 43 Urb. Law. 949 (2011); NAHB, NAHB's Model Green Home Building Guidelines (2005) (available at http://www.nahb.org/publication); David Moffat, New Urbanism's Smart Code, 16:2 Places (2004); PPRC, Green Building: Codes and Standards, http://www.pprc.org/pubs/greencon/code__std.cfm.

[6] Kelly, Fair Housing, Good Housing or Expensive Housing: Are Building Codes Part of the Problem or Part of the Solution?, 29 J. Marshall L. Rev. 349 (1996).

[7] Kelly, Fair Housing, Good Housing or Expensive Housing: Are Building Codes Part of the Problem or Part of the Solution?, 29 J. Marshall L. Rev. 349, 354 (1996).

[8] McGrew and Bates, Code Enforcement: The Federal Role, 14 Urb. Law. 1, 2 (1982). A statutory definition of housing codes reads as follows: "any code or rule intending post construction regulation of structures which would include but not be limited to: standards of maintenance, condition of facilities, condition of systems and components, living conditions, occupancy, use, and room sizes." Fla. Stat. Ann. § 553.71(4).

[9] See, e.g., Florida Building Codes Act, Fla. Stat. Ann. § 553.70.

[10] See, e.g., Energy Building Regulations: The Effect of the Federal Performance Standards on Building Code Administration and Conservation of Energy in New Buildings, 13 U.C. Davis L. Rev. 330, 336–7 nn. 32–35 (1980).

[11] Pub. L. No. 94–385, 90 Stat. 1144, 42 U.S.C.A. §§ 6831 to 6840.

[12] Conservation and Efficient Use of Energy: Hearings Before a Subcomm. of the House Comm. on Government Operations, 93rd Cong., 1st Sess. 33–35 (1973). Performance standards are also regularly used in the U.S. National Conf. of States on Building Costs & Standards, Inc., Survey on Utilization of Systems Analysis Designs in State Energy Conservation Codes (1979).

[13] An interesting example of these "consequences" is reflected in Florida's strengthening of its coastal construction building standards. See Fla. Stat. Ann. §§ 161.54 to 161.56.

as setback provisions were first found in building codes.[14] Height limits were also originally imposed in building codes rather than in zoning codes.[15]

Recently, localities have imposed standards on building codes that are more oriented on sustainability and environmental impact. Many states are now requiring, or at least encouraging new buildings and renovations to meet a model code standard developed by a third party.[16] These standards were developed to be voluntary and encourage competition in sustainable building, incorporating factors that affect building practices as well as electrical, mechanical and plumbing systems.[17] The most popular in the United States is the Leadership in Energy and Environmental Design (LEED) standard. Another system, the Green Globes rating system, was developed in Canada but has gained a foothold in the United States.

Because the model code standards were developed to be voluntary, incorporating them into mandatory state and local codes can be problematic. The leading sustainable building groups, including the US Green Building Council (USGBC), which created the LEED standards, have banded together and recently released Standard 189.1, which is written in code language and intended for use by government entities.[18]

The model codes use both specification and performance requirements in their approach to construction. The six elements the sustainable model codes focus on are optimization of site, energy efficiency, water conservation, building materials that reduce pollution, better indoor air quality, and optimized operational and maintenance practices.[19]

Another land use control aspect of building codes is the requirement frequently contained in them for building permits and certificates of occupancy. The issuance of a building permit is usually the last point at which the local government can exercise leverage regarding the type of development that will be permitted on the land, and the certificate of occupancy is the last permission needed to use the new improvements. Consequently, land use control authorities use these permits to check compliance with various land use controls.[20] Local governments can also use the issuance of these permits as the point at which to assess and collect payments for capital facilities required to service the new development.[21]

---

[14] See, e.g., *Klinger v. Bicket,* 117 Pa. 326, 11 A. 555 (1887) (upholding prohibition of wood building in fire zone).

[15] See *Welch v. Swasey,* 214 U.S. 91, 29 S. Ct. 567, 53 L. Ed. 923 (1909) (allowing regulation of building height).

[16] Howe, LEED Standards in Green Building Laws, 2008 Emerging Issues 412 (July 7, 2008).

[17] Bennett, Howe and Newman, Current Critical Issues in Environmental Law: Green Buildings and Sustainable Development, 2008 Emerging Issues 282, (May 16, 2008).

[18] ASHRAE.org, ICC, ASHRAE, USGBC, and IES Announce Nation's First Set of Model Codes and Standards for Green Building in the U.S. http://www.ashrae.org/pressroom/detail/1748.

[19] Bennett, Howe and Newman, Current Critical Issues in Environmental Law: Green Buildings and Sustainable Development, 2008 Emerging Issues 282, (May 16, 2008).

[20] See § 8:7 infra.

[21] See infra § 9:9.

§ 8:2 Model Codes

A. *Traditional Models*

After passage of the Housing Act of 1954, local governments were expected to develop and implement both housing and building codes to qualify for federal urban renewal and public housing programs. Qualification for these programs required that the city submit a "workable program" to the administrator. As a result, between 1955 and 1968, housing and building code adoption increased 100% nationally.[22] Due to the complexity of building regulation, only the largest jurisdictions attempted to develop their own unique building codes. Therefore, most state and local building codes were usually based on nationally recognized model codes.

A number of model building codes were developed. They included the National Building Code of the American Insurance Association, the Uniform Building Code of the International Conference of Building Officials, the Southern Standard Building Code of the Southern Building Code Conference and the Basic Building Code of the Building Officials Conference of America.[23] Later, widely used supplemental codes were developed that included: the National Electric Code, prepared by the National Fire Protection Association; the ASHRAE documents for heating, ventilating and air conditioning, named for its sponsor, the American Society of Heating, Refrigeration and Air Conditioning Engineers; and the National Plumbing Code, developed by the American Society of Mechanical Engineers.[24]

The Uniform Building Code, the Southern Standard Building Code, and the Basic Building Code were regional in effect, though to delineate the boundaries one would need to refer to individual state and local laws. The Southern Standard Building Code, for example, was generally used in Florida, Georgia, Alabama, South Carolina, North Carolina, Virginia, Tennessee, Mississippi, and Texas, and the Uniform Building Code sponsored by the International Conference of Building Officials was used in California.

Traditional model codes generally reflected the state of the art of building rather than scientific engineering data and were therefore easily amended by localities with differing views. The organizations which promulgated the model codes often lacked funds to support all their provisions with sound engineering data, and in some cases even urged local deviations. Additionally, the update processes for the model codes were independent of one another. Thus, approval of a new technology or design under one of the national codes did not ensure its approval by the other code groups.[25] Often, instead of accepting these model codes intact, local governments make revisions, additions, deletions, and amendments, which in an overwhelming majority of cases were

---

[22] U.S. Nat'l Comm'n on Urban Problems, Building the American City 227 (1968). The workable program requirement was repealed in 1974 with passage of the Housing and Community Development Act of 1974, 42 U.S.C.A. §§ 5301 to 5308. See Galvan, Note: Rehabilitating Rehab Through State Building Codes, 115 Yale L.J. 1744 (2006) (traditional building codes impede rehabilitation efforts in center cities).

[23] See e.g., the U.S. Dep't of Housing & Urban Dev., Final Report of HUD Review of Model Building Codes (2000) that identifies the variances between the design and construction requirements of the Fair Housing Act and four model building codes.

[24] Kelly, Fair Housing, Good Housing or Expensive Housing? Are Building Codes Part of the Problem or Part of the Solution?, 29 J. Marshall L. Rev. 349, 351 (1996).

[25] Kelly, Fair Housing, Good Housing or Expensive Housing? Are Building Codes Part of the Problem or Part of the Solution?, 29 J. Marshall L. Rev. 349, 351 (1996).

more restrictive in nature.[26] This resulted in considerable variety in codes from one locale to another even in regard to those based on the same model.

Not only did the model building codes vary in terms of general construction requirements, but they varied in scope, so that they may or may not have included provisions for setbacks from other buildings and streets, multiple dwelling laws (which apply to apartment houses and boarding houses), health codes that deal with plumbing, sewerage, drainage, light and ventilation, mobile home codes and fire codes. If these kinds of provisions were not in the basic building code they were usually covered by separate local ordinances. In addition, there were sometimes separate boiler codes, electrical codes, elevator codes, heating codes and mechanical codes.

The complexities and confusion that often resulted from the sometimes random choice of a particular model and the resulting need for national models led to the formation in 1994 of the International Code Council (ICC), a nonprofit organization dedicated to developing a single set of comprehensive and coordinated national model construction codes. The founders of the ICC were the organizations responsible for the three most popular original model codes discussed above, namely, Building Officials and Code Administrators International, (BOCA), International Conference of Building Officials (ICBO), and Southern Building Code Congress International, (SBCCI). As the ICC has stated, "although regional code development has been effective and responsive to our country's needs, the time came for a single set of codes. The nation's three model code groups responded by creating the International Code Council and by developing codes without regional limitations—the International Codes."[27]

The Codes currently provided by ICC include:

2012 International Building Code®

2012 International Residential Code for One- and Two-Family Dwellings®

2012 International Fire Code®

2012 International Energy Conservation Code®

2012 International Existing Building Code®

2012 ICC® Performance Code for Buildings and Facilities

2012 International Fuel Gas Code®

2012 International Green Construction Code™ [28]

2012 International Mechanical Code®

---

[26] U.S. Dep't of Housing & Urban Dev., Final Report of the Task Force on Housing Costs 35 (May 1978).

[27] http://www.iccsafe.org.

[28] An option to this code is Standard 189.1 [which] provides a "total building sustainability package" for those who "strive to design, build and operate green buildings. From site location to energy use to recycling, this standard sets the foundation for green buildings by addressing site sustainability, water use efficiency, energy efficiency, indoor environmental quality, and the building's impact on the atmosphere, materials and resources." This Code has been prepared by ASHRAE and the U.S Green Building Council. http://www.ashrae.org/resources—publications/bookstore/standard-189-1.

2012 International Plumbing Code®

2012 International Private Sewage Disposal Code®

2012 International Property Maintenance Code®

2012 International Swimming Pool and Spa Code™

2012 International Wildland-Urban Interface Code®

2012 International Zoning Code®

The codes are extremely comprehensive and are coordinated with each other thereby solving a serious flaw that existed in regard to previous model building codes.

Although most promulgation and enforcement of building and housing codes has been done at the local level, state and federal governments, through legislation and responsible administrative bodies, have played a role in causing the marked increase in the number of building and housing codes enacted by local governments.[29]

B. Smart Growth and New Urbanism Codes

Traditional building codes and their replacements have somewhat limited goals. They focus primarily on ensuring the quality of construction of individual buildings. Recently "green" codes and "smart" codes have been introduced with wider scope and loftier goals. Green codes focus on a number of environmental issues in regard to design and construction but emphasize primarily the energy efficiency and environmental friendliness of buildings from both a construction and a maintenance standpoint.[30] As discussed above,[31] there was federal legislation on point enacted in the 1970's—namely The Energy Conservation Standards for New Building Act of 1976. Presently, green codes and green certification programs have become key in regard to design and construction standards in many states.

An International Energy Conservation Code has been drafted and promoted by the Building Codes Assistance Project (BCAP) which is a joint initiative of the Alliance to Save Energy, the American Council for an Energy-Efficient Economy, and the Natural Resources Defense Council. This code establishes minimum regulations for energy efficient buildings and uses prescriptive and performance basis approaches.[32] The current (2012)[15] version has just been promulgated but earlier versions have already been adopted wholly or in part in several states.[33]

---

[29] See Code Enforcement: The Federal Role, 14 Urb.Law. 1, 2 (1982); Klass, State Standards for Nationwide Products Revisited: Federalism, Green Building Codes, and Appliance Efficiency Standards, 34 Harv. Envtl. L. Rev. 335 (2010).

[30] See Anderson, Legal and Business Issues of Green Building, 79-AUG Wis. Law. 10 (2006); Perzan, What You Should Know About Green Building, 20-Nov CBA Rec. 38 (2006)

[31] See § 8:1 supra.

[32] The Code is available online at http://www.iccsafe.org.

[15] http://www.energycodes.gov/status/2012__Final.stm.

[33] Current state adoptions are listed and detailed on the "Status of State Energy Codes" page of the BCAP website: http://www.bcap-energy.org.

There is also a "voluntary, consensus-based, market-driven building standards system" developed by the US Green Building Council (USGBC),[34] which is becoming increasingly popular. The program promotes conservation of energy, efficiency of design and choice of materials, and the reduction of the impact of building and construction on the environment.[35] The USGBC considers itself the nation's "foremost coalition of leaders from every sector of the building industry working to promote buildings that are environmentally responsible, profitable and healthy places to live and work." The Council has more than 16,000 member organizations and a network of 78 regional chapters.

The U.S. Green Building Council's core purpose is to "transform the way communities as well as individual structures are designed, built and operated, enabling an environmentally and socially responsible, healthy, and prosperous environment that improves the quality of life." The Leadership in Energy and Environmental Design (LEED) Green Building Rating System has become the nationally accepted benchmark for the design, construction, and operation of high performance green buildings. LEED promotes a whole-building approach to sustainability by recognizing performance in five key areas of human and environmental health: sustainable site development, water savings, energy efficiency, materials selection, and indoor environmental quality.[36]

Trailing behind the popularity of LEED in the United States, another model code, Green Globes, is migrating south from Canada. Incorporated into the Minnesota, Washington and Maryland development laws, Green Globes have an online component, and are generally known to be slightly less complicated than LEED standards, though possibly less comprehensive.[37]

Smart codes include energy efficiency, environmentalism, and sustainability but they have even loftier goals than green codes. They seek to improve quality of life from numerous perspectives and are designed to implement the social and planning goals of the new urbanism movement.[38] The clarion call for the Smart Code[39] as a completely new genre of urban planning codes was sounded by Andres Duany, one of its coauthors and the founder of new urbanism:

What is needed is a fundamentally different vision of how cities should be coded The Smart Code exemplifies how the principles of new urbanism and environmentalism can be mutually protected and enhanced. It is strongly aligned with the notion of "smart growth," a planning and environmentalist movement based on the goals of environmental protection and sustainable development.[40]

---

[34] http://www.usgbc.org.

[35] See LEED Green Building Rating System at http://www.usgbc.org.

[36] http:/1/www.usgbc.org.

[37] Bennett, Howe and Newman, Current Critical Issues in Environmental Law: Green Buildings and Sustainable Development, 2008 Emerging Issues 282, (May 16, 2008).

[38] See § 9:1 infra.

[39] Duany, Plater-Zyberk & Co., Smart Code (2001).

[40] Duany and Talen, Making The Good Easy: The Smart Code Alternative, 29 Fordham Urb. L.J. 1445, 1446 (2002). This seminal article is updated and extended by Emerson, Making Main Street Legal Again: The SmartCode Solution to Sprawl, 71 Mo. L. Rev. 637 (2006). See also Geller, The Legality of Form-Based Zoning Codes, 26 J. Land Use & Envtl. L. 35 (2010); Pollard, Smart Growth: The Promise, Politics and Potential Pitfalls of Emerging Growth Management Strategies, 19 Va. Envtl. L.J. 247 (2000).

The role of the Smart Code is not just to supplement conventional zoning and subdivision regulations, as is often the case with green codes, but to replace them with a very different approach to land use planning and regulation. As Duany has stated, "our current codes are based on a theory of urbanism that is decidedly anti-urban. They separate land uses, decrease densities, and increase the amount of land devoted to car travel, prohibiting the kind of urbanism that typifies our most beloved urban places."[41]

While zoning is primarily "proscriptive," the smart codes are intended to be "prescriptive" by being designed to encourage development consistent with new urbanism and sustainability principles and to prevent rather than encourage urban sprawl.[42] These codes largely reject the use-based zoning at the heart of Euclidian zoning and substitute a form-based code[43] with an additional layer of considerations based on the transect concept. In fact, the transect concept is the key to understanding the philosophy behind a smart code. "A transect is an ecological concept that visually demonstrates how different natural environments are ordered on a progressive scale from rural to urban habitats. When applied to a zoning system, transect defines where a particular form of a building is properly situated within a progression of six rural to urban environments called transect zones."[44]

§ 8:3   Relation to Zoning

Many provisions of traditional building codes have been incorporated into modern zoning ordinances, though it is common to find similar provisions either in building codes or zoning codes or both. For example, fire prevention ordinances which prohibited wooden buildings in certain areas of the city were a kind of precursor to zoning which excludes buildings used for certain purposes, such as commercial or industrial, from parts of a city for reasons of public health, safety, or welfare. The yard requirements of modern zoning ordinances are similar to the setback requirements under some fire and building codes. Heights of buildings are controlled under zoning though at an earlier time and sometimes even today, they are controlled under building codes, including "zoned" building codes that provide for different heights in different areas of the city.[45] Zoning bulk regulations dealing with the portion of yard covered and density of popula-

---

[41] Pollard, Smart Growth: The Promise, Politics and Potential Pitfalls of Emerging Growth Management Strategies, 19 Va. Envtl. L.J. 247 (2000).

[42] See Andres Duany, Elizabeth Plater-Zyberk & Jeff Speck, Suburban Nation: The Rise of Sprawl and the Decline of the American Dream (2000); Buzbee, Urban Sprawl, Federalism, and the Problem of Institutional Complexity, 68 Fordham L. Rev. 57 (1999).

[43] Quindal C. Evans, The Smartcode: Understanding a Modern Trend, 51 No. 10 DRI For Def. 22 (2009); Robert Sitkowski, An Introduction to Form-Based Codes, SM 004 ALI-ABA 475 (Aug. 2006); Sitkowski and Ohm, Form-Based Land Development Regulations, 38 Urb. Law. 1 (2006); Jerry Weitz, Form-Based Codes: A Supportive But Critical Perspective, Practicing Planner (Fall 2005).

[44] Emerson, Making Main Street Legal Again: The SmartCode Solution to Sprawl, 71 Mo. L. Rev. 637, 642 (2006). See Andres Duany & Emily Talen, Transect Planning, 68 Am. Plan. Ass'n J. 247 (Summer 2002); Duany, Introduction to the Special Issue: The Transect, 7 J. Urb. Design 251 (2002); Bower, The Sectors of the Transect, 7 J. Urb. Design 313 (2002); Volk and Zimmerman, American Households On (and Off) the Urban-to-Rural Transect, 7 J. Urb. Design 341 (2002). Duany's Smart Code, note 20 supra, contains numerous diagrams and illustrations essential to fully understanding the concept.

[45] *Brougher v. Board of Public Works of City and County of San Francisco,* 107 Cal. App. 15, 290 P. 140 (1st Dist. 1930).

tion overlap housing code coverage. A building permit frequently can be issued only after compliance with building and zoning ordinances and other ordinances as well.[46]

It is often important to distinguish between building code ordinances and zoning ordinances. In Florida, for example, a zoning ordinance is invalid if notice requirements are not complied with, whereas building regulations are not held to such strict notice prerequisites to be valid. The court, in *Fountain v. Jacksonville,*[47] held invalid an ordinance which required structural modifications on buildings located near air installations to reduce internal noise, because procedural requirements in promulgating the ordinance were not followed. The city's argument that the standard was more akin to a building code than a zoning amendment met with little success.[48] In another case, because the court construed an off-street parking requirement to be a building rather than a zoning ordinance matter,[49] the court upheld a variance that did not otherwise meet the criteria for a zoning variance.

Green codes also often overlap and supplement traditional zoning ordinances and may even be included within them. Smart codes, on the other hand, are designed to replace traditional Euclidean zoning ordinance either in their entirety or in certain designated areas of a jurisdiction.[50]

§ 8:4   Unauthorized and Unconstitutional Applications of Codes

As with other land use regulations, the two major routes for attacking the application of a building or development code are to allege that the regulation is not authorized by a statute or home rule power or that it is unconstitutional. For example in *Safer v. Jacksonville,*[51] a Florida district court of appeal held that enabling legislation behind the housing code was valid, but that the specific code provisions (one requiring each dwelling unit to contain a sink, lavatory, tub or shower connected with potable hot water, and another code provision requiring at least two conveniently located electrical outlets per habitable room) were not demonstrably related to the health or safety of tenants, generally. The court concluded that the provisions were not authorized by the statute. Challenges to the position taken by the court in *Safer,* both in Florida and other jurisdictions, generally have failed and the requirement that specific provisions be demonstrably related to health and safety remains intact.[52]

Regulations can also be challenged as unreasonable exercises of the police power and therefore unconstitutional.[53] The issue has most often been raised when the codes

---

[46] For a discussion of the role that building codes have played in Houston, a city without zoning, see Lewyn, How Overregulation Creates Sprawl (Even in a City Without Zoning), 50 Wayne L. Rev. 1171, 1177–91 (2004).

[47] *Fountain v. City of Jacksonville,* 447 So. 2d 353 (Fla. 1st DCA 1984).

[48] Fountain, 447 So. 2d at 354.

[49] *Siller v. Board of Sup'rs of City and County of San Francisco,* 58 Cal. 2d 479, 25 Cal. Rptr. 73, 375 P.2d 41 (1962); cf. *Off Shore Rest. Corp. v. Linden,* 30 N.Y.2d 160, 331 N.Y.S.2d 397, 282 N.E.2d 299 (1972).

[50] See § 8:2 supra. See also Wolf, A Yellow Light For "Green Zoning": Some Words of Caution About Incorporating Green Building Standards into Local Land Use Law, 43 Urb. Law. 949 (2011).

[51] *Safer v. City of Jacksonville,* 237 So. 2d 8 (Fla. 1st DCA 1970). See also *Early Estates, Inc. v. Housing Bd. of Review of City of Providence,* 93 R.I. 227, 174 A.2d 117(1961).

[52] E.g., *Stallings v. City of Jacksonville,* 333 So. 2d 70 (Fla. 1st DCA 1976); *City of St. Louis v. Brune,* 515 S.W.2d 471, 79 A.L.R.3d 701 (Mo. 1974).

[53] See e.g., Turner, Paradigms, Pigeonholes, and Precedent: Reflections on Regulatory Control of Residential Construction, 23 Whittier L. Rev. 3 (2001).

are applied to older buildings.[54] The property owner often loses these battles as in *Queenside Hills Realty Co. v. Saxl,*[55] a leading case. While the lodging house involved in the case met the standards of the codes when it was built, it did not have the wet pipe sprinkling system required by a new code. The court upheld the application of the new code requirements to the building and indicated that the legislature may decide the level of protection required for safety from fire and that if a building is unsafe per a legislatively established standard, it must be made safe, whatever the cost, or closed, despite loss of value. The building's owners raised an equal protection issue, since the sprinkling system was only applied to pre-1944 lodging houses; the Court held that the legislature could properly draw such lines because the risk in older buildings is greater.

While the courts often compare the cost of compliance with the value of the building, a more relevant consideration might be the cost of compliance as compared to the value of the building after compliance. For example, if a sprinkling system cost $25,000 in a building worth $30,000 and after compliance the building would still be worth only $30,000, the requirement might be viewed as too onerous on the owner. On the other hand, public interest in safety might nonetheless justify the requirement. If the building is worth $50,000 after compliance, a court might be much more disposed to uphold the regulation.

Courts often hold zoning ordinances that operate retroactively on nonconforming buildings unconstitutional and typically come to a contrary conclusion on housing codes. There are several possible reasons for the difference. Zoning was primarily adopted to control prospective development and nonconformities were typically protected under early zoning ordinances because of a fear that zoning would be held unconstitutional if applied retroactively. Courts began to believe that themselves, and some still do.[56] Housing codes, on the other hand, regulate the minimum conditions for occupancy, not development, and are applied retroactively to rid buildings of nonconformities caused by deterioration, obsolescence or changes in minimum housing requirements.

Moreover, most housing code standards are directly related to the public health and safety. Suppose the Court in *Queenside Hills Realty* had held the statute violated the due process clause as applied, and subsequently a fire occurred which could have been prevented by elimination of the nonconformity. The courts are reluctant to risk such results. Many zoning standards are less directly grounded on health and safety concerns. Substantial personal injury is unlikely if a building were built two feet closer than a newly imposed setback line permitted. The property owner often loses an attack

---

[54] See Galvan, Rehabilitating Rehab through State Building Codes, 115 Yale L.J. 1744 (2006) (traditional codes fail to adequately address rehab; states should adopt mandatory rehab codes).

[55] *Queenside Hills Realty Co. v. Saxl,* 328 U.S. 80, 66 S. Ct. 850, 90 L. Ed. 1096 (1946). See also *McCallin v. Walsh,* 64 A.D.2d 46, 407 N.Y.S.2d 852 (1st Dep't 1978), order aff'd, 46 N.Y.2d 808, 413 NY.S.2d 922, 386 N.E.2d 833 (1978).

[56] See supra §§ 4:31 to 4:40 (non- conforming uses).

on the housing code provisions,[57] unless the requirements deal with peripheral matters rather than matters basic to health and safety.[58]

If building and housing codes were "zoned," so that one code did not apply to all housing in the jurisdiction, problems of unreasonable application to older housing might be reduced. Opponents of uniform codes argue that one set of minimum standards in a normally diverse community ignores legitimate differences between neighborhoods resulting from age, structure type and socio-economic factors. Some localities are developing separate codes for historic buildings and districts.[59] Though different standards may lessen the impact of enforcing codes in the more deteriorated neighborhoods, they may be difficult to support. Zoned codes might be judicially accepted if they are based on substantial distinctions, reasonably related to the goal sought to be achieved and evenly applied.[60] Differential enforcement may be a feasible way to deal with differences in a community's housing. If it is utilized it should be acceptable as long as enforcement is uniform in the selected areas.[61] On the other hand, if enforcement of code provisions is not uniform, not based on substantial distinctions nor related to acceptable goals, a violation of equal protection may be found. In *Dowdell v. Apopka,*[62] disparate provision of municipal services, such as paved roads, running water and sewer systems, between black and white neighborhoods led to a finding of intentional discrimination based on race. Typically, however, building and housing codes are not zoned. It has been argued that they could be, with very low jurisdiction-wide requirements, which could be variably increased on a neighborhood basis.[63]

Building and development codes can also be challenged on the basis that they are so vague that they constitute an unlawful delegation of legislative power.[64] This can be a problem particularly with form-based codes:

> Form-based land development regulations must . . . comport with the principles of procedural due process, i.e., they must contain sufficiently detailed and meaningful standards in order to alert applicants to what is expected of them while allowing sufficient discretion in the decision-making body to determine the approval of an application. Otherwise, these regulations will fall prey to the void for vagueness doctrine.[65]

---

[57] *Kaukas v. City of Chicago,* 27 Ill. 2d 197, 188 N.E.2d 700 (1963); *City of Chicago v. Sheridan,* 40 Ill. App. 3d 886, 353 N.E.2d 270 (1st Dist. 1976); *Adamec v. Post,* 273 N.Y. 250, 7 N.E.2d 120, 109 A.L.R. 1110 (1937); *Miller v. Foster,* 244 Wis. 99, 11 N.W.2d 674, 153 A.L.R. 845 (1943).

[58] *City of Columbus v. Stubbs,* 223 Ga. 765, 158 S.E.2d 392 (1967); *Barrett v. Hamby,* 235 Ga. 262, 219 S.E.2d 399 (1975).

[59] For a discussion of the interaction between California's Uniform Building Code and its State Historical Building Code, see Daniel Curtin & Cecily Talbert, California Land Use and Planning Law 227 (26th ed 2006). See also §§ 12:1 et seq., infra.

[60] See *Brennan v. City of Milwaukee,* 265 Wis. 52, 60 N.W.2d 704 (1953) and Abbott, Housing Policy, Housing Codes and Tenant Remedies: An Integration, 56 B.U. L. Rev. 1, 105 (1976) for enumerated conditions.

[61] Polaka, Housing Codes and Preservation of Urban Blight-Administrative and Enforcement Problems and Proposals, 17 Vill. L. Rev. 490, 519 (1972).

[62] *Dowdell v. City of Apopka, Florida,* 698 F.2d 1181, 36 Fed. R. Serv. 2d 72 (11th Cir. 1983).

[63] Babcock and Bosselman, Citizen Participation: A Suburban Suggestion for the Central City, 32 L. & Contemp. Prob. 221 (1967).

[64] See § 5:3, supra.

[65] Robert Sitkowski, An Introduction to Form-Based Codes, SM 004 ALI-ABA 475, 483 (Aug. 2006). The author contrasts *Anderson v. City of Issaquah,* 70 Wash. App. 64, 851 P.2d 744 (Div. 1 1993) (vague design

§ 8:5   State and Federal Preemption

Many states have adopted statewide building codes, most of which are mandatory.[66] The issue arises as to whether or not local codes and ordinance may differ from the state adopted codes. In *Oregon v. Troutdale*,[67] the court held that the provision of the state building code permitting "single-wall" construction did not preempt a city ordinance which required "double-wall" construction in new buildings within the city. The court determined that because the construction standards regulated builders rather than municipal government, the city could adopt building code requirements in addition to or more stringent than the statewide code, but not incompatible with its provisions. State regulations were to establish basic uniform standards which would reasonably safeguard health, safety, welfare and comfort. In an appropriate case, however, the need for uniformity of the law may be a sufficient basis for legislative preemption at state level.

In California, the administrative code allowed a city or county to determine changes or modifications in the state's building requirements where appropriate because of local conditions.[68] "Local conditions" had been construed rather loosely, until 1977, when the California attorney general defined local conditions as those which could be broadly labeled as geographical or topographical, excluding local political, economic or social concerns as destructive of any attempt to achieve statewide uniformity. Code uniformity reduces housing costs, increases the efficiency of the private housing construction industry and helps meet housing needs of the state.[69] Uniform codes are generally based on professional expertise, research and testing not routinely available to local agencies.[70] Evidence of the desirability of uniformity can be seen in the development of model codes and their subsequent adoption as law by state legislatures.

Federal mobile home construction and safety standards were established by the Secretary of HUD pursuant to the National Mobile Home Construction and Safety Standards Act of 1974,[71] which has subsequently been retitled the Manufactured Home Construction and Safety Standards Act. Whenever a federal manufactured home construction and safety standard is in effect, no state or political subdivision shall have authority to enact or maintain any standard which is not identical to the federal standard.[72]

Federal preemption is much less a potential problem now than before enactment of the 1974 Housing and Community Development Act.[73] Congress was dissatisfied with code enforcement under the "workable program," and the new act entitled indi-

---

standards unconstitutional) and *Novi v. City of Pacifica,* 169 Cal. App. 3d 678, 215 Cal. Rptr. 439 (1st Dist. 1985) (some vagueness inherent and acceptable in design standards).

[66] 5 Housing & Dev. Rep. 754 (1977). See also See e.g., the U.S. Dep't of Housing & Urban Dev., Final Report of HUD Review of Model Building Codes (2000).

[67] *State, By and Through Haley v. City of Troutdale,* 281 Or. 203, 576 P.2d 1238 (1978).

[68] Cal. Health & Safety Code § 17958.5. See Daniel Curtin & Cecily Talbert, California Land Use and Planning Law 227 (26th ed 2006).

[69] See Hutton, Note: Toward Better and More Uniform Building Efficiency Codes, 28 Va. Envtl. L.J. 121 (2010). But see Kelly, Fair Housing, Good Housing or Expensive Housing? Are Building Codes Part of the Problem or Part of the Solution?, 29 J. Marshall L. Rev. 349 (1996).

[70] 60 Ops. Cal. Atty. Gen. 234 (1977).

[71] 42 U.S.C.A. § 5403(a). See § 8:2 supra.

[72] 42 U.S.C.A. § 5403(d), Supremacy of Federal Standards.

[73] 42 U.S.C.A. §§ 5301 to 5308.

vidual communities to decide for themselves the most appropriate building and housing standards. HUD now encourages development of more effective standards through the National Institute of Building Sciences,[74] a private organization chartered by the statute.

More recently, the federal government established the Building Energy Performance Standards (BEPS).[75] Many traditional building codes did not take climatic variations or energy use into account, but only regulated design and construction of buildings, principally for protecting the public health and welfare.[76] Congress chose to effect energy conservation in buildings through existing codes,[77] based on the presumption that it would be more efficient and economical to use building code officials to enforce the standards rather than to develop an alternative mechanism. The department of energy was responsible for promulgating energy conservation standards for new buildings while HUD was required to formulate cost-effective "weatherization" standards for existing housing rehabilitated with federal funds.

Most states had already adopted building energy conservation standards recommended in the Energy Policy and Conservation Act of 1975[78] which made funds available to each state for development of a conservation plan meeting certain enumerated requirements.[79]

§ 8:6   Building Code Enforcement

Municipal or state building codes are usually enforced by the commissioner of buildings or similar official under powers delegated by the city's charter or state constitution or statutes.[80] The building code usually requires submission of plans for the project for approval by the building official. Forms are provided, and the application must include a description of the work and its location. For new construction or major alterations, the application must include a lot diagram showing compliance with local zoning, foundation plans, floor and roof plans, detailed architectural, structural and mechanical drawings. The code officials examine the plans submitted for compliance with the code, and other applicable laws and regulations.

If plans comply, then they are approved in writing and notice is given to the applicant. When plans fail to comply, the application and plans will be rejected in writing

---

[74] H.R. Rep. No. 93–1279 (1974). "The National Institute of Building Sciences (NIBS) was authorized by the U.S. Congress in the Housing and Community Development Act of 1974, Public Law 93–383. In establishing NIBS, Congress recognized the need for an organization that could serve as an interface between government and the private sector. The Institute's public interest mission is to: improve the building regulatory environment; facilitate the introduction of new and existing products and technology into the building process; and disseminate nationally recognized technical and regulatory information." NIBS website, http://www.nibs.org.

[75] Building Energy Standards Act of 1976, as amended, 42 U.S.CA. §§ 6801 to 6873. In 1981, these standards were made voluntary. 42 U.S.C.A. §§ 6801 to 6873.

[76] See § 8:2 supra.

[77] 42 U.S.C.A. § 6831 et seq., but conservation measures may be implemented in other ways. Energy efficient buildings may be encouraged by tax credits, e.g., 26 U.S.C.A. § 23.

[78] 89 Stat. 871, 42 U.S.C.A. § 6201.

[79] These standards were based on ASHRAE guidelines-prescriptive standards which were much more easily enforced than BEPS could be. Aderman, Energy Standards for New Buildings, 11 Nat. J. 1084 (1979). See § 8:2 supra.

[80] A look at the Florida code provides a common example of the mechanics of operation. See Fla. Stat. Ann. §§ 553.70 to 553.895.

with reasons clearly stated. Rejected applications may be revised and resubmitted until standards are met. Minor alterations (not affecting health, fire or structural safety of the building) and ordinary repairs (replacement or renewal) of existing work during ordinary maintenance usually do not require plan approval. Application for plan approval and the work permits are often separate processes, but may be applied for all at once.

To insure that health and safety requirements are met during the building process, the building official is authorized to enter and inspect any premises or building to check for compliance with code and other applicable laws. Necessary tests are conducted at the direction of the building official, and the expense is borne by the owner or lessee of the property.

Final inspection is made upon completion of the work by a building official, and the architect, engineer or other supervisor of the work may be present also. The owner must be notified of any failures of the work to comply with code provisions. A certificate of occupancy will be issued when a building is found to substantially conform to applicable laws and regulations, and to the approved plans and code provisions. A temporary certificate of occupancy can be issued for 60–90 days if occupancy of the building (or relevant portion) will not endanger public safety during that period.[81]

In *Camara v. Municipal Court*[82] and *See v. Seattle*[83] the Supreme Court of the United States held that building inspectors must have either consent or a search warrant to look for violations of a housing code having criminal penalties. These cases only inconvenience administration and present no impossible barriers to enforcement. In *Marshall v. Barlow's, Inc.,*[84] which involved an inspection by an OSHA agent of business premises, the Supreme Court upheld the warrant requirement as established in *Camara* and *See.*

Despite a generally favorable judicial response to upholding the constitutionality of building codes and their enforcement, enforcement problems remain. In many cities a multiplicity of agencies deals with the problem: different agencies for different parts of the code, different agencies for new buildings, for old buildings, for administration, for compliance. Inspectors are inadequate in number and frequently are not well trained.[85] Inspections, re-inspections, orders, extension of time to comply with orders, partial compliance being equated with good faith and the hope that compliance may be obtained short of court proceedings all delay the time prior to imposition of judicial sanctions. Since criminal sanctions are involved, process may be difficult to serve, procedures are slow and the burden of proof difficult.

---

[81] For a discussion of building code enforcement in California see Daniel Curtin & Cecily Talbert, California Land Use and Planning Law Ch.19 (26th ed. 2006); Turner, Paradigms, Pigeonholes, and Precedent: Reflections on Regulatory Control of Residential Construction, 23 Whittier L. Rev. 3 (2001).

[82] *Camara v. Municipal Court of City and County of San Francisco,* 387 U.S. 523, 87 S. Ct. 1727, 18 L. Ed. 2d 930 (1967).

[83] 387 U.S. 541, 87 S.Ct. 1737, 18 L. Ed. 2d 943 (1967).

[84] *Marshall v. Barlow's, Inc.,* 436 U.S. 307, 98 S. Ct. 1816, 56 L. Ed. 2d 305, 6 O.S.H. Cas. (BNA) 1571, 1978 O.S.H. Dec. (CCH) P 22735, 8 Envtl. L. Rep. 20434 (1978).

[85] Howe, Code Enforcement in Three Cities: An Organizational Analysis, 13 Urb. Law. 65, 74 (1981). See also Comptroller General of the U.S., Enforcement of Housing Codes: How It Can Help Achieve the Nation's Housing Goal (1972).

The courts have shown great reluctance to impose criminal sanctions for failure to comply with repair orders. Such penalties are neither effective nor do they create an economic incentive for the landowner to comply with the codes. As a result judicial proceedings are often suspended when the defendant shows some last minute efforts at compliance, sentences are suspended or fines when imposed are small. Failure of the judiciary to impose jail sentences and the tendency to avoid stiff sanctions result in a system in which landowners include numerous petty fines in calculating their costs of doing business.[86] While the courts are willing to broadly uphold the constitutionality of housing codes, they are not as willing to uphold convictions for violations.[87]

Vacation and demolition orders are also available as enforcement mechanisms. Though most codes have provisions allowing local governments considerable powers in regard to enforcement, vacation and demolition are not very frequently used.[88]

Another issue which may arise in the process of code enforcement is that of discriminatory[89] or disparate enforcement. The latter issue is especially complicated since enforcement is usually considered to be discretionary with the proper official. "At times, a violator will claim as a defense that the relevant laws are not being enforced against similarly situated people. However the courts generally have rejected this argument . . . . In such cases there is no denial of due process or equal protection."[90] However, in *Squaw Valley Development Co. v. Goldberg,* the Ninth Circuit Court of Appeals imposed the requirement that the more aggressive enforcement against one violator must bear some rational relation to a state interest.[91]

In a related code enforcement issue, municipalities are more frequently being held liable for negligent inspections of both new construction and existing housing, due to the erosion of sovereign immunity and the public duty doctrine.[92] In *Manors of Inverrary XII Condominium Association v. Atreco-Florida, Inc.,*[93] a Florida district court of appeal held that a building inspector's approval of a building permit and on-

---

[86] See, e.g., Grad, New Sanctions and Remedies in Housing Code Enforcement, 3 Urb. Law. 577 (1971); Love, Landlord's Liability for Defective Premises, Caveat Lessee, Negligence or Strict Liability?, 49 Wis. L. Rev. 38 (1975).

[87] See, e.g., *People v. Rowen,* 9 N.Y.2d 732, 214 N.Y.S.2d 347, 174 N.E.2d 331 (1961).

[88] J. Hartman, Housing and Social Policy 67 (1975). But see *Devines v. Maier,* 728 F.2d 876 (7th Cir. 1984). For a recent dramatic instance of demolition because housing units were constructed pursuant to building permits which violated requirements for consistency with the local government's comprehensive plan, see *Pinecrest Lakes, Inc. v. Shidel,* 795 So. 2d 191 (Fla. 4th DCA 2001); § 2:13, supra.

[89] See, e.g., *Espanola Way Corp. v. Meyerson,* 690 F.2d 827 (11th Cir. 1982); *Amen v. City of Dearborn,* 718 F.2d 789 (6th Cir. 1983).

[90] Daniel Curtin & Cecily Talbert, California Land Use and Planning Law 471–72 (27th ed. 2007) (citing *City and County of San Francisco v. Burton,* 201 Cal. App. 2d 749, 20 Cal. Rptr. 378 (1st Dist. 1962) (Unintentional discriminatory enforcement not a defense.); *Sutherland v. City of Fort Bragg,* 86 Cal. App. 4th 13, 102 Cal. Rptr. 2d 736 (1st Dist. 2000) (fire chief's duty to enforce discretionary).

[91] *Squaw Valley Development Co. v. Goldberg,* 375 F.3d 936, 58 Env't. Rep. Cas. (BNA) 2013, 34 Envtl. L. Rep. 20051 (9th Cir. 2004).

[92] Stone and Rinker, Governmental Liability for Negligent Inspections, 57 Tul. L. Rev. 328 (1982). See Note: Municipal Liability for Negligent Building Inspection, 65 Iowa L. Rev. 1416 (1980); Robinson, Rebuilding the Wall of Sovereign Immunity: Municipal Liability for Negligent Building Inspections, 37 U. Fla. L. Rev. 343 (1985); Markowitz, Municipal Liability for Negligent Inspection and Failure to enforce Safety Codes, 15 Hamline J. Pub. L. & Pol'y 181 (1994); Kubes, The Design Professional's Project Self Certification: A Key to Efficiency or Liability?, 26 Construction L. 5 (2006) (Fla. Stat. Stat. § 553.791(17) requires local building code enforcement agency to develop and maintain an audit process for the building code inspection services by private providers).

[93] *Manors of Inverrary XII Condominium Ass'n, Inc. v. Atreco-Florida, Inc.,* 438 So. 2d 490 (Fla. 4th DCA 1983).

site inspections prior to issuance of a certificate of occupancy were operational, thus the sovereign immunity doctrine did not protect the municipality from liability for the negligence of the inspector in approving the plans, specifications, and construction, none of which met the requirements of the applicable building code.[94] The Wisconsin Supreme Court held a city liable for damages caused by fire because the inspector should have foreseen that his negligent inspection might result in harm.[95] After an inspection and recommendation for demolition of a building had been made but no action taken by the city or owner, when the building collapsed and two children were killed, a city in New York was found liable for failure to carry out its statutory duty.[96] The *United States Supreme Court, in Block v. Neal,*[97] held Farmers Home Administration liable under the Tort Claims Act, for failure to properly inspect a house during construction. Defects found in the house were attributable to the negligent inspection and did not fall within the misrepresentation exception to the Act. Government can be protected from the danger of excessive damages by enacting statutes which put a ceiling on the amount of damages recoverable against it.[98] The government can also be exempted from liability for failure to inspect or negligent inspection if the property is not owned by the government.[99]

§ 8:7 Building Permits and Certificates of Occupancy

Until recently, the issuance of building and certificate of occupancy permits was considered a non-discretionary or ministerial act.[100] The applicant was entitled to them as long as she had complied with applicable building codes and construction procedures.[101] Today, however, "courts no longer treat the issuance of building permits as ministerial only. Rather, courts consistently uphold local regulations that treat the issuance of building permits as discretionary, which allows cities to impose conditions on their issuance . . . ."[102]

Today, issuance is frequently made dependent upon compliance by the applicant with numerous other requirements—especially those requiring the payment of infrastructure finance regulatory payments such as impact and linkage fees. The issuance of these permits has thus become a focal point of the enforcement and implementation

---

[94] Manors of Inverrary XII Condominium Ass'n, Inc., 438 So. 2d at 494.

[95] *Coffey v. City of Milwaukee,* 74 Wis. 2d 526, 247 N.W.2d 132 (1976).

[96] *Runkel v. City of New York,* 282 A.D. 173, 123 N.Y.S.2d 485 (2d Dep't 1953). See also *Gannon Personnel Agency, Inc. v. City of New York,* 57 A.D.2d 538, 394 N.Y.S.2d 5 (1st Dep't 1977); *Campbell v. City of Bellevue,* 85 Wash. 2d 1, 530 P.2d 234 (1975); compare *Quinn v. Nadler Bros., Inc.,* 92 A.D.2d 1013, 461 N.Y.S.2d 455 (3d Dep't 1983), order aff'd, 59 N.Y.2d 914, 466 N.Y.S.2d 292, 453 N.E.2d 521 (1983).

[97] *Block v. Neal,* 460 U.S. 289, 103 S. Ct. 1089, 75 L. Ed. 2d 67 (1983).

[98] See, e.g., Fla. Stat. Ann. § 768.28(5); Ill.—S.H.A. ch. 85, ¶ 2–102; Mont. Code Ann. §§ 2–9–101 to 2–9–105; Or. Rev. Stat. § 30.270; Utah Code Ann. § 63–30–34; Wis. Stat. Ann. § 893.80(3).

[99] Cal. Gov't Code § 818.6; Ill.—S. H.A. ch. 85, ¶ 2–105 and 2–207; Ind. Code § 34–4–16.5–3(11); Nev. Rev. Stat. § 41.033; N.J. Stat. Ann. 59:2–6; Utah Code Ann. § 63–30–10(4) (1953).

[100] *Prentiss v. City of South Pasadena,* 15 Cal. App. 4th 85, 18 Cal. Rptr. 2d 641 (2d Dist. 1993) (California Environmental Quality Act did not apply as issuance of building permit free of historical architectural conditions was a "ministerial project."); *Incorporated Village of Atlantic Beach v. Gavalas,* 81 N.Y.S.2d 322, 599 N.Y.S.2d 218, 615 N.E.2d 608 (1993) (building permit issuance was not an agency action for which an Environmental Impact Statement was required since underlying ordinance did not entrust municipal building inspector with type of discretion which would allow grant or denial to be based on environmental concerns).

[101] D. Curtin & C. Talbert, California Land Use and Planning Law 519 (26th ed. 2006).

[102] Incorporated Village of Atlantic Beach v. Gavalas, 81 N.Y.2d 322, 599 N.Y.S.2d 218, 615 N.E.2d 608 (1993), citing *Avco Community Developers, Inc. v. South Coast Regional Com.,* 17 Cal. 3d 785, 132 Cal. Rptr. 386, 553 P.2d 546 (1976).

of various growth management programs.[103] As discussed earlier in this treatise,[104] whether or not a developer is entitled to the issuance of a building permit also raises vested rights issues.[105]

---

[103] See infra § 9:8.

[104] See § 5:28 supra.

[105] For a state by state discussion of cases on point, see Kushner, Subdivision Law & Growth Management § 10:15 (2d ed.).

Chapter 9

GROWTH MANAGEMENT AND SMART GROWTH*

Analysis

§ 9:1   The Growth Management and Smart Growth Concepts

A. *Evolution of Growth Management and Smart Growth*

The traditional land use control devices—zoning and subdivision control—have always had at least a potential effect on the growth rate and patterns of growth for those local governmental entities which employ them. For example, zoning codes which include density allocations for the permitted use zones set a theoretical maximum population figure for the jurisdiction. Subdivision control ordinances likewise affect allowable population limits and the speed at which development occurs by setting minimum lot sizes and requiring construction of capital facilities before plat approval can be obtained or before building permits will be issued. Nonetheless, controlling the maximum population of a community and the rate at which growth will occur is at best a minor goal of traditional zoning and subdivision control ordinances.

---

* For more detailed discussion and more extensive citations of authority of the issues covered in this chapter, see Juergensmeyer and Roberts, Land Use Planning and Development Regulation Law, Practitioner Treatise Series (3rd ed. 2012).

The growth management plans which came in vogue in the 1970s and 1980s utilized many traditional land use control techniques but for the primary purpose of regulating the pace and extent of growth.[1] Thus, the issues of how much growth should occur and *when* it should occur became as important as the traditional height, bulk and use aspects of Euclidean zoning's preoccupation with *where* development will be permitted.

The decision of various communities to manage growth has been prompted by a variety of interrelated factors—many laudable and some suspect. Key factors include concern for the effects of growth on environmentally sensitive areas and scarce environmental resources,[2] crowding of public facilities, the economic and social effects of the energy crisis and the steady decrease of nonrenewable energy stores, the decrease of federal money allocations to local and state governments for a wide variety of land use and public facilities programs, the high unemployment rate in the late 1970s and early 1980s, and an acceleration of the rate of growth in the so-called "sunbelt" states. However when one evaluates these factors, the growth management movement of recent years has had the effect of making land use planning and control law a more popular and controversial topic at the grass roots level than it has ever been before. "Manage Growth," "Stop Growth," "Smart Growth," "Make Growth Pay For Itself," and "Support the Population Cap" have become familiar bumper sticker slogans. There is little if any doubt that exclusionary motives including even racial and economic discrimination lurk behind some of the proposals [3] but at the very least the controversies which envelope nearly all growth control proposals have brought much needed public interest and attention to the land use planning and control process. In fact, it seems quite possible that growth management and its evolved form—smart growth—provide the primary theme and coherence for land use regulation and environmental protection in the 21st century.[4]

In looking ahead, it should be noted that three interrelated concepts are becoming intertwined with the concept of growth management: carrying capacity, impact analysis and sustainable development.[5] The origin of all of these sometimes overlapping concepts is environmental law.

---

[1] An extensive overview and analysis of these programs and their legal implications are found in the Urban Land Institute's Management and Control of Growth Series, to wit: Urban Land Institute, Management and Control of Growth Vol. I (1975), Vol. II (1975), Vol. III (1975), Vol. IV (1978); Urban Land Institute, The Permit Explosion: Coordination of the Proliferation (1976); Urban Land Institute, Growth and Change in Rural America (1979); Arthur C. Nelson and James B. Duncan, Growth Management Principles and Practices (1995); Jerry Weitz, Sprawl Busting: State Programs to Guide Growth (1999); James A. Kushner, Subdivision Law and Growth Management (2d ed. 2006); Robert H. Freilich, From Sprawl to Smart Growth: Successful Legal, Planning, and Environmental Systems (1999); John DeGrove, Planning Policy and Politics: Smart Growth and the States (2005); Gregory K. Ingram et al., Smart Growth Policies: An Evaluation of Programs and Outcomes (2009).

[2] See Freilich and Davis, Saving the Land: The Utilization of Modern Techniques of Growth Management to Preserve Rural and Agricultural America, 13 Urb. Law. 27 (1981). Leerssen, Smart Growth and Green Building: An Effective Partnership to Significantly Reduce Greenhouse Gas Emissions, 26 J. Envtl. L. & Litig. 287 (2011).

[3] The "wolf of exclusionary zoning hides under the environmental sheepskin worn by the stop-growth movement." Bosselman, Can the Town of Ramapo Pass a Law to Bind the Rights of the Whole World?, 1 Fla. St. U. L. Rev. 234, 249 (1973. See also §§ 6:1 et seq., supra.

[4] See supra § 1:3.

[5] Ziegler, Urban Sprawl, Growth Management and Sustainable Development in the United States: Thoughts on the Sentimental Quest for a new Middle Landscape, 11 Va. J. Soc. Pol'y & L. 26 (2003).

"Carrying capacity" is used to determine environmental criteria upon which to ground land use decisions and refers to the extent to which land in its natural or current state can be developed without destruction of the ecosystem.[6] Generally today, carrying capacity is just one way of evaluating the impact of development.

"Impact analysis" in its current usage is no doubt a transfer of the concepts involved in environmental impact studies conducted pursuant to environmental protection statutes.[7]

The seminal conceptual examination of impact analysis was done by Fred Bosselman, who defined impact analysis as "the process of examining a particular land development proposal and analyzing the impact it will have on a community."[8] Bosselman suggests that the acceptance of impact analysis techniques reflects two trends in government policy toward land use regulation:

(1) Regulation should respond to specific development proposals: The policy that the formulation of land use controls should be delayed until the developer's intentions are known has been reflected in the weakening of legal support for the principle that a developer should be entitled to develop if his proposal is consistent with pre-established regulations adopted pursuant to a comprehensive plan.

(2) Development standards should be predictable: The policy that a greater degree of predictability ought to be found in the local process of responding to development proposals, has been reflected in the increasing uneasiness of courts toward local regulations that lack a "scientific" basis.

The use of impact analysis in regard to infrastructure funding is discussed below.[9] Three even newer ways of translating the impact analysis concept into land use regulation are "linkage," "mitigation," and "transfer." Again, Fred Bosselman has provided the definitions and examples:

Linkage is a system by which a developer who wants to build one thing is required to also build something else; e.g., an office developer is required to build housing.

Mitigation is a system by which a developer who will cause some adverse environmental impact is required to counterbalance that impact by creating an equivalent benefit; e.g., a project that will destroy wetlands is required to create equivalent wetlands elsewhere. Transfer is a system by which a certain type or degree of development is made conditional on the extinguishment of an equivalent right to undertake such development elsewhere; e.g., a height increase is made contingent on acquisition of air rights over a historic structure somewhere else.

---

[6] The term "carrying capacity" is also sometimes used to refer to the ability of the infrastructure in a given area to support new development: for example the excess or unused sewage treatment or water treatment capacity of the existing private and/or governmental facilities. See J. Juergensmeyer, Florida Land Use Law § 26 (2d ed. 1999).

[7] See Schaenman & Muller, Land Development: Measuring the Impacts, Urban Land Institute, Management and Control of Growth, Vol. II 494 (1975).

[8] Bosselman, Linkage, Mitigation and Transfer: Will Impact Analysis Become the Universal Antidote to Land Use Complaints? (1985).

[9] See infra § 9:9.

Although the future course of growth management and smart growth is far from certain, concentration on the impact of development would seem to be an essential ingredient of any growth management or smart program.[10]

"Sustainable development," in its broadest context, is a concept of social change in which the population and intended functions of a community can be maintained into the indefinite future without degrading community institutions, the means of production, systems of infrastructure, the resource base, and natural and man-made environments. Sustainable development embraces the environment as a mainstream scientific and economic factor in all policy, planning, and decision-making. The concept has been applied in a variety of contexts and to denote a wide range of issues, including urban sprawl, new economic development, inner-city and "brown field" redevelopment, local small business, a strong local economy, environmental justice, ecosystem management, resource recycling, agriculture, biodiversity, lifestyles, "green" buildings, energy conservation, and pollution prevention.[11]

While the terms "sustainable" and "development" each have a variety of meanings alone, together they are apt to suggest many varying ideas to the people who employ them. Thus, the implementation of sustainable development initiatives is problematic. Nonetheless, the concept is increasingly a subject of intense discussion among policy-makers and community groups, and is likely to remain an issue in land use planning in the 21st century, and thus to become an additional concern for land use planning and control law, particularly in the area of growth management.[12]

B.   Smart Growth and Urban Sprawl

After World War II, American soldiers came home to start families and enjoy the American dream they had fought so hard to protect. These new families wanted the economic prosperity of urban employment and at the same time desired to experience open spaces and other benefits associated with rural living. Indeed, residing in the country and working in the city was made easy and even encouraged by the government during these times. The Eisenhower Interstate Highway system solved the transportation problem for these outlying communities and allowed more residential development to occur further and further from urban centers.[13] Additionally, federal home loans and federal tax law encouraged the purchase of new suburban homes by making it possible for more people to obtain mortgages and by allowing a deduction for mortgage interest.[14] Euclidian Zoning, itself, is considered one of the culprits in the spread of sprawl since use districting forbid or discouraged the inclusion of commercial and professional uses in or close to residential developments thereby increasing auto-

---

[10] Weitz, The Next Wave in Growth Management, 42/143 Urb. Law. 407 (2011).

[11] See, generally, Symposium on Sustainable Development, 31 Willamette L. Rev. 261 (1995); Ziegler, American Cities and Sustainable Development in the Age of Global Terrorism: Some Thoughts on Fortress America and the Potential for Defensive Dispersal II, 30 Wm. & Mary Envtl. L. & Pol'y Rev. 95 (2005); Lewyn, Sprawl in Europe and America, 46 San Diego L. Rev. 85 (2009).

[12] See Rothrock, Oregon's Goal Five: Is Ecologically Sustainable Development Reflected, 31 Willamette L. Rev. 449 (1995); Tarlock, Local Government Protection for Biodiversity: What Is Its Niche?, 60 Chi. L. Rev. 555 (1993).

[13] Freilich and Peshoff, The Social Costs of Sprawl, 29 Urb. Law. 183, 184 (1997).

[14] Tom Daniels, When City and County Collide (1999).

mobile dependency and the resulting need for new roads.[15] Another reason for the mass exodus from cities was the so-called "white flight" that began during the civil rights movement and contributed to racially segregated housing developments.[16] These changes in development patterns are what have become known as urban sprawl because these new automobile-dependent communities are created in areas that were previously undeveloped or designated for agriculture and therefore likely lack the infrastructure needed to support them.[17]

Defining "sprawl" is not without some difficulty because of varying views of its causes and effects but a generally accepted definition is:

> Sprawl refers to a particular type of suburban growth—it is development that expands in an *unlimited and noncontiguous (leapfrog) way outward* from the solidly built-up core of a metropolitan area. In terms of land use type, sprawl can define both *residential and nonresidential* development. In sprawled areas, residential development comprises primarily single-family housing, including significant numbers of distant units scattered in outlying areas. Non residential development includes shopping centers, strip retail outlets along arterial roads, industrial and office parks, and freestanding industrial and office buildings, as well as schools and other public buildings.[18]

Urban sprawl can have many negative impacts on an area. Air quality can suffer because individuals living in car-dependent communities on the urban fringe will have long commutes, which will add to the volatile organic compounds and nitrogen oxides that combine to form ground level ozone.[19] Highway systems can become overly congested, resulting in wasted time and added stress.[20] Valuable undeveloped land is consumed, which destroys needed green space to maintain watershed integrity and wildlife habitat.[21] Additionally, minority communities are often disproportionately affected by urban sprawl, increasing segregation in most urban public schools.[22]

Nonetheless, urban sprawl is not without its defenders or at least those who point out the societal benefits that accompany the costs. They stress the low density life style that it permits on an affordable basis. In other words, the American dream of a single family dwelling with a picket fence and flower garden in the front and a tree house for

---

[15] See Hall, Divide and Sprawl, Decline and Fall: A Comparative Critique of Euclidian Zoning, 68 U. Pitt. L. Rev. 915 (2007); Note: Putting a Stop to Sprawl: State Intervention as a Tool for Growth Management, 62 Vand. L. Rev. 979 (2009).

[16] Buzbee, Urban Sprawl, Federalism, and the Problem of Institutional Complexity, 68 Fordham L. Rev. 57, 64 (1999).

[17] See, generally, Robert H Freilich, From Sprawl to Smart Growth: Successful Legal, Planning, and Environmental Systems (1999).

[18] Robert W. Burchell, State of the Cities and Sprawl 3 (Mar. 9, 2000) (unpublished manuscript presented at the Rocky Mountain Land Use Institute's Ninth Annual Land Use Conference, "The Costs and Benefits of Sprawl"). See also Juergensmeyer, An Introduction to Urban Sprawl, 17 Ga. St. L. Rev. 923 (2001).

[19] Gallagher, The Environmental Social, and Cultural Impacts of Sprawl, 15-SPG Nat. Resources & Env't. 219 (2001).

[20] Freilich and White, Transportation Congestion and Growth Management: Comprehensive Approaches to Resolving America's Major Quality of Life Crisis, 24 Loy. L.A. L. Rev. 915, 919–920 (1991).

[21] Griffith, The Preservation of Community Green Space: Is Georgia Ready to Combat Sprawl with Smart Growth?, 35 Wake Forest L. Rev. 563, 567 (2000).

[22] Bullard, Johnson and Torres, The Costs and Consequences of Suburban Sprawl: The Case of Metro Atlanta, 17 Ga. St. L. Rev. 935, 939 (2001).

the kids in the back is affordable to considerably more Americans if housing is built in distant suburbs.[23]

Whatever the cost benefit ratio, the negative effects of urban sprawl increasingly concern Americans and many urban planners and others who seek ways to reverse the ever accelerating spread of sprawl offer "smart growth" as an antidote.[24] The term "smart growth" was popularized by Maryland Governor Paris Glendening's 1997 smart growth initiatives.[25] However, smart growth is not easily defined because it means something different in different jurisdictions, and communities have their own particular goals or challenges associated with future growth.[26] In general, smart growth represents everything that sprawl is not. It is planning that considers both environmental protection and economic growth while resulting in sustainable developments that increase the quality of life.[27] Principles usually associated with smart growth include:[28]

1. Mixed land uses

2. Communities where transportation options include walking, biking, and mass transit

3. Decreasing traffic congestion[29]

4. Density[30]

5. Protecting open space, wetlands, and prime agricultural land[31]

6. Urban revitalization[32]

7. Decreasing taxes and costs of infrastructure[33]

---

[23] Helling, Advocate for a Modern Devil: Can Sprawl Be Defended?, 17 Ga. St. L. Rev. 1063 (2001). See also, Joseph Persky and Wim Wiewel, When Corporations Leave Town: The Costs and Benefits of Metropolitan Job Sprawl (Lincoln Institute Report).

[24] Arthur C. Nelson, Smart Growth or Business as Usual? Which Is Better at Improving Quality of Life and Central City Vitality?, 2000 Dep't of Housing and Urban Dev. 83; Ziegler, Urban Sprawl, Growth Management and Sustainable Development in the United States: Thoughts on the Sentimental Quest for a New Middle Landscape, 11 U. Va. J. Soc. Pol'y & L. 26 (2003).

[25] Salkin, Smart Growth At Century's End: The State of The States, 31 Urb. Law. 601 (1999). The smart growth movement is not without its skeptics. Young, The Tao of Smart Growth: The Way That Can Be Named Is Not the Way, 41 No. 4 Plan Canada 29 (Oct.-Dec. 2001); Siegan, Smart Growth and Other Infirmities of Land Use Controls, 38 San Diego L. Rev 693 (2001).

[26] Pollard, Smart Growth: The Promise, Politics, and Potential Pitfalls of Emerging Growth Management Strategies, 19 Va. Envtl. L.J. 247 (2000).

[27] Ohm, Reforming Land Planning Legislation at the Dawn of the 21st Century: The Emerging Influence of Smart Growth and Livable Communities, 32 Urb. Law. 181 (2000).

[28] A parallel list endorsed by Minnesota's Smart Growth Network (1000 Friends of Minnesota) is found at John DeGrove, Planning Policy and Politics: Smart Growth and the States 2 (2005).

[29] Salkin, Smart Growth at Century's End: The State of the States, 31 Urb. Law. 601 (1999); Bolen, Brown, Kiernan, and Konschink, Smart Growth: A Review of Programs State by State, 8 Hastings W.-Nw. J. Envtl. L. & Pol'y 145 (2002); Maya, Transportation Planning and the Prevention of Urban Sprawl, 83 N.Y.U. L. Rev. 879 (2008).

[30] Pollard, Smart Growth: The Promise, Politics, and Potential Pitfalls of Emerging Growth Management Strategies, 19 Va. Envtl. L.J. 247 (2000).

[31] Griffith, Green Infrastructure, The Imperative of Open Space Preservation, 42/43 Urb. Law. 259 (2011); Morris, Conservation Easements and Urban Parks: From Private to Public Use, 51 Nat. Resources J. 357 (2011).

[32] Pollard, Smart Growth: The Promise, Politics, and Potential Pitfalls of Emerging Growth Management Strategies, 19 Va. Envtl. L.J. 247 (2000).

The American Planning Association has adopted a definition of smart growth:

Smart growth means using comprehensive planning to guide, design, develop, revitalize and build communities for all that have a unique sense of community and place; preserve and enhance valuable natural and cultural resources, equitably distribute the costs and benefits of development, expand the range of transportation, employment and housing choices in a fiscally responsive manner; value long-range, regional considerations of sustainability over short term incremental geographically isolated actions; and promotes public health and healthy communities. Compact, transit accessible, pedestrian-oriented, mixed use development patterns and land reuse epitomize the applications of the principles of smart growth.[34]

It would seem that the goals of smart growth could be implemented through the same tools that traditional growth management uses. These techniques include timed growth programs,[35] urban service boundaries, and requiring adequate infrastructure before development.[36] The current momentum of the smart growth movement is focused, however, on "redoing" traditional growth management and stresses the need for new legislation embodying and facilitating growth management principles. The American Planning Association reports that "more than 2,000 land use reform bills [were] introduced in statehouses across the country between 1999 and 2001. Of these, approximately 20 percent have been enacted."[37] The American Planning Association has sought to further this astounding revision of existing land use laws by publishing a "monumental" (over 1400 pages!) work entitled *Growing Smart Legislative Guidebook: Model Statutes for Planning and the Management of Change* (2002 Edition), which has 2 volumes of accompanying work papers and its own user manual.[38] According to recent surveys, state smart growth activities now require an impressive number of pages to even summarize.[39]

C. New Urbanism

From a planning perspective, the Smart Growth movement is closely allied to the "New Urbanism" movement currently in vogue with urban designers and urban planners.[40] One of the leaders of this movement is Andres Duany whose many publications

---

[33] Nolon, Local Land Use Controls That Achieve Smart Growth, 31 Envtl. L. Rep. 11025 (2001); John R. Nolon, Well Grounded: Using Local Land Use Authority to Achieve Smart Growth (2001).

[34] American Planning Association Policy Guide on Smart Growth (adopted April 4, 2002 by Chapter Delegate Assembly and ratified by the Board of Directors April 15, 2002).

[35] See supra § 9:2.

[36] The only traditional growth management technique that is incompatible with current ideas of smart growth may be population caps because smart growth does not advocate cessation in development. Ohm, Reforming Land Planning Legislation at the Dawn of the 21st Century: The Emerging Influence of Smart Growth and Livable Communities, 32 Urb. Law. 181 (2000).

[37] American Planning Association, Planning for Smart Growth: 2002 State of the States (Summary Report 2).

[38] Salkin, The Smart Growth Agenda: A Snapshot of State Activity at the Turn of the Century, 21 St. Louis. U. Pub. L. Rev. 271 (2002); Bolen, Brown, Kiernan, Konschnik, Smart Growth: A Review of Programs State by State, 8 Hastings W.-Nw. J. Envtl. L. & Pol'y 145 (2002). A brief summary of leading state smart growth and growth management programs may be found in § 9:14, infra.

[39] Jerry Weitz, Growing Smart User Manual (APA 2002). The Guide-book, Work Papers, and Manual are available in hard copy and on the APA website: http://www.planning.org.

[40] See Charter of the New Urbanism (Michael Leccese and Kathleen McCormick, eds. 2000); John A. Dutton, New American Urbanism: Re-Forming the Suburban Metropolis (2000). See William Fulton, The New Urbanism: Hope or Hype for American Communities? (Lincoln Institute Policy Focus Report 1996);

and "cutting-edge" urban designs have become synonymous with smart growth. His "principles" of smart growth stress urban configuration and architectural designs that reconfigure sprawling suburbs into communities of "real" neighborhoods.[41] New Urbanism challenges and seeks to replace many of the traditional tenets of land use planning and control law.[42] The increasing popularity of "smart codes" designed to replace traditional zoning and subdivision regulation approaches will no doubt accelerate this trend.[43]

§ 9:2   Growth Management and Smart Growth Programs

Land use control planners and attorneys are still searching for effective and permissible ways of formulating and implementing growth management and smart growth programs. Several signals have emerged.[44] The most important of these is that "timed" or "phased" growth control measures are more palatable for courts and the electorate than population caps. One early commentator identified and discussed five primary motivations for regulating the timing and pace of urban development: (1) to economize on the costs of municipal facilities and services; (2) to retain control over the eventual character of development; (3) to maintain a desirable degree of balance among various uses of land; (4) to achieve greater detail and specificity in development regulations; and (5) to maintain a high quality of community services and facilities.[45]

The first major victory before the courts for pro-growth management forces occurred in litigation contesting the phased growth plan developed by Ramapo, New York. This plan used a residential development timing technique for the avowed purpose of eliminating premature subdivision, urban sprawl, and development without adequate municipal facilities and services. The plan did not rezone or reclassify any land into different residential or use districts but provided that any person engaged in residential development must obtain a special permit.

> The standards for the issuance of special permits are framed in terms of the availability to the proposed subdivision plat of five essential facilities or services, specifically: (1) public sanitary sewers or approved substitutes; (2) drainage facilities; (3) improved public parks or recreation facilities, including public schools; (4) State, county, or town roads—major, secondary, or collector; and (5) firehouses. No special permit shall issue unless the proposed residential development has accu-

---

Gindroz, New Urbanism and Smart Growth: City Life and New Urbanism, 29 Fordham Urb. L.J. 1419 (2002). See also Congress for the New Urbanism, Who Is CNU, http://www.cnu.org/who__we__are.

[41] Duany's major publications on point include: Andres Duany, Jeff Speck, Elizabeth Plater-Zyberk, Smart Growth Manual (2002); Andres Duany, et al, Suburban Nation: The Rise of Sprawl and the Decline of the American Dream (2010). His firm's website, http://www.dpz.com gives considerable information about new urbanism and smart growth.

[42] See Sitkowski and Ohm, Enabling the New Urbanism, 34 Urb. Law. 935 (2002); The Influence of New Urbanism on Local Ordinances: The Twilight of Zoning?, 35 Urb. Law. 783 (2003).

[43] See § 8:2, supra; Duany and Talen, Making the Good Easy: The Smart Code Alternative, 29 Fordham Urb. L.J. 1445 (2002); Emerson, Making Main Street Legal Again: The Smart Code Solution to Sprawl, 71 Mo. L. Rev. 637 (2006).

[44] See, generally, DeGrove, Balanced Growth: A Planning Guide for Local Government (1991); Kelly, Managing Growth: Policies, Techniques, and Impacts (1993); Bollens, State Growth Management: Intergovernmental Frameworks and Policy Objectives, 58 J. Am. Plan. Ass'n 454 (1992); John DeGrove, Planning Policy and Politics: Smart Growth and the States (2005); Daniel R. Mandelker, ed., Planning Reform in the New Century (2005).

[45] Fagin, Regulating the Timing of Urban Development, 20 L. & Contemp. Prob. 298 (1955). See also, Freilich and White, Transportation Congestion and Growth Management: Comprehensive Approaches to Resolving America's Major Quality of Life Crisis, 24 Loy. L.A. L. Rev. 915 (1991).

mulated 15 development points, to be computed on a sliding scale of values assigned to the specified improvements under the statute.[46]

A developer, by agreeing to provide those improvements that would bring the proposed plat within the number of development points needed could advance the date of subdivision approval. Also applications to the "Development Easement Acquisition Commission" for a reduction in assessed valuation were authorized.

In essence the "timed" or "phased" growth programs, like Ramapo's, generally limit the number of residential and/or commercial units which can be built in a specified period of time. Along with the Ramapo, New York plan, other prototypes for this approach were developed in Florida,[47] and Colorado.[48] These programs are generally tied to the availability of public services and capital improvements. Sometimes a point system is established according to which a developer or the parcel of land sought to be developed must have a certain number of points before development is allowed. Points are earned or awarded on the basis of availability of public services and/or design criteria.[49]

A second type of growth management program is the "population cap."[50] Under the population cap approach the local government entity sets the maximum number of dwelling units which will be allowed to be built in the jurisdiction. Perhaps the most famous of these is the Boca Raton plan in Florida where the city sought to establish an absolute cap.[51] Equally famous, though somewhat different, is the Petaluma plan in California,[52] which set a cap on the number of dwelling units that could be built within a five-year period.[53]

---

[46] *Golden v. Planning Bd. of Town of Ramapo,* 30 N.Y.2d 359, 368, 334 N.Y.S.2d 138, 285 N.E.2d 291 (1972). The primary legal architect of the plan was Professor Robert Freilich who discusses it at length in Robert H. Freilich, From Sprawl to Smart Growth: Successful Legal, Planning, and Environmental Systems (1999). See also Bosselman, Can the Town of Ramapo Pass a Law to Bind the Rights of the Whole World?, 1 Fla. St. U. L. Rev. 234 (1973).

[47] See J. Juergensmeyer, Florida Land Use Law § 21 (2d ed. 1999) (Looseleaf); D. Godschalk, D. Brower, L. McBennett, B. Vestal & D. Herr, Constitutional Issues of Growth Management, ch. 20 (Sanibel, FL) (1979).

[48] See, D. Godschalk, D. Brower, L. McBennett, B. Vestal & D. Herr, Constitutional Issues of Growth Management, ch. 18 (Boulder, CO) (1979). See *Robinson v. City of Boulder,* 190 Colo. 357, 547 P.2d 228, 6 Envtl. L. Rep. 20418 (1976) (overruled by, Board of County Com'rs of Arapahoe County v. Denver Bd. of Water Com'rs, 718 P.2d 235 (Colo. 1986)).

[49] The refinement of the "point system" is usually attributed to attorney Kirk Wickersham, Jr. See Wickersham, The Permit System of Managing Land Use and Growth, Urban Land Institute, Management and Control of Growth, Vol. IV (1978).

In 1983, the Town of Ramapo eliminated the point system due to slow growth rates in the New York Metropolitan area. See Geneslaw and Raymond, Planning (June 1983) at 8. See also Robert H Freilich, From Sprawl to Smart Growth: Successful Legal, Planning, and Environmental Systems (1999).

[50] See infra § 9:3. See also Lamm and Davison, Legal Control of Population Growth and Distribution in a Quality Environment: The Land Use Alternative, 49 Denver L.J. 1 (1972).

[51] *City of Boca Raton v. Boca Villas Corp.,* 371 So. 2d 154 (Fla. 4th DCA 1979) (cap invalid). See J. Juergensmeyer, Florida Land Use Law § 21.07 (2d ed. 1999); D. Godschalk, D. Brower, L. McBennett, B. Vestal & D. Herr, Constitutional Issues of Growth Management, ch. 19 (Boca Raton, FL) (1979).

[52] See *Construction Industry Ass'n of Sonoma County v. City of Petaluma,* 522 F.2d 897, 8 Env't. Rep. Cas. (BNA) 1001, 5 Envtl. L. Rep. 20519 (9th Cir. 1975); D. Godschalk, D. Brower, L. McBennett, B. Vestal & D. Herr, Constitutional Issues of Growth Management, ch. 17 (Petaluma, CA) (1979).

[53] For litigation over a 280-unit per annum cap, see *Sustainable Growth Initiative Committee v. Jumpers, LLC,* 122 Nev. 53, 128 P.3d 452 (2006) (cap consistent with comprehensive plan).

A third form of growth control delineates the area or areas for staged future urban growth, outside of which urban development is restricted, deferred, or prohibited.[54] The provision of municipal services usually occurs only within the boundaries of the growth areas. This method is frequently labeled "urban service boundaries" or "urban growth boundaries" and, like the Ramapo plan, was pioneered by Professor Freilich.[55] The state planning programs of California,[56] Oregon,[57] Arizona,[58] Minnesota,[59] and Tennessee [60] provide for such urban growth boundaries.[61]

A fourth approach to growth control is to forego the establishment of ultimate or periodic numbers but to avoid, deter, or overcome many problems associated with growth by conditioning the issuance of building permits or plat approval on the existence of public improvements and capital facilities or requiring that developers pay fees which will be used by the proper governmental authority to provide the roads, schools, parks, sewer and water facilities, and/or police protection which will be needed because of the new development.[62] This approach is often referred to as a "Concurrency Requirement,"[63] or an adequate public facilities requirement (often referred to as APF).[64]

Developing, along with these various approaches to growth management, are the increased usage of the so-called "temporary" growth control measures such as development moratoria and withheld municipal services.[65]

Of the four approaches, programs employing concurrency or adequate public facilities requirements have been identified by one commentator as "the most basic, most useful and most easily defensible."[66] It is important, however, that any determinations

---

[54] See, generally, Easley, American Planning Ass'n, Planning Advisory Service Rep. No. 440, Staying Inside the Lines: Urban Growth Boundaries (1992); Epstein, Where Yards are Wide: Have Land Use Planning and Law Gone Astray?, 21 Wm & Mary Envtl. L. & Pol'y Rev. 345 (1997); Robert H. Freilich, From Sprawl to Smart Growth: Successful Legal, Planning, and Environmental Systems (1999).

[55] See Robert Freilich, Battling Sprawl: Making Smart Growth Work (1999).

[56] See *Shea Homes Ltd. Partnership v. County of Alameda,* 110 Cal. App. 4th 1246, 2 Cal. Rptr. 3d 739 (1st Dist. 2003).

[57] See Or. Rev. Stat. § 199.410; see also Knapp and Nelson, The Regulated Landscape: Lessons on State Land Use Planning from Oregon, Ch. 2 (1992); Nelson and Duncan, Growth Management Principles and Practices (1995).

[58] Salkin, Squaring the Circle on Sprawl: What More Can We Do? Progress Toward Sustainable Land Use in the States, 16 Widener L. Symp. J. 787 (2007).

[59] See Minn. Stat. Ann. § 473.861 (requiring a regional urban growth area for a five county area around metropolitan Minneapolis and St. Paul).

[60] 1998 Tenn. Pub. Act 1101; S.B. 3278/HB 3295 (Tenn.); University of Tennessee Institute for Public Service, Growth Policy, Annexation, and Incorporation Under Public Act 1101 (1998).

[61] Washington also requires designation of areas within which urban growth will not be permitted. See Wash. Rev. Code Ann. § 36.70A.110(1).

[62] See infra §§ 9:7, 9:8, 9:9.

[63] Florida imposed "concurrency" requirements as part of its mandatory state planning law: "public facilities and services needed to support development shall be concurrent with the impacts of such development . . . . " Fla. Stat. Ann. § 163.3177(10)(h). See Pelham, Transportation Concurrency, Mobility Fees, and Urban Spawl in Florida, 43/42 Urb. Law. 105 (2011). For recent developments in regard to the Florida Growth Management system, see infra § 9:15.

[64] In 1990, Washington began requiring local governments to link development approval and provision of facilities. Wash. Rev. Code Ann. ch. 36.70A. See Smith, Planning for Growth, Washington Style, in State and Regional Comprehensive Planning: Implementing New Models for Growth Management (Buchsbaum and Smith eds., 1993); Walsh and Pearce, The Concurrency Requirement of the Washington State Growth Management Act, U. Puget Sound L. Rev. 1025 (1993).

[65] See infra §§ 9:6 and 9:7; Layman, Concurrency and Moratoria, 71 Fla. B.J. 49 (Jan. 1997).

[66] Kelly, Zoning and Land Use Controls, § 4.01[2] (1996). See also Pelham, Timing Controls and Adequate Public Facilities: From the Ramapo Plan to Florida's Statewide Concurrency System: Ramapo's Influ-

of adequacy or inadequacy of the public facilities be rational, preferably having some quantifiable basis upon which the determinations are made, to insure that the program is well designed, that deficiencies are accurately identified, and that new development will in fact be served by the provision of the required facilities.[67] This approach allows local governments to establish a direct causal link to fundamental health, safety and welfare issues related to essential public facilities. In addition, it allows the developer to assess the feasibility of curing the inadequacies if necessary for development to proceed.

Negotiation between regulatory agencies and developers is one of the hallmarks of growth management programs—especially those based on the fourth approach. Also, it is one of the characteristics which distinguishes growth management from traditional zoning oriented land use regulation.[68] In many jurisdictions negotiation is based on practice or on the nature of the infrastructure finance requirements or point systems approaches that form a part of the jurisdiction's growth management program. A few jurisdictions, however, have provided statutory framework for negotiation through the enactment of Development Agreements Acts.[69]

A "Development Agreement"[70] is a voluntary, bargained for, agreement entered into between a developer and a land use control authority—usually a local government. Conceptually, it combines contract and police power based regulatory principles. The primary purpose of the agreement from the developer's perspective is to vest her rights to develop in exchange for promises made to the local government in regard to infrastructure finance, clustering, maintenance of open space, environmental mitigation, design, or other obligations. The local government agrees to "freeze" its regulations for an extended period of time in order to get the developer committed on one or more of the points just mentioned.[71]

Practically all of the land use regulation and control concepts discussed in this book can be of service to the diversity of approaches to growth management.[72] Moratoria, withheld or delayed governmental services, infrastructure financing, impact fees, transferable development rights, carrying capacity, impact analysis, and sustainable development will be highlighted in this chapter. Nonetheless, other concepts such as farmland preservation, building codes, building permits, comprehensive planning, conditional zoning, conservation easements, eminent domain, environmental controls, height restrictions, historic districts, holding zones, planned unit developments, subdi-

---

ence on Infrastructure Planning, 35 Urb. Law. 113 (2003); Weaver, Concurrency, Concurrency Alternatives, Infrastructure, Planning and Regional Solution Issues, 12 U. Fla. J.L. & Pub. Pol'y 251 (2001).

[67] See Pelham, Timing Controls and Adequate Public Facilities: From the Ramapo Plan to Florida's Statewide Concurrency System: Ramapo's Influence on Infrastructure Planning, 35 Urb. Law. 113 (2003); see also Durden, Layman, and Ansbacher, Waiting for the Go: Concurrency, Takings, and the Property Rights Act, 20 Nova L. Rev. 661 (1996).

[68] Consider, for example, the traditional prohibition of contract zoning. See supra § 5:11.

[69] Citations to the statutes may be found supra § 5:31.

[70] See Development Agreements: Practice, Policy and Prospects, (Porter and Marsh, eds.,1989); Johnson and Ziegler, Development Agreements: Analysis, Colorado Case Studies, Commentary, Rocky Mountain Land Use Institute (1993); Curtin, Development Agreement Practice in California and Other States, 22 Stetson L. Rev. 761 (1993); Kent, Forming a Tie That Binds: Development Agreements in Georgia and the Need for Legislative Clarity, 30-Fall Environs Envtl. L. Pol'y J. 1 (2006).

[71] Development agreements are discussed in detail in § 5:31, supra.

[72] See 1 Management and Control of Growth 24–31 (Scott ed., 1975) for an extensive list of regulatory concepts. See also Note: The Constitutionality of State Growth Management Programs, 18 J. Land Use & Envtl. L.145 (2002).

vision control, and zoning may be employed to manage urban growth. As consulting the index will indicate, these other concepts are explored at greater length throughout this treatise.

§ 9:3   Power of Local Government to Establish Growth Management and Smart Growth Programs

To the extent that a unit of local government uses traditional land use control measures such as zoning or subdivision control or minor variations thereof, the "power" issue is no different nor more difficult than that encountered by local governments in other land use planning and control activities. The police power automatically possessed by the local government on home rule power theories or specifically delegated to it pursuant to zoning enabling acts suffices.[73]

Many growth management programs and devices, however, involve often controversial approaches and tools, relatively new to land development control. The small number of decisions emanating from the courts of last resort in most jurisdictions coupled with scant guidance on some of the most basic federal constitutional issues from the United States Supreme Court leave planners and attorneys with inadequate guidance.[74]

The lack of clear judicial precedent has led many local governments to seek special legislative delegation or approval from their state legislatures. Still another approach employed by units of local government to buttress the legal status of their growth management activities is to submit their growth management plans or policies to referendum by the electorate.[75]

The use of a referendum in this area seems to stem from the decision of the Supreme Court of the United States in *James v. Valtierra.*[76] In this 1971 decision, the Supreme Court reversed a three-judge panel's holding that article 34 of the California Constitution which required voter approval of proposed low rent housing projects violated equal protection principles. The Court refused to impose the compelling state interest criteria because it found that article 34 made no distinction based on race, and declined to extend the compelling state interest test to classifications based on wealth. The Court placed great stress on the referendum as a procedure for democratic decision-making, saying, "referendums demonstrate devotion to democracy, not to bias, discrimination, or prejudice."[77]

Taking the lead from this statement, the questionable idea developed that submission of a growth management program to referendum and voter approval helps insu-

---

[73] For a state by state summary of statutes and cases authorizing growth management programs, see James Kushner, Subdivision Law and Growth Management §§ 1.17 and 1.22 (2d 2006). See also supra §§ 3:1 et seq.; Juergensmeyer and Gragg, Limiting Population Growth in Florida and the Nation: The Constitutional Issues, 26 U. Fla. L. Rev. 758 (1974).

[74] Attkisson, Putting a Stop to Sprawl: State Intervention as a Tool for Growth Management, 62 Vand. L. Rev. 979 (2009). See D. Godschalk, D. Brower, L. McBennett, B. Vestal & D. Herr, Constitutional Issues of Growth Management (1979); Bosselman, Growth Management and Constitutional Rights-Part I: The Blessing of Quiet Seclusion, 8 Urb. L. Ann. 3 (1974).

[75] See § 5:5, supra, for a detailed discussion of current cases involving initiative and referendum issues.

[76] *James v. Valtierra*, 402 U.S. 137, 91 S. Ct. 1331, 28 L. Ed. 2d 678 (1971).

[77] James, 402 U.S. at 141; see also *City of Eastlake v. Forest City Enterprises, Inc.*, 426 U.S. 668, 96 S. Ct. 2358, 49 L. Ed. 2d 132 (1976), on remand 48 Ohio St.2d 47, 356 N.E.2d 499 (1976).

late such programs from equal protection, "exclusionary," discriminatory and related attacks. The Petaluma, Sanibel and Boca Raton plans were submitted to referendum and approved by the electorate. The first two have survived attack in the courts and the third has not.[78]

Another source of power for local governments to practice growth management stems from state legislative and constitutional environmental protection provisions. Several states, including Florida, Illinois, Massachusetts, Michigan, Montana, New Mexico, New York, North Carolina, Pennsylvania, Rhode Island and Virginia have provisions in their state constitution guaranteeing their citizens a healthful environment.[79] Arguably a local government is required by such constitutional provisions or he state statutes implementing them to exercise their land use control powers in such a way as to protect environmentally sensitive land or endangered resources. This "duty" might be used as a justification of at least some elements of a growth management program. The court decisions at this point are sparse and indecisive.

A final justification for growth management by a unit of local government may be founded on mandated local government planning and the consistency requirement. As discussed elsewhere,[80] in several states, local governments are required to engage in comprehensive planning and to exercise their land use control powers consistently with those plans. The elements required to be included in the comprehensive plans inevitably raise growth management issues. A Florida court has held that the Local Government Comprehensive Planning Act which mandates the comprehensive planning also constitutes a source of power for local governments since all of their actions must be consistent with their plans.[81]

§ 9:4   Constitutional Limitations on the Power of Local Governments to Establish Growth Management Programs

One of the leading publications dealing with constitutional issues and growth control lists the following federal constitutional challenges to growth management programs: (1) the general due process challenge, (2) the takings challenge, (3) the regional welfare challenge, (4) the equal protection challenge, and (5) the right to travel challenges.[82]

Growth management programs are land use planning and control activities and are therefore exercises of the police power just as much as zoning or subdivision control. The general limitations, which apply to all exercises of the police power, apply to

---

[78] See supra § 9:2. On the subject of referenda in land use control, see supra §§ 3:10 and 5:5.

[79] See, generally, Godschalk, supra note 2, ch. 8.

[80] See supra §§ 2:12 to 2:13.

[81] *Home Builders and Contractors Ass'n of Palm Beach County, Inc. v. Board of County Com'rs of Palm Beach County*, 446 So. 2d 140 (Fla. 4th DCA 1983). See, *Mendota Golf, LLP v. City of Mendota Heights*, 708 N.W.2d 162 (Minn. 2006); *Ash Grove Cement Co. v. Jefferson County*, 283 Mont. 486, 943 P.2d 85 (1997); Linsk, Hole-in-One for Land Use Control: Endorsing the Dominance of Comprehensive Plans—Mendota Golf, LL.P v. City of Mendota Heights, 33 Wm. Mitchell L. Rev. 627 (2007).

[82] See D. Godschalk, D. Brower, L. McBennett, B. Vestal & D. Herr, Constitutional Issues of Growth Management (1979). Note: The Constitutionality of State Growth Management Programs, 18 J. Land Use & Envtl. L. 145 (2002). The following slightly more comprehensive list with state by state statutory and case law citations is found in Kushner, Subdivision Law & Growth Management Ch. 3 (2d ed.): Need for enabling legislation under state constitutional planning power, substantive due process, the right to travel, the takings clause, exclusionary zoning, equal protection clause, The Fair Housing Act, antigrowth control legislation, and antitrust legislation.

growth management. There is an especially close parallel between the limitations placed upon exclusionary zoning activities and the potential limitations placed on growth management programs. These general and specific limitations are discussed elsewhere.[83]

Several constitutional hurdles that growth management programs must survive that manifest themselves a bit differently in a growth control controversy than in a regular zoning dispute include the arguments that growth control measures constitute takings or are denials of substantive due process or equal protection. They are discussed elsewhere.[84]

A constitutional claim not usually made against other land use control devices is the constitutional right to travel, which is sometimes raised as an objection to growth controls. When local government limits growth, the argument goes, fewer houses are built and some people are excluded from settling in the town. Professor Siegan, for example, believes that "[e]recting barriers to travel and occupancy interferes with a free society's ideals of mobility and opportunity"[85] Absent a vital and pressing need, which he finds generally lacking, growth controls should not be allowed.

The courts, however, have not found that growth controls improperly impinge on a right to travel, or more specifically, a right to migrate to another state, or to a particular community within a state. The Supreme Court of California rejected a right to travel objection to an ordinance that prohibited the issuance of building permits until the city met its infrastructure needs.[86] The court reasoned that since "[m]ost zoning and land use ordinances affect population growth and density, to insist that such zoning laws are invalid unless the interests supporting the exclusion are compelling in character . . . would result in wholesale invalidation of land use controls and endanger the validity of city and regional planning."[87]

The right to travel is one of those "doctrinal messes" in constitutional law.[88] The parameters of the right are unclear. The Supreme Court has used it to strike down residency requirements that affect one's ability to vote and obtain welfare benefits,[89] but refused to find that it bars residency requirements for divorce. The constitutional source of the right has been disputed. In *Saenz v. Roe*,[90] the Court noted three components to the right to travel: "the right of a citizen of one State to enter and to leave another State, the right to be treated as a welcome visitor rather than an unfriendly alien

---

[83] See supra § 6:6.

[84] See §§ 10:1 et seq. infra (§ 10:8 regarding growth control moratoria; § 10:12, substantive due process, and § 10:14, equal protection).

[85] Siegan, Conserving and Developing the Land, 27 San Diego L. Rev. 279, 284 (1990).

[86] *Associated Home Builders etc., Inc. v. City of Livermore,* 18 Cal. 3d 582, 135 Cal. Rptr. 41, 557 P.2d 473, 7 Envtl. L. Rep. 20155, 92 A.L.R.3d 1038 (1976).

[87] CEEED, *California Coastal Zone Conservation Com.,* 43 Cal. App. 3d 306; *Associated Home Builders etc., Inc. v. City of Livermore,* 18 Cal. 3d 582, 135 Cal. Rptr. 41, 53, 557 P.2d 473, 485, 7 Envtl. L. Rep. 20155, 92 A.L.R.3d 1038 (1976).

[88] See, generally, Zubler, The Right to Migrate and Welfare Reform: Time for Shapiro v. Thompson to Take a Hike, 31 Val. U. L. Rev. 893 (1997). See also Wilhelm, Note: Freedom of Movement at a Standstill? Toward the Establishment of a Fundamental Right to Intrastate Travel, 90 B.U. L. Rev. 2461 (2010).

[89] *Dunn v. Blumstein,* 405 U.S. 330, 336, 92 S. Ct. 995, 999, 31 L. Ed. 2d 274 (1972) (right to vote in state elections on equal basis with other citizens); *Shapiro v. Thompson,* 394 U.S. 618, 89 S. Ct. 1322, 22 L. Ed. 2d 600 (1969) (overruled in part by, Edelman v. Jordan, 415 U.S. 651, 94 S. Ct. 1347, 39 L. Ed. 2d 662 (1974)) (welfare benefits).

[90] *Saenz v. Roe,* 526 U.S. 489, 119 S. Ct. 1518, 143 L. Ed. 2d 689, 61 Soc. Sec. Rep. Serv. 75 (1999).

when temporarily present in the second State, and, for those travelers who elect to become permanent residents, the right to be treated like other citizens of that State."[91] The source of the first right, that of free interstate movement, is unclear, and the *Saenz* Court declined to identify its source, since it was not implicated in the case. The second and the third, the Court held, come from the Privileges and Immunities Clause of the Fourteenth Amendment. In *Saenz*, the Court dealt with the third component and invalidated a durational residency requirement for welfare benefits as a violation of the Privileges and Immunities Clause.

Whether, or the degree to which, the right to travel includes a right to intrastate travel, the important question for challenges to growth management techniques, is unclear.[92] If such a right were found to exist, it might be treated as a fundamental right and be protected by strict scrutiny, or it might be seen as a matter of equal protection, in which event it would be subject to the intent test and likely low scrutiny.[93] In the context of exclusionary zoning, Professor Schragger contrasts the dramatic difference between cases like *Saenz* with the case of *Warth v. Seldin*,[94] in which the Court denied standing to residents of a state to challenge the zoning laws of a city in which they did not reside. As Schragger says, under *Saenz*, "the choice to move from one state to another * * * is a right that cannot be burdened even by a slight differential in welfare benefits for a period of one year, * * * while [under *Warth*] the assertion of a right to be able to choose to live in [a particular city within a state] is consigned to the pile of mere preference."[95] The problem, he laments, is that we lack a constitutional doctrine of local citizenship.

It is, thus, doubtful that the Supreme Court would find that a growth control measure violates the constitution.[96] In the first place, as noted above, showing the requisite standing to raise a right to travel argument under the Court's restrictive standing rules applicable to zoning challenges would be difficult.[97] Secondly, and on the merits, the Court has upheld other types of zoning ordinances that have similar potential exclusionary effects. In *Village of Belle Terre v. Boraas*,[98] the Court rejected the argument that a village's narrow definition of "single-family" for zoning purposes violated the right to travel of a group of unrelated college students from living together. In *Village of Arlington Heights v. Metropolitan Housing Development Corp.*,[99] the Court implicitly endorsed economic exclusionary zoning when it upheld the exclusion of multi-family housing from a suburb of Chicago. While *Arlington Heights* specifically addressed, and found wanting, the claim that the application of the ordinance violated the equal protection clause due to its racially discriminatory effect, the Court ignored the possibility that the ordinance affected other rights.

---

[91] Saenz, 526 U.S. at 500, 119 S. Ct. 1526.

[92] Commentators disagree. See Siegan, Smart Growth and Other Infirmities of Land Use Controls, 38 San Diego L. Rev. 693, 706 (2001) and Schragger, The Limits of Localism, 100 Mich. L. Rev. 371 (2001).

[93] See discussion infra § 10:14.

[94] 422 US. 490, 95 S. Ct. 2197, 45 L. Ed. 2d 343 (1975).

[95] Schragger, The Limits of Localism, 100 Mich. L. Rev. 371, 469 (2001).

[96] See Denny, supra note 3, at 1276 (agreeing that it is unlikely that Court would apply strict scrutiny to such a challenge).

[97] See infra § 10:14.

[98] *Village of Belle Terre v. Boraas*, 416 U.S. 1, 7, 94 S. Ct. 1536, 39 L. Ed. 2d 797, 6 Env't. Rep. Cas. (BNA) 1417, 4 Envtl. L. Rep. 20302 (1974).

[99] *Village of Arlington Heights v. Metropolitan Housing Development Corp.*, 429 U.S. 252, 263, 97 S. Ct. 555, 562, 50 L. Ed. 2d 450 (1977).

One short-lived success for the right to travel argument came when the district court in the *Petaluma* case found that city's quota on housing violated the right to travel.[100] The Ninth Circuit, however, overturned the decision on appeal, finding the plaintiff builder's association lacked standing to raise the rights of unknown third parties.[101] State courts interpreting state constitutions may differ. Though it has not styled it as a right to travel, the Pennsylvania Supreme Court's decision in *National Land & Investment Co. v. Kohn*[102] limits local zoning that affects the ability of persons living in the region to move to a community. On the other hand, the Supreme Court of Florida has summarily rejected the allegation that impact fees violate the right to travel by increasing home cost.[103] In short, as Professor Kushner has observed, "the right to travel has simply not materialized as a significant restraint on local growth management and land use controls."[104]

§ 9:5   Growth Management Through Regional Planning and Regulation

In our nation of over 80,000 governments, which together need to add at least 1.6 million new units of housing each year, problems associated with urban sprawl and unmanaged growth cross political boundaries.[105] Local governments are often not well-equipped to deal with these trans-jurisdictional issues because their abilities and agendas are limited; therefore, a regional perspective is needed for effective planning.[106] Regions have been defined as "geographic areas with problems of public policy or administration for which no existing unit of government is organized."[107] The purpose of a regional agency should be to discover the region's needs and move to meet these needs or encourage the local governments to do so.

The failure of many state and local governments to implement growth management and smart growth programs adequate to solve the sprawl oriented problems of major metropolitan areas has resulted in a resurgence of interest in and proposals for regional governments with planning and development regulation authority on a metropolitan wide basis.[108] A leading local government law expert has envisioned this development thusly:

---

[100] See discussion of *Petaluma,* supra § 9:2.

[101] *Construction Industry Ass'n of Sonoma County v. City of Petaluma,* 375 F. Supp. 574, 6 Env't. Rep. Cas. (BNA) 1453, 4 Envtl. L. Rep. 20454 (N.D. Cal. 1974), judgment rev' on other grounds 522 F.2d 897, 8 Env't. Rep. Cas. (BNA) 1001, 5 Envtl. L. Rep. 20519 (9th Cir. 1975). See also *Northern Illinois Home Builders Ass'n, Inc. v. County of Du Page,* 165 Ill. 2d 25, 208 Ill. Dec. 328, 649 N.E.2d 384, 397 (1995) (developer lacked standing).

[102] *National Land & Inv. Co. v. Kohn,* 419 Pa. 504, 215 A.2d 597 (1965), discussed in more detail supra § 6:2.

[103] *Contractors and Builders Ass'n of Pinellas County v. City of Dunedin,* 329 So. 2d 314, 317 (Fla. 1976).

[104] James Kushner, Subdivision Law and Growth Management § 3.4 (2d ed. 2006).

[105] Andrew M. Cuomo, "Toward A New Template," in Susan M. Wachter, R. Leo Penne & Arthur C. Nelson, editors, Bridging the Divide Making Regions Work for Everyone, U.S. Department of Housing and Urban Development (2000).

[106] Harr, Regionalism and Realism in Land-Use Planning, 105 U. Pa. L. Rev. 515 (1957); Griffith, Regional Governance Reconsidered, 21 J.L. & Pol. 505 (2005).

[107] Bruce D. McDowell, The Practice of State and Regional Planning, Regional Planning Today, Ch. 6 (1986).

[108] Griffith, Regional Governance Reconsidered, 21 J.L. & Pol. 505 (2005). See also, Aoki, All the King's Horses and All the King's Men: Hurdles to Putting the Fragmented Metropolis Back Together Again?

A transformation of American cities and outlying regions will occur during the twenty-first century as the citizenry responds to the political, economic, equitable, and environmental challenges posed by the continuing rapid growth many metropolitan areas will face. Today's regionally based economies further necessitate convergence with a political structure on the same scale. Although voters prefer local autonomy over land use, education, and fiscal resource decision making, federal and state authorities may increasingly seek regional solutions to provide the services and infrastructure needs that can best be met in a larger area of operation. Eventually, the region may also become the platform from which economic, equity-oriented, and environmental policy decisions will be made.[109]

The necessity for a regional approach has been exacerbated and complicated by the development of megapolitan clusters or transmetropolitan areas which extend beyond traditional metropolitan areas and often cover several metropolitan areas and states. A recent examination of this phenomenon identifies 23 such areas in the United States the largest of which extends from Virginia northward through Washington, D.C. and Baltimore, Philadelphia and New York, and on through Hartford and Boston, finally ending with Portland, Maine.[110] The challenge this growth pattern presents to land use control law, which has traditionally been centered at the local government level, is formidable.

Neither regional planning nor regional land use planning and control authorities are new. In fact, several regional planning organizations exercise considerable power and influence. The Tahoe Regional Planning Agency is well known for both as can be seen in two recent Supreme Court decisions: *Suitum v. Tahoe Regional Planning Agency*[111] and *Tahoe-Sierra Preservation Council v. Tahoe Regional Planning Agency*.[112] The Tahoe Agency is unusual in that it was created in 1969 by interstate compact (between California and Nevada) which offers a viable but infrequently considered format for metropolitan areas which sprawl across state boundaries.[113] A slightly different interstate model is that of The Columbia River Gorge National Scenic Area created by Act of Congress in 1986 to establish a partnership between the Federal Government, the States of Washington and Oregon, and 50 units of their local governments.[114] Still another well-known and innovative regional authority is New Jersey's Pinelands National Reserve[115] created by federal[116] and state legislation.[117]

Statewide Land Use Planning, Portland Metro and Oregon's Measure 37, 21 J.L. & Pol. 397 (2005); Jackson, The Need for Regional Management of Growth: Boulder, Colorado, as a Case Study, 37 Urb. Law. 299 (2005).

[109] Griffith, Regional Governance Reconsidered, 21 J.L. & Pol. 505, 558, 559 (2005).

[110] Arthur C. Nelson & Robert E. Lang, Megapolitan America: A New Vision for Understanding America's Metropolitan Geography (2011).

[111] *Suitum v. Tahoe Regional Planning Agency*, 520 U.S. 725, 117 S. Ct. 1659, 137 L. Ed. 2d 980, 44 Env't. Rep. Cas. (BNA) 1673, 27 Envtl. L. Rep. 21064 (1997).

[112] *Tahoe-Sierra Preservation Council, Inc. v. Tahoe Regional Planning Agency*, 535 U.S. 302, 122 S. Ct. 1465, 152 L. Ed. 2d 517, 54 Env't. Rep. Cas. (BNA) 1129, 32 Envtl. L. Rep. 20627, 10 A.L.R. Fed. 2d 681 (2002).

[113] The Agency's website provides detailed information about past and current activities of the Agency as well as a copy of the Interstate compact itself (Pub. L. No. 96–551, 94 Stat. 3233). See http://www.trpa.org.

[114] 16 U.S.C.A. § 544. See *Columbia River Gorge United-Protecting People and Property v. Yeutter*, 960 F.2d 110, 22 Envtl. L. Rep. 20947 (9th Cir. 1992) (act described and held valid). See also Blair, The Columbia River Gorge National Scenic Area: The Act, Its Genesis, and Legislative History, 17 Envtl. L. 863 (1987); Watters, The Columbia River Gorge National Scenic Act, 23 Envtl. L. 1127 (1993).

[115] See http://www.nps.gov/pine.

[116] 16 U.S.CA. § 471i.

A regional planning agency may be completely advisory, having no direct control over the local government's land use control decisions, or it may be granted certain powers to require actions from local governments to be consistent with the region's plan.[118] Agencies that are only advisory have the advantage of being less controversial because they do not usurp power from the local governments, which have traditionally exercised control over land use planning.[119] These types of agencies also have the disadvantage of not being able to require local conformance with the region's goals and plans.[120] However, it is still possible for these regional agencies to use incentives that will encourage local governments to act consistently with the region's plan.[121]

An important element of regional planning is how the region is organized. Metropolitan areas or river basins are typical examples of how regions can be organized. Metropolitan areas are often chosen for regional planning because they consist of numerous individual governments whose citizens often impact other governments through commuting, employment, recreation, shopping, and entertainment more than they impact their own, making the entire area operate like one unit.[122] River basins are chosen as regions because a single watershed consists of not only the bodies of water, but also the entire landmass that provides the drainage for the water body;[123] therefore, sustainability of water resources depends on adequate management of the entire watershed.[124]

Georgia is an example of a state which has created regional planning agencies and authorities.[125] One of these is the Atlanta Regional Commission which dates its origins to 1947 and is thought to be the oldest regional planning authority in the country.[126] It is the regional planning and intergovernmental coordination agency for a 10 county area and the City of Atlanta.[127] The Georgia Regional Transportation Authority was created in 1999[128] to combat Atlanta's land-based transportation and air quality problems, which are the result of unprecedented growth (from 1970 to 1996, the Atlanta area was the second-fastest growing city in the nation).[129] Additionally, Georgia has

---

[117] N.J. Stat. Ann. 13-18A.

[118] For an example of required consistency between the local governments and region see Nicholas, Steiner, Growth Management and Smart Growth in Florida, 35 Wake Forest L. Rev. 645 (2000).

[119] Alexander, Inherent Tensions Between Home Rule and Regional Planning, 35 Wake Forest L. Rev. 539 (2000).

[120] Porter, Reinventing Growth Management For The 21st Century, 23 Wm. & Mary Envtl. L. & Pol'y Rev. 705 (1999).

[121] Winstead, Smart Growth, Smart Transportation: A New Program To Manage Growth With In Maryland, 30 Urb. Law. 537 (1998).

[122] Briffault, Localism and Regionalism, 48 Buff. L. Rev. 1 (2000).

[123] Adler, Addressing Barriers to Watershed Protection, 25 Envtl. L. 973 (1995).

[124] Bruce D. McDowell, The Practice of State and Regional Planning, Regional Planning Today, Ch 6 (1986).

[125] See the Georgia Planning Act of 1989, Ga. Code Ann. § 36–70–3. See http://www.gadata.org/information_services/reg1.htm. Compare Florida's Regional Planning Councils Act, Fla. Stat. Ann. § 186.501. See http://www.ncfrpc.org. The Utah experience through Envision Utah presents a very different model. See Note: Old Regionalism, New Regionalism, and Envision Utah: Making Regionalism Work, 118 Harv. L. Rev. 2291 (2005).

[126] The history, organization, funding, and powers and responsibilities of the Agency are set forth in detail at its website: http://www.atlantaregional.com.

[127] Its powers and responsibilities do not cover the entire Atlanta metropolitan area which has approximately 166 local governments—28 counties and 138 cities.

[128] See Ga. Code Ann. §§ 50–32–1 et seq.

[129] Nelson, New Kid in Town: The Georgia Regional Transportation Authority and Its Role in Managing Growth in Metropolitan Georgia, 35 Wake Forest L. Rev. 625 (2000).

created the Metropolitan North Georgia Water Planning District to develop a regional water policy for Atlanta's limited water supply.[130] Georgia's ability to require mandatory planning is not clear because the state's constitution grants the "power of zoning" to "the governing authority of each county and of each municipality,"[131] and Georgia is a state with large political support for home rule.[132] However, the state's constitution also provides that the state's legislative branch may "establish procedures for the exercise of such power."[133] It is not yet clear whether the Georgia Regional Transportation Authority and the Metropolitan North Georgia Water Planning District will have the political support necessary for a regional approach to be successful.[134]

§ 9:6   Moratoria and Interim Controls

Implementation of an effective growth management plan may require the adoption of a development approval moratorium or some interim control to preserve the status quo while the plan is created and implemented.[135] Without a moratorium on development, building activity may occur that will defeat the plan's purposes before it is enacted. The publicity that will necessarily be a part of the planning process may in fact trigger a race by developers to build or at least achieve a vested right to build before new controls, which they fear may be more intrusive than current ones, are adopted. Since effective interim controls must be enacted without the usual notice and hearing that accompany the adoption of land use controls not all jurisdictions allow their use. Legal principles and judicial decisions relevant to the imposition of a moratorium are discussed elsewhere in this treatise.[136]

§ 9:7   Capital Improvement Programming[137]

As discussed earlier,[138] a potentially effective growth management approach is the use of the timing and location of public facilities to guide and shape a community's development. By deciding where to put water lines, sewers, roads, and other public facilities, and by deciding when to put them there, a community is not only making public

---

[130] Ga. Code Ann. §§ 12–5–570 to 12–5–586; see generally Griffith, Smart Governance for Smart Growth: The Need for Regional Governments, 17 Ga. St. U. L. Rev. 1019 (2001).

[131] Ga. Const. Art. IX, § II.

[132] See Alexander, Inherent Tensions Between Home Rule and Regional Planning, 35 Wake Forest L. Rev. 539 (2000). See Welch, Containing Urban Sprawl: Is Reinvigoration of Home Rule the Answer?, 9 Vt. Envtl. L. 131 (2008).

[133] Welch, Containing Urban Sprawl: Is Reinvigoration of Home Rule the Answer?, 9 Vt. Envtl. L. 131 (2008).

[134] Bross, Smart Growth in Georgia: Micro-Smart and Macro-Stupid, 35 Wake Forest L. Rev. 609 (2000).

[135] Kushner, Smart Growth: Urban Growth Management and Land-Use Regulation Law in America, 32 Urb. Law. 211, 212 (2000).

[136] See supra § 4:20 for a discussion of interim zoning, § 5:28 regarding vested rights, and infra § 10:8 regarding constitutional issues.

[137] Much of the text of §§ 9:7 and 9:8 is based on Thomas H. Roberts, Funding Public Capital Facilities: How Community Planning Can Help, ch. 1 of The Changing Structure of Infrastructure Finance (J. Nicholas ed. 1985). Excerpted with permission of Thomas H. Roberts.

[138] See supra § 9:2. Leading cases analyzing the withholding or delaying of governmental services as a growth management approach include *Associated Home Builders etc., Inc. v. City of Livermore,* 18 Cal. 3d 582, 135 Cal. Rptr. 41, 557 P.2d 473, 7 Envtl. L. Rep. 20155, 92 A.L.R.3d 1038 (1976); *Dateline Builders, Inc. v. City of Santa Rosa,* 146 Cal. App. 3d 520, 194 Cal. Rptr. 258 (1st Dist. 1983); *Smoke Rise, Inc. v. Washington Suburban Sanitary Commission,* 400 F. Supp. 1369, 8 Env't. Rep. Cas. (BNA) 1350, 6 Envtl. L. Rep. 20389 (D. Md. 1975); *Robinson v. City of Boulder,* 190 Colo. 357, 547 P.2d 228, 6 Envtl. L. Rep. 20418 (1976) (overruled by, Board of County Com'rs of Arapahoe County v. Denver Bd. of Water Com'rs, 718 P.2d 235 (Colo. 1986)).

investment decisions but, more important, is setting a pattern and establishing a framework for the much larger amount of private development that will be influenced by these public decisions. By consciously locating and timing such investments not only in response to present needs but also as a catalyst for future growth and change, a community can exercise a great deal of leverage on its development pattern. Planners generally refer to this approach as Capital Improvement Programming.

A Capital Improvement Program (CIP) is an annually compiled schedule of public construction activity covering the next five or six years, stating what public improvements will be built, where they will be built, and when, along with costs, sources of funding, and other pertinent information. It is an organized way for a community to discuss what it wants to do, what it can afford to do, what its priorities are, and how the projects will be coordinated.

The idea of capital improvements programming has been around for a long time. In fact, it evolved at about the same time in the history of American urban planning as land use regulation. In older cities such as Baltimore, Philadelphia, Pittsburgh, and Cleveland, the capital improvements program became the centerpiece of the planning program. In most places, however, communities moved more readily into the regulatory side of planning than they did into orderly fiscal planning, budgeting, and public investment programming. Urban planning in the United States today would certainly be much stronger if both the public regulatory and public investment sides of the coin had evolved together. In recent years, with the stress that has been placed first on growth management and on managing scarce fiscal resources, the time has become ripe for public capital investment planning to blossom.

Many states now require a capital improvement element in local government comprehensive plans—either as an absolute requirement or as a prerequisite for the exercise of various powers. The Georgia definition of a capital improvement element is typical:

> "Capital improvements element" means a component of a comprehensive plan . . . which sets out projected needs for system improvements during a planning horizon established in the comprehensive plan, a schedule of capital improvements that will meet the anticipated need for system improvements, and a description of anticipated funding sources for each required improvement.[139]

Hence, even though capital improvements planning is an old idea, its widespread and institutionalized use as part of the comprehensive planning process has been a long overdue innovation in most cities and counties. Moreover, the imaginative combination of regulatory and investment concepts, such as through the imposition of impact fees as a form of development regulation, is an even more innovative aspect of community planning.

The current year of the multi-year capital improvements program can become the basis for that year's annual operating budget. Also each year the capital improvements program is recompiled, dropping the first year and adding a new fifth (or sixth) year. Hence, a capital improvements program can serve as a policy implementation link be-

---

[139] Ga. Code Ann. § 36–71–2(2).

tween a long-range plan such as the comprehensive plan or one of the functional components thereof, and the actual line-item budgeting of funds for carrying out the plan.

Included among the many benefits of capital improvements programming are the following:

1. It can insure that plans for needed community facilities will actually be carried out by translating them into "bite-sized" chunks.

2. It allows various capital improvement proposals to be tested against sets of policies. Certain proposed projects may be someone's pet ideas but may not survive the tests of relevance, feasibility, or need.

3. It permits the multiyear scheduling of capital improvements that require more than one year to construct.

4. It provides an opportunity to acquire future public sites and rights-of-way before the costs go up.

5. It provides an opportunity for long-range financial planning and management.

6. It stabilizes tax rates through debt management.

7. It avoids costly and embarrassing instances of poor timing and noncoordination, such as paving a street and then tearing it up to install a sewer, or completing a school building before the water line reaches it.

8. It provides an opportunity for citizen participation and the involvement of specific interest groups in public matters that affect them.

9. It fosters better overall management of city or county affairs.

In a broader sense, capital improvements programming can also help a community establish the maximum amount of debt that it wishes to incur. It can focus on the various types of financing devices that can or should be resorted to, including traditional ones such as revenue bonds and special assessments, or some of the newer, innovative ones such as tax increment financing or impact fees.

Capital improvement programming is also an invaluable growth management tool. It can help determine whether, where, and how various parts of the community will develop. It can set priorities—for example, between the extension of public services into the urban fringe and the filling in and strengthening of services within substantially developed areas. In fact, the "concurrency" approach to growth management discussed earlier [140] is a way of requiring capital improvement programming and then using it to determine what development projects will be allowed. Florida [141] and Wash-

---

[140] See § 9:2, supra.

[141] "Florida's concurrency system is the nation's most comprehensive and innovative attempt to integrate capital improvements programs into the local comprehensive planning process." Pelham, Timing Controls and Adequate Public Facilities: From the Ramapo Plan to Florida's Statewide Concurrency System: Ramapo's Influence on Infrastructure Planning, 35 Urb. Law. 113, 132 (2003). For current plans to dismantle Florida's concurrency system, see Thomas G. Pelham, "Florida's Comprehensive Planning System Encounters Stormy Weather," State and Local Law News, vol. 34, no. 4, at 1 (June, 2011).

ington [142] are states that have adopted concurrency, and therefore capital improvement programming plays a major role in their smart growth and growth management programs.[143]

§ 9:8   Infrastructure Finance[144]

Traditionally the responsibility to provide so-called "infrastructure" has fallen to local government. Potable water, waste water collection and treatment, solid waste collection and disposal, streets, parks, and public schools generally fall into the category of "infrastructure." These services are required for the community to function in a manner that the public health, safety and welfare are protected. There is no doubt that growing communities require expanded water and waste water facilities, new schools additional fire stations and the like. The issue which has arisen is how are these services to be paid for?

It might seem that when a community experiences population growth, it would be a financial boon to all concerned—more people, more jobs, more trade, and more dollars being imported into the county and recirculated within the county. This, then, should lead to a larger tax base, more tax revenues, and more opportunity for local government to provide and pay for the public facilities that people want and need, possibly even more efficiently and at a higher level of quality than before.

Unfortunately, it doesn't usually happen that way. It is true that new outside money comes in, in the form of payroll, investments, and purchases. It is also true that the level of county government activity increases: there is more development to regulate, more public facilities to build, more community services to provide, and more taxes to collect. But generally the public revenues don't come in fast enough or in the right way to cover growing public costs. So things get out of joint: public costs go up, the availability and quality of public services go down, and the burden of additional costs is unfairly distributed, or at least that is how it is perceived by the citizenry.

Typically, there are four kinds of money shortage problems that arise in a local government experiencing growth, particularly rapid growth:

1.   Not enough increased revenue to cover increased expenses.

2.   Not enough revenues early enough to cover front-end costs of new public facilities (negative cash flow).

3.   Not enough revenue available in the right places or for the right purposes.

4.   Inequitable distribution of the cost burden.

---

[142] See Freilich, Garvin and White, Economic Development and Public Transit: Making the Most of the Washington Growth Management Act, 16 U. Puget Sound L. Rev. 949, 964 (1993) (concurrency management in Washington is an adjunct to capital improvement programming).

[143] Other states place emphasis on various implications of capital improvement programming. For example in Georgia, local government must have capital improvement programs in order to enact impact fees. Ga. Code Ann. § 36–71–3.

[144] See, generally, Rosenberg, The Changing Culture of American Land Use Regulation: Paying for Growth with Impact Fees, 59 SMU L. Rev. 177, 182 (2006); Arthur C. Nelson, James C. Nicholas & Julian C. Juergensmeyer, Impact Fees: Principles and Practice of Proportionate Share Development Fees Ch. 7 (2009). Thomas H. Roberts, Funding Public Capital Facilities: How Community Planning Can Help, Ch. 1 of The Changing Structure of Infrastructure Finance (J. Nicholas ed. 1985).

Problem 1, not enough increased revenue to cover increased expenses, can be caused by (1) inelastic revenue sources, (2) undependability of grant sources, or (3) the voters' refusal to countenance higher taxes.

An inelastic revenue source is one that does not grow fast enough to compensate for the offsetting effects of increased service demands or inflation. A sales tax, for example, is a fairly elastic response to the effects of inflation, because it grows in direct proportion to sales receipts, which in turn grow in direct proportion to inflation. In contrast per-gallon fuel taxes are a good example of inelastic taxes, because the revenue they produce does not increase as the cost of fuel increases, nor does it increase as fuel efficiency (that is, mileage per gallon) increases. Typical local governmental revenues, such as the ad valorem real property tax or business licenses and fees, may or may not be elastic, depending upon how careful local government officials are to see that property assessments and other components of revenue are periodically updated. Inasmuch as various types of development (such as residential, commercial, and industrial development) rarely produce real estate tax revenues in direct proportion to the services they consume, it is also important that local government constantly keep a close watch on the relative amounts of the various types of development it is experiencing (or permitting or encouraging) and also on the total mixture of revenues (that is, general property taxes, special assessments, user charges, business licenses, and other fees) that each type of development is producing.

Undependability of grant sources can be a serious cause of revenue shortages in local government. Federal and state funding policies can change quickly; and although federal aid can be a useful source of funding, it can also lead a local government to over commit itself, only to find that the grants it anticipated are not forthcoming because of a change in the political or fiscal climate, leading to a change in the law or in authorization or appropriation levels. If the grants are forthcoming, they may not come when they were supposed to, or the amount may be computed conservatively or inequitably.

A third typical cause of revenue shortages in growing localities is voters' opposition to higher taxes. "Taxpayer revolts" can be caused by general economic conditions or by specific dissatisfaction with the effects of growth, and they can result in the defeat of bond issues, pressure on public officials to keep taxes low, or replacement of officials at the polls with new ones who say they will keep taxes down. In any case, the result is less revenue to meet mounting expenses.

Problem 2, cash flow problems—that is, not having money in hand early enough to cover front-end costs—are the bane of any growing community, and particularly local governments confronted with rapid growth and development. Although new real estate development adds value to the tax roll, which will eventually produce more tax revenue for the city or county, these funds are not available ahead of time when they are needed to provide new public facilities. The traditional answer to this timing problem is to borrow the money by issuing bonds and paying them off over the life of a facility, usually several decades. There are limitations on this procedure, including legal debt limits, refusal by the voters or the elected officials to incur the debt, lack of identifiable or predictable future revenues to pledge (as in the case of revenue bonds), and a reluctance to charge all taxpayers for growth costs inflicted by new growth (as in the case of general obligation bonds).

Problem 3, not enough revenue available in the right places or for the right purposes, is another funding problem typically experienced by a locality faced with new growth. In this case the amount of available funds grows, but not in such a way as to make funds available for specific purposes. One example is the revenue produced by user charges within a special taxing district or public service district, which cannot be drained off and used for some other purpose—nor should it be, however meritorious the other purpose.

Other examples include various federal and state assistance programs which make funding available only for certain projects or categories. Not only are such limitations unresponsive to local needs and priorities, but they can also tempt local governments into compounding their financial problems, for example by accepting a grant to construct a capital facility, without paying adequate attention to the true life-cycle cost of the facility, including long-term operating and maintenance costs.

Problem 4 is the inequitable distribution of the cost burden. It is common for taxpayers to feel that they are being unfairly treated in one way or another, and this feeling is almost always exacerbated in a growing area, where residents may feel that they are being made to pay not only for their own services but for the expense of accommodating newcomers as well. Sometimes this situation is brought on by the high front-end cost of new development, discussed as problem 2 above. Sometimes it is caused by the fact that the new residents demand and receive a higher level or quality of services than was provided before, such as more libraries or better garbage collection, and the higher costs of these improved services are shared by all. Sometimes taxes rise simply because of an increase in per capita costs brought on by higher densities or a larger or more complex population, as in the case of police protection costs.

Inequitable tax burdens can also occur in a growing area when one unit of government provides services to another unit of government or to the citizens of another unit. An example is the provision of sewer or water service by a municipality to the surrounding area. There is always a strong risk that the providing government may charge too much or too little for the service, creating an inequity in either case. The most common situation is for the providing government to charge enough to cover the direct costs of the service but not enough to cover the full range of indirect costs of urban impacts that go along with it. Conflicting interpretations of these complex fiscal interrelationships can easily lead to public disagreements about who is subsidizing whom.

Whenever citywide or county-wide revenue sources are used to pay for the impact of new development, such as by paying off general obligation bonds or by covering increased annual operating costs, the original residents often feel that their taxes are being raised to pay for the costs of new development; and sometimes they are. (It is also often true, however, that much of the original residential development is subsidized by commercial and industrial property tax to begin with.) Although these same residents may often benefit financially from the new growth as a result of increased economic activity in the area (new jobs, more trade, new markets for services), these benefits are not proportionally distributed. Thus a retiree or a farmer, for example, may benefit less than a merchant or insurance agent, but his taxes go up nevertheless.

As often as not, these four types of revenue shortage problems occur in combined and overlapping fashion or with additional complications. For instance, the demand for a particular public service may grow evenly in proportion to the growth rate, whereas the provision of the service may have to grow in periodic increments. Fire protection is a common example: once a fire station is constructed, equipped, and manned, it can service a certain number of additional residences that are built within its service radius without a corresponding increase in cost. However, at some point a second station or additional equipment must be provided to handle additional demand beyond the capacity or reach of the original station. Hence, while the growth may occur evenly, the public cost of servicing that growth occurs in periodic jumps, making it more difficult to allocate costs and raise revenues in a manner that is viewed as equitable by all concerned. In short, new development often brings surprises in the form of unanticipated public costs.

New development produces additional capital costs, and it also produces increased operating and maintenance costs. This discussion deals with capital costs because they constitute the large, conspicuous, early expenditures that are most directly associated with new development, whereas operating and maintenance costs tend to be absorbed into government-wide operations and funded by the locality-at-large for the benefit of the locality-at-large. However, as discussed above, new development can also increase public service costs for current and new residents alike, and this should not be overlooked in an examination of the total effects of new development.

Two distinct types of capital facility impact costs resulting from new development can be identified. The two categories are site-related (or intradevelopment) costs and non-site-related (or extradevelopment) costs. Site-related costs are the regular capital costs that occur within a development or that are intimately and directly related to a development. In the typical case of a residential subdivision these include, at a minimum, local streets and drainage. As the density or size of a subdivision increases, sanitary sewers, water lines, more substantial drainage facilities and related rights-of-way, and neighborhood park and playground facilities become customary on-site or site-related improvements. In addition, street lights and sidewalks may be viewed as normal improvement costs, depending upon conditions. In short, whatever it takes to convert raw land into fully groomed, finished building sites, according to whatever standards the local government seeks to attain for its people, should be viewed as site-related costs and should be funded as such. Non-site-related costs are those that affect the community at large. More frequently now, non-site related infrastructure is analyzed as "system improvements" and site-related infrastructure is considered as "project improvements" but the essence of the dichotomy remains unchanged.[145]

§ 9:9   Developer Funding of Infrastructure

A common concern of most growth management programs is the availability and financing of public facilities. In the past, general revenues, special assessments and service districts, and ad hoc negotiations with developers have been the usual methods of finance. An ever increasing number of local governments—even those without full scale growth management programs—have adopted policies and programs designed to make new development and not existing residents bear the cost of new capital improvements such as schools, roads, parks, public safety facilities, and sewer and water

---

[145] See § 7:10, supra.

treatment facilities necessitated by the new development.[146] Three major categories of developer funding requirements can be identified: (1) Required Dedications, (2) Impact Fees, and (3) Linkage and Mitigation Fees.

A.   *Required Dedications*

Required dedications or payments in lieu thereof were the original approach to developer funding of infrastructure and developed in connection with subdivision regulations. Their history and current usage are discussed in detail above in Chapter 7 on Subdivision Regulation. A brief summary of required dedications and in-lieu fees will be given at this point to facilitate the discussion of impact fees and linkage and mitigation programs. The reader is referred to Chapter 7's more detailed discussion [147] but reminded that required dedications are becoming more and more entwined with impact fees which are discussed below.

The first land use regulation developed to shift the capital expense burden to the developer and new residents was the required dedication. Local governments conditioned their approval of a subdivision plat upon the developer's agreement to provide and dedicate such improvements as streets and drainage ways. Required dedications for these intradevelopment, or site-related capital improvements are now a well accepted part of subdivision regulation and are generally approved by the courts if reasonable.[148]

The "in lieu" fee developed as a refinement of required dedications. For example, to require each subdivision to dedicate land to educational purposes would not solve the problem of providing school facilities for developing suburban areas, because the sites would often be inadequate in size and inappropriately located. The in lieu fee solves this problem by substituting a money payment for dedication when the local government determines the latter is not feasible.

B.   *Impact Fees*

In one form or another, impact fees now exist in nearly all states and are a common technique used to generate revenue for capital funding necessitated by new development. To date, approximately 27 states have enacted impact fee enabling legislation [149] and in most other states impact fees are enacted pursuant to home rule powers or

---

[146] Infrastructure finance in general is discussed in supra § 9:8. Impact fees and infrastructure finance have become increasingly popular topics for books and law review articles. The major publications relied upon in the preparation of this section include Juergensmeyer and Blake, Impact Fees: An Answer to Local Governments Capital Funding Dilemma, 9 Fla. St. U. L. Rev. 415 (1981); Juergensmeyer, Funding Infrastructure: Paying the Costs of Growth Through Impact Fees and other Land Regulation Charges, Ch. 2 of The Changing Structure of Infrastructure Finance (J. Nicholas ed. 1985); James C. Nicholas, Arthur C. Nelson and Julian C. Juergensmeyer, A Practitioner's Guide to Development Impact Fees (1991) [Hereinafter cited as Practitioner's Guide]; J. Juergensmeyer, The Development of Regulatory Impact Fees: The Legal Issues, Ch. 8 of Development Impact Fees (Nelson ed. 1988); Nicholas, The Calculation of Proportionate Share Impact Fees, 408 A.P.A. Plan Advisory Ser. Rep. (1988); Frank and Rhodes, Development Exactions (1987); Development Impact Fees: Policy Rationale, Practice, Theory, and Issues (Nelson ed. 1988); Nelson, Paying for Growth's Impacts: A Guide to Impact Fees (1992); Bauman and Ethier, Development Exactions and Impact Fees: A Survey of American Practices, 50 L. & Contemp. Prob. 51 (1987).

[147] See § 7:8, supra.

[148] See § 7:8, supra.

[149] A list of states and citations to their enabling acts is given later in this section. See Arthur C. Nelson, James C. Nicholas & Julian C. Juergensmeyer, Impact Fees: Principles and Practice of Proportionate Share Development Fees Ch. 4 (2009).

pursuant to individual local government enablement. Impact fees are charges levied by local governments on new developments in order to pay a proportionate share of the capital costs of providing public infrastructure to those developments. In the Georgia Development Impact Fee Act, a typical impact fee enabling statute, an "impact fee" is defined as "a payment of money imposed upon development as a condition of development approval to pay for a proportionate share of the cost of system improvements needed to serve new growth and development,"[150]

Impact fees play an increasing role in the efforts of local governments to cope with the economic burdens of population growth such as the need for new parks, roads, schools, jails, public buildings, libraries, sewer, water treatment and storm water facilities, and public safety buildings and equipment. Exactly which infrastructure items may be financed through impact fees can be limited in those states with impact fee enabling acts, as the following table illustrates:[151]

Figure 1
FACILITIES ELIGIBLE FOR IMPACT FEES BY STATE

State	Roads	Water	Sewer	Storm Water	Parks	Fire	Police	Library	Solid Waste	School
Arizona (cities)	■	■	■	■	■	■	■	■		
Arizona (counties)	■	■	■		■	■	■			
Arkansas (cities)	■	■	■	■	■	■	■			
California	■	■	■	■	■	■	■	■	■	■
Colorado	■	■	■	■	■	■	■	■	■	
Florida	■	■	■	■	■	■	■	■		■
Georgia	■	■	■	■	■	■	■	■		
Hawaii	■	■	■	■	■	■	■	■	■	■
Idaho	■	■	■	■	■	■	■			
Illinois	■									
Indiana	■			■						
Maine	■	■	■		■	■	■	■	■	■
Montana	■	■	■	■	■	*	■	*		*
Nevada	■	■	■	■	■	■	■	■		**
New Hampshire	■	■	■	■	■	■	■	■	■	■
New Jersey	■	■	■	■						
New Mexico	■	■	■	■	■	■	■			
Oregon	■	■	■	■	■					***
Pennsylvania	■									
Rhode Island	■	■	■	■	■	■	■	■	■	■
South Carolina	■	■	■	■	■	■	■			
Texas (cities)	■	■	■	■						
Utah	■	■	■	■	■	■	■			
Vermont	■	■	■	■	■	■	■	■	■	■
Virginia****	■									
Washington	■				■	■				■
West Virginia	■	■	■	■	■	■	■		■	
Wisconsin (cities)	■	■	■	■	■	■	■	■	■	

* can be imposed by super-majority vote of city council or unanimous vote of county commission
** school construction tax up to $1,600 per unit authorized in districts with populations up to 50,000 (NRS 387.331)
*** development tax of up to $1.00/sq. ft. for residential and $0.50/sq. ft. for nonresidential may be imposed by school districts
**** impact fees may be imposed on by-right residential subdivision of agriculturally-zoned parcels for a broad array of facilities under certain circumstances
Source: Clancy Mullen, *Summary of State Impact Fee Acts*, October 2011 (www.impactfees.com - state information)

---

[150] Georgia Development Impact Fee Act, Ga. Code Ann. § 36–71–2(8).

[151] The charts and tables that follow were prepared in November 2011 by Clancy Mullen, AICP, of Duncan Associates of Austin, Texas. They are reproduced by permission from Clancy Mullin and Duncan Associates. Up-dated material may be obtained from the firm's website: http://www.impactfees.com.

Figure 2.
NATIONAL AVERAGE IMPACT FEES
PER SINGLE FAMILY UNIT

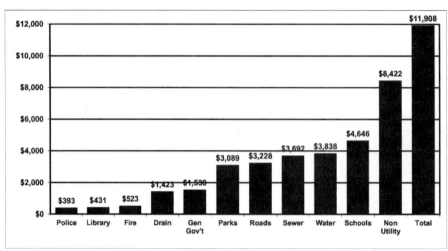

Figure 3.
AVERAGE IMPACT FEES BY LAND USE

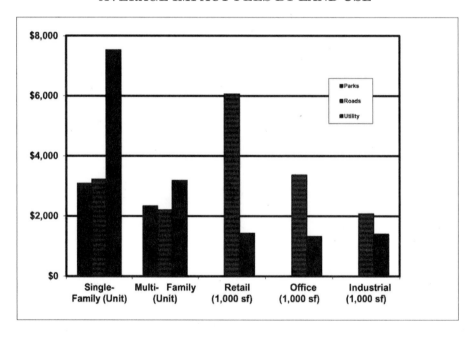

Figure 4.
AVERAGE NON-UTILITY IMPACT FEE PER SINGLE FAMILY UNIT BY STATE 2011

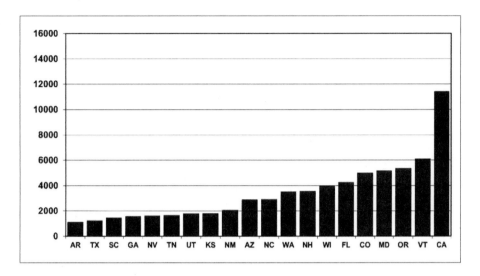

Although the impact fee owes its origin to the impact analysis concepts of environmental law, it is functionally similar to the in lieu fee, discussed above, in that both are required payments for capital facilities. In fact, the terms are sometimes used interchangeably.[152] The impact fee concept, however, is a much more flexible cost shifting tool. Because in lieu fees are predicated on dedication requirements, they can only be used where required dedications can be appropriately utilized. In the case of sewer and water facilities, public safety facilities, and similar capital outlays, required dedications are not always an appropriate device to shift a portion of the capital costs to the development, because one facility (and parcel of land) can service a very wide area and there is little need for additional land in extending these services.

The distinction between in lieu fees and impact fees results in several decided advantages for impact fees. First, impact fees can be used to fund types of facilities and capital expenses which are not normally the subject of dedication requirements and in lieu fees, and can more easily be applied to facilities to be constructed outside the development (extradevelopment or nonsite-related) as well as those inside the development (intradevelopment or site-related). Second, impact fees can be applied to developments platted before the advent of required dedications or in lieu fees and thus impose on incoming residents their fair share of these capital costs. A third advantage is that impact fees can be applied to condominium, apartment, and commercial developments which create the need for extradevelopment capital expenditures, but generally escape dedication or in lieu fee requirements because of the small land area involved or the inapplicability of subdivision regulations. Finally, impact fees can be collected at

---

[152] A hybrid form of the two has developed in Virginia where "proffers" combine many aspects of impact fees and in lieu type payments that are negotiated and yet based on schedules relating to infrastructure provision costs.

the time building permits or certificates of occupancy are issued and when growth creating a need for new services occurs, rather than at the time of platting.[153]

1.   Economic Analysis[154]

In the early days of impact fees, the 1960's and 1970's, there was extensive debate over whether the economic underpinnings of impact fees are applicable to government activities other than utility type services. Those who argued for restricting the concept to utility type services based their reasoning on the existence of a physical connection between the benefited unit and the facilities to be constructed with the fees collected. Moreover, they argued that utility type services are "closed ended" in that only those who pay the fee and receive the service benefit from the capital expansion as distinct from non-payers receiving a benefit. An "open ended" system, such as a road or park, is different, they argued. In such "open ended" systems it is either impossible or impractical to exclude non-payers from benefiting from the capital improvement.

The reasoning on the other side was that local governments face a host of capital expansion costs which may be reasonably anticipated because of new development: (1) if the present system of roads or parks has to be expanded to meet the needs of new development, (2) if the fees imposed were no more than what the local government unit would incur in accommodating the new users of the road or park system, and (3) if the fees are expressly earmarked and spent for road and park expansion, then the same economic logic applies as it does to utility type services.

These two positions are often characterized as the "exclusiveness of benefit" analysis and the "but not for" analysis. Those who adhere to the exclusiveness of benefit position argue that only those facilities which can be provided for the exclusive benefit of the individual paying the cost are fit candidates for impact fees. The premise of their argument is that if there is a public benefit from the expansion of a public facility, i.e., some individuals who do not pay for the expansion may use the facility, then individual payments would have to be classified as a tax rather than a fee. Such payments being taxes follows from the premise that there may be benefits flowing to individuals who have not paid for the facility. Thus, according to this position, only those public facilities which possess the capability to exclude nonpayers (or free-riders) are fit candidates for impact fees.

---

[153] Thus, the so-called pre-platted lands problem can be avoided. The "pre-platted lands" problem refers to the situation, especially prevalent in various sunbelt states, in which thousands and thousands of acres of land were platted during the land booms in the earlier part of the twentieth century before required dedications and exactions were standard. Those lands can frequently be sold and developed without the local government having any way of obtaining the dedications exactions or in lieu fees that would be obtained if the land were being platted today. See Juergensmeyer, Drafting Impact Fees to Alleviate Florida's Pre-platted Lands Dilemma, 7 Fla. Envtl. & Urb. Issues 7 (Apr. 1980); Schnidman and Baker, Planning for Platted Lands: Land Use Remedies for Lot Sale Subdivisions, 11 Fla. St. U. L. Rev. 505 (1983).

Impact fees are also collected at one or more of the following stages of development: (1) rezoning, (2) platting, (3) development order issuance, (4) building permit issuance, and (5) certificate of occupancy issuance. Collecting them late in the development process is best for the developer since he has no (or low) finance charges to pay on the impact fee amount. Local governments prefer collecting the fee as early as possible in the development process so that funds will be available to start construction in time to provide infrastructure when the development is completed. The conflicting preference of payors and payees has been resolved in most jurisdictions by providing for payment at the time a building permit is issued.

[154] The economic analysis given below is based on Chapters 1, 5, 8 & 9 of Arthur C. Nelson, James C. Nicholas & Julian C. Juergensmeyer, Impact Fees: Principles and Practice of Proportionate Share Development Fees Ch. 7 (2009).

The argument is based, in part, on the economic theory of externalities. An externality is an effect of an action by one individual upon another. Externalities can be either positive or negative. If an externality is positive it is seen as a social benefit and if it is negative it is seen as a social cost. The majority of regulations promulgated under the police power are attempts by government to stop the creation of negative externalities, i.e., to stop individuals from creating social costs. An example of such an exercise would be prohibition of excessive noise. Such a prohibition is not to benefit those who would have to suffer the noise but rather to stop others (noise makers) from causing harm. The opposite is where an individual is required to create a social benefit. An example would be a municipal concert hall. The requiring of individuals to provide, in whole or in part, a concert hall is not for the prevention of harm to the public. Rather, it is to benefit the public.

While there is no question that government is empowered to undertake such actions, requirements for individual financial participation in the creation of social benefits are exercises of the taxation powers of government rather than regulations under the police power. Given that a public park is not for the exclusive benefit of those who paid for it, it would follow, based upon the exclusiveness of benefit principle, that any requirement for individuals to financially contribute to a public park would be an act of taxation rather than of regulation. Returning to the theory of externalities; requirements to prohibit negative externalities (social costs) are considered to be regulatory under the police power to protect the public while requirements to create social benefits are seen as taxation to benefit the public. In this way the right and/or ability to exclude non-payers is very important to whether an assessment to expand a public facility will be seen as a regulatory fee or a tax.

Those who subscribe to the "but not for" argument take a different tack. Their premise is that if the facilities would not have to expand but for new development, then new development should be required to pay for that expansion. Use and benefit are seen differently in this position. It is not, herein, a matter of who uses or receives benefit from the particular facility but rather what (or who) caused the need for the facility. This line of reasoning views the theory of externalities differently. Take the example of a public park. If new development results in population growth that overcrowds the public parks, a social cost will have been created. This social cost is the loss of public use of the public park. A regulation to prevent the imposition of such public costs would have to be seen, therefore, as an exercise of the police power. While both sides of this argument would agree that requirements to create a public benefit would be an exercise of the taxation powers, the divergence comes in what constitutes a public cost.

The conservative position, characterized herein as the exclusive benefit argument, holds that public costs are only those direct impositions of harm such as excessive noise. The "but not for" position sees the loss of an existing public benefit as being a social cost. Thus, one side would argue that requiring impact fees for facilities such as parks would be taxation because the entire public, rather than only those who pay, will receive the benefit (use). The counter argument is that failure of park expansion will impose a public cost. Inasmuch as new development is the source of this public cost then regulations to prohibit such a cost would be exercises of the police power and a fee. These two positions can be argued ad infinitum but fortunately for the development of impact fees most courts have accepted the "but not for" approach.

The Florida courts addressed this issue early in the development of impact fees in that state. In *Hollywood, Inc. v. Broward County,*[155] the court wrote:

> [B]enefit accruing to the community generally does not adversely affect the validity of a development regulation ordinance as long as the fee does not exceed the cost of the improvements required by the new development and the improvements adequately benefit the development which is the source of the fee.

The Wisconsin and Utah courts have also addressed this matter. In *Jordan v. Village of Menomonee Falls,*[156] the court wrote:

> In most instances it would be impossible for the municipality to prove that the land required to be dedicated for a park or school site is to meet a need solely attributable to the anticipated influx of people in the community to occupy this particular subdivision. On the other hand, the municipality might well be able to establish that a group of subdivisions approved over a period of several years had been responsible for bringing into the community a considerable number of people making it necessary that the land dedications required of the subdividers be utilized for school, park and recreational purposes for the benefit of such influx. In the absence of contravening evidence this would establish a reasonable basis for finding that the need for the acquisition was occasioned by the activity of the subdivider.

The Utah court looked at the same issue in *Call v. West Jordan.*[157] In *Call* the court dealt directly with the issue of exclusiveness of benefit as a criterion to separate regulatory fees from taxes. The court wrote:

> We agree that the dedication should have some reasonable relationship to the needs created by the subdivision. . . . But it is so plain as to hardly require expression that if the purpose of the ordinance is properly carried out, it will redound to the benefit of the subdivision as well as the general welfare of the whole community. The fact that it does so, rather than solely benefiting the individual subdivision, does not impair the validity of the ordinance.[158]

In these various cases the courts are saying that the fact the entire community may use or enjoy the facilities is not the important point. Rather, what is important is that the need for the facility is occasioned by new development and that new development itself benefits. But, it is clear that the new development need not be the exclusive recipient of the benefits. Thus, the courts are aligned with the "but not for" position. The message here is clear—exactions can benefit the entire community as long as the need for the exaction is reasonably related to the needs of new development and as long as new development itself benefits from that exaction.

Thus, the two main economic analysis principles of impact fee assessment may be stated as (1) the cost imposed through the fee must flow reasonably from those costs to be borne by local government which are reasonably attributable to new development and (2) new development must benefit from the expenditure of the fees collected.

---

[155] *Hollywood, Inc. v. Broward County,* 431 So. 2d 606, 612–613 (Fla. 4th DCA 1983).

[156] *Jordan v. Village of Menomonee Falls,* 28 Wis. 2d 608, 617, 137 N.W.2d 442, 447 (1965).

[157] *Call v. City of West Jordan,* 606 P.2d 217, 219 (Utah 1979), on reh'g, 614 P.2d 1257 (Utah 1980).

[158] Call, 606 P.2d at 220.

2. Impact Fees and Comprehensive Planning

The increased emphasis being placed on the need and even requirement for consistency between comprehensive plans and land use regulatory activities of local governments makes necessary, or at least wise, the inclusion of language in comprehensive plans which will authorize and support impact fees. The following language is suggested as the embodiment of the planning principles inherent in impact fees:

1.   Land development shall not be permitted unless adequate capital facilities exist or are assured.

2.   Land development shall bear a proportionate cost of the provision of the new or expanded capital facilities required by such development.

3.   The imposition of impact fees and dedication requirements are the preferred methods of regulating land development in order to assure that it bears a proportionate share of the cost of capital facilities necessary to accommodate that development and to promote and protect the health, safety, and general welfare.[159]

Principle III ties directly to the capital improvement program (CIP) element of comprehensive plans.[160] Without such an element or planning process and the levels of service for infrastructure items which they should establish, it is difficult if not impossible to determine the proportionate share of new development.[161] Impact fees programs established without a CIP to underpin them are particularly vulnerable to attack under the rational nexus requirements discussed below.

The intergovernmental co-ordination elements of comprehensive plans are also increasingly important in regard to impact fee programs. Considerable controversy has arisen in Florida over whether municipalities are subject to the impact fee programs enacted by their counties.[162] Although the constitutional framework in a given state for its local governments may determine the outcome of the conflict, intergovernmental coordination, or lack thereof, can also play a key role.[163]

---

[159] The impact fee "Magna Charta" language was drafted by Julian C. Juergensmeyer, James C. Nicholas, Thomas H. Roberts and is published in The Changing Structure of Infrastructure Finance 15 (J. Nicholas, ed.1985).

[160] See supra § 9:7.

[161] See Arthur C. Nelson, James C. Nicholas & Julian C. Juergensmeyer, Impact Fees: Principles and Practice of Proportionate Share Development Fees Ch. 7 (2009)).

[162] See City of Ormond Beach v. County of Volusia, 535 So. 2d 302 (Fla. 5th DCA 1988); Seminole County v. City of Casselberry, 541 So. 2d 666 (Fla. 5th DCA 1989).

[163] In Cherokee County v. Greater Atlanta Homebuilders Ass'n, Inc., 255 Ga. App. 764, 566 S.E.2d 470 (2002), Cherokee County's impact fee program adopted pursuant to the Georgia Development Impact Fee Act, was challenged on equal protection grounds because the fees were imposed only on development within the unincorporated area of the County but also benefited development in the incorporated areas. The Court upheld the fees and stated: "The county's authority to require development approval through a building permit, however, is restricted to development in unincorporated portions of the county. OCGA § 36–13–1. Thus, the General Assembly has limited Cherokee County's authority to impose impact fees to the unincorporated portions of the county. It has authorized but not required counties to enter into intergovernmental agreements with municipalities to jointly collect impact fees to pay for system improvements benefiting both. OCGA § 36–71–11 . . . . The county has imposed an impact fee on all new developments within the unincorporated portions of the county, which is all it has the power to do. It has not made a 'classification' exempting incorporated developments from the fees, for by statute the county simply has no power or control over developments in municipal limits. The reason new developments in municipalities do not pay the fees is not because of any legislative distinction or action by the county, but results from decisions by the municipal-

3. Evolution of Impact Fees

In the early stages of impact fee development, they were subjected to two principal attacks: (1) First, impact fees were challenged as unreasonable regulations which were not acceptable exercises of the police power which made them "disguised" and unauthorized taxes. (2) Second they were attacked on the theory that they were not authorized by state statute or constitutional provision and therefore were void as *ultra vires* acts of the governmental entities which had enacted them.[164]

The characterization of impact fees as land use regulations or taxes presents a complex problem which has already been analyzed above in the economic analysis discussion in this section. Because impact fees are functionally similar to dedications and to other land use planning and growth management tools, the regulation tag appears appropriate but their revenue raising nature and purpose also makes them look very much like taxes to some judges.

The choice a court makes in "tagging" the impact fee "regulatory fee" or "tax" will often be determinative of its validity.[165] If the tax label is adopted, the impact fee will be invalidated unless express and specific statutory authorization for the tax exists. Even if statutory authorization is present, constitutional limitations on taxation may still invalidate the statute. Alternatively, if the impact fee is construed as a police power regulation, very broad legislative delegation should suffice. Once past this statutory hurdle, the clear trend among state courts is to validate such developer funding requirements as a valid exercise of the police power. Not surprisingly, therefore, most state courts have summarily labeled impact fees as either a tax or regulation in a result-oriented fashion that avoids an adequate theoretical or policy-directed explanation. Nonetheless, the problem will not go away and several recent cases return to the fee v. tax or the ultra vires problem resolved in most states by judicial decision or impact fee enabling statutes.[166]

There are two rationales either implicit or expressly cited in those decisions which apply the tax label to impact fees. The first is a simplistic observation that impact fees are a positive exaction of funds and are therefore a tax.[167] This criterion is an untena-

---

ities not to impose such fees and not to enter into optional intergovernmental agreements with the county regarding such." 566 S.E. 2d 470, 474.

[164] Compare *McCarthy v. City of Leawood*, 257 Kan. 566, 894 P.2d 836 (1995) with *Home Builders Ass'n of Cent. New York v. County of Onondaga*, 151 Misc. 2d 886, 573 N.Y.S.2d 863 (Sup 1991).

[165] See Heyman and Gilhool, The Constitutionality of Imposing Increased Community Costs on New Subdivision Residents Through Subdivision Exactions, 73 Yale L.J. 1119, 1146–55 (1964).

[166] Recent decisions on point include Mayor and Bd. of Aldermen, *City of Ocean Springs v. Homebuilders Ass'n of Mississippi, Inc.*, 932 So. 2d 44, 61 (Miss. 2006) (impact fees void because taxes); *Home Builders Ass'n of Greater Des Moines v. City of West Des Moines*, 644 N.W.2d 339 (Iowa 2002), as amended, (May 31, 2002) (impact fees taxes not regulatory fees); *Home Builders Ass'n of Lincoln v. City of Lincoln*, 271 Neb. 353, 711 N.W.2d 871 (2006) (impact fees "taxes" but city authorized by its charter to collect them); *Durham Land Owners Ass'n v. County of Durham*, 177 N.C. App. 629, 630 S.E.2d 200, 208, 209 Ed. Law Rep. 528 (2006), writ denied, review denied, 360 N.C. 532, 633 S.E.2d 678 (2006) (County lacked authority to impose impact fee—no discussion of fee v. tax.); *Home Builders Ass'n of Dayton & the Miami Valley v. Beavercreek*, 89 Ohio St. 3d 121, 2000-Ohio-115, 729 N.E.2d 349, 97 A.L.R.5th 657 (2000) (impact fee valid under City's powers pursuant to Ohio Constitution; *City of Olympia v. Drebick*, 156 Wash. 2d 289, 126 P.3d 802 (2006) (Wash Sup. Ct. held City's transportation impact fee really excise tax and therefore not subject to dual rational nexus requirements).

[167] For a brief discussion of the role property taxes play in growth management programs, see Arthur C. Nelson, And Then There Were Property Taxes: A Primer on Property Taxes, Economic Development, and Public Policy Urban Land Institute Working Paper Series, Paper 661 (July 1998).

ble basis for distinction because it exalts form over function. It ignores similar police power regulations which mandate that the developer expend great amounts of funds for streets, sewers, and other capital improvements within the development. Any distinction between impact fees and similar police power regulations made on the basis that impact fees are imposed prior to the issuance of building permits rather than as part of the plat approval process is a distinction without a difference.[168] The other rationale used to label impact fees as taxes is the theory that funds for education, recreation, and public safety purposes cannot be raised under the police power. This assertion is based on the conviction that such facilities should be financed solely from general revenues provided by the community as a whole and is discussed above.[169]

The second and often dispositive objection to impact fees has been that they were not authorized by state statute or constitutional provision and therefore were void as *ultra vires* acts of the governmental entities which had enacted them. As discussed above, the authority or ultra vires issue has been intertwined with the impact fees as taxes issue, and as such has already been analyzed.

The judicial resistance to impact fees in some states has lead for curative or preventive reasons to the enactment of impact fee enabling statutes in many states. They are discussed below. Although they differ considerably in scope and content, they share a common purposes of clarifying—sometimes by restricting—the power of local governments to enact impact fee. Nonetheless, several states without authorization or enabling statutes have found authority in home rule power, planning and consistency requirements, or on the theory that impact fees are land use regulations and that a local government with general land use regulatory authority may enact them as part of that power.

An authority problem which remains is that of whether the power of a local government to enact impact fees extends to all types of infrastructure or is limited to certain infrastructure items. Jurisdictions with impact fee authorization statutes generally have no problem with this issue since their statutes usually contain a list of permissible impact fees. In those states without such a list or without any statutory provisions on impact fees, educational facilities have been the most troublesome to courts.[170]

In Florida, a jurisdiction with impact fees dating back to the 1960's but without an impact fee authorization statute until 2006,[171] the battle over whether local governments can enact school impact fees based on their general land use regulatory powers has been particularly intense. It was finally resolved in favor of school impact fees by the Supreme Court of Florida's 1991 decision in *St. Johns County v. Northeast Fla. Builders Ass'n*.[172] The court found no preemption or prohibition in the Florida Constitution or statutes relating to educational funding. The court also rejected the argument

---

[168] See supra § 7:8.

[169] It is interesting to note that the United States Internal Revenue Service has ruled that impact fees incurred in connection with the construction of a residential rental building are capitalized costs allocable to the building under §§ 263(a) and 263A of the Internal Revenue Code. Rev. Rul. 2002–9.

[170] See Siemon and Zimet, Who Should Pay for Free Public Schools in an Expensive Society?, 20 Stetson L. Rev 725 (1991).

[171] Fla. Stat. Ann. § 163.31801 (2006). See Smith and Juergensmeyer, Development Impact Fees 2006: A Year in Review, 59 Plan. & Envtl. L. 3 (2007).

[172] *St. Johns County v. Northeast Florida Builders Ass'n, Inc.*, 583 So. 2d 635, 69 Ed. Law Rep. 636 (Fla. 1991). The case is discussed at length in J. Juergensmeyer, Florida Land Use Law § 22 (2d ed.1999).

that a school impact fee violates the "free" or "uniform" provisions of the Florida Constitution relevant to public education.[173]

A decision by the *Supreme Court of Colorado, Board of Cty. Com'rs, Douglas County v. Bainbridge, Inc.,*[174] runs counter to the current judicial trend. Although the Colorado court found, as did the Florida court, that the state's legislature had not preempted school finance, it held the school impact fees invalid on the theory that the provision in the Colorado statutes permitting counties to collect in lieu fees at the subdivision platting stage of development controls the maximum school related fees that can be collected and that counties have no implied powers to require additional infrastructure funding for schools at the time of building permit or certificate of occupancy issuance.[175]

4.   Impact Fees as Reasonable Exercises of the Police Power: The Dual Rational Nexus Test

As has been indicated, most state courts have recognized impact fees as permissible exercises of the police power. Once a jurisdiction's courts or legislative enactments have established this principle, the focus of controversy shifts to the standard of reasonableness which must be met since all exercises of the police power must be "reasonable."

In the early development stage of impact fees, two landmark decisions placed an almost insurmountable burden on local governments in this regard. In *Pioneer Trust & Savings Bank v. Mount Prospect,*[176] a developer challenged the validity of an ordinance requiring subdividers to dedicate one acre per 60 residential lots for schools, parks, and other public purposes. In determining whether required dedications or money payments for recreational or educational purposes represented a reasonable exercise of the police power, the Illinois Supreme Court propounded the "specifically and uniquely attributable" test. The court focused on the origin of the need for the new facilities and held that unless the village could prove that the demand for additional facilities was "specifically and uniquely attributable" to the particular subdivision, such requirements were an unreasonable regulation not authorized by the police power. Thus, where schools had become overcrowded because of the "total development of the community" the subdivider could not be compelled to help fund new facilities which his activity would necessitate.

A related and equally restrictive test was delineated by the New York court in the short-lived decision of *Gulest Associates, Inc. v. Newburgh.*[177] In that case developers attacked an ordinance which charged in lieu fees for recreational purposes. The

---

[173] However, the Florida Supreme Court has since refined this holding by ruling that where a residential development has no potential to increase school enrollment, public school impact fees are unwarranted. *Volusia County v. Aberdeen at Ormond Beach, L.P.,* 760 So. 2d 126, 137 (Fla. 2000).

[174] *Board of County Com'rs of Douglas County, Colo. v. Bainbridge, Inc.,* 929 P.2d 691, 115 Ed. Law Rep. 123 (Colo. 1996), as modified on denial of reh'g, (Jan. 13, 1997).

[175] The Colorado school finance statute was amended prior to the decision in the case to prohibit future school impact fees. Board of County Com'rs of Douglas County, Colo., 929 P.2d 691.

[176] *Pioneer Trust and Sav. Bank v. Village of Mount Prospect,* 22 Ill. 2d 375, 176 N.E.2d 799 (1961).

[177] *Gulest Associates, Inc. v. Town of Newburgh,* 25 Misc. 2d 1004, 209 N.Y.S.2d 729 (Sup 1960), order aff'd, 15 A.D.2d 815, 225 N.Y.S.2d 538 (2d Dep't 1962) and (disapproved of by, Jenad, Inc. v. Village of Scarsdale, 18 N.Y.2d 78, 271 N.Y.S.2d 955, 218 N.E.2d 673 (1966)). The *Gulest* decision was overruled in *Jenad, Inc. v. Village of Scarsdale,* 18 N.Y.2d 78, 271 N.Y.S.2d 955, 218 N.E.2d 673 (1966).

amounts collected were to be used by the town for "'neighborhood park, playground or recreational purposes including the acquisition of property.'"[178] The court held that the fee was an unreasonable regulation tantamount to an unconstitutional taking because the funds collected were not used solely for the benefit of the residents of the particular subdivision charged, but rather could be used in any section of town for any recreational purposes. In essence, the *Gulest* "direct benefit" test required that funds collected from required payments for capital expenditures be specifically tied to a benefit directly conferred on the homeowners in the subdivision which was charged. If recreational fees were used to purchase a park outside the subdivision, the direct benefit test was not met and the ordinance was invalid.

The *Pioneer Trust* and *Gulest* tests became difficult to reconcile with the planning and funding problems imposed on local governments by the constant acceleration of suburban growth. This restrictiveness also became difficult to rationalize with the judicial view of zoning ordinance as presumptively valid. Consequently, courts were not convinced of the practical or legal necessity of such stringent standards for the validation of required payments for extradevelopment or system capital funding.

At first, in turning away from the restrictive standards of *Gulest* and *Pioneer Trust,* state courts developed divergent and conflicting police power criteria for assessing the validity of extradevelopment or system capital funding fees.[179] The test which quickly became the standard view of state courts was suggested by the *Wisconsin Supreme Court in Jordan v. Village of Menomonee Falls.*[180] A two part "rational nexus" test of reasonableness for judging the validity of impact fees can be discerned in the decision. In response to a developer's attack upon the ordinance as both unauthorized by state statute and as an unconstitutional taking without just compensation, the *Jordan* court addressed the constitutionality of in lieu fees for educational and recreational purposes. After concluding that the fee payments were statutorily authorized, the court focused first on the *Pioneer Trust* "specifically and uniquely attributable" test.

The Wisconsin Supreme Court expressed concern that it was virtually impossible for a municipality to prove that money payment or land dedication requirements were assessed to meet a need solely generated by a particular subdivision. Suggesting a substitute test, the court held that money payment and dedication requirements for educational and recreational purposes were a valid exercise of the police power if there was a "reasonable connection" between the need for additional facilities and the growth generated by the subdivision. This first "rational nexus" was sufficiently established if the local government could demonstrate that a series of subdivisions had generated the need to provide educational and recreational facilities for the benefit of this stream of new residents. In the absence of contrary evidence, such proof showed that the need for

---

[178] Jenad, Inc., 218 N.E.2d at 730.

[179] See, *Jordan v. Village of Menomonee Falls,* 28 Wis. 2d 608, 137 N.W.2d 442 (1965); *Call v. City of West Jordan,* 606 P.2d 217 (Utah 1979), on reh'g, 614 P.2d 1257 (Utah 1980). It is somewhat ironic that the Illinois court has now interpreted the *Pioneer Trust* test to be met by proportionate share impact fee programs which meet the rational nexus test. See *Northern Illinois Home Builders Ass'n, Inc. v. County of Du Page,* 165 Ill. 2d 25, 208 Ill. Dec. 328, 649 N.E.2d 384 (1995).

[180] *Jordan v. Village of Menomonee Falls,* 28 Wis. 2d 608, 137 N.W.2d 442 (1965).

the facilities was sufficiently attributable to the activity of the particular developer to permit the collection of fees for financing required improvements.[181]

The *Jordan* court also rejected the *Gulest* direct benefit requirement, declining to treat the fees as a special assessment. Therefore, it imposed no requirement that the ordinance restrict the funds to the purchase of school and park facilities that would directly benefit the assessed subdivision. Instead, the court concluded that the relationship between the expenditure of funds and the benefits accruing to the subdivision providing the funds was a fact issue pertinent to the reasonableness of the payment requirement under the police power.

The *Jordan* court did not expressly define the "reasonableness" required in the expenditure of extradevelopment capital funds; however, a second "rational nexus" was impliedly required between the expenditure of the funds and benefits accruing to the subdivision. The court concluded that this second "rational nexus" was met where the fees were to be used exclusively for site acquisition and the amount spent by the village in constructing additional school facilities was greater than the amounts collected from the developments creating the need for additional facilities.

This second "rational nexus" requirement inferred from *Jordan,* therefore, is met if a local government can demonstrate that its actual or projected extradevelopment or system capital expenditures earmarked for the substantial benefit of a series of developments are greater than the capital payments required of those developments. Such proof establishes a sufficient benefit to a particular subdivision in the stream of residential growth such that the payment requirements may be deemed to be reasonable under the police power. The concept of benefits received is clearly distinct from the concept of needs attributable. As the *Jordan* court recognized, the benefit accruing to the new development, although it need not be direct, is a necessary factor in analyzing the reasonableness of impact fee payment requirements.[182]

Simply stated, the rational nexus test, i.e., the dual rational nexus test, has two components: (1) Impact fees may be no more than the government's infrastructure costs which are reasonably attributable to the new development, and (2) The new development required to pay impact fees must benefit from the expenditure of those fees.

With the adoption by most state courts of the dual rational nexus test, the focus of impact fee controversies shifted to the calculation of impact fees so as to meet the first prong of the test. Since the test provides that a developer can be charged no more than her proportionate share of the cost of new infrastructure, the calculation process must take into account not only the cost of the new infrastructure that the new development requires but credits for payments that have been or will be made by the developer outside the impact fee program. Furthermore, the developer cannot be required to pay for the unmet infrastructure costs of previously permitted development.

---

[181] Jordan, 137 N.W.2d at 447. See *Northern Illinois Home Builders Ass'n, Inc. v. County of Du Page,* 165 Ill. 2d 25, 208 Ill. Dec. 328, 649 N.E.2d 384 (1995) (Pioneer Trust test met by proportionate share impact fee program.).

[182] Northern Illinois Home Builders Ass'n, Inc., 649 N.E.2d at 448.

The Supreme Court of Utah in *Banberry Dev. Corp. v. South Jordan City*,[183] addressed these issues in the following language that has become widely accepted throughout the country for its specificity and clarity in giving the rules to follow in order to meet the first prong of the dual rational nexus test:

[To] comply with the standard of reasonableness, a municipal fee . . . must not require newly developed properties to bear more than their equitable share of the capital costs in relation to benefits conferred.

To determine the equitable share of the capital costs to be borne by newly developed properties, a municipality should determine the relative burdens previously borne and yet to be borne by those properties in comparison with the other properties in the municipality as a whole; the fee in question should not exceed the amount sufficient to equalize the relative burdens of newly developed and other properties.

Among the most important factors the municipality should consider in determining the relative burden already borne and yet to be borne by newly developed properties and other properties are the following, suggested by the well-reasoned authorities cited below: (1) the cost of existing capital facilities; (2) the manner of financing existing capital facilities (such as user charges, special assessments, bonded indebtedness, general taxes, or federal grants); (3) the relative extent to which the newly developed properties and the other properties in the municipality have already contributed to the cost of existing facilities (by means such as user charges, special assessments, or payments from proceeds of general taxes); (4) the relative extent to which the newly developed and the other properties in the municipality will contribute to the cost of existing capital facilities in the future; (5) the extent to which the newly developed properties are entitled to a credit.[184]

5. Impact Fees and Other Developer Funding Requirements Under Federal Constitutional Law

Once the development of impact fee law had become clarified and relatively uniform in the state courts,[185] the Supreme Court of the United States decided two cases that set out the federal constitutional standards which must be met by programs requiring developer funding of infrastructure by way of required dedications or physical exactions: *Nollan v. California Coastal Commission*[186] and *Dolan v. City of Tigard*.[187] A look at *Dolan* will provide the opportunity to consider the effect of both cases on the rational nexus standards for impact fees.

In *Dolan v. City of Tigard*,[188] the Supreme Court of Oregon used the "reasonable relationship" test to uphold the validity of the city's requirement that a landowner ded-

---

[183] *Banberry Development Corp. v. South Jordan City*, 631 P.2d 899 (Utah 1981). See also *Lafferty v. Payson City*, 642 P.2d 376 (Utah 1982).

[184] 631 P.2d at 903–04.

[185] Subject, of course, to differing statutory provisions in the various state enabling acts.

[186] *Nollan v. California Coastal Com'n*, 483 U.S. 825, 107 S. Ct. 3141, 97 L. Ed. 2d 677, 26 Env't. Rep. Cas. (BNA) 1073, 17 Envtl. L. Rep. 20918 (1987). The case is also discussed infra at § 10:5.

[187] *Dolan v. City of Tigard*, 512 U.S. 374, 114 S. Ct. 2309, 129 L. Ed. 2d 304, 38 Env't. Rep. Cas. (BNA) 1769, 24 Envtl. L. Rep. 21083 (1994). The case is also discussed infra at § 10:5.

[188] *Dolan v. City of Tigard*, 317 Or. 110, 854 P.2d 437 (1993), judgment rev'd, 512 U.S. 374, 114 S. Ct. 2309, 129 L. Ed. 2d 304 (1994).

icate land for improvement of a storm drainage system and for a bicycle/pedestrian pathway. The Oregon court considered its usage of the "reasonable relationship" test consistent with the "essential nexus" language contained in *Nollan*. In a 5–4 decision, the Supreme Court of the United States reversed the Oregon decision. Chief Justice Rehnquist, writing for the majority, first explained that the Court granted certiorari to resolve a question left open by *Nollan* "of what is the required degree of connection between the exactions imposed by the city and the projected impacts of the proposed development."[189]

The Chief Justice went on to characterize the attack by the landowner Dolan on the constitutional validity of the city's actions as being grounded in the contention that the Supreme Court in *Nollan* "had abandoned the 'reasonable relationship' test in favor of a stricter 'essential nexus' test"[190] and further commented that the Supreme Court of Oregon had read *Nollan* "to mean that an exaction is reasonably related to an impact if the exaction serves the same purpose that a denial of the permit would serve."[191]

The majority had no problem, as it had in *Nollan,* finding an essential nexus between governmental action and the governmental interest furthered by the permit condition and therefore reached the second issue, i.e., "whether the degree of the exactions demanded by the city's permit conditions bear the required relationship to the projected impact of petitioners proposed development."[192]

In answering this question, the majority opinion first turned to state court decisions because, as Chief Justice Rehnquist phrased it, "they have been dealing with this question a good deal longer than we have . . . . " The examination of state court decisions began with *Billings Properties, Inc. v. Yellowstone County* and *Jenad, Inc. v. Scarsdale*.[193] Without any discussion of what the standard used was in those cases or why it was deficient, the majority opinion rejected the standard used as "too lax to adequately protect petitioner's right to just compensation if her property is taken for a public purpose."[194]

The opinion next turned to a case previously discussed in this section, *Pioneer Trust & Savings Bank v. Mount Prospect,*[195] and, in a comment of considerable potential importance to local governments which enact impact fee programs, concluded that the Federal Constitution does *not* require such exacting scrutiny as the *Pioneer Trust* court's *specific and uniquely attributable test* requires.

The Chief Justice then turned to state court decisions of which he approved. One of these is *Jordan v. Menomonee Falls,*[196] the important Wisconsin decision that established the dual rational nexus test and is discussed at length earlier in this section. Surprisingly, the Chief Justice did not refer to the *Jordan* test by its usual name but

---

[189] *Dolan v. City of Tigard,* 512 U.S. 374, 114 S. Ct. 2309, 2312, 129 L. Ed. 2d 304, 38 Env't. Rep. Cas. (BNA) 1769, 24 Envtl. L. Rep. 21083 (1994).

[190] Dolan, 114 S. Ct. at 2315.

[191] Dolan, 114 S. Ct. at 2315.

[192] Dolan, 114 S. Ct. at 2318.

[193] Discussed above.

[194] Dolan, 114 S. Ct. at 2319.

[195] Note that the case has been re-interpreted by the Illinois courts in Northern Ill. *Northern Illinois Home Builders Ass'n, Inc. v. County of Du Page,* 165 Ill. 2d 25, 208 Ill. Dec. 328, 649 N.E.2d 384 (1995).

[196] *Jordan v. Village of Menomonee Falls,* 28 Wis. 2d 608, 137 N.W.2d 442 (1965).

instead referred to it as a "form" of the reasonable relationship test. This part of the decision seems to leave us with the specific and uniquely attributable test being stricter than the Constitution requires, the "generalized statements as to the necessary connection between the required dedication and the proposed development" required by a few state courts being *too lax,* and the form of the reasonable relationship test adopted by a majority of state courts as the constitutionally acceptable standard.

Instead of calling the "acceptable test" the "dual rational nexus test" the court comes up with a new label, to wit:

> We think the "reasonable relationship" test adopted by a majority of the state courts is closer to the federal constitutional norm than either of those previously discussed. But we do not adopt it as such, partly because the term "reasonable relationship" seems confusingly similar to the term "rational basis" which describes the minimal level of scrutiny under the Equal Protection Clause of the Fourteenth Amendment. We think a term such as "rough proportionality" best encapsulates what we hold to be the requirement of the Fifth Amendment. No precise mathematical calculation is required, but the city must make some sort of individualized determination that the required dedication is related both in nature and extent to the impact of the proposed development.[197]

To the extent that *Dolan* applies to impact fees, the majority may have actually liberalized the standard required of local governments in most states since the Chief Justice concludes that "No precise mathematical calculation is required, but the city must make some effort to quantify its findings in support of . . . [its] dedication requirement."[198] As discussed throughout this section, most state courts and statutes require local governments enacting impact fee and other exaction programs to have precise mathematical calculations and to make considerable efforts to quantify their findings.

Arizona and California courts and a few others [199] have considered the applicability of *Nollan* and *Dolan* to developer funding fees.[200] The Arizona and California cases intertwine. The Arizona Court of Appeals in *Home Builders Ass'n of Central Arizona v. City of Scottsdale,*[201] deduced that the United States Supreme Court's remand of *Ehrlich v. Culver City* [202] (a case in which the city required a developer to pay an impact type fee for recreational facilities when it sought approval to build apartments to replace a private tennis club) for reconsideration in light of the *Dolan* decision implied that the *Dolan* tests can apply to impact fee cases. However, the court of appeals proceeded to distinguish *Dolan* and determined that a *Dolan* analysis was not appropriate in the *Scottsdale* case:

> Unlike Tigard's ordinance, Scottsdale's (ordinance) allows its staff no discretion in setting the fees which are based upon a standardized schedule. The fees are tailored to the type of development involved and are uniform within each class of de-

---

[197] 512 U.S. 374, 391, 114 S. Ct. 2309, 2319–20, 129 L. Ed. 2d 304 (1994).

[198] 512 U.S. 374, 391, 114 S. Ct. 2309, 2319–20, 129 L. Ed. 2d 304 (1994).

[199] See list of cases supra § 10:5.

[200] See also infra § 10:5.

[201] *Home Builders Ass'n of Cent. Arizona v. City of Scottsdale,* 183 Ariz. 243, 902 P.2d 1347 (Ct. App. Div. 1 1995), opinion approved in part, 187 Ariz. 479, 930 P.2d 993, 44 Env't. Rep. Cas. (BNA) 1447 (1997).

[202] *Ehrlich v. City of Culver City,* 512 U.S. 1231, 114 S. Ct. 2731, 129 L. Ed. 2d 854 (1994).

velopment. Because the fees are standardized and uniform, and because the ordinance permits no discretion in its application, a prospective developer may know precisely the fee that will be charged. The Scottsdale ordinance, therefore, does not permit a Dolan-like ad hoc, adjudicative determination.[203]

Although, the Supreme Court of Arizona unanimously affirmed the court of appeals decision,[204] the court saw the *Dolan* issue somewhat differently, It agreed with the language just quoted but added:

> We note, however, that there may be good reason to distinguish the Dolan adjudicative decision from the Scottsdale legislative one. Ehrlich v. City of Culver City * * * dramatically illustrates the differences between the two exactions. * * * On remand from the United States Supreme Court for reconsideration in light of Dolan, the California Supreme Court held the record insufficient to show that the fee was roughly proportional to the public burden of replacing recreational facilities that would be lost as a result of rezoning Ehrlich's property. The California court suggested that the Dolan analysis applied to cases of regulatory leveraging that occur when the landowner must bargain for approval of a particular use of its land . . . . The risk of that sort of leveraging does not exist when the exaction is embodied in a generally applicable legislative decision.
>
> Dolan may also be distinguished from our case on another ground. There, the city demanded that Mrs. Dolan cede a part of her property to the city, a particularly invasive form of land regulation that the court believed justified increased judicial protection for the landowner. Here, Scottsdale seeks to impose a fee, a considerably more benign form of regulation.[205]

As indicated in the quoted language from the *Scottsdale* case above, following remand of its decision in *Ehrlich* by the Supreme Court of the United States, the California Court of Appeal, in a divided and unpublished decision, reaffirmed its earlier ruling in favor of Culver City. In a long, rambling decision made especially confusing by the "concurring in part—dissenting in part" statements of several justices, the Supreme Court of California reversed and remanded.[206]

The holding starts out with a direct statement responsive to the speculation over the impact of *Dolan,* to wit:

> We conclude that the tests formulated by the high court in its Dolan and Nollan opinions for determining whether a compensable regulatory taking has occurred under the takings clause of the Fifth Amendment to the Federal Constitution apply under the circumstances of this case, to the monetary exaction imposed by Culver City as a condition of approving plaintiffs request that the real property in suit be rezoned to permit the construction of a multi-unit residential condominium. We thus reject the city's contention that the heightened takings clause stand-

---

[203] 183 Ariz. 243, 902 P.2d 1347, 1352 (1995).

[204] 187 Ariz. 479, 930 P.2d 993 (1997), cert. denied 521 U.S. 1120, 117 S. Ct. 2512, 138 L. Ed. 2d 1015 (1997).

[205] 187 Ariz. 479, 930 P.2d 993 (1997), cert. denied 521 U.S. 1120, 117 S. Ct. 2512, 138 L. Ed. 2d 1015 (1997).

[206] 12 Cal.4th 854, 50 Cal.Rptr.2d 242, 911 P.2d 429 (1996), cert. denied 519 U.S. 929, 117 S. Ct. 299, 136 L. Ed. 2d 218 (1996).

ard formulated by the court in Nollan and Dolan applies only to cases in which the local land use authority requires the developer to dedicate real property to public use as a condition of permit approval.[207]

Unfortunately for those seeking a clear answer to the speculation over the meaning of *Dolan,* the California court ties its above-quoted conclusion to its interpretation of the California Mitigation Fee Act.[208]

The Supreme Court of California revisited the issue in *San Remo Hotel v. City and County of San Francisco*[209] which involved the required payment of a substantial in lieu fee pursuant to the San Francisco Residential Hotel Unit Conversion and Demolition Ordinance regulating the conversion and demolition of single room occupancy units. The court held that the heightened scrutiny requirements of Nollan/Dolan did not apply because the in lieu fee was generally applicable and non discretionary.

The Supreme Court of Washington weighed in on the applicability of Nollan/Dolan principles to impact fees. In *City of Olympia v. Drebick,*[210] the amicus parties argued that Nollan/Dolan was the applicable standard and had been violated. The court totally and no doubt properly rejected this contention but with an analysis much less clear than some of its sister state supreme courts such as those of Arizona and California.[211] The Washington Court of Appeals had found Nollan/Dolan not only applicable to the impact fees in question but also found the fees in violation of them. The state supreme court disagreed and opined as follows:

> [T]he dissent takes the . . . view that local governments must base GMA impact fees on individualized assessments of the direct impacts each new development will have on each improvement planned in a service area . . . . The dissent does not explain that neither Nollan nor Dolan concerned the imposition of impact fees but addressed instead the authority of a local government to condition development approval on a property owner's dedication of a portion of land for public use; nor does the dissent mention that neither the United States Supreme Court nor this court has determined that the tests applied in Nollan and Dolan to evaluate land exactions must be extended to the consideration of fees imposed to mitigate the direct impacts of a new development, much less to the consideration of more general growth impact fees imposed pursuant to statutorily authorized local ordinances.[212]

---

[207] 12 Cal.4th 854, 50 Cal.Rptr.2d 242, 911 P.2d 429 (1996), cert. denied 519 U.S. 929, 117 S. Ct. 299, 136 L. Ed. 2d 218 (1996).

[208] Gov. Code, section 66000 et seq.

[209] *San Remo Hotel L.P. v. City And County of San Francisco,* 27 Cal. 4th 643, 117 Cal. Rptr. 2d 269, 41 P.3d 87, 32 Envtl. L. Rep. 20533 (2002).

[210] *City of Olympia v. Drebick,* 156 Wash. 2d 289, 126 P.3d 802 (2006) (Wash Sup. Ct. held City's transportation impact fee really excise tax and therefore not subject to dual rational nexus.). For a discussion of the Drebick case, see Smith and Juergensmeyer, Development Impact Fees 2006: A Year in Review, 59 Plan. & Envtl. L. 3 (2007).

[211] *See* TAKING SIDES ON THE TAKINGS ISSUES: PUBLIC AND PRIVATE PERSPECTIVES, Chpts 13–15 (Thomas E. Roberts, ed. 2002).

[212] 126 P. 3d at 807–08.

The debate continues over whether or to what extent Nollan/Dolan principles [213] of essential nexus and rough proportionality apply to all or some impact fees or only to required dedications—i.e., physical exactions.[214] Four principal positions have emerged. Some advocate the full application of takings principles including Nollan/Dolan to impact fees and all other forms of exactions.[215] Others consider that Nollan/Dolan should be applied only to mandatory dedications of land.[216] A third position is that Nollan/Dolan should apply to administratively determined impact fees but not to those legislatively set.[217] This approach centers on the Ehrlich decision by the Supreme Court of California which is discussed earlier in this section.[218] A fourth view of the issue is that impact fees, and perhaps all exactions, should not be subject of the Nollan/Dolan test because in virtually all states they are subject to the dual rational nexus test which is more stringent than Nollan/Dolan and guarantees that exactions which meet the dual rational nexus test could not be takings.[219]

6.   *Impact Fee Enabling Acts*

At least 27 states have statutory provisions authorizing or enabling impact fees. These statutory y provisions range from a few short paragraphs which generally authorize all or certain local governments to adopt impact fees programs, Arizona, for example, or briefly "solve" a very specific impact fee issue, Florida, for example, to lengthy and comprehensive impact fee codes that cover most impact fee issue in considerable detail, Texas, Georgia and New Mexico, for example. The chart below lists the states with impact fee statutes and gives citations to their acts.[220]

---

[213] Nollan and Dolan are discussed in depth at §§ 10:3, 10:4, and 10:5 supra. See also; Ziegler, Development Exactions and Permit Decisions: The Nollan, Dolan and Del Monte Dunes Decisions, 34 Urb. Law. 155 (2002).

[214] See the discussion of Nollan/Dolan and Lingle at §§ 10:4 and 10:5 supra.

[215] See F. Bosselman, "*Dolan* Works, Takings Sides on Taking Issues, Ch. 14 (T. Roberts, ed. 2002)." The *Dolan* test is well established: it is logical in its outcome and it seems to work reasonably well for both developers and local governments. Let's not complicate the legal picture unnecessarily by imposing illogical limitations on the type of exactions to which the Dolan test applies." F. Bosselman, "*Dolan* Works, Takings Sides on Taking Issues, Ch. 14 (T. Roberts, ed. 2002).

[216]See Stroud, A Review of Del Monte Dunes v. City of Monterrey and Its Implications for Local Government Exactions, 15 J. Land Use & Envtl. L. 195 (1999)

[217] See D. Curtin & C. Talbert, "Applying *Nollan/Dolan* to Impact Fees: A Case for the *Ehrlich* Approach, TAKING SIDES ON THE TAKINGS ISSUES: PUBLIC AND PRIVATE PERSPECTIVES, Chpt 13 (Thomas E. Roberts, ed. 2002).

[218] As Curtin & Talbert view that case: "The Ehrlich court held that if a city bases a development or impact fee on an ordinance or rule of general applicability, the fee will be within the city's police power and will not be subject to the heightened constitutional scrutiny of the Nollan/Dolan nexus test. However, if an impact fee is adjudicatively imposed on an individual property owner, it will be subject to heightened scrutiny under the *Nollan/Dolan* test." F. Bosselman, "*Dolan* Works, Takings Sides on Taking Issues, Ch. 14 (T. Roberts, ed. 2002).

[219] J. Juergensmeyer & J. Nicholas, Impact Fees Should Not Be Subjected to Takings Analysis, Taking Sides on the Takings Issues: Public and Private Perspectives, Chpt 15 (Thomas E. Roberts, ed. 2002). "No takings analysis of dual rational nexus-based impact fees is appropriate or necessary. If an impact fee is valid, i.e., it satisfies the dual rational nexus test, then it cannot destroy property rights. If an impact fee violates the nexus test . . . it is invalid." F. Bosselman, "*Dolan* Works, Takings Sides on Taking Issues, Ch. 14 (T. Roberts, ed. 2002).

[220] The Chart was prepared in 2011 by Clancy Mullen, AICP, of Duncan Associates of Austin, Texas. It is reproduced by permission of Clancy Mullen and Duncan Associates. Updated material may be obtained from the Duncan Associates website: http://www.impactfees.com.

State	Year	Citation
Arizona	1988	Ariz. Rev. Stat. Ann. § 9–463.05 (cities), § 11–1102 et seq. (counties)
Arkansas	2003	Ark. Code Ann. § 14–56–103 (cities only)
California	1989	Cal. Gov't Code §§ 66000 et seq. (mitigation fee act), § 66477 (Quimby Act for park dedication/fee-in-lieu), § 17620 et. seq. (school fees)
Colorado	2001	Colo. Rev. Stat. §§ 29–20–104.5, 29–1–801804 (earmarking requirements), § 22–54–102 (school fee prohibition)
Florida	2006	Fla. Stat. Ann. § 163.31801
Georgia	1990	Ga. Code Ann. §§ 36–71–1 et seq.
Hawaii	1992	Haw. Rev. Stat. §§ 46–141 et seq., 264–121 et seq.
Idaho	1992	Idaho Code §§ 67–8201 et seq.
Illinois	1987	605 Ill. Comp. Stat. Ann. §§ 5/5–901 et seq.
Indiana	1991	Ind. Code Ann. §§ 36–7–4–1300 et seq.
Maine	1988	Me. Rev. Stat. Ann. tit. 30-A, § 4354
Montana	2005	Mont. Code Ann. Ch. 6, Part 16
Nevada	1989	Nev. Rev. Stat. § 278B
New Hampshire	1991	N.H. Rev. Stat. Ann. § 674:21
New Jersey	1989	N.J. Stat. Ann. §§ 27:1C-1 et seq., 40:55D-42
New Mexico	1993	N.M. Stat. Ann. §§ 5–8–1 et seq.
Oregon	1991	Or. Rev. Stat. §§ 223.297 et seq.
Pennsylvania	1990	Pa. Stat. Ann. tit. 53, §§ 10502-A et seq.
Rhode Island	2000	R.I. Gen. Laws § 45–22.4
South Carolina	1999	S.C. Code Ann. §§ 6–1–910 et seq.
Texas	1987	Tex. Loc. Gov't Code Ann. §§ 395.001 et seq.
Utah	1995	Utah Code Ann. §§ 11–36–101 et. seq.
Vermont	1989	Vt. Stat. Ann. tit. 24, §§ 5200 et seq.
Virginia	1990	Va. Code Ann. §§ 15.2–2317 et seq.
Washington	1991	Wash. Rev. Code Ann. §§ 82.02.050 et seq.
West Virginia	1990	W. Va. Code §§ 7–20–1 et seq.
Wisconsin	1993	Wis. Stat. § 66.0617

7. Impact Fee Implementation Issues

Now that the authority and tax v. regulation issues have been largely resolved in most jurisdictions—or at least the battle lines clearly drawn—other legal issues are taking the spotlight. These include (1) the credits issue, (2) the capital versus non-capital expenditures problem, (3) equal protection issues, (4) exclusionary considerations, (5) service or benefit areas, and (6) allocation of school, library, and park fees to nonresidential uses.

The credits issue, discussed above in connection with Utah's *Banberry* case and the problem of calculating impact fees so as to comply with the first prong of the dual rational nexus test, is of particular concern to the development industry. In a certain sense it is not only a logical extension of the problem of applying the rational nexus test but it re-raises the issue of how to reconcile taxes which can be or were used for building infrastructure and which were or are being paid on the same development that is charged impact fees.[221]

The capital expenditures versus non capital expenditures problem is not new but its previous resolution is being questioned. From the very beginning, commentators have limited the expenditure of impact fees to capital infrastructure items. To spend them on operation and maintenance or for items with a very short "life" has been considered improper and most impact fee ordinances and authorization statutes are very careful and precise in their definition of "capital."[222] A few jurisdictions are beginning to question whether or not the restrictions to "capital" expenditures might not be relaxed. Often it is difficult for local governments to spend impact fee moneys if they can only be used for capital and the local government has no source of revenue to repair and maintain the infrastructure items once they are constructed. The development industry sometimes would prefer to see maintenance and repair included in the impact fee expenditures list rather than not have the infrastructure item preserved.[223]

The equal protection issue arises because different types of development are charged different fees and developments permitted prior to the enactment of an impact fee program pay no such fees. Neither of these occurrences has found much sympathy from the courts thus far[224] but if discriminatory intent rather than impact analysis based differences can be shown a court may be more sympathetic.

The existence of discriminatory intent would not only raise the equal protection issue but would fit in with concerns over the exclusionary effect of impact fees and other developer funding of infrastructure devices. A comment in this regard by the New Jersey Supreme Court in *New Jersey Builders Ass'n v. Bernards Township,*[225] focuses the issue:

> The variety of governmental devices used to impose public facility costs on new development reflect a policy choice that higher taxes for existing residents are less desirable than higher development costs for builders, and higher acquisition costs for new residents. An obvious concern is that the disproportionate or excessive use of development exactions could discourage new development or inflate housing prices to an extent that excludes large segments of the population from the available market.[226]

---

[221] See Nicholas, The Calculation of Proportionate Share Impact Fees, 408 APA. Plan Advisory Serv.Rep (1998).

[222] See James C. Nicholas, Arthur C. Nelson and Julian C. Juergensmeyer, A Practitioner's Guide to Development Impact Fees Ch. 16 (1991).

[223] James C. Nicholas, Arthur C. Nelson and Julian C. Juergensmeyer Impact Fees: Principles and Practice of Proportionate-Share Development Fees Ch. 13 (2009).

[224] *Northern Illinois Home Builders Ass'n, Inc. v. County of Du Page,* 251 Ill. App. 3d 494, 190 Ill. Dec. 559, 621 N.E.2d 1012 (2d Dist. 1993), judgment aff'd in part, rev'd in part on other grounds, 165 Ill. 2d 25, 208 Ill. Dec. 328, 649 N.E.2d 384 (1995) (concluding no equal protection violation from differing fees); *Ivy Steel & Wire Co., Inc. v. City of Jacksonville,* 401 F. Supp. 701 (M.D. Fla. 1975).

[225] *New Jersey Builders Ass'n v. Mayor and Tp. Committee of Bernards Tp., Somerset County,* 108 N.J. 223, 528 A.2d 555 (1987).

[226] New Jersey Builders Ass'n, 528 A.2d at 560.

The debate over this aspect of impact fees is just beginning [227] and the potentially regressive nature of impact fees is now receiving some analysis and proposals for making them less regressive. For example, in some jurisdictions residential impact fees are calculated on a square footage rather than a per unit basis so as to recognize the lower impact of smaller and therefore usually less expensive homes and thereby lower the impact fees they must pay.[228] Many jurisdictions are trying to mitigate the exclusionary impact by exempting low and moderate income housing and other socially desirable developments from impact fees [229] although this raises another problem since the resulting shortfall in the impact fee accounts may threaten the adequacy of the impact fee revenues to fund the needed infrastructure.[230]

When it comes to the expenditure of impact fee funds, most of the controversy has been over *how* the money can be spent—i.e. what capital expenditures can be covered by impact fee monies. Recently in many jurisdictions, the conflict is over *where* money can be spent. Benefit districts have been used since the early days of impact fees to guarantee that the second prong of the dual rational nexus test will be met. The concept is that if infrastructure is built too far away from the development that is charged the impact fee there will be little if any benefit conferred on those who pay the fees. Several impact fee statutes require that local governments establish service areas or benefit districts and confine expenditures to the benefit area from which impact fees are collected but the local government is usually authorized to create one or more service areas. Many local governments, at least from the perspective of the development community, create one jurisdiction-wide district without adequate attention to guaranteeing that monies will be spent close enough to the developments which pay the fees to ensure receipt of benefit. In Olympia, Washington, for example the city established a jurisdiction-wide benefit district for its transportation impact fee program which meant that the benefit area was 17 square miles. Nonetheless, the Supreme Court of Washington rejected the feepayors complaint that the size of the area invalidated the fee.[231] The Georgia Development Impact Fee Act was recently amended in an attempt to restrict the expenditure of impact fee funds to the proximity of the major feepayors.[232]

A final recently important issue is what land uses can be charged what impact fees. Transportation impact fees are generally imposed on all types of development—residential, commercial, and industrial—because it is impossible to think of any development that does not generate and attract traffic. But, although most jurisdictions impose park, library, and school impact fees only on residential developments, all three

---

[227] See Arthur C. Nelson, Lisa K Bowles, Julian C. Juergensmeyer, & James C. Nicholas, A Guide to Impact Fees and Housing Affordability (2008); Burge and Ihlanfeldt, The Effects of Impact Fees on Multifamily Housing Construction, 46 Jr. Reg. Sci. 5 (2006); Been, Exit as a Constraint on Land Use Exactions: Rethinking the Unconstitutional Conditions Doctrines, 91 Colum. L. Rev. 473 (1991); Sterk, Competition Among Municipalities as a Constraint on Land Use Exactions, 45 Vand. L. Rev. 831 (1992).

[228] See Lisa K. Bowles and Arthur C. Nelson, Impact Fees: Equity and Housing Affordability: A Guidebook for Practitioners (U.S.Dep't HUD, April 2007).

[229] See White, Development Fees and Exemptions for Affordable Housing: Tailoring Regulations to Achieve Multiple Public Objectives, 6 J. Land Use Envtl. L. 25 (1990); Larson and Zimet, Impact Fees: Et Tu, Illinois, 21 J. Marshall L. Rev. 489 (1988).

[230] The Georgia impact fee act seeks to solve this problem by allowing specified exemptions but only if the "exempt development's proportionate share of the system improvements is funded through a revenue source other than development impact fees." Ga. Code Ann. § 36–71–4(3). See James C. Nicholas, Arthur C. Nelson and Julian C. Juergensmeyer, A Practitioner's Guide to Development Impact Fees Ch. 10 (1991).

[231] *City of Olympia v. Drebick,* 156 Wash. 2d 289, 126 P.3d 802 (2006), cert. denied, 127 S. Ct. 436, 166 L. Ed. 2d 330 (U.S. 2006).

[232] Georgia Legislature, HB 232 (2007 Sess.).

types of infrastructure are frequently "used" by businesses either directly or indirectly. For example, businesses often use recreational facilities for company picnics and athletic teams for all employees whether or not they are residents of the jurisdiction where the recreational facilities or community centers are located, or indirectly, by sponsoring athletic events or teams. The same can be said for libraries and particularly for schools.

School impact fees are high on local governments' wish lists and low on developer acceptability lists.[233] One reason for their controversial nature is that they are frequently the highest of all impact fees charged due to spiraling educational facility costs. Another reason that they are seldom popular with homebuilder groups is that they are usually paid exclusively by residential development projects and not spread across a broader development spectrum. Which types of developments should and can be charged educational facilities impact fees involve controversies even within the residential use categories. Age restricted residential developments often request and receive exemptions from school impact fees on the theory that they will not increase the number of school age children.

In the Supreme Court of Florida's *Aberdeen* case,[234] an "age" deed-restricted retirement development sought and obtained exemption from the local school impact fee on the theory that no school children would be "generated" by the development. School boards, when deciding whether or not age restricted residential developments and nonresidential uses should be charged educational facilities impact fees, are confronted with a number of issues. Will the age related restrictions be enforced or enforceable under state law as the Supreme Court of Florida seems to have assumed would be the case in that state? Even if it can or must be assumed that age restricted residential developments will produce no school age children they will nonetheless place demands on educational infrastructure because of the myriad community uses currently made of school facilities. Exactly what those uses are can vary from locale to locale. Prime candidates include using schools for adult education, community meetings and activities, private sector training programs, emergency shelters, voting places, and also the use of school athletic and playground facilities by adults as individuals and as participants in commercially sponsored athletic teams. Additionally, local businesses may make considerable use of school library and computer facilities. The list goes on and on but the point is clear that school facilities are not used just by school children.

One problem with requiring "adult only" residential communities and/or commercial and industrial facilities to bear a portion of school infrastructure costs through school impact fees is that the "formulae" used by most local governments to calculate school impact fees emphasize exclusively student generation numbers and student station costs. Jurisdictions which wish to impose school impact fees on age restricted residential developments and nonresidential developments will need to calculate school impact fees in a way that accurately assesses the demands that all types of development place on the need for school infrastructure.[235]

---

[233] See Derek J. Williams, Rethinking Utah's Prohibition on School Impact Fees, 22 J. Land Resources & Envtl. L. 489 (2002).

[234] *Volusia County v. Aberdeen at Ormond Beach, L.P.*, 760 So. 2d 126 (Fla. 2000).

[235] See Smith and Juergensmeyer, Development Impact Fees 2006: A Year in Review, 59 Plan. & Envtl. L. 3 (2007).

C. *Linkage and Mitigation Fees*

The success of impact fees in raising funds for infrastructure items such as roads, parks, schools, jails, public buildings, and other "hard" or traditional infrastructure items has led many local governments to explore the possibility of using them for so-called "soft" or "social" infrastructure such as child care facilities, low affordable housing,[236] art in public places, and environmental mitigation programs.[237]

Developer funding requirements designed to raise capital funds for the "soft" or "social" infrastructure items are usually referred to as "linkage fees" and are viewed as the latest form of exaction.[238] Linkage fees charge commercial developers a fee to provide for expanded services that are incurred by the community because of the new development.

> Underlying every linkage program is the fundamental concept that new downtown development is directly "linked" to a specific social need. The rationale is fairly simple: Not only does the actual construction of the commercial buildings create new construction jobs, but the increased office space attracts new businesses and workers to fill new jobs. The new workers need places to live, transit systems, day care facilities, and the like. From the perspective of linkage proponents, the new commercial development is directly linked both to new employment opportunities and to increased demand for improved municipal facilities and services.[239]

The judicial attitude toward linkage programs has been somewhat mixed with the greatest enthusiasm coming from the California and New Jersey courts. One of the earliest "linkage" programs was San Francisco transit fee imposed on downtown commercial development.[240] It was upheld in *Russ Building Partnership v. City and County of San Francisco.*[241] In *Commercial Builders v. City of Sacramento,*[242] the court upheld a

---

[236] See Arthur C. Nelson, Lisa K Bowles, Julian C. Juergensmeyer, & James C. Nicholas, A Guide to Impact Fees and Housing Affordability (2008); Lisa K. Bowles and Arthur C. Nelson, Impact Fees: Equity and Housing Affordability: A Guidebook for Practitioners (U.S.Dep't HUD, April 2007); Juergensmeyer, Infrastructure and the Law: Florida's Past, Present and Future, 23 J. Land Use & Envtl. L. 441 (2008). For discussion of inclusionary zoning for low and moderate cost housing, see supra § 6:7.

[237] See Ledman, Local Government Environmental Mitigation Fees: Development Exactions, The Next Generation, 45 Fla. L. Rev. 835 (1993); Bosselman and Stroud, Mandatory Tithes: The Legality of Land Development Linkage, 9 Nova L.J. 381 (1985); Mudge, Impact Fees for Conversion of Agricultural Land: A Resource-Based Development Policy for California's Cities and Counties, 19 Ecology L.Q. 63 (1992); Alterman, Evaluating Linkage and Beyond: Letting the Windfall Genie Out of the Exactions Bottle, 34 Wash. U. J. Urb. & Contemp. L. 3 (1988); Merrill and Lincoln, Linkage Fees and Fair Share Regulations: Law and Method, 25 Urb. Law. 223 (1993).

[238] "[L]inkage refers to a variety of programs that require developers to contribute toward new affordable housing, employment opportunities, child care facilities, transit systems and the like, in return for the city's permission to build new commercial developments." C. Andrew and D. Merriam, Defensible Linkage, Ch. 19, Development Impact Fees p. 227 (Nelson, ed. 1988).

[239] C. Andrew and D. Merriam, Defensible Linkage, Ch. 19, Development Impact Fees p. 228. See also, Kayden and Pollard, Linkage Ordinances and the Traditional Exactions Analysis: The Connection between Office Development and Housing, 50 L. & Contemp. Probs. 127 (1987).

[240] *Terminal Plaza Corp. v. City and County of San Francisco,* 177 Cal. App. 3d 892, 223 Cal. Rptr. 379 (1st Dist. 1986) (upholding fees charged against conversion of single room occupancy hotels) was decided earlier but received considerably less attention.

[241] *Russ Bldg. Partnership v. City and County of San Francisco,* 199 Cal. App. 3d 1496, 246 Cal. Rptr. 21 (1st Dist. 1987), review granted and opinion superseded, 236 Cal. Rptr. 403, 735 P.2d 444 (Cal. 1987), order modified, 237 Cal. Rptr. 456, 737 P.2d 359 (Cal. 1987) and aff'd in part, rev'd in part, partial publication ordered, 44 Cal. 3d 839, 244 Cal. Rptr. 682, 750 P.2d 324 (1988). See also *San Remo Hotel L.P. v. City And County of San Francisco,* 27 Cal. 4th 643, 117 Cal. Rptr. 2d 269, 41 P.3d 87, 32 Envtl. L. Rep. 20533 (2002), upholding linkage fee for demolition of low cost housing. See also discussion supra at § 6:7.

city ordinance which conditioned nonresidential building permits upon the payment of a fee for housing to offset expenses associated with the influx of low-income workers for the new project. The developers argued that the ordinance was a taking because it placed the burden of paying for the housing upon the new development without a sufficient showing that nonresidential development contributed to the need for new low-income housing in proportion to that burden. The court found no taking, however, as the fee was enacted only after a study revealed that the need for low-income housing would rise as a direct result of demand from workers on the new development. The court found that "[t]he burden assessed against the developers thus bears a rational relationship to a public cost closely associated with such development."[243] The court seemingly broadened its holding beyond the imposition of a fee for low-income housing when it stated that "[a] purely financial exaction, then, will not constitute a taking if it is made for the purpose of paying a social cost that is reasonably related to the activity against which the fee is assessed."[244]

Perhaps the most famous linkage case thus far decided is the New Jersey case, *Holmdel Builders Ass'n v. Township of Holmdel*,[245] which upheld the imposition of fees on commercial and non-inclusionary residential developments for the construction of low income housing per the local government's responsibilities under the *Mt. Laurel* doctrine.[246]

Not all linkage fee programs have fared as well as those just discussed. In *San Telmo Assoc. v. City of Seattle*,[247] the Supreme Court of Washington had before it a Seattle housing preservation ordinance which provided that property owners who wished to demolish low income housing units had to replace a specified percentage of the housing to be demolished with other suitable housing or contribute to the city's low income housing replacement fund. The court found the requirement to constitute an unauthorized tax.

The list of issues raised in regard to the validity of linkage fees is almost identical to the list of issues regarding the validity of impact fees.[248] These include authority of the local government to enact linkage programs,[249] illegal tax rather than land use regulation,[250] violation of due process, equal protection or takings provisions of U.S.

---

[242] *Commercial Builders of Northern California v. City of Sacramento*, 941 F.2d 872 (9th Cir. 1991).

[243] Commercial Builders of Northern California, 941 F.2d at 874.

[244] Commercial Builders of Northern California, 941 F.2d at 876. The *Commercial Builders* court also rejected the developers' contention that *Nollan* requires a more stringent taking standard, holding that "*Nollan* does not stand for the proposition that an exaction ordinance will be upheld only where it can be shown that the development is directly responsible for the social ill in question. Rather, *Nollan* holds that where there is no evidence of a nexus between the development and that problem that the exaction seeks to address, the exaction cannot be upheld." Commercial Builders of Northern California, 941 F.2d at 876.

[245] *Holmdel Builders Ass'n v. Township of Holmdel*, 121 N.J. 550, 583 A.2d 277 (1990).

[246] See supra § 6:6 for a discussion of *Mt. Laurel* I and *Mt. Laurel* II, and § 6.7 for discussion of inclusionary zoning.

[247] *San Telmo Associates v. City of Seattle*, 108 Wash. 2d 20, 735 P.2d 673 (1987). See also *Sintra, Inc. v. City of Seattle*, 119 Wash. 2d 1, 829 P.2d 765 (1992) (ordinance was found to be an illegal tax, and when the city persisted in applying the ordinance to other property, court found behavior which led to § 1983 damages).

[248] See supra § 9:9.

[249] See *Holmdel Builders Ass'n v. Township of Holmdel*, 121 N.J. 550, 583 A.2d 277 (1990).

    Bonan v. City of Boston, 398 Mass. 315, 496 N.E.2d 640 (1986) (court did not reach issue of authority which was raised by lower court).

[250] *San Telmo Associates v. City of Seattle*, 108 Wash. 2d 20, 735 P.2d 673 (1987).

and state constitutions,[251] and the standard to be applied to govern the reasonableness of the exercise of the police power.

In this last regard, *Holmdel* is of particular interest since it held that linkage programs for low income housing need not meet the rational nexus test:

> We conclude that the rational-nexus test is not apposite in determining the validity of inclusionary zoning devices generally or of affordable housing development fees in particular. * * * Inclusionary zoning through the imposition of development fees is permissible because such fees are conducive to the creation of realistic opportunities for the development of affordable housing; development fees are the functional equivalent of mandatory set-asides; and it is fair and reasonable to impose such fee requirements on private developers when they possess, enjoy, and consume land, which constitutes the primary resource for housing.[252]

Whether linkage programs will develop on a parallel course to impact fees and become a reflection of them as far as the legal issues and standards are concerned is one of the current but unresolved issues of growth management law.

A similar issue exists in regard to environmental mitigation fees which are assessments made by local governments against new development to reimburse the community for the new development's proportionate negative impact on the community's environment.[253] A major distinction between mitigation fees on the one hand and impact and linkage fees on the other is that mitigation fees are resource based and impact and linkage fees are service or facility based. Mitigation fees have a direct correlation between the loss and the replacement of a resource while impact fees concern the provision of services necessitated by new development. Also, impact fees are imposed to help defray governmental costs while mitigation fees are imposed to protect against public harm by preserving or protecting natural resources.[254]

The goal of an environmental mitigation fee is to move away from the on-site regulatory framework and toward a more broad-based and long-range approach to environmental protection. Historically, mitigation of the ecological impact of development has been addressed on a case-by-case basis. Each individual development or polluting facility has been required to minimize its own impact on site, or mitigate its impact through some regulation approved means. This can result in fragmented scraps of habitat that may not assure an adequate critical mass, and it may not be the best place for the habitat in the long term. Through the use of an environmental mitigation fee, solu-

---

[251] For a full discussion of due process, equal protection, and taking challenges, see Merrill and Lincoln, Linkage Fees and Fair Share Regulations: Law and Method, 25 Urb. Law. 223 (1993).

[252] 121 N.J. 550, 583 A.2d 277, 288.

[253] See Nicholas and Juergensmeyer, Market Based Approaches to Environmental Preservation: Mitigation Fees and Beyond, 43 Nat. Resources L.J. 837 (2003); Ledman, Local Government Environmental Mitigation Fees: Development Exactions, The Next Generation, 45 Fla. L. Rev.835 (1993); Nicholas, Juergensmeyer and Basse, Perspectives Concerning the Use of Environmental Mitigation Fees as Incentives in Environmental Protection, Part I 7 Env. Liab. 27 (1999), Part II 7 Env. Liab. 71 (1999). The labels "environmental mitigation fees" and "environmental linkage fees" are often used interchangeably. See Nelson, Nicholas and Marsh, Environmental Linkage Fees are Coming, 58 Plan. 1, 2 (1992).

[254] Nicholas and Juergensmeyer, Market Based Approaches to Environmental Preservation: Mitigation Fees and Beyond, 43 Nat. Resources L.J. 837 (2003). See also, Robin A. Kramer, Mitigation Fees for Environmental, Agricultural and Open Space Preservation, The Center for American and International Law Institute on Planning, Zoning and Eminent Domain (Dec. 9, 2004).

tions are more readily available. To achieve these solutions requires long range planning of environmental goals as well as an expanded concept of "environment."

As has been the case with traditional impact fees, environmental mitigation fees need very careful impact analysis in order to make them feasible and defensible. An effective and legally defensible environmental mitigation fee program, like a valid impact fee program, will require three things:

· First, the specification of a level of service;

· Second, incorporation into a comprehensive plan; and,

· Third, the adoption of regulations that maintain the level of service in accordance with that comprehensive plan.

Assuming that the mitigation fee imposed does not exceed the cost of regulation, however, the standard impact fee formula would seem appropriate to determine the environmental mitigation fee for that project. At this point, the developer would have three choices. First, the developer can simply pay the environmental mitigation fee and proceed with the project. The funds derived from these fees would be used to purchase habitat that has been identified in the comprehensive plan or for pollution prevention and clean up projects also identified in a pollution control element of the plan. Second, the developer can reduce the environmental impact of the project to a point at which the activity is still profitable but the environmental impact is significantly less and thereby reduce the amount of payment required pursuant to the mitigation fee. Third, the polluter can pay another firm to mitigate the impact elsewhere. The last option is very similar to tradeable emissions programs and wetlands mitigation programs.

From a legal perspective, mitigation fees should be considered exercises of the police power and subject to the same standard of "reasonableness" as impact fees—namely, the dual rational nexus test.[255] As far as the first prong of that test is concerned, new development can be charged no more than a proportionate share of the impact cost of that development on the environment or the preservation of the environment. The next step is to ensure that a regulatory program is established so as to accomplish the environmental goals for which the fee is collected. The second prong of the dual rational nexus test is the one in which planning is critical. In order or a mitigation fee program to function as it should, long range plans and goals should be established in a comprehensive plan. The dilemmas encountered when such a plan is not in place can be seen in the Connecticut Supreme Court case of *Branhaven Plaza. v. Inland Wetlands Commission of Branford.*[256]

In Branhaven, a developer wanted to build a convenience store on a parcel of land with some very minor and very small wetland areas. Initially, the developer offered to build a bigger wetland offsite (mitigate). The local government agreed, but then changed its mind over fears that there were flood control problems with the proposal. In response to this, the developer offered to spend $25,000 to construct an offsite wetland and to donate to the local government $25,000 worth of engineering services. The

---

[255] See § 9:9, supra.

[256] *Branhaven Plaza, L.L.C. v. Inland Wetlands Com'n of Town of Branford*, 251 Conn. 269, 740 A.2d 847 (1999). See Salzman and Ruhl, Currencies and Commodification of Environmental Law, 53 Stan. L. Rev. 607 (2000).

local government agreed, but many people in the community objected to the building of the convenience store on the grounds that only paying money to be able to destroy the on-site wetlands was an inadequate and unacceptable way of satisfying the mitigation requirements. The court struck down the fee on the basis that there were no comprehensive plans and goals for how the money was to be spent. Neither the developer, nor the planning commission, nor the local government authority had formulated a proposal for the creation of new wetlands or the enhancement of existing wetlands.

The future of environmental mitigation programs is far from certain but combined with impact fees and linkage fees they offer local and regional governments an opportunity to comprehensively shift the costs and impacts of development to new growth rather than requiring existing residents to bear such burdens.[257]

§ 9:10   Transferable Development Rights Programs

A.   *General Theory: Mitigating Potential Wipeouts*

Euclidean zoning and related land use regulations necessarily create uneven impacts on landowners. Landowners in areas where higher intensity development is encouraged economically benefit, while landowners in areas where land is protected from development are hurt.[258] A fairer system would allow all landowners to benefit from an area's development, and require all benefited landowners to pay the costs associated with the preservation and protection of sensitive land in the area.

Transferable Development Right (TDR) programs are frequently incorporated into growth management programs because they offer that alternative by separating the need to preserve a particular parcel of land and the right of the landowner to develop that land. The advantage of the TDR is that it provides a means to economically benefit owners of sensitive land by a means other than development of that land or the payment of public funds and thereby to mitigate the adverse economic effect of many land use regulations. Indeed, TDR programs can be used for a wide variety of purposes,[259] such as preserving agricultural land,[260] preserving environmentally important areas,[261] preserving historic landmarks and buildings,[262] reducing development on steep slopes, concentrating new development within the limits of public transportation, protecting view corridors, controlling beachfront development, reducing potential landslides, controlling riverfront development, preserving open space,[263] and decreasing impervious surfaces.[264]

---

[257] James C. Nicholas, Arthur C. Nelson and Julian C. Juergensmeyer Impact Fees: Principles and Practice of Proportionate-Share Development Fees Ch. 12 (2009).

[258] This phenomenon is often referred to as "windfalls and wipeouts" and the attempts to remedy it as "land value capture and compensation programs." The classic analysis of it is D. Hagman and D. Misczynski, eds, Windfalls for Wipeouts: Land Value Capture and Compensation (1978).

[259] Arthur C. Nelson, Rick Pruetz & Doug Woodruff, The TDR Handbook: Designing and Implementing Transfer of Development Rights Programs (2012). For a list of TDR programs in the United States, see Jerold S. Kayden, A Review of Transferable Development Rights (TDR) Programs in the United States, SG040 ALI-ABA 409 (2001).

[260] See infra § 12:8.

[261] See Juergensmeyer, Nicholas, and Leebrick, Transferable Development Rights and Alternatives After Suitum, 30 Urb. Law. 441, 462–464 (1998).

[262] See infra § 13:11

[263] See infra § 9:11.

[264] See Green and Alby, Watershed Planning, 1 U. Denv. Water L. Rev. 75 (1997).

There are economic benefits which arise from protecting environmental quality. By requiring landowners of non-sensitive land to buy development rights from the owners of sensitive land, the government is forcing developers to "internalize" the costs associated with land development. The traditional zoning oriented approach to development regulation permits private landowners that are benefited from environmental amenities not to consider the social costs of destroying environmental or similar benefits enjoyed by a community. If places are made for bald eagles, the community is better for it. If those places are lost, the community, as well as the bald eagles, are worse for it. TDRs create a greater social efficiency by forcing the developers that benefit from land preservation to recognize the costs associated with such preservation.

Thus, from an economic analysis perspective, TDR programs deal with the failure of the market to equate social benefits and costs with private costs and benefits. Under Euclidean zoning, significant costs are created by development that are not borne by the development. At the same time, owners of environmentally sensitive land are forced to provide a significant benefit to society without getting compensated. This creates a failure in the market in which the development is being priced too low (because it is not internalizing the costs it creates) and the owners of sensitive lands are not getting the values they deserve.[265]

Under Euclidean zoning, local governments must either buy sensitive land or regulate it heavily and risk a takings challenge.[266] To prevent takings challenges that drain the public fisc, local governments often grant some development on each parcel through some type of a variance or similar procedure. This results in urban sprawl, environmental resource depletion, and public safety problems. The constitutional and budgetary limitations of zoning thus limit the effectiveness of land protection programs. By separating the development potential of the parcel from the land itself, and creating a market in which that development potential can be separately purchased, TDR programs provide value to the owners of preserved properties and may avoid takings challenges without threatening the effectiveness of the preservation plan.[267]

B.   How TDRs Work

TDR programs separate the development potential of a parcel from the land itself, and create a market where that development potential can be sold. Planning agencies then identify areas they wish to protect and other areas which are suitable for development.[268] An effective TDR program will have delineated sending and receiving

---

[265] See Frederick Goddard, Economic Theory for Analysis of Natural Resources and the Environment 23 (1993). For a different approach arguing that TDR programs are largely unsuccessful because they should require low density development and not high density development to purchase development rights, see Bruening, The TDR Siren Song; The Problems with Transferable Development Rights Programs and How to Fix Them, 23 J. Land Use & Envtl. L. 423 (2008).

[266] Regulatory takings are considered in §§ 10:1 et seq. See also, Ziegler, Partial Taking Claims, Ownership Rights in Land and Urban Planning Practice: The Emerging Dichotomy Between Uncompensated Regulation and Compensable Benefit Extraction Under the Fifth Amendment Takings Clause, 22 Utah J. Land Res & Envtl. L. 1 (2002).

[267] It would follow that if TDRs are not considered in the takings calculus, development regulating entities would lose a significant incentive to use a program which is more fair and efficient than current, regulation-based land use control. This is the dilemma posed by the *Suitum* case discussed below in this section.

[268] See Stinson, Note and Comment, Transferring Development Rights: Purpose, Problems, and Prospects in New York, 17 Pace L.Rev. 319, 328–29 (1996).

zones.[269] Since the need to protect sensitive land is often the impetus for TDR arrangements, identifying the land from which development potential will be sent, the sending zones, is relatively simple.[270] Local governments quite often have a difficult time, politically and practically, identifying receiving zones that will then have more dense development than would otherwise be allowed.[271]

Sending zones,[272] as the name suggests, are simply zones or areas that will export development potential. The sending areas should be identified as areas for limited development within the context of a comprehensive plan.[273] The plan could designate an area for limited development for any number of reasons: habitat preservation,[274] wetland protection, erosion control,[275] protection of historic resources,[276] and agricultural land retention.[277]

Generally sending area property owners are required to record a covenant running with the land permanently removing certain development rights. Once a landowner in a sending zone has received her TDRs, she no longer has the right to develop the land in the manner or manners restricted by the general regulations and the restrictions contained in the covenant.[278] However, the regulating agency prepares, or at least should prepare, a list of residual uses of the land after the TDRs have been sold. This accomplishes two things: 1) it helps protect against a takings claim if TDRs are not considered relevant to the takings analysis;[279] and 2) it helps determine the "non-development" value of the land. Non-development uses might include agriculture, beekeeping, bird watching, primitive camping and other recreational use. A recently discovered popular residual use of wetlands near metropolitan areas is as "antenna farms." The land can also be used in a "mitigation bank" system.[280]

In order to achieve fairness, the TDRs must have a meaningful economic value. To make sure a market is created, there must be a balance between sending and receiving

---

[269] See Tripp and Dudek, Institutional Guidelines for Designing Successful Transferable Development Rights Programs, 6 Yale J. Reg. 369, 376 (1989).

[270] See James C. Nicholas, Hackensack Meadowlands Development Commission's Program of Transferable Development Rights 10–11 (Oct. 1997) [hereinafter Hackensack proposal].

[271] See Tierney, Bold Promises but Baby Steps: Maryland's Growth Policy to the Year 2020, 23 U.Balt.L.Rev. 461, 496 (1994). See also Hackensack proposal, at 10–11.

[272] Arthur C.Nelson, Rick Pruetz & Doug Woodruff, The TDR Handbook: Designing and Implementing Transfer of Development Rights Programs Ch. 8 (2012).

[273] Solloway, Note: Preserving Our Heritage: Tools To Cultivate Agricultural Preservation in New York State, 17 Pace L. Rev. 591, 626–27 (1997).

[274] See *Glisson v. Alachua County,* 558 So. 2d 1030 (Fla. 1st DCA 1990) (considering a TDR scheme designed, in part, to protect wildlife habitat).

[275] See *Suitum v. Tahoe Regional Planning Agency,* 520 U.S. 725, 117 S. Ct. 1659, 137 L. Ed. 2d 980, 44 Env't. Rep. Cas. (BNA) 1673, 27 Envtl. L. Rep. 21064 (1997).

[276] See *Suitum,* Amicus brief of City of New York, 1997 WL 10278.

[277] See Tierney, Bold Promises but Baby Steps: Maryland's Growth Policy to the Year 2020, 23 U.Balt.L.Rev. 461, 496 (1994).

[278] See Stinson, Note and Comment, Transferring Development Rights: Purpose, Problems, and Prospects in New York,17 Pace L.Rev. 319, 329 (1996).

[279] See *Lucas v. South Carolina Coastal Council,* 505 U.S. 1003, 112 S. Ct. 2886, 120 L. Ed. 2d 798, 34 Env't. Rep. Cas. (BNA) 1897, 22 Envtl. L. Rep. 21104 (1992). For a discussion of takings generally, see infra §§ 10:2 to 10:11.

[280] See supra § 9:9.

zones.[281] If there are too many TDRs on the market, the price falls and the fairness of the TDR scheme is questionable. Additionally, if receiving area property owners need not acquire TDRs in order to attain their desired level of intensity, then there will be no demand for those rights and their economic value will be zero. Ideally, each owner of restricted land would get enough TDRs to mitigate the development value loss and the value of the use of those TDRs in the receiving area will deliver that value to the sending area property owners.

Receiving zones[282] are regions set aside by the regulating jurisdiction to accept development potential from restricted land elsewhere in the jurisdiction.[283] To maintain a market for the TDRs from the sending zone, receiving zones must be growing areas with a market demand for increased density.[284] In a free market, the value of the TDRs will be set near the marginal value of that increased density.[285] However, if landowners in receiving zones can increase density through variances or rezoning, those administrative procedures are, in effect, competing with TDRs. If it costs less to go through the administrative process for a rezoning, the TDR market will flounder. Local governments instituting TDR programs should be careful not to cannibalize the TDR program by providing administrative alternatives to the market. Additionally, if receiving areas are already "over-zoned," marginal increases in land development intensity will have no economic value and so also will TDRs have no economic value.

In summary, the following factors are key in evaluating the potential success of a TDR program:

1.   The agency must have legal authority to implement the program.

2.   It must also have the expertise to design and implement the program and it must monitor the program carefully.

3.   The program should be the only way to exceed the prior density levels.

4.   The program must have clear objectives.

5.   The program should address problems of regional significance.

6.   The TDRs must have an economic value and there must be incentives for a market to develop. The receiving areas must have strong growth sufficient to absorb the TDRs. The agency should consider the estimated demand and value of TDRs so that there is balance between the supply of TDRs and their demand. The agency should make sure that the estimated value (price) of TDRs is less than the marginal value of increased density in the receiving areas.

---

[281]See Stinson, Note and Comment, Transferring Development Rights: Purpose, Problems, and Prospects in New York,17 Pace L.Rev. 319, 341-342 (1996); Virginia McConnell, Elizabeth Kopits & Margaret Walls, Using Markets for Land Preservation: Results of a TDR Program, 49 Jr Env. Planning & Management 631 (2006) (Calvert County, MD. Program).

[282] Arthur C.Nelson, Rick Pruetz & Doug Woodruff, The TDR Handbook: Designing and Implementing Transfer of Development Rights Programs Ch. 9 (2012).

[283] See Tierney, Bold Promises but Baby Steps: Maryland's Growth Policy to the Year 2020, 23 U.Balt.L.Rev. 461, 496-97 (1994).

[284] See Stinson, Note and Comment, Transferring Development Rights: Purpose, Problems, and Prospects in New York,17 Pace L.Rev. 319, 347-348 (1996).

[285] See Tripp and Dudek, Institutional Guidelines for Designing Successful Transferable Development Rights Programs, 6 Yale J. Reg 369, 376 (1989).

7.   The original allocation of TDRs to sending area properties should be simple and equitable.

8.   Agencies should try to minimize the complexity, confusion and costs associated with the acquisition, transfer and use of TDRs.

9.   Agencies should clearly articulate the development allowed in the receiving areas, both with and without TDRs.

10.   Agencies must consider what to do with developments that have already begun the development process prior to the implementation of the TDR scheme.

11.   Agencies should consider the infrastructure needs associated with increased growth in the receiving areas and make those infrastructure needs budgetary priorities.

12.   Agencies must define the sending zones clearly.

13.   Agencies should clearly describe those residual or remaining uses for the land after the TDRs have been severed.[286]

C.   *Legal Issues*

The first case in which the Supreme Court considered transferable development rights was the Penn Central case.[287] The Court there upheld the historic landmark commission's denial of the plaintiff's lessee's request to construct a tower over its Grand Central Station. Although the Court found no taking it went on to discuss the TDRs available under the New York historic preservation program to the plaintiff by way of mitigation of the economic effects of the restriction. In regard to the TDRs (actually transferable density rights), Justice Brennan opined that "[w]hile these rights may well not have constituted 'just compensation' if a 'taking' had occurred, the rights nevertheless undoubtedly mitigate whatever financial burdens the law has imposed on appellants and, for that reason, are to be taken into account in considering the impact of regulation."[288]

Proponents of TDR programs have interpreted this language to mean that the value of TDRs is to be considered as part of the "has there been a taking" analysis—in other words, the value of the TDRs is relevant to the value of the property rights left to the landowner after the restrictions at issue. Under this analysis, the landowner is envisioned as being able to make an off-site use of her land through the exercise of the rights on other land. Others consider that Justice Brennan's language does not make

---

[286] Juergensmeyer, Nicholas, and Leebrick, Transferable Development Rights and Alternatives After Suitum, 30 Urb. Law. 441, 456–457 (1998). See Machemer and Kaplowitz, A Framework for Evaluating Transferable Development Rights Programmes, 45 J. Envtl. Plan. & Mgt. 773 (2002) (comparing Manheim Township, Pa., Montgomery County, MD, & New Jersey Pinelands TDR programs); Beetle, Are Transferable Development Rights a Viable Solution to New Jersey's Land Use Problems?: An Evaluation of TDR Programs Within the Garden State, 34 Rutgers L.J. 513 (2003).

[287] *Penn Cent. Transp. Co. v. City of New York,* 438 U.S. 104, 98 S. Ct. 2646, 57 L. Ed. 2d 631, 11 Env't. Rep. Cas. (BNA) 1801, 8 Envtl. L. Rep. 20528 (1978). The case is analyzed in depth at § 10:4. Leading early state court decisions include *Fred F. French Investing Co., Inc. v. City of New York,* 39 N.Y.2d 587, 385 N.Y.S.2d 5, 350 N.E.2d 381, 6 Envtl. L. Rep. 20810 (1976) (not upheld); *City of Hollywood v. Hollywood, Inc.,* 432 So. 2d 1332 (Fla. 4th DCA 1983) (upheld).

[288] 438 U.S. 104, 170.

clear whether TDRs can be used to determine if a taking has occurred or if they only can be considered as part of the just compensation that must be paid for a taking

In *Suitum v. Tahoe Regional Planning Agency,* the Supreme Court was faced with this exact issue, but decided the case on the narrower ground of ripeness.[289] However, Justice Scalia authored a concurring opinion in which Justices O'Connor and Thomas joined that clearly stated TDRs should only be considered as a means of payment and not considered when determining whether there is a taking.[290] Since the Court explicitly rejected the opportunity to decide whether TDRs should be considered in the takings analysis, the takings role of TDRs remains unclear.[291]

Many of the issues discussed above may be covered in relevant state statutes. Currently approximately 25 states have TDR enabling legislation. The three main principles covered in these laws are authorization of the authority to convey development rights, identification of the types of resources that TDR ordinances can be used to preserve, and the voluntary or involuntary nature of TDR programs in that state. At least eight states currently have active TDR programs but no enabling act.[292]

§ 9:11   Green Space Protection

Maintaining a sufficient amount of undeveloped land is of critical importance when designing a growth management program because undeveloped land or green space is necessary to meet agricultural needs, preserve wildlife habitat, maintain water quality, provide areas for outdoor recreation, allocate space for alternative transportation corridors, and promote sustainability.[293] Additionally, green space can slow urban sprawl and increase property values.[294] Establishing greenbelt zones can be an important component of urban service boundary programs.[295]

A jurisdiction has many different options it can choose from to protect green space if it is unable or unwilling to preserve open space through zoning regulations. First, land can be obtained in fee simple by a government through either voluntary purchase or through the exercise of the eminent domain power. Second, green space can be preserved through conservation easements, which permanently restrict the land's devel-

---

[289] *Suitum v. Tahoe Regional Planning Agency,* 520 U.S. 725, 733, 734, 117 S. Ct. 1659, 137 L. Ed. 2d 980, 44 Env't. Rep. Cas. (BNA) 1673, 27 Envtl. L. Rep. 21064 (1997). For a graphic representation of the practical difference between the Souter and Scalia positions, see Arthur C.Nelson, Rick Pruetz & Doug Woodruff, The TDR Handbook: Designing and Implementing Transfer of Development Rights Programs Ch. 10 (2012).

[290] Suitum, 520 U.S. at 747–750.

[291] Suitum, 520 U.S. at 733, 734. See Holloway and Guy, The Utility and Validity of TDRs Under the Takings Equation Under Legal Theory, 11 Penn. St. Envtl. L. Rev. 45 (2002); Miller, Transferable Development Rights in the Constitutional Landscape: Has Penn Central Failed to Weather the Storm?, 39 Nat. Resources J. 459 (1999).

[292] Arthur C.Nelson, Rick Pruetz & Doug Woodruff, The TDR Handbook: Designing and Implementing Transfer of Development Rights Programs Ch. 11 (2012) (tables indicate the state enabling acts and their citation and focus).

[293] Griffith, Green Infrastructure: The Imperative of Open Space Preservation, 42/43 Urb. Law. 259 (2011); Freilich and Popowitz, The Umbrella of Sustainability: Smart Growth, New Urbanism, Renewable Energy and Green Development in the 21st Century, 42 Urb. Law. 1 (2010).

[294] Buzbee, Sprawl's Political-Economy and the Case for a Metropolitan Green Space Initiative, 32 Urb. Law. 367 (2000); Buzbee, Smart Growth Micro-Incentives and the Tree-Cut Tax Case, 17 Ga. St. L. Rev. 999 (2001). See also, Jeffrey A. Zinn, State Policies to Manage Growth and Protect Open Spaces (2004).

[295] For a discussion of greenbelt zones, see Comment: Preservation of Open Space Through Scenic Easements and Greenbelt Zoning, 12 Stan. L. Rev. 638 (1960).

opment.[296] The primary issue for a local or regional government which decides to embark on green space preservation through either of these approaches is how to obtain the money to pay for the land or easements. Possible sources of funds in some jurisdictions include a special purpose local option sales tax and environmental mitigation impact fees.[297]

In some jurisdictions there are state funded programs whereby the state pays for the land or easements either wholly or in cooperation with the local authorities. One example of a state green space program is the Georgia Green Space Commission.[298] The commission has the duty of formulating a strategy to protect 20% of the state's land "as connected and open green space which can be utilized for informal recreation activities and protection of natural resources."[299] Further, the commission is given funds to distribute to local governments if the government formulates a plan to permanently protect 20% of its land as green space.[300]

Sometimes green space can be protected without spending any tax dollars or regulatory fees because private landowners can be encouraged or required to donate the right to develop their property to a local governmental entity or a private public interest land trust or similar organization and in return the land owner can receive tax benefits[301] or transferable development rights.[302] Many local governments formulate green space preservation programs on a public/private partnership basis with the Trust for Public Lands (TPL) "a national, nonprofit, land conservation organization that conserves land for people to enjoy as parks, community gardens, historic sites, rural lands, and other natural places . . . ."[303] The Trust not only raises private money for land and conservation easement acquisition but also assists local governments in formulating programs for public financing.[304] The American Farmland Trust (AFT), a national, non-profit organization formed in 1980, engages in comparable programs designed specifically to preserve farmland through purchase and conservation easement

---

[296] Morrisette, Conservation Easements and the Public Good, Preserving the Environment on Private Lands, 41 Nat. Resources J. 373 (2001); Griffith, Green Infrastructure: The Imperative of Open Space Preservation, 42/43 Urb. Law. 259 (2011). See infra §§ 12:7, 13:12, 15:13.

[297] Griffith, The Preservation of Community Green Space: Is Georgia Ready to Combat Sprawl With Smart Growth?, 35 Wake Forest L. Rev. 563, 572 (2001). For further discussion of environmental mitigation impact fees in this treatise, see § 9:10, supra.

[298] Ga. Code Ann. § 36–22–3.

[299] Ga. Code Ann. § 36–22–1.

[300] Griffith, The Preservation of Community Green Space: Is Georgia Ready to Combat Sprawl With Smart Growth?, 35 Wake Forest L. Rev. 563, 572 (2001). Georgia's most ambitious project which incorporates green space is the Atlanta Beltline which is a comprehensive redevelopment and mobility project which will provide a network of public parks, multi-use trails and transit along a historic 22-mile railroad corridor circling downtown and connecting 45 neighborhoods directly to each other. See http://www.beltline.org.

[301] See Laurie Fowler & Hans Neuhauser, A Landowner's Guide: Conservation Easements for Natural Resource Protection, Ga. Envtl. Pol'y Inst. & Ga. Land Tr. Serv. Ctr., Resource Paper GA. #16 (2d ed. 1998); Baldwin, Conservation Easements: A Viable Tool for Land Preservation, 32 Land & Water L. Rev. 89 (1997); Hocker, Land Trusts: Key Elements In the Struggle Against Sprawl, 15-SPG Nat. Resources & Envtl. 244 (2001); Hollingshead, Conservation Easements: A Flexible Tool for Land Preservation, 3 Envtl. L. 319 (1997); White, "Extra" Tax Benefits for Conservation Easements: A Response to Urban Sprawl, 18 Va. Envtl. L.J. 103 (1999).

[302] See § 9:10 supra.

[303] Trust for Public Lands website, http://www.tpl.org.

[304] "Since 1972, TPL has worked with willing landowners, community groups, and national, state, and local agencies to complete more than 4,250 park and conservation projects nationwide, protecting more than 3 million acres. Since 1994, TPL has helped states and communities generate more than $34 billion in new conservation-related funding." http://www.tpl.org.

programs.[305] One source of funds for farmland preservation is The Farm and Ranch Lands Protection Program which is a voluntary federal conservation program which provides matching funds for the purchase of permanent conservation easements on farm and ranch land. The program was originally established by the Federal Agriculture Improvement and Reform Act of 1996 and reauthorized and expanded by the Farm Security and Rural Investment Act of 2002.[306]

A discussed earlier,[307] conservation and cluster subdivisions are residential or mixed-use developments in which a significant portion of the tract being subdivided is designated as undivided and permanently preserved open space.[308] The lots to be built on are clustered on the remainder of the tract. They are inspired by cluster communities[309] and golf course developments but they are innovative in that the protected open space areas may be forests, meadows, wetlands, aquifer recharge areas, gardens, or even working farms. Conservation subdivisions are of recent origin and in their current format are attributable to planning implementation of smart growth and new urbanism principles.

A newly popular resurgence of land banks, discussed in the following section, provides another source of land for green space through the conversion of foreclosed and abandoned properties.[310]

§ 9:12   Land Banks

Land banking has been practiced in Europe and parts of Canada for many years and consists of local governments buying undeveloped land on the urban outskirts so as to control its time and type of development. Some traditional land banking programs also have farmland preservation as a goal.[311] Modern urban land banks are public or private nonprofit organizations that take control of foreclosed or abandoned properties through various measures to ensure that they are sold or developed in a manner that best serves the long-term interests of the surrounding community. The U.S. Department of Housing and Urban Development defines a land bank as "a governmental or nongovernmental nonprofit entity established, at least in part, to assemble, temporarily manage, and dispose of vacant land for the purpose of stabilizing neighborhoods and encouraging re-use or redevelopment of urban property."[312] The primary objective of all land bank initiatives is to acquire and maintain properties that have been rejected by

---

[305] The AFT website is http://www.Farmland.org. For further discussion in this treatise of farmland preservation programs, see §§ 13:1 seq., infra.

[306]   7   U.S.C.A.   § 7201.   See   http://www.nrcs.usda.gov/wps/portal/nrcs/main/national/programs/easements/farmranch.

[307] § 7:9 supra.

[308] S. Wenger & L. Fowler, Conservation Subdivision Ordinances, Atlanta Regional Commission Community Choices Toolkit: Conservation Subdivisions (2002). They are also sometimes referred to as "open space communities." See R. Kaplan, M. Austin & S. Kaplan, Open Space Communities: Resident Perceptions, Nature Benefits, and Problems with Terminology, 70:3 J.Am.Plan.Ass'n, 300 (2004).

[309] See §§ 7:15 and 13:10 infra.

[310] Frank S. Alexander, *Land Banks and Land Banking,* 10 (2011).

[311] See § 13:13 infra.

[312] Notice of Allocations, Application Procedures, Regulatory Waivers Granted to and Alternative Requirements for Emergency Assistance for Redevelopment and Abandoned and Foreclosed Homes Grantees Under the Housing and Economic Recovery Act, 2008, 73. Fed. Reg. 58,330, 58,332 (Oct. 6 2008), revised by 74 Fed. Reg. 29,223, 29,224 (June 19, 2009).

the open market and left as liabilities for neighboring property owners and the community at large.[313]

The establishment of a land bank is facilitated if the state has enacted comprehensive land bank enabling legislation.[314] As of 2011, 15 states had existing land bank enabling statutes.[315] The core legal authority to be authorized by statute is the power to acquire, manage and dispose of property.[316] Land bank statutes are permissive, not mandatory, leaving to the local governments the ultimate decision of whether or not to form a land bank authority. Land banks may be formed through ordinances adopted by a local government [317] or interlocal agreements between multiple local governments with overlapping tax districts.[318]

The state enabling statute will dictate the form and structure of a land bank, as well as its authority to acquire, manage and dispose of properties, while interlocal agreements between the participating local governments dictate the structure of the board of directors and in what manner they will govern the operations of the land bank.[319] The formal legal structure is determined by the allocation of powers and authority between the state and local governments in the state enabling statute: land banks can exist as independent public legal entities created at the local level,[320] as independent authorities authorized by the state,[321] or as private non-profit entities. A land bank will be governed by its own board of directors, which can be made up of either private citizens, elected officials or employees of the participating local governments.

The local governments that create land banks are responsible for establishing their broad operational goals and priorities, which will guide the authorities' efforts in identifying appropriate properties and future uses, and acquiring and disposing of properties. Land banks must establish clear and precise goals and functions, in order to avoid the strong tendency to look to land banks as a clear-all for all problems related to vacant, abandoned and tax-delinquent properties. The dominant goals shared by existing land banks are: (1) to eliminate the harms caused by vacant, abandoned and tax-delinquent properties; (2) eliminate barriers to returning the properties to productive use; (3) conveying properties to new owners for productive use; and (4) holding properties for future use.[322] At the ground level, an important policy goal for land banks has been the creation of affordable housing stock for the surrounding community.[323] In furtherance of this goal, most land banks—such as St. Louis Land Bank's pri-

---

[313] Frank S. Alexander, *Land Banks and Land Banking,* 10 (2011).

[314] Schilling, Code Enforcement and Community Stabilization: The Forgotten First Responders to Vacant and Foreclosed Homes, 2 Alb. Gov't L. Rev. 101, 118–19 (2009).

[315] Alabama, Alaska, California, Georgia, Indiana, Kansas, Kentucky, Louisiana, Maryland, Michigan, Missouri, Montana, Nebraska, Ohio, and Texas. See Frank S. Alexander, *Land Banks and Land Banking,* 95 (2011) for statutory citations and a model Act.

[316] Frank S. Alexander, Land Banks and Land Banking, 44 (2011).

[317] *See* Kan. Stat. Ann. § 12–5902(a).

[318] *See* Ky. Rev. Stat. Ann. § 65.355(1).

[319] Frank S. Alexander, *Land Banks and Land Banking,* 54 (2011).

[320] See Ky. Rev. Stat. Ann. § 65.355(1).

[321] See Mo. Rev. Stat. § 92.875.

[322] Frank S. Alexander, *Land Banks and Land Banking* 58.

[323] Frank S. Alexander, *The Brookings Institution Metropolitan Policy Program, Land Banking as Metropolitan Policy,* 7 (2008).

ority to public agencies for public use projects and the Atlanta Land Bank's priority to neighborhood non-profit entities for creation of low-income housing—provide public agencies and non-profit community development corporations a right of first refusal for any property in the land bank.[324]

Land banks may use various approaches to acquire properties. Some automatically receive title to all properties not sold at tax foreclosure auctions for the minimum bid, while other may receive, but are not automatically given, such properties. A land bank may have the authority to tender the minimum bid at a tax foreclosure sale and will acquire it if there is no higher bid.[325] Additional means by which land banks may acquire properties include purchase of publicly owned properties, acceptance of properties through voluntary donations and transfers from private owners, and acquisition or lease on the open market.[326] Land banks must also be granted authority to manage all aspects of the properties they acquire, whether through existing local government departments such as Code Enforcement or by entering into property management contracts with private third parties.[327] Enabling statutes must also grant land banks authority to dispose of properties. The nature of these vacant and abandoned properties necessitate flexibility in the terms and conditions under which they can be sold to third parties, but oftentimes existing state and local laws already exist to control the pricing and disposition of publicly owned properties. The enabling state legislation may expressly exempt land banks from these disposition requirements and allow local governments to establish their own disposition policies through interlocal agreements.[328]

The need to manage vacant urban properties has risen in urban communities that struggle with economic development in the face of a declining industrial base, suburban flight of business and residents, and rundown and vacant properties.[329] The wave of foreclosures as a result of the sub-prime mortgage collapse is but the most recent crisis adding to many cities' expanding inventories of vacant properties.[330] The presence of vacant and abandoned properties is considered "a symptom of central city decline . . . [which is now] a problem in its own right," which studies reveal has a significant impact on neighboring property values.[331] In Philadelphia, Pennsylvania, a study has shown that properties located within 150 feet of a single abandoned property lost an average of $7,627 in value, while properties on the same block lost an average of $6,500 in value.[332] Local governments also incur significant costs in their efforts to maintain vacant properties. Philadelphia spends more than $1.8 million per year, and in Ohio, a 2008 study of eight cities revealed that vacant and abandoned properties

---

[324] Alexander, Land Bank Strategies for Renewing Urban Land, 14 J. Affordable Hous. & Community Dev. L. 140, 155–57 (2005).

[325] Ga. Code Ann. § 48–4–64(a).

[326] Frank S. Alexander, *Land Banks and Land Banking*, 45 (2011).

[327] Frank S. Alexander, *Land Banks and Land Banking*, 46.

[328] Frank S. Alexander, *Land Banks and Land Banking*, 47. *See* Ga. Code Ann. § 48–4–63(c); Ky. Rev. Stat. Ann. § 65.370(7).

[329] Jennifer S. Vey, T*he Brookings Institution Metropolitan Policy Program, Restoring Prosperity: The State Role in Revitalizing America's Older Industrial Cities*, 10 (2007).

[330] Alan Mallach, *The Brookings Institution Metropolitan Policy Program, Tackling the Mortgage Crisis: 10 Action Steps for State Government*, 1–3 (2008).

[331] Accordino and Johnson, Addressing the Vacant and Abandoned Property Problem, 22 J. Urb. Aff. 225, 301–315 (2000).

[332] Frank S. Alexander, *The Brookings Institution Metropolitan Policy Program, Land Banking as Metropolitan Policy*, 11 (2008).

cost local governments $15 million per year in city service expenses and result in lost tax revenue of approximately $49 million.[333]

The idea behind contemporary urban land banks arose when urban planners suggested that cities and towns acquire vacant, unimproved properties at the edges of urban markets in an effort to direct long-term growth management planning and control urban sprawl.[334] Land banks provided an alternative method of public land use planning through the artificial control of the local market for land, but these early entities—which operated more like "land reserves" than banks—came under intense scrutiny and political opposition, including takings challenges asserting that it was unconstitutional for the government to take private property and hold it for an indeterminate period without an established redevelopment goal.[335]

The first generation of land banks—located in the five metropolitan areas of St. Louis, Cleveland, Louisville, Atlanta, and Flint, Michigan—developed with a common purpose of converting abandoned, tax-delinquent properties to productive use in areas in where there was a significant lack of market access to these properties due to burdensome property tax foreclosure laws. Common foreclosure laws requiring public auction tax sales and mandating minimum bids hindered the transfer of properties for which the tax liens exceeded fair market value and encouraged sales to private investors who often failed to invest in improvements or pay subsequent years' taxes, while state law often required that properties not sold at auction defaulted to local government control.[336] The result was that the local governments were left with ownership of the most costly, unmarketable properties due to the significant delinquent taxes owed and the generally low market value attributable to the citywide economic decline. Additionally, archaic and inefficient local tax foreclosure proceedings and tax liens further stymied efforts to purchase and develop the vacant properties, as investors sought clear and marketable title prior to acquisition.[337] As Frank S. Alexander, the leading legal scholar on land banks, has noted, "One of the primary reasons that normal market forces do not reach vacant, abandoned, and tax delinquent property is that there are numerous defects or clouds on the title to the property. If title to property is not marketable, it usually is not insurable, and if not insurable it has little if any value to prospective owners."[338]

Faults in first generation land banks revealed four systemic limitations that were to be corrected by the second generation: (1) the lack of multiple sources of finances; (2) amendment to the property tax foreclosure process; (3) the ability to transfer properties with insurable and marketable title; and that (4) land banks must be created by intergovernmental collaboration, especially where property taxes are levied by separate municipal and county entities. In recent years, state legislatures have enacted new land banking statutes that reform their tax foreclosure proceedings in an effort to es-

---

[333] Schilling, Code Enforcement and Community Stabilization: The Forgotten First Responders to Vacant and Foreclosed Homes, 2 Alb. Gov't L. Rev. 101, 111 (2009).

[334] Stoebuck, Suburban Land Banking, 1986 U. Ill. L. Rev. 581, 584 (1986).

[335] Frank S. Alexander, *Land Bank Strategies for Renewing Urban Land,* 14 J. Affordable Hous. & Community Dev. L. 140, 143 (2005).

[336] Frank S. Alexander, *Land Banks and Land Banking,* 19 (2011).

[337] Frank S. Alexander, *Land Bank Authorities: A Guide for the Creation and Operation of Local Land Banks*, 14–15, Local Initiatives Support Corp. (2005).

[338] Frank S. Alexander, *Land Bank Authorities: A Guide for the Creation and Operation of Local Land Banks*, 18.

tablish more effective land bank authorities. The reforms necessary to foster the establishment of land banks include: (1) the creation of judicial foreclosures which will provide a final judicial decision and deliver the property with clear and insurable title; (2) decreasing tax foreclosure time periods; and (3) creating no-bid land transfers to the land bank whereby the property is automatically transferred to the land bank if the minimum bid at a foreclosure sale is not met.[339] State statutes may also permit "conduit transfers"—utilized by the Atlanta Land Bank—which allow land bank authorities to extinguish or reduce delinquent taxes if the property is transferred to a Community Development Corporation, nonprofit or for-profit developer that agrees to develop the property for a specific use.[340]

Beyond streamlined tax foreclosure proceedings and transfer of clear title, in order to best achieve their goals, land banks require a dedicated or internally generated source of funding and powers and authority grounded in intergovernmental agreements.[341] Funding for land bank authorities may come from three primary sources: contributions from local governments, proceeds from the sale of property, or future tax revenues.[342] Land banks may be funded by budget allocations by participating local governments, but relying solely on general revenue funding tends to be effective only when incremental costs are low and may create budget uncertainty from year to year. Reliance on general revenue funding also may prove challenging because land banks are often necessarily cooperative endeavors between multiple local governments, which can create tension regarding whether each parties' financial benefit is commensurate with its annual contribution.[343]

Existing land bank statutes permit the authority to retain proceeds from the sale of properties in order to cover expenses and fund operations.[344] Additional sources of funding include tax recapture, which redirects some portion of the property taxes generated in the future by land bank properties that have been returned to the tax rolls; a delinquent revolving tax fund, which involves the local government or land bank borrowing sufficient funds to pay the entire amount of delinquent taxes to the local government and receives control of all delinquent tax liens, including the right to enforce and to receive interest and penalties on such liens.[345] In 2004, Michigan enacted the most sweeping land bank authority statute in the country, the Land Bank Fast Track Authority Act, which sought to address each of the four systemic limitations found in the first generation.[346]

---

[339] *See* 1893 Mich. Pub. Acts 206, as amended by 1999 Mich. Pub. Acts 123; Mich. Comp. Laws. Ann. §§ 211.1 et. seq.

[340] *See* Ga. Code Ann. § 48–4–64(c).

[341] Frank S. Alexander, *Land Banks and Land Banking,* 18–19 (2011).

[342] Frank S. Alexander, *Land Bank Authorities, A Guide for the Creation and Operation of Land Banks,* 9 (2005).

[343] Frank S. Alexander, *Land Banks and Land Banking,* 48 (2011).

[344] *See* Ga. Code Ann. § 48–4–64(d); Kan. Stat. Ann. § 12–5910.

[345] Frank S. Alexander, *Land Banks and Land Banking* at 51.

[346] *See* Mich. Pub. Acts 258; Mich. Comp. Laws Ann. § 124.751. See also Frank S. Alexander, *Land Bank Authorities: A Guide for the Creation and Operation of Local Land Banks,* 25–26, Local Initiatives Support Corp. (2005).

RED FIELDS TO GREEN FIELDS

Related to Land Banking is Red fields to Green fields ("RFTGF"), a research initiative exploring solutions to the increasing glut of vacant, abandoned and bank-owned commercial properties crowding American sidewalks in the wake of the economic recession of the late 2000s. Red Fields to Green Fields (RFTGF) is an ambitious proposal for public and private underwriting of redevelopment of failed properties into green spaces. The idea behind RFTGFs is simple: (1) acquire financially distressed properties (real estate that is "in the red" where the property value is less than the outstanding debt); and convert them into public parks and adjacent land "banked" for future sustainable development.[347]

Currently, a glut of vacant, non-performing and bank-owned properties stand stagnant on the balance sheets of thousands of financial institutions of all sizes, restricting those institutions ability to make new loans. The inability to obtaining financing in turn discourages small business growth and stymies the revitalization of the abandoned properties. The initiative focuses on the feasibility of acquiring financially distressed properties (real estate "in the red") in major U.S. cities and converting them into green space, particularly public parks and adjacent land "banked" for future sustainable development.[348]

The idea is to remove these functionally obsolescent physical structures from banks' balance sheets by using a land bank and parkland acquisition fund provided by the nation's banking system and led by the Federal Reserve, Treasury, and FDIC.[349] Financial institutions would then have the liquidity to support new growth, and underused, obsolete commercial properties could be transitioned into green spaces until such a time that the market could responsibly support new development.[350] Additional funding mechanisms could include options such as tax credits, leveraged with local equity capital.[351] Once the properties are placed in the land bank, public-private partnerships would buy distressed properties and remove buildings, using loans from the Land Bank Fund—a portion of the site would be become parkland the rest would be redeveloped into new commercial use, from which proceeds would be used to retire the loans. The clear benefit of the initiative would be the removal of bad loans from banks' books, as well as job creation in all phases of the process. In the end, Red field to Green field sites will result in the removal of dilapidated buildings, increased property values and a greater sense of community in the surrounding community.

§ 9:13   Transit Oriented Developments

Transit Oriented Development, or "TOD," refers to the reemergence and growing trend of creating livable communities centered around railway and other mass-transit systems.[352] "Transit-Oriented Development is compact, mixed use development near

---

[347] http://rftgf.org/joomla/.

[348] http://rftgf.org/joomla/.

[349] http://rftgf.org/joomla/.

[350] http://rftgf.org/joomla/.

[351] http://rftgf.org/joomla/.

[352] http://www.transitorienteddevelopment.org/. See Freilich, The Land Use Implications of Transit-Oriented Development: Controlling the Demand Side of Transportation Congestion & Urban Sprawl, 30 Urb. Law. 547 (1998); Bernick and Freilich, Transit Villages and Transit-Based Development: The Rules Are More Flexible: How Government Can Work with the Private Sector to Make It Happen, 30 Urb. Law. 1 (1998).

new or existing public transportation infrastructure that serves housing, transportation and neighborhood goals. Its pedestrian-oriented design encourages residents and workers to drive their cars less and ride mass transit more."[353] Also known as Transit Oriented Design or Car-Free Developments, this part of the Smart Growth movement attempts to create compact, walkable communities in an effort to make possible a higher quality of life without complete dependence on a car for mobility and survival.[354]

Many factors are playing into this new trend of development. As the Urban Land Institute has noted, Transit Oriented Development as an approach to combat traffic congestion and protect the environment has caught on all across the country. The trick for real estate developers has always been identifying the hot transportation system. Today, highways are out; urban transit systems are in.[355] Perhaps the recent focus on TOD is, in part, due to the growing distaste for suburbia and the strip mall-type developments that come with it. Or, perhaps, it is simply the result of collective tastes desiring more walkable lifestyles away from traffic congestion. No matter the reason, a shift can be seen throughout the country towards a widespread desire for a more quality urban lifestyle. Changing structures of modern families (i.e., more singles and empty-nesters) is also playing into this new approach to growth and development. Growing national support for Smart Growth and a new focus on Federal policy are also influential. All of these factors are serving to drive the trend toward TOD.[356]

Some common characteristics or ideals if transit oriented developments are:

• Walkable design with pedestrian walkways being the highest priority is one of the primary goals of a successful TOD project;

• Train station, or other mass-transit station, as a prominent feature of town center is a common component of TODs;

• Ideally, surrounding this town center station would be a regional node containing a mixture of uses in close proximity, including office, residential, retail, and civic uses;

• High density, high-quality development, ideally within 10-minute "walk circle" surrounding the central transit station;

• Collector support transit systems including trolleys, streetcars, light rail, and buses, cable cars, etc.;

• The TOD would contain lanes for the easy use of bicycles, scooters, and roller-blades as daily support transportation systems; and

---

[353] APTA: American Public Transportation Association, www.apta.com.

[354] Kushner, Car-Free Housing Developments: Towards Sustainable Smart Growth and Urban Regeneration Through Car-Free Zoning, Car Free Redevelopment, Pedestrian Improvement Districts, and New Urbanism, 23 UCLA J. Envtl. L. & Pol'y 1 (2005).

[355] See the Urban Land Institute website, http://www.uli.org.

[356] Kushner, Car-Free Housing Developments: Towards Sustainable Smart Growth and Urban Regeneration Through Car-Free Zoning, Car Free Redevelopment, Pedestrian Improvement Districts, and New Urbanism, 23 UCLA J. Envtl. L. & Pol'y 1 (2005).

• Reduced and managed parking inside 10-minute "walk circle" around the central station.[357]

Proponents of TOD suggest that the benefits of such developments far outweigh the option of sprawling development where automobiles are the primary means of transportation. Amongst the suggested benefits of TOD, and perhaps most important, though difficult to measure, is a higher quality of life. Better places to live, work, and play are claimed to result. Greater mobility with ease of moving around more freely and increased transit ridership[358] should result, which should bring reduced traffic congestion and driving. With reduced automobile use would come reduced car accidents and related injuries and reduction in greenhouse gases.[359] Further, proponents of TOD argue that these developments will bring about reduced household spending on transportation, resulting in more affordable housing.

Various changes in a local government's land use regulations may be essential to facilitate TOD. Normally, mixed use development authorization must be permitted for a successful TOD. If the jurisdiction follows the traditional Euclidean separation of use districts this will be the essential change. The provisions allowing mixed use must also permit or even require adequate densities to make the development both economically feasible and an adequate attractor and generator of transit traffic since the goal is to encourage a concentrated development pattern of development. Since high density is so important, many jurisdictions choose to offer density bonuses to developers so as to use market values as inducements.

Having a TOD ordinance and TOD zones or overlay districts is advisable not only to establish mixed use and high density features but also to vary the usual setback and related requirements. As Professor Freilich has explained:

TOD ordinances have several features that distinguish them from conventional zoning regulations. First TOD ordinances often feature *maximum* setback ("build-to" lines) rather than minimum setbacks. By bringing buildings closer to the street, TOD ordinances attempt to generate pedestrian activity and to force parking and other automobile related facilities to the rear of buildings. Second, the frontage and lot size requirements in TODs are reduced in order to encourage higher densities. These may be coupled with zero lot line provisions which allow homes to be sited with no side setback on the lot side. Third, TOD ordinances often require urban design amenities such as colonnades, front porches, and rear parking in order to stimulate pedestrian activity at the street level.[360]

---

[357] http://www.transitorienteddevelopment.org/.

[358] Dumbaugh, Overcoming Financial and Institutional Barriers to TOD: Lindberg Station Case Study, 7 Jr. Pub. Transp. 43 (2004) (suggesting transit ridership is increased for those who live within two miles of a transit station, with a greatly increased number for those living within 1/4 mile.). For a discussion of the success of car-free developments in Europe, see Kushner, Car-Free Housing Developments: Towards Sustainable Smart Growth and Urban Regeneration Through Car-Free Zoning, Car Free Redevelopment, Pedestrian Improvement Districts, and New Urbanism, 23 UCLA J. Envtl. L. & Pol'y 1 (2005).

[359] "According to recent cost-benefit analyses of regional efforts to reduce GHGs, transit-oriented development is among the best—producing large reductions in greenhouse gasses for relatively little expense." Silverman, Green Transportation: Roadblocks and Avenues for Promoting Low-Impact Transportation Choices, 43 Urb. Law. 775 (2011).

[360] Robert H. Freilich, The Land Use Implications of Transit-Oriented Development: Controlling the Demand Side of Transportation Congestion & Urban Sprawl, 30 Urb.Law. 547, 555 (1998).

Whatever format—zone or overlay—a jurisdiction chooses, it must make certain that its comprehensive plan includes TOD concepts and goals and that they are consistent with other provisions of the local plan and such ancillary documents as Official Maps.

§ 9:14   Growth Management and Smart Growth: Leading State Programs

Throughout this chapter the reader can find discussions and references concerning the growth management and smart growth programs of many states. The following "thumbnail" sketches are designed to succinctly summarize the legal and planning frameworks for growth management and smart growth in some of the "leading growth management" states and to give references to recent discussions and evaluations of them.[361]

A.   *Arizona*

Arizona's population has more than tripled since 1960 and is projected to double between 1990 and 2020. Concern over this rapid growth led Arizona to pass the Growing Smarter Act in 1998. The Growing Smarter Act requires that all municipalities and counties regularly readopt comprehensive plans, that four new elements—open space, growth areas, environmental planning, and cost of development—be included in each comprehensive plan, and that all subsequent zoning actions conform with the comprehensive plans.[362] Moreover, the Act provides $200 million over an 11-year period in matching funds for the purchase of open space.[363] The Growing Smarter Act also created the Growing Smarter Commission for the purpose of establishing and recommending changes to the state's land use laws.[364]

The Commission's recommendations led to the passage of the Growing Smarter Plus Act in 2000. The Growing Smarter Plus Act made several changes to the Growing Smarter Act of 1998. One such change authorized counties and municipalities to set urban growth boundaries. Additionally, the Growing Smarter Plus Act required that counties and municipalities adopt a citizen review process for rezoning actions, that a fifth element—water resources—be added to future comprehensive plans, an encouragement to counties and municipalities to develop coordinated regional plans, and a requirement that a municipality have a plan to provide infrastructure to an area with-

---

[361] See also §§ 2:1 et seq., supra, "Comprehensive Plans and the Planning Process." For detailed topic by topic discussions of the growth management and smart growth programs in various states, see, John M. DeGrove, Planning Policy and Politics: Smart Growth and the States (2005) [hereinafter DeGrove] (Oregon, Florida, New Jersey, Maine, Rhode Island, Vermont, Georgia, Maryland, & Washington); Jerry Weitz, Sprawl Busting: State Programs to Guide Growth (1999) [hereinafter Weitz] (Florida, Georgia, Oregon and Washington); Salkin, The Smart Growth Agenda: A Snapshot of State Activity at the Turn of the Century, 21 St. Louis U. Pub. L. Rev. 271 (2002) [hereinafter Salkin]; Bolen, Brown, Kiernan and Konschnik, Smart Growth: A Review of Programs State by State, 8 Hastings W.-Nw. J. Envtl. L. & Pol'y 145 (2002) [hereinafter Bolen et al].

[362] Rick Heffernon & Rob Melnick, *Growth Management and Open Space Protection in Arizona: Current Tools and Progress,* 2001 Morrison Inst, for Pub. Pol'y 2, *available at* http://morrisoninstitute.asu.edu/publications-reports/IssuesInBriefGPL__GrowthMgmtOpenSpaceProtect-CurrToolsProg. At the time the Growing Smarter Act was passed, Arizona law already required municipalities to adopt comprehensive plans containing nine elements. See Ariz. Rev. Stat. 9–461.05 (1996).

[363] William Blackstone, Growing Smarter in Arizona, SE11 ALI-ABA 505 (1999).

[364] Rick Heffernon & Rob Melnick, *Growth Management and Open Space Protection in Arizona: Current Tools and Progress,* 2001 Morrison Inst, for Pub. Pol'y 2,

in 10 years as a prerequisite to its annexation.[365] In 2001, by executive order, Governor Jane Dee Hall established the Growing Smarter Oversight Council to monitor the implementation of the Growing Smarter Acts and to identify problems and suggest legislative responses.[366] In 2006, the Council published a list of "Guiding Principles" to help counties and municipalities implement the Growing Smarter Acts and craft comprehensive plans.[367]

The future of growth management in Arizona has been called into question by the enactment in 2006, through the initiative process, of the Arizona Private Property Protection Act (Proposition 207) which requires compensation for diminution in value caused by land use regulations. It is patterned after Oregon's Measure 37.[368] Indeed, an analysis performed several years after the law's enactment seems to confirm that the law has had a chilling effect on growth management regulation in Arizona.[369]

B. *California*

California, particularly the Los Angeles region, is the poster child for unchecked growth in the United States. The population of the state has increased dramatically since the end of World War II. Between 1940 and 2010, California's population rose from just under seven million people to over 37 million.[370] Because much of California's growth occurred during the decades after World War II, California confronted the need to control its growth earlier than most other states and its local governments were some of the first in the nation to enact growth control measures.[371]

Growth management regulation in California has been more at the local government and regional entities level than at the state level.[372] Though state law requires every city and county to develop a comprehensive plan addressing seven elements— land use, circulation, housing, conservation, open space, noise, and safety—the law is not adequately enforced and, in 2000, over 175 cities and 26 counties were found to be out of compliance with it.[373] Additionally, unlike states such as Florida and Colorado,

---

[365] Rick Heffernon & Rob Melnick, *Growth Management and Open Space Protection in Arizona: Current Tools and Progress,* 2001 Morrison Inst, for Pub. Pol'y 2,

[366] Salkin, Squaring the Circle on Sprawl: What More Can We Do? Progress Toward Sustainable Land Use in the States, 16 Widener L. Symp. J. 787 (2007).

[367] Salkin, Squaring the Circle on Sprawl: What More Can We Do? Progress Toward Sustainable Land Use in the States, 16 Widener L. Symp. J. 787 (2007).

[368] Sparks, Note: Land Use Regulation in Arizona After the Private Property Rights Protection Act, 51 Ariz. L. Rev. 211, 211–216 (2009); Ariz. Rev. Stat. § 12–1134. Diminution in value; just compensation provides: "A. If the existing rights to use, divide, sell or possess private real property are reduced by the enactment or applicability of any land use law enacted after the date the property is transferred to the owner and such action reduces the fair market value of the property the owner is entitled to just compensation from this state or the political subdivision of this state that enacted the land use law." See infra § 10:11 for a discussion of Measure 37.

[369] Sparks, Note: Land Use Regulation in Arizona After the Private Property Rights Protection Act, 51 Ariz. L. Rev. 211, 219–222 (2009).

[370] U.S. Census Bureau, State and County Quick Facts, California, http://quickfacts.census.gov/qfd/states/06000.html (last visited Nov. 4, 2011). U.S. Census Bureau, Resident Population and Apportionment of the U.S. House of Representatives, California, http://www.census.gov/dmd/www/resapport/states/california.pdf (last visited Nov. 4, 2011).

[371] The Petaluma plan and litigation are discussed at § 9:2 supra.

[372] Daniel J. Curtin and Cecily T. Talbert, California Land Use and Planning Law Ch. 15 (26th ed. 2006). See also, Salkin at 275; Bolen el al. at 145.

[373] Cal. Gov. Code §§ 65300 to 65302 (2011); California Smart Growth Caucus, Report, available at http://www.assembly.ca.gov/sgc/sgbriefing__book.htm#Defined.

the state's planning office does not provide any financial or technical help to local governments in formulating a comprehensive plan.[374] Finally, the state itself does not have a comprehensive state plan. State agencies are excused from compliance with local government comprehensive plans and each agency is given leeway to develop its own "functional plan," that agency's plan for future development, which does not have to be consistent with plans from other state agencies.[375]

There have been some smart growth successes on the state level, however. The Williamson Act of 1965 has been successful at protecting over 15 million acres of open space within the state through state purchased conservation easements.[376] Additionally, the California Coastal Commission, set up to manage land use in the coastal region, has been quite successful even though it delegates considerable authority to local commissions that are properly constituted and which have established approved local mandatory plans.[377]

Recently, California has made potentially significant strides in its growth management program with passage of the Sustainable Communities and Climate Protection Act of 2008.[378] Aimed at reducing greenhouse gas emissions, the act divides the state into regions, sets emissions standards for each region and mandates that each region develop a Sustainable Communities Strategy (SCS) which utilizes transportation investment, land use controls and housing policies to meet those set emissions standards.[379] A potential major shortcoming of the new law, however, is that it does not require local governments to comply with the SCS nor tie receipt of their state transportation funding to land use decisions which are consistent with it. This has many commentators fearful that the new law will be a paper tiger.[380]

C. Colorado

Colorado is the country's eighth largest state by land area and twenty-second in the nation by population. However, since 1970, the population has risen from 2.2 million people to over five million people and this growth in population has shown no signs of slowing down.[381] Though Colorado is known for its vast open spaces and soaring peaks, a whopping 80% of the state's population lives along the Front Range, a 40 mile wide band that follows the eastern edge of the Rocky Mountains. The massive growth

---

[374] California Smart Growth Caucus, Report, available at http://www.assembly.ca.gov/sgc/sgbriefing __book.htm#Defined.

[375] California Smart Growth Caucus, Report, available at http://www.assembly.ca.gov/sgc/sgbriefing__ book.htm#Defined.

[376] Cal. Gov't Code §§ 51200 to 51297.4 (2011); The California Land Conservation (Williamson) Act, 2010 Status Report 2 (2010), http://www.conservation.ca.gov/dlrp/lca/stats__reports/Documents/ 2010%20Williamson%20Act%20Status%20Report.pdf.

[377] Cal. Gov't Code §§ 30000 to 30900 (2011); see Kushner, Subdivision Law & Growth Management § 6:24 (2d ed.).

[378] The text of the act, otherwise known as SB 375, can be found at http://www.leginfo.ca.gov/pub/07– 08/bill/sen/sb__0351–0400/sb__375__bill__20080930__chaptered.pdf (last visited Nov. 2, 2011).

[379] http://www.leginfo.ca.gov/pub/07–08/bill/sen/sb__0351–0400/sb__375__bill__20080930__chaptered. pdf (last visited Nov. 2, 2011).

[380] For a sample of these concerns see Bill Fulton, California Planning and Development Report, Bill Fulton's Blog, SB 375 Is Now Law—But What Will It Do? (Oct. 1, 2008), http://www.cp-dr.com/node/2140; Ethan Elkind, Legal Planet: the Environmental Law and Policy Blog, The Myth of SB 375 (Sept. 23, 2010), http://legalplanet.wordpress.com/2010/09/23/the-myth-of-sb-375/.

[381] See 2010 United States Census, Colorado, http://2010.census.gov/2010census/popmap/ (last visited Oct. 13, 2011).

in this area has led Colorado to be ranked the 16th worst congested state in the nation.[382]

Despite several governors who have attempted reform, Colorado lacks a comprehensive statewide growth management program to tackle this rapid growth. Rather, under the Local Government Land Use Control and Enabling Act of 1974, growth management is a problem which is regulated locally by county and municipal governments.[383] The state does actively participate in some areas of growth management control, however. For example, the Land Use Commission and the Department of Local Affairs have the authority to regulate "areas and activities of state interest."[384] The state government, however, uses this power primarily to arbitrate disputes between local governments on projects that have a regional impact. Also, by executive order in 2001, Governor Owens created the Office of Smart Growth within the Department of Local Affairs.[385] The purpose of this agency is to help local governments voluntarily adopt smart growth practices.

Though the Colorado state government has largely stayed out of growth management regulation, Colorado has been relatively successful at managing its growth. Much of this is due to the strong tradition of local regulation in Colorado. In 2001, for example, county and municipal governments in the Denver metropolitan region bonded together to sign the Mile High Compact, creating the Denver Regional Council of Governments (DCROG). The DCROG's Metro Vision 2035 plan, a comprehensive growth management plan for the region which has been voluntarily adopted by the Mile High Compact governments, sets an urban growth boundary for the region, provides a plan for the establishment of green space and sets out a plan for the expansion of mass transit throughout the region.[386] Commentators also point to market forces resulting from the unique geography of the Front Range region as a reason for Colorado's success in managing its growth. One of these market forces is the aridity of the Front Range region and the resulting requirement that local governments pipe water from the western side of the Continental Divide. This necessitates cost sharing among local governments and, in turn, fosters cooperation.[387] The second factor is the general desire among the population to live near the mountains. This concentrates development and acts as a sort of natural urban growth boundary.[388]

D. *Florida*

Florida began its growth management program in the early 1970s by enacting several statutes that regulated areas of critical state concern and developments of regional impact, established water management districts and regional planning councils,

---

[382] Gregory K. Ingram et al., Smart Growth Policies: An Evaluation of Programs and Outcomes 201 (2009).

[383] Local Government Land Use Control Enabling Act, Colo. Rev. Stat. §§ 29–20–101 to 29–20–108 (2011).

[384] Areas and Activities of State Interest Act, Colo. Rev. Stat. §§ 24–65. 1–101 to 24–65.1–502 (2011).

[385] Colo. Rev. Stat. § 24–32–3201. The website for that office is http://dola.colorado.gov/dlg/osg/index.htm.

[386] Denver Regional Council of Governments, Metro Vision 2035 Plan (2011), http://www.drcog.org/documents/2011%20MV%202035%20Plan%20for%20Web5–12–11.pdf.

[387] Gregory K. Ingram et al., Smart Growth Policies: An Evaluation of Programs and Outcomes 207 (2009).

[388] Gregory K. Ingram et al., Smart Growth Policies: An Evaluation of Programs and Outcomes 207 (2009).

and required local governments to adopt and act consistently with comprehensive plans.[389] Some of the early legislation was patterned after the American Law Institute's Model Land Development Code.[390]

In 1985, the Growth Management Act (GMA)[391] was passed to improve the effectiveness of the existing Florida system by strengthening the planning and plan consistency requirements and by adding "teeth" to Florida growth management planning by requiring concurrency—i.e., a requirement that public facilities and other infrastructure be present before development permits can be issued.[392] A companion bill adopted a State Comprehensive Plan thereby making Florida one of only a few states with a state comprehensive plan adopted as a statute.[393] In 1993, further amendments were made to the major growth management acts—particularly the Local Government Comprehensive Planning and Land Development Regulation Act [394] clarifying and strengthening state, regional and local planning and consistency and concurrency requirements.

Thus, by the mid 1990s Florida's growth management program reached a high level of comprehensiveness and maturity vis-a-vis that of most other states.[395] The Florida system is often encapsulated with the term "top-down" consistency and concurrency based comprehensive planning. In essence, the system requires all land development permissions to comply with concurrency and consistency requirements. The consistency requirement is especially broad since it means that land development permits must be consistent not only with the mandated local government comprehensive plan but that that plan must be consistent with regional policy plans and the local and regional plans must be consistent with the State Comprehensive Plan.[396] In addition,

---

[389] The following articles contain recent reviews of the Florida growth management system and its evolution: Gregory K. Ingram et al., Smart Growth Policies: An Evaluation of Programs and Outcomes 153–65 (2009); Jeffrey A. Zinn, State Policies to Manage Growth and Protect Open Spaces 93–95 (2004); Nicholas and Steiner, Growth Management and Smart Growth in Florida, 35 Wake Forest L. Rev. 645 (2000); Dawson, The Best Laid Plans: The Rise and Fall of Growth Management in Florida, 11 J. Land Use & Envtl. L. 325 (1996); Pelham, Restructuring Florida's Growth Management System: Alternative Approaches to Plan Implementation and Concurrency, 12 U. Fla. J.L. & Pub. Pol'y 299 (2001); Rhodes, Florida Growth Management: Past Present, Future, 9 Fla. Coastal L. Rev. 107 (2007); Pelham, Transportation Concurrency, Mobility Fees, and Urban Sprawl in Florida, 42/43 Urb. Law. 105 (Fall 2010/Winter 2011); Thomas G. Pelham, Florida's Comprehensive Planning System Encounters Stormy Weather, State and Local Law New, vol. 34, no. 4 at 1 (June 2011).

[390] The Act patterned on the Model Code was ambitiously titled The Environmental Land and Water Management Act of 1972 [Fla. Stat. Ann. § 380]. The original act and its evolution are discussed in Julian C. Juergensmeyer, Florida Land Use Law ch. 25 (2d ed. 1998)

[391] The Growth Management Act of 1985, Laws of Florida Ch. 85–55, was not designed to be a "freestanding" piece of legislation but instead a series of amendments to 12 chapters of the Florida Statutes thereby unifying but leaving in place the pre-existing structure of separate growth management acts.

[392] Ewing, Florida's Growth Management Learning Curve, 19 Va. Envtl. L.J. 375 (2000); Rhodes, Concurrency: Problems, Practicalities, and Prospects, J. Land Use & Envtl. L. 241 (1991); Weaver, Concurrency, A Growth Management Tool, 12 U. Fla. J.L. & Pub. Pol'y 251 (2001). See § 9:2 supra (explaining the concurrency requirement).

[393] Laws of Florida Ch. 85–57, codified as Fla. Stat. Ann. § 187.

[394] Fla. Stat. Ann. § 163, Pt.II. The 1993 revisions were contained in Laws of Florida, Ch. 93–22206. Additional changes were made by the 2002 Florida Legislature. See Committee Substitute for Senate Bills 1906 and 550; see Roth and Feagin, 2002 Reforms to Growth Management, 2002 Fla. B.J. 57 (July/August 2002).

[395] For recent evaluations of Florida's Growth Management Act see Pelham, Powell and Stroud, Twenty Years Later: Three Perspectives on the Evolution of Florida's 1985 Growth Management Act, 58 Plan. & Envtl. L. 3 (2006).

[396] Sakowicz, Note: Urban Sprawl: Florida's and Maryland's Approaches, 19 J. Land Use & Envtl. L. 377 (2004).

development permission for projects in areas of critical state concern or of the type or magnitude deemed to be of regional impact are subjected to additional procedures designed to recognize state and regional—and not just local—interests and concerns.

Despite the maturity of Florida's growth management program, Florida has not been as successful at controlling growth as some other states. This is the result of many factors—not the least of which is the massive population growth the state has undergone in the last few decades. However, there has also been a clear lack of political support for the program. For instance, there has been only inconsistent state infrastructure investment in proportion to that required by population growth making it all but impossible for many local governments to achieve concurrency.[397] As a result of these shortfalls, 70% of Florida's new population growth since the state began its growth management program occurred in new urban or rural areas.[398]

In 2011 The Florida Legislature, through the enactment of new planning legislation [H.B 2707 and SB 2156][399] virtually gutted the Florida growth management system. The effect of this new legislation is best described by Thomas Pelham, who twice served as Secretary of the Florida Department of Community Affairs and was one of the key architects of the Florida system:

> The state **land planning agency, DCA,** was **dismantled. Its Division** of Comprehensive Planning will become the Division of Community Development, with reduced staff, in a new Department of Economic Opportunity in the Governor's Office.
>
> State review of virtually all local plan amendments will be greatly expedited and limited to adverse impacts on undefined state and regional resources and facilities. Most of Chapter 9J-5, the compliance rules for local plans and amendments, is repealed. The new Division will no longer make compliance decisions and is not required to even make comments on plan amendments, with some exceptions. The Division's role in the review and approval of large scale development in rural areas under the sector plan and rural land stewardship planning processes are also significantly restricted.
>
> The statutory requirements for local plans are greatly weakened. The fundamental requirements that local plans be financially feasible and based on demonstrated need and energy efficiency are eliminated, and the anti-sprawl requirements are weakened. Concurrency requirements for transportation, schools, and parks and recreation are no longer mandatory.
>
> The current statutory limitation of local plan amendments to two cycles a year is eliminated. Local governments are prohibited from requiring public referenda or supermajority votes for approval of plan amendments. Numerous local governments currently have such requirements.

---

[397] Pelham, *A Historical Perspective for Evaluating Florida's Evolving Growth Management Process,* in Charles E. Connerly, Timothy Stewart Chapin, Harrison T. Higgins, Growth Management in Florida: Planning for Paradise 14 (2007).

[398] Gregory K. Ingram et al., Smart Growth Policies: An Evaluation of Programs and Outcomes 159 (2009).

[399] HB 2707, 2011 Leg., Reg. Sess. (Fla. 2011); SB 2156, 2011 Leg., Reg. Sess. (Fla. 2011).

Citizen enforcement of the planning laws will be more difficult. If a third party challenger with standing appeals a local plan amendment, the challenger will have to overcome the very difficult fairly debatable standard.[400]

E. Georgia

The greater Atlanta metropolitan area has been called the "poster child" of urban sprawl and is widely known for having congested, time-consuming commutes.[401] In response, the state has tried a host of programs to manage its explosive growth. In 1989, the Georgia General Assembly passed the Georgia Planning Act,[402] which took a bottom-up approach to planning instead of a top-down approach similar to states like Oregon and Florida.[403] The legislature decided this approach, which requires regional and local planning in order for local governments to qualify for state infrastructure funding, was better suited to Georgia, which is a strong private property rights state with a home rule provision in its state constitution.[404] In 2011, however, the Georgia Planning Act was nearly gutted by a bill which would have removed the requirement for local governments to adopt comprehensive plans in order to receive state infrastructure funding. Though the bill, SB 86, was passed by the legislature, it was vetoed by Governor Nathan Deal.[405]

Additionally, Georgia has created the Georgia Regional Transportation Authority (GRTA) to manage transportation and air quality problems associated with the Atlanta metropolitan area.[406] GRTA is granted the power to disapprove of any development that will have an impact inside its jurisdiction and can discontinue state highway funds if local governments fail to comply with its regional plan.[407] While hailed as innovative in land use planning circles upon its creation in 1999, many commentators feel that GRTA has largely failed to live up to expectations—primarily due to a lack of political will to adequately exercise its powers.[408] Other pertinent state programs include: the Georgia Green Space Commission, created in 2000 for the purpose of permanently protecting 20% of the state's land as green space through the use of incentives [409] and the Metropolitan North Georgia Water Planning District, created to develop and implement "regional and watershed-specific plans" for all water-related issues inside its jurisdiction.[410]

---

[400] Thomas G. Pelham, "Florida's Comprehensive Planning System Encounters Stormy Weather," State and Local Law News, vol. 34, no. 4, at 1 (June, 2011).

[401] Nelson, New Kid in Town: The Georgia Regional Transportation Authority and Its Role in Managing Growth in Metropolitan Georgia, 35 Wake Forest L. Rev. 625 (2000); Bullard, Johnson and Torres, The Costs and Consequences of Suburban Sprawl: The Case of Metro Atlanta, 17 Ga. St. U. L. Rev. 935 (2001).

[402] Ga. Code Ann. § 45–12–202.

[403] See DeGrove at Ch. 6; Bolen et al at 158; Jerry Weitz, Sprawl Busting (1999).

[404] Jerry Weitz, Sprawl Busting (1999). See Alexander, Inherent Tensions Between Home Rule and Regional Planning, 35 Wake Forest L. Rev. 539 (2000).

[405] Ryan Harbin, Adam Sonenshine, State Government, 28 Ga. St. U. L. Rev. 305 (2011).

[406] Ga. Code Ann. § 50–32–1 (2011).

[407] Griffith, Smart Governance for Smart Growth: The Need for Regional Governments, 17 Ga. St. U. L. Rev. 1019, 1048–1049 (2001).

[408] Robert H. Freilich, Robert J. Sitkowski, Seth D. Mennillo, From Sprawl to Sustainability: Smart Growth, New Urbanism, Green Development, and Renewable Energy 108–09 (2d ed. 2010).

[409] Griffith, Smart Governance for Smart Growth: The Need for Regional Governments, 17 Ga. St. U. L. Rev. 1019, 1047 (2001); see Griffith, The Preservation of Community Green Space: Is Georgia Ready to Combat Sprawl with Smart Growth?, 35 Wake Forest L. Rev. 563 (2000).

[410] Ga. Code Ann. § 12–5–572 (2011).

In 2010, the Georgia Legislature passed the Georgia Transportation Investment Act.[411] The act divided the state into 12 regions and tasked each region with developing a list of transportation improvements—a substantial portion of which will be mass transit projects—to be put up for referendum. As of the writing of this publication, each region has developed its list of improvements and voters are expected to vote on these lists during a special election in the summer of 2012.

F. Hawaii

Hawaii has a strong tradition of statewide land use management. In 1961, only two years after becoming a State, Hawaii passed the nation's first comprehensive statewide land use classification and regulation, i.e. zoning system.[412] The system is still basically in effect today even though "rezoning" must conform to a later enacted state plan.[413] Hawaii divides its lands into four classes of districts including urban, agricultural, conservation, and rural. Zoning in each of these categories is reserved for the counties with the exception of land in a conservation district which is managed exclusively by the Hawaii Department of Land and Natural Resources. It is important to note that the four counties are Hawaii's only units of local government. Additionally, state law mandates that all county zoning must be done consistently with the county's comprehensive plan.[414] Under the system, landowners have only two ways of changing the use of their land; (1) by obtaining an amendment to district boundaries or (2) by acquiring a special permit.[415]

Though the Hawaii growth management program has seen little change in the years since it was adopted, a bill was recently introduced into the Hawaii Legislature which would have created a task force to study and recommend updates to the Hawaii State Plan.[416] However, the bill did not pass the Legislature.[417]

G. Maine

Maine began to experience growth pains in the mid 1980s and, in 1988, the state legislature adopted the Comprehensive Planning and Land Development Act which is also referred to as the Growth Management Act of 1988.[418] The Act contains 10 statutory state goals that are comprehensive in scope. For example the goals include encouraging orderly growth while protecting the state's rural character, making efficient use of infrastructure, preventing sprawl, protecting natural resources, encouraging

---

[411] The text of the act can be found at Georgia General Assembly, 2009–10, HB 277, http://www1.legis.ga.gov/legis/2009_10/versions/hb277_HB_277_AP_10.htm (last visited Nov. 4, 2011).

[412] Codified at Haw. Rev. Stat. §§ 205–1 et seq. (2011); see also McPherson, Vanishing Sands: Comprehensive Planning and The Public Interest in Hawaii, 18 Ecology L.Q. 779 (1991).

[413] The state plan was adopted via the Hawaii State Planning Act passed in 1978. It is codified at Haw. Rev. Stat §§ 226–1 et seq. See also David Callies, Regulating Paraside: Land Use Controls in Hawaii (2d ed.); Keith, The Hawaii State Plan Revisited, 7 U. Haw. L. Rev. 29 (1985).

[414] Haw. Rev. Stat. §§ 226–1 et seq. (2011); see Bolen et al. at 160.

[415] Haw. Rev. Stat. §§ 205–3.1 and 205–6 (2011). For more information on Hawaii's growth management system see Robert H. Freilich, Robert J. Sitkowski, Seth D. Mennillo, From Sprawl to Sustainability: Smart Growth, New Urbanism, Green Development, and Renewable Energy 93–94 (2d ed. 2010); Jeffrey A. Zinn, State Policies to Manage Growth and Protect Open Spaces 66–68 (2004).

[416] For the last version of the bill see HB 1529, http://www.capitol.hawaii.gov/session2011/Bills/HB1529_HD1_.HTM (last visited Nov. 8 2011).

[417] Hawaii State Legislature, Measure Status, HB 1529 HD2 SD1, http://www.capitol.hawaii.gov/measure_indiv.aspx?billtype=HB&billnumber=%201529 (last visited Nov. 8, 2011).

[418] Me. Rev. Stat. Ann. tit. 30-A, §§ 4311 to 4350A.

affordable housing, promoting outdoor recreation, etc.[419] The Act also established a governance system that creates growth management roles at the state, regional, and local levels. A state entity, the Office of Comprehensive Planning, was charged with giving assistance to local governments and with creating a process for it and regional councils to review local growth management programs for consistency with state planning goals.[420] Local governments were not required to obtain certification of their programs but funding incentives were established to encourage them to do so.

Before Maine's system could be fully implemented, an economic downturn led to a weakening of political support that, in turn, led to discontinuance of the program in 1991. Nonetheless, the state continued to exercise considerable land use regulatory power because it has land use regulatory power over unincorporated areas.[421] In 1992, the statute was basically reinstated and a long struggle to re-energize the program began. By 2000, political support had increased to the point that various smart growth agenda items were added to the basic program between then and 2004.[422]

In 2007 and in response to the problem of big box stores opening up on the outskirts of small towns, devastating traditional town centers, the Maine Legislature passed the Maine Informed Growth Act.[423] The Act requires that a retailer wanting to develop a big box store pay for a comprehensive impact analysis of the development's impact on the community and, if an undue adverse impact is found, that the development be barred from going forward.[424]

H. Maryland

Maryland is considered by many to be the birthplace of smart growth.[425] The keystone of Maryland's current smart growth program is Governor Parris Glendening's 1997 Smart Growth Initiatives, a collection of five bills (four of which were enacted) aimed at implementing the broad land use policy goals set out by the legislature in 1992.[426] The center piece of the Glendening Initiatives was the Smart Growth Areas Act. The Smart Growth Areas Act aims to concentrate development into "Priority Funding Areas" (PFAs). These areas include existing municipalities and other areas which meet certain state designated criteria. What sets Maryland apart from other states, however, is the mechanism through which it attempts to achieve this goal. Instead of mandating that local governments comply with the act, the Smart Growth Areas Act awards state funding for growth related expenditures to county governments which plan and focus growth within these PFAs. In order to qualify for funding, county governments must craft a comprehensive plan for the PFAs in its jurisdiction and then submit that plan to the Maryland Department of Planning for review and comment. It

---

[419] Me. Rev. Stat. Ann. tit. 30-A, § 4312.

[420] Me. Rev. Stat. Ann. tit. 30-A, §§ 4341 to 4344 (repealed Dec. 23, 1991).

[421] Me. Rev. Stat. Ann. tit. 12, § 683.

[422] DeGrove at 135–159; Bolen et al. at 167; Salkin at 289.

[423] Me. Rev. Stat. Ann. tit. 30-A, §§ 4365 to 4372; see also Weitz, Future Directions: The Next Wave in Growth Management, 42/43 Urb. Law. 407, 415–16 (2010).

[424] Me. Rev. Stat. Ann. tit. 30-A, §§ 43656 to 4369.

[425] See Glendening, Maryland's Smart Growth Initiative: The Next Steps, 29 Fordham Urb. L.J. 1493 (2002) (author was Governor during adoption of smart growth legislation); Sakowicz, Urban Sprawl: Florida's and Maryland's Approaches, 19 J. Land Use & Envtl. L. 377 (2004); James R. Cohen, Maryland's "Smart Growth": Using Incentives to Combat Sprawl, Urban Sprawl: Causes, Consequences and Policy Responses 293 (Gregory D. Squires, ed. 2002). Smart growth programs and principles are discussed at § 9:1 supra.

[426] Economic Growth, Resource Protection, and Planning Act, Md. Ann. Code art. 66B, § 3.01 (2011).

should be noted that the Maryland Department of Planning has no power to approve or disapprove of a local government's comprehensive plan. Rather, it only has the power to approve funding based on the comprehensive plan submitted by the county government.[427]

Recent research has shown the Maryland growth management model to be largely ineffective at restricting growth to PFAs.[428] Indeed, according to a Maryland Department of Planning study of development patterns in the state, between 1997 and 2007 there was no increase in the share of improved residential parcels inside PFAs. Additionally, there has been no consistent reduction in the percentage of residential acres developed outside of PFAs.[429] Part of the blame for this failure lies with the state's relatively weak enforcement powers—the state has no authority to override local government land use decisions but can only refuse to allocate state funds to growth related projects in PFAs. However, many commentators also blame the political atmosphere in the state upon the transition of power from Governor Parris Glendening to Governor Robert Ehrlich in 2003. Though never repealing any of the 1997 laws, Governor Ehrlich refused to adequately support the state's growth management program. He also refused to direct state funds to PFAs in a way entirely consistent with the Smart Growth Areas Act and made a failed attempt to abolish the Office of Smart Growth.[430]

I.   New Jersey

In 1985 the New Jersey Legislature passed the New Jersey State Planning Act.[431] The State Planning Act created the New Jersey State Planning Commission and tasked the Commission with adopting a comprehensive state plan. The first New Jersey State Plan was adopted in 1992 and an amended version adopted in 2001.[432] The overall focus of the New Jersey State Plan is to focus growth and infrastructure development within urban centers, towns, regional centers, villages and hamlets.[433] The effectiveness of the State Planning Act has been questioned, however, as it does not mandate that local governments follow the State Plan. Rather, the State Plan is simply intended to provide local governments guidance in making development related decisions.[434] In this vein of local government taking the lead on land use decisions, local governments are encouraged by the state to participate in a process called cross-acceptance. In this process, local governments may file a cross-acceptance report which identifies inconsistencies between the State Plan and the various regional, county and

---

[427] Gregory K. Ingram et al., Smart Growth Policies: An Evaluation of Programs and Outcomes 168–74 (2009).

[428] Lewis, Knaap, Sohn, Managing Growth with Priority Funding Areas: A Good Idea Whose Time Has Yet to Come, 75 No. 4 J. Am. Plan. Ass'n 457 (2009); Hanlon, Marie Howland & Michael McGuire, *Hotspots for Growth: Land Use Change and Priority Funding Areas Policy in A Transitional County in the U.S.* (2010), *available at* http://www.smartgrowth.umd.edu/articles/HanlonEtAl_030110.pdf. *But see* Shen, Zhang, Land Use Changes in a Pro-smart Growth State: Maryland USA, A 39 Env't & Plan. 1457 (2007).

[429] Maryland Department of Planning, Smart Growth Goals, Measures and Indicators, http://www.mdp.state.md.us/OurWork/smartGrowthIndicators.shtml (last visited Oct. 15, 2011).

[430] Gregory K. Ingram et al., Smart Growth Policies: An Evaluation of Programs and Outcomes 173–74 (2009).

[431] N.J. Stat. Ann. 52:18A-196 et seq.

[432] Jeffrey A. Zinn, State Policies to Manage Growth and Protect Open Spaces 93–95 (2004); Gregory K. Ingram et al., Smart Growth Policies: An Evaluation of Programs and Outcomes 178–80 (2009).

[433] See New Jersey Department of State, New Jersey State Plan, http://www.nj.gov/state/planning/plan.html (last visited Oct. 17, 2011).

[434] Gregory K. Ingram et al., Smart Growth Policies: An Evaluation of Programs and Outcomes 178–80 (2009).

municipal plans. The New Jersey State Planning Commission is also authorized to provide endorsements to municipalities, counties, and regional planning commissions whose plans are consistent with the State Plan.[435]

Although state programs for growth management in New Jersey have been, at best, marginally effective, New Jersey has developed some strong and effective regional growth management programs. The two most impressive programs are the Pinelands Commission and the New Jersey Meadowlands Commission.[436] The Pinelands Commission was created in 1979 to protect the sensitive environmental resources within and surrounding the Pinelands National Reserve. In its initial years, the Commission used its power to review proposed developments to ensure their consistency with its comprehensive management plan. Now, the Commission shares this power with local governments which have brought their ordinances into compliance with the Pineland Commission's Comprehensive Plan.[437] Similarly, the New Jersey Meadowlands Commission (NJMC) was created in the late 1960s in order to reclaim and revive the Meadowlands after decades of industrial use. Within its jurisdiction, the NJMC exercises the zoning power instead of the county and municipal governments and ensures that all land use decisions are done in accordance with its comprehensive plan.[438]

J. Oregon

Oregon was the first state to adopt comprehensive growth management legislation. Passed in 1973, the Oregon Land Use Act requires all local governments to formulate a comprehensive plan, requires that all land use decisions by these local governments be consistent with their comprehensive plans, mandates state review of these comprehensive plans and, if necessary, enforcement against non-compliant local governments, and sets up an appeals system.[439] Additionally, the act created the Land Conservation and Development Commission ("LCDC"), a commission created for the purpose of determining whether locally prepared plans are consistent with the state's planning goals.[440] LCDC has adopted 19 goals and guidelines for planning, including goal 14, which is urbanization. Goal 14's stated purpose is "to provide for an orderly and efficient transition from rural to urban land use."[441] Under this goal, LCDC requires that all cities establish urban growth boundaries. These urban growth boundaries determine which areas can be developed for urban uses and which areas cannot and is the most famous and most important component of Oregon's land use planning scheme.[442]

While Oregon's growth management program is primarily centered around the relationship between the state and local governments, there have been a few effective regional programs. The most notable is the Metro program in the Portland metropolitan area. Consisting of three counties and 24 local governments, Metro is responsible

---

[435] Gregory K. Ingram et al., Smart Growth Policies: An Evaluation of Programs and Outcomes at 183.

[436] See DeGrove at Ch. 4; Bolen et al at 192; Salkin at 299.

[437] For more information see New Jersey Pinelands Commission, http://www.state.nj.us/pinelands/ (last visited Oct. 17, 2011).

[438] New Jersey Pinelands Commission, http://www.state.nj.us/pinelands/ (last visited Oct. 17, 2011).

[439] Or. Rev. Stat. § 197.005–860 (2011); See also Gerrit Knaap & Arthur C. Nelson, The Regulated Landscape: Lessons on State Land Use Planning from Oregon, Ch. 1 (1992).

[440] Or. Rev. Stat. § 197.005–860 (2011); See also DeGrove at Ch. 2; Salkin at 304; Bolen et al. at 304.

[441] Or. Rev. Stat. § 197.005–860 (2011); See also DeGrove at Ch. 2; Salkin at 304; Bolen et al. at 304.

[442] Or. Rev. Stat. § 197.005–860 (2011). Also, see § 9:2 for description of urban growth boundaries.

for developing a comprehensive plan for the region and, when necessary, amending and resetting the area's urban growth boundary.[443]

Oregon's growth management program is the most famous and, arguably, most successful growth management program in the country. Since the program went into effect, Oregon has seen intense urbanization and a substantial decrease in development outside of urban growth boundaries. Indeed, the amount of developed land per capita has been steadily declining and, between 1982 and 1997, Oregon converted just 1% of its farmland to other uses.[444] For a while, however, the future of Oregon's growth management system looked bleak as a result of the enactment of Measure 37. Measure 37 required that compensation be paid to certain land owners whose property values were lowered by Oregon's growth management restrictions.[445] Indeed, by 2007, over seven thousand Measure 37 claims had been filed against either local governments or the state.[446] Since neither the state nor local governments could afford to pay for the reduction in property values caused by their growth management restrictions, most of these restrictions were waived and growth was permitted to continue unchecked.[447] This interruption in Oregon's growth management program, however, has been mitigated somewhat by the 2007 passage of Measure 49 which removes some of the more damaging aspects of Measure 37.[448]

K. Tennessee

Like many southern states, Tennessee experienced rapid growth during the 1990s. In an effort to control this growth, legislation was introduced which resulted in the passage of the Growth Policy Act of 1998.[449] Under this Act, counties and municipalities were instructed to develop joint growth management plans for combating sprawl. In these plans, local governments were required to set urban growth boundaries for areas of existing growth, designate areas for future growth, and delineate all other areas as rural areas.[450] The Growth Management Policy Act's results have been mixed. Some observers contend that the Act has been ineffective in controlling sprawl.[451] One

---

[443] Jeffrey A Zinn, State Policies to Manage Growth and Protect Open Space 102 (2004); Gregory K. Ingram et al., Smart Growth Policies: An Evaluation of Programs and Outcomes 192 (2009).

[444] Shelia A. Martin & Katie Shriver, Institute of Portland Metropolitan Studies, Portland State University, Documenting the Impact of Measure 37: Selected Case Studies 3 (Jan. 2006), http://www.pdx.edu/ sites/www.pdx.edu.ims/files/ims__M37brainerdreport.pdf; Gregory K. Ingram et al., Smart Growth Policies: An Evaluation of Programs and Outcomes 195 (2009).

[445] Or. Rev. Stat. § 195.300–336 (2011). The Measure was upheld by the Supreme Court of Oregon in *MacPherson v. Department of Administrative Services,* 340 Or. 117, 130 P.3d 308 (2006). See Sullivan and Richter, A Taste of Ashes—The MacPherson Decision and the Future of Oregon's Planning Program, 58 Plan. & Envtl. Law. 3 (2006); Sullivan, Through a Glass Darkly: Measuring Loss under Oregon's Measure 37, 39 Urb. Law. 563 (2007); Blumm and Grafe, Enacting Libertarian Property: Oregon's Measure 37 and Its Implications, 85 Denv. U. L. Rev. 279 (2007–2008). See also discussion infra § 10:11.

[446] Portland State University, College of Urban and Public Affairs: Institute of Portland Metropolitan Studies, Measure 37 Database, http://www.pdx.edu/ims/measure-37-database (last visited Nov. 1, 2011).

[447] Shelia A. Martin & Katie Shriver, Institute of Portland Metropolitan Studies, Portland State University, Documenting the Impact of Measure 37: Selected Case Studies 3 (Jan. 2006), http://www.pdx.edu/ sites/www.pdx.edu.ims/files/ims__M37brainerdreport.pdf.

[448] Oregon Department of Land Conservation and Development, Ballot Measures 37 (2004) and 49 (2007) Outcome and Effects 34 (Jan. 2011), http://www.oregon.gov/LCD/docs/publications/M49__2011–01–31.pdf.

[449] Tenn. Code. Ann. § 6–58–101–117 (2011).

[450] Jeffrey A. Zinn, State Policies to Manage Growth and Protect Open Spaces 112–14 (2004).

[451] Seong-Hoon, Chen, and Yen, Urban Growth Boundary and Housing Prices: The Case of Knox County, Tennessee, 38 Rev. Reg'l Stud. 29, 29 (2008); Seong-Hoon Cho et al., The Impact of Urban Growth Boundaries on Land Development in Knox County, Tennessee: A Comparison of Two-State Probit Least Squares

reason often cited is that many local governments' growth management plans, while complying with the letter of the law, are not formulated to actually control growth. For instance, many municipalities simply set their urban growth boundaries at the city limits, effectively rendering that urban growth boundary ineffective. Nonetheless, supporters of the Act contend that the Growth Policy Act's use of urban growth boundaries, such as those found in Oregon and Washington legislation, constitutes a progressive first step for growth management in Tennessee.[452]

L. Texas

Growth management regulation in Texas is largely anemic. Texas has no statewide growth management program, and any growth management regulation which does occur is done at the regional or local level. From a regional planning perspective, there are three notable regional planning programs: Envision Central Texas, Vision North Texas and Blueprint Houston. The most successful and powerful is Envision Central Texas, a planning agreement among five counties in the Austin Metropolitan Region which aims to acquire green space, fund infrastructure improvements, build cultural facilities, and encourage the construction of affordable housing.[453] To achieve its goals, Envision Central Texas uses funds generated from a bond issuance which was overwhelmingly approved by voters in a 2005 election. Less effective but nonetheless important are Vision North Texas, representing the Dallas-Fort Worth Metropolitan Region, and Blueprint Houston, representing the city of Houston. These entities are regional planning organizations with the goal of setting out an optional planning vision for transportation, land use, water management and other growth related issues within each region.[454] Neither of these programs, however, are funded or exercise any real regional planning power.[455]

In 1997, the state legislature passed legislation allowing cities and regional planning entities the power to formulate comprehensive plans as well as the authority to require consistency between these comprehensive plans and local land use decisions.[456] A minority of cities have used this power to enact growth management regulation for the purpose of curbing suburban sprawl. Additionally, some larger cities such as Dallas and Houston have begun construction on extensive public transportation networks. Nonetheless, despite the increasing urbanization of Texas and largely due to the anti-regulation political climate, Texas remains a nonentity when it comes to growth management regulation.[457]

---

and Multilayer Neural Network Models, 39 J. Agric. & Applied Econ. 701 (Dec. 2007); Douglas R. Porter, *Tennessee's Growth Policy Act: Purposes, Implementation, and Effects on Development,* Growth Management Institute (July 2002).

    [452] Douglas R. Porter, Tennessee's Growth Policy Act: Purposes, Implementation, and Effects on Development, Growth Management Institute (July 2002).

    [453] Envision Central Texas, About Us, http://envisioncentraltexas.org/index.php (last visited Dec. 23, 2011).

    [454] Vision North Texas, http://www.visionnorthtexas.org/activities.html (last visited Dec. 23, 2011); Blueprint Houston, http://www.blueprinthouston.org/ (last visited Dec. 23, 2011).

    [455] Gregory K. Ingram et al., Smart Growth Policies: An Evaluation of Programs and Outcomes 224–25 (2009).

    [456] Tex. Loc. Gov't Code Ann. § 213.

    [457] Gregory K. Ingram et al., Smart Growth Policies: An Evaluation of Programs and Outcomes 178–80 (2009); Jeffrey A. Zinn, State Policies to Manage Growth and Protect Open Spaces 114–15 (2004).

M.　Utah

Like many western states, Utah has seen significant growth over the last several decades. As an initial stab at controlling this growth, the state legislature passed the Utah Land Use Act of 1974 which was designed to create a land use commission. However, upon enactment, opponents successfully spun the Act as an infringement on private property rights and, shortly thereafter, the legislature repealed the Act.[458]

Utah did not address its growth issues again until the 1990s. Runaway growth in the Wasatch Front Region (the area surrounding Salt Lake City) prompted community political and business leaders to form Envision Utah, a public private partnership for quality growth with a consensus building rather than an agenda driven approach to controlling growth in the region.[459] Its Quality Growth Strategy, arrived at through intensive public input, provides a recommended guide on which governments, businesses and individuals in the region are encouraged to base their planning decisions.[460] It encourages the creation of more walkable communities, the creation of a true regional transportation system, the fostering of transit oriented developments and the preservation of more green space.[461] Indeed, for many of these goals, Utah has become a national model over the last decade. For instance, Utah has significantly expanded its mass transit offerings since the late 1990s and now has in place an extensive light rail and commuter rail system. In May 2011, the Brookings Institute ranked Salt Lake City as the third best city in the country for connecting people to their jobs with mass transit.[462]

Though the Envision Utah movement was a mostly privately funded endeavor, the excitement it generated encouraged the state to participate in the goals it set out. In 1999, the state legislature enacted the Quality Growth Act which created the Critical Land Conservation Fund and the Quality Growth Commission.[463] The Conservation Fund allows local governments and other parties to use monies from the fund to preserve open space by purchasing parcels of land and conservation easements.[464] The Quality Growth Commission, though it is not given any regulatory power, advises the state legislature on growth related issues, administers the Critical Land Conservation Fund and helps local governments craft growth management oriented policies.[465]

---

[458] Craig M. Call, A Utah Citizen's Guide to Land Use Regulation: How it Works and How to Work It (2005); Jeffrey A Zinn, State Policies to Manage Growth and Protect Open Space 102 (2004).

[459] The group's website is http://www.envisionutah.org. See Note: Old Regionalism, New Regionalism, and Envision Utah: Making Regionalism Work, 118 Harv. L. Rev. 2291 (2005).

[460] Envision Utah, The Quality Growth Strategy, http://envisionutah.org/eu__about__eu__ qualitygrowthstrategy__main.html (last visited Nov. 16, 2011).

[461] Envision Utah, The Quality Growth Strategy, http://envisionutah.org/eu__about__eu__ qualitygrowthstrategy__main.html (last visited Nov. 16, 2011).

[462] Lee Davidson, *Utah Transit Among Best to Connect People and Jobs,* Salt Lake City Tribune, May 11, 2011, *available at* http://www.sltrib.com/sltrib/money/51794064–79/transit-jobs-lake-salt.html.csp.

[463] 1999 Utah Laws 24, § 120.

[464] Utah Code Ann. § 11–38–302 (2011).

[465] Utah Code Ann. § 11–38–302 (2011). Smith, Quality Growth Act, 1999 Utah L. Rev. 1168 (1999); Bolen et al 218; Salkin at 308.

N. Vermont[466]

Vermont has a strong tradition of growth management and environmental stewardship. Act 250,[467] the state's first growth management law, was passed in 1970 and requires that most new developments affecting 10 or more acres or involving 10 or more housing units be reviewed by one of nine District Environmental Commissions on a case-by-case basis in order to receive a building permit. To be approved, each new development must be consistent with 10 state criteria designed to maintain air and water quality, prevent erosion, prevent traffic congestion, ensure infrastructure is not overly burdened, and protect scenic and historical areas. Each of these criteria serves more as guidelines than as requirements because a permit can be issued by a Commission even if all criteria are not met.[468] It should be noted that local governments also retain control over unwanted development because local building permits can be denied even if a state permit has been granted.

Act 200,[469] the second major Vermont growth management act, was passed in 1988 and requires regional planning throughout the state, mandates certain criteria for local governments which choose to enact comprehensive plans, and requires that all state agencies adopt plans which are in conformity with regional and local plans. Since Act 200's passage, Vermont has implemented a host of other growth management programs including the Vermont Downtown Program and the Growth Centers Program, both aimed at promoting new growth in traditional downtowns and other areas of existing development.

O. Washington[470]

In 1990, Washington adopted the Growth Management Act [471] and then strengthened it through amendment in 1991. The Growth Management Act is considered to be one of the most aggressive growth management laws in the nation and requires counties and cities with populations over 50,000 with 17% decennial population growth and all counties and cities with 20% decennial population growth to prepare comprehensive plans and set urban growth areas. In addition, these comprehensive plans are to be implemented and to be consistent with 14 state goals for guiding growth. which include consideration of transportation, housing, economic development, natural resource industries, property rights and the environment.[472] Furthermore, all cities and counties are required to protect land classified as critical areas.[473]

---

[466] DeGrove at 184–207; Gay, State Solutions to Growth Management: Vermont, Oregon, and a Synthesis, 10 Natural Res. & Envtl. 13 (1996); Bolen et al. 308; Salkin at 309.

[467] Vt. Stat. Ann. tit. 10, §§ 6001 to 6093 (2011).

[468] Dreisewerd, Staving Off the Pillage of the Village: Does in Re Wal-Mart Stores, Inc. Offer Hope to Small Merchants Struggling for Economic Survival Against Box Retailers?, 54 Wash. U. J. Urb. & Contemp. L. 323, 332 (1998).

[469] Vt. Stat. Ann. tit. 24, §§ 4301 to 4476 (2011).

[470] Jerry Weitz, Sprawl Busting (1999); DeGrove at Ch. 8; Bolen et al at 224; Salkin at 310; Jeffrey A. Zinn, State Policies to Manage Growth and Protect Open Spaces 118–20 (2004).

[471] Wash. Rev. Code Ch. 36.70A (2011).

[472] The State of Washington, Growth Management Hearings Board, http://www.gmhb.wa.gov/Reader.aspx?pg=About.htm (last visited Dec. 21, 2011).

[473] Lloyd, Accommodating Growth or Enabling Sprawl? The Role of Population Growth Projections in Comprehensive Planning Under the Washington State Growth Management Act, 36 Gonz. L. Rev. 73, 145 (2001).

§ 9:15   Growth Management: The Canadian Context[474]

A.   *Placing Ourselves in the Constitutional Universe*

Canada is a federal state in which all of the powers one would normally attribute to sovereignty are divided between the federal government on one hand, and the provincial governments on the other. This division of powers was originally effected by an Act of the Parliament of the United Kingdom and has, through successive Acts of the United Kingdom Parliament, and subsequent repatriation to Canada of those Acts in 1982 remained substantially unchanged. In this regard, "civil rights and property," "local matters," and "local government," are all matters that fall within the jurisdiction of the provinces. As a result, except in respect of federal lands and undertakings, and in respect of subject matters exclusively assigned by the division of powers to the federal government, planning law and takings law is most actively engaged at the provincial level. The federal government most certainly has power of expropriation in respect of matters fully within federal constitutional competence (for example, ports, harbours, aviation, shipping, defence, navigable waters, et al.), and in the exercise of such compulsory purchase powers, it is the master of its own procedures. As to land use law, while the federal government has exclusive control over the use of and development of land owned by it, and can in respect of private lands render them immune from provincial land use laws where a federal agency has approved or licensed the use of such lands for a purpose wholly within federal jurisdiction (i.e., airports, nuclear power facilities, et al.), the real focus of planning and land use regulation (including growth management) lies within exclusive provincial competence.

B.   *Growth Management*

Growth management control, originating in formal fashion in American jurisdictions during the 1990's, is the most current evolution of big picture planning in Canada. While official community plans or master plans fit well within discrete local geopolitical units at the urban and regional level, growth management control casts its ultimate ambition much wider. Growth management plans, while popular at the local level, are most effective on a regional or even supra-regional basis. The nature of the problems they address mandate a scope that is not defined by political boundaries but rather by factors evidencing regional geographic environmental and economic interdependence.

As the nomenclature suggests, the major purpose is to manage growth by distributing its impacts throughout a region in a manner that serves public interests that lie beyond the boundaries of individual local governments. Conservation of environmentally sensitive areas and water sheds, preservation of agricultural lands, efficient provision of costly public infrastructure including public transportation, densification of settlement patterns close to public facilities and employment, more efficient use of power

---

[474] The authors express their gratitude to Raymond Young QC for the preparation of this section. Mr. Young is a land use and local government lawyer who is a partner in the Vancouver, British Columbia, law firm of Young, Anderson, Barristers and Solicitors. He is also an adjunct professor of planning law at the University of British Columbia's Faculty of Law and School of Community and Regional Planning. For additional discussion by him of growth management in Canada, see Young, Vancouver: Made in America, Eh?, 17 Ga. St.L.Rev. 1109 (2001); Young, Canadian Law of Expropriation, 68 Sask. L. Rev. 345 (2005); Young, Canadian Commentary on Constructive Expropriation Law Under NAFTA Article 1110, 43 Alberta L. Rev. 1001 (2006).

grids and consequent cost saving in massive power generation projects in the hinterlands, are all recognized goals of growth management.

As with many planning and land-use initiatives, the concept of growth management, or perhaps more accurately, its formal identification by that terminology comes to Canada carrying the imprint of American practice, experience and commentary. A review of Canadian planning and land-use control schemes indicates that in many provinces the enabling authority for achieving growth management objectives, and the tools to do so, have been in place for some time. What has been lacking, and what the American experience reveals, is the recognition of growth management control as a defined and separate component of both planning and land-use regulatory programs. The identification of growth management, in particular control in relation to the timing, sequence and extent of growth in a regional context, as a discernable and legitimate element of planning, has focused attention on new roles for existing planning and regulatory tools. At least two jurisdictions in Canada have formally identified and reorganized their land-use legislation to integrate growth management at the regional level and even supra-regional levels. As will be apparent from what follows, the tasks in Canada to implement growth management strategies—aside from promotion of their utility—are to create effective regional planning authorities to re-employ the extensive land-use control powers local government already have, and to re-deploy such powers to the regional level for growth management purposes.

C. Power of Local Government to Establish Growth Management Programs

Canada does not have a home rule system. Local government power and authority originates only from express and specific delegation from the provincial government. In metropolitan areas, politically subdivided into numerous autonomous municipalities, often all that is necessary in order to arm and implement a growth management scheme is either the creation of an over-arching regional government with express regional planning and land-use authority, or some form of direct provincial control over the approval of comprehensive plans at the local government level, accompanied by provincial overarching planning coupled with mandatory consistency with provincially established or regionally negotiated objectives and policies relating to regional growth.

Constitutionally, land-use control is much less constrained in Canada than in the United States. Elected legislatures are supreme except when they trench upon constitutionally protected rights. Property ownership is not expressly protected in the Constitution. Residual remnants of the doctrine of vested rights, and some ordinary statute law requiring compensation for takings of property, provide general protection from outright seizure; however, in all jurisdictions the exercise of planning and zoning powers has been protected by no compensation provisions found in the local enabling statutes. Such provisions operate effectively to protect the exercise of regulatory power, but usually contain an exception where land is restricted to public use. Theoretically it is possible that land may be so restricted that no use whatsoever, is permitted; however, with the exception of short term statutorily enabled moratoria, such zoning restrictions in Canada have not survived challenge either on grounds of unreasonableness or improper purpose (i.e., that the real purpose of sterilization of all private use was to effectively dedicate the land to a public use).

The Canadian Constitution does contain mobility rights (right to move between provinces), and at least one court has commented that even though the wording of the constitutional provision speaks to inter-provincial mobility, it would be surprising if Canadians did not similarly enjoy intra-provincial mobility rights. It is unlikely that any growth management program that focused on timing, sequence and proportionality in the distribution of growth throughout a region, as opposed to straying into absolute population controls, would ever breach the mobility rights provision of the constitution. In contrast, any provincial legislation authorizing local governments or regions to impose absolute population caps, and a consequent development freeze, might itself, given proper evidence of its effect, be unconstitutional.

D. *Statutory Growth Management Programs*

While many provinces are beginning to consider and even to promote growth management as an important planning initiative, only a few have as yet formally enacted legislation to identify it and to implement it as a coherent and essential planning initiative. There are two distinct statutory models amongst the emerging current Provincial approaches to establishing growth management at the regional and urban levels in Canada. Both British Columbia and Ontario have been early innovators in introducing growth management as a local government power and as a major component of comprehensive planning and land use control schemes.

1) British Columbia

The leading jurisdiction in Canada is British Columbia which in 1996 enacted a comprehensive legislative scheme enabling, (and in some cases, requiring) growth management strategies to be developed at a regional level and providing for their legal effect on the planning authority and capital expenditure programs of constituent local governments within the region. The legislative scheme is highly permissive, allowing regional governments to take the initiative in preparing regional growth strategies. It is also a statutory scheme that is not at all a command and control or top down model. It is an approach that depends on consultation, consensus, mediation and ultimately arbitrated agreement (if necessary) between the originating regional government and the constituent and separate municipalities within that region.

The British Columbia legislation states that the general purpose of a required growth management strategy is, "to promote human settlement that is socially, economically and environmentally healthy and that makes efficient use of public facilities and services, land and other resources, and to guide decisions in growth, change and development within its region." A regional growth strategy is required to work towards:

(a) avoiding urban sprawl and ensuring that development takes place where adequate facilities exist or can be provided in a timely, economic and efficient manner;

(b) settlement patterns that minimize the use of automobiles and encourage walking, bicycling and the efficient use of public transit;

(c) the efficient movement of goods and people while making effective use of transportation and utility corridors;

(d) protecting environmentally sensitive areas;

(e) maintaining the integrity of a secure and productive resource base, including the agricultural and forest land reserves;

(f) economic development that supports the unique character of communities;

(g) reducing and preventing air, land and water pollution;

(h) adequate, affordable and appropriate housing;

(i) adequate inventories of suitable land and resources for future settlement;

(j) protecting the quality and quantity of ground water and surface water;

(k) settlement patterns that minimize the risks associated with natural hazards;

(l) preserving, creating and linking urban and rural open space including parks and recreation area;

(m) planning for energy supply and promoting efficient use, conservation and alternate forms of energy; and

(n) good stewardship of land, sites and structures with cultural heritage value.

The enactment at the regional level of a growth management strategy is permissive, although the provincial government may require any region to prepare and adopt one. If adopted, a regional growth management strategy must cover a period of 20 years and provide:

(a) a comprehensive statement on the future of the region, including the social, economic and environmental objectives of the board in relation of the regional district;

(b) population and employment projections for the period covered by the regional growth strategy;

(c) to the extent that these are regional matters, actions proposed for the regional district to provide for the needs of the projected population in relation to

    (i) housing,

    (ii) transportation,

    (iii) regional district services,

    (iv) parks and natural areas, and

    (v) economic development.

The growth management strategy enabling legislation provides for mandatory consultation is required to be early and ongoing and must provide at a minimum for consultation with citizens, affected local governments, first nations, school districts, water and sewer boards (if any) and the provincial and federal governments and their respective agencies. Regional governments funding for up to 50% of the cost of preparing and developing the regional growth strategy, and the Province will also appoint facilitators during the consultation processes where the Province recognizes that such assistance is desirable.

Before a regional government can formally adopt a regional growth strategy, the strategy must be accepted by all affected local governments in the region. If an affected local government within the region is unwilling to accept the required growth strategy, the dispute involving that local government and the region goes first to a facilitator and then to binding arbitration. A number of options for binding arbitration are provided for, and where the regional government of the constituent local governments in the region cannot agree, the province chooses. This process of gaining acceptance of each of the constituent local governments in the region is not an all-party process, rather the region negotiates and then arbitrates (if necessary) singularly, or in groups, around issues that various constituent local governments refuse to accept. Options involve peer panel (that is other politicians selected by the Minister from other regions), final proposal arbitration by a single arbitrator, or alternatively, full arbitration by a single arbitrator where the arbitrator is not bound to one of the proposals submitted by the region or any non-accepting local government.

Once adopted by the region, the regional growth strategy requires that all regional government legislation adopted and services and facilities undertaken must be consistent with the strategy. Similarly, all enactments of single purpose agencies such as water boards and sewer boards must be consistent with the regional growth management strategy. Municipalities within the region have two years after the adoption of a regional growth strategy to embed in their local government comprehensive plans a regional context statement setting out how that local comprehensive plan is to be made consistent with the regional growth management strategy. If the region and the local government cannot agree on the regional context statement, then the dispute is settled by the same options for arbitration provided for settling the regional growth strategy. Under the general statutory rules relating to the legal effect of a local government's comprehensive plan, the local government cannot adopt any bylaws or undertake any works or services inconsistent with its comprehensive plan. Under the legislation, the Province retains the power to establish policy guidelines for all processes and content related to the development and adoption of regional growth strategies and local comprehensive plans.

2) Ontario

Ontario has chosen to impose a top down statutory model that places the Province itself in a pivotal role in the development of growth management strategies. This central role for the Provincial government reflects a long tradition in Ontario of local planning and land use regulations being subject to Provincial oversight in respect to the substance of local government exercise of planning and zoning powers. In Ontario, substantive elements of both planning and zoning regulation are subject to a Provincial tribunal (the Ontario Municipal Board) which has certain jurisdiction to examine and weigh the merit of planning and land use decisions made by elected councils of local governments. The role of the OMB in respect of its merit based oversight of local government action goes far beyond the normal judicial remedies (ultravires and procedural due process) to which superior courts are limited. In the tradition of such pivotal policy oversight in land use matters, it is no surprise that Ontario's Places to Grow Act 2005, reserves the central role to the Province in growth management control.

The Places to Grow Act 2005 has as its key purpose the guiding of long-term goals and decision making about growth in a manner that provides for multi-municipality and multi-regional coordination of growth regardless of the local geo-political boundaries involved. It focuses on directing planning at the local level to reflect and harmonize growth in a large geographic perspective in order to integrate and coordinate important planning approaches across multiple local jurisdictions. The growth strategy aims to promote a rational basis and integrated scheme of decision making that makes efficient use of infrastructure, promotes environmental sustainability and a culture of conservation while building "strong communities" and maintaining a "robust economy."

Under Ontario's growth management legislation, the Province itself initiates and designates parts of the Province as a "growth planning area." In keeping with the "top-down" model of the scheme, the Province prepares the growth management plan. There are extensive provisions for consultation with local governments and other stakeholders during the preparation of the growth management plan. Upon completion by the Province of a growth management plan, the responsible Provincial Minister must give notice to the public generally, and to municipalities and planning authorities in the areas covered by the growth management plan. The Province may choose or not to have a public hearing process after giving of notice—either on specific matters addressed in the growth management plan or on the plan generally. Such plan will ultimately be approved by the cabinet and a date is fixed for its coming into force. The legal effect of such growth management plan is that within a specified period each municipality and planning authority in the area of the plan must amend their "official plan" to conform to the growth plan. Where a municipality or planning authority fails to comply, the Province may negotiate, but ultimately retains the authority to unilaterally amend the local plan. In addition, moving forward, all planning decisions made by municipalities and other planning bodies subsequent to the approval of the growth plan must conform to the growth plan.

A growth plan may address the following:

(a) population projection and allocations;

(b) identity of priority growth areas, emerging and future growth areas over specified time periods;

(c) different growth strategies for various parts of the growth area;

(d) policies, goals and criteria in relation to:

   (i) intensification and density,

   (ii) land supply for residential, employment and other uses,

   (iii) expansions and amendments to the boundaries of areas of settlement,

   (iv) the location of industry and commerce,

   (v) the protection of sensitive and significant lands, including agricultural lands, and water resources,

   (vi) non-renewable resources,

(vii) the conservation of energy,

(viii) infrastructure development and the location of infrastructure and institutions,

(ix) transportation planning,

(x) municipal waste management planning,

(xi) the co-ordination of planning and development among municipalities,

(xii) growth-related capital spending and financing,

(xiii) affordable housing,

(xiv) community design,

(xv) specified actions to be taken by municipalities to implement or achieve the policies or goals;

(e) such other policies, goals or matters that the Minister considers advisable.

At the present time, Ontario has prepared and approved a growth plan for a major region of the Province referred to as the "Golden Horseshoe." The area encompasses a substantial portion of the urbanized area of the Province situate on and around Lake Ontario involving 27 urban centres with a population of eight Million people. Recently the Province has completed and released a growth plan for a second major portion of the Province known as the Growth Plan for Northern Ontario. It applies to a vast area of 800,000 square kilometres—close to 90% of the land mass of the Province. The Plan covers 114 municipalities and 106 First Nation communities.

E.   Land Use Control/Regulatory Takings

As mentioned at the beginning of this section, there is no constitutional entrenchment in Canada of, "property rights" or a right not to be deprived of property by any means. In respect of land, and in the context of land use regulation, the principle of sovereignty of parliament applies. The primary tenet of parliamentary sovereignty is that no rule of law is so fundamental or basic that it is beyond the reach of Parliament to alter, restrict, or abolish. Consequently, there is no law that Parliament cannot make provided that it is not contrary to the Constitution. In Canadian terms when we refer to Parliament we do so in the context of federalism and the division of powers between the federal and the provincial parliaments discussed at the beginning of this section.

That a citizen ought not to be deprived of property without compensation is a well-known and firmly accepted common-law principle of statutory interpretation. At its highest it can be said that there is a strong prima facie presumption that Parliament does not intend to take the property of a subject without fair compensation. Such presumption falls within a class of core common law principles that have been scrupulously protected by common law judges, and jealously guarded by the electorate alert to governmental erosion of what are, "popularly" accepted as property rights. This of course is not to detract from the fact that in real terms, as well as in terms of the law, a high social value is placed in Canadian society on the ownership of property and these values are reflected in both a political and legal commitment to compensate.

There is no doubt that the absolute application of the principle of parliamentary sovereignty would support the taking of property without compensation. If any elected government could politically bring itself to do so in express terms, such legislation would be valid. The operation of a strong presumption in favour of fair compensation has ensured that any legislation that would seek to advance such result would have to be clear, express, and unambiguous since the presumption is a strong one—it is, however, only a presumption underlying an interpretive canon.

Takings in the context of land use regulation—that is resulting from over-regulation—present problems as difficult as those raised in the United States, where the right not to be deprived of property without fair compensation has been raised to a constitutional level. An analysis of Canadian takings cases discloses two primary principles:

1. for there to be a finding that a taking has occurred there must first be a deprivation of property or an interest in it; and

2. there must be a corresponding acquisition or "constructive acquisition" of that property or interest by the government, or some augmentation of a governmental property interest in a form that is reasonably referable to the deprivation.

Thus, a mere reduction in the incidents of land ownership by land use regulation, in particular, the common law right to use property any way the owner wishes subject only to the law of nuisance (protection of the use and enjoyment of proximate land occupiers), and the conversion of such reduction by general land use regulation into an amorphous public benefit, does not constitute a taking.

To go further with this discussion, it is necessary in Canada to distinguish between the exercise of sovereign power (by either the federal or provincial governments), and the exercise of delegated power (power delegated, for example, from the province to a local government to exercise zoning authority). The former is not subject to judicial review except to the extent there is constitutional breach (either a division of powers dispute, or a breach of the Charter of Rights and Freedoms). Acts of Parliament are supreme unless the Constitution is somehow engaged. In contrast, a local government is not a sovereign body. It is created by an act of the provincial parliament and its powers, including its land use powers are delegated to it. Delegatees have no inherent power (Dillon's Rule). It is a fundamental principle of delegation that a delegatee only has such powers as are delegated to it. In the land use field to date, no sovereign parliament has delegated to local governments the authority to take land without compensation.

In the context of planning and land use control, the basic delegation of actual regulatory power (zoning) is an authority to enact laws to regulate the use of land. In Canada, courts have interpreted this delegation as a power to regulate private land for private uses. To regulate land so that it can only be used for public purposes so as to sterilize its private utility altogether has been interpreted to be beyond the power delegated. Canadian courts have framed this ground of judicial review as one of discerning the intent of the Parliament when delegating such power. They have concluded that if the Parliament had intended that private land could be regulated in a way that exclusively dedicated it to public use, or sterilized it of all use, the Parliament would have to say so in clear and express language. Absent such clear delegation, the courts have defined this excess of jurisdiction as, "bad faith"—namely using the power for a purpose that the legislature never intended it to be used. The effect of a finding of bad faith by a court is the invalidity of the regulation. Land use regulations enacted by delegatees having planning or zoning powers are commonly quashed on such basis. There can be no taking found because such a finding would implicitly admit of an extension of the jurisdiction of the delegatee. If a delegate has no authority to take land, it has no authority to pay compensation for taking.

The matter is qualitatively different where the legislation that over-regulates to the point of sterilization is an Act of the Parliament itself. Such Act is a sovereign act, an exercise of sovereign power and not delegated power. Unless Parliament has over-reached constitutionally, it is not open to a reviewing court to set aside a sovereign act. The role of the court is merely to interpret such legislation. Again if the legislation is ambiguous, the strong presumption in favour of compensation will assert itself as the court grapples with the question of whether there was a legislative, "intent to take without compensation." If a taking is found, and if there is no reason that the presumption in favour of compensation should not operate, then compensation is payable. If the legislation expressly negates compensation, or must necessarily do so by implication, then there will be and could be a regulatory taking without compensation.

F.　Developer Funded Infrastructure

To the extent that growth management includes concerns for funding public infrastructure necessary to sustain growth while maintaining the quality of life and public services expected by the community, public exactions have long been a part of planning and land-use control regulation in Canada. Again, the police power and home rule concept are irrelevant to the Canadian experience. The authority to levy exactions can only arise by direct and express delegation of power from the Province to the local government. No constitutional issues as to the substantive legitimacy of such exactions as takings whether as dedications without compensation or as fees and charges has ever arisen. What constitutional questions have arisen have been division of power issues between the federal power to tax directly and indirectly, and the more limited power of the Provinces to impose direct taxes only. The Provincial delegation of the power to provide for development, exactions and impact fees to local governments even though often clearly likely to be passed on to the consumer (and thus be indirect) have been upheld constitutionally as not being indirect taxes because they are not taxes at all. Rather the court has distinguished them as fees and charges "adhesive to a regulatory scheme." The key distinguishing feature in such context between a tax and a charge/fee being that a charge or fee ought not to raise more revenue than is necessary to fund the specific regulatory purpose. Thus so long as the fees or charges are rationally related to, are calculated on reasonable growth projections, do not rise above the cost of the specific public infrastructure requirements identified by growth projections, and are levied proportionately to burden, they are constitutional and a Province can delegate such authority to local governments.

In British Columbia for instance, impact fees are statutorily authorized for capital recovery of the costs of roads, sewers, water, drainage and parkland. Such charges must be approved by a provincial official, the calculations of cost recovery for public facilities must be based on growth contemplated by the comprehensive plan and the specific calculations themselves and the related public infrastructure on which they are based must be open to the public for inspection. The statute requires that no impact fees can be levied unless the development imposes new capital cost burdens either directly or indirectly, and that the fees and charges must be similar for developments that impose similar general capital burdens on the local government. The Statute requires that the monies collected must be kept in special reserve funds and may only be expended for the purpose for which they were collected. Illegal expenditure of such monies results in disqualification from office of elected officials voting in favour of such improper expenditure, and electors may sue on behalf of the municipal corporation for recovery of illegal expenditures from the elected officials that voted in favour of such expenditure.

Dedication of land for streets, roads and parks without compensation has long been a common feature of subdivisions requirements in Canadian jurisdictions. Provision of school sites is becoming more common. While streets and roads must be dedicated as reasonably necessary—that is, without a fixed limit, it is common by statute that park and school site dedication are capped at a percentage of the area being subdivided. Also, some Provincial legislative schemes provide that developers may provide cash in lieu of land dedication.

G. *Linkage and Mitigation*

As discussed above, impact fees have been formalized by express statutory authority in many Canadian jurisdictions. This allows such impact fees to be imposed and collected as part of the development process (usually either at subdivision or building permit issuance) where the owner has a right to develop under the current plan and land-use regulations. Where an owner has no right to use land for the intended purpose pursuant to the existing land-use regulations, such owner requires a zoning amendment, and at worst both a plan amendment and a zoning amendment. In either case, such acts are legislative and solely at the discretion of the planning and zoning authority. In Canada this will almost always be the elected local government to whom the province has delegated the power to enact bylaws establishing comprehensive plans and regulatory zoning regulations. It is not open to a court in Canada to compel by order the doing of a discretionary legislative act except where a constitutionally protected right is at issue. A court may for innumerable public law reasons, ranging from substantive jurisdictional defects to breach of natural justice (fair procedure) set aside and quash a plan amendment or a zoning amendment, but may not order the plan or the zoning bylaw to be amended. There is no constitutional right to a higher and better use, or to a different use.

To take an example, it may be that a municipal council will not be willing to rezone inner city land for high income condominiums where such rezoning will accelerate and lead to unacceptable depletion of scarce low income rentals and other affordable inner city housing. Barring Provincial legislation to the contrary, the elected council is entitled to take that legislative position forever. In such context, it is common in Canada for landowners to come forward voluntarily and offer to mitigate the impacts of their proposed activities in relation to public interest concerns of the municipal council. Many arrangements of a consensual nature are made and can in jurisdictions such as British Columbia be documented and registered to run with the land by way of statutorily created covenants that do not require the public body to own a dominant tenement, and which can include both positive and negative obligations.

Linkage and mitigation can also be addressed by legislation in several Canadian jurisdictions delegating to local governments to bonus. One example of this in British Columbia is the authority to impose a base density and a sliding density scale in a zone and to thus bonus owners who provide either linkage amenities or mitigation works and services as specified in the density formula.

Chapter 10

CONSTITUTIONAL LIMITATIONS ON LAND USE CONTROLS*

Analysis

I. INTRODUCTION

II. FIFTH AMENDMENT TAKINGS

III. DUE PROCESS AND EQUAL PROTECTION

IV. FIRST AMENDMENT

V. COMMERCE CLAUSE, ANTITRUST, AND WASTE CONTROL

---

* For more detailed discussion and more extensive citations of authority of the issues covered in this chapter, see Juergensmeyer and Roberts, Land Use Planning and Development Regulation Law, Practitioner Treatise Series (3rd ed. 2012).

I.   INTRODUCTION

§ 10:1   Introduction

A.   *The Property Conflict in American Society*

Alexis de Tocqueville found "the love of property" "keener" in the United States than elsewhere, and observed that Americans "display less inclination toward doctrines that in any way threaten the way property is owned."[1] In the context of property in land, this affinity takes different forms, what Fred Bosselman calls multiple land ethics. Likely most prominent is the land ethic of opportunity, the view of land as things, parcels and interests, used to create wealth.[2] However, as Bosselman notes, other land ethics influence Americans' views of property. In tension with the ethic of opportunity is the land ethic of responsibility, which views parcels of property as interdependent parts of an ecological and social whole.[3] These conflicting land ethics result in intense conflict over the extent to which government may affect private property rights for the greater good of society. The battleground for this jurisprudential issue is the constitutional law of land use, not only the Fifth Amendment takings clause, but also guarantees of due process, equal protection, free speech, and religious freedom. Given that property is the oldest branch of the common law, the legal fundamentals of property ownership are surprisingly vague. Any law student would feel much more comfortable defining crime, tort, or contract than property, possession, or ownership.[4] Precise meanings for these property concepts do not in fact exist, and this complicates the resolution of land use conflicts between individual property rights and the social interest. The absence of consistent standards has made the constitutional protection of property susceptible to change, as different social and judicial outlooks have gained power over time. Justice Holmes' statement that "[e]very opinion tends to become a law"[5] has proved especially true concerning constitutional land use issues.

The endpoints on the line of opposing views in this area are a "proacquisitive position," which favors individual wealth, and a "prosocial position," which argues for su-

---

[1] Alexis de Tocqueville, Democracy in America 614 (J. Mayer & M. Lerner, eds.1966).

[2] See Bosselman, Four Land Ethics: Order, Reform, Responsibility, Opportunity, 24 Envtl. L. 1429 (1994).

[3] See Humbach, Law and a New Land Ethic, 74 Minn. L. Rev 339 (1989).

[4] See, generally, Rose, Possession as the Origin of Property, 52 U. Chi. L. Rev. 73 (1985).

[5] *Lochner v. New York,* 198 U.S. 45, 76, 25 S. Ct. 539, 547, 49 L. Ed. 937 (1905) (Holmes, J., dissenting).

premacy of the common good. The proacquisitive position sees the value of land in what it can produce for the individual. Adherents sometimes describe this right as "inherent in human nature" or part of the "natural law." Differences exist among these adherents. Richard Epstein espouses a libertarian position arguing that the Fifth Amendment's just compensation requirement should protect against all government efforts of redistribution of personal or real property.[6] Justice Scalia rejects the libertarian view, favoring a utilitarian approach, and gives enhanced protection to real property over personal and intangible property.[7]

The prosocial position is a manifestation of the social function theory of ownership first popularized as a jurisprudential theory of ownership by Leon Duguit.[8] Under the social function theory, the ownership of property is not absolute or immutable but a changing concept, constantly redefined to permit ownership of property to fill whatever role society assigns it at a given time.[9] The individual has an obligation not to use property in violation of the public right. Economic losses may result, but the value of a parcel of land "has no economic value in the absence of the society around it."[10] As Justice Jackson put it, "not all economic interests are 'property rights'; only those economic advantages are 'rights' which have the law back of them."[11] Private property rights exist because the law says they exist and the law controls because it has coercive power behind it.

The independence and interdependence of land parcels are other lenses through which to view the conflict over property. Some theorists begin with land as independent from society. They divide land into parcels for people to use. As Eric Freyfogle observes, if one views land as a commodity, then property is not the land or "the thing itself, but the owner's power over the thing."[12] So viewed, property "lose[s] its tethers with any particular spot on the landscape [and becomes] an imaginary ideal [where] an owner's legal rights transcen[d] the details of place."[13]

Others see land in an ecologically and socially interdependent context. Wetlands, for example, are part of an ecosystem where they receive the water flowing from uplands, filter pollutants from the water, provide spawning grounds for fish, and prevent downstream floods by slowing water flows. Artificial parceling of adjacent wetlands creates rights in owners that are secondary to the primary natural function. Similarly, a building long a part of a neighborhood may become so much a feature of the built environment that its preservation justifies preventing the owner from leveling it.

Commentators have described these independent and interdependent positions, respectively, as those of a "transformative economy" and an "economy of nature."[14]

---

[6] Richard A. Epstein, Takings: Private Property and the Power of Eminent Domain (1985).

[7] See Bosselman, Four Land Ethics: Order, Reform, Responsibility, Opportunity, 24 Envtl. L. 1429 (1994).

[8] Mirow, The Social Obligation Norm of Property: Duguit, Hayem, and Others, 12 Fla. J. Int'l L. 191 (2010).

[9] See Freyfogle, Context and Accommodation in Modern Property Law, 41 Stan. L. Rev. 1529 (1989).

[10] *Penn Central Transp. Co. v. City of New York,* 42 N.Y.2d 324, 397 N.Y.S.2d 914, 918, 366 N.E.2d 1271 (1977).

[11] *U.S. v. Willow River Power Co.,* 324 U.S. 499, 502, 65 S. Ct. 761, 764, 89 L. Ed. 1101 (1945).

[12] Freyfogle, The Owning and Taking of Sensitive Lands, 43 UCLA L. Rev. 77, 97 (1995).

[13] Id.

[14] Joseph Sax, Property Rights and the Economy of Nature: Understanding Lucas v. South Carolina Coastal Council, 45 Stan. L. Rev. 1433, 1442 (1993).

They contrast anthropocentrism with biocentrism, and natural law with the law of nature. The division can be seen on the Supreme Court as well. Justice Scalia endorsed the former view in *Lucas v. South Carolina Coastal Council* quoting with approval Lord Coke, who said "For what is land but the profits thereof?"[15] Justice Blackmun endorsed the latter view in *Sierra Club v. Morton,* by quoting John Donne: "No man is an Hand, intire of itselfe; every man is a piece of the Continent * * *."[16]

Expectations play an important role in defining property rights, but how expectations are shaped and how they are affected by new learning and changed circumstances is not clear. The history of property law is important in determining expectations of rights in land, but differences of opinion exist over what history shows. Some say that history supports freedom to use land without much in the way of legislative interference.[17] Under this view, landowners may do as they wish with their property limited only by the common law nuisance requirement that they do no harm to others.

Others say that legislative restrictions on land use that went well beyond the common law of nuisance were found with some frequency in colonial and the early post-Revolutionary times.[18] Chief Justice Rehnquist observed that "zoning and permitting regimes are a longstanding feature of state property law,"[19] and must shape a landowner's expectations beyond the limitations of nuisance law.

Whether one view among these several will dominate seems unlikely. The pendulum seems not to swing back and forth between these views but to swirl around the midpoint. Whether one view ought to dominate is a question that proponents of each view should ask themselves. Minimizing public rights may impair our cultural and historical resources and may devastate our natural resources, upsetting critical ecological balances. Minimizing private rights may mean destabilizing investment in land[20] and eroding individual liberties.[21] And yet, maximizing private rights may cause further inequality of wealth. Perhaps, "in a democratic society the existence of multiple ethics must be accepted."[22]

B.   Overview of the Constitutional Issues

The most contentious and difficult constitutional land use issue involves the reach of the Fifth Amendment's provision that private property shall not be "taken for public use without just compensation." This clause is the basis for the regulatory takings doc-

---

[15] *Lucas v. South Carolina Coastal Council,* 505 U.S. 1003, 1017, 112 S. Ct. 2886, 2894, 120 L. Ed. 2d 798 (1992).

[16] *Sierra Club v. Morton,* 405 U.S. 727, 760 n.2, 92 S. Ct. 1361, 1378, 31 L. Ed. 2d 636 (1972) (Blackmun, dissenting).

[17] See Pilon, Property Rights, Takings, and a Free Society, 6 Harv. J.L. & Pub. Pol'y 165 (1983).

[18] See Hart, Land Use Law in the Early Republic and the Original Meaning of the Takings Clause, 94 NW. U. L. Rev. 1099 (2000).

[19] *Tahoe-Sierra Preservation Council, Inc. v. Tahoe Regional Planning Agency,* 535 U.S. 302, 122 S. Ct. 1465, 1494 (2002) (Rehnquist, C.J., dissenting).

[20] Rose, A Dozen Propositions on Private Property, Public Rights, and the New Takings Legislation, 53 Wash. & Lee L. Rev. 265, 297 (1996).

[21] See Ellickson, Liberty, Property, and Environmental Ethics, 21 Ecology L.Q. 397 (1994) urging accommodation.

[22] Bosselman, Four Land Ethics: Order, Reform, Responsibility, Opportunity, 24 Envtl. L. 1429, 1511 (1994).

trine used to identify police power actions affecting property that are the functional equivalent of physical appropriations. The question, as we will see, often becomes one of line drawing under the reasoning of Justice Holmes that "if regulation goes too far it will be recognized as a taking."[23]

Many constitutional land use concerns, however, do not fall on Holmes' Fifth Amendment scale, but implicate the 14th Amendment. Substantive due process looks to the benefits that a regulation confers on society to decide whether the regulation is within the scope of government authority and examines whether its goal is accomplished in a rational manner. Procedural due process oversees the methods of adjudicating rights of landowners, requiring that an opportunity be given to challenge deprivations of property before an impartial decisionmaker. Further, the guarantee of equal protection limits government regulation from irrational classifications, and has the most force when ordinances affect the rights of suspect classes or the exercise of fundamental rights of some in ways different from others.

First Amendment protections of free speech and religion also curtail the power of government to regulate land use. The First Amendment is especially relevant concerning ordinances that regulate signs, sex-oriented businesses, and religious uses.

II. FIFTH AMENDMENT TAKINGS

§ 10:2   Framing the Takings Issue

A.   *Direct v. Indirect Government Actions as Takings*

The Fifth Amendment's requirement that property cannot be taken for a public use without just compensation, applied to the states through the 14th Amendment,[24] is the centerpiece of constitutional land use law. In this Chapter, we deal with when indirect government actions, physical invasions and regulatory impacts, implicate the takings clause. We deal with government initiated condemnation actions in Chapter 16.

The Supreme Court's opinions dealing with the question of when land use regulations constitute takings have not set a clear course and the area has often been depicted as muddled and ad hoc. While it remains ad hoc in its application, it is doctrinally less confusing than it once was. Furthermore, since the takings issue deals with one of the most contentious matters in American society, it is not surprising that the Supreme Court has struggled to establish useful guidelines. If the Court were to establish hard line rules, it is unlikely they would survive our inclination to avoid extremes. The Court's takings law also pays deference to our federal system by recognizing the important role states have in defining property. The complexity of the issue has drawn

---

[23] *Pennsylvania Coal Co. v. Mahon,* 260 U.S. 393, 415, 43 S. Ct. 158, 160, 67 L. Ed. 322 (1922).

[24] The Fifth Amendment's takings clause is today viewed as having been applied to the states through the 14th Amendment in *Chicago, B. & Q.R. Co. v. City of Chicago,* 166 U.S. 226, 17 S. Ct. 581, 41 L. Ed. 979 (1897). *Dolan v. City of Tigard,* 512 U.S. 374, 382, 114 S. Ct. 2309, 2316, 129 L. Ed. 2d 304 (1994). Chicago, B. & Q. R.R., though, does not mention the Fifth Amendment. *Dolan, 512 U.S. at 406, 114 S. Ct. at 2327* (Stevens, J., dissenting).

the attention of many writers and an enormous amount of literature exists addressing what is, or what ought to be, the law.[25]

This part of Chapter 10 focuses primarily on the regulatory takings issue by tracing its path through the major Supreme Court decisions, and then dealing with salient problem areas, such as the meaning of investment-backed expectations, the definition of property for purposes of a takings claim, the remedy available, and rules of ripeness. We treat the related topics of eminent domain, public use, and just compensation in Chapter 16.

The takings issue is concerned with whether, and if so when, the Fifth Amendment requirement that just compensation be paid when the government "takes" property should be applied when the government "regulates" property. The physical connotation of the word "take" argues against applying the clause to regulatory impacts. It also seems to be agreed that the founders intended to require compensation only for physical expropriations of property.[26] Yet, the Court has "not * * * read [the takings clause] literally,"[27] but, over the years, has interpreted the word "take" to include the effect of regulations in some instances. This has given rise to the doctrine of regulatory takings, or, in terms perhaps more familiar to the legal ear, the doctrine of constructive takings.[28]

The touchstone of the Fifth Amendment is to prevent government "from forcing some people to alone bear public burdens which, in all fairness and justice, should be borne by the public as a whole."[29] The touchstone of the regulatory takings doctrine within the Fifth Amendment is "to identify regulatory actions that are functionally equivalent to a direct appropriation of or ouster from private property."[30] Under the doctrine courts must determine when a regulation that is otherwise a valid exercise of the police power should be converted into an exercise of the power of eminent domain. Since the Constitution does not prohibit the taking of property, crossing the line from the police power to the eminent domain power does not invalidate the regulation. Rather, it means that compensation is due.

B. Inverse Condemnation

Aptly named, the action in inverse condemnation is the procedural context in which the regulatory takings issue arises. Direct appropriations under the power of eminent domain occur by condemnation proceedings brought by the state against a property owner. These direct condemnation proceedings establish that the taking is for a public use or purpose and assess just compensation to be paid to the owner. In contrast, the takings issue explored here arises from the consequences of government action with respect to property, unaccompanied by an offer of compensation or an action

---

[25] Two early, influential articles are Michelman, Property, Utility, and Fairness: Comments on the Ethical Foundations of "Just Compensation," 80 Harv. L. Rev. 1165 (1967) and Sax, Takings and the Police Power, 74 Harv. L. Rev. 36 (1964).

[26] See *Lucas v. South Carolina Coastal Council,* 505 U.S. 1003, 1015 n.15, 112 S. Ct. 2886, 2893, 120 L. Ed. 2d 798 (1992).

[27] *Penn Cent. Transp. Co. v. City of New York,* 438 U.S. 104, 142, 98 S. Ct. 2646, 2668, 57 L. Ed. 2d 631 (1978) (Rehnquist, J., dissenting).

[28] Some courts speak of "constructive takings." See, e.g., *R.W. Docks & Slips v. State,* 244 Wis. 2d 497, 628 N.W.2d 781 (2001).

[29] *Armstrong v. United States,* 364 U.S. 40, 49, 80 S. Ct. 1563, 1569, 4 L. Ed. 2d 1554 (1960).

[30] *Lingle v. Chevron U.S.A. Inc.,* 544 U.S. 528, 529, 125 S. Ct. 2074, 161 L. Ed. 2d 876 (2005).

to condemn. When a government dams a river, flooding upstream property, or zones land for open space so that no economically viable use can be made of it, no offer of compensation precedes the act. An owner who thinks the action has effected a taking and that compensation ought to be paid has the burden to initiate suit against the government.

C. Judicial Takings

There is some support for the proposition that judicial decisions can take property within the meaning of the Fifth Amendment.[31] No court has so held,[32] but a plurality of Supreme Court justices support the premise. In *Stop the Beach Renourishment Inc. v. Florida Dept. of Environmental* Protection,[33] the Court addressed, but did not decide, the question. In that case, property owners contended that the Florida Supreme Court had taken their property by construing the state's statutory and common law in such a way as to abolish a well established property right. The US Supreme Court found that the Florida court had not done so, but in dicta, a plurality of justices said that the Fifth Amendment is "concerned simply with the act, and not with the governmental actor . . . [and that it] would be absurd to allow a State to do by judicial decree what the Takings Clause forbids it to do by legislative fiat."[34] Justice Kennedy disagreed. In concurring, he opined that only the executive and legislative branches had the power to make the policy decisions as to when the state should spend its money. "[T]hese are matters for the political branches-the legislature and the executive-not the courts. Courts, unlike the executive or legislature, are not designed to make policy decisions about 'the need for, and likely effectiveness of, regulatory actions.'"[35] Justice Kennedy went on to suggest that a judicial decision that eliminated an established property right could violate due process. Two differences that flow from the approaches include the deference given to state court decisions and the remedy.[36]

§ 10:3 Physical Invasions as Takings

A. The Loretto Per Se Test

Governmentally induced physical invasions trigger special concern since the Court treats the right to exclude as the paramount property right.[37] The fact that land was invaded has been critical in numerous cases where takings have been found, such as where a government dam caused flooding of upstream property,[38] where military planes engaged in frequent, low-level flights over land wreaking havoc with the chicken farm below,[39] and where the government required the owner of a pond, which had

---

[31] See Echeverria, Stop the Beach Renourishment: Why the Judiciary Is Different, 35 Vt. L. Rev. 475, 482–83 (2010); Barros, The Complexities of Judicial Takings, 45 U. Rich. L. Rev. 903, 955 (2011).

[32] See *Burton v. American Cyanamid Co.*, 775 F. Supp. 2d 1093, 1099 (E.D. Wis. 2011). See also Blumm and Dawson, The Florida Beach Case and the Road to Judicial Takings, 35 Wm. & Mary Envtl. L. & Pol'y Rev. 713, 770 (2011).

[33] *Stop the Beach Renourishment, Inc. v. Florida Dept. of Environmental Protection,* 130 S. Ct. 2592, 177 L. Ed. 2d 184 (2010).

[34] 130 S. Ct. at 2601. See Byrne, Stop the Stop the Beach Plurality!, 38 Ecology L.Q. 619 (2011).

[35] 130 S. Ct. at 2613.

[36] See infra §§ 10:6 and 10:9.

[37] See *Kaiser Aetna v. U. S.,* 444 U.S. 164, 176, 100 S. Ct. 383, 391, 62 L. Ed. 2d 332 (1979).

[38] *Pumpelly v. Green Bay & Mississippi Canal Co.,* 80 U.S. 166, 20 L. Ed. 557 (1871).

[39] *U.S. v. Causby,* 328 U.S. 256, 66 S. Ct. 1062, 90 L. Ed. 1206 (1946).

been made navigable by dredging, to allow entry to the boating public.[40] While the vast majority of cases relevant to land use law involve non-invasive regulations, regulations do sometimes result in physical invasions. For example, subdivision approvals that call for developers to provide land to be used for streets, parks, sidewalks, and schools may implicate the physical takings doctrine.

In *Loretto v. Teleprompter Manhattan CATV Corp.,*[41] the Court established a per se takings test for physical invasions. The City of New York required lessors of residential property to permit the installation of cable television facilities on their buildings. When a cable company installed a metal box on the roof of Loretto's apartment building and ran cable wires down its side, Loretto alleged a taking had occurred. The intrusion was minor. The boxes were small, the wires thin, and neither interfered with Loretto's use of her property. Nonetheless, the Court held that a permanent physical occupation of property by a third party pursuant to state authority is a taking, regardless of the scope or economic impact of the intrusion. Noting that the right to exclude is "one of the most treasured strands in an owner's bundle of property rights,"[42] the Court held that the fact that a permanent invasion has occurred is determinative. The strength of the public interest and the overall impact on the property's value are not relevant.

Labeling its ruling "narrow,"[43] the *Loretto* Court exempted temporary physical invasions from its per se test, using two cases decided shortly before *Loretto* as examples where the per se test was not applicable. In *Kaiser Aetna v. United States,*[44] the government imposed a navigational servitude on a once non-navigable pond made navigable with government permission. The servitude allowed public use of the pond. Noting the physical character of the invasion, albeit temporary, and the property owner's expectations of private use, on balance the Court found a taking. In *PruneYard Shopping Center v. Robins,*[45] no taking was found where state law required shopping center owners to allow third parties to exercise speech and petitioning rights. The Court found the invasion was temporary and limited in nature and that it did not seriously interfere with the owner's expectations.[46]

In *Nollan v. California Coastal Commission,*[47] the Court expanded the definition of permanent for purposes of the per se *Loretto* rule. There, the state coastal commission required the Nollans to deed an easement allowing the public to walk along the beachfront side of their ocean lot in return for permission to build a larger house. At first blush, *Loretto* appeared inapplicable since the invasion was not a permanent occupation. The Court, nonetheless, found *Loretto* applied. While acknowledged that the easement did not allow people permanently to station themselves on the land, it said a classic right of way easement to pass back and forth is permanent for purposes of the rule of *Loretto*.

---

[40] *Kaiser Aetna v. U. S.,* 444 U.S. 164, 176, 100 S. Ct. 383, 391, 62 L. Ed. 2d 332 (1979).

[41] *Loretto v. Teleprompter Manhattan CATV Corp.,* 458 U.S. 419, 102 S. Ct. 3164, 73 L. Ed. 2d 868 (1982).

[42] Loretto, 458 U.S. 419., quoting from *Kaiser Aetna, 444 U.S. at 179–180, 100 S. Ct. at 393.*

[43] 458 U.S. at 441, 102 S. Ct. at 3179.

[44] *Kaiser Aetna v. U. S.,* 444 U.S. 164, 100 S. Ct. 383, 62 L. Ed. 2d 332 (1979).

[45] *PruneYard Shopping Center v. Robins,* 447 U.S. 74, 100 S. Ct. 2035, 64 L. Ed. 2d 741 (1980).

[46] If an invasion is not permanent, the *Penn Central* test controls. See discussion infra § 10:6.

[47] *Nollan v. California Coastal Com'n,* 483 U.S. 825, 107 S. Ct. 3141, 97 L. Ed. 2d 677 (1987).

A second aspect of *Nollan* acknowledged an exception to *Loretto* of great significance to land use regulations. Interpreted literally, *Loretto* raised the specter that conditions imposed in the permitting process that resulted in physical occupations, such as subdivision exactions of land for schools or roads, were per se takings. A straightforward application of the *Loretto* per se rule would have meant that a taking had occurred in *Nollan* without further inquiry, but the Court said that requiring the easement as a condition for issuing a land use permit would avoid the conclusion that a taking had occurred if the state could show that a nexus existed between the effects of the landowner's proposed development and the land that was being exacted for easement use.[48] The nexus was found wanting in *Nollan,* but the principle rescued many land use controls.[49]

The narrow nature of the *Loretto* per se test was confirmed by the Court in *Yee v. City of Escondido.*[50] There, the combination of state landlord-tenant law and a local rent control ordinance gave mobile home tenants the right to continue to occupy the land on which their homes sat at below market rents for so long as the terms of their leases were met and the landlord continued to use the land for rental purposes. Some lower courts had held these types of controls to be physical takings, but in *Yee* the Supreme Court disagreed and refused to give *Loretto* an expansive reading. "[R]equired acquiescence" of an owner was necessary to invoke the per se test and that was not present in *Yee* where the lessors had voluntarily opened their land to the lessees. Furthermore, the lessors were not required to rent in perpetuity. They could terminate the leases by changing the use.[51]

B.   Non-Trespassory Invasions

Harm from a government operation that is nuisance-like, but does not result in a physical invasion, generally is not found to be a taking. For example, in cases where noise from airplane overflights caused harm to the use of the land below, a critical fact for the courts has been that the noise invaded the land from above. The Supreme Court found a taking in such a case in *United States v. Causby.*[52] Though the *Causby* opinion used nuisance language to describe the harm suffered, lower courts have seized on the fact that *Causby* involved overflights to deny compensation in cases where the noise came from adjacent land.[53]

Non-trespassory harm may be a taking if the harm is peculiar to the land, and not community wide in nature. In *Richards v. Washington Terminal Co.,*[54] a landowner complained of injury from smoke, dust, cinders, and gases emitted from an adjoining railroad. To the extent that the invasions were indirect or the harm general, the Court found no taking. The burden suffered was one shared in common with the community

---

[48] See further discussion of the nexus test infra § 10:5.

[49] See, e.g., *Sparks v. Douglas County,* 127 Wash. 2d 901, 904 P.2d 738 (1995).

[50] *Yee v. City of Escondido, Cal.,* 503 U.S. 519, 112 S. Ct. 1522, 118 L. Ed. 2d 153 (1992).

[51] Lower courts have, for the most part, adhered to a narrow reading of *Loretto. See, e.g., Herzberg v. County of Plumas,* 133 Cal. App. 4th 1, 34 Cal. Rptr. 3d 588 (2005); *Tuthill Ranch, Inc. v. U.S.,* 381 F.3d 1132 (Fed. Cir. 2004); *Kingsway Cathedral v. Iowa Dept. of Transp.,* 711 N.W.2d 6 (Iowa 2006); *CRV Enterprises, Inc. v. U.S.,* 626 F.3d 1241 (Fed. Cir. 2010). But see *Casitas Mun. Water Dist. v. U.S.,* 543 F.3d 1276, 1294 (Fed. Cir. 2008).

[52] *U.S. v. Causby,* 328 U.S. 256, 66 S. Ct. 1062, 90 L. Ed. 1206 (1946).

[53] *Batten v. U. S.,* 306 F.2d 580 (10th Cir. 1962); *Branning v. U. S.,* 228 Ct. Cl. 240, 654 F.2d 88 (1981).

[54] *Richards v. Washington Terminal Co.,* 233 U.S. 546, 34 S. Ct. 654, 58 L. Ed. 1088 (1914).

and not compensable. However, a taking was found with respect to harm suffered from a tunnel built by the railroad next to plaintiff's property, which used a fanning system that forced the gases and dust collected in the tunnel directly onto plaintiffs land.

An injured landowner unable to show a taking may have an action in tort.[55] Where vibrations from a highway construction project damaged a building to the point where it was not economically feasible to repair it, the Iowa supreme court held there was no taking.[56] The court recognized that a permanent invasion could create a servitude that would constitute a taking, but the activity creating the vibrations was temporary in nature. Still, the landowner, the court said, could sue in tort.

Some state courts, relying on state constitutions, find takings in a wider range of instances involving non-trespassory invasions than is true under the federal constitution. In large part this is based on provisions contained in nearly one-half of the states' constitutions that require compensation where land is "taken or damaged."[57] In *Thornburg v. Port of Portland,* for example, the court found a taking where airport noise came from adjacent land rather than from above.[58]

§ 10:4   Regulatory Impacts as Takings

A.   *The Early Cases: Mugler and Pennsylvania Coal*

In the 1887 decision of *Mugler v. Kansas,*[59] the Supreme Court rejected the idea that an improper or excessive use of the police power became a taking. In *Mugler,* a state alcohol prohibition law rendered a brewery practically worthless. When the brewery owner argued that his property had been taken and that he should receive compensation, the Court labeled the argument an "inadmissible"[60] interpretation of the constitution. The view of the *Mugler* Court was that regulations under the police power were not burdened by a requirement of compensation. Rather, they were to be reviewed solely under the substantive due process standard that required the Court to uphold a law if it promoted a legitimate public end in a rational way. If the test was met, that was the end of the matter.

The Court's expansion of the takings clause to include regulations is generally viewed as having arisen in the 1922 decision, *Pennsylvania Coal v. Mahon.*[61] A Pennsylvania statute prohibited mining beneath residential areas in such a way as to cause mine subsidence. Subsidence or cave-ins from mining were common throughout the Pennsylvania anthracite coal region, and had led to numerous deaths and widespread property damage. When a coal company announced its intention to mine under the Mahons' house, they sought an injunction. The coal company claimed that the statute was an unconstitutional taking of mineral rights since the statute effectively prohibited it from excavating the coal that the company had expressly reserved to itself in conveying the land to the Mahons' predecessor in title.

---

[55] *Hansen v. U.S.,* 65 Fed. Cl. 76 (2005) (exploring the overlap between a tort and a taking).

[56] *Kingsway Cathedral v. Iowa Dept. Of Transp.,* 711 N.W.2d 6 (Iowa 2006).

[57] See *Felts v. Harris County,* 915 S.W.2d 482, 484 n.4 (Tex. 1996) (listing 22 states in addition to Texas with such damage language).

[58] *Thornburg v. Port of Portland,* 244 Or. 69, 415 P.2d 750 (1966).

[59] *Mugler v. Kansas,* 123 U.S. 623, 8 S. Ct. 273, 31 L. Ed. 205 (1887).

[60] Mugler 123 U.S at 664, 8 S. Ct. at 298.

[61] *Pennsylvania Coal Co. v. Mahon,* 260 U.S. 393, 43 S. Ct. 158, 67 L. Ed. 322 (1922).

The Court agreed with the coal company. The majority opinion, written by Justice Holmes, showed the strong influence of its author's pragmatic view of private contract law: that contracts, and by extension the mineral rights that the coal company had reserved, are legal duties inextricably bound up with "the consequences of [their] breach."[62] To Holmes, contracts were legal relationships in which a party had simply but inextricably agreed either to perform or "suffer in this way or that by judgment of the court."[63] With this outlook, the Fifth Amendment takings issue resolved itself. Holmes considered the issue a "question of degree,"[64] and warned that "[w]e are in danger of forgetting that a strong public desire to improve the public condition is not enough to warrant achieving the desire by a shorter cut than the constitutional way of paying for the change."[65] The famous, or perhaps infamous, test he established was that "while property may be regulated to a certain extent, if regulation goes too far it will be recognized as a taking."[66] In this case the statute went too far since it made it commercially impracticable to mine certain coal that had been expressly reserved by contract to advance a purpose that Holmes regarded as predominantly private in nature.

Pennsylvania Coal left numerous problems in its wake. The generality of the "too far" test was one. Diminution in value, Holmes said, was one factor to be used to determine how far a regulation could go. However, it was not clear what the diminution was in *Pennsylvania Coal*. The Court also did not say what factors other than diminution in value are relevant. Holmes also did not cite, much less discuss, *Mugler,* leaving its validity unclear, and likely extending its life. In dissent, Justice Brandeis made it clear that he regarded *Mugler* as inconsistent with the Court's holding,[67] and *Mugler* has been cited favorably in some subsequent court opinions.

Some authors have suggested that *Pennsylvania Coal* was simply wrongly decided.[68] Others have argued that the decision does not rest on the takings clause but on substantive due process grounds, and that it only uses its takings language metaphorically.[69] Lending support to the argument that *Pennsylvania Coal* was a due process case is the fact that compensation, the mandated remedy of the Fifth Amendment, was neither sought nor awarded, and with good reason: the state was not a party to the case. Since both litigants were private, the entire discussion of the Fifth Amendment takings clause, some suggest, may be regarded as dictum.[70] Even treating the case as a taking, the issue of the appropriate remedy for a regulatory taking was left hanging for decades.[71]

These uncertainties over *Pennsylvania Coal* explain the references to "so-called regulatory takings" prevalent in opinions and articles. The confusion stems in large

---

[62] Holmes, The Path of the Law, 10 Harv. L. Rev. 457, 458 (1897).

[63] Holmes, The Path of the Law, 10 Harv. L. Rev. 457, 458 (1897).

[64] *Pennsylvania Coal,* 260 U.S. at 415, 43 S. Ct. at 160.

[65] Pennsylvania Coal, 260 U.S. at 416, 43 S. Ct. at 160.

[66] Pennsylvania Coal, 260 U.S. at 416, 43 S. Ct. at 160.

[67] 260 U.S. at 418, 43 S. Ct. at 161.

[68] See Byrne, Ten Arguments for the Abolition of the Regulatory Takings Doctrine, 22 Ecology L.Q. 89 (1995).

[69] See Williams, Jr., Smith, Siemon, Mandelker and Babcock, The White River Junctions Manifesto, 9 Vt. L. Rev. 193, 208–14 (1984).

[70] Id., at 209–10.

[71] See infra § 10:9.

part from the striking similarity of the takings test to the substantive due process test.[72] While the due process test applied in *Mugler* did not consider the degree of loss suffered by the property owner to be relevant, that factor worked its way into the Court's later statements of the rule. In the 1894 decision of *Lawton v. Steele,* for example, the Court said the validity of a police power regulation depends on whether the measure promotes the public interest by a means reasonably necessary to accomplish the purpose, which "is not unduly oppressive upon individuals."[73] The subsequent *Pennsylvania Coal* decision restated the *Lawton* substantive due process test in takings language. The result has been a confusion of tongues and minds.[74] Determining whether courts have used, or ought to use, substantive due process or the takings clause to adjudicate disputes over allegedly excessive land use controls was long debated.[75] It is now settled: excessive police power measures affecting property rights are actionable under the Fifth Amendment takings clause.

The view of the 1920s Court with respect to the questions surrounding the regulatory takings doctrine of *Pennsylvania Coal* is difficult to judge since, in the years shortly after the case, the Court ignored it in several important decisions, preferring to deal with alleged regulatory excesses as substantive due process matters. A few years after *Pennsylvania Coal* the Court decided the landmark case of *Village of Euclid v. Ambler Realty Co.,*[76] holding that zoning on its face did not violate the substantive due process guarantee to be free from arbitrary state action. Though the opinion echoed Holmes' idea that the validity of police power measures involve questions of degree, saying that "[t]he line which in this field separates the legitimate from the illegitimate assumption of power is not capable of precise delimitation,"[77] it cited neither the takings clause nor *Pennsylvania Coal.*

Two years after *Euclid* the Court decided another land use case, again failing to cite *Pennsylvania Coal.* In *Nectow v. City of Cambridge,*[78] the Court looked at zoning as applied to a particular tract, and found it invalid on due process grounds. The Court held that the zoning of the tract for residential use did not, under the circumstances, promote the public interest.[79] Despite the lack of reference to the Fifth Amendment in the *Euclid* and *Nectow* opinions, on occasion, the Court has loosely referred to them as takings cases, further confusing the line between substantive due process and takings.[80] Some confusion occasionally appears in judicial decisions, yet it ought not. The Court has definitively held that claims of excessive regulation are cognizable under the Fifth Amendment.[81]

---

[72] This issue is dealt with also infra § 10:12.

[73] *Lawton v. Steele,* 152 U.S. 133, 137, 14 S. Ct. 499, 501, 38 L. Ed. 385 (1894).

[74] See *Metromedia, Inc. v. City of San Diego,* 453 U.S. 490, 498 n.7, 101 S. Ct. 2882, 2887, 69 L. Ed. 2d 800 (1981).

[75] See infra § 10:12.

[76] *Village of Euclid, Ohio v. Ambler Realty Co.,* 272 U.S. 365, 47 S. Ct. 114, 71 L. Ed. 303 (1926).

[77] 272 U.S. at 387, 47 S. Ct. at 118.

[78] *Nectow v. City of Cambridge,* 277 U.S. 183, 48 S. Ct. 447, 72 L. Ed. 842 (1928).

[79] City of Cambridge, 277 U.S. at 188, 48 S. Ct. at 448. See infra § 10:12.

[80] *Penn Cent. Transp. Co. v. City of New York,* 438 U.S. 104, 131, 98 S. Ct. 2646, 2662, 57 L. Ed. 2d 631 (1978).

[81] *First English Evangelical Lutheran Church of Glendale v. Los Angeles County, Cal.,* 482 U.S. 304, 107 S. Ct. 2378, 96 L. Ed. 2d 250 (1987).

B.   The Modern Era: Penn Central, Agins, and Lingle

The next important regulatory takings decision, *Penn Central Transportation Co. v. New York City,*[82] came in 1978, more than 50 years after *Pennsylvania Coal.* New York City declared Grand Central Station an historic landmark, requiring the owner to seek municipal permission to make changes in the structure. After the designation, Penn Central leased the airspace above the station to a developer who planned to build a 55-story office complex. When the railroad and its lessees sought a certificate of appropriateness from the city's landmark commission, permission was denied with the uncharitable characterization that the proposed tower was an "aesthetic joke." The railroad claimed its inability to build in the airspace was a taking.

The Court admitted that the takings issue was "a problem of considerable difficulty," and that there was no "'set formula' for determining when 'justice and fairness' require that economic injuries caused by public action be compensated by the government, rather than remain disproportionately concentrated on a few persons."[83] While the Court admitted the test involved "essentially ad hoc, factual inquiries," it attempted to be more concrete in its analysis than Holmes had been in *Pennsylvania Coal.* It listed three factors for consideration: (1) the economic impact on the claimant, (2) the extent to which the regulation interfered with investment-backed expectations, and (3) the character or extent of the government action.

In weighing these factors, the Court held that the landmarking did not effect a taking because it left the station exactly as it had been, it did not amount to a physical invasion of the property, and it did not interfere with the original investment-backed expectations of the owners. The railroad argued a total loss of use had occurred by focusing on the airspace alone. The Court, however, said the relevant measure was the whole parcel, and with respect to it, the record showed that the railroad was able to earn a reasonable return under its present use. The Court also said there was no proof of loss of all airspace. A smaller tower might be approved, and the transferable development rights available to the station owner mitigated the loss.

While *Penn Central's* ad hoc test can be faulted for lack of precision and predictability, the Court unnecessarily made matters worse in *Agins v. City of Tiburon,*[84] where it held that an ordinance designed to preserve open space did not constitute a facial taking of five acres of unimproved land by limiting the owner to building from one to five houses. The difficulty with *Agins* was not its result, which is easy to understand since the owners, not having submitted a plan for approval, made no showing that they suffered any significant loss. The problem with *Agins* was that in its general statement of takings principles, the Court, without acknowledging and apparently not realizing it, moved the substantive due process test of *Nectow* and *Euclid* into the Fifth Amendment, saying that "[t]he application of a general zoning law to particular property effects a taking if the ordinance does not substantially advance legitimate state interests [citing *Nectow*], or denies an owner economically viable use of his land [citing *Penn Central*]."[85] Digging the hole even deeper, the Court added that "[a]lthough no precise

---

[82] *Penn Cent. Transp. Co. v. City of New York,* 438 U.S. 104, 98 S. Ct. 2646, 57 L. Ed. 2d 631 (1978).

[83] 438 U.S. at 124, 98 S. Ct. at 2659.

[84] *Agins v. City of Tiburon,* 447 U.S. 255, 100 S. Ct. 2138, 65 L. Ed. 2d 106 (1980) (overruled by, Lingle v. Chevron U.S.A. Inc., 544 U.S. 528, 125 S. Ct. 2074, 161 L. Ed. 2d 876 (2005)).

[85] 447 U.S. at 260, 100 S. Ct. at 2141.

rule determines when property has been taken * * *, the question necessarily requires a weighing of private and public interests."[86] With *Agins,* the Court's regulatory takings doctrine truly earned the sobriquet of muddled.

A major course correction occurred in 2005, when the Court overruled *Agins* in the unanimous decision of *Lingle v. Chevron, USA, Inc.*[87] In a refreshingly frank opinion, the Court admitted what critics had long contended, that the "substantially advances. . . formula prescribes an inquiry in the nature of a due process, not a takings, test, and that it has no proper place in our takings jurisprudence."[88] The *Agins'* "substantially advances" means-end formula, said the Court, addresses a question that is a condition precedent to a takings claim, which is whether a regulation is effective in achieving a legitimate goal. If a law fails to promote a legitimate end, as was true for example in *Nectow,* it is invalid and it makes no sense to proceed to discuss whether compensation is due under the Fifth Amendment.

The "substantially advances" test does not answer the question of whether the regulation forces the property owner "alone [to] bear public burdens which, in all fairness and justice, should be borne by the public as a whole."[89] A law could easily pass due process muster by substantially advancing a legitimate state interest, and yet unfairly make a landowner suffer the burden. Thus, the *Lingle* Court reasoned that it "reveals nothing about the magnitude or character of the burden a particular regulation imposes upon private property rights. Nor does it provide any information about how any regulatory burden is distributed among property owners."[90] *Lingle's* importance lies in the doctrinal clarity it brings to the takings issue. It eliminates, or should eliminate, the confusion between due process and takings that has existed since the 1922 *Pennsylvania Coal* decision.

C.   The Takings Tests

Lingle lays out an analytic framework to assess a potential takings claim. Assuming one can establish a constitutionally protected property interest, a takings claim must fall into one of three categories: (1) a physical takings claim under the *Loretto* doctrine, with an exception for legitimate land exactions imposed as conditions for development permission under *Nollan,*[91] (2) a regulatory takings claim under *Lucas,* requiring compensation for a total loss of economic value, unless excepted by background principles of property or nuisance law, or, (3), when the economic impact is less than total, a regulatory takings claim under *Penn Central.* These tests "share a common touchstone," the Court says, which is "to identify regulatory actions that are functionally equivalent to a direct appropriation of or ouster from private property."[92]

It has become common for courts and commentators to refer to the *Nollan-Dolan* doctrine as constituting an independent category of takings claims. *Lingle* also lists it as a separate test, and in its closing remarks, the Court refers to "a land-use exaction

---

[86] 447 U.S. 255, 260, 100 S. Ct. 2138, 2141, 65 L. Ed. 2d 106 (1980).

[87] *Lingle v. Chevron U.S.A. Inc.,* 544 U.S. 528, 125 S. Ct. 2074, 161 L. Ed. 2d 876 (2005).

[88] *Lingle,* 544 U.S. at 540, 125 S. Ct. at 2083.

[89] *Armstrong v. United States,* 364 U.S. 40, 49, 80 S. Ct. 1563, 4 L. Ed. 2d 1554 (1960).

[90] *Lingle,* 544 U.S. at 542, 125 S. Ct. at 2084.

[91] The Court spoke of four tests. As we explain below, one of the four was the *Nollan* exactions test, which we think is better viewed as a defense to a *Loretto* permanent physical occupation claim.

[92] Lingle, 544 U.S. at 548, 125 S. Ct. at 2087.

violating the standards set forth in *Nollan* and *Dolan.*"[93] The exactions problem, however, cannot stand alone. The opinion makes clear that the genesis of *Nollan* (and its sequel *Dolan)* was an affirmative defense to a per se physical takings claim, and, for that reason, we list it as an exception to the *Loretto* test. In its analysis of *Nollan* and *Dolan,* the *Lingle* Court noted that in both cases "the Court began with the premise that, had the government simply appropriated the easement in question, this would have been a per se physical taking."[94] The physical invasion is the taking, but the government's justification, if it meets the *Nollan* nexus, excuses the government from paying compensation.

The question of the standard of review the Court uses in regulatory takings claims is in a confused state because of the Court's *pre-Lingle* injection of due process considerations into the takings equation. In applying the *Penn Central* ad hoc test, the Court has used a deferential standard of review. This was true in *Penn Central* itself, where the Court deferred to New York City's goal of protecting historic landmarks and its method of achieving that goal and in *Agins,* where the Court accepted at face value the city's goal to preserve open space. Later in *Keystone,* the Court deferred to Pennsylvania's method of controlling surface subsidence from coal mining. Those cases, however, all involved the use of due process factors as part of the takings test. With *Lingle,* reviewing the means and ends of government action is no longer proper in a takings claim.

In an inverse condemnation action, the plaintiff accepts the validity of the government action and must show that the burden of the action falls disproportionately on her. The issue of deference to legislative action does not arise. It is the court's job to determine what the burden is and whether it is too severe in its impact on the plaintiff.

Intermediate scrutiny is used in a takings suit when the government attempts to show its action, which would otherwise be a per se taking under *Loretto* or *Lucas,* is exempt from the command to pay compensation. In these cases, the burden is placed on the state to satisfy the nexus defense to physical exactions under *Nollan.*[95] In a *Lucas* categorical taking case, once the plaintiff establishes a total economic loss, the burden switches to the government to show its regulation is justified under background principles of state property or nuisance law.[96] Though the *Lucas* Court did not speak in terms of levels of scrutiny, the switching of the burden and the Court's admonition that the state court provide an "objectively reasonable application of relevant precedents"[97] demonstrates that deference is not appropriate.

§ 10:5   Exactions: *Nollan* and *Dolan* Tests

Certain permanent physical occupations that would be takings under the *Loretto* doctrine [98] may be excused if the state can show that the land exaction is a condition for the granting of development permission and that, qualitatively and quantitatively, the exaction is reasonably necessary to prevent or counteract anticipated adverse pub-

---

[93] Lingle, 544 U.S. at 548, 125 S. Ct. at 2087.

[94] Lingle, 544 U.S.at 546, 125 S. Ct. at 2086.

[95] See infra § 10:5.

[96] See infra § 10:6.

[97] See *Lucas, 505 U.S. at 1032, n.28.*

[98] *Loretto v. Teleprompter Manhattan CATV Corp.,* 458 U.S. 419, 102 S. Ct. 3164, 73 L. Ed. 2d 868 (1982).

lic effects of the proposed development. The leading case is *Nollan v. California Coastal Commission*,[99] where the Court ostensibly applied the now defunct "substantially advances" test of *Agins v. City of Tiburon*.[100] Though *Agins* is dead, the rule of *Nollan* is alive and well, but we find a close reading suggests it lives on only as an exception to *Loretto's* physical takings test.[101] However, others continue to press the argument that *Lingle* and *Nollan* affirmed or created a separate takings test of much broader reach.[102]

When the Nollans, owners of a beachfront lot, sought permission to build a larger house, the state coastal commission conditioned the permit on the granting of an easement to allow the public to walk along the beachfront side of the lot. The state-asserted interest was to protect the public's ability to see the beach from the street, to prevent congestion on the beach, and to overcome psychological barriers to the use of the beach resulting from increased shoreline development. The Court had no quarrel with the legitimacy of the state's goals, but disagreed that the lateral access easement along the beachfront would promote them. Stressing the word "substantially" in the *Agins* formula, the Court employed heightened scrutiny and found the interests asserted by the state would not have been substantially advanced by the easement sought. *Nollan's* articulation of the *Agins* "substantially advances" test insisted that when the state conditions development permission on the owner dedicating property to public use it may only do so without paying compensation if there is a nexus between the land to be taken and the anticipated adverse public effects of the proposed development. The word "substantially" was given emphasis by the Court to make it clear that low-level, rational basis scrutiny is insufficient to test the strength of the nexus.

Even if a causal connection between the adverse impact of the development project and the condition is established, it still must be shown that the amount exacted is proportional to the anticipated impact of the development. That issue was dealt with in *Dolan v. City of Tigard*[103] where the owner of a plumbing and electric supply store sought a permit to double the store's size and pave the parking lot. For flood control reasons, the city required the owner to convey to it an affirmative easement on the portion of her lot lying within the 100-year floodplain adjacent to a creek and an easement on an additional 15-foot strip of land for a pedestrian and bicycle path. The two requirements amounted to approximately 10% of Dolan's property.

The *Dolan* Court held that once the *Nollan* nexus test is met, the state must show that the extent of the exaction is proportional. The *Dolan* Court agreed that the paving of the parking lot would increase stormwater runoff and exacerbate flooding problems, justifying the city in requiring some mitigation response by the owner. However, it was not clear to the Court why the city asked for an easement permitting the public to use Dolan's floodplain land. Physical access by the public generally was not necessary to control flooding. The Court agreed that the store's expansion might lead to more traffic, so that asking the owner to help the city cope with traffic problems made sense. Yet, the city had only found that the pedestrian/bicycle pathway *could offset* this increased demand. That was not good enough for the Court. The city needed to quantify the traf-

---

[99] *Nollan v. California Coastal Com'n,* 483 U.S. 825, 107 S. Ct. 3141, 97 L. Ed. 2d 677 (1987).

[100] See discussion supra § 10:4.

[101] See the discussion of *Lingle,* supra § 10:4.

[102] See discussion infra § 10:9.

[103] *Dolan v. City of Tigard,* 512 U.S. 374, 114 S. Ct. 2309, 129 L. Ed. 2d 304 (1994).

fic increase, at least in some general way, to show that the pathway *would offset* some of the traffic.

Dolan adopted what it called a rule of "rough proportionality" to set "outer limits" as to how a city may achieve what the Court called the "commendable task of land use planning."[104] While the burden is on the government to show a degree of connection, the Court did not demand a "precise mathematical calculation, but [rather] some sort of individualized determination that the required dedication is related both in nature and extent to the impact of the proposed development."[105] Though *Dolan's* phrasing of "rough proportionality" was new, the Court acknowledged that its test is the same as the dedication test followed by the vast majority of state courts.

In overruling *Agins,* the *Lingle* Court retained the holdings of *Nollan* and *Dolan* but disclaimed the "substantially advances" rationale used in those opinions. While recognizing that "it might be argued that [the *Agins]* formula played a role in [those] decisions * * *, the rule those decisions established is entirely distinct"[106] from *Agins'* "substantially advances" test. Rather, the Court says, those cases "involved dedications of property so onerous that, outside the exactions context, they would be deemed per se physical takings"[107] under the *Loretto* doctrine. Thus, whether an exaction is justified, and thus exempt from *Loretto's* per se takings rule, depends on whether the exaction is a condition for the granting of development permission and that, qualitatively and quantitatively, the exaction is reasonably necessary to prevent or counteract anticipated adverse public effects of the proposed development.

A number of courts have addressed whether *Nollan* and *Dolan's* intermediate scrutiny takings test should be extended to regulations that do not cause physical invasions, such as impact fees, with the majority holding in the negative.[108] Prior to Lingle, lower courts differed on the question. By tying *Nollan/Dolan* to *Loretto* and in disclaiming use of the "substantially advances test" to explain them, *Lingle* appears to answer that question in the negative.[109] Without a threatened physical invasion, there is nothing to trigger *Loretto,* and no need for the government to raise the *Nollan-Dolan* nexus defenses. One commentator criticizes the Court's focus on physical invasions as a "technicality in a modern world where value is fungible and economic considerations dominate our thinking."[110] Yet, the Court remains committed to the idea that the right to exclude is, as Justice O'Connor says in *Lingle,* perhaps the most fundamental of all property interests.[111]

A second reason that monetary charges do not raise takings issues is that nothing is taken for which the state could pay just compensation. As one court said, "applying the Takings Clause to regulations that merely require the payment of money is like saying the government can take money, but only if it pays it back. It is far more logical

---

[104] Dolan, 512 U.S. at 395, 114 S. Ct. at 2322.

[105] Dolan, 512 U.S. at 395, 114 S. Ct. at 2322.

[106] *Lingle,* 544 U.S. at 547, 125 S. Ct. at 2086.

[107] Lingle, 544 U.S. at 547, 125 S. Ct. at 2087.

[108] Finding *Nollan/Dolan* applicable to non-possessory exactions, see, e.g., *Home Builders Ass'n of Dayton & the Miami Valley v. Beavercreek,* 89 Ohio St. 3d 121, 729 N.E.2d 349 (2000); *Ehrlich v. City of Culver City,* 12 Cal. 4th 854, 50 Cal. Rptr. 2d 242, 911 P.2d 429 (1996).

[109] See *St. Johns River Water Management Dist. v. Koontz,* 77 So. 3d 1220 (Fla. 2011).

[110] Nelson, Lingle v. Chevron USA, Inc., 20 Harv. Envtl. L. Rev. 281, 290 (2006).

[111] See discussion supra § 10:3.

to conclude that a regulation of this sort"[112] violates due process by employing an irrational means and declare the fee void, than to let the government "take" the money and then require it to "pay" the money as compensation.[113]

Nollan and *Dolan* arose in adjudicatory settings, and the courts have grappled with whether the doctrine of those cases applies to legislative action as well. The legislative-adjudicatory question arises because exactions are imposed on development in two distinct settings that may call for different levels of review. As Chief Justice Rehnquist said in *Dolan,* the burden is on a challenger to prove the invalidity of a generally applicable law, but where an adjudicative decision is made, the burden switches to the government.[114] Where property owners must bargain on a case by case basis, in what is essentially an adjudicatory setting, the safeguards of the open legislative process are lost, and concern arises that the individual may be compelled to give more than a fair share.[115] Taking their cue from *Dolan's* emphasis on the fact that the case involved an adjudicative decision, most courts have found heightened scrutiny inapplicable to broad-based legislative conditions.[116] Other courts take the position that heightened scrutiny applies to legislative as well as adjudicative acts.[117]

Dolan's discussion of legislative versus adjudicatory action is, as was true in *Penn Central* and *Agins,* based on due process factors and the distinction may not survive *Lingle. Lingle* does not expressly deal with the question, but it does note that *Nollan* and *Dolan* involved adjudicatory actions. That, however, may not have been intended to limit those cases but to simply describe what happened in them. The case does say that the focus is to be on the burden the property suffers as opposed to the legitimacy of the law. Whether the exaction arises from legislative or adjudicatory action a landowner must give up an easement and thus suffers the same burden. The question remains open and likely will continue to be disputed until the Court answers it.

§ 10:6   The Economic Impact Test

In *Pennsylvania Coal v. Mahon*[118] and *Penn Central Transportation Co. v. City of New York,*[119] the Court treated the economic impact of a regulation as an important, if not the primary, factor in determining whether a taking had occurred. Those cases, however, provided little guidance as to how much of an economic impact was tolerable and how other factors should be considered. They also left unanswered the question as

---

[112] *Small Property Owners of San Francisco v. City and County of San Francisco,* 141 Cal. App. 4th 1388, 47 Cal. Rptr. 3d 121, 130 n.6 (2006).

[113] *West Linn Corporate Park, L.L.C. v. City of West Linn,* 349 Or. 58, 85, 240 P.3d 29, 44 (2010).

[114] *Dolan,* 512 U.S. at 391, n.8, 114 S. Ct. at 2320.

[115] See Reznik, Note: The Distinction Between Legislative and Adjudicative Decisions in *Dolan v. City of Tigard,* 75 N.Y.U. L. Rev. 242 (2000

[116] See e.g., *McClung v. City of Sumner,* 548 F.3d 1219, 1224 (9th Cir. 2008). A complete listing of cases can be found in the Practitioner's Edition of this work: Juergensmeyer and Roberts, Land Use Planning and Development Regulation Law (3rd ed.2012).

[117] *Home Builders Ass'n of Dayton & the Miami Valley v. Beavercreek,* 89 Ohio St. 3d 121, 729 N.E.2d 349 (2000) (impact fees). A complete listing of cases can be found in the Practitioner's Edition of this work: Juergensmeyer and Roberts, Land Use Planning and Development Regulation Law (3rd ed.2012).

[118] *Pennsylvania Coal Co. v. Mahon,* 260 U.S. 393, 415, 43 S. Ct. 158, 160, 67 L. Ed. 322 (1922), discussed supra § 10:4.

[119] *Penn Cent. Transp. Co. v. City of New York,* 438 U.S. 104, 98 S. Ct. 2646, 57 L. Ed. 2d 631 discussed supra § 10:4.

to whether the nuisance or nuisance-like character of a use justified a total deprivation of economic value or use.

A. *Categorical Taking by Total Economic Deprivation: Lucas*

In 1992, the Supreme Court established a categorical rule for economic impact cases in *Lucas v. South Carolina Coastal Council*.[120] The owner of two beachfront lots was unable to build due to the application of a setback rule adopted to deter sand dune loss and beach erosion. Accepting the state trial court's finding that the lots subject to the regulation were valueless, the Court held that where a regulation deprives real property [121] of all economically viable use a taking occurs unless the state can prove that the regulation does no more to restrict use than what the state courts could do under background principles of property law or the law of private or public nuisance.[122]

Lucas rejected case law that suggested that regulations causing serious public harm, but falling short of being common law nuisances, could not be takings. *Mugler v. Kansas,* the 1887 case where the Supreme Court dismissed out of hand a takings claim brought by the owner of a brewery who was shut down when the state went dry and went on to hold that the ordinance did not violate due process, has sometimes been viewed as espousing the rule that a regulation that prevents serious public harm is not a taking. This is sometimes labeled the "nuisance-like exception." The Court applied the notion in *Keystone Bituminous Coal Ass'n v. DeBenedictis,* saying that the "state has not 'taken' anything when it asserts its power to enjoin the nuisance-like activity."[123] *Keystone* also spoke of "uses of property that are tantamount to public nuisances" and found a statute preventing mining coal so as to cause subsidence was not a taking, in part, because it prevented a serious public harm.

Lucas rejected the idea that a regulation preventing serious public harm that approached, but did not constitute, a common law nuisance, was immunized from a takings claim. Thus, *Lucas* reaffirmed the age old principle that no one has a property right to commit a nuisance or to breach other background principles of property law. Regulations that fall short of either of those findings and that deprive an owner of all economic use are takings.

To take advantage of the *Lucas* categorical rule, one must show a total loss. In *Palazzolo v. Rhode Island,*[124] the Court rejected the argument that a 93.7% diminution in value was a categorical taking. The property owner alleged that his property, most of which was wetlands, had a value of $3,150,000 if developed with 74 single-family homes. However, as restricted by the state's wetlands laws, the claimant could only build one home, leaving his parcel with a value of $200,000, or, as he put it, "a few crumbs of value." These "few crumbs," however, were sufficient to render *Lucas* inapplicable, as the Court found that the right "to build a substantial residence on an 18 acre parcel does not leave the property 'economically idle.'"[125]

---

[120] *Lucas v. South Carolina Coastal Council,* 505 U.S. 1003, 112 S. Ct. 2886, 120 L. Ed. 2d 798 (1992).

[121] The *Lucas* categorical rule only applies to real property. 505 U.S. at 1028, 112 S. Ct. at 2900.

[122] 505 U.S. at 1027, 112 S. Ct. at 2899.

[123] *Keystone,* 480 U.S. 470, 492 n.20.

[124] *Palazzolo v. Rhode Island,* 533 U.S. 606, 121 S. Ct. 2448, 150 L. Ed. 2d 592 (2001).

[125] 121 S. Ct. at 2465.

The invocation of *Lucas* may depend upon whether one must show a deprivation of all economically viable use or of all value. A regulation, for example, might prohibit all developmental use of land but not deprive the land of all value. The problem lies in whether, when, and how to distinguish between "use" and "value," concepts that are so closely intertwined. Courts, including the Supreme Court in *Lucas,* have used the terms interchangeably in takings cases.[126] The *Lucas* Court also assumed the land to be valueless. In *Tahoe-Sierra Preservation Council, Inc. v. Tahoe Regional Planning Agency,* the Court said that anything less than a "complete elimination of value" requires a *Penn Central* analysis.[127] Where unimproved land cannot be developed due to regulation, but the land has more than token value for recreational or some other use, *Lucas'* categorical rule will not apply.[128]

Establishing a prima facie *Lucas* taking is realistically only possible if the court treats the portion of the land affected by the regulation as the denominator by which to measure the loss. If, however, as is usually the case, the whole parcel rule is used,[129] a categorical taking will not be found. Defining the relevant portion of land to measure loss then is effectively outcome-determinative in many, if not most, cases.

The *Lucas* Court's "categorical" rule is not really categorical. As is true with the so-called "categorical" *Loretto* rule regarding permanent physical occupations, *Lucas* uses the term as a burden switching tool. A prima facie case is made where a law denies all economically beneficial use or value and no "case-specific inquiry into the public interest advanced in support of the restraint [occurs]."[130] However, when the property owner shows a total deprivation of all economically beneficial use, the burden switches to the government, which must show that property or nuisance law justifies the restriction to avoid paying compensation.

B.   *Background Principles*

Where a total deprivation of economically beneficial use occurs, the state can insulate itself from paying compensation only if the prohibition "inhere[s] in the title itself, in the restrictions that background principles that the State's law of property and [private or public] nuisance already place upon land ownership."[131] Read narrowly, this means that legislatures cannot impose new limitations that effect total economic deprivations unless the state courts could impose the same limit under the common law. Some justices have suggested, however, that land use zoning and permitting regimes qualify as background principles.[132] Furthermore, the test is not limited to a backward look at what the state courts have held in specific cases pursuant to the common law. The principles, not holdings, of state law control, and the power of the courts under the common law is not fixed. Thus, the *Lucas* Court acknowledged that new prohibitions may be imposed if deemed necessary by virtue of changed circumstances or new knowledge. The Lucas Court reserved its right to review state court interpretations of

---

[126] Unless specifically noted otherwise, we also use the terms interchangeably.

[127] *Tahoe-Sierra Preservation Council, Inc. v. Tahoe Regional Planning Agency,* 535 U.S. 302, 122 S. Ct. 1465, 152 L. Ed. 2d 517 (2002).

[128] *Tahoe-Sierra,* 122 S. Ct. at 1483.

[129] See discussion infra § 10:8.

[130] *Lucas,* 505 U.S. at 1015, 112 S. Ct. at 2893.

[131] 505 U.S. at 1029, 112 S. Ct. at 2900.

[132] *Tahoe-Sierra Preservation Council, Inc. v. Tahoe Regional Planning Agency,* 535 U.S. 302, 344, 122 S. Ct. 1465, 1490, 152 L. Ed. 2d 517 (2002) (Rehnquist, C.J., dissenting).

state property law, saying that state courts can only engage in "objectively reasonable application[s] of relevant precedents."[133] The burden is on the claimant to prove the existence of the right alleged to have been taken.

The Supreme Court applied the rule in *Stop the Beach Renourishment Inc. v. Florida Dept. of Environmental Protection,*[134] where coastal property owners contended that the state supreme court's interpretation of Florida's law relating to beach ownership effected a taking. The issue arose due to the state's beach restoration program implemented in response to the loss of dry sand due to erosion. On restored beaches, the statute established a fixed erosion control line. The sand added by restoration, generally seaward from the statutory line, created new land, which, under the statute, belongs to state. Beachfront property owners claimed that under the state's common law, the boundary between public and private ownership of tidal lands was the ordinary high tide mark and that new land created by the state landward of the ordinary high tide line belonged to the private owners, giving them direct access to the ocean. When the state's fixed line fell landward of the ordinary high tide line, the beachfront property owners lost the right to claim title to the new land and lost direct access to the water. The Florida court held that under the common law, these claimed rights were superseded by the state's right to fill submerged land. In a unanimous decision, the US Supreme Court found the state court's ruling consistent with the background principles of state property law.

In another case, the Court declined review of an Oregon Supreme Court opinion, which recognized a public right of access on private beach property based on the doctrine of custom, precluding the conclusion that public entry was a taking.[135] The Court also let stand the Hawaii Supreme Court's ruling that private property owners must allow native Hawaiians to enter private land to exercise native gathering rights.[136]

In other decisions construing background principles, the Colorado Supreme Court held that its doctrine of nuisance law could preclude the spread of radioactive contamination,[137] and the Federal Circuit has found that the federal navigation servitude is a background principle under *Lucas.*[138] State courts have differed, as they presumably are entitled to do, on whether filling wetlands violates their background principles.[139]

The role that statutes play as background principles is unclear. Some contend that statutes may only qualify as background principles to the extent that they codify state common law (by which they mean judicially developed rules), while others contend that statutes may reflect newly developed principles responding to changing circumstances. Expanding the scope further, Chief Justice Rehnquist observed that "zoning and per-

---

[133] *Lucas,* 505 U.S. at 1032, n.18, 112 S.Ct. at 2902.

[134] *Stop the Beach Renourishment, Inc. v. Florida Dept. of Environmental Protection,* 130 S. Ct. 2592, 177 L. Ed. 2d 184 1505 (2010).

[135] *Stevens v. City of Cannon Beach,* 317 Or. 131, 854 P.2d 449 (1993).

[136] *Public Access Shoreline Hawaii by Rothstein v. Hawai'i County Planning Com'n by Fujimoto,* 79 Haw. 425, 903 P.2d 1246 (1995). But see *Severance v. Patterson,* 2012 WL 1059341 (Tex. 2012).

[137] *State, Dept. of Health v. The Mill,* 887 P.2d 993 (Colo. 1994).

[138] *Palm Beach Isles Associates v. U.S.,* 208 F.3d 1374 (Fed. Cir. 2000).

[139] Compare *K & K Const., Inc. v. Department of Natural Resources,* 217 Mich. App. 56, 551 N.W.2d 413 (1996), decision rev'd on other grounds, 456 Mich. 570, 575 N.W.2d 531 (1998).

mitting regimes are a longstanding feature of state property law,"[140] indicating that limiting background principles to the common law is too narrow an approach.

In *Palazzolo v. Rhode Island,* the Court held that "a regulation that otherwise would be unconstitutional absent compensation is not transformed into a background principle of the State's law by mere virtue of the passage of title,"[141] but the Court acknowledged a role for statutes when it said that it had "no occasion to consider the precise circumstances when a legislative enactment can be deemed a background principle of state law or whether those circumstances are present here."[142] Prior to *Palazzolo,* a number of state courts had found that restrictions embodied in statutes that pre-dated a challenger's acquisition of title were background principles that defeated a takings claim.[143] To the extent that those decisions rest on the idea that the mere passage of title converts a statute into a background principle, they are no longer valid.

C.   *The Penn Central Multifactor, Ad Hoc Test*

If a regulation's economic effect is less than total, the *Penn Central* multi-factor test is used to determine whether a taking has occurred. Under *Penn Central,* as discussed above,[144] economic impact is but one factor to consider. Other factors include the extent to which the regulation interferes with investment-backed expectations and the character or extent of the government action. *Penn Central* did not indicate the relative weight of these factors, choosing instead to speak of takings cases as "ad hoc factual inquiries." As the Court said in the oft-quoted case of *Armstrong v. United States,* "these inquiries are informed by the purpose of the Takings Clause, which is to prevent the government from 'forcing some people alone to bear public burdens which, in all fairness and justice, should be borne by the public as a whole.'"[145]

Penn Central is the test most likely to be applied to a regulatory takings claim. Claims rarely qualify for the more landowner-favorable rules of *Lucas* or *Loretto* (with the exception of cases raising the *Nollan* nexus defense). *Penn Central* also has been endorsed by the Court in its most recent takings cases.[146] Not only is it the most likely to be used by a court, it is rare for a property owner to prevail under it. Professor Ely sums up *Penn Central's* test by observing that its "indeterminate factors provide little guidance to individuals and, in practice, are heavily balanced in favor of the government and against compensation."[147]

(1) Economic Impact

The economic impact factor, other than where it is shown to be a total diminution in value, is critical to a claim but not determinative. Standing alone, partial economic

---

[140] *Tahoe-Sierra Preservation Council, Inc. v. Tahoe Regional Planning Agency,* 535 U.S. 302, 122 S. Ct. 1465, 1494, 152 L. Ed. 2d 517 (2002) (Rehnquist, C.J., dissenting).

[141] *Palazzolo v. Rhode Island,* 533 U.S. 606, 629, 121 S. Ct. 2448, 2464, 150 L. Ed. 2d 592 (2001).

[142] Palazzolo, 533 U.S. 606.

[143] See infra § 10:7.

[144] Supra § 10:4.

[145] *Armstrong v. United States,* 364 U.S. 40, 49, 80 S. Ct. 1563, 4 L. Ed. 2d 1554 (1960).

[146] See *Lingle v. Chevron U.S.A. Inc.,* 544 U.S. 528, 529, 125 S. Ct. 2074, 161 L. Ed. 2d 876 (2005).

[147] See Ely, Jr., "Poor Relation" Once More: The Supreme Court and the Vanishing Rights of Property Owners, 2005 Cato Sup. Ct. Rev. 39 (2005), text accompanying notes 35–36 and 70–71.

loss does not result in a taking. In *Palazzolo v. Rhode Island,*[148] the Court rejected the argument that a 93.7% diminution in value was a categorical taking. While there is no absolute number, to aid the claimant's case at all, the diminution, as *Palazzolo* illustrates, must be close to total. Comparing *Lucas* and *Penn Central,* one court concluded that the latter provides "an avenue of redress for a landowner whose property retains value that is slightly greater than de minimis, * * * [but the results of cases demonstrate] that the level of interference must be very high."[149]

One such case is *Florida Rock Industries, Inc. v. United States,* where the Court of Federal Claims found a taking relying primarily on a 73% deprivation in value.[150] More often than not, a percentage of loss is not calculated in written opinions. To most appellate courts, the lack of a record proving a percentage loss will be assumed to be insubstantial and treated as dispositive or the case will be remanded.

(2) Character of the Government Action

The "character or extent of the government action" factor has been read by many courts to open up the inquiry into an assessment of the "purpose and importance of the public interest,"[151] which then must be weighed against the loss. Whether this is what the *Penn Central* Court intended is doubtful. After stating the "character" factor, the Court gave as an example the temporary physical invasion that occurred in *United States v. Causby.*[152] The matter soon became muddled. In *Agins v. City of Tiburon,* the Court said "the question [of when a taking has occurred] necessarily requires a weighing of private and public interests."[153] Shortly after, but without citing to, *Agins,* the Court began to speak of the "multifactor balancing test prescribed by this Court's recent Takings Clause decisions."[154] Until *Lingle,* the Supreme Court retained what appeared to be a standard that integrated the balancing aspect of *Agins* with the *Penn Central* factors. Lower courts followed suit.

Lingle, in overruling the *Agins'* substantially advances test, eliminates evaluation of the legitimacy of the regulation, and a judicial balancing of interests should follow it to the dustbin of Supreme Court errors. In *Lingle,* the Court did not refer to a multifactor balancing test. Rather, when reciting the *Penn Central* factors, the *Lingle* Court gave a physical invasion as its example of the character factor. Just as the challenger cannot argue an illegitimate regulatory purpose or use of irrational means in presenting its case, the government ought not be able to argue the importance of its regulation's purpose in defense. By extricating due process from the takings question, the Court seems to have returned to its position in *Pennsylvania Coal v. Mahon,* where it said that "a strong public desire to improve the public condition is not enough to warrant achieving it by a shorter cut than the constitutional way of paying for the

---

[148] *Palazzolo v. Rhode Island,* 533 U.S. 606, 121 S. Ct. 2448, 150 L. Ed. 2d 592 (2001).

[149] *Animas Valley Sand and Gravel, Inc. v. Board of County Com'rs of County of La Plata,* 38 P.3d 59 (Colo. 2001).

[150] *Florida Rock Industries, Inc. v. U.S.,* 45 Fed. Cl. 21 (1999).

[151] *Loveladies Harbor, Inc. v. U.S.,* 28 F.3d 1171, 1176 (Fed. Cir. 1994).

[152] *Penn Central,* 438 U.S. at 124.

[153] *Agins v. City of Tiburon,* 447 U.S. 255, 260, 100 S. Ct. 2138, 65 L. Ed. 2d 106 (1980), overruled, Lingle v. Chevron U.S.A. Inc., 544 U.S. 528, 125 S. Ct. 2074, 161 L. Ed. 2d 876 (2005).

[154] *Loretto v. Teleprompter Manhattan CATV Corp.,* 458 U.S. 419, 102 S. Ct. 3164, 73 L. Ed. 2d 868 (1982).

change."[155] *Lingle's* emphasis on physical invasions is in accord with *Pennsylvania Coal,* which the Court has characterized as a case involving "a physical restriction"[156] of land.

Nuisance law may be used to measure the strength of the public interest.[157] For example, in *Rose Acre Farms, Inc. v. United States,*[158] the court reasoned that *Lingle* did not diminish consideration of the strength of the public interest in health and safety regulations. The court held that a government restriction on *egg* sales, which caused the loss of egg-laying chickens that tested positive for the presence of salmonella bacteria, was not a regulatory taking. While the court couched its decision in *Penn Central* terminology, the decision may be better explained as holding that endangering the health and safety is a nuisance.

The balancing conundrum stems from the awkward transition that courts face in moving from the police power to the eminent domain power in regulatory takings cases. At bottom, the issue of balancing returns to the blend of substantive due process and takings law. *Lingle* goes a long way towards separating the two, but it is likely that some mixing will continue so long as the *Penn Central* test remains vague.

§ 10:7 Investment-Backed Expectations

Investment-backed expectations entered takings lexicon in *Penn Central,* where the Court listed it as one factor to consider under its ad hoc approach to takings determinations. Though the term was new, the Court traced its source to *Pennsylvania Coal v. Mahon.* While some initially saw in this concept "new support for landowner takings claims, * * *, the factor has become, instead, a shield for government."[159] Use of the expectations test has its critics, who point out that limiting a landowner's use under the concept of expectations runs counter to property rights as natural rights.[160] The idea, however, finds support in utilitarian theory,[161] and the Court recently reaffirmed it as part of the takings inquiry in *Palazzolo v. Rhode Island.*[162] Interference with investment-backed expectations does not constitute a taking by itself. Economic loss still must be considered.

The Court has not defined "investment-backed expectations," but some guidance as to its meaning can be gleaned from the Court's applications. In *Penn Central,* the Court found that the railroad's belief that it could use the airspace above the railroad terminal did not qualify as a "distinct investment-backed expectation." It was sufficient for takings purposes, held the Court, that the railroad's primary expectation of using Grand Central Station as a railroad terminal and office building, established by 65 years of use, was unaffected by the landmark designation. That the railroad built the

---

[155] *Pennsylvania Coal Co. v. Mahon,* 260 U.S. 393, 416, 43 S. Ct. 158, 160, 67 L. Ed. 322 (1922).

[156] *Andrus v. Allard,* 444 U.S. 51, 67, 100 S. Ct. 318, 327 n.22, 62 L. Ed. 2d 210 (1979).

[157] See § 14:1 et seq. infra.

[158] *Rose Acre Farms, Inc. v. U.S.,* 559 F.3d 1260 (Fed. Cir. 2009), cert. denied, 130 S. Ct. 1501, 176 L. Ed. 2d 109 (2010).

[159] Daniel R. Mandelker, The Notice Rule in Investment-Backed Expectations at 21, in Taking Sides on Takings Issues: Public and Private Perspectives (T. Roberts ed.2002).

[160] See, e.g., Eagle, The Rise and Fall of "Investment-Backed Expectations," 32 Urb. Law. 437 (2000).

[161] See Michelman, Property, Utility, and Fairness: Comments on the Ethical Foundations of "Just Compensation" Law, 80 Harv. L. Rev. 1165 (1967).

[162] *Palazzolo v. Rhode Island,* 533 U.S. 606, 121 S. Ct. 2448, 150 L. Ed. 2d 592 (2001).

station with columns to support a 20-story tower did not give rise to an expectation to build a 50-story tower.

In *Pennsylvania Coal,* expectations played a role where the state's anti-subsidence statute abrogated an express contractual reservation of the right to remove coal free from liability for damage to the surface. The fact that *Pennsylvania Coal* was a private dispute where the surface owner bought the land with notice of the prior severance of the mineral rights suggests a high degree of expectation on both sides to the contract that the coal could be removed without liability for surface damage.

A year after *Penn Central,* in *Kaiser Aetna v. United States,*[163] the Court applied the concept, this time referring to "reasonable", as opposed to "distinct," investment-backed expectations.[164] There, a developer dredged a non-navigable pond to create a private marina. With consent of the government's Corps of Engineers, the developer cut a channel to the ocean. Ten years later, when a dispute arose between the Corps and the marina, the Corps advised the marina that since the once non-navigable pond had been rendered navigable, it was subject to public use as an incident of the navigational servitude. Noting the physical character of the invasion, albeit temporary, and the property owner's expectations of private use based on the initial government consent or acquiescence, the Court found imposition of the navigation servitude would be a taking.

Lucas says that a landowner's reasonable expectations are used to determine the relevant parcel by which to measure deprivation of value.[165] Whether expectations are to be used beyond that is disputed.[166] Under *Lucas* the landowner can shift the burden to the state with a showing of total economic deprivation, and in contrasting total and partial economic deprivation cases, the *Lucas* majority acknowledges that investment-backed expectations are "keenly relevant" to the latter.[167] The negative inference is that expectations, if not irrelevant, then at least are less relevant to the former. While *Palazzolo* held that constructive notice of the law in force upon acquisition of title is not an automatic bar to a *Lucas* or a *Penn Central* takings claim, it did not eliminate use of expectations in determining the force of the state's background principles defense. Indeed, in *Tahoe-Sierra Preservation Council, Inc. v. Tahoe Regional Planning Agency,* Chief Justice Rehnquist observed that "zoning and permitting regimes [dating back to colonial times] are a longstanding feature of state property law and part of a landowner's reasonable investment-backed expectations."[168]

In applying the expectations test under *Penn Central,* one writer has concluded the factor that most often used to deny takings claims based on expectations is purchasing after the enactment of the challenged law. "Beyond that," he says, "there is no readily identifiable pattern to state court investment-backed expectations decisions,

---

[163] *Kaiser Aetna v. U. S.,* 444 U.S. 164, 100 S. Ct. 383, 62 L. Ed. 2d 332 (1979).

[164] Kaiser Aetna, 444 U.S at 175, 100 S. Ct. at 390.

[165] 505 U.S. at 1019, 112 S. Ct. at 2895 n. 7.

[166] Expectations not to be considered, see *Cane Tennessee, Inc. v. U.S.,* 62 Fed. Cl. 703 (2004) and *Palm Beach Isles Associates v. U.S.,* 208 F.3d 1374 (Fed. Cir. 2000). To be considered, see *Good v. U.S.,* 189 F.3d 1355 (Fed. Cir. 1999) and *Gazza v. New York State Dept. of Environmental Conservation,* 89 N.Y.2d 603, 657 N.Y.S.2d 555, 679 N.E.2d 1035 (1997).

[167] 505 U.S. at 1019, 112 S. Ct. at 2895 n. 8.

[168] *Tahoe-Sierra Preservation Council, Inc. v. Tahoe Regional Planning Agency,* 535 U.S. 302, 122 S. Ct. 1465, 1495, 152 L. Ed. 2d 517 (2002) (Rehnquist, C.J., dissenting).

except that they tend to evolve, with each new set of facts, to challenge the reasonableness of the claimant's investment-backed expectations."[169]

A. Purchase Price as Basis of Expectation

Courts have generally refrained from allowing the purchase price of land to qualify as an investment-backed expectation. An example is the case of *Haas & Co. v. City of San Francisco*,[170] where a developer acquired land in the Russian Hill neighborhood of San Francisco and proposed to erect two apartment buildings, one of 25 stories, the other of 31. The land was zoned to allow high-rises and sat amid low-rise buildings. Perhaps foreseeably, neighbors' objections sparked a "battle for Russian Hill,"[171] and ultimately the land was downzoned to a 40-foot height limit, consistent with neighboring uses. The land had been purchased for $1.6 million, was worth $2 million zoned for high-rises, and valued at $100,000 when zoned at the 40-foot limit. These "disappointed expectations" based on what was paid for the land did not create a taking.[172] In effect, the deal was what it seemed, "too good to be true." As the *Lucas* Court said, one buys property with the understanding that it is subject to the police power of the state and "necessarily expects the use of his property to be restricted, from time to time, by various newly enacted measures."[173]

B. Notice of Pre-Existing Law, Foreseeability, and Regulatory Risk

Constructive notice of the law in force upon acquisition of title, though it is not an automatic bar to a takings claim, is a factor in the assessment of reasonable expectations. Even where a law does not pre-date acquisition of ownership, foreseeability of impending change and knowledge of the regulatory climate may so diminish expectations as to defeat a takings claim.

Prior to *Palazzolo,* a number of lower federal and state courts had held that a landowner cannot complain of a taking based on restrictions to which the land was subject at the time of purchase. They reasoned that the hardship was self-imposed and that allowing recovery would confer a windfall benefit. Courts based their holdings in part on *Lucas v. South Carolina Coastal Council*,[174] where the Court said that the state need not pay an owner compensation if the "proscribed use interests were not part of [the owner's] title to begin with,"[175] and that owners' understandings of the state's power over land are shaped by the "'bundle of rights' they acquire when they obtain title to property."[176]

In *Palazzolo v. Rhode Island*,[177] the Court rejected this reading of *Lucas.* The *Palazzolo* Court held that a takings claim is not barred by the mere fact that the

---

[169] Breemer, Playing the Expectations Game: When Are Investment-Backed Land Use Expectations (Un)Reasonable in State Courts?, 38 Urb. Law. 81, 110 (2006).

[170] *William C. Haas & Co., Inc. v. City and County of San Francisco, Cal.*, 605 F.2d 1117 (9th Cir. 1979).

[171] See Robert C. Ellickson and A. Dan Tarlock, Land-Use Controls, Cases and Materials 334 to 338 (1981) for a description of the struggle.

[172] *Haas,* 605 F.2d at 1121.

[173] *Lucas,* 505 U.S. at 1027, 112 S. Ct. at 2886.

[174] *Lucas v. South Carolina Coastal Council,* 505 U.S. 1003, 112 S. Ct. 2886, 120 L. Ed. 2d 798 (1992).

[175] 505 U.S. at 1027, 112 S. Ct. at 2899.

[176] See *M & J Coal Co. v. U.S.*, 47 F.3d 1148, 1153 (Fed. Cir. 1995).

[177] *Palazzolo v. Rhode Island,* 533 U.S. 606, 121 S. Ct. 2448, 150 L. Ed. 2d 592 (2001).

claimant took title after the regulations of which he complains were enacted. The state had argued that its wetlands statutes, upon enactment, became background principles of property law which could ban all economically viable use of land without triggering the need to compensate post-enactment titleholders. The Supreme Court said it need not consider when new legislation might be deemed a background principle of law that would defeat a takings claim. It sufficed, the Court said, to hold that a "regulation that would otherwise be unconstitutional absent compensation is not transformed into a background principle * * * by mere virtue of the passage of title."[178]

While *Palazzolo* holds that the mere passage of title does not automatically bar a takings claim, the claimant's notice of existing regulations is likely a factor to be considered. Justice O'Connor, concurring in *Palazzolo,* said that the Court's "holding does not mean that the timing of the regulation's enactment relative to the acquisition of title is immaterial to the *Penn Central* analysis. Indeed, [she said,] it would be just as much error to expunge this consideration from the takings inquiry as it would be to accord it exclusive significance."[179]

In some instances, due to existing law or other circumstances, a court may find that the claimant knew or should have known when she bought the land that development likely would not be permitted.[180] In *Good v. United States,*[181] for example, the court found the "regulatory climate" that existed when property was acquired put the claimant on notice that development might not be allowed.

§ 10:8   Defining Property and the Relevant Parcel

State law creates and defines property.[182] The Constitution protects property, whether it be real or personal, tangible or intangible. In construing the protection afforded property, the Supreme Court often uses the Hofeldian bundle of rights theory of property [183] and holds that the "destruction of one strand of the bundle does not constitute a taking because the aggregate must be viewed in its entirety."[184] In the context of alleged regulatory takings of real property, the choice of a broad or narrow approach will often be outcome determinative. Choosing only the portion of land affected by a regulation increases the prospects of a total diminution in value. That, in turn, invokes the *Lucas* categorical takings rule. Defining the relevant unit of property is a process bound up with the overall test of when "fairness and justice" require that compensation be paid.[185] The Supreme Court's approach has been to employ a broad view,[186] often characterized as the "whole parcel" approach.

---

[178] 121 S. Ct. at 2464.

[179] 121 S.Ct at 2466. See, e.g., *Guggenheim v. City of Goleta,* 638 F.3d 1111 (9th Cir. 2010), cert. denied, 131 S. Ct. 2455, 179 L. Ed. 2d 1210 (2011).

[180] *Kirby Forest Industries, Inc. v. U.S.,* 467 U.S. 1, 104 S. Ct. 2187, 81 L. Ed. 2d 1 (1984).

[181] *Good v. U.S.,* 189 F.3d 1355 (Fed. Cir. 1999).

[182] *Board of Regents of State Colleges v. Roth,* 408 U.S. 564, 577, 92 S. Ct. 2701, 2709, 33 L. Ed. 2d 548 (1972).

[183] See Hohfeld, Fundamental Legal Conceptions as Applied in Judicial Reasoning, 23 Yale L.J. 16 (1913).

[184] *Andrus v. Allard,* 444 U.S. 51, 66, 100 S. Ct. 318, 327, 62 L. Ed. 2d 210 (1979).

[185] The entitlement approach to property under procedural and substantive due process, which severely limits landowner claims, does not apply to Fifth Amendment takings. See infra § 10:12. See also Mandelker, Entitlement to Substantive Due Process: Old Versus New Property in Land Use Regulation, 3 Wash. U. J.L. & Pol'y 61, 66 (2000).

A. The Whole Parcel Rule

Hoping to take advantage of the categorical *Lucas* rule and avoid the *Penn Central* multi-factor test, landowners generally ask courts to adopt the position that the relevant parcel is solely the land for which the permit is sought. The courts, however, generally have refused to do so. Instead, in most cases, courts have measured economic impact by reference to the whole parcel.[187]

The Supreme Court began with a narrow approach in *Pennsylvania Coal*. While the majority did not specifically discuss the segmentation issue, it appeared to treat the coal that had to be left in place to comply with the statute as the relevant measure for its "too far" test. In dissent Justice Brandeis objected to this segmentation of rights.[188] For the majority, however, looking only at the affected coal may have been deemed fair since the case arose in the context of a private dispute where the surface owner bought the land with notice of the prior severance. This suggests a high degree of expectation on both sides to the contract that the coal could be removed. In the later case of *Keystone Bituminous Coal v. DeBenedictis,* the Court viewed *Pennsylvania Coal* as having used a broader approach to defining property. Thus, *Keystone* read the statement of Justice Holmes that the statute had made it "commercially impracticable to mine certain coal" to reflect a finding that the company's mining operations as a whole could not be conducted profitably if the coal affected by the Kohler Act had to be left in place.[189]

In the modern takings era that began with *Penn Central,* the Court has broadly defined the relevant parcel of property for regulatory takings cases involving economic impact. In *Penn Central,* the railroad claimed a total economic loss of its airspace above Grand Central Station by application of the landmark designation. The railroad, however, was wrong to limit the focus to the airspace above the terminal, for, as the Court said, "'Making' jurisprudence does not divide a single parcel into discrete segments, [but] focuses on the nature and extent of the interference in the parcel as a whole."[190] Viewing the whole parcel, the loss of the airspace still left the railroad with a reasonable use of the existing building.

In *Keystone,* where the Court faced a statute virtually identical to the one invalidated in *Pennsylvania Coal,* it rejected the coal companies' plea to use the coal that had to be left in place (the "support estate") as the measuring unit. Without saying so, the *Keystone* majority adopted Justice Brandeis' dissenting view in *Pennsylvania Coal.* The Court thought it unreasonable to allow the coal companies to claim a total loss where only 2% of their coal was required to be left in place. No evidence existed to show that mining would be unprofitable. The support estate, though a separate property right under state law, had no value apart from ownership of the surface or mineral estate, and thus the Court refused to focus on it alone.

---

[186] *Andrus v. Allard,* 444 U.S. 51, 66, 100 S. Ct. 318, 327, 62 L. Ed. 2d 210 (1979).

[187] See, e.g., *Coast Range Conifers, LLC v. State ex rel. Oregon State Bd. of Forestry,* 339 Or. 136, 117 P.3d 990 (2005) (40 acre tract used as denominator rather than the nine acres which could not be logged to protect bald eagle habitat). For a complete listing, see Juergensmeyer and Roberts, Land Use Planning and Development Regulation Law §10.8 (Practitioner's Edition 3rd ed.2012).

[188] 260 U.S. 393, 419, 43 S. Ct. 158, 161 (Brandeis, dissenting).

[189] *Keystone Bituminous Coal Ass'n v. DeBenedictis,* 480 U.S. 470, 107 S. Ct. 1232, 94 L. Ed. 2d 472 (1987).

[190] 438 U.S. at 130–31, 98 S. Ct. at 2662.

The Court has suggested that the broad approach has its limits. In a *Lucas* footnote, the Court voiced disapproval of what it styled the "extreme" approach used by the New York Court of Appeals' in the *Penn Central* case. The state court had looked to all the land owned by the railroad in the vicinity of Grand Central Station as the relevant property unit.[191] *Lucas* did not disapprove of the Court's own combination of surface and air rights *Penn Central.*

The Court injected some doubt as to the strength of the whole parcel rule when, in *Palazzolo v. Rhode Island,*[192] it referred to this *Lucas* footnote as an indication of "discomfort with the logic of the [whole parcel] rule."[193] But less than a year later, the Court strongly endorsed the whole parcel approach in a case rejecting temporal segmentation.[194]

The Court confirmed the whole parcel approach in *Tahoe-Sierra Preservation Council, Inc. v. Tahoe Regional Planning Agency,*[195] but does not likely mean that the broadest characterization of property always will be used. A rigid rule does not fit with the spirit of *Tahoe-Sierra* that takings be judged by specific reference to the facts of each case, attempting to determine when fairness and justice require compensation. As the *Lucas* Court said, the question may be answered by examining "how the owner's reasonable expectations have been shaped by the State's law of property—i.e., whether and to what degree the State's law has accorded legal recognition and protection to the particular interest in land * * *."[196]

B. *Temporal Segmentation: Moratoria*

Interim development controls that temporarily freeze land development raise the segmentation issue in the temporal context. The general rule is that one is guaranteed a reasonable use over a reasonable period of time, and that the mere loss of the present right to use land is not a taking. A statement by the Court in *First English Evangelical Lutheran Church v. County of Los Angeles*[197] to the effect that temporary takings that deny all use are no different than permanent takings led some to argue that a temporary denial of all use was a categorical *Lucas* taking of the entire present right to use property. The fact that *First English* involved a moratorium, while irrelevant to the holding in the case, fueled the argument. While the lower courts refused to treat moratoria as per se takings, landowners pressed the argument in the Supreme Court.

The Supreme Court flatly rejected this reading of *First English,* holding, in *Tahoe-Sierra Preservation Council, Inc. v. Tahoe Regional Planning Agency,*[198] that a moratorium prohibiting all use of land did not effect a facial taking. *First English,* the Court said, was strictly a remedy case. Not only did *First English* not decide that moratoria

---

[191] *Lucas,* 505 U.S. at 1016, n.7, 112 S. Ct. at 2894.

[192] *Palazzolo v. Rhode Island,* 533 US. 606, 121 S. Ct. 2448, 150 L. Ed. 2d 592 (2001).

[193] Palazzolo, 121 S. Ct. at 2465.

[194] See discussion infra part B of this section.

[195] *Tahoe-Sierra Preservation Council, Inc. v. Tahoe Regional Planning Agency,* 535 U.S. 302, 122 S. Ct. 1465, 152 L. Ed. 2d 517 (2002).

[196] *Lucas v. South Carolina Coastal Council,* 505 U.S. 1003, 1016 n.7, 112 S. Ct. 2886, 2894, 120 L. Ed. 2d 798 (1992).

[197] *First English Evangelical Lutheran Church of Glendale v. Los Angeles County, Cal.,* 482 U.S. 304, 318, 107 S. Ct. 2378, 2388, 96 L. Ed. 2d 250 (1987), discussed infra § 10:9 in detail.

[198] *Tahoe-Sierra Preservation Council, Inc. v. Tahoe Regional Planning Agency,* 535 U.S. 302, 122 S. Ct. 1465, 152 L. Ed. 2d 517 (2002).

were takings, but, to the extent that *First English* addressed the issue, it suggested that landowners must tolerate normal delays in the land use permitting process without compensation.[199]

Tahoe-Sierra also rejected the landowners' reading of *Lucas*. Treating the fact that *Lucas* involved a permanent restriction as irrelevant, the landowners argued that a moratorium that denies all economically viable use is a categorical *Lucas* taking. In *Tahoe-Sierra,* however, the Court said that the permanence of the regulation in *Lucas* was critical to the premise of the opinion that the takings clause protected against the "obliteration of value."[200] The mere fact that one is delayed for a period of time does not rise to that level of severity. Regulations are only to be converted into constructive takings in instances where they are truly excessive, and these instances, *Lucas* and *Tahoe-Sierra* say, will be extremely rare. Since *Tahoe-Sierra,* as was true before, courts generally uphold moratoria unless there is evidence of bad faith or foot-dragging.

§ 10:9   The Compensation Remedy

A.   *Invalidation or Compensation*

One might think the remedy for a Fifth Amendment taking is obvious: just compensation. The answer is, indeed, compensation for direct condemnations and inverse condemnation actions based on physical invasion. Yet, a question debated for many years was whether regulatory takings required or at least allowed a compensation award. It was not until 1987 that the answer came when, in *First English Evangelical Lutheran Church v. County of Los Angeles,*[201] the Court held that the remedy for a regulatory taking, as with a physical taking, is compensation. In so holding, the Court put to rest the long debated issue of whether the "regulatory taking" theory used by the Court in *Pennsylvania Coal* was grounded in the Fifth Amendment's takings clause or in the 14th Amendment. If grounded in the former, compensation would be the mandatory and sole remedy. If the latter, invalidation would be a constitutionally adequate remedy.

Prior to *First English* several state courts and many commentators had viewed the police power and the eminent domain powers as different in kind, not simply in degree. Under this view, an overreaching exercise of the police power was invalid on substantive due process grounds but was not, by its overreaching, converted into an exercise of eminent domain. This view was consistent with *Pennsylvania Coal,* which was a case between private parties where the remedy was to deny injunctive relief, not to order that compensation be paid. Thus, the "takings" language of the *Pennsylvania Coal* was considered "metaphorical."[202]

While local governmental bodies and agencies are clearly liable, it has been suggested that states may have 11th Amendment immunity from takings clause liability. Several states have argued that the Supreme Court's expansion of states' sovereign

---

[199] Tahoe-Sierra Preservation Council, Inc., 535 U.S. 302. See also Frank Michelman, Takings, 1987, 88 Colum. L. Rev. 1600, 1621 (1988).

[200] 535 U.S. 302, 122 S. Ct. 1465, 1483, 152 L. Ed. 2d 517 (2002).

[201] *First English Evangelical Lutheran Church of Glendale v. Los Angeles County, Cal.*, 482 U.S. 304, 107 S. Ct. 2378, 96 L. Ed. 2d 250 (1987).

[202] See discussion of the metaphor theory in *Williamson County Regional Planning Com'n v. Hamilton Bank of Johnson City,* 473 U.S. 172, 197, 105 S. Ct. 3108, 3122, 87 L. Ed. 2d 126 (1985).

immunity in cases like *Alden v. Maine* [203] confirm that it trumps the Fifth Amendment in state and federal court. However, the courts to address the matter hold, in *post-Alden* decisions, that the Fifth Amendment abrogates state sovereign immunity in state court.[204] These holdings make sense given that allowing immunity in state and federal courts would effectively nullify the Fifth Amendment's takings clause as applied to the states.[205]

The rightly maligned *Agins v. City of Tiburon* [206] opinion increased the already existing confusion regarding the remedy for a taking. By saying that an ordinance that does not substantially advance a legitimate state interest is a taking, the natural inference is that the injured party can, indeed must, seek compensation. However, government cannot acquire property in such a manner by simply paying for it. Did *Agins* mean, then, that invalidation is a proper remedy or that invalidation is an alternative takings remedy? As the *Lingle* Court noted in overruling *Agins,* the "the notion that such a regulation [that does not substantially advance a legitimate state interest] nevertheless 'takes' private property for public use merely by virtue of its ineffectiveness or foolishness is untenable."[207] As Chief Justice Rehnquist has said:

> This basic understanding of the [Fifth] Amendment makes clear that it is designed not to limit the governmental interference with property rights per se, but rather to secure compensation in the event of an otherwise proper interference amounting to a taking.[208]

The remedy for an act that violates due process is invalidation. The difference between a due process violation and a Fifth Amendment taking is not mere semantics. First, heightened scrutiny applies to some takings claims, but not to due process claims. Second, when an ordinance is declared void, compensation cannot be the remedy since there is no taking.

When an ordinance is invalidated as an improper exercise of the police power, the harm sustained for the period the ordinance applied to the property is not compensable under the Fifth Amendment. As Chief Justice Rehnquist's quoted language above points out, a pre-condition to finding a taking and awarding compensation is that, there has been "an otherwise *proper interference*" with property rights. Unauthorized government actions cannot be takings because they do not meet the public use or public purpose requirement of the Fifth Amendment. Before it was overruled, *Agins* fostered confusion on this point with its statement that an ordinance that does not substantially advance a state interest is a taking.

A regulation that is invalid under state law can be remedied pursuant to state law. The government or its agents may be liable in damages under some theory, like

---

[203] *Alden v. Maine,* 527 U.S. 706, 119 S. Ct. 2240, 144 L. Ed. 2d 636 (1999).

[204] See, e.g., *Manning v. N.M. Energy, Minerals & Natural Resources Dept.,* 140 N.M. 528, 144 P.3d 87 (2006). For more extensive discussion, see Juergensmeyer and Roberts, Land Use Planning and Development Regulation Law §10.9 (Practitioner's Edition 3rd ed.2012).

[205] See Seamon, The Asymmetry of State Sovereign Immunity, 76 Wash. L. Rev. 1067, 1080 (2001).

[206] *Agins v. City of Tiburon,* 447 U.S. 255, 100 S. Ct. 2138, 65 L. Ed. 2d 106 (1980) abrogated by, Lingle v. Chevron U.S.A. Inc., 544 U.S. 528, 125 S. Ct. 2074, 161 L. Ed. 2d 876 (2005).

[207] *Lingle,* 544 U.S. at 543, 125 S. Ct. 2084.

[208] *First English Evangelical Lutheran Church of Glendale v. Los Angeles County, Cal.,* 482 U.S. 304, 314–315, 107 S. Ct. 2378, 96 L. Ed. 2d 250 (1987).

state tort law. Such a regulation might also be a violation of due process, which would lead to invalidation and possibly damages under the federal civil rights statute.[209]

It has been argued that invalidation, not compensation, is the proper remedy when an exaction or other condition imposed on a landowner as the price for acquiring a development permit violates the *Nollan/Dolan* test.[210] Bringing a facial takings claim challenging an affordable housing set-side, the plaintiff developer in *Alto Eldorado Partnership v. County of Santa* Fe [211] argued that *Lingle* created a new takings test applicable in the context of unconstitutional conditions, which authorized a court to invalidate a condition found improper under *Nollan/Dolan*. The court rejected the argument finding it "akin to the now-defunct 'substantially advances' theory previously available to challenge any regulatory taking."[212]

B. *Permanent or Temporary Taking: The State's Choice*

A court cannot use the Fifth Amendment to invalidate a law that takes property so long as it promotes a public purpose, since the Constitution does not proscribe the taking of property. A court can only award compensation. Even then, the government, as defendant in the inverse condemnation action, not the court, decides whether the compensation should be paid on the basis of a permanent taking or a temporary taking. The government has the option of keeping the regulation in place and paying compensation for a permanent taking, or rescinding the excessive regulation and paying only for the period of the take.

Compensation is due for the period of time that the taking endured, and the beginning point in calculating compensation depends on whether the challenge is facial or as-applied. With a facial challenge, the date of enactment starts the compensation meter running since by definition it is the mere enactment of the law that effects the taking. With an as-applied challenge, the enactment date does not start the meter running because the landowner suffers no harm from enactment alone. The beginning date generally will be when the action is ripe and the statute of limitations begins to run.[213]

In order for a takings claim to be ripe, an owner must obtain a final decision as to what uses will be allowed by following the local permitting processes.[214] The time that passes in obtaining a final decision is not compensable since subjecting a landowner to a permitting process does not effect a taking.[215] If the government elects to rescind the regulation when the court finds that it has gone "too far," the date of rescission is the taking's ending point. If the government elects to keep the law in place, the question is moot since the taking becomes permanent.

---

[209] See discussion of 42 U.S.C.A. § 1983 infra at §§ 10:23 to 10:29.

[210] See discussion supra, § 10:5.

[211] *Alto Eldorado Partnership v. County of Santa Fe,* 634 F.3d 1170 (10th Cir. 2011), cert. denied, 132 S. Ct. 246, 181 L. Ed. 2d 141 (2011).

[212] 634 F.3d at 1178.

[213] See, generally, Stein, Pinpointing the Beginning and Ending of a Temporary Regulatory Taking, 70 Wash. L. Rev. 953 (1995).

[214] *Williamson County Regional Planning Com'n v. Hamilton Bank of Johnson City,* 473 U.S. 172, 105 S. Ct. 3108, 87 L. Ed. 2d 126 (1985).

[215] *U.S. v. Riverside Bayview Homes, Inc.,* 474 U.S. 121, 127, 106 S. Ct. 455, 458, 88 L. Ed. 2d 419 (1985).

It is often assumed that the compensation required by the Fifth Amendment means money, but the Court has not held that to be the case. In dealing with non-traditional, constructive takings, non-monetary compensation might be adequate in some cases. Transferable development rights, for example, may qualify as a constitutional form of compensation.[216]

C.   Measuring Compensation

In the regulatory context, a distinction is drawn between permanent and temporary takings. Where the regulation permanently renders property worthless, courts generally adopt the market value test, which provides that the measure of just compensation is the market value of the property at the time of the taking. When a regulation diminishes but does not destroy the market value of property a "modified market value" test has been used.[217]

Where government elects to rescind the regulation and pay compensation for only a temporary taking, various measures of damages have been used. Rental return is probably the most frequently used. It requires the calculation of the rent the parties would have negotiated for the period of the taking. Other methods include use of the option price, where compensation that equals the market value of an option to buy the land during the take is awarded, and before and after valuation. Lost profits are not recoverable.[218]

D.   Injunctive or Declaratory Relief

Injunctive relief generally is not available to enjoin an alleged taking of private property for a public use, duly authorized by law, since a suit for compensation can be brought against the sovereign subsequent to the taking.[219] However, if a court finds a taking for a private use, injunctive or declaratory relief is proper.[220] In the unusual situation where monetary relief would be ineffective, the Court has found that equitable and declaratory relief may be in order. In *Eastern Enterprises v. Apfel,*[221] coal companies sued to avoid having to pay money into a miners retirement fund. Finding the act's imposition of retroactive liability to constitute a taking, a four justice plurality found equitable relief appropriate. The plurality thought it made no sense to have the coal company comply with the law by paying money into the fund (and thus complete the taking) only to turn around and order the fund to give the money back to the coal company as compensation. As Justice Kennedy pointed out in his concurrence, this feature itself suggests that majority erred in viewing the problem through the lens of the takings clause rather than the due process clause. This exception allowing injunctive relief is possibly applicable in the land use context if the Court were to find that impact fees were subject to a Fifth Amendment takings analysis.[222]

---

[216] *Suitum v. Tahoe Regional Planning Agency,* 520 U.S. 725, 750, 117 S. Ct. 1659, 137 L. Ed. 2d 980 (1997) (Scalia, J. concurring). See supra § 9:9 for a discussion of transferable development rights.

[217] See detailed discussion infra § 16:10.

[218] For more extensive discussion of compensation issues, see Juergensmeyer and Roberts, Land Use Planning and Development Regulation Law, Ch. 16 (Practitioner's Edition 3rd ed.2012).

[219] *Ruckelshaus v. Monsanto Co.,* 467 U.S. 986, 1016, 104 S. Ct. 2862, 81 L. Ed. 2d 815 (1984). See also supra, § 10:9A.

[220] *Samaad v. City of Dallas,* 940 F.2d 925 (5th Cir. 1991).

[221] *Eastern Enterprises v. Apfel,* 524 U.S. 498, 118 S. Ct. 2131, 141 L. Ed. 2d 451 (1998).

[222] See discussion supra § 10:5.

§ 10:10 Ripeness and Forum Selection for Takings Claims

A. *Generally*

Special ripeness and forum selection requirements apply to Fifth Amendment takings claims. They stem from *Williamson County Regional Planning Commission v. Hamilton Bank,*[223] where the Court held that for a cause of action to be ripe, the state action must be final, and to achieve finality a meaningful development application must be made. Second, with respect to takings claims, a claimant must seek compensation from the state. Suits brought under the due process and equal protection clauses are generally subject to the final decision rule but not the compensation rule.[224]

Many takings claims are brought under Section 1983 of the Civil Rights Act under which a plaintiff need not exhaust state judicial or administrative remedies before seeking redress.[225] While exhaustion of administrative remedies is not required under 1983, finality of decision is. Confusion between the two has lead to the filing of numerous unripe cases, with much wasted time and expense.

Ripeness requirements are based on jurisdictional[226] and prudential concerns.[227] While the Supreme Court has said that *Williamson County's* requirements are prudential,[228] the parameters of what is jurisdictional and what is prudential are not clear.[229] The Court has found the final decision rule met in several cases,[230] but has not ruled on the specific steps necessary to meet the compensation requirement other than to say that compensation must be pursued if the state has an adequate procedure.[231]

B. *The Leading Cases: Williamson County and MacDonald*

In *Williamson County Regional Planning Commission v. Hamilton Bank of Johnson City,*[232] a developer received preliminary plat approval in 1973 for a cluster home development from the planning commission. Over the next few years, the commission reapproved the preliminary plans on several occasions. In 1977, the county changed the density provisions of its zoning. The commission rejected revised plats submitted in 1980 and 1981 for numerous reasons, some based on the new law and some based on the old law. The developer then brought suit in federal court.

---

[223] *Williamson County Regional Planning Com'n v. Hamilton Bank of Johnson City*, 473 U.S. 172, 105 S. Ct. 3108, 87 L. Ed. 2d 126 (1985).

[224] See infra § 10:10.

[225] Section 1983 is covered infra §§ 10:22 to 10:28.

[226] *Alto Eldorado Partnership v. County of Santa Fe*, 634 F.3d 1170, 1173 (10th Cir. 2011), cert. denied, 132 S. Ct. 246, 181 L. Ed. 2d 141 (2011).

[227] *Suitum v. Tahoe Regional Planning Agency*, 520 U.S. 725, 734, 117 S. Ct. 1659, 1665, 137 L. Ed. 2d 980 (1997).

[228] *Lucas v. South Carolina Coastal Council*, 505 U.S. 1003, 112 S. Ct. 2886, 120 L. Ed. 2d 798 (1992).

[229] See *Guggenheim v. City of Goleta*, 638 F.3d 1111 (9th Cir. 2010), cert. denied, 131 S. Ct. 2455, 179 L. Ed. 2d 1210 (2011), discussing the issue in depth.

[230] See *Suitum v. Tahoe Regional Planning Agency*, 520 U.S. 725, 734, 117 S. Ct. 1659, 1665, 137 L. Ed. 2d 980 (1997); *Lucas v. South Carolina Coastal Council*, 505 U.S. 1003, 112 S. Ct. 2886, 120 L. Ed. 2d 798 (1992); *Palazzolo v. Rhode Island*, 533 U.S. 606, 121 S. Ct. 2448, 150 L. Ed. 2d 592 (2001). See also discussion infra § 10.10.

[231] See discussion infra § 10.10.

[232] *Williamson County Regional Planning Com'n v. Hamilton Bank of Johnson City*, 473 U.S. 172, 105 S. Ct. 3108, 87 L. Ed. 2d 126 (1985).

The Court found the action unripe, noting that a takings claim is premature until the "government entity charged with implementing the regulation has reached a final decision."[233] This had not occurred since the developer had not "sought variances that would have allowed it to develop the property according to its proposed plat."[234] The Court noted that the Board of Zoning Appeals had the authority to grant variances dealing with five of the eight objections, and that the commission itself had the power to grant variances to solve the other objections.

A second problem was that the landowner had not used the inverse condemnation process available in state court. Even assuming the restrictions were so severe that they constituted a taking, the Constitution is not violated unless compensation is not paid. *Williamson County* said that if the state has an adequate inverse condemnation remedy, suit must be filed in state court. Two years later, in *First English,*[235] the Court held that states were obligated to provide such a remedy.

A year after *Williamson County,* the Court decided *MacDonald, Sommer & Frates v. Yolo County.*[236] There, the developer submitted a preliminary plan to subdivide its residentially zoned land into 159 lots for single family and multi-family housing. After the planning commission rejected the plan due to inadequacies in access, police protection, water and sewer services, the developer filed suit in state court asserting that its property was being condemned to open space.

The Court found the action was not ripe since the developer had not obtained a final decision as to what kind of development would be allowed. The developer failed to convince the Court that it had, with its one application, done enough. "Unfair procedures, [or] futile [ones]" need not be pursued, said the Court, but the "rejection of exceedingly grandiose development plans does not logically imply that less ambitious plans will receive similarly unfavorable reviews."[237]

C. *Seeking a Final Decision*

Williamson County and *MacDonald* require that a challenger obtain a final decision on a meaningful application for development to make an as-applied takings action ripe. Physical takings claims are not subject to the final decision requirement since the physical invasion itself establishes what has been taken. Likewise, a property owner making a facial takings claim is not subject to the final decision rule since, by definition, the mere enactment of the law, and not its application, takes the property.[238]

The final decision requirement is theoretically distinct from the requirement of exhaustion of administrative remedies, but in practice the distinction blurs. The former addresses whether one must seek some confirmation by the initial decisionmaker that a denial is final, and the latter addresses whether one is obligated to climb the administrative ladder to seek review of that final decision. For ripeness purposes, resort to a board of adjustment, for example, is required if the board possesses the power to waive

---

[233] 473 U.S. 172, 186, 105 S. Ct. 3108, 3116, 87 L. Ed. 2d 126 (1985).

[234] 473 U.S. at 188, 105 S. Ct. at 3117.

[235] See discussion supra § 10:9.

[236] *MacDonald, Sommer & Frates v. Yolo County,* 477 U.S. 340, 106 S. Ct. 2561, 91 L. Ed. 2d 285, 16 Envtl. L. Rep. 20807 (1986).

[237] MacDonald, Sommer & Frates, 477 U.S. at 351 n. 8, 9.

[238] *Yee v. City of Escondido, Cal.,* 503 U.S. 519, 112 S. Ct. 1522, 118 L. Ed. 2d 153 (1992).

or grant a variance from a regulation, but is not required if the board has only the power to review the application of the regulation. *Williamson County* provides an example. The Court said the property owner had to seek permission of both the board of adjustment and the planning commission for variances because both bodies had the power to relieve the property owner of the alleged hardships. But, the Court said the developer would not be required to appeal the planning commission's rejection of the plat to the board of adjustment since the board had the power only to review, not participate in, that decision.

Identifying the government actor or agency that must make the final decision, what the Court calls the "initial decisionmaker,"[239] can be troublesome. Case law instructs that it is a mistake to view the term "initial decisionmaker" narrowly. In seeking a final decision, if a variance or other procedure exists that might permit the project to proceed, it must be used unless applying would be futile. Resort to the legislative body may be necessary in addition to seeking a variance, where the current zoning classification is dated. This follows from the reason that drives the rule, which is to give the governing body a "realistic opportunity and reasonable time within which to review its zoning legislation vis-a-vis the particular property."[240]

When the *MacDonald* Court suggested that the denial of "exceedingly grandiose" plans did not mean that "less ambitious plans" would also be rejected, it created an obligation of reapplication in situations where the initial application is not a realistic one. Determining when that obligation arises is a guessing game with but few rather unhelpful clues. The Court, for example, referred to the *MacDonald* 159 lot subdivision as an "intense type of residential development," and intimated that the "'five Victorian mansions'" sought in *Agins v. City of Tiburon* [241] and the nuclear power plant in *San Diego Gas & Electric Co. v. City of San Diego* [242] were of the grandiose variety. The proposed 55 story office tower atop Grand Central Station in the *Penn Central* case was also likely "grandiose" in the ripeness sense, since the Court there noted that the landmark commission might have approved, and might yet approve, a smaller tower.

A reapplication requirement creates a dilemma. Using *Penn Central* as an example, if one were pursuing the Grand Central Station project, one might apply for a 40-story tower after failing to get approval for the 55 story proposal. If the 40-story proposal is rejected, one then might seek 25 stories. At some point the downsizing will render the project economically unattractive, but if the developer gains approval of a lesser request, it presumably waives any objection to losses based on the prior denials.

The requirement of repeated downsizing requests, drawn from *MacDonald,* goes beyond the *Williamson County* Court's concern for a final decision based on the proposed development to become a de facto rule that dictates negotiation and compromise by the developer. The goal changes from ripeness to litigation avoidance. If the parties compromise, there will be no suit. This lightens the courts' dockets, but it also deprives the developer of the ability to challenge perceived overreaching by the government in the initial denial.

---

[239] 473 U.S. at 193, 105 S. Ct. at 3120.

[240] *Hernandez v. City of Lafayette,* 643 F.2d 1188, 1200 (5th Cir. 1981).

[241] *Agins v. City of Tiburon,* 447 U.S. 255, 100 S. Ct. 2138, 65 L. Ed. 2d 106 (1980).

[242] *San Diego Gas & Elec. Co. v. San Diego,* 450 U.S. 621, 101 S. Ct. 1287, 67 L. Ed. 2d 551 (1981).

While *Lucas* shows that one need not pursue applications for relief that the authorities lack the power to give,[243] likelihood of success is not the test. Relief must be pursued if it is theoretically possible that it can be granted.[244] Suspicions as to local hostility or even oral statements by local officials generally cannot be relied upon to release one from the obligation of making formal application.[245] The rule is not ironclad. If the legislation is recent, there may be no reasonable likelihood that the legislative body will change its mind and it is more likely that a rezoning or variance need not be sought. A recent downzoning itself may be evidence of futility.[246] Extraordinary delay or bad faith in permit processing can render a claim ripe, but courts do not readily find either.[247]

Statutory solutions to final decision ripeness are possible. Florida, for example, forces a final decision by compelling a municipality to issue a ripeness determination after a property owner files notice of intent to sue under the state's statutory takings remedy. If a determination is not issued within 180 days, the government's prior action is treated as the final decision.[248]

D. *Seeking Compensation from the State Courts*

All takings claims, except those alleging a taking for a private use,[249] are subject to the requirement that the property owner seek compensation from the state by way of an action in inverse condemnation. This includes physical [250] and regulatory claims, both facial [251] and as-applied. The reason is inherent in the Fifth Amendment, which does not proscribe the taking of property, but mandates that owners be compensated. This mandate is satisfied by post-taking compensation.[252]

The 1985 *Williamson County* ruling requires takings claimants to seek compensation from the state courts "if the state provides an adequate procedure for seeking just compensation." The initial impact of this requirement was limited, since, at that time, there were several states that did not have a compensation remedy. In 1987, however, the Court held in *First English Evangelical Lutheran Church v. County of Los Angeles* [253] that the self-executing nature of the Fifth Amendment required a compensation remedy. The only remaining question is whether the remedy is adequate. In almost all cases it is.

The burden on the property owner to establish inadequacy of the state's compensation remedy is difficult to carry. Uncertainty and perceived hostility do not equal in-

---

[243] *Lucas* is discussed supra § 10:6.

[244] *Williamson County,* 473 U.S. at 197, 105 S. Ct. at 3122.

[245] *Wheeler v. City of Wayzata,* 511 N.W.2d 39 (Minn. Ct. App. 1994).

[246] *Resolution Trust Corp. v. Town of Highland Beach,* 18 F.3d 1536 (11th Cir. 1994), reh'g en banc granted, opinion vacated, 42 F.3d 626 (11th Cir. 1994).

[247] *Wyatt v. U.S.,* 271 F.3d 1090 (Fed. Cir. 2001).

[248] Fla. Stat. Ann. § 70.001(4).

[249] *Montgomery v. Carter County, Tennessee,* 226 F.3d 758 (6th Cir. 2000).

[250] *Daniel v. County of Santa Barbara,* 288 F.3d 375, 382 (9th Cir. 2002).

[251] See *Southern Pacific Transp. Co. v. City of Los Angeles,* 922 F.2d 498, 505 (9th Cir. 1990).

[252] *Williamson County,* 473 U.S. at 194, 105 S. Ct. at 3120.

[253] *First English Evangelical Lutheran Church of Glendale v. Los Angeles County, Cal.,* 482 U.S. 304, 107 S. Ct. 2378, 96 L. Ed. 2d 250 (1987).

adequacy.[254] The procedure need not be statutorily authorized.[255] Self-executing provisions of state constitutions, even if untested, must be pursued.[256] It is sufficient that the courts of the state will hear the claim even if the contours of the action are unclear.[257] In rare instances, futility can be established by proving that the state courts have rejected takings claims that are on all fours with the challenger's case. Since takings claims are usually highly fact specific and subject to an ad hoc analysis this will not often occur, but it does happen.

The Supreme Court has said that *Williamson County's* requirements are prudential,[258] but the parameters of what is jurisdictional and what is prudential are not clear.[259] While the Court has found the final decision rule met in several cases, it has not ruled on the specific steps necessary to meet the compensation requirement other than to say that compensation must be pursued if the state has an adequate procedure. While one court has held that the compensation requirement is jurisdictional,[260] other courts have assumed it is prudential.[261]

Once a property owner has pursued the compensation remedy, the law of res judicata and issue preclusion will usually preclude a Fifth Amendment claim from being maintained in federal court. Adjudication of the claim in state court bars a subsequent suit in federal court under the full faith and credit statute.[262] Over the years numerous lower courts have so held,[263] and the Supreme Court confirmed this rule in *San Remo Hotel, L.P. v. City and County of San Francisco.*[264] That the decision was unanimous was not surprising. There is no justification for duplicative litigation (and no Justice offered one) that would allow a federal district court to second guess a decision of a state court, thereby undermining the integrity of the courts, not to mention overusing limited resources.

Collateral attack of the state court judgment is not available in federal district court. A property owner who is dissatisfied with the results obtained from the state court is limited to appealing directly to the United States Supreme Court. While there is disagreement over whether the action pursued in state court is a federal or state-based claim, under even the latter view, once litigated, rules of issue preclusion likely

---

[254] See, e.g., *Colony Cove Properties, LLC v. City of Carson,* 640 F.3d 948 (9th Cir. 2011), cert. denied, 132 S. Ct. 456, 181 L. Ed. 2d 308 (2011).

[255] *Southview Associates, Ltd. v. Bongartz,* 980 F.2d 84 (2d Cir. 1992).

[256] *Peters v. Village of Clifton,* 498 F.3d 727 (7th Cir. 2007).

[257] *Coles v. Granville,* 448 F.3d 853 (6th Cir.2006).

[258] See § 10.10.

[259] See *Guggenheim v. City of Goleta,* 638 F.3d 1111 (9th Cir. 2010), cert. denied, 131 S. Ct. 2455, 179 L. Ed. 2d 1210 (2011), discussing the issue in depth.

[260] *Snaza v. City of Saint Paul,* 548 F.3d 1178, 1182 (8th Cir. 2008).

[261] *Guggenheim v. City of Goleta,* 638 F.3d 1111 (9th Cir. 2010), cert. denied, 131 S. Ct. 2455, 179 L. Ed. 2d 1210 (2011).

[262] 28 U.S.C.A. § 1738. *San Remo Hotel, L.P. v. City and County of San Francisco, Cal.,* 545 U.S. 323, 125 S. Ct. 2491, 162 L. Ed. 2d 315 (2005).

[263] See, e.g., *Griffin v. State of R.I.,* 760 F.2d 359 (1st Cir. 1985); *Peduto v. City of North Wildwood,* 878 F.2d 725 (3d Cir. 1989).

[264] *San Remo Hotel, L.P. v. City and County of San Francisco, Cal.,* 545 U.S. 323, 125 S. Ct. 2491, 162 L. Ed. 2d 315 (2005).

will bar a suit in federal court on the federal claim since the issues being tried in state court would be the same.[265]

Mixing the state compensation rule with preclusion rules has paradoxical consequences due to the custom courts have of referring to the state compensation rule as one of ripeness. Viewing the matter through the lens of ripeness, one expects a suit to lie in federal court after doing what is required in state court. Yet, engaging in the process necessary to give rise to the claim also terminates it. The ripeness label is misleading and its continued use by courts is unfortunate.

The continuing vitality of the state compensation requirement is in some doubt. Four justices issued a concurring opinion in *San Remo,* indicating dissatisfaction with it. *Williamson County's* interpretation of the Fifth Amendment, while defensible, is not unassailable. It is defensible in that while a federal forum is denied, such denial does not violate the constitution. Our dual system presumes state court competency. Furthermore, state courts have greater experience in land use matters than federal courts, and they are interpreting their own law.

On the other hand, neither the language of the Fifth Amendment nor the rationale of inverse condemnation compels the conclusion that compensation must first be sought from the state by way of litigation. The cause of action could be said to arise when the action complained of is final under prong one of *Williamson County,* or the Court could modify the prong two rule to say that the cause of action arises when the property owner simply demands compensation and the state refuses to pay.[266] Practically, it may not matter since those few claimants who manage to get to federal court seem to fare as poorly as takings claimants do in state court.

If the matter is thought to be in need of change, the Court has two solutions: rewrite the law of res judicata and full faith and credit or rewrite the law of the Fifth Amendment. *San Remo* tells us the former will not happen. The *San Remo* concurrence, however, suggests that the Court might take the latter option. Also, word may come from Congress, which has considered *Williamson County's* State Court Compensation Requirement from time to time.

§ 10:11 Takings Legislation

Over the past two decades, many states considered, and a few adopted, legislation commonly labeled "takings legislation." These efforts, often voter-initiated, do not define a constitutional taking, which is a job for the judicial branch, but rather impose procedural steps to be followed in the adoption and application of land use regulations or establish new causes of action for landowners requiring compensation for any reduction in property value or, in some instances, a more modest reduction in property value than required by the courts under the Fifth Amendment. These takings bills generally have been reactions against the takings law developed in the courts, which, from the viewpoint of the proponents, is perceived as underprotective of the property rights of

---

[265] See Roberts, Procedural Implications of Williamson County/First English Takings Litigation: Reservations, Removal, Diversity, Supplemental Jurisdiction, *Rooker-Feldman,* and Res Judicata, 31 Envtl. L. Rep. 10353, 10355 (2001).

[266] A demand letter, nothing more, might suffice. At least one lower court has so held. See *Dickinson Leisure Industries, Inc. v. City of Dickinson,* 329 F. Supp. 2d 835 (S.D. Tex. 2004).

landowners. Two distinct types of bills have been considered: takings impact or assessment bills and compensation bills.

A. Impact or Assessment Laws

Takings impact legislation requires specified state agencies or local governmental entities to assess the likely economic effect of any proposed law that might affect land values. The catalyst for takings impact laws was Executive Order 12630 issued in 1988 by President Reagan, which uses a process roughly analogous to the environmental impact statement required for federal action under the National Environmental Policy Act.[267]

The executive order directs federal agencies to prepare a takings implication assessment (TIA) to determine whether proposed actions are likely to effect a taking, to estimate the cost to the agency of paying compensation, and to consider less intrusive alternatives.[268] A TIA must be prepared at each step of the rule making process, and be submitted to the Office of Management and Budget for review. While the order uses Fifth Amendment takings terminology, it directs agencies to use a definition of a taking that does not restate existing case law. Instead, the order uses a definition characterized by its principal drafter as a "'conservative view' of takings law * * * resolving * * * uncertainty in favor of the affected individual rights."[269] The TIA is designated as an internal management tool, and is not subject to judicial review.

A dozen or so states require takings impact assessments.[270] These obligate state agencies, and in some instances local governments, to conduct a study of all proposed rules to determine their potential impact on property values, but they vary widely in specifics. Unlike the federal executive order, state statutes normally do not direct the use of legislative takings standards, but direct agencies to refer to existing case law. Exemptions may also exist. For example, under the Texas statute, government enforcement actions are exempt as are actions protecting groundwater.[271]

It is questionable whether the benefits of these risk assessment laws outweigh the high costs of compliance. The people, paper, and time that it takes to comply could significantly slow government action. If the requirements are sufficiently onerous, the regulators simply may not take action. That, of course, may be the result that proponents desire. The government may also realize some savings by not having to pay compensation awards for precipitous, ill-considered regulations. Individuals who are left unregulated will benefit, but their neighbors and the public generally will be harmed if the process induces excess timidity in regulators.

Since impact acts require a determination of whether a proposed action is a taking on its face, a "mission impossible" in one sense, they may not be too onerous. The test for a facial taking is that a challenger must show that the mere enactment of a law ef-

---

[267] 42 U.S.C.A. §§ 4321 to 4361.

[268] Exec. Order No. 12630, 53 Fed. Reg. 8859 (Mar. 15, 1988).

[269] Mark L. Pollot, The Effect of the Federal Takings Executive Order, Land Use Law & Zoning Dig. 3, 5 (May 1989) (author was principal draftsman of executive order). See also McElfish, Jr., The Takings Executive Order: Constitutional Jurisprudence or Political Philosophy?, 18 Envtl. L. Rep. 10474 (Nov. 1988).

[270] See, e.g., Del. Code Ann., tit. 29, § 605. See listing in Coursen, Property Rights Legislation: A Survey of Federal and State Assessment and Compensation Measures, 26 Envtl. L. Rep. 10239, 10249 (May 1996).

[271] See *Bragg v. Edwards Aquifer Authority*, 71 S.W.3d 729 (Tex. 2002).

fects the taking, and one must decide that there is no set of circumstances under which the law can constitutionally be applied. That is a tall order for a challenger to meet, and it is relatively easy to state that an act is not facially a taking.

B. Compensation Laws

Compensation bills have been introduced in many states over the past two decades, but have passed in only a few. These bills generally require that compensation be paid when property owners suffer any, or a specific percentage of, diminished value as a result of government regulation. By initiative in 2004, voters in Oregon enacted the most extreme version of such a statute. Known as Measure 37, the act requires compensation for the enforcement of a land use regulation that has the effect of causing any reduction in value.[272] Government can opt to waive the law rather than pay. The state supreme court upheld the law [273] in 2007. Then, the people, having second thoughts, enacted Measure 49, significantly modifying Measure 37. Measure 49 allows rural landowners to build one to 10 houses under various scenarios, but, prohibits larger subdivisions and commercial and industrial development. Section 197.352 (1) now provides that "[i]f a public entity enacts one or more land use regulations that *restrict the residential use of private real property or a farming or forest practice* and that reduce the fair market value of the property, then the owner of the property shall be entitled to just compensation * * *."[274]

A resurgence of property-rights advocacy followed the 2005 decision in *Kelo v. City of New London*,[275] where the Supreme Court reaffirmed use of relaxed judicial review of legislative public use determinations under the Fifth Amendment.[276] This led to "anti-Kelo" ballot initiatives in a dozen or so states in the November, 2006 elections. In a few states regulatory takings were tacked onto to these public use initiatives. They followed generally the Oregon statute, enhancing compensation requirements. Initiatives in Washington, Idaho, and California failed, while one in Arizona passed.[277]

In 1995, Florida enacted the Bert J. Harris Private Property Rights Protection Act, which creates a new cause of action for governmental regulations that inordinately burden real property.[278] Florida's use of the "inordinate burden" standard, rather than a set percentage of lost value, is a major difference from other states' compensation laws. The question of when the burden reaches the point of being inordinate is judicial. The Florida act is significantly different procedurally from traditional inverse condemnation claims. Under the Florida act, if an application for development permission is rejected, a property owner can file a notice of claim. The government must then advise the property owner of the permissible land uses by issuing a so-called ripeness decision. If the government fails to issue such a determination within six months, the mat-

---

[272] Or. Rev. Stat. §§ 197.352 et seq.

[273] *MacPherson v. Department of Administrative Services*, 340 Or. 117, 130 P.3d 308 (2006).

[274] Language in italics reflect Measure 49's change. See Sullivan and Bragar, The Augean Stables: Measure 49 and the Herculean Task of Correcting an Improvident Initiative Measure in Oregon, 46 Willamette L. Rev. 577, 620 (2010).

[275] *Kelo v. City of New London, Conn.*, 545 U.S. 469, 125 S. Ct. 2655, 162 L. Ed. 2d 439 (2005).

[276] See infra § 16:3.

[277] Echeverria and Hansen-Young, The Track Record on Takings Legislation: Lessons from Democracy's Laboratories, 28 Stan. Envtl. L.J. 439, 444–445 (2009).

[278] Fla. Stat. Ann. § 70.001(2).

ter is deemed ripe.[279] The statute also requires government to initiate a settlement process.

In contrast to Florida's inordinate burden standard, other states use fixed percentage reductions. The Texas statute, also adopted in 1995, defines a statutory taking as a market value reduction of 25% of the portion of land affected permanently or temporarily by governmental action.[280] The act applies to most state agency actions, but only covers municipalities when they are acting extraterritorially. Actions taken that are reasonably necessary to fulfill obligations mandated by state or federal law are also exempt. The government has the choice between an invalidation and compensation remedy. Louisiana provides a cause of action for governmental actions that result in a diminution in value of 20% or more of agricultural or forestry property. [281] The Mississippi statute sets 40% as the triggering loss in value and it applies only to forest land.[282]

The future of compensation laws is uncertain. Their effect on the efficacy of land use planning, on the government treasury, and on the perceived fairness to non-compensated neighbors remains to be seen. Their one-sided nature is disheartening. While they proceed from the belief that judicially-developed takings law underprotects the property owner, compensation laws, which government will likely waive rather than pay due to inadequate financial resources to pay, may underprotect the neighbors of the now-unregulated property owner and the public. An arguable deficiency with these efforts to treat property owners more fairly is the notable omission of any effort to recapture for the public the windfall gains conferred on landowners by virtue of public improvements and government regulation. We discuss the windfalls and wipeouts dilemma of land use regulation in Chapter 3 and commend it to you at this point.

III. DUE PROCESS AND EQUAL PROTECTION

§ 10:12 Substantive Due Process

Substantive due process limits the exercise of the police power by requiring that a land use regulation promote the health, safety, morals, or general welfare by a rational means. It protects against arbitrary or capricious actions,[283] which "'may not take place no matter what procedural protections accompany them' * * *."[284] Substantive due process stems from natural law theories of the 17th and 18th centuries under which all men were thought to be possessed of certain fundamental rights that no government should infringe. While the doctrine's legitimacy as a federal constitutional right has long been contested, legal historian James Ely concludes that it draws "upon a heritage of liberty firmly fixed in the matrix of American legal thought."[285]

---

[279] Fla. Stat. Ann. § 70.001(5)(a). See *Sosa v. City of West Palm Beach,* 762 So. 2d 981 (Fla. 4th DCA 2000) (dismissing claim for failure to file an appraisal in support of claim).

[280] Tex. Gov't Code Ann. § 2007.002(5).

[281] La. Rev. Stat. Ann. § 3:3622.

[282] Miss. Code Ann. §§ 49–33–1 to 49–33–17.

[283] *Village of Arlington Heights v. Metropolitan Housing Development Corp.*, 429 U.S. 252, 263, 97 S. Ct. 555, 562, 50 L. Ed. 2d 450 (1977).

[284] *Harris v. City of Akron,* 20 F.3d 1396, 1405 (6th Cir. 1994).

[285] Ely, Jr., The Oxymoron Reconsidered: Myth and Reality in the Origins of Substantive Due Process, 16 Const. Comment. 315, 345 (1999).

The use of substantive due process to overturn legislative action has waxed and waned over the course of our constitutional history. The doctrine was a high hurdle for governmental regulations to clear during the first part of the twentieth century when the Court, viewed as acting as a kind of superlegislature, gave little deference to the other branches of government. Starting in 1934 with *Nebbia v. New York,*[286] the Court turned away from using substantive due process as a device to frustrate the legislative will. The high court and other courts today may articulate substantive due process as a theoretical constraint on government action, but, by according great deference to the legislative branch, most courts do not use it to strike down legislation unless fundamental rights are affected. Usually unsuccessful and still controversial, substantive due process continues to be a basis of complaint in many land use cases, and for a time, it appeared dressed in the garb of takings claims.[287]

A.   Major Supreme Court Cases: The 1920s and 1970s

In 1926, the Supreme Court upheld a comprehensive zoning ordinance against a substantive due process challenge in *Village of Euclid v. Ambler Realty Co.*[288] The Court's general endorsement of zoning opened the doors to the widespread adoption of land use controls. Prior to *Euclid,* state courts divided on the constitutionality of zoning. While most had upheld zoning, some had found zoning's interference with free market forces to be an arbitrary invasion of property rights.[289] Thus, *Euclid* was a critical confrontation between unrestricted development rights and the ability of cities to plan and manage growth.

Euclid's zoning ordinance divided the village into six use districts and zoned Ambler Realty's land into one industrial and two residential classifications. The realty company challenged the ordinance on its face claiming that the mere existence of the ordinance greatly reduced the value of its land and thus deprived it of its rights under the 14th Amendment. The Court disagreed, finding the zoning ordinance was a legitimate police power regulation due to the public interest in segregating incompatible land uses. *Euclid* set a deferential tone: "If the validity of the legislative classification for zoning purposes be fairly debatable, the legislative judgment must be allowed to control."[290] The Court attributed no significance to the 75% diminution in the landowner's property value as a result of the adoption of the ordinance. The *Euclid* Court, however, did issue a warning that when zoning came to be challenged in an as-applied rather than facial context, it might be found arbitrary.

Two years later the Court fulfilled its *Euclid* warning, finding a zoning ordinance invalid on substantive due process grounds. In *Nectow v. City of Cambridge,*[291] a landowner lost a contract to sell a large parcel of land because the city had zoned a small strip of the property for residential use. While a master appointed by the lower state court had found no justification for placing the boundary through Nectow's land, rather than down the middle of the street, the state supreme court was unwilling to second guess where the zoning boundary had been set and upheld the zoning. The Supreme

---

[286] 291 U.S. 502, 54 S. Ct. 505, 78 L. Ed. 940 (1934).

[287] See discussion supra §§ 10:4 and 10:5.

[288] *Village of Euclid, Ohio v. Ambler Realty Co.,* 272 U.S. 365, 47 S. Ct. 114, 71 L. Ed. 303 (1926).

[289] Compare *Goldman v. Crowther,* 147 Md. 282, 128 A. 50 (1925) (zoning unconstitutional) and *Lincoln Trust Co. v. Williams Bldg. Corporation,* 229 N.Y. 313, 128 N.E. 209 (1920) (zoning valid).

[290] 272 U.S. at 388, 47 S. Ct. at 118.

[291] *Nectow v. City of Cambridge,* 277 U.S. 183, 48 S. Ct. 447, 72 L. Ed. 842 (1928).

Court, however, followed the master's findings and held that zoning the tract for residential use was arbitrary in that it did not promote the public interest.

With the pro-free market, anti-regulation attitude of the Supreme Court in the 1920s, it is tempting to think that *Nectow's scrutiny* was the norm and *Euclid's deference* the anomaly. But, in the land use area that was not the case. In three other cases in the late 1920s, the Court used *Euclid's* deferential test to sustain land use controls in as-applied, substantive due process challenges.[292] After the *Euclid* Court set the stage for relaxed due process review of land use controls, it left the development of constitutional land use law to the state courts during the next half-century. In the 1970s the Supreme Court reentered the land use field.

In 1974, the Court declined an opportunity to reinvigorate substantive due process in *Village of Belle Terre v. Boraas.*[293] An ordinance allowed only single family use and defined a family as either any number of related persons or not more than two unrelated adults. The effect, and likely purpose, of the ordinance was to prevent groups of students from a nearby university from living together in the small village. When the village ordered a landowner who rented his house to six unrelated students to cease and desist, he brought suit on several grounds, urging the Court to find "that social homogeneity is not a legitimate interest of government."[294] The ordinance likely would have failed had any type of exacting scrutiny been applied, but it survived because the Court used the deferential rational basis test. The Court saw the ordinance as merely regulating social and economic affairs, and not implicating any fundamental rights or affecting any suspect class. Several state courts, refusing to accept the *Belle Terre* Court's deferential posture, have invalidated ordinances with restrictive family definitions relying on state constitutional provisions of substantive due process or privacy.[295]

Three years later, substantive due process rose phoenix-like in *Moore v. City of East Cleveland.*[296] *Moore,* like *Belle Terre,* involved a regulation aimed at allowing only "single families" in single homes. The ordinance's complex definition of family precluded the plaintiff from living with her son and two grandsons (who were also first cousins). Aware of the quagmire it was stepping into, a plurality of the Court entered the "treacherous field" of substantive due process to strike down the ordinance because the special sanctity of the family was at stake. The Court found the ordinance to be an "intrusive regulation of the family," distinguishing it from the *Belle Terre* ordinance, which affected only unrelated persons. Under strict scrutiny review, the city could establish no compelling justification for "slicing deeply into the family" in order to reduce congestion or crime.

Moore is a limited revival of substantive due process. At most, the Court is likely to use the strict scrutiny of *Moore* only when a fundamental right or suspect class is affected by a land use control. The difficulty of enticing the Court to use substantive

---

[292] *Zahn v. Board of Public Works of City of Los Angeles,* 274 U.S. 325, 47 S. Ct. 594, 71 L. Ed. 1074 (1927) (upholding exclusion of business from residential zone); *Gorieb v. Fox,* 274 U.S. 603, 47 S. Ct. 675, 71 L. Ed. 1228 (1927), and *Miller v. Schoene,* 276 U.S. 272, 48 S. Ct. 246, 72 L. Ed. 568 (1928).

[293] *Village of Belle Terre v. Boraas,* 416 U.S. 1, 94 S. Ct. 1536, 39 L. Ed. 2d 797 (1974).

[294] *Belle Terre,* 416 U.S. at 3, 94 S. Ct. at 1538.

[295] *City of Santa Barbara v. Adamson,* 27 Cal. 3d 123, 164 Cal. Rptr. 539, 610 P.2d 436 (1980); *State v. Baker,* 81 N.J. 99, 405 A.2d 368 (1979); *Charter Tp. of Delta v. Dinolfo,* 419 Mich. 253, 351 N.W.2d 831 (1984).

[296] *Moore v. City of East Cleveland, Ohio,* 431 U.S. 494, 97 S. Ct. 1932, 52 L. Ed. 2d 531 (1977).

due process is reflected in the fact that only five justices voted in *Moore* to overturn a state court conviction of a grandmother for allowing a second grandchild to live with her upon the death of his mother.

B.   Relationship to 14th Amendment Equal Protection and Procedural Due Process Guarantees

Perhaps due to its amorphous nature, substantive due process tends to be confused with other constitutional guarantees such as equal protection, procedural due process, the First Amendment, and, most particularly, the takings clause. While the general test for equal protection challenges and substantive due process challenges is the same, the two guarantees differ. Equal protection examines the rationality of governmental classifications of people and property while substantive due process concerns the rationality of the restraints. Procedural due process is concerned with whether the method of application of a law is fair, and substantive due process deals with whether the result is fair. While distinct in theory, these due process claims sometimes merge in judicial analysis. Finally, conduct that is challenged as arbitrary, such as the denial of a permit in retaliation against a developer for seeking judicial review of a city's zoning laws, might also be viewed as a violation of free speech rights.

C.   Relationship to Fifth Amendment Regulatory Takings Doctrine

The relationship between substantive due process and regulatory takings has been confusing. There are two areas of confusion. One is whether the excessive economic impact caused by an otherwise valid law can constitute either a Fifth Amendment taking or a violation of due process. The other is whether a law that fails to substantially advance a legitimate state interest can be either a Fifth Amendment taking or a violation of due process. The answer to the first is most likely, "no." Excessive economic impact is likely only actionable under the Fifth Amendment. The answer to the second is "no." A statute's failure to advance a legitimate state interest is only actionable under the due process clause.

This first area of confusion is understandable since the formulations of the two constraints, except for remedy, has at times been almost identical. While substantive due process is most often expressed as imposing a requirement that a law promote a legitimate public end in a rational manner,[297] the Court has said on occasion that substantive due process also means that laws ought not be unduly oppressive upon the affected class.[298] The claim has even been labeled a "due process taking."[299] This "unduly onerous" prong of substantive due process, which first surfaced in 1894,[300] created no doctrinal problem until *Pennsylvania Coal v. Mahon*[301] when the Court used the same idea to suggest that excessive regulations, those that went "too far," were Fifth Amendment takings.

---

[297] See *Honeywell, Inc. v. Minnesota Life and Health Ins. Guar. Ass'n*, 110 F.3d 547, 554 (8th Cir. 1997).

[298] *Nollan v. California Coastal Com'n*, 483 U.S. 825, 845, 107 S. Ct. 3141, 3153, 97 L. Ed. 2d 677 (1987) (dissenting opinion).

[299] *City of Monterey v. Del Monte Dunes at Monterey, Ltd.*, 526 U.S. 687, 753, 119 S. Ct. 1624, 1660, 143 L. Ed. 2d 882 (1999).

[300] *Lawton v. Steele*, 152 U.S. 133, 137, 14 S. Ct. 499, 501, 38 L. Ed. 385 (1894).

[301] *Pennsylvania Coal Co. v. Mahon*, 260 U.S. 393, 43 S. Ct. 158, 67 L. Ed. 322 (1922).

Faced with a regulation alleged to be excessive in its impact on an individual, a court might find that the regulation is unduly onerous and thus void under substantive due process or that it goes "too far" and becomes a taking under *Pennsylvania Coal,* requiring the payment of compensation.[302] Under the due process clause, the remedy generally will be injunctive relief and possibly damages,[303] while just compensation is the mandatory remedy under the takings clause.[304] Low level scrutiny is applied to substantive due process challenges, but higher scrutiny *may* apply to takings claims.[305]

This apparent choice to sue under the Fifth Amendment or the 14th Amendment is illusory. The Court has held in other areas that where there is an explicit textual source in the constitution it must be used to determine liability rather than generalized notions of substantive due process.[306] If, as several lower courts have held, the Fifth Amendment takings clause qualifies as sufficiently explicit under this theory, substantive due process claims that are duplicative of takings claims, what we refer to as the "unduly onerous" substantive due process claim, should be subsumed by the Fifth Amendment.[307] Given the Court's recognition of the regulatory takings doctrine, there is no justification for a duplicative test under substantive due process.

Not all substantive due process claims are subsumed. Those claims premised on arbitrary state action, which allege that an act is an invalid police power measure, are not duplicative of takings claims and must be distinguished from claims that an action has an unduly onerous economic impact. The latter, duplicative claim should fade into obscurity, but the former should not since it is independent from a takings claim. For example, a property owner's complaint that a regulation was adopted solely in response to neighbor prejudices,[308] or in retaliation against a developer for seeking judicial review of a city's actions,[309] or that development permission was denied in bad faith [310] might be held to violate substantive due process on grounds of arbitrariness. Lacking legitimate public purposes, such state actions would not be characterized as takings and would never be sustainable with the payment of just compensation. Rather, the actions would be invalidated.

These complaints of arbitrary action bring us to the second area of confusion. For a time, such complaints were actionable as takings. The culprit was the troublesome case of *Agins v. City of Tiburon.*[311] In 1980, the *Agins* Court injected the substantive due process requirement that an action must "substantially advance a legitimate state interest" into the Fifth Amendment's takings clause and it became a test separate from the *Pennsylvania Coal/Penn Central* economic impact test. Twenty-five years later the Court acknowledged its mistake.

---

[302] *Eberle v. Dane County Bd. of Adjustment,* 227 Wis. 2d 609, 595 N.W.2d 730, 744 n.29 (1999).

[303] Damages may be awarded under § 1983. See infra § 10:25.

[304] But see § 10:9 for limited use of injunctive relief.

[305] See supra §§ 10:5 and 10:6.

[306] *Whitley v. Albers,* 475 U.S. 312, 106 S. Ct. 1078, 89 L. Ed. 2d 251 (1986); *Graham v. Connor,* 490 U.S. 386, 109 S. Ct. 1865, 104 L. Ed. 2d 443 (1989).

[307] *Graham* "precludes the use of 'substantive due process' analysis when a more specific constitutional provision governs." *City of Cuyahoga Falls, Ohio v. Buckeye Community Hope Foundation,* 538 U.S. 188, 200–01, 123 S. Ct. 1389, 1397, 155 L. Ed. 2d 349 (2003) (Scalia, J., concurring).

[308] *Marks v. City of Chesapeake, Va.,* 883 F.2d 308 (4th Cir. 1989).

[309] *Carr v. Town of Dewey Beach,* 730 F. Supp. 591 (D. Del. 1990).

[310] *Woodwind Estates, Ltd. v. Gretkowski,* 205 F.3d 118 (3d Cir. 2000).

[311] *Agins v. City of Tiburon,* 447 U.S. 255, 100 S. Ct. 2138, 65 L. Ed. 2d 106 (1980).

In *Lingle v. Chevron, USA, Inc.,*[312] the Court overruled *Agins.* In a surprisingly frank opinion, the Court admitted what critics had long contended, that the "substantially advances" "formula prescribes an inquiry in the nature of a due process, not a takings, test, and that it has no proper place in our takings jurisprudence."[313] The "substantially advances" means-end formula, said the Court, addresses a question that is a condition precedent to a takings claim, which is whether a regulation is effective in achieving a legitimate goal. If a law fails to promote a legitimate end, it is invalid and it makes no sense to proceed to discuss whether compensation is due under the Fifth Amendment.

D. Substantive Due Process Today: A Tool of Limited Use

The degree of deference a court affords the challenged government action is critical to the outcome of a claim of substantive due process. The Supreme Court recognizes a "right to be free from arbitrary or irrational zoning actions,"[314] but, in the absence of a fundamental right, the review is deferential. As Professor Ely observes, "the Supreme Court has not invalidated an economic regulation as violative of due process since 1937."[315] The lesson one might take is that it is wise not to have high expectations when asserting a substantive due process claim. While some thought the Supreme Court's decision in *Lingle v. Chevron U.S.A. Inc.* might reinvigorate substantive due process that has not proven to be the case. Substantive due process claims not based on fundamental rights continue to be rejected.[316]

Substantive due process is violated where the complained of action "shocks the conscience."[317] Some courts use language apparently attempting to illustrate how difficult it is to meet that test, requiring the action to be "egregiously unacceptable,"[318] or "truly horrendous."[319] These tests reflect the lack of judicial appetite in the federal courts to use substantive due process to revive *Lochner*-type judicial interference with the legislative and executive branches.[320]

While it is rare for a landowner to prevail on a substantive due process claim, the doctrine is tenacious, and the test so vague,[321] that on occasion some courts will find violations of substantive due process.[322] In contrast to federal courts, which by and large shun what they perceive of as sitting as zoning board of appeals, some state

---

[312] *Lingle v. Chevron U.S.A. Inc.,* 544 U.S. 528, 125 S. Ct. 2074, 161 L. Ed. 2d 876 (2005). See § 10:5.

[313] Lingle, 544 U.S. at 540, 125 S. Ct. 2083.

[314] *Village of Arlington Heights v. Metropolitan Housing Development Corp.,* 429 U.S. 252, 263, 97 S. Ct. 555, 562, 50 L. Ed. 2d 450 (1977).

[315] James W. Ely Jr., "Poor Relation" Once More: The Supreme Court and the Vanishing Rights of Property Owners, Cato Sup. Ct. Rev., 2004–2005, at 39.

[316] See Byrne, Due Process Land Use Claims after *Lingle,* 34 Ecology L.Q. 471, 477–478 (2007).

[317] *County of Sacramento v. Lewis,* 523 U.S. 833, 846, 118 S. Ct. 1708, 1717, 140 L. Ed. 2d 1043 (1998); *Torromeo v. Town of Fremont, NH,* 438 F.3d 113 (1st Cir. 2006).

[318] *Licari v. Ferruzzi,* 22 F.3d 344, 347 (1st Cir. 1994).

[319] *SFW Arecibo, Ltd. v. Rodriguez,* 415 F.3d 135, 141 (1st Cir. 2005).

[320] See Levy, Escaping Lochner's Shadow: Toward a Coherent Jurisprudence of Economic Rights, 73 N.C. L. Rev. 329 (1995).

[321] Wilson, A Forty-Foot Boat and Two Girls' Equals Damages: Recent Constitutional Claims for Damages in Land-Use Litigation, 37 Urb. Law. 561, 564 (2005).

[322] Many are colored by political, religious, racial, or crass socio-economic discrimination, but some involve solely economic harm. See, e.g., *JSS Realty Co., LLC v. Town of Kittery, Maine,* 177 F. Supp. 2d 64 (D. Me. 2001).

courts actively oversee land use law through due process. Courts that do intervene are more likely to find delaying and deceptive conduct by the government as arbitrary [323] than to second guess the wisdom of zoning land for a particular purpose.[324] However, an erroneous interpretation or application of state law does not constitute a violation of due process.[325]

The degree of deference accorded to the government may also depend on whether the challenged action is legislative or administrative. The difference is important since a court may hypothesize a rational basis for a legislative action but insist on actual proof for administrative action.[326] While all courts agree that review of economic claims is deferential, some treat all zoning actions, including variances, as legislative for the purposes of reviewing the substance of an action.[327] Other courts divide acts along more traditional lines and confer less deference to administrative acts.[328] Even then, the review is described as "extremely narrow."[329]

E.   The Property Interest Required

In addition to varying degrees of receptivity to the merits of arbitrary and capricious substantive due process claims, a conflict exists among the courts as to the property interest sufficient to invoke such a claim.[330] While ownership of an interest in land is sufficient for some courts,[331] most courts require a property owner to establish a right or entitlement in a permit.[332] The showing is difficult to make since an entitlement exists only if there is a strong likelihood or virtual assurance that the permit will be issued.[333] If the regime vests the decisionmaker with discretion, there is no entitlement. Since land use permitting processes generally do confer discretion on the authorities, a developer who seeks, or needs, to establish a property right in a permit loses its case at the outset.[334] If one has no right to a permit, there is no need to determine whether the action denying it was arbitrary.

Property rights in permits sometimes are found.[335] Where a zoning code's special exception procedure for residential use district required the board to issue a permit if

---

[323] See, e.g., *Mission Springs, Inc. v. City of Spokane*, 134 Wash. 2d 947, 954 P.2d 250 (1998).

[324] *New Port Largo, Inc. v. Monroe County*, 95 F.3d 1084 (11th Cir. 1996).

[325] See, e.g., *Torromeo v. Town Of Fremont, NH*, 438 F.3d 113 (1st Cir. 2006).

[326] *Shelton v. City of College Station*, 780 F.2d 475 (5th Cir.1986).

[327] Shelton, 780 F.2d at 479.

[328] See list and discussion of cases in *Pearson v. City of Grand Blanc,* 961 F.2d 1211, 1220 (6th Cir. 1992).

[329] Pearson, 961 F.2d 1211.

[330] See *George Washington University v. District of Columbia*, 318 F.3d 203, 207 (D.C. Cir. 2003) (surveying law of other circuits, though missing the 7th circuit as joining the 3rd Circuit in adopting the minority view) and *Pearson v. City of Grand Blanc*, 961 F.2d 1211, 1220 (6th Cir. 1992).

[331] See, e.g., *Polenz v. Parrott,* 883 F.2d 551, 555 (7th Cir. 1989). For list of other cases, see Juergensmeyer and Roberts, Land Use Planning and Development Regulation Law §10.8 (Practitioner's Edition 3rd ed.2012).

[332] See. e.g., *RRI Realty Corp. v. Incorporated Village of Southampton*, 870 F.2d 911 (2d Cir. 1989). For list of other cases, see Juergensmeyer and Roberts, Land Use Planning and Development Regulation Law §10.8 (Practitioner's Edition 3rd ed.2012).

[333] *Regency Outdoor Advertising, Inc. v. City of Los Angeles*, 39 Cal. 4th 507, 46 Cal. Rptr. 3d 742, 139 P.3d 119 (2006). For list of other cases, see Juergensmeyer and Roberts, Land Use Planning and Development Regulation Law §10.8 (Practitioner's Edition 3rd ed.2012).

[334] *Kelley Property Development, Inc. v. Town of Lebanon*, 226 Conn. 314, 627 A.2d 909 (1993).

[335] *Woodwind Estates, Ltd. v. Gretkowski*, 205 F.3d 118 (3d Cir. 2000).

the qualifying criteria are met, the court found a property owner could challenge denial on substantive due process grounds.[336] In another case, a court found a property interest in the exercise of an option to buy land, which conferred equitable title under state law.[337] A vested right acquired under the state's zoning law may also be regarded as a property interest.[338] Even then, the owner must still show an arbitrary denial to prevail. If the state has a rational reason for its action, it will not violate due process. Courts applying a deferential standard of review are not likely to find a violation of due process.[339] Some courts, using more scrutiny, have held that the denial of a permit to which an applicant was entitled is a violation of substantive due process.[340]

The entitlement test for property stems from what were once called the Supreme Court's "new property" cases that dealt with procedural due process rights in certain government benefit programs.[341] This new property theory is used in the land use area to shrink property rights for substantive due process purposes. This is doubly odd since the right to use land has not historically been thought of as a government benefit, and even if it were, the new property cases expanded procedural due process protection. The problem with the entitlement test comes when it is used as the sole source of property rights. If those courts using the entitlement theory as the exclusive route to stating a claim are correct, the government can insulate its land use regulations from judicial review simply by adopting discretionary processes. As the Seventh Circuit observed, "a single local ordinance providing that 'we may put your land in any zone we want, for any reason we feel like' would abolish all property rights in land overnight."[342] The Supreme Court should set the matter straight.

F.   Finality and Ripeness

Finality and ripeness issues with respect to substantive due process claims are similar to those discussed previously with regard to Fifth Amendment takings claims.[343] In *Williamson County Regional Planning Commission v. Hamilton Bank of Johnson City,*[344] the Court imposed a two-fold requirement on regulatory takings claims. Under prong one, the landowner must obtain a final decision from the government as to what land uses will be allowed. Prong two requires the landowner pursue compensation in state court.

In *Williamson County,* the Court applied the final decision ripeness rule to substantive due process claims that allege, in a manner identical to the Fifth Amendment, that a regulation is unduly onerous, a so called "due process takings" claim. Thus, where the substantive due process claim is seen as a disguised takings claim dressed up in due process to language to avoid *Williamson County,* it will not work.[345] The point

---

[336] See *George Washington University v. District of Columbia,* 318 F.3d 203 (D.C. Cir. 2003).

[337] *Forest Properties, Inc. v. U.S.,* 39 Fed. Cl. 56 (1997), judgment aff'd, 177 F.3d 1360 (Fed. Cir. 1999).

[338] *Nasierowski Bros. Inv. Co. v. City of Sterling Heights,* 949 F.2d 890, 892 (6th Cir. 1991).

[339] *Decarion v. Monroe County,* 853 F. Supp. 1415 (S.D. Fla. 1994).

[340] See, e.g., *Walz v. Town of Smithtown,* 46 F.3d 162 (2d Cir. 1995).

[341] *Goldberg v. Kelly,* 397 U.S. 254, 90 S. Ct. 1011, 25 L. Ed. 2d 287 (1970); *Perry v. Sindermann,* 408 U.S. 593, 92 S. Ct. 2694, 33 L. Ed. 2d 570 (1972).

[342] River Park, Inc. v. City of Highland Park, 23 F.3d 164, 166 (7th Cir. 1994).

[343] See discussion supra § 10.10.

[344] *Williamson County Regional Planning Com'n v. Hamilton Bank of Johnson City,* 473 U.S. 172, 105 S. Ct. 3108, 87 L. Ed. 2d 126 (1985).

[345] *Deniz v. Municipality of Guaynabo,* 285 F.3d 142 (1st Cir. 2002).

ought not matter since it is unlikely that such a cause of action will continue to be recognized.[346]

Most courts have held that the final decision ripeness requirement applies to as-applied, arbitrary and capricious substantive due process claims.[347] The rule is not applicable to facial claims.[348]

The requirement that compensation be sought in state court for a Fifth Amendment takings claim rightly has been held not to apply to substantive due process claims based on arbitrary conduct.[349] The same result is achieved by other courts, which take the position that a cause of action for any due process claim, substantive or procedural, is not complete until state postdeprivation remedies have been used.[350] In *Zinermon v. Burch,*[351] a five-member majority of the Court, in dicta, said that a substantive due process claim is actionable regardless of potentially adequate state remedies. Numerous courts have followed this statement, but some lower courts have concluded that one must show that state remedies are inadequate in order to state a substantive due process claim.[352] It has also been held that no violation of substantive due process can occur where the victim of the deprivation has in fact received an adequate post-deprivation hearing.[353]

§ 10:13 Procedural Due Process

The Fifth and 14th Amendments prohibit government from depriving "any person of life, liberty or property without due process of law."[354] Judicial refinement of what process is "due" for what degree of deprivation and for what personal and property interests has been going on for decades. The guarantee offers both substantive and procedural protection. In contrast to substantive due process, which looks primarily at why a deprivation occurred, procedural due process asks how the deprivation came to be.

Procedural due process rights do not attach to legislation of general applicability.[355] Thus, a critical question is whether to characterize a land use decision as legislative or quasi-judicial.[356] If a rezoning is deemed legislative, the due process clause does not require that affected persons be given notice or a hearing.[357] State law may provide for some type of notice and hearing, but the constitution does not. The same question, with possibly different results, may also be asked for the purposes of deciding which

---

[346] See discussion supra § 10:12.

[347] See, e.g., *Signature Properties Intern. Ltd. Partnership v. City of Edmond,* 310 F.3d 1258 (10th Cir. 2002). For list of other cases, see Juergensmeyer and Roberts, Land Use Planning and Development Regulation Law §10.8 (Practitioner's Edition 3rd ed.2012).

[348] *County Concrete Corp. v. Town of Roxbury,* 442 F.3d 159 (3d Cir. 2006).

[349] *Southview Associates, Ltd. v. Bongartz,* 980 F.2d 84, 96 (2d Cir. 1992).

[350] See discussion infra § 10:13 regarding *Parratt* doctrine.

[351] *Zinermon v. Burch,* 494 U.S. 113, 125, 110 S. Ct. 975, 983, 108 L. Ed. 2d 100 (1990).

[352] *New Burnham Prairie Homes, Inc. v. Village of Burnham,* 910 F.2d 1474, 1481 (7th Cir. 1990).

[353] *Archuleta v. Colorado Dept. of Institutions, Div. of Youth Services,* 936 F.2d 483 (10th Cir. 1991).

[354] For a general discussion of procedural due process, see John E. Nowak and Ronald D. Rotunda, Constitutional Law, Ch. 13 (8th ed.2010).

[355] *Bi-Metallic Inv. Co. v. State Bd. of Equalization,* 239 U.S. 441, 36 S. Ct. 141, 60 L. Ed. 372 (1915).

[356] *Pearson v. City of Grand Blanc,* 961 F.2d 1211, 1220 (6th Cir. 1992).

[357] *Pro-Eco, Inc. v. Board of Com'rs of Jay County, Ind.,* 57 F.3d 505, 512 (7th Cir. 1995).

acts can be put to a referendum vote,[358] and whether personal immunity from liability exists.[359] Also, an act may be regarded as legislative for the purposes of substantive due process, yet quasi-judicial for procedural due process questions.[360]

Procedural due process rights attach to administrative or quasi-judicial decisionmaking. In land use, the decisions of the various zoning boards of adjustment and planning commissions typically are viewed as administrative or quasi-judicial. Actions by local legislative bodies pose problems. Site specific rezonings present the major difficulty since they often constitute applications of previously adopted policies to particular parcels. For that reason many courts treat these nominally legislative acts as quasi-judicial.[361] If a rezoning is quasi-judicial, due process rights attach. While the mere fact that a generally applicable law is triggered by a specific development proposal does not render it quasi-judicial,[362] an action aimed solely at one landowner may be so treated.[363] Decisions of zoning enforcement officers on permit requests are often viewed as routine, nondiscretionary actions, which do not require a hearing. This is true where the administrative officer determines objective facts that do not involve an element of discretion.[364]

The controversy over defining the requisite property interest that exists in the substantive due process cases[365] also exists in the procedural due process cases. As noted in the prior discussion, ownership of the land is sufficient for a few courts, but most courts require an entitlement under state law to that which is sought. The entitlement views poses a major hurdle in land use disputes since courts require a showing that the granting of a permit is a virtual certainty.

Where one seeks permission to use land in which one has an ownership interest or seeks due process protection for a zoning change aimed specifically and only at one's land and is told by the courts that she does not possess a property right because the state has discretion in adjudicating her request, the result is problematical as it suggests that "a single local ordinance providing that 'we may put your land in any zone we want, for any reason we feel like' would abolish all property rights in land overnight."[366] Where the challenger owns no land but possesses a mere license to use land,[367] or has a contract to buy land,[368] or a mere expectation of municipal support for a development project,[369] no property right exists. However, a right vested under state law may qualify. For example, the right to maintain a nonconforming use has been held to be protected by due process.[370]

---

[358] See supra § 5:5.

[359] See infra § 10:26.

[360] *Shelton v. City of College Station,* 780 F.2d 475, 482 (5th Cir. 1986).

[361] See discussion supra § 5:9.

[362] *L C & S, Inc. v. Warren County Area Plan Com'n,* 244 F.3d 601 (7th Cir. 2001).

[363] *Club Misty, Inc. v. Laski,* 208 F.3d 615 (7th Cir. 2000).

[364] *Jefferson Utilities, Inc. v. Jefferson County Bd. of Zoning Appeals,* 218 W. Va. 436, 624 S.E.2d 873, 874 (2005).

[365] See discussion supra § 10:12.

[366] *River Park, Inc. v. City of Highland Park,* 23 F.3d 164, 166 (7th Cir. 1994).

[367] *Federal Lands Legal Consortium ex rel. Robart Estate v. U.S.,* 195 F.3d 1190 (10th Cir. 1999).

[368] *Bryan v. City of Madison, Miss.,* 213 F.3d 267 (5th Cir. 2000).

[369] *Macone v. Town of Wakefield,* 277 F.3d 1 (1st Cir.2002).

[370] *Mator v. City of Ecorse,* 301 Fed. Appx. 476 (6th Cir. 2008).

Where a property right exists and the action taken is quasi-judicial in nature, the process that is due varies. The essence of procedural due process requires notice and an opportunity to be heard before an impartial decisionmaker, but the specifics are determined according to the particular situation. When a legislative body holds a hearing to rezone a specific parcel (in effect a quasi-judicial hearing) the landowner is entitled to individual notice. The fact that an act violates state law does not constitute a per se violation of due process. The right to cross-examine may or may not be allowed. There is no right to pre-trial discovery. Ex parte telephone conferences preceding a hearing, where the names of the callers and the substance of the comments received were not disclosed, have been held to violate due process.

The process that may be required does not always have to be given prior to the deprivation. Post-deprivation remedies available in state court suffice to meet the constitutional requirement where the deprivation occurs as the result of random or unpredictable actions.[371]

Courts differ as to whether procedural due process claims are subject to the final decision ripeness requirement that is applied to takings claims.[372] The requirement to seek compensation in state courts, an express component of a takings claim, ought to have no application to a procedural due process claim unless the claim is a disguised takings claim. However, if the deprivation occurs as the result of random or unpredictable actions and if a post-deprivation remedy is available in state court, then the *Parrott* doctrine requires that the state process be used.[373]

§ 10:14 Equal Protection

A. Introduction

The 14th Amendment's equal protection clause is "to secure every person * * * against intentional and arbitrary discrimination."[374] The guarantee that "all persons similarly situated should be treated alike"[375] is often implicated in land use law since the essence of many controls, particularly Euclidean zoning, is to classify land and people. In cases dealing with zoning's effect on economic interests, the restraint has been illusory since such ordinances traditionally have been reviewed under a highly deferential standard.

The rational basis test used by the Supreme Court to test social and economic legislation under the equal protection clause borders on being a rule of non-review. As the Court has said:

[E]qual protection is not a license for courts to judge the wisdom, fairness, or logic of legislative choices. In areas of social and economic policy, a statutory classifica-

---

[371] *Parratt v. Taylor,* 451 U.S. 527, 101 S. Ct. 1908, 68 L. Ed. 2d 420 (1981), overruled on other grounds by, Daniels v. Williams, 474 U.S. 327, 106 S. Ct. 662, 88 L. Ed. 2d 662 (1986); *Zinermon v. Burch,* 494 U.S. 113, 110 S. Ct. 975, 108 L. Ed. 2d 100 (1990) (*Parratt* inapplicable where deprivation caused by conduct pursuant to established procedure).

[372] No: *Wedgewood Ltd. Partnership I. v. Township of Liberty, Ohio,* 456 F. Supp. 2d 904 (S.D. Ohio 2006). Yes: *Dougherty v. Town of North Hempstead Bd. of Zoning Appeals,* 282 F.3d 83 (2d Cir. 2002).

[373] *Parratt v. Taylor,* 451 U.S. 527, 101 S. Ct. 1908, 68 L. Ed. 2d 420 (1981).

[374] *Village of Willowbrook v. Olech,* 528 U.S. 562, 564, 120 S. Ct. 1073, 1075, 145 L. Ed. 2d 1060 (2000).

[375] *City of Cleburne v. Cleburne Living Center,* 473 U.S. 432, 439, 105 S. Ct. 3249, 87 L. Ed. 2d 313 (1985).

tion that neither proceeds along suspect lines nor infringes fundamental constitutional rights must be upheld against equal protection challenge if there is any reasonably conceivable state of facts that could provide a rational basis for the classification. * * * Where there are 'plausible reasons' for Congress' action, 'our inquiry is at an end.' * * * [A] legislative choice is not subject to courtroom fact-finding and may be based on rational speculation unsupported by evidence or empirical data.[376]

This rational or conceivable basis test is not applicable if a zoning ordinance categorizes uses on the basis of a suspect class (race, national origin, and, to a lesser extent, alienage) or a fundamental interest (such as religion, speech, privacy, right to travel, or right to vote). In that event, strict scrutiny applies, which requires a compelling governmental interest to justify the law. When strict scrutiny is applied courts almost always strike down the law in question. A middle ground of intermediate scrutiny looks for a purpose substantially related to an important governmental interest. This intermediate standard appears most often in gender and legitimacy-based classifications. An elevated, or meaningful, rational basis test may be used in a narrow set of cases dealing with the unpopular and vulnerable. While greater than deferential review, the review of these claims has not risen to the intermediate level of review.

Challenges to local government treatment of parties seeking development permission can often be framed in equal protection or substantive due process terms. The resemblance of the two is particularly noticeable in claims involving allegations of municipal delay and harassment.[377] The two are similar in that most courts apply the *Williamson County* ripeness requirement to both.[378] Yet, a major difference of equal protection over substantive due process is that there is no need to establish a property interest when asserting a denial of equal protection.

In examining the willingness of courts to strike zoning classifications, one should not overlook state courts' use of the doctrine of spot zoning since the doctrine is built on equal protection considerations of unjustified and dissimilar treatment between parcels.[379] The same is true for cases based on the uniformity provision of the Standard State Zoning Enabling Act.

B. *Deferential Review: Belle Terre*

The classic application of judicial deference to a zoning ordinance is *Village of Belle Terre v. Boraas*.[380] The challenged ordinance differentiated between related and unrelated persons. It allowed only "families" to live in single-family homes and defined "family" to include any number of related persons but not more than two unrelated adults. The effect, and likely purpose, of the ordinance was to prevent groups of students from a nearby university from living together in single-family houses in the small village. A landowner who rented his house to six unrelated students brought suit on several grounds, urging the Court to find "that social homogeneity is not a legitimate interest of government."

---

[376] *F.C.C. v. Beach Communications, Inc.*, 508 U.S. 307, 313–16, 113 S. Ct. 2096, 2101–2102, 124 L. Ed. 2d 211 (1993).

[377] See supra § 10:12.

[378] See *County Concrete Corp. v. Town of Roxbury*, 442 F.3d 159 (3d Cir. 2006).

[379] See, e.g., *Kinzli v. City of Santa Cruz*, 539 F. Supp. 887, 894 (N.D. Cal. 1982).

[380] *Village of Belle Terre v. Boraas*, 416 U.S. 1, 94 S. Ct. 1536, 39 L. Ed. 2d 797 (1974).

The Court was not troubled by the law since it saw the ordinance as merely regulating social and economic affairs, and not implicating any fundamental rights or affecting any suspect class. In an opinion by Justice Douglas, the Court cast aside any constitutional objection, stating:

> The regimes of boarding houses, fraternity houses and the like present urban problems. More people occupy a given space; more cars rather continuously pass by; more cars are parked; noise travels with crowds.

> A quiet place where yards are wide, people few, and motor vehicles restricted are legitimate guidelines in a land use project addressed to family needs * * *. The police power is not confined to elimination of filth, stench, and unhealthy places. It is ample to lay out zones where family values, youth values, and the blessings of quiet seclusion, and clean air make the area a sanctuary for people.[381]

Seeking the application of strict scrutiny, the *Belle Terre* plaintiffs claimed that the village's ordinance infringed their right to travel, but the Court dismissed the claim with a curt statement that the law was not aimed at transients. The right to travel argument has also been raised in challenges to growth management programs, but without success.[382]

Plaintiffs' argument found a sympathetic ear with Justice Marshall who, in dissent, viewed the ordinance as affecting fundamental rights of association and privacy, which required strict scrutiny. Had strict scrutiny been applied, the ordinance likely would have failed. Several state courts have refused to accept the *Belle Terre* Court's deferential posture in the context of zoning excluding unrelated persons. Applying greater scrutiny, they have invalidated such ordinances relying on state constitutional provisions of equal protection,[383] substantive due process and privacy rights.[384]

C. *Meaningful Rational Basis Review: Cleburne*

The Court broke from its practice of applying a deferential standard of review in equal protection challenges to land use regulations in *City of Cleburne v. Cleburne Living Center, Inc.*[385] The Court found a violation of the equal protection clause where a city zoning ordinance excluded group homes for the mentally retarded from a zone where apartment houses, fraternity and sorority houses, hospitals, and nursing homes for the aged were permitted. The Court was urged to classify the mentally retarded as a "quasi-suspect" class, so as to trigger intermediate scrutiny, but it refused to do so. Nonetheless, the Court proceeded to find the ordinance invalid by examining, and refuting, the reasons the city offered for handling housing for the mentally retarded under a special classification. The Court said it was using the rational basis test, but it was not the toothless test of *Belle Terre*. Rather, it was what Justice Kennedy calls

---

[381] 416 U.S. at 5, 94 S. Ct. at 1539.

[382] See discussion supra § 9:4.

[383] *Kirsch v. Prince George's County,* 331 Md. 89, 626 A.2d 372 (1993).

[384] *City of Santa Barbara v. Adamson,* 27 Cal. 3d 123, 164 Cal. Rptr. 539, 610 P.2d 436 (1980); *State v. Baker,* 81 N.J. 99, 405 A.2d 368 (1979).

[385] 473 U.S. 432, 105 S. Ct. 3249, 87 L. Ed. 2d 313 (1985).

"meaningful rational basis,"[386] or as others call it, more colloquially, "rationality with a bite."[387]

Courts have not extended *Cleburne* to mere social and economic interests, but have used it to demand evidence of rationality when unpopular, vulnerable, or sensitive groups are affected. Developers, asserting economic interests, have been unable to convince courts to apply *Cleburne-like* scrutiny to permit denials.[388] A shelter for battered women and a day care center were also refused such scrutiny.[389] *Cleburne* scrutiny was applied to a residential substance abuse center.[390] Courts have differed over whether halfway homes for prisoners deserve more exacting scrutiny.[391] *Cleburne* scrutiny also was used to find a substantive due process violation where a palm reader was denied a permit based on the religious objections of neighbors.[392]

In short, "meaningful rational basis" review is difficult to obtain. One court, uneasy with the notion of implying enhanced scrutiny from the *Cleburne* Court's declaration that it was simply applying the rational basis test, asserted that "despite the hue and cry from all sides, *[Cleburne]* may not signal the birth of a new category of equal protection review."[393] "Perhaps," the court continued, "after considering all other conceivable purposes, the [*Cleburne* Court] found that "a bare * * * desire to harm a politically unpopular group," was the only conceivable basis for the city's action."[394]

D. Opening the Door to Claims Involving Socio-Economic Rights: Olech

Developers' contentions that permit denials violate equal protection are often and easily rejected under the rational basis test. This is true in both state [395] and federal courts.[396] Rare is the trial judge who cannot find a conceivable basis for a challenged governmental action, and, when that rare event occurs, the unimaginative judge is likely to be reversed on appeal.[397] Where permits have been granted or denied for personal or political reasons, courts sometimes have found equal protection violations.[398] Until recently, however, even these cases usually have failed.

A potential break from this tradition came in a terse, per curiam ruling by the Supreme Court in the "class of one" *Village of Willowbrook v. Olech* case.[399] Olech sued the Village of Willowbrook seeking damages for the village's alleged denial of her right

---

[386] *Kelo v. City of New London,* 545 U.S. 469, 125 S. Ct. 2655, 2670, 162 L. Ed. 2d 439 (2005).

[387] *Cervantes v. Guerra,* 651 F.2d 974, 982 (5th Cir. 1981).

[388] *Jacobs, Visconsi & Jacobs, Co. v. City of Lawrence, Kan.,* 927 F.2d 1111 (10th Cir. 1991) (shopping center).

[389] *Doe v. City of Butler,* 892 F.2d 315 (3d Cir. 1989) (shelter case based on substantive due process but test the same); *Howard v. City of Garland,* 917 F.2d 898 (5th Cir.1990) (day care).

[390] *Open Homes Fellowship, Inc. v. Orange County,* 325 F. Supp. 2d 1349, 1358 (M.D. Fla. 2004).

[391] *Bannum, Inc. v. City of St. Charles,* 2 F.3d 267 (8th Cir. 1993) (no); *Bannum, Inc. v. City of Louisville, Ky.,* 958 F.2d 1354 (6th Cir. 1992) (yes).

[392] *Marks v. City of Chesapeake,* 883 F.2d 308 (4th Cir. 1989).

[393] *Powers v. Harris,* 379 F.3d 1208, 1224 (10th Cir. 2004).

[394] Harris, 379 F.3d 1208.

[395] *Security Management Corp. v. Baltimore County,* 104 Md. App. 234, 655 A.2d 1326 (1995).

[396] *Crowley v. Courville,* 76 F.3d 47 (2d Cir. 1996).

[397] *Front Royal and Warren County Indus. Park Corp. v. Town of Front Royal,* 922 F. Supp. 1131, 1152 n.30 (W.D. Va. 1996), rev'd on other grounds, 135 F.3d 275 (4th Cir. 1998).

[398] See, e.g., *Cordeco Development Corp. v. Santiago Vasquez,* 539 F.2d 256 (1st Cir. 1976).

[399] *Village of Willowbrook v. Olech,* 528 U.S. 562, 120 S. Ct. 1073, 145 L. Ed. 2d 1060 (2000).

to equal protection. The essence of her complaint was that when she asked the village to hook her house to the public water line, the village demanded that she convey a 33-foot easement. Others similarly situated had only been asked to grant a 15-foot easement. The reason for the disparate treatment, she alleged, was that she had previously successfully sued the village for stormwater damage, and that the village, seeking revenge, was motivated by ill will.

The Court held that Olech stated an equal protection claim. It mattered not that she was a "class of one," or that she asserted no fundamental right or that she claimed no membership in a suspect class. It is sufficient, said the Court, that she "alleges that she has been intentionally treated differently from others similarly situated and that there is no rational basis for the difference in treatment."[400] Though Olech had alleged that the village was motivated by ill will, the Court said the village's subjective motivation did not matter. Her complaint was sufficient without such allegation.

In a concurring opinion, Justice Breyer, worried that the Court's ruling could be read as "transforming run-of-the-mill zoning cases into cases of constitutional right,"[401] sought to limit these "class of one" cases to those involving allegations of ill will or vindictive action. While none of the other Justices joined Breyer, some lower courts have followed his view. Most notable is the Seventh Circuit, which initially, in a somewhat rogue fashion, adopted Justice Breyer's concurrence and held that to make out a prima facie class of one case a plaintiff must present evidence that "the cause of the differential treatment of which the plaintiff complains [is] a totally illegitimate animus toward the plaintiff by the defendant."[402] The Seventh Circuit now poses an alternative test, which requires, after alleging intentional, differential treatment, that the plaintiff show that the cause of the differential treatment is a totally illegitimate animus or, finally in line with the per curiam opinion in *Olech,* that there is no rational basis for the difference in treatment.[403] Other courts have taken the per curiam opinion at face value and assumed that motive is irrelevant,[404] while some have casually assumed *Olech* presents nothing new in the way of equal protection jurisprudence.[405] Some require illegitimate animus[406] and others have thus far avoided deciding the issue.[407] As one court has observed, "most circuits have proceeded cautiously in applying the theory, sensitive to Justice Breyer's warning against turning even quotidian exercises of government discretion into constitutional causes."[408]

Many plaintiffs stumble over the requirement that they show that there are others who are similarly situated.[409] The showing is difficult. As one court has said, for any

---

[400] Olech, 528 U.S.. at 564, 120 S. Ct. at 1074.

[401] 528 U.S. at 566, 120 S. Ct. at 1075.

[402] *Hilton v. City of Wheeling,* 209 F.3d 1005, 1008 (7th Cir. 2000).

[403] *Nevel v. Village of Schaumburg,* 297 F.3d 673, 681 (7th Cir. 2002).

[404] *City Recycling, Inc. v. State,* 257 Conn. 429, 778 A.2d 77 (2001).

[405] *Bryan v. City of Madison,* 213 F.3d 267 (5th Cir. 2000).

[406] *Petersen v. Riverton City,* 2010 UT 58, 243 P.3d 1261 (Utah 2010).

[407] See, e.g., *Bizzarro v. Miranda,* 394 F.3d 82, 88 (2d Cir. 2005).

[408] *Lindquist v. City of Pasadena,* 656 F. Supp. 2d 662, 681 (S.D. Tex. 2009), judgment aff'd, 669 F.3d 225 (5th Cir. 2012).

[409] *Baron v. Frederickson,* 419 F. Supp. 2d 1056 (W.D. Wis. 2006).

development project to be similarly situated, "it must be prima facie identical in all relevant respects."[410]

Under both *Olech* and the Seventh Circuit's original limited reading of *Olech,* equal protection claims can more easily survive a motion to dismiss than has been the case in the past.[411] More significantly, they also may survive a summary judgment motion as well,[412] enabling landowners to submit their claims to a jury.[413] This occurred in *Cruz v. Town of Cicero.*[414] The district court had denied the town's motion for summary judgment despite the fact that the town had conceivable, rational reasons to deny the development permission requested. The town, said the district court, had not offered sufficient proof. The case went to the jury, which awarded the developer $402,000. The Seventh Circuit affirmed the jury verdict on the basis that the jury could have found that the town acted for totally illegitimate reasons.[415]

E.   *Discrimination Based on Race*

Discrimination against persons on the basis of race through land use controls has a long history in this country and it continues to be practiced though in less subtle ways than was once the case.

Municipalities adopted ordinances restricting where people could live on the basis of race at the beginning of the twentieth century when blacks began migrating to cities from the rural south. In *Buchanan v. Warley,*[416] the Court found that an ordinance that established zones on racial lines violated the due process property right of "a white man to dispose of his property to a person of color if he saw fit * * *."[417] Racially restrictive zoning, however, persisted for decades in defiance of *Buchanan.* Racial segregation was also promoted by federal housing practices. In the 1930s, when the federal government began loan guarantees to save the housing industry, it required that racially restrictive covenants be put in deeds for transactions to qualify.[418]

In the 1977 decision of *Village of Arlington Heights v. Metropolitan Housing Development Corporation,*[419] the ability to attack zoning ordinances restricting multifamily developments as racially discriminatory was dealt a major blow by the Supreme Court. There, a developer wished to build a federally subsidized public housing project on land zoned for single family use. Arlington Heights refused to rezone the land, invoking a buffer policy which allowed multifamily zoning only when it could serve as a buffer between single family use and industrial use. The developer, whose site did not meet that criterion, attacked the action on equal protection grounds.

---

[410] *Campbell v. Rainbow City,* 434 F.3d 1306, 1314 (11th Cir. 2006).

[411] See, e.g., *Northwestern University v. City of Evanston,* 2001 WL 219632, *3 (N.D. Ill. 2001).

[412] *Maguire Oil Co. v. City of Houston,* 69 S.W.3d 350 (Tex. App. 2002).

[413] *Valley Outdoor, Inc. v. City of Riverside,* 446 F.3d 948 (9th Cir. 2006).

[414] *Cruz v. Town of Cicero,* 275 F.3d 579 (7th Cir. 2001).

[415] 275 F.3d at 589.

[416] *Buchanan v. Warley,* 245 U.S. 60, 38 S. Ct. 16, 62 L. Ed. 149 (1917).

[417] Warley, 245 U.S. at 80, 38 S. Ct. at 20.

[418] See Drinan, Untying the White Noose, 94 Yale L.J. 435, 437 (1984).

[419] *Village of Arlington Heights v. Metropolitan Housing Development Corp.,* 429 U.S. 252, 97 S. Ct. 555, 50 L. Ed. 2d 450 (1977). See also *City of Cuyahoga Falls v. Buckeye Community Hope Foundation,* 538 U.S. 188, 123 S. Ct. 1389, 155 L. Ed. 2d 349 (2003).

The Court upheld Arlington Heights' refusal to rezone, holding that the equal protection clause requires proof of discriminatory intent rather than effect. Intent is much harder to prove than effect. Even though the failure of Arlington Heights to rezone would have a disproportionate impact on racial minorities, the Court held that this could only be used as evidence of intent. Discriminatory intent could be proved by showing a "clear pattern" of discriminatory effect even if the ordinance is neutral on its face. The usefulness of that approach must be questioned, however, since the Court ignored the "clear pattern" of Arlington Heights' lily-white complexion.

A second way to prove discriminatory intent under the *Arlington Heights* test is to show substantive departures from established zoning policy. Because Arlington Heights had always been zoned in a highly exclusionary manner and had applied its buffer policy in a substantially uniform manner, plaintiffs could not challenge the failure to rezone on that ground. If a city, upon learning that a racially integrated housing project is being considered for a tract that is zoned for high density housing, quickly downzones the land to low density use, the requisite intent to discriminate may be shown.[420] Communities may take from *Arlington Heights* the lesson that if the little or no land is zoned for high density housing by right they may effectively immunize themselves from liability on equal protection grounds.

Land use claims based on racial discrimination under the federal constitution's equal protection clause generally will fail. While an allegation of racial discrimination will trigger strict scrutiny, intent must be shown to establish and typically that is difficult to do. This, however, by no means ends the matter. Racial discrimination in zoning can be challenged without proof of intent under the federal Fair Housing Act, where a showing of effect is sufficient to raise a prima facie case.[421]

F.   *Discrimination Based on Wealth*

Discrimination on the basis of wealth is practiced by zoning for single-family use only (thus excluding multifamily use), precluding manufactured housing, and requiring large lots or houses so as to exclude all but the upper economic strata. These practices, which generally fall under the rubric of exclusionary zoning, are dealt with in depth in Chapter 6. At this point we limit our discussion to their equal protection implications.

Economic segregation was approved in *Euclid v. Ambler Realty Co.,*[422] where the Court upheld the exclusion of apartment houses from single-family districts with the unflattering view that apartments in districts of "private houses" were "mere parasites" stealing light and open space and were "near to being nuisances" endangering children in single-family detached housing.[423] Fifty years later, *Arlington Heights* reinforced this holding by implicitly finding that the village's exclusion of multi-family use did not violate equal protection.

Allegations based on the failure to provide adequate housing opportunities or on wealth discrimination do not trigger strict scrutiny. The Court has held that housing is

---

[420] See. e.g., *Scott v. Greenville County,* 716 F.2d 1409 (4th Cir.1983).

[421] *Huntington Branch, N.A.A.C.P. v. Town of Huntington,* 844 F.2d 926 (2d Cir. 1988). See discussion of Fair Housing Act supra § 6:8.

[422] *Village of Euclid, Ohio v. Ambler Realty Co.,* 272 U.S. 365, 47 S. Ct. 114, 71 L. Ed. 303 (1926).

[423] Ambler Realty Co., 272 U.S. at 394, 47 S. Ct. at 120.

not a fundamental right [424] and poverty not a suspect classification.[425] The standard of review is rational basis, and this makes an equal protection claim a likely loser from the outset. As the Court observed in *Arlington Heights,* the developer did not base its complaint on the "generous *Euclid* test."[426] The only reason the developer got anywhere in *Arlington Heights* was due to the allegation of racial discrimination. While equal protection claims based on economic discrimination will likely fail, such exclusionary zoning practices are actionable under the statutory or constitutional law of a number of states.[427]

G. Standing

Federal standing law is a further limit on the availability of equal protection attacks on exclusionary land use ordinances. The most important standing decisions are *Warth v. Seldin*[428] and *Arlington Heights v. Metropolitan Housing Development Corp.*[429]

Warth involved a challenge to the exclusionary nature of the zoning ordinance of Penfield, a suburban town adjacent to Rochester, New York. There were four categories of plaintiffs: low income nonresidents unable to find housing in Penfield; taxpayers in Rochester bearing a disproportionate share of low income costs; Penfield residents denied benefits of living in an integrated community; and associations representing contractors unable to construct low-income housing in Penfield. The Court denied standing to all of them because none could show how they were personally injured by the ordinances. For example, with respect to the nonresidents who could find no affordable housing in the area, the Court noted that there was inadequate proof that the injury they suffered would be remedied by judicial intervention. Elimination of exclusionary zoning practices would not necessarily lead to the construction of affordable housing. The Court said two showings were necessary. First, there must be but-for causation, that is there must be "specific, concrete facts" proving harm to plaintiffs. Second, the plaintiffs must show a possibility of redress to them by the Court's intervention. The *Warth* test is hard to meet, for, as the dissent noted, the opinion "tosses out of court almost every conceivable kind of plaintiff" in an exclusionary zoning case.[430]

Standing was found in *Arlington Heights* due to rare circumstances. A religious order had sold land at a below market price to a developer of federally subsidized housing. The developer was granted standing on the basis of its preliminary expenditures on the project and its interest in providing low cost housing in areas where it was scarce. Additionally, a black employee of a nearby plant alleged that he was unable to find affordable housing near his place of work. Because his claim was based on a particular project and not speculation as to possible future projects (as in *Warth*), the black plaintiff proved an injury in fact. In most exclusionary zoning cases, there will be no specific project, and under the rule of *Warth,* standing in federal courts will be lack-

---

[424] *Lindsey v. Normet,* 405 U.S. 56, 92 S. Ct. 862, 31 L. Ed. 2d 36 (1972).

[425] *San Antonio Independent School Dist. v. Rodriguez,* 411 U.S. 1, 93 S. Ct. 1278, 36 L. Ed. 2d 16 (1973).

[426] 429 U.S. at 263, 97 S. Ct. at 562.

[427] These cases are discussed supra § 6:6.

[428] *Warth v. Seldin,* 422 U.S. 490, 95 S. Ct. 2197, 45 L. Ed. 2d 343 (1975).

[429] *Village of Arlington Heights v. Metropolitan Housing Development Corp.,* 429 U.S. 252, 97 S. Ct. 555, 50 L. Ed. 2d 450 (1977).

[430] 422 U.S. at 520, 95 S. Ct. at 2216.

ing. State courts, which need not apply Article III standing rules, may grant standing in such cases.[431]

IV. FIRST AMENDMENT

§ 10:15 First Amendment Issues

Land use controls implicate rights protected by the First Amendment most frequently in the regulation of billboards and other signs, sexually oriented adult businesses, and religious uses. The extent, even existence, of such protection has not always been clear. When a lower court confronting a zoning regulation that banned live entertainment opined that "'First Amendment guarantees were not involved [since the case dealt] solely with a zoning ordinance,'"[432] and based its opinion on Supreme Court precedent,[433] the Supreme Court said the court had misread the law. The zoning power, said the Court, is not "infinite and unchallengeable,"[434] and it is the nature of the right affected, not the power being exercised, that dictates the level of judicial review. While strict scrutiny tests the validity of controls that impinge fundamental rights, not all First Amendment rights rise to that level. This is particularly true of adult use zoning that affects non-obscene sexually oriented speech and sign controls that affect commercial speech. Courts are likely to review more closely regulations that affect noncommercial speech and religious uses.

§ 10:16 Retaliatory Conduct

The First Amendment right to free speech and to petition the government may be implicated in land use disputes where the government is alleged to have retaliated against those seeking zoning changes or opposing zoning changes.[435]

Generally, to prevail on constitutional retaliation claim plaintiff must prove (1) that he engaged in constitutionally-protected activity; (2) that government responded with retaliation; and (3) that protected activity caused the retaliation.[436] Stating a retaliation claim is difficult and many plaintiffs fail at that stage.[437] Proof of motive is necessary. In one case, a developer alleged that the mayor had retaliated against him because he ran, albeit unsuccessfully, for mayor himself. To prove his allegation, the developer only offered the opinion of former city official that mayor influenced the commission when it denied developer a permit. This opinion evidence was insufficient to submit the matter to a jury.[438] Retaliatory claims may also be filed under the due process clause.[439]

---

[431] A plaintiff may be able to take advantage of broader state court standing rules since state courts are not obligated to follow *Warth*.

[432] *Schad v. Borough of Mount Ephraim*, 452 U.S. 61, 64, 101 S. Ct. 2176, 2180, 68 L. Ed. 2d 671 (1981).

[433] *Young v. American Mini Theatres, Inc.*, 427 U.S. 50, 96 S. Ct. 2440, 49 L. Ed. 2d 310 (1976).

[434] *Schad*, 452 U.S. at 64, 101 S. Ct. at 2180.

[435] *White v. Lee*, 227 F.3d 1214 (9th Cir. 2000).

[436] *Eichenlaub v. Township of Indiana*, 385 F.3d 274, 282 (3d Cir. 2004).

[437] See *Baumgardner v. Town of Ruston*, 712 F. Supp. 2d 1180 (W.D. Wash. 2010).

[438] *Campbell v. Rainbow City*, 434 F.3d 1306 (11th Cir. 2006).

[439] See discussion supra § 10:12. The due process clause, however, may be less attractive since it requires that the plaintiff have a protected property interest.

§ 10:17 Sign Controls

The regulation of signs for reasons of traffic safety and aesthetics has a long history in this country. Though commonplace, the First Amendment requires that it tread a narrow path between regulating too much speech and too little speech.[440] The more expansive the control and the more speech that it affects, the more likely it will be found to deny avenues of protected communication and violate the First Amendment. The obvious answer to regulating too much speech is to fine-tune the regulation to minimize its impact on speech by exempting some types of signs. However, this choice is problematical since the narrower the control, the more likely it will be found improperly to favor one type of speech over another.

A. *Commercial and Non-Commercial Speech: Billboards and Other Signs*

Constitutional litigation over sign regulations is of recent origin since it was not until 1976 that the Supreme Court held that the First Amendment protected commercial speech. Even then, the protection conferred was limited. Commercial speech, said the Court, was not "wholly outside" the First Amendment.[441] With this tepid welcome, the door was opened to the outdoor advertising industry, and a barrage of billboard litigation followed with challenges based on the First Amendment and the Fifth Amendment's takings clause.[442]

Metromedia, Inc. v. City of San Diego[443] is the case with which analysis should begin. The San Diego ordinance at issue in *Metromedia* banned all billboards with two categories of exceptions. First, it had 12 exemptions for such matters as informational and governmental messages, commemorative historical plaques, religious symbols, time and temperature signs, and temporary political campaign signs. Second, it exempted on-site commercial signs. This ban on off-site commercial billboards cutting the lifeline of the outdoor advertising industry guaranteed a challenge. The Court upheld the restrictions on commercial speech but invalidated the restrictions on noncommercial speech. In doing so, the Court produced five separate opinions, making it a difficult case from which to draw guidance.

Justice White's plurality opinion upheld the restriction on commercial speech under the four-part test of *Central Hudson Gas & Electric Corp. v. Public Service Commission.*[444] To be valid, a restriction on commercial speech must (1) concern a lawful activity and not be misleading; (2) the asserted governmental interest must be substantial. If the answers to (1) and (2) are yes, (3) the regulation must directly advance the governmental interest asserted; and (4) the regulation cannot be more extensive than is necessary to serve that interest. The plurality found all four parts satisfied. The two goals furthered by the ordinance, traffic safety and aesthetics, were considered substantial. Acknowledging that the ordinance was underinclusive in that the permitted on-site commercial billboards were "equally distracting and unattractive," the

---

[440] See, generally, Kramer, Current Decisions on State and Federal Law in Planning and Zoning, Part I, 33 Urb. Law. 561, 633 (2001).

[441] *Virginia State Bd. of Pharmacy v. Virginia Citizens Consumer Council, Inc.*, 425 U.S. 748, 761, 96 S. Ct. 1817, 1825, 48 L. Ed. 2d 346 (1976).

[442] On takings issues, see supra, §§ 10:2 to 10:11.

[443] *Metromedia, Inc. v. City of San Diego*, 453 U.S. 490, 101 S. Ct. 2882, 69 L. Ed. 2d 800 (1981).

[444] *Central Hudson Gas & Elec. Corp. v. Public Service Commission of New York*, 447 U.S. 557, 100 S. Ct. 2343, 65 L. Ed. 2d 341 (1980).

Court nonetheless held the classification constitutional. The city "may [have] believe [d]", said the Court, that off-site billboards posed "a more acute problem" than on-site signs, and since the affected speech was commercial, favoring one kind of commercial speech over another was permissible.[445]

The noncommercial speech aspects of San Diego's zoning law received greater scrutiny and did not fare well. The ordinance allowed only on-site *commercial* messages.[446] Because the ordinance failed to provide also for on-site *noncommercial* messages (which would be no more distracting or unattractive than commercial billboards), that portion of the law was found facially unconstitutional. This was considered impermissible content-based regulation and not a reasonable time, place, or manner restriction. "Insofar as the city tolerates billboards at all," said the Court, "it cannot choose to limit their content to commercial messages."[447]

Despite varying analytical approaches, all the Justices in *Metromedia* agreed that aesthetics is a legitimate and substantial governmental interest in the evaluation of restraints on First Amendment speech rights. They reaffirmed that view in *Members of the City Council of the City of Los Angeles v. Taxpayers for Vincent,*[448] where they held that the city could ban political posters from public property to further its interest in traffic safety and aesthetics so long as the ordinance did not discriminate between types of speech. While *Metromedia* and *Vincent* make it clear that aesthetic concerns support restraints on both commercial and noncommercial speech, a municipality runs the risk of undermining its assertion of aesthetics as a goal to the extent that it grants exemptions.

While the Court remains split on the value to assign to commercial speech, the 1993 decision in *City of Cincinnati v. Discovery Network, Inc.*[449] shows that the gap between commercial and noncommercial speech has narrowed since *Metromedia*. In *Discovery,* the Court invalidated a ban on commercial newsracks, and in so doing, applied its commercial speech test with more force than had previously been the case. In 1989, Cincinnati gave permission to publishers of newspapers that contained almost exclusive commercial content to place their newsracks on public property. Experiencing a quick change of mind, one year later the city began enforcing an "outdated" ordinance against "commercial handbills" out of a newly developed concern for safety and aesthetics.[450]

The *Discovery* Court put the burden on the city to show a reasonable fit between its concededly legitimate safety and aesthetic goals and its means. It was incumbent on the city to show that its regulation of speech was no more extensive than necessary. Under the intermediate scrutiny test of *Central Hudson,*[451] the city failed to carry the burden. The "outdated" handbill ordinance was designed to prevent litter not newsracks, and the city had made no recent effort to assess the gains in safety and aes-

---

[445] 453 U.S. at 507, 101 S. Ct. at 2892.

[446] An on-site sign may be defined as one identifying the use occurring on the premises where it is located. See *Outdoor Systems, Inc. v. City of Mesa,* 997 F.2d 604 (9th Cir.1993).

[447] 453 U.S. at 513, 101 S. Ct. at 2895.

[448] *Members of City Council of City of Los Angeles v. Taxpayers for Vincent,* 466 U.S. 789, 104 S. Ct. 2118, 80 L. Ed. 2d 772 (1984).

[449] *City of Cincinnati v. Discovery Network, Inc.,* 507 US. 410, 113 S. Ct. 1505, 123 L. Ed. 2d 99 (1993).

[450] Discovery Network, Inc., 507 US. at 416, 113 S. Ct. at 1510.

[451] Discovery Network, Inc., 507 US. at 415–30, 113 S. Ct. at 1509–17.

thetics from the ordinance against the restraint on speech. Finally, the effort enabled the city to eliminate only 62 of some 2,000 newsracks. The *Discovery* opinion did not leave cities without means of regulating newsracks and other forms of commercial speech, but it required them to do their homework and refine their methods.

The application of intermediate scrutiny in *Discovery* demonstrated increased, but reserved, support for commercial speech. The majority declined to go along with Justice Blackmun who, in concurring, urged the Court to treat truthful, commercial speech on par with noncommercial speech. The majority also characterized its holding as narrow, emphasizing that the city's distinction between commercial and noncommercial speech had "absolutely no bearing on the interests it asserted."[452] *Discovery's* intermediate scrutiny also was limited to ordinances that distinguish between commercial and non-commercial speech, suggesting that the more stringent regulation of off-site commercial billboards is not to be subjected to higher scrutiny.

Off-site commercial billboard bans, as approved in *Metromedia,* survived *Discovery's* increased protection of commercial speech. In *Discovery,* Cincinnati relied principally on the *Metromedia* plurality's relaxed treatment of commercial speech. Just as San Diego did not have to prove that off-site commercial billboards were more harmful than on-site billboards, Cincinnati suggested that the Court ought not require it to show that the newsracks it banned were more harmful than those permitted. This argument, said the Court, "seriously underestimate [d] the value of commercial speech."[453] When reminded of the lack of concern for commercial speech shown in *Metromedia,* the Court distinguished Cincinnati's and San Diego's ordinances. Cincinnati drew distinctions between commercial and noncommercial speech, which are subject intermediate scrutiny. In contrast, the portion of San Diego's ordinance that was approved distinguished between types of commercial speech. Such distinctions apparently must only satisfy low level scrutiny.

Defining and distinguishing between off-site and on-site signs is fraught with difficulty in the context of noncommercial speech. A common onsite sign definition is one "'located on the same premises as the use that sign identifies or advertises.'"[454] What, then, is a sign proclaiming "Jesus Saves"? Can it only be located at the site of a church? Where would a sign admonishing "No Wetlands, No Seafood" be permitted? In *Southlake Property Associates, Ltd. v. City of Morrow,*[455] the Eleventh Circuit held that noncommercial signs are onsite wherever located. In the court's view, since such signs express abstract ideas, they are located wherever the ideas are expressed. Classifications of speech as commercial or noncommercial are likewise difficult, and may be viewed as content-based. The banned newspapers in *Discovery,* for example, contained some noncommercial content. A message that "Jesus: The Reason for the Season" seems, at first blush, non-commercial, but it might be commercial advertising "if the color scheme and font indicate a business."[456] While courts uphold the on-site/off site distinction, it is widely criticized by commentators.[457]

---

[452] 507 U.S. at 428, 113 S. Ct. at 1516.

[453] 507 U.S. at 418, 113 S. Ct. at 1510.

[454] *Outdoor Systems, Inc. v. City of Mesa,* 997 F.2d 604 (9th Cir.1993).

[455] Southlake Property Associates, Ltd. v. City of Morrow, 112 F.3d 1114 (11th Cir. 1997).

[456] Menthe, Writing on the Wall: The Impending Demise of Modern Sign Regulation Under the First Amendment and State Constitutions, 18 Geo. Mason U. Civ. Rts. L.J. 1, 6 (2007).

[457] Id.; Blaesser and Weinstein, Federal Land Use Law & Litigation § 5:22 (2011).

As noted above, cities can violate the First Amendment by regulating too much speech or too little speech. Drafting sign codes that will pass muster is a challenging task. A way to avoid regulating too much speech is to exempt some types of signs. However, exemptions based on content are subject to strict scrutiny and often fail.[458] An ordinance that bans or regulates equally all signs may be valid as a time, place, and manner restriction even as applied political signs.[459] Limited exemptions are more likely to be upheld than wholesale ones. Thus, a court upheld an ordinance exempting public signs, hospital signs, legal notices, railroad signs and danger signs from the permitting process and fee schedule imposed on all others.[460] Notably, the signs were required to comply with all other rules, such as those on size and placement. The court also upheld the ordinance's allowance of temporary signs for 90 days prior to an election. The sign's content was not regulated. It did not have to address an issue in the upcoming election but whatever message the property had to share, it could be shared only in the three months prior to the election.[461]

B. Residential Yard Signs

Yard signs scattered through residential neighborhoods tell neighbors and passers by a number of things: for whom the posting resident thinks they should vote, what position the resident takes on various public issues, which houses are for sale and which ones have sold, and who is painting or remodeling houses in the neighborhood. They also may identify who lives in a home and advertise a home occupation. Though less intrusive than the traditional billboard, yard signs nonetheless are targets of regulations based on traffic safety and visual clutter concerns.

When a New Jersey town enacted a zoning ordinance prohibiting posting "for sale" signs to limit panic selling or "white flight," the Supreme Court wasted no time in striking down the control as a free speech violation in *Linmark Assoc, Inc. v. Township of Willingboro.*[462] The ordinance was not a mere restriction of time, place, and manner because reasonable alternatives for landowners wishing to sell were not available, and it was not content-neutral. Though the speech regulated was commercial, the "for sale" messages were vital community information.

In *City of Ladue v. Gilleo,*[463] a residential suburb of St. Louis banned virtually all signs except "for sale" signs and few others. Margaret Gilleo's 8.5 inch by 11 inch window sign proclaiming that she was "For Peace in the Gulf was not among the exceptions, and she sued to enjoin enforcement of the act against her. Describing the case as "in some respects * * * the mirror image"[464] of *Linmark,* the Court held that the city banned "too much" speech. The Court, noting the nation's historic respect for "liberty in the home,"[465] viewed noncommercial sign posting from one's home as an important, unique, and "venerable means of communication." For the Court the regulation was essentially a total ban on this "distinct medium of expression," and left persons with no

---

[458] See, e.g., *Solantic, LLC v. City of Neptune Beach,* 410 F.3d 1250 (11th Cir. 2005).

[459] *La Tour v. City of Fayetteville, Ark.,* 442 F.3d 1094 (8th Cir. 2006).

[460] *G.K. Ltd. Travel v. City of Lake Oswego,* 436 F.3d 1064, 1076 (9th Cir. 2006).

[461] G.K. Ltd. Travel, 436 F.3d at 1077–78.

[462] *Linmark Associates, Inc. v. Willingboro Tp.,* 431 U.S. 85, 97 S. Ct. 1614, 52 L. Ed. 2d 155 (1977).

[463] *City of Ladue v. Gilleo,* 512 U.S. 43, 114 S. Ct. 2038, 129 L. Ed. 2d 36 (1994).

[464] 512 U.S. at 48, 114 S. Ct. at 2042.

[465] 512 U.S. at 58, 114 S. Ct. at 2047.

reasonable options to communicate quickly, directly, and cheaply with their neighbors. The Court in *Ladue* did not deprive cities of all power to regulate noncommercial signs on residential property. While cities cannot likely ban such signs, reasonable regulations that deal with location, size, number and color are acceptable.

By choosing to deal with the Ladue ordinance as an instance of regulating "too much" speech, the Court left hanging the validity of regulations that choose among types of speech, and thus may regulate "too little" speech. The question is significant since most sign control ordinances fall into this category. While case law is mixed, a critical factor in the validity of a selective law is the degree to which the subject of an exempted sign relates to the activities on or near the land on which it is located. The more direct the relationship, the higher the likelihood that courts will uphold it. For example, highway directional signs must appear at intersections and warning signs at dangerous curves. Even if a city bans all other signs, a compelling interest in traffic safety exists in allowing the highway signs.[466] Both *Metromedia* and *Ladue* support the idea that signs identifying activities on-site find favor over off-site signs.[467] The on-site commercial billboard in *Metromedia* held an attraction for the Court that the off-site board lacked. *Ladue* also recognized the home as a place where noncommercial signs have greater justification than commercial ones. Unlike Gilleo's personal antiwar message, commercial signs have less claim to be located in residential areas, and ought to be subject to greater regulation.[468]

§ 10:18 Regulating the Sex Business

Sexually oriented businesses (known among some regulators as SOBs) such as adult video stores, strip clubs, and massage parlors are regulated separately and more stringently than other entertainment venues. Yet, singling out adult uses for special treatment raises free speech concerns. While the First Amendment does not protect obscene speech, it does protect non-obscene, sexually oriented speech.[469]

The reason typically given for singling out adult uses is that they "attract an undesirable quantity and quality of transients"[470] resulting in an increase in crime, especially prostitution. As a consequence, when adult uses move into an area, the expectation or indeed fear is that property values will drop, and that those neighbors who are able to do so will move elsewhere. Whether these "secondary effects" are caused by adult uses is not conceded by the adult entertainment industry, which claim that the moving force behind such regulations is dislike of the message conveyed, not a supposed secondary effect.[471]

Adult businesses generally must be licensed prior to opening. A city's licensing scheme needs to be carefully drawn so as to not run afoul of the First Amendment prior restraint doctrine. To avoid that error, licensing procedures may not give unbridled discretion to the official charged with processing permits,[472] and they must provide for

---

[466] *Ackerley Communications of Massachusetts, Inc. v. City of Cambridge*, 88 F.3d 33 (1st Cir. 1996).

[467] Defining on-site versus off-site can pose problems. See *Outdoor Systems, Inc. v. City of Mesa,* 997 F.2d 604 (9th Cir.1993).

[468] *Ackerley*, 88 F.3d 33.

[469] See generally, Ziegler, Rathkopf's The Law of Zoning and Planning § 24:11 (4th ed.).

[470] *Young v. American Mini Theatres*, 427 U.S. 50, 55, 96 S. Ct. 2440, 2445, 49 L. Ed. 2d 310 (1976).

[471] See Fee, The Pornographic Secondary Effects Doctrine, 60 Ala. L. Rev. 291 (2009).

[472] *FW/PBS, Inc. v. City of Dallas*, 493 U.S. 215, 110 S. Ct. 596, 107 L. Ed. 2d 603 (1990).

prompt administrative and judicial review and determination.[473] Special rules for adult businesses are not required. A state's ordinary judicial review rules will suffice "so long as the courts remain sensitive to the need to prevent First Amendment harms and administer those procedures accordingly."[474]

Adult use zoning is usually done through either a "keep your distance" or "concentration" method. The "keep your distance" ordinance requires that adult uses locate within a certain minimum distance from certain sensitive land uses like schools, religious uses and residential areas. An ordinance may also have a "scatter" component, imposing a minimum distance between adult uses to disperse the negative effects that accompany them. The concentration method lumps all such businesses in one area, sometimes called a "combat zone."[475] Property values in that zone may deteriorate, but the rest of the city is spared.

The scattering or dispersal method came under review in *Young v. American Mini Theatres,*[476] where a Detroit ordinance prohibited the location of an adult movie theater within 1,000 feet of another such theater or 10 other establishments thought to produce similar effects. In a divided opinion, the Court upheld the ordinance, finding it was a valid exercise of the city's zoning power and not an impermissible prior restraint on free speech. The city did not aim the regulation at suppressing ideas. Documented studies of the effects of the regulated uses supported the law, which had the legitimate purpose of maintaining neighborhood character. The ordinance did not significantly foreclose opportunities for the regulated uses because the market, the Court said, was "essentially unrestrained."[477] In language that reflects the Court's ambiguous feelings toward the zoning of adult uses, Justice Stevens for the plurality declared that

> [e]ven though we recognize that the First Amendment will not tolerate the total suppression of erotic materials * * * few of us would march our sons and daughters off to war to preserve the citizen's right to see "specified sexual activities" exhibited in the theaters of our choice. Even though the First Amendment protects communication in this area from total suppression, we hold that the state may legitimately use the content of these materials as the basis for placing them in a different classification from other motion pictures.[478]

The Court upheld the "keep your distance" technique in *City of Renton v. Playtime Theatres,*[479] and, in doing so, expanded local control over adult uses beyond that allowed in *Young.* Renton, a Seattle suburb, banned adult theaters from locating within 1,000 feet of any residential zone, single or multi-family dwelling, park, school, or church. The effect of the distance limitation was to limit adult theaters to an area of 520 acres, 5% of the city.

The *Renton* Court faced the question of whether to classify the ordinance as content-based or content-neutral. If the former, strict scrutiny is applied and if the latter,

---

[473] *City of Littleton v. Z.J. Gifts D-4, L.L.C.,* 541 U.S. 774, 124 S. Ct. 2219, 159 L. Ed. 2d 84 (2004).

[474] 541 U.S. at 781, 110 S. Ct. at 224.

[475] See *Northend Cinema, Inc. v. City of Seattle,* 90 Wash. 2d 709, 585 P.2d 1153 (1978).

[476] *Young v. American Mini Theatres, Inc.,* 427 U.S. 50, 96 S. Ct. 2440, 49 L. Ed. 2d 310 (1976).

[477] American Mini Theatres, Inc., 427 U.S. at 62, 96 S. Ct. at 2448.

[478] American Mini Theatres, Inc., 427 U.S. at 70, 96 S. Ct. at 2452.

[479] *City of Renton v. Playtime Theatres, Inc.,* 475 U.S. 41, 106 S. Ct. 925, 89 L. Ed. 2d 29 (1986).

intermediate scrutiny is used.[480] While Renton's adult use ordinance was content-based (one determined affected theaters by asking what kind of movies they played), the Court treated the ordinance as content-neutral because it found that the predominant intent was directed at the secondary effects of the message, not the message itself. As a content-neutral ordinance, it would pass constitutional muster if it served a substantial governmental interest and did not unreasonably foreclose other avenues of communication. Renton's ordinance met the test.

The *Renton* Court's determination that adult use ordinances are content-neutral has caused some confusion. Coupled with the Court's general language of deference to such legislation,[481] the opinion has, in the view of some, led to the use of a watered-down intermediate scrutiny. In *City of Los Angeles v. Alameda Books, Inc.*,[482] Justice Kennedy, in his concurrence, labeled *Renton's* test "something of a fiction," observing that it is "perhaps more confusing than helpful." "These ordinances" he said, "are content-based, and we should call them so."[483] Kennedy did not, however, suggest that strict scrutiny be applied, but argued that an exception be applied to content-based ordinances regulating adult uses. Essentially, Justice Kennedy countered *Renton's* implicit suggestion that a watered-down intermediate scrutiny would suffice with the position that real intermediate scrutiny be used.

While courts are supposed to closely review an ordinance to determine whether it serves a substantial government interest, is narrowly tailored, and does not unreasonably limit alternate avenues of communication,[484] the mandate of the Supreme Court is not strong. Justice Kennedy would raise the bar. He suggests, for example, focusing on proportionality, saying that a city may not reduce secondary effects by reducing speech in the same proportion. "The premise, [he said, is] that businesses * * * will for the most part disperse rather than shut down."[485]

To pass muster, when challenged a city must provide some evidence that its ordinance is designed to, and does, deal with secondary effects. The burden is on the government to show a connection between the regulated business and the alleged secondary effects.[486] "Shoddy data or reasoning" will not suffice.[487] The burden, while real,[488] is not heavy.[489] The City of Renton, for example, had conducted no studies on the effects of adult theaters. Instead, the city relied on studies of nearby Seattle. First-hand studies were not required said the Court, holding that a city meets its First Amendment burden if it relies on evidence that it reasonably believes relevant to the problem against which it is legislating.

---

[480] See, generally, Wright, Content-Based and Content-Neutral Regulation of Speech: The Limitations of a Common Distinction, 60 U. Miami L. Rev. 333 (2006).

[481] E.g., "finding of 'predominate intent' more than adequate." *City of Renton v. Playtime Theatres, Inc.,* 475 U.S. 41, 48, 106 S. Ct. 925, 929, 89 L. Ed. 2d 29 (1986).

[482] *City of Los Angeles v. Alameda Books, Inc.,* 535 U.S. 425, 122 S. Ct. 1728, 152 L. Ed. 2d 670 (2002).

[483] Id., 535 U.S. 425, 445, 122 S. Ct. 1728, 1741.

[484] See *Illusions—Dallas Private Club, Inc. v. Steen,* 482 F.3d 299 (5th Cir. 2007) (burden "very light"). But see *R.V.S., L.L.C. v. City of Rockford,* 361 F.3d 402, 410 (7th Cir. 2004).

[485] 535 U.S. at 450, 122 S. Ct. 1742.

[486] Fee, The Pornographic Secondary Effects Doctrine, 60 Ala. L. Rev. 291 (2009).

[487] 535 U.S. at 438, 122 S. Ct. at 1736.

[488] *R.V.S., L.L.C. v. City of Rockford,* 361 F.3d 402, 411 (7th Cir. 2004).

[489] See *Abilene Retail No. 30, Inc. v. Board of Com'rs of Dickinson County,* 492 F.3d 1164 (10th Cir. 2007).

Overbreadth and vagueness concerns arise in defining covered activities. An ordinance regulating "any business which offers to members of the public entertainment featuring or in any way including specified sexual activities [as further defined]," was held not to apply to a house in a residential area that hosted an internet web site displaying camera images of nude women where the customers did not come to the house.[490]

While the *Renton* Court confirmed the rule that legislation that has suppression of speech as its purpose is presumptively invalid, the City of Renton avoided being found to have harbored intent to suppress because the Court accepted the lower court's finding that the city's "predominate intent" was to deal with secondary effects. This, said the Court, "was more than adequate to establish that the city's [goal] was unrelated to suppression * * *."[491] The relevance of motive is murky. While the Court has long said that it "will not strike down an otherwise constitutional statute on the basis of an alleged illicit motive,"[492] *Renton's* language suggests that actual motive is relevant and that the Court might regard a mixed motive as content-neutral or content-based.

Reasonable alternative avenues of communication must be left open. In *Renton,* the Court found that 520 acres equaling 5% of the city "easily" met the test.[493] Unlike Detroit, where the market opportunities were essentially unrestrained, the court of appeals found that none of the land was commercially viable for a theater. That, said the *Renton* Court, was not relevant. While "practically none" of the land was for sale or lease, the theater operators had "to fend for themselves in the real estate market * * *."[494] Numerous courts have confronted the question of whether the reasonable alternatives requirement has been met. Typically, even though the burden is on the government,[495] the requirement has been met. Yet, there are instances where cities go too far.[496]

While *Renton's* relaxed application of the reasonable alternative requirement allows local government to limit adult uses to unattractive land in small sections of town, total exclusion is suspect. An ordinance that prohibited any form of "live entertainment," including but not limited to nude dancing, was struck down by the Court in *Schad v. Borough of Mount Ephraim.*[497] More recently, the Court sustained a total ban on public nudity in *Erie v. Pap's A.M.*[498] Thus, while *Renton* requires a reasonable opportunity to operate an adult theater within the city, a total ban on public nudity is valid. Validity, then, depends in part upon the type of conduct or entertainment being regulated.

---

[490] *Voyeur Dorm, L.C. v. City of Tampa*, 265 F.3d 1232 (11th Cir. 2001).

[491] Playtime Theatres, Inc., 475 U.S. at 48, 106 S. Ct. at 929.

[492] *City of Erie v. Pap's A.M.*, 529 U.S. 277, 292, 120 S. Ct. 1382, 146 L. Ed. 2d 265 (2000).

[493] *Renton,* 475 U.S. at 41.

[494] Renton, 475 U.S. at 41.

[495] See *J & B Entertainment, Inc. v. City of Jackson, Miss.*, 152 F.3d 362 (5th Cir. 1998).

[496] *Young v. City of Simi Valley*, 216 F.3d 807 (9th Cir. 2000).

[497] *Schad v. Borough of Mount Ephraim*, 452 US. 61, 101 S. Ct. 2176, 68 L. Ed. 2d 671 (1981).

[498] *City of Erie v. Pap's A.M.,* 529 U.S. 277, 120 S. Ct. 1382, 146 L. Ed. 2d 265 (2000).

§ 10:19 Religious Uses

A. *Religious Uses and Their Neighbors*

In zoning's early years, regulators viewed religious uses as "inherently beneficial" to residential areas and treated them favorably.[499] Minimal friction existed with their neighbors. Generally, they served persons living close by and their buildings were fairly unobtrusive. The presence of a religious organization, typically a church or synagogue, provided a moral tone for a neighborhood, and its building was a center of community activity. In the rare event that a city tried to exclude religious uses from residential areas, courts found such exclusions arbitrary.[500]

Times have changed. The so-called "mega-church" trend leads to land use projects of sizeable dimensions with frequent and varied activities, whose intrusiveness in a neighborhood is difficult to ignore and sometimes hard to appreciate. When activities expand beyond traditional worship (itself a loaded term) to include housing for elderly members, day-care centers, radio and television broadcasting, combined residential-worship use, and homeless shelters, the prospects of neighborhood conflict increase. Neighbors also may find little benefit to a place of worship if the congregation has no ties to the neighborhood. In our ever more mobile society with our sprawling pattern of development, this increasingly is the case. Intolerance or suspicion of diverse faiths may also play a role in community acceptance when the new neighbor is not the traditional church or synagogue, but a religious organization new to the area.

Some or all of these factors have led some communities to regulate religious land uses more stringently than in the past. Often, this simply means treating such uses on a par with other institutional uses since, as with much land development, they produce secular problems of noise, traffic, parking, storm runoff, and erosion. At times, and particularly with religious groups that are not familiar to a community, religious land uses may be treated more harshly than other, similar uses. In either case, increasing regulation provokes an increase in First Amendment free exercise challenges. We begin this chapter by examining constitutional free exercise issues. Then we consider the Religious Land Use and Institutionalized Persons Act (RLUIPA).[501]

In contrast to free exercise, zoning ordinances that exempt religious uses from controls or otherwise treat them more favorably than similar secular uses may be challenged on establishment clause grounds. The dilemma then for regulators is to deal with the Catch 22 of the First Amendment: regulating religious uses may lead to free exercise claims but not regulating religious uses may lead to establishment clause claims. We close this section on religious land use discussing the establishment clause.

B. *Free Exercise Clause*

Land use controls must accommodate religious practices under the command of the free exercise clause, at least to some degree. Long ago, the Court held that while the free exercise clause absolutely protects religious beliefs, government can regulate

---

[499] See, e.g., *Pine Knolls Alliance Church v. Zoning Bd. of Appeals of Town of Moreau,* 5 N.Y.3d 407, 804 N.Y.S.2d 708, 838 N.E.2d 624 (2005).

[500] See *State ex rel. Lake Drive Baptist Church v. Village of Bayside Bd. of Trustees,* 12 Wis. 2d 585, 108 N.W.2d 288, 300 (1961). See also discussion of state court treatment of religious uses, supra § 4:27.

[501] For other coverage of religious uses, see supra § 4:28.

religious conduct.[502] However, in 1963, the Court held in *Sherbert v. Verner*[503] that government regulation of conduct that substantially burdens the free exercise of religion cannot be sustained unless it promotes a compelling interest and uses the least restrictive means to advance this interest.

Developments after *Sherbert* followed a "crooked path,"[504] as the Court unevenly applied its new strict scrutiny test. Lower courts characterized the Supreme Court's case law as "fluid precedent," in an area "'dotted with unanswered questions.'"[505] In the *Sherbert* era, however, the courts consistently found that land use regulations did not substantially burden the free exercise of religion and were thus not subject to the compelling interest test.[506]

In *Messiah Baptist Church v. County of Jefferson,*[507] the county denied a special permit to construct a church in a district zoned for agricultural uses for reasons dealing with access, erosion, and the lack of fire protection. The Tenth Circuit held that the construction of a house of worship on the particular tract of land was not integrally related to the church's beliefs. The church made no showing that alternative sites were unavailable, and while exclusion from the agricultural district where land values were lower may have made the practice of religion more expensive, that incidental burden did not violate the free exercise clause. In a similar case, where a city excluded religious uses from low density residential zones, the *Sixth Circuit in Lakewood, Ohio Congregation of Jehovah's Witnesses v. City of Lakewood,*[508] held that the First Amendment did not "require the City to make all land or even the cheapest or most beautiful land available to churches."[509] And in *Grosz v. City of Miami Beach,*[510] the city prevented a rabbi from conducting organized religious services in his home. Other places conducive to worship, which would not infringe on the quiet of the neighborhood, were available in town.

Religious exercise claims in the land use context, which had already typically failed under *Sherbert,* became even more tenuous in 1990 when the Court held in *Employment Division v. Smith* [511] that the strict scrutiny test of *Sherbert* does not apply to claims challenging neutral laws of general applicability. Following *Smith,* courts, treating zoning ordinances as laws of general applicability, refused to apply strict scrutiny

---

[502] *Reynolds v. U.S.,* 98 U.S. 145, 25 L. Ed. 244, 1878 WL 18416 (1878).

[503] *Sherbert v. Verner,* 374 U.S. 398, 83 S. Ct. 1790, 10 L. Ed. 2d 965 (1963).

[504] Eisengruber and Sager, Congressional Power and Religious Liberty After City of Boerne v. Flores, 1997 Sup. Ct. Rev. 79, 101 (1997).

[505] *Messiah Baptist Church v. County of Jefferson,* 859 F.2d 820, 823 (10th Cir. 1988).

[506] *Lakewood, Ohio Congregation of Jehovah's Witnesses, Inc. v. City of Lakewood,* 699 F.2d 303 (6th Cir. 1983); *Messiah Baptist Church v. County of Jefferson,* 859 F.2d 820 (10th Cir. 1988); *Grosz v. City of Miami Beach,* 721 F.2d 729 (11th Cir. 1983).

[507] *Messiah Baptist Church v. County of Jefferson,* 859 F.2d 820 (10th Cir. 1988).

[508] *Lakewood, Ohio Congregation of Jehovah's Witnesses, Inc. v. City of Lakewood,* 699 F.2d 303 (6th Cir. 1983).

[509] Id. at 307.

[510] *Grosz v. City of Miami Beach,* 721 F.2d 729 (11th Cir. 1983).

[511] *Employment Div. v. Smith,* 494 U.S. 872, 110 S. Ct. 1595, 108 L. Ed. 2d 876 (1990).

and upheld the exclusion of a church from a commercial district[512] and the designation of a church as an historic landmark.[513]

If a state has a system of individualized exceptions to an otherwise generally applicable law, *Smith* does not apply and government needs a compelling reason not to extend the exception to a religious use. Some courts have found variances and special permit processes to be systems of individualized exemptions.[514] This is an arguable proposition. While a variance is a standard zoning tool to grant exemptions, the relevant factors are land based, not personal.[515] Variance law is neutral with respect to whether the user claims religious motivations for wanting an exemption or other personal hardships.[516]

The Court clarified the reach of *Smith* in *Church of Lukumi Babalu Aye, Inc. v. City of Hialeah,*[517] where it said that *Smith* did not grant government the power to target religious practices. In *City of Hialeah,* the Court found that a city violated the First Amendment when it applied its zoning, health, and animal cruelty ordinances prohibiting the ritual slaughter of animals to specifically target one church's religious conduct. Applying the compelling interest test, the Court found that the ordinances were not narrowly tailored to achieve the city's interests. Thus, under *City of Hialeah,* an ordinance that is neutral on its face will be subjected to strict scrutiny if its application is shown to have been motivated by religious animus.

Concerned that the Supreme Court's interpretation of the First Amendment provided inadequate protection to religious exercise, Congress enacted legislation in 1993 and 2000 designed to restore the protection it thought the First Amendment should provide.

C. *Legislation Protecting Religious Land Uses*

Religious Freedom Restoration Act (RFRA)

The decision in *Employment Division v. Smith*[518] provoked outcry from some who somewhat dramatically denounced it as the end of religious freedom. Decisions in land use cases were cited as examples of a need for greater protection of religious liberty. In response, Congress enacted the Religious Freedom Restoration Act of 1993 (RFRA).[519] The act purported to restore the compelling interest test of *Sherbert,* but four years after it was enacted, the Court invalidated it as it applied to the states. In *City of*

---

[512] *Cornerstone Bible Church v. City of Hastings,* 948 F.2d 464 (8th Cir.1991).

[513] *Rector, Wardens, and Members of Vestry of St. Bartholomew's Church v. City of New York,* 914 F.2d 348 (2d Cir. 1990).

[514] See *Korean Buddhist Dae Won Sa Temple of Hawaii v. Sullivan,* 87 Haw. 217, 953 P.2d 1315, 1345 n.31 (1998).

[515] See supra § 5:17.

[516] See *Tran v. Gwinn,* 262 Va. 572, 554 S.E.2d 63, 68 (2001).

[517] *Church of the Lukumi Babalu Aye, Inc. v. City of Hialeah,* 508 U.S. 520, 533–35, 113 S. Ct. 2217, 2227, 124 L. Ed. 2d 472 (1993).

[518] 494 U.S. 872, 110 S. Ct. 1595, 108 L. Ed. 2d 876 (1990).

[519] 42 U.S.C.A. §§ 2000bb et seq.

Boerne v. Flores,[520] the Court found RFRA an unconstitutional exercise of Congress' remedial powers under Section Five of the 14th Amendment.[521]

Religious Land Use and Institutionalized Persons Act (RLUIPA)

Attempting to overcome the Court's objections to RFRA, Congress enacted the Religious Land Use and Institutionalized Persons Act of 2000 (RLUIPA).[522] RLUIPA's main provision is that government shall not "impose or implement a land use regulation in a manner that imposes a substantial burden on the religious exercise of a person, including a religious assembly or institution, unless the government demonstrates that imposition of the burden on that person, assembly, or institution (A) is in furtherance of a compelling governmental interest; and (B) is the least restrictive means of furthering that compelling governmental interest."[523] The provision applies where "the substantial burden is imposed in the implementation of a land use regulation or system of land use regulations, under which a government makes, or has in place formal or informal procedures or practices that permit the government to make, individualized assessments of the proposed uses for the property involved."[524]

The act also contains an "equal terms" section, which provides that "[n]o government shall impose or implement a land use regulation in a manner that treats a religious assembly or institution on less than equal terms with a nonreligious assembly or institution."[525] RLUIPA applies only to land use regulations, defined as "zoning or landmarking law[s]."[526] It does not apply to exercises of the eminent domain power,[527] or the annexation power.[528]

In order to avoid RFRA's fate, Congress designed RLUIPA differently in two respects. First, the act is based on the power under the spending and commerce clauses in addition to the enforcement power in the 14th Amendment.[529] Second, avoiding RFRA's broad coverage, RLUIPA is limited in reach to land use regulations and to institutionalized persons. Several courts have found that these changes solve the defects the Court found in *Boerne,* and held RLUIPA constitutional under the 14th Amendment [530] and under the commerce clause.[531]

RLUIPA has generated myriad lawsuits. Several reasons explain this. Municipal codes may not have been updated to account for RLUIPA. Local legislators and administrators may not be well informed, if informed at all, about the obligations imposed on them by the act. Mostly, though, the litigation reflects the tension between expanding

---

[520] 521 U.S. 507, 117 S. Ct. 2157, 138 L. Ed. 2d 624 (1997).

[521] RFRA still applies to the federal government. *Gonzales v. O Centro Espirita Beneficente Uniao do Vegetal,* 546 U.S. 418, 126 S. Ct. 1211, 163 L. Ed. 2d 1017 (2006).

[522] 42 U.S.C.A. §§ 2000cc et seq. See Hamilton, Federalism and the Public Good: The True Story Behind the Religious Land Use and Institutionalized Persons Act, 78 Ind. L.J. 311 (2003).

[523] 42 U.S.C.A. § 2000cc.

[524] 42 U.S.C.A. § 2000cc (a)(2)(C).

[525] 42 U.S.C.A. § 2000cc-(b)(1).

[526] 42 U.S.C.A. § 2000cc-5 (5).

[527] *City and County of Honolulu v. Sherman,* 110 Haw. 39, 129 P.3d 542 (2006).

[528] *Vision Church v. Village of Long Grove,* 468 F.3d 975 (7th Cir. 2006).

[529] See *Guru Nanak Sikh Soc. of Yuba City v. County of Sutter,* 456 F.3d 978 (9th Cir.2006).

[530] See *World Outreach Conference Center v. City of Chicago,* 591 F.3d 531 (7th Cir. 2009).

[531] See, e.g., *Westchester Day School v. Village of Mamaroneck,* 504 F.3d 338 (2d Cir. 2007).

religious land uses and their neighbors. There has been a surge in the expansion of existing religious organizations' buildings and activities. Also, new religious organizations, or ones new to the community, have appeared. The inevitable clash then occurs with those who live near the land where this activity is proposed or has occurred. Finally, the fact that attorney's fees are available under RLUIPA likely spurs some of the litigation.

Activities Protected

The act's language is quite broad. This is particularly true of its definition of protected religious exercise as "any exercise of religion, whether or not compelled by, or central to, a system of religious belief."[532] It also provides that the "use, building, or conversion of real property for the purpose of religious exercise shall be considered to be religious exercise of the person or entity that uses or intends to use the property for that purpose."[533] These definitions cover acts well beyond free exercise case law.[534]

Activities found to constitute "religious exercises" have been held to include a religious organization's community center providing recreational and other nonreligious services,[535] a temporary encampment for homeless persons,[536] and a religious school's classroom expansion.[537] On the other hand, an apartment complex was held not covered.[538] Likewise, a cemetery,[539] Alcoholics Anonymous meetings,[540] and the holding of boxing matches to raise money [541] were denied protection. Despite the omission of a requirement that the religious exercise be taken pursuant to a "sincerely held" religious belief, several courts have implied one,[542] relying upon First Amendment case law, supported by legislative history.[543] The sincerity of a belief is treated as a question of fact. In one case, a jury found a church had failed to prove its desire to open a day care center was based on a sincere exercise of religion.[544]

Deciding what constitutes a sincere religious exercise is a dicey matter, which courts avoid in at least two ways. A court inclined to favor the plaintiff may avoid interpreting RLUIPA's "exercise" definition by asking whether the activity is a permitted accessory use under the local ordinance.[545] If it is, a RLUIPA claim is moot.[546] A court

---

[532] 42 U.S.C.A. § 2000cc-5(7)(A).

[533] 42 U.S.C.A. § 2000cc-5(7)(B).

[534] See discussion in *Civil Liberties for Urban Believers v. City of Chicago*, 342 F.3d 752, 761 (7th Cir. 2003).

[535] *World Outreach Conference Center v. City of Chicago*, 591 F.3d 531 (7th Cir. 2009).

[536] *City of Woodinville v. Northshore United Church of Christ*, 166 Wash. 2d 633, 644, 211 P.3d 406, 411 (2009).

[537] *Westchester Day School v. Village of Mamaroneck*, 504 F.3d 338, 351 (2d Cir. 2007).

[538] *Greater Bible Way Temple of Jackson v. City of Jackson*, 478 Mich. 373, 733 N.W.2d 734 (2007).

[539] *St. John's United Church of Christ v. City of Chicago*, 502 F.3d 616 (7th Cir.2007).

[540] Glenside Center, Inc. v. Abington Tp. Zoning Hearing Bd., 973 A.2d 10 (Pa. Commw. Ct. 2009).

[541] *Scottish Rite Cathedral Ass'n v. City of Los Angeles*, 156 Cal. App. 4th 108, 67 Cal. Rptr. 3d 207 (2007).

[542] See, e.g., *Grace United Methodist Church v. City of Cheyenne*, 451 F.3d 643 (10th Cir. 2006).

[543] See *Grace United Methodist Church v. City of Cheyenne*, 235 F. Supp. 2d 1186, 1193 (D. Wyo. 2002).

[544] *Grace United Methodist Church v. City of Cheyenne*, 451 F.3d 643 (10th Cir. 2006).

[545] See Jay M. Zitter, Annot. What constitutes accessory or incidental use of religious or educational property within zoning ordinance, 11 A.L.R.4th 1084.

[546] *Jirtle v. Board of Adjustment for the Town of Biscoe*, 175 N.C. App. 178, 622 S.E.2d 713 (2005) (food pantry qualified as an accessory building or use of church, and RLUIPA question not reached).

finding no substantial burden may simply assume without discussion that the activity is covered.[547]

Exclusion of homeless shelters and related activities like soup kitchens from residential areas have met mixed results under the First Amendment.[548] and under RLUIPA.[549] A number of courts gloss over the question of whether sheltering the homeless is a religious exercise and uphold reasonable permit requirements.[550]

Protection of home prayer meetings may depend on the number of participants and frequency of the meetings.[551] Where zoning ordinances are applied to prohibit small groups from gathering in homes for religious services, courts have found free exercise violations.[552] In one case, a group of 15 to 20 persons that met by appointment was protected,[553] while, in another, a group of 70 to 150 persons at weekday services was not.[554]

"Substantial Burden" Under RLUIPA

Most RLUIPA challenges are based on the provision that prohibits the imposition of a substantial burden on religious exercise. Legislative history indicates that "substantial burden" was intended to adopt the *pre-Smith v. Employment Division* test from *Sherbert.*[555] While the lower courts do rely on pre-*Smith* Supreme Court case law,[556] a complicating factor is that the test now applies to the new and broader definition of religious exercise.[557]

In *Civil Liberties for Urban Believers (C.L.U.B.) v. City of Chicago,*[558] the Seventh Circuit held that a substantial burden "is one that necessarily bears direct, primary, and fundamental responsibility for rendering religious exercise—including the use of real property for the purpose thereof within the regulated jurisdiction generally—effectively impracticable."[559] The court modified this strict test in *Sts. Constantine and Helen Greek Orthodox Church, Inc. v. City of New Berlin,*[560] noting that the C.L.U.B. opinion does not impose an absolute rule that there is no other land than that which the applicant owns on which it can build. For example, the court said that the substantial burden showing can be met where a religious user establishes that it must choose

---

[547] *City of Hope v. Sadsbury Tp. Zoning Hearing Bd.*, 890 A.2d 1137 (Pa. Commw. Ct. 2006).

[548] Not protected, *First Assembly of God of Naples, Florida, Inc. v. Collier County, Fla.*, 20 F.3d 419 (11th Cir. 1994). But see *Fifth Ave. Presbyterian Church v. City of New York*, 293 F.3d 570, 575 (2d Cir. 2002).

[549] *Westgate Tabernacle, Inc. v. Palm Beach County*, 14 So. 3d 1027, 1032 (Fla. 4th DCA 2009).

[550] *Family Life Church v. City Of Elgin*, 561 F. Supp. 2d 978 (N.D. Ill. 2008).

[551] *Murphy v. Zoning Com'n of Town of New Milford*, 148 F. Supp. 2d 173 (D. Conn. 2001).

[552] *State v. Cameron*, 100 N.J. 586, 606, 498 A.2d 1217, 1227 (1985).

[553] *Kali Bari Temple v. Board of Adjustment of Tp. of Readington*, 271 N.J. Super. 241, 638 A.2d 839 (App. Div. 1994).

[554] *Muslim Center of Somerset County, Inc. v. Borough of Somerville Zoning Bd. of Adjustment*, 2006 WL 1344323 (N.J. Super. Ct. Law Div. 2006).

[555] Civil Liberties for Urban Believers, 342 F.3d at 761.

[556] *Midrash Sephardi, Inc. v. Town of Surfside*, 366 F.3d 1214, 1226 (11th Cir. 2004).

[557] See text supra accompanying notes 532–534.

[558] *Civil Liberties for Urban Believers v. City of Chicago*, 342 F.3d 752 (7th Cir. 2003).

[559] Id. at 761.

[560] *Sts. Constantine and Helen Greek Orthodox Church, Inc. v. City of New Berlin*, 396 F.3d 895 (7th Cir. 2005).

between selling its land and finding another suitable parcel or establishes that it is being subjected to unreasonable delay by having to make multiple or new permit requests where it has already agreed to the zoning authority's mitigating conditions. The court has also held that the burden is relative to the weakness of the burdened.[561]

The Eleventh Circuit refused to adopt the Seventh Circuit's "effectively impracticable" test as it stood before the *Sts. Constantine* opinion, finding it too onerous on plaintiffs. It adopted what it considered to be the majority rule that "a substantial burden is one which actually inhibits religious practice by virtue of a land use decision."[562] The court said that a chilling effect is insufficient. "The governmental conduct being must actually inhibit religious activity in a concrete way."[563] The court went on to find that a zoning ordinance prohibiting synagogues from being located in a business district, relegating them solely to a two-family residential district did not violate the substantial burden provision. That Orthodox Jews, who do not use automobiles on the Sabbath, would have to walk extra blocks to reach the synagogue was not a substantial burden.[564] Numerous courts follow the Eleventh Circuit's reasoning focusing on whether there was significant pressure which actually inhibited religious exercise.[565]

The Ninth Circuit's interpretation is that for a land use regulation to impose a substantial burden, "it must be 'oppressive' [and] must impose a significantly great restriction or onus upon such exercise."[566] In *Guru Nanak Sikh Society of Yuba City v. County of Sutter,*[567] the court held that a board's denial of a conditional use permit, which would have allowed Guru Nanak to establish a Sikh Temple in an agricultural district, placed a substantial burden on religious exercise. In particular, the court noted that the board had denied the permit despite the applicant's willingness to accept various conditions on use and that it had denied a previous permit application to build on a smaller residential lot. The board's actions, said the court, gave the impression that it would never grant Guru Nanak a permit.

The substantial burden provision only applies where "the implementation of a land use regulation or system of land use regulations, under which a government makes, or has in place formal or informal procedures or practices that permit the government to make, individualized assessments of the proposed uses for the property involved." Such "individualized assessments" are typically the common variance and special permit processes.

The government can overcome the finding of a substantial burden by proving that its action furthers a compelling governmental interest and is the least restrictive means of furthering that interest. While not easy to show, it is not impossible. Requiring a church install an automatic sprinkler system advanced a compelling interest in safety.[568] Protecting neighborhood safety were compelling reasons for a town to prohib-

---

[561] *World Outreach Conference Center v. City of Chicago*, 591 F.3d 531 (7th Cir. 2009).

[562] *Midrash Sephardi, Inc. v. Town of Surfside*, 366 F.3d 1214, 1227 (11th Cir. 2004).

[563] Midrash Sephardi, Inc., 366 F.3d 1214.

[564] See also *Konikov v. Orange County,* 410 F.3d 1317 (11th Cir. 2005).

[565] See Alden, Reconsidering RLUIPA: Do Religious Land Use Protections Really Benefit Religious Land Users?, 57 UCLA L. Rev. 1779, 1792 (2010).

[566] *San Jose Christian College v. City of Morgan Hill*, 360 F.3d 1024, 1034 (9th Cir. 2004).

[567] *Guru Nanak Sikh Soc. of Yuba City v. County of Sutter*, 456 F.3d 978 (9th Cir. 2006).

[568] *Peace Lutheran Church and Academy v. Village of Sussex*, 246 Wis. 2d 502, 631 N.W.2d 229 (Ct. App. 2001).

it a group of 25 people from holding weekly prayer meetings at an individual's house.[569] On the other hand, several courts have found adverse traffic and increased activities were not compelling interests.[570] While these examples give a sense of how courts handle the issue, there can be no hard and fast list of what is and what is not a compelling interest since the decision turns on the facts of each case, particularly the nature of the surrounding uses.

Even where a compelling interest is found, the means chosen to implement it must be the least restrictive. Thus, assuming a compelling interest, one court found the least restrictive means test not met where the city required religious uses to leave a 200 foot setback and limit building lot coverage to 4% to protect density and setback concerns.[571] In another case, a village's denial of a permit to address anticipated traffic increases was held not the least restrictive means where the concerns could have been mitigated by approving the application subject to conditions relating to traffic management, bus schedules, and enrollment caps for the school.[572] A compelling government interest in creating a redevelopment zone, which led to a prohibition of religious uses within a limited commercial district, was the least restrictive means of furthering a compelling interest in creating an artistic and dynamic business center.[573]

Equal terms

Even if an act does not place a substantial burden on religious exercise, it may run afoul of RLUIPA's "equal terms" section, which provides that "[n]o government shall impose or implement a land use regulation in a manner that treats a religious assembly or institution on less than equal terms with a nonreligious assembly or institution."[574] The section the clause falls under is entitled "discrimination and exclusion," which separately bans unequal terms treatment, discrimination, and exclusion, all of which seemingly overlap. Presumably the equal terms provision means something different than discrimination. One answer is that discrimination requires a showing of intent; the act must be done "on the basis of religion."[575]

The courts have had difficulty in developing a test for an equal terms challenge, as seen in the decisions of the 3rd and 7th Circuits, which vie with the 11th Circuit. The Eleventh Circuit requires a showing that the non-religious use with which the religious use is compared is an assembly as that term is commonly understood by standard dictionary definitions.[576] If the religious and non-religious uses are both understood as assemblies then the court applies strict scrutiny to determine whether the uses are treated equally. In *Konikov v. Orange County*,[577] the court held that requiring a group meeting for religious purposes to seek a permit, yet not require that of other similar

---

[569] *Murphy v. Zoning Com'n of Town of New Milford*, 148 F. Supp. 2d 173 (D. Conn. 2001), held unripe, 402 F.3d 342 (2d Cir. 2005).

[570] See, e.g., *Mintz v. Roman Catholic Bishop of Springfield*, 424 F. Supp. 2d 309, 323 (D. Mass. 2006).

[571] *Mintz v. Roman Catholic Bishop of Springfield*, 424 F. Supp. 2d 309 (D. Mass. 2006).

[572] *Westchester Day School v. Village of Mamaroneck*, 504 F.3d 338 (2d Cir. 2007).

[573] *The Lighthouse Institute for Evangelism, Inc. v. City of Long Branch*, 406 F. Supp. 2d 507, 516 (D.N.J. 2005), judgment aff'd in part, vacated in part, 510 F.3d 253 (3d Cir. 2007).

[574] 42 U.S.C.A. § 2000cc-(b)(1)

[575] 42 U.S.C.A. § 2000cc-(b)(2). See *River of Life Kingdom Ministries v. Village of Hazel Crest*, 611 F.3d 367, 382 (7th Cir. 2010) (Sykes, J. dissenting).

[576] *Midrash Sephardi, Inc. v. Town of Surfside*, 366 F.3d 1214 (11th Cir. 2004).

[577] *Konikov v. Orange County*, 410 F.3d 1317 (11th Cir. 2005).

assemblies, such as a Cub Scout group meeting, violated the equal terms provision of RLUIPA.

The Third Circuit holds that "a regulation will violate the equal terms provision only if it treats religious assemblies or institutions less well than secular assemblies or institutions that are similarly situated *as to the regulatory purpose.*"[578] The Seventh Circuit follows the 3rd Circuit, but, finding itself uncomfortable with the subjective nature of the purpose test, changes "as to the regulatory purpose" to "[according] to any accepted zoning criterion."[579] The objection to the 11th Circuit's approach is that it "reads the language of the equal-terms provision literally: a zoning ordinance that permits any 'assembly,' as defined by dictionaries, to locate in a district must permit a church to locate there as well[.]"[580] The Third and Seventh Circuit court cases upheld the exclusion of non-commercial uses from areas designated for economic development.

State Religious Freedom Acts

Legislative activity involving religious land use is not limited to Congress. A number of states have their own religious freedom acts that direct courts to closely review actions burdening such uses.[581] Such a law is unnecessary in some states where, by statute, religious uses are exempt to some degree from land use controls.[582] Local governments also may make their own decision to exempt religious uses from zoning.[583]

By statute in Massachusetts, zoning may not prohibit the use of land or structures for religious purposes, but may subject such uses to "reasonable regulations concerning the bulk and height of structures and determining yard sizes, lot area, setbacks, open space, parking and building coverage requirements."[584] When a Mormon church applied to construct an 83 foot steeple atop the roof of its temple, some neighbors objected. The town granted the church a variance and the neighbors sued in federal and state court claiming a violation of the establishment clause. Since church members said the steeple was an integral part of its building, the court held a limitation on it would be unreasonable. Consequently, the variance was not only justified, it was required.[585]

D. Establishment Clause

The desire to avoid treading on free exercise rights requires government to walk a tightrope. Zoning regulations may lead to a free exercise violation, yet zoning exemptions may lead to establishment clause violations. Developing case law allows government to lean fairly far toward favoring religious uses without violating the establishment clause. Some municipalities, likely overreacting to RLUIPA, are prone to go far-

---

[578] *Lighthouse Institute for Evangelism, Inc. v. City of Long Branch*, 510 F.3d 253, 266 (3d Cir. 2007) (emphasis the court's)

[579] *River of Life Kingdom Ministries v. Village of Hazel Crest*, 611 F.3d 367, 371 (7th Cir. 2010).

[580] *Id.*, 611 F.3d 367, 369.

[581] See Gildin, A Blessing in Disguise: Protecting Minority Faiths Through State Religious Freedom Non-Restoration Acts, 23 Harv. J.L. & Pub. Pol'y 411 (2000), listing eight states with such acts.

[582] See, e.g., Mass. Gen. Laws ch. 40A, § 3.

[583] Granting preferential treatment raises the flip side of the coin as it may constitute an establishment clause violation. See infra § 10:19.

[584] Mass. Gen. Laws ch. 40A, § 3.

[585] *Martin v. Corporation of Presiding Bishop of Church of Jesus Christ of Latter-Day Saints*, 434 Mass. 141, 747 N.E.2d 131 (2001).

ther than necessary to give religious uses preferential treatment over like, secular uses.

Under *Lemon v. Kurtzman,*[586] to survive an establishment clause challenge, an ordinance must have a secular purpose, must not have as its primary effect the advancement of religion, and must not foster an excessive entanglement with religion. In *Larkin v. Grendel's Den,*[587] the Court invalidated an ordinance that gave a "church" a veto power over an application for a liquor license for an establishment within 500 feet of the church. The ordinance had a valid secular purpose of insulating religious uses from the disruptive activities that accompany the use of alcohol, but the Court held that by vesting veto authority in the religious organization, the ordinance both advanced religion and resulted in an excessive church-state entanglement.

While the Supreme Court has held that RLUIPA does not violate the establishment clause in the context of prisoners' religious rights,[588] it has not addressed the land use prong of the statute. Some lower courts have held that RLUIPA does not violate the establishment clause in land use cases.[589]

In the lower courts, recent cases reflect a trend toward the view that favorable zoning treatment is justified where its primary purpose is to minimize governmental interference with religious uses.[590] Construing various local laws that give preferential treatment to religious land uses, these courts have held that government is entitled to act out of a so-called "benevolent neutrality," which is viewed as having a secular purpose of supporting, but not promoting, religion.[591] This support is valid if the legislature rationally thinks that the exemption will protect against a potential burden on free exercise.[592]

V. COMMERCE CLAUSE, ANTITRUST, AND WASTE CONTROL

§ 10:20 Commerce Clause-Based Limitations

The commerce clause is both a source of power for federal land use controls and a negative restraint on state and local land use laws. Such federal laws as the Surface Mining Control and Reclamation Act,[593] the Clean Water Act,[594] particularly the Section 404 wetlands controls, and the Endangered Species Act [595] are direct regulations of private land use activities based in whole or in part on the commerce clause. The Religious Land Use and Institutionalized Persons Act,[596] based in part on the commerce clause, is a direct limitation on state and local government's land use regulation of re-

---

[586] *Lemon v. Kurtzman,* 403 U.S. 602, 91 S. Ct. 2105, 29 L. Ed. 2d 745 (1971).

[587] *Larkin v. Grendel's Den, Inc.,* 459 U.S. 116, 103 S. Ct. 505, 74 L. Ed. 2d 297 (1982).

[588] *Cutter v. Wilkinson,* 544 U.S. 709, 125 S. Ct. 2113, 161 L. Ed. 2d 1020 (2005).

[589] See, e.g., *Midrash Sephardi, Inc. v. Town of Surfside,* 366 F.3d 1214 (11th Cir. 2004).

[590] See, e.g., *Boyajian v. Gatzunis,* 212 F.3d 1 (1st Cir. 2000).

[591] *Boyajian v. Gatzunis,* 212 F.3d 1, 6 (1st Cir. 2000).

[592] *East Bay Asian Local Development Corp. v. State of California,* 24 Cal. 4th 693, 102 Cal. Rptr. 2d 280, 293–294, 13 P.3d 1122, 1134 (2000).

[593] 30 U.S.C.A. §§ 1201 et seq.

[594] 33 U.S.C.A. §§ 1251 et seq.

[595] 16 U.S.C.A. §§ 1531 et seq.

[596] 42 U.S.C.A. §§ 2000cc et seq.

ligious uses. Commerce clause-based acts promoting communications functions, such as satellite dishes and cellular telephones, indirectly affect land use in that they partially preempt local zoning.[597]

While the constitutionality of these and other such acts was once assumed in light of the Supreme Court's traditional deference to congressional determinations that interstate commerce was affected, recent cases eliminate that facile assumption. In several cases, the Court has shown a renewed interest in scrutinizing federal commerce clause-based legislative intervention into state and local affairs.[598] In this context, the Court has observed that the regulation of land use is "'a function traditionally performed by local governments.'"[599] The specific acts listed above are considered elsewhere.[600]

The coverage below deals with limitations on the freedom of local government to regulate land use that may arise from federal antitrust laws based on the commerce clause and with limitations on state and local laws that affect the interstate shipment of waste that arise from the negative or dormant commerce clause.

§ 10:21 Antitrust: Local Government Immunity

Land use regulations frequently have anticompetitive effects that raise possible federal antitrust liability concerns. The facts of *City of Columbia v. Omni Outdoor Advertising, Inc.*[601] illustrate the problem. When a new outdoor advertising company tried to break into the local market of Columbia, South Carolina, it ran into significant opposition. Much of the opposition allegedly came from a local company that controlled 95% of the billboard business in town. Eventually, the city enacted a restrictive billboard measure that had the effect of banning most new billboards and allowing most existing ones to continue in place. The law clearly favored the hometown business and disadvantaged the outsider. The outside company brought suit against the city and the competitor, alleging their conduct constituted a conspiracy in restraint of trade under the Sherman Act.[602]

In a broad ruling favoring municipalities, the Court held that the city was immune from liability under the state action doctrine of *Parker v. Brown*.[603] In *Parker*, the Court had held that sovereign immunity shielded a state from liability for anticompetitive action. Subsequently, the Court held that municipalities acquired derivative immunity only when they were carrying out clearly articulated state policies.[604] The antitrust immunity doctrine requires a delegation that authorizes the suppression of competition, and in *Omni* the Court found the state's delegation of zoning power to the city

---

[597] See discussion supra § 4:25.

[598] *U.S. v. Morrison*, 529 U.S. 598, 120 S. Ct. 1740, 146 L. Ed. 2d 658 (2000); *U.S. v. Lopez*, 514 U.S. 549, 115 S. Ct. 1624, 131 L. Ed. 2d 626 (1995).

[599] *Solid Waste Agency of Northern Cook County v. U.S. Army Corps of Engineers*, 531 U.S. 159, 173, 121 S. Ct. 675, 684, 148 L. Ed. 2d 576 (2001).

[600] For coverage of wetlands, see §§ 11:9 to 11:13; endangered species, § 11:17; Surface Mining Control and Reclamation Act, Religious Land Use Act, § 10:19; Telecommunications Act, § 4:25.

[601] *City of Columbia v. Omni Outdoor Advertising, Inc.*, 499 U.S. 365, 111 S. Ct. 1344, 113 L. Ed. 2d 382 (1991).

[602] 15 U.S.C.A. § 1.

[603] 317 U.S. 341, 63 S. Ct. 307, 87 L. Ed. 315 (1943).

[604] *City of Lafayette v. Louisiana Power & Light Co.*, 435 U.S. 389, 98 S. Ct. 1123, 55 L. Ed. 2d 364 (1978).

"amply met" the test. The billboard regulations were enacted pursuant to state law modeled after the Standard State Zoning Enabling Act that allowed the city to regulate the location of uses. "The very purpose of zoning regulation," the Court said, "is to displace unfettered business freedom."[605]

Omni went on to hold that the immunity existed even if the local action exceeded the delegated authority. Under the law of most states, while it is recognized that zoning may affect competition, zoning for the purpose of controlling competition is illegal.[606] For antitrust purposes, however, the delegated authority is interpreted more broadly so as to minimize federal interference with state law. Thus, even if the City of Columbia had enacted the billboard law with the intent of suppressing competition in violation of state law, it would not have mattered.

While the *Parker* doctrine protected the city from liability, the *Noerr-Pennington* doctrine saved the hometown competitor.[607] *Noerr-Pennington* prevents persons from being penalized for exercising their First Amendment right to petition the government. Private parties can urge the government to enact anticompetitive laws, which are to their economic benefit, without fear of antitrust liability. There is, however, a sham exception. If the anticompetitive tool is the government process itself, and not the outcome, liability may ensue. Filing a frivolous lawsuit or objection in a pending action with no expectation of winning, but simply to harass and delay a competitor, is not protected by the First Amendment. In *Omni,* the alleged anticompetitive action was not the lobbying effort but the result, and, thus, the private party was immune. The *Noerr-Pennington* defense was extended to public officials immunizing them from § 1983 liability in *Manistee Town Center v. City of Glendale.*[608]

Before *Omni* there had been some question as to whether there were conspiracy exceptions to *Parker* and *Noerr-Pennington* immunity. The *Omni* Court said "no" to both. The Court was unwilling to allow even a narrow conspiracy exception for corruption. If bribery of local officials is involved, other federal and state laws will apply.

Treble damages, as well as injunctive and declaratory relief, are available against private parties for antitrust violations under the Clayton Act.[609] Local governments, however, are immune from monetary liability. Shortly after a $28.5 million treble damage verdict against a Chicago suburb, Congress enacted the Local Government Antitrust Act of 1984.[610] It forbids antitrust damage claims against local governments and their officials: "no damages, interest on damages, costs or attorney's fees may be recovered under Section 4, 4A, or 4C of the Clayton Act * * * from any local government, or official or employee thereof acting in an official capacity."[611] Both the plain language of the Section and the legislative history of the Act make clear that a local government is

---

[605] *City of Columbia v. Omni Outdoor Advertising, Inc.,* 499 U.S. 365, 372, 111 S. Ct. 1344, 1350, 113 L. Ed. 2d 382 (1991).

[606] See §3.18.

[607] *Eastern R. R. Presidents Conference v. Noerr Motor Freight, Inc.,* 365 U.S. 127, 81 S. Ct. 523, 5 L. Ed. 2d 464 (1961) and *United Mine Workers of America v. Pennington,* 381 U.S. 657, 85 S. Ct. 1585, 14 L. Ed. 2d 626 (1965).

[608] *Manistee Town Center v. City of Glendale,* 227 F.3d 1090 (9th Cir. 2000).

[609] 15 U.S.C.A. §§ 12 to 26.

[610] 15 U.S.C.A. §§ 34 to 36.

[611] 15 U.S.C.A. § 35(a).

absolutely immune from antitrust damage claims even though the local government may have acted beyond its authority or in bad faith.

In summary, private parties lobbying for land use measures are potentially liable for antitrust treble damage claims, unless they can bring themselves within the *Noerr-Pennington* doctrine. Local governments exercising land use authority will generally be protected by the *Parker* doctrine. In the rare case where they are not, they are still immune from damage claims, as are their public officials when acting in their official capacity. Local governments remain subject to injunctive relief, and compliance with injunctions may in some cases be expensive. Still, with *Omni,* this threat is not great. As Professor Wolf has observed, "local land use regulators who engag[e] in arguably anticompetitive activities [are] no longer pursuing a high-risk activity."[612] These developments, taken together with the expansion of 11th Amendment immunity, make it clear, as Thomas Sullivan concludes in a study of the past 50 years of federal-state relationships in the regulation of competition, "that the multifaceted protections afforded to local government actors leave little room for the federal antitrust laws to affect land use issues."[613]

§ 10:22 State and Local Efforts to Control Waste Disposal

The siting of waste disposal facilities virtually assures controversy. Potential neighbors who do not want them in their "backyards" will likely protest zoning and siting decisions on various state law grounds.[614] In turn, the regulated user may also object to restrictive local laws. Generally, however, subjecting facilities to special permitting processes and imposing distance controls, two common features of local law, are valid. Constitutional difficulties arise when state or local government choose the parochial options of excluding waste facilities, discouraging the importation of waste by charging higher fees, or in the reverse, hoarding waste for the benefit of local business. When government opts for one of these paths, the disadvantaged businesses have a potent ally in the dormant commerce clause.

A state cannot isolate itself from interstate trade. State or local laws that unduly burden or discriminate against interstate commerce violate the dormant commerce clause. Though waste may have no value, the fact that one must pay for its disposal converts waste into an article of commerce. And, with the mountains of waste that we produce, the business of transporting and processing waste is a big business.

The Supreme Court has invalidated numerous state and local efforts to exclude waste from out of state. When New Jersey, finding itself running short of landfill space, banned the import of waste from out of state, the Court held the discriminatory treatment unconstitutional.[615] When Alabama imposed a higher fee on waste generated out of state, the Court found it also to be unconstitutionally discriminatory.[616] When Michigan delegated to its counties the power to exclude waste generated outside the

---

[612] Wolf, Euclid at Threescore Years and Ten: Is This the Twilight of Environmental and Land-Use Regulation?, 30 U. Rich. L. Rev. 961, 981 (1996).

[613] Sullivan, Antitrust Regulation of Land Use: Federalism's Triumph over Competition, the Last Fifty Years, 3 Wash. U. J.L. & Pol'y 473, 511 (2000).

[614] See § 6:9 regarding LULUs.

[615] *City of Philadelphia v. New Jersey,* 437 U.S. 617, 98 S. Ct. 2531, 57 L. Ed. 2d 475 (1978).

[616] *Chemical Waste Management, Inc. v. Hunt,* 504 U.S. 334, 112 S. Ct. 2009, 119 L. Ed. 2d 121 (1992).

county, the Court invalidated a county ordinance that took up the state's invitation.[617] The Court reasoned that local governmental units can no more discriminate than the state itself. The fact that the ordinance banned in-state waste along with out-of-state waste did not save it.

Some states and communities ban the export of waste. Those efforts too have failed. Keeping waste at home is important to maintain a supply for local disposal sites. When Clarkstown, New York needed a new transfer station to sort waste, but apparently could not afford to build it, a local developer agreed to build and operate the facility in return for the town's promise to provide a minimum waste flow and allow the charging of a high tipping fee. To assure a flow of waste, the town adopted an ordinance that required all waste generated in town or brought to town to be taken to the private facility. In *C & A Carbone, Inc. v. Town of Clarkstown,*[618] the Court held the ordinance invalid. Hoarding waste for the benefit of one local private operator was classic protectionism that the commerce clause was designed to prevent.

On the other hand, the Court has upheld a flow-control ordinance that requires waste to be delivered to a public processing facility. So long as there is no discrimination between in-state and out-of-state business, state and local government may regulate waste disposal in the public interest.[619]

In recent years Congress has considered a number of bills seeking to overcome the Court's interpretation of the commerce clause. Most of the bills authorize bans against out of state waste or allow the charging of higher fees.[620] If passed, such legislation would dispense with the commerce clause problem, but there would remain a potential equal protection challenge.

VI. LITIGATION ISSUES AND SECTION 1983

§ 10:23 Choice of Forum: Some General Considerations

The Civil Rights Act of 1871, Section 1983 of Title 42 of the United States Code, provides a cause of action for damages and equitable relief for violations of constitutional and federal statutory rights. Originally interpreted as providing redress for only "personal rights," in 1972 that the Supreme Court expressly held that property rights fell within the purview of § 1983.[621] With two other developments in the 1970s (the availability of attorney's fees and the holding that municipalities were persons under the act),[622] land use claims under § 1983 became legally available and financially viable.

Federal and state courts have concurrent jurisdiction over § 1983 actions, an option to keep in mind since constitutional land use claims, particularly those involving

---

[617] *Fort Gratiot Sanitary Landfill, Inc. v. Michigan Dept. of Natural Resources,* 504 U.S. 353, 112 S. Ct. 2019, 119 L. Ed. 2d 139 (1992).

[618] *C & A Carbone, Inc. v. Town of Clarkstown,* 511 U.S. 383, 114 S. Ct. 1677, 128 L. Ed. 2d 399 (1994).

[619] *United Haulers Ass'n, Inc. v. Oneida-Herkimer Solid Waste Management Authority,* 550 U.S. 330, 127 S. Ct. 1786, 167 L. Ed. 2d 655 (2007).

[620] See Weinberg, Congress, the Courts, and Solid Waste Transport: Good Fences Don't Always Make Good Neighbors, 25 Envtl. L. 57 (1995).

[621] *Lynch v. Household Finance Corp.,* 405 U.S. 538, 92 S. Ct. 1113, 31 L. Ed. 2d 424 (1972).

[622] Civil Rights Attorney's Fees Award Act, 42 U.S.C.A. § 1988 and *Monell v. Department of Social Services of City of New York,* 436 U.S. 658, 98 S. Ct. 2018, 56 L. Ed. 2d 611 (1978).

the Fifth and 14th Amendments, have received a cool welcome in many federal courts. The Court of Appeals for the First Circuit, for example, has repeatedly emphasized that "federal courts do not sit as a super zoning board or a zoning board of appeals."[623] The Seventh Circuit said of a land use claim: "[i]f the plaintiffs can get us to review the [decision], we cannot imagine what zoning dispute could not be shoehorned into federal court * * *, there to displace or postpone consideration of some worthier object of federal judicial solicitude."[624]

The antipathy of these federal courts toward land use claims perhaps explains in part their enthusiastic application of several rules that permit them to reduce their role and their caseload. Several of these rules have been discussed in preceding sections, such as the adoption of a narrow view of what constitutes a protectable property interest,[625] a strict application of the ripeness finality doctrine,[626] a requirement that takings claimants seek compensation in state court,[627] and an expansive reading of the *Parrott* post-deprivation remedy doctrine regarding due process claims.[628] Federal courts have also demonstrated a willingness to abstain in land use cases.[629] Whether a particular state court is more or less hospitable to land use claims than the local federal court, however, is a moot question in many cases since the state court will be the only forum legally or sensibly available.

§ 10:24 Section 1983 of the Civil Rights Act

A. *Procedural, Not Substantive, Protection*

Section I of the Civil Rights Act of 1871, 42 U.S.C.A. § 1983, is the procedural vehicle for much constitutional land use litigation. Section 1983 states in full:

> Every person who, under color of any statute, ordinance, regulation, custom, or usage, of any state or territory, subjects or causes to be subjected, any citizen of the United States or other person within the jurisdiction thereof to the deprivation of any rights, privileges, or immunities secured by the Constitution and laws, shall be liable to the party injured in an action at law, suit in equity, or other proper proceeding for redress.[630]

Enacted as implementing legislation under section five of the 14th Amendment, § 1983 was designed to protect the civil rights of the newly freed slaves. Moving far beyond its original purpose, § 1983 has practically become a federal tort law, and a large body of case law has developed surrounding the use of this statutory avenue for the protection of federal rights.[631]

---

[623] *Raskiewicz v. Town of New Boston,* 754 F.2d 38, 44 (1st Cir. 1985).

[624] *Coniston Corp. v. Village of Hoffman Estates,* 844 F.2d 461, 467 (7th Cir. 1988).

[625] See § 10:12.

[626] See § 10.10.

[627] See § 10.10.

[628] See §§ 10:12 to 10:13.

[629] See § 10:27.

[630] 42 U.S.C.A. § 1983.

[631] See Mary Massaron Ross and Edwin P. Voss, Jr., Sword and Shield: A Practical Approach to Section 1983 Litigation (3d ed. 2006).

Section 1983 creates no substantive rights. It is an enabling statute, providing a procedural vehicle for a person to secure damages or injunctive relief for the violation of federal constitutional or statutory rights. One must establish the deprivation of a right secured by the constitution or laws of the United States. In land use, generally this will involve the Fifth Amendment's requirement of compensation for the taking of property, free speech or religious rights under the First Amendment, or due process or equal protection violations under the 14th Amendment. The substantive law of those provisions, not § 1983, determines when an action lies.

The § 1983 cause of action is particularly important since the option of bringing suit directly on the constitutional provision in question may not exist or, if it does, may be less attractive. While the Fifth Amendment's takings clause is self-executing, and an action in inverse condemnation lies to permit the recovery of just compensation,[632] whether direct actions are available for other constitutional rights is not clear. The Court has held that direct suits are available against the federal government for conduct violative of the Fourth Amendment [633] and the due process clause of the Fifth Amendment.[634] Direct actions against state or local governments based on the 14th Amendment may or may not be implied.[635] The availability of a suit based on § 1983 usually obviates the question.[636]

Federal statutes that create private causes of action, such as the Fair Housing Act[637] and the Telecommunications Act, may preclude § 1983 suits. Generally, this is true if the statute contains a comprehensive remedial scheme. While the "ordinary inference" is that the statutory remedy is exclusive, it can be overcome by textual indication, express or implicit, that the remedy is to complement, rather than supplant, § 1983."[638]

In *City of Rancho Palos Verdes v. Abrams,*[639] the Court held that § 1983 was not available to enforce the rights created by the Telecommunications Act.[640] There, the plaintiff, having been denied a permit to construct a radio tower on his property, brought suit in federal court seeking an injunction under the Telecommunications Act and damages under § 1983. The plaintiff preferred § 1983 since the Telecommunications Act does not include a damage remedy or allow attorney's fees. However, the act has its own special features that suggested exclusivity, such as the requirement that courts hear suits on an expedited basis and within a 30 day limitation period. Allowing enforcement of the Telecommunications Act through § 1983 would, said the Court, "dis-

---

[632] *First English Evangelical Lutheran Church of Glendale v. Los Angeles County,* 482 U.S. 304, n.9, 107 S. Ct. 2378, 96 L. Ed. 2d 250 (1987).

[633] *Bivens v. Six Unknown Named Agents of Federal Bureau of Narcotics,* 403 U.S. 388, 91 S. Ct. 1999, 29 L. Ed. 2d 619 (1971).

[634] *Davis v. Passman,* 442 U.S. 228, 99 S. Ct. 2264, 60 L. Ed. 2d 846 (1979).

[635] See *Rogin v. Bensalem Tp.,* 616 F.2d 680 (3d Cir. 1980).

[636] Some courts have held that the existence of § 1983 precludes a direct action. See *Azul-Pacifico, Inc. v. City of Los Angeles,* 973 F.2d 704 (9th Cir. 1992).

[637] 42 U.S.C.A. § 3613(a)(1)(A).

[638] *City of Rancho Palos Verdes, v. Abrams,* 544 U.S. 113, 125 S. Ct. 1453, 1459, 161 L. Ed. 2d 316 (2005).

[639] Id.

[640] 47 U.S.C.A. § 332(c)(7).

tort the scheme of expedited judicial review and limited remedies created by [the Act.]"[641]

In certain instances § 1983 may be used along with other federal statutory rights of action. The Religious Land Use and Institutionalized Persons Act [642] creates a right of action for a person seeking to enforce religious land use rights. RLUIPA statutory claims are often combined with § 1983 claims asserting First Amendment violations.[643] Both statutes authorize attorney's fees.[644]

B.   Stating a Claim Under § 1983

A § 1983 action requires that the complained of conduct (1) have resulted in (a), the deprivation of (b), a right, privilege or immunity secured by the constitution or laws of the United States and (2), have been committed by a person acting "under color of state law." Both intentional and negligent deprivations may be actionable, but no single standard of care applies in all § 1983 cases; rather, the standard of care demanded depends on the specific constitutional or statutory right under consideration. With respect to violations of due process, for example, the Court noted in *Daniels v. Williams* [645] that to prevail in a § 1983 claim a plaintiff must prove a violation of an underlying constitutional right. Mere negligence is not sufficient conduct upon which to base a 14th Amendment due process claim.[646]

C.   Deprivation

To state a claim, plaintiff must prove that the defendant *deprived* the plaintiff of a "right, privilege or immunity secured by the constitution or laws of the United States * * *."[647] The deprivation element is usually expressed in terms of a violation of an express right created by the constitution or statute. While the complaint must assert that a specific right was infringed, there is no heightened pleading standard under § 1983.[648] Conclusory allegations, however, may not be sufficient.[649]

In cases under the Bill of Rights, the question of deprivation is usually self-evident. A violation of the Fourth Amendment is complete when an illegal search occurs and by such a search the government deprives the individual of a protected right. However, as the Supreme Court pointed out in *Parrott v. Taylor*,[650] alleged violations of the due process clause require a different analysis. Under that clause, the deprivation of a property right, is not per se a deprivation of a constitutional right. It is only when the deprivation of the property right is accomplished without due process that it be-

---

[641] 125 S. Ct. at 1461.

[642] 42 U.S.C.A. § 2000cc-2(a).

[643] See, e.g., *Fifth Ave. Presbyterian Church v. City of New York*, 293 F.3d 570 (2d Cir. 2002).

[644] RLUIPA does not make reference to attorney's fees but Congress, when enacting RLUIPA, also amended 42 U.S.C.A. § 1988, to allow attorney's fees in RLUIPA cases.

[645] *Daniels v. Williams*, 474 U.S. 327, 106 S. Ct. 662, 88 L. Ed. 2d 662 (1986).

[646] Williams, 474 U.S. 327.

[647] 14 U.S.C.A. § 1983.

[648] *Leatherman v. Tarrant County Narcotics Intelligence and Coordination Unit*, 507 U.S. 163, 113 S. Ct. 1160, 122 L. Ed. 2d 517 (1993).

[649] *Barrington Cove Ltd. Partnership v. Rhode Island Housing and Mortg. Finance Corp.*, 246 F.3d 1 (1st Cir. 2001).

[650] *Parratt v. Taylor*, 451 U.S. 527, 101 S. Ct. 1908, 68 L. Ed. 2d 420 (1981), overruled on other grounds by, Daniels v. Williams, 474 U.S. 327, 106 S. Ct. 662, 88 L. Ed. 2d 662 (1986).

comes a deprivation of a constitutional right. Because due process can, depending on the circumstances, be provided either before or after the deprivation of property, simple proof of a deprivation of property will not suffice to show a constitutional deprivation. Rather, in order to sustain a claim, it is necessary to show that state law fails to afford adequate pre- or post-deprivation remedies.

D.　Under Color of State Law

An individual government official's actions are "under color of state law" when the government official acts within the scope of his or her duties.[651] The "color of requirement of § 1983 means the same thing as state action under the 14th Amendment.[652] An official's actions are also actionable if taken "while clothed with the authority of state law."[653] As stated by the Supreme Court, "[m]isuse of power, possessed by virtue of state law and made possible because the wrongdoer is clothed with the authority of state law, is action taken 'under color of state law.'"[654] In addition, activities pursued under a municipal ordinance are sufficient to meet the "under color of state law" requirements.[655] Thus, state or local officials act "under color of state law" when they either act within the scope of their duties or misuse power granted to them by the state.

Plaintiffs have frequently sought to make the government entity itself answer for the actions of its offending officials and employees. One method tested by plaintiffs is the doctrine of *respondeat superior*. At common law, "[a] master is subject to liability for the torts that servants commit while acting in the scope of their employment."[656] Plaintiffs, however, have enjoyed little success in applying this doctrine to civil rights claims, and most courts hold that the doctrine has no place in the civil rights field.[657] The result is that, in order to recover against the government entity, the plaintiff must show that the "conduct" was conduct of the entity itself. However, since the entity can act only through its officials and employees, the line between direct liability and *respondeat superior* liability is not always easy to draw.

Private parties acting by order or consent of the state may be liable under § 1983. The question arises with respect to lessees of government property, licensees, homeowner associations, neighborhood groups, permit holders, and government contractors or consultants. To meet the color of law requirement, the private party's action must have been made possible because she "was clothed with the authority of the state,"[658] or as the courts often say, that the act was "fairly attributable to the state." It is the relationship between the action taken and the government that matters, not the relationship between the private actor and the government.[659]

Lessees of state property, for example, may act under color of law. In one case, a court found that a private organization that leased a city park, a traditional public fo-

---

[651] *Monroe,* 365 U.S. at 167, 81 S. Ct. at 473.

[652] *U.S. v. Price,* 383 U.S. 787, 794 n.7, 86 S. Ct. 1152, 16 L. Ed. 2d 267 (1966).

[653] Monroe, 365 U.S. at 184, 81 S. Ct. at 482.

[654] *U.S. v. Classic,* 313 U.S. 299, 326, 61 S. Ct. 1031, 1043, 85 L. Ed. 1368 (1941).

[655] *Home Tel. & Tel. Co. v. City of Los Angeles,* 211 U.S. 265, 29 S. Ct. 50, 53 L. Ed. 176 (1908).

[656] Restatement of the Law of Agency, Second, § 219.

[657] *Williams v. Vincent,* 508 F.2d 541 (2d Cir.1974).

[658] *West v. Atkins,* 487 U.S. 42, 108 S. Ct. 2250, 101 L. Ed. 2d 40 (1988).

[659] *Young v. Halle Housing Associates, L.P.,* 152 F. Supp. 2d 355, 364 (S.D. N.Y. 2001).

rum, acted as the state where the city virtually ceded all power to the organization.[660] In another, a court held that a street festival organizer given nonexclusive power over certain city streets, also a traditional public forum, did not become a state actor because the city retained ultimate control of the streets.[661] The difference between the two is that the lease in the former case authorized the lessee to create rules for public access, while the lease in the latter case required the lessee to comply with all directives of the police department.

Most efforts to sue private parties are unsuccessful. In *City of Cuyahoga Falls v. Buckeye Community Hope Foundation,*[662] the Supreme Court held that comments by citizens in the petitioning process attempting to repeal an ordinance allowing the construction of a low-income housing project do not constitute state action. In addition to lobbying, cases also against homeowners' associations, permit holders, government contractors, and recipients of federal funding generally fail.[663]

E. Acting under Custom or Policy

Municipal corporations and other political subdivisions, which act under color of state law, are directly liable, if an alleged injury or deprivation is the "natural consequence of [an official] policy or custom."[664] There is no precise definition of "policy," but a single action by a city official may suffice. In *Pembaur v. City of Cincinnati,*[665] the Court held that a municipality is liable "where and only where a deliberate choice to follow a course of action is made from among various alternatives by the official or officials responsible for establishing final policy with respect to the subject matter in question."[666]

In land use cases, a municipality may be liable not only through the adoption of a zoning ordinance, but also by taking other official action, such as where a city council denies a building permit.[667] The action of a building inspector taken pursuant to authority from the board of adjustment has been held to be official policy.[668] The powers granted to a planning director and to a planning commission also have been held sufficient to cause their actions in issuing permits to be official policy for § 1983 liability purposes.[669] However, where a mayor vetoed a zoning ordinance in an attempt to bribe a developer, it was held not to be official policy of the city.[670] The mayor was not a policymaker in zoning matters, and the city council overrode the veto.

---

[660] *Lee v. Katz,* 276 F.3d 550 (9th Cir. 2002).

[661] *Lansing v. City of Memphis,* 202 F.3d 821 (6th Cir. 2000).

[662] *City of Cuyahoga Falls v. Buckeye Community Hope Foundation,* 538 U.S. 188, 123 S. Ct. 1389, 155 L. Ed. 2d 349 (2003).

[663] See Roberts, The Section 1983 Land Use Case, Sword and Shield Revisited: A Practical Approach to Section 1983 § 7.4 (Massaron Ross and Voss, eds. 2006).

[664] *Smith v. Ambrogio,* 456 F. Supp. 1130, 1135 (D. Conn. 1978).

[665] *Pembaur v. City of Cincinnati,* 475 U.S. 469, 106 S. Ct. 1292, 89 L. Ed. 2d 452 (1986).

[666] Pembaur, 475 U.S. at 483, 106 S. Ct. at 1300.

[667] *Bateson v. Geisse,* 857 F.2d 1300 (9th Cir.1988).

[668] *Video Intern. Production, Inc. v. Warner-Amex Cable Communications, Inc.,* 858 F.2d 1075 (5th Cir. 1988).

[669] *Hutchison v. City of Huntington,* 198 W. Va. 139, 479 S.E.2d 649 (1996).

[670] *Manor Healthcare Corp. v. Lomelo,* 929 F.2d 633 (11th Cir. 1991).

§ 10:25 Exhaustion of Remedies

Generally, a plaintiff need not exhaust state judicial or administrative remedies before seeking redress in under § 1983. The section provides a remedy that is supplementary to any state remedies, and the Court has held that requiring exhaustion would thwart the purpose of the statute.[671] There are, however, significant qualifications to this rule in the land use context.

One qualification to the non-exhaustion rule deals with finality. While exhaustion of administrative remedies is not required, finality of decision is.[672] Exhaustion of remedies refers to use of procedures to provide redress to an injured party. Finality asks whether the government has reached a definitive position that inflicts injury. While "conceptually distinct,"[673] as the Court says, the distinction blurs in practice. Under the final decision rule, multiple applications for development may need to be made and a variance sought to render a case ripe.[674] Confusion between finality and exhaustion has lead to numerous unripe cases being filed in federal court.[675] This final decision ripeness requirement applies to as-applied takings claims, as well as to substantive due process claims and equal protection claims.

Resort to state court is also necessary for Fifth Amendment takings claims in most cases. Since the Fifth Amendment is satisfied by post-taking compensation, the Court has held that a property owner must use available state procedures. Characterizing the case as a § 1983 case does not avoid this requirement. While the Court has phrased the requirement of seeking compensation from the state in terms of ripeness, the preclusive effects accorded to a state court judgment generally will bar a subsequent suit in federal court.[676]

A similar requirement exists for procedural due process claims. As with the Fifth Amendment, a post-deprivation remedy by way of a cause of action in state court may cure a potential due process violation. Under *Parrott v. Taylor*[677] and *Hudson v. Palmer*,[678] a damage action for random, unauthorized acts of state officials must be pursued in state court. Again, once a state court adjudicates an issue, the federal courts must give it full faith and credit.[679] The Supreme Court has suggested that the *Parratt-Hudson* rule applies only to procedural due process,[680] but some courts have applied it to substantive due process as well.[681]

---

[671] *Patsy v. Board of Regents,* 457 U.S. 496, 102 S. Ct. 2557, 73 L. Ed. 2d 172 (1982).

[672] *Williamson County Regional Planning Com'n v. Hamilton Bank of Johnson City*, 473 U.S. 172, 105 S. Ct. 3108, 87 L. Ed. 2d 126 (1985).

[673] 473 U.S. at 192, 105 S. Ct. at 3119.

[674] See discussion § 10.10.

[675] See Roberts, Ripeness and Forum Selection in Fifth Amendment Takings Litigation, 11 J. Land Use & Envtl. L. 37 (1995).

[676] See discussion supra § 10.10.

[677] *Parratt v. Taylor,* 451 U.S. 527, 101 S. Ct. 1908, 68 L. Ed. 2d 420 (1981), overruled on other grounds by, Daniels v. Williams, 474 U.S. 327, 106 S. Ct. 662, 88 L. Ed. 2d 662 (1986).

[678] *Hudson v. Palmer,* 468 U.S. 517, 104 S. Ct. 3194, 82 L. Ed. 2d 393 (1984).

[679] 28 U.S.C.A. § 1738.

[680] See, e.g., *Albright v. Oliver,* 510 U.S. 266, 313, 114 S. Ct. 807, 127 L. Ed. 2d 114 (1994) (Stevens, J. dissenting) (*Parratt* is categorically inapplicable to substantive due process).

[681] *Weimer v. Amen,* 870 F.2d 1400 (8th Cir.1989) (finding *Parratt* applicable).

§ 10:26 Relief Available Under § 1983

Section 1983 provides that the offending person is liable "in an action at law, suit in equity, or other proper proceeding for redress."[682] The choice of remedy lies within the discretion of the court, and depends on the circumstances of the case.[683]

A. Actual Damages

Actual damages are recoverable under § 1983, but they must be proven. They will not be presumed.[684] Where mitigation is possible, the plaintiff must take reasonable, affirmative steps to reduce damages.[685] When a plaintiff is unable to prove actual damages, nominal damages are available.[686]

B. Punitive Damages

Punitive damages may be allowed under § 1983.[687] Because federal standards apply, punitive damages may be awarded in states that do not allow them.[688] They are available against individual defendants,[689] but not against municipalities.[690] However, municipal immunity to punitive damages may be waived and, where a statute so provides, a municipality may be liable to indemnify its employees against punitive damage awards.[691] Actual damages need not be shown in order to sustain a punitive damage award,[692] but the defendant's conduct must have been willful or in gross disregard of the plaintiffs rights.[693] Some courts require a showing of malice or bad faith.[694]

C. Equitable Relief

Where otherwise proper, injunctions and other equitable relief are generally available under § 1983. Preliminary injunctions are also available where they are necessary to preserve the status quo and to prevent irreparable harm.[695]

D. Attorney's Fees

The Civil Rights Attorney's Fees Awards Act of 1976 enables courts to award attorney's fees to prevailing parties in § 1983 actions. The amount of an award is within the discretion of the trial court. The Supreme Court has held that the 11th Amendment is not a bar to awarding attorney's fees against states and political subdivisions of

---

[682] 42 U.S.C.A. § 1983.

[683] *Adickes v. S. H. Kress & Co.,* 398 U.S. 144, 232, 90 S. Ct. 1598, 1642, 26 L. Ed. 2d 142 (1970).

[684] *Carey v. Piphus,* 435 U.S. 247, 98 S. Ct. 1042, 55 L. Ed. 2d 252 (1978).

[685] *Meyers v. City of Cincinnati,* 14 F.3d 1115 (6th Cir. 1994).

[686] *Tatum v. Houser,* 642 F.2d 253 (8th Cir.1981).

[687] *Merritt v. De Los Santos,* 721 F.2d 598 (7th Cir.1983).

[688] *Garrick v. City and County of Denver,* 652 F.2d 969 (10th Cir. 1981).

[689] *Smith v. Wade,* 461 U.S. 30, 103 S. Ct. 1625, 75 L. Ed. 2d 632 (1983).

[690] *City of Newport v. Fact Concerts, Inc.,* 453 U.S. 247, 101 S. Ct. 2748, 69 L. Ed. 2d 616 (1981).

[691] *Kolar v. Sangamon County,* 756 F.2d 564 (7th Cir. 1985).

[692] *Ryland v. Shapiro,* 708 F.2d 967 (5th Cir. 1983).

[693] Bunn v. Central Realty of Louisiana, 592 F.2d 891 (5th Cir.1979).

[694] *DeLaCruz v. Pruitt,* 590 F. Supp. 1296 (N.D. Ind. 1984).

[695] *Wright v. Chief of Transit Police,* 527 F.2d 1262 (2d Cir. 1976).

states.[696] Nor is legislative [697] or judicial immunity a bar to such awards.[698] The federal government and its agencies, however, are immune to such awards.[699]

Because the purpose of the Civil Rights Attorney's Fees Awards Act is to open the judicial system to persons with civil rights grievances, "prevailing plaintiffs" are entitled to attorney's fees. In determining whether a plaintiff is a "prevailing party," the question is whether the plaintiff has been successful on a central issue; the plaintiff need not prevail on all issues. However, a prevailing party is only potentially eligible for attorney's fees and the court must consider the extent of the recovery obtained. If a party seeks substantial damages and recovers only nominal damages, an attorney's fee will not necessarily be awarded.[700] "When a plaintiff recovers only nominal damages because of his failure to prove an essential element of his claim for monetary relief, the only reasonable fee is usually no fee at all."[701] A final judgment is not necessary for an award of attorney's fees. Both favorable settlements and consent decrees are outcomes upon which attorney's fees may be based.

The court decides the question of whether one is a "prevailing party," and defendants, including municipal employers, have in some instances been held to be prevailing parties and entitled to attorney's fees.[702] Defendants are considered prevailing parties only when they can prove that the plaintiffs underlying claim is "frivolous, unreasonable, or groundless."[703]

§ 10:27 Immunities

If a court finds that a deprivation of a constitutional right has occurred, money damage actions may nonetheless be barred by immunities. Immunity rules differ for governmental entities and individuals. There are also distinctions between absolute immunity and qualified immunity.

While § 1983 makes no reference to immunity defenses, the Supreme Court has implied one if it existed at common law at the time § 1983 was adopted and if implying such an immunity would be consistent with the purposes of § 1983. The Court reasoned that a tradition of some immunity was so deeply rooted in our law that "congress would have specifically so provided had it wished to abolish the doctrine."[704]

A. *Governmental Immunities*

Local governments have no immunity from money damage awards. In 1978 the Court held in *Monell v. New York City Dept. of Social Services* [705] that local governments were "persons" subject to § 1983, but it did not decide whether they might never-

---

[696] *Hutto v. Finney,* 437 U.S. 678, 98 S. Ct. 2565, 57 L. Ed. 2d 522 (1978).

[697] *Gates v. Collier,* 616 F.2d 1268 (5th Cir. 1980).

[698] *Rheuark v. Shaw,* 477 F. Supp. 897 (N.D. Tex. 1979), judgment aff'd in part, rev'd in part, 628 F.2d 297 (5th Cir. 1980).

[699] *Smith v. Puett,* 506 F. Supp. 134 (M.D. Tenn. 1980).

[700] *Farrar v. Hobby,* 506 U.S. 103, 113 S. Ct. 566, 121 L. Ed. 2d 494 (1992).

[701] 506 U.S. at 116, 113 S. Ct. at 575.

[702] See *Campbell v. Cook,* 706 F.2d 1084 (10th Cir. 1983).

[703] *Hensley v. Eckerhart,* 461 U.S. 424, 103 S. Ct. 1933, 76 L. Ed. 2d 40 (1983).

[704] *Pierson v. Ray,* 386 U.S. 547, 554, 87 S. Ct. 1213, 1218, 18 L. Ed. 2d 288 (1967).

[705] *Monell v. Department of Social Services of City of New York,* 436 U.S. 658, 98 S. Ct. 2018, 56 L. Ed. 2d 611 (1978).

theless in some instances be immune from money damages for their violations of the statute. In 1980 in *Owen v. City of Independence*,[706] the Court held that because no qualified immunity existed at common law at the time § 1983 was enacted, no qualified immunity could be implied. The Court has also held that state sovereign immunity rules cannot be applied to protect local government from liability in suits brought in state court.[707] Punitive damages are an exception. Municipalities are absolutely immune from such awards.[708] While some have questioned whether *Monnell* and *Owens* preclude governmental immunity for legislative actions, it seems established that no immunity exists.[709]

The state, in contrast to municipalities, is absolutely immune from suit in federal court for money damages under the 11th Amendment.[710]

B. *Absolute Individual Immunities: Legislative and Quasi-Judicial*

Public officials who are sued in their individual capacities may be able to assert absolute or qualified immunity. Judges, legislators, and prosecutors (when initiating and presenting the state's case) all have absolute immunity.[711] In the land use context, absolute immunity arises typically with respect to those claiming to have acted in a legislative capacity. Courts use a functional test to determine whether an action is legislative for the purposes of conferring absolute immunity,[712] and they may not inquire into the motive of the actor.[713]

Absolute legislative immunity extends to local[714] and regional legislators[715] and to mayors acting legislatively.[716] While city officials who possess legislative power will lose absolute immunity if they are found to have acted administratively,[717] they may still be entitled to qualified immunity.[718]

While many zoning ordinances, including rezonings, will qualify as legislative, site-specific actions may not. The Third Circuit breaks the question into two parts of substance and procedure. The substantive component requires that the action taken makes general policy or involves the community at large. Decisions that involve the application of pre-existing policy or apply to only a small number of persons will normally be viewed as non-legislative.[719] The procedural component requires that the action be taken through established legislative procedures.[720] Classification of an act as

---

[706] 445 U.S. 622, 100 S. Ct. 1398, 63 L. Ed. 2d 673 (1980).

[707] *Howlett v. Rose,* 496 US. 356, 110 S. Ct. 2430, 110 L. Ed. 2d 332 (1990).

[708] *City of Newport v. Fact Concerts, Inc.,* 453 U.S. 247, 101 S. Ct. 2748, 69 L. Ed. 2d 616 (1981).

[709] See *Goldberg v. Town of Rocky Hill,* 973 F.2d 70 (2d Cir.1992).

[710] *Lake Country Estates, Inc. v. Tahoe Regional Planning Agency,* 440 U.S. 391, 99 S. Ct. 1171, 59 L. Ed. 2d 401. See also supra § 10:9, n. 6.

[711] Id. (granting immunity to members of board of regional authority formed by interstate compact).

[712] See *Orange Lake Associates, Inc. v. Kirkpatrick,* 21 F.3d 1214 (2d Cir. 1994).

[713] *Bogan v. Scott-Harris,* 523 U.S. 44, 118 S. Ct. 966, 140 L. Ed. 2d 79 (1998).

[714] *Bryan v. City of Madison, Miss.,* 213 F.3d 267 (5th Cir. 2000).

[715] 440 U.S. 391, 99 S. Ct. 1171, 59 L. Ed. 2d 401 (1979).

[716] *Bogan v. Scott-Harris,* 523 U.S. 44, 118 S. Ct. 966, 140 L. Ed. 2d 79 (1998).

[717] *Mission Springs, Inc. v. City of Spokane,* 134 Wash. 2d 947, 954 P.2d 250 (1998).

[718] *Scott v. Greenville County,* 716 F.2d 1409 (4th Cir. 1983).

[719] *Acierno v. Cloutier,* 40 F.3d 597 (3d Cir. 1994).

[720] See *Key West Harbour Development Corp. v. City of Key West,* 738 F. Supp. 1390 (S.D. Fla. 1990).

non-legislative, while eliminating absolute legislative immunity, may give rise to absolute quasi-judicial immunity. Non-legislative actions may be referred to as "administrative" or "quasi-judicial," and while the label is not determinative, if a city official action is deemed to have acted judicially or quasi-judicially, absolute immunity attaches.[721] Thus, members of zoning boards of appeal, who perform such adjudicatory functions as taking testimony, making credibility determinations, and applying the applicable law to their fact determinations, who are free from direct political influence, and who must adhere the demands of procedural due process, are awarded absolute quasi-judicial immunity.[722] The same immunity has been extended to members of legislative bodies when acting judicially.[723] As the Third Circuit puts it, "regardless of his job title, if a state official must walk, talk, and act like a judge as part of his job, then he is as absolutely immune from lawsuits arising out of that walking, talking, and acting as are judges who enjoy the title and other formal indicia of office."[724]

C. *Qualified Individual Immunity*

The test for qualified immunity is set out in *Harlow v. Fitzgerald:*[725]

[G]overnment officials performing discretionary functions generally are shielded from liability for civil damages insofar as their conduct does not violate clearly established statutory or constitutional rights of which a reasonable person would have known.[726]

The qualified immunity of *Harlow* may be used by various executive officials, including local school board members, prison officials, police officers, and building and zoning officers.

Harlow created an objective standard, and dispensed with the requirement of prior case law that had required a showing that the official had acted with a good faith belief of legality. This revision of the test for qualified immunity is especially valuable to local officials because it may encourage early dismissal of § 1983 cases, before the officials are subjected to the burdens and costs of lengthy litigation.[727]

Qualified immunity can be defeated by showing malice, ill will or wanton conduct on the part of the official charged. An example is *Walz v. Town of Smithtown,*[728] where the town's highway superintendent told landowners that he would issue them a permit for excavation of a highway to enable them to connect to the public water supply if they would convey a 15-foot strip of their property to the town. This action was held to violate substantive due process, and no qualified immunity existed. The highway official, said the court, could not have reasonably believed that he had the discretion to deny permits "as a means of extorting land."[729]

---

[721] *Antoine v. Byers & Anderson, Inc.,* 508 U.S. 429, 432, 113 S. Ct. 2167, 124 L. Ed. 2d 391 (1993).

[722] *Zapach v. Dismuke,* 134 F. Supp. 2d 682 (E.D. Pa. 2001).

[723] *Dotzel v. Ashbridge,* 438 F.3d 320 (3d Cir. 2006).

[724] *Dotzel v. Ashbridge,* 438 F.3d 320, 325 (3d Cir. 2006).

[725] *Harlow v. Fitzgerald,* 457 U.S. 800, 102 S. Ct. 2727, 73 L. Ed. 2d 396 (1982).

[726] Fitzgerald, 457 U.S. at 818, 102 S. Ct. at 2738.

[727] *Harlow v. Fitzgerald,* 457 U.S. 800, 102 S. Ct. 2727, 73 L. Ed. 2d 396 (1982).

[728] *Walz v. Town of Smithtown,* 46 F.3d 162 (2d Cir. 1995).

[729] Walz, 46 F.3d at 169.

§ 10:28 Abstention

The exercise of abstention may frustrate one who seeks to challenge a local land use action in federal court. While the Supreme Court says that "[a]bstention from the exercise of federal jurisdiction is the exception, not the rule,"[730] and that abstention is an "extraordinary and narrow exception to the duty of a district court to adjudicate a controversy properly before it,"[731] lower federal courts have used the *Pullman, Burford, Younger* and *Colorado River* doctrines to abstain from adjudicating § 1983 claims in the land use area fairly often.

Under the *Pullman* abstention doctrine,[732] a federal district court may refrain from deciding constitutional questions that hinge on difficult state law issues, if a constitutional ruling would be avoided by resolution in state court of those state issues. When a federal court invokes the *Pullman* abstention doctrine, the federal action is not dismissed. Rather, it is stayed pending decision in the state court of the uncertain state law issues.

A number of courts relying on the *Pullman* abstention doctrine have held that adjudication of state law issues in land use cases would alleviate the necessity of addressing federal constitutional questions.[733] Where it is clear that no state law interpretation would eliminate the need to address the federal constitutional questions, *Pullman* abstention is inappropriate.[734]

Under *Burford* abstention, a federal court may decline to hear a case where a federal decision of the case would risk interfering with complex state regulatory schemes concerning important state policies for which expeditious and adequate judicial review is afforded in state courts.[735] In applying *Burford,* municipal policy may receive less deference from the courts than state policy.[736] *Burford* abstention is only appropriate "where relief being sought is equitable or otherwise discretionary."[737] Under *Burford,* plaintiffs are not able to preserve their right to return to federal court once a decision has been rendered at the state level. Rather, the federal action is dismissed. While the Supreme Court has sparingly used *Burford,* lower courts find it attractive.

Courts differ over what comprises a complex regulatory scheme in land use cases for the purposes of *Burford* abstention. The Eleventh Circuit holds that zoning decisions must be vested in a "single forum" to qualify.[738] The fact that an enabling act provides that a city "may" appoint a board of adjustment, as the standard act does, has also been held to reveal a lack of state interest in uniformity. In contrast, the Fourth Circuit says that abstention is proper if the state has a comprehensive regulatory scheme and that there is no requirement that a specialized state agency exist to resolve

---

[730] *Colorado River Water Conservation Dist. v. U. S.,* 424 U.S. 800, 814, 96 S. Ct. 1236, 1244, 47 L. Ed. 2d 483 (1976).

[731] *Allegheny County v. Frank Mashuda Co.,* 360 U.S. 185, 188–189, 79 S. Ct. 1060, 1063, 3 L. Ed. 2d 1163 (1959).

[732] *Railroad Commission of Tex. v. Pullman Co.,* 312 U.S. 496, 61 S. Ct. 643, 85 L. Ed. 971 (1941).

[733] See *Wedgewood Ltd. Partnership I. v. Township of Liberty,* 456 F. Supp. 2d 904 (S.D. Ohio 2006).

[734] See, e.g., *Neufeld v. City of Baltimore,* 964 F.2d 347 (4th Cir. 1992).

[735] *Burford v. Sun Oil Co.,* 319 U.S. 315, 63 S. Ct. 1098, 87 L. Ed. 1424 (1943).

[736] See *Saginaw Housing Com'n v. Bannum, Inc.,* 576 F.3d 620, 626 (6th Cir. 2009).

[737] *Quackenbush v. Allstate Ins. Co.,* 517 U.S. 706, 116 S. Ct. 1712, 135 L. Ed. 2d 1 (1996).

[738] *Nasser v. City of Homewood,* 671 F.2d 432, 440 (11th Cir. 1982).

zoning disputes.[739] Courts that are reluctant to use the *Burford* doctrine standing alone in land use cases may apply it in combination with the *Pullman* doctrine.

A third abstention doctrine comes from *Younger v. Harris.*[740] Under the *Younger* doctrine, if a parallel proceeding in a state court is pending and that proceeding involves largely the same issues as the federal proceeding, the federal court may dismiss or stay the case.[741] *Younger's* goal is to avoid friction between state and federal courts. However, the mere pendency of a parallel state court proceeding is insufficient to trigger *Younger*. Before abstaining, the court must determine that the relief sought in federal court would in some manner directly interfere with ongoing state judicial proceedings.[742] As with *Burford* abstention, the proceeding in the federal court is dismissed, and the plaintiff does not retain the right to return to federal court once the state court has issued a decision.[743]

The *Younger* abstention doctrine is applied in land use cases where a pending state court proceeding involves the same issues as the federal proceeding.[744] In *Community Treatment Centers, Inc. v. City of Westland,*[745] the court, applying *Younger,* noted that it was "well-established that for abstention purposes, the enforcement and application of zoning ordinances and land-use regulations is an important state and local interest."[746] In that case, an organization sought a special use permit to operate prerelease center for federal prisoners. When the city denied the permit, the organization sued in state court, and while that action was pending, it sued in federal court. By the time the district court ruled on the defendant's motion to dismiss, the case had been appealed to the state intermediate appellate court. Federal interference with the state proceedings was deemed inappropriate.[747] Where the state proceeding is brought by private interest groups, the state's interest in protecting its executive function of law enforcement may not be implicated.[748]

Younger abstention has been rejected when it appears that irreparable harm will ensue. For example, one court refused to apply *Younger* abstention when an action was pending in state court since it found that the residents of a group home for recovering alcoholics would suffer irreparable harm if they lost their home through the state court proceeding before the federal court could act on their constitutional claim.[749] In another case, the court found that *Younger* abstention could not be invoked where a city started a criminal action in state court against a plaintiff who had a federal action pending against the city in which the district court had already held an evidentiary hearing.[750]

---

[739] *Browning-Ferris, Inc. v. Baltimore County*, 114 F.2d 77, 80 (4th Cir. 1985).

[740] *Younger v. Harris*, 401 U.S. 37, 91 S. Ct. 746, 27 L. Ed. 2d 669 (1971).

[741] *Coles v. Granville*, 448 F.3d 853 (6th Cir.2006) (dismissal proper under *Younger*).

[742] *Younger v. Harris*, 401 U.S. 37, 91 S. Ct. 746, 27 L. Ed. 2d 669 (1971).

[743] *Colorado River*, 424 U.S. 800, 816, 96 S. Ct. 1236, 1245–46, 47 L. Ed. 2d 483 (1976).

[744] See *Ebiza, Inc. v. City of Davenport*, 434 F. Supp. 2d 710 (S.D. Iowa 2006).

[745] 970 F. Supp. 1197 (E.D. Mich. 1997).

[746] Id. at 1223.

[747] See also *Lambeth v. Miller*, 363 Fed. Appx. 565, 568 (10th Cir. 2010).

[748] *Potrero Hills Landfill, Inc. v. County of Solano*, 657 F.3d 876, 879 (9th Cir. 2011).

[749] *Sullivan v. City of Pittsburgh, Pa.*, 811 F.2d 171 (3d Cir. 1987).

[750] *For Your Eyes Alone, Inc. v. City of Columbus, Ga.*, 281 F.3d 1209 (11th Cir. 2002).

A final doctrine that deserves mention stems from *Colorado River Water Conservation District v. United States,*[751] where the Court held that a federal court should decline to exercise jurisdiction in limited circumstances where state proceedings are pending so as to avoid duplicative litigation. In contrast to the above three abstention doctrines, which are concerned with comity and federalism, the rule of *Colorado River* is based on considerations of judicial economy.[752] "There cannot be *Colorado River* abstention in a close case; . . . there must be the 'clearest of justifications.'"[753] In most land use cases where a *Colorado River* dismissal has been sought, the courts have refused the request.[754]

§ 10:29 Res Judicata and *Rooker-Feldman*

Attempting to litigate issues in federal court already the subject of state court litigation may barred by one or both of two statutes: The full faith and credit statute, 28 U.S.C.A. § 1738, and 28 U.S.C.A. § 1257, which vests appellate jurisdiction solely in the Supreme Court.

Surprisingly, it is necessary to state the obvious: res judicata will bar a suit in federal court on issues already litigated in state court. Some doubt has existed about the applicability of claim and issue preclusion with regard to takings claims due to the Supreme Court's unfortunate labeling as a "ripeness" matter the requirement that a takings claimant seek compensation in state court. Until a claim for compensation has been litigated in a state court inverse condemnation suit, a takings claim in federal court, under the language of *Williamson County, is* premature. In that case, the Court ignored the preclusion implications of its so-called ripeness requirement. We discuss the misleading nature of *Williamson County's* language earlier in this chapter.[755]

Over the two decades since the decision in *Williamson County,* numerous courts, sometimes apologizing to plaintiffs for the "ripeness" rule enticing them file suit in federal court, have held that once a property owner pursued the compensation remedy, the law of res judicata and issue preclusion preclude a Fifth Amendment takings claim from being maintained in federal court.[756] Any doubt that remained was clarified by the Supreme Court in 2005, when it confirmed what the lower courts had done in dismissing cases on res judicata grounds with its holding to that effect in *San Remo Hotel, L.P. v. City and County of San Francisco.*[757]

Another potential bar to suit in federal court comes from the Supreme Court's reading of 28 U.S.C.A. § 1257, which vests appellate jurisdiction solely in the Supreme Court. The *Rooker-Feldman* doctrine[758] construes the statute as prohibiting federal dis-

---

[751] 424 U.S. 800, 96 S. Ct. 1236, 47 L. Ed. 2d 483 (1976).

[752] Gibson, Private Concurrent Litigation in Light of Younger, Pennzoil, and Colorado River, 4 Okla. City U. L. Rev. 185, 259 (1989).

[753] *Gentry v. Wayne County,* 2010 WL 4822749, *6 (E.D. Mich. 2010) (extensive discussion of issue).

[754] See, e.g., *Baskin v. Bath Tp. Bd. of Zoning Appeals,* 15 F.3d 569 (6th Cir. 1994); *Lake Lucerne Civic Ass'n, Inc. v. Dolphin Stadium Corp.,* 878 F.2d 1360 (11th Cir. 1989). But see *Tyrer v. City of South Beloit,* 456 F.3d 744 (7th Cir. 2006).

[755] See supra § 10.10.

[756] *Saboff v. St. John's River Water Management Dist.,* 200 F.3d 1356 (11th Cir. 2000).

[757] *San Remo Hotel, L.P. v. City and County of San Francisco,* 545 U.S. 323, 125 S. Ct. 2491, 162 L. Ed. 2d 315 (2005).

[758] See *Rooker v. Fidelity Trust C.,* 263 U.S. 413, 44 S. Ct. 149, 68 L. Ed. 362 (1923) and *District of Columbia Court of Appeals v. Feldman,* 460 U.S. 462, 103 S. Ct. 1303, 75 L. Ed. 2d 206 (1983).

tricts from serving as courts of appeal of state court judgments. Thus, district courts are prohibited from hearing cases when the decision they are asked to make would effectively reverse a state court decision.

Rooker-Feldman enjoyed a burst of popularity beginning in the early 1990s. One study found courts relied on the doctrine to find jurisdiction lacking in more than 500 cases during the 1990s alone.[759] These cases spanned a host issues, including a number of land use cases. A cynic would suggest that the use of the doctrine was fueled at least in part by the desire of federal courts to reduce their caseload.[760] The binge ended with the Supreme Court's 2005 decision in *Exxon Mobil Corp. v. Saudi Basic Industries Corp*,[761] where the Court significantly limited the doctrine. Returning the doctrine to the rationale of the cases upon which is based, the Court "confined the doctrine * * * to cases brought by state-court losers complaining of injuries caused by state-court judgments rendered before the district court proceedings commenced and inviting district court review and rejection of those judgments."[762]

Res judicata and abstention are close relatives, but not twins, of *Rooker-Feldman*. *Rooker-Feldman* goes to the subject matter jurisdiction of the district court and may be raised at any time by either party or sua sponte by the court.[763] In this respect, the doctrine differs from the affirmative defenses of collateral estoppel or res judicata. Res judicata is waivable. Subject matter jurisdiction is not. The *Rooker-Feldman* determination of jurisdiction based on federal law comes first; and, if jurisdiction exists, res judicata or collateral estoppel may follow as an affirmative defense.[764] What *Rooker-Feldman* does not bar, preclusion doctrines may.

Rooker-Feldman also differs from abstention, though the two often are raised together. While courts sometimes loosely refer to *Rooker-Feldman*[765] as an abstention doctrine,[766] the label is misused since a court can only abstain if it has the power to act in the first place, and application of *Rooker-Feldman* is a determination that subject matter jurisdiction is lacking.[767]

---

[759] Sherry, Judicial Federalism in the Trenches: The *Rooker-Feldman* Doctrine in Action, 74 Notre Dame L. Rev. 1085, 1088 (1999).

[760] See discussion supra § 10:23.

[761] *Exxon Mobil Corp. v. Saudi Basic Industries Corp.,* 544 U.S. 280, 125 S. Ct. 1517, 161 L. Ed. 2d 454 (2005).

[762] Saudi Basic Industries Corp., 544 U.S. at 284, 125 S. Ct. 1521–22.

[763] *Garry v. Geils,* 82 F.3d 1362, 1364 (7th Cir. 1996).

[764] *Long v. Shorebank Development Corp.,* 182 F.3d 548, 553 (7th Cir. 1999).

[765] See discussion supra § 10:22.

[766] *Johnson v. De Grandy,* 512 U.S. 997, 1004, 114 S. Ct. 2647, 2654, 129 L. Ed. 2d 775 (1994).

[767] See, e.g., *Ankenbrandt v. Richards,* 504 U.S. 689, 704, 112 S. Ct. 2206, 119 L. Ed. 2d 468 (1992).

Chapter 11

REGULATION AND PROTECTION OF ENVIRONMENTALLY SENSITIVE LANDS*

Analysis

I.   INTRODUCTION

I.   INTRODUCTION

§ 11:1   Introduction

Although scarcely a concern before the 1960s, environmental aspects of land use control have become a primary consideration of land use planners. Even during the environmental renaissance of the 1960s, land use planning and control did not receive the attention focused on air and water pollution. Air and water were viewed as public

---

* For more detailed discussion and more extensive citations of authority of the issues covered in this chapter, see Juergensmeyer and Roberts, Land Use Planning and Development Regulation Law, Practitioner Treatise Series (3rd ed. 2012).

trusts to be shared by all. Land was considered a matter of private property generally out of governmental reach. That attitude has changed markedly in the last several decades, nowhere more dramatically than in regard to environmentally related land use regulations.

Environmental laws on the federal level prior to the late 1960s were almost non-existent. Those laws that did exist focused primarily on public lands that were set aside as protected areas, such as the Wilderness Act of 1964, or on special species such as the bald eagle.[1] Development and industrialization were allowed to continue unabated, regardless of the adverse effects on the environment. Broad federal legislation started in 1969 with the National Environmental Policy Act (NEPA),[2] which imposed a duty on federal agencies to weigh the environmental consequences of their actions. Although not a true national planning measure, NEPA brought an environmental consciousness to federal agency decisionmaking that had not previously existed. Then came the Clean Air Act of 1970 and Clean Water Act of 1972.[3] Though they primarily concern pollution abatement, they affect land use decisionmaking, as land use planners must consider these federal acts when evaluating proposed development with possible pollution problems.

State environmental regulation, as on the federal level, came about beginning in the late 1960s and early 1970s. While most land use regulations come from local governments, state environmental controls have a major impact on local land use decisionmaking.

The protection of environmentally sensitive lands rather than pollution control is the subject in this chapter: (1) wetlands, (2) coastal zones, (3) floodplains, and (4) habitat for endangered species.

The basic problem in all environmental land use decisions is that land is a finite resource. There must be room not only for houses, shopping malls, and paper mills, but also for wetlands, beaches, barrier islands and snail darters. Industrial and economic growth is considered desirable, but so are clean air and water. As a result, there is a great divide between those who believe in a landowner's right to develop her land so as to maximize her benefit and those who place greater weight on the value of protecting the environment. Development on environmentally sensitive land must be cautiously done. Both future and present needs have to be considered. While a residential subdivision in a prime aquifer-recharging wetland may expand a local government's tax base, the bargain may prove Faustian when drinking wells dry up. Somewhere a balance must be struck.

This chapter deals primarily with federal controls, but state environmental controls also play a major role in land use planning. Furthermore, local governments have responded, often by necessity, by including environmental and sensitive lands regulations into the approval process. The end result is a comprehensive multi-tiered system of interlocking federal, state, and local controls.

---

[1] Bald Eagle Protection Act of 1940, 16 U.S.C.A. § 668 et seq.

[2] Pub. L. No. 91–190, 83 Stat. 852, codified at 42 U.S.C.A. §§ 4321 to 4361 (1995).

[3] See W.H. Rodgers, Jr. Environmental Law Treatise, Vols. 1–4 (2011 Supp.).

The overlap in these interlocking regulations can lead to complicated jurisdictional problems. Of even greater concern may be the complications arising from policy conflict. Zoning development away from one environmentally sensitive area may add development pressure to another. These jurisdictional and policy conflicts are part and parcel of the approach governments at all levels have taken to the problem of environmental land use.

II. WETLANDS

§ 11:2 Definition and Importance of Wetlands

To many people the word "wetlands" conjures up images of dismal, dank, mosquito-ridden, snake-infested, miasmic swamps to either be avoided or paved over. Indeed, this notion has been so prevalent in our nation's collective subconscious that we have destroyed over 50% of our wetland resources.[4] They were lost beneath the crunching blow of drag lines and dredges making way for subdivisions, trailer parks, agribusiness and dumps. For some this may seem just fine: the best swamp is a drained swamp. That delusional view, however, is fading as we realize that wetlands are vital to the national interest economically, as well as ecologically. Major efforts are now directed at reversing the losses through the creation of new wetlands as well as wetland restoration.[5]

Saltwater marshes are the most biologically productive lands on earth, producing more than twice the biomass of our most fertile hayfields. Such estuarine areas also serve an essential role as nurseries for seven of the 10 most commercially valuable fish and shellfish consumed in this country. Fresh water wetlands play an important (critical, in some areas) role in aquifer recharge, pollution control (through a remarkably efficient system of capture and filtration), flood control, prevention of soil erosion and as wildlife habitat. Absent adequate wetlands protection, there will occur a dramatic drop in fish, shellfish, wildlife, and timber production nationwide with a corresponding rise in flood damage, soil loss, fresh water depletion (accompanied by salt water intrusion in coastal areas) and general environmental degradation as pollutants concentrate.

With wetlands' value identified and need for protection recognized, the first hurdle toward sensible management is definitional. There is simply no standard, all inclusive definition of a wetland that meets all needs. Marshes, swamps, bogs, some types of hardwood forested areas, sloughs, wet meadows, natural ponds, potholes and river overflow areas have all been described as wetlands. Basically, the term "wetlands" is generic and refers to areas supporting vegetation capable of withstanding wet conditions. This occurs where land levels are low and ground water levels are high.

§ 11:3 Federal Regulation

Wetlands protection is characterized by a strong federal and state regulatory presence. From a "do as you please" attitude, wetlands development has become dominated by an array of state and federal regulations and permit requirements. In addition, many states with substantial wetlands acreage have local regulations tied in with

---

[4] U.S. Fish and Wildlife Service, Wetlands Status and Trends (1991).

[5] See US Fish and Wildlife Status and Trends of Wetlands in the Coterminous United States 2004–2009, http://www.fws.gov/wetlands/.

the broader federal and state programs. Because permits at all levels must be obtained before any form of development may occur in a wetland area it is important to understand the regulatory interplay in the permitting process and the federal, state, and local jurisdictions involved.

A.   *The Rivers and Harbors Act of 1899*

The granddaddy of all wetland regulations was not designed to conserve wetlands at all. When President McKinley signed the Rivers and Harbors Act of 1899, his intent was to protect navigable waters to keep them safe for shipping.[6] Thus, jurisdiction was provided over "navigable waters" alone. Navigation, not water quality, was the concern. Nevertheless, the Corps of Engineers and the courts found in § 10's prohibition of the obstruction or alteration of "navigable waters" a basis for protecting both.

While many environmentally sensitive wetlands are not covered by the definition of navigability used by the Corps of Engineers,[7] some larger areas are. The Fifth Circuit Court of Appeals in *Zabel v. Tabb* verified § 10's applicability to wetlands regulation.[8] There, two developers applied for a permit to dredge and fill in the navigable waters of Boca Ciega Bay, near St. Petersburg, Florida, in order to build a trailer park. The project was denied the necessary permits by the Corps of Engineers. Under normal circumstances (at that time) the matter would probably have ended there. However, the permit denial was issued solely on the basis of environmental concerns since the project would neither interfere with navigation nor flood control. The developers cried foul in that they believed the Corps had no authority to deny a dredge and fill permit on purely environmental grounds, and the district court agreed with them. In a sweeping opinion, Judge John R. Brown reversed the district court and held that the Corps had indeed such power, and could base its permitting decisions either partially or wholly on ecological reasons. The Supreme Court has confirmed that § 10 should receive broad construction.[9] However, use of the Rivers and Harbors Act to protect wetlands has diminished with increasingly heavy reliance on § 404 of the Clean Water Act.[10]

B.   *Section 10 Jurisdiction*

Federal jurisdiction under § 10 is complicated by water level changes. Jurisdiction over tidal water extends to the mean high water line.[11] The mean high water line is calculated by using tidal cycle data. The ordinary high water mark, which defines federal jurisdiction in nontidal waters is not so easily determined. As defined by regulation,

> [t]he "ordinary high water mark" on non-tidal rivers is the line on the shore established by the fluctuations of water and indicated by physical characteristics such

---

[6] 33 U.S.C.A. §§ 401 to 418.

[7] The Army Corps of Engineers defines "navigable waters" under the act as "those waters that are subject to the ebb and flow of the tide and/or are presently used, or have been used in the past, or may be susceptible for use to transport interstate or foreign commerce." 33 C.F.R. § 329.4.

[8] *Zabel v. Tabb*, 430 F.2d 199 (5th Cir. 1970).

[9] *U.S. v. Alaska*, 503 U.S. 569, 112 S. Ct. 1606, 118 L. Ed. 2d 222 (1992).

[10] With the adoption of § 404 of the Clean Water Act, see discussion infra § 11:12, jurisdiction under § 10 of the Rivers and Harbors Act is exercised less frequently. However, § 10 is still useful in situations where, for instance, a § 404 exemption applies and § 10 is the only protection left. See, e.g., *Save Our Sound Fisheries Ass'n v. Callaway*, 387 F. Supp. 292, 305 (D.R.I. 1974).

[11] 33 C.F.R. § 329.12(a)(2).

as a clear, natural line impressed on the bank; shelving; changes in the character of soil; destruction of terrestrial vegetation; the presence of litter and debris; or other appropriate means that consider the characteristics of the surrounding areas.[12]

Because of the definitional complexity of § 10, identifying jurisdictional lines in nontidal lakes and rivers (whose shore areas are often classified as wetlands) is accomplished by using eyewitness accounts, photographs, and surveys of biological and physical data.

One important land use aspect of § 10 jurisdiction concerns artificial canals. Real estate developers have used these canals for decades to attract buyers looking for "waterfront" property with lake or ocean access. These canals often run into § 10 problems when constructed within tidal areas. Greater jurisdictional uncertainties occur when canals are constructed in inland waters not subject to tidal flow.[13]

A tactic of developers to escape § 10 jurisdiction is to build a series of unconnected canals.[14] Unconnected canals are not "navigable" and are thus not regulated by § 10. These canals invariably become connected, allowing ocean or lake access, through somewhat mysterious activities, sometimes undertaken late at night with the aid of bulldozers and draglines. Indeed, these canals are occasionally opened up by environmental officials worried about the adverse ecological effects resulting from stagnant water.

§ 11:4   Section 404 of the Clean Water Act

A.   Corps of Engineers' 404 Jurisdiction

It was not until 1972 with passage of the Clean Water Act[15] that wetlands gained real protection. As with the 1899 Rivers and Harbors Act,[16] the term "navigable waters" is the jurisdictional touchstone for § 404, the wetlands provision of the Act, but the term here is defined to mean "waters of the United States."[17] With this broad language, § 404's proscription of the "discharge of any dredged or fill material into navigable waters at specified disposal sites"[18] without a permit from the Corps of Engineers covers wetlands. Upon adoption, the agency in charge of implementing the Act, the Corps of Engineers, did not initially consider wetlands as protected. This is not remarkable. Had the drafter of § 404 been expressly charged with the task of drafting a wetlands protection bill the language chosen is not the language one would expect to find. A better job could have been done. Nonetheless, congressional history and Supreme Court recognition of the need to regulate wetlands in order to carry out the purposes of the Clean Water Act confirm that § 404's discharge provision covers wetlands.

---

[12] 33 C.F.R. § 329.11(a)(1).

[13] See *National Wildlife Federation v. Alexander*, 613 F.2d 1054, 1066 (D.C. Cir. 1979), appeal after remand 665 F.2d 390 (D.C.Cir. 1981) (§ 10 held not to apply).

[14] *U.S. v. Sexton Cove Estates, Inc.*, 526 F.2d 1293 (5th Cir. 1976).

[15] 33 U.S.C.A. § 1344.

[16] The Rivers and Harbors Act of 1899 is discussed at § 11:11.

[17] 33 U.S.C.A. § 1362 (7).

[18] 33 U.S.C.A. § 1144.

After the passage of the 1972 Act, the Corps of Engineers read § 404 to cover only traditionally navigable waters. Then in 1975, a district court found the Corps' limitation an unlawful act in derogation of its responsibilities under § 404 and ordered the Corps to adopt a broader definition.[19] The Corps complied, adopting regulations expressly regulating wetlands. In 1977 Congress reviewed the Corps' new definition and refrained from narrowing it. The Supreme Court, reciting this history, deferred to the Corps' regulations covering wetlands, emphasizing the need to regulate wetlands in order to carry out the purposes of the Clean Water Act "to restore and maintain the chemical, physical, and biological integrity of the Nation's waters."[20]

The current definition of "waters of the United States" used by the Corps and the Corps' definition of wetlands reflect the earlier judicial mandates and congressional acquiescence. Thus, jurisdiction is extended to:

1) all waters which are currently used, or were used in the past, or may be susceptible to use in interstate commerce including waters subject to the ebb and flow of the tide;

2) all interstate wetlands;

3) all other waters such as intrastate lakes, rivers, streams (including intermittent streams), mudflats, sandflats, wetlands, sloughs, prairie potholes, wet meadows, playa lakes, or natural ponds, the use, degradation or destruction of which could affect interstate or foreign commerce;

4) all impoundments of waters otherwise defined as waters of the United States under the definition;

5) tributaries of waters in paragraphs (1) and (4);

6) the territorial seas;

7) wetlands adjacent to waters identified in paragraphs (1) through (6);

8) waters of the United States do not include prior converted cropland.[21]

The Corps defines wetlands as:

[T]hose areas that are inundated or saturated by surface or ground water at a frequency and duration sufficient to support, and that under normal circumstances do support, a prevalence of vegetation typically adapted for life in saturated soil conditions. Wetlands generally include swamps, marshes, bogs, and similar areas.[22]

These definitions of jurisdictional reach and of wetlands have been the subject of much litigation in the lower courts and three Supreme Court decisions. The first Su-

---

[19] *Natural Resources Defense Council, Inc. v. Callaway*, 392 F. Supp. 685 (D.D.C. 1975).

[20] 33 U.S.C.A. § 1251. See *U.S. v. Riverside Bayview Homes, Inc.*, 474 U.S. 121, 132, 106 S. Ct. 455, 462, 88 L. Ed. 2d 419 (1985).

[21] Our listing deletes, without ellipses, some language deemed unnecessary to show the basic coverage. See 33 C.F.R. § 328.3(a)(3).

[22] 33 C.F.R. § 328.3(b).

preme Court case, *U.S. v. Riverside Bayview Homes, Inc.*,[23] supported a broad reading of the statute's jurisdictional reach and the Corps' authority, while the two more recent cases, Solid Waste Agency of *Northern Cook County v. United States Army Corps of Engineers*,[24] and *Rapanos v. United States*,[25] take a narrower view.

In Riverside Bayview the Court held that wetlands adjacent to navigable waters were covered by the Act. Faced with what the Court acknowledged was the difficult task of deciding where water ended and land began, the Corps' regulation of the wetlands here made sense in light of the purpose of the Act "to restore "to restore and maintain the chemical, physical, and biological integrity of the Nation's waters."[26] The key to jurisdiction was not navigability but ecological integrity of the aquatic system.

Riverside Bayview left open the question of whether waters, including wetlands, that are not physically adjacent to a navigable body of water, so-called "isolated waters or wetlands," are covered. The Court partially addressed it *Solid Waste Agency of Northern Cook County v. United States Army Corps of Engineers (SWANCC)*.[27] In that case, the Court held that the Corps' extension of the statutory definition of "navigable waters" to include intrastate waters used as habitat by migratory birds exceeded its authority under the statute (a statutory reading the dissent called "miserly").[28] Distinguishing *Riverside Bayview Homes*, the isolated ponds here lacked a "'significant nexus,' to waters that are or were navigable in fact or that could reasonably be so made.[29]

Despite the anti-regulatory tone of the majority in *SWANCC*, most courts have read *SWANCC* narrowly as solely invalidating the migratory bird rule. These courts have continued to find non-adjacent wetlands with a hydrological connection to navigable water to be within the Corps' jurisdiction.[30] The propriety of that view came into question in *Rapanos v. United States*,[31] where the Court confronted the degree of connectivity required of non-adjacent wetlands to other regulated surface waters to come within the CWA's jurisdictional grant. There were two companion cases. One case involved wetlands that were adjacent to manmade drainage ditches, which emptied into a series of non-navigable tributaries and which flowed for up to 20 miles before connecting to the nearest navigable in fact waterway. In the other case the wetlands were separated by a berm from a manmade drainage ditch. Occasionally, the water would overflow the berm into the ditch, emptying into another ditch, which connected to a creek, which emptied into a navigable lake one mile away. The Court split 4–1–4 on the question of whether the connection to navigable waters in the cases was sufficient. A four justice plurality led by Justice Scalia said no, a four justice dissent led by Justice Stevens said yes, and a concurring opinion by Justice Kennedy said maybe.[32]

---

[23] *U.S. v. Riverside Bayview Homes, Inc.*, 474 U.S. 121, 106 S. Ct. 455, 88 L. Ed. 2d 419 (1985).

[24] *Solid Waste Agency of Northern Cook County v. U.S. Army Corps of Engineers*, 531 U.S. 159, 121 S. Ct. 675, 148 L. Ed. 2d 576 (2001).

[25] *Rapanos v. U.S.*, 547 U.S. 715, 126 S. Ct. 2208, 165 L. Ed. 2d 159 (2006).

[26] *Riverside Bayview*, 474 U.S. at 132, 106 S. Ct. at 462.

[27] *SWANCC*, 531 U.S. 159, 121 S. Ct. 675, 148 L. Ed. 2d 576 (2001).

[28] 121 S. Ct. at 693.

[29] U.S. Army Corps of Engineers, 531 U.S. 167, 172, 121 S. Ct. 675.

[30] See, e.g., *U.S. v. Deaton*, 332 F.3d 698 (9th Cir. 2001). For more cases, see Juergensmeyer and Roberts, Land Use Planning and Development Regulation Law §11.4 (Practitioner's Edition 3rd ed.2012).

[31] *Rapanos v. U.S.*, 547 U.S. 715, 126 S. Ct. 2208, 165 L. Ed. 2d 159 (4th Cir. 2003).

[32] As was the case in *SWANCC*, the *Rapanos* Court avoided the commerce clause issue.

In his plurality opinion, Justice Scalia took a narrow stance on the grant of jurisdiction. Driving his analysis of the statute was his view that states rights in regulating land use were at risk of being overrun by federal power. He decried the breath of the Corps' rule noting the entire land area of the United States lies in some drainage basin."[33] He would limit jurisdiction to relatively permanent, standing or flowing bodies of water. In his view, the only type of wetlands subject to regulation are those "with a continuous surface connection to bodies that are 'waters of the United States' in their own right."[34]

At the other end of the spectrum the four dissenting justices found the Corps' interpretation of the statute permissible. Driving their opinion was the deference they believed was due to the executive branch in interpreting statutory grants of authority.

Justice Kennedy occupied the middle, finding the plurality's interpretation of the statute "unduly dismissive" of the public interests served by the protection of wetlands.[35] The dissent's concession of authority to the Corps, he thought, read the adjective "navigable" out of the act. Stressing that the statute should be interpreted to carry out the purpose of the act in protecting water quality, Kennedy's test focused on the nexus between the wetlands and the navigable waters. "If the wetlands, either alone or in combination with similarly situated lands in the region, significantly affect the chemical, physical, and biological integrity of other covered waters more readily understood as 'navigable,' they should be covered. When, in contrast, wetlands' effects on water quality are speculative or insubstantial, they fall outside the zone fairly encompassed by the statutory term 'navigable waters.'"[36]

The lower courts now grapple with the multiple views of the justices in *Rapanos*. Most courts have adopted Justice Kennedy's significant nexus test,[37] but, as one court has said, "if *Raponos* represents a fractured viewpoint on CWA jurisdiction, the Courts of Appeals' attempts to apply *Rapanos* have only compounded the fracture."[38] Proceeding on a case by case basis without specific guidance under the nexus test basically leaves the parties where they were before the decision.

B.   Filling and Draining Wetlands

Section § 404 requires a permit for the discharge of dredged or fill materials into wetlands covered by the Act. Dredged material is defined as any material that is excavated or dredged from waters of the United States.[39] Fill material is defined as any material used to replace an aquatic area with dry land.[40] Activities that do not involve discharges are not regulated by the Corps even if they have negative effects on wetlands.[41] Thus, the CWA does not expressly ban draining a wetland.

---

[33] 126 S. Ct. at 2215.

[34] 126 S. Ct. at 2227.

[35] 547 U.S. at 777.

[36] 547 U.S. at 2248.

[37] See, e.g., *U.S. v. Donovan*, 661 F.3d 174 (3d Cir. 2011), cert. denied, 132 S.Ct. 2409 (2012). *Precon Development Corp., Inc. v. U.S. Army Corps of Engineers*, 633 F.3d 278 (4th Cir. 2011).

[38] *U.S. v. Roberts*, 86 Fed. R. Evid. Serv. 1570 (M.D. Tenn. 2011) (discussing the various views).

[39] 33 C.F.R. § 323.2(c).

[40] 33 C.F.R. § 323.2(e). Also see 33 C.F.R. § 323.2(f).

[41] See *U.S. v. Pozsgai*, 999 F.2d 719 (3d Cir. 1993).

Draining was effectively banned by the Corps' adoption of a regulation in 1993, which defined the "discharge of dredged material as . . . any addition of dredged material into, *including any redeposit* of dredged material within, the waters of the United States."[42] Since it is difficult to drain or dredge a wetland without some of the material being taken out falling back in, once it falls back it, it is a discharge into the wetlands. This new rule came to be known as the "incidental fallback rule," or the "Tulloch Rule."[43] The District of Columbia Court of Appeals invalidated it in *National Mining Association v. United States Army Corps of Engineers.*[44] Noting that the statute authorizes regulation of deposits of pollution, the court reasoned that with incidental fallback more material is removed than what falls back in and that this net withdrawal could not reasonably constitute an "addition" of a pollutant to the waters of the U.S.[45]

After the *National Mining* decision, the Corps issued a new rule that gave the decision a narrow reading. The new regulations replaced "any redeposit of dredged material" with "redeposit of dredged material other than incidental fallback."[46] However, the regulation defines incidental fallback as "the redeposit of small volumes of dredged material that is incidental to excavation activity in waters of the United States when such material falls back to substantially the same place as the initial removal,"[47] a difficult standard to meet. A district court invalidated the new rule finding the Corps guilty of doing what it had been warned not to do, that is "parsing the language of [prior] decisions . . . to render a narrow definition of incidental fallback that is inconsistent with an objective and good faith reading [of the appellate court decision]."[48]

In *United States v. Deaton*,[49] the Fourth Circuit disagreed with reasoning of *National Mining* and found sidecasting, which involves deposit of dredged material from a wetland back into that same wetland, constitutes a discharge under the Act. The landowner had argued that the word "addition" means putting something in that wasn't there before, and, with sidecasting, there is no net increase in material in the wetland. While this makes sense superficially, the court, considering the language and purpose of the statute, disagreed. The statute, said the court, prohibits the addition of pollutants, not material. The act of removal of dirt and vegetation converted it to "dredged spoil," a statutory pollutant. While the material had previously been present in an undisturbed state, by sidecasting,[50] it was returned in a disturbed state. Disturbances of soil trigger potential environmental harm and the statute justifiably regulates sidecasting.

C.   *Statutory Exemptions from Section 404*

Section 404 applies to the discharge of dredge or fill material. It does not cover any wastewater or pollutant discharged for waste disposal purposes.[51] Certain dredge or fill

---

[42] 33 C.F.R. § 323.2(d)(1) (emphasis added). 33 C.F.R. § 323.2(d)(l)(iii).

[43] See Kalo, "Now Open for Development?": The Present State of Regulation of Activities in North Carolina Wetlands, 79 N.C. L. Rev. 1667, 1695 (2001).

[44] *National Min. Ass'n v. U.S. Army Corps of Engineers*, 145 F.3d 1399 (D.C. Cir. 1998).

[45] U.S. Army Corps of Engineers, 145 F.3d at 1404.

[46] 33 C.F.R. § 323.2(d)(2).

[47] 33 C.F.R. § 323.2(d)(2)(ii).

[48] *National Ass'n of Home Builders v. U.S. Army Corps of Engineers*, 2007 WL 259944 (D.D.C. 2007).

[49] *U.S. v. Deaton*, 332 F.3d 698 (4th Cir. 2003).

[50] *U.S. v. Cundiff*, 555 F.3d 200, 213–14 (6th Cir. 2009).

[51] 33 C.F.R. § 323.2(d)(2)(i).

activities are specifically exempted by statute. Those include the discharge of dredged or fill material from "normal" farming, silviculture, ranching and other specified activities, usually of a temporary or emergency nature.[52] However, if land has not been farmed for so long that drainage is necessary, the exemption does not apply.[53]

These exceptions do not apply if the activity results in changing navigable waters to a new use or if circulation of the affected waters is changed or reduced. The court in *Avoyelles Sportsmen's League, Inc. v. Alexander (Avoyelles I)*,[54] construed these exemptions narrowly in a challenge brought under § 404 concerning an operation converting wetland forest to agricultural use. The court reasoned the exemption for farming applied only to ongoing activity and not the type of clearing operation (hardwood wetland to soybean fields) in dispute. The court concluded that the "normal farming" exemption from § 404 does not extend to projects that convert wetlands to dry lands.

D. Permits: General and Individual

The Corps of Engineers issues two types of permits under § 404 that allow dredge and fill activities that otherwise would violate the CWA. General permits may be issued by the Corps for routine activities that typically have minimal adverse environmental effects.[55] These permits may be issued on a state, regional, or nationwide basis and activities so permitted generally do not require individual permits. The Corps generally reviews these permits every five years for reissuance, modification or termination. For example, in 2000 the Corps reduced the nationwide permit (NWP) that allowed the filling of 10 wetland acres to one-half acre.[56] While public review is held on the creation of the general permit, once the permit is issued, a landowner need only ask for an authorization to engage in the permitted activity, saving time and paperwork.

General permits, particularly NWPs, are controversial. Since the authorization process is less onerous than with individual permits,[57] landowner-developers like them and want them expanded while environmental groups dislike them and press for their contraction.

E. Individual Permits

Individual permits are required when discharges are not exempt or are not permitted by a general permit. The individual permitting process is based on guidelines issued by both the Corps of Engineers and the Environmental Protection Agency. When the Corps receives an application, the proposed activity is initially reviewed to see if it is in "the public interest." Factors considered include conservation, economics, aesthetics, fish and wildlife values and general environmental concerns, among others.[58] The regulatory presumption is that wetlands are vital areas that constitute a productive and valuable public resource, the unnecessary alteration or destruction of

---

[52] 33 U.S.C.A. § 1144(f).

[53] 33 C.F.R. § 323.4(a)(l)(ii).

[54] *Avoyelles Sportsmen's League v. Alexander*, 473 F. Supp. 525 (W.D. La. 1979); 33 U.S.C.A. § 1144(f)(1)(b).

[55] 33 U.S.C.A. § 1144(e)(1).

[56] *National Ass'n of Home Builders v. U.S. Army Corps of Engineers*, 453 F. Supp. 2d 116 (D.D.C. 2006).

[57] See *Sierra Club v. U.S. Army Corps of Engineers*, 464 F. Supp. 2d 1171 (M.D. Fla. 2006).

[58] 33 C.F.R. § 320.4(a)(2).

which should be discouraged as contrary to the public interest. If an activity is determined by the Corps not to be in the "public interest," a permit will not be issued.

Even if an activity is found not to be against the "public interest," the Corps must still follow certain permitting guidelines set out by the Environmental Protection Agency as authorized by § 404(b). If proposed activity would cause or contribute to "significant degradation" of waters of the United States no permit may be issued. Effects leading to a finding of significant degradation include:

(1) Significantly adverse effects of the discharge of pollutants on human health or welfare, including but not limited to effects on municipal water supplies, plankton, fish, shellfish, wildlife, and special aquatic sites.

(2) Significant adverse effects of the discharge of pollutants on life stages of aquatic life and other wildlife dependent on aquatic ecosystems . . . .

(3) Significantly adverse effects of the discharge of pollutants on aquatic ecosystem diversity, productivity, and stability . . . .

(4) Significantly adverse effects of discharge of pollutants on recreational, aesthetic, and economic values.[59]

Section 404(b)(1) dictates that the filling of wetlands cannot occur if there is a practicable alternative available with less adverse effects. An applicant has the burden to show that there are no practicable alternatives.[60] In evaluating practicable alternatives, availability, cost, logistics, and technology are considered. Therefore, practicable alternatives must be both feasible and available.

Section 404(b)(1) also distinguishes water dependent activities from those that are not. Non-water dependent activities are those activities that do not have to be located on or around water, such as housing or office facilities. For non-water dependent activities there is a presumption that practicable alternatives are available.[61]

Furthermore, no permit may be issued where the discharge of dredged or fill material violates any state water quality standard, toxic effluent standard, jeopardizes a threatened or endangered species, or harms a marine sanctuary. When reviewing a permit application possibly affecting a threatened or endangered species, the Corps will consult interested state wildlife agencies as well as the United States Fish and Wildlife Service. If no exemption exists, a finding by the Secretary of the Interior concerning the discharge's impact on the species or their habitat will be considered final by the Corps.[62]

Both state and federal fish and wildlife services can be of considerable importance in dredge and fill permit applications. The Corps must give "great weight" to these agencies' determinations when wildlife may be affected by development in a wetland area.[63] While the Corps may ignore state or federal wildlife agency recommendations,

---

[59] 40 C.F.R. § 230.10(c).

[60] Section 404(b)(1); *Bersani v. U.S. E.P.A.*, 489 U.S. 1089, 109 S. Ct. 1556, 103 L. Ed. 2d 859 (1989).

[61] 40 C.F.R. § 230.10(a)(3).

[62] 40 C.F.R. § 230.30(c).

[63] 33 C.F.R. § 230.4(c).

the Environmental Protection Agency may block any permit authorization by the Corps.[64]

F. *Mitigation*

A permit may be accompanied by conditions, one of which may include mitigation. The national goal endorsed by the Corps is for "no net loss of wetlands."[65] Therefore, the Corps may require changes to the plans of a project and will usually require some kind of mitigation to offset or reduce the adverse effects to wetlands.

The Corps considers three methods of mitigation. They include: avoidance, minimization, and compensation. In evaluating the appropriate form of mitigation, the Corps will first determine if avoiding negative adverse effects to wetlands is altogether possible.[66] If all out avoidance is not possible, then the Corps will determine if the adverse effects can be minimized. This may require alterations of the development plans.[67]

The last resort, and the most controversial, is the use of compensatory mitigation.[68] Compensatory mitigation involves the creation of new wetlands, rehabilitation of degraded wetlands, or the conservation of existing functional wetlands. Generally, compensatory mitigation must take place within the watershed where the adverse effects were caused. The amount of mitigation depends upon the nature of the mitigation. Generally, one to one ratios are the minimum. For example, for each acre of wetlands destroyed, another acre of wetlands must be created, rehabilitated or preserved. The ratios differ according to the type of mitigation used. In cases where wetlands are created, it may be required that two or three acres be created for every acre destroyed. However, developers are only required to monitor and maintain these sites for two years after creation. Many of them ultimately fail.[69]

Mitigation banking is another approach to mitigating adverse effects to wetlands.[70] Under this system, third parties create, restore, or acquire functional wetlands. The third party then sells mitigation credits to developers who need them to compensate for adversely affecting wetlands by their development. Generally, as in compensatory mitigation, the mitigation bank must be located within the watershed where the adverse effects occur. The advantage to this form of mitigation is that the third party is usually more knowledgeable about wetland creation and preservation than most developers and this leads to more successful mitigation projects.[71]

---

[64] 33 U.S.C.A. § 1144(c).

[65] See Memorandum of Agreement Between EPA and Dept. of Army Concerning the Determination of Mitigation Under the Clean Water Action Section 404(b)(1), Guidelines, 55 Fed. Reg. 9210, 9211 (Mar. 12, 1990).

[66] 40 C.F.R. § 230.10(a) and (d).

[67] The Effects of Wetland Mitigation Banking on People, SL091 ALI-ABA 161 (2006).

[68] *Norman v. U.S.*, 63 Fed. Cl. 231 (2004).

[69] See National Academy of Sciences/National Research Council, Compensating for Wetland Losses under the Clean Water Act (2001).

[70] See Gardner et al., Compensating for Wetland Losses Under the Clean Water Act (Redux): Evaluating the Federal Compensatory Mitigation Regulation, 38 Stetson L. Rev. 213 (2009).

[71] See Environmental Law Institute eli.org, for studies of mitigation banking. Nicholas and Juergensmeyer, Market Based Approaches to Environmental Preservation: To Environmental Mitigation Fees and Beyond, 43 Nat. Resources L.J. 837 (2003). See also § 9:8 supra.

G. Cost of the Permitting Process

Landowner-developers complain that the time and cost of the wetland permitting process is too high. One study, quoted by Justice Scalia in *Rapanos*, estimates that "the average applicant for an individual permit spends 788 days and $271,596 in completing the process, and the average applicant for a nationwide permit spends 313 days and $28,915—not counting costs of mitigation or design changes."[72] In dissent, Justice Stevens, citing the same study, notes that "for 80% of permits the mean cost is about $29,000 (with a median cost of about $12,000) [and that] only for less than 20% of the permits—those for projects with the most significant impacts on wetlands—is the mean cost around $272,000 (and the median cost is $155,000)."[73]

While the federal § 404 process is formidable, only a third of the process may have been completed. In some jurisdictions state and local permits may also be acquired, and states and localities may have stricter guidelines than those followed by the Corps.[74]

§ 11:5   State Regulation

State regulation of wetlands runs the gamut from none to extensive. By one count, 21 states regulate coastal wetlands and 17 states directly regulate inland wetlands.[75] Local governments may also regulate wetlands, usually indirectly through zoning to protect shoreland or other sensitive lands. Definitions, scope, and permitting processes vary widely.

States that rely on the federal 404 process instead of enacting their own laws may find themselves underprotected when federal law is weakened. This occurred in North Carolina, which found the state helpless to prevent the draining of wetlands when a federal court in 1998 overturned a Corps of Engineers' regulation dealing with redeposit of dredged materials.[76] After the decision, the state announced that its regulations implementing a 1996 law on draining wetlands would be ready for enforcement by March, 1999. That left a window of opportunity, which was not missed by. developers.[77]Indeed, a company in the business of draining wetlands bought space on a billboard, with the advertising slogan of "Don't Delay, Drain Today." With the unclear state of the federal 404 process and the political volatility of the issue, states concerned with wetlands preservation should look out for themselves.

§ 11:6   Wetlands Takings Claims

Denials of § 404 permits have generated many takings claims. State and local denials have done so as well. This is unsurprising since the consequence of a denial may mean there is no economically viable use of the wetland. As for the taking of property by regulation, wetlands are not unique and our earlier discussion of regulatory takings

---

[72] Sunding and Zilberman, The Economics of Environmental Regulation by Licensing: An Assessment of Recent Changes to the Wetland Permitting Process, 42 Nat. Resources J. 59, 63, 74 (2002).

[73] 126 S. Ct. 2208, 2258–2259, 165 L. Ed. 2d 159 (2006).

[74] See infra § 11:5 for discussion of state controls.

[75] Linda A. Malone, Environmental Regulation of Land Use, § 4:29 (2011). See also Ziegler, Rathkopf's The Law of Zoning and Planning § 7:01 et seq. (4th ed.).

[76] See discussion supra § 11:12.

[77] Kalo, "Now Open for Development?": The Present State of Regulation of Activities in North Carolina Wetlands, 79 N.C. L. Rev. 1667, 1702, n.168 (2001).

law covers this issue.[78] There are two recurring questions that arise in many wetlands takings cases, which we will briefly mention. First, is defining the unit of property against which to measure the economic loss. If only the affected wetlands are considered, the chances of proving a per se taking under the *Lucas* holding are good. That, however, does not generally occur since the "parcel as a whole" rule is typically applied and most applicants have uplands in addition to wetlands that leave them with some economically viable use. However, if a showing of a total loss is made, the next question that generally arises is whether alteration of the wetlands violates a background principle of property or nuisance law. If it does, there can be no taking of a property right since the landowner does not have the property right he claims.

III. COASTAL ZONES

§ 11:7   Coastal Zone Values

The intense population pressures exerted upon coastal areas combined with their inherent fragility make them an extreme challenge to land use regulators. In recent years unfettered construction in the coastal zone has been greatly curtailed due to issues ranging from protection of sea turtles to prevention of erosion. The destruction wrought by Hurricanes Katrina and Rita in New Orleans and other areas along the Gulf Coast in 2005 vividly illustrated that curtailment and changes in construction have nonetheless been inadequate or not widespread. The battle between protection and use will inevitably continue as more and more people populate the coastal regions. A 2003 study estimates the percentage of the nation's population that resides within the coastal and Great Lakes counties exceeds 50%.[79]

Coastal zones are comprised of two separate types of environmentally sensitive lands. Wetlands, in the form of estuarine areas, form a substantial percentage of the coastal zone. Virtually all coastal states protect estuarine wetlands through coastal zone management programs or comprehensive plans, while only a few protect inland wetlands as such.

The other environmentally sensitive aspect of coastal zones is the substance most often identified with the coast—sand. Sand bars and dunes play an important role in protecting inland areas from flooding and coastal areas from severe storm damage and erosion. That role, however, can only be played when sufficient vegetation is present to secure the sand from undue erosion. Coastal construction alters the natural erosion pattern and hastens its rate.

It is estimated that 90% of the nation's beaches are eroding.[80] The Atlantic coast has receded an average of two to three feet per year, while the Gulf coast has receded

---

[78] See discussion supra §§ 10.1 to 10.11.

[79] See America's Living Oceans, Pew Oceans Commission Report (2003), http://www.pewtrusts.org/our_work_report_detail.aspx?id=30009; Coastal and Great Lakes counties account for only 17% of the nation's total land area. See http://coastalmanagement.noaa.gov/.

[80] See The Coastlines Project, http://coastlinesproject.wordpress.com/2011/09/05/as-beach-erosion-accelerates-remedies-are-costly-and-few-katia-update-after-11am/.

an average of six feet annually.[81] Further exacerbating the problem of erosion is the accelerating sea level rise from climate changes.[82]

Erosion enhanced by poorly planned development has disastrous effects on coastal property. Unless the lessons of Hurricane Katrina are learned quickly, the combined effects of erosion and sea level rise will result in many coastal communities being subject to "inundation, increased frequency and severity of storms and wave surge, increased rates of shoreline erosion, wetlands inundation and recession, modification of dynamic coastal physical properties, and damage to or reduction of shoreline protective structures and facilities."[83]

Thus, the concern of coastal zone management is that development not unduly interfere with natural coastal processes. Where needed, moratoria are placed on building permits. More commonly, coastal setback lines, density restrictions and construction standards are established. Just how and through what authority coastal zone regulation is accomplished is the subject of the following section.

§ 11:8   Takings Claims

Stringent regulation of development along the coast may severely diminish economically viable uses available to owners. This, in turn, will lead to the filing of Fifth Amendment takings claims. As is true with wetlands discussed above, coastal lands are not unique in this regard and our earlier discussion of regulatory takings law covers this issue.[84]

§ 11:9   Legislative Responses to Coastal Management Needs

A.   *The Coastal Zone Management Act*

Shoreline regulation was historically a local concern until coastal energy resources (such as offshore oil and gas) became economically and politically important on a national level. The National Coastal Zone Management Act of 1972 (CZMA)[85] was the nation's first attempt to develop a comprehensive coastal zone protection plan. The drive to extract offshore oil and gas led to a federal/state conflict over jurisdiction and revenue collection. Through the CZMA Congress attempted to defuse the growing polarization between the federal government and the states over these resource management issues. As such, the Coastal Act relies on joint federal/state cooperation and funding.

The CZMA's genesis came from a two-year presidential commission study of maritime resources published in 1969. Commonly called the Stratton Commission, the report of the Commission on marine science, engineering and resources highlighted the importance of shoreline areas. At that time, with 17% of the country's land area lying

---

[81]   Robert   Stewart,   Coastal   Erosion,   http://oceanworld.tamu.edu/resources/oceanography-book/coastalerosion.htm.

[82] Coastal Zones and Sea Level Rise, U.S.E.P.A., http://epa.gov/climatechange/effects/coastal/index.html.

[83] One study estimates that within the next 60 years, shoreline erosion will claim one in four U.S. homes within 500 feet of the shore, costing coastal property owners roughly $530 million per year. Evaluation of Erosion Hazards, The Heinz Center (2000), http://www.fema.gov/pdf/library/erosion.pdf.

[84] See discussion supra §§ 10.1 to 10.11.

[85] 16 U.S.C.A. §§ 1451 et seq.

within coastal counties, over 40% of the nation's population lived in that coastal land.[86] The Commission recommended a federally supported, state administered Coastal Management Act. The resulting CZMA was enacted after four years of Congressional attention on October 27, 1972.

The CZMA proceeds under a two-tiered process whereby states obtain federal financial assistance for coastal zone protection by

1) developing a comprehensive, long-range coastal management plan meeting federal statutory criteria; and

2) getting approval for that plan followed by state implementation.

To meet the CZMA's requirements for matching funds, the state program must comply with the act's statutory coastal management program in the judgment of the Secretary of Commerce. The pieces of the federal pie each coastal state seeks are the CZMA's grants covering development and implementation of state coastal programs. The program development grants (which help states devise their plans) are known as § 305 grants, and the state implementation grants (which help put the plans into practice) are called § 306 grants. Thirty-four of the 35 coastal and Great Lake states and territories have programs approved under CZMA. These states and territories comprise over 90% of the nation's coastline and include the shores of the Great Lakes.

The structure and scope of coastal zone management programs vary widely from state to state. Congress intended this diversity as a means of reflecting individual state concerns. Each state plan must, however, include the following:

1) an identification of the boundaries of the coastal zone subject to the management program;

2) a definition of what shall constitute permissible land and water uses within the coastal zone which have a direct and significant impact on the coastal waters;

3) an inventory and designation of areas of particular concern within the coastal zone;

4) an identification of the means by which the state proposes to exert control over the land and water uses referred to in paragraph 2) including a listing of relevant constitutional provisions, legislative enactments, regulations and judicial decisions;

5) broad guidelines on priority of uses in particular areas, including specifically those uses of lowest priority;

6) a description of the organizational structure proposed to implement the management program, including the responsibility and interrelationships of local, areawide, state, regional, and interstate agencies in the management process;

---

[86] See discussion supra §11.7.

7) a definition of the term "beach" and a planning process for the protection of, and access to, public beaches and other public coastal areas of environmental, recreational, historical, aesthetic, ecological, or cultural value;

8) a planning process for energy facilities likely to be located in, or which may significantly affect, the coastal zone, including, but not limited to, a process for anticipating and managing the impacts from such facilities;

9) a planning process for (A) assessing the effects of shoreline erosion (however caused), and (B) studying and evaluating ways to control, or lessen the impact of, such erosion, and to restore areas adversely affected by such erosion.[87]

Importantly, state programs must have viable coordinating mechanisms with local governments and designate a specific state agency to administer the program. States with approved programs are assured that federal actions are consistent with state coastal management programs.[88]

Section 307 of the CZMA provides for federal/state consistency. The section requires that activities affecting the coastal zone supported or conducted by federal agencies must be consistent with approved state programs to the "maximum extent practicable." Of most importance to the private developer is the subsection providing that private activities significantly affecting land and water uses in the coastal zone and which require federal licenses and permits must be consistent with the state's approved program.[89] The state must approve the applicant's certification of consistency for the federal license or permit to be granted. However, the Secretary of Commerce may overturn a state's determination of inconsistency if the Secretary finds that consistency does in fact exist.[90] Finally, federal agencies may not approve state or local applications for federal assistance for activities significantly affecting the coastal zone if they are inconsistent with the state's approved coastal management program.[91]

Congress reviewed the entire CZMA in 1980 to determine whether it should be reauthorized. The result was a series of amendments referred to as the Coastal Management Improvement Act of 1980.[92] Greater clarity in the policy behind the CZMA was made through additions in the statement of congressional findings (found in § 302). These policies again reflect a strong desire to manage and protect coastal resources through joint federal/state cooperation. The resources themselves, from fisheries to defense installation sitings, are spelled out in considerable detail. The § 306 implementation grant process was revised so that each complying state must use a greater proportion of the grant money (up to 30%) to implement these policies spelled out by Congress in § 302.

---

[87] 16 U.S.C.A. § 1455(d)(2).

[88] 16 U.S.C.A. § 1456(c). Thirty-four of the 35 coastal and Great Lake states and federal territories have federally approved coastal zone management programs. http://coastalmanagement.noaa.gov/programs/coast_div.html.

[89] 16 U.S.C.A. § 1456(c)(3).

[90] 16 U.S.C.A. § 1456(v)(3).

[91] 16 U.S.C.A. § 1456(d).

[92] These amendments are listed in their entirety in 16 U.S.C.A. § 1451 et seq.

The 1980 amendments included a new section of activities entitled the "Coastal Resource Improvement Program."[93] This section assumed the states were ready to move from planning into implementation and management. It provides states with incentives to implement their management programs in view of specific objectives and results. In general, the section gives federal assistance to states in "meeting low-cost construction, land acquisition, and shoreline stabilization costs associated with the designation of areas of preservation and restoration, the revitalization of urban waterfronts and parks, and public access to coastal acres."[94]

Section 306A(b)(l), the preservation subsection, is based on an assumption that through low-cost construction, environmentally sensitive areas could be protected and increased public access established. Such objectives could be reached by building paths through dunes (environmentally sensitive areas in themselves) to channel public access to beach areas. These paths or trails could be accompanied by signs, exhibits, and other "small scale construction programs" complementing a state's coastal zone management program.

In locales already developed, § 306A(a) provides assistance in urban waterfront and port development. The program stresses public access to port areas, rehabilitation of piers, bulkhead restoration and piling removal or replacement to the extent such activities comport with the policies behind the CZMA. Grants under this section could be used to devise urban waterfront redevelopment programs not eligible for any other federal funding.

In 1990, the CZMA was amended by the Coastal Zone Act Reauthorization Amendments (CZARA). The amendments dealt primarily with two issues. The consistency provision was amended to read "[e]ach Federal agency activity within or outside the coastal zone . . . shall be carried out in a manner which is consistent to the maximum extent practicable with the enforceable policies of approved state management programs."[95] With this amendment, Congress overturned the United States Supreme Court's ruling in *Secretary of the Interior v. California*.[96] This amendment ensures that all federal activities that affect the coastal zone, whether they take place in or out of the zone, are covered under the consistency provisions.

Section 6217 of the CZARA addresses the problem of coastal nonpoint source pollution.[97] Each state that has an approved coastal management program is required "to develop and implement management measures for nonpoint source pollution to restore and protect coastal waters, working in close conjunction with other State and local authorities."[98] Each state coastal nonpoint pollution control program must contain the following:

1) Identification of land uses which individually or cumulatively may cause or contribute significantly to a degradation of coastal waters;

---

[93] 16 U.S.C.A. § 1455a. See H.R. Rep. No. 97–628 (1982).

[94] H.R. Rep. No. 97–628 (1982).

[95] 16 U.S.C.A. § 1456(c)(1)(A).

[96] *Secretary of the Interior v. California*, 464 U.S. 312, 104 S. Ct. 656, 78 L. Ed. 2d 496 (1984).

[97] Pub. L. No. 101–508, § 6217, 104 Stat. 1388–314 to 1388–319 (1990).

[98] 16 U.S.C.A. § 1455b(a)(1).

2) Identification of critical coastal areas adjacent to coastal waters within which any new land uses or substantial expansion of existing land uses shall be subject to management measures;

3) Management measures to implement and to continue revision of additional management measures to maintain water quality standards and to protect designated uses;

4) Provisions for technical and other assistance to local governments and the public for implementing management measures;

5) Opportunities for public participation in all aspects of the program;

6) Mechanisms to improve coordination among State agencies and between State and local officials responsible for land use and environmental programs;

7) A proposal to modify the boundaries of the State Coastal Zone in response to evaluation of whether the State's coastal boundary extends inland to the extent necessary to control the land and water uses that have a significant impact on coastal waters of the state.[99]

The requirement for modification of the coastal boundary under number seven above may result in land use controls reaching further inland than prior to CZARA. The guidelines focus on five specific causes of nonpoint source pollution: 1) agricultural runoff; 2) silvicultural or forestry runoff; 3) urban runoff, including developed and developing areas; 4) marinas and recreational boating; and 5) hydromodification, including channelization, dams, and erosion of streambanks and shorelines.

B.   The Coastal Barrier Resources Act

The passage of the Coastal Barrier Resources Act (CBRA)[100] in 1982 gives additional protection to coastal zones. Coastal barriers are islands or spits consisting chiefly of sand that have the effect of protecting landward areas from direct wave action.[101] Because they consist of unstable sediments and serve as "natural storm protection buffers," coastal barriers are particularly ill suited for development.[102] Yet, by providing financial assistance in the form of subsidies and flood insurance, the federal government actively encouraged coastal barrier development for years.[103] The purpose of the Coastal Barrier Resources Act was to restrict development through the termination of federal assistance in undeveloped coastal barriers.

The Act is quite simple in its approach. It first sets up a "Coastal Barrier Resources System" consisting of all undeveloped coastal barriers located on the Atlantic and Gulf Coasts.[104] This system is carefully mapped and the boundaries set.[105] With

---

[99] 16 U.S.C.A. § 1455b(b).

[100] 16 U.S.C.A. §§ 3501 et seq. See Jones, The Coastal Barrier Resources Act: A Common Cents Approach to Coastal Protection, 21 Envtl. L. 1015 (1991).

[101] 16 U.S.C.A. § 3502(1)(A).

[102] 16 U.S.C.A. § 3501(a)(3).

[103] 16 U.S.C.A. § 3501(a)(4).

[104] 16 U.S.C.A. § 3503.

[105] 16 U.S.C.A. § 3503. Boundary modification is made through § 3503(c).

some exceptions,[106] "no new expenditures or new financial assistance may be made available under authority of any federal law for any purpose within the [Coastal Barrier Resource] System."[107] Thus, any state-permitted development will have to pay its own way.

In *Bostic v. United States*, the Fourth Circuit affirmed the legality of CBRA's denial of federal subsidies.[108] In *Bostic*, plaintiffs challenged the designation of their property as part of an undeveloped coastal barrier. They claimed that this designation disqualified certain construction on the property for federal flood insurance and denied them substantive due process. The court held that clear statutory language and history suggested that property designated on a map as "an undeveloped coastal barrier" illustrates a clear intent to include that property as such. The court also ruled that the designation bore a rational relation to the Act's objectives since withdrawing federal flood insurance from certain development on less developed portions of particular islands "prevents wasteful subsidies for construction that would not be feasible if developers had recourse only to the private insurance market."[109]

In 1990, the Coastal Barrier Improvement Act (CBIA) amended the Coastal Barrier Resources Act.[110] CBIA added nearly 820,000 new acres, tripling the acreage under the initial system. Most of these lands were aquatic habitat associated with the original coastal barriers.[111] CBIA also requires the heads of the federal agencies to report and certify compliance directly with the Interior Department and congressional committees.[112]

The CBRA has several advantages, including: 1) combining environmental protection and federal deficit reduction capabilities; 2) provision of alternatives to property acquisition when funds are limited; 3) avoiding takings claims since denial of subsidies takes away only a privilege and not a right; 4) promotion of State and local land use programs since these entities retain their authority to make decisions about what takes place on CBRA land.

C. *Coastal Zone Regulation: An Uncertain Future*

Coastal zone protection of environmentally sensitive lands is, as illustrated by the preceding discussions, a complicated process. Federal, state, and local plans, policies, and laws must all be consulted before development may take place in coastal areas. Whether such a mish-mash of competing jurisdictions can reach the desired goal of comprehensive, cohesive, and consistent management has not yet been demonstrated.

If more federal budget cutbacks occur, future coastal management and protection will be more and more a state and local activity. That has the possibility of destroying many years of progress in protecting sensitive coastal lands. At the same time, a dra-

---

[106] Exceptions include energy exploration and exploitation, maintenance of existing channels and roads and necessary military activities. 6 U.S.C.A. § 3505.

[107] 6 U.S.C.A. § 3504(a).

[108] *Bostic v. U.S.*, 753 F.2d 1292 (4th Cir. 1985).

[109] Bostic, 753 F.2d at 1294.

[110] Pub. L. No. 101–591, 104 Stat. 2931.

[111] Jones, The Coastal Barrier Resources Act: A Common Cents Approach to Coastal Protection, 21 Envtl. L. 1015, 1048 (1991).

[112] 16 U.S.C.A. § 3506(b).

matic cutback in federal disaster relief would shift the economic burden to those who create the risk. State and local governments must assume greater responsibility for their actions in allowing unwise development. Individuals and businesses need to confront building decisions without the aid of subsidized insurance. The question of the "moral hazard" must be confronted: "namely, to what extent does the likelihood of generous federal assistance serve to diminish the natural caution that individuals, communities, and businesses might otherwise exercise in adjusting to natural hazards in their investment and locational decisions?"[113]

IV. FLOOD PLAINS

§ 11:10 Flood Plain Use and Abuse

Flood plains are areas adjacent to rivers, streams, or other water bodies subject to periodic flooding of some degree. They form an important component of a particular geographic area's watershed. Over geologic time, floods are as natural as the river channel itself. The river channel and flood plain combine to form the drainage pathway for each watershed.

Flood plains are of three basic types. The most common are those associated with major rivers whose flooding is characterized by slow water movement over low land gradients, such as the Mississippi and Nile. Because the land is flat, a large amount of flood prone development occurs in this type of flood plain. The other flood plain types are those located in mountain valleys and coastal areas.

A. Flood Plain Values

Flood plains serve much the same purposes as wetlands.[114] In fact, many wetlands are part of flood plains. Historically, the most important human flood plain benefit has been agricultural.[115] Floodwater deposition of silt and nutrients allowed the Nile and Tigris and Euphrates Rivers to serve as "cradles of civilization."[116] Agricultural practices were designed to match the rise and fall in floodwaters. When the waters were in normal flood stage, crops were not endangered because they were not yet planted. People were not endangered because they were smart enough to not build on land subject to yearly flooding. The lesson has not been learned. Today, in an unfortunate commentary on our intelligence, there over six million homes built on flood hazard areas in this country.[117]

B. Development in Flood Plains

In contrast to the practices of years gone by, today's society has moved from an agricultural orientation to one divorced from the cycles of the seasons. Residential and commercial development, along with agricultural use, is now widespread in flood plain areas. Annual flooding is a grim reminder that development in flood-prone areas poses high risk to life, property and the environment. This development is often due to igno-

---

[113] Rutherford H. Platt, Disasters and Democracy: The Politics of Extreme Natural Events 9 (1999).

[114] See supra § 11:2.

[115] Kusler & Platt, Physical Characteristics of Flood Plains and Wetlands, Conference on Local Options for Flood Plain and Wetlands Management, at I-31, I-49.

[116] Kusler & Platt, at I-50.

[117] Kusler & Platt, I-50.

rance or nonchalance concerning flood hazards. Draining, dredging, filling, diking and impoundment building are all used to create habitable land in flood plains. If done with foresight (i.e., building houses on stilts or earth embankments) and away from the most hazardous areas, some development can successfully occur in flood plains. If not, situations as ironic as that found in the Everglades region of South Florida can happen. There, a 50-mile sheet flow of floodplain water was reduced by development to a 12-foot wide spillway.[118] Because the Everglades' extremities are bordered with levees and canals to protect residential and agricultural development, the water forced through this spillway is too much for the natural absorption processes of the reduced surface area of the Everglades to accept. Thus, the water management control districts involved must make the choice between destroying Everglades habitat as the water rises or opening up the levees and flooding the developed land.[119]

C. *Flood Plain Regulation*

The three principal approaches to flood hazard protection are: (1) regulation, (2) incentive programs, and (3) condemnation. Regulation is often accomplished through zoning setback restrictions [120] and is frequently combined with incentive programs such as those established by the National Flood Insurance Act of 1968 and the Federal Disaster Protection Act of 1973.[121] If regulation, with or without incentives, fails, a governmental entity may choose to obtain title to, or the development rights of, flood prone lands through voluntary sale or compulsory purchase through the exercise of the power of eminent domain.[122]

Flood plain mapping must occur before land use regulations can properly control development. Once mapped, the appropriate local or state authorities can apply specific zoning laws.[123] Mapping reveals to these authorities, among other things, two flood plain areas of note for land use purposes; floodways and flood fringes. Floodways are the unobstructed stream channel and overbank areas where flooding is most common. Structural development of any sort is generally prohibited there. Flood fringes are adjacent to floodways and are subject to less flooding and less damage (or potential damage) when floods do occur. A variety of land uses are permitted in flood fringe areas provided precautions such as elevation are taken.[124]

The National Flood Insurance Program,[125] which provides protection at premium rates below market, is a key component in flood plain protection. Local governments must have a comprehensive flood plain plan in order for buildings in the flood plain to be eligible for federal flood insurance.[126] Without such insurance, lenders will usually not finance development or support resale of property in flood prone areas. The pro-

---

[118] Nat'l Conference of State Legislatures, Land Management: Sustaining Resource Values, 63, 64 (Oct. 1983).

[119] Kusler & Platt, at I-50.

[120] See § 4:12 supra.

[121] 42 U.S.C.A. §§ 4001 et seq.

[122] See, generally, Malone, Environmental Regulation of Land Use § 7; 5 Water and Water Rights, Ch. 60 (Robert E. Beck ed. 1991).

[123] Malone, Environmental Regulation of Land Use § 7 at 23.

[124] Malone, Environmental Regulation of Land Use § 7.

[125] 42 U.S.C.A. §§ 4001 et seq. See http://www.floodsmart.gov/floodsmart/pages/index.jsp, the official website of the national program. See also Ziegler, Rathkopf's The Law of Zoning and Planning § 7:24 (4th ed.).

[126] 42 U.S.C.A. § 4011.

gram has many critics.[127] One critic suggests the NFIP price premiums accurately based on risk, eliminate subsidies on vacation homes, second homes and repetitive loss properties and update flood maps.[128] Another suggests repeal of the program, forcing the private sector to realize the cost of insuring vulnerable property.[129] Every few years reforms are considered but often are not enacted. For example, in 2006, the House passed the Flood Insurance Reform and Modernization Act of 2006, HR 4973, which was to phase in market premium rates on vacation homes and non-residential property. It did not become law.

A major problem resulting from the federal program and federal disaster relief in general is that individuals and local communities do not pay the bulk of the bill when a disaster strikes. The federal government does. This creates a disincentive for individuals to locate their buildings in safe spots and for local governments to enact effective flood regulations. They can allow development in flood prone areas without too much worry about the cost of possible loss of property in the event of a flood. Development pressures and short-term thinking cause some communities to follow this, the easier path.[130]

Although closely related to regulations protecting wetlands, flood plain protection has been more readily accepted by courts. This is probably true because the public hazard of flooding is dramatically illustrated by almost annual flood disasters. The harm accruing to the public through wetlands destruction is less obvious.[131] Flood plain regulations are the oldest and most extensive of all sensitive land programs.[132] The important role that wetlands play in flood control was not recognized until more recently.

Even though flood plain land use ordinances sometimes result in severe economic impact on the land's value to the owner, the courts generally uphold them [133] and reject takings claims. For instance, in *Turnpike Realty Co. v. Town of Dedham*,[134] the Massachusetts high court upheld a flood plain ordinance so severely restricting development that the restricted land was reduced in value from $431,000 to $53,000. In *Usdin v. State*,[135] a New Jersey court upheld a restrictive flood plain ordinance on ecological

---

[127] See Brown, Dealing with Disasters, 20 Prob. & Prop. 34 (Oct. 2006). See also Griffith, The National Flood Insurance Program: Unattained Purposes, Liability in Contract, and Takings, 35 Wm. & Mary L. Rev. 727 (1994).

[128] Spinelli, Reform of the National Flood Insurance Program: Congress Must Act Before the Next Natural Disaster, 39 Real Est. L.J. 430, 463 (2011).

[129] McMillan, Federal Flood Insurance Policy: Making Matters Worse, 44 Hous. L. Rev. 471, 505 (2007).

[130] See Rutherford H. Platt, Disasters and Democracy: The Politics of Extreme Natural Events 28 (1999).

[131] This is true even though wetlands serve as one of nature's best flood protection devices.

[132] J. Kusler, Regulating Sensitive Lands 22 (1980). At least 24 states and 17,000 local governments have flood plain programs, usually adopted in order to qualify for federal flood insurance. J. Kusler, Regulating Sensitive Lands 22 (1980).

[133] See, e.g., *Gove v. Zoning Bd. of Appeals of Chatham*, 444 Mass. 754, 831 N.E.2d 865 (2005); *Turner v. County of Del Norte*, 24 Cal. App. 3d 311, 101 Cal. Rptr. 93 (1972); *Vartelas v. Water Resources Commission*, 146 Conn. 650, 153 A.2d 822 (1959); *Iowa Natural Resources Council v. Van Zee*, 261 Iowa 1287, 158 N.W.2d 111 (1968); *First English Evangelical Lutheran Church v. County of Los Angeles*, 210 Cal. App. 3d 1353, 258 Cal. Rptr. 893 (1989).

[134] *Turnpike Realty Co. v. Town of Dedham*, 362 Mass. 221, 284 N.E.2d 891 (1972).

[135] *Usdin v. State, Dept. of Environmental Protection, Division of Water Resources*, 173 N.J. Super. 311, 414 A.2d 280 (Law Div. 1980), judgment aff'd, 179 N.J. Super. 113, 430 A.2d 949 (App. Div. 1981).

grounds, stating that a landowner's rights must be balanced against ecological harm prevented by the regulation.[136]

If all pecuniary value of a landowners' property is lost due to flood plain regulations, courts may well find a presumptive *Lucas*-type taking.[137] However, even if all economic value is destroyed, the state may be able to avoid paying compensation if it can show that it would be a nuisance to build in the flood plain or otherwise be contrary to background principles of state property or nuisance law.[138]

V. ENDANGERED SPECIES AND HABITAT PROTECTION

§ 11:11 Importance of Habitat Protection

Land use, be it agricultural, residential, commercial or industrial, urban or rural, refers to human uses of the land that alter the natural environment. Almost any use of land harms the natural ecosystem to some degree.[139] Too much human activity in the wrong place destroys the ecosystem on which we depend to survive. The increase in land development and consequent loss of native plant and animal life and habitat over the past century has led to the adoption of federal and state laws to regulate, and in some instances prohibit, development where it would unduly threaten certain species or vital ecosystems.

The realization that land development threatened irreparable damage to the natural world coupled with recognition of the interdependence of life forms led the scientific community to recognize the need for a broad approach to ecosystem management.[140] The law followed with regimes to implement needed protection. The law, however confronts difficulties in doing what science tells us may be required. Legal boundaries divide the land into states, and create parcels of land owned and controlled by separate persons. These artificial lines create jurisdictional powers and constitutional, statutory and common law rights in the owners of these parcels that are drawn without regard to nature. Consequently, the land preservation and wildlife laws that we have do not, with a few exceptions, protect ecosystems.

A host of state and federal laws attempt in a piece meal fashion to preserve land or protect particular species. Several federal statutes are species-related, like the Bald Eagle Protection Act,[141] the Wild-Free Roaming Horses and Burros Act,[142] and the Mi-

---

[136] Usdin, 173 N.J. Super. at 319, 414 A.2d at 288. See also Singer, Flooding the Fifth Amendment: The National Flood Insurance Program and the "Takings" Clause, 17 B.C. Envtl. Aff. L. Rev. 323, 370 (1990). Of course, if no real flood danger is shown, a court unwilling to defer the finding of the legislative and executive bodies may find an ordinance to be arbitrary. *Sturdy Homes, Inc. v. Redford Tp.*, 30 Mich. App. 53, 186 N.W.2d 43 (1971).

[137] See § 10:6A.

[138] *Lucas v. South Carolina Coastal Council*, 505 U.S. 1003, 112 S. Ct. 2886, 120 L. Ed. 2d 798 (1992); *Just v. Marinette County*, 56 Wis. 2d 7, 201 N.W.2d 761 (1972); *First English Evangelical Lutheran Church v. County of Los Angeles*, 210 Cal. App. 3d 1353, 258 Cal. Rptr. 893 (1989). See Singer, Flooding the Fifth Amendment: The National Flood Insurance Program and the "Takings"Clause, 17 B.C. Envtl. Aff. L. Rev. 323, 370 (1990).

[139] National Aeronautics and Space Administration. See http://sedac.ciesin.columbia.edu/tg/guide_main.jsp.

[140] See definitions and discussion of ecosystems at Silviculture Laboratory, Univ. of Washington, http:/depts.washington.edu/sfrsilva/index.html.

[141] 16 U.S.C.A. §§ 668 et seq.

[142] 16 U.S.C.A. §§ 1331 et seq.

gratory Bird Treaty Act,[143] but have only an incidental effect on protecting the habitat of the species protected. The federal Wilderness Act of 1964[144] is an early example of land preservation, but it is limited to federal public lands. The Marine Mammal Protection Act[145] and the Fisheries Conservation Act[146] protect fish habitat.

The federal law that does the most in terms of habitat protection, and ecosystem management is the Endangered Species Act.

§ 11:12 The Endangered Species Act as a Land Use Control Device

A. ESA Overview

The Endangered Species Act (ESA)[147] has proved to be a useful land use control tool in environmentally sensitive areas. The United States Supreme Court described the Act as "the most comprehensive legislation for the preservation of Endangered Species ever enacted by any Nation."[148] Enacted "to provide a means whereby the ecosystems upon which endangered species and threatened species depend may be conserved,"[149] the ESA can halt or require the alteration of development that threatens wild plant or animal species listed by the Secretary of the Interior as threatened or endangered.[150]

Section 4 authorizes the Secretary to list species of plants, fish, and wildlife as threatened or endangered.[151] Some 1300 species are listed as either threatened or endangered.[152] Section 3 of the ESA defines an "endangered species" as one that is "in danger of extinction throughout all or a significant portion of its range."[153] A threatened species is one that "is likely to become an endangered species within the foreseeable future throughout all or a significant portion of its range."[154] Whether a particular species falls within one of these categories is determined on "the basis of the best scientific and commercial data available."[155] The Act exempts insects that present an overwhelming risk to humans.[156]

---

[143] 16 U.S.C.A. §§ 703 et seq.

[144] 16 U.S.C.A. § 1131(a).

[145] 16 U.S.C.A. § 1361 ("certain species and population stocks of marine mammals are, or may be, in danger of extinction or depletion as a result of man's activities; . . . such species and population stocks should not be permitted to diminish beyond the point at which they cease to be a significant functioning element in the ecosystem of which they are a part, and, consistent with this major objective, they should not be permitted to diminish below their optimum sustainable population").

[146] 16 U.S.C.A. § 1801 ("conservation and management of the fishery resources of the United States is necessary to prevent overfishing, to rebuild overfished stocks, to insure conservation, to facilitate long-term protection of essential fish habitats, and to realize the full potential of the Nation's fishery resources").

[147] 16 U.S.C.A. §§ 1531 to 1543.

[148] *Tennessee Valley Authority v. Hill*, 437 U.S. 153, 180, 98 S. Ct. 2279, 57 L. Ed. 2d 117 (1978).

[149] 16 U.S.C.A. § 1531(b).

[150] The process to be followed by the Secretary in adding or subtracting a species from the act's domain is found at 16 U.S.C.A. § 1533(a), (b).

[151] 16 U.S.C.A. § 1533(a)(1). See Morse, Listing Under the Endangered Species Act: How Low Can You Go?, 47 Idaho L. Rev. 559 (2011).

[152] 588 species of animals and 794 species of plants listed in the United States as of December 2011. There are also foreign listings. For currently listed plants and animals, see http://www.fws.gov/endangered/.

[153] 16 U.S.C.A. § 1532(6).

[154] § 1532(20).

[155] § 1533(b)(1)(A).

[156] § 1533(b)(1)(A).

The land use element in the Endangered Species Act is § 4. This section reflects ecological reality; there is no use in protecting a plant or wildlife species if that species has no place to live. Section 4 authorizes the Secretary of Interior to designate areas of "critical habitat" for specified species.[157] Section 3 of the ESA defines critical habitat for a threatened or endangered species as the "specific areas within the geographical area occupied by the species, at the time it is listed."[158] If the designation of the critical habitat is not determinable at the time the species is listed, the Secretary may do so up to one year after the species is listed.[159] Even areas outside the geographical area can be determined as critical habitat if the Secretary determines such areas as essential for the species' conservation.[160] A critical habitat is limited, however, and "shall not include the entire geographical area which can be occupied"[161] by the species. As important as the designation of critical habitat is for a species, and while designation is supposed to be concurrent with the listing of that species, that often does not happen. Critical habitat has been designated for only 610 species.[162] The main reason that FWS gives for not designating critical habitat is that it is not "prudent."

B. Section 9 "Takes"

Section 9 is the triggering mechanism of the ESA. Section 9 prohibits the taking of any protected species by government or private parties.[163] Under § 3 to "take" includes to "harass, harm, pursue, hunt, shoot, wound, kill, trap, capture, or collect, or attempt to engage in any such conduct."[164] The keyword for land use issues is "harm," which the Secretary defines as "an act which actually kills or injures wildlife, but such act may include significant habitat modification or degradation where it actually kills or injures wildlife by significantly impairing essential behavioral patterns, including breeding, feeding, or sheltering."[165] The Secretary also defines "harass" broadly as "an intentional or negligent act or omission which creates the likelihood of injury to wildlife by annoying it to such an extent as to significantly disrupt normal behavioral patterns."[166]

C. Incidental Takings and Habitat Conservation Plans

Sections 7(b)(4) and 10(a) allow for "incidental takings" of protected species. An incidental taking is defined as "a taking [that is] otherwise prohibited, if such taking is incidental to, and not the purpose of, carrying out of an otherwise lawful activity."[167] The process of attaining an incidental taking permit differs slightly between a taking involving a federal action and one involving a private action.[168]

---

[157] 16 U.S.C.A. § 1533(a)(3)(A).

[158] 16 U.S.C.A. § 1532(5)(A)(i).

[159] 16 U.S.C.A. § 1533(b)(6)(C)(ii).

[160] 16 U.S.C.A. § 1532(5)(A)(ii).

[161] 16 U.S.C.A. § 1532(5)(C).

[162] See http://ecos.fws.gov/tess__public/CriticalHabitat.do?nmfs=1.

[163] § 1538(a)(1). States and their political subdivisions are persons subject to the act.

[164] § 1532(19).

[165] 50 C.F.R. 17.3. The Supreme Court upheld the Secretary's definition of "harm" in *Babbitt v. Sweet Home Chapter of Communities for a Great Oregon*, 515 U.S. 687, 115 S. Ct. 2407, 132 L. Ed. 2d 597 (1995).

[166] 50 C.F.R. 17.3.

[167] 50 C.F.R. 17.3.

[168] See, e.g., *Arizona Cattle Growers' Ass'n v. U.S. Fish and Wildlife, Bureau of Land Management*, 273 F.3d 1229 (9th Cir. 2001) for a description of process used for federal requests.

A proposed federal action, such as the review for a § 404 Dredge and Fill Permit, will trigger § 7 of the Act. The proponent federal agency, such as the Army Corps of Engineers, must [169] first consult with the U.S. Fish and Wildlife Service (FWS) or the National Marine Fisheries Service (NMFS) to determine whether any protected species may be present in the area of the proposed development and that the action is not likely to jeopardize the continued existence of any such species. The FWS or the NMFS then must issue a written statement that details how the proposed action would affect the species or its critical habitat.[170] If the service finds the action will jeopardize a species or its critical habitat, the service suggests, if possible, "reasonable and prudent alternatives" to the agency's proposal.[171] The federal agency may then follow the service's suggestions, which may include the right to an incidental take. If the agency chooses not to follow the alternatives offered or if no alternatives are offered and the project will be halted, the agency can apply to the Endangered Species Committee for an exemption arguing that the public interest served by its project outweighs the predicted jeopardy of the species or its habitat.[172]

Section 10 applies to non-federal requests for incidental take permits. To secure a permit, the applicant must submit a habitat conservation plan (HCP) to the FWS or NMFS that shows the expected effects, the steps that will be taken to minimize and mitigate any taking, show that the taking will not appreciably reduce the likelihood of the survival of the species, and what alternative actions were considered and why they were not adopted.[173] The Services must also be assured that there will be adequate funding for the conservation plan.[174] The permit may be issued subject to terms and conditions that the Secretary deems necessary.[175] Furthermore, the Services may revoke a permit if the permittee is not complying with the terms and conditions of the permit.[176] Under a "no surprises" policy, the FWS and NMFS assure permit holders that if circumstances change so as to render the HCP inadequate to conserve listed species, the Services will not impose additional conservation and mitigation requirements that would increase costs or further restrict the use of natural resources beyond the original plan.[177] Under a Permit Revocation Rule, the Services will not revoke an

---

[169] The duty may not apply to discretionary actions. *National Ass'n of Home Builders v. Defenders of Wildlife*, 551 U.S. 644, 127 S. Ct. 2518, 168 L. Ed. 2d 467 (2007). See Karpa, Loose Canons: The Supreme Court Guns for the Endangered Species Act in National Association of Home Builders v. Defenders of Wildlife, 35 Ecology L.Q. 291 (2008).

[170] 16 U.S.C.A. § 1536(b)(3)(A). See, e.g., *Home Builders Ass'n of Northern Cal. v. U.S. Fish and Wildlife Service*, 616 F.3d 983 (9th Cir. 2010), cert. denied, 131 S. Ct. 1475, 179 L. Ed. 2d 301 (2011). Despite the importance of protecting critical habitat, some argue that the FWS and NMFS have failed to discharge their statutory obligations by following a "policy of disinterest." Robbins, Recovery of an Endangered Provision: Untangling and Reviving Critical Habitat Under the Endangered Species Act, 58 Buff. L. Rev. 1095, 1107 (2010).

[171] See *Arizona Cattle Grower's Ass'n,* 273 F.3d at 1238.

[172] 16 U.S.C.A. § 1536(s). While an agency may petition the so-called "God Squad" for an exemption, this rarely happens—and is even more rarely granted.

[173] 16 U.S.C.A. § 1536(a). See, e.g., Douglas Wheeler and Ryan Rowberry, Habitat Conservation Plans and the Endangered Species Act, Ch. 11, Endangered Species Act: Law, Policy and Perspectives (2nd ed.) (2010); Duggan, Incidental Extinction: How the Endangered Species Act's Incidental Take Permits Fail to Account for Population Loss, 41 Envtl. L. Rep. News & Analysis 10628 (2011), arguing that "a close examination of relevant regulations shows that crucial components of the approval process lack the scientific clarity and regulatory direction to deal with modern Incidental Take Permits. Specifically, current and future populations are grossly overestimated because of regulatory deficiencies."

[174] 16 U.S.C.A. § 1539(a)(2)(B)(iii).

[175] 16 U.S.C.A. § 1539(a)(2)(B).

[176] 16 U.S.C.A. § 1539(a)(2)(C).

[177] 50 C.F.R. § 17.22. See also *Spirit of Sage Council v. Kempthorne,* 511 F. Supp. 2d 31 (D.D.C. 2007).

incidental take permit unless continuation of the permit puts a listed species in jeopardy of extinction.

Similarly and where the ESA is seen by local government and their constituent developers as intruding on matters of local control, a "candidate conservation agreement" may be used.[178] Under these agreements state and local governments along with private parties agree to provide some protection to as yet unlisted, candidate species, avoiding the listing process and all that goes with it.[179]

D. *Constitutionality as Applied to Development on Private Land*

The Supreme Court has not addressed the constitutionality of applying the ESA to private land. The commerce clause is a, and perhaps the only, source of power by which the ESA can regulate private land. The Property Clause of Article IV of the constitution confers power on Congress to regulate activity on the public lands.[180] This power extends in some instances to adjacent lands,[181] but not to private land in general. As is true of the Property Clause, the treaty power may support the ESA's extension to private land in narrow circumstances.[182]

The Supreme Court's relatively new activism in invalidating congressional enactments sought to be justified on the commerce clause power [183] sparked speculation that the ESA might be found unconstitutional.[184] Yet, four federal courts of appeal have upheld the Act,[185] and no court has held to the contrary. A brief look at two of the cases shows the courts' rationales. *National Association of Home Builders v. Babbitt*[186] involved the Delhi Sands flower-loving fly (the Fly), which has its home and last remaining habitat in San Bernardino County, California. The day before the county was to begin construction of a hospital, the Fly was listed as endangered. The listing suspended construction, which was to occur on Fly habitat. Eventually, the hospital was built 250 feet north of the original site. The Fish and Wildlife Service then held up a highway realignment necessitated by the new siting of the hospital, contending that it

---

[178] See Announcement of Final Policy for Candidate Conservation Agreements with Assurances, 64 Fed. Reg. 32,726 (June 17, 1999); Safe Harbor Agreements and Candidate Conservation Agreements with Assurances, 64 Fed. Reg. 32,706 (June 17, 1999).

[179] See Ortiz, Candidate Conservation Agreements as a Devolutionary Response to Extinction, 33 Ga. L. Rev. 413 (1999).

[180] *Kleppe v. New Mexico*, 426 U.S. 529, 96 S. Ct. 2285, 49 L. Ed. 2d 34 (1976).

[181] See Keiter, Taking Account of the Ecosystem on the Public Domain: Law and Ecology in the Greater Yellowstone Region, 60 U. Colo. L. Rev. 923 (1989).

[182] See White, Comment: The Endangered Species Act's Precarious Perch: A Constitutional Analysis Under the Commerce Clause and the Treaty Power, 27 Ecology L.Q. 215 (2000).

[183] See *U.S. v. Lopez*, 514 U.S. 549, 115 S. Ct. 1624, 131 L. Ed. 2d 626 (1995); *U.S. v. Morrison*, 529 U.S. 598, 120 S. Ct. 1740, 146 L. Ed. 2d 658 (2000).

[184] See, e.g., Kmiec, Rediscovering a Principled Commerce Power, 28 Pepp. L. Rev. 547 (2001).

[185] *Alabama-Tombigbee Rivers Coalition v. Kempthorne*, 477 F.3d 1250, 1271 (11th Cir. 2007), cert. denied 552 US. 1097, 128 S.Ct. 877, 169 L.Ed.2d 725 (2008); *GDF Realty Investments, Ltd. v. Norton*, 326 F.3d 622, 641 (5th Cir. 2003), cert. denied, 545 U.S. 1114, 125 S.Ct. 2898, 162 L.Ed.2d 294 (2005); *Gibbs v. Babbitt*, 214 F.3d 483 (4th Cir. 2000), cert. denied sub nom Gibbs v. Norton, 531 U.S. 1145, 121 S.Ct. 1081, 148 L.Ed.2d 957 (2001); *National Ass'n of Home Builders v. Babbitt*, 130 F.3d 1041 (D.C. Cir. 1997), cert. denied 524 U.S. 937, 118 S.Ct. 2340, 141 L.Ed.2d 712 (1998). See also *Rancho Viejo, LLC v. Norton*, 323 F.3d 1062 (D.C. Cir. 2003), cert. denied, 540 U.S. 1218, 124 S.Ct. 1506, 158 L.Ed.2d 153 (2004) (commercial housing project substantially related to interstate commerce such that ESA's application to protect the intrastate arroyo toad was constitutional). The Ninth Circuit upheld the Bald Eagle Protection Act finding that its extinction would substantially affect interstate commerce by foreclosing any possibility of several types of commercial activity. *U.S. v. Bramble*, 103 F.3d 1475 (9th Cir. 1996).

[186] *National Ass'n of Home Builders v. Babbitt*, 130 F.3d 1041 (D.C. Cir. 1997).

would encroach on the corridor the Fly needs to travel between colonies. At that point, the County, along with the home builders association, challenged the power of Congress to dictate land use on the basis of the Fly's connection to interstate commerce.

The challenge was a broad one. The plaintiffs did not seek to show that the regulations implementing the ESA imposed an economic burden on them. Their attack was simply that whether the Fly became extinct was none of the federal government's business. The Court of Appeals found that the taking of the Fly could be regulated as activity substantially affecting interstate commerce to prevent destructive interstate competition.[187] A concurring judge found the ESA's action stopping the hospital to be a constitutional exercise of commerce clause power in that it prevented destruction of biodiversity, which, since it is critical to our continued existence, is critical to interstate commerce.[188]

In *Gibbs v. Babbitt* [189] a man convicted in a federal prosecution for shooting a red wolf, which he feared might threaten his cattle challenged the authority of the Fish and Wildlife Service to promulgate a regulation limiting the taking of red wolves on private land. The regulation was upheld by the Court of Appeals for the Fourth Circuit. The *Gibbs* court found that the future effect of the "taking" of the red wolf could possibly have far reaching effects on interstate commerce, including effects on "interstate commerce through tourism, trade, scientific research, and other potential economic activities."[190] The court conceded that the taking of one red wolf may not be substantial, but takings of the wolves in the aggregate would have a sufficient impact on interstate commerce to uphold the regulation.

The Court of Appeals relied on Congressional power to protect the environment when upholding the application of the Endangered Species Act:

> It is well established, however, that Congress can regulate even private land use for environmental and wildlife conservation. Courts have consistently upheld Congress's authority to regulate private activities in order to conserve species and protect the environment . . . . Given the history of federal regulation over wildlife and related environmental concerns, it is hard to imagine how this anti-taking regulation trespasses impermissibly upon traditional state functions—either control over wildlife or local land use . . . . If we struck down this regulation under the commerce power, we would throw into question much federal environmental legislation. This would be a portentous step, leaving many environmental harms to be dealt with through state tort law. Such a movement might well subject interstate companies to a welter of conflicting obligations. If Congress is constitutionally forbidden from even enacting uniform environmental rules, the confusion for interstate commercial enterprises might increase exponentially.[191]

Despite these lower court holdings in favor of the ESA, what the Supreme Court would say were it to take such a case is by no means clear. Arguing against the Act is that many species do not move across state boundaries (at least while they are alive).

---

[187] *Babbitt*, 130 F.3d at 1048.

[188] *Babbitt*, 130 F.3d at 1059 (Henderson, J., concurring).

[189] *Gibbs v. Babbitt*, 214 F.3d 483 (4th Cir. 2000), *cert. denied sub nom. Gibbs v. Norton*, 531 U.S. 1145, 121 S. Ct. 1081, 148 L. Ed. 2d 957 (2001).

[190] 214 F.3d. at 497.

[191] *Babbitt*, 214 F.3d at 500–02.

While tourism is significant for some species, it is non-existent for many. There is a strong national interest in species and habitat protection but some argue that this rationale has no logical stopping point and would permit the federal government to regulate activities traditionally regulated by the states.[192] Finally, when Congress passed the ESA in 1973 it did not make the kind of findings that may now be necessary. The question of when the Supreme Court will demand congressional findings to support commerce clause enactments and when the Court will reject findings that are made is unclear.[193] The fact that the Court has denied certiorari in all of the cases and that there is no conflict among the circuits argues against a strong expectation that the Court will address the question.

E. Fifth Amendment Takings under the ESA

A property owner may also claim that the ESA applies in such a way as to constitute a Fifth Amendment taking. A number of cases involve physical takings claims based on damage inflicted on private land by protected species. The claims have generally failed on the ground that the government neither owns the wildlife nor controls its movements.[194] The reasoning is arguably specious since it is, after all, the government that protects the animal from harm, granting it the power to kill cattle and other livestock.

Despite the general complaints or perceptions that the ESA as applied frequently deprives landowners of economic use of their land, there have been very few regulatory takings cases reported under the ESA. Those that have been reported have been unsuccessful.[195] Most fail due to application of the "whole parcel" rule.[196] The reason for the lack of lawsuits can hardly be attributable to the procedural hurdles of takings law or to its substance, as some have suggested. After all, in other areas, landowners feeling the weight of government regulation are not hesitant to sue. For example, there are a great many reported takings cases involving wetlands regulations. In recent years, takings claims have likely been avoided by the Interior Department's fairly aggressive use of habitat conservation plans allowing landowners to take species under limited circumstances. Whatever the reason for the scarcity of cases, when they do arise, they are subject to the law discussed in detail in Chapter 10.[197]

Regulations affecting water use raise separate questions. The United States Court of Federal Claims and the Federal Circuit have confronted several challenges to federal actions that seek to maintain instream flow for protected fish species by diverting water that farmers and ranchers rely upon or ordering them to curtail their water use. When the water rights rise to the level of property rights, a takings claim may be as-

---

[192] See *Home Builders v. Babbitt*, 130 F.2d at 1064 (dissent of J. Sentelle). A counter-point is that in contrast to land use regulation, which has been traditionally local, the federal government has long been active in the area of wildlife regulation. See Kmiec, Rediscovering a Principled Commerce Power, 28 Pepp. L. Rev. 547, 575 (2001).

[193] Buzbee and Schapiro, Legislative Record Review, 54 Stan. L. Rev. 87, 111 (2001) ("*Lopez* and *Morrison* duet established that findings might be necessary, but were certainly not sufficient. The question remains what kind of legislative materials, if any, will satisfy the Court's scrutiny.").

[194] See. e.g., *Christy v. Hodel*, 857 F.2d 1324 (9th Cir. 1988).

[195] *Allegretti & Co. v. County of Imperial*, 138 Cal. App. 4th 1261, 42 Cal. Rptr. 3d 122 (2006); *State v. Sour Mountain Realty, Inc.*, 276 A.D.2d 8, 714 N.Y.S.2d 78 (2000).

[196] See supra § 10:8. See, e.g., *Seiber v. U.S.*, 364 F.3d 1356 (Fed. Cir. 2004).

[197] See supra §§ 10.2 to 10.11.

serted. In *Casitas Municipal Water District v. United States*,[198] the Bureau of Reclamation ordered the Water District to construct a fish ladder necessary for the survival of the steelhead trout and to decrease its diversion of water from the river for the operation of the ladder. The water district complained that the loss of water was a physical taking. The Federal Circuit agreed, holding *Loretto* controlled. The government had "commandeer[ed] the water for a public use-preservation of an endangered species. [In so doing,] Casitas' right to use that water is forever gone."[199]

---

[198] *Casitas Mun. Water Dist. v. U.S.*, 543 F.3d 1276 (Fed. Cir. 2008). But see *CRV Enterprises, Inc. v. U.S.*, 626 F.3d 1241 (Fed. Cir. 2010). For an unfavorable view of *Casitas*, see Dake, Trout of Bounds: The Effects of the Federal Circuit Court of Appeals' Misguided Fifth Amendment Takings Analysis in Casitas Municipal Water District v. United States, 36 Colum. J. Envtl. L. 59 (2011).

[199] *CRV Enterprises, Inc.*, 626 F.3d at 1294. See also *Tulare Lake Basin Water Storage Dist. v. U.S.*, 49 Fed. Cl. 313 (2001).

Chapter 12

AESTHETIC REGULATION AND HISTORIC PRESERVATION*

Analysis

I. AESTHETIC REGULATION AND ARCHITECTURAL CONTROL

I. AESTHETIC REGULATION AND ARCHITECTURAL CONTROL

§ 12:1   Introduction

What is beauty? Our individual preferences are conditioned by educational, social and environmental factors. What is pleasing to the eye depends upon to whom the eye belongs. As David Hume, a Scottish philosopher, has said, beauty in things exists in the mind that contemplates them. Thus, as a basis for regulation of land uses, statutes and ordinances grounded *solely* on furthering of aesthetic purposes have been, at least until recently, difficult to justify.[1]

In land use control lore, an aesthetic control attempts to preserve or improve the beauty of an area. All zoning is to a certain extent based on the desire for beauty. Some of this country's first planning efforts arose from what was called the "city beautiful" movement.[2] In one of the earliest zoning decisions, the Supreme Court of the United

---

* For more detailed discussion and more extensive citations of authority of the issues covered in this chapter, see Juergensmeyer and Roberts, Land Use Planning and Development Regulation Law, Practitioner Treatise Series (3rd ed. 2012).

[1] See Pearlman, Linville, Phillips, and Prosser, Beyond the Eye of the Beholder Once Again: A New Review of Aesthetic Regulation, 38 Urb. Law. 1119 (2006) (state by state analysis).

[2] See § 2:4.

States in *Village of Euclid v. Ambler Realty Co.*,[3] validated zoning as a reasonable exercise of the police power, taking the view that law must respond to the changing demands and needs of urban areas. After *Euclid* and until 1954, however, aesthetics alone was not considered a valid purpose for land use measures. Courts required that such measures be coupled with more traditional grounds to be sustained.[4]

In 1954, Justice Douglas noted in *Berman v. Parker*[5] that public safety, health, morality, peace and quiet, law and order—which are some of the more conspicuous examples of the traditional application of the police power—merely illustrate the scope of the power and do not limit it. He further observed that the concept of public welfare includes values which are "spiritual as well as physical, aesthetic as well as monetary. It is within the power of the legislature to determine that the community should be beautiful as well as healthy."[6] Subsequently, in *People v. Stover*,[7] the New York Court of Appeals determined that aesthetic purposes would support a restriction on the use of land. More recent cases extend legal support for the validity and necessity of aesthetic considerations in natural resource allocation and land use planning.[8]

Consideration of aesthetics in the promulgation of federal regulations was essentially guaranteed in 1969, with passage of the National Environmental Policy Act.[9] NEPA made consideration of aesthetic objectives a fundamental part of national policy by requiring an assessment of a project's impact on the built environment. Congress intended that creation and maintenance of a productive harmony between man and the environment be a national goal, to the end that the nation may be assured safe, healthy, productive, and aesthetically and culturally pleasing surroundings.[10] Enforcement of NEPA by courts has led to enactment of similar statutes in several states.[11]

---

[3] *Village of Euclid, Ohio v. Ambler Realty Co.*, 272 U.S. 365, 47 S. Ct. 114, 71 L. Ed. 303, 4 Ohio L. Abs. 816, 54 A.L.R. 1016 (1926).

[4] See, e.g., *Board of Sup'rs of James City County v. Rowe*, 216 Va. 128, 216 S.E.2d 199 (1975) (protecting property values); *Cochran v. Preston*, 108 Md. 220, 70 A. 113 (1908) (height restrictions in Washington Monument vicinity upheld on safety and aesthetic grounds).

[5] *Berman v. Parker*, 348 U.S. 26, 75 S. Ct. 98, 99 L. Ed. 27 (1954).

[6] Parker, 348 U.S. at 29, 75 S. Ct. at 100.

[7] *People v. Stover*, 12 N.Y.2d 462, 240 N.Y.S.2d 734, 191 N.E.2d 272 (1963) (regulation requiring removal of clothesline from front yard).

[8] See, e.g., *Members of City Council of City of Los Angeles v. Taxpayers for Vincent*, 466 U.S. 789, 805, 104 S. Ct. 2118, 2129, 80 L. Ed. 2d 772 (1984) (holding that "[i]t is well settled that the state may legitimately exercise its police powers to advance [a]esthetic values"); *Metromedia, Inc. v. City of San Diego*, 453 U.S. 490, 507–08, 101 S. Ct. 2882, 2892–93, 69 L. Ed. 2d 800, 16 Env't. Rep. Cas. (BNA) 1057, 11 Envtl. L. Rep. 20600 (1981) (plurality opinion) (concluding that the appearance of the city constitutes a substantial governmental goal); *Flippen Alliance for Community Empowerment, Inc. v. Brannan*, 267 Ga. App. 134, 601 S.E.2d 106 (2004) (Holding that zoning, even if based merely on aesthetic interests, is a reasonable and proper exercise of the police power.); *Kuvin v. City of Coral Gables*, 62 So. 3d 625, 640 (Fla. 3d DCA 2010), review denied, 64 So. 3d 118 (Fla. 2011) (Holding that "[t]he City may constitutionally pass ordinances to enhance or maintain the aesthetic appeal of the community and to protect the City's residential neighborhoods against the lingering presence of commercial-looking vehicles.").

[9] National Environmental Policy Act of 1969, 42 U.S.C.A. §§ 4321 to 4370.

[10] 42 U.S.C.A. § 4331.

[11] E.g., Cal. Pub. Res. Code § 21000(b); Minn. Stat. Ann. § 116B.02; N.Y. Envtl. Conserv. Law § 8-0101–0117. This sort of cause and effect situation is mirrored to some extent by the experience with the National Historic Preservation Act, and subsequently enacted similar state laws. See § 12:6, infra.

In spite of the jurisprudential support given aesthetic control as a valid regulatory goal in recent years, problems still exist.[12] Courts are repeatedly forced to determine whether a particular aesthetic regulation is a proper use of the police power.[13] Questions also arise when the adequacy of due process, in either the creation or application of the aesthetic control, is called into question.[14] Measures based on visual compatibility principles, analogous to zoning rationale, are fairly easy to sustain, but if the compatibility requirements are vague, overbroad or ambiguous, serious due process and First Amendment problems may be indicated.[15] Sign control ordinances are particularly susceptible to First Amendment attacks. Another charge that may be leveled at an aesthetics-based regulation is that the affected property has been taken without compensation.[16]

On the whole, the courts' shift in favor of aesthetic-based regulation recognizes that pleasing surroundings are protectable as part of the public welfare.[17] Commentators have suggested that zoning ordinances enacted primarily for aesthetic objectives should be recognized as a legitimate means of implementing community values.[18] This would enable courts to discontinue upholding ordinances prohibiting uses that are aesthetically offensive, such as billboards, under the fiction that they constitute public health and safety hazards.[19]

This first part of this chapter explores regulation of aesthetic values in two specific areas, sign control and architectural regulation. In each of these areas, aesthetic considerations loom large and particular attention must be given to the ways in which aesthetics relate to the public health, safety and welfare.

§ 12:2   Sign Control

Billboard and sign regulation is not a new phenomenon. People have long protested the unsightliness of billboards, and legislatures have attempted to appease them from time to time—"The story of billboards in America is . . . characterized by an ongoing struggle between an expanding industry and a resistant public."[20] Courts, however, in the early part of the twentieth century, were not receptive to these moves. In the 1905 case of *City of Passaic v. Paterson Bill Posting, Advertising & Sign Painting Co.*, the court invalidated an ordinance which imposed setback and height restrictions, reasoning that aesthetic considerations were matters of luxury, and necessity alone

---

[12] See Karp, The Evolving Meaning of Aesthetics in Land Use Regulation, 15 Colum. J. Envtl. L. 307 (1990).

[13] See Validity and construction of zoning ordinance regulating architectural style or design of structure, 41 A.L.R.3d 1397, 1401–03.

[14] Validity and construction of zoning ordinance regulating architectural style or design of structure, 41 A.L.R.3d 1397, 1401–03.

[15] Shawn Rice, Zoning Law: Architectural Appearance Ordinances and the First Amendment, 76 Marq.L.Rev., 439, 448-51 (1993); Costonis, Law and Aesthetics: A Critique and a Reformulation of the Dilemmas, 80 Mich. L. Rev. 355, 360–361 (1981). See supra §§ 10:2, 10:3.

[16] See §§ 10:3 to 10:11 for takings law.

[17] "Presently, the majority of courts allow regulations based on aesthetic considerations alone." Stevenson, Aesthetic Regulations: A History, 35 Real Est. L.J. 519 (2007).

[18] Costonis, Law & Aesthetics: A Critique and a Reformulation of the Dilemmas, 80 Mich. L. Rev. 355 (1982).

[19] See Michael Pace, Note, Aesthetic Regulation: A New General Rule, 90 W.Va.L.Rev. 581, 592-93 (1987). See also Dukeminier, Zoning for Aesthetic Objectives: A Reappraisal, 20 Law & Contemp. Probs. 281 (1955).

[20] Burnett, Judging the Aesthetics of Billboards, 23 J.L. & Pol. 171, 174 (2007).

justified exercise of the police power.[21] Some later opinions were not quite so rigidly set, and courts allowed regulation of signs for traffic safety and health purposes or to preserve the scenery obliterated by the erection of signs.[22]

More recently, courts have recognized aesthetic concerns as being a valid justification for use of the police power. An early opinion sustaining aesthetic values as sufficient grounds for a community to ban all off-premise signs was *Cromwell v. Ferrier*.[23] The New York Court of Appeals reasoned that exercise of the police power should extend to those aesthetic considerations which bear substantially on the economic, social, and cultural patterns of a community or district. "Advertising signs and billboards . . . often are egregious examples of ugliness . . . just as much subject to reasonable controls . . . as enterprises which emit offensive noises, odors or debris."[24] But elsewhere, an ordinance which attempted to require property owners to provide for "beauty, attractiveness, aesthetics and symmetry in commercial signs . . . " was invalidated.[25] The court distinguished between ordinances with a primary goal of furthering aesthetics, and those with other immediate goals, only secondarily considering aesthetics. The latter were a valid use of the police power, while the former were not.[26] It seems that a majority of states now hold that a regulation based solely upon aesthetic considerations is legitimate.[27]

There are many ways to impose restrictions on signs, ranging from total exclusion from a given area, to limitation of location, size, height, and setback from the street. Distinctions are made between on-and off-premise signs, between those located in urban or residential areas, and between commercial and noncommercial signs. The First Amendment protection afforded speech often comes into play when a statute or ordinance is not carefully drafted and infringes on the protected right. If similarly situated signs are categorized or treated differently by the ordinance, an equal protection problem may exist. The constitutional issues relevant to sign control are covered in depth earlier in this treatise.[28]

§ 12:3   Architectural Control

Ordinances that provide for architectural design review intended to control the appearance of building are increasing in popularity.[29] Architectural design review is

---

[21] *City of Passaic v. Paterson Bill Posting, Advertising & Sign Painting Co.*, 72 N.J.L. 285, 62 A. 267, 268 (N.J. Ct. Err. & App. 1905).

[22] *St. Louis Gunning Advertisement Co. v. City of St. Louis*, 235 Mo. 99, 137 S.W. 929 (1911), dismissed, 231 U.S. 761, 34 S. Ct. 325, 58 L. Ed. 470 (1913).

[23] *Cromwell v. Ferrier*, 19 N.Y.2d 263, 279 N.Y.S.2d 22, 225 N.E.2d 749, 21 A.L.R.3d 1212 (1967).

[24] *Cromwell*, 19 N.Y.2d at 272.

[25] *Mayor and City Council of Baltimore v. Mano Swartz, Inc.*, 268 Md. 79, 299 A.2d 828, 4 Env't. Rep. Cas. (BNA) 2034, 3 Envtl. L. Rep. 20232 (1973).

[26] *Cromwell*, 19 N.Y.2d at 272.

[27] Sarah L. Goss, Nat'l Park Serv. & Nat'l Ctr. for Preservation Law, Propriety of Using the Police Power for Aesthetic Regulation: A Comprehensive State-by-State Analysis (1992).

[28] See supra § 10:17.

[29] See Regan, You Can't Build That Here: The Constitutionality of Aesthetic Zoning and Architectural Review, 58 Fordham L. Rev. 1013, 1019 (1990); Weinberg, Zoning for Aesthetics—Who Decides What Your House Will Look Like?, 28 Zoning & Plan. L. Rep. No. 9 (Oct. 2005); American Planning Association, Planning Advisory Service and Lane Kendig, Too Big Boring or Ugly: Planning and Design Tools to Combat Monotony, The Too-Big House, And Teardowns, (PAS Report 528, 2004); Garvin and Leroy, Design Guidelines: The Law of Aesthetic Controls, 55 Land Use L. & Zoning Dig. 3 (Apr. 2003).

one example of zoning based on aesthetics.[30] Like sign regulation, the standards or criteria to be applied may be included in the zoning scheme or may be enacted separately. Typically, a board is established to review designs in accordance with enumerated criteria including compatibility with surrounding area, the effect of allowing the design on neighboring property values and certain common stylistic features. Some boards also attempt to prevent monotony by requiring that the designs not be too similar while other boards may require conformity or harmony with the community's existing or even desired architecture. These boards consider all proposed buildings in a district and hold the authority to disapprove a design and deny a building permit if the requirements of the ordinance are not met.[31]

In 1954, dictum by the Supreme Court in *Berman v. Parker* [32] introduced an expanded conception of the public welfare that included aesthetics.[33] Before the *Berman* decision most courts held that architectural design review regulations could not be based solely on aesthetics. Many courts invalidated land use regulations based purely on aesthetics because they objected to the subjective nature of aesthetics. Courts also worried that majorities could use aesthetic regulation to impose their tastes on minorities. Additionally, judges were concerned that the use of the police power to promote aesthetics infringed on private property rights.[34] In spite of these concerns, Justice Douglas in *Berman* opined that "[i]t is within the power of the legislature to determine that the community should be beautiful as well as healthy, spacious as well as clean, well-balanced as well as carefully patrolled."[35] Today, a majority of states allow architectural design review regulations based solely on aesthetic considerations.[36] The remaining states are either undecided or require more than a pure aesthetic basis in order to justify architectural design review ordinances.[37]

An early case upholding architectural design review is *State ex rel. Saveland Park Holding Corp. v. Wieland.*[38] The ordinance under scrutiny provided that a building permit would not be issued if the building were so at variance with existing structures that it would cause substantial depreciation in property values. Although the express purpose of the ordinance was to protect property values, the court characterized it as being based on aesthetics, and upheld it on both grounds.[39]

---

[30] Regan, You Can't Build That Here: The Constitutionality of Aesthetic Zoning and Architectural Review, 58 Fordham L. Rev. 1013, 1015 (1990).

[31] Rice, Zoning Law: Architectural Appearance Ordinances and the First Amendment, 76 Marq. L. Rev. 439, 446 (1993).

[32] *Berman v. Parker*, 348 U.S. 26, 75 S. Ct. 98, 99 L. Ed. 27 (1954).

[33] Bunting, Unsightly Politics: Aesthetics, Sign Ordinances, and Homeowners Speech in City of Ladue v. Gilleo, 20 Harv. Envtl. L. Rev. 473, 479 (1996).

[34] Bunting, Unsightly Politics: Aesthetics, Sign Ordinances, and Homeowners Speech in City of Ladue v. Gilleo, 20 Harv. Envtl. L. Rev. 473, 478 (1996).

[35] *Berman v. Parker*, 348 U.S. 26, 33, 75 S. Ct. 98, 102–03, 99 L. Ed. 27 (1954).

[36] Shawn Rice, Zoning Law: Architectural Appearance Ordinances and the First Amendment, 76 Marq.L.Rev., 439, 445 (1993).

[37] County of Contra Costa, 21 Cal. App. 4th 330 (1993).

[38] *State ex rel. Saveland Park Holding Corp. v. Wieland*, 269 Wis. 262, 69 N.W.2d 217 (1955). Cf. *Hankins v. Borough of Rockleigh*, 55 N.J. Super. 132, 150 A.2d 63 (App. Div. 1959) (ordinance invalid as applied).

[39] See supra § 3:14 regarding preservation of values.

A classic case sustaining an architectural review board decision is *Reid v. Architectural Bd. of Review*.[40] The board had disapproved a permit for a single-story, 10-foot high house built of glass and concrete in a rough U-shape, which rambled through a grove of trees on a lot surrounded by a 10-foot fence. While the house otherwise complied with zoning requirements, it was to be built in an area of stately, older, two-and-a-half story houses. The architectural review board concluded that it should not be built, for it did not comply with the ordinance which required that the buildings maintain the high character of community development and protect real estate from impairment or destruction of value. The court held that maintenance of a high character of community appearance was within the scope of the general welfare, and while aesthetics alone would not be sufficient to sustain the ordinance, it was not enacted solely for that purpose.

Not surprisingly, these cases also involved the issue of whether the standards were adequate to guide administrative decisions. The purported standards in both ordinances were vague, but the courts did not find them so vague as to be an improper delegation of authority.

A third major case in this milieu is *State ex rel. Stoyanoff v. Berkeley*.[41] The court upheld a denial of a building permit by an architectural review board on grounds that the proposed building would not fit the architectural character of the neighborhood, and would reduce the property values of neighboring homes. The proposed residence was to be a pyramid-like structure with a flat top, and triangular windows or doors at the corners. This was found to have an adverse aesthetic impact in a community of conventional residences of rather substantial value.

An interesting complement to these three cases is *LaSalle National Bank v. Evanston*.[42] The city refused to change a zoning designation and allow building of high-rise apartments near Lake Michigan, partly on the grounds that the building would disrupt the city's attempt to effect a gradual tapering of building heights toward the open lakefront and park area, which was used for recreational purposes. The court found that aesthetic qualities were properly cognizable, and when coupled with reasonable restrictions on population density, the refusal to rezone was valid.[43]

Currently, the focus of architectural controls has shifted somewhat to the McMansions trend [44] and implementation of new urbanism concepts. Maximum house size regulations as an ingredient of architectural control are fairly new and are a response to the building of so-called monster homes, also called McMansions or starter castles, which are generally considered those from 5,000 square feet and up.[45] Caps are

---

[40] *Reid v. Architectural Bd. of Review of City of Cleveland Heights*, 119 Ohio App. 67, 26 Ohio Op. 2d 178, 92 Ohio L. Abs. 271, 192 N.E.2d 74 (8th Dist. Cuyahoga County 1963).

[41] *State ex rel. Stoyanoff v. Berkeley*, 458 S.W.2d 305, 41 A.L.R.3d 1386 (Mo. 1970).

[42] *La Salle Nat. Bank v. City of Evanston*, 57 Ill. 2d 415, 312 N.E.2d 625 (1974).

[43] See also *Landmark Land Co., Inc. v. City and County of Denver*, 728 P.2d 1281, 17 Envtl. L. Rep. 20640 (Colo. 1986) (upholding height limit to preserve mountain views from several city parks).

[44] See § 4:14, supra for a discussion of house size controls.

[45] See, generally, Garvin and LeRoy, Design Guidelines: The Law of Aesthetic Controls, 55 Land Use L. & Zoning Dig. 3 (Apr. 2003); Knack, Cutting Monster Houses Down to Size, 65 Planning 1, 4 (Oct.1999). McMansions can soar to the truly super-sized. In one case, a proposed 29-bedroom, 40-bathroom, 55,000 square foot home with a 75 car garage and a 10,000 square foot playhouse on a 63 acre tract led to the adoption of an ordinance limiting houses to 20,000 square feet. The ordinance came too late to prevent this proposal as the court found the owner had a vested right to complete his house. *Association of Friends of*

set on houses by local government who believe that such hefty houses have an adverse impact on the supply of affordable housing and are out of place with the character of the area. Some local governments also impose maximum square footage caps on "big box" commercial buildings.[46] Putting aside vested rights problems, limits on building size have generally been upheld by the courts. Architectural controls designed to implement new urbanism principles are currently in vogue and promise to greatly expand the reach and use of architectural controls. As discussed earlier,[47] new urbanism is design oriented and architectural controls are deemed necessary to achieve walkable, cohesive communities with "retro" features such as front porches, mixed use convenience, and the like.[48]

Although it is possible that the legitimacy of aesthetic regulation may vary with the kind of aesthetic control at issue, the courts have not made distinctions on these grounds. Statutes and ordinances perceived to be based exclusively or primarily upon aesthetic considerations have been either sustained or struck, according to the perception of validity of such regulation in a given jurisdiction. Decisions upholding ordinances based solely on aesthetics continued to grow in number, and in 1984, the Supreme Court affirmed aesthetics as a proper basis for the exercise of the state police power for the general welfare in *Members of City Council of City of Los Angeles v. Taxpayers for Vincent.*[49] Nonetheless, some courts still persist in requiring that additional grounds, such as protection of property values, density control, promotion of tourism, and protection of the public health and safety, be present.[50]

In addition to the general considerations affecting the validity of architectural controls, two constitutional issues frequently appear. Ordinances establishing procedures for architectural design review must set forth standards which are not unduly vague. The creation of standards that are not unduly vague can be a challenging task for legislatures given the subjective nature of aesthetics.[51] Such measures must also be narrowly drawn and must further a sufficiently substantial governmental purpose to avoid running afoul of First Amendment considerations.

The vagueness-due process challenge was raised in both *Saveland Park* and *Reid*, but each court held that the standards involved were adequate to support the factual determinations made in those cases.[52] Other courts have held architectural design ordinances to be unconstitutionally vague when the standards were not adequate to con-

---

Sagaponack v. Zoning Bd. of Appeals of the Town of Southampton, 287 A.D.2d 620, 731 N.Y.S.2d 851 (2d Dep't 2001).

[46] See § 4:14, supra.

[47] See § 9:1, supra.

[48] See French, Cities Without Soul: Standards for Architectural Controls with Growth Management Objectives, 71 U. Det. Mercy. L. Rev. 267 (1994).

[49] *Members of City Council of City of Los Angeles v. Taxpayers for Vincent*, 466 U.S. 789, 805, 104 S. Ct. 2118, 2129, 80 L. Ed. 2d 772 (1984) ("It is well settled that the state may legitimately exercise its police powers to advance aesthetic values.").

[50] See, e.g., *Village of Hudson v. Albrecht, Inc.*, 9 Ohio St. 3d 69, 458 N.E.2d 852, 857 (1984); Rice at 444, supra note 3.

[51] See Regan, You Can't Build That Here: The Constitutionality of Aesthetic Zoning and Architectural Review, 58 Fordham L. Rev. 1013, 1025 (1990);

[52] See *Reid v. Architectural Bd. of Review of City of Cleveland Heights*, 119 Ohio App. 67, 26 Ohio Op. 2d 178, 92 Ohio L. Abs. 271, 192 N.E.2d 74 (8th Dist. Cuyahoga County 1963); *State ex rel. Saveland Park Holding Corp. v. Wieland*, 269 Wis. 262, 69 N.W.2d 217 (1955). Compare *Historic Green Springs, Inc. v. Bergland*, 497 F. Supp. 839, 14 Env't. Rep. Cas. (BNA) 2057, 11 Envtl. L. Rep. 20034 (E.D. Va. 1980).

trol the exercise of the reviewing board's discretion.[53] Proper standards are necessary for reasonable implementation of aesthetic zoning because they help avoid the abuse of discretion inherent in decisions based on aesthetics.[54] When standards incorporated into an ordinance are sufficiently certain that they can be understood by the regulated group, implemented by the administering agency, and applied by the reviewing court, the chances that the ordinance will survive judicial scrutiny are greatly increased.[55] Standards may be found in the consistency or patterns of community preference.[56] For example, communities may favor billboard controls[57] or preservation of historic-architectural "ensembles" such as New Orleans' Vieux Carre.[58] Thus, the presence of expressly articulated standards is exceedingly important. When combined with separation of powers considerations and the judiciary's inability to determine community aesthetic values, such standards will often warrant granting a legislative presumption of validity to an architectural control.[59]

Aesthetic regulation based on the offensiveness of the expression or architectural design can amount to censorship, and thus raise freedom of expression concerns.[60] While the Supreme Court has not addressed the question of whether architecture is speech, many support the idea that it is a form of protected expression.[61] Permit denials, such as those in *Reid*, *Stoyanoff* and *Saveland Park*, are in a sense content-based restrictions on expression rather than simply time, place and manner regulations. A connection between the offensive expression and a threat to a substantial governmental interest may be sufficient to rebut a First Amendment challenge. The question becomes one of how to define a community's burden of proving that failure to regulate "design as expression" would threaten a substantial governmental interest. In *Penn Central*,[62] the Court found that the interest in preserving landmarks was sufficiently

---

[53] *R.S.T. Builders, Inc. v. Village of Bolingbrook*, 141 Ill. App. 3d 41, 95 Ill. Dec. 423, 489 N.E.2d 1151 (3d Dist. 1986); *De Sena v. Board of Zoning Appeals of Inc. Village of Hempstead*, 45 N.Y.2d 105, 408 N.Y.S.2d 14, 379 N.E.2d 1144 (1978); *Anderson v. City of Issaquah*, 70 Wash. App. 64, 851 P.2d 744 (Div. 1 1993).

[54] See Tappendorf, Architectural Design Ordinances, SM004 ALI-ABA 497 (2006) (ALI-ABA Continuing Legal Education August 17–19, 2006, Land Use Institute Designing and Implementing an Effective Compliance Program for Mutual Funds, Investment Advisers, and Broker-Dealers, Cosponsored by the Center for Urban and Environmental Solutions, Florida Atlantic University.).

[55] See, e.g., *Morristown Road Associates v. Mayor and Common Council and Planning Bd. of Borough of Bernardsville*, 163 N.J. Super. 58, 394 A.2d 157 (Law Div. 1978).

[56] See, generally, Costonis, Law and Aesthetics: A Critique and Reformulation of the Dilemmas, 80 Mich. L. Rev. 355 (1982).

[57] *United Advertising Corp. v. Borough of Metuchen*, 42 N.J. 1, 198 A.2d 447 (1964); *People v. Goodman*, 31 N.Y.2d 262, 338 N.Y.S.2d 97, 290 N.E.2d 139 (1972).

[58] *Maher v. City of New Orleans*, 516 F.2d 1051, 5 Envtl. L. Rep. 20524 (5th Cir. 1975).

[59] See *Metromedia, Inc. v. City of San Diego*, 453 U.S. 490, 101 S. Ct. 2882, 69 L. Ed. 2d 800, 16 Env't. Rep. Cas. (BNA) 1057, 11 Envtl. L. Rep. 20600 (1981). See also Garvin and Jourdan, Through the Looking Glass: Analyzing the Potential Legal Challenges to Form-Based Codes, 23 J. Land Use & Envtl. L. 395, 411 (2008).

[60] "Nothing to my mind could be worse imposition than to have some individual, even temporarily, deliberately fix the outward forms of his concept of beauty upon the future of a free people or even of a growing city." Frank Lloyd Wright, In the Cause of Architecture, Second Paper (May 1914), reprinted in Hugh Dunlan & Martin Filler, eds., Architectural Record 125 (1975).

[61] Shawn Rice, Zoning Law: Architectural Appearance Ordinances and the First Amendment, 76 Marq.L.Rev., 439, 450 (1993) See also Nivala, Constitutional Architecture: The First Amendment and the Single Family House, 33 San Diego L. Rev. 291, 316 (1996).

[62] *Penn Cent. Transp. Co. v. City of New York*, 438 U.S. 104, 98 S. Ct. 2646, 57 L. Ed. 2d 631, 11 Env't. Rep. Cas. (BNA) 1801, 8 Envtl. L. Rep. 20528 (1978).

substantial to withstand a takings claim. Whether the rationale would stand in the face of a First Amendment challenge is yet an unresolved issue.[63]

Restrictive covenants are alternatives to the public regulation of aesthetics. Restrictive covenants are land use controls that deprive from private agreement to restrict the use of land.[64] The general absence of state action reduces, but does not eliminate, First Amendment considerations.[65] Currently, many states allow aesthetic control through restrictive covenants. Many states approve these covenants if they are exercised reasonably and in good faith. Additionally, courts have been less stringent in scrutinizing aesthetic standards in covenants, thus providing a flexible, yet private answer to aesthetic regulation.[66]

II. HISTORIC PRESERVATION

§ 12:4 Introduction

In the opening discussion of aesthetics and architectural regulation, our first concern was with defining beauty or that which is "aesthetically pleasing."[67] Now, we must pose an equally difficult question, what is the meaning of *historic*? Does it mean "old" or "significant in history" or both? Whatever definition is formulated, the most essential aspect of the concept is *why* we preserve, protect and restore "historic" resources.

Professor Robert Stipe's list of reasons for preserving historic resources deserves to be and has become a classic.

First, we seek to preserve because our historic resources are all that physically link us to our past. Some portion of that patrimony must be preserved if we are to recognize who we are, how we became so and, most important, how we differ from others of our species. * * * Second, we strive to save our historic and architectural heritage simply because we have lived with it and it has become part of us. The presence of our physical past creates expectations and anticipations that are important parts of our daily lives. We tend to replace them only when they no longer have meaning, when other needs are more pressing, and do so with caution, knowing how our environment creates us and how we create our environment.

Third, we save our physical heritage partly because we live in an age of frightening communication and other technological abilities, as well as in an era of increasing cultural homogeneity. In such a situation we subconsciously reach out for any opportunity to maintain difference and uniqueness.

Fourth, we preserve historic sites and structures because of their relation to past events, eras, movements and persons that we feel are important to honor and understand. * * * Nostalgia and patriotism are important human emotions for

---

[63] See Nivala, Constitutional Architecture: The First Amendment and the Single Family House, 33 San Diego L. Rev. 291 (1996) (arguing that the exterior design of a private home is constitutionally-protected expression of the inhabitants).

[64] See Regan, You Can't Build That Here: The Constitutionality of Aesthetic Zoning and Architectural Review, 58 Fordham L. Rev. 1013, 1030 (1990); See infra §§ 15:4 to 15:9 regarding private controls.

[65] See infra § 15:10, regarding constitutional issues.

[66] Regan, You Can't Build That Here: The Constitutionality of Aesthetic Zoning and Architectural Review, 58 Fordham L. Rev. 1013, 1029-30 (1990);

[67] See supra § 12:1.

preservation, and important human emotions must be served. But the important point is that the historic associations inherent in preserved structures and sites should encourage much more than mere nostalgia and patriotism. They are potential sources of imagination and creativity in our attempts to understand and appreciate the past—a past distant from us, but a time that can still offer much to guide us.

Fifth, we seek to preserve the architecture and landscapes of the past simply because of their intrinsic value as art. * * * Sixth, we seek to preserve our past because we believe in the right of our cities and countryside to be beautiful. Here, with much regret, we must reorganize the essential tawdriness of much contemporary design and construction. Much of it is junk; it assaults our senses. We seek to preserve the past, not only because it is unique, exceptional, architecturally significant or historically important, but also because in most cases what replaces it will be inhuman and grotesque. Potentially, of course, many old buildings could be demolished and replaced with contemporary structures of equal functional or aesthetic value. Yet, recent experience has shown that this is not likely, and until it is we shall preserve our past in order to preserve what is left of our pleasing and humane urban and rural landscape.

Finally, and most important of all, we seek to preserve because we have discovered—all too belatedly—that preservation can serve an important human and social purpose in our society. Ancestor worship and aesthetic motivations are no longer enough: our traditional concern with great events, great people and great architects will not serve society in any full measure. The problem now is to acknowledge that historic conservation is but one aspect of the larger problem, basically an environmental one, of enhancing, or perhaps providing for the first time, a quality of human life.[68]

§ 12:5   History of Historic Preservation in the United States

Historic preservation [69] in the United States began in the mid 1800's with a private attempt to rescue Mt. Vernon from an uncertain fate. At the time the only means for protecting a landmark of historical significance was private purchase by preserva-

---

[68] Robert Stipe, Why Preserve Historic Resources?, Legal Techniques in Historic Preservation (1972).

[69] In the preface to the well-respected work, A Handbook on Historic Preservation Law, the editor, Christopher Duerksen, addresses what is meant by preservation law:

'Just what is "preservation law"? It is a collage, cutting across and drawing from several other established areas of law: land use and zoning, real property, taxation, local government, constitutional, and administrative. In many ways preservation law, particularly at the local level, is closest to land use and zoning; the rules are very similar. For example, the standards that dictate governmental behavior in enacting and administering zoning ordinances are virtually identical to those applicable to local landmark and historic district laws, and the constitutional doctrines governing regulation of private property are similar.

For discussions of the development of historic preservation law in the United States and abroad, see generally Callies, Historic Preservation Law in the United States, 32 Envtl. L. Rep. 10348 (2002); Sax, Is Anyone Minding Stonehenge? The Origins of Cultural Property Protection in England, 78 Cal. L. Rev 1543 (1990); Sax, Heritage Preservation as a Public Duty: Abbe Gregoire and the Origins of an Idea, 88 Mich. L. Rev 1142 (1990); Rose, Preservation and Community: New Directions in the Law of Historic Preservation, 33 Stan. L. Rev. 473 (1981). For an overview of historic preservation law prepared by the National Trust for Historic Preservation, see Julia H. Miller, A Layperson's Guide to Historic Preservation Law: A Survey of Federal, State, and Local Laws Governing Historic Resource Protection (2004).

tionists. The focus was generally local, and aimed at preventing destruction of a single building.[70]

Congress injected itself into the preservation field some time later when it began purchasing Civil War battlefield sites. This action resulted in *United States v. Gettysburg Electric Railway Co.*,[71] which involved condemnation of private property for the creation of a national battleground memorial. The Court rejected the narrow view that the condemnation was not for a valid public purpose, and held that preservation of an important monument to the country's past was a proper purpose. Thus, the tool of eminent domain was established as a valid method for protecting our historical heritage.

A more complicated and less well settled question was that of whether government regulatory powers could be similarly employed to limit uses or structures not inherently noxious, particularly without payment of compensation to the owner. Although regulation is now a well-recognized preservation technique, early decisions were not as broad minded about the application of the police power for such purposes. One of the first steps toward a more expansive use of regulatory power came in *Welch v. Swasey*,[72] where the United States Supreme Court upheld a Boston ordinance limiting building heights under the state police power, notably for fire prevention. Seventeen years later, the Court, in *Village of Euclid v. Ambler Realty*,[73] validated a zoning regulation which reduced the plaintiff's property value by almost 75%. The Court found that the burden was imposed in a nondiscriminatory manner, and the benefits accrued to all property owners as well; thus the regulation was reasonable. With this expansive view of the police power, these cases laid the groundwork that allowed preservation programs to grow.

About the same time, the use of the historic district as a preservation tool was gaining considerable support not just for economic but for architectural reasons. In 1931, Charleston, South Carolina, enacted the first law that was effective to protect an historic area, the city's pre-civil war district. The Vieux Carre, in New Orleans, was established pursuant to a Louisiana Constitutional amendment in 1936,[74] and in 1939, San Antonio passed a preservation law. By 1956, still only a handful of cities had enacted such laws. They were very controversial, but despite owner opposition, nearly all challenges to historic district ordinances were rejected.[75]

---

[70] See C. Hosmer, Presence of the Past (1965).

[71] *U.S. v. Gettysburg Electric R. Co.*, 160 U.S. 668, 16 S. Ct. 427, 40 L. Ed. 576 (1896). See also *Roe v. State of Kansas ex rel. Smith*, 278 U.S. 191, 49 S. Ct. 160, 73 L. Ed. 259 (1929).

[72] *Welch v. Swasey*, 214 U.S. 91, 29 S. Ct. 567, 53 L. Ed. 923 (1909).

[73] *Village of Euclid, Ohio v. Ambler Realty Co.*, 272 U.S. 365, 47 S. Ct. 114, 71 L. Ed. 303, 4 Ohio L. Abs. 816, 54 A.L.R. 1016 (1926).

[74] See La. Const. Art. 14, § 22A (creating the Vieux Carre Commission to preserve such buildings in the district as it deems to have archaeological and historical significance). For a discussion of the role that historic preservation concepts and regulations have played in rebuilding New Orleans after Katrina, see Christoff, House of the Setting Sun: New Orleans, Katrina, and the Role of Historic Preservation Laws in Emergency Circumstances, 5 Geo. L.J. 781 (2007).

[75] *City of New Orleans v. Impastato*, 198 La. 206, 3 So. 2d 559 (1941) (upholding Vieux Carre Ordinance); *Opinion of the Justices to the Senate*, 333 Mass. 773, 128 N.E.2d 557 (1955) (upholding creation of historic district commissions in Boston and Nantucket); *Fabiano v. City of Boston*, 49 Mass. App. Ct. 281, 730 N.E.2d 311 (2000); *Billy Graham Evangelistic Ass'n v. City of Minneapolis*, 667 N.W.2d 117 (Minn. 2003); *Bruley v. City of Birmingham*, 259 Mich. App. 619, 675 N.W.2d 910 (2003); *Roman Catholic Bishop of Springfield v. City of Springfield*, 760 F. Supp. 2d 172 (D. Mass. 2011).

§ 12:6   Preservation at the Federal Level

Federal legislation has also played an important role in the advancement of preservation.[76] In 1906, Congress passed the Antiquities Act,[77] allowing the President to designate national monuments, primarily from federally-owned sites. Ten years later, the National Park Service was created, and it soon became the primary focus for federal preservation efforts. In 1935, Congress enacted the Historic Sites Act,[78] which for the first time conceived of historic preservation as national policy. In addition, the Act extended the Department of Interior's authority beyond federally owned properties to identify and survey historic sites throughout the country. This program later became the frame-work for the National Register of Historic Places. Not much later came the National Trust for Historic Preservation Act,[79] which facilitated private participation in preservation by creating a non-profit congressionally chartered corporation.[80] Finally, in 1966, Congress passed the National Historic Preservation Act (NHPA),[81] which has become the basis for most of the administrative and protective devices, as well as the financial incentives, through which national preservation policy is now implemented.

The National Historic Preservation Act (NHPA)[82] provides the authority for a number of activities which implement the federal historic preservation program:[83] i) the National Register of Historic places, identifying and listing historic and cultural resources;[84] ii) an expanded national register to include sites of state and local significance, establishing standards for evaluating historic significance;[85] iii) the matching grants-in-aid program, encouraging preservation activities at the state and local levels;[86] iv) the Advisory Council on Historic Preservation, providing information on historic properties to the executive and other federal agencies;[87] and v) the "section 106" review process, for protection of federal resources.

Under the act, "historic resources of federal interest" are broadly defined, so that not only nationally significant properties, but those important at local and state levels as well, are eligible for designation.[88] Listing on the National Register qualifies a prop-

---

[76] For an overview of federal historic preservation law prepared by the National Trust for Historic Preservation, see Julia H. Miller, A Layperson's Guide to Historic Preservation Law: A Survey of Federal, State, and Local Laws Governing Historic Resource Protection (2004).

[77] 16 U.S.C.A. §§ 431 et seq.

[78] 16 U.S.C.A. § 461 et seq. See *Preservation Coalition of Erie County v. Federal Transit Admin.*, 129 F. Supp. 2d 551 (W.D. N.Y. 2000).

[79] 16 U.S.C.A. § 468.

[80] The website for the National Trust for Historic Preservation is: http://www.nationaltrust.org/.

[81] 16 U.S.C.A. § 470 et seq.

[82] Pub. L. No. 89–665, 80 Stat. 915, codified at 16 U.S.C.A. §§ 470 et seq.

[83] See, generally, Callies, Historic Preservation Law in the United States, 32 Envtl. L. Rep. 10348 (2002); C. Duerksen ed., A Handbook on Historic Preservation 214 (1983); Julia H. Miller, A Survey of Federal, State, and Local Laws Governing Historic Resource Protection, Preservation Information 1 (1997).

[84] 16 U.S.C.A. § 470a. An important aspect of the National Register is the National Historic Landmarks Program. Operated under the auspices of the National Park Service, the program provides for designation and protection of national landmarks. Once designated, a national landmark receives even greater protection from the impact of federal projects than even the § 106 review process provides. See 16 U.S.C.A. § 470a(a)(l)(B).

[85] 16 U.S.C.A. § 470a(a)(2). The criteria are found at 36 C.F.R. § 60.4.

[86] 16 U.S.C.A. § 470a(c).

[87] 16 U.S.C.A. §§ 470i to 470j.

[88] 36 C.F.R. § 60.4. The National Register criteria for evaluation are:

erty for participation in most of the federal incentive and protective programs.[89] Most properties find their way onto the Register through local initiative, followed by a process of state review and nomination in accordance with federal criteria.[90]

The National Historic Preservation Fund [91] provides matching grants to the states to carry out the purposes of the NHPA. The monies are used to conduct statewide surveys, prepare nominations to the National Register, and develop state preservation plans. In addition, the funds are used to support the necessary administrative structure of state programs, and financially assist the restoration of Register properties within the state.[92] This portion of the act has been a great impetus in establishing historic preservation at the state level, and its requirements for participation in the grants program have led to greater administrative uniformity among state activities.

The Advisory Council on Historic Preservation (ACHP) is a cabinet level body which advises the president and Congress on preservation matters. It also comments on federal projects which may impact on historic properties, and aids in coordinating activities of federal agencies affecting preservation.[93] Its principal role, however, is the review and comment responsibility under section 106 of the Act.[94]

Section 106 [95] brings together all elements of the federal preservation program to provide the basic federal legal protection for historic properties. Federal agencies must seek the council's comments for any action they wish to pursue which may affect a property either on or eligible for inclusion on the National Register of Historic Places. Like NEPA,[96] the provision mandates that an evaluation and analysis process be followed prior to approval of federal projects affecting historic properties. However, the ACHP's recommendations are not binding, and a proposed action may proceed once the review process is completed, regardless of a disfavorable recommendation. This does

---

The quality of significance in American history, architecture, archeology, engineering, and culture is present in districts, sites, buildings, structures, and objects that possess integrity of location, design, setting, materials, workmanship, feeling, and association and

(a) that are associated with events that have made a significant contribution to the broad patterns of our history; or

(b) that are associated with the lives of persons significant in our past; or

(c) that embody the distinctive characteristics of a type, period, or method of construction, or that represent the work of a master, or that possess high artistic values, or that represent a significant and distinguishable entity whose components may lack individual distinction; or

(d) that have yielded, or may be likely to yield, information important in prehistory or history. Id.

[89] 16 U.S.C.A. § 470f.

[90] Properties may become eligible for inclusion on the register when nominated by: 1) a State Historic Preservation Officer, qualified local government, or individual, 2) the head of a federal agency, 3) the Secretary of the Interior, by designating the property as a National Landmark, or 4) by Congress. See Duerksen, supra note 6, at 197.

[91] 16 U.S.C.A. § 470h. See also 16 U.S.C.A. § 470a(d).

[92] Due to recent cutbacks in funding, most federal money is now being spent on surveying and documentation of historic sites and structures, and little money is available for the less critical programs. The Trust's various funding programs, most of which come from private donations, include: National Preservation Endowment, National Trust Loan Funds, National Trust Community Investment Corporation, Save America's Treasures, Federal Rehabilitation Tax Credit, Transportation Enhancements Funding, Historic Preservation Fund, National Park Service, Lowe's Charitable and Educational Foundation Preservation Fund, Profiles of Preservation Revolving Funds

[93] 16 U.S.C.A. § 470j.

[94] 16 U.S.C.A. § 470f.

[95] 16 U.S.C.A. § 470f.

[96] 42 U.S.C.A. §§ 4321 to 4370d.

not mean section 106 review is entirely without teeth. Even a determination of whether it is necessary to comply can take several years to complete. It is important to note that the Section 106 review process is applicable only to federal agencies and agencies proceeding with federally funded projects. Thus, state or local regulation is necessary to impose any sort of review process on projects affecting historic properties that are proposed by state or local governments, or by private individuals.

Two other federal statutes are important in establishing the federal structure for national historic preservation: the National Environmental Policy Act (NEPA) and the Department of Transportation Act (DTA). NEPA requires consideration of impact on cultural environment as part of the environmental impact statement process.[97] Section 4(f) of the Department of Transportation Act contains some of the strongest language of all federal acts relevant to historic preservation because it *prohibits* federal approval or funding of transportation projects that require the use, direct or indirect, of historic sites unless there is no feasible or prudent alternative and the project includes all possible planning to minimize harm to the site.[98]

In addition to the NHPA, NEPA, and DTA, several other federal statutes provide a number of other tools and incentives to preservationists. They include the Coastal Zone Management Act,[99] the Surface Mining Control and Reclamation Act,[100] and the Archeological Resources Protection Act.[101] Several statutes provide federal aid for preservation through loans, grants and use of surplus government buildings.[102] The Public Buildings Cooperative Use Act [103] directs the General Services Administration to give preference to use of historic buildings for federal offices.

The Tax Reform Act of 1976 and the Economic Recovery Tax Act of 1981 created federal tax incentives, reflecting a shift in the policy of the Internal Revenue Code from penalizing to encouraging property owners to invest in preservation.[104] To qualify for a rehabilitation investment credit, a taxpayer must incur qualified expenses for rehabilitation of a certified historic structure. This eligibility determination relies heavily on the State Historic Preservation Officer's (SHPO) review of a lengthy application and recommendation to the regional office of the Secretary of the Interior. Any property or district on the National Register is automatically certified historic, and property within a registered district may also be certified if the enabling ordinance and the ordinance

---

[97] 42 U.S.C.A. § 4321 (it is the continuing responsibility of the Federal Government to use all practical means . . . to . . . preserve important historic, cultural, and natural aspects of our national heritage).

[98] 49 U.S.C.A. § 303. See Julia Miller, A Survey of Federal, State, and Local Laws Governing Historic Resource Protection 7 (2004).

[99] See e.g., The National Coastal Zone Management Act, 16 U.S.C.A. §§ 1451 to 1465. For an insightful analysis of the CZMA as applied to Preservation objectives, see generally Schmitz, The Coastal Zone Management Act's Role in Historic Preservation, Vol. 4 No. 6 Preserv'n L. Rep. (Dec. 1985).

[100] 30 U.S.C.A. § 1201 ("[N]o surface mining operations . . . shall be permitted which will adversely affect any . . . places included in the National Register of Historic Sites unless approved jointly by the regulatory authority and the Federal, State, or local agency with jurisdiction over the . . . historic site."). Section 106 does not apply directly to individual mining permits issued by the states in spite of a Congressional amendment to that effect in 1992. See *National Min. Ass'n v. Fowler*, 324 F.3d 752 (D.C. Cir. 2003); Julia Miller, A Survey of Federal, State, and Local Laws Governing Historic Resource Protection 10 (2004).

[101] 16 U.S.C.A. § 470. See Julia Miller, A Survey of Federal, State, and Local Laws Governing Historic Resource Protection 19 (1997).

[102] E.g., 42 U.S.C.A. §§ 5304(h), 5318 (Block Grants and Urban Development Action Grants).

[103] 40 U.S.C.A. § 611(c) (1997).

[104] Tax Reform Act of 1976, 26 U.S.C.A. §§ 167, 168 (permitting accelerated depreciation); Economic Recovery Tax Act of 1981, 26 U.S.C.A. §§ 44, 48(g) (allowing investment tax credits).

creating the district qualify under National Register Criteria. Once the structure is certified, the proposed rehabilitation work itself must also be reviewed and certified. In making the review, the SHPO follows the Department of Interior's "Standards for Rehabilitation and Guidelines for Rehabilitating Historic Buildings," to determine whether the work is consistent with the historic character of the building.[105] Finally, to qualify for the tax benefits, the building must have been "substantially rehabilitated."[106] In the 1986 tax reform act, Congress limited the availability and amount of the credit.[107]

The legal role of the federal government, in spite of all of the federal acts discussed above, is largely confined to regulating its own activities with respect to historic properties. Despite their limitations, the federal legislation has had a marked catalytic effect on programs at state and local levels. All states and territories have now enacted historic preservation laws, and hundreds of historic districts or landmark commissions have been created.[108]

§ 12:7   State Historic Preservation Law

The 1980 amendments to the National Historic Preservation Act (NHPA) greatly increased the states' role under the federal preservation scheme. The diminished federal involvement, while reducing funding, has given states the opportunity to assume greater responsibility for preservation and to better respond to the individual needs of the state. Over the past 50 years, every state and more than 500 municipalities have enacted laws to encourage or require the preservation of buildings and areas with historical or aesthetic importance. *Penn Cent. Transp. Co. v New York City.*[109] Various types of laws have been utilized: grants of power to local governments to preserve historic resources through zoning, establishment of historic districts and commissions, creation of state agencies with preservation powers, state registers of historic places, environmental policy acts which consider the adverse effects of government actions on historic resources, and even inclusion of historic preservation policy in a few state constitutions.[110]

States can delegate regulatory authority in several ways. Most provide localities with power to enact historic district zoning, and some allow for landmark designa-

---

[105] See 36 C.F.R. § 67.7.

[106] 26 U.S.C.A. § 47(c)(1)(A)(i).

[107] See White and Keating, Historic Preservation and Architectural Control Law, 24 Urb. Law. 865 (1992); Cheverine and Hayes, Rehabilitation Tax Credit: Does is Still Provide Incentive?, 10 Va. Tax Rev. 167 (1990). The current status of the rehabilitation tax credit is summarized thusly by the National Trust: "Federal law provides a federal income tax credit equal to 20% of the cost of rehabilitating a historic building for commercial use. To qualify for the credit, the property must be a certified historic structure—that is, on the National Register of Historic Places or contributing to a registered historic district. (Nonhistoric buildings built before 1936 qualify for a 10% tax credit.) A substantial rehabilitation is necessary, and the work must meet the Secretary of the Interior's Standards for Rehabilitation . . . At present, individuals rehabilitating a historic property for their primary residence do not qualify for this tax credit." http://www.nationaltrust.org/funding/nonprofit.html#federal.

[108] See Directory of American Preservation Commissions III (S. Dennis ed. 1981); Beckwith, Appendix of State & Territorial Historic Preservation Statutes and Session Laws, 11 N.C. Cent. L.J. 308 (1980).

[109] *Penn Cent. Transp. Co. v. City of New York*, 438 U.S. 104, 98 S. Ct. 2646, 57 L. Ed. 2d 631, 11 Env't. Rep. Cas. (BNA) 1801, 8 Envtl. L. Rep. 20528 (1978).

[110] E.g., La. Const. Art. VI, § 17; Cal. Const. Art. XIII, § 8; Md. Const. Art. 51; Mo. Const. Art. III, § 48; N.Y. Const. Art. XIV, § 4. See Callies, Historic Preservation Law in the United States, 32 Envtl. L. Rep. 10348 (2002). For an overview of state historic preservation laws prepared by the National Trust for Historic Preservation, see Julia H. Miller, A Layperson's Guide to Historic Preservation Law: A Survey of Federal, State, and Local Laws Governing Historic Resource Protection (2004).

tion.[111] The standard zoning power generally can be used to protect historic areas and to require special standards and review procedures for actions proposed within them. Regulations which designate landmarks or establish historic districts have generally been upheld by courts as a valid use of local authority to promote the general welfare.[112]

Most states authorize local preservation bodies to acquire historic properties.[113] They may be acquired not only in fee simple but in less-than-fee interests, such as facade or conservation easements.[114] Acquisition power also includes that of eminent domain which results in condemnation for a public purpose and payment of just compensation. Localities also have the responsibility of raising funds to foster preservation and maintain the properties under their dominion.[115]

Acquisition of full ownership of property is expensive and often has the effect of removing property from the local tax base. These drawbacks have limited its use as a preservation tool. On the other hand, enabling local governments or other bodies to accept preservation easements, or enter into and enforce partial acquisition contracts and covenants, results in less cost but offers many of the same protective benefits.[116]

Another technique enjoying some recent success is the use of a revolving funds program to purchase, or to acquire options on historic properties. Once purchased, a structure is sold to a new owner who covenants to maintain the building's historic character. The money realized from this sale is then reused to purchase and protect other historic structures.

---

[111] Zax, Protection of the Built Environment: A Washington D.C. Case Study in Historic Preservation, 19 B.C. Envtl. Aff. L. Rev. 651 (1992). See e.g., Cal. Gov't Code §§ 50280 to 50290; Colo. Rev. Stat. §§ 24–80–1201 to 24–80–1202; D.C. Code §§ 5.801 to 5.805; Fla. Stat. Ann. §§ 380.501 to 380.515; Haw. Rev. Stat. §§ 46–4.5, 246–34; N.Y. Gen. Mun. Law § 96-a.

[112] See, e.g., *Estate of Tippett v. City of Miami*, 645 So. 2d 533 (Fla. 3d DCA 1994) (where landowner claimed that creation of historic district that included her property was an unconstitutional taking); *Figarsky v. Historic Dist. Commission of City of Norwich*, 171 Conn. 198, 368 A.2d 163, 6 Envtl. L. Rep. 20654 (1976) (denial of demolition permit by historic commission upheld where local preservation ordinance incorporated by reference state enabling statute); *A-S-P Associates v. City of Raleigh*, 298 N.C. 207, 258 S.E.2d 444 (1979) (approving legislative grant of authority to locality for creation of historic district); *City of Santa Fe v. Gamble-Skogmo, Inc.*, 73 N.M. 410, 389 P.2d 13 (1964) (city had sufficient authority to impose criminal sanctions for violations of preservation ordinance).

[113] Beckwith, Developments in the Law of Historic Preservation and a Reflection on Liberty, 12 Wake Forest L. Rev. 93 (1976).

[114] *U.S. v. Albrecht*, 496 F.2d 906 (8th Cir. 1974). A preservation easement may be created by purchase or donation. Put simply, it is an agreement between a landowner and a locality or charitable organization giving the latter the right to monitor and protect the architectural and historic integrity of the property. The concept represents a statutory departure from the common law's hostility toward easements in gross and is quite similar to conservation easements used to protect agricultural and environmentally sensitive lands. See also § 13:12, infra and § 15:3, infra.

[115] See, e.g., Fla. Stat. Ann. § 704.06; Mich. Comp. Laws Ann. § 5.3395; N.Y. Gen. Mun. Law §§ 119-aa to 119-dd.

[116] The advantages are primarily financial. Because the cost of a typical facade easement is around 10% of the structure's value, the amount of money normally required to purchase just one historic structure can now be used to protect 10 structures (assuming similar value) through acquisition of only a preservation easement. An added benefit is that the cost of maintenance and repairs is borne by the owner, further lessening the locality's financial commitment. Finally, federal tax incentives in the form of charitable deductions for donation of easements make this preservation technique especially popular with property owners. See, generally, Lord, The Advantages of Facade Easements, Legal Techniques in Historic Preservation, National Trust for Historic Preservation in the U.S., 35 (1971).

Some states have enacted tax laws to aid and promote historic preservation. Among the available methods are granting localities specific power to reduce tax burdens on historic properties [117] and giving tax credits for restoration of buildings in historic districts.[118] The state may in some cases provide financing to the locality to the extent revenues are reduced. Under such a scheme, if a structure is subsequently destroyed or put to incompatible use, the owner repays taxes saved.[119] One of the greatest barriers to use of this device by state and local government is the fear of lost revenue.[120]

There are also laws or programs in several states within state environmental policy acts (SEPA), which require extensive review of planned activities. These acts essentially mirror the policy and provisions of NEPA.[121] In nearly every SEPA, historic properties are included within the definition of the environment, and a permit to demolish a registered property would probably come under review. This is an important supplement to preservation at the state level because activities which would be generally outside the scope of other laws may be covered by a SEPA.[122]

Although most states, with or without a SEPA, have adopted their own version of § 106 of the NHPA, there are some exceptions which make it essential to check the exact language of the relevant state statute. Florida, for example, has modeled its statute after the stronger § 4f of the DTA.[123]

§ 12:8   Historic Preservation at the Local Level

The most important preservation work occurs at the local level, and it is here that the major issues are encountered and resolved.[124] It was from a local regulation which allowed designation of landmarks in New York City that *Penn Central Transportation Co. v. New York*[125] arose. There, the Supreme Court of the United States affirmed community power to adopt ordinances which control what owners of historic buildings can do with their properties.

It is no accident that local regulation plays such an important role in our preservation scheme. As noted above,[126] the NHPA provides protection from only the potentially intrusive projects of federal government agencies. Thus, even if a locality is listed

---

[117] Or. Rev. Stat. §§ 358.475 to 358. 565.

[118] Ala. Code § 11–68–5(11) (1996).

[119] Wilson and Winkler, Response of State Legislation to Historic Preservation, 36 Law & Contemp. Probs. 329 (1971).

[120] Cheverine and Hayes, Rehabilitation Tax Credit: Does It Still Provide Incentives, 10 Va. Tax Rev. 167 (1990); Silver, Note: Federal Tax Incentives for Historic Preservation: A Strategy for Conservation and Investment, 10 Hofstra L. Rev. 887 (1982); Powers, Tax Incentives for Historic Preservation, 12 Urb. Law. 103 (1980).

[121] Johnson, NEPA and SEPA's in the Quest for Environmental Justice, 30 Loy. L.A. L. Rev. 565 (1997).

[122] NEPA and NHPA, again, only regulate federal use of its own property or major federal actions with significant effect on the environment. A SEPA would catch state activities which otherwise would fall through the cracks in federal law.

[123] Fla. Stat. Ann. § 267.061.

[124] For an overview of historic preservation law at the local government level prepared by the National Trust for Historic Preservation, see Julia H. Miller, A Layperson's Guide to Historic Preservation Law: A Survey of Federal, State, and Local Laws Governing Historic Resource Protection (NTHP 2000, rev. 2008).

[125] *Penn Cent. Transp. Co. v. City of New York*, 438 U.S. 104, 98 S. Ct. 2646, 57 L. Ed. 2d 631, 11 Env't. Rep. Cas. (BNA) 1801, 8 Envtl. L. Rep. 20528 (1978).

[126] See supra, § 12:8.

on the National Register of Historic Places, additional protection is needed to prevent alteration or demolition of historic properties by private individuals or state and local governments. This protection usually comes in the form of a local preservation ordinance.

Generally, local regulatory schemes are fairly simple and are usually considered to be just another type of zoning control. A preservation program is typically initiated by a locality through appropriate enabling legislation, which establishes a preservation overlay zone, sets forth criteria for inclusion in the district, and creates some sort of a preservation review board. Under the scheme, owners of designated historic properties must seek board approval prior to proceeding with any proposed alterations to the property. The amount of authority vested in a review board varies and may extend to cover demolition and new construction or may be limited to regulating exterior alterations.[127]

As might be expected, legal challenges—including the takings challenge—are frequently raised and litigated at this stage.[128] Owners of designated property, dissatisfied with the review board's denial of a certificate of appropriateness,[129] often question the sufficiency of due process in both the creation[130] and application of the preservation ordinance. Many localities have successfully anticipated the problem and have thwarted such attacks through careful ordinance drafting. Seeking to avoid vagueness challenges, localities often incorporate NHPA review standards, for which a considerable body of interpretive case law already exists. Safety valves, allowing for exception to the regulatory scheme where economic hardship would occur, are another means of dealing with a potential takings challenge.

A good preservation or landmarks control program commonly contains three elements: 1) a survey, to establish the basis for designation and regulation; 2) a means of providing technical and economic assistance, to aid historic property owners, and 3) some sort of synchronization with the jurisdiction's comprehensive plan, zoning ordinances or other regulatory programs.[131]

The 1980 amendments to the NHPA emphasized surveys and inventories. Under the amended act, states must maintain surveys to be eligible for National Register

---

[127] See Mallard, Avoiding the "Disneyland Facade": The Reach of Architectural Controls Exercised By Historic Districts Over Internal Features of Structures, 8 Widener L. Symp. J. 323 (2002).

[128] See, e.g., *Penn Cent. Transp. Co. v. City of New York*, 438 U.S. 104, 98 S. Ct. 2646, 57 L. Ed. 2d 631, 11 Env't. Rep. Cas. (BNA) 1801, 8 Envtl. L. Rep. 20528 (1978).

See also, Byrne, Regulatory Takings Challenges to Historic Preservation Laws After Penn Central, 15 Fordham Envt'l L. Rev. 313 (2004).

[129] A certificate of appropriateness is a fundamental requirement of any preservation ordinance. It is essentially a requirement that proposed changes to an historic structure within a designated district be reviewed by a preservation commission to ensure that the changes are in harmony with the character, significant features, and atmosphere of the structure or area. See, generally, Recommended Model Provisions for a Preservation Ordinance, National Trust for Historic Preservation (1983), reprinted as Appendix A in a Handbook on Historic Preservation Law (C. Duerksen, ed. 1983).

[130] *Metropolitan Dade County v. P.J. Birds, Inc.*, 654 So. 2d 170 (Fla. 3d DCA 1995) (upholding designation of portion of tourist attraction as historic site); *Caspersen v. Town of Lyme*, 139 N.H. 637, 661 A.2d 759 (1995) (holding that zoning ordinance was properly enacted).

[131] A Handbook on Historic Preservation Law 37 (C. Duerksen, ed. 1983).

nomination and federal funding programs.[132] Surveys are also useful in providing direction to a preservation program. Using a well-documented survey as a guide, a community can carefully and rationally select those areas or structures it deems most worth protecting.[133] An added benefit is that such documentation provides a record of the designation decision, useful in the event of a court challenge.[134]

While most historic preservation plans tend to focus on what a property owner may do with his designated property, another successful approach used in addition to a regulatory scheme is to provide landmark owners technical and economic assistance. The idea is to defuse economic concerns weighing against preservation and make participation easier on historic property owners. In *Penn Central*,[135] New York City used a transferable development rights (TDR)[136] system to mitigate the financial effects of building permit denial. Other measures include financial assistance through reduction of property taxes, direct grant or revolving fund programs, and donation of facade easements qualifying for federal tax deductions, as well as educational programs, providing technical assistance through publications and workshops.[137]

Coordination of a preservation program is important legally, since a growing number of states require local governments to have comprehensive plans which include a preservation element.[138] This is especially important when a preservation ordinance comes under attack in court. If a local government can demonstrate that preservation is part of its overall plan to promote general community welfare, the local preservation ordinance stands a much better chance of surviving judicial scrutiny.

Commentators have suggested that, in order to avoid invalidating early zoning ordinances, courts often held that the existence of comprehensive plans could be implied from the combined effect of zoning ordinances, regulations and maps.[139] Although none really existed, the finding of a comprehensive landmarks program was important to the success of New York's Landmarks Program in *Penn Central*.[140] By looking at the local landmarks law and the properties designated under it, the Supreme Court was able to satisfy the requirement, albeit by legal fiction, that zoning be "in accordance with a comprehensive plan."[141]

---

[132] Pub. L. No. 96–515, §§ 201(a), 202, codified at 16 U.S.C.A. § 470a (requiring the states to maintain a statewide inventory and permitting the Secretary of the Interior to make 70% grants for state and local surveys).

[133] *South of Second Associates v. Georgetown*, 196 Colo. 89, 580 P.2d 807 (1978). The ordinance here designated the whole town an historic district. The Colorado Supreme Court struck the law because the local commission treated areas within the district differently, indicating district boundaries should have been more precise.

[134] *Bohannan v. City of San Diego*, 30 Cal. App. 3d 416, 106 Cal. Rptr. 333 (4th Dist. 1973); *Manhattan Club v. Landmarks Preservation Commission of City of New York*, 51 Misc. 2d 556, 273 N.Y.S.2d 848 (Sup 1966).

[135] *Penn Cent. Transp. Co. v. City of New York*, 438 U.S. 104, 98 S. Ct. 2646, 57 L. Ed. 2d 631, 11 Env't. Rep. Cas. (BNA) 1801, 8 Envtl. L. Rep. 20528 (1978).

[136] See § 9:10 supra.

[137] See A Handbook on Historic Preservation Law 42, 43 (C. Duerksen, ed. 1983).

[138] See, e.g., Fla. Stat. Ann. § 163.3177(6)(f)(l)(e) which includes preservation as a mandatory element of a local comprehensive plan.

[139] Haar, In Accordance with a Comprehensive Plan, 68 Harv. L. Rev. 1154 (1955).

[140] A Handbook on Historic Preservation Law 35 (C. Duerksen, ed. 1983).

[141] 438 U.S. at 132, 133, 98 S. Ct. at 2663. See also § 2:14.

In addition to the legal benefits it provides, a coordinated preservation program has some practical advantages as well. A well-ordered preservation plan will make acquisition of federal funding easier for local governments.[142] Synchronization of building, fire, and housing codes with preservation policies can do much for the success of a local program, since building officials usually consider safety of the building first, and only secondarily look to its special aesthetic or historic qualities.[143]

Because most preservation ordinances are implemented through overlay zoning, it is especially important that the plan be consistent with the applicable zoning. Problems arise when a preservation ordinance forbids alteration or demolition of a certain landmark but the zoning classification provides an incentive to tear it down by permitting a more lucrative use. Downzoning may work to ease this sort of development pressure.[144] To be truly effective, historic preservation must go beyond mere design and move broadly into the zoning realm by considering, in addition, such matters as density of development and permitted uses.[145] This integration will help satisfy concerns expressed by courts, notably the Supreme Court in *Penn Central*, about comprehensiveness, and further strengthen the legal status of preservation in general.

A final issue that merits discussion in regard to local preservation programs and the ordinances which establish them is that of owner consent or owner objection.[146] The issue has become increasingly important since an owner objection provision was added to the National Historic Preservation Act by the 1980 amendments. Pursuant to that provision, owners must be given an opportunity to object to the listing of their property in the National Register and if they do object, the property may not be listed.[147] There is no requirement that state and local programs must include such provisions but landowner opposition is particularly difficult to overcome at the local level.

---

[142] E.g., NEPA requires an environmental impact statement which includes consideration of the project's effect on aesthetics and the built environment. *Citizens to Preserve Overton Park, Inc. v. Volpe*, 401 U.S. 402, 91 S. Ct. 814, 28 L. Ed. 2d 136, 2 Env't. Rep. Cas. (BNA) 1250, 1 Envtl. L. Rep. 20110 (1971) (abrogated by, Califano v. Sanders, 430 U.S. 99, 97 S. Ct. 980, 51 L. Ed. 2d 192 (1977)); *WATCH (Waterbury Action to Conserve Our Heritage Inc.) v. Harris*, 603 F.2d 310, 9 Envtl. L. Rep. 20565 (2d Cir. 1979).

[143] Some progress was made in this vein when the National Trust for Historic Preservation, the American Institute of Architects and the Building Officials and Code Administrators joined forces and amended the Basic Building Code to provide specifically for restoration of landmarks. See B.O.C.A., Basic Building Code § 576.1 (1981).

[144] *Acierno v. Cloutier*, 40 F.3d 597 (3d Cir.1994); *New Castle County, DE v. National Union Fire Ins. Co. of Pittsburgh, PA*, 243 F.3d 744, 97 A.L.R. 5th 747 (3d Cir. 2001); *Amdur v. City of Chicago*, 638 F.2d 37 (7th Cir. 1980).

[145] C. Weaver & R. Babcock, City Zoning: The Once and Future Frontier, 120, 121 (1979).

[146] See, generally, E.L. Hunt, J. McPherson and C. Brinson, Historic Preservation in Florida Ch. 5 (1988).

[147] 16 U.S.C.A. §§ 470 et seq. See 36 C.F.R. § 60.6.

Chapter 13

AGRICULTURAL LAND PROTECTION AND PRESERVATION*

Analysis

§ 13:1 Agricultural Land and Land Use Planning and Development Regulation Law[1]

Planners and land use attorneys for many years gave very little attention to farmland or agricultural uses. Although many, if not most, zoning ordinances included an agricultural land use category, farmland was generally viewed from the urban land regulation perspective as a temporary use designation or holding category. As the urban area expanded, farmland was to "give way" to residential, commercial or industrial uses. For planners, agricultural lands were those left blank or white on the land use

---

* For more detailed discussion and more extensive citations of authority of the issues covered in this chapter, see Juergensmeyer and Roberts, Land Use Planning and Development Regulation Law, Practitioner Treatise Series (3rd ed. 2012).

[1] The authors appreciate the assistance of the late Professor James Wadley of Washburn University School of Law and Professor Arthur C. Nelson of the University of Utah in the preparation of several portions of this Chapter in the first edition and of Professor Wadley in the revision of portions of this chapter for the second edition.

map unless they were already surrounded by development in which case the holding category concept was applied.[2]

Today, both planners and attorneys increasingly recognize the importance and even necessity for including agricultural lands as a permanent land use category in plans and land development control codes. In fact, there is growing recognition of the need to extend special preservation and protection concepts to farmland for many of the same reasons that historic[3] and environmentally sensitive areas[4] are accorded special treatment and protection.[5]

By according special treatment to agricultural lands, societal needs to preserve food, fiber and fuel production are fulfilled and urban needs for open space and buffer zones are also met. The accomplishment of these goals is usually sought through use of the same planning and land use control tools encountered in other subject areas such as zoning, subdivision control, districting, clustering, transferable development rights, and private restrictions. Special modifications of the usual approaches and concepts are frequently required and are analyzed in the sections which follow.

The growing interest in what is called "Agritourism" and recent cases regarding the recreational use of farmland[6] suggest that there is still a vital interest in our society regarding the value of farmland or open space in close proximity to urban areas. On the other hand, recent developments with respect to the ability of states to protect farmland by restricting corporate ownership of such lands[7] or with respect to shielding farmland from nuisance liability,[8] both traditional farmland preservation tools, suggest that emphasis will likely shift to more conventional land use planning and management tools to accomplish those same goals.

Additionally, interest in urban agriculture has grown dramatically in recent years. Urban agriculture encompasses a variety of farming activities involving the production of food in or near cities including home gardening, gardening on vacant land often in rundown industrial areas, and roof-top gardening. It includes the raising of chickens and, less often, goats, bees, and pigs. The yield of produce and animal products may be for personal, cooperative or charitable use, as well as for sale on-site or at farmer's markets.[9]

§ 13:2   The *Historic* Need to Protect Farmland

Until relatively recently, interest in protecting farmland near urban areas was grounded largely in concerns about food, fiber, and fuel production capability. That is, there was a substantial fear that if too much agricultural land was converted to non-

---

[2] Roberts, Getting Ready for the Ag Revolution, 49 Planning 4 (June 1983).

[3] See §§ 12 et seq.

[4] See §§ 11 et seq.

[5] See Holloway and Guy, Emerging Regulatory Emphasis on Coordinating Land Use, Soil Management and Environmental Policies to Promote Farmland Preservation, Soil Conservation and Water Quality, 13 Zoning & Plan. L. Rep. 49 (1990).

[6] See § 13:3, infra.

[7] See § 13:3, infra.

[8] See § 13:3, infra.

[9] See § 13.16, infra.

farm uses, the nation's capacity to produce adequate supplies of food would be jeopardized and food costs would rise.

These fears were based on two facts. First, major amounts of farmland were being converted to non-farm uses. Second, the characteristics of ideal agricultural land and of ideal development land are almost identical-i.e., level, relatively free from vegetation, good drainage, accessible to transportation, and in large parcels. Consequently, a severe threat to farmland was considered to exist particularly on the urban fringe due to the competition between developers and farmers for use of the same land.[10] Normal economic conditions place a much higher value on land used for development than on land used for agricultural production thus predetermining the victory of development interests over agricultural interests if only economic factors determine the outcome of the conflict. On the theory that large scale conversion of agricultural lands to urban uses threatened the future of the national or local agricultural sector, land use control authorities became interested in imposing restrictions or providing incentives to prevent or deter conversion of agricultural lands to nonagricultural uses. The need for and justification of such farmland protection programs was therefore especially grounded on the perceived high rate of conversion.[11]

Data regarding trends in the aggregate agricultural land base have supported the concern that much farm land was being lost from agricultural production. For example, according to one estimate, 35,000 acres are lost every week to developments.[12] In 1978, the United States Department of Agriculture's Soil Conservation Service (now the Natural Resources Conservation Service) research indicated that roughly five million acres of rural land are lost yearly through urban development, through isolation as a result of urban development, and through destruction for the benefit of new water supply projects.[13]

Rural lands are being urbanized at rates that exceed the population growth rate. The loss of farmland is more severe in some areas of the country than others. Between 1950 and 1972, 17 states lost 20% of their taxable farmland, nine states more than 30%, four states more than 40%, and the states of New Hampshire and Rhode Island lost more than 50%. The overall result of continued suburban migration has been the loss of 119 million acres of farmland between 1954 and 1974. This is equal to an area three times the size of New England.[14]

---

[10] The most valuable agricultural land is cropland of which there were 335 million acres in 2010 down from 382 million acres in 1992. Statistical Abstract, Table 857 (2012). About 50 million acres of this land is within 50 miles of the 100 largest urbanized areas. O. Furuseth and J. Pierce, Agricultural Land in Urban Society (1982). Most of the cropland is found within the suburban and exurban counties of metropolitan areas. Nelson, The Analytic Basis for an Effective Prime Farmland Landscape Preservation Scheme in the U.S.A., 6 Jr. Rural Stud. 337 (1991).

[11] The need for farmland preservation is controversial and the statistics differ considerably depending on which "side" is using them. The exaggeration of these statistics has been alleged by the Urban Land Institute which "believes that pressures for farmland preservation are based on inaccurate and incomplete information and on assertions and distortions rather than on rational analysis." Urban Land Institute, Has the "Farmland Crisis" Been Overstated?: Recommendations for Balancing Urban and Agricultural Land Needs, 1983 Zoning & Plan. L. Handbook 235, 266 (1983) [hereinafter cited as Urban Land Institute].

[12] H.R. Rep. No. 95–1400.

[13] H.R. Rep. No. 95–1400 at 8. This figure varies greatly depending on the source. See, e.g., Merriam, Making TDR Work, 56 N.C. L. Rev. 77 (1978) (1.4 million acres); Roe, Innovative Techniques to Preserve Rural Land Resources, 5 Envtl. Aff. 419 (1976) (one million acres); National Agricultural Lands Study, Final Report (1981) (three million acres) [hereinafter cited as Final Report].

[14] Bonner and Sidor, Issues in Land Use, 1975 Land Resources Today 4 (January 1975).

Recent studies confirm that much of the nation's best farmland has been lost to farming.[15] The U.S.D.A. Agricultural Fact Book reported that between 1989 and 1994, the number of acres of land in farming dropped from 991.2 million to 794.8 million.[16] This computes into an average loss of 3.3 million acres per year.[17] Nonetheless nearly one-half of the land of the United States is considered farmland and the food and farming business contributes more than $1 trillion to the U.S. economy, more than 13% of the nation's gross domestic product, and employs about 17% of the national labor force.[18] With the recently increased demands on the agricultural sector to greatly expand production of some crops for the production of ethanol and other renewable fuels and to serve as sites for various renewable energy production facilities such as wind farms, the loss of agricultural land promises to attract more and more attention.[19] The American Farmland Trust recently reported that "The most recent NRI [USDA's National Resource Inventory], covering the 25-year period between 1982 and 2007, reveals that more than 23 million acres of America's agricultural land have been lost to development—an area the size of Indiana. According to the NRI, not a single state in the continental United States was left untouched. In fact, the most fertile land was developed at a disproportionately high rate. Thirty-eight percent of the agricultural land developed nationwide was prime, the land that is best suited to produce food and other agricultural crops."[20]

§ 13:3   The *Changing* Need to Protect Farmland

Although the interest in farmland preservation historically originated from concerns about the impact of the high rate of conversion of farmland upon food production capability, there seems to be little evidence that the nation is suffering to the degree anticipated. While uncertainties remain,[21] growing evidence suggests that increases in productivity and new technologies have actually increased food production capacity and that the nation as a whole has more such capacity now than it did 10 or 20 years ago when far more land was in agriculture.[22] Nevertheless, there remains a high level of interest in farmland preservation throughout the nation. This can be explained in part by uncertainties that persist over the consequences of converting farmland and by the fact that farming marginal lands may be environmentally harmful.[23] It is also diffi-

---

[15] Farmland Lost in Urban Sprawl, Chicago Tribune, Oct. 26, 1996 (p. 11) (based on data from Northern Illinois University.)

[16] USDA Fact Book 16 (1996).

[17] Between 1982 and 1992, more than 41 million acres of agricultural land was converted to urban or low density nonrural uses (such as hobby farms and ranchettes). (Compare Statistical Abstract of the United States 1995 reporting the 1992 Census of Agriculture with Statistical Abstract of the United States 1985 reporting the 1982 Census of Agriculture.) This equates to nearly two acres of land lost for each new resident added. Given the historical rate of farmland conversion, by the middle of the 21st Century the United States could move from being an exporter of food to an importer. American Farmland Trust, Farming on the Fringe (1997). As the best farmland is lost, marginally productive land is brought into resource uses through heavy applications of chemicals but with potentially adverse environmental consequences. Platt, The Farmland Conversion Debate, 37 Prof. Geographer 433 (1982).

[18] Paster, Preservation of Agricultural Lands Through Land Use Planning Tools and Techniques, 44 Nat. Resources J. 283 (2004).

[19] The website of the American Farmland Trust gives current local and national data in regard to farmland loss and preservation. See http://www.farmland.org/.

[20] http://farmland.org/programs/protection/American-Farmland-Trust-Farmland-Protection-Farmland-by-the-numbers.asp.

[21] See supra § 13:2.

[22] See, e.g., B. Delworth Gardiner, Plowing Ground in Washington: The Political Economy of U.S. Agriculture (Pacific Research Institute for Public Policy, San Francisco 1995).

[23] See supra § 13:2.

cult to gauge worldwide demand for American agricultural commodities and the extent to which American agriculture will be called upon to decrease American dependence on fossil fuels by production of renewable energy. A major reason for continued interest, however, is a shift in focus from fears over losing food production capability toward a fear of losing the advantages which come from having cities surrounded with open, less developed areas.

In this shifting paradigm, four different emerging concerns tend to dominate decision-making regarding farmland preservation: (1) the demographics of farming are changing so that small farms on the urban fringe are particularly vulnerable to urban pressures and therefore need to be protected in order to preserve the attractiveness and amenities of rural lifestyles;[24] (2) that farmers within the urban fringe are increasingly the targets of nuisance actions generated by changing conditions in the vicinity; (3) that urban residents are discovering the need for open space as an element of psychological well-being and quality of life and therefore benefit from less developed areas surrounding urban areas; and (4) the interest of urban dwellers in open space is extending to include recreational use.

A. *Changing Demographics and Corporate Farming*

Farm demographics have significantly changed from the midpart of the 20th century.[25] There are far fewer farms, farmers on the whole are much older, there is great disparity in production between large and small farms and there appears to be a significant move in the direction of corporate agriculture. This has caused concerns that agriculture may be moving from a popular base to an industrial base which, in turn, has fueled fears that food production capability will become so concentrated in the hands of relatively few producers that food monopolies will likely result.[26] For example, it has been predicted that within the next several years traditional seed companies will disappear. There will be only four grain consortiums and two vegetable consortiums. These entities will supply the inputs and control marketing, processing, and distribution of crops.[27] Already only 20% of the farms produce over 85% of the nation's agricultural output.[28] Further, there is a sense that the change in farming from family dominated farms to corporate agriculture is destroying the attractive values of rural America. As a result, there is much interest in trying to preserve the small farm structure of farm-

---

[24] This is sometimes referred to as the "Impermanence Syndrome." When farmers see urban families moving into agricultural areas, they begin calculating their exit strategy from farming. It usually takes the form of making no further investments in capital such as barns, irrigation systems, and reproducing livestock. The effect is that because of the perceived threat of invasion by urban sprawl, many more farmers than would actually be put out of business from conversion decide to reduce production. David Berry, Ernest Leonardo, and Kenneth Bieri, The Farmer's Response to Urbanization, Regional Science Research Institute Discussion Paper Series No. 92 (Regional Science Research Institute, University of Massachusetts, Amherst, MA. 1976.

[25] Coulthard, The Changing Landscape of America's Farmland: A Comparative Look at Policies Which Help Determine the Portrait of Our Land—Are There Lessons We Can Learn from the EU?, 6 Drake J. Agric. L. 261 (2002) (Discussion of the historic role of the family farm in our heritage in contrast to its contribution to today's economy and the USDA's initiative to save small farms.).

[26] See, generally, Hamilton, Tending the Seeds: The Emergence of a New Agriculture in the United States, 1 Drake J. Agric. L. 7 (1996); Hamilton, Plowing New Ground: Emerging Policy Issues in a Changing Agriculture, 2 Drake J. Agric. L. 181 (1997); Wadley, Small Farms: The USDA, Rural Communities and Urban Pressures, 21 Washburn L.J. 478 (1982).

[27] Doan's Agricultural Report, Sept. 12, 1997.

[28] B. Gardner, Plowing Ground in Washington: The Political Economy of U.S. Agriculture, 119 (Pacific Research Institute for Public Policy, San Francisco) (1995).

ing.[29] One key to keeping small farm agriculture strong is the ability of small farms to compete successfully with larger, often corporate, entities.

These demographic concerns have prompted a number of jurisdictions to adopt restrictions on the types of businesses which are allowed to own farmland or engage in farming.[30] "Nine states have these restrictions, prohibiting the use of the corporate form on approximately 312 million acres of farmland, which is approximately seventy-seven percent of the land in those states, and approximately one-third of all farmland in the United States."[31] Typically, these statutes permit only non-corporate entities to engage in agriculture. For corporations to own farmland or operate farms, they typically must be family-farm or small-farm corporations. The rationale behind these statutes is that the smaller farms need protection against not only the direct pressures of large scale agriculture but also against indirect pressures on farmland.

The goal of these statutes seems to be to preserve the small farms which are, in many if not most cases, the ones which are also the most vulnerable to the economic pressures of the urban fringe. Thus, it is thought that by keeping the small farms intact a popular-based agriculture can be maintained. While these approaches are not directly targeted toward preserving farmland within the urban fringe, they are designed to keep small farms in farming and to better resist the conversion pressures that result from the inability to compete with larger operations. In many areas, as a matter of state policy, these programs are coupled with efforts to help small farms find production alternatives, such as organic gardening or specialty crops, which thrive well only in close proximity to urban areas.

With respect to the strategy of protecting farmland by restricting corporate ownership three court decisions need to be considered because they call the strategy into question. *South Dakota Farm Bureau, Inc. v. Hazeltine*,[32] and *Jones v. Gale*[33] involve cases where the courts struck down anti-farm corporation statutes as violating the dormant commerce clause. In Hazeltine, the Court recognized that protecting the fami-

---

[29] See Future Directions in Rural Development Policy: Findings and Recommendations of the National Commission on Agriculture and Rural Development Policy (December 1990). This Commission was mandated by the Food Security Act of 1985 and its report was presented to the President in 1989.

[30] See e.g. Kan. Stat. Ann. §§ 17–5901 et seq. Similar restrictions are found in North Dakota, South Dakota, Nebraska, Iowa, Michigan, Missouri, Oklahoma, Wisconsin and Minnesota. Oklahoma and Nebraska include these restrictions in their constitutions. Neb. Const. Art. XII, § 8(1); Okla. Const. Art. XXII, § 2; See Slayton, A Legislative Experiment in Rural Culture: The Anti—Corporate Farming Statutes, 59 UMKC L. Rev. 679 (1991); Smart and Hoberg, Corporate Farming in the Anti—Corporate Farming States, Nat'l Center for Agric.Res. & Info. (1989); J. Wadley, Agriculture and Farm Law, § 47.10 in Thompson on Real Property (Thomas ed.) (1994); Pietila, "We're Doing This to Ourselves": South Dakota's Anticorporate Farming Amendment, 27 J. Corp. L. 149 (2001) (Discussion of the initiation and passing of South Dakota's constitutional amendment that severely restricts corporate investment in agricultural production.).

[31] Schutz, Corporate Farming Measures in a Post-Jones World, 14 Drake J. Agric. L. 97 (2009).

[32] *South Dakota Farm Bureau, Inc. v. Hazeltine*, 340 F.3d 583, 33 Envtl. L. Rep. 20260, 125 A.L.R.5th 665 (8th Cir. 2003).

[33] *Jones v. Gale*, 470 F.3d 1261, 1270 (8th Cir. 2006) (striking down Nebraska's restriction). See Schutz, Corporate Farming Measures in a Post-Jones World, 14 Drake J. Agric. L. 97 (2009); Schutz, Nebraska's Corporate Farming Law and Discriminatory Effects Under the Dormant Commerce Clause, 88 Neb. L. Rev. 50 (2009); Validity, Construction and Application of Constitutional and Statutory Provisions Regarding Corporate Farming, 15 A.L.R. 5th 147 (2005).

ly farm was a legitimate purpose but held the state had failed to demonstrate that it had no other effective alternative.[34]

B. *Nuisance Protection and Right to Farm Legislation*

Concerns regarding the vulnerability of farms to nuisance-type problems resulting from the influx of urban residents into formerly rural or agricultural areas have triggered two different kinds of responses which bear on the question of farmland preservation. First, every state now has what are popularly called "right-to-farm" laws.[35] These laws, in one way or another, seek to shield farmers from nuisance claims that might result from normal farming operations.[36] They are typically enacted on a jurisdiction-wide basis[37] and tend to codify the "coming to the nuisance defense." Second, some jurisdictions have sought to minimize the extent to which urban immigrants into rural areas can pressure farming operations to conform to the newly emerging notions of what the area should be like by enacting exemptions from zoning authority in favor of farms.[38] In these states, farms that are established in an area are considered as a matter of law not to be nuisances provided they were there before the arrival of the complainant or are being conducted in accordance with established agricultural practices.[39]

As just stated, every state has adopted some version of the so-called "right to farm" laws which are specifically designed to give agricultural operations some measure of protection against nuisance complaints of the type that often arise as a result of having non-agricultural uses intermixed with agricultural land use activity.[40] Right to Farm statutes tend to be one of three major types: (1) those that establish a specific time within which nuisance claims arising because of changes in the neighborhood must be brought against an agricultural operation,[41] (2) those which create a rebuttable presumption that the operation is not a nuisance when it is in compliance with federal or state laws,[42] and (3) those that exempt particular kinds of agricultural operations.[43]

---

[34] The Court did note that the federal government had made a compelling case for preserving the family farm in a 1998 report from USDA entitled *A Time to Act: Report of the USDA National Comm'n on Small Farms* (1998) but held that the state had not demonstrated that the measures proposed by the federal government were likely to be ineffective.

[35] For a list of citations to the 50 statutory provisions, see Centner, Creating an "Undeveloped Lands Protection Act" for Farmlands, Forests, and Natural Areas, 17 Duke Envt'l L. & Pol'y F. 1 (2006) [hereinafter, Centner].

[36] See infra § 14:6.

[37] Since they are state-wide in their applicability, their effect on local zoning power is often controversial. "Right to farm legislation can supplement but not replace zoning because only zoning prevents or minimizes conflicts. Disallowing a nuisance suit does not prevent the conflict—it only suppresses a remedy potentially more damaging than the conflict itself." Walker, Whole Hog: The Pre-emption of Local Control by the 1999 Amendment to the Michigan Right to Farm Act, 36 Val. U. L. Rev 461, 493 (2002).

[38] See. e.g., Kan. Stat. Ann. § 19–2921.

[39] See, e.g., Kan. Stat. Ann. §§ 2–3201 et seq.

[40] See Hamilton and Bolte, Nuisance Laws and Livestock Production in the United States: A Fifty-State Analysis, 10 J. Agric. Tax'n & L. 99 (1988).

[41] See, e.g. Ala. Code § 6–5–127 (a). Other States of this type include Arkansas, Colorado, Connecticut, Florida, Georgia, Idaho, Illinois, Indiana, Louisiana, Maryland, Mississippi, New Hampshire, New Mexico, North Carolina, North Dakota, South Carolina, Texas and Virginia.

[42] See e.g. Mich.Stat.Ann. § 12:122(3); Mich. Comp. Laws. Ann §§ 286.471 to 286.474; Laurent, Michigan's Right to Farm Act: Have Revisions Gone Too Far?, 2002 L. Rev. Mich. St. U. Det. C. L. 213 (2002). Oth-

The statutes, in various degrees, attempt to codify the "coming to the nuisance" defense[44] in situations where the challenge comes from landowners who have moved into a heretofore agricultural area but who object to various, often inherent, aspects of agricultural operations, such as odor, noise, or machinery uses that seem to be threatening to a more urban lifestyle. The rationale behind these statutes, as they relate to farmland preservation, seems to be that since nuisance claims pose a major threat to small farms in urban fringe areas, to the extent to which those farms can be shielded from the costs and risks of such claims, those farms will more likely survive as viable farms.

A key to invoking the protection offered by these statutes in many cases seems to be how "changed circumstances" are defined for purposes of the application of the statute. In most cases, courts have interpreted these statutes within the context of "extension of non-agricultural land uses, residential or otherwise, into existing agricultural areas."[45] Where there is such an intrusion, the statutes may be invoked to protect the agricultural use. Some jurisdictions apply this concept rather rigidly. In one case, the court refused to protect a hog operation that was developed after the plaintiff moved into the area.[46] The time is generally treated as beginning to run when the farming operation begins or from the date of a substantial change in the operation.[47] Alternatively, the plaintiff must base the complaint on a violation of any Federal, State or local statute or regulation. In cases where the existence of the farming operation predates the arrival of the complainant, the burden appears to be on the complainant to establish that the operation is conducted in violation of the law or that the complaint is filed in a timely manner with regard to a substantial change in the operation. There appears to be a presumption that farming operations that are not considered nuisances when they commence do not become such simply because someone later moves near the operation.

Nonetheless, a Washington court[48] recently refused to protect a farming operation that had been in existence for more than 50 years from complaints raised by a neighbor who moved in after the farm had been established. In this case, the farm started out as an apple orchard. It was converted into a cherry orchard after the complainant built a house near the farm. The problem complained of was the use of propane cannons that were used to scare birds away from the cherries. This activity began after the complainants built their house. While the law otherwise allows crop conversion without jeopardizing status as a farm, the court held that the nuisance statute requires that

---

er states with this type of legislation include Arizona, Connecticut, Kansas, Maine, Massachusetts, New York, Oklahoma, Vermont, and Washington.

[43] See, e.g. Kan. Stat. Ann. § 47–1505 (dealing with feed lot operations).

[44] See *Vicwood Meridian Partnership v. Skagit Sand and Gravel*, 123 Wash. App. 877, 98 P.3d 1277 (Div. 2 2004) (court treated composting as a necessary component of a mushroom operation and hence entitled to the benefit of the protective statute).

[45] *Herrin v. Opatut*, 248 Ga. 140, 281 S.E.2d 575 (1981).

[46] *Flansburgh v. Coffey*, 220 Neb. 381, 370 N.W.2d 127 (1985).

[47] See *Home v. Haladay*, 1999 PA Super 64, 728 A.2d 954 (1999).

[48] *Davis v. Taylor*, 132 Wash. App. 515, 139 Wash. App. 715, 132 P.3d 783 (Div. 3 2006), review dismissed, cause remanded, 161 P.3d 379 (Wash. 2007).

the conversion occur prior to local development. Thus, new or expanded activities are not immune from nuisance liability.[49]

Another issue relates to whether farmers are protected vis a vis other farmers. In a Kansas case, *Finlay v. Finlay*,[50] a farmer complained that another farmer was maintaining a nuisance upon his land. The farmer against whom the complaint was brought argued that the operation was shielded by the state's "Protection of Farmland and Agricultural Activities Act." The court held that the provisions of the statute protecting the farmer from nuisance claims could only be invoked against non-farmers and had no effect on claims brought by one farmer against another. In this regard, there seems to be a growing trend to interpret these statutes as designed to have relevance only in nuisance disputes between farmers and non-farmers.[51]

For a long time, the view seemed to be that right to farm statutes did not radically alter the law of nuisance.[52] That view was challenged in *Bormann v. Board of Supervisors*,[53] where the Supreme Court of Iowa found the Iowa version of Right to Farm statutes unconstitutional. The court's rationale was that the immunity from nuisance liability effectively imposed an easement on the neighbors to bear the burden of an activity that otherwise would likely be prevented as a nuisance. Since there was no compensation paid to the adjoining landowner in connection with that burden, an unconstitutional taking occurred. The Iowa Supreme Court later came to the same conclusion in regard to a statutory provision conferring nuisance immunity on animal feeding operations in *Gacke v. Pork Xtra*.[54] However, recent cases from Idaho[55] and Minnesota[56] have found no deprivation of property to result from application of Right to Farm statutory provisions.

Nonetheless, given the uncertainty of the constitutional status of nuisance protection for agricultural operations from Right To Farm legislation, Professor Centner has proposed an "Undeveloped Lands Protection Act" as "a new anti-nuisance paradigm for the protection of lands used as farmland, forestry, and natural areas." The Act is de-

---

[49] See White, Beating Plowshares into Townhomes: The Loss of Farmland and Strategies for Slowing Its Conversion to Nonagricultural Uses, 28 Envtl. L. 113 (1998); Richardson, Downzoning, Fairness and Farmland Protection, 19 J. Land Use & Envtl. L. 59 (2003).

[50] 18 Kan. App.2d 479, 856 P.2d 183 (1993).

[51] *State v. Finley*, 18 Kan. App. 2d 419, 854 P.2d 315 (1993); See also *Buchanan v. Simplot Feeders, Ltd. Partnership*, 134 Wash. 2d 673, 952 P.2d 610 (1998).

[52] See J. Wadley, Agriculture and Farm Law, Ch. 47 of Thomson on Real Property at 97 (Thomas ed. 1994).

[53] *Bormann v. Board of Sup'rs In and For Kossuth County*, 584 N.W.2d 309, 29 Envtl. L. Rep. 20235 (Iowa 1998) (statutory provision at issue was "A farm or farm operation located in an agricultural area shall not be found to be a nuisance regardless of the established date of operation or expansion of the agricultural activities of the farm or farm operation." Iowa Code Ann. § 352.11(l)(a)). See Centner at 4; Centner, Anti-nuisance Legislation: Can the Derogation of Common Law Nuisance Be a Taking?, 30 Envtl. L. Rptr. 10253 (2000); Centner, Governments and Unconstitutional Takings: When Do Right-to-Farm Laws Go Too Far?, 33 B.C. Envtl. Aff. L. Rev. 87 (2006); Gittins, Bormann Revisited; Using the Penn Central Test to Determine the Constitutionality of Right-to-Farm Statutes, 2006 BYU L. Rev. 1381 (2006).

[54] *Gacke v. Pork Xtra, L.L.C.*, 684 N.W.2d 168 (Iowa 2004) (Statutory provision at issue was "An animal feeding operation, as defined in section 455B.161, shall not be found to be a public or private nuisance under this chapter or under principles of common law, and the animal feeding operation shall not be found to interfere with another person's comfortable use and enjoyment of the person's life or property under any other cause of action." Iowa Code Ann. § 657.11(2).). See Centner, Governments and Unconstitutional Takings: When Do Right-to-Farm Laws Go Too Far?, 33 B.C. Envtl. Aff. L. Rev. 87, 115 (2006).

[55] *Moon v. North Idaho Farmers Ass'n*, 140 Idaho 536, 96 P.3d 637 (2004).

[56] *Overgaard v. Rock County Bd. of Com'rs*, 2003 WL 21744235 (D. Minn. 2003).

signed to supplement existing right to farm legislation by offering special protection for natural resources.[57]

In addition to "right-to-farm" statutes, some states have sought to shield farms from nuisance-type pressures in other ways. Where the pressures seem likely to be exacerbated by changing neighborhoods, a number of jurisdictions have sought to protect small farms through zoning exceptions. Typical of this approach is the Kansas statute:[58]

No zoning regulation shall apply to the use of land for agricultural purposes nor for the erection and maintenance of agricultural buildings so long as such agricultural buildings are used for agricultural purposes and no other. Dwellings, garages and other similar accessory buildings shall not be considered as agricultural buildings. All buildings, including agricultural buildings may be regulated as to set-back requirements from public roads so as to protect the future use and improvement of such roads.

The rationale of these zoning exemption approaches appears to be that if the land can be shielded from the pressures to conform to the land use patterns that arise when non-agricultural development occurs in areas that were formerly dominantly agricultural in nature, the farm operations will be more likely to remain in those areas. Otherwise, the costs associated with making the structures conform to the zoning codes or the risks attendant upon becoming a non-conforming use under the code might well persuade a farmer to convert the use of the land to a non-agricultural use.[59]

In these jurisdictions, the question usually will be whether the operation is truly an agricultural one or not. This question arises from the propensity of zoning codes to treat intensive agricultural operations as commercial rather than agricultural. It was held, for example, that a piggery was not a farming operation in *Town of Mt. Pleasant v. Van Tassell*.[60] Thus small farms may be given the benefit of the exception whereas the larger, more commercial oriented ones may not.

In two Iowa cases, the zoning exemption was invoked to protect large, commercial hog operations. In *Racine Police & Fire Commission v. Budish*[61] and *Kuehl v. Cass County*,[62] the Iowa Supreme Court considered facilities which would accommodate between 2,000 and 5,000 hogs as excluded from the zoning. In doing so, the court overturned a long-standing precedent, *Farmegg Products, Inc. v. Humboldt County*.[63] It specifically rejected the argument that to be exempt as an agricultural use, the facility

---

[57] The Act is set out at Centner, App.2.

[58] Kan. Stat. Ann. § 19-2960(d).

[59] In *Ladner v. Hancock County*, 899 So. 2d 899 (Miss. Ct. App. 2004) (Unpublished), the court upheld the authority of the county to regulate the construction of a residence on unincorporated agricultural county land even though the landowner planned to use the residence as part of the agricultural purposes on the property.

[60] *Town of Mount Pleasant v. Van Tassell*, 7 Misc. 2d 643, 166 N.Y.S.2d 458 (Sup 1957), judgment aff'd, 6 A.D.2d 880, 177 N.Y.S.2d 1010 (2d Dep't 1958). But see *Fields v. Anderson Cattle Co.*, 193 Kan. 558, 396 P.2d 276 (1964) where two feedlots for cattle and sheep within 700 feet of the city limits were not considered to be commercial but were agricultural uses.

[61] *Racine Police & Fire Comm'n v. Budish*, 121 Wis. 2d 696, 359 N.W.2d 181 (Ct. App. 1984).

[62] *Kuehl v. Cass County*, 555 N.W.2d 686 (Iowa 1996).

[63] *Farmegg Products, Inc. v. Humboldt County*, 190 N.W.2d 454 (Iowa 1971) (disapproved of by, Kuehl v. Cass County, 555 N.W.2d 686 (Iowa 1996)).

must be used in conjunction with a traditional agricultural use otherwise in existence. That view had been the basis for excluding "commercial" agricultural uses since they were not considered "traditional" in nature. Under the new view, not only will small farms near urban areas benefit from the exception, larger ones will as well. This may pose problems for jurisdictions that are interested in farmland preservation primarily because of the connection between small farms and "open space." Jurisdictions of this type might find that "commercial" or "industrial" agriculture threatens their views of desirable "open space." Other jurisdictions, that are interested in farmland preservation because of the connection between farming and food production, may have difficulty as well with the idea of protecting non-traditional, large scale commercial farms as part of their preservation strategy even though they are the primary contributors to food production, simply because their size and scale suggests that they may not need the same degree or level of protection as do smaller farms. As such, they may be forced to rethink whether they are going to hold on to traditional views of agriculture or protect agriculture regardless of its format.

C. *Agricultural Land as Open Space*

An important motivation for preserving and protection agricultural land is its role as open space. The availability of open space for urban dwellers is closely aligned to psychological well-being and quality of life. Thus, regardless of any fears regarding food supplies or cost, the fact that an area surrounding or within an urban area is undeveloped or open warrants efforts to keep that area in that condition.[64] In this sense, farms function as public open space[65] which is to be tenaciously protected. When farmland is protected under this guise, the benefit seems to work both ways—to the urban resident now living in or near the countryside, quality of life is improved because of the psychological effects of open space. The farmer who is thereby allowed to continue to farm also benefits because there is some evidence that the ability to control how one's land is used is particularly important to farmers and is therefore one measure of their quality of life.[66]

A recently significant role that agricultural lands play as open space is that of serving as the site for renewable energy installations—particularly wind farms. A recent controversy over construction of wind farms in the Flint Hills area of Kansas reveals the conflicting agricultural and legal considerations in this increasingly important use of farmland.[67] Objections to wind farms in that area are based on aesthetic, nuisance,[68] and ecological considerations and have led to legislative proposals for moratoria, repeal of renewable energy property tax exemptions, and comprehensive county

---

[64] See Hiss, The Experience of Place (1991); Langdon, A Better Place to Live: Reshaping the American Suburb (1994); see Krannich, A Modern Disaster: Agricultural Land, Urban Growth and the Need for a Federally Organized Comprehensive Land Use Planning Model, 16 Cornell J.L. & Pub. Pol'y 57 (2006).

[65] Hiss, The Experience of Place at 146 (1991).

[66] Wadley and Falk, *Lucas* and Environmental Land Use Control in Rural Areas: Whose Land is It Anyway, 19 Wm. Mitchell L. Rev. 331, 359 (1993): "Modern theorists have suggested various reasons why psychological well-being may be jeopardized due to excessive government intrusion into property use and enjoyment . . . ."

[67] Dietz, Turbines vs. Tallgrass: Law, Policy, and a New Solution to Conflict over Wind Farms in the Kansas Flint Hills, 54 U. Kan. L. Rev. 1131 (2006).

[68] For nuisance based litigation in another jurisdiction, see *Rassier v. Houim*, 488 N.W.2d 635 (N.D. 1992); Bliss, Tilting at Wind Turbines: Noise Nuisance in the Neighborhood after Rassier v. Houim, 69 N.D. L. Rev. 535 (1993) (no nuisance found).

zoning and conditional use restrictions. Litigation has also ensued.[69] A key argument by landowner supporters of wind farms is that restrictions precluding them would constitute a taking of property rights.[70]

As urban residents have become increasingly interested in the existence of nearby open space, their interest has broadened to include hopes to use such open areas for recreational purposes even if privately owned. Because of the high public cost associated with the creation of recreational opportunities in most areas, local and state governments have sought ways to encourage or induce individual landowners to make their lands available for recreational use by others. Perhaps the most popular means by which landowners with "open space" are encouraged to make that land available for recreational activities are the so-called "recreational use" statutes. These statutes, found in most states,[71] reduce the liability exposure of landowners for injuries suffered by recreational use entrants by requiring that the landowner not be obligated to protect the recreational entrant beyond any duties that might be owed to a trespasser.

Each statute defines the land that is covered by that statute. In some statutes, it may be broadly defined.[72] In others, the view may be confined strictly to agricultural land or open space.[73] The statutes will also define what is considered "recreational use." This may include such activities as hunting, fishing, swimming, boating, camping, picnicking, hiking, pleasure driving, nature study, water skiing, winter sports, and viewing historical, archeological, scenic or scientific sites.[74] With respect to particular uses, the intent of the entrant seems irrelevant as does the landowner's understanding of the entrant's purpose, or possibly even the entrant's presence because the policy behind the statute seems to be to "avoid entry into a thicket entangled with speculation as to the motives of the landowner in permitting the use of the land."[75] In fact, most statutes do not require that the landowner give permission to the entrant to be on the

---

[69] *Flint Hills Tallgrass Prairie Heritage Foundation v. Scottish Power, PLC*, 2005 WL 427503 (D. Kan. 2005), judgment aff'd, 147 Fed. Appx. 785 (10th Cir. 2005) (dismissed on basis plaintiff failed to establish constitutional right to salubrious environment, cause of action under Migratory Bird Treaty Act, or basis for equitable relief to preserve natural resources treasures).

[70] Dietz, Turbines vs. Tallgrass: Law, Policy, and a New Solution to Conflict over Wind Farms in the Kansas Flint Hills, 54 U. Kan. L. Rev. 1131, 1143–1152 (2006). See also Challenges Under State Law to Wind Energy Facilities and Laws Regulating or Prohibiting Such Facilities, 64 A.L.R.6th 601; The Power of Wind: Current Legal Issues in Siting for Wind Power, 61 No. 5 Plan. & Envtl. L. 3 (2009); Wind Farms and NIMBYS: Generating Conflict, Reducing Litigation, 20 Fordham Envtl. L. Rev. 427 (2010).

[71] These statutes are largely patterned after model proposals developed by the Council of State Governments. See Council of State Governments, Public Recreation on Private Lands: Limitations on Liability, 24 Suggested State Legislation 150 (1965). Statutes have been adopted by most states, including Alabama, Arkansas, California, Colorado, Delaware, Georgia, Hawaii, Idaho, Illinois, Indiana, Iowa, Kansas, Kentucky, Louisiana, Maine, Maryland, Massachusetts, Michigan, Minnesota, Mississippi, Montana, Nebraska, Nevada, New Hampshire, New Jersey, North Dakota, Ohio, Oklahoma, Oregon, Rhode Island, South Carolina, South Dakota, Tennessee, Texas, Utah, Washington, West Virginia, Wisconsin, and Wyoming.

[72] See, e.g. Kan. Stat. Ann. § 58–3202, covering land, roads, water, watercourses, private ways and buildings, structures, and machinery and equipment that is attached to realty.

[73] See, e.g. Or. Rev. Stat. § 105.655 (now repealed). See also *Tijerina v. Cornelius Christian Church*, 273 Or. 58, 539 P.2d 634 (1975).

[74] Kan. Stat. Ann. § 58–3202(c).

[75] *Fisher v. U.S.*, 534 F. Supp. 514 (D. Mont. 1982).

property.[76] On the other hand, the statutes generally require that there be no charge imposed for the privilege of entry.[77]

These statutes play an important role in the overall farmland preservation scheme. Although they are not particularly focused on ensuring that agricultural activities continue on the land, they serve to encourage the existence of "open space" in close proximity to urban centers while at the same time seeking to remove an important possible source of conflict between urban and rural landowners. These statutes clearly contemplate that agricultural activities on the land do not need to cease for the land to be eligible for recreational use. Nor is agricultural activity considered to be inconsistent with non-agricultural recreational activities. Indeed, the statutes contemplate that if agricultural uses can continue, not only will the land be maintained in an economically productive manner; it will also be maintained in a condition that will make it attractive as a site for recreational activities. Further, since there does not seem to be any requirement that the recreational use be considered by the landowner to be an important aspect of the land configuration, the outcome engendered by these statutes encourages the continued existence of attractive lands near urban areas with the prospect that recreational opportunity will be available as a bonus to both the landowner and the entrant. Finally, by reducing the prospect of the farmer having to pay damages to someone who may enter the land for recreational activities and be harmed as a result of farming activities (such as farm machinery left in the field) the statutes seem to attempt to shore up a significant aspect of the farm economic situation. Not only does the farmer not have to change farming practices to accommodate recreation, the farmer does not have to worry about the increase in liability that inherently arises as a result of being geographically near or accessible to urban population.

The concept of public recreational use of agricultural land has begun to evolve toward models of "ecotourism" and "agritourism." A number of states have now adopted statutes relating to "agritourism." A model statute of this type is the Kansas "Agritourism Promotion Act"[78] in which the Kansas Legislature adopted a policy of promoting "rural tourism and rural economic development by encouraging owners and operators of farms, ranches, and rural attractions, including historic, cultural, and natural attractions, to invite members of the public to view, observe and participate in such operations and attractions for recreational or entertainment purposes."[79]

"Agritourism activity" is typically defined to include "any activity which allows members of the general public, for recreational, entertainment or educational purposes, to view or enjoy rural activities, including, but not limited to, farming activities, ranching activities or historic, cultural or natural attractions. An activity may be an agritourism activity whether or not the participant pays to participate in the activity. An activity is not an agritourism activity if the participant is paid to participate in the activity."[80]

---

[76] See, e.g., *Johnson v. Stryker Corp.*, 70 Ill. App. 3d 717, 26 Ill. Dec. 931, 388 N.E.2d 932 (1st Dist. 1979).

[77] Kansas is somewhat of an exception in that owners of agricultural land can impose a charge whereas owners of non-agricultural land cannot. Kan. Stat. Ann. § 58–3206(b).

[78] Kan. Stat. Ann. §§ 74–50, 74–165.

[79] Kan. Stat. Ann. § 74–166.

[80] Kan. Stat. Ann. § 74–167.

Once properly registered as an agritourism activity, the statute creates an effective assumption of risk defense against claims from anyone injured while engaged in the agritourism activity. Notably, these acts are considered to be available in addition to, rather than a replacement for, the state's recreational use liability limitation statutes. Although not limited to the urban fringe area, these statutes would be considered particularly useful to encourage the opening up of farmland close to urban areas for recreational activity.

As already indicated, both recreational use statutes and agritourism statutes are quite sympathetic to the liability concerns of farmers associated with allowing others onto agricultural land for recreational purposes. The goal of statutes addressing this problem is to shield landowners from liability in order that such land may remain available for use by the public. In other words, these statutes are a type of farmland protection albeit not directly targeting the use of farmland for agricultural purposes. Nonetheless, the protection from liability conferred on farmers is not unlimited. In the recent case of *Leet v. City of Minot*,[81] the North Dakota Supreme Court held that although the North Dakota Legislature had intended in its Recreation Use Immunity Statute to define "recreational purposes" broadly enough to "cover all recreational activities," some activities may still be excluded. In this case, the individual had been injured by a falling curtain while he was on the premises as an employee of a vendor preparing for an activity at the facility the following day. The court held that "the plain language of the statute is not so broad as to include a person present on the property for purposes of the person's employment."[82] Therefore, despite the conclusion that the statute was to be interpreted broadly, it could not encompass all activities so the injured party was considered to be on the premises for employment and not for a recreational purpose.[83]

The multifunctionality of farmland is currently viewed as even more complex than its value as open space, its recreational value and its role in providing sites for renewable energy installations. As Professor Ruhl has stated, ecologists and economists now "see farms as housing the natural capital capable of providing a stream of diverse goods and services, including ecosystem services such as increased biodiversity, carbon sequestration, pollination, groundwater recharge, and improvement of water quality."[84]

§ 13:4   Farmland Preservation in Farm States

[Section appears only in practitioner's treatise]

§ 13:5   Making Farmland Preservation Work

Farmland protection programs, if they are to be successful, must respond to the factors which determine the conversion of farmland to non-agricultural uses.[85] Many forces and factors are involved.

---

[81] *Leet v. City of Minot*, 2006 ND 191, 721 N.W.2d 398 (N.D. 2006).

[82] Leet v. City of Minot, 721 N.W.2d 398, 406 (2006).

[83] See also Butcher, The Forgotten Intent of the Williamson Act: Regulation of Non-Contracted Lands, 12 Hastings W-Nw. J. Envtl. L. & Pol'y 37 (2005).

[84] Ruhl, Agriculture and Ecosystem Services: Strategies for State and Local Governments, 17 N.Y.U. Envtl. L.J. 424, 426 (2008).

[85] Stanislaus County California now conditions conversions of farmland to residential use on the developer obtaining agricultural easements on other farmland within that county. The requirement was upheld in

A primary factor contributing to the loss of prime agricultural land is increasing land values.[86] The farmer on the urban fringe is placed in an especially uncomfortable position. Although possessing a different understanding of the land, of the relationship of people to the land, and of the problems and costs of land ownership, the farmer may not hold such affection for the soil that he will hold out in the face of massive profits. The temptation to sell is undoubtedly connected to the proximity of the farmland to the urban fringe. Since average suburban land values are dramatically higher when utilized for building purposes than for cultivation or grazing, the farmer is likely to take his profits and leave farming altogether.[87]

Another factor that must be considered in evaluating preservation alternatives is the changing nature of farmland ownership. Urbanites, investors, syndicates, retirees, and corporations have entered the agricultural land market in increasing numbers. In 1976 alone, 35% of farmland purchases were made by local non-farmers, non-county residents, and others.[88] Investors, both foreign and domestic, appear to view land acquisition as a hedge against inflation. Urbanites and retirees, on the other hand, purchase suburban and rural land to escape the pace of urban life. Developers purchase rural land because it provides large, contiguous, relatively inexpensive parcels of land for commercial, industrial, recreational, and housing developments. Finally, farmers and agricultural corporations purchase additional acreage to take advantage of economies of scale. On the other side of rural land demand is the slowly disappearing family farm. The family farmer is confronted with factors such as an inability to compete against the large agricultural corporations coupled with pressure to sell at a profit.[89]

As the foregoing discussion suggests, whether or not a farmer will sell his land to buyers for non-agricultural use is determined by the interrelationship of complex socio-economic factors. These include: (1) demographic factors, such as the farmer's age and state of health and whether or not he has children who want to be farmers; (2) economic factors, including not only the fair market value of the land but also the profit that can be made from the land if it is farmed (these two factors are determined by such considerations as income tax, estate tax, transportation costs, energy costs, and the like); (3) transitional factors, such as the landowner's interest in pursuing a non-farm occupation or moving to another climate; and (4) so called secondary factors, such as nuisance complaints by non-farm neighbors about farm odors and pesticides, decrease in the availability of farm labor, supplies, and services, and increase in government regulation of farming activities.[90]

The quest for farmland preservation must be balanced against the needs and demands of the non-farm public and against the direct and indirect social costs that any viable program will involve. A multitude of land use planning concepts is currently in

---

Building Industry Assn. of Cent. California v. County of Stanislaus, 190 Cal. App. 4th 582, 118 Cal. Rptr. 3d 467 (5th Dist. 2010), review denied, (Feb. 16, 2011). See Juergensmeyer, Implementing Agricultural Preservation Programs: A Time to Consider Some Radical Approaches?, 20 Gonz. L. Rev. 701 (1984–85).

[86] In a five year period the average per-acre price for all farmland increased approximately 65%. R. Gloudemans, Use Value Farmland Assessments: Theory, Practice and Impact 4 (1974).

[87] Healy and Short, New Forces in the Market for Rural Land, 46 Appraisal J. 190 (1978) (suburban land values average 1,800% more when utilized for building purposes than agricultural uses).

[88] Healy and Short, New Forces in the Market for Rural Land, 46 Appraisal J. 190 (1978).

[89] Farm Unit Size: Preservation of the Family Farm, J. Juergensmeyer & J. Wadley, Agricultural Law § 4.1 (1982).

[90] See Keene, Agricultural Land Preservation: Legal and Constitutional Issues, 15 Gonz. L. Rev. 621 (1980); Juergensmeyer, The Future of Government Regulation of Agriculture, 3 No. Ill. L. Rev. 253 (1984).

vogue as potential "solutions" to the problem. They include zoning, cluster zoning, compensable regulation plans, negative easements and purchase of development rights, land banking, large lot zoning, open space zoning, planned unit developments, purchase and leaseback programs, agricultural service districts, transferable development rights, differential taxation, eminent domain, public rights of first refusal, and public and private land trusts.[91]

Planners who see the goal of farmland preservation to be the protection of open space rather than the protection of the farm production base may not see that there is still a significant farm interest in farmland preservation. They may therefore seriously discount the extent to which farmers may see their own need to change their economic base as more important to them than farmland preservation may be to those who simply desire to preserve open space. As a result, farmers may be very interested in engaging in the very things the preservation efforts are designed to eliminate. There is a common assumption among planners and the public at large that farmland preservation programs will inherently appeal to farmers. It often comes as a great surprise when farmers are among the first to withdraw or withhold their support from the programs. It is also probably assumed that if the land can be kept in farming, farmers will be interested in farming it. This ignores the extent to which farmers resent any transfers of control over land use decision making to a non-farm dominated body. The unfortunate reality is that some of the most effective preservation efforts are the most intrusive into those decisions and are therefore the most resisted by the farmers themselves.[92]

For virtually any farmland preservation programs to succeed, some consideration must be given to a much neglected aspect of farm economics. If it is desired that land in a particular area remain in farming, it is important that the farming activity be economically feasible. In a very vital sense, the farm must have access to the inputs needed to make the venture successful as well as have a market for the produce. Two things tend to jeopardize this. First, when planners pursue an agenda that is grounded on a concern not directly related to farming (such as open space preservation), there seems to be a tendency to link the program to other environmental interests such as habitat protection or tree preservation. This engenders a much different perspective relative to the agricultural land and seems to make the program restrictive of any practice that is seen as having the capacity of "destroying" the natural condition of the area. This is often interpreted in the farming sector as an effort to "rescue the area before it is too late" as if no legitimate activity is or can occur in the area. In this setting, even many agricultural practices that may be considered vital to the economic success of the farming operation are no longer tolerable. Under such circumstances, the farm may be literally "open-spaced" to death.

The other factor which jeopardizes farmer support for farmland preservation programs is the impact of general development in the area. This is an aspect of farm economics that is not always recognized in the development of farmland preservation plans and is what farm economists would call "critical mass." In order for a single farm to survive, there have to be enough other farms in the area to warrant the presence of

---

[91] An increasingly popular concept, which has important land use regulation consequences but is primarily a fortification of the "coming to the nuisance" defense, is the so-called "right to farm" laws. See supra § 13:3.

[92] J. Wadley, Agriculture and Farm Law, §§ 47.07 in Thompson on Real Property (Thomas ed.) (1994).

vital support services. To have access to seed suppliers, fertilizer dealers, farm implement dealers and service areas, produce distributors and so forth, it is vital to have enough farms that those industries will remain in the area. If they leave, the farmer will need to go further afield to find the inputs or the marketing outlets that are needed. This may greatly increase the costs to the farmer and make the enterprise less viable. In this sense, there is an observable domino effect. If some farmers leave farming, others will leave. If too many leave, the support structure leaves as well. If the support structure leaves, other farmers may be forced to leave farming no matter how well conceived the preservation program is. The economic reality is that it may no longer be feasible to continue farming in that area. For years, the data has suggested that for every five farms to go out of production, one support industry leaves.[93] Most planning approaches do not consider the relationship between farms and the vast support structure that farming needs as part of the agricultural area to be preserved.

It should also be remembered that farmland preservation viewed from a societal land use planning perspective involves complex competing needs and values. Land preserved for farmland is not available for urban expansion and consequently may have serious consequences in regard to the cost and availability of housing, commercial centers and industrial sites.[94]

§ 13:6   Farmland Defined

An obvious prerequisite to the structuring of farmland protection programs is the identification of the land and uses deemed to merit protection. If the protective legislation or enactment defines agricultural real estate generally in terms of rural or open space lands, the protective blanket may be so broad as to include lands that have no real value for cultivation and grazing. If, alternatively, agricultural land is defined narrowly, buffer lands that effectively separate farmland from the urban fringe may not be protected. The importance of seeking a definition of agricultural lands does not lie in developing a hard and fast meaning for the term or in developing any hierarchy of definitional preference. The true value of such an inquiry is found in the realization that the definition of agricultural land is only one variable of many that must be assessed in any given land preservation and use plan.[95]

The definition of "agricultural land" used in the National Agricultural Lands Study follows:

"Agricultural lands" are lands currently used to produce agricultural commodities, including forest products, or lands that have the potential for such production. These lands have a favorable combination of soil quality, growing season, moisture supply, size and accessibility. This definition includes about 590 million acres of land that has no potential for cultivated crop use but is now in agricultural uses

---

[93] Wadley, The Future of Government Regulation: Biting the Hand that Feeds Us?, 3 No. Ill. L. Rev. 299 (1983).

[94] Alterman, The Challenge of Farmland Preservation: Lessons from a Six—Nation Comparison, 63 J. Am. Plan. Ass'n 220, 224 (Spring 1997).

[95] For a more detailed discussion of "agriculture," "farming," "farmers," and "farmland," see J. Wadley, Agriculture and Farm Law, §§ 47.05 in Thompson on Real Property (Thomas ed.) (1994); Construction and application of terms "agricultural," "farm," "farming," or the like, in zoning regulations, 38 A.L.R.5th 357.

including range, pasture, or forest land. There were 1.361 billion acres of agricultural land in 1977.[96]

Another typical definition of "farmland" is "a piece of land consisting of a fixed number of acres which is used primarily to raise or produce agricultural products, and the customary buildings which accompany such activities."[97] The U.S. Department of Commerce in its 1969 census indicated that "farmland as defined in that census included all land contained within the physical boundaries of a farm including cropland, woodland, and pasture."[98]

Since many farmland preservation efforts concentrate on the protection of "prime farmland," that concept also merits definition. The U.S. Department of Agriculture's Natural Resources Conservation Service (NRCS) defines "prime farmland" as:

land that has the best combination of physical and chemical characteristics for producing food, feed, forage, fiber, and oilseed crops, and is also available for these uses (the land could be cropland, pastureland, rangeland, forest land, or other land, but not urban built-up land or water). It has the soil quality, growing season, and moisture supply needed to economically produce sustained high yields of crops . . . . In general, prime farmlands have an adequate and dependable water supply from precipitation or irrigation, a favorable temperature and growing season . . . and few or no rocks . . . . Prime farmlands are not excessively erodible or saturated with water for a long period of time, and they either do not flood frequently or are protected from flooding.[99]

A popular land use oriented definitional approach is to define "farmland" as "a parcel of land used for agricultural activities" and to then define "agriculture" as:

The production, keeping or maintenance for sale, lease or personal use of plants and animals useful to man, including but not limited to: forages and sod crops; grains and seed crops, dairy animals and dairy products; poultry and poultry products; livestock, including beef cattle, sheep, swine, horses, ponies, mules, or goats, or any mutations or hybrids thereof, including the breeding and grazing of any or all of such animals; bees and apiary products; fur animals; trees and forest products; fruits of all kinds, including grapes, nuts and berries; vegetables; nursery, floral, ornamental and greenhouse products; or lands devoted to a soil conservation or forestry management program.[100]

Although farmland and farming are generally defined in terms of the uses to which the land is put, it is not inappropriate to consider also the nature of the individual or the entity who engages in farming as well as the level or intensity of the use.[101] The value of such a consideration is to avoid the possibility that land may be "kept in farming" even though it is occupied and used by individuals who have no significant economic interest in the farming activity. This would be the case, for example, with

---

[96] National Agricultural Lands Study, Final Report xx (1981).

[97] Rohan, Agricultural Zoning, 3 Zoning & Land Use Controls 17 (1978).

[98] Comment: Preservation of Florida's Agricultural Resources Through Land Use Planning, 27 U. Fla. L. Rev. 130 (1974).

[99] 7 C.F.R. § 657.5(a).

[100] H. Moskowitz & C. Lindbloom, The Illustrated Book of Development Definitions 23–24 (1981).

[101] J. Wadley, Agriculture and Farm Law, §§ 47.07 in Thompson on Real Property (Thomas ed. 1994).

those who own "country ranch estates" of approximately 10 acres in size who claim all of the tax benefits of differential assessment yet cannot engage in any significant agricultural activity on a tract that size other than perhaps the maintenance of hobby animals such as horses. If the definition of farmland is simply a soil-based definition or requires the keeping of animals that are useful to man, the land may well qualify for agricultural treatment even though it may be the intention of the jurisdiction to exclude it.

Similarly, if there is no consideration of the intensity of the use, activities which probably should be treated as commercial activities might well fall within the scope of farming. Many land use ordinances such as zoning codes appear to take the position that if the "farming" activity is sufficiently "commercial" in nature, it should not be treated the same as more traditional and therefore less intense uses. In these situations, agricultural activity is perceived to be a low to moderate density use by nature whereas more intense activities should be considered commercial in nature. If that is the case in other aspects of the land use regulatory scheme in the jurisdiction, the definitions used for farmland preservation programs should operate in the same paradigm. Otherwise, the different programs may work at cross purposes.

§ 13:7   Land Use Planning and Farmland Protection

The increased usage and importance of comprehensive land use planning at all levels of government are discussed elsewhere in this book. True comprehensive land use planning is recent in origin. Even more recent is the inclusion in the scope of planning activities of farmland preservation and protection considerations. This phenomenon is occurring at all governmental levels-federal, state, regional and local.

A.   Federal

The concern of federal agencies with the agricultural lands preservation and protection problem represents a relatively recent and significant change of position. In 1974, a U.S. Department of Agriculture (USDA) study concluded that "although thousands of acres of farmland are converted annually to other uses * * * we are in no danger of running out of farmland."[102]

A shift in USDA policy began the next year. By 1976, the Secretary of Agriculture announced a new USDA policy aimed at discouraging federal government activities that would convert prime agricultural land to other uses and at encouraging state and local authorities to advocate the protection of such land. In 1979, USDA issued a revised and considerably stronger policy directed toward committing USDA agencies to intercede with all other federal government agencies when conversion of prime farmland is threatened.[103]

The second most significant federal government policy revision in regard to farmland preservation, was the action taken in 1976 by the Council on Environmental Quality (CEQ) directing all federal agencies to consider the loss of prime farmland

---

[102] U.S. Dep't of Agriculture, Econ.Res.Sem., Our Land and Water Resources: Current and Prospective Supplies and Uses, Misc.Publ. No. 1,290 (Wash.D.C. U.S.G.P.O. 1974). See F. Schnidman, Agricultural Land Preservation: The Evolving Federal Role, ALI—ABA, Land Use Regulation and Litigation 100 (1984).

[103] Report to the Congress by the Comptroller General, Preserving America's Farmland—A Goal the Federal Government Should Support, (CED-79-109) 7 (1979).

when preparing the environmental impact statements (EIS) required by the National Environmental Policy Act of 1969.[104] Compliance was purely voluntary under the 1976 action but in 1980 CEQ made the requirement mandatory.[105]

In spite of the changes in federal agency policies, federal government programs were still considered the cause of the loss of thousands of acres of prime agricultural land annually. Continuing concern over such government activities led to the establishment in June 1979 of the National Agricultural Lands Study (NALS) to assess and propose remedies for the problem.[106] The recommendations contained in the final report of the NALS are broad and extensive and directed toward five objectives: (1) information sharing by state and local governments concerning successful agricultural lands preservation programs; (2) articulation of a national policy on agricultural lands preservation and its implementation; (3) federal support of state and local government programs; (4) financial assistance for protection programs; and (5) clarification of land information base statistics and data.

To help accomplish these five goals, the study makes five categories of recommendations. The first category concerns the characteristics of successful agricultural lands preservation programs and how they can serve as guidelines for development of new programs. The suggestions are: (a) that agricultural lands preservation programs should be combined with a comprehensive growth management system; (b) that state governments should assume an active role in the programs; (c) that protection programs should be adopted before development patterns foreclose some or many options; (d) that accurate information should be used in developing the programs; (e) that able political leadership should be sought as a key element of success; (f) that agricultural land protection programs should support the economic viability of agriculture in the area; and (g) that considerable attention should be given to assuring that protection programs are legally defensible.

The second category of recommendations relates to "national policy and federal agency initiatives." Most of these recommendations are vague and general. The three remaining categories of recommendations are technical assistance and education, financial assistance, and information and research needs.

At least partially in response to the NALS recommendations, Congress enacted the Farmland Protection Policy Act (FPPA)[107] as part of the Food and Agriculture Act of 1981. This Act required USDA to develop criteria for identifying the effects of federal programs on farmland conversion and required all divisions and units of the federal government to use the criteria to identify and take into account the adverse effects of federal actions on preservation of farmland and how to avoid such adverse effects.

The Secretary of Agriculture's rule for implementation of the FPPA established criteria for identifying the effects of federal programs on conversion of agricultural lands to non-agricultural uses.[108] Five "land evaluation criteria" were established pursuant to which parcels will be evaluated and assigned a score from 0 to 100 represent-

---

[104] Report to the Congress by the Comptroller General, Preserving America's Farmland—A Goal the Federal Government Should Support, (CED-79-109) 35 (1979).

[105] CEQ, Memoranda for Heads of Agencies of August 11, 1980.

[106] Report to the Congress by the Comptroller General, at 49–52.

[107] Pub. L. No. 97–98, 7 U.S.C.A. §§ 4201 to 4209.

[108] 7 C.F.R. § 658.1.

ing the value of the land as farmland in comparison to other land in the area. This "scoring" was to be performed by the NRCS. The federal agency whose action might lead to conversion of the agricultural land was required to assess the suitability of the tract in question for protection by using 12 "site assessment criteria."[109]

The Federal government is also a source of funds for farmland preservation through conservation easements.[110] The Farm and Ranch Lands Protection Program is a voluntary federal conservation program which provides matching funds for the purchase of permanent conservation easements on farm and ranch land. The program was originally established by the Federal Agriculture Improvement and Reform Act of 1996 and reauthorized and expanded by the Farm Security and Rural Investment Act of 2002.[111]

In addition to attempting to change federal agency policies regarding farmland conversions, the federal government has sought to encourage farmers to keep their land in farming by reducing capital gains and estate tax burdens on the farmland. Although certainly relevant to the issue of farmland preservation, such provisions are outside the scope of this treatise.

B. State and Regional

Not many states have state comprehensive plans[112] but Oregon and Florida are notable examples of those who do. Farmland and agricultural land use policies are given considerable attention in the plans of both states.

In fact, preservation of agricultural land is said to have been the primary motivation behind the adoption of the Oregon comprehensive planning statute.[113] The goals and guidelines for Oregon's agricultural lands are now formulated as follows:[114]

---

[109] 7 C.F.R. § 658.5.

[110] "See § 13:2, infra.

[111] 7 U.S.C.A. § 7201. See Eitel, The Farm and Ranch Lands Protection Program: An Analysis of the Federal Policy on United States Farmland Loss, 8 Drake J. Agric. L. 591 (2003).

[112] See §§ 2:1 et seq., supra;

[113] Or. Admin. R. 660–15–000(3) (1997); T. Pelham, State Land Use Planning and Regulation 158 (1979). See also Juergensmeyer, Introduction: State and Local Land Use Planning and Control in the Agricultural Context, 25 S.D. L. Rev. 463 (1980). In evaluating Oregon's regulatory and planning provisions designed to preserve agricultural lands, the recent adoption of Measure 37, a private property compensation statute for certain landowners whose property values are decreased by land use planning and regulation and its judicial approval in MacPherson v. Department of Administrative Services, 340 Or. 117, 130 P.3d 308 (2006), have created doubt in regard to the future of the current Oregon system. See Aoki, Briscoe, and Hovland, Trading Spaces: Measure 37, MacPherson v. Department of Administrative Services, and Transferable Development Rights as a Path out of Deadlock, 20 J. Env't. L.& Litig. 273 (2005); Sullivan and Eber, The Long and Winding Road: Farmland Protection in Oregon 1961–2009, 18 San Joaquin Agric. L. Rev. 1 (2008–2009); Blumm and Grafe, Enacting Libertarian Property: Oregon's Measure 37 and Its Implications, 85 Denv. U. L. Rev. 279 (2007).

[114] Or. Admin. R. 660–15–000(3) (1997). The implementation of Oregon's agricultural lands preservation goal is discussed in Rochette, Prevention of Urban Sprawl: The Oregon Method, 3 Zoning & Plan. L. Rep. 25 (1980). See also Rothrock, Oregon's Goal 5: Is Ecologically Sustainable Development Reflected?, 31 Willamette L. Rev. 449 (1995). Key Oregon cases on point are Lane County v. Land Conservation and Development Com'n, 138 Or. App. 635, 910 P.2d 414 (1996), opinion adhered to as modified on reconsideration on other grounds, 140 Or. App. 368, 914 P.2d 1114 (1996), decision rev'd, 325 Or. 569, 942 P.2d 278 (1997); Department of Land Conservation and Development v. Curry County, 132 Or. App. 393, 888 P.2d 592 (1995); Department of Land Conservation and Development v. Coos County, 117 Or. App. 400, 844 P.2d 907 (1992).

Goal 3: Agricultural Lands

To preserve and maintain agricultural lands.

> Agricultural lands shall be preserved and maintained for farm use, consistent with existing and future needs for agricultural products, forest and open space and with the state's agricultural land use policy expressed in Or. Rev. Stat. §§ 215.243 and 215.700.

Uses

> Counties may authorize farm uses and those non-farm uses defined by commission rule that will not have significant adverse effects on accepted farm or forest practices.

Implementation

> Zoning applied to agricultural land shall limit uses which can have significant adverse effects on agricultural and forest land, farm and forest uses or accepted farming or forest practices.

Counties shall establish minimum sizes for new lots or parcels in each agricultural land designation. The minimum parcel size established for farm uses in farmland zones shall be consistent with applicable statutes. If a county proposes a minimum lot or parcel size less than 80 acres, or 160 acres for rangeland, the minimum shall be appropriate to maintain the existing commercial agricultural enterprise within the area and meet the requirements of Or. Rev. Stat. § 215.243.

Counties authorized by Or. Rev. Stat. § 215.316 may designate agricultural land as marginal land and allow those uses and land divisions on the designated marginal land as allowed by law.

LCDC shall review and approve plan designations and revisions to land use regulations in the manner provided by Or. Rev. Stat. Ch. 197.

Definitions

Agricultural Land—in western Oregon is land of predominantly Class I, II, III and IV soils and in eastern Oregon is land of predominantly Class I, II, III, IV, V and VI soils as identified in the Soil Capability Classification System of the United States Soil Conservation Service, and other lands which are suitable for farm use taking into consideration soil fertility, suitability for grazing, climatic conditions, existing and future availability of water for farm irrigation purposes, existing land-use patterns, technological and energy inputs required, or accepted farming practices. Lands in other classes which are necessary to permit farm practices to be undertaken on adjacent or nearby lands, shall be included as agricultural land in any event.

More detailed soil data to define agricultural land may be utilized by local governments if such data permits achievement of this goal.

Agricultural land does not include land within acknowledged urban growth boundaries or land within acknowledged exceptions to Goals 3 or 4.

* * *

Guidelines

A.   Planning

1.   Urban growth should be separated from agricultural lands by buffer or transitional areas of open space.

2.   Plans providing for the preservation and maintenance of farm land for farm use should consider as a major determinant the carrying capacity of the air, land and water resources of the planning area. The land conservation and development actions provided for by such plans should not exceed the carrying capacity of such resources.

B.   Implementation

1.   Non-farm uses permitted within farm use zones under Or. Rev. Stat. §§ 215.213(2) and (3) and 215.283(2) and (3) should be minimized to allow for maximum agricultural productivity.

2.   Extension of services, such as sewer and water supplies into rural areas should be appropriate for the needs of agriculture, farm use and non-farm uses established under Or. Rev. Stat. §§ 215.213 and 215.283.

3.   Services that need to pass through agricultural lands should not be connected with any use that is not allowed under Or. Rev. Stat. §§ 215.203, 215.213, and 215.283, should not be assessed as part of the farm unit and should be limited in capacity to serve specific service areas and identified needs.

4.   Forest and open space uses should be permitted on agricultural land that is being preserved for future agricultural growth. The interchange of such lands should not be subject to tax penalties.

The point was made in discussing growth management[115] that the lack of regional planning in most states is a detriment to effective solutions to combating sprawl. The same is particularly true in regard to protecting agricultural land from the consequences of urban expansion. In fact, many see the lack of regional planning as one of the major factors in the current loss of farmland.[116]

As discussed above,[117] virtually every state has adopted one or more statutes designed to protect agricultural operations from nuisance actions. These statutes may

---

[115] § 9:5, supra.

[116] Levy and Melliar-Smith, The Race for the Future: Farmland Preservation Tools, 18 Nat. Resources & Env't 15 (2003).

[117] See § 13:3 supra.

impair the ability of local governments to "control" farming operations through zoning and other land use control measures.[118]

C.   Local

Another relevant development in the land use control area is the requirement via state legislation that all units of local government formulate and adopt comprehensive plans that meet state specified standards. The important implementation mechanism in such statutes is the consistency requirement,[119] whereby the state statute requires all subsequent land use regulations by local governments to be consistent with local, and regional or state, if any, comprehensive plan.

A specifically required element of such a plan normally includes planning for agricultural lands and related activities. Florida's Local Government Comprehensive Planning and Land Development Regulation Act provided from the beginning for a "future land use plan element designating proposed future general distribution, location, and extent of"[120] agricultural uses as well as the requirement that each local government comprehensive plan contain an "open space element."[121]

The Florida Act has been recently amended to encourage the creation of rural land stewardship areas "within which planning and economic incentives are applied to encourage the implementation of innovative and flexible planning and development strategies and creative land use planning techniques . . . . "[122] These areas are to " be used to further the following broad principles of rural sustainability: restoration and maintenance of the economic value of rural land; control of urban sprawl; identification and protection of ecosystems, habitats, and natural resources; promotion of rural economic activity; maintenance of the viability of Florida's agricultural economy; and protection of the character of rural areas of Florida."[123] One of the most significant and motivating results of creating rural land stewardship areas is the portion of the new statutory provision which authorizes the creation of "transferable rural land use credits" or "stewardship credits" which are a slight variation of the transferable development rights concept.[124] In 2006 Florida adopted an Agricultural Lands and Practices Act and created a special concept of "agricultural enclave."[125]

---

[118] See § 13:7 infra; Walker, Whole Hog: The Pre-emption of Local Control by the 1999 Amendment to the Michigan Right to Farm Act, 36 Val. U. L. Rev 461, 493 (2002).

[119] See supra § 2:14.

[120] Fla. Stat. Ann. § 163.3177(6)(a).

[121] Fla. Stat. Ann. § 163.3177(6)(e).

[122] Fla. Stat. Ann. § 163.3177(11)(d)(l).

[123] Fla. Stat. Ann. § 163.3177(11)(d)(2). "A rural land stewardship area shall be not less than 10,000 acres and shall be located outside of municipalities and established urban growth boundaries, and shall be designated by plan amendment." Fla. Stat. Ann. § 163.3177(11)(d)(4).

[124] See § 13:11 infra for a discussion of TDRs in the agricultural lands preservation context and § 9:10 supra, for a general discussion of TDRs.

[125] 163.3162(33) "Agricultural enclave" means an unincorporated, undeveloped parcel that:

(a) Is owned by a single person or entity;

(b) Has been in continuous use for bona fide agricultural purposes, as defined by s. 193.461, for a period of 5 years prior to the date of any comprehensive plan amendment application;

(c) Is surrounded on at least 75% of its perimeter by:

1. Property that has existing industrial, commercial, or residential development; or

2. Property that the local government has designated, in the local government's comprehensive plan, zoning map, and future land use map, as land that is to be developed for industrial, commercial, or residen-

Perhaps the greatest role local government comprehensive plans can play is pulling it all together. Professor Arthur C. Nelson has observed that agricultural land preservation works best, and may work only, if the best elements of all techniques are choreographed. A local comprehensive plan must state the public interest in preserving such land, which is accomplished usually by citing the economic contributions and taking notice that because urban and agricultural land uses are fundamentally incompatible they must be clearly separated. Zoning is used to provide for the market demand for rural lifestyles but in locations and in a manner that does not interfere with agricultural activities that are expected of the remaining agricultural area. Property taxation based only on agricultural productivity and not urban uses is applied to those areas that are subject to exclusive agricultural zoning; the logic would be sensible since these lands would be for most practical purposes removed from the urban land market and speculation for conversion would be reduced if not eliminated. Right-to-farm laws would supplement these efforts. While no single technique is effective by itself (and can be counterproductive), the combination of techniques allows them to be mutually reinforcing.[126]

D.   *Resolving Land Use Conflicts on the Urban Fringe*

Studies have suggested that there is a predictable pattern associated with the conversion of land from rural to urban oriented uses in the fringe areas surrounding metropolitan areas. In many instances, the first thing to occur is that land costs begin to rise and speculation enters the picture. This causes ad valorem and other taxes associated with the land to rise. Soon, the development value of the land exceeds the production value of the land. As urban-oriented development occurs near the farmland, pilfering and destruction of crops and concerns over livestock increase. Complaints about noise, odor, dust, and farm machinery on roads and highways begin to come to local governments and increased political pressure tends to be brought against the agricultural uses to take action to address matters that tend to be considered nuisances. When the farmers become convinced that the area will inevitably become urban, they tend to stop investing in farm improvements. As further development occurs, a number of the more vulnerable farmers will leave and, as a consequence, the support industries, such as feed mills, machinery dealers, and suppliers tend to find that they no longer have the critical mass of farms that they require in order to survive and they also start to leave the area or migrate to regional locations. It is about this time that the decision is made to convert the land to non-farm use. If this conversion process continues uninterrupted, an area that was once predominantly farmland will become predominantly dedicated to urban uses.

---

tial purposes, and at least 75% of such property is existing industrial, commercial, or residential development;

(d) Has public services, including water, wastewater, transportation, schools, and recreation facilities, available or such public services are scheduled in the capital improvement element to be provided by the local government or can be provided by an alternative provider of local government infrastructure in order to ensure consistency with applicable concurrency provisions of s. 163.3180; and

(e) Does not exceed 1,280 acres; however, if the property is surrounded by existing or authorized residential development that will result in a density at buildout of at least 1,000 residents per square mile, then the area shall be determined to be urban and the parcel may not exceed 4,480 acres.

[126] See Arthur C. Nelson and James B. Duncan, Growth Management Principles and Practices (1995). See also Ruhl, Agriculture and Ecosystem Services: Strategies for State and Local Governments, 17 N.Y.U. Envtl. L.J. 424, 426 (2008).

One of the most difficult aspects associated with addressing the problem of farm-land preservation is that the conversion process may have reached such an advanced stage that there is no real prospect of halting the conversion. This seems particularly to be the case where there has been a change in ownership in advance of a change in land use, where the new owner has purchased the property with a view toward making the use change at a more opportune time. In these situations, the conflicts between farm land users and non-farm landowners tend to diffuse themselves because the conflicts actually accelerate the conversion.

A number of cases have held that state or regional efforts to protect farmland from the intrusion of urban uses preempt other kinds of local decision-making. For example, in one case,[127] the state's right to farm law was held to preempt municipal land use authority over a farming operation. Similarly, it has been held that the Growth Management Plan, under which an area had been designated as agricultural, prevented a change in use of that land from agricultural to athletic fields and recreational use.[128]

What is perhaps more likely is that the dispute resolution process will be left to private actions—most likely of the nuisance variety. Here, there has been a noticeable propensity to confine the so-called right to farm laws to the urban-rural conflict. Several recent cases have interpreted so-called right to farm laws as creating a shield only against nuisance claims brought by nonagricultural landowners but not as protecting the activity from complaints raised by other agricultural landowners.[129]

§ 13:8   Zoning of Farmland

In spite of recent changes and innovations in the land use control area, zoning remains the most frequently used and potentially the most effective land use control device to protect and preserve agricultural lands.[130] Nonetheless, serious limitations exist on the effectiveness of zoning, in its traditional format, as a solution to the preservation problem.[131]

The key characteristic of use categories under traditional or Euclidean zoning is that all use zones are "cumulative," meaning that all higher, i.e., more preferred, uses are permitted in "lower" categories. Since the urban planners who traditionally drafted zoning ordinances were development oriented, "agricultural use" was ranked at or near the bottom, meaning that uses ranked "higher" were frequently permitted in agricultural zones no matter how inconsistent or competing they were with agricultural activities. Even those traditional zoning ordinances that allow only agricultural and specified other uses in agricultural zones permit so many inappropriate uses that the result is the same.

---

[127] *Township of Franklin v. Hollander,* 338 N.J. Super. 373, 769 A.2d 427 (App. Div. 2001), judgment aff'd, 172 N.J. 147, 796 A.2d 874 (2002).

[128] *King County v. Central Puget Sound Growth Management Hearings Bd.,* 142 Wash. 2d 543, 14 P.3d 133 (2000).

[129] See, e.g. *State v. Finley,* 18 Kan. App. 2d 419, 854 P.2d 315 (1993); *Buchanan v. Simplot Feeders, Ltd. Partnership,* 134 Wash. 2d 673, 952 P.2d 610 (1998).

[130] See, generally, Paster, Preservation of Agricultural Lands Through Land Use Planning Tools and Techniques, 44 Nat. Resources J. 283 (2004).

[131] See Arthur C. Nelson and James B. Duncan, Growth Management Principles and Practices (1995); Berry, The Effects of Urbanization on Agricultural Activities, 3 Growth & Change 2–8 (1978); Rasche, Protecting Agricultural Lands in Oregon: An Assessment of the Exclusive Farm Use Zone System, 77 Or. L. Rev. 993 (1998).

Modern zoning ordinances are increasingly noncumulative in nature: all or specified use zones are to be devoted exclusively to the designated use, and even so-called "higher" uses are excluded. Given the failures of cumulative zoning to protect agricultural lands as discussed above, it is not surprising to find that in many zoning ordinances of recent vintage land zoned for agricultural purposes can be devoted only to agricultural and closely related uses.[132]

Exclusive agricultural zoning, unlike agricultural zoning under cumulative ordinances, not only restricts the landowner of agricultural land but confers protection to the farmer by excluding incompatible uses.[133] Such zoning, in theory at least, is a definitive tool for preserving agricultural lands and preventing their conversion to nonagricultural uses. Even if land speculators purchase farmland and take it out of agricultural production, strict enforcement of the zoning code should prevent any development on or changes of the land that would affect its ultimate suitability for agricultural production.

The problems encountered in using exclusive agricultural use zoning as a farmland preservation tool result not from zoning principles but from zoning practice. The farmer himself may find the stringency of the zoning protection economically unacceptable, and he or his vendees may resort to the normal avenues for zoning flexibility—variances, special exceptions, and rezonings—to obtain permission for profitable but ultimately incompatible uses, thus undermining if not defeating the protective goals of such zoning approaches.[134] Since exclusive agricultural use zones are relatively new,[135] little judicial attention has been given to them but most courts which have considered the issue have upheld them.

One case in which the local government's non-exclusive agricultural zoning plan was not upheld provides some judicial guidelines for local governments. In *Hopewell Township Board of Supervisors v. Golla*,[136] the Supreme Court of Pennsylvania was confronted with a zoning code provision which permitted the owner of a tract of land in an agricultural zone to use the undivided tract as a farm with only one single-family dwelling or to establish as many as five contiguous residential lots of no more than 1 ½ acres and a single family dwelling on each lot. Plaintiffs did not challenge the agricultural zoning classification but only the reasonableness of the restrictions placed on their own land. The court held that this approach to farmland preservation placed an unreasonably severe limitation on permissible land uses and that it had an arbitrary and discriminatory impact on different landowners since under the ordinance the owner of a small tract of land could devote a larger percentage of his tract to residential development than the owner of a large tract. The court suggested a cure for the ordinance's defects by stating: "were the ordinance to permit the dedication of the 1 ½ acre lot to a single family residence per each X number of acres in the tract, this scheme

---

[132] See supra § 4:8.

[133] See, generally, Keating, Exclusionary Zoning: In Whose Interests Should the Police Power be Exercised?, 23 Real Est. L.J. 304 (1995).

[134] See supra § 5:1.

[135] Exclusive agricultural use zoning is used throughout Hawaii and Oregon but in very few other areas. Arthur C. Nelson and James B. Duncan, Growth Management Principles and Practices (1995).

[136] *Hopewell Tp. Bd. of Sup'rs v. Golla*, 499 Pa. 246, 452 A.2d 1337 (1982). The case is analyzed at Berger, Agricultural Zoning Held Invalid, 7 APA Plan. & L. Div. Newsl. 10 (May 1983). See also Kaufmann, Comment: Agricultural Zoning in Pennsylvania: Will Growth Pressure Prevail?, 91 Dick. L. Rev. 289 (1986).

would have a more equitable effect and would avoid impacting landowners on an arbitrary basis."[137]

§ 13:9   Agricultural Districts

Agricultural districting is designed to bring about through voluntary compliance and local initiative the same quality of protection for farmland as that afforded by exclusive agricultural zoning.[138] It was pioneered in California,[139] New York,[140] and Virginia.[141] Agricultural landowners whose lands meet specified acreage minimums can voluntarily form special districts.[142] Such status, depending on the exact provisions of the relevant statute, creates a binding agreement between the landowner and local authorities for a specified number of years during which the landowner receives special tax treatment and freedom from eminent domain. The authority of public agencies to install growth-stimulating public services in the area is limited and special assessments against the land are forbidden. Local governments often are forbidden to exercise zoning power within the district.[143] If nonagricultural uses are made of the land during the "contract" period, heavy tax penalties are incurred.[144]

The major advantage and appeal of the agricultural districting approach to farmland preservation lies in its emphasis on voluntary compliance and local initiative. Other strengths, compared to previously and subsequently discussed approaches, include the retention of land ownership by the farmer, the stringent restrictions are voluntary in nature and allow land use without raising taking issue problems, and its emphasis on local control, which thereby at least theoretically makes it responsive to

---

[137] 499 Pa. 246, 452 A.2d 1337, 1344 (1982).

[138] See Myers, The Legal Aspects of Agricultural Districting, 55 Ind. L.J. 1, 2 (1979), reprinted in 2 Agric. L.J. 627 (1981); Safran, Contracting For Preservation: An Overview of State Agricultural District Programs, 27 Zoning & Plan. L. Rep. 1 (2004).

[139] The precursor and inspiration for all agricultural districting acts is said to be California's Land Conservation Act, Cal. Gov't Code §§ 51200 to 51295, which is known popularly as the Williamson Act. For discussions of the Williamson Act and California's Agricultural Land Preservation Act of 1995, see McGurty, The State of Agricultural Land Preservation in California in 1997: Will the Agricultural Land Stewardship Program Solve the Problems Inherent in the Williamson Act?, 7 San Joaquin Ag. L. Rev. 135 (1997); Daniel J. Curtin and Cecily T. Talbert, California Land Use and Planning Law at 228 (26th ed. 2006). The concept of the Williamson Act was recently expanded in California by the adoption of the Farmland Security Zone Act, Cal. Gov't Code §§ 51296 to 51297.4 (2001). See O'Brien, California's Farmland Security Zone: A New Incentive for the Preservation of Existing Farmland, 11 S. J. Agric. L. Rev. 135 (2001).

[140] N.Y. Agric. & Mkts. Law §§ 300 to 307. See Nolon, The Stable Door is Open: New York's Statutes to Protect Farm Land, 67 N.Y. St. B. J. 36; Salkin, New York Zoning Law and Practice § 14:03 (4th ed.).

[141] Agricultural and Forestal Districts Act, Va. Code Ann. §§ 15.1–1506 to 15.1–1513 (1997). At least three additional states have enacted agricultural district statutes. See. 505 Ill. Comp. Stat. 57/1; Iowa Code Ann. § 358A.27; Md. Code Ann., Agric., § 2–501 et seq. For an overview of agricultural districting legislation, see Duncan, Toward a Theory of Broad—Based Planning for the Preservation of Agricultural Land, 24 Nat. Resources J. 51, 96–113 (1984).

[142] Any owner of agricultural land who meets the statutory acreage requirements (in New York the greater of 500 acres or 10% of the land to be included in the district and in Virginia at least 200 acres) may apply to the local governing body that then seeks the opinion of a planning body, holds public hearings, and then adopts, modifies, or rejects the proposal. The details of the New York and Virginia procedure are discussed in Myers, supra note 1.

[143] See *Inter-Lakes Health, Inc. v. Town of Ticonderoga Town Bd.,* 13 A.D.3d 846, 786 N.Y.S.2d 643 (3d Dep't 2004) (court held the state's Agriculture and Markets Law preempted local zoning ordinances regarding agricultural activities on property located in agricultural districts).

[144] In New York, for example, conversion to nonagricultural uses during the contract period results in a penalty equal to five times the tax saved in the last year in which the land benefitted from an agricultural assessment, plus interest. N.Y. Agric. & Mkts. Law § 306.

local needs and problems.[145] Given these advantages, the popularity of this approach to farmland preservation is not surprising. By 1978 approximately one-half of the farmland in the state of New York was in agricultural districting.[146]

In spite of this popularity, the approach is not without its problems and disadvantages. The obvious disadvantage is the feature that already has been pointed out as a basis for the concept's appeal—i.e., it is entirely voluntary. Studies indicate that the effectiveness of the approach is limited by the fact that only those lands relatively free from urban fringe development pressures, that is to say, those lands that need protection the least, are placed in districts. Secondly, the special tax treatment, which constitutes the major advantage to the landowner, hampers the revenue raising authority of local governments and provides dubious incentives to retain agricultural district status. Finally, the limitations placed on governmental power in regard to regulation of the land in question and the location of public facilities, may hamper local government comprehensive planning and result in less desirable growth patterns in the long run.

§ 13:10 Clustering, Planned Unit Developments, Conservation Subdivisions, and Minimum Lot Size

One of the most serious dilemmas encountered by owners of agricultural land occurs when adjacent land is developed for residential, commercial or other non-farm uses. Once such development occurs, the farmer usually finds himself subjected to intense economic pressures to convert his farm to non-agricultural use because of the increase in value which results from neighboring development. The farmer also frequently discovers that his land no longer is well-suited to agricultural uses, since the normal odors, noises, and pollutants accompanying many agricultural activities are now nuisances in the eyes of his new neighbors.[147] Cluster zoning, planned unit developments, and open space zoning are land use control techniques designed to alleviate such consequences of development by providing a land buffer on or between the developed land and the neighboring farmland.

Cluster zoning involves development of a tract of land in order to meet density maximums for the tract as a unit but places improvements on the tract so as to allow the preservation of open space or buffer areas on all or certain borders.[148] As a result, new development need not abut agricultural land, and the development/farming conflict is lessened.[149]

Local governmental use of the cluster concept to provide a buffer between areas of development and of agriculture is relatively simple in the sense that little or no change in basic zoning codes is necessary to allow such an approach. Most courts have recognized the permissibility of such an approach, even pursuant to Euclidean ordinances, since no variation of overall density or of permissible uses occurs. The developer who is required or encouraged to cluster his planned improvements is not usually in a position

---

[145] See Geier, Agricultural Districts and Zoning: A State—Local Approach to a National Problem, 1980 Ecology L.Q. 655 (1980).

[146] Myers, The Legal Aspects of Agricultural Districting, 55 Ind. L.J. 1, 2 (1979), reprinted in 2 Agric. L.J. 627 (1981

[147] See § 13:3, supra and §§ 14:1 et seq., infra.

[148] See Stroud, The Farm and the City, 9 Fla. Envtl. & Urb. Issues 4 (1981); Pivo, Small, and Wolfe, Rural Cluster Zoning: Survey and Guidelines, 42 No. 9 Land Use L. & Zoning Dig. 1, 3 (1990).

[149] See supra § 4:11.

to assert constitutionally based objections since he is not denied the right to develop the overall density established by the local land use regulation. In fact, developers frequently seek permission to cluster since there often are economies of design and construction to such a development arrangement.[150]

The planned unit development (PUD) is grounded upon the cluster concept but constitutes both a refinement of that concept and a departure from traditional Euclidean zoning approaches. The PUD combines uses within a development so that various housing types—for example, high-rise apartments, townhouses, single family dwellings, and condominiums—co-exist with open spaces, recreational areas, convenience type commercial uses, and business/professional uses.[151]

The use of a PUD for the development of land adjacent to agricultural lands offers various protective aspects. As with clustering, buffer areas that are not built upon can be placed between new improvements and neighboring farmland. Furthermore, unlike clusters, the provision for various commercial, recreational, or business/professional facilities within the PUD means that adjacent farmland is not needed as a location for supportive services that inevitably accompany development. By providing for such non-residential uses, the PUD offers greater protection for adjacent agricultural land than does simple cluster zoning. Although PUDs frequently receive even greater developer enthusiasm than clusters, local land use control authorities are often less enthusiastic about the PUD since its combination of uses is in conflict with one of the sacred cows of traditional zoning—separation of uses. Additionally, approval for use of PUDs frequently requires the existence of floating zones[152] within the zoning jurisdiction.

Conservation subdivisions are residential or mixed-use developments in which a significant portion of the tract being subdivided is designated as undivided and permanently preserved open space. The lots to be built on are clustered on the remainder of the tract. They are inspired by cluster communities and golf course developments but they are innovative in that the protected open space areas may be forests, meadows, wetlands, aquifer recharge areas, gardens, or even working farms. They thus differ dramatically from the conventional, sometimes called "cookie cutter," approach to subdivision where the entire tract is divided in to buildable lots usually of uniform size with any open space being provided by setback lines within the privately owned lots or home owner association owned active recreational areas. Conservation subdivisions are of recent origin and in their current format are attributable to planning implementation of smart growth and new urbanism principles.[153] The Pennsylvania Supreme Court recently rejected takings and exclusionary zoning claims raised as objections to conservation subdivision restrictions designed to protect prime agricultural and environmentally sensitive lands.[154]

Open space zoning is a more drastic way of providing the type of open space or land buffer between new development and neighboring agricultural land that results almost automatically from clusters and PUDs. The technique is much simpler; however, since land bordering agricultural areas is designated in the relevant comprehensive

---

[150] See supra §§ 7:17 to 7:22.

[151] See supra § 7:17.

[152] See supra § 4:16.

[153] Conservation subdivisions are discussed in § 7:9, supra.

[154] *In re Petition of Dolington Land Group*, 576 Pa. 519, 839 A.2d 1021 (2003).

plan as being unavailable for development and is zoned for only recreational or other nondevelopment uses.[155] The problem presented by open space zoning is that the economic value of land so zoned is nearly destroyed, thereby entitling the landowner to contest the zoning designation as an unconstitutional taking of property without compensation.[156]

Another related zoning technique frequently advocated as an agricultural lands preservation device is "large lot" zoning. By establishing high minimum lot area requirements such as 1 acre, 5, 10, 15, 18, or, in one case,[157] 160 acres, residential development of rural land is discouraged by increasing the cost of, and thereby decreasing the demand for, such property. Furthermore, if the land is developed, the low density of such developments only slightly affects the continued suitability of adjacent or nearby land for agricultural use. The major disadvantage of using large lot zoning to protect agricultural land is the same encountered with open space zoning: the economic value may be so greatly decreased as to raise the taking issue. The exclusionary effects of large lot requirements provide still another basis for contesting their validity.[158]

§ 13:11 Transferable Development Rights

The application of the transferable development rights (TDR) approach to agricultural land preservation is of relatively recent origin.[159]

The TDR approach designates certain land areas within a given jurisdiction as subject to severe regulations and designates other land areas within the jurisdiction as appropriate for development. Owners of the severely restricted land are allowed to sell their rights to develop, which they cannot exercise because of the land use restrictions, to the owners of land permitted to be developed. The purchasing landowners may be required to purchase the rights of the restricted landowners before they may develop, or the purchase of development rights may authorize them to develop at greater density than otherwise would be permitted. Transferable Development Rights are discussed at length in § 9:10, supra.

Although considerable support exists for using the TDR concept as an agricultural lands preservation device, the National Agricultural Lands Study treated the idea rather negatively.[160] In evaluating the usefulness of TDRs, it first should be noted that the statistics used by the NALS are now out of date and actual experience with TDRs is considerably broader and more positive.[161] Furthermore, whatever complexities and difficulties are encountered in regard to implementation of TDR programs, their key potential advantage over virtually all other approaches to agricultural lands preservation is that restricted landowners receive compensation for their losses without the

---

[155] The important interrelationship between agricultural land preservation and open space protection is discussed at § 13:3, supra.

[156] See supra §§ 10:4 to 10:8.

[157] *Wilson v. McHenry County,* 92 Ill. App. 3d 997, 48 Ill. Dec. 395, 416 N.E.2d 426 (2d Dist. 1981).

[158] See supra § 6:2.

[159] See McEleney, Using Transferable Development Rights to Preserve Vanishing Landscapes and Landmarks, 83 Ill. B. J. 634 (1995). Feitshans, PDRs and TDRs: Land Preservation Tools in a Universe of Voluntary and Compulsory Land Use Planning Tools, 7 Drake J. Agric. L. 305 (2002); Arthur C. Nelson, Rick Pruetz & Doug Woodruff, The TDR Handbook: Designing and Implementing Transfer of Development Rights Programs Chapters 14 & 15 (2012).

[160] National Agricultural Lands Study, Final Report 61 (1981).

[161] See § 9:10.

need for expenditure of public funds.[162] The compensation comes from payments made in an open market context by landowners economically benefited by land use restrictions. In short, TDRs allow payment of compensation without cost to the taxpayer.

Finally, as far as the acceptability of the TDR concept is concerned, the basic principle is a familiar one to farmers. As Professor Torres has observed:[163]

> While in urban areas transferable development rights may be looked upon as a novel land planning device, in farm country the notion that the productive capacity of one area may be severed and transferred to another area is at least as old as the Agricultural Adjustment Act.[164] Depending on the crop being farmed, acreage allotments have traditionally been transferable between farms . . . . One crop that farmers, especially those farmers in developing areas, hope to harvest is the appreciated non-farm development value of their holdings . . . . TDRs function much like the transfer of acreage allotments between . . . holders of development potential . . . . Like crops, development potential becomes merely another cash valued commodity.

The judicial reaction to TDR programs is discussed elsewhere in this book.[165] The initial approval of the TDR concept by the Supreme Court in *Penn Central*[166] has been somewhat clouded by the Supreme Court's decision in *Suitum v. Tahoe Regional Planning Agency.*[167] Although TDR Programs themselves received favorable comment, the Court left undecided whether the alternate use and value TDRs provide are to be considered in reaching a decision as to whether or not a taking has occurred or only in deciding how much compensation has been paid if a taking is found.[168]

§ 13:12 Conservation Easements

Conservation easements merit special attention as an agricultural lands preservation technique, even though their use is sometimes part of a transferable development rights plan or of the land banking or public and private trusts approach.[169] Their current use and popularity is due at least in part to the programs promoted and funding provided by the Trust for Public Lands (TPL) and the American Farmland Trust. TPL is "a national, nonprofit, land conservation organization that conserves land for people

---

[162] Bozung, Transferable Development Rights: Compensation for Owners of Restricted Property, 1984 Zoning & Plan. L. Handbook 207.

[163] Torres, Helping Farmers and Saving Farmland, 37 Okla. L. Rev. 31, 40 (1984).

[164] 7 U.S.C.A. § 1281 et seq.

[165] See § 9:10.

[166] *Penn Cent. Transp. Co. v. City of New York,* 438 U.S. 104, 98 S. Ct. 2646, 57 L. Ed. 2d 631 (1978).

[167] *Suitum v. Tahoe Regional Planning Agency,* 520 U.S. 725, 117 S. Ct. 1659, 137 L. Ed. 2d 980, 44 Env't. Rep. Cas. (BNA) 1673, 27 Envtl. L. Rep. 21064 (1997).

[168] See Nicholas, Juergensmeyer and Leebrick, Transferable Development Rights and Alternatives After *Suitum,* 30 Urb. Law. 441 (1998).

[169] For an analysis of conservation easements and an early bibliography, see National Trust for Historic Preservation, Information Sheet No. 25, Establishing an Easement Program to Protect Historic, Scenic and National Resources (Washington, D.C. 1980). See also Thompson and Jay, An Examination of Court Opinions on the Enforcement and Defense of Conservation Easements and Other Conservation and Preservation Tools: Themes and Approaches to Date, 78 Denv. U. L. Rev. 373 (2001)For a discussion of federal conservation easement programs, see Jordan, Perpetual Conservation: Accomplishing the Goal Through Preemptive Federal Easement Programs, 43 Case W. Res. L. Rev. 401 (1993); Hamilton, Legal Authority for Federal Acquisition of Conservation Easements to Provide Agricultural Credit Relief, 35 Drake L. Rev. 477 (1985–86); See Eitel, The Farm and Ranch Lands Protection Program: An Analysis of the Federal Policy on United States Farmland Loss, 8 Drake J. Agric. L. 591 (2003).

to enjoy as parks, community gardens, historic sites, rural lands, and other natural places . . . . "[170] The Trust not only raises private money for land and conservation easement acquisition but also assists local governments in formulating programs for public financing.[171] The American Farmland Trust (AFT), a national, non-profit organization formed in 1980, engages in comparable programs designed specifically to preserve farmland through purchase and conservation easement programs.[172]

A conservation easement is created when a landowner restricts his rights to develop his own land in ways that would be incompatible with its use as farmland. The landowner burdens his land in the form of a negative restriction, thereby creating a negative easement in favor of other parcels of land or for the benefit of public or private agricultural lands preservation organizations. Unless the negative restriction is in some way limited, it will bind all future owners of the land.[173]

Although such arrangements are generally referred to as conservation or preservation "easements," the same goals can be accomplished from a property law viewpoint through real covenants or equitable servitudes.[174] Perhaps the greatest advantage to the use of conservation easements is that the farmer remains owner of all interests in the land in question except the right to use the property in a manner inconsistent with the restriction.

The institution of conservation easement programs is proceeding at an impressive pace. At least 34 states have adopted such measures.[175] The federal government also utilized the theory of voluntary negative easements in its creation of the Conservation Reserve Program. Pursuant to the Program, the Secretary of Agriculture had authority to contract with the owners and operators of specified farmlands to assist them in conserving and improving the soil and water resources on their land.[176] The Conservation Reserve Program was replaced by the Farm and Ranch Lands Protection Program which is a voluntary federal conservation program which provides matching funds for the purchase of permanent conservation easements on farm and ranch land. The program was originally established by the Federal Agriculture Improvement and Reform Act of 1996 and reauthorized and expanded by the Farm Security and Rural Investment Act of 2002.[177]

---

[170] Trust for Public Lands website, http://www.tpl.org.

[171] "Since 1972, TPL has worked with willing landowners, community groups, and national, state, and local agencies to complete more than 3,000 land conservation projects in 46 states, protecting more than two million acres. Since 1994, TPL has helped states and communities craft and pass over 330 ballot measures, generating almost $25 billion in new conservation-related funding." http://www.tpl.org.

[172] The website for the American Farmland Trust is http://www.farmland.org.

[173] See Brown, A Time to Preserve: A Call for Formal Private-Party Rights in Perpetual Conservation Easements, 40 Ga. L. Rev. 85 (2005).

[174] See infra § 15.6.

[175] State-by-State Roundup of 1983 Preservation Actions, 4 Am. Farmland 3 (Mar. 1984). See, e.g., Agricultural Land Stewardship Program Act of 1995, Cal. Agric. Code § 931 (creating state fund which provides grants for acquisition of agricultural conservation easements).

[176] Conservation Reserve Program, 16 U.S.C.A. § 3831. See also Watson, Jr., Symposium, Changing Structures and Expectations in Agriculture Conservation Reserve Program: What Happens to the Land After the Contracts End?, 14 N. Ill. U. L. Rev. 733 (1994); Hamilton, State Initiatives to Supplement the Conservation Reserve Program, 37 Drake L. Rev. 251 (1987–88); Grossman, Exercising Eminent Domain Against Protected Agricultural Lands: Taking a Second Look, 30 Vill. L. Rev. 701 (1985).

[177] 7 U.S.C.A. § 7201. See Eitel, The Farm and Ranch Lands Protection Program: An Analysis of the Federal Policy on United States Farmland Loss, 8 Drake J. Agric. L. 591 (2003); Morrow, Agri-Environmentalism: A Farm Bill for 2007, 38 Tex. Tech. L. Rev. 345 (2006).

One of the most innovative uses of agricultural easements in found in Stanislaus County, California which now conditions conversions of farmland to residential use on the developer obtaining agricultural easements on other farmland within that county. The requirement was upheld in *Building Industry Ass'n v. County of Stanislaus.*[178]

§ 13:13 Land Banking and Farmland Trusts

The agricultural lands preservation technique of land banking involves purchase of farmland by governmental or public organizations for the purpose of insuring that the land remains in agricultural production. The use of land banking to control urban land development patterns has long been practiced in Europe,[1] but one of the most ambitious uses of the concept in the agricultural context has occurred in Canada, particularly in the province of Saskatchewan.[179]

In recent years, several American states have expressed interest in the Canadian land bank idea and considered the possible applicability of the concept to this country.[180] To date, however, there has been no widespread acceptance of the idea. Where it has been adopted, it has been used principally as a device by which farmland may be made available to specific groups of individuals rather than as a farmland preservation technique. It is also significant to note that interest in the idea has been more intense at the state or local level and is only very recently finding significant support at the federal level.[181]

The American Law Institute (ALI) Model Land Development Code defines land banking as a "system in which a governmental entity acquires a substantial fraction of the land in a region that is available for future development for the purpose of controlling the future growth of the region . . . ."[182] The ALI definition requires that: (1) the land being acquired does not become committed to a specific future use at the time of acquisition and (2) the land being acquired is sufficiently large in amount to have a substantial effect on urban growth patterns.

Two aspects of the ALI definition are inapplicable when land banking is used to preserve farmland. First there is a commitment to a specific future use at the time of acquisition—namely, continuation of agricultural uses.

---

[178] *Building Industry Assn. of Cent. California v. County of Stanislaus,* 190 Cal. App. 4th 582, 118 Cal. Rptr. 3d 467 (5th Dist. 2010), review denied, (Feb. 16, 2011).

[1] A. Strong, Land Banking: European Reality, American Prospect (1979). See also Callies and Grant, Paying for Growth and Planning Gain: An Anglo—American Comparison of Development Conditions, Impact Fees, & Development Agreements, 23 Urb. Law. 221 (1991); Lapping and Forster, Farmland and Agricultural Policy in Sweden: An Integrated Approach, 7 Int'l Regional Sci. Rev. 3 (1982).

[179] Young, The Saskatchewan Land Bank, 40 Saskatchewan L. Rev. 1 (1975). See also, Fitch & Mock, Land Banking, in The Good Earth of America 134 (Harris ed.1974); Note: Public Land Banking: A New Praxis for Urban Growth, 23 Case W. Res. L. Rev. 897 (1972). The statutory authority for the Saskatchewan land bank was repealed in 1983.

[180] See Kamm, Note: Public Trust, Farmland Protection, and the Connecticut Environmental Protection Act, 23 Conn. L. Rev. 811 (1991). What have recently received wide-spread acceptance in the United States are the modern urban land banks which are public or private nonprofit organizations that take control of foreclosed or abandoned properties through various measures to ensure that they are sold or developed in a manner that best serves the long-term interests of the surrounding community. Thus far, the emphasis is almost exclusively on urban properties and their only relevance to farmland protection is that some are redirected to serve as sites for urban agricultural plots. See § 9:12 supra and Frank S. Alexander, *Land Banks and Land Banking,* (2011).

[181] See J. Juergensmeyer & J. Wadley, Agricultural Law § 4.14 (1982).

[182] ALI Model Land Development Code Commentary on Art. 6 at 254 (1975).

Secondly, the ALI definition presumes government involvement. In many instances in which farmland is "banked" for preservation purposes a government entity is involved. However, land banking for farmland preservation purposes is done on a private as well as a public basis. In fact, the major land banking efforts of agricultural lands preservation advocates are directed to private trusts.[183]

The private land trust is a charitable organization that acquires and holds interests in agricultural land for preservation purposes. To qualify as charitable, the trust must exist for a charitable purpose and operate for the benefit of an indefinite group of persons. Additionally, the trust must satisfy various state laws relating to charitable organizations and numerous federal and state tax laws and regulations in order to qualify for receipt of tax deductible or tax exempt "charitable" donations.

Land trusts[184] need not be organized as "trusts" in the technical legal meaning of the term. In fact, "land trusts" can and do exist as (1) unincorporated associations, (2) charitable trusts, or (3) charitable corporations. The last two of these—charitable trusts and charitable corporations—are clearly the preferable form of organization. The charitable corporation format has been chosen by the most significant agricultural lands trust—the American Farmland Trust (AFT).[185]

§ 13:14 Preferential Assessment and Differential Taxation

The major source of revenue for most local governments is the ad valorem tax levied on real property. In most states, agricultural land is given special treatment regarding ad valorem taxes or "property taxes," as they are often called. The justification given for "special treatment" or the "differential taxation" approach usually combines two arguments.

The first argument is farmland preservation. Agricultural land tax breaks save farmers money, and make agricultural activities more profitable, consequently giving farmers an economic incentive to continue farming. The second justification given for treating farmers differently for property tax purposes is that agricultural activities do not make the demands on governmental services that urban land uses make. Farmers therefore are entitled to tax breaks because they otherwise would be paying more than their fair share of the costs of governmental services. Under this justification, any farmland preservation effects are merely incidental.

Whatever the justification given, the differential taxation or preferential assessment approach is commonly used. In fact, all 50 states[186] have statutory and/or constitutional provisions falling under generally accepted definitions of differential taxation

---

[183] See McVickar, Land Trusts: A Growing Conservation Institution, 21 Vt. B. J. & L. Dig. 33 (1995).

[184] Cheever, Public Good and Private Magic in the Law of Land Trusts and Conservation Easements: A Happy Present and a Troubled Future, 73 Denv. U. L. Rev. 1077 (1996).

[185] The American Farmland Trust was incorporated in 1980 pursuant to the District of Columbia Nonprofit Corporation Act. See American Farmland Trust, Statement of Purpose (1980). The Trust's website is http://www.farmland.org/.

[186] "All fifty states have some form of tax relief provisions for agricultural land. Most common are preferential-assessment statutes, which assess land at reduced value when used for agriculture, and deferred taxation programs, which provide lower assessment for farmland but require partial or total repayment of tax savings if the land is converted to other uses." Cordes, Agricultural Zoning: Impacts and Future Directions, 22 N. Ill. U. L. Rev. 419, ft/nt 4 (2002). For a listing of all 50 state statutes, see American Farmland Trust, State Farmland Protection Statutes by Category (Table), at http://www.farmlandinfo.org/fic/laws/fpkeytab.html.

or preferential assessment. Not surprisingly, differential taxation is also one of the issues most frequently written about in all of agricultural law.[187] It is also one of the most controversial. The most recent evaluations suggest that differential taxation for ad valorem tax purposes has had little, if any, effect on keeping land in agricultural production.[188] Differential taxation for estate, gift, and inheritance tax purposes is considered much more important and considerably more effective in accomplishing preservation goals.[189] Perhaps the most balanced evaluation of differential taxation programs is that of the National Agricultural Lands Study—Final Report:

> Although many states have used property tax relief as a tool in protecting agricultural land, only a small fraction of farm estates or farms which enjoy the tax benefits of differential assessment meet all the conditions necessary to make this incentive effective. The benefits of reduced taxation, however, are conferred broadly, with no proof required of each recipient that the public policy of protecting farmland is being promoted. For this reason, tax policy is often viewed as a shotgun approach. Furthermore, unless differential assessment programs are combined with agricultural zoning and/or with agreements that restrict the land to agricultural use and/or purchase of development rights, there is no assurance that the beneficiaries of tax reduction or abatement will keep their land in agricultural use. Owners may simply enjoy reduced taxes until the time comes when they want to sell.

> In isolation, then, differential assessment is largely ineffective in reducing the rate of conversion of agricultural land. It does not discourage the incursion of non-farm uses into stable agricultural areas; it simply enables owners of land under development pressure to postpone the sale of their land until they are ready to retire. The incentives are not keyed into actual need, except in the case of the tax credit programs of Wisconsin and Michigan.

> Nevertheless, differential taxation is a valuable component of a comprehensive agricultural land protection program. As a matter of equity, if a program prevents agricultural land from being developed, the owner should pay taxes only on its agricultural use value.[190] Further, benefits such as these may serve as incentives to

---

[187] Some of the classic discussions include J. Wershow, Florida Agricultural Law, at chs. 2 & 3 (1981); Cooke and Power, Preferential Assessment of Agricultural Land, 47 Fla. B. J. 636 (1973); Currier, An Analysis of Differential Taxation as a Method of Maintaining Agricultural and Open Space Land Uses, 30 U. Fla. L. Rev. 832 (1978).

[188] "The most typical taxation methods employed by local governments are differential assessments, deferred taxation, and restrictive agreements. Under the pure differential assessment method, agricultural land is taxed at a value that reflects only its agricultural use, despite its development potential. Because this method has no penalty provision for converting farmland to nonfarm uses, it is merely a financial buffer for current farmers, yet has limited value for preventing conversion. Under deferred taxation schemes, all of the tax savings which resulted from the differential tax must be repaid upon conversion of the land from agricultural purposes. This penalty tax, or recapture of lost taxes, is likely to become a cost of business for developers or farmers whose profit from the sale far exceeds any penalty." See White, Beating Plowshares into Townhomes: The Loss of Farmland and Strategies for Slowing its Conversion to Nonagricultural Uses, 28 Envtl. L. 113, 115–116 (1998).

[189] See, e.g., H.R. Rep. No. 104–520 (1996) (providing farmers with protection against estate taxes in order to encourage the transfer of farms from generation to generation).

[190] There has been considerable recent litigation exploring the purpose of use value taxation as a means of encouraging landowners to keep land in agricultural use. See, e.g. *Jones v. Department of Forests, Parks and Recreation,* 177 Vt. 81, 2004 VT 49, 857 A.2d 271 (2004) (holding that the use value appraisal program is designed to provide a tax incentive for landowners to maintain the property in agricultural uses).

encourage farmers to participate in integrated agricultural land protection programs.[191]

§ 13:15 Constitutional Limitations on Farmland Protection Programs

The power of state and local governments to use land use planning and control techniques to protect and preserve agricultural lands is based on the police power. It is therefore subject to the same constitutional limitations and requirements that apply to all exercises of the police power.

The issues of constitutional limitation are explored elsewhere in this book.[192] The reader should consider carefully the following interrelated concepts in judging the constitutional validity of farmland preservation programs: (1) the takings issue, (2) the arbitrary, capricious, and unreasonable standard, (3) the requirement of conformity to comprehensive plans, (4) the unlawful delegation of legislative authority issue, and (5) the exclusionary zoning prohibition.[193]

Several aspects of the relationship between the public interest and farming activities suggests that most farmland preservation approaches will survive attacks grounded on complaints that the restrictions constitute a taking.[194] As a general rule, there is no constitutionally protected right to make the "highest and best" use of the land.[195] Thus a restriction denying the owner of the land an opportunity to develop the property to some use that is more economically valuable would not necessarily constitute a taking as long as there was some viable use opportunity left.[5] Further, there is no constitutionally protected right to farm[196] nor is there a proprietary interest in farming per se.[197] Likewise, a jurisdiction can mandate particular conservation measures without effecting a taking.[198]

In that same vein, it has been held that farmers are not a "discrete, insular minority" for purposes of "equal protection" determinations.[199] Thus restrictions that distinguish between the kinds of business entities that can own farms or engage in farming

---

[191] National Agricultural Lands Study: Final Report 55 (1981). See also Duncan, Toward a Theory of Broad—Based Planning for the Preservation of Agricultural Land, 24 Nat. Resources J. 61, 78–96 (1984); Dunford, A Survey of Property Tax Relief Programs for the Retention of Agricultural and Open Space Lands, 15 Gonz. L. Rev. 675 (1980).

[192] See supra §§ 10:1 et seq.

[193] Regarding the taking issue, see § 10:2; arbitrary and capricious conduct, § 10:12; conformity to comprehensive plans, §§ 2:11 to 2:14; unlawful delegation, § 5:3; exclusionary zoning, §§ 6:1 et seq.

[194] For a general discussion of the issue, see Cordes, Takings, Fairness and Farmland Preservation, 60 Ohio St. L.J. 1033 (1999).

[195] *City of Miami v. Zorovich*, 195 So. 2d 31 (Fla. 3d DCA 1967): "A zoning ordinance is not invalid merely because it prevents the owner from using the property in the manner which is economically most advantageous. If the rule were otherwise, no zoning could ever stand."

[5] See *Lucas v. South Carolina Coastal Council*, 505 U.S. 1003, 112 S. Ct. 2886, 120 L. Ed. 2d 798 (1992).

[196] *U.S. v. Garth*, 773 F.2d 1469 (5th Cir. 1985). In regard to the constitutionality of right to farm legislation which grants immunity from certain possible nuisance actions, see § 13:3, supra; Centner, Governments and Unconstitutional Takings: When Do Right-to-Farm Laws Go Too Far?,33 B.C. Envtl. Aff. L. Rev. 87 (2006).

[197] *Woodbury County Soil Conservation Dist. v. Ortner*, 279 N.W.2d 276 (Iowa 1979).

[198] *U.S. v. Garth*, 773 F.2d 1469 (5th Cir. 1985).

[199] See, e.g. *MSM Farms, Inc. v. Spire*, 927 F.2d 330 (8th Cir. 1991).

have been considered rationally related to the broad public purpose of keeping farmland in the hands of small, family farms.[200] Indeed, the courts seem to give considerable deference to state interests that promote a popular based agriculture that is proximate to urban areas.[201]

On the other hand, because of the strong federal presence regarding regulation of the agricultural sector, there is potential that there will be conflicts between federal program objectives and those of particular preservation programs or strategies. Federal regulation of agriculture as an industry is grounded in the Commerce Clause of the federal constitution.[202] This raises the possibility that the state programs might be considered preempted by the federal regulation or considered to be an impermissible interference with interstate commerce if the farmland program is too restrictive as to farming practices or opportunities to use the farmland in particular ways.[203] For example, given the flexibility in the current farm program regarding the kinds of farming activities the farmer may engage in, some changes permitted under the federal program may be denied to the farmer under the impact of a local zoning ordinance program where the change might jeopardize the ability of the farm to qualify as a nonconforming use under a zoning code. In such a case, the state program may deter farmers from participating fully in the federal program.

§ 13:16 Urban Agriculture

Urban agriculture encompasses a variety of farming activities involving the production of food in or near cities including home gardening, gardening on vacant land often in rundown industrial areas, and roof-top gardening. It includes the raising of chickens and, less often, goats, bees, and pigs. The yield of produce and animal products may be for personal, cooperative or charitable use, as well as for sale on-site or at farmer's markets.

Interest in urban agriculture has grown dramatically in recent years. The local food movement, as it is often called, stems from several sources, primarily health and environmental. Sparked in part by books such as Michael Pollan's The Omnivore's Dilemma, locavores, as they are known, either grow their own food in their backyards or in nearby vacant land or create a market demand for such goods. Economic considerations play a major role as home gardens may aid in reducing the food budget and provide fresh produce to needy families. Finally, the constant search of ways to revitalize deteriorating areas has led communities to encourage the use of vacant land in such areas for farming purposes, particularly with the development of community garden organizations. Numerous national and local organizations in many communities across

---

[200] MSM Farms, Inc. v. Spire, 927 F.2d 330 (8th Cir. 1991).

[201] *Wickard v. Filburn,* 317 U.S. Ill, 63 S. Ct. 82, 87 L. Ed. 122 (1942).

[202] See, generally, *Federal Land Bank of Wichita v. Bott,* 240 Kan. 624, 732 P.2d 710 (1987).

[203] For a discussion of commerce clause problems with state regulation of corporate farming, see Choster, Buying the Farm: The Eighth Circuit declares South Dakota's Anti-corporate Farming Amendment Violates the Dormant Commerce Clause, 11 Mo. Envtl. L. & Pol'y Rev. 184 (2004); Redlin and Redlin, Amendment E, Rural Communities and the Family Farm, 49 S.D. L. Rev. 787 (2004); Banks, The Past, Present and Future of Anti-Corporate Farming Laws in South Dakota: Purposeful Discrimination or Permissive Protectionism, 49 S.D. L. Rev. 804 (2004); Benz, Saving Old McDonald's Farm After South Dakota Farm Bureau, Inc. v. Hazeltine: Rethinking the Role of the State, Farming Operations, the Dormant Commerce Clause, and Growth Management Statutes, 46 Nat. Resources J. 793 (2006).

the country have formed to encourage and assist those interested in eating locally produced food.[204]

While growing crops at home for sale and raising chickens have a long history in this country, with the advent of zoning, the increasing affluence of the population, and changes in agricultural practices, such farming waned. Euclidean zoning's emphasis on the sanctity of the single family home and the purity of the residential zone excluded practices such as raising chickens or stabling horses that, while often not common law nuisances, were found nuisance-like. The ease of transporting produce from large farms at some distance from population centers at relatively low cost made the efforts of growing one's own food less attractive. Periods of economic necessity saw an increase in local farming. During the Great Depression federal, state and local governments promoted and subsidized "relief gardens," also called "welfare garden plots."[205] During World War II, the federal government championed so-called "victory gardens" to ease the effects of rationing. The US Department of Agriculture estimated "that more than 20 million victory gardens were planted. Fruit and vegetables harvested in these home and community plots was estimated to be 9–10 million tons, an amount equal to all commercial production of fresh vegetables"[206] during the war years. When rationing ended, victory gardens disappeared.

When interest in urban agriculture revived during the last quarter of the 20th century, proponents often found that local land use ordinances often stood in their way. Zoning codes have long prevented or limited urban agricultural activities. Crops may be raised, but not sold. Generally, home gardening will not qualify as an allowed home occupation since it involves outdoor activity.[207] In addition to use restrictions, traditional bulk and area requirements may impede successful small scale farming. Height limitations, aesthetic design requirements, and fencing regulations may make the use of greenhouses or the building of chicken coops impossible.[208] Other than in rural agricultural zones, the raising of animals may be prohibited.

Today, pressure from locavores and their many community organizations moves cities to update codes to accommodate, or indeed encourage, urban agriculture. In 2010, Seattle adopted comprehensive legislation to promote the local food movement.[209] The code allows "urban farms" and "community gardens" in all zones. It defines a community garden as "a use in which land managed by a public or nonprofit organization, or group of individuals, is used to grow plants or harvest food or ornamental crops from them for donation or for use by those cultivating the land and their households."[210] An urban farm is a "use in which plants are grown for sale of the plants or their products, and in which [they] are sold at the lot where they are grown or off site, or both, and in which no other items are sold. Examples include flower or vegetable

---

[204] See resources noted by the US Dept of Agriculture on its Community Supported Agriculture website, http://www.nal.usda.gov/afsic/pubs/csa/csa.shtml. See also, e.g., Sprouts in the Sidewalk, http://www.nal.usda.gov/afsic/pubs/csa/csa.shhttp://sidewalksprouts.wordpress.com/; Your Backyard Farmer (Portland, OR) http://www.yourbackyardfarmer.com/.

[205] http://sidewalksprouts.wordpress.com/history/relief-garden/.

[206] Farming the 1940s. http://www.livinghistoryfarm.org/farminginthe40s/crops_02.html.

[207] See § 4:4.

[208] See Voigt, Pigs in the Backyard or the Barnyard: Removing Zoning Impediments to Urban Agriculture, 38 B.C. Envtl. Aff. L. Rev. 537 (2011).

[209] Seattle Municipal Code § 23.42.051.

[210] Seattle Municipal Code, § 23.84A.002 "A" 3.

raising, orchards and vineyards."[211] Farmer's markets are permitted in more areas. Generally, the code liberalizes restrictions on fences and accessory structures. Rooftop greenhouses are allowed with a 15 foot exemption from height controls. The code increases the number of chickens allowed per lot from three to eight, but, as with many such codes, it prohibits roosters. Seattle's code is considered a model of clarity in contrast to the piecemeal efforts of many cities.[212]

Another source of action in the urban agriculture movement comes from efforts to revitalize deteriorating areas. Most cities, certainly large ones, suffer from the blight of vacant land and abandoned buildings in aging industrial areas, which attract crime, pose health and fire hazards, and generally reduce property values. Adapting those areas to agricultural use is seen as a way of instilling a positive sense of community while, at the same time, bringing locally grown produce to the market.

The problem is particularly acute in cities such as Detroit, Buffalo, Philadelphia, and Cleveland.[213] In 2009, some 15,000 houses in Cleveland were estimated as vacant. Detroit has more than 75,000 abandoned residential structures and some neighborhoods are more than 50% vacant.[214] These "shrinking cities" are unlikely to return to the industrial giants they once were.[215] Enticing new, alternative development, particularly green development, including urban agriculture is touted as one means of rebirth.[216]

At the current time, urban agriculture is largely affected only by local government land use regulations but both federal and state legislation and proposed legislation also have some relevance. At the federal level, The Farm Security and Rural Investment Act of 2002 contains some provisions relating to urban agriculture.[217] The act authorizes a Community Food Projects Competitive Grants Program which aims to put funds in low income communities that have difficulty accessing healthy and nutritious food. In 2010 the Greening Food Deserts Act was introduced in the U.S. House of Representatives.[218] If enacted, the Act would create a Department of Urban Agriculture and an Urban Agriculture Outreach Program. Ambitious bills have also been introduced at the state level. In Georgia, for example, The Georgia Right to Grow Act was introduced during the 2010 legislative session.[219] The purpose of this bill was to forbid local governments to prohibit or require permits for the raising of food crops, chickens, rabbits and milk goats in certain urban areas.

---

[211] Seattle Municipal Code, § 23.84A.002 "A" 5.

[212] See Voigt, supra, at 560.

[213] Choo, Plowing over, 97 ABA J. 43 (Aug. 2011).

[214] Mogk, Kwiatkowski and Weindorf, Promoting Urban Agriculture as an Alternative Land Use for Vacant Properties in the City of Detroit: Benefits, Problems and Proposals for a Regulatory Framework for Successful Land Use Integration, 56 Wayne L. Rev. 1521, 1523–24 (2010).

[215] LaCroix, Urban Agriculture and Other Green Uses: Remaking the Shrinking City, 42 Urb. Law. 225 (2010).

[216] See Mogk, Kwiatkowski and Wendorf, Promoting Urban Agriculture as an Alternative Land Use for Vacant Properties in the City of Detroit: Benefits, Problems and Proposals for a Regulatory Framework for Successful Land Use Integration, 56 Wayne L. Rev. 1521, 1523–24 (2010) and LaCroix, Urban Agriculture and Other Green Uses: Remaking the Shrinking City, 42 Urb. Law. 225 (2010).

[217] 7 U.S.C.A. § 2034 (2010).

[218] Greening Food Deserts Act, H.R. Rep. No. 111–4971 (2010).

[219] Georgia General Assembly. H.B 842 (2010).

Chapter 14

NUISANCES*

Analysis

Sec.

§ 14:1   Introduction

Courts use nuisance law to resolve land use disputes by determining which use belongs in a neighborhood and which does not. Developed shortly after the Norman Conquest, nuisance law served for centuries as the primary device to regulate land use between neighbors.[1] Today, many states define nuisance by statute, generally in terms not dissimilar to the common law.[2] As a land use control device, nuisance law has its shortcomings. Sometimes labeled "judicial zoning," decision making is ad hoc and after the fact, affording no advance notice to persons who wish to invest in land use activities that they will be safe from a nuisance action. By the early twentieth century, comprehensive legislative controls emerged in the belief that a more finely-tuned system was needed to accommodate disputes and provide advance notice to the community of how land would be used.

While comprehensive zoning has decreased reliance on nuisance law, it remains important. In the first place, some rural areas remain unzoned, leaving nuisance law as the only land use control available. Furthermore, nuisance law serves as a supplementary tool. If the local legislative body fails to deal with incompatible development through zoning, persons may seek protection through nuisance law. Finally, the common law of nuisance is a critical determinant in defining property for the purposes of constitutional protection and the need of government to pay compensation when it overregulates land use.[3]

---

* For more detailed discussion and more extensive citations of authority of the issues covered in this chapter, see Juergensmeyer and Roberts, Land Use Planning and Development Regulation Law, Practitioner Treatise Series (3rd ed. 2012).

[1] Beuscher and Morrison, Judicial Zoning Through Recent Nuisance Cases, 1955 Wis. L. Rev. 440, 442. Nuisance law also has roots in Roman law.

[2] See, e.g., Cal. Civ. Code § 3479; Ind. Code Ann. § 32–30–6–6; N.D. Cent. Code § 42–01–01.

[3] See discussion supra §§ 10:4 and 10:6.

Common law nuisances are classified as public or private, and as nuisances per se or nuisances in fact (or per accidens). Most land use disputes are private nuisance in fact claims since they involve conflicts between neighbors and they typically turn on questions of locale. A public nuisance is an unreasonable interference with a right common to the public that impairs the health, safety, morals or comfort of the community. It may, but need not, be conduct proscribed by statute.[4] A public nuisance is usually continuing in nature or produces a long term or permanent effect, and the actor has reason to know of that effect on the common right.[5]

A private nuisance is an unreasonable interference with another's use and enjoyment of land. A landowner has a property right to be free from unreasonable invasions that substantially affect the use and enjoyment of his land. Conversely, a landowner has the duty not to use his property so as to cause an unreasonable harm to his neighbor. An invasion must be intentional and unreasonable, or unintentional and otherwise actionable under rules of negligence, constitute reckless conduct or involve abnormally dangerous situations.[6] A nuisance is a non-trespassory invasion of a private interest, and confers upon the court the power to attempt to internalize the social costs of certain uses of property. This principle was recognized as early as the seventeenth century in England. *William Aldred's Case*[7] was a private nuisance action brought to enjoin the operation of a pig sty next door to the plaintiff's dwelling. The court found the sty to be a nuisance. "Infecting and corrupting the air" was an invasion of the plaintiff's property rights.

Although theoretically distinct, the difference between public and private nuisances may be of little practical significance in providing an injured party a cause of action. A public nuisance is often also a private nuisance, and legislatures and courts[8] sometimes grant private parties rights to sue under public nuisance doctrine where special damages are shown.[9]

A nuisance per se is an activity, occupation, or structure that is a nuisance at all times and under any circumstances regardless of location. It is so as a matter of law. An activity that is licensed or permitted by statute cannot be a public nuisance.[10] A nuisance in fact is an activity, operation or structure that constitutes a nuisance only because of its location, surroundings, or manner of operation.

Most nuisances are nuisances in fact because most harm producing activity is lawful somewhere and even socially productive. A halfway house for prisoners, for example, is not a nuisance per se.[11] It might be a nuisance in fact in a residential area if a court finds that its utility does not outweigh the harm to other interests.

Over time, changing values and advances in technology have caused some shifting of the rights that inure in property ownership.[12] Whatever the relative values of the

---

[4] *Flo-Sun, Inc. v. Kirk,* 783 So. 2d 1029 (Fla. 2001).

[5] Restatement Second, Torts § 821B.

[6] Restatement Second, Torts § 822.

[7] *William Aldred's Case,* 9 Coke 57b, 77 Eng.Rep. 816 (K.B. 1611).

[8] *Towne v. Harr,* 185 Mich. App. 230, 460 N.W.2d 596 (1990).

[9] See infra §§ 14:3 and 14:5.

[10] *North Carolina, ex rel. Cooper v. Tennessee Valley Authority,* 615 F.3d 291 (4th Cir. 2010).

[11] See *Smith v. Gill,* 293 Ala. 736, 310 So. 2d 214 (1975).

[12] See, e.g., *State of Ill. ex rel. Scott v. Butterfield,* 396 F. Supp. 632 (N.D. Ill. 1975) (airport noise).

competing uses, the initial assignment of legal rights does not determine which use ultimately prevails. By granting one party the legal right to prevent interference by the other, the courts attempt a value-maximizing accommodation of the conflict. In some cases, the costs of transferring the property right are so high that voluntary transfer is not feasible. Placing liability on the party who causes the damage will not always be the most efficient solution of the conflict. The common law of nuisance attempts to obtain optimal resource use by assigning property rights to the more valuable use between conflicting land uses.[13]

§ 14:2 Public Nuisances

A public nuisance is an activity that interferes with the rights of the public.[14] This often involves acts that injure the public health or safety, but also includes more intangible injuries to the public morals. While often unsuccessful,[15] public nuisance complaints have been lodged against such activities as power plant emissions,[16] interference with the ingress and egress to and from a public street,[17] excessive noise from a nightclub,[18] maintenance of an electric transmission line resulting in injury to cultural sites on an Indian reservation,[19] and using property for the illegal use of drugs or prostitution.[20] A homeless shelter and alcohol crisis center have been found to not be public nuisances.[21]

The difference between a public and private nuisance is the nature of the interest invaded. A public nuisance invades public rights, and a private nuisance invades private rights. Often conduct is actionable on both grounds. Generally, cases of air pollution and water pollution will be both. However, if the air pollution harms a limited number of people, and not the public generally, it is only a private nuisance.[22] Some conduct can be a public, but not a private, nuisance. Blocking the view of a competitor's business, for example, was held not to be a private nuisance, but, since it was a traffic hazard, it was a public nuisance.[23]

In contrast to a private nuisance, a public nuisance need not involve an invasion of property rights. The injury is to the community, not the individual landowner. Private parties injured by pollution sometimes turn to public nuisance law for relief seeking perceived benefits in longer statutes of limitations and a more favorable measure of

---

[13] R. Posner, Economic Analysis of the Law 16 (1972).

[14] See Walker and Cottingham, An Abridged Primer on the Law of Public Nuisance, 30 Tulsa L.J. 355 (1994).

[15] Many public nuisance claims fail on statutory immunity grounds and failure to show special damages. See West Keynote, Public Nuisances, k59 to k96.

[16] *North Carolina, ex rel. Cooper v. Tennessee Valley Authority,* 615 F.3d 291 (4th Cir. 2010).

[17] *Kempton v. City of Los Angeles,* 165 Cal. App. 4th 1344, 81 Cal. Rptr. 3d 852 (2008).

[18] *Capitol Properties Group, LLC v. 1247 Ctr. Street, LLC,* 283 Mich. App. 422, 770 N.W.2d 105 (2009).

[19] *Quechan Indian Tribe v. U.S.,* 535 F. Supp. 2d 1072 (S.D. Cal. 2008).

[20] *Keshbro, Inc. v. City of Miami,* 801 So. 2d 864 (Fla. 2001).

[21] *DeStefano v. Emergency Housing Group, Inc.,* 281 A.D.2d 449, 722 N.Y.S.2d 35 (2001).

[22] *Padilla v. Lawrence,* 101 N.M. 556, 685 P.2d 964 (Ct. App. 1984) (odors were not a public nuisance, but were a private nuisance).

[23] *44 Plaza, Inc. v. Gray-Pac Land Co.,* 845 S.W.2d 576 (Mo. Ct. App. 1992).

damages.[24] Much of today's environmental regulation protecting the air, water, and land from pollution through the exercise of the police power is public nuisance-based.[25]

The state,[26] through its police power, can declare an activity to be a public nuisance that was not a public nuisance at common law,[27] or it may rely on what was a public nuisance at common law.[28] While the legislature can declare what is a public nuisance and the executive can prosecute and attempt to enjoin such activities, the question of whether a public nuisance exists is for the courts to determine.[29] Further, government action in the prosecution of a statutory or common law public nuisance is subject to constitutional limitations.[30]

An activity that is licensed or permitted by statute cannot be a public nuisance.[31] However, some courts require an "'unequivocal legislative intent'" to find a use immune.[32] This immunity does not extend to private nuisance. If a state confers private nuisance immunity on an activity, it may constitute a constitutional taking of the neighbor's right to be from a nuisance. This issue arises with right-to-farm laws.[33]

§ 14:3   Public Nuisance Remedies

Public nuisances, which historically developed as crimes against the state, may be abated by the state, acting in the public interest.[34] In the absence of a statutory provision, the state need not compensate an owner for the destruction or damage of property incurred in abatement.[35] Also, the state can charge the cost of abatement to the responsible party.[36] Most states have enacted criminal statutes declaring maintenance of a public nuisance a misdemeanor.[37] An individual affected by a public nuisance may be able to remove it without suffering liability.[38] While courts early on expressed some reluctance to enjoin public nuisances on the ground that equity did not intervene in

---

[24] See Walker and Cottingham, An Abridged Primer on the Law of Public Nuisance, 30 Tulsa L.J. 355 (1994), discussing primarily Oklahoma law and questioning whether these advantages, if they in fact exist, will be available to private parties through public nuisance suits.

[25] See *CEEED v. California Coastal Zone Conservation Com.,* 43 Cal. App. 3d 306, 118 Cal. Rptr. 315, 324 (1974). Schwartz and Goldberg, The Law of Public Nuisance: Maintaining Rational Boundaries on a Rational Tort, 45 Washburn L.J. 541 (2006).

[26] In addition, many states have enacted legislation permitting municipalities to define what uses constitute a public nuisance. See § 14:1. See also Vernon's Ann. Texas art. 1175(19).

[27] *Lawton v. Steele,* 152 U.S. 133, 14 S. Ct. 499, 38 L. Ed. 385 (1894).

[28] *City of Chicago v. Festival Theatre Corp.,* 91 Ill. 2d 295, 63 Ill. Dec. 421, 438 N.E.2d 159 (1982).

[29] *Sharon Steel Corp. v. City of Fairmont,* 175 W. Va. 479, 334 S.E.2d 616 (1985).

[30] *Lawton v. Steele,* 152 U.S. 133, 14 S. Ct. 499, 38 L. Ed. 385 (1894). In general, see supra §§ 10:1 et seq.

[31] *North Carolina, ex rel. Cooper v. Tennessee Valley Authority,* 615 F.3d 291 (4th Cir. 2010). Operating without a necessary permit is a public nuisance. *City of Claremont v. Kruse,* 177 Cal. App. 4th 1153, 100 Cal. Rptr. 3d 1 (2d Dist. 2009) (medical marijuana dispensary opened without a permit).

[32] *Tally Bissell Neighbors, Inc. v. Eyrie Shotgun Ranch, LLC,* 355 Mont. 387, 393–94, 228 P.3d 1134, 1139–40 (2010).

[33] See discussion infra §§ 14:6 and 14:7.

[34] *Copart Industries, Inc. v. Consolidated Edison Co. of New York, Inc.,* 41 N.Y.2d 564, 394 N.Y.S.2d 169, 362 N.E.2d 968 (1977).

[35] *Miller v. Schoene,* 276 U.S. 272, 48 S. Ct. 246, 72 L. Ed. 568 (1928). But see discussion of *Lucas v. South Carolina Coastal Council,* 505 U.S. 1003, 112 S. Ct. 2886, 120 L. Ed. 2d 798 (1992), supra § 10:6.

[36] *4M Holding Co., Inc. v. Town Bd. of Town of Islip,* 81 N.Y.2d 1053, 601 N.Y.S.2d 458, 619 N.E.2d 395 (1993).

[37] See supra § 8:7.

[38] See Cal. Civ. Code § 3495.

criminal conduct,[39] today courts generally allow injunctive relief in favor of the state in cases of public nuisances.[40] The injunction, however, is not a substitute for criminal enforcement. For example, while prostitution solicitation on neighborhood streets was enjoinable as a public nuisance, an injunction that banned certain persons believed to be pimps and prostitutes from the city streets during certain hours was held to be overbroad.[41]

Most courts and some statutes recognize a private cause of action in tort for an individual who suffers special injuries, different in kind rather than degree from those of the general public.[42] In a private suit, the plaintiff can generally recover damages despite the public character of the nuisance.[43] Upon a showing of special injury, injunctive relief in favor of a private individual is usually available in a case of public nuisance.[44] Where the complained of conduct is both a public and a private nuisance and the primary objective is to stop the conduct, the availability of injunctive relief in a public nuisance suit is attractive since courts often will not grant such relief in a private nuisance suit.[45]

§ 14:4   Private Nuisances

A private nuisance is an unreasonable interference with the use and enjoyment of land. The underlying principle is that one should not use one's property to the injury of the property of another.[46] Factors applied in determining whether a nuisance exists include the use being made of the plaintiffs property, the use being made of the defendant's property, the character of the neighborhood, and the frequency and extent of the injury.[47] Other things considered include the social value of the respective uses, the suitability of the uses to the character of the locality, and the ability of the plaintiff or the defendant to avoid or prevent the harm.[48] As these general statements suggest, nuisance cases are highly fact specific, making it risky to predict the outcome of litigation.[49]

Though none of the above factors is controlling, the principal question is that of locale: is it reasonable for the defendant to be doing what it is doing *where* it is doing it? For that reason, nuisance law is considered judicial zoning, with the court playing the role of the planner, deciding whether the complained of use is proper for the area. Thus, a residential use in a residential area is generally protected against subsequent encroachment by business or industrial interests.[50] Conversely, where an area is not

---

[39] See *Michigan ex rel. Wayne County Prosecutor v. Bennis,* 447 Mich. 719, 527 N.W.2d 483 (1994).

[40] *People ex rel. Gallo v. Acuna,* 14 Cal. 4th 1090, 60 Cal. Rptr. 2d 277, 929 P.2d 596 (1997).

[41] *City of New York v. Andrews,* 186 Misc. 2d 533, 719 N.Y.S.2d 442 (2000).

[42] *532 Madison Ave. Gourmet Foods, Inc. v. Finlandia Center, Inc.,* 96 N.Y.2d 280, 727 N.Y.S.2d 49, 750 N.E.2d 1097 (2001).

[43] Proof of substantial injury must be shown. *Hartford v. Womens Services, P.C.,* 239 Neb. 540, 477 N.W.2d 161 (1991).

[44] *Callanan v. Gilman,* 107 N.Y. 360, 14 N.E. 264 (1887); *Birke v. Oakwood Worldwide,* 169 Cal. App. 4th 1540, 87 Cal. Rptr. 3d 602 (2d Dist. 2009). Some statutes expressly authorize an abatement remedy in favor of private parties. See, e.g., Cal. Civ. Code § 3491.

[45] See *Boomer v. Atlantic Cement Co.,* 26 N.Y.2d 219, 309 N.Y.S.2d 312, 257 N.E.2d 870 (1970).

[46] *Lussier v. San Lorenzo Valley Water Dist.,* 206 Cal. App. 3d 92, 100, 253 Cal. Rptr. 470, 473 (1988).

[47] See Restatement Second, Torts, §§ 827 and 828.

[48] Restatement Second, Torts, §§ 827 and 828.

[49] See *Pestey v. Cushman,* 259 Conn. 345, 788 A.2d 496 (2002).

[50] *Schlotfelt v. Vinton Farmers' Supply Co.,* 252 Iowa 1102, 109 N.W.2d 695 (1961).

predominately residential, judges tend to permit whatever use they deem appropriate to the area, emphasizing the business necessity or social desirability of the defendant's activity.[51]

Courts also consider potential future development as well as present use to decide whether a particular use is a nuisance.[52] Being the first to locate in an area does not preclude a court from deciding that the area is better suited to other types of uses. Land users are in effect charged with foreseeing how an area will develop. A pig farmer who locates on the outskirts of town may have to move when population growth comes his way.[53] A homeowner, who buys when an area is essentially undeveloped, may be forced to tolerate heavy industry in her neighborhood if the area is now prime for industrial use.[54] While application of that rule may seem harsh, to rule otherwise might preclude development. Courts are generally loath to have that occur. The "coming to the nuisance" defense that courts often intone suggests that the first one to arrive fixes forever the character of the area. The defense, however, is rarely determinative and some courts do not even recognize it.[55] For those that do, it is but a factor to consider.[56]

Typical actionable interferences involve physical discomfort,[57] such as foul odors from a hog farm,[58] dust from a cement plant,[59] safety concerns from an airport,[60] and noise from a bar,[61] or other outdoor recreational facility.[62] While most courts insist, as the Illinois supreme court states, on there being a "perceptible element that would influence the physical senses,"[63] other courts have found that interference with an occupant's peace of mind will sometimes suffice.[64]

In the case of funeral homes, most courts will enjoin the activity in residential areas based on the perceived psychological injury stemming from the "constant reminder of death."[65] Also, uncontrolled and intrusive nudity on a public beach adjacent to private property has been held to constitute a private nuisance.[66] In other contexts, courts have held that mental discomfort and depressed feelings are not actionable.[67] Generally, a fear or public perception of contamination is not actionable as a nuisance.[68] While a threat to safety from a prisoner halfway house in residential areas may suffice to

---

[51] *Daniel v. Kosh,* 173 Va. 352, 4 S.E.2d 381 (1939).

[52] See, e.g., *Oak Haven Trailer Court, Inc. v. Western Wayne County Conservation Ass'n,* 3 Mich. App. 83, 141 N.W.2d 645 (1966), judgment aff'd, 380 Mich. 526, 158 N.W.2d 463, 26 A.L.R.3d 647 (1968).

[53] *Pendoley v. Ferreira,* 345 Mass. 309, 187 N.E.2d 142 (1963).

[54] *Bove v. Donner-Hanna Coke Corp.,* 236 A.D. 37, 258 N.Y.S. 229 (1932).

[55] *Hoffman v. United Iron and Metal Co., Inc.,* 108 Md. App. 117, 671 A.2d 55, 66 n.11 (1996).

[56] *Miller v. Rohling,* 720 N.W.2d 562 (Iowa 2006).

[57] See, e.g., *Adams v. Snouffer,* 88 Ohio App. 79, 82, 87 N.E.2d 484, 486 (1949); *Jordan v. Luippold,* 189 Okla. 189, 191, 114 P.2d 917, 918 (1941).

[58] *Pendoley v. Ferreira,* 345 Mass. 309, 187 N.E.2d 142 (1963).

[59] *Boomer v. Atlantic Cement Co.,* 26 N.Y.2d 219, 309 N.Y.S.2d 312, 257 N.E.2d 870 (1970).

[60] *Emerald Development Co. v. McNeill,* 82 Ark. App. 193, 120 S.W.3d 605 (2003).

[61] *61 West 62 Owners Corp. v. CGM EMP LLC,* 77 A.D.3d 330, 906 NY.S.2d 549 (2010).

[62] *Evans v. Lochmere Recreation Club, Inc.,* 176 N.C. App. 724, 627 S.E.2d 340 (2006).

[63] *In re Chicago Flood Litigation,* 176 Ill. 2d 179, 223 Ill. Dec. 532, 680 N.E.2d 265, 278 (1997).

[64] *Mark v. State ex rel. Department of Fish and Wildlife,* 191 Or. App. 563, 84 P.3d 155 (2004).

[65] *Powell v. Taylor,* 222 Ark. 896, 263 S.W.2d 906, 907 (1954).

[66] See *Mark v. State ex rel. Department of Fish and Wildlife,* 191 Or. App. 563, 84 P.3d 155 (2004). See also Nagle, Moral Nuisances, 50 Emory L.J. 265 (2001).

[67] *In re Chicago Flood Litigation,* 176 Ill. 2d 179, 223 Ill. Dec. 532, 680 N.E.2d 265 (1997).

[68] *Ramirez v. Akzo Nobel Coatings, Inc.,* 153 Ohio App. 3d 115, 791 N.E.2d 1031 (2003).

show a nuisance,[69] a similar finding with respect to a group home for the disabled would likely violate the federal Fair Housing Act.[70]

Historically, activities that offend aesthetic sensibilities, such as interferences with sight or view, were not considered nuisances.[71] While many courts still resist recognition of aesthetic harms, there are those which accept such claims.[72] Visual blight, such as debris,[73] and wrecked cars,[74] can be the basis for a nuisance finding without regard to the invasion of another human sense.[75] Blighted conditions created simply for spite are more easily found actionable.[76] While the unsightliness of a neighboring wind farm may not support a nuisance claim, complaints of noise and anxiety from strobe light effects may lead the court to find that the plaintiffs stated a private nuisance claim.[77] The reluctance of courts to find an aesthetic injury as a sufficient basis for suit troubles some who argue that the courts' fear of engaging in subjective determinations of beauty is misplaced. The question, they say, is not beauty, but visual dissonance from the social and cultural character of the neighborhood.[78] The subjectivity concern can be overcome by evidence of an actual diminution in the value of property. A counter concern is the potential infringement of free expression if neighbors can compel conformity to their idea of the way things should look.[79]

An invasion of another's interest in the use and enjoyment of property is a basis for liability, regardless of the care or skill exercised to avoid injury. Showing that the conduct is negligent is not necessary, reckless or ultrahazardous.[80] An otherwise lawful use may constitute a nuisance if it is part of a general scheme to annoy a neighbor, or if the main purpose of the use is to prevent a neighbor from the enjoyment of her own property.[81]

§ 14:5 Private Nuisance Remedies

Compensatory damages, measured by the character and extent of the injury to the plaintiffs property interest, are always recoverable. Where an interference is permanent, a plaintiff may join claims for both past and prospective injuries in a single cause of action.[82] The general measure of damages is the difference between the fair market value of the property with and without the presence of the nuisance. Otherwise, suc-

---

[69] See, e.g., *Arkansas Release Guidance Foundation v. Needier,* 252 Ark. 194, 477 S.W.2d 821 (1972).

[70] See *Smith v. Gill,* 293 Ala. 736, 310 So. 2d 214 (1975).

[71] *Rankin v. FPL Energy, LLC,* 266 S.W.3d 506 (Tex. App. 2008).

[72] *Rattigan v. Wile,* 445 Mass. 850, 841 N.E.2d 680 (2006).

[73] *Allison v. Smith,* 695 P.2d 791 (Colo. App. 1984).

[74] *Foley v. Harris,* 223 Va. 20, 286 S.E.2d 186 (1982).

[75] See *Coty v. Ramsey Associates, Inc.,* 149 Vt. 451, 546 A.2d 196 (1988).

[76] *Rattigan v. Wile,* 445 Mass. 850, 841 N.E.2d 680 (2006).

[77] *Burch v. Nedpower Mount Storm, LLC,* 220 W. Va. 443, 647 S.E.2d 879 (2007). See Butler, Headwinds to a Clean Energy Future: Nuisance Suits Against Wind Energy Projects in the United States, 97 Cal. L. Rev. 1337 (2009).

[78] See Coletta, The Case for Aesthetic Nuisance: Rethinking Traditional Judicial Attitudes, 48 Ohio St. L.J. 141 (1987).

[79] Krasilovsky, A Sculpture is Worth a Thousand Words: The First Amendment Rights of Homeowners Publicly Displaying Art on Private Property, 20 Colum.-VLA J.L. & Arts 521 (1996).

[80] *Morgan v. High Penn Oil Co.,* 238 N.C. 185, 77 S.E.2d 682 (1953); Restatement Second, Torts § 822.

[81] *Martin v. Moore,* 263 Va. 640, 561 S.E.2d 672 (2002).

[82] *Northern Indiana Public Service Co. v. W.J. & M.S. Vesey,* 210 Ind. 338, 200 N.E. 620 (1936).

cessive actions must be brought for actual, not prospective, losses.[83] Where the nuisance is abatable, the temporary damage awarded is the loss in rental value.[84] If a defendant acts with malice, a court may allow punitive damages.[85] Where the legal remedy is inadequate, a plaintiff may seek an injunction. An injunction is possible where the injury is irreparable, even if the consequential damages are small.[86]

Most courts will balance the relative hardships in deciding whether to enjoin the activity. If the hardship to the defendant and the community is considerable, compared to harm to the plaintiff, the court may deny injunctive relief and award money damages.[87] *Boomer v. Atlantic Cement Co.*[88] is a leading case involving this remedy. The defendant's cement operation, located near an established residential area, caused dust and ground tremors that disturbed neighboring houses. The court found a nuisance but, after balancing the benefits of the defendant's presence in the community, its investment and the number of people it employed against the damage suffered by the plaintiffs, the court denied the injunctive relief requested by the plaintiffs. Instead, the court awarded them permanent damages.

This remedial balancing in equity is the second balancing test that occurs in a nuisance case. Initially, a court balances the parties' actions by using the factors listed above[89] to determine whether the defendant's activity is an unreasonable interference with the plaintiffs use. If it is, then damages are appropriate. A second balancing test must follow if injunctive relief is sought. The result of that balancing may be a determination that despite the unreasonable interference with plaintiffs use of her land, the defendant's activity is more important and must be allowed to continue.

In earlier times, courts issued injunctions as a matter of course when they found a nuisance existed.[90] This is a less frequent occurrence today, however, as a short-term economic view may outweigh the interests of the injured property owner.[91] The *Boomer* court, for example, simply could not bring itself to enjoin an operation of such immediate financial importance to the community. Short term protection of the local economy, however, may result in long term harm to the community caused by the defendant's unenjoined activity. Still, an inflexible rule that an injunction will issue as a matter of course may not work to protect the environment long term. A court, required to issue an injunction but fearful of the short term economic consequences of shutting down an industry, may simply not find a nuisance on the merits.[92] When an injunction is issued, a court may make it temporary and conditional where the defendant can reduce or abate the interference by reasonable changes in the conduct of his activities.[93]

---

[83] *Santa Fe Partnership v. ARCO Products Co.,* 46 Cal. App. 4th 967, 54 Cal. Rptr. 2d 214 (1996).

[84] *Hammond v. City of Warner Robins,* 224 Ga. App. 684, 482 S.E.2d 422, 427 (1997).

[85] *Coty v. Ramsey Associates, Inc.,* 149 Vt. 451, 546 A.2d 196 (1988).

[86] *Becker v. State,* 363 Md. 77, 767 A.2d 816 (2001).

[87] *Varjabedian v. City of Madera,* 64 Cal. App. 3d 199, 134 Cal. Rptr. 305 (1976).

[88] *Boomer v. Atlantic Cement Co.,* 26 N.Y.2d 219, 309 N.Y.S.2d 312, 257 N.E.2d 870 (1970).

[89] See supra § 14:4.

[90] *Hulbert v. California Portland Cement Co.,* 161 Cal. 239, 118 P. 928 (1911).

[91] See Smith, Re-Validating the Doctrine of Anticipatory Nuisance, 29 Vt. L. Rev. 687 (2005).

[92] According to Professor Ellickson, this is what occurred under New York's pre-*Boomer* rule, when the state followed a pro-injunction rule. *Bove v. Donner-Hanna Coke Corp.,* 236 A.D. 37, 258 N.Y.S. 229 (1932). See Ellickson, Alternatives to Zoning: Covenants, Nuisance Rules, and Fines as Land Use Controls, 40 U. Chic. L. Rev. 681, 720 (1973).

[93] *McCleery v. Highland Boy Gold Mining Co.,* 140 F. 951 (C.C.D. Utah 1904).

In perhaps a one-of-a-kind case, the court in *Spur Industries, Inc. v. Del E. Webb Development Co.*,[94] found a cattle feedlot to be a nuisance in a suit brought by a developer who had leapfrogged developable land near Phoenix to acquire cheaper land farther out to create a large residential development. The residents of the development, the court found, should not suffer the health risk of living amid the flies and odor from the feedlot. The feedlot operator salvaged something as the court, in an unusual remedy twist, required the developer to indemnify the defendant for the cost of moving its feedlot. In such cases, the farmer's land may rise in value as it will now be attractive for residential use, though this is likely of little solace to the farmer.

Damages and conditional injunctions may be the most efficient remedies for a nuisance. An award of damages against a nuisance serves to internalize the costs and permits the defendant to make his own cost-benefit analysis of preventive measures. Conditional injunctions may facilitate the termination of a nuisance whose harm a plaintiff values greater than recoverable damages. This situation is most common where the plaintiff is hypersensitive to injury or has come to the nuisance.[95]

Proof of a connection between plaintiff's injuries and defendant's act is often difficult to obtain. Effects of hazardous waste disposal, for example, may not become obvious for many years.[96] A dearth of scientific knowledge of the effects of chemicals and other waste products can make it very difficult for plaintiffs to carry their burden of proof.[97]

Public nuisance[98] or combined public and private nuisance[99] actions have been more successful than private nuisance actions alone in effecting abatement or recovering damages by private parties. In some cases, defendant's activity may be found to pose imminent danger to public health and safety, enjoined, and ordered cleaned up at the defendants' expense.[100]

Where there are multiple industrial users in the vicinity of the plaintiff's property, proving that the activity of any one of the users in and of itself creates enough harm to constitute a nuisance is difficult.[101] Solving cumulative harms from multiple users usually requires legislative action. The Clean Air Act, for example, can set standards for a given industry or enable the EPA to set standards for specific areas to control air pollution problems that nuisance law cannot remedy.

---

[94] *Spur Industries, Inc. v. Del E. Webb Development Co.,* 108 Ariz. 178, 494 P.2d 700 (1972).

[95] Id.

[96] See, e.g., *U.S. v. Price,* 523 F. Supp. 1055 (D.N.J. 1981).

[97] See, e.g., Adler, Science, Politics, and Problem Solving: Principles and Practices for the Resolution of Environmental Disputes in the Midst of Advancing Technology, Uncertain or Changing Science, and Volatile Public Perceptions, 10 Penn St. Envtl. L. Rev. 323 (2002).

[98] *City of Philadelphia v. Stepan Chemical Co.,* 544 F. Supp. 1135 (E.D. Pa. 1982); *McCastle v. Rollins Environmental Services,* 514 F. Supp. 936 (M.D. La. 1981).

[99] *Chappell v. SCA Services, Inc.,* 540 F. Supp. 1087 (CD. Ill. 1982).

[100] *Wood v. Picillo,* 443 A.2d 1244 (R.I. 1982).

[101] See Homer, Comment: Indivisible Injury Negligence and Nuisance Cases-Proving Causation Among Multiple-Source Polluters: A State-By-State Survey of the Law for New England, and a Proposal for a New Causation Framework, 3 Pierce L. Rev. 75 (2004).

§ 14:6   Agricultural Operations as Nuisances: The Right to Farm

Farming and other agricultural operations are frequent targets of public and private nuisance suits brought by residential neighbors. Over the past century, as the population has moved into the countryside, the conflicts between the two have grown. While the plaintiffs have usually been late arrivals to the area, the farmers' use of the defense that the plaintiffs "came to the nuisance"[102] has often not been successful.[103]

Hog farms and cattle feedlots are often targets of nuisance claims. When urban growth reaches the farmer's doorstep, courts have found that it is the farmer who must leave to make way for places for people to live. Courts have declared these uses nuisances even though their use of the land conforms to applicable health and safety standards and is otherwise reasonable and consistent with traditional uses in the area.[104] Such farming operations are, in effect, high risk ventures, and the farmer must foresee that he is living on borrowed time.[105] The foreseeability powers courts attribute to persons may be rather great.[106]

In response to concerns about the loss of an enormous amount of our most valuable farmland, which is, or was, on the fringe of densely settled urban areas,[107] legislatures have acted in several ways to protect against further loss. Among a variety of agricultural preservation techniques,[108] a particularly popular one is the abolition of the right to bring a nuisance action against farm operations. In the last quarter of the 20th century, all states adopted "right to farm" statutes that represent codifications of the "coming to the nuisance" defense.[109]

Most statutes provide that agricultural operations that have been in existence longer than one year cannot become either public or private nuisances by virtue of changed conditions in the surrounding area, if they were not nuisances when the agricultural operations began and if they are property managed.[110] Farm expansions of varying degrees may be allowed. Some go so far as to allow unlimited expansion.[111] Some statutes list exceptions to the rule.[112] Negligent operations typically are not exempt,[113] Inevitably, questions arise as to the kinds of operations that qualify,[114] and whether changes in use qualify for protection.[115] Some states protect all agricultural operations,[116] while others protect operations used for specific purposes, such as pro-

---

[102] Restatement Second, Torts § 840D.

[103] See supra § 14:4.

[104] See, e.g., *Pendoley v. Ferreira,* 345 Mass. 309, 187 N.E.2d 142 (1963).

[105] See *Spur Industries, Inc. v. Del E. Webb Development Co.,* 108 Ariz. 178, 494 P.2d 700 (1972).

[106] See *Pendoley v. Ferreira,* 345 Mass. 309, 187 N.E.2d 142 (1963).

[107] See A. Ann Sorensen et al., American Farmland Trust, Farming on the Edge (1997).

[108] Agricultural preservation is discussed in detail supra §§ 13:1 et seq.

[109] See, e.g., Cal. Civ. Code § 3482.5; Fla. Stat. Ann. § 823.14; Neb. Rev. Stat. §§ 2–401 to 2–404. See also supra § 15:2.

[110] S.D. Code Ann. § 21–10–25.2.

[111] See Centner, Governments and Unconstitutional Takings: When Do Right-to-Farm Laws Go Too Far?, 33 B.C. Envtl. Aff. L. Rev. 87, 103 (2006).

[112] Fla. Stat. Ann. § 823.14.

[113] N.D. Cent. Code § 42–04–02.

[114] *Modern Continental Const. Co., Inc. v. Building Inspector of Natick,* 42 Mass. App. Ct. 901, 674 N.E.2d 247 (1997).

[115] See, e.g., *Durham v. Britt,* 117 N.C. App. 250, 451 S.E.2d 1 (1994).

[116] N.D. Cent. Code § 42–04–02.

duction of milk, eggs, or livestock.[117] The statutes also may bar local government from enacting zoning laws that would force the closure of an existing agricultural operation.[118]

Whether right to farm statutes are successful in protecting farm operations is open to question. One study found that they have been less effective than some hoped.[119] Concentrated animal feedlot operations, known as CAFOs, are particularly controversial. The EPA defines CAFOs as large, medium and small.[120] A large CAFO is one that has more than 1,000 cows, or 2,500 hogs, or 125,000 chickens. Many CAFOs greatly exceed these numbers. It is doubtful that legislators enacting the right to farm statutes in the 1970s and 80s intended to protect what some call what some call factory farms.[121]

§ 14:7   Legislative Changes of Common Law Nuisance

The common law of nuisance is subject to legislative change, but such change, in turn, is subject to the same constitutional limitations that apply to any exercise of the police power.[122] While it has been said that "within constitutional limits not exactly determined, the legislature may change the common law of nuisances, and may move the line either way, so as to make things nuisances which were not so, or to make things lawful which were nuisances,"[123] the Supreme Court has said that "while the legislature may legalize what otherwise would be a public nuisance, it may not confer immunity from action for a private nuisance of such a character as to amount in effect to a taking of private property for public use."[124] The constitutional limits arise in two settings. First, the legislature is limited in its ability to legalize a private nuisance, and second, it is said that the police power may not extend to declaring activities nuisances that are not nuisances in fact.[125] In examining these issues, distinguishing between public and private nuisances is important.

A question that arises frequently is whether zoning or other regulatory permission to engage in an activity precludes a finding of nuisance. When a zoning ordinance authorizes a certain use, that use cannot, by definition, constitute a nuisance per se. Courts also hold that a permitted use cannot constitute a public nuisance.[126] By statute, for example, California provides that "[n]othing which is done or maintained under the express authority of a statute can be deemed a nuisance,"[127] but the courts interpret the statute narrowly. Mere legislative authorization for use does not excuse the use from being found a nuisance in the manner of its operation.[128] Thus, a sewage discharge permit issued by the state department of environmental protection did not insu-

---

[117] Md. Code Ann., Cts. & Jud.Proc. § 5-308(a).

[118] See, e.g., Idaho Code § 22–4504.

[119] See Bahls, Preservation of Family Farms—The Way Ahead, 45 Drake L. Rev. 311, 317 (1997).

[120] http://www.epa.gov/npdes/regulations/cafo__final__rule__preamble2008.pdf.

[121] See Centner, Nuisances from Animal Feeding Operations: Reconciling Agricultural Production and Neighboring Property Rights, 11 Drake J. Agric. L. 5, 10 (2006).

[122] See supra §§ 10:1 et seq.

[123] *Commonwealth v. Parks,* 155 Mass. 531, 532, 30 N.E. 174, 174 (1892).

[124] *Richards v. Washington Terminal Co.,* 233 U.S. 546, 553, 34 S. Ct. 654, 657, 58 L. Ed. 1088 (1914).

[125] *City of Scottsbluff v. Winters Creek Canal Co.,* 155 Neb. 723, 53 N.W.2d 543 (1952).

[126] *North Carolina, ex rel. Cooper v. Tennessee Valley Authority,* 615 F.3d 291 (4th Cir. 2010).

[127] Cal. Civ. Code § 3482.

[128] *Barnes v. City of Thompson Falls,* 294 Mont. 76, 979 P.2d 1275 (1999).

late a town from private nuisance liability.[129] California also precludes injunctive relief by private persons against a use conducted in an appropriate zone that does not employ harmful methods of operation.[130] The statute, however, does not preclude the recovery of damages.

Courts widely hold that a zoning ordinance permitting a use does not in and of itself immunize the use from being held to be a private nuisance in fact. However, the weight given by a court to the existence of an ordinance affects the question of whether a given use constitutes a private nuisance. The character of the area is an important factor in determining whether a nuisance in fact exists. Also, the existence of a zoning ordinance permitting or precluding uses is significant in determining the character of the area. Most courts regard proof of the existence of a zoning ordinance to be admissible as evidence of the character of the district and bearing on the question of whether a nuisance exists.[131] While some courts declare the zoning classification to be a persuasive factor, it is not conclusive.[132]

Judicial refusal to allow the legislative body to license a nuisance has constitutional underpinnings. The Court, in *Richards v. Washington Terminal Company*,[133] discussed the question of legalization of a nuisance. There, a landowner suffering from the operation of an adjoining railroad track and tunnel, sought damages from the railroad in a nuisance action. The Court held that to the extent that the complainant suffered from the gases and dust of the normal operation of the railroad, the injury was noncompensable. Since Congress had authorized the construction, they had legalized the nuisance, and to the extent that the passing of the locomotives indirectly diminished the property's value, it was a burden common to all. There was, however, evidence that the tunnel had been constructed so that a fanning system forced gases and dust from the tunnel onto the plaintiffs land at a single point. The Court held that the plaintiff could collect damages from the railroad for this "peculiar harm" that he alone suffered. In reaching its decision, the Court stated in dicta that "while the legislature may legalize what otherwise would be a public nuisance, it may not confer immunity from action for a private nuisance of such a character as to amount in effect to a taking of private property for public use."[134] To paraphrase Justice Holmes, the parameters of this limit have not been set.[135] What can be said is that legislative authorization of a nuisance is subject to the same limitations as any other legislative action.

Whether legislative abrogation of a neighbor's private nuisance action is a taking of the neighbor's property under the Fifth Amendment arises in the context of right to farm statutes discussed above.[136] While the property owner loses a discrete property right, the right to sue, she keeps possession of her land. In most instances there will

---

[129] *Walsh v. Town of Stonington Water Pollution Control Authority,* 250 Conn. 443, 736 A.2d 811 (1999).

[130] Cal. Civ. Proc. Code § 731a.

[131] Id.

[132] *Armory Park Neighborhood Ass'n v. Episcopal Community Services,* 148 Ariz. 1, 712 P.2d 914 (1985).

[133] *Richards v. Washington Terminal Co.,* 233 U.S. 546, 34 S. Ct. 654, 58 L. Ed. 1088 (1914). See, generally, Ball, The Curious Intersection of Nuisance and Takings Law, 86 B.U. L. Rev. 819 (2006).

[134] *Richards,* 233 U.S. at 553, 34 S. Ct. at 657.

[135] "Within constitutional limits not exactly determined, the legislature may change the common law as to nuisances, and may move the line either way, so as to make things nuisances which were not so, or to make things lawful which were nuisances." *Commonwealth v. Parks,* 155 Mass. 531, 532, 30 N.E. 174, 174 (1892) (Holmes, J).

[136] See § 14:6. For detailed takings law analysis see supra §§ 10:1 et seq.

not be a total economic loss. The immunity in effect confers an affirmative easement on the farmer to cast pollutants of odors, noise, or dust on the neighbors land. If this is characterized as a physical invasion, then the prospects of succeeding in a takings claim are brighter. Even treated as a physical invasion, a court would have to find it was permanent in nature to make it a categorical taking.[137] Finally, the expectations of the plaintiff may or may not suggest a taking. The person who buys land downwind of a hog farm will be hard pressed to prevail arguing that he has a reasonable investment backed expectation to expect clean air. If the farm comes later, the neighbor has a nuisance action since most statutes do not confer the immunity from suit until the passage of one year.

The Supreme Court of Iowa in *Bormann v. Board of Supervisors In and For Kossuth County,*[138] found that the right to farm statute facially took property by granting an agricultural use an affirmative easement to cast noise, odor, dust, or fumes onto a neighbor's land without providing compensation. While the court initially examined the case as falling into the Supreme Court's physical invasion takings cases, the court held that the statute authorized a non-trespassory invasion. The court relied on the *Richards* case discussed above to find the non-trespassory invasion a taking. The United States Supreme Court has yet to decide how the dicta of *Richards* fits into modern takings analysis, and in particular, whether a non-trespassory invasion can constitute a per se taking under *Loretto* or *Lucas,* or should be subject to the *Penn Central* line of cases and determined in an as applied challenge.[139]

In contrast to the Iowa court, the Supreme Court of Idaho found that while smoke from the burning of post harvest straw from a grass seed growing operation was a nuisance, the state's immunity law barred suit. The court found no taking of the injured neighbor's right to be free from a nuisance.[140] Examining the issue as a potential regulatory, as opposed to physical, taking, the court found there was not a deprivation of all reasonable use. Also, the court held that, unlike the Iowa *Bormann* case, the Idaho immunity statute did not create an easement on the neighbors land.

The flip side of the question is whether mere evidence of a violation of a zoning ordinance is a nuisance per se. It is sometimes said that the legislature cannot declare an activity to be a nuisance that is not in fact a nuisance. Yet, it is a common practice of state and local legislatures to declare that the violation of a land use regulation, such as a zoning ordinance or building and safety code, constitutes a nuisance. For example, the Michigan enabling statute for municipal zoning provides that "* * * uses violating any provision of local ordinances or regulations * * * are nuisances per se."[141] While the statute eliminates the necessity that a plaintiff establish a nuisance in fact before being entitled to relief,[142] the type of nuisance contemplated is a public nuisance and enforcement by private party requires proof of special damages.[143]

---

[137] If the activity was seasonal, that might not fit the Supreme Court's rule. See infra § 10:3.

[138] *Bormann v. Board of Sup'rs In and For Kossuth County,* 584 N.W.2d 309 (Iowa 1998).

[139] See supra § 10:3.

[140] *Moon v. North Idaho Farmers Ass'n,* 140 Idaho 536, 96 P.3d 637 (2004). See also *Lindsey v. DeGroot,* 898 N.E.2d 1251, 1258 (Ind. Ct. App. 2009).

[141] Mich. Comp. Laws Ann. § 125.294.

[142] *Bruggeman v. Minster,* 42 Mich. App. 177, 201 N.W.2d 344, 345 (1972).

[143] *Towne v. Harr,* 185 Mich. App. 230, 460 N.W.2d 596 (1990).

Whatever the legislation, it cannot be arbitrary or capricious. It must comply with the limits imposed by the due process clause.[144] For example, it would be unconstitutional for a legislative body to declare perfectly good houses to be nuisances because the legislative body wanted them removed so it could acquire the property at less cost through eminent domain. However, if an ordinance is reasonable, government may abate activity declared a statutory nuisance, though without the statutory declaration a court might not find a nuisance in fact.[145] The same result may be reached by courts which nominally require that the activity constitute a nuisance in fact, but defer to the legislative judgment that the required harm exists.[146] The question is not the label, but whether the state action is rational and fair.

Local governments may be able to pass nuisance prevention ordinances without fully complying with the requirements imposed on zoning enactments in those states that grant broad police powers to local governments.[147] However, if state zoning enabling statutes use broad language in describing the types of land use controls authorized by the statute, an ordinance exercising such type of control may arguably be required to comply with zoning procedures even though it does not purport on its face to be a zoning law.[148] In the absence of statutory guidance, some courts look to the nature and purpose of the specialized measure.[149] If it deals with zoning concepts or its effect is to regulate the use of land, then compliance with zoning procedural safeguards may be necessary.

---

[144] See supra § 10:12.

[145] *Farmington, Tp. Oakland County v. Scott,* 374 Mich. 536, 132 N.W.2d 607 (1965).

[146] See *City of Bakersfield v. Miller,* 64 Cal. 2d 93, 48 Cal. Rptr. 889, 410 P.2d 393 (1966).

[147] See supra § 3:7.

[148] See *City of Escondido v. Desert Outdoor Advertising, Inc.,* 8 Cal. 3d 785, 106 Cal. Rptr. 172, 505 P.2d 1012 (1973).

[149] See *Landmark Land Co., Inc. v. City and County of Denver,* 728 P.2d 1281 (Colo. 1986).

Chapter 15

PRIVATE LAND USE CONTROLS*

Analysis

I. INTRODUCTION

I.   INTRODUCTION

§ 15:1   Introduction

Prior to the 20th century, privately created restrictions, along with nuisance law,[1] dominated the control of land use. Public controls, which began at least as early as Elizabethan England,[2] gradually came to the foreground, and now dominate. While overshadowed by zoning, private controls persisted. They were particularly important

---

* For more detailed discussion and more extensive citations of authority of the issues covered in this chapter, see Juergensmeyer and Roberts, Land Use Planning and Development Regulation Law, Practitioner Treatise Series (3rd ed. 2012).

[1] See §§ 14:1 et seq. for a discussion of nuisance law.

[2] 31 Eliz. I C 7 (Statutes at Large, Vol.6 at 409).

in the post-World War II development of large scale subdivisions,[3] and have experienced resurgence in use in recent years with the increase in common interest communities. Private controls complement public controls in two areas: (1) as restrictions in traditional subdivisions and in planned communities to control use more stringently than zoning does, and (2) as methods used by private organizations and government to limit land use for various preservation purposes.

More than 30 million people live in residential communities subject to private restrictions. The use limitations imposed by these restrictions, which may be quite invasive, are enforced by property owners' associations whose powers resemble those of local governments.[4] The desire to protect homeowners from arbitrary controls and the historical canon favoring free land use may lead courts to interpret such provisions narrowly.

Freedom of contract and equity are countervailing concerns. People who buy within privately regulated communities do so voluntarily and either expressly agree to such limits or buy with record notice of preexisting restrictions. There is strong public interest in protecting the expectations of the neighbors who seek to enforce the restrictions, and little equity in favor of those who bought with notice of the restrictions.[5]

Private controls, like public controls, may have an exclusionary impact on nonresidents.[6] Gated communities, which may literally wall out the nonresident, may also exclude the public from the use of publicly created resources that lie within the enclave.[7]

It falls to the legislatures and courts to decide whether and when people should be left to live with their own bargains that have turned sour, and whether and when private parties should be able to band together to form communities that exclude others.

Governments also use private controls as alternatives to the exercise of the police power. This is particularly true with the preservation of sensitive lands where government may acquire conservation easements by voluntary purchase, by gift, or by the exercise of the power of eminent domain.

Several forms of controls, either singly or in combination, are available to control land use by private agreement: defeasible estates, easements, and promises respecting the use of the land. We will first examine the devices that may be used, and then turn to the public policy issues.

---

[3] See Korngold, The Emergence of Private Land Use Controls in Large-Scale Subdivisions: The Companion Story to Village of Euclid v. Ambler Realty, 51 Case Wes. Res. L. Rev. 617 (2001).

[4] In 2001, there were reportedly 231,000 community associations in the country, compared 130,000 at the end of the 1980s, and 500 in 1965. Approximately one-half of all new homes built in major metropolitan areas fall within community associations. Franzese, Does It Take a Village?Privatization, Patterns of Restrictiveness and the Demise of Community, 47 Vill. L. Rev. 553, 554, n. 4 (2002).

[5] *Green v. Lawrence,* 2005 ME 90, 877 A.2d 1079 (Me. 2005).

[6] See Callies, Franzese, Guth, *Ramapo* Looking Forward: Gated Communities, Covenants, and Concerns, 35 Urb. Law. 177 (2003). §§ 6:1 et seq. supra covers the exclusionary impact of public controls.

[7] See *Citizens Against Gated Enclaves v. Whitley Heights Civic Assn.,* 23 Cal. App. 4th 812, 28 Cal. Rptr. 2d 451 (1994).

II. TYPES OF PRIVATE CONTROLS

III. PUBLIC INTEREST IN, AND USE OF, PRIVATE CONTROLS

§ 15:10 Constitutional Limitations

The constitutional provisions that restrain government in the exercise of the police power generally will not apply to private covenants due to the absence of state action. Several caveats are in order. First, a noteworthy exception is that judicial enforcement of racial covenants is state action for the purposes of the Chapter 2. Second, federal statutes, based on the 13th Amendment or the commerce clause, apply to private covenants without the need for state action. Third, state constitutions may ban private conduct that is outside the reach of the federal constitution. Fourth, state public policy enunciated judicially or legislatively, may make private covenants unenforceable.

In *Shelley v. Kraemer*,[8] the Supreme Court confronted companion cases from Missouri and Michigan where state courts, at the request of white neighbors, had enjoined black purchasers from occupying the homes they had purchased based on racially restrictive covenants. The Court held the state court injunctions were state action for purposes of the 14th Amendment and that the equal protection clause precluded enforcement of the racially restrictive covenants. Two questions that arise with respect to the reach of *Shelley* are whether it applies to the enforcement of covenants that discriminate on grounds other than race and whether it applies to property interests other than covenants.

---

[8] *Shelley v. Kraemer,* 334 U.S. 1, 68 S. Ct. 836, 92 L. Ed. 1161 (1948).

The Supreme Court has not extended the *Shelley* doctrine beyond racial covenants, and it is improbable that it would do so if the issue were presented to it. The reason is that carried to the extreme, an extension would mean that the judicial enforcement of any private contract would be state action for purposes of the 14th Amendment, eviscerating the state action requirement. In several non-land use cases, the Court has given a restrictive reading to the state action doctrine.[9] The Court does not seem likely to eliminate the distinction between private and public discrimination.

Several state courts, however, have applied *Shelley* to non-racial covenants. In one case, a court found arbitrary enforcement of an adults-only covenant to violate equal protection.[10] State courts have differed over whether a private covenant prohibiting buildings for religious use violates the First Amendment.[11] The Colorado supreme court, without citing *Shelley* or discussing the need for state action, applied a substantive due process restriction to private covenants regulating architectural design.[12]

The type of property interest at issue may also determine the applicability of *Shelley*. The rights of the covenant beneficiaries in *Shelley* were not self-executing. They needed judicial action to prevail. However, courts have held *Shelley* inapplicable where possessory title is acquired by automatic reversion to the holder of a possibility of reverter following the breach of a fee simple determinable. In *Charlotte Park and Recreation Commission v. Barringer,*[13] land for park use was granted to a city pursuant to language held to create a fee simple determinable that nonwhites not be allowed entry. In a declaratory judgment action, the court held that if the city were to breach the condition, title would revert automatically without state court involvement. Since the state courts would not be involved in moving title from one party to another, there was no state action.

Under the *Barringer* rationale, a right of re-entry following a fee simple subject to a condition subsequent is different because title does not vest automatically on breach. The owner must exercise the right of re-entry and, if unable to gain possession voluntarily, would need to secure state court aid. *Shelley* would preclude the court from helping. Use of this arcane distinction between the two types of future interests is lamentable. It is also manipulable in that the language used to create the defeasible fee is often unclear and requires judicial construction. Despite the nicety of the distinction, it did not bother the Supreme Court sufficiently in *Barringer* to grant certiorari.[14]

Another possible avenue to subject private covenants to those constitutional provisions that require state action is the theory used in *Marsh v. Alabama,*[15] where the Court held that the First Amendment applied to land owned by a company that had assumed virtually all of the responsibilities of a local government. The Court, however, has been strict in applying the *Marsh* company town rule, requiring that the private property be used as the functional equivalent of a local government.[16] For application

---

[9] See, e.g., *Flagg Bros., Inc. v. Brooks,* 436 U.S. 149, 98 S. Ct. 1729, 56 L. Ed. 2d 185 (1978) (private sale of goods under UCC).

[10] *White Egret Condominium, Inc. v. Franklin,* 379 So. 2d 346 (Fla. 1979).

[11] *Ginsberg v. Yeshiva of Far Rockaway,* 45 A.D.2d 334, 358 N.Y.S.2d 477 (1974).

[12] *Rhue v. Cheyenne Homes, Inc.,* 168 Colo. 6, 449 P.2d 361 (1969).

[13] *Charlotte Park and Recreation Commission v. Barringer,* 242 N.C. 311, 88 S.E.2d 114 (1955).

[14] See also *Evans v. Abney,* 396 U.S. 435, 90 S. Ct. 628, 24 L. Ed. 2d 634 (1970).

[15] *Marsh v. State of Ala.,* 326 U.S. 501, 66 S. Ct. 276, 90 L. Ed. 265 (1946).

[16] See *Hudgens v. N. L. R. B.,* 424 U.S. 507, 96 S. Ct. 1029, 47 L. Ed. 2d 196 (1976).

to a private community this requires that there be a community organization that supplies the full range of services including fire and police protection, schools, utilities, and mail service. Even with the spread of gated communities, this is not often the case.

Though federal constitutional protection may be lacking, private covenants may violate state constitutional provisions. This may occur either because the state constitution applies to private conduct, or if it requires state action, that the state courts use a less onerous test than the federal one.[17] In New Jersey, for example, the free speech guarantee in the state constitution protects against unreasonably restrictive conduct by private parties.[18] Also, the right of privacy guarantee of the California constitution applies to private conduct.[19]

§ 15:11 Legislative and Judicial Public Policy Constraints

A. Federal Statutes

The existence of federal civil rights statutes diminishes the need to find a direct constitutional basis to complain about arbitrary or discriminatory enforcement of private covenants. These statutes apply to private covenants in both racial and non-racial contexts without the need for state action.

The Civil Rights Act of 1866, 42 U.S.C.A. § 1982 provides, in part, that:

All citizens of the United States shall have the same right as is enjoyed by white citizens * * * to * * * purchase [or] lease * * * real * * * property.[20]

In *Jones v. Alfred H. Mayer Company*,[21] the Court held the statute constitutional under the 13th Amendment, which has no state action requirement. While *Mayer* dealt with a refusal to sell, the statute also bars an effort to enforce a private racial covenant to block a sale of property. Though the language of the statute refers to the manner of transfer and not use, the Court has held that the right to purchase language of the statute includes the right to be free from race-based private covenants.[22]

Express race-based covenants are not used, or at the most rarely used, in real estate transactions today,[23] but racial discrimination has not disappeared from our society, and it can be accomplished by discriminatory application of facially neutral covenants. One instance when racial discrimination may occur is where a community association has a right of first refusal to purchase any lot or unit offered for sale. Though the covenant is facially neutral, if the association or a member exercises the right based on the prospective purchaser's color, it will violate § 1982.[24]

---

[17] See *Laguna Publishing Co. v. Golden Rain Foundation,* 131 Cal. App. 3d 816, 182 Cal. Rptr. 813 (1982).

[18] *Committee For A Better Twin Rivers v. Twin Rivers Homeowners' Ass'n,* 192 N.J. 344, 929 A.2d 1060 (2007).

[19] *Nahrstedt v. Lakeside Village Condominium Assn.,* 8 Cal. 4th 361, 33 Cal. Rptr. 2d 63, 878 P.2d 1275 (1994).

[20] 42 U.S.C.A. § 1982.

[21] *Jones v. Alfred H. Mayer Co.,* 392 U.S. 409, 88 S. Ct. 2186, 20 L. Ed. 2d 1189 (1968).

[22] *Hurd v. Hodge,* 334 U.S. 24, 68 S. Ct. 847, 92 L. Ed. 1187 (1948).

[23] They still appear in older deeds in the chain of title of many properties.

[24] See *Phillips v. Hunter Trails Community Ass'n,* 685 F.2d 184 (7th Cir.1982).

While § 1982 is limited in that it applies only to racial discrimination and only protects citizens,[25] the Fair Housing Act is broader. It covers discrimination based on race, color, religion, sex, familial status, national origin, and handicap.[26] The Act also protects "any person." It does not require citizenship. The Act makes it illegal "to refuse to sell or rent * * * or otherwise make unavailable or deny"[27] a dwelling on the basis of the protected categories. That language encompasses "a wide array of housing practices, [including] restrictive covenants."[28] Litigation over restrictive covenants under the Act arises most frequently with respect to efforts by neighbors to block or close down group homes for the mentally retarded[29] or for others protected under the Act's "handicap" provisions.[30] The Fair Housing Act, covered in detail elsewhere in this treatise,[31] also applies to private conduct without state action.[32]

Upset by reports of homeowners' associations banning the display of the American flag, Congress enacted the Freedom to Display the American Flag Act of 2005, which provides that no residential real estate management association may adopt or enforce any rule that would restrict a member from displaying the flag on residential property.[33]

B. State Statutes and Common Law

Private restrictions that are contrary to public policy as expressed by state statute[34] or by judicial interpretation of state public policy[35] are unenforceable. Several states, for example, have statutes that declare void private covenants that preclude the use of property for group homes or communal living arrangements for disabled persons.[36] Some statutes may only apply prospectively. If the ban applies retroactively, a question that arises is whether legislation can validly terminate preexisting property and contract rights without running afoul of the due process, takings or contract clauses of the constitution. Generally, the courts have addressed the issue under the contract clause,[37] and while they have differed in their responses, most have found no constitutional impairment.[38] The reasoning is that the effect on the contract right is minimal and that even if viewed as substantial, the state's interest in promoting fair housing justifies the impairment.

---

[25] The "white citizens" language is applied with a historical, not anthropological, definition of race. See *Shaare Tefila Congregation v. Cobb,* 481 U.S. 615, 107 S. Ct. 2019, 95 L. Ed. 2d 594 (1987).

[26] Section 1982 has some advantages. It applies to all property transactions, real and personal, not just housing. And, unlike the Fair Housing Act, it has no exemptions.

[27] 42 U.S.C.A. § 3604(a).

[28] *Casa Marie, Inc. v. Superior Court of Puerto Rico for Dist. of Arecibo,* 988 F.2d 252, 256 (1st Cir. 1993).

[29] *Deep East Texas Regional Mental Health and Mental Retardation Services v. Kinnear,* 877 S.W.2d 550 (Tex. App. 1994).

[30] *Canady v. Prescott Canyon Estates Homeowners Ass'n,* 204 Ariz. 91, 60 P.3d 231 (Ct. App.2002).

[31] See supra §§ 4:7 and 6:8.

[32] *Williams v. Matthews Co.,* 499 F.2d 819 (8th Cir. 1974).

[33] 4 U.S.C.A. § 5.

[34] See *Hoye v. Shepherds Glen Land Co., Inc.,* 753 S.W.2d 226 (Tex. App. 1988).

[35] *McMillan v. Iserman,* 120 Mich. App. 785, 327 N.W.2d 559 (1982).

[36] See, e.g., Cal. Gov't Code § 12955(1) and N.C. Gen. Stat. § 168–22.

[37] One case found a taking. *Clem v. Christole, Inc.,* 548 N.E.2d 1180 (Ind. Ct. App. 1990).

[38] *Barrett v. Dawson,* 61 Cal. App. 4th 1048, 71 Cal. Rptr. 2d 899 (1998).

The view more likely to prevail under current constitutional doctrine is that no taking occurs because the loss of the right to enforce the covenant is but a small part of the landowner's bundle of rights. Furthermore, the loss of the covenant is likely not total since it will usually still be of value to bar other uses, such as commercial uses, not covered by the statute.[39] A similar rationale is used to validate such statutes under the contract clause.[40] Still, the matter is not free from doubt. The loss of the specifically bargained for contract right may create expectations that a court thinks should be paid for if eliminated by the state.[41]

The increasingly intrusive nature of restrictions imposed in common interest communities is troublesome. For example, by private contract homeowners may agree to prohibit the posting of political signs. A municipal ordinance to that effect would likely be unconstitutional. Homeowners, the ones who would violate the restriction as well as the ones who themselves will abide by the restriction and expect others to do the same, have notice when they buy into the community, providing a strong equitable basis for upholding the valid contractual arrangement. Still, even freedom of contract has its limitations. In order to curtail homeowner associations' excessive zeal, increased judicial scrutiny under accepted common law limitations has been suggested.[42]

In addition to the common law rule that invalidates covenants in violation of public policy, the common law generally imposes a reasonableness limitation.[43] The test is similar to that of substantive due process: a covenant will be invalidated if it is arbitrary or capricious and bears no reasonable relationship to the purposes of the association.[44] In *Chateau Village North Condominium Association v. Jordan,*[45] for example, the court held a blanket policy against keeping pets arbitrary.[46] In *Rhue v. Cheyenne Homes, Inc.* the court subjected an architectural compatibility covenant to a test of reasonableness.[47] Examining the reasons given by the review board, the court upheld the refusal to permit a Spanish-style house in an area of ranch style and split level houses.[48]

The common law policy against restraints on alienation may also be used to deny enforcement to provisions in condominium and homeowner association bylaws that restrict the ability of members to convey their interest in property.[49]

---

[39] Aggregation of property rights, examining the effect of a regulation on the whole bundle, is the norm. See supra § 10:8.

[40] *Deep East Texas Regional Mental Health and Mental Retardation Services v. Kinnear,* 877 S.W.2d 550, 566 (Tex. App. 1994).

[41] See supra § 10:7 regarding role of expectations in takings law.

[42] Fleming, Note: Regulation of Political Signs in Private Homeowner Associations: A New Approach, 59 Vand. L. Rev. 571 (2006).

[43] Some states do so by statute. See Tex. Prop. Code Ann. § 202.004(a).

[44] See supra § 10:12.

[45] *Chateau Village North Condominium Ass'n v. Jordan,* 643 P.2d 791 (Colo. App. 1982).

[46] But see *Nahrstedt v. Lakeside Village Condominium Assn.,* 8 Cal. 4th 361, 33 Cal. Rptr. 2d 63, 878 P.2d 1275 (1994).

[47] *Rhue v. Cheyenne Homes, Inc.,* 168 Colo. 6, 449 P.2d 361 (1969).

[48] See also *McHuron v. Grand Teton Lodge Co.,* 899 P.2d 38 (Wyo. 1995).

[49] See *R.H. Macy & Co., Inc. v. May Dept. Stores Co.,* 337 Md. 323, 653 A.2d 461 (1995).

§ 15:12 Public Use of, or Benefit from, Private Restrictions for Preservation Purposes

Many preservation interests can be accomplished by private land restrictions. These include land preserved for agricultural use, historical sites, environmentally sensitive lands, wilderness, and open space for aesthetic purposes. In recent years, government agencies and private groups have used such restrictions to preserve more than four million acres of land.[50]

Generally, governments may acquire conservation easements by purchase, gift, or eminent domain.[51] Acquisition of a limited interest, rather than the fee, has the advantage of reducing the cost to the acquirer and of keeping the land in productive, although limited, economic use. From the government perspective, this provides a continued, if diminished, tax revenue. From the private perspective, when the state takes the interest involuntarily by eminent domain, the ability to retain possession and use the property for limited purposes may be of some solace to the condemnee. Gift and estate tax advantages may also accrue to the private owner who donates an easement.

While fitting these interests within common law devices such as covenants, equitable servitudes and easements is easy, there is reluctance to do so since each may pose problems of enforcement. The arrangements often employ language of promise, but if styled as a negative covenant or equitable servitude, they will not be enforceable against subsequent transferees of the burdened land if, as often happens, the covenant is in gross. Rejection of the often criticized rule that calls for a dominant estate, or a liberal definition of the dominant estate would overcome the problem. The public interest in preservation ought to counter any concern with the restraint on alienability, but if a dominant estate is needed, it is not a difficult stretch to find that highway land benefits aesthetically by restrictions on adjacent land or that an agreement limiting land to agricultural use benefits other land in the community. Still, the specter of the anti-in gross rule is a deterrent. Potential privity problems also arise if the arrangement is treated as a covenant.[52]

A better, but not risk-free, option is to treat the interest as a negative easement in gross. There is no problem with the burden passing to a transferee of the servient estate. Negative easements, however, may be limited in subject matter to the four categories allowed at early common law. There is also the common law rule that may persist in some states that the benefit of the easement in gross is not assignable. Thus, if the Nature Conservancy acquires an easement in gross but wishes to transfer enforcement rights to a governmental agency, it could not do so.

The label "conservation easement" has grown to be the most commonly used term, but the enforceability of the arrangement, regardless of labels, may still turn on how a court views the matter in light of the common law rules noted above. To promote use of conservation efforts, several states have passed statutes dispensing with the common law requirements. A North Carolina statute, for example, provides that:

(a) No conservation or preservation agreement shall be unenforceable because of

---

[50] McLaughlin, Conservation Easements: Perpetuity and Beyond, 34 Ecology L.Q. 673 (2007).

[51] *Kamrowski v. State,* 31 Wis. 2d 256, 142 N.W.2d 793 (1966).

[52] See discussion supra § 15:4.

(1) Lack of privity of estate or contract, or

(2) Lack of benefit to particular land or person, or

(3) The assignability of the benefit to another holder as defined in this Article.[53]

Other states have statutes authorizing conservation agreements without regard to how they are named.[54]

§ 15:13 Public Use of Private Restrictions to Complement Zoning

Restrictive covenants may be used by a municipality to complement zoning ordinances and provide individualized treatment to an area for which a zoning change is sought. For example, a municipality may reclassify land to a less restricted use if the applicant for rezoning agrees to special limitations on the use of the rezoned property that are not imposed on other land included in the same classification. The municipality and the landowner will execute and record an agreement complying with the statute of frauds.

The process is not recommended. First, neighbors may challenge it as contract zoning,[55] resulting in a declaration either that the rezoning stands but the covenant is void as ultra vires, or if the covenant is seen as tainting the entire process, that the rezoning itself is void. While a few courts have approved the device as a legitimate manner of exercising the zoning power and achieving flexibility,[56] it may result in uncertainty about how the land can be used since one looking at the zoning records alone might find no reference to the covenant.[57]

A better approach, if the jurisdiction recognizes conditional zoning as valid, is to put the restriction in the rezoning ordinance. Not only is it discoverable by those examining the records in the zoning office, but the publicity attendant to making it part of the rezoning amendment detracts from the perception of wrongdoing that may arise when the parties bury the restriction in the private land records. If the state has not recognized conditional zoning, there are other ways to achieve flexibility.[58]

A similar process that in form may avoid the contract zoning problem has the developer execute a covenant to the objecting neighbors.[59] The covenant limits use more strictly than the new rezoning classification and should be enforceable by the owner of the neighboring land against the developer and subsequent purchasers. A court, however, might find that silencing the neighbors by purchase is contrary to public policy

---

[53] N.C. Gen. Stat. § 121–38.

[54] See, e.g., Alaska Stat. §§ 34.17. 030, 34.17.040(a).

[55] *Hartnett v. Austin,* 93 So. 2d 86 (Fla. 1956). See supra § 5:11 for discussion of contract and conditional zoning.

[56] *Sylvania Elec. Products, Inc. v. City of Newton,* 344 Mass. 428, 183 N.E.2d 118 (1962).

[57] *Haymon v. City of Chattanooga,* 513 S.W.2d 185 (Tenn. Ct. App. 1973) (owners of land entered into a covenant with board of zoning appeals that if the board would rezone the land, the owners would maintain a buffer zone of 200 feet and subsequent owners, without knowledge of the covenant, obtained amendment reducing the buffer zone to 100 feet, the covenant, the ordinance enacted in consideration thereof, and the amending ordinance were void as against public policy); *Cederberg v. City of Rockford,* 8 Ill. App. 3d 984, 291 N.E.2d 249 (1972).

[58] See supra § 4:15.

[59] See, e.g., *Johnson v. Myers,* 226 Ga. 23, 172 S.E.2d 421 (1970).

and therefore unenforceable, or that the covenant tainted the rezoning, resulting in its invalidation.

Where private parties enter into an otherwise valid covenant, a city might be able to enforce the covenant although it was not a party to the covenant by way of third-party beneficiary principles.[60] While the common law might support such a suit, a statute authorizing the suit helps. A Wisconsin statute, for example, allows for public enforcement if a covenant was imposed by demand of the public body, or if the agreement names a public body as a beneficiary of the promise.[61]

A Texas statute provides that municipalities that do not have zoning may sue to enjoin or abate violations of recorded private restrictions.[62] The legislation gives cities like Houston, which do not have zoning, a method for exerting limited police power control over land use. Questions have been raised as to the constitutionality of the Texas act, the most serious being that it represents an unlawful delegation of legislative authority to the nongovernmental parties who created the restriction.[63] Objections have also been raised that the device represents control without planning and that enforcement of private restrictive covenants without planning or standards can be no better than haphazard.[64]

Restrictive covenants also play a role in public land use planning in that planners may be able to achieve objectives beyond the scope of their regulatory powers by persuading developers to include restrictive covenants in the deeds to property contained in a subdivision. If the government requires the covenants, the contract zoning issued discussed above applies. In instances when the police power is found not to justify certain controls, courts have encouraged landowners to enter into private schemes to achieve their goals.[65]

Redevelopment agencies may impose restrictions on property returned to private uses in the implementation of an urban renewal project. Enforcement problems, however, may arise after the public agency disposes of land that benefits from the restriction. In those jurisdictions that hold that the benefit of a covenant cannot be held in gross, the agency cannot enforce a covenant unless it retains some land that the covenant benefits.[66]

§ 15:14 Conflict Between Private Restrictions and Zoning

Private and public controls may differ with respect to property use. For example, a prior covenant may restrict property to a residential use while a subsequent zoning ordinance allows a business use.[67] In that event, courts universally hold that the ordinance does not abrogate the restrictive covenant. A would-be violator of a covenant

---

[60] See *State ex rel. Zupancic v. Schimenz,* 46 Wis. 2d 22, 174 N.W.2d 533 (1970).

[61] Wis. Stat. § 236.293.

[62] Tex. Loc. Gov't Code Ann. § 230.003.

[63] See Allen, Municipal Enforcement of Deed Restrictions: An Alternative to Zoning, 9 Hous. L. Rev. 816 (1972).

[64] Comment: Municipal Enforcement of Private Restrictive Covenants: An Innovation in Land—Use Control, 44 Tex. L. Rev. 741 (1966).

[65] *National Land & Inv. Co. v. Kohn,* 419 Pa. 504, 215 A.2d 597 (1965).

[66] See discussion supra § 15:6.

[67] See *Dolan v. Brown,* 338 Ill. 412, 170 N.E. 425 (1930).

cannot seek refuge behind the permission of zoning authorities. Thus, where a restrictive covenant and zoning ordinance both established 30 foot setbacks and the city granted a variance from the ordinance, the neighbors could still enforce the setback through the covenant.[68] A number of courts, while following this general rule, have admitted evidence of the zoning ordinance to show a change in neighborhood conditions has occurred that would render enforcement of the covenant inequitable.[69]

Courts and commentators often say that in the event of conflict between public and private controls, the more restrictive of the two governs. In most cases, however, there is no conflict. When a restrictive covenant requires residential use of the property and the zoning classification is commercial in a cumulative zoning scheme, there is technically no conflict between the private and the public restriction since residential use—as a "higher" use—is permitted in "lower" use zones.

In the case of conflict, where, for example, a lot is privately restricted to residential use but is zoned for exclusive commercial use, the police power will prevail.[70] Thus, a zoning ordinance that prohibited an accessory use on property trumped a private easement that allowed the use.[71] Some courts have questioned whether a refusal to enforce the covenant would be an unconstitutional impairment of contract rights,[72] but usually the strength of the public purpose behind the zoning law is likely to justify any impairment of contract.[73] A property owner might also argue that a ruling giving effect to the ordinance is a taking of property requiring compensation. The issue has arisen most often with statutes that retroactively void covenants that exclude group homes. The mere fact that covenants are property rights does not establish a regulatory taking. As discussed above, the issue of whether a taking occurs is usually not measured by reference to the loss of a single property right, but by the property as a whole.[74]

§ 15:15 Condemnation

Public agencies frequently acquire less than fee interests in land, such as easements. They also acquire land burdened by such interests in favor of third parties.[75] In either case, whether the agency holds the benefit or burden of the restriction, its rights and duties generally are the same as those of private parties.[76] If the government condemns property burdened by a covenant or easement, generally it must abide by such restriction or condemn it and pay compensation.[77]

---

[68] *McDonald v. Emporia-Lyon County Joint Bd. of Zoning Appeals,* 10 Kan. App. 2d 235, 697 P.2d 69 (1985).

[69] *Rofe v. Robinson,* 415 Mich. 345, 329 N.W.2d 704 (1982).

[70] *Grubel v. MacLaughlin,* 286 F. Supp. 24 (D.V.I. 1968).

[71] *Baccouche v. Blankenship,* 154 Cal. App. 4th 1551, 65 Cal. Rptr. 3d 659 (2007).

[72] *Mains Farm Homeowners Ass'n v. Worthington,* 121 Wash. 2d 810, 854 P.2d 1072, 1078 (1993).

[73] *Deep East Texas Regional Mental Health and Mental Retardation Services v. Kinnear,* 877 S.W.2d 550, 566 (Tex. App. 1994).

[74] See, e.g., *Annison v. Hoover,* 517 So. 2d 420 (La. Ct. App. 1987). See supra §§ 10:1 et seq.

[75] See infra §§ 16:1 et seq. regarding the acquisition of restricted property by eminent domain.

[76] See *City of Reno v. Matley,* 79 Nev. 49, 378 P.2d 256 (1963).

[77] See infra § 16:3.

Chapter 16

THE POWER OF EMINENT DOMAIN*

Analysis

I. INTRODUCTION

I. INTRODUCTION

§ 16:1 The Power of Eminent Domain

As sovereigns, the federal and state governments possess the inherent power to take property for public use. Local governments possess no inherent eminent domain power, but they are generally delegated the power by state legislatures. While many

---

* For more detailed discussion and more extensive citations of authority of the issues covered in this chapter, see Juergensmeyer and Roberts, Land Use Planning and Development Regulation Law, Practitioner Treatise Series (3rd ed. 2012).

courts strictly construe delegations of the power to condemn,[1] some state constitutions may confer eminent domain power on municipalities through home rule provisions.[2]

The Fifth Amendment limits the power of eminent domain by providing that "private property [shall not] be taken for public use, without just compensation." The Supreme Court applies the Fifth Amendment takings clause to the states by incorporation through the 14th Amendment,[3] and all state constitutions, or state courts employing judicial concepts of "natural justice," impose similar limitations on state government.[4]

Other constitutional guarantees may trump the exercise of eminent domain. For example, while property used for religious purposes can be taken for a public use, there is some support for the position that the First Amendment or a state constitutional counterpart will, in the absence of a compelling governmental interest, bar the use of the eminent domain power if its exercise will unduly interfere with religious activity.[5] Similarly, a property owner may be able to challenge the use of the eminent domain power when done in retaliation for the property owner's exercise of the right to free speech.[6]

Eminent domain plays an important role in the implementation of land use planning objectives, particularly in the acquisition of land for urban renewal projects and industrial parks. States also employ eminent domain to acquire historic sites,[7] and to purchase conservation easements for open space, scenic views, and agricultural preservation.[8]

§ 16:2   The Eminent Domain Power and the Police Power

Courts and commentators have long debated the relationship between the police power and the power of eminent domain. Most theoreticians see them as distinct. The police power is a power of regulation while the power of eminent domain is one of the taking, seizing, or conscription of private property for public use. Yet, the course of the law has been to merge or blur these regulatory and acquisitory powers.

As we discuss in Chapter 10,[9] the Supreme Court has read the "takings" language of the Fifth Amendment broadly to hold that exercises of the police power that go "too far" or otherwise impose an unfair burden on a landowner may be treated as exercises of the power of eminent domain, requiring the payment of compensation. These con-

---

[1] See, e.g., *Department of Transp. v. Stapleton,* 97 P.3d 938 (Colo. 2004); *In re Petition of City of Long Beach,* 119 Wash. App. 628, 82 P.3d 259 (2004).

[2] *Town of Telluride v. San Miguel Valley Corp.,* 185 P.3d 161 (Colo. 2008).

[3] There is dispute about the history of incorporation of the public use and just compensation clause. See *Chicago, B. & Q.R. Co. v. City of Chicago,* 166 U.S. 226, 239, 17 S. Ct. 581, 585, 41 L. Ed. 979 (1897) but see *Dolan v. City of Tigard,* 512 U.S. 374, 405, 114 S. Ct. 2309, 2326, 129 L. Ed. 2d 304 (1994) (Stevens, J., dissenting).

[4] See e.g., *Raleigh & G. R. Co. v. Davis,* 19 N.C. 451 1837 WL 468 (1837) as an example of this latter method. In almost all other states, the limitation is express.

[5] *Pillar of Fire v. Denver Urban Renewal Authority,* 181 Colo. 411, 509 P.2d 1250 (1973). See also Saxer, Eminent Domain Actions Targeting First Amendment Land Uses, 69 Mo. L. Rev. 653 (2004).

[6] *Rolf v. City of San Antonio,* 77 F.3d 823 (5th Cir.1996).

[7] See supra § 12:9.

[8] See supra § § 13:12 and 15:12.

[9] See supra § 10:4.

structive or regulatory takings, litigated by way of inverse condemnation actions, are the focus of Chapter 10. While there is some overlap, this chapter concentrates primarily on direct exercises of the eminent domain power.

II. PROPERTY, PUBLIC USE, AND CONDEMNATION ISSUES

§ 16:3   Compensable Property Rights

The "property" for which compensation must be paid includes personal as well as real property, future as well as present interests, intangible as well as tangible property, and nonpossessory as well as possessory interests. Not all interests associated with property are compensable. In addition to the interests discussed below, an option to purchase land, for example, is not compensated when terminated by eminent domain.[10] Likewise, a personal, covenant, one that does not touch or concern the land, is not compensable.[11]

A. *Easements, Covenants and Servitudes*

While it is widely agreed that traditional affirmative easements are property rights within the meaning of the Fifth Amendment for which compensation must be paid when they are taken,[12] courts differ over whether compensation must be paid to one who loses the right to enforce the benefit of a negative easement, covenant or equitable servitude as a consequence of eminent domain.[13]

The majority rule is that negative easements, covenants, and equitable servitudes, though they may arise out of contract, are compensable property interests. As such, their loss must be paid for by the condemning authority.[14] Since covenants and servitudes are in many respects the functional equivalent of easements, the majority rule treats like-interests in a like-fashion.[15] Awarding compensation when a servitude is destroyed as a part of a taking of the fee, is akin to allowing government to acquire negative easements by eminent domain.[16] They also may be specifically terminated by eminent domain,[17] and compensation may be mandated by statute.[18]

Some courts hold that negative rights are merely contractual rights that do not rise to the level of property interests for which compensation must be paid when destroyed by eminent domain.[19] One court, adopting the non-compensable rule, expressed the concern that recognition of compensable property rights in restrictive servitudes

---

[10] *San Jose Parking, Inc. v. Superior Court,* 110 Cal. App. 4th 1321, 2 Cal. Rptr. 3d 505 (2003).

[11] *Alternative Networking, Inc. v. Solid Waste Authority of Palm Beach County,* 758 So. 2d 1209 (Fla. 4th DCA 2000).

[12] See *U.S. v. Welch,* 217 U.S. 333, 30 S. Ct. 527, 54 L. Ed. 787 (1910).

[13] *School Dist. No. 3 of Charleston County v. Country Club of Charleston,* 241 S.C. 215, 127 S.E.2d 625 (1962).

[14] *Morley v. Jackson Redevelopment Authority,* 632 So. 2d 1284 (Miss. 1994).

[15] See supra § 15:8.

[16] *Department of Transp. v. Callender Const. Co.,* 305 Ill. App. 3d 396, 238 Ill. Dec. 538, 711 N.E.2d 1199 (1999).

[17] *Housing and Redevelopment Authority of City of Saint Paul v. ExxonMobil Oil Corp.,* 2006 WL 997699 (Minn. Ct. App. 2006).

[18] See, e.g., Va. Code Ann. § 10.1–1010(F).

[19] *Arkansas State Highway Commission v. McNeill,* 238 Ark. 244, 381 S.W.2d 425 (1964).

would impose an "intolerable burden" in the event of the condemnation of part of a large subdivision where each lot owner benefited from a restrictive covenant.[20] Another court disagreed, opining that the before and after market value rule would limit liability of the government to those who could prove a diminution in value. With a large subdivision, "only those landowners immediately adjoining or in close proximity to the lot taken" would be injured and "the public use of other condemned lots may result in only negligible damages to other lot owners."[21]

If a state court recognizes the beneficial interest in a covenant or servitude as property, condemnation of the servient estate will not necessarily lead to compensation to the covenant holder. If the condemnation does not conflict with the covenant[22] or does not harm the owner of the right,[23] no compensation is due. Also, a statute declaring a covenant void may be, but is not necessarily, a taking. Unlike the loss of an affirmative easement, there is no physical ouster when one loses the right to enforce a covenant. One example is a statute declaring void covenants that bar group homes for the disabled. Certain factors may militate against the finding of a taking. The covenant may still have value since it may be enforceable against other uses. Furthermore, the loss of the right of enforcement may leave other property rights in the benefited lot, which, considered as a whole, lessen the overall impact on the owner to the point that no taking results.[24]

B. Access and View as Property Rights

Courts recognize a right of access in property abutting a public street.[25] There is no right to demand that government provide public access to a landlocked parcel, but, once having provided access, there is a right not to have it withdrawn or unreasonably diminished. The origin of this right is unclear. Some suggest the state, in building a highway, creates property rights in the abutting property, or that by payment of taxes property owners acquire a property interest.[26] Courts intuitively seem to recognize that once access is provided, property owners have a legitimate expectation that it will continue. As Professor Stoebuck suggests, it may come down to a sense that it would be unfair to landlock someone by removing access.[27]

The right of access is not to maintain the status quo, but to require that compensation be paid where there is a substantial loss of access as a result of governmental action. If reasonable access remains, there is no taking.[28] Courts differ as to what con-

---

[20] *Board of Public Instruction of Dade County v. Town of Bay Harbor Islands,* 81 So. 2d 637, 643 (Fla. 1955).

[21] *Leigh v. Village of Los Lunas,* 137 N.M. 119, 108 P.3d 525 (Ct. App. 2004).

[22] *Albrecht v. State Highway Commission,* 363 S.W.2d 643 (Mo. 1962).

[23] *School Dist. No. 3 of Charleston County v. Country Club of Charleston,* 241 S.C. 215, 127 S.E.2d 625 (1962).

[24] See discussion supra § § 10:8 and 15:12.

[25] *Brownlow v. O'Donoghue Bros.,* 276 F. 636 (App. D.C. 1921); *People v. Ricciardi,* 23 Cal. 2d 390, 144 P.2d 799 (1943).

[26] Or, it may be based on necessity. See *Riddle v. State Highway Commission,* 184 Kan. 603, 339 P.2d 301, 307 (1959).

[27] Stoebuck, The Property Right of Access Versus the Power of Eminent Domain, 47 Tex. L. Rev. 733, 736 (1969).

[28] *Cohen v. City of Hartford,* 244 Conn. 206, 710 A.2d 746 (1998).

stitutes a substantial loss, and cases vary widely among the states.[29] Generally, there is no right to have traffic pass by in any particular place nor is there a right to a commercially advantageous traffic flow.[30] Some courts, however, hold that the landowner has a right of access not only to the immediately abutting street, but also from that street to advantageous intersections and to the general system of streets. Therefore, compensation may be due when the closing of an intersection makes the abutting street a cul de sac,[31] when direct access is lost, or street grade changed.[32]

The interests of an abutting owner in a public way are subject to reasonable interference by police power action without compensation.[33] For example, the public interest in safety and convenience is considered to outweigh the abutting owner's interests when it requires reasonable, temporary obstruction of the way during repairs.[34] Insertion of a median strip can also be done without compensation.[35]

Many courts also recognize an implied negative easement to light, air, and view from the property to the public street it abuts.[36] As with the right of access, the derivation of these rights is not clear, but they appear to be "appendages" to the right of access.[37] Since American jurisdictions have universally rejected the English doctrine of ancient lights, and do not generally recognize implied negative easements,[38] it is odd that many do so in the eminent domain context. Recognition of this fact led the Nevada Supreme Court to repudiate the doctrine of implied negative easements in the context of eminent domain.[39]

In contrast to a right to *view from the property,* there is no right to be *seen from the street.* The latter, while an interest of great commercial value, is not a compensable property right.[40] Thus, in a common scenario, where a city's beautification efforts in planting trees along a highway cut off the public's ability to see billboards, the loss was not actionable. If however, a partial taking occurs, it may be proper to consider the loss of visibility in determining the diminution in value of the remaining property.

In some states, a riparian owner has a right to an unobstructed view of the water. When a county built a bridge blocking a riparian's view of a channel, the court found a physical taking. Though the bridge did not rest on the plaintiffs property, the court reasoned that the bridge physically invaded the view corridor that was part of the plaintiffs property rights.[41]

---

[29] See Montague, The Circuitous Route Taken to Deny Property Owners Damages in Access Cases: Where Has All the Fairness Gone?, 32 Urb. Law. 523 (2000).

[30] *City of Wichita v. McDonald's Corp.,* 266 Kan. 708, 971 P.2d 1189 (1999).

[31] *Bacich v. Board of Control of California,* 23 Cal. 2d 343, 144 P.2d 818 (1943).

[32] *Brumer v. Los Angeles County Metropolitan Transp. Auth.,* 36 Cal. App. 4th 1738, 43 Cal. Rptr. 2d 314 (1995).

[33] *City of Wichita v. McDonald's Corp.,* 266 Kan. 708, 971 P.2d 1189 (1999).

[34] *Farrell v. Rose,* 253 N.Y. 73, 170 N.E. 498 (1930).

[35] *County of Anoka v. Blaine Bldg. Corp.,* 566 N.W.2d 331 (Minn. 1997).

[36] *Grossman Investments v. State by Humphrey,* 571 N.W.2d 47 (Minn. Ct. App. 1997).

[37] *Gilich v. Mississippi State Highway Com'n,* 574 So. 2d 8, 12 (Miss. 1990).

[38] *Kruger v. Shramek,* 5 Neb. App. 802, 565 N.W.2d 742 (1997).

[39] *Probasco v. City of Reno,* 85 Nev. 563, 459 P.2d 772 (1969).

[40] *Regency Outdoor Advertising, Inc. v. City of Los Angeles,* 39 Cal. 4th 507, 46 Cal. Rptr. 3d 742, 139 P.3d 119 (2006) (extensive discussion of issue).

[41] See *Center Townhouse Corp. v. City of Mishawaka,* 882 N.E.2d 762 (Ind. Ct. App. 2008).

C. *Compensation for Divided Fees*

Though a fee may be divided into several interests all of which are compensable, such as a leasehold and a reversion, courts value the property for purposes of eminent domain as an undivided fee. The interest holders then apportion the award according to their respective rights.[42] The undivided fee rule is applied even though the aggregate value of the separate interests is greater than the value of the property as a whole.[43] Unusual circumstances may lead a court to apply the "aggregate-of-interests" formula where the government pays each owner of each individual interest its fair market value regardless of whether the total payment is more or less than the value of the fee if it had been owned by one person.[44]

§ 16:4   Public Use

The Fifth Amendment requires compensation for the taking of property for a "public use." While the phrase "public use" suggests physical use by the public, most courts have interpreted it broadly to mean public purpose, and the United States Supreme Court has held that any conceivable public purpose qualifies. The term "public use" is, the Court has said, "coterminus with the scope of [the] sovereign's police powers."[45]

A. *Taking for a Public Use or Purpose*

Over the years the courts have defined the public use limitation differently. Early in our nation's history the power was not extensively used. However, as the scope of governmental activity expanded and the unoccupied lands in both public and private domains dwindled, and as the exercise of the power of eminent domain became more frequent, courts were frequently called upon to decide whether to give the term a narrow or broad reading. In doing so, courts had little history to rely upon since the historical record suggests that the founding fathers lacked a clear vision of the reach of the public use clause.[46] As Justice Thomas has written, it "was a hotly contested question in state courts throughout the 19th and into the 20th century."[47] By the middle of the 19th century, if there was no actual use by the public there was some likelihood the condemnation would not pass muster.[48] However, courts then began to create exceptions to accommodate uses established in the earlier period, such as mill acts that authorized a private riparian owner to build a mill dam interfering with a neighbor's riparian rights on payment of compensation for such interference.[49] Further exceptions to meet the country's changing needs were recognized so that the exceptions began to swallow the rule by the end of the nineteenth century. The 20th century witnessed the

---

[42] *City of Roeland Park v. Jasan Trust,* 281 Kan. 668, 132 P.3d 943 (2006).

[43] *Sowers v. Schaeffer,* 155 Ohio St. 454, 99 N.E.2d 313 (1951).

[44] See *County of Clark v. Sun State Properties, Ltd.,* 119 Nev. 329, 72 P.3d 954 (2003).

[45] *Hawaii Housing Authority v. Midkiff,* 467 U.S. 229, 240, 104 S. Ct. 2321, 2329, 81 L. Ed. 2d 186 (1984).

[46] See Johnson, Reconciling Originalism and the History of the Public Use Clause, 79 Fordham L. Rev. 265, 319 (2010).

[47] *Kelo v. City of New London,* 545 U.S. 469, 513–14, 125 S. Ct. 2655, 2682, 162 L. Ed. 2d 439 (2005) (dissenting opinion).

[48] *Gravelly Ford Canal Co. v. Pope & Talbot Land Co.,* 36 Cal. App. 556, 178 P. 150 (1918).

[49] *Head v. Amoskeag Mfg. Co.,* 113 U.S. 9, 5 S. Ct. 441, 28 L. Ed. 889 (1885).

demise of the "physical use by the public" test in the federal courts, which read "public use" to mean "public purpose."[50]

The leading federal public use cases are *Berman v. Parker,*[51] *Hawaii Housing Authority v. Midkiff,*[52] and *Kelo v. City of New London,*[53] In *Berman,* the Court upheld a condemnation for urban renewal purposes despite the fact that unblighted property would be taken from one private owner and sold to another. The Court reasoned that the exercise of the power of eminent domain was simply a means to an end. So long as the objective of the action was within the government's police power, the means of implementation did not matter.

In *Midkiff,* the Court upheld Hawaii's land redistribution program. Land in Hawaii was concentrated in a few owners. To alleviate the evils of oligopolic land ownership, the Hawaiian legislature created a system of forced sales of the residential property of large landowners. Relying on *Berman,* the Court put it bluntly: the public use requirement of the Fifth Amendment is "coterminus with the scope of [the] sovereign's police powers,"[54] and any conceivable public purpose suffices.

In *Kelo,* homeowners challenged the taking of their property for inclusion in a 90 acre redevelopment project to aid the economically depressed city of New London, Connecticut. The plan, prepared by a private organization and funded by the state, called for a mixed-use development of public and private facilities. The city approved the plan and commenced property acquisition by purchase or eminent domain. Some property owners balked, claiming the taking was for a private use.

Relying on *Berman* and *Midkiff,* the Court sustained the city's condemnation, finding that the redevelopment project was a public use within the meaning of the Fifth Amendment. In addition to numerous uses by the public, such as a Coast Guard museum, a walkway, and parking area, the city's plan was designed to bring jobs to the city, generate tax revenue, help build momentum for downtown revitalization, and to create leisure and recreational opportunities on the waterfront and in the park. Promoting economic development was a traditional function government, and the Court saw "no principled way of distinguishing economic development from the other public purposes" it had approved over the years.

A purely private taking of the property of one to transfer it to another, the Court noted, is not authorized. The Court said that a taking for "the sole reason that [a private beneficiary of a taking] will put the property to a more productive use and thus pay more taxes . . . would certainly raise a suspicion that a private purpose was afoot. Such a one-to-one transfer of property, executed outside the confines of an integrated development plan, is not presented in this case."[55]

---

[50] *Kelo v. City of New London,* 545 U.S. 469, 513–14, 125 S. Ct. 2655, 2682, 162 L. Ed. 2d 439 (2005) (Justice Thomas, dissenting opinion.). See also Comment: The Public Use Limitation on Eminent Domain: An Advance Requiem, 58 Yale L.J. 599 (1949).

[51] *Berman v. Parker,* 348 U.S. 26, 75 S. Ct. 98, 99 L. Ed. 27 (1954).

[52] *Hawaii Housing Authority v. Midkiff,* 467 U.S. 229, 104 S. Ct. 2321, 81 L. Ed. 2d 186 (1984).

[53] *Kelo v. City of New London, Conn.,* 545 US. 469, 125 S. Ct. 2655, 162 L. Ed. 2d 439 (2005).

[54] *Midkiff,* 467 U.S. at 240, 104 S. Ct. at 2329.

[55] Kelo, 125 S. Ct. at 2666–67.

The core of federal constitutional law found in *Kelo, Berman,* and *Midkiff* is that a public purpose satisfies the public use requirement and that deference is given to the legislature's assessment of what constitutes a public purpose. However, while *Berman* and *Midkiff were* unanimous, the more recent *Kelo* decision was 5–4. Notably the majority did not reiterate the highly deferential standard of review of those cases, but cautioned against one to one transfers, suggesting some degree of scrutiny would be applied to such transfers. Justice Kennedy, concurring, thought that a "meaningful rational basis" should be used. "A court confronted with a plausible accusation of impermissible favoritism to private parties[,he said,] should treat the objection as a serious one and review the record to see if it has merit, though with the presumption that the government's actions were reasonable and intended to serve a public purpose."[56] He went on to find that such a careful and extensive inquiry had in fact been made by the state trial court. The dissent of Justice O'Connor, joined by three justices, would have barred economic development transfers unless initiated to cure pre-existing ills, like the blighted area involved in the *Berman* case.

The *Kelo* Court, perhaps in an effort to diminish the impact of what it knew would be a controversial decision, stressed the power of the states to define their takings clauses more narrowly than that which applies to the Fifth Amendment.[57] Indeed, even prior to *Kelo,* numerous state courts have construed their constitution's public use clauses more narrowly than the United State Supreme Court. The *Kelo* decision sparked a nationwide debate over the propriety of using eminent domain to take property for economic development. Within a few years, 43 states amended their constitutions or passed statutes in varying ways, either prohibiting its use for economic development or requiring a super-majority of the legislature to authorize such a taking.[58] Citizens in 10 states passed initiatives in response to *Kelo.* One critic finds only three, Arizona, Louisiana, and Oregon, to provide significant limits on eminent domain.[59] Florida has adopted the most stringent limitation on the use of eminent domain. The state now bans the transfer of "ownership or control of property acquired" by eminent domain to "a natural person or private entity, by lease or otherwise," except for common carriers or public roads.[60] It also prohibits the use of eminent domain "for the purpose of preventing or eliminating slum or blight conditions."[61] In a number of states, the legislative responses have been criticized as being ineffective, often containing large loopholes so that the efforts have been little more than window dressing[62] or leaving in place definitions of blight that "include any area where there are obstacles to 'sound growth' or conditions that constitute an 'economic or social liability.'"[63] As one commentator has said, "[w]hatever one's view of the merits of the remedial effort, the sheer volume of post-*Kelo* legislation is a testament to the health of the federalism that lies at the foundation of our system of government."[64]

---

[56] Id., 125 S. Ct. at 2669.

[57] 545 U.S. at 489.

[58] 50 State Report Card: Tracking Eminent Domain Reform Legislation Since *Kelo,* December 2008, http://www.castlecoalition.org/about/component/content/57?task=view. See also Somin, The Limits of Backlash: Assessing the Political Response to *Kelo,* 93 Minn. L. Rev. 2107 (2009) (noting 22 are largely symbolic).

[59] Id., Somin at 2143–44.

[60] Fla. Stat. Ann. § 73.013.

[61] Fla. Stat. Ann. § 73.014.

[62] Somin, supra at 2136 (2009).

[63] Id.

[64] Lopez, Revisiting *Kelo* and Eminent Domain's "Summer of Scrutiny," 59 Ala. L. Rev. 561, 609 (2008).

Also, in recent years, numerous state courts have addressed the question of whether economic development qualifies as a public use under their state constitutions. In contrast to the recent spate of constitutional amendments and statutes, the results in the courts are varied.[65] Ohio and Oklahoma rejected the *Kelo* view of public use.[66] In two controversial decisions, the New York Court of Appeals upheld condemnations for economic development deferring to agency determinations of blight.[67]

B. *Taking for Private Use*

Although the Constitution does not explicitly prohibit the taking of private property for private use, the Court reads it as doing so implicitly.[68] Even the payment of just compensation will not validate a private taking.[69] While no one disputes the illegitimacy of private takings, the source of the bar is disputed.[70] Most courts gloss over the text of the Fifth Amendment and simply assume that it is the Fifth Amendment that proscribes private takings.[71] The difficulty in relying on the Fifth Amendment, however, is its plain language, which does not say that property can only be taken for public use. Rather, it provides that when government takes property for a public use, it must pay just compensation.[72] Some authorities point to the due process clause as the source of the ban against private takings.[73] The source of the wrong is important since procedural differences exist between actions based on the takings clause and on the due process clause.[74]

---

[65] Against-economic development as a public use, see *County of Wayne v. Hathcock, All* Mich. 445, 684 N.W.2d 765 (2004); *Norwood v. Horney,* 110 Ohio St. 3d 353, 853 N.E.2d 1115 (2006).

[66] *Norwood v. Horney,* 110 Ohio St. 3d 353, 853 N.E.2d 1115 (2006); *Board of County Com'rs of Muskogee County v. Lowery,* 136 P.3d 639 (Okla. 2006).

[67] *Kaur v. New York State Urban Development Corp.,* 15 N.Y.3d 235, 907 N.Y.S.2d 122, 933 N.E.2d 721 (2010).

[68] See *Hawaii Housing Authority v. Midkiff,* 467 U.S. 229, 104 S. Ct. 2321, 81 L. Ed. 2d 186 (1984).

[69] *Thompson v. Consolidated Gas Utilities Corp.,* 300 U.S. 55, 57 S. Ct. 364, 81 L. Ed. 510 (1937).

[70] See Julius L. Sackman, 2A Nichols' The Law of Eminent Domain, § § 7.01[3] to 7.01[5]a (3d rev.ed.1995).

[71] *Hawaii Housing Authority v. Midkiff,* 467 U.S. 229, 104 S. Ct. 2321, 81 L. Ed. 2d 186 (1984).

[72] See Rubenfeld, Usings, 102 Yale L.J. 1077, 1119 (1993).

[73] *Forseth v. Village of Sussex,* 199 F.3d 363, 369 (7th Cir. 2000).

[74] *Armendariz v. Penman,* 75 F.3d 1311, 1324 (9th Cir. 1996). See discussion supra § § 10:10 and 10:12.

Table of Cases

___

Index

References are to Pages
